UNDERSTANDING HUMAN DIGNITY

PROCEEDINGS OF THE BRITISH ACADEMY • 192

UNDERSTANDING HUMAN DIGNITY

Edited by
CHRISTOPHER McCRUDDEN

Published for THE BRITISH ACADEMY
by OXFORD UNIVERSITY PRESS

UNIVERSITY PRESS

Great Clarendon Street, Oxford OX2 6DP
United Kingdom

Oxford University Press is a department of the University of Oxford.
It furthers the University's objective of excellence in research, scholarship,
and education by publishing worldwide. Oxford is a registered trade mark of
Oxford University Press in the UK and in certain other countries

© The British Academy 2013

The moral rights of the authors have been asserted

Database right The British Academy (maker)

First published 2013
Paperback edition 2014

All rights reserved. No part of this publication may be reproduced,
stored in a retrieval system, or transmitted, in any form or by any means,
without the prior permission in writing of Oxford University Press,
or as expressly permitted by law, or under terms agreed with the appropriate
reprographics rights organization. Enquiries concerning reproduction
outside the scope of the above should be sent to the Publications Department,
The British Academy, 10 Carlton House Terrace, London SW1Y 5AH

You must not circulate this book in any other form
and you must impose this same condition on any acquirer

British Library Cataloguing in Publication Data
Data available

Library of Congress Cataloging in Publication Data
Data available

ISBN 978-0-19-726582-6

Contents

Acknowledgements		ix
Preface by the Rt Hon. the Baroness Hale of Richmond		xv
Preface by Archbishop Vincent Nichols		xix
Notes on Contributors		xxv

1. In Pursuit of Human Dignity: An Introduction to Current Debates 1
   CHRISTOPHER McCRUDDEN

Part I Historical Perspectives   **59**

2. *Dignité/Dignidade*: Organizing against Threats to Dignity in Societies after Slavery 61
   REBECCA J. SCOTT

3. *Würde des Menschen*: Restoring Human Dignity in Post-Nazi Germany 79
   CHRISTOPH GOOS

4. The Secret History of Constitutional Dignity 95
   SAMUEL MOYN

5. Constructing the Meaning of Human Dignity: Four Questions 113
   CATHERINE DUPRÉ

6. Human Dignity: Experience and History, Practical Reason, and Faith 123
   DAVID HOLLENBACH

Part II Dignity Critiques   **141**

7. Dignity: The Case Against 143
   MICHAEL ROSEN

8. Socio-Economic Rights, Basic Needs, and Human Dignity: A Perspective from Law's Front Line 155
   CONOR GEARTY

| 9. | The Triple Dilemma of Human Dignity: A Case Study
CHRISTOPH MÖLLERS | 173 |
| 10. | Dignity Rather Than Rights
JOHN MILBANK | 189 |

Part III Theological Perspectives — 207

11.	Dignity, Person, and *Imago Trinitatis* JAMES HANVEY	209
12.	Human Dignity and the Image of God JANET SOSKICE	229
13.	Dignity as an Eschatological Concept DAVID WALSH	245
14.	The Vanishing Absolute and the Deconsecrated God: A Theological Reflection on Revelation, Law and Human Dignity TINA BEATTIE	259
15.	A Christian Theological Account of Human Worth DAVID P. GUSHEE	275

Part IV Philosophical Perspectives — 289

16.	Human Dignity and the Foundations of Human Rights JOHN TASIOULAS	291
17.	In Defence of Human Dignity: Comments on Kant and Rosen THOMAS E. HILL, JR.	313
18.	Citizenship and Dignity JEREMY WALDRON	327
19.	Human Dignity, Human Rights, and Simply Trying to Do the Right Thing ROGER BROWNSWORD	345

Part V Judicial Perspectives — 359

| 20. | Human Dignity: The Constitutional Value and the Constitutional Right
AHARON BARAK | 361 |

CONTENTS

21.	Dignity in a Legal Context: Dignity as an Absolute Right DIETER GRIMM	381
22.	Human Dignity in the Jurisprudence of the European Court of Human Rights JEAN-PAUL COSTA	393

Part VI Applications — **403**

23.	Justifying Freedom of Religion: Does Dignity Help? JULIAN RIVERS	405
24.	Which Dignity? Which Religious Freedom? PATRICK RIORDAN	421
25.	From *Imago Dei* to Mutual Recognition: The Evolution of the Concept of Human Dignity in the Light of the Defence of Religious Freedom SERGIO DELLAVALLE	435
26.	'A Communion in Good Living': Human Dignity and Religious Liberty beyond the Overlapping Consensus JOEL HARRISON	451
27.	Dignity and Disgrace: Moral Citizenship and Constitutional Protection EDWIN CAMERON	467
28.	The Dignity of Marriage CHRISTOPHER TOLLEFSEN	483
29.	Response to Tollefsen and Cameron ROBERT P. GEORGE	501
30.	Dignity and the Duty to Protect Unborn Life REVA SIEGEL	509
31.	Is Dignity Language Useful in Bioethical Discussion of Assisted Suicide and Abortion? DAVID ALBERT JONES	525
32.	Dignity, Choice, and Circumstances DENISE RÉAUME	539
33.	Human Dignity, Interiority, and Poverty CLEMENS SEDMAK	559

34. Dignity as Perception: Recognition of the Human Individual and the Individual Animal in Legal Thought   573
JOSEPH VINING

Part VII Ways Forward? 591

35. The Good Sense of Dignity: Six Antidotes to Dignity Fatigue in Ethics and Law   593
MATTHIAS MAHLMANN

36. Human Rights, Human Dignity, and Human Experience   615
PAOLO G. CAROZZA

37. The Concept of Human Dignity: Current Usages, Future Discourses   631
BERNHARD SCHLINK

38. Discourses of Dignity   637
GERALD L. NEUMAN

39. Dignified Disciplinarity: Towards a Transdisciplinary Understanding of Human Dignity   649
ALEXANDRA KEMMERER

Select Bibliography   659
Tables of Cases, and Other Legal Authorities   699
Index   713

Acknowledgements

TO A CONSIDERABLE EXTENT, this book is the outcome of a conference held in Rhodes House, Oxford, in June 2012. It largely results from discussions there in which a decidedly multidisciplinary group, including historians, legal academics, judges, political scientists, theologians, and philosophers were brought together to discuss the concept of human dignity from their various disciplinary perspectives.

Some of the main issues that the group were asked to consider include the following fundamental theoretical questions: Is there a minimum core to the meaning of human dignity? Is a person's human dignity to be assessed subjectively from his or her point of view, or 'objectively'? Can human dignity be understood in purely secular terms, or is it (as Michael Perry has claimed in respect of human rights) 'ineliminably religious'?[1] Can there be a shared meaning of human dignity where there is religious and ideological pluralism? What ontological claims are implied by appeals to human dignity?

Other questions were more directed at the implications of dignity for relations between individuals, and between individuals and the state: What are the implications of such ontological claims for the ways in which we should behave towards each other? What are its implications for the ways in which the state should treat those who fall under its authority?

An important set of questions posed considered the relationship between human dignity, human rights, and other values: What is the relationship between human dignity and human rights? Is human dignity more appropriately seen as attaching to some rights rather than others? What is the relationship between human dignity and other values and principles connected with rights, such as autonomy, freedom, equality, social solidarity, and identity? What is the weight and status of human dignity? Does human dignity have a status superior to that of other values? Is it absolute, or can it be balanced against other values? Does human dignity essentially serve community or individual goals? Can it also serve moralistic and paternalistic goals? Is human dignity necessarily an emancipatory idea? Is it rights-supporting or rights-constraining?

We also considered how, if at all, the concept of human dignity helps us to deal with claims made in relation to several issues that are among the most

---

[1] Michael J. Perry, *The Idea of Human Rights: Four Inquiries* (Oxford and New York, Oxford University Press, 1998), ch.1, 'Is the Idea of Human Rights Ineliminably Religious?', 11–41.

divisive current political and social questions: the claims of right involved in the issue of abortion; the vexed topic of assisted suicide ('death with dignity'); non-discrimination and minority rights; and claims of socio-economic rights, such as health care. Does dignity apply only to sentient humans, or can it apply to animals, dead humans, and human foetuses? What is the relation between the idea of dignity and what appears to be voluntary self-degradation (for example, in some instances of prostitution and pornography)? How far, if at all, can a person waive his or her human dignity? Does human dignity determine the boundaries of religious pluralism?

A further set of questions considered were more institutional, or related to the relationship between disciplines: How appropriate is the use of the concept of human dignity for judicial decision-making? What is the role of courts and legal authorities in developing and elaborating the concept of human dignity? What role, if any, should human dignity play in adjudicating conflicts of human rights, philosophical and legal?

Readers, at this point, may feel that this list is so daunting, and raises such complex issues, that we are in danger of not being able to see the forest for the trees. The aim of my Introduction is to provide a guide, a map, through the thicket. It situates the subsequent chapters within an overview of the terrain that currently constitutes debates about the use of dignity. While no such mapping exercise is ever entirely innocent, the strategy adopted in the Introduction might be misinterpreted as attempting to tackle more than it does. I have not attempted to put forward my own comprehensive account of dignity (that is for another day, perhaps). I have sought, rather, to probe the potential weaknesses of the positions advanced, mostly based on the rich conversations that took place at the conference, at least in some contexts taking on the role of a devil's advocate.

Having a sense of the origins of the book should explain why it has some of the characteristics that set it apart from other recent and forthcoming discussions of dignity. The conference, and this book, represent the coming together of three strands of thinking. The first was academic: as we shall see, there has been an extraordinary explosion of scholarly writing about the concept of human dignity, often showing a degree of ignorance of equivalent writing in cognate disciplines. One aim of the conference, and of this book, is to reflect on intra-disciplinary debates about dignity in law, philosophy, history, politics, and theology, as well as expose those working within these disciplines to some of the richness of debates occurring in the other disciplines with which they might be less familiar.

The origins of the conference, and of this book, are also personal. In my own work on the theory and practice of human rights, funded by the

Leverhulme Trust, I have become increasingly intrigued by the concept of human dignity. In 2008, I published a lengthy article examining its use.[2] On the basis of a comparative examination of the use of human dignity by courts in human rights adjudication, I argued that the use of dignity, beyond a basic minimum core, did not provide a universalistic, principled basis for judicial decision-making in the human rights context, in the sense that there was little common understanding of what dignity requires substantively within or across jurisdictions. The meaning of dignity, I suggested, is therefore context-specific, varying significantly from jurisdiction to jurisdiction and (often) over time within particular jurisdictions. Indeed, instead of providing a basis for principled decision-making, dignity seems open to significant judicial manipulation, increasing rather than decreasing judicial discretion. That is one of its significant attractions to both judges and litigators alike. Dignity provides a convenient language for the adoption of substantive interpretations of human rights guarantees which appear to be intentionally, not just coincidentally, highly contingent on local circumstances.

Despite that, however, I argued that the concept of human dignity plays an important role in the development of human rights adjudication, not in providing an agreed content to human rights but in contributing to particular methods of human rights interpretation and adjudication. I did *not* argue that a coherent extra-legal conception of dignity that could form the basis of a common transnational legal approach was impossible. I accepted that it could be, therefore, that the interpretation of dignity within Catholic social doctrine, or within a social democratic framework, or within an Islamic framework, or within the Jewish tradition, or based on Kant, might fulfil this role. But I thought that none of these currently provided a consensus conception of the legal use of dignity, and I was sceptical whether any of these could really provide a secure foundation for its judicial application in the future. When any one of these conceptions is adopted, dignity loses its attractiveness as a basis for generating consensus with those who do not share that tradition. The conference and this book were, at least partly, intended to test these arguments and take the discussion further.

The third strand of thinking was more practical. For some time, there has been a palpable tension, perhaps particularly in the USA, between some understandings of human rights and some religious understandings of what constitutes the common good. The controversies over President Obama's health care reforms, in particular whether certain medical procedures forbidden by

---

[2] Christopher McCrudden, 'Human dignity and judicial interpretation of human rights', *European Journal of International Law* 19 (2008), 655–724.

the Catholic Church should nevertheless be imposed on all hospitals that receive federal funding (including Catholic hospitals), is one prominent example. Frequently, these tensions have been exposed to a heightened degree in litigation where issues of individual rights have been involved. A relatively recent example is the now extensive British litigation concerning assisted suicide. This trend is now also appearing in Europe to a greater extent than previously. The Bishops' Conference of the Catholic Church in England and Wales has been considering for some time how best to contribute to public and legal debates on these issues in ways that are constructive and effective. The visit of Pope Benedict XVI to England and Scotland in 2010, during which he called for a dialogue between faith and reason, stimulated further thinking. This resulted in the idea that one way of engaging with current human rights debates was to consider the deeper theoretical foundations of human rights, particularly the idea of human dignity, which is claimed to serve both as a foundation of international and European human rights, and also of Catholic social teaching. The Bishops' Conference was instrumental in driving forward the plans for the conference.

Organizing a conference and producing a book from that conference incurs many debts of gratitude, which it is only right to acknowledge. Apart from the contributors to the book, who deserve praise and thanks beyond measure for coping with tight deadlines with no complaints, I am particularly grateful to Jeremy Waldron FBA, who co-organized the conference with me. Conor Gearty FBA was of immense help at the planning stage in advising how to make the conference work, and subsequently in the preparation of the book. My debt to him, both intellectual and personal, is considerable. Archbishop Peter Smith, James Hanvey SJ, and Charles Wookey advised extensively on the original concept of the conference and were involved at each stage in ensuring that it took place. The chairs of the various conference sessions expertly guided the discussion. The staff of the Catholic Bishop's Conference of England and Wales, especially Julia Flanagan and Arabella MacDonald, handled the day-to-day organizational arrangements. I am most grateful to them all. The conference was supported by a wide array of different groups and organizations: the British Academy, the Catholic Bishops Conference of England and Wales, the University of Oxford, the Pontifical Academy of Sciences, and Queen's University Belfast. In addition, several donors enabled the conference to invite a wide array of distinguished participants from far-flung places. I would like to acknowledge and thank the following donors to the conference: the Edith Bessie Gibson Trust, the British Province of the Society of Jesus, Porticus Trust, Peter Harper, and Atlantic Trading Charitable Trust. I am particularly grateful to Archbishop Vincent Nichols and Lady

Hale, not only for chairing part of the Conference but also for each contributing a Preface to this volume. Brigid Hamilton-Jones was responsible for expertly guiding the book through the British Academy publications process. Elizabeth Stone was a magnificent editor and deserves considerable credit for successfully bringing the book to publication. My family were subjected to an almost constant barrage of discussion about human dignity at the dinner table, and responded as generously as always by helping to clarify my thoughts. The book was conceived and completed whilst I held a Leverhulme Major Research Fellowship, without which it could not have been written.

Christopher McCrudden
Oxford, 1 July 2013

Preface

Brenda Hale

ACCORDING TO STROUD'S JUDICIAL DICTIONARY, dignity means a status. 'Dignities may be divided into superior and inferior; as the titles of duke, earl, baron, and so on are the highest names of dignity; and those of baronet, knight, serjeant at law, etc. the lowest.' A dignity in the church involves having a jurisdiction as well as a spiritual function: so a parson or vicar does not hold a dignity but a bishop, dean, or archdeacon does. Succession law still excludes adopted and children of unmarried parents from those entitled to succeed to hereditary 'dignities and titles of honour'.

That is the sort of meaning a lawyer can understand. It may be old fashioned but it is a precise description of a status attached to a particular individual, a status which by definition only a few can have. It is very like a property right. So how did we get from that exclusive and hierarchical view of dignity to Article 1 of the Universal Declaration of Human Rights: 'Everyone is born free and equal in dignity and rights'? Equal rights we may understand, but what do we mean by equal dignity? Is it just the reason why everyone has equal rights or is it something separate and distinct from those rights? If so, what is it?

More puzzling still, what does it mean to say that there is a right to dignity? Thus Article 1(1) of the German Basic Law declares: 'Human Dignity shall be inviolable. To respect and protect it shall be the duty of all state authority.' The Israeli Basic Law: Human Dignity and Liberty translates this into a negative obligation in section 2: 'There shall be no violation of the life, body or dignity of any person as such'; and a positive obligation in section 4: 'All persons are entitled to protection of their life, body and dignity.' Here, dignity is not just the reason why all people have rights: it is a right in itself which must have a specific content if it is to have any meaning at all. But what should that content be? Should it be pitched at a minimum level of respect for humanity—freedom from torture or inhuman and degrading treatment, for example? Or, and this is the big question, does human dignity mean that all people must be treated as well as valued equally? Does dignity now mean equality? The Supreme Court of Israel thinks that it does.

The law may eventually have reached this point, but the lawyers did not invent such a major shift in political thinking. The people did that.

Freedom-fighters, levellers, feminists even, who knew that they were not being accorded their proper respect as human beings and sometimes called this dignity. Philosophers and theologians supplied the thinking behind it. But how did they get from the hierarchical to the universal view of human worth? From the idea that God ordained the rich man in his castle and the poor man at his gate to the idea that such differences are made by man and not by God? And have they all got there? Surely there are some differences that are ordained by God, if only in the hierarchy of an apostolic church which does not yet admit that women may have that dignity. So what does it mean to say that man is made in the image of God? Or is it, as some would say, the other way round?

These are big questions, and no one discipline can claim to have all the answers. But it helps to get together to discuss them seriously. So it was a great privilege, as well as a great education, to be present at the Rhodes House conference in July 2012, along with historians, philosophers, judges from Germany, Israel, South Africa, and the European Court of Human Rights, theologians from the Christian (primarily Roman Catholic) tradition, and legal scholars from around the world. Having spent a little time myself wondering what we could possibly mean by a right to dignity in a world where hospital patients could be left without food, water, pain relief, or help with their bodily functions, I hoped the conference might supply me with some answers. I cannot say that it did. It supplied me with a great deal of information which I did not have before and more to think about than I could ever have imagined.

The trouble with judging is that you do not have the luxury of doubt and indecision. You have to make up your mind one way or another. There has to be an answer to the case. That is why so many judicial decisions seem unsatisfactory to deep-thinking critics—either the result, or the reasoning, or both, fail to take account of the complexity of the issues, or to reflect a coherent world view, or to appreciate the deeper consequences of deciding a particular way. So it was a mistake on my part to hope for answers.

What I did find was a breadth and depth of scholarship and thought, a richness of debate, and above all for the most part a deep respect for one another's points of view. I did learn one thing—that we have moved away from dignity as hierarchy to dignity as reciprocity—you must respect my human dignity as much as I must respect yours (even if I don't or you don't). But there could be reciprocity of respect between people who are very far from equal. So the content of what we have to respect in one another remains something of a mystery.

So congratulations to Christopher McCrudden for arranging the conference and bringing such a diverse group of people together without their coming to blows and for editing this magnificent collection of essays. They may not have supplied the answers, but he has certainly enabled us to organize our thoughts more coherently on this immensely challenging but also immensely important subject.

Brenda Hale
The Rt Hon. the Baroness Hale of Richmond
Justice of the Supreme Court of the United Kingdom

Preface

Vincent Nichols

WHAT IS IT IN virtue of which we can say that each person has an intrinsic human dignity? Where does this transcendent value come from? For the Christian, and for many of other religions too, this transcendent value is from God. But one does not need to be a religious believer to affirm, from reflection on experience, that other people matter and make a claim upon us, and that 'human dignity' is the idea which best encapsulates the universal truth of that claim, with the moral force that it carries.

We can see this if we reflect on the extraordinary scenes played out in 2011 in the countries of the Middle East. In Tunisia the slogan was 'Dignity, Bread and Freedom'. And I was struck by this account from an Egyptian journalist, Nawara Najem, of how the crowds suddenly decided to risk being shot and refuse to be intimidated. She said: 'Why did the people not fear death? No one knows. It was not only religion. It was not only poverty. It was not only despair. Perhaps the answer is human dignity. No force, however tyrannical, is able to deprive human beings of this.'[3]

Ideas of human dignity have had a long history, going back to Cicero. Down the centuries, the idea has continued to play a part in moral discourse, in particular through Kantian philosophy, in which dignity resides only in humanity insofar as it is capable of morality.[4] These uses of dignity are relatively well known. Less well known, perhaps, is that the concept of human dignity has also had a central place within Catholic theology and philosophy. It has featured particularly in reflections and debates about social injustice, in discussion about slavery, and in the articulation of the rights of indigenous peoples by the Salamanca school of Dominicans following the Spanish colonizations of Latin America. In these contexts the recognition of the human dignity of 'the other' was the first and fundamental step to moral and spiritual change, and to recognizing as injustices the oppression they were suffering. Then, in the nineteenth century, through reflection on the dignity of work and the rights of the poor, we find Pope Leo XIII in his 1891 encyclical *Rerum Novarum* establishing human dignity as the foundational principle for the de-

---

[3] *The Guardian*, 20 February 2011.
[4] Kant, *Groundwork of the Metaphysics of Morals* (Ak. 4:435).

velopment of the modern social doctrine of the Church.[5] Subsequently this has been developed into a rich corpus of teaching by successive popes.

In the immediate aftermath of the Second World War there was a strong desire to articulate a binding set of universal principles to which all could agree and which would serve as a permanent bulwark against arbitrary action by any state power. This desire was shared by a broad coalition of countries and faiths, and the Catholic Church played a significant role alongside others in the discussions that led up to the formulation of the United Nations Universal Declaration of Human Rights. The use of the term 'human dignity' in the Declaration was possible because it seemed to encapsulate an idea of the intrinsic worth and value of every human life which served as a foundation for the legitimacy of human rights, whilst at the same time not presupposing any particular theological or philosophical basis for those rights. Affirming the centrality of 'human dignity' was possible from the perspective of both religious faith and secular rationality.

Today, the widespread contemporary use of human dignity both in law and in ethics is under the spotlight, particularly in the areas of law and medical ethics. The underlying consensus about what human dignity means or requires is increasingly in question. Rival moral conceptions of freedom, autonomy, and the role of the state, the nature of human identity and what makes human life worth living, lie just beneath the surface. The way in which in our pluralist society we develop and hold onto a shared understanding of such a key concept can have an immense influence on the quality of moral and social development of people, and in particular on the practical development of law.

So, when it was suggested by Christopher McCrudden that the Catholic Bishops' Conference of England and Wales might collaborate with Oxford University (where Professor McCrudden was Professor of Human Rights before moving to Queen's University Belfast) in organizing a major interdisciplinary conference on understanding human dignity, Archbishop Peter Smith and I had no hesitation in strongly supporting the idea. We felt that such a dialogue was extremely important and timely. It would offer an open, frank, serious intellectual engagement between the worlds of religious faith and secular reason, through the lenses of history, law, theology, and philosophy.

During his visit to the UK in 2010, Pope Benedict XVI reflected on the relationship between faith and secular reason, and how each needs the insights of the other. A key paragraph of the historic speech he gave in Westminster Hall reads as follows:

---

[5] See http://www.vatican.va/holy_father/leo_xiii/encyclicals/documents/hf_l-xiii_enc_15051891_rerum-novarum_en.html.

The Catholic tradition maintains that the objective norms governing right action are accessible to reason, prescinding from the content of revelation. According to this understanding, the role of religion in political debate is not so much to supply these norms, as if they could not be known by non-believers—still less to propose concrete political solutions, which would lie altogether outside the competence of religion—but rather to help purify and shed light upon the application of reason to the discovery of objective moral principles. This 'corrective' role of religion vis-à-vis reason is not always welcomed, though, partly because distorted forms of religion, such as sectarianism and fundamentalism, can be seen to create serious social problems themselves. And in their turn, these distortions of religion arise when insufficient attention is given to the purifying and structuring role of reason within religion. It is a two-way process. Without the corrective supplied by religion, though, reason too can fall prey to distortions, as when it is manipulated by ideology, or applied in a partial way that fails to take full account of the dignity of the human person. Such misuse of reason, after all, was what gave rise to the slave trade in the first place and to many other social evils, not least the totalitarian ideologies of the twentieth century. This is why I would suggest that the world of reason and the world of faith—the world of secular rationality and the world of religious belief—need one another and should not be afraid to enter into a profound and ongoing dialogue, for the good of our civilization.

As Archbishops, we saw the 2012 conference—and this book which has resulted from it—as a direct response to Pope Benedict's strong encouragement of such a dialogue. The chapters in this volume, together with the outstanding introduction by Professor McCrudden, take that dialogue in many different directions. The conversation is multifaceted, direct, and sometimes extremely sharp when profound differences are laid bare in areas of current controversy. There are challenges here for everyone, and there is much rich food for further thought and reflection, including for the Church itself, which must always be attentive, as Pope Benedict said, to what it might learn from the voice of secular reason.

If I were to single out one area of contemporary debate in our society where different understandings of human dignity are shaping the debate, it would be the care of the elderly and most vulnerable. In the United States of America, the State of Oregon legalized physician-assisted suicide in November 1997 under the heading of the 'Death with Dignity Act'. The 2012 official report on the operation of Oregon's physician-assisted suicide law revealed that the three most frequently mentioned end-of-life concerns of those who died by physician-assisted suicide were loss of autonomy (93.5 per cent), decreasing ability to participate in activities that made life enjoyable (92.2 per cent), and loss of dignity (77.9 per cent). In fact, Oregon's Public Health Division records that the majority (82 per cent) of those who have ended their lives in this way in the fifteen years since the Act was first implemented have attributed their decision to a 'loss of dignity'.[6]

These are distressing and debilitating experiences and not in any way to be minimized. Yet what we are seeing here is the use of the term 'dignity' as a profoundly subjective notion. If I am the only person who can decide whether or not my life has any dignity, and if I decide it no longer does, and if I need the help of others to end it, then they should have a duty to help me to do so. It is no accident that in Britain the main campaign group for the legalization of euthanasia and assisted suicide changed its name from the Voluntary Euthanasia Society to 'Dignity in Dying'. The underlying rationale in these situations is that individual personal autonomy is what matters above all else.

While this autonomy is of real importance it can only be a decisive factor if the true meaning of human dignity has been abandoned. It is striking that the 2012 campaign within the British health and social care sector, which aimed to improve the quality of care provided to those with chronic illness or dementia, was called 'Dignity in Care'. In contrast with 'Dignity in Dying', underlying this campaign is the view that, whilst the sense of personal autonomy is important, it is not the only source of value. Rather, recognition is given to the fact that one's sense of dignity is immensely influenced by the social environment of care, and the wider context of social and cultural values in which we live; an ethic of respect and care for others can enhance a person's sense of self worth and dignity. Human dignity in its fullest sense emerges from social relationships. The experience of loving care can transform the subjective experiences of the loss of dignity or the loss of self-respect.

As James Hanvey SJ points out in his fine chapter in this volume, Christian anthropology is profoundly helpful in this respect, for it affirms that our humanity is found and fulfilled precisely in relationships with others, and fundamentally with God. It is not surprising that in this vital arena of care of the vulnerable it is in the quality of social relationships that a richer understanding of human dignity is to be found. Indeed, for those who have dementia, there is a powerful sense in which their dignity is held by others who care for them. And for those who are wholly incapable of conscious awareness, we can affirm that their human dignity is still upheld by the love shown by others and by the unchanging love of God for them which is never withdrawn.

This social dimension of human dignity, which arises from our nature as social beings, helps to explain why we lose something extremely important

---

[6] Oregon's Death With Dignity Act: 2012 Annual Report, Oregon Public Health Division, available at http://public.health.oregon.gov/ProviderPartnerResources/EvaluationResearch/DeathwithDignityAct/Documents/year15.pdf.

if we try to reduce the value of human dignity to simply protecting personal autonomy. Nor is it sufficient to equate treating people 'with dignity' to requiring merely that we show them 'respect'. Respect for others is of course important but it too is socially conditioned. We easily think of respect in terms of those who 'earn' or 'deserve' it and of those who do not. In this sense we can 'earn' respect. But we cannot 'earn' human dignity. Respect cannot be a substitute for human dignity because a person's intrinsic human dignity is the very reason we want to treat them with respect. A society in which there is a strong sense that people matter has a bulwark against the temptation to devalue particular groups or people, including those suffering from acute dementia or the elderly.

In thinking about human dignity in relation to specific issues of policy or law we can easily find ourselves focusing on what needs to be protected or safeguarded. The area of social care is a good example of where this approach is profoundly important. But there is a deeper richness in the idea of human dignity we may not yet have grasped, something that is profoundly creative and emancipatory, something that stimulates a desire and an openness to a common understanding. The protestors in the Arab spring uprisings in 2011 seized on the idea of human dignity precisely because it offered a promise of a new future. It carried a latent power and potential, an intimation of the deepest truth about humanity made in the image and likeness of God. As Christians we bring our faith to a world in need of healing and hope, and through dialogue and engagement with others, and an openness to learn from the insights of others, we seek to gain a deeper understanding of where that truth about humanity may yet be leading us all.

This fascinating book, covering an immense canvas, helps us all to think harder about what is at stake. I hope it will provoke and stimulate further dialogue. In particular, recognizing that the theological contributions were largely from a Catholic perspective, I hope that it may encourage a deeper dialogue on human dignity from the perspectives of different faiths and Christian denominations. This book provides an excellent foundation for such further exploration.

Archbishop Vincent Nichols

Notes on Contributors

Aharon Barak is a Professor of Law at the Interdisciplinary Center in Herzliya and a lecturer in law at the Hebrew University of Jerusalem, the Yale Law School, the University of Alabama Law School, and the University of Toronto Faculty of Law. Barak was President of the Supreme Court of Israel from 1995 to 2006. Before that, he served as a Justice on the Supreme Court of Israel (1978–95), and as the Attorney General of Israel (1975–8). He studied law, international relations and economics at the Hebrew University of Jerusalem, and obtained his Bachelor of Laws in 1958. After military service, he returned to the Hebrew University, where he completed his doctoral dissertation with distinction in 1963. Between 1966 and 1967, Barak studied at Harvard University. In 1968, he was appointed as a professor at the Hebrew University of Jerusalem, and in 1974–5 served as Dean of its Law Faculty. In 1975, he was awarded the Israel Prize for legal research. In the same year, he became a member of the Israel Academy of Sciences and Humanities. In 1978, he became a foreign member of the American Academy of Arts and Sciences. Between 1975 and 1978 he served as Attorney General of Israel. Barak was appointed by Israeli Prime Minister Menachem Begin in 1978 as the legal advisor to the Israeli delegation for negotiating the Camp David Accords.

Tina Beattie is Professor of Catholic Studies and Director of the Digby Stuart Research Centre for Religion, Society and Human Flourishing at the University of Roehampton in London. Her research interests are in Catholic theology and gender, Lacanian theory, human rights and women's rights, and the theology, art, and symbolism of the Virgin Mary. Her latest book is *Theology after Postmodernity: Divining the Void* (2013). In addition to her academic publications, she writes for *The Tablet*, *The Guardian* online and the online journal *Open Democracy*, and she is a frequent contributor to BBC Radio 4.

Roger Brownsword is Professor of Law at King's College London. His books include (with Deryck Beyleveld) *Human Dignity in Bioethics and Biolaw* (2001) and *Consent in the Law* (2007); *Contract Law: Themes for the Twenty-First Century* (2006); *Rights, Regulation and the Technological Revolution* (2008); and (with Morag Goodwin) *Law and the Technologies of the Twenty-First Century* (2012). He is a member of the editorial board of the *Modern Law Review*, the general editor of the *Understanding Law* series of books, and the founding general editor, with Han Somsen, of *Law, Innovation and Technology*. From 2004 to 2010 he was a member of the Nuffield Council on Bioethics; currently he chairs the Ethics and Governance Council of UK Biobank.

Edwin Cameron is a Justice of the Constitutional Court of South Africa. He studied at Stellenbosch and Oxford. In the 1980s, he was an anti-apartheid lawyer. In 1994, President Mandela appointed him a judge of the High Court. He was a judge in the Supreme Court of Appeal for eight years before being appointed to South Africa's highest court in 2009. Apart from his memoir, *Witness to AIDS* (2005), he has written books on the law of trusts, labour law, and gay and lesbian lives in South Africa. He is an honorary Bencher of the Middle Temple, London and holds honorary degrees in law from King's College, London, Wits University, the University of St Andrews, and Oxford.

Paolo G. Carozza is Professor of Law and Director of the Kellogg Institute for International Studies at the University of Notre Dame, where he also directs the Law School's JSD programme in international human rights law and the Program on Law and Human Development. From 2006 to 2010, he was a member of the Inter-American Commission on Human Rights and served as its President in 2008–9. Professor Carozza's research and writing covers areas in human rights, comparative constitutional law, European and Latin American legal traditions, public international law, and law and human development.

Jean-Paul Costa was President of the European Court of Human Rights from January 2007 to November 2011. From January 2012, he has served as President of the International Institute of Human Rights, founded by René Cassin. He previously served as Vice-President of the Court (2011), a Section President (2000), and a Judge of the Court with respect to France, from 1998 to 2011. Born in Tunis in 1941, he received his Diploma from the Institute of Political Studies of Paris, Master of Law from the Faculty of Law in Paris, and Diploma of Superior Studies (post-graduate) in Public Law. He was a student at ENA (Ecole nationale d'administration, Paris) and has been a member of the Conseil d'Etat since 1966. His teaching career includes being Associate University Professor of Public Law in Orleans and Pantheon-Sorbonne Faculties of Law (1989–98), and the presentation of numerous courses and lectures delivered in the universities of more than twelve countries. He was President of the commission for access to administrative documents (1993–8). He has received honorary doctorates from the Universities of Bucharest, Košice, and Brno. He is the author of four books and numerous articles.

Sergio Dellavalle is Professor of General Theory of Public Law, Department of Law, Turin, Associate Member of the Cluster of Excellence 'Normative Orders' of the University of Frankfurt, and Co-director (with Prof. Dr Armin von Bogdandy) of the research project 'Paradigms of Public Order' at the Max Planck Institute for Comparative Public Law and International Law, Heidelberg. His main fields of research are the Philosophy of Law, Political Philosophy, and International Law Theory. Among his publications are: 'The necessity of international law against the A-normativity of neo-conservative thought', in Russell Miller and Rebecca Bratspies (eds), *Progress in International Law* (2008), 95–118; 'Universalism renewed', *German Law Journal* 10:1 (2009), 5–29 (with Armin von Bogdandy); and 'Beyond particularism', *European Journal of International Law* 21:3 (2010), 765–88.

Catherine Dupré is a Senior Lecturer in Law, University of Exeter. She studied law in France and Germany, and obtained her PhD from the European University Institute (Florence, Italy). She is a comparatist working in the field of constitutional law and human rights. Her interest in human dignity goes back to her study of this concept's role in Hungarian constitutional case law (*Importing the Law in Post-communist Transitions, the Hungarian Constitutional Court and the Right to Human Dignity*, 2003). Her current research focuses on the connections between dignity and European constitutionalism since 1945, a project for which she was awarded a Leverhulme Research Fellowship (2010–11). She has taught at the University of Birmingham and at the University of Wales Aberystwyth, and has held visiting professorships at Paris La Sorbonne and at the Institute of Political Studies in Toulouse.

Conor Gearty FBA is professor of human rights law at LSE and a Barrister in Matrix Chambers from where he practises law. His books include *Liberty and Security* (2013); (with Virginia Mantouvalou) *Debating Social Rights* (2011); (with Costas Douzinas (eds)), *The Cambridge Companion to Human Rights Law* (2012); *Principles of Human Rights Adjudication* (2004); and *Civil Liberties* (2007). He has appeared in human rights cases in the House of Lords, the Court of Appeal and the Administrative Court. From 2002 to 2009 he was inaugural Rausing Director of LSE's Centre for the Study of Human Rights. He is now Director of LSE's Institute of Public Affairs.

Robert P. George is McCormick Professor of Jurisprudence and Director of the James Madison Program in American Ideals and Institutions at Princeton University, and Visiting Professor of Law at Harvard University. He serves on the

US Commission on International Religious Freedom, and previously served on the President's Council on Bioethics and as a presidential appointee to the US Commission on Civil Rights. He was a Judicial Fellow at the Supreme Court of the United States, where he received the Justice Tom C. Clark Award. He is a recipient of the United States Presidential Citizens Medal and the Honorific Medal for the Defense of Human Rights of the Republic of Poland.

Christoph Goos has been an Assistant Professor at the Institute of Public Law at the University of Bonn since 2010. He studied law at the University of Heidelberg (1st Legal State Examination, 2000) and completed his legal clerkship at the Higher Regional Court of Bamberg (2nd Legal State Examination, 2002). Subsequently, he served as assistant to Professor Christian Hillgruber at the universities of Erlangen and Bonn. In 2009, he received a PhD in jurisprudence (summa cum laude) from Bonn University with an award-winning thesis on the German Basic Law's legal concept of human dignity. He is currently working on his habilitation thesis on the disciplinary law in state and church.

Dieter Grimm studied law and political science in Germany, France and the United States. He holds a law degree and the degree of Dr iur from the University of Frankfurt (Germany) and an LLM degree from Harvard Law School (1965). He is currently Professor of Law at Humboldt University Berlin and a Permanent Fellow of the Wissenschaftskolleg zu Berlin, Institute for Advanced Study, whose Director he was from 2001 to 2007. From 1987 to 1999, he served as Justice of the Federal Constitutional Court of Germany. He has held visiting appointments at Yale Law School, Harvard Law School, NYU Law School, University of Toronto, University of Haifa, and University of Rome. Dieter Grimm is a member of the Academia Europaea, of the Berlin-Brandenburgische Akademie der Wissenschaften and of the American Academy of Arts and Sciences. He holds a Doctor of Laws honoris causa from the University of Toronto and University of Göttingen. He was decorated with the highest class of the German Order of Merit and is Commander of the French Order of Merit.

David P. Gushee is Distinguished University Professor of Christian Ethics and Director of the Center for Theology and Public Life at Mercer University. Professor Gushee is the author, co-author, or editor of fifteen books, primarily in ethics, including *Righteous Gentiles of the Holocaust* (1994/2003) and *Kingdom Ethics* (2003), and most recently *A New Evangelical Manifesto* (2012) and *The Sacredness of Human Life* (2013). A noted evangelical scholar, activist, and commentator on issues of faith and public life on the lecture circuit and for outlets such as *USA Today* and *Huffington Post*, Dr Gushee resides with his wife Jeanie in Atlanta, Georgia.

The Rt Hon. the Baroness Hale of Richmond FBA is a Justice of the Supreme Court of the United Kingdom. Lady Hale became the United Kingdom's first woman Lord of Appeal in Ordinary in January 2004, after a varied career as an academic lawyer, law reformer, and judge. She is now the first woman Justice of the Supreme Court. After graduating from Cambridge in 1966, she taught law at Manchester University from 1966 to 1984, also qualifying as a barrister and practising for a while at the Manchester Bar. She specialised in Family and Social Welfare law, was founding editor of the *Journal of Social Welfare and Family Law*, and co-authored (with David Pearl) a pioneering casebook on *The Family, Law and Society*. In 1984 she was the first woman to be appointed to the Law Commission. Important legislation resulting from the work of her team at the Commission includes the Children Act 1989, the Family Law Act 1996, and the Mental Capacity Act 2005. She also began sitting as an assistant recorder. In 1994 she became a High Court judge, the first to have made her career as an academic and public servant rather than a practising barrister. In 1999 she was the second woman to be promoted to the Court of Appeal, before becoming the first woman Law Lord. She retains her links with the academic world as Chancellor of the University of Bristol, Visitor of Girton College, Cambridge, and Visiting Professor of Kings College London.

James Hanvey SJ holds the Lo Schiavo Chair in Catholic Social Thought at the University of San Francisco. He has been Head of the Department of Theology at Heythrop College (University of London) and the founding director of the Heythrop Institute for Religion, Ethics and Public Life. He has published widely in theology and spirituality.

Joel Harrison is an Associate-in-Law at Columbia Law School, New York and has recently been awarded a DPhil by Oxford University. He received his undergraduate legal education at the University of Auckland. He then served as Clerk to the Hon. Justice Grant Hammond, Court of Appeal of New Zealand, followed by one year as a Legal and Policy Advisor at the New Zealand Law Commission. He has also taught as Teaching Fellow at Victoria University of Wellington, and as Tutor in Constitutional Law at Lady Margaret Hall while Oxford Graduate Teaching Assistant in Public Law.

Thomas E. Hill, Jr. is Kenan Professor at the Department of Philosophy of the University of North Carolina, Chapel Hill. He graduated magna cum laude from Harvard University, was awarded a Rhodes Scholarship to Oxford University, and received his PhD from Harvard University in 1966. He has taught at Johns Hopkins University and Pomona College, was a visiting associate professor at Stanford University, and from 1968 to 1984 he was at the University of California, Los Angeles, where he served as acting chair of the department from 1983 to 1984. He has written extensively in ethics, the history of ethics, and political philosophy. Publications include *A Blackwell Guide to Kant's Ethics* (2009), a new edition of *Kant: Groundwork for the Metaphysics of Morals*, co-edited with Arnulf Zweig (2003); *Human Welfare and Moral Worth: Kantian Perspectives* (2002); *Respect, Pluralism and Justice: Kantian Perspectives* (2000); *Dignity and Practical Reason in Kant's Moral Theory* (1992); and *Autonomy and Self-Respect* (1991). His most recent book is *Virtue, Rules, and Justice: Kantian Aspirations* (2012). Also noteworthy is the forthcoming 'Rational foundations of human dignity in Kantian approaches', in Marcus Duewell, Jens Braarvig, Roger Brownsword, and Dietmar Miethready (eds), *The Cambridge Handbook of Human Dignity* (forthcoming). He was elected a Fellow of the American Academy of Arts and Sciences in 2003 and in 2013 elected to be President of the American Philosophical Association, Eastern Division, for 2014–15.

David Hollenbach SJ holds the University Chair in Human Rights and International Justice at Boston College, where he teaches Christian social ethics. He also regularly teaches at Hekima College of The Catholic University of Eastern Africa, Nairobi, Kenya. He holds a PhD from Yale University, was President of the Society of Christian Ethics, and assisted the United States Catholic Bishops in drafting their 1986 pastoral letter on Catholic Social Teaching and the US Economy. In 1998, he received the John Courtney Murray Award for outstanding contributions to theology from the Catholic Theological Society of America. His books include *The Common Good and Christian Ethics* (2002).

David Albert Jones is Director of the Anscombe Bioethics Centre, Research Fellow in Bioethics at Blackfriars Hall, Oxford, and Visiting Professor at St Mary's University College, Twickenham. Prof. Jones is Vice-chair of the Ministry of Defence Research Ethics Committee, examiner for the Diploma on Medicine and Philosophy run by the Society of Apothecaries, and a member of the National Reference Group of the Liverpool Care Pathway. His publications include *The Soul of the Embryo* (2004), *Approaching the End* (2007) and the co-edited volume *Chimera's Children* (2012).

Alexandra Kemmerer is Academic Coordinator of Recht im Kontext and Co-Director of its programme *Rechtskulturen: Confrontations beyond Comparison* at the Wissenschaftskolleg zu Berlin and Humboldt University Law School. She is a member of the Frankfurt Bar and has been a researcher at the University of Würzburg, Faculty of Law, a law clerk with the European Commission's Delegation to the United Nations, New York, and a senior research fellow and head of the section 'Law, Politics, Institutions' at the Simon Dubnow Institute for Jewish History and Culture at the University of Leipzig. She has been a research scholar at the EUI, Florence, and visits regularly at the University of Michigan Law School where she will be a Grotius Fellow in 2013–14. Her research interests include international law, European public law, constitutional theory, comparative constitutional law, context(s) of law, and the media theory and communicative praxis of law. Currently, her research concentrates on transnational citizenship in Europe and on the history of European and International Law as a history of ideas. As biographer of Eric Stein, she is particularly interested in interrelations between biography, doctrine, and theory. She serves on the editorial boards of the *German Law Journal* and of *Zeitschrift für Ideengeschichte*, and is contributing editor of *Verfassungsblog*. Her reviews, essays and other writings regularly appear, inter alia, in the *Frankfurter Allgemeine Zeitung*.

Christopher McCrudden FBA is Professor of Human Rights and Equality Law at Queen's University Belfast, and William W. Cook Global Law Professor at the University of Michigan Law School. He is a graduate of Queen's University Belfast (1970–4). He was awarded a Harkness Felllowship in 1974 and spent two years at Yale Law School (1974–6), and then at Oxford University as a doctoral student, beginning at Nuffield College (1976–7). He was elected by Balliol College to a Junior Research Fellow (1977–80) during his doctoral studies. He was elected as Fellow and Tutor in Law at Lincoln College, and CUF Lecturer in the Oxford Law Faculty in 1980, becoming Professor of Human Rights Law at Oxford in 1998. He is a barrister at the English Bar (Gray's Inn) and has been called to the Northern Ireland Bar; he is a Non-Resident Tenant at Blackstone Chambers in the Temple. He is the author of *Buying Social Justice* (2007), a book about the relationship between public procurement and equality, for which he was awarded a Certificate of Merit by the American Society of International Law in 2008, and *Courts and Consociations* (2013, with Brendan O'Leary). He serves on the editorial boards of several journals, including the *Oxford Journal of Law and Religion*, the *Oxford Journal of Legal Studies*, the *International Journal of Discrimination and the Law*, and the *Journal of International Economic Law*, and is co-editor of the *Law in Context* series (Cambridge University Press). In 2006, Queen's University, Belfast, awarded him an honorary LLD. He was elected a fellow of the British Academy in 2008. In 2011, he was awarded a three-year Leverhulme Major Research Fellowship.

Matthias Mahlmann holds the Chair of Legal Theory, Legal Sociology and International Public Law at the Faculty of Law, University of Zurich in Switzerland. He is a Recurrent Visiting Professor at the Central European University in Budapest and was a visiting professor at the Hebrew University, Jerusalem and the Georgetown University Law Center, Washington DC. He has been a legal advisor and consultant to various public bodies including the Swiss Federal Government, the German Parliament, and the Commission of the European Union. Recent books include *Elemente einer ethischen Grundrechtstheorie* (*Elements of an Ethical Theory of Human Rights*, 2008); *Rationalismus in der praktischen Theorie* (*Rationalism in Practical Theory*, 2nd edn, 2009); *Rechtsphilosophie und Rechtstheorie* (*Legal Philosophy and Legal Theory*, 2nd edn, 2012.)

John Milbank is Research Professor of Religion, Politics and Ethics and Director of the Centre of Theology and Philosophy at the University of Nottingham. He holds a DD from Cambridge. He joined the Department of Theology in September 2004. He previously held a chair at the University of Virginia, a Readership at Cambridge with a Supernumerary Fellowship at Peterhouse, and a Teaching Fellowship at Lancaster. He is the author of several books of which the most well known is *Theology and Social Theory* and the most recent *Being Reconciled: Ontology and Pardon*. He is one of the editors of the *Radical Orthodoxy* collection of essays. He is the chairperson of the postliberal think tank *Respublica,* a regular commentator on the ABC 'Religion and Culture' website, and an occasional broadcaster.

Christoph Möllers Dr jur. (Munich), LLM (Chicago) is a Professor of Public Law and Jurisprudence, Faculty of Law, Humboldt University Berlin. He was a Fellow at NYU School of Law and at the Wissenschaftskolleg zu Berlin (Institute for Advanced Study), and Visiting Professor at Paris II and CEU Budapest. He is a member of the Berlin-Brandenburg Academy of Sciences. Since January 2011, he has been a judge at the Superior Administrative Court in Berlin. Since April 2012, he has been a Permanent Fellow at the Institute for Advanced Study. His main interests include German, European and comparative constitutional law, regulated industries, democratic theory in public law, and the theory of normativity. His book *The Three Branches* was published in 2013.

Samuel Moyn is a professor of history at Columbia University. His research interests are in modern European intellectual and human rights history. He is editor of the journal *Humanity*. He has a PhD from the University of California-Berkeley (2000) and a JD from Harvard Law School (2001). His most recent book is *The Last Utopia: Human Rights in History* (2010), and he is also author of 'Do human rights treaties make enough of a difference?', in the *Cambridge Companion to Human Rights Law* (2012).

Gerald L. Neuman is the J. Sinclair Armstrong Professor of International, Foreign, and Comparative Law at Harvard Law School, and co-director of the school's Human Rights Program. He earned his JD degree at Harvard Law School (1980), and a PhD in Mathematics at MIT (1977). He previously taught at the University of Pennsylvania Law School (1984–92) and Columbia Law School (1992–2006). His publications include the casebook *Human Rights* (2009); *Strangers to the Constitution: Immigrants, Borders and Fundamental Law* (1996); 'Human dignity in United States constitutional law', in Dieter Simon and Manfred Weiss (eds), *Zur Autonomie des Individuums: Liber Amicorum Spiros Simitis* (2000); 'On Fascist honour and human dignity: a sceptical response', in Christian Joerges and Navraj Ghaleigh (eds), *Darker Legacies of Europe* (2003); 'Human rights and constitutional rights: harmony and dissonance', *Stanford Law Review* 55 (2003), 1863; and 'Talking to ourselves', *European Journal of International Law* 16 (2005), 139. Since 2011, he has been a member of the UN Human Rights Committee, which monitors compliance with the International Covenant on Civil and Political Rights.

Archbishop Vincent Nichols is the eleventh Archbishop of Westminster. Born in Crosby, Liverpool, he studied for the priesthood at the English College in Rome from 1963 to 1970, gaining licences in philosophy and theology at the Gregorian University. He was ordained priest in Rome in 1969 for the Archdiocese of Liverpool. In 1971, he was appointed assistant priest in St Mary's Parish, Wigan and chaplain to the Sixth Form College and St Peter's High School. In January 1980, he was appointed director of the Upholland Northern Institute, where he was responsible for the in-service training of the clergy, pastoral and religious education courses. In January 1984, he was appointed general secretary of the Bishops' Conference in England & Wales. From 1989 to 1996, he was moderator of the Steering Committee of the Council of Churches for Britain and Ireland. He was appointed auxiliary bishop to Westminster, with responsibility for North London, in 1992. In 1998, he was appointed chair of the Bishops' Conference department for Catholic Education and Formation and also chair of the Catholic Education Service. In 2000, Bishop Nichols was appointed Archbishop of Birmingham, and in 2009 he was installed as Archbishop of Westminster.

Denise Réaume is Professor of Law at the University of Toronto. She was appointed to the Faculty of Law of the University of Toronto in 1982 and promoted to full professor in 1996. She holds law degrees from Oxford, where she attended Balliol College, and Queen's University in Ontario, as well as a degree in history from Queen's University. She currently holds a visiting appointment at Oxford University, and has been a Visiting Professor at the University of Saskatchewan, the University of Victoria, and the University of British Columbia. Professor Réaume teaches in the areas of tort law and discrimination law. Her current research projects include work on private sector discrimination law and constitutional equality rights. Among her publications are: 'Defending the human rights codes from the *Charter*', *Journal of Law & Equality* 9 (2012), 67; 'Dignity, equality, and second generation rights', in Margot Young, Susan B. Boyd, Gwen Brodsky, and Shelagh Day (eds), *Poverty: Rights, Social Citizenship and Legal Activism* (2007); and 'Discrimination and dignity', in Christopher McCrudden (ed.), *Anti-Discrimination Law* (2004), reprinted from *Louisiana Law Review* 63 (2003), 645.

Patrick Riordan SJ teaches political philosophy at Heythrop College, University of London. He has previously worked in Dublin, and as visiting professor in the Philippines, where he contributed to debates on capital punishment, law and morality, constitutional change, and 'people power'. His current research interests are Religion in Public Life, the Philosophy of Justice, and the Common Good. Recent publications include *A Grammar of the Common Good: Speaking of Globalization* (2008), and 'Human happiness as a common good: clarifying the issues', in *The Practices of Happiness. Political Economy, Religion and Wellbeing* (2011).

Julian Rivers has been Professor of Jurisprudence at the University of Bristol Law School since 2007. He teaches European and domestic constitutional and administrative law, human rights law and jurisprudence. His research interests lie mainly in the area of legal and constitutional theory, with particular interests in legal reasoning and the relationship between law and religion, in which areas he has published widely. In 2010, he published *The Law of Organized Religions: Between Establishment and Secularism*. He is a member of the Editorial Advisory Board of the *Ecclesiastical Law Journal*, and an editor-in-chief of the *Oxford Journal of Law and Religion*.

Michael Rosen has been Professor of Political Theory in the Government Department of Harvard University since 2006. He studied PPE as an undergraduate in Oxford (1970–4) before studying in Frankfurt and returning to complete his doctorate under Charles Taylor at Oxford (1980). He taught at Harvard, Oxford and University College London before becoming Fellow and Tutor in Philosophy at Lincoln College, Oxford (1990). He has worked on a wide variety of topics in philosophy, social theory and the history of ideas but is particularly interested in nineteenth- and twentieth-century European philosophy and in contemporary Anglo-American political philosophy. His research is unified by his attention to two issues: the relationship between philosophy, history, and politics, as well as the relationship between the Anglo-American tradition of philosophy and continental European philosophy. Rosen's most recent book is entitled *Dignity: Its History and Meaning* (2012). Among his other publications are *On Voluntary Servitude: False Consciousness and the Theory of Ideology* (1996). With Brian Leiter, he edited the *Oxford Handbook of Continental Philosophy* (2007).

Bernhard Schlink is a professor of public law and legal philosophy and a writer; he was also Justice of the Constitutional Court of the State of North-rhein-Westfalia. He teaches at Humboldt University in Berlin and at the Benjamin N. Cardozo School of Law in New York. His scholarly publications include *Weimar: A Jurisprudence of Crisis*, with A. Jacobson (2000), *Guilt about the Past* (2009), *Polizei- und Ordnungsrecht*, with B. Pieroth and M. Kniesel (7th edn, 2012), and *Grundrechte*, with B. Pieroth (28th edn, 2012).

Rebecca J. Scott is Distinguished University Professor of History and Professor of Law at the University of Michigan. She and Jean Hébrard are co-authors of *Freedom Papers: An Atlantic Odyssey in the Age of Emancipation* (2012). Her essay 'Paper thin: freedom and re-enslavement in the diaspora of the Haitian Revolution', *Law and History Review* (November 2011) received the 2012 Surrency Prize from the American Society for Legal History. She holds an AB from Radcliffe College, an MPhil from the LSE, and a PhD from Princeton. She is currently writing on the phenomenon of illegal enslavement in the nineteenth century and the present.

Clemens Sedmak is the F. D. Maurice Professor for Moral and Social Theology at King's College London; he is also the Director of the Center for Ethics and Poverty Research at the University of Salzburg. Sedmak, born in 1971, is originally from Austria, where he has taught Philosophy at the Universities of Innsbruck and Salzburg. He has been awarded an APART Fellowship by the

Austrian Academy of Sciences and a START Award by the Austrian Science Fund. He has served as Visiting Professor at the Ateneo de Manila University, at the University of Notre Dame, Indiana, and as Johann Gottfried Herder Chair Holder at the University of Jena, Germany.

Reva Siegel is the Nicholas deB. Katzenbach Professor of Law at Yale University. She draws on legal history to explore questions of law and inequality, and to analyse how courts interact with representative government and popular movements in interpreting constitutions. Her publications include *Before Roe v. Wade: Voices That Shaped the Abortion Debate before the Supreme Court's Ruling* (with Linda Greenhouse, 2012) and *Processes of Constitutional Decisionmaking* (with Brest, Levinson, Balkin, and Amar, 2006), and others at http://www.law.yale.edu/faculty/siegelpublications.htm. Professor Siegel is a member of the American Academy of Arts and Sciences, and on the board of the American Constitution Society.

Janet Martin Soskice is Professor of Philosophical Theology at the University of Cambridge and a Fellow of Jesus College. She is a past President of both the Catholic Theological Association of Great Britain and the Society for the Study of Theology. Among her recent works are *The Kindness of God* (2008), *Sisters of Sinai* (2009), and *Creation and the God of Abraham*, ed. with David Burrell, Carlo Cogliati, and William Stoeger (2010).

John Tasioulas is Quain Professor of Jurisprudence in the Faculty of Laws, University College London. He received degrees in philosophy and law from the University of Melbourne and a DPhil in Philosophy from the University of Oxford, where he was a Rhodes Scholar. He was a Reader in Moral and Legal Philosophy at the University of Oxford and a Fellow of Corpus Christi College, Oxford (1998–2010). He is the co-editor of *The Philosophy of International Law* (2010), and is currently working on a monograph on the philosophy of human rights.

Christopher O. Tollefsen (PhD Emory University) is Professor of Philosophy at the University of South Carolina; he has twice been a visiting fellow in the James Madison Program at Princeton University. He has published over sixty articles, book chapters, and reviews on bioethics and natural law ethics, and is the author, co-author, or editor of five recent books, including *Biomedical Research and Beyond: Expanding the Ethics of Inquiry*, and, with Robert P. George, *Embryo: A Defense of Human Life*. Tollefsen sits on the editorial board of a number of journals and is the editor of the Springer book series *Catholic Studies in Bioethics*.

Joseph Vining is Hutchins Professor of Law Emeritus at the University of Michigan. He received a BA in zoology from Yale University, an MA in history from Cambridge University, and a JD from Harvard University. He is a Fellow of the American Academy of the Arts and Sciences, and has been a Senior Fellow of the National Endowment for the Humanities and a Rockefeller Foundation Bellagio Fellow. His work includes *Legal Identity* (1978), *The Authoritative and the Authoritarian* (1986), *From Newton's Sleep* (1995), and *The Song Sparrow and the Child* (2004).

Jeremy Waldron FBA is University Professor at New York University School of Law and also Chichele Professor of Social and Political Theory at Oxford University (All Souls College). Professor Waldron has written and published extensively in jurisprudence and political theory on topics such as democracy, constitutionalism, security and terrorism, and cosmopolitanism. His Tanner lectures, *Dignity, Rank, and Rights*, were published by OUP in 2012. He is also the author of *The Dignity of Legislation* (1999), *Torture, Terror and Trade-offs* (2010) and *The Harm in Hate Speech* (2012), based on his 2009 Holmes Lectures at Harvard Law School. He was elected a Fellow of the British Academy in 2011 and a Member of the American Academy of Arts and Sciences in 1998. In April 2011, he was awarded the American Philosophical Society's Phillips Prize for lifetime achievement in jurisprudence.

David J. Walsh is Professor of Politics at The Catholic University of America in Washington DC where his teaching and research responsibilities are in the field of political theory broadly conceived. His focus has been on the question that the modern world poses for itself at its deepest level: does modernity possess the moral and spiritual resources to survive? The search for an answer has led him to the existential recovery of truth that emerged from the totalitarian crisis, the limited affirmation of truth contained within liberal political principles, and the discovery of practice as the horizon of thought in modern philosophy. The trilogy on modernity includes *After Ideology*, *The Growth of the Liberal Soul*, and *The Modern Philosophical Revolution*. He is currently completing a study of the new philosophical language required of any account of the person, tentatively titled *Politics of the Person*.

1

In Pursuit of Human Dignity: An Introduction to Current Debates

Christopher McCrudden

THE CONCEPT OF HUMAN DIGNITY has probably never been so omnipresent in everyday speech, or so deeply embedded in political and legal discourse. In debates on welfare reform, or in addressing the effects of the current economic crisis, appeals to dignity are seldom hard to find. When Nelson Mandela spoke against poverty, for example, he spoke in terms of a 'right to dignity and a decent life'.[1] The concept of dignity is not only a prominent feature of political debate, but also, and increasingly, of legal argument. Indeed, since the European Court of Human Rights, among others, tells us that human dignity is the foundation of all human rights,[2] it is clear that human dignity will continue to be a central element in legal argument into the future.

The power of the concept of human dignity is unquestionable. It appears to present a simple command to all of us: that we (individually and collectively) should value the human person, simply because he or she is human. But are we all singing from the same hymn sheet when we use the concept of human dignity, and is it a problem if we are not? Human dignity often seems to be used on both sides of many of the most controversial political debates: on issues such as abortion, assisted suicide, genetic experimentation, freedom of expression, and gay rights, human dignity is invoked to justify apparently conflicting positions. Does this demonstrate that the concept is hopelessly vague and excessively prone to manipulation? Or does the existence of dignity arguments on both sides of controversial debates simply demonstrate the complexity of moral argument? Addressing the fundamentals of human dignity, and thereby furthering our understanding of how we might better comprehend the concept, has never seemed more opportune.

---

[1] Nelson Mandela speech, Trafalgar Square, London, 3 February 2005, http://news.bbc.co.uk/1/hi/uk_politics/4232603.stm.
[2] See Jean-Paul Costa, Chapter 22, this volume, 402.

Why now?

The use of the language of dignity is not, of course, a new phenomenon, so why does the discussion about human dignity appear to have become so much more intense over the last few years?[3] As an issue in the history of ideas, the reason for the relatively recent pervasiveness of dignity discourse is interesting and problematic. Several explanations have been advanced, relying on the relative failures of alternative ethical approaches to gain sufficient traction. Dignity's role is to supply a value, or a set of values, that other approaches do not.

One explanation for the increasing importance and salience of debates about dignity relates to the discourse of human rights in general. With the increased political salience of human rights, and the increased use in litigation of human rights language, has come increasing attention to the theoretical underpinnings of human rights. This has tended to demonstrate how contested the foundations of human rights are. The familiar story is that when the Universal Declaration of Human Rights was being drafted in 1948, the participants were able to agree on what they were against, but not on *why* they were against these violations.[4] Human dignity, so the story goes, was inserted as a placeholder when those drafting the Declaration failed to agree on any single foundation.

Since the 1970s at least, the human rights enterprise has become both more powerful and more controversial, legally, politically, and ethically, and this absence of a clear agreement on the foundations has threatened to undermine the project. Many human rights instruments invoke dignity rhetorically, sometimes consciously to bridge agreement on concrete rights and deeper foundations without achieving agreement on the latter. As practical use of concrete rights proceeds, nagging questions about foundations come to the surface and beg for further discussion. From this has come the urge to revisit the concept of human dignity, in order to examine whether it is more than a placeholder and whether it can provide the needed foundational principle.

---

[3] Samuel Moyn, for example, points to the exceptional burst of interest in dignity in Anglophone liberal philosophy in the last five years: Chapter 4, this volume. Thomas Hill is more sceptical of the alleged prior neglect of dignity among contemporary philosophers, see Thomas Hill, Chapter 17, this volume.

[4] See Jacques Maritain, writing in the introduction to a symposium held by UNESCO in 1948: 'It is related that at one of the meetings of a Unesco National Commission where Human Rights were being discussed, someone expressed astonishment that certain champions of violently opposed ideologies had agreed on a list of those rights. "Yes," they said, "we agree about the rights *but on condition that no one asks us why.*" That "why" is where the argument begins.' Jacques Maritain, 'Introduction', in *Human Rights: Comments and Interpretations*, symposium edited by UNESCO (New York, Columbia University Press, 1949).

A specific example of dignity's greater visibility in the context of debates about human rights can be seen in the area of bioethics. Developments in the life sciences, in biotechnology particularly, have provoked deep moral concerns about the direction and the practice of this science.[5] In the German-speaking world, this debate became particularly intense from around 2000, when issues concerning stem-cell research and other issues of biotechnology generated considerable public and scholarly debate. Dignity is seen, potentially, as placing limits on some developments in these areas of scientific development. This is particularly the case in those areas of biotechnology that relate to genetic engineering and other technologies involving human enhancement. Human enhancement is identified as problematic, it is said, because it compromises human dignity.[6]

These concerns have led to a plethora of legal instruments and official reports that identify human dignity as a cornerstone principle that must be safeguarded.[7] The 2005 UNESCO Declaration on Bioethics and Human Rights, for example, provides, in its section dealing with human dignity, that the 'interests and welfare of the individual should have priority over the sole interest of science or society'.[8] For many of its detractors and proponents, human dignity acts as more of a complete limit than other ethical viewpoints, a 'conversation stopper'.[9] The relative effectiveness of human dignity in that regard has led to considerable resistance to the use of dignity by some scientists working in these areas.

Dignity's history

What, if anything, does the study of history bring to our attempt to understand the various meanings accorded to the concept of human dignity? More specifically, where there are disagreements among historians about dignity's

---

[5] Roger Brownsword, Chapter 19, this volume.
[6] Michael J. Sandel, *The Case against Perfection: Ethics in the Age of Genetic Engineering* (Cambridge, MA, Harvard University Press, 2009), 24.
[7] For example, (United States) President's Council on Bioethics Washington, *Human Dignity and Bioethics: Essays Commissioned by the President's Council on Bioethics* (The President's Council on Bioethics, Washington DC, March 2008); Convention for the Protection of Human Rights and Dignity of the Human Being with regard to the Application of Biology and Medicine: Convention on Human Rights and Biomedicine, CETS No. 164 (Oviedo Convention).
[8] Universal Declaration on Bioethics and Human Rights, General Conference of UNESCO, 33rd Session, 19 October 2005, Article 3(2).
[9] See Dieter Birnbacher, 'Ambiguities in the concept of Menschenwürde', in K. Bayertz (ed.), *Sanctity of Life and Human Dignity* (Kluwer, 1996), 107 (quoting Keenan).

history, what is at stake in these debates? The first point to bear in mind is that the history of human *rights* is itself a relatively new scholarly phenomenon. Recent historical debates over the sources of human rights have tended to concentrate on four periods. There is a lively debate on whether rights discourse has its origins in the idea of natural rights in the Middle Ages, with the canonists and Roman law to the fore.[10] Some argue that the decades of the French and American Revolutions of the late eighteenth century is the critical period, while others emphasize the 1940s and the development of the Universal Declaration of Human Rights. Most recently, several scholars have emphasized the 1970s as marking a decisive shift in the embedding of human rights theory and practice. Samuel Moyn sees developments in the 1970s as marking a significant break from the past. He emphasizes the discontinuities, and resists the notion that the development of human rights should be seen as linear.[11] In particular, Moyn argues that it is mistaken to see the development of human rights in the late twentieth century as inevitable, resisting a teleological explanation, and pointing to the many contingencies and choices that arose along the way when a different road could have been taken.

Given the close connection between human rights and human dignity, there has also been an understandable tendency, in this recent history, simply to regard the two ideas as different sides of the same coin, and a separate history of human dignity has yet to be written. Where should such a history of human dignity, as opposed to a history of human rights, start?

Several different approaches suggest themselves. One approach is to identify the original use of dignity as high status, and stress the increasing challenges to distinctions attached to such high status in the period of the Enlightenment. We see in the immediate aftermath of the French Revolution the abolition of aristocratic 'dignities', and increasing disapproval of dignity in the sense of the bearing or demeanour associated with aristocratic status.[12] Another approach is to date the emergence of human dignity from when it became a legal concept distinguishable from, but intertwined with, human rights. Moyn, Christoph Goos, and Rebecca Scott provide the opening salvos for such a history. Scott identifies 1848, and the decree that abolished slavery in the French empire on the basis of its incompatibility with human dignity, as an important breakthrough, as this seems to be the first mention

---

[10] Contrast, for example, Michel Villey, *Critique de la Pensée Juridique Moderne* (Paris, Dalloz, 1985) with Brian Tierney, *The Idea of Natural Rights* (Atlanta, GA, Scholars Press, 1997).
[11] Samuel Moyn, *The Last Utopia: Human Rights in History* (Cambridge, MA, Belknap Press of Harvard University Press, 2010).
[12] See, for example, Jeremy Waldron, *Dignity, Rank, and Rights, with Commentaries by Wai Chee Dimnock, Don Herzog, Michael Rosen*, ed. Mier Dan-Cohen (Oxford, Oxford University Press, 2012).

of dignity in its modern sense in a major legal text.[13] Or perhaps we should begin later, in 1919, which saw both the creation of the International Labour Organization and its emphasis on dignified working conditions, and the adoption of the Weimar Constitution with its mention of dignity in the broader context of securing socio-economic justice. Or perhaps the critical date is 1937 and the adoption of the Irish Constitution, with its inclusion of dignity in the Preamble,[14] or 1949, with the adoption of the German Basic Law.[15] Or was it, perhaps, 1948, with the adoption of the Universal Declaration of Human Rights and its multiple uses of dignity, initiating the use of dignity in international human rights texts? There are various ways of justifying each of these dates.

Why do such debates about the origins of dignity in public discourse matter? The word 'dignity' has been used in different contexts and semantic fields, and its scope and meaning are not identical. A key distinction is between popular uses of dignity and dignity used in theoretical or legal contexts. Some of the controversies that this raises are fairly typical of debates in current historiography more generally. Should the history of dignity be seen, for example, as a top-down or bottom-up process, contrasting Scott (bottom-up, vernacular) with Goos and Moyn (top-down, legal, and theoretical)? Clearly a bottom-up approach is more likely to avoid the 'intellectual elitism' that is said to follow when the focus is on the use of the term by great authors, and certainly it is less likely to underestimate the importance of the struggles of non-intellectuals.[16]

The issues of particular relevance to this book are those historical controversies that shed light on how we can begin to understand the use to which the concept of human dignity has been put. The use of dignity in the German Basic Law and the Universal Declaration, for example, differs from that in the anti-slavery texts. In the latter, dignity is used as a reason or a justification for the abolition of slavery. In the case of the German Basic Law and the Universal Declaration, in contrast, dignity appears as a protected good itself. As Catherine Dupré argues, the history of human dignity can have different starting dates and, depending on the choice of dates, we construct a different narrative as a result.[17]

Dealing with the historical use of dignity discourse seems particularly challenging because historians are necessarily embarking on a theoretically and politically loaded project. That may appear, perhaps, to be less critical if

---

[13] Rebecca J. Scott, Chapter 2, this volume.
[14] Samuel Moyn, Chapter 4, this volume.
[15] Christoph Goos, Chapter 3, this volume.
[16] Matthias Mahlmann in discussion at the conference and Chapter 35, this volume.
[17] Catherine Dupré, Chapter 5, this volume.

all that the historian is doing is identifying the appearance of a particular word in particular texts (although, even then, identifying a non-English term as being equivalent to 'dignity' brings with it important ideological challenges). Where historians are not just looking for words or terms, however, but looking for the presence of an idea in human history,[18] then the historian is more clearly likely to come to the project with an already formulated view of what the concept of human dignity involves.

Even the apparently more restricted enterprise of identifying the historical appearance of the word 'dignity' carries with it significant theoretical challenges, particularly if the enterprise is seen as attempting to discover 'first use' of a word that describes an inherent quality and an inherent value that resides in human beings that deserves respect. If dignity can be dated in this way, and if dignity emerged quite recently, then the implication is therefore that there are grounds to doubt its objective credentials. True, a certain language may be invented to discuss this aspect of human reality, but if 'dignity' is 'invented' then does this challenge the idea that it is timeless? If it could be shown to be invented, then we would have an account of the use of dignity language that did not reveal it to be responsive to the subject matter to which some think it is meant to be responsive.

But is this not to fall into the genetic fallacy? It does not follow that an idea is not timeless merely because it has been named only recently in history as an idea. A less controversial approach would be to locate the use of a term identifying a particular set of understandings, without saying that this use 'invented' that particular set of understandings. For example, if one reads the nineteenth-century slave narratives, powerful claims are made by the slaves themselves as to their subjectivity, but this intuition may or may not have been articulated as a claim for dignity.

The issue then arises as to whether the same thing is being historicized. We shall see that there are different ways of thinking about dignity: as something institutional (in which case the issue for historians is when the word was used by particular institutions, such as judicially, legislatively, constitutionally), or as a concept that captures a set of understandings (in which case other words might be used to capture that set of understandings, say subjective personality), or we might be interested simply in the use of the word (in which case the word might be used for several different purposes). A rich history of dignity would combine these differing approaches, and we need to be aware that the explicitly historical chapters in this book are presented only as fragments of that richer history.

---

[18] Matthias Mahlmann in discussion at the conference and in Chapter 35, this volume.

Short of producing this richer history, what is at stake for current controversies about dignity? The first issue that the chapters address implicitly is the extent to which there is a continuity of the use of dignity language. Scott argues that in certain shared contexts, for example in slave labour either in its classical form, or in the form of modern slavery, dignity plays an importantly similar role, with a relatively similar meaning in both situations. Scott's inquiry is set in the context of slavery, but it is of relevance more generally in the discussion of work and working conditions. Moyn, on the other hand, has a very different understanding of the process. As part of his wider project of stressing the discontinuities between what might be seen as sparks of human rights thinking and today's human rights movement, Moyn stresses the foundation of Ireland's adoption of dignity in the 1937 Constitution in Catholic social teaching, and the links between this and the development of conservative Christian Democracy, rather than seeing it as the beginning of anything that would lead, he argues, to the very different phenomenon of international human rights of the type that emerged in the 1970s.[19]

The second area of current controversy that these histories touch on is how far Kantian or Catholic thinking influenced the adoption of dignity in various constitutional texts. We shall see that both strands of thought are of importance in current debates, but this question of their historical influence is of importance not least because it is relevant to the question of how far a conception of dignity as meaning an inner transcendent core of value was the 'original' meaning in particular contexts.

Goos indicates that the subsequent importance of the Kantian understanding of dignity in the German constitutional debates in the late 1940s was not so important as has been thought. Moyn's argument is that Catholic thought was influential not only in Ireland, but also in the development of dignity in the German state constitutions such as in Bavaria. But Goos appears sceptical as to how far Catholic thought was critical in the German federal constitutional debates either. Goos's careful archival research shows that while some considered that dignity was best viewed as a 'non-interpreted thesis' (to be explained below, but essentially meaning a placeholder),[20] others regarded it as something quite specific, and in particular they viewed it as an idea of 'inner freedom', which we can define as the freedom from compulsion to act against one's own convictions. Goos agrees with Moyn that the Jewish Holocaust itself was not critical in stimulating the adoption of a language

---

[19] Moyn, *The Last Utopia*.
[20] Theodor Heuss referred to human dignity as a 'non-interpreted thesis'. See Horst Dreier, in Dreier (ed.), *Grundgesetz. Kommentar, Band I, Artikel 1–19*, 3rd edn (Tübingen, Mohr Siebeck, 2013), Article 1, Abs. 1, margin no. 53.

of human dignity, at least in the German constitutional debates, but that the experiences of the Nazi concentration camps in general were critical in the adoption of this idea of dignity as 'inner freedom'. David Hollenbach[21] and Matthias Mahlmann[22] are much more sceptical of Moyn's denial of the importance of the Holocaust in this respect.

Different conceptions of dignity: a preliminary sketch

It is clear, even from what has already been said, that there are significantly different conceptions of human dignity in play historically, and in current use. It is useful to try to systematize these different usages at this point, even in a preliminary way, before discussing the implications of some of them in more detail. We can identify, for example in the context of Scott's discussion of slavery, how a person's human dignity was seen as requiring that people should be *treated with dignity*, meaning that respect should be shown to them as individuals. Other uses are apparent too; for example, indignity was seen as being present when human persons were reduced to the status of animals—human beings were seen as having a normative moral status different in kind from that of other animals and other living things. We shall see that this second idea of dignity has two important implications: that dignity is seen as involving questions of appropriate *status*, an approach that has become a central view in some recent philosophical discussion. Jeremy Waldron, for example, sees dignity as currently concerned with raising everyone to the rank and status that only aristocrats formerly enjoyed.[23] The emphasis on *in*dignity also suggests that dignity may be best understood by focusing on the negative rather than on the positive, and this has given rise to an argument that indignity is primarily about humiliation, as Avishai Margalit suggests.[24] There is clearly an important question to be considered regarding the relationship between treatment with respect and according a common (higher) level of status to individuals, an issue explored by Michael Rosen.[25]

In Goos's discussion, we can identify several additional and competing conceptions of dignity: human dignity as derived from man being made in the image of God (*imago Dei*); the view ascribed to Kant that dignity requires

---

[21] David Hollenbach Chapter 6, this volume.
[22] Matthias Mahlmann, Chapter 35, this volume.
[23] Waldron, *Dignity, Rank, and Rights*. See also Jeremy Waldron, Chapter 18, this volume.
[24] Avishai Margalit, 'Human dignity between kitsch and deification', in Christopher Cordner (ed.), *Philosophy, Ethics, and a Common Humanity: Essays in Honour of Raimond Gaita* (New York, Routledge, 2011), 106–20.
[25] Michael Rosen, *Dignity: Its History and Meaning* (Cambridge, MA, Harvard University Press, 2012).

us to treat people as ends in themselves rather than simply as means to an end; the idea of dignity as 'inner freedom'; and (in both Goos and Moyn) dignity as a concept that captures the idea that all human beings are morally considerable simply by being human, indeed that all persons have incommensurable value—the view that Rosen describes as involving a belief that human beings (and only human beings) possess an 'inner transcendental kernel' that is valuable.[26]

Moyn usefully distinguishes between the use of dignity as applied to the human person from what he terms 'corporatist' conceptions of dignity, where dignity is attached to institutions like Parliament or the Church, an understanding that is perhaps rooted in the older eighteenth- and nineteenth-century meaning of dignity as distinction and status. We shall see that Christopher Tollefsen considers that many different things (animate and inanimate) can be seen as having 'a dignity', and that we can refer to the dignity of legislation, for example, or the dignity of labour.[27] Is the same conception of dignity in play in these contexts as when we speak of *human* dignity? To what extent is it appropriate to refer to the dignity of marriage, as Tollefsen himself does; or to the dignity of animals, an issue that Joseph Vining considers?[28] And to what extent is dignity a useful tool of analysis when we consider the question of the religious freedom of churches and the freedom of church members considered collectively, the issue that Julian Rivers considers?[29] Waldron has referred to the *dignity of legislation*[30] and the *dignity of citizenship*,[31] and others have referred, on occasion, to the dignity of courts, or the dignity of the nation state, or the dignity of ambassadors. The issue, then, is whether the idea of dignity that we would apply to *persons* is the same as that which we would apply to institutions such as marriage.

It certainly seems likely that the underpinning of human dignity attached to ordinary men, women, and children, differs significantly from claims that might be made of the dignity of some particular political arrangement or institution. The fact that dignity can be attached to institutional *competitors*, for instance, supports the argument that different values may support different corporatist uses of dignity; so we talk about the dignity of monarchy *and* the dignity of democracy; we can talk about the dignity of legislation *and* the dignity of constitutional courts striking down legislation. One could argue

---

[26] Rosen, *Dignity*, 69.
[27] Christopher Tollefsen, Chapter 28, this volume.
[28] Joseph Vining, Chapter 34, this volume.
[29] Julian Rivers, Chapter 23, this volume.
[30] Jeremy Waldron, *The Dignity of Legislation* (Cambridge, Cambridge University Press, 1999).
[31] Jeremy Waldron, Chapter 18, this volume.

in favour of some corporatist applications of dignity on what are thought to be dignitarian grounds based on personhood (such as the dignity of labour), but there is no necessary guarantee that an argument that attaches dignity to an institution will always be supported by such dignitarian values. Utilitarian values, for example, sustain the dignity of the market; values concerned with liberty might underpin the dignity of Churches. We should not assume in what follows, therefore, that arguments that relate to *human* dignity necessarily support broader conceptions of corporatist dignity.

The fact that dignity is used in many contexts far removed from those traditionally associated with human rights is important for another reason. We will observe how frequently the two concepts are seen to be connected by many of the contributors to this volume; indeed, we shall see how some argue that a principle criterion for assessing how convincing a particular interpretation of 'dignity' is, is to see whether that conception of dignity would provide a convincing justification for the broad range of human rights currently contained in regional and international human rights instruments.[32] It is worth bearing in mind that all such arguments will assume a necessary connection between human rights and human dignity, a connection that needs to be convincingly argued for rather than assumed. We shall consider subsequently what the relationship between human rights and human dignity might be in more detail, and we shall see how controversial that claim is. We should not assume that 'dignity' (or 'human dignity') is coterminus with 'human rights'. Nor, if we are to understand the meaning and function of 'dignity', should we see it only through the lens of human rights.

Dignity-critique: power politics

We can glean from these historical chapters that the concept of dignity is not ideologically fixed in its meaning, thus allowing the term to be used by those with quite different perspectives; dignity may be adopted by those with a religious perspective, or a secular philosophical perspective, or a political perspective. This is the sense in which Theodor Heuss referred to dignity as a 'non-interpreted thesis', a concept 'that is not fixed in its meaning and can therefore marry otherwise opposing views'.[33] What are the implications of this?

---

[32] An issue discussed by John Tasioulas, Chapter 16, this volume.
[33] Doris Schroeder, 'Human rights and human dignity: an appeal to separate the conjoined twins', *Ethical Theory and Moral Practice* 15:3 (2012), 323, at 326.

As many contributors show, dignity can often function as a placeholder, accepting that there is no actual or possible agreed articulation of its content. Indeed, some may wish to avoid any too-critical analysis of the concept, preferring to advert to the core mystery of the person, an intuition that reveals the ethical demands for respect. Some will undoubtedly be impatient with inconclusive and potentially never-ending debates, and may prefer to opt for a placeholder idea of dignity without even that content. However, the absence of analysis and critical reflection on the meaning of and reasons for the assertion of human dignity could then leave a vacuum to be filled. This too has its dangers, which Jürgen Habermas would identify as the likely colonization of the life-world by strategic rationality, potentially distorting the recognition of human dignity and the protection of the rights founded on it. In other words, the interests of the law, or of politics, would shape the meaning of dignity in practice, not always with benign consequences.

For Costas Douzinas, dignity is an empty or flawed signifier, and a hegemonic battle is taking place to capture the concept for one particular ideology.[34] All abstract universals, he argues, tend to be hegemonized for a period of time by particulars that struggle to call themselves universal.[35] Whether the claimed universal is the sacredness of life, or free will, or autonomy, or humanity, each is trying to hegemonize the universal, in other words to turn their particularity into a universal validity. Dignity, then, simply provides another vocabulary for asserting conflicting claims. For Douzinas, only a political and moral commitment to a groundless humanity, continuously open to redefinition, to localized struggles of resistance and revolt, and to an undetermined future can release us from the oppressive power and violence of abstract concepts such as human rights or human dignity.[36]

Tina Beattie provides a detailed critique of Douzinas. Her analysis is that, in common with much postmodern theory, Douzinas presents a pessimistic view of the human condition, 'which could be seen as the secular derivative of the doctrine of original sin', and 'the distant heir to Augustinianism and the theologies of the Reformation, although shorn of their themes of judgment and redemption'. She sees Douzinas as advocating utopian revolution, and asks whether such revolutions reduce, or actually stimulate, the oppressive power and violence that he professes to abhor.[37] She adopts John Gray's

---

[34] Costas Douzinas, *Human Rights and Empire: The Political Philosophy of Cosmopolitanism* (Abingdon, Routledge-Cavendish, 2007), 8.
[35] Douzinas, *Human Rights and Empire*, 196.
[36] Douzinas, *Human Rights and Empire*, 290.
[37] Tina Beattie, Chapter 14, this volume.

argument that utopian revolutions have been the seedbed of every kind of terror, fascism, and genocide since the Enlightenment.[38]

A less dramatic way of reading Douzinas, however, is to see his argument as concerned with the centrality of politics in the definition and application of concepts such as human dignity, and that we ignore political power at our peril. The debate that this generates is manifold, but one particularly important element is whether certain elite uses of dignity, particularly perhaps in the legal context, lead to unacceptable constraints on democratic decision-making. Conor Gearty argues that because the concept of dignity comes and goes, varying over time, and because there are so many competing versions of it, it is not a concept that should be overseen by the courts.[39] For Gearty, the competing versions of dignity, which cannot easily be reconciled, prompt the question: who should decide between these competing versions? For Gearty, those kinds of issues in which dignity is so often brought to bear (the right to die, abortion, etc.) are issues that should be decided in a representative assembly. They need to be concretized in legislation, and the judgements made should be provisional rather than permanent.

Douzinas and Gearty thus significantly develop the more sceptical tone of the discussion of dignity already identified with Moyn and Rosen, and they level several charges, echoing those set out by Rosen:[40] that dignity in the hands of the judges is potentially anti-democratic; that dignity is subject to abuse at the hands of the powerful; that it is conceptually muddy; and that it can end up being used on both sides of the argument. There are two difficulties with these arguments. One is that some of the characteristics of dignity these sceptics identify as problematic are seen by others as positive advantages. For example, is muddiness an advantage or a defect? While Moyn considers the current imprecision in the use of dignity is a defect, for others it is a sign that the concept is alive and functioning well (for example, Scott appears to welcome a certain lack of certainty in the use of dignity). Or we might think, with Aharon Barak, that imprecision is neither defect nor strength, but rather just a fact of normative life with which judges, like other institutional players who have responsibility for determining the terms of our joint existence, must grapple.[41] A second difficulty with some of these criticisms is that these objections to dignity may simply be criticisms that are no different from those

---

[38] John Gray, *Black Mass: Apocalyptic Religion and the Death of Utopia* (London and New York, Penguin Books, 2008). See also John Gray, *Heresies: Against Progress and Other Illusions* (London, Granta, 2004).
[39] Conor Gearty, Chapter 8, this volume.
[40] Michael Rosen, Chapter 7, this volume.
[41] Aharon Barak, Chapter 20, this volume.

commonly applied to other concepts. Waldron, for example, considers that we should not be afraid of the possibility that dignity might be used on both sides of some important questions.[42] He argues that this is also true of liberty; indeed, it is true of almost every major value. Instead of being a criticism, it is a tribute to dignity that it might be engaged on both sides.

Dignity's functions

In light of this flexibility in its substantive meaning, the utility of dignity may lie more in the functions that it fulfils rather than in any uniqueness of meaning as a basic moral concept. Several of the contributors to this book focus, therefore, on the different *functions* of dignity. We have already encountered several functions that the concept of human dignity may fulfil. There is its political function as a flag under which the dispossessed unite and fight for freedom, equality, and basic resources. In this context, dignity becomes a useful vehicle for an expanding idea of empathy. In addition to Scott's case study of post-slavery organization, a good example of this is provided by Edwin Cameron's description of the use of dignity in providing a tool for combating discrimination on the grounds of sexual orientation in post-apartheid South Africa.[43] There is also human dignity as an institutional notion employed in a constitutional structure that confers on judges a certain discretion to make moral judgements, fleshing out the constitutional protection of human rights, proving a mechanism for providing some basic protection from political give and take, and also from utilitarian calculation.[44] If this is extended to the view about what law and legal actors *ought* to do, Denise Réaume appears to take a similar approach. For her, judges *ought* to use dignity this way.[45]

Although Bernhard Schlink, as we shall see, is sceptical whether dignity brings any significant added substantive meaning to many legal debates, he nevertheless argues that there is an important *functional* justification for holding onto human dignity as a concept.[46] Dignity, he argues, functions as *Sehnsuchtsbegriff*, a concept that encapsulates our yearning for a recognition and protection of humans that is not up for grabs (political grabs, balancing grabs).

---

[42] Jeremy Waldron, in discussion at the conference.
[43] Edwin Cameron, Chapter 27, this volume.
[44] Although, of course, the way in which any particular legal system structures the way in which courts interpret 'dignity' in this context is likely to differ. Contrast Barak, Chapter 20, this volume, with Dieter Grimm, Chapter 21, this volume.
[45] Denise Réaume, Chapter 32, this volume.
[46] Bernhard Schlink, Chapter 37, this volume.

It is characteristic of *Sehnsuchtsbegriff* that the *Sehnsucht*, the yearning that the concept of human dignity encapsulates, will never be fulfilled and that it will be often severely disappointed, but that we need it anyway. Because we all long for this recognition and protection, even though we do so in different ways, as moral philosophers, as lawyers, or as theologians, dignity functions as a concept around which we can meet and discuss. As we have seen, this was one of the underlying rationales for choosing the issue of dignity as the basis for the multidisciplinary conference that forms the basis for this book.

Schlink's argument hints at an important function that dignity may play, a function that has attracted recent scholarly attention and is also significantly reflected by other contributors to this book. This is the use of dignity as a vehicle for attempting to secure consensus in the face of disagreement about comprehensive positions or starting points. Rather than regarding dignity as a conversation stopper,[47] dignity becomes an occasion for dialogue, partly because it is a 'non-interpreted' thesis that nevertheless appeals to some undefined set of yearnings. Thus, in the scholarly literature and, indeed, in some of the jurisprudence and constitutional doctrine, it is sometimes said that one of the functional values that the concept of dignity fulfils is to provide a language in which conflicting values, and even conflicting rights, can be brought into relationship with each other, and this is reflected in several contributions.

For Reva Siegel[48] (and Paolo Carozza, using somewhat different language),[49] the possible good of dignity might be to keep 'agonists' in one conversation, rather than to supply technical directions about how these conflicting values and rights are to be accommodated.[50] Observing the structure of struggle around dignity, Siegel argues that a conversation among agonists, each of whom is committed to dignity, at least involves a common fidelity to dignity, even as they profoundly disagree about its entailments and about the forms of human flourishing to which dignity may refer. So, on that view, dignity's virtue is not that it provides answers but that it may create the conditions for the task of trying to look for an answer to, or at least an accommodation of, conflicting values and rights. Others are be more sceptical about the depth or acceptability of any integrative function that dignity may serve. For David Albert Jones, dignity plays a limited role in securing agreement in debates over abortion, where there is fundamental disagreement over the status of the

---

[47] Dieter Birnbacher's much-quoted observation that human dignity is a 'conversation stopper', see footnote 9.
[48] Reva Siegel, Chapter 30, this volume.
[49] Paolo Carozza, Chapter 36, this volume.
[50] 'Agonists' refers, in brief, to those who are sceptical about the likelihood that politics can surmount the most basic societal divisions, and that the principal issue is how to manage such divisions.

foetus.[51] There seems little point in keeping agonists in conversation when their conversation is premised on a false belief that they agree about anything in the first place.[52] It is a question of empirical judgement whether dignity actually does do any work in terms of helping us reconcile or accommodate competing claims.

Dignity as foundation and the foundations of dignity

Before considering those who take a different approach, seeing dignity as more than simply an empty vessel open to capture, or primarily as a functionally useful device for allowing dialogue between those who fundamentally disagree, an important distinction should be made. We have identified previously that for some the primary issue is whether and how far dignity provides a suitable foundation for other things, particularly for human rights law and practice. So, one critical set of debates is concerned with the issue of dignity as foundational. There is, however, an additional issue which others are more concerned to explore, which concerns the foundations of dignity; in other words, what is dignity based on and are these foundations secure? The latter set of debates can lead to frustration for those concerned with the former set of debates, because it seems to result in a never-ending cycle of explorations of foundations. For some concerned with the use of dignity as a foundation for human rights, as we have seen, the attraction of dignity is the extent to which it is a 'conversation stopper', a concept that neither requires nor permits any further digging. Those engaged in the exploration of the foundations of dignity, however, resist this approach, seeking to open up these foundations to further scrutiny and contestation.

Catholic debates: revisionism and anti-revisionism

Many religions consider dignity central to their understanding of what it means to be human, and there has been much recent writing exploring dignity from the perspective of various Christian traditions as well as from Jewish and Islamic perspectives.[53] The contributors to this book tend to focus mainly

---

[51] David Albert Jones, Chapter 31, this volume.
[52] Robert P. George, Chapter 29, this volume.
[53] See, for example, Behrouz Yadollahpour, 'Human dignity and its consequences in the Holy Qur'an', 2011 International Conference on Sociality and Economics Development, IPEDR vol. 10 (2011), 551; Susannah Heschel, 'Human dignity in Judaism', and Stephan Schaede, 'Ban on anthropological im-

(but not exclusively) on Catholic perspectives, if they consider religious arguments.[54] In recent years, the Catholic Church has been engaged in discussions about the nature and basis of human rights, drawing on the rich tradition of thinking about 'human dignity' by Catholic theologians. We are, then, not only at a key juncture as regards the legal and philosophical framework of human rights but also as regards its theological foundations. Theologians are increasingly engaging in discussions on how the notion of human dignity is to be understood from a religious perspective.

In this book, as was pointed out earlier, it is particularly the Catholic which is the most developed theological perspective. James Hanvey introduces the theology controversies and locates the Catholic approach,[55] including the idea of the human person being made in the image of God (*imago Dei*). Janet Soskice picks up on the importance of *imago Dei* and develops some of the implications.[56] David Walsh introduces the idea of eschatology[57] as a way of accessing the transcendence of the person in the context of debates about how to understand human dignity.[58] Tina Beattie extends this debate with the notion of the desacralized God.[59] David Gushee challenges the underlying assumptions of the engagement and offers an alternative approach.[60]

In order to understand these and other theologically oriented contributions in this book, it may be useful to set them in the context of some of the broader debates within the Catholic Church over human rights. Going back to 1948, as Moyn suggests, the founding documents of the internationalist strand of the modern human rights movement were influenced by Catholic thinking; not only by Catholic thinking, of course, because there were undoubtedly many influences in the drafting of the Universal Declaration. Given this diversity of viewpoints, the strategy adopted by those drafting the Declaration was to put to one side the deeply contested problems of where human rights come from, and what their foundations are, in favour of reaching a consensus about what specific fundamental rights could find universal acceptance. The role of Pope

---

ages and human dignity: some theological remarks', both presented at The Concept of Human Dignity in a Transatlantic Perspective: Foundations and Variations: A Berlin Dialogue on Transatlantic Legal Culture(s), Wissenschaftskolleg zu Berlin, 16–18 November 2011.

[54] See, in particular, David P. Gushee, Chapter 15, this volume.
[55] James Hanvey, Chapter 11, this volume.
[56] Janet Soskice, Chapter 12, this volume.
[57] The *Oxford English Dictionary* defines eschatology as: 'The department of theological science concerned with "the four last things: death, judgement, heaven and hell"', but its application here identifies the transcendence of all limits as the distinguishing feature of the person.
[58] David Walsh, Chapter 13, this volume.
[59] Beattie, Chapter 14, this volume.
[60] Gushee, Chapter 15, this volume.

John XXIII is critical in providing a bridge between this post-Second World War human rights discourse and the *magisterium* (the teaching of the Church), culminating in *Pacem in Terris*, the papal encyclical that did more than any other single document to signal a rapprochement between Catholic teaching and human rights developments at that time. This was subsequently confirmed and developed by the Second Vatican Council ('Vatican II') in *Gaudium et Spes*[61] and *Dignitatis Humanae*.[62]

During the 1960s, there was a significant opening up to human rights thinking. Why the Catholic Church was willing to adopt human rights thinking is still the subject of considerable historical investigation and interest, but in part it is likely that the human rights agenda was seen as having sufficient overlap with Church positions on issues of justice, welfare, and the common good to be worthy of support; that the Church's decline as a secular power resulted in greater self-awareness of the Church's moral voice in the world, a voice that could be articulated in the language of human rights; and that Catholic understandings of freedom of religion and conscience were partly articulated in human rights terms. It is also probable that the influential involvement of Catholics in the drafting of both the Universal Declaration of Human Rights and the European Convention on Human Rights in the late 1940s was seen as giving a seal of approval to the process, further underpinning the presumption that human rights would have little disruptive effect on Church doctrine and practice (not least because of the apparently strong protection for religious freedom within these human rights documents).

Given this apparent rapprochement, what needs to be explained is why there is now such a widely shared view inside and outside the Church that significant gaps have opened up between the Catholic *magisterium* and aspects of human rights thinking.[63] Now, more than sixty years after the Universal Declaration, deep questions are resurfacing as human rights language in law, philosophy, and theology, providing the arena in which rival conceptions of the human person and the common good of society become articulated and debated, in particular in the areas relating to gender and sexual orientation, but also in contexts relating to the beginning and end of life.

---

[61] For a discussion of the significance of these documents, see Hollenbach, Chapter 6, this volume, and Beattie, Chapter 14, this volume.
[62] Vatican Council II, *Dignitatis Humanae (Declaration of Religious Freedom)*, no. 2, in Walter M. Abbott and Joseph Gallagher (eds), *The Documents of Vatican II* (New York, America Press, 1966).
[63] For a preliminary attempt to identify where the tension lies, see Christopher McCrudden, 'Legal and Roman Catholic conceptions of human rights: convergence, divergence and dialogue?', *Oxford Journal of Law and Religion* 1 (2012), 185–201.

Support for human rights can be seen as an example of the difficulty the Church faces in reacting to aspects of modernity. Bernard Lonergan's 1967 essay is a useful starting point.[64] In it, he contrasts two modes of thinking about meaning, those characteristic of 'classical' and those characteristic of 'modern' culture, with the former being ahistorical and essentialist, secure in having a clear and accepted meaning, while the latter is more historical and inductive. Catholic moral theology, born in the former, is now confronted, according to Lonergan, with the latter world of meaning. Lonergan anticipated a split in Catholic theology in which 'a scattered left' develops, 'captivated by now this, now that new development, exploring now this and now that new possibility', in contrast with 'a solid right that is determined to live in a world that no longer exists'.[65]

John Langan, although using the terms 'revisionist' and 'anti-revisionist', has acknowledged a similar intuition.[66] The main factors making for revisionism are: the importance of historical conscientiousness; the general theological awareness that doctrine develops; the desire for a more culturally and psychologically sensitive pastoral practice; and the social distance between ecclesial authority and the profession of theology. The main factors making for anti-revisionism are: an essentialist, rule-oriented, and significantly biologistic conception of natural law as developed in neo-scholasticism, with a strong emphasis on its immutability and universality; and the assertion of papal authority in moral matters since the mid-nineteenth century (in the First Vatican Council), with a preoccupation on infallibility and the irreversibility of Church teaching.

This discussion is relevant for the issues of dignity because it puts into perspective several intellectual developments that took root in the late 1960s and contributed to opening up the perceived gap between the human rights movement and the Catholic Church. One of these involves developments within secular human rights and human dignity discourse itself, particular in the area of equality. With the increasing emphasis on racial and gender equality from the 1960s onwards, morphing into a more general concern to enable individual identities to be valued and protected, equality discourse took on a strongly individualistic, autonomy-based, anti-essentialist, and constructivist quality.

---

[64] Bernard Lonergan, 'Dimensions of meaning', in Frederick E. Crowe (ed.), *Collection: Papers by Bernard Lonergan, SJ* (New York, Herder and Herder, 1967), 252. I am grateful to James Hanvey, SJ for drawing this to my attention.
[65] Lonergan, 'Dimensions of meaning', 245.
[66] Personal communication on file with the author.

There are, of course, several different meanings that may be intended by the use of the term 'essentialist'. I use it here to refer to the idea that 'definitions are descriptions of the essential properties of things, and that one can evaluate attempts at definitions in terms of the falsity or truth of the descriptions given by them'.[67] Essentialism is now most used in the social sciences as a description of a position that is regarded as outdated, a term of criticism rather than approbation. As Simon Blackburn explains, 'Essentialism is used in feminist writing of the view that females (or males) have an essential nature (e.g. nurturing and caring versus being aggressive and selfish), as opposed to differing by a variety of accidental or contingent features brought about by social forces.'[68] Often such 'essentialism' is seen as based on biological determinism. It is this understanding that anti-essentialism seeks to challenge, viewing institutions and roles as socially constructed and provisional. In particular, *social identities* are seen as socially constructed and changeable. Human rights discourse and, to a notable extent, human rights law, has significantly (but by no means uniformly) adopted an anti-essentialist understanding of 'equality as dignity'.[69]

These revisionist and anti-revisionist approaches have both affected doctrine and practice within the Catholic Church since then, and to the extent that these approaches differ this has contributed to internal tensions. Some of these effects will be considered in a moment, but in one respect at least those adopting opposed positions within the Church do not differ. Both approaches are based on interpretations of 'natural law'; and those who adopt these approaches do not consider that either is narrowly 'religious', as both appeal to reason and the natural order. Before turning to consider some aspects of these debates, it should be also noted that there are four main sources of Catholic doctrine in addition to the *magisterium*, including biblical revelation, natural law, tradition, and human experience. This multiplicity of sources means that, taken together, they can be interpreted in a variety of ways that tell different stories about what that religion requires. Perhaps of particular significance, it means that these sources require sophisticated interpretation, and an important source of such interpretation is the work of current theologians.

---

[67] Entry on 'essentialism' in John Scott and Gordon Marshall, *A Dictionary of Sociology* (Oxford, Oxford University Press, 2009), http://www.oxfordreference.com/views/ENTRY.html?subview=Main&entry=t88.e745.

[68] Entry on 'essentialism' in Simon Blackburn, *The Oxford Dictionary of Philosophy* (Oxford, Oxford University Press, 2008), http://www.oxfordreference.com/views/ENTRY.html?subview=Main&entry=t98.e1139.

[69] T. Modood, 'Anti-essentialism, multiculturalism and the "recognition" of religious groups', *The Journal of Political Philosophy* 6 (1998), 378.

'New natural law' as anti-revisionism

Another set of intellectual developments affecting the relationship between the Catholic Church and human rights thinking concerns the idea of 'natural law', and the relationship between attempts to understand the concept of dignity and 'natural law'.[70] Although, as we have seen, 'natural law' is one of the sources of the Catholic *magisterium*, that does not make natural law 'religious', which is to confuse the idea of 'natural law' with the (other) beliefs of (some of) its adherents. The criticism has been made, understandably in some cases, that those espousing 'natural law' may interpret it in such a way as simply to justify the existing Catholic *magisterium*, rather than using natural law as an independent basis for assessing and contributing to the evolution of the *magisterium*, but the former is a misuse of 'natural law'. Those who purport to interpret 'natural law' do so, they say consistently, on the basis of practical reason, and those interpreting it and the conclusions they reach are therefore open to being criticized on the basis of practical reason.

Significant developments have taken place in discussions of 'natural law', which some would characterize as 'anti-revisionist'. From the early 1960s, there was a sustained attempt to rethink and reformulate the foundations of 'natural law' in a way that grew from and was seen by its proponents as consistent with Thomist approaches. One of the most influential of these attempts was what came to be called, originally by its critics but increasingly its proponents,[71] 'new natural law'.[72] 'New natural law', as articulated by a group of scholars around Germain Grisez, and including John Finnis and Robert George, became in practice a controversial anti-revisionist approach within the Church. 'New natural law' was seen by some elements of the Church hierarchy, particularly in the USA, as supportive of the more traditional elements of some of the existing *magisterium* and in turn to be supported and encouraged, particularly after the bitter controversy that arose within the Church on the publication of *Humanae Vitae*, the Papal Encyclical that continued the

---

[70] There is a large and complex literature on the meaning and implications of natural law. See, for example, the chapters by John Finnis and Brian Bix in Jules Coleman and Scott J. Shapiro (eds), *The Oxford Handbook of Jurisprudence and Philosophy of Law* (Oxford, Oxford University Press, 2002), at 1 and 61 respectively.

[71] Russell Hittinger, *A Critique of the New Natural Law Theory* (South Bend, IN, University of Notre Dame Press, 1987).

[72] See, for example, Nicholas C. Bamforth and David A. J. Richards, *Patriarchal Religion, Sexuality, and Gender: A Critique of New Natural Law* (Cambridge, Cambridge University Press, 2008). Hittinger's *Critique of the New Natural Law Theory* is from a Catholic and (arguably more orthodox than the new natural law) Thomist perspective.

prohibition on Catholics using contraception.[73] 'New natural law' is, however, a complex phenomenon, and not one that can be easily pigeonholed.

From the perspectives of those writing in the 'new natural law' tradition, represented in this book by George[74] and Tollefsen,[75] religious approaches to dignity and approaches based on natural law and practical reason must be kept quite distinct. Echoing Galileo's claim that the Church teaches how to go to heaven, not how the heavens go,[76] while deriving a moral norm is the business of practical reason, to the extent that that moral norm is dependent on science, then scientific understanding is determinative. Taken on its own, however, the scientific claim does not deliver the moral norm, otherwise there would be a considerable danger of falling into the naturalistic fallacy. For example, on issues such as when life begins, Tollefsen does not consider that there is any answer from a religious perspective to this question; indeed, for Tollefsen that is the wrong place to look for an answer. Instead, he argues, one should consider what scientists say on issues of embryology and embryological development. In the context of debates about abortion, whether we should regard the foetus as a 'human being' initially involves consideration of the scientific issues around the behaviour of the new organism (the human embryo) brought into being by the union of gametes (fertilization). The Church can teach that it is wrong to kill an innocent human being, but the scientific claim about when a human being's life begins is essential for applying that teaching at life's earliest stages.

Tollefsen's understanding of dignity, as we have noted earlier, is that it refers to a particular kind of excellence that each thing has. From this perspective, a lot of different things can be seen as having dignity. *Human* dignity involves recognition of the excellence that persons have; their inherent worth as persons. The issue is this: what is the basis on which such an idea of intrinsic dignity should be based? He considers that a capacities-based approach establishes the basis for intrinsic dignity in this sense. However, as Emily Jackson argued,[77] if humans are special because of their special characteristics, then what are the implications? Animals like dolphins, whales, and the great apes share some of those special characteristics, whereas persistently vegetative human beings do not. Why are the lives of animals not also in some sense sacred?

Tollefsen further distinguishes an ethical sense of dignity from a political sense of dignity. The ethical sense of dignity has two aspects: a task aspect

---

[73] As opposed to 'natural family planning', which is regarded as acceptable.
[74] Robert P. George, Chapter 29, this volume.
[75] Christopher Tollefsen, Chapter 28, this volume.
[76] G. Galilei, *Lettere* (Torino, Einaudi, 1978), 128–35.
[77] In discussion at the conference.

(what we need to live up to in order to realize the demands of our dignity) and the constraints that our dignity places on others. Similarly, the 'political aspect' of dignity has a task aspect (the politics that we need in order to fully realize our dignity as persons in community with others), and the constraints that our dignity, as both individuals and in community with others, creates relative to the state. Perhaps more straightforwardly, this conception of dignity thus entails both rights and obligations.

One structural feature that these instantiations of dignity, whether applied to things or to humans, have in common (other than both referring to an idea of excellence) is that if something can be excellent, or is excellent by nature, it can also typically fail with regard to its characteristic activity of excellence. It can fail with regard to what Tollefsen characterises as its 'task'. So, for example, if we think of the 'dignity of labour', we should view it not just as involving issues of what kinds of constraint that creates for other people, it should also involve consideration of what kind of obligations it creates for the people who are engaged in labour.

Catholic 'revisionism'

Hollenbach illustrates well elements of a more 'revisionist' approach within the Catholic tradition.[78] For Hollenbach, Vatican II appealed both to the creation of all persons in the image of God, based on revelation, and to the results of the use of human intelligence, to provide a basis for dignity. The grounds for human dignity based in revelation and those reached inductively based on practical reason illuminate each other rather than standing in conflict. Hollenbach argues that the interaction of reason and faith in shaping the Catholic understanding of dignity is a historical process, leading to notable revisions in the Catholic stance, and it will continue to do so. His strong emphasis on practical reason means that the Catholic Church should not be reaching premature decisions about complex questions of bioethics, for example, when there has not been a sufficient experience combined with reasoned reflection upon it to reach a conclusion about what human dignity demands.

This approach involves several different elements, all of which are controversial. An anti-revisionist critique of Hollenbach would argue that there is a tension between, on the one hand, being inductive, being responsive to history, and to the developmental aspects of Catholic understanding of how

---

[78] Hollenbach, Chapter 6, this volume.

dignity applies, and, on the other, retaining the appeal of dignity as universal. Indeed, going further, Hollenbach might be criticized for surrendering the religious to the secular, advocating that the Church should simply follow the movements of culture. Dignity would then become determined by society, with the Church simply tidying up afterwards.

This criticism assumes, however, that the Church is not now and has not always been deeply engaged with secular culture in developing its understanding of Church teaching, sometimes for the good and sometimes in unfortunate ways. Christianity started off in the first century AD, for example, with a very strong opposition to torture, but through the appropriation of Roman law came not only to endorse torture but to practise it. There are also examples, however, of progressive influences from secular culture that (sometimes grudgingly) led to significant changes in Church teaching, notably the acceptability of women in the workplace, and their right to be treated equally at work. So, too, the Church eventually reversed its position on torture, again influenced by developments in secular politics, and now declares that torture is one of the most fundamental violations of dignity of the person—an offence against God.

This change in teaching, in both cases, was influenced by the complex interaction between the Church and secular culture that led to changing understandings of dignity and its implications. For Hollenbach, the moral is not that the Church should refuse to engage with culture, but that its conclusions as to what to understand from that culture should be modest, and in particular that the Church should be very careful about coming to premature absolutes in situations where human experience is still fast evolving. For Hollenbach, this approach echoes Thomas Aquinas's awareness of the implications of natural law: that the most fundamental principles of natural law are evident to all reasonable people and are changeless, but that the *applications* of these fundamental principles may not be at all self-evident and are changeable.

Women, sexual orientation, and marriage

Given these differences between 'revisionist' and 'anti-revisionist' approaches, it is not surprising that Catholic understandings of the role of women and of the behaviour of gay men and women, as reflected in the writing of Catholic theologians, reflect a considerably greater plurality of viewpoints than those outside the Church sometimes appear to recognize; in particular, there are different understandings of the meaning and implications of dignity for such issues. To suggest otherwise is to impoverish a vibrant and (most importantly) *continuing* discussion within the Church. The major difference, for the purposes of this discussion at least, is in anthropological understanding. One key issue is that of sexual 'complementarity'. There is debate within the Church as to the appropriate understanding of this 'complementarity', and the result is a sharp dispute, *within* the Church, over what is required to ensure human flourishing. In the contributions to this book we see this tension vividly on display.

Dignity language is used on both sides of the internal debate,[79] and there is sharp disagreement as to what human dignity requires. Sometimes a revisionist understanding of dignity is evident, particularly in the social teaching of the *magisterium*, and sometimes an anti-revisionist approach to dignity is evident, particularly in some of the teaching of the *magisterium* in areas touching on gender and sexual orientation. The use of dignity within Catholic discourse (understood broadly) is sometimes confusing, often uncertain, and always evolving.

On the issue of same-sex marriage, for example, and whether the idea of 'marriage' should be used only in the context of the 'conjugal' (or as some would say 'procreative') conception of marriage, George's position is that this should not be a debate about religion.[80] No religion invented the conjugal conception of marriage. Religions can recognize it; they can give expression to it in their revelation, as the Hebrew Bible does in Genesis; but they did not create it. So, too, the state through the legal system cannot create it, although again the state can recognize it. The state can also abolish it by law, but the state cannot eliminate the reality, as he sees it, that marriage in this form and structure is a basic good of the human person. This idea of conjugal marriage is also supported, he argues, by other norms associated with marriage that have a long historical pedigree, including sexual fidelity, monogamy, and permanence of commitment.

As it is based on practical reason and human experience, one way of responding is to question how coherent the results of the reasoning undertaken by 'new natural lawyers' are. For example, we can consider whether the

---

[79] It is also used differently even within the various competing approaches. For example, different authors within 'new natural law' place somewhat different emphasis on the importance and centrality of dignity to their enterprise. John Finnis, treats it very briefly, for example in *Aquinas: Moral, Political, and Legal Theory* (Oxford, Oxford University Press, 1998), 176–80, whereas Patrick Lee and Robert George have given the concept much more extensive treatment and importance; see, for example, 'The nature and basis of human dignity', *Ratio Juris* 21 (2008), 173.

[80] For Robert George's views on the conjugal conception of marriage, see Sherif Girgis, Robert P. George, and Ryan T. Anderson, 'What is marriage?', *Harvard Journal of Law and Public Policy* 34 (2010), 245. This paper elicited criticisms from Kenji Yoshino, Andrew Koppelman, and Barrie Deutsch, among others. George and his co-authors responded to those criticisms in a series of online exchanges, and have turned these articles into a book which includes responses to critics, published as Sherif Girgis, Ryan T. Anderson, and Robert P. George, *What is Marriage?: Man and Woman: A Defense* (New York, Encounter Books, 2012).

procreative view of marriage is coherent by considering its possible implications, and challenge its apparent roots in long historical practice. From Tollefsen's and George's perspective, would it be wrong, for example, for those who are knowingly infertile or post-menopausal to marry? More importantly, if a person in a relationship with another has a condition such that they could not perform penetrative sex, would they be wrong to marry? Does it matter if consummation only became a condition of a valid marriage in the Middle Ages, meaning that the tradition has changed quite dramatically from an earlier tradition when celibate spiritual marriage was often seen as an ideal? Other questions may be raised about the implications of the argument that marriage is a basic good: if marriage is a basic good, why is it threatened by the extension of the same rights under law to same-sex people? Why does a 'procreative marriage' gain in strength from denying the right to marry to people who would choose a different understanding of marriage?[81]

However, for those supporting the retention of the concept of sexual complementarity in the conception of marriage, a set of questions arise if the idea of sexual complementarity as essential to marriage were to be abandoned. How is it that marriage is to continue to be understood as inherently a *sexual* partnership, as opposed to a partnership that might just as well be integrated around other (non-sexual) activities or mutual interests, depending on the subjective preferences of the spouses? What ground of principle can be adduced for regarding marriage as a union of two persons as opposed to three or more in polyamorous sexual relationships? What ground of principle can be identified (if any can be) for honouring the norms of monogamy, sexual exclusivity (fidelity), and a commitment to the permanence of the marital bond? Why should law and the state recognize and regulate marriages at all, as they have historically done, rather than treat them as private matters, the way they treat other friendships?

Beyond revisionism and anti-revisionism: Christian personalism

The dichotomy between revisionism and anti-revisionism is useful as a heuristic device, but can easily be overdone. Langan's reading of Lonergan can itself be contested. As described previously, Langan translates Lonergan's 'scattered left' and 'solid right' into the language of 'revisionism' and 'anti-

---

[81] These issues are similar to those raised by critics of the original article and are addressed in the forthcoming book of the same name, see previous footnote. John Finnis has also addressed some of these issues in his 'Sex and marriage: some myths and reasons', in *Collected Essays*, vol. 3: *Human Rights and Common Good* (Oxford, Oxford University Press, 2011), 353–88.

revisionism' (I have further exemplified Hollenbach as the former and 'new natural law' as the latter). But in the passage from which it is drawn, Lonergan criticizes both the 'scattered left' (as being too relativistic and uninterested in continuity) and the 'solid right' (as reactionary and living in the past). In describing the debate within the Catholic Church simply in terms of revisionism versus anti-revisionism, one may lose sight of the fact that both positions are open to criticism. Lonergan himself, crucially, proposes that 'what will count is a perhaps not numerous centre, big enough to be at home in both the old and the new, painstaking enough to work out one by one the transitions to be made, strong enough to refuse half-measures and insist on complete solutions even though it has to wait'. Neither 'revisionists' nor 'anti-revisionists' succeed in getting the whole picture right, and what some seek is 'to be at home in both the old and the new'.

This unease about dichotomy may explain why it is difficult to locate the popes in office immediately before Pope Francis (John Paul II and Benedict XVI) comfortably in either camp. (Pope Francis's approach may differ; it is too soon to tell.) These recent popes have been seen as representing a distinctly different theoretical approach that has been termed 'Christian personalism', which attempts to bridge the classical and the modern forms of thought in a way that is faithful to the notion of essence and to the notion of history. Walsh's chapter is implicitly in this tradition,[82] but Joel Harrison[83] and Clemens Sedmak[84] are the most explicitly 'personalist' in perspective, and readers unfamiliar with this tradition may welcome a brief account of why it is important to the issue of human dignity.

There is a very considerable variety of 'personalist' metaphysical approaches. The particular type of personalism that is the focus of attention here is in the form of 'Christian personalism' or Thomistic personalism, and is associated with French Catholic debates during the interwar period, in particular those involving Jacques Maritain. Thomas Williams has identified the core of personalism as a school of thought or intellectual movement that 'focuses on the reality of the person ... and on his unique dignity, insisting on the radical distinction between persons and all other beings (nonpersons)'.[85] But there is more to it than that. Williams sets out the distinctive characteristics of personalism as not only including 'an insistence on the radical difference between persons and nonpersons' and 'an affirmation of the dignity

---

[82] David Walsh, Chapter 13, this volume.
[83] Joel Harrison, Chapter 26, this volume.
[84] Clemens Sedmak, Chapter 33, this volume.
[85] Thomas D. Williams, *Who Is My Neighbor?: Personalism and the Foundations of Human Rights* (Washington DC, Catholic University of America Press, 2005), 108.

of persons' but also 'a concern for the person's subjectivity, attention to the person as object of human action to be treated as an end and never as a mere means, and particular regard for the social (relational) nature of the person'. Personalism, therefore, has been viewed not only as an important influence in strengthening the use of the concept of dignity within Catholicism but also, via Maritain, in contributing to the development of the Universal Declaration on Human Rights, in particular its emphasis on human dignity.

Today, personalism is seen as helping to bridge revisionism and anti-revisionism. In France during the interwar years, personalism was seen as bridging another divide. It 'arose as a reaction to impersonalist modes of thought which were perceived as dehumanizing',[86] whether based on radical collectivist ideologies, such as Communist and Marxist materialism, deterministic ideologies such as Nazism or racism, or radical individualism as espoused by utilitarians and Nietzsche. For Maritain, personalism was 'a phenomenon of reaction against two opposite errors (totalitarianism and individualism)'.[87] The rejection of totalitarianism is seen in the emphasis given to subjectivity (with its view of persons as free and responsible moral subjects, giving rise to the responsibility of others to respect this), and the prohibition on treating others as means rather than ends, with strong echoes of Kant.[88] The rejection of radical individualism is seen in the identification of the person in relationships, as a social being in community with others.

Maritain espoused a variety of 'personalism', although he distanced himself increasingly from some of those who claimed to be 'personalist' after the Second World War, particularly Edward Mounier. His disagreement with Mounier is of importance because it illustrates an important point about 'personalism': that the balance that personalism sought to retain between individualism and community left it open to 'capture' by *both* the political left and the political right. The communitarian left and right can claim that personalism supports an authoritarian world view;[89] the libertarian right and left can

---

[86] Thomas D. Williams and Jan Olof Bengtsson, 'Personalism', in *Stanford Encyclopedia of Philosophy*, online.

[87] John J. Fitzgerald, *The Person and the Common Good* (South Bend, IN, University of Notre Dame Press, 1985), 12–13.

[88] Robert P. Kraynak, 'The influence of Kant on Christian theology: a debate about human dignity and Christian personalism: a response to Derek S. Jeffreys', *Journal of Markets and Morality* 7:2 (2004), 533.

[89] Kevin Schmiesing puts the point well in *A History of Personalism* (1 December 2000), available at SSRN, at 17: 'Because the nature of personhood demanded sociality, Mounier believed that coercion might be employed to achieve that end. His idea of freedom as not merely the ability to choose, but the act of choosing rightly, lent itself to being distorted into a political principle that permitted governmental intervention to force citizens "to act freely". The importance of interpersonal cooperation and

claim that it supports autonomy. Maritain dissented from the direction that Mounier took personalism in the 1940s and 1950s because he considered that Mounier had taken personalism too far towards collectivism in the form of French communism.[90] But personalism could equally well have become the basis for a *rapprochement* between *conservative* forces and Catholic intellectuals. The very strength of personalism, its centredness, may be its fatal weakness, capable of veering from one to the other extreme when tested. The same weakness may be evident in its current use as a bridge between both 'revisionism' and 'anti-revisionism'.

Beyond practical reason: revelation, *imago Dei*, experience, mystery

Thus far, the emphasis has been squarely on those contributors who focus on the use of practical reason. Gushee's argument draws from an alternative Christian tradition that is Protestant and evangelical, focusing more on revelation and on divine command than Hollenbach, Tollefsen, and George.[91] Gushee sets the discussion of dignity in the context of a consideration of the sacredness of human life. For him, the sacredness of human life is rooted in the will of God. No reason is given for why God should decide to value human beings. It is not based on anything intrinsic about humans or their capacity (in contrast to Tollefsen). He does not argue that the value of a human being is not fixed or exalted, simply that its fixity and elevation is based on divine decision, command, and love, rather than on something about the human being itself that imbues it with intrinsic value. One reason for this move on Gushee's part is the danger that as soon as we identify a particular aspect of the human being as that which confers intrinsic value or dignity, its absence in a particular individual can then be taken as warrant for treating that human as less than sacred. Gushee's approach is thus a direct challenge to the capacities-based approach to human dignity suggested by Tollefsen. The obligations that flow from Gushee's approach are no less important. A person who believes Gushee's account is called to respond by adopting a posture that begins with reverence for the person, and by accepting responsibility for human life. It includes offering due respect and care to each human being that

---

the destructive nature of individualism, moreover, justified the use of state power for the purpose of enforcing social values in the economic sphere.'

[90] For a perspective on this controversy see John Hellman, 'The opening to the left in French Catholicism: the role of the personalists', *Journal of the History of Ideas* 34:3 (1973), 381.

[91] Gushee, Chapter 15, this volume.

we encounter and extends further to specific obligations to protect human life and to foster human flourishing.

The contrasts between Gushee's and Hollenbach's approaches are intriguing, and take us into complex debates. For Gushee, the sacredness of human life is simply a divine decision, and this appears to indicate a significant difference between Hollenbach and Gushee. Second, there is a distinct difference in the role that revelation plays, with Gushee emphasizing the importance of biblical sources for his argument, and Hollenbach concentrating more on practical reason. Third, unlike Hollenbach, Gushee does not consider that it is particularly helpful to draw on the concept of *imago Dei*, or at least not one based on the image of God as presented in Genesis.

As regards the role of *imago Dei*, the issue is to what extent, if at all, this provides an adequate basis for the intrinsic value of the human person. Traditionally, the core Christian notion of human dignity is to be found in the image of God, and Soskice considers that there are significant advantages in the concept of '*imago Dei*' over 'sanctity of life' as a guiding theological notion in end-of-life issues, for example.[92] *Imago Dei* is seen within Catholic teaching, in particular, as pointing in the direction of human beings as free and rational, and it is this that distinguishes human persons from others. Each and every person has an intrinsic value because of that. Sergio Dellavalle's critique of *imago Dei* points to the principal disadvantage of *imago Dei*'s close relationship with religion being its possible parochialism: an idea of dignity based on this understanding is accessible only to the adherents of a religious group, and seems to exclude others.[93]

There are, of course, several religions that have used the idea of the *imago Dei* in connection with developing an understanding of human dignity, but often in very different ways. Margalit introduces a Jewish reading of the Hebrew Bible's description of man being created in the image of God, in which human beings, and only human beings, are seen as icons of God.[94] This does not lead, however, to humans having intrinsic value because only God has intrinsic value. The value of humans is the reflected glory that human beings have, but they do not have intrinsic value. They have a value only as icons of something else that deserves adoration.[95]

---

[92] Soskice, Chapter 12, this volume.
[93] Sergio Dellavalle, Chapter 25, this volume.
[94] Margalit, 'Human dignity between kitsch and deification', 106–20.
[95] It is an interesting question whether the relational aspect that Margalit identifies necessarily rules out an idea that humans cannot have intrinsic value.

For Hanvey, an account based on the account of creation in Genesis presents an impoverished understanding of *imago Dei*.[96] Like Gushee, Hanvey prefers a broader reading of the canon that gives multiple sources for a claim to divinely conferred human dignity, one not just based on Genesis. A reading based only on Genesis does not take sufficiently into account the very substantial change in our understanding of *imago Dei*, rooted in Christian tradition, particularly the teachings of Augustine, who links the idea of *imago Dei* with the idea of the Trinity, that is the idea that God is three 'persons' in unity. If one believes that God is Trinity, then in what sense are humans, created in the image of God, also Trinitarian? For Hanvey, in contemplating and reflecting on the nature of the 'persons' in the Trinity, the concepts of reciprocity, mutuality, and equality can all be derived, thus contributing significantly to a richer understanding of human dignity. For Hanvey, then, the human person is not an icon in the sense used by Margalit. The human person is not a *representative* of God—or a carrier or cipher of God's holiness; the human person from the Christian perspective possesses the *imago Dei* as part of their being. It can be debased, it can be effaced; but it cannot be lost, and this, according to Hanvey, carries a meaning that is ontologically stronger than that presented by Margalit.

There are much deeper divisions between the contributors than over the meaning and the role of *imago Dei*. At this point, we can return to consider criticisms that have been levelled at dignity, including by Rosen.[97] Several criticisms identify what, if they are true, are unambiguously dark aspects that appear to be specific to dignity: that it is a kind of façade; that it provides a false consolation for inequality; that it is a Trojan horse for religiously inspired attacks on various aspects of liberalism, such as equality; and that dignity justifies attacks on autonomy, understood as the power of choice.[98] Often linking these criticisms of dignity is the frequently expressed view that the relationship between organized and hierarchical religions and the use of dignity has been in the past, and remains currently, somewhat problematic.

As we have seen, Douzinas argues that human rights and dignity are historically contingent terms, with significant shifts in their meaning depending on their contexts, and always vulnerable to co-option on the side of abusive power.[99] In particular, Christianity's universalization of the term 'human', he argues, has lent legitimacy to the West's colonial violence, and this has contin-

---

[96] James Hanvey, Chapter 11, this volume.
[97] Rosen, Chapter 7, this volume.
[98] The use of dignity-language in new natural law would be likely to feature as an example of the dark side of dignity by critics of that approach.
[99] Douzinas, *Human Rights and Empire*.

ued even when human dignity became secularized. Beattie contrasts Douzinas and Gushee.[100] For Douzinas, Christianity is part of the problem, and Marxist, Nietzschean, and Freudian perspectives offer a vantage point for criticism. However, for Beattie, Douzinas may be thought to be too monochrome and pessimistic in his telling of history, for he fails to acknowledge how often Christianity has inspired the very kind of revolutionary visions for which he calls. Gushee, on the other hand, while recognizing that history offers plenty of harrowing examples of Christianity abandoning its own best theology and ethics, nevertheless considers Christianity to offer the solution, and Nietzsche and Nihilism to be the problem.[101] The task of the Christian intellectual is, Gushee suggests, to retrieve the richness of the sacredness of human life from the thinner versions that secularism offers.

The contrasts between Hollenbach and Gushee also raise directly the relationship between debates within theology and debates external to theology, and the relative importance of revelation to each. Gushee argues that the norms regarding the sacredness of human life are rooted in the Old and New Testaments, which includes the idea of the image of God in Genesis but goes beyond it. This is a richer, thicker concept than secular conceptions of dignity, he argues. Leaving to one side whether the sacredness of human life is rooted in biblical texts, there is a significant difference between them as to whether secular conceptions of dignity are being developed that may have their own richness without being mere pale imitations of the religious. The principal issue dividing Hollenbach and Gushee involves a disagreement over the appropriate relationship between the sacred and the profane in theological development.

Walsh argues that there are movements of the Spirit in the world outside Church and religion, and part of the way the Church has been called to account is by moral advances within secularization, especially within the realm of rights and dignity.[102] The language of rights and dignity, he argues, has become an external moral challenge to Christianity. For Hanvey also,[103] secularization is not necessarily seen as bad, since it too is to be regarded as the work of the Holy Spirit, and the Church is obliged to follow the Good wherever it occurs. Hanvey argues that theology should develop its own self-critique. Vital to that self-critique are secular liberal understandings of dignity. Theology needs a secular understanding as well as a theological understanding if it is to keep true to itself. Beattie goes further, in calling for 'the abroga-

---

[100] Beattie, Chapter 14, this volume.
[101] Gushee, Chapter 15, this volume.
[102] Walsh, Chapter 13, this volume.
[103] Hanvey, Chapter 11, this volume.

tion of the idolatry of power that has been perpetuated through theology itself, in … [an] unholy alliance between patriarchal and/or imperial domination and Christianity's God'.[104]

It would be misleading, however, to underemphasize the tensions between secular philosophical and religious understandings of dignity. Vining's contribution is a good starting point for exploring this tension.[105] He suggests that the individual we perceive is something more than the product exclusively of two factors usually identified (genetic and environment, nature and nurture, as those terms are now widely used). There is, he suggests, a third element, either implicit or sometimes given a name, which goes beyond reason, thus challenging those who see reason as the only way of approaching the concept of persons or of their dignity.

Hanvey's contribution is also a challenge to an over-concentration on the role of reason in theology.[106] For Hanvey, theology must always begin in humility before a truth that it cannot fully grasp and a reality that it cannot fully know or exhaust. It is always a struggle to understand. Although Hanvey clearly values rational argument, he argues that theology should never forget the limits of reason. The fact that theology cannot grasp the mystery of what it seeks to understand is not an occasion of despair, or an occasion of self-criticism. Nor is the understanding that human dignity is in some sense a mystery in any way a conversation stopper; dignity's capacity for inexhaustible meaning allows, encourages, indeed *requires* further conversation.

An emphasis on 'mystery' is also embedded in Sedmak's contribution.[107] Sedmak adopts an understanding of human dignity as a requirement to treat people as human beings rather than as objects. Treating people as objects leads to two particular problems: first, we lose the sense of what he terms the 'interiority of the person'. Rather than seeing the depth of the person, one sees the person as if he or she was a table or a chair. Second, he suggests, we lose an appreciation of the importance and the role of vulnerability, and we end up abusing the most vulnerable. Appreciating vulnerability provides an insight into our own human nature. Thinking about our own vulnerability gives us a deep first-person insight into how we are, who we are, and what human beings in general are. Vulnerability also provides a litmus test: how we deal with the most vulnerable members of society tests our commitment to dignity. Interiority, for Sedmak, can give us a deeper sense of self-respect, but it also, and this

---

[104] Beattie, Chapter 14, this volume.
[105] Vining, Chapter 34, this volume.
[106] Hanvey, Chapter 11, this volume.
[107] Sedmak, Chapter 33, this volume.

is the link to Hanvey's reflections, gives us a sense of the inner structure of the person, and of the person's *mystery*.

We have seen earlier that one of the criticisms levelled at dignity by secular thinkers is that dignity is based on a religious understanding of the person, and of the person's relationship with the divine. In terms of the contributions to this book, that key issue is raised most prominently by those contributors writing about the relationship between dignity and freedom of religion. For Rivers,[108] for example, dignity needs a theological referent to do the work of protecting freedom of religion, and one that probably needs to be grounded in some sort of minimal theism if it is to escape the current trend towards autonomy-based justifications for state burdening of religious practice. Freedom of religion needs more than merely the capacity to construct a subjective understanding of the divine; it needs to presuppose the capacity actually to relate to the divine.

Philosophical debates

References to 'mystery' and to 'minimal theism' have important implications for the relations between theological and philosophical understandings of dignity. John Tasioulas, for example, distinguishes between religious propositions that are accessible to natural reason from those that are not, and asks what is the added value of a faith that cannot be vindicated by natural reason.[109] In particular, even if there is an added value that religion brings to dignity, does it have a valid political role to play if it is specifically based on faith considerations that cannot be backed up by natural reason? From Tasioulas's philosophical perspective, religious reasons can be relevant in understanding human dignity but only to the extent that they can be 'cashed out' in terms of reasons (the term is his). In any political context, one would have to say that texts embodying dignity language contain something that can be expressed, and defended rationally. Talk of 'mystery' clearly complicates this analysis.

Scepticism of dignity because it is seen as dependent on religious understandings of the person is also seen when it is viewed as dependent on a metaphysics that is not explicitly religious. Rosen, for example, is dismissive of Immanuel Kant's understanding of dignity for this reason, viewing Kant as conceiving of dignity as a 'transcendental kernel'.[110] The problem for Rosen is

---

[108] Rivers, Chapter 23, this volume.
[109] Tasioulas, in discussion at the conference.
[110] Rosen, *Dignity*.

that this would mean that Kant derives his ethical belief from unsupportable, obscure, and non-empirical metaphysics. Thomas Hill, however, challenges this assessment as incorrect.[111] Although he accepts that there is a 'widely shared impression' that Kant's understanding of dignity is 'hopelessly mired in an obscure and untenable metaphysics', and that this is 'understandable', this view is nevertheless misguided. Kant's understanding of dignity, argues Hill, is not a mysterious metaphysical 'kernel' from which we derive our belief in the moral law and its practical applications. Not even in his so-called 'metaphysics of morals' does Kant actually try to base morals on metaphysics, as traditionally conceived.

In this consideration of different ways of understanding human dignity, we have moved decisively to consider those contributors who focus on attempts to pin down more precisely what they see as the substantive content of human dignity, and who view it as having significant added value in normative ethics. Jones, for example, argues that dignity adds something uniquely valuable to debates on assisted suicide and abortion that is not reducible to other principles.[112] We shall be looking now at how contributors from the disciplines of philosophy and law consider this, but before turning to these individual disciplines and the debates within each of them, it may be useful to set out several broad alternative approaches that are frequently adverted to in these disciplines.

Broadly, three alternative approaches to the study of normative ethics are often distinguished. One approach, well known at least in outline, emphasizes the consequences of actions, and often involves the adoption of a utilitarian approach to problem-solving, asking whether one or other solution will maximize well being (however that is conceived). A second approach, which is commonly characterized as a 'deontological' approach, emphasizes duties, or rules, and sometimes rights. A deontological perspective would consider whether a proposed solution to a problem involves acting according to one or more appropriate moral obligations. A third approach, relatively neglected in modern ethics but attracting increased interest in recent years, as discussed by Soskice,[113] is termed 'virtue ethics'. This is the view that says that what is fundamental in ethics is not principles of conduct but excellences of character (virtues), and the emphasis is on the exercise of these virtues, which its proponents would say are more broadly conceived than in consequentialism or deontology; these virtues are not only important, they are foundational. Each

---

[111] Thomas Hill, Chapter 17, this volume.
[112] Jones, Chapter 31, this volume.
[113] Soskice, Chapter 12, this volume.

of these broad approaches (consequentialism, deontology, and virtue ethics) is more in the nature of a group of theories rather than one central theory, and this (very) brief outline raises serious issues, of course, which go far beyond the topic of this book. These complex issues need not detain us, however, not least because none of the philosophical contributors to this book fits entirely comfortably within any of these three commonly identified approaches when discussing dignity.

Tasioulas's approach to dignity is grounded in a richly developed philosophical approach that is offered as an alternative to all of these.[114] Both Kantianism (as a form of deontology) and utilitarianism are, he considers, act-focused theories, concentrating on the question of what is the right act to perform. For Tasioulas, there is a prior question: how to view things correctly before one proceeds to action. On this distinction hangs much of Tasioulas's analysis, and it is therefore important to point out that the distinction is a controversial one, in the sense that not all would support his apparently sharp distinction between acting and preparing to act.

Assuming that there is such a distinction, however, how should we describe Tasioulas's position? There is no generally accepted term for this perspective, distinct from deontology, consequentialism, and virtue ethics, but the one that Tasioulas has used in the past (as has James Griffin) is 'teleology'.[115] Unlike classic deontology, for example in Kant, teleological views treat the human good as basic in morality, and believe that moral norms are in some sense derived from considerations about the good. Unlike consequentialism, teleological views do not assert that only consequences, and not the intrinsic nature of acts, matter morally. Unlike virtue ethicists, virtues are not morally foundational, even though they are important. What *is* foundational for teleology is considerations of human good and human flourishing.

Tasioulas's philosophical conception of dignity is that it is an intrinsically valuable status possessed by all human beings simply in virtue of their humanity, and discoverable by ordinary moral reasoning or through natural reason. One of the things one needs to see correctly before acting, he argues, is the intrinsic value of other people, in other words their human dignity. All human beings have an intrinsic worth as human beings, and their interests count equally and are not to be subject to certain kinds of interpersonal trade-offs. There is undoubtedly a distance to travel from that perception to the identification of what the precise practical implications of this insight are, and this requires practical wisdom, but at least it seems to satisfy the need to

---

[114] Tasioulas, Chapter 16, this volume.
[115] See John Tasioulas, 'Taking rights out of human rights', *Ethics* (2010), 675–8.

produce a comprehensive theory that incorporates the idea that human rights are grounded in dignity. Where Tasioulas differs from other proponents of this idea is in his insistence that dignity alone is insufficient to justify the familiar schedule of human rights, and that in addition we have to invoke universal human interests as grounding values.

At the level of moral reason in a purely formal sense, virtue also figures in Roger Brownsword's reflections on human dignity, but, like Tasioulas, he would not consider himself to be a virtue ethicist.[116] For Brownsword, 'the moral' (whether as in a 'moral community' or a 'moral way of life') commits its adherents to trying to do the right thing for the right reason. For moral persons, the focal virtue, we might say, is to try to do the right thing for the right reason.[117] However, once we declare our favoured criterion in relation to doing the right thing, Brownsword adopts a deontological approach (specifically a Gewirthian rights approach):[118] we should try to respect the rights of others (this being the right thing) for the reason that this is the right thing to do.[119]

The demand that human dignity be respected can be equated with the 'moral' in this sense. For Brownsword, this moral command is unlikely to have any real chance of being followed in practice unless there is a supportive societal context. He considers that the context in which we try to do the right thing for the right reason is currently unsupportive in two respects. The first is that the colonizing effect of the risk society and its risk-focused discourse makes it difficult to raise certain sorts of moral concerns.[120] The second arises from the fact, as he sees it, that new technologies present regulators with huge opportunities to manage environments that fundamentally change the way in which individuals are directed and channelled, so that even if we do the right thing we are no longer doing it freely or for the right reason. In this respect, we may see one of Brownsword's primary concerns in practice is a concern with autonomy.[121]

---

[116] Roger Brownsword, Chapter 19, this volume.

[117] Roger Brownsword, 'Human dignity, biolaw, and the basis of moral community', *Journal International de Bioethique* 21 (2010), 21–40.

[118] Alan Gewirth, 'Human dignity as the basis of rights', in Michael J. Meyer and William A. Parent (eds), *The Constitution of Rights: Human Dignity and American Values* (1992), 10–28; Alan Gewirth, 'Are there any absolute rights?', in J. Waldron (ed.), *Theories of Rights* (Oxford, Oxford University Press, 1984), 91–109.

[119] Roger Brownsword, *Rights, Regulation, and the Technological Revolution* (Oxford, Oxford University Press, 2008).

[120] Roger Brownsword, 'Human dignity and nanotechnologies: two frames, many ethics', *Jahrbuch für Recht und Ethik* 19 (2011), 429–39.

[121] Roger Brownsword, 'Lost in translation: legality, regulatory margins, and technological management', *Berkeley Technology Law Journal* 26 (2011), 1321–65.

Dignity as freedom or autonomy is a popular conception of dignity, particularly in the USA. There is a stronger version of this argument, and a weaker version. Some appear to consider that dignity is simply autonomy (the strong argument), while others would not put the argument that strongly, considering it to be one strand that is worth emphasizing in particular contexts. Siegel considers that one of the crucial ways in which those in favour of decriminalizing abortion in the United States and Germany conceptualized their claim was in this form.[122] So, too, we can see in the argument advanced by Cameron that a similar conception of dignity, one based on the importance of protecting particularly important choices, was adopted in the context of claims that criminalizing same-sex sexual conduct in post-apartheid South Africa was unconstitutional.[123] Similarly, social and economic rights are sometimes seen as necessary because they attend to those material needs of the human individual that help to guarantee an individual's authentic capacity to choose; this also arises in Réaume's discussion.[124] In all these instances, human dignity is seen as in a certain sense protecting and instantiating a dimension of human autonomy.

One prominent philosophical version of this has been advanced by Griffin, who in a recent important book argued that human dignity is not a kind of basic moral status, the intrinsic worth of being a human being (as Tasioulas interprets it), but rather consists in one particular interest, an interest in freedom.[125] Tasioulas outlines several difficulties with this approach, but there are essentially two.[126] First, it seems to present an impoverished understanding of the grounds of human rights to see them as purely protecting freedom. So, from Griffin's perspective, the reason why torture constitutes a violation of human rights is that it undermines the capacity of the person tortured to make decisions and stick to them. Tasioulas considers that the fact that torture is incredibly painful is not, in Griffin's argument, relevant to it being a violation of human rights, and that this is fundamentally mistaken. Second, Tasioulas argues, a focus exclusively on freedom means that human rights standards do not protect human beings incapable of agency.

An emphasis on dignity as freedom and autonomy alone also appears to pose significant difficulties as a foundation for a significantly robust understanding of freedom of religion. The chapters by Rivers, Dellavalle, Riordan,

---

[122] Siegel, Chapter 30, this volume.
[123] Cameron, Chapter 27, this volume.
[124] Réaume, Chapter 32, this volume.
[125] James Griffin, *On Human Rights* (Oxford, Oxford University Press, 2008).
[126] John Tasioulas's extended critique of Griffin's position is 'Taking rights out of human rights', *Ethics* 120 (2010), 647–78.

and Harrison explore this theme. Rivers sets out the area of debate, and Dellavalle, Riordan, and Harrison make a case for three different options for addressing the issue: a richer notion of the good of religion (Riordan), a richer notion of moral autonomy and discursive community (Dellavalle), and a broadened theologically informed notion of the human person (Harrison).[127]

Dellavalle examines received accounts of the human on which the assertion of dignity has been grounded.[128] As we have seen, he finds wanting the familiar theological notion of the human as *imago Dei* since it tends to invoke a particular religious experience of a specific community in relation to its God, which is not accessible to members of other communities. Dellavalle also considers the modern account of the human in terms of autonomy and conscience to be inadequate, since while it can ground an important value of toleration and a protection of a sphere of negative liberty, it does not offer a basis for recognition in the sense of a positive valuing of the plurality of religious expressions. It is this theme of recognition that moves Dellavalle to favour a communicative understanding of the human, following Habermas among others. But is Dellavalle's preferred communication action account vulnerable to the same kind of criticisms he has himself aimed at the *imago Dei* model, namely the inevitable exclusion of those who do not share the enlightenment rationality presupposed by Habermas or the skills of articulate debate? Could an account of an ideal type of discourse supplant the actual discourse between proponents of different positions on the meaning of dignity, in particular as it grounds the promotion and protection of the freedom of religion?

Taking a different tack, Patrick Riordan also finds flaws in the grounding of dignity in the exercise of autonomous choice.[129] Drawing on Ronald Dworkin's account of dignity as rooted in the human freedom to make life-shaping choices, Riordan highlights the implications of this for the further level of debate in the grounding of rights. This grounding of dignity can possibly result in the elimination of the freedom of religion as a distinct right among the list of basic human rights, since religion is interpreted as one life choice among others, and given the freedoms of conscience, of speech, and of assembly, requires no distinctive protection. Countering this tendency, Riordan argues for an ontological grounding of dignity in an account of the kind of being that humans are, one more open to the distinctiveness of religion as a form of life, not reducible to a choice. But is Riordan's hoped-for ontology

---

[127] I am grateful to Julian Rivers for this summary.
[128] Dellavalle, Chapter 25, this volume.
[129] Patrick Riordan, Chapter 24, this volume.

sufficiently robust to resist the charges of essentialism directed at previous attempts?

Rivers also reacts against the narrowing of the understanding of religion when the freedom of religion is understood in terms of a dignity founded on individual freedom.[130] He points to two dangers arising from this tendency. When religion is interpreted as a personal life-choice, nowadays often labelled one's spirituality, it becomes privatized and is deprived of political and legal relevance. The second dimension of religion in danger of being excluded is its social and communal nature. Religion is institutionalized in various forms, and as such plays a significant part in civil society, but when its communal and institutional nature is denied, religion is disarmed as a countervailing power to the influence of the state.

Harrison similarly argues that the autonomy account of dignity, and consequently religious liberty, undermines religious groups as sites of authority pursuing particular social ends beyond self-determination.[131] In contrast to Dellavalle's communicative understanding, he contends that religious liberty discourse faces competing political and social imaginaries (drawing from Charles Taylor). He argues that the autonomy-centred vision of dignity, focusing on equal concern and respect, construes society and religious groups as existing for the facilitation of individual interests. He then points to an alternative vision of dignity, drawn from Christian personalism. Here, persons are understood as a gift, cohering in groups outside the state in pursuit of desirable and even transcendental ends.

What are the implications for practical decision-making of these and other critiques of autonomy-based dignity beyond the debate on freedom of religion? One effect is likely to be that previous justifications based in autonomy may have to be rethought more widely. Sedmak would have us emphasize much more the importance of relationality rather than autonomy in our understanding of dignity.[132] Socio-economic rights would be rethought, for example, as protecting *relational* aspects of human flourishing in order to maximize the recognition and protection of our dignity, rather than as protecting the exercise of autonomy.[133] This is not to say that a relational approach is incapable of coexisting with all understandings of autonomy. A focus on

---

[130] Rivers, Chapter 23, this volume.
[131] Harrison, Chapter 26, this volume.
[132] Sedmak, Chapter 33, this volume.
[133] A point made by Paolo Carozza in oral discussion. A World Bank study in 1999, *'Can Anyone Hear Us?'*, emphasized how poverty encourages relationships to break down, with increased incidence of household breakdown, friendship breakdown, marriage breakdown, parental–children relationship breakdown; all examples where economic deprivation leads to a breakdown of relationality.

autonomy does not have to adopt a conception of the individual as ruggedly individualistic. Indeed, one can argue that autonomy often results from the existence of certain kinds of supportive relationships.

Whether consistent with autonomy or not, relationality may be useful in other contexts. For Rivers, for example, underestimating the importance of relationality is central to the weakness of current conceptions of dignity as a legal foundation for freedom of religion. Harrison takes this further, arguing that a personalist understanding of the person as 'gift' points towards a stronger associational account of religious liberty. It might also help us appreciate different ways of reinterpreting famous instances in which dignity is perceived as unduly antagonistic to autonomy interests, where dignity sometimes appears as a restriction on liberty for paternalistic reasons (for example, prohibiting dwarf-throwing).[134] On closer inspection these may appear to be more about restricting the perceived adverse impact of a social practice on *other* people who belong to a category that is subject to discrimination or low status. The prohibition based on dignity is to protect that larger category, rather than paternalistically trying to tell the individual whose actions are restricted that the society knows best for them.

As we saw earlier, Sedmak adopts an understanding of human dignity as a requirement to treat people as human beings rather than as objects, emphasizing how important the loss of the 'interiority of the person' can be. But how central should ideas of subjectivity be to the concept of dignity? To argue that one should pay attention to subjective experience is not necessarily to argue that this is all that matters. When somebody neglects another person, whether it is neglecting their hunger or leaving them naked in a wheelchair outside the bathroom of an old people's home, it is arguable that this is more than simply a failure to respect the 'interiority of the person'. The essence of the concern with dignity, some argue, is the indignity being offered to the human being who is naked or hungry, whether that human being is conscious of the indignity or not. For some, and we see this in Margalit's discussion of humiliation,[135] what dignity does is not just protect people from the experience of a collapse of self-esteem or being ignored but from the actual harm itself. So when an army jeep drags a corpse around the square of a village, wouldn't we consider this as inhuman treatment of the parents and an infringement of

---

[134] Conseil d'Etat, 27 October 1995, Commune de Morsang-sur-Orge, no. 136727, Rec. Lebon 372, *Commune de Morsang-sur-Orge v Société Fun Production et M Wackenheim*. See further: Communication No. 854/1999, *Wackenheim v France*, UN Doc. CCPR/C/75/D/854/1999 (2002).
[135] Margalit, 'Human dignity between kitsch and deification', 106–20.

the dignity of the dead man?[136] Shouldn't we also treat with dignity those who have lost consciousness and those with dementia, who possess no interiority?

Does the idea of humiliation come closer to the core sense of what dignity involves, as argued by Margalit? Notice four implications of the move to consider humiliation as a key to understanding dignity. First, we have moved away from the idea that the search for dignity involves trying to understand what it is about humans that involves intrinsic value, towards a different understanding, what some have called 'attributed dignity', where the issue is rather how we regard other people and act towards them. The second implication of a move to humiliation is that we have moved from a positive understanding of dignity towards a negative understanding of dignity: those who support humiliation as the key stress the importance of considering what constitutes *in*dignity, rather than trying to understand what constitutes dignity. The third implication is that concentrating on humiliation involves an expressive conception of indignity. That is to say, we should act towards others not just in ways that are objectively good, in some mechanistic and impartial way, but in ways that are expressive of respect, somewhat similar to the meaning of dignity that Rosen adopts.[137] The fourth implication is that there is a strong emphasis in the humiliation approach of considering what duty requires rather than what rights require.

Several potential problems with this understanding of dignity might be identified. First, if dignity is thought to be the foundation of human rights, humiliation cannot be a comprehensive foundation for rights. If what one is trying to think through is the idea of dignity and its relation to human rights, adopting a humiliation-based understanding quickly demonstrates that all those who say that human rights have a foundation in dignity are mistaken, because one cannot derive all those rights from dignity, understood as humiliation. So if one is trying to make best sense of human rights practice, an alternative understanding of dignity is necessary.[138] Second, we have seen that humiliation involves a duty-based perspective, but this raises the further question of *why* we owe that duty to other human beings. Why do we have a duty not to humiliate them? In particular, do those who believe in attributed dignity have to believe also in some notion of intrinsic dignity in order to identify to whom the duty not to humiliate is owed? Is it possible to believe in attributed dignity without also accepting intrinsic dignity?

---

[136] *Tachiona v Mugabe*, 169 F.Supp 2d 259, 313 (SDNY 2001).
[137] Rosen, *Dignity*. For a discussion of expressive approaches to dignity, see Tarunabh Khaitan, 'Dignity as an Expressive Norm: Neither Vacuous nor a Panacea', *Oxford Journal of Legal Studies* 32 (2012), 1.
[138] A point made in oral comments by John Tasioulas.

So far, we have considered three main ways in which different contributors have sought to capture the idea of human dignity: as the concept we use to describe the intrinsic value of the person; as essentially protecting autonomy; and as that which a person has when not humiliated by others. The fourth principal philosophical understanding of dignity considered in this book is as a protected status or, more accurately perhaps, the attribution of dignity as the expression of moral status. Viewing this understanding as truer to its historical roots, Waldron argues in his recent book that modern understandings of dignity take the intuition that dignity is about status and combine it with modern commitments to equality.[139] In his chapter in this book, Waldron returns to consider how to navigate between an egalitarian idea of human dignity and the idea of *dignitas*, connected with hierarchy, rank, and office.[140] One possible way of bridging the gap between the two, he argues, is to talk of *the dignity of the citizen*. In modern republics and democracies, he suggests, the dignity of the citizen extends to a large sector of the population and connotes something about the general quality of the relation between the government and the governed. Though the dignity of the citizen and human dignity are not the same concept, he argues that they are congruent in many respects; and the former casts considerable light on the latter.

Rosen is sceptical of Waldron's equal status-based conceptions of dignity. Quoting Gilbert and Sullivan's *The Gondoliers* ('When everybody's somebody then nobody's anybody'), he argues that levelling up is often pretty meaningless. For Waldron, however, this criticism misses the mark.[141] We can easily imagine situations where high-ranking people in society have a vote, low-ranking people don't, and then we decide to give the vote to everybody. We decide to treat everybody as having the high rank. Or, to take another example, high-ranking people are punished humanely and allowed to give evidence freely in court, but low-ranking people are punished savagely and give evidence only under torture, and then we decide to confer the high rank on everybody.

It is unclear, however, how far this response deals with Rosen's criticism of Waldron. Adopting an egalitarian, status-based conception of dignity requires a decision as to which of the characteristics of high status are going to be attributed to people when everybody has this high status. Clearly, if those with high status have previously required their dignity to be recognized by having people kowtow to them, then we are unlikely to want to generalize that

---

[139] Waldron, *Dignity, Rank, and Rights*.
[140] Waldron, Chapter 18, this volume.
[141] Jeremy Waldron, in discussion at the conference.

requirement to everyone. In addition, the idea that we can generalize high-status privileges may misunderstand the nature of the privilege in question; at least some privileges require there to be inequality. So which aspects of a high status are the ones that are essential to that high status, and therefore part of one's dignity? Finally, equal status is seldom presented as a comprehensive theory of dignity, even by its supporters, and the equal status idea may itself be based on the notion of an inner kernel of value, which is then recognized by according equal status.

Human dignity and human rights

The philosophical debates frequently touch on the relationship between dignity and human rights, and it is to a more systematic consideration of this relationship that we now turn. What is the added value that dignity might bring to discussion about the foundations of human rights, if, indeed, it has any value at all? The previous paragraphs made certain assumptions that now require further consideration: that there is a foundational vacuum in human rights, and that this is problematic and should be addressed; that human dignity and human rights are connected, and that this relationship may provide a foundation for more specific ethical principles articulated in the form of rights. What should we make of these arguments?

Initially, we need to consider a preliminary, more pragmatic, question. Assuming that there is a significant absence of agreement on the foundations of human rights, and that human rights are generally thought to be 'a good thing', should this absence of agreement be unmasked? On the one hand, one may take the position that, powerful though myths may be, not making clear the foundations of human rights is more likely to undermine the human rights project in the longer term than is exposing the existing uncertainties about what those foundations might be. Not all agree, however, and some appear to adopt a different strategy: that we should just deliberately fool ourselves (and, by implication, others) into believing that there are such foundations of belief; we should call a halt to unmasking and start remasking.[142]

A related issue is what standard such foundations would have to meet in order to fulfil the task required of them. Richard Rorty has, in the eyes of some,[143] inflated the idea of what a foundational explanation for human rights

---

[142] See Gearty, Chapter 8, this volume, in which he raises but then discounts remasking as a tempting but not an effective solution.
[143] John Tasioulas, 'The legal relevance of ethical objectivity', *American Journal of Jurisprudence* 47 (2002), 211.

would require: that it would have to be the sort of explanation which anyone would automatically come to see the truth of if confronted with it; and that it would have to be the sort of explanation which would guarantee the historical success of human rights.[144] For others, talk about foundations simply means that if one believes in human rights as a rational animal, one should have good reasons for one's belief, and one should not have beliefs that one cannot justify. Adopting this less inflated standard may address the dilemma sketched out in the previous paragraph. For those who consider that we should fool ourselves and others into believing that human rights have foundations, the question then is why we would want to do this? We might say to them: you think human rights are a good thing; well then, you must have reasons for that belief, otherwise you will not be able to distinguish yourself from those you are using human rights to criticize; what are those reasons? With that brief excursus, let us return to consider dignity.

Even assuming that discussion about the foundations of human rights is useful, how useful is the concept of human *dignity* in this discussion? Does dignity language supply any additional substantive meaning? For Schlink, in legal contexts, the answer is often not.[145] When specific problems and cases involving alleged violations of human rights are addressed, he cannot see that dignity adds any additional substantive meaning to the unfolding or solving of the case. There may, in his view, be nothing wrong with using the rhetoric of dignity in discussing problem cases, but there is nothing necessarily lost when we just talk about freedom, religious liberty, the right to life, or equality by themselves, without dignity. If we just talk about these specific freedoms or about equality, and do it carefully and comprehensively, then we often don't miss any important aspect of the issue. He recognizes that there are exceptions to this in practice, where dignity is used as a specific legal concept and judges therefore are required to consider dignity as the principal legal concept in issue, such as in Israel and Germany; but in general he considers that dignity adds no substantive meaning to a legal human rights debate that other concepts cannot supply. Some would go even further in discounting the importance of dignity for conceptions of human rights, seeing dignity as little more than a shorthand way of speaking of human rights collectively, adding nothing substantive.

---

[144] Richard Rorty, 'Human rights, rationality, and sentimentality', in Stephen Shute and Susan Hurley (eds), *On Human Rights: The Oxford Amnesty Lectures 1993* (New York, Basic Books, 1993).
[145] Schlink, Chapter 37, this volume.

Others profoundly disagree. Two broad approaches have proved particularly interesting, one represented by Tasioulas,[146] the other by John Milbank.[147] Both argue that there is an important substantive relationship between the concepts of human rights and human dignity, but beyond that their disagreement is profound.

Tasioulas argues, as we have seen earlier, that human dignity is a basic moral status, not a human interest or good. It is a vital ground supporting the idea of human rights, but it cannot be the sole ground of human rights. More specifically, human dignity has to operate in tandem with a rich conception of the elements of human flourishing or basic human goods, including knowledge, friendship, and achievement, among others. How these different elements fit together is not entirely clear, however. Is it the case that Tasioulas sees some particular human rights as grounded in dignity but other rights as founded in knowledge or friendship? If so, which are the rights founded in dignity, and why? Are the rights founded in dignity in some sense more important than others, or more paradigmatic than others?

Tasioulas's position means that he has to steer a middle course between two more extreme alternatives. One alternative is presented by those who say that human dignity is the exclusive basis of human rights: that it is the *only* value we need to appeal to in order to generate anything like a recognizable list of human rights. The other more extreme position, which Tasioulas also rejects, argues that the project of deriving any human rights from human dignity is unpersuasive. One cannot generate human rights from anything like human dignity, and therefore we should abandon the notion of human dignity entirely; and in particular we should not think of it as something that we necessarily need to appeal to in defending human rights (a position similar to that advocated by Schlink).

By contrast, Milbank suggests a radically different approach to the relationship between human dignity and human rights. He suggests that not only do human rights not derive from human dignity but that dignity and rights are concepts that are in some considerable tension with each other. For Milbank, dignity is something with roots in premodernity, having to do with status and not something derived from a kind of isolated a priori subjective individual, and that dignity is incompatible therefore with any idea of subjective rights. While, in the Middle Ages, more and more rights for subjects are discussed, these are not grounded in subjectivity. His distinction between dignity and rights, between dignity as status and notions of subjective freedom,

---

[146] Tasioulas, Chapter 16, this volume.
[147] John Milbank, Chapter 10, this volume.

counterposes the two concepts rather than, as with Tasioulas, viewing rights as derived (even partly) from dignity. Milbank's analysis, contrasting rights and dignity, appears to depend, however, on a particular characterization of rights as 'subjective', a characterization that not all rights theorists would accept.

Even if one does not agree with the stronger form of Milbank's claim, that there is a necessary and fundamental conflict between the concept of rights and a concept of dignity, we can see that there is, at least, sometimes an uneasy relationship between those two.[148] Certainly, one cannot move in a facile way from an idea of dignity to the derivation of ideas of rights and vice versa; and dignity may not always necessarily find its best expression and protection in the language of rights. Riordan, for instance, argues that religion and religious liberty can be understood broadly or narrowly, and that the notion of dignity used for the grounding of rights can result in a significant restriction in the understanding of the right to religious freedom, even to the point of its elimination as a distinctive right. Dignity may, therefore, cut across rights, and we may ask whether this may not actually be a good thing, keeping human rights concepts from becoming unquestioned, and supplying a possible critique of human rights. Dignity may, indeed, outstrip rights. It may, then, function in some way as a ground for rights but also a ground for the critique of rights. Thus, for example, those who consider that dignity protects the integrity of the human person may be able to use the concept of dignity to criticize an interpretation of rights that is too cramped to protect that person, or to criticize a claimed extension of rights that seems not to reflect or protect human dignity. So dignity may help to provide a certain kind of critical distance from rights, reducing the tendency to fetishize rights in contemporary society. This does not, however, necessarily undermine the argument that dignity is a (partial, at least) foundation for rights. If dignity is part of the foundation, it can provide a basis for criticism of current interpretations of specific rights.

Clearly, the relationship between human dignity and human rights is intensely related to one's understanding of rights, as the discussion of Milbank illustrates, but also to the conception of dignity that one has. If, for example, one has a conception of indignity that is rooted in the idea of shaming someone or in the closely related idea of humiliation, as we have seen is Margalit's understanding, then it is easy to see that dignity in that sense cannot provide the basis for all human rights. If I steal your car, I trample on your property rights (assuming that property rights are human rights) but I do not hurt your dignity, in this sense.

---

[148] This paragraph draws extensively on an oral contribution to the discussion by Paolo Carozza.

All this also has important implications for the extent to which, even if we agree that dignity is a foundation for rights, dignity provides any guide for action. The more general and open-ended one's conception of dignity, the more steps removed we are from being able to specify the contours of rights: rights with what content, whose responsibility it is to accord those rights, what kind of remedy for rights violations is appropriate, and how does the state fit in? Even if we all agreed on the foundations and meaning of human dignity, there would still be a rich difference of understandings about how exactly that principle should be instantiated in specific contexts, with respect to specific persons, and in specific cultures.

Legal debates

There appear to be two levels in the debates around dignity. One level of debate, the foundational level, concerns the grounding of the concept of dignity in some anthropological, historical, philosophical, theological, or ontological account of what Dellavalle calls the pre-legal,[149] or what Habermas calls the life-world.[150] Another level of debate concerns whether, and if so how, dignity provides a guide for action, and this frequently involves the role that dignity plays in the legal sphere: the way in which declarations, conventions, and legislation on rights appeal to dignity. So much is this the case that the concept of dignity itself becomes incorporated within the legal resources on which judges and lawyers draw.

It is the intimate connection between the concept of dignity and legal texts and practices that may appear to reveal the need for the second level of analysis and debate. This distinction is, however, problematic. For heuristic reasons, this introduction has so far distinguished between reasoning of the type carried out by philosophers and theologians from what lawyers and judges do. At one level this distinction is important, and the previous paragraph reflects the fact that there are importantly different institutional contexts in which these different actors reason. But we should not overemphasize the differences. In important respects, law involves foundational moral reasoning of a type that is very similar to that which philosophers and theologians engage in.

---

[149] Dellavalle, Chapter 25, this volume.
[150] Jürgen Habermas, *The Theory of Communicative Action*, vol. 2: *Life-World and System: A Critique of Functionalist Reason*, trans. Thomas McCarthy (Boston, MA, Beacon Press, 1987).

This has important implications for our understanding of dignity because many of the moral and ethical issues that philosophers and theologians are concerned to explore are the same as those that judges, for example, will have to grapple with in their use of dignity, and the heuristic device of concentrating on differing disciplinary approaches should not blind us to that. As importantly, to the extent that judges and legal scholars are not only 'doing legal interpretation' but are also, perhaps particularly in this area, also 'doing moral reasoning', their methods and the arguments they engage with contribute to the societal context in which philosophers and theologians also operate. To put the point briefly: legal (and perhaps particularly judicial) interpretation is not only influenced by but also contributes to moral reasoning.[151]

As has already been made plain, there are many areas of legal controversy in which dignity-based arguments arise, ranging from issues of torture, to discrimination, privacy, forced labour, and freedom of religion, thereby demonstrating the breadth of the concept's relevance in legal contexts. Enough has been said to show that there is a considerable number of different conceptions of dignity in the legal context, and that these both overlap and may conflict. Given this, it is not surprising that dignity arguments are often present on both sides of contested legal issues, thus also demonstrating the versatility of dignity 'talk' in the legal as well as in the philosophical and theological contexts. Indeed, where legal interpretation is seen as adopting a particular understanding of dignity, as Rivers argues that judicial decisions do (if only covertly) in freedom of religion cases, this is seen as problematic, and a greater diversity of meaning of dignity is advocated.

Perhaps one of the most contentious legal areas in which dignity has been drawn on concerns abortion. Siegel's account of the political struggles that led to abortion's constitutionalization in Germany and the USA is a useful case study of these aspects of dignity.[152] She indicates that competing conceptions of dignity, what she terms 'dignity as liberty', 'dignity as equality', and 'dignity as life', are useful (if rough) ways of identifying the competing legal claims made by the different actors in these jurisdictions over a significant period of time. Some feminists argued that under then prevailing social arrangements, laws criminalizing abortion violated dignity as liberty, taking away from women control over decisions concerning their bodily health, sexual relations, family relations, economic independence, and participation in political life, while simultaneously appealing to dignity as equality, viewing

---

[151] I am grateful to Samantha Besson for making this point.

[152] Siegel, Chapter 30, this volume. Another example is how Tollefsen's dignity of procreative marriage is counterpointed by Cameron's dignity-based argument in favour of same-sex marriage.

laws vesting decision about abortion in doctors' committees as degrading to women, by treating women as the kind of decision-makers who lack moral competence to make decisions. In contrast, those endeavouring to preserve the law criminalizing abortion adopted an apparently different conception of dignity, appealing to dignity as life, emphasizing that life has dignity whether the foetus has gained consciousness or not. This conception of dignity is not concerned with coercion, humiliation, or instrumentalization but rather, through the regulation of birth, sex, and death, with the symbolic reaffirmation of the sacredness of life.

In considering how law deals with these different understandings of dignity, and more generally what role dignity plays in the legal context and in legal scholarship, a preliminary question must be identified. Should the law be primarily concerned with expressing values, or with the practical effect of the law? One of the central issues in the German constitutional debates over abortion that Siegel discusses concerned this issue. Jackson has pointed to the relevance of a recent global review of abortion published in *The Lancet* for considering this issue more widely.[153] Perhaps counter-intuitively, the review suggests that the abortion rate is higher in countries with restrictive abortion laws than it is where the law is more liberal. Why this matters, she suggests, is that the illegality of abortion may not mean that it doesn't happen; it may mean that it happens more frequently and unsafely, resulting not only in the death of the foetus, but also in serious harm or death for the woman.

More broadly, does the context in which dignity is operationalized (political, moral, or legal; legislative or judicial) affect our understanding of the concept? Christoph Möllers argues for an affirmative answer: that when human dignity becomes used as an argument in the *judicial* context, for example, many things change.[154] In particular, the idea that human dignity is something like an incompletely theorized argument, which may well be a highly successful strategy to use in a context where political compromise is necessary (as in an international treaty), becomes highly problematic when we start to apply the concept of dignity to solve a particular legal problem before a court. Because of this, Möllers argues, although human dignity might be a good term to put into preambles, or into general parts of treaties, it is probably not very helpful to include dignity in a legal instrument that is intended to be a regulatory tool, placing dignity on an equal footing with individual rights such as freedom of expression, freedom of religion, or property rights.

---

[153] Emily Jackson, in discussion at the conference, referring to Gilda Sedgh, Susheela Singh, Iqbal H. Shah, Elisabeth Ahman, Stanley K. Henshaw, and Akinrinola Bankole, 'Induced abortion: incidence and trends worldwide from 1995 to 2008', *The Lancet*, 379:9816 (18 February 2012), 625–32.
[154] Christoph Möllers, Chapter 9, this volume.

We do not have to accept Möllers's scepticism, echoing Gearty, of the utility of dignity in adjudication to take his point that the institutional context in which dignity is used matters. This intuition not only seems valid when we contrast the political and legal contexts in which dignity is put, but also when we contrast the differing legal contexts with each other. Barak[155] and Dieter Grimm[156] both emphasize these differing contexts in which dignity is used and the necessity of distinguishing between them if the legal use of the term is to be properly appreciated.

Several different legal contexts can be identified. We can distinguish the use of dignity in the context of constitutional drafting as compared with the use of dignity in the ordinary legislative context. We need also to distinguish the use of dignity in the drafting context (whether constitutional or legislative) from appeals to dignity in litigation and adjudication. Finally, in some other legal contexts, such as the European Convention on Human Rights, dignity does not feature in the text at all (the implications of which are explored by Jean-Paul Costa).[157] In these contexts, dignity may function as a value, or principle, or policy deeply instantiated within the legal system, and something to which the legal system has committed itself, and to which actors in the system refer. Quite different uses of dignity might be intended by the different origins of the legal instantiation of dignity in these different contexts. Goos shows, for example, that the different origins of dignity in the German Länder and the German Federal Republic makes a single 'constitutional' understanding of dignity difficult to sustain, even within Germany.[158]

Of those contributors who address the legal use of dignity, most discuss its interpretation by judges in the context of constitutional litigation. In this context, as Barak argues, the concept is employed in a constitutional structure that confers on judges a certain discretion to make judgments, fleshing out the constitution. It is useful to identify the major debates that are usually encountered in this context. The first is whether dignity is a right, or a principle, or a value. The second issue is whether dignity embodies a negative or a positive obligation: to what extent is dignity conceptualized as simply a negative right against other persons or the state, and to what extent is it conceptualized as a positive obligation (particularly on the state)? If it is a negative obligation, how narrow is it—just a prohibition on humiliating others, or more? If it is a positive obligation, how broad is it? Réaume considers whether socio-economic rights are generated, for example.

---

[155] Barak, Chapter 20, this volume.
[156] Grimm, Chapter 21, this volume.
[157] Costa, Chapter 22, this volume.
[158] Goos, Chapter 3, this volume.

Important as these considerations are, however, we will not consider them further here. In fact, two other sets of issues dominate the internal debate in this book: the absolute or qualified nature of dignity, and the relevance of philosophical or theological understandings of dignity in the legal context. It is to these that we now turn.

Is dignity qualified or absolute? Barak asserts that the use of dignity in the Israeli context, where dignity is a right as well as a principle, is qualified rather than absolute, and is of broad application. Grimm addresses the use of dignity mostly in the German context, where dignity is predominantly seen as a principle, absolute and confined (although Rosen queries the extent to which dignity is actually seen in Germany as an absolute right, as opposed to being a source of rights, and queries whether the conception adopted in Germany is in fact a restricted conception of dignity).[159]

What are the implications of dignity being interpreted as imposing absolute duties, without exception? Barak identifies one particular consequence: that it is more likely that dignity will have to be defined more narrowly. Where dignity is absolute, the more broadly it is defined, the more the courts will be prevented from balancing competing values. Grimm identifies several additional consequences of treating dignity as absolute. Only one right in a legal system can be absolute, he argues. If we want to have two legal rights both with the quality of being absolute rights, unless both are specified in a very narrow way, for example by imposing only negative duties, it is likely that these two rights will conflict. If the judge has to decide which one prevails in all circumstances, the other is no longer absolute; if hierarchical priority is sometimes given one of these rights but at other times the other right, then neither is absolute.

Several contributors consider the implications somewhat more theoretically. For Dupré there is a third, possibly more attractive, effect of making dignity absolute: that it creates conflicts with other human rights, which requires us to rethink what we understand as the importance of the opposing right—dignity conceived in this way keeps rights continually on their toes, we might say.[160] For Beattie, however, making dignity absolute in the German legal context has a paradoxical effect. By enacting dignity into law and making it subject to judicial interpretation in a specifically German context, she tentatively suggests that this smuggles into German law the right to define not only dignity but also the human according to its terms of inclusion and

---

[159] Rosen, *Dignity*, at 100ff.
[160] Catherine Dupré in discussion at the conference.

exclusion, 'and thus it cannot avoid reinstating the conditions which made the death camps possible'.[161]

The major legal effect of creating an absolute right, however, is that proportionality and balancing cannot be used: Barak regards this as a major disadvantage, while Grimm regards it as a major advantage. We can test the implications of the exclusion of balancing through an example.[162] Suppose that the results of the experiments on twins carried out as part of the pseudoscientific research by Mengele in Auschwitz and Birkenau came into your possession. Let us suppose, further, that the results were compiled in an orderly way and that there was useful information that would indisputably benefit others. Should we be allowed to use the information? Or, in the name of human dignity, should its use be prohibited? Or consider whether the use of evidence obtained under torture should be able to be used in court. Do these test the limits of the acceptability of an absolute understanding of dignity?

These hypothetical cases may illustrate a significant difference between the moral and the legal contexts in which dignity is interpreted. There might be reasons for enshrining things as absolute requirements in law, even though in pure moral reasoning we might not have such an absolute requirement. There are important institutional effects in having a more nuanced principle involved, which might make an absolute prohibition more acceptable in a legal context. Suppose that torture evidence was the only way that we could save the actual torture victim from being killed or being subjected to further torture? We might say that it is an absolute *moral* requirement that torture should not be used, but this will strike some as problematic—they would want at least to have a debate about the issue as a matter of morality. But does that necessarily mean that in the *legal* context we should be similarly worried about an absolute prohibition? The notion that a *court* should engage in a balancing exercise with regard, for example, to the use of torture evidence or the use of evidence from evil experimentation may strike some as so fundamentally out of tune with the function of courts as to be properly prohibited whatever the consequences, even though they may recognize that as a *moral* issue there is room for debate.

There is one further internal debate between the contributors, which arises out of the previous paragraph: to what extent should we regard law and legal interpretation as autonomous systems of reasoning and judgement? We should immediately distinguish, however fuzzily, between the making of law and its interpretation. In a democracy, the domain of politics is where debates

---

[161] Beattie, Chapter 14, this volume.
[162] Originally suggested by Avishai Margalit at the conference.

about what the law should be primarily take place. Theologians, philosophers, lawyers, and all other kinds of citizens have the possibility of contributing to these political debates, and may indeed have an impact on the content of legislation. The law that judges and lawyers interpret and apply is already shaped by certain influences, therefore, which at times may be philosophical and even theological. How far should judges consider that they should incorporate philosophical or theological understandings, in particular of dignity, into legal interpretation?

This is essentially the same debate that arises whenever the relationship between law and morality is under discussion, and the usual divisions therefore seem to emerge when the normative concept is dignity. For Barak, the judge's role is clearly one of interpreting a legal concept, but one with a heavy moral content, one that can best be approached by understanding the society whose laws the judge is interpreting. Two possible problems arise from this position. First, if legal interpretation is so contextual, does that mean that the legal meaning of dignity is also highly contextualized, and if so, what does this do to the idea of dignity being universal? Second, where does the difference lie between law and political sociology in a context where the judge's role is to understand society, as well as law?

Although Grimm argues that it is necessary for lawyers and judges to have a general intellectual understanding of the concept of dignity in order to apply it, he questions whether philosophical or theological understandings of the term can be used to help elucidate the meaning of dignity in the legal context. He considers that the transfer of dignity from the philosophical and theological to the legal disconnects the notion from its original roots and sources, regarding law as a relatively autonomous system. Within the operation of the legal system only legal arguments count. Extra-legal sources are irrelevant unless and until they are translated into a legal argument, which must fit the legal environment in which the concept is being interpreted. What counts as a legal argument may be contested and it may change over time, but the decision as to what counts can only be taken inside and not outside the legal system itself. For Beattie, this is exactly the problem.[163] 'In co-opting the word "dignity"', she argues, 'the law also drains it of any alternative meaning.' In order to legitimate its use of the concept, law must 'empty ... words of all their historical references and ideological inscriptions'.

If the relationship between law and philosophy is problematic for lawyers, it is also problematic for philosophers. There are certain benefits of engaging with lawyers in attempting to understand the nature of dignity. Both Waldron

---

[163] Beattie, Chapter 14, this volume.

and Rosen, in remarkably different ways it is true, have identified how their philosophical explorations benefited from exposure to legal debates because lawyers focus on concrete cases, and on issues of decision.[164] The potential disadvantage, as suggested by Tasioulas,[165] is that precisely this focus on the bottom line may lead to a certain kind of impatience, where the only purpose of philosophy is seen as its utility in helping to resolve the difficult practical cases with which lawyers and judges are confronted. For philosophers, no ethical principle by itself resolves a difficult practical issue. It is one thing for the principle to be taken into account, but what resolves the matter is the use of judgement. A purely ethical understanding of human dignity is likely still to need to be supplemented if it is to be workable or operational, and one of the important roles that law performs is to give more specific content to rather vague concepts at the ethical level. The specificity of law works hand in hand with the vagueness of philosophy or moral reasoning, because moral reasoning often needs to be supplemented in this way.

Inductive method, consensus, and dialogue

Common to all the disciplines represented in this book is the methodological problem of how we should go about identifying the meaning and function of dignity. Hollenbach suggests that there are essentially two choices: a deductive approach, in which reasoning works from the more general to the more specific, and (his own preference) an inductive approach in which reasoning works the other way, moving from specific observations to broader generalizations and theories, paying attention to what diverse communities think about how persons should be treated and seeking to determine where agreement may be possible across communities.[166] This involves reasoned reflection on the experience of what it is to be human, and in particular reasoned reflection on what happens when these factors are denied. For Hollenbach, the overlapping consensus that has emerged over the past fifty years at the international level on what human rights require did not happen by accident; there were good reasons for it. This illustrates the use of practical reason to reflect inductively on experience in order to reach consensus on at least some of the most important requirements.

---

[164] Rosen, *Dignity*, and Waldron, *Dignity, Rank, and Rights*.
[165] The remainder of the paragraph summarizes a point he made in discussion at the conference.
[166] Hollenbach, Chapter 6, this volume.

Nor is the issue of what is the appropriate methodology to adopt limited to the philosophical and theological spheres. Réaume, although not explicitly drawing on the concept of practical reason, also eschews proceeding by way of grand theory down to concrete legal cases, and adopts an inductive approach: identifying the ideas about dignity that are seeping out of the pores of the legal system, when law is called to respond to certain kinds of situations.[167]

More generally, one of the themes of Barak's chapter is the methodology courts use to determine what human dignity involves in particular situations.[168] One of the characteristic methods identified in Barak's chapter and reflected in the practice of courts around the world, is that in discussions of what dignity requires courts sometimes look at what courts in other jurisdictions are doing. There has been much discussion of what exactly the function of comparison and the use of comparative law is in this context. One of the answers might be that the function of comparison in the human dignity area, where courts look at what other courts are doing, is that they might be engaging in 'practical reasoning', leading to a consensus that emerges out of contestation.

Hollenbach, it should be noted, combines two methodological elements. First, as has been mentioned, he favours an inductive rather than a deductive approach, but in addition he attempts to use this inductive method to identify where there appears to be a consensus, and then wants to rely on that consensus as a basis for arguing that this provides grounds for generating a normative obligation to further that consensus. It is thus a somewhat similar method to that adopted by courts when drawing on the experience of other courts. It is also similar to approaches that have sought to find ways of resolving fundamental political disputes by searching for an 'overlapping consensus' among the disputing parties.

This idea of an 'overlapping consensus', most clearly identified with John Rawls, has come in for convincing criticism, much of which need not detain us here. In so far as the second element of Hollenbach's strategy does share a family resemblance with Rawls, it is subject to similar criticisms, particularly if one sees consensus as fully formed and not open to further development or refinement. Why would a given consensus be seen as a powerful basis for deciding what dignity requires, given that there may be a sexist consensus or a homophobic consensus, and we would not think that this should generate the norms required by dignity? But if we say we should only take into account 'enlightened' opinion, is that assuming the very concept we are seeking to

---

[167] Réaume, Chapter 32, this volume.
[168] Barak, Chapter 20, this volume.

identify? Or if, as Hollenbach suggests, practical reason can lead to historical development, the consensus may itself be a developing reality.

Carozza also addresses the methodological question, and indeed sees it as central to the debate about dignity.[169] Unlike Hollenbach, he is sceptical of a consensus approach in the sense identified. Although he considers that the practical or overlapping consensus methods that Maritain advocated in drafting the Universal Declaration of Human Rights were highly successful in many ways, he queries whether we can follow the same path today, relying on a practical consensus around dignity to achieve similarly positive results. Constructing the human rights project solely on the grounds of a practical overlapping consensus, he argues, has contributed to several serious problems over the past six decades: problems of institutional weakness, problems of non-compliance, problems of ideological capture, the masking of fundamental differences, and heavy bureaucratization and proceduralization. All these, he believes, are in one way or another related to the original structure of the discourse. The relatively recent resort to human dignity is in part a consequence of the limits of the human rights project itself, where the disagreement we have had since its origin is now pushed back onto the question of human dignity. So we cannot, he argues, rely on a practical consensus as our method of resolving the meaning of human dignity, because we have already learned that this method is unstable and unsustainable.

Is there a way forward? Langan distinguishes between two different ways of understanding the inductive approach: where inductive reasoning is used to identify consensus, and where it is used to generate respectful dialogue.[170] His understanding is that in much contemporary discussion in this area the latter is the preferable position to adopt. What he advocates is a dialogical view of reasoning, in which learning from other individuals, learning from other communities, and other traditions is an important part of the process, not necessarily for the purpose of generating agreement (indeed, honest dialogue may well lead to a sharper sense of the points of disagreement), but in order to be able to state the position of the other side without offering a travesty, and thereby to lead to higher levels of mutual respect and the increased possibility of dialogue.

Carozza's approach, and Hollenbach's as well, seem relatively similar to such a dialogic approach. We can rely on a strategy of practical consensus, Carozza argues, if we understand that in the original human rights project its use was not meant to be an end point but was intended instead to be the

---

[169] Carozza, Chapter 36, this volume.
[170] In discussion at the conference.

starting point for a reasoned reflection and dialogue about the requirements of justice and the protection of the human. Carozza suggests that we need to engage now in a more fundamental reflection on human experience that goes to the origin of our understanding of our own humanity. For Carozza, dignity discourse invites openness to the posing of the question of what it is to be human in our public and communal discourse. Such a dialogue is all the more important because, as we have noted, some consider that there is something irreducible about the human person that cannot be fully captured (Sedmak and others, as we have seen, use the word 'mystery'). This means that there is always going to be a need for discussion, the likelihood of disagreement, and a certain under-determination. The very nature of what we are talking about—the human person—means that we should never presume to be able to specify dignity beyond contestation.

Conversations and dialogue

The purpose of the conference, and of this book, is to engage in exactly this dialogue about human dignity, and to stimulate further productive discussion about human dignity and about what it means to be human. What has emerged from the course of this set of introductory remarks? There are at least three conversations identifiable in the book, and this introduction has identified these different strands and pinpointed the particular issues that arise within, as well as the ways in which the discussion crosses, these strands. One conversation is within and between the different disciplines represented, between lawyers and lawyers, for example, and between philosophers and theologians. The second conversation is that between the secular and the religious understandings of human rights and human dignity. The third conversation is a serious debate within Catholicism, one that has importance for the other two conversations as well.

The group brought together in this book is distinctly multidisciplinary, but does the dialogue go beyond multidisciplinarity? What, indeed, is the purpose of bringing these different disciplines together? Gerald Neuman argues that the advantages of dialogue across disciplines concerning human dignity should not distract us from the reality that different intellectual disciplines have different discourses and methods.[171] Philosophical and religious traditions can contribute insights to debates within the legal discourses (and vice

---

[171] Gerald L. Neuman, Chapter 38, this volume.

versa, I suggest), but those insights need to be translated into terms that are accessible to outsiders to those traditions.

Alexandra Kemmerer distinguishes several different types of engagement involving different disciplines.[172] Adopting the terminology she suggests, we can say that the purpose of this book is not to engage in an *inter*disciplinary approach; the aim is not, in other words, to seek some sort of shared position about human dignity among secular and religious people, lawyers, and philosophers. Agreeing with Kemmerer, the aim of the book is more in the nature of a *trans*-disciplinary engagement, in which the aim of the dialogue between the different disciplines is to generate a process of transcending, transgressing, and transforming, rather than integrating, blending, or hybridizing.

This introduction has sought to sketch the contours of each set of debates, and how they interrelate with each other, but it is a reasonable question to ask whether these dialogues are successful. It may be useful, finally, to consider some criteria for what would constitute 'success', if only for the future. For a real dialogue to be successful, at least three conditions seem to be vital. First, a dialogue will only take place if those in dialogue come to the conversation with sufficient confidence in their own positions to be able to open up to others. Second, since a dialogue is a conversation that involves differing positions, with which comes the tendency to regard the other as hostile, for a dialogue to be successful, those taking part need to recognize that there may nevertheless be some value in what the other is saying. Third, those in dialogue have to be prepared to question their own starting points; we can't simply assume the correctness of our deepest beliefs, but have to be open to the possibility that we are wrong. Readers will form their own view on whether any or all of these criteria have been met in what follows. In my view, these conditions were largely met, and the resulting book attempts to reflect the richness of the dialogue that resulted.

---

[172] Alexandra Kemmerer, Chapter 39, this volume.

Part I

Historical Perspectives

2

Dignité/Dignidade: Organizing against Threats to Dignity in Societies after Slavery

Rebecca J. Scott[1]

ONE OF THE MOST striking modern historical occurrences of the term 'dignity' in a legal text appears in the preamble to the 1848 decree abolishing slavery in the French empire:

> Considérant que l'esclavage est un attentat contre la dignité humaine; qu'en détruisant le libre arbitre de l'homme, il supprime le principe naturel du droit et du devoir ; qu'il est une violation flagrante du dogme républicain : Liberté, Égalité, Fraternité …
>
> Considering that slavery is an assault upon human dignity; that in destroying man's free will, it destroys the natural source of law and duty; that it is a flagrant violation of the republican creed: Liberty, Equality, Fraternity …[2]

Written into a key text, the term 'dignity' became increasingly available for borrowing and invocation in subsequent struggles. Like other normative terms of the kind that philosophers characterize as 'thick', however, the concept 'dignity' necessarily carries descriptive as well as evaluative content. That is to say, its use does not only mark something as positive, it also implies ways in which the action or comportment is thought to be good.[3] The nature

---

[1] I thank Elizabeth Anderson, Pedro Cantisano, Mark Elliott, Malick Ghachem, Ángela Maria de Castro Gómez, Keila Grinberg, Jean M. Hébrard, Don Herzog, Thomas Holt, Silvia Lara, Beatriz Mamigonian, Christopher McCrudden, Mariana Dias Paes, Cristiano Paixão, Marieke Polfliet, Peter Railton, João José Reis, and Patricia Sampaio for suggestions and discussion. In Brazil, I owe a particular debt to Luís Camargo, Attorney General of the Ministério Público do Trabalho (MPT), for having invited me to participate in a panel at the November 2012 gathering of MPT attorneys working on issues of contemporary slavery, and to Jonas Moreno and Cristiano Paixão for arranging that visit. The meeting also included anthropologist Ricardo Rezende Figueira and several *auditores fiscais* from the Ministério do Trabalho e Emprego, who were equally generous with their ideas.
[2] For the full French-language text of the decree of 27 April 1848, see http://www.assemblee-nationale.fr/histoire/esclavage/decret1848.asp. All English translations are mine.
[3] On 'thick' normative terms see Bernard Williams, who summarizes the idea in this way: 'The way these notions are applied is determined by what the world is like (for instance, by how someone has behaved), and yet, at the same time, their application usually involves a certain valuation of the situation'.

of that descriptive content in social practice, in turn, emerges as we examine vernacular as well as elite understandings of the term in particular historical circumstances.[4]

This chapter is not an attempt to join the fractious debate over philosophical first principles or juridical first usages of the term 'dignity'. Instead, it explores the tight connection between the institution of slavery and the giving of specific meanings to the concept of dignity, in particular times and particular places. To explore the dynamics of the intertwined process of creating and drawing upon meaning for the terms 'dignity' and 'slavery', I examine two historical movements that emerged after formal abolition.

As slavery became widely recognized as emblematic of a fundamental violation of human dignity, practices associated with slavery could themselves be seen to carry a potential threat to dignity, even without any further ownership of property in persons. The late nineteenth-century popular campaign against legally mandated racial segregation, particularly as it unfolded in the state of Louisiana, drew upon a language of dignity, sometimes echoing the uses in earlier French radical thought of the term *dignité*. Louisiana's white supremacists had often portrayed segregation regulations and statutes as aimed merely at maintaining familiar customs, public comfort, and public order. Those who opposed the statutes nonetheless saw an intentional dignitary offence, precisely because of the ways in which legally mandated segregation reproduced forms of humiliation practised against free persons of colour under slavery. The meaning—and the marking—involved in the practice of forced separation could, in their view, best be understood with reference to the slaveholding past, as constituting a project of white supremacy for the post-emancipation future.[5]

One hundred years later, in Brazil, the link between dignity and slavery has re-emerged in jurisprudence and in a social movement. Forms of highly constrained and degrading labour, stimulated in part by westward expansion and in part by new forms of export agriculture and the deregulation of private enterprise, are now increasingly referred to as constituting *trabalho escravo*, slave labour. To characterize contemporary labour practices as 'slavery' has involved severing the term 'slavery' from legally authorized ownership. It

---

Bernard Williams, *Ethics and the Limits of Philosophy* (Cambridge, MA, Harvard University Press, 1985), 128–30.

[4] Christopher McCrudden has pointed out that the specific meanings imputed to the term human rights are necessarily local, even if the larger concept often implies universality. Christopher McCrudden, discussion, Conference on Law and Human Rights in Global History, University of Michigan, April 2012. The same could be said of the concept of dignity.

[5] For a subtle essay on the process of 'marking', see Thomas C. Holt, 'Marking, race-making, and the writing of history', *American Historical Review* 100 (February 1995), 1–20.

has also required moving beyond the question of consent, since debt rather than mere force often serves as a key mechanism of control. Those charged with investigating and penalizing such labour practices increasingly invoke (among other things) the guarantee of dignity written into the 1988 Brazilian constitution. The link to historical experiences of nineteenth-century slavery thus passes through the concept of human dignity, closing the obvious gap in time and space that separates the chattel slavery that was abolished in 1888 from the rural labour processes that have come to be identified as contemporary slavery.

Although both the nineteenth-century Louisiana experience and the contemporary Brazilian process highlight the relationship between the concept of 'dignity' and that of 'slavery', the lines of interpretation and reinterpretation go in opposite direction in the two cases. In post-1862 Louisiana, an awareness of the slave past made salient the affront to dignity contained in what might otherwise seem to be mere customary modes of allocating seats on trains and in theatres. In contemporary Brazil, specific working conditions have come to be seen as in themselves an assault on human dignity—often because they include actions that assimilate human beings to animals, or prevent workers from leaving the property of the employer. For prosecutors, in turn, these practices become indicia of the presence of legally prohibited *trabalho escravo* (slave labour) or *trabalho em condicões análogas às de escravo* (labour in conditions analogous to those of slavery). The ancient term 'slavery' has thus been brought back into wide usage through its link to the more recent term 'dignity', making it possible to give a specific name to a perceived harm.

Louisiana, 1862–96

Although by the mid-nineteenth century chattel slavery had been abolished in many jurisdictions in the Americas (including Haiti, most of the new Latin American republics, the French Caribbean colonies, the British Caribbean, and many northern states of the USA), it nonetheless remained central to the economies of Cuba, Brazil, and the southern states of the USA. The sharp conflict between the perceived security needs of the slaveholding states and a growing abolitionism stimulated rigorous restrictions on the public discussion of race and slavery, and led to a multiplication of laws stigmatizing and constraining not only slaves but also free persons of colour. Claims by free persons of colour to individual dignity and voice would run directly against long-standing prohibitions on the fomenting of discontent that might imperil slavery itself.⁶

The texts of France's 1848 Revolution, including the decrees of abolition, nonetheless found an audience deep in the Gulf South. A substantial population of men and women in the city of New Orleans spoke French and English, a legacy both of the city's French colonial background and of the arrival of thousands of immigrants from France and from the Francophone Caribbean during the first half of the nineteenth century. The 1848 French texts offered a powerful invocation of abolition, human dignity, broad citizenship for freed people, and an open embrace of what the French government itself designated as 'social equality'.⁷ Living in a slaveholding metropolis, free persons of colour in New Orleans were obliged to show great discretion as they developed their own political thought, but these ingredients were now within reach for those who chose to adopt or adapt them.⁸

Once Union forces occupied the city of New Orleans in April 1862, the questions of abolition, equal rights, and an expanded suffrage became subject to wide debate. Although the federal government had uttered no definitive judgement on the future of the institution of slavery, with the issuance of the preliminary and then the definitive Emancipation Proclamation, the direction of change was clear. Each further advance by Union forces would now bring formal freedom to those who had been held as slaves in Confederate territory.

Into the newly opened space of public discussion that had emerged under Union occupation came a group of activist men of colour who founded a French-language newspaper which they titled *L'Union*, aiming at a readership among the Afro-Creole men and women of colour who formed the backbone of the city's artisanal classes, particularly in the building trades and cigar-making.⁹ The editors quickly began enunciating a strong defence of equal rights, drawing freely on the figures and language of the French 1848ers.

---

⁶ On struggles in the US Congress over the public expression of abolitionism, and over the right of free persons of colour to petition the Congress, see William Lee Miller, *Arguing About Slavery: John Quincy Adams and the Great Battle in the United States Congress* (New York, Random House, 1995). Statutes in Louisiana criminalized any action or speech tending to encourage discontent among free persons of colour. See the discussion in Rebecca J. Scott and Jean M. Hébrard, *Freedom Papers: An Atlantic Odyssey in the Age of Emancipation* (Cambridge, MA, Harvard University Press, 2012), 76.

⁷ On reactions in New Orleans to the events of 1848 in France, see Caryn Cossé Bell, *Revolution, Romanticism, and the Afro-Creole Protest Tradition in Louisiana, 1718–1868* (Baton Rouge, Louisiana State University Press, 1997), 160–86.

⁸ There was, of course, no necessary relationship between one's colour category and one's politics, and some free persons of colour were deeply involved with slavery itself. It was nonetheless from the community of free persons of colour that much of the political thought of Louisiana's Reconstruction era emerged. See Scott and Hébrard, *Freedom Papers*, chapters 6 and 7.

⁹ On the long-standing traditions of Afro-Creole activism, see Bell, *Revolution*.

Their first evocation of the concept of dignity appeared within a matter of weeks. In a stirring essay titled 'La Liberté', an author who signed his name F. B****** quoted the poet Alphonse de Lamartine on liberty, and applied the message specifically to the question of the hour: the abolition of slavery and the equality of men. To deny liberty, the author insisted, was to deny all grandeur and dignity to man. His essay echoed the 1848ers' linking of slavery to the loss of free will, and of abolition to human dignity.[10]

The Afro-Creole activists of New Orleans exhorted the nation to go much further than the president's Proclamation, and to abolish slavery entirely. The distinction between emancipation as an act of military necessity (as Lincoln had necessarily framed it) and freedom as a fundamental right (as the editors of *L'Union* would see it) was crucial for tens of thousands of residents of the state of Louisiana. Under the terms of the Proclamation, slavery would be abolished in territory deemed to be in rebellion, but could continue to exist in areas already under Union control. New Orleans and the sugar parishes of the state's bayou country were indeed under Union control in January 1863, hence exempt from the formal effects of the Proclamation.

The logic that lay behind the limits on the Proclamation was complex, and included Lincoln's concerns about the boundaries of executive power and the nature of his authority as a wartime commander-in-chief. Permanently destroying 'property'—for it seemed that such was the effect of declaring slaves to be henceforward and forever free—raised serious questions under the laws of war as previously understood, laws that seemed only to permit confiscation for the duration of the hostilities.[11] For the Afro-Creole radicals who took the text of 1848 as their model, by contrast, the claim was simple: slavery was by its nature a direct affront to human dignity, and could not be allowed to continue in a self-respecting republic.[12]

One thinker whose writings appealed strongly to the editors of *L'Union* was Eugène Pelletan, a charismatic French journalist and 1848er who had directly addressed the question of slavery. In early April 1863, *L'Union* printed multiple excerpts from Pelletan's pamphlet *Adresse au roi Coton* ('Address to King Cotton'). The text provided Francophone readers with a brief history that contrasted the continuance of slavery in the United States

---

[10] See 'La Liberté', signed F. B******, *L'Union* (New Orleans), 18 October 1862, 1. It seems likely that the author was the eloquent activist François Boisdoré.

[11] On the connection of the Proclamation to the Laws of War, see the analysis in chapter 7 of John Witt, *Lincoln's Code: The Laws of War in American History* (New York, Free Press, 2012).

[12] On the politics of the newspaper, see the account by a Belgian 1848er who had collaborated on it: Jean-Charles Houzeau, 'Le journal noir, aux Etats-Unis, de 1863 à 1870 (1)', *Revue de Belgique* 11 (1872), 5–28.

with a stirring account of the abolition of slavery by the French republicans in 1848. In that summary, Pelletan emphasized the Republic's 'tendresse pour la dignité humaine'—its careful concern for human dignity—in order to explain the context of abolition.[13]

In the months after the federal Emancipation Proclamation of 1863, the practical effects of Union occupation continued to undermine the social relations of slavery in Louisiana, and the activists put increasing pressure on the Union high command to cease recognizing any property rights in persons.[14] The rapid breakdown of slavery in turn nourished a growing activism. In July 1863, *L'Union* collaborated with the recruitment of a regiment of men of colour, whose service was needed to defend the city against a possible Confederate attack. Questions of honour, dignity, equal rights, and patriotism were fused as the various leaders of the activist community assembled in Economy Hall and called their brothers to arms.[15]

A regiment was quickly assembled, drawing both on free men of colour and on men whose status as slave or free was by this point indeterminate. For the leaders who proposed to assume officer status in the regiment, recruitment provided an occasion on which to fuse the bedrock claim to dignity and universal human rights—'les droits qui appartiennent à tous les hommes' ('the rights which belong to all men')—with an expansive claim to honour and respect as soldiers. Even for mere privates, it offered the possibility of fighting directly against the Confederacy, and of making it clear that they were willing to perform the duties of a citizenship that they believed was already theirs by right.[16]

---

[13] On Pelletan, see chapter 4 of Sudhir Hazareesingh, *Intellectual Founders of the Republic: Five Studies in Nineteenth-Century French Republican Political Thought* (Oxford, Oxford University Press, 2001). The 'Adresse au Roi Coton', including the quoted phrase, appears in *L'Union* (New Orleans) on 11 April 1863.

[14] On slavery in Louisiana in these months see Rebecca J. Scott, *Degrees of Freedom: Louisiana and Cuba after Slavery* (Cambridge, MA, Harvard University Press, 2005), chapter 2.

[15] The account of the meeting at Economy Hall appears in 'Assemblée à la Salle d'Economie', *L'Union*, 30 June 1863. Paul Trévigne referred specifically to the *dignité* of those there assembled.

[16] The phrase is from the speech by Anthony Fernandez reported in 'Assemblée', cited above. This essay is not the place to try to disentangle claims to dignity from claims to honor and respect. (On this question see Jeremy Waldron, *Dignity, Rank, and Rights*, ed. Meir Dan-Cohen (Oxford, Oxford University Press, 2012), including the response by Don Herzog.) It may be enough for our purposes to notice that earlier in the war, some men of colour in New Orleans had thought that their honour actually required volunteering for Confederate service, lest they be thought cowardly and unpatriotic. Needless to say, such service (generally brief and unarmed) did not earn from the Confederates recognition of the dignity of persons of colour more generally. Many of these soldiers subsequently joined Union units. See Justin Nystrom, *New Orleans after the Civil War: Race, Politics, and a New Birth of Freedom* (Baltimore, MD, Johns Hopkins University Press, 2010), chapter 1.

Soon the risks of retaliation against claims of this kind became quite clear. The very sight of men of colour in uniform provoked conflicts on public transportation, as both pro-Confederate townspeople and unsympathetic white Union soldiers acted to expel the offending passengers. Most of the members of the Union high command, moreover, were not ready to see men of colour as commissioned officers. General Nathaniel Banks moved to force the original captains from their posts.[17]

The results were complex. For some individual men of colour, the affronts to personal honour and dignity imposed by the Union high command and by many in the white population of the city were simply intolerable. Lieutenant Joseph Tinchant, who had helped to recruit a company of the 6th Louisiana Volunteers, was by 1864 ready to take his distance from the struggle. He gathered his family, and began to plan to join two of his brothers in Mexico, where he could try his hand at trade in a country that enforced no colour bar.[18]

For Joseph Tinchant's younger brother Édouard, by contrast, the affronts were a stimulus to further action. Édouard, who had served as a private in that same regiment, penned a vigorous call to his fellow 'sons of Africa' to support the struggle to end slavery once and for all, and to resist all such affronts on public transportation. In the course of these battles over access to public space, the concept of equal rights expanded beyond civil and political rights to encompass what would soon come to be called 'public rights', including the right to respectful and equal treatment in all places of public resort, without discrimination or separation on the grounds of colour.[19]

This right to such equal treatment was a radical demand, and one that its enemies portrayed as an unacceptable pursuit of 'social equality'—a polemical term freighted with associations of sexuality and promiscuous association. Édouard Tinchant, however, combined ideals of personal honour as a veteran with claims to formal respect for all. Despite the disrespect shown by Union general Nathaniel Banks to officers of colour, Private Edouard Tinchant, who had himself been shoved off a streetcar, could use the military structure for his own purposes, appealing successfully to his commanding officer to insist that a man in the Union uniform, whether he was white or black, should not

---

[17] See the discussion of Banks's policy in James G. Hollandsworth, Jr, *The Louisiana Native Guards: The Black Military Experience during the Civil War* (Baton Rouge, Louisiana State University Press, 1995), 43–4.

[18] See Scott and Hébrard, *Freedom Papers*, chapters 6–8.

[19] See Édouard Tinchant, 'Communiqué', *La Tribune de la Nouvelle-Orléans*, 21 July 1864. On the construct of 'public rights' see Rebecca J. Scott, 'Public rights, social equality, and the conceptual roots of the Plessy challenge', *Michigan Law Review* 106 (March 2008), 777–804.

be subjected to the disrespect shown by the white sergeant who had delivered the shove.[20]

By the autumn of 1864, the newspaper *L'Union* had been reconfigured into a larger-circulation bilingual daily paper, the New Orleans *Tribune*. Edited by the local activist Paul Trévigne, in collaboration with a Belgian émigré, Jean-Charles Houzeau, the *Tribune* spoke to a wide audience, conveying the concerns of both the long-free and the newly freed in Louisiana, and from there all the way to Washington. With the end of the war, and the extension of the vote to men of colour in Louisiana by congressional action, the activist community could go further still. Under the broad suffrage conferred by the federal Reconstruction Acts, elections took place in 1867 to elect delegates to a Constitutional Convention that would produce a document under which Louisiana could rejoin the Union.

Reflecting both the newly cross-racial electorate, and the careful electoral strategy of the activists themselves, the resulting body of delegates was composed in nearly equal numbers of men described as white and men described as black or coloured. They drafted a radical constitution, one whose Bill of Rights guaranteed the same 'civil, political and public rights' to all citizens, and whose Article 13 asserted equal rights to access to public transportation and all businesses offering service to the public under state or municipal licence.[21]

For a decade, law in the state was formally governed by this Constitution and subsequent enabling legislation. The link between public rights and dignity became explicit during the debate on the provisions of the enforcement statutes. The editors of the *Tribune* insisted that punitive as well as actual damages should be imposed on those who practised forced segregation, noting that 'the real injury lies in the *indignity* done to the passenger'.[22] A significant number of lawsuits were indeed brought and won under Article Thirteen and the subsequent enabling statutes that had established a specific cause of action in cases of refusal of service on the basis of colour.[23]

Louisiana's experiment in challenging these indignities met with opposition both in the US Supreme Court and in the local Democratic Party. By

---

[20] Édouard Tinchant, 'Communiqué'.
[21] The debates are conveyed, in part, in *Official Journal of the Proceedings of the Convention for Framing a Constitution for the State of Louisiana* (New Orleans, LA, J. B. Roudanez, 1867–8). Further information appears in *La Tribune* during the weeks that the convention was in session.
[22] Emphasis in the original. 'The bill to enforce Article Thirteen', *The New Orleans Tribune* (12 February 1869), 1.
[23] For cases adjudicated in the courts of first instance, see most recently Beth Kressel, 'Creating "what might have been a fuss": the many faces of equal public rights in reconstruction-era Louisiana', in *Louisiana History*, forthcoming.

1879, the ascent of white-supremacist forces in the state had reversed many of the gains of the 1860s and early 1870s, and the *Tribune* had closed its doors. The activists of the *Tribune* nonetheless remained an inspiration to the next generation, and their principled claims of equal rights in the name of liberty and dignity constituted a bedrock on which subsequent campaigns would be built.[24]

White supremacists (and they openly identified themselves as such) had their own memories of the period of Reconstruction, which they saw as having violated their inherent right to rule over the state's residents of African descent. Once the threat of federal reintervention had passed, Louisiana's Democratic Party moved to enact explicit segregationist statutes. In 1891, they achieved passage of a state law requiring the provision of 'equal but separate' accommodations on trains, and the mandatory sending of each passenger to the car in which he or she 'belonged' on the basis of race and colour.[25]

A few Afro-Creole veterans of the Reconstruction-era struggles promptly joined forces with a larger group of younger activists to form the Citizens' Committee for the Repeal of the Separate Car Act. Their goal was to challenge the constitutionality of the new law. The strategy that the committee chose was to combine mass meetings and popular mobilization with the development of legal test cases, one by Daniel Desdunes to test the law with reference to interstate travel, and another by Homer Plessy to test the law with reference to intrastate travel.[26]

The story of the committee's legal challenges is well known, having reached the US Supreme Court as the case of *Plessy v. Ferguson*. The committee's claims to equal access to public transportation were once again portrayed by their opponents as efforts to use the power of the state to gain an unearned 'social equality', even though as a matter of fact the committee was now seeking to fend off, rather than call for, state action. In response, the committee insisted that dignified treatment in the public sphere was a matter of equal citizenship, not social presumption.[27]

The lead attorney for Homer Plessy, Albion W. Tourgée, penned one after another eloquent defence of equality in the face of what he described as the 'spirit of caste'. Tourgée counterposed forced segregation with 'that divine

---

[24] The US Supreme Court ruled Louisiana's anti-discrimination statute unconstitutional insofar as it interfered with the commerce clause of the US Constitution, to which the court on this occasion gave a surprisingly broad reading. See *Hall v Decuir* 95 U.S. 485 (1877).

[25] On the circumstances of the passage of the law, see Keith Weldon Medley, *We as Freemen: Plessy v Ferguson* (Gretna, LA, Pelican Publishing, 2003).

[26] For discussions of the process by which the case of *Plessy v Ferguson* emerged, see Medley, *We as Freemen*.

[27] The nature of the committee and of its arguments is discussed in Scott, 'Public rights'.

equality which prescribe[s] one rule of Christian conduct for all'. Implicitly invoking dignity by speaking of its opposite, humiliation, Tourgée defined the core evil of slavery as 'the degradation of manhood and the legalized defilement of womanhood'.[28]

Tourgée emphasized the link between the campaign for equal treatment and the refusal of distinctions established under slavery, referring to the Separate Car Act's 'two grand divisions of humanity'—'white' and 'coloured'—as 'a new ethnology by prejudice based on the lessons of slavery'.[29] Alongside the formal reasoning laid out by the attorneys and organizers in the case, there was also a bedrock of local, vernacular understandings of dignity on which that reasoning rested. It is not easy to capture the thoughts of Alice Hampton, a schoolteacher in the Donaldsonville Academy who raised money to support the legal challenge, or of Pierre Carmouche, a blacksmith from Ascension Parish who contributed on behalf of a local True Friends Association. But it is clear that support for the legal challenge to dignitary offences went well beyond the urban activists who had organized the committee.[30] Sometimes we can even catch a glimpse of the concepts with which persons of very modest means analysed their own predicaments. One routine legal document provides a hint of the wider adherence to the construct of dignity. Louis Martinet, a key figure in the committee, earned his living as a public notary, operating in daily dialogue with those among his neighbours who sought his services to give legal form to their transactions. The documents that he drafted for those neighbours have been preserved in his ledgers, reflecting some of the ways in which women and men from the artisan and working-class households of New Orleans sought to fend off the humiliations of a society in which the theory and practice of white supremacy had rapidly gained ascendance.[31]

On 3 April 1890, a small group of women came to Martinet to draft and record the founding document for a mutual aid association that they wished to constitute. They proposed to join together to provide mutual aid in sickness,

---

[28] These phrases come from the pamphlet *The Violation of a Constitutional Right, published by Authority of the Citizens' Committee* (New Orleans, LA, The Crusader Print, 1893), 20, 22. The richness of Tourgée's thought has been revealed by the recent work of Mark Elliott, including *Color-Blind Justice: Albion Tourgée and the Quest for Racial Equality from the Civil War to Plessy v Ferguson* (New York, Oxford University Press, 2006).

[29] The quotation is from Tourgée's oral argument, reprinted in Mark Elliott and John David Smith, *Undaunted Radical: The Selected Writings and Speeches of Albion W. Tourgée* (Baton Rouge, Louisiana State University Press, 2010), 329.

[30] For Alice Hampton, see 'Young lady's noble work for the stocking', from the *Crusader* (c. 12–20 July 1895), clipping in *Crusader* Clippings File, Special Collections, Library of Xavier University of New Orleans. On Carmouche, see Scott, *Degrees of Freedom*, 90–1.

[31] These papers are held in the New Orleans Notarial Archives Research Center (NONARC).

and assistance with the costs of a proper burial in case of death. They called the society Dignité, expressing their sense of the multiple risks to their own dignity in a society only a few decades removed from slavery. Indeed, each act of the society was to be marked with the word '*Dignité*', from a stamp that they pledged to have made for that purpose.[32]

In these uses of the term 'dignity', and the associated efforts to fend off humiliation, we can see something of the conceptual universe of men and women who had emerged from a condition of vulnerability, some of them as slaves, others as free persons of colour with sharply limited civil rights. Both the formal status and the practical conditions of slaves and of *gens de couleur libres* had often been defined by humiliations large and small. Part of the meaning of freedom, then, was the replacement of these humiliations with a claim to dignity, in the sense of treatment in the public sphere as bearers of rights and persons worthy of respect.

We might observe that in this context the term 'dignity' was used to reject practices whose logic emerged directly from that of a slaveholding society, encompassing both the exclusion of men and women of colour from public life, and the exclusion of such men and women from various forms of public transportation and lodging. Not confined to the sphere of politics, the word '*dignité*' as used by the women who ventured to Notary Martinet's office also reflected the hope that through mutual aid one might escape some of the humiliations of poverty, particularly at the moment of death.

Written into the 1868 state constitution (and expunged in its 1879 successor), the entitlement to 'public rights' had rested on the idea of an equal claim to dignity in the public sphere, picking out certain actions and designating them as impermissible. 'Public rights' thus provided an alternative to the familiar triad of civil, political, and *social* rights, a framing that had tended to weaken the force of dignitary claims by associating them with the sphere of social rights or, more ominously, with 'social equality', the label given to assertions portrayed as unworthy of any legal recognition. Through conjoined efforts in formal politics and in informal mutual association in post-slavery Louisiana, 'dignity' had taken its place in public debate as a term carrying descriptive weight and meaning, capable of linking features of lived experience with a definite, diagnostic, normative concept.

---

[32] 'Chartre 'La Dignité' Société D'Assistance Mutuelle', 3 October 1890, Act no. 6, vol. 1, 1890, Notarial Acts of Louis Martinet, NONARC.

Brazil, 1970–2012

In the last decades, there has emerged a new variation on the association of the term 'dignity' with a repudiation of the powers once exercised over those held as slaves. Brazil was, famously, the last country in the Americas to abolish chattel slavery, finally terminating the ownership of property in men and women in 1888. One hundred years later, upon the emergence of democracy following an extended period of dictatorship, Brazil's Constituent Assembly in 1987–8 drafted a constitution in which commitment to 'the dignity of the human person' figures as the third fundamental principle of the state, coming after sovereignty and citizenship.[33]

If we were to attempt a strict constitutional history, we would likely find that the invocation of 'dignity' in the Brazilian text owes more to the German *Grundgesetz* of 1949 than to a memory of slavery.[34] By offering up this powerful normative term alongside a list of workers' rights and landowners' obligations, however, the Constitution opened a door to a new way of framing the debate over conditions of labour. This re-framing of the critique of working conditions, moreover, pre-dated the drafting of the Constitution, though it accelerated after its adoption.

In 1940, the government of President Getúlio Vargas had written into the penal code an explicit reference to slavery, albeit modified by the phrase 'analogous to', presumably borrowed from the language of the League of Nations and the International Labour Organization. Article 149 of the 1940 Penal Code read: 'To reduce someone to a condition analogous to that of a slave. Penalty: Imprisonment for from two to eight years.' The new post-1988 Constitutional regime, then, could already count on a long-standing statutory basis for the prosecution of labour practices 'analogous to' slavery. As the incidence of sharply degrading labour conditions become more widely recognized in the 1990s and early 2000s, Article 149 of the Penal Code was modified to provide a clarification of the phrase 'labour analogous to that of a slave': 'either to submit someone to forced labour or to *jornadas exhaustivas* [debilitating work days], or to subject a person to degrading working conditions, or to restrict by whatever means a person's mobility on ground of debt contracted with the employer or employer's representative'.[35]

---

[33] For the full text of the Constitution, with indication of subsequent amendments, see the official site of the Brazilian state: http://www.planalto.gov.br/ccivil_03/constituicao/constitui%C3%A7ao.htm.

[34] I am indebted to Cristiano Paixão of the Faculty of Law of the University of Brasilia for this suggestion. Personal communication, 21 May 2012.

[35] I am drawing here on the careful discussion of the process of 'resignification' of the term *trabalho escravo* offered by Ángela de Castro Gómez in 'Trabalho análogo a de escravo: construindo um prob-

Already in the 1970s, during the dictatorship, social justice missions of the Catholic Church had taken a leading role in the investigation of farms and other isolated locales in which employers were suspected of subjecting workers to conditions constituting or analogous to slavery.[36] After the end of the dictatorship, successive Brazilian governments—including those of Itamar Franco, Fernando Henrique Cardoso, Luis Inácio Lula da Silva, and Dilma Roussef—in turn supported efforts to enforce the federal regulations through the imposition of penalties on offending employers.

In the mid-1990s, the campaign against contemporary slavery took on greater formality with the formation of what were called Mobile Inspection Groups, organized under the auspices of the Ministry of Labour and Employment in collaboration with the Public Ministry of Labour. When they receive credible information suggesting the possibility of conditions of *trabalho escravo* (slave labour), inspectors from the Ministry of Labour and Employment and attorneys from the Public Ministry of Labour are deployed to reach the site before evidence can be suppressed.[37] Given the physical risks to these teams, they are now generally accompanied by members of the Federal Police. The 'mobile groups' are authorized to take immediate legal action leading to the liberation of workers held in conditions 'analogous to slavery', and the attorneys can bring charges against the offending employers before the labour courts.[38]

The government has also compiled and made public a *lista suja* (dirty list), naming enterprises that have been found to be employing *trabalho escravo*. The list provides a daunting inventory of cane growers, charcoal manufacturers, cattle raisers, and others. The *lista suja* itself, by associating specific companies and their owners with the word 'slavery', also operates as a market-based deterrent, enabling non-governmental organizations to call on other enterprises to refuse to do business with the offending companies.[39]

The workers liberated each year by the mobile groups number in the thousands. Those engaged in the campaign against *trabalho escravo* freely use the

---

lema', *História Oral* 11(January–December 2008), 11–41.

[36] A detailed anthropological study of the phenomenon of contemporary debt labour, carried out by a scholar with a background of years of activism in this domain, is Ricardo Rezende Figueira, *Pisando Fora da Própria Sombra: A Escravidão por Dívida no Brasil Contemporâneo* (Rio de Janeiro, Civilização Brasileira, 2004).

[37] For a review of policies and procedures, see the *Manual de combate ao trabalho em condições análogas às de escravo* (Brasilia, Ministério do Trabalho e Emprego, 2012).

[38] Updated information on the campaign is available from the website of the Ministério Público do Trabalho (www.mpt.gov.br/) and from the site http://trabalhoescravo.org.br.

[39] The non-governmental organization Repórter Brasil provides a searchable inventory of enterprises on the list: http://www.reporterbrasil.com.br/listasuja/resultado.php.

term dignity, and invoke workers' rights to the dignity of being issued official identification papers and of having labour contracts properly formalized. Indeed, the acts of liberation are often accompanied by the conferral on the spot of a *carteira*, the government-issued booklet in which are recorded terms of employment and identifying information.[40]

The meaning of 'dignity' in this context seems to be double. First, it captures a dimension of human dignity that has been familiar for centuries, one that invokes a key moral line between human beings and animals.[41] Certain conditions of work are seen as 'humiliating and degrading' precisely because they blur the line between humans and animals, subjecting men, women, and children to conditions that are essentially those of farm animals—obliging them to sleep on dirt floors, or directly in the field under plastic, and providing only untreated river water to drink. (This connection between the phrase 'humiliating and degrading' and the concept of human dignity is one that is also found elsewhere, notably in the 1949 Geneva Convention on prisoners of war, which prohibits 'outrages upon personal dignity, in particular humiliating and degrading treatment'.)[42]

Second, the phrase *trabalho escravo* anchors this dimension of human dignity in a metaphor that has a powerful historical resonance in the country that was the last in the nineteenth-century Americas to abolish slavery, and whose population is now categorized as majority black and brown. The first line of the preface to the classic 1883 abolitionist text by Joaquim Nabuco, *O Abolicionismo*, reads: 'In our country there already exists, fortunately,

---

[40] One prosecutor managed recently to obtain a court settlement obliging an offending company to pay for the cost of running in the local newspaper large announcements that emphasize each worker's right to dignity, and to have a *carteira* with his or her terms of labour properly recorded. (From interviews by the author at the meetings of the MPT attorneys in Brasilia, November 2012.)

[41] Formal jurisprudence on slavery in Brazil, drawing on Roman law, used the term *dignidade humana* in addressing the question of the rights over children born to an enslaved woman whose usufruct had been conferred on someone other than the owner. The great jurist Perdigão Malheiro held that such children were not in fact 'fruits' of their mother, to be reaped by the holder of the usufruct, but should instead remain property of the owner. The reason to refuse ownership of the children to the usufructuary was, in his view, that conferring it would be a violation of human dignity, for it would treat the mother as if she were a mare or other animal. This policy and this reasoning, however, conferred no rights on either the mother or the child; it simply allocated ownership rights as between contending third parties. See Agostinho Marques Perdigão Malheiro, *A Escravidão no Brasil: Ensaio Historico-Juridico-Social*, part 1, section 70 (Rio de Janeiro, Typographia Nacional, 1866), 86–7. I thank Mariana Dias Paes, a master's student in law at the University of São Paulo, for having spotted this reference.

[42] Detailed information on specific cases can be found on the websites http://trabalhoescravo.org.br/ and http://www.reporterbrasil.org.br/ . These phrases in the Geneva Convention are analysed, for a somewhat different purpose, in Michael Rosen, *Dignity: Its History and Meaning* (Cambridge, MA, Harvard University Press, 2012), 59.

a certain national consciousness—still in formation, to be sure—which is introducing into our legislation the element of human dignity, and for which slavery, although inherited from the past, is a true mark of Cain that Brazil carries on its forehead.'[43] Those subjected to humiliating and degrading labour practices in the twenty-first century are not defined by colour, but the unacceptability of their exploitation may be particularly vivid to those for whom the social memory of historical slavery is strongest.[44]

The connection between *trabalho escravo* and affronts to human dignity has been rendered particularly vivid in a prizewinning study by Ricardo Rezende Figueira, who served as a Catholic priest for a decade in the rural state of Pará before initiating his doctoral work in anthropology and sociology. His massively documented study, *Pisando Fora da Propria Sombra* (*Stepping outside One's Own Shadow*), is built on interviews with workers, labour recruiters, family members left behind, and the employers themselves. Resolutely unromantic, and at the same time deeply principled, Figueira carefully analyses the ways in which individuals experience the labour conditions associated with debt servitude. He draws particular attention to the moral pressure that is imposed upon indebted workers to force them to submit to degrading conditions, moral pressure that is in turn often backed up by direct threats of violence.[45]

Figueira provides a detailed description of the lack of sanitary facilities, the constant debilitating labour, the risk and reality of injury or death, and the moments of specific humiliation, including the refusal of medical care, the blocking of all exits from the place of labour, and, in one particularly vivid episode, an employer's refusal to allow a dying worker to return to his family. Like the women in New Orleans in 1890 who joined together to assure that they would have the resources for a proper funeral, the workers on this farm perceived the refusal of decent consideration to a dying person as a violation of fundamental human dignity. They may previously have believed themselves to be morally bound by the debts that the system was designed to perpetuate, and by their promise to earn something before returning to their families. But the indignity imposed upon their fellow worker triggered protest

---

[43] Joaquim Nabuco de Araújo, *O Abolicionismo* (1883; reprint São Paulo, Publifolha, 2000). I thank Keila Grinberg for having called this quotation to my attention. The actual dynamics of abolition were in operation well before Nabuco's book appeared, and involved many actors beside himself, as several authors (including Grinberg) have argued. See, most recently, Elciene Azevedo, *O Direito dos Escravos: Lutas Jurídicas e Abolicionismo na Província de São Paulo* (Campinas, São Paulo, Editora da Unicamp, 2010).

[44] This connection seemed clear in the debates on the floor of the Chamber of Deputies on 22 May 2012, broadcast on the television channel Câmara.

[45] Figueira, *Pisando Fora*.

against the underlying dehumanization inherent in the larger labour practices in which they had become entangled.[46]

The link between dignity as a moral precept and dignity as a value underlying the protection the state owes to those under its jurisdiction emerges quite clearly in the context of current debates and prosecutions in Brazil. The work of members of the Catholic Church, and of the teams from the two labour ministries, brings in an alternative source of authority that can challenge local landowners and the local authorities with whom landowners are often in close collaboration. The 'mobile teams' of inspectors and attorneys have in the process built on their experience in the field in order to transform the phrase 'degrading and humiliating labour' from an apparently unspecified normative statement into a legally recognizable category of behaviour that the state should act to halt.[47]

The issue of *trabalho escravo* surged into public view in Brazil in May 2012, when a long-standing proposal for an amendment to the federal constitution came up for a vote in the Chamber of Deputies. The proposed constitutional amendment (referred to as PEC 438/2001) would impose a penalty of expropriation of property on employers convicted of using *trabalho escravo*. Advocates of the amendment mobilized broad support, but faced delaying tactics from what was referred to as the *bancada ruralista*, a group of deputies representing landowners' interests who opposed the amendment in the name of the absolute right of property. These deputies argued that the terms of the proposed amendment were impermissibly vague, and they evoked the risk of a rogue prosecutor who would seize land on false pretences.[48]

In the course of the nationally televised debates, the word 'dignity' resonated again and again in the speeches of supporters of the amendment. In the final vote in the Chamber, on 22 May, opponents initially held out by staying off the floor to block the achievement of a quorum. At the last minute, the necessary votes were obtained to pass the amendment, but only through a promise from the government that a serious discussion yielding a proposal for 'infra-constitutional' legislation would be forthcoming to clarify the language of the amendment itself. The matter then went to the Brazilian Senate.[49]

---

[46] Figueira, *Pisando Fora*, 356.

[47] Ángela de Castro Gómez, in 'Trabalho análogo', emphasizes the role of these practical efforts in helping to refine the definition of *trabalho escravo*.

[48] For the official record of the long legislative history of the amendment, see http://www.camara.gov.br/proposicoesWeb/fichadetramitacao?idProposicao=36162.

[49] The transcript of the debates can be consulted at camara.gov.br, in the Diário of the Câmara for 23 May 2012, beginning on 18181.

In an insightful recent essay on the history of the concept of *trabalho escravo* in Brazil, the historian Ángela de Castro Gómez has traced in detail the way in which the term 'slave labour' has come to be 're-signified', to use her phrase. The new usage, she suggests, is metaphorical, but metaphorical in the strongest sense, giving meaning to one thing by drawing attention to the way in which it is like something quite different. The worker subjected to *trabalho escravo*, Gómez concludes, is referred to as a slave precisely in order to say that he or she is *not* a slave, for slavery cannot by law exist in Brazil. The practice of *trabalho escravo*, and its inherent affront to human dignity, is thus named in order to assist in its extinction. The Afro-Creole activists of nineteenth-century Louisiana, who a century earlier had combined their equal rights litigation with a commitment to the dignity of labour, would have understood.[50]

In these two periods—across two continents and two centuries—the term 'dignity' became a key link between specific experiences of exploitation or humiliation, and a normative diagnosis that evoked the previous institution of chattel slavery. Far from being a term confined to abstract political philosophy, it thus became a vital part of how people saw the harms and hopes of their own lives.

---

[50] On the overlap between the supporters of the Plessy challenge and the organizers of the Knights of Labor in Louisiana, see Scott, *Degrees of Freedom*, 78, 90, 91.

3

Würde des Menschen: Restoring Human Dignity in Post-Nazi Germany

Christoph Goos

A 'non-interpreted thesis'

THE GENESIS OF THE German Basic Law's human dignity article[1] has so far played a rather marginal role in the interpretation of this provision.[2] The numerous commentators have focused on the deeper philosophical or religious 'roots' of the concept.[3] However, hardly anybody has considered the question of what the 'mothers and fathers of the Basic Law',[4] the sixty-five delegates from the State Parliaments assembled as Parliamentary Council in Bonn between September 1948 and May 1949,[5] could have meant by the term 'Würde des Menschen'.

---

[1] Article 1, paragraph 1 of the Grundgesetz für die Bundesrepublik Deutschland, 23 May 1949, Bundesgesetzblatt I, 1 (German Basic Law) states: 'Die Würde des Menschen ist unantastbar. Sie zu achten und zu schützen ist Verpflichtung aller staatlichen Gewalt.' 'The dignity of man is inviolable. To respect and protect it is the duty of all state authority.'
[2] See also Martin O'Malley, 'A performative definition of human dignity', in Nikolaus Knoepffler et al. (eds), *Facetten der Menschenwürde* (Freiburg and München, Karl Alber Verlag, 2011), 75–101, at 75: '[t]he principle's historical aspect is downplayed'.
[3] See, most recently, Josef Isensee, 'Würde des Menschen', in Detlef Merten and Hans-J. Papier (eds), *Handbuch der Grundrechte in Deutschland und Europa, vol. IV: Grundrechte in Deutschland: Einzelgrundrechte I* (Heidelberg, C. F. Müller, 2011), §187 margin numbers 55–84; Nils Teifke, *Das Prinzip Menschenwürde* (Tübingen, Mohr Siebeck, 2011), 36–46; important clarifications at Stephan Schaede, 'Würde—eine ideengeschichtliche Annäherung aus theologischer Perspektive', in Petra Bahr and Hans Michael Heinig (eds), *Menschenwürde in der säkularen Verfassungsordnung. Rechtswissenschaftliche und theologische Perspektiven* (Tübingen, Mohr Siebeck, 2006), 7–69.
[4] BVerfGE (Entscheidungen des Bundesverfassungsgerichts) 103, 142–64, at 158: 'Mütter und Väter des Grundgesetzes'.
[5] See Werner Heun, *The Constitution of Germany. A Contextual Analysis* (Oxford, Hart Publishing, 2011), 9–24; Michael F. Feldkamp, *Der Parlamentarische Rat 1948–1949. Die Entstehung des Grundgesetzes* (Göttingen, Vandenhoek & Ruprecht, 1998); Erhard H. M. Lange, *Die Würde des Menschen ist unantastbar. Der Parlamentarische Rat und das Grundgesetz* (Heidelberg, Decker & Müller, 1993).

There might be several reasons for this. First and foremost, the German Federal Constitutional Court held already in one of its very first decisions that not the subjective notions of the framers but the 'objectified will of the legislator' or the 'will of the law' was crucial for the interpretation of legal provisions.[6] Second, there was and there is still a widespread assumption that the records of the Parliamentary Council's proceedings were unproductive with regard to the meaning of the legal term of 'dignity of man'. Finally, these records were only partially published in 1949. The records of the proceedings of the 'Committee dealing with Basic Issues', where Article 1 of the Basic Law was mainly and intensely discussed, were not published until 1993.[7] Until then, one had to manage with a summary, written by three staff members of the Parliamentary Council and published in the first volume of the new series of the Yearbook for Public Law in 1951.[8] This summary, entitled 'History of Origins of the Provisions of the Basic Law', is outstanding, and it is still a treasure chest for anyone who wants to learn more about the genesis of the Basic Law.[9] It is not exhaustive, however. The seven pages about Article 1 contain only one clue to a possible positive understanding of the term 'dignity of man': it is the famous but ambiguous dictum of Theodor Heuss that human dignity was a 'non-interpreted thesis'.[10] This statement was often quoted and taken as evidence that the framers had deliberately chosen a term that was meant to be freely interpretable or maybe even inaccessible to any kind of interpretation.[11] This false assumption did not remain without consequences.

---

[6] BVerfGE 1, 299–322, at 312.
[7] Deutscher Bundestag and Bundesarchiv (eds), *Der Parlamentarische Rat 1948–1949. Akten und Protokolle, Band 5, Ausschuss für Grundsatzfragen*, bearbeitet von Eberhard Pikart und Wolfram Werner (Boppard am Rhein, Harald Boldt Verlag, 1993).
[8] Klaus-Berto von Doemming, Rudolf W. Füsslein and Werner Matz, 'Entstehungsgeschichte der Artikel des Grundgesetzes', *Jahrbuch des öffentlichen Rechts der Gegenwart*, neue Folge, 1 (1951), 1–941.
[9] A second edition, completed by a concise introduction written by Peter Häberle, has been published recently: Peter Häberle (ed.), *Entstehungsgeschichte der Artikel des Grundgesetzes. Neuausgabe des Jahrbuch des öffentlichen Rechts der Gegenwart Band 1* (Tübingen, Mohr Siebeck, 2010).
[10] Von Doemming, Füsslein and Matz, 'Entstehungsgeschichte der Artikel des Grundgesetzes', 49: 'Die Würde des Menschen stehe in seinem [Heuss'] Vorschlag als nicht interpretierte These'.
[11] See, for instance, Jutta Limbach, 'Der Mensch wird nie ohne Makel sein', *Frankfurter Allgemeine Zeitung* (25 February 2002), 51: 'non-interpretable thesis', my translation; Doris Schroeder, 'Human rights and human dignity. An appeal to separate the conjoined twins', *Ethical Theory and Moral Practice* 15 (2012), 323–35, at 326.

Loss of meaning

What is meant by 'Würde des Menschen', usually translated as 'dignity of man' or 'human dignity'?[12] 'Ironically, we do not know what human dignity is, but we know exactly whether human dignity is violated or not', states the author of a popular textbook on German constitutional law.[13] In the 1950s, things were different.[14] 'Having dignity means: being a personality', formulated Günter Dürig, maybe the most influential German constitutionalist of the time, in 1952.[15] In his opinion, a person 'ripens' to a personality by affirming and serving the values the person is 'essentially' related to, namely the eternal 'You' of God, the 'You' of the others, and the 'We' of the community. The subject of the fundamental right guarantees of the Basic Law is, according to Dürig, 'always the responsible person, never the bondless individual'. None of the fundamental right guarantees protected the 'subhuman'.[16] Consequently, Dürig and others were convinced that the use of violence, drugs, and psycho-technical means could be allowed and perhaps even constitutionally required in the interrogation of 'hardboiled' lawbreakers.[17] On the other hand, Dürig 'shuddered' to think about issues like artificial insemination with the help of a sperm donor. He had not the slightest doubt that such acts violated human dignity 'as such'.[18]

Dürig's deliberations shaped and dominated the interpretation of Article 1 of the Basic Law for years. Fundamental criticism did not emerge until the mid-1960s. In 1964, Peter Badura pointed out that the common value-based and personalistic interpretation of the first article of the Basic Law did not see men as they are but in the way they should be, according to the ethical ideal of the autonomous personality. However, those people not corresponding to

---

[12] Martin O'Malley rightly emphasizes that 'Dignity is not simply Würde', see O'Malley, 'Dignity in US bio-ethics debate: needs Würde', in Christine Baumbach and Peter Kunzmann (eds), *Würde—dignité—godnosc—dignity: Die Menschenwürde im internationalen Vergleich* (München, Herbert Utz Verlag, 2010), 253–76, at 254–61.
[13] Friedhelm Hufen, *Staatsrecht II. Grundrechte*, 3rd edn (München, Verlag C. H. Beck, 2011), §10 margin number 29, my translation.
[14] For detailed references, see Christoph Goos, *Innere Freiheit. Eine Rekonstruktion des grundgesetzlichen Würdebegriffs* (Göttingen, V&R unipress, 2011), 21–30.
[15] Günter Dürig, 'Die Menschenauffassung des Grundgesetzes', *Juristische Rundschau* 6 (1952), 259–63, at 259, my translation.
[16] Dürig, 'Die Menschenauffassung des Grundgesetzes', 261, my translation.
[17] Günter Dürig, 'Der Grundrechtssatz von der Menschenwürde', *Archiv des öffentlichen Rechts* 81 (1956), 117–57, at 128; Friedrich Klein, in Hermann von Mangoldt/Friedrich Klein, *Das Bonner Grundgesetz*, 2nd edn (Berlin and Frankfurt am Main, Verlag Franz Vahlen, 1957), Article 1, Note III 5 a.
[18] Dürig, 'Der Grundrechtssatz von der Menschenwürde', 130.

this ideal because of their behaviour or their constitution needed to be protected. Paradoxically, the personalistic understanding of human dignity was forced to give reasons for the dignity of these people, as if they were a problematic borderline case. And even worse: this interpretation made it possible to exclude the most vulnerable people from the protection of Article 1 of the Basic Law. Badura therefore argued that one should no longer theorize about the moral personality of man but rather agree on a casuistry of clear infringements of human dignity.[19] His proposal was later called the 'negative interpretation method',[20] and it did not last long until Baduras's approach became the prevailing opinion. Günter Dürig, changeable as a chameleon, relented in the early 1970s and declared, as if he had never claimed anything else: 'One should not presume to interpret the principle of human dignity positively, but you can say what violates it.'[21]

A positive definition of human dignity was considered dispensable, because—this is how Dürig formulated it—'after the experience of our people, there is a very precise consensus about how a political and social order should look and how it should not look'.[22] This assumption, however, soon proved illusory. In 1982, the first German test-tube baby was born, and it soon became apparent that it would be impossible to reach an agreement about the status of the embryo *in vitro* and the constitutional review of these new opportunities. Human dignity was therefore not the appropriate word, Peter Lerche concluded. According to him, human dignity could only defend its contours if one limited the use of the concept to those topics consented to by the community, and *in vitro* fertilization was, obviously, not one of these.[23] In the mid-1990s, Horst Dreier proposed to 'free' the abortion debate 'from the

---

[19] Peter Badura, 'Generalprävention und Würde des Menschen', *Juristenzeitung* 19 (1964), 337–44, at 340–1.
[20] See Hans-Georg Dederer, 'Die Garantie der Menschenwürde (Art. 1 Abs. 1 GG). Dogmatische Grundfragen auf dem Stand der Wissenschaft', *Jahrbuch des öffentlichen Rechts der Gegenwart* 57 (2009), 89–124, at 105–7.
[21] Günter Dürig, 'Zur Bedeutung und Tragweite des Art. 79 Abs. III GG', in Hans Spanner et al. (eds), *Festgabe für Theodor Maunz zum 70. Geburtstag am 1. September 1971* (München, Verlag C. H. Beck, 1971), 41–53, at 44–5, my translation.
[22] Günter Dürig, 'Zur Bedeutung und Tragweite des Art. 79 Abs. III GG', 44, my translation.
[23] Peter Lerche, 'Verfassungsrechtliche Aspekte der Gentechnologie', in Rudolf Lukes and Rupert Scholz (eds): *Rechtsfragen der Gentechnologie. Vorträge anläßlich eines Kolloquiums Recht und Technik—Rechtsfragen der Gentechnologie in der Tagungsstätte der Max-Planck-Gesellschaft 'Schloß Ringberg' am 18., 19. und 20. November 1985* (Köln, Carl Heymanns Verlag, 1986), 88–111, at 100.

heavy burden of Article 1, paragraph 1 of the Basic Law' as well, because, even in this case, there was no consensus in sight.[24]

In the first edition of his legal commentary on the Basic Law, which was published in 1996, Dreier listed slavery, servitude, deportation, stigmatization, and torture as examples of self-evidently and universally consented violations of Article 1, para. 1 of the Basic Law.[25] Nevertheless, only a few years later, a German police officer threatened a kidnapper with considerable pain to find out the whereabouts of a kidnapped child. All the courts later concerned with this tragical case stated clearly and without exception that this was a violation of the kidnapper's dignity, even though the police officer had tried to save the life of an innocent child.[26] However, German constitutionalists began to discuss seriously if the so-called 'rescue torture' could be allowed by Article 1 of the Basic Law.[27] Critical observers anxiously diagnosed that the inviolability of human dignity seemed no longer as obvious as before. The findings of the Federal Constitutional Court concerning the dignity of innocent passengers on board a hijacked aircraft in the Aviation Security Act decision[28] were also discussed controversially.[29] A kind of 'tiredness with dignity' and a tendency to solve problematic cases without using Article 1 of the Basic Law could not be overlooked. 'After the knowing about the meaning of human dignity has faded away, it is now also becoming increasingly unclear to us why we still need it', the German constitutionalist Uwe Volkmann remarked.[30]

---

[24] Horst Dreier, 'Menschenwürdegarantie und Schwangerschaftsabbruch', *Die Öffentliche Verwaltung* 48 (1995), 1036–40, at 1040, my translation.
[25] Horst Dreier, in Dreier (ed.), *Grundgesetz. Kommentar, Band I, Artikel 1–19*, 1st edn (Tübingen, Mohr Siebeck, 1996), Article 1, Abs. 1, margin no. 80.
[26] See, most recently, Oberlandesgericht Frankfurt/Main, 1 U 201/11 of 10 October 2012, http://www.lareda.hessenrecht.hessen.de; European Court of Human Rights, *Gafgen v Germany*, *European Human Rights Reports*, 52 (2011), 1–57; Bundesverfassungsgericht, 1 BvR 1807/07 of 19 February 2008, http://www.bverfg.de.
[27] For discussion of this topic, see Helmut Goerlich (ed.), *Staatliche Folter, Heiligt der Zweck die Mittel?* (Paderborn, mentis Verlag, 2007); Gerhard Beestermöller and Hauke Brunkhorst (eds), *Rückkehr der Folter. Der Rechtsstaat im Zwielicht?* (München, Verlag C. H. Beck, 2006).
[28] BVerfGE 115, 118–66, at 152–4.
[29] For an overview, see Oliver Lepsius, 'Human dignity and the downing of aircraft. The German Federal Constitutional Court strikes down a prominent anti-terrorism provision in the new air-transport security Act', *German Law Journal* 7 (2006), 761–76, at 766–74; Felix Müller and Tobias Richter, 'Report on the Bundesverfassungsgericht's (Federal Consitutional Court) jurisprudence in 2005/2006', *German Law Journal* 9 (2008), 161–93, at 184–93; both with further references.
[30] Uwe Volkmann, 'Nachricht vom Ende der Gewissheit', *Frankfurter Allgemeine Zeitung* (24 November 2003), 8, my translation; see also Tim Wihl, 'Wahre Würde. Ansätze zu einer Metatheorie der Menschenwürdetheorien', in Carsten Bäcker and Sascha Ziemann (eds), *Junge Rechtsphilosophie* (Stuttgart, Franz Steiner Verlag, 2012), 187–200, at 200: 'dispensable as a legal term', my translation.

Rediscovering the original meaning

What was meant by 'dignity of man'?[31] During the first meetings of the Plenary Assembly of the Parliamentary Council, rather non-specific 'dignity-talk' prevailed: Delegates from all parties emphasized that freedom and dignity were the 'highest goods' and that it would be the main task of the Council to secure them again. However, some delegates already distinguished explicitly between 'freedom' and 'dignity'. Adolf Süsterhenn, for instance, one of the most influential Christian Democratic members of the Council,[32] stated that human dignity, 'inner freedom', and the 'inner value' of the personality remained 'fine words' as long as the individuals had no possibility to make use of these capacities in their daily lives.[33] Helene Wessel, one of the two delegates of the Catholic Centre party, emphasized in a very similar way the necessity to convey to the Germans the notion of 'true liberty', the freedom for individual development. She used the terms of 'human dignity' and 'freedom rights', differentiating between the ability to make one's own decisions and the freedom to act and to enter into relationships with others.[34]

The distinction between 'inner' and 'outer' freedom can also be found in the deliberations of the Committee dealing with Basic Issues that was responsible for the phrasing of the fundamental rights catalogue. The records of the proceedings of this committee show that the already mentioned dictum on human dignity as a 'non-interpreted thesis' was not at all meant to be a carte blanche for any arbitrary interpretation. Theodor Heuss[35] repeatedly criticized an early draft version of Article 1 ('The dignity of man rests on eternal, inherent

---

[31] Article 1 German Basic Law was mainly discussed during the fourth meeting of the Committee dealing with Basic Issues on 23 September 1948 (see Deutscher Bundestag and Bundesarchiv (eds), *Der Parlamentarische Rat 1948–1949. Akten und Protokolle, Band 5, Ausschuss für Grundsatzfragen*, 62–75) and during its twenty-second and twenty-third meeting on 18 November 1948 (see 584–609). For further and more detailed references, see Goos, *Innere Freiheit*, 75–94. Compare also Christoph Möllers, 'Democracy and human dignity: limits of a moralized conception of rights in German constitutional law', *Israel Law Review* 42 (2009), 416–39, at 417–21; Christoph Enders, 'A right to have rights—the German constitutional concept of human dignity', *NUJS Law Review* 3 (2010), 253–64, at 254–5; both with further references.

[32] For further information, see Christoph von Hehl, *Adolf Süsterhenn (1905–1974). Verfassungsvater, Weltanschauungspolitiker, Föderalist* (Düsseldorf, Droste Verlag, 2012).

[33] Deutscher Bundestag and Bundesarchiv (eds), *Der Parlamentarische Rat 1948–1949. Akten und Protokolle, Band 9, Plenum*, bearbeitet von Wolfram Werner (München, Harald Boldt Verlag, 1996), 185.

[34] Deutscher Bundestag and Bundesarchiv (eds), *Der Parlamentarische Rat 1948–1949, Akten und Protokolle, Band 9, Plenum*, 209.

[35] For further information, see, most recently, Peter Merseburger, *Theodor Heuss. Der Bürger als Präsident. Biographie* (München, Deutsche Verlags-Anstalt, 2012); Ernst-Wolfgang Becker, *Theodor Heuss. Bürger im Zeitalter der Extreme* (Stuttgart, Kohlhammer Verlag, 2011).

rights') for the very reason that he considered the reference to 'eternal, inherent rights' as too ambiguous.[36] He recalled his proposal ('The dignity of man is placed under the protection of the state order'),[37] and explained that the dignity of man was a 'non-interpreted thesis' in it.[38] He added that he wanted to choose the wording of this Article in a way 'that one could comprehend theologically, another philosophically, another ethically'.[39] Helene Weber, one of the four mothers of the Basic Law, agreed: 'The individual is free to take religious, ethical or historical insights as his or her starting point. However, it is most significant that we, at this historical moment, begin our Constitution with the concept of human dignity.'[40] Adolf Süsterhenn likewise declared: 'One sees human dignity rooted in humanity, another in the Christian conviction that men and women are created in the image of God. However, we agree in the concept of human dignity as the highest value in our worldliness.'[41] The members of the Committee dealing with Basic Issues agreed that the concept of human dignity has different roots and origins, and that there are several good reasons for protecting human dignity constitutionally. With regard to its foundation, the human dignity Article remained a 'non-interpreted thesis'.

However, the records also show that the mothers and fathers of the Basic Law did their very best to clarify the substantive meaning of the legal term of human dignity. Carlo Schmid, one of the most influential Social Democratic members of the Parliamentary Council,[42] demanded right at the beginning of the consultations: 'Dignity of man—that should be defined!'[43] The wording of Article 1 should be considered carefully, because 'in its systematic relevance, it is the key to the whole'.[44] Ludwig Bergsträsser contradicted this

---

[36] Deutscher Bundestag and Bundesarchiv (eds), *Der Parlamentarische Rat 1948–1949. Akten und Protokolle, Band 5, Ausschuss für Grundsatzfragen*, 67 and 72.

[37] Deutscher Bundestag and Bundesarchiv (eds), *Der Parlamentarische Rat 1948–1949. Akten und Protokolle, Band 5, Ausschuss für Grundsatzfragen*, 52 and 67, my translation.

[38] Deutscher Bundestag and Bundesarchiv (eds), *Der Parlamentarische Rat 1948–1949. Akten und Protokolle, Band 5, Ausschuss für Grundsatzfragen*, 72, my translation.

[39] Deutscher Bundestag and Bundesarchiv (eds), *Der Parlamentarische Rat 1948–1949. Akten und Protokolle, Band 5, Ausschuss für Grundsatzfragen*, 67, my translation.

[40] Deutscher Bundestag and Bundesarchiv (eds), *Der Parlamentarische Rat 1948–1949. Akten und Protokolle, Band 5, Ausschuss für Grundsatzfragen*, 69, my translation.

[41] Deutscher Bundestag and Bundesarchiv (eds), *Der Parlamentarische Rat 1948–1949. Akten und Protokolle, Band 5, Ausschuss für Grundsatzfragen*, 915, my translation.

[42] For further information, see Petra Weber, *Carlo Schmid 1896–1979. Eine Biographie* (Frankfurt am Main, Suhrkamp Verlag, 1998); Carlo Schmid, *Erinnerungen*, 3rd edn (Bern, München, Wien, Scherz Verlag, 1979).

[43] Deutscher Bundestag and Bundesarchiv (eds), *Der Parlamentarische Rat 1948–1949. Akten und Protokolle, Band 5, Ausschuss für Grundsatzfragen*, 66, my translation.

[44] Deutscher Bundestag and Bundesarchiv (eds), *Der Parlamentarische Rat 1948–1949. Akten und Protokolle, Band 5, Ausschuss für Grundsatzfragen*, 64, my translation.

immediately when Hermann von Mangoldt, the chairman of the Committee dealing with Basic Issues, complained that one could hardly get a concrete idea about the meaning of the legal term of human dignity: 'Human dignity forbids any compulsion to act against one's own conviction. For me, this seems to be one of the most important features of human dignity. Human dignity forbids that someone is beaten. Human dignity is, in other words, the freedom from compulsion to act against one's convictions.'[45] Theodor Heuss insisted: 'Human dignity must rest in itself. It must not be derived from any governmental position.'[46] Carlo Schmid called human dignity 'a quality, an attribute that determines the human and that distinguishes humans from other creatures.'[47] Schmid, well versed in philosophy and theology, referred to Martin Luther's concept of the 'freedom of the Christian'[48] and the inherent dignity that, according to the late Stoic philosopher Epictetus, remains even to the galley slave forged to his bench:[49] 'For me', Schmid explained, 'the dignity of man recognizes this attribute of man as an honour.'[50]

Inner freedom

This 'attribute' or capability that Carlo Schmid referred to can be described as 'inner freedom'.[51] Martin Luther protested vehemently as the German peasants demanded in 1525 in their *Twelve Articles* that they did not want to be serfs any longer because the scripture said that Christ had freed them. 'That is', declared Luther, 'making Christian freedom a completely physical matter.' 'A slave can be a Christian', Luther wrote in his famous *Admonition to Peace*, 'and have Christian freedom, in the same way that a prisoner or a sick

---

[45] Deutscher Bundestag and Bundesarchiv (eds), *Der Parlamentarische Rat 1948–1949. Akten und Protokolle, Band 5, Ausschuss für Grundsatzfragen*, 607.

[46] Deutscher Bundestag and Bundesarchiv (eds), *Der Parlamentarische Rat 1948–1949. Akten und Protokolle, Band 5, Ausschuss für Grundsatzfragen*, 588, my translation.

[47] Deutscher Bundestag and Bundesarchiv (eds), *Der Parlamentarische Rat 1948–1949. Akten und Protokolle, Band 5, Ausschuss für Grundsatzfragen*, 72.

[48] Deutscher Bundestag and Bundesarchiv (eds), *Der Parlamentarische Rat 1948–1949. Akten und Protokolle, Band 14, Hauptausschuss*, bearbeitet von Michael F. Feldkamp (München, R. Oldenbourg Verlag, 2009), 1290.

[49] Deutscher Bundestag and Bundesarchiv (eds), *Der Parlamentarische Rat 1948–1949. Akten und Protokolle, Band 5, Ausschuss für Grundsatzfragen*, 72; Deutscher Bundestag and Bundesarchiv (eds), *Der Parlamentarische Rat 1948–1949. Akten und Protokolle, Band 14, Hauptausschuss*, 1290.

[50] Deutscher Bundestag and Bundesarchiv (eds), *Der Parlamentarische Rat 1948–1949. Akten und Protokolle, Band 14, Hauptausschuss*, 1290, my translation.

[51] See Goos, *Innere Freiheit*, 95–157.

man is a Christian, and yet not free.'[52] Luther distinguished carefully between the 'inner' man and his liberty and the 'outward' man.[53] For Epictetus, one's outer, external, social, and political freedom is also not essential: If a liberated slave—to quote one of the examples he uses in his *Discourses*—falls in love with the wrong girl or makes himself dependent on other people for the sake of his professional advancement, he might fall into a far more abject slavery than the one he has escaped: 'Finally, when he crowns it off by becoming a senator, becoming a slave in fine company, then he experiences the poshest and most prestigious form of enslavement.'[54] For Epictetus, those are free who are able to distinguish between the things in their power and the things that are not in their power: 'I must die. But must I die bawling? I must be put in chains—but moaning and groaning too? I must be exiled; but is there anything to keep me from going with a smile, calm and self-composed?'[55]

Liberal thinkers like Isaiah Berlin doubt that this inner freedom deserves the name of freedom at all, because it is 'compatible with a very high degree of political despotism'.[56] One might also ask if 'inner freedom' really needs to be protected by law.[57] Isn't the galley slave, chained but free anyway, the best example that the 'inner freedom' of man is inviolable in the truest sense of the word? In fact, there is still a dispute in the literature as to whether the first sentence of Article 1 ('The dignity of man is inviolable') is to be understood descriptively or prescriptively.[58] 'It should be inviolable!', declared Ludwig

---

[52] Martin Luther, 'Admonition to peace', trans. Charles M. Jacobs, revised Robert C. Schultz, in Robert C. Schultz (ed.), Helmut T. Lehmann (gen. ed.), *Luther's Works*, vol. 46, *The Christian in Society III* (Philadelphia, PA, Fortress Press, 1967), 3–43, at 39.

[53] See Christoph Goos, 'Wirtschaft und Freiheit in den Bauernkriegsartikeln. Verfassungshistorische Anmerkungen zu Artikel 2, 3, 11: Freiheit von Zehnt, Leibeigenschaft und Todfallabgaben', in Görge K. Hasselhoff and David von Mayenburg (eds), *Die Zwölf Artikel von 1525 und das 'Göttliche Recht' der Bauern—rechtshistorische und theologische Dimensionen* (Würzburg, Ergon Verlag, 2012), 77–98, at 94–7; Martin Heckel, 'Luthers Traktat "Von der Freiheit eines Christenmenschen" als Markstein des Kirchen- und Staatskirchenrechts', *Zeitschrift für Theologie und Kirche*, 109 (2012), 122–52; Eberhard Jüngel, *Zur Freiheit eines Christenmenschen. Eine Erinnerung an Luthers Schrift* (München, Chr. Kaiser Verlag, 1991).

[54] Epictetus, 'Discourses' IV.1.39, in Robert Dobbin (trans. and ed.), *Epictetus: Discourses and Selected Writings* (London, Penguin Books, 2008), 177.

[55] Epictetus, 'Discourses' I.1.22, 7; for further information, see, for example, Anthony A. Long, *Epictetus. A Stoic and Socratic Guide to Life* (Oxford, Clarendon Press, 2004), 207–30; Richard Sorabji, 'Epictetus on *proairesis* and self', in Theodore Scaltsas and Andrew S. Mason (eds), *The Philosophy of Epictetus* (Oxford, Oxford University Press, 2010), 87–98.

[56] Isaiah Berlin, *Liberty: Incorporating Four Essays on Liberty* (Oxford, Oxford University Press, 2002), 32.

[57] See, however, particularly instructively, Clemens Sedmak's reflections on interiority and the uniqueness of the inner life of human beings and the political dimension of interiority: Chapter 33, this volume.

[58] See Teifke, *Das Prinzip Menschenwürde*, 73–4.

Bergsträsser when this question arose in the debates of the Parliamentary Council.[59] Hermann von Mangoldt said, and this was universally consented: 'After the things we have witnessed during the Nazi era, the legal protection of human dignity must be one of our main concerns.'[60]

The mothers and fathers of the Basic Law had experiences in mind like those transmitted by the later Hanoverian bishop Hanns Lilje, the psychoanalyst Bruno Bettelheim and the Viennese psychiatrist and philosopher Viktor Frankl. Lilje, for instance, reports of a shocking encounter with the severely tortured Carl Friedrich Goerdeler: 'The Gestapo had made a ruin out of him. He made his comments in a mechanical, soulless manner, as if he said nothing but the things they taught him. His eyes had lost their former brightness, and they gave away that, in addition to the usual torture, even drugs and other bad things had done their work.'[61] After having spent approximately one year in the concentration camps at Dachau and Buchenwald, Bettelheim described it as being one of the goals of the Gestapo 'to break the prisoners as individuals'.[62] 'The last vestiges of personality were erased there', reported Viktor Frankl.[63] In a nightmarish study, the German philosopher Reinhold Aschenberg characterizes the Nazi concentration camps as 'institutions of de-subjectification': 'These laboratories emit large numbers, masses of human beings whose subjectivity slowly fades until they, while still alive, totally lose it.'[64] The Nazi system as a whole can be described as a major project of de-subjectifying man—in the concentration camps, the mass organizations, at school, and in university, even at home, by a certain kind of infant education that caused avoidant personality disorders—with the well-known, devastating consequences.[65]

Only a few could preserve and prove their inner freedom under such circumstances. It can be shown that the desire for 'true intellectual freedom' was one of the motivations, the 'complete protection of freedom of spirit' one of the goals of the conspirators, especially for the students and professors around

---

[59] Deutscher Bundestag and Bundesarchiv (eds), *Der Parlamentarische Rat 1948–1949. Akten und Protokolle, Band 5, Ausschuss für Grundsatzfragen*, 913, my translation.
[60] Deutscher Bundestag and Bundesarchiv (eds), *Der Parlamentarische Rat 1948–1949. Akten und Protokolle, Band 5, Ausschuss für Grundsatzfragen*, 52, my translation.
[61] Hanns Lilje, *Im finstern Tal* (Nürnberg, Laetare Verlag, 1947), 50, my translation.
[62] Bruno Bettelheim, 'Individual and mass behavior in extreme situations', *The Journal of Abnormal and Social Psychology* 38 (1943), 417–52, at 418.
[63] Viktor E. Frankl, 'Homo patiens' (1950), in Frankl, *Der leidende Mensch*, 3rd edn (Bern, Verlag Hans Huber, 2005), 161–241, at 176, my translation.
[64] Reinhold Aschenberg, *Ent-Subjektivierung des Menschen. Lager und Shoah in philosophischer Reflexion* (Würzburg, Königshausen & Neumann, 2003), 278, my translation.
[65] See Goos, *Innere Freiheit*, 127–38.

Sophie and Hans Scholl and Helmuth von Moltke and his Kreisau circle:[66] 'Delp, Gerstenmaier and I only thought', Moltke wrote to his wife a few days before he was executed. 'And the Nazis fear the mere thought of these three lonely men so much that they want to cut off all that is infected with it.'[67] During the Nazi time, even freedom of thought, even inner freedom, had been threatened and proven to be fragile. For the fathers and mothers of the Basic Law there was no question that it had to be protected by law in the future. Not yet the Jewish tragedy, as Samuel Moyn rightly points out,[68] but this is the reason why they decided to begin with the sentence: 'The dignity of man is inviolable'.

Nevertheless, this conception might seem to be inadequate because it only applies to the 'inner' freedom of man. However, the inseparable connection between inner and outer freedom was not only intensely discussed in the Parliamentary Council. It is stated in the following paragraph of Article 1 of the Basic Law: 'The dignity of man is inviolable. To respect it and to protect it is the duty of all state authority. The German people therefore acknowledge inviolable and inalienable human rights as the basis of every community, of peace and of justice in the world.' Human dignity and human rights can be distinguished and they must be distinguished, but they must not be separated.[69] The basic rights are guaranteed for the sake of human dignity, 'since', according to Hermann von Mangoldt, 'every single article protects a bit of the freedom that is necessary to guarantee human dignity'.[70] It was precisely in this sense that Carlo Schmid stated it at the Hamburg SPD Party Congress in May 1950: 'Epictetus once expressed that even the slave chained to his oar was free if he had the right attitude. But, comrades, we do not want to be satisfied with this freedom of the galley slave. We do not only want the opportunity to have this inner freedom. We also want to have the opportunity for a freedom that enables us to develop all human capacities in the outside world.'[71]

---

[66] See Goos, *Innere Freiheit*, 116–27.
[67] Helmuth J. von Moltke, 'Letter of 10 January 1945', in Günter Brakelmann (ed.), *Helmuth James von Moltke. Im Land der Gottlosen. Tagebuch und Briefe aus der Haft 1944/45* (München, Verlag C. H. Beck, 2009), 328–35, at 334, my translation.
[68] Samuel Moyn, Chapter 4, this volume.
[69] See Goos, *Innere Freiheit*, 205–9.
[70] Deutscher Bundestag and Bundesarchiv (eds), *Der Parlamentarische Rat 1948–1949. Akten und Protokolle, Band 5, Ausschuss für Grundsatzfragen*, 91, my translation.
[71] Carlo Schmid, in *Protokoll der Verhandlungen des Parteitages der SPD vom 21. bis 25. Mai 1950 in Hamburg* (Frankfurt am Main, n.d.), 257, my translation.

Dignity and the 'weak subject'

One might ask, however, if 'inner freedom' is not just another noble ideal that excludes many people, for example little children, the mentally disabled, people suffering from Alzheimer's disease, and, of course, the unborn and the deceased.[72] It is completely inconceivable that the mothers and fathers of the Basic Law wanted Article 1 paragraph 1 to be interpreted like this. To me, it therefore seems appropriate to further develop their conception in a way that these problematic cases can also be covered.[73] The records show clearly that the framers carefully chose the wording of Article 1 of the Basic Law. They discussed and discarded the wordings dignity of human 'existence', 'essence', or 'life', and unanimously decided for the dignity of 'man'. Helene Weber explained: 'This term covers everything and highlights neither the purely biological nor the purely spiritual. In short, it is exhaustive.'[74] On the other hand, the records also indicate that the framers did not use the term 'Würde des Menschen' as a not further substantiated value attribution to the motto 'every human being is somehow valuable'. They used it to describe a very specific, vulnerable quality of man.

Considering this, it seems obvious to me that dignity as 'inner freedom' should be understood in the broadest possible sense. One should particularly avoid overemphasizing aspects like reason or rationality in positive definitions of the Basic Law's legal term of human dignity. The conception of the Italian Renaissance philosopher Giovanni Pico Della Mirandola, for instance, enthusiastically received by some German constitutionalists since the 1990s,[75] would not be adequate in describing the meaning of the Basic Law's human dignity Article. For Pico, the human is characterized by the ability to lead his life according to his own design, to interpret and assimilate culture: 'its status

---

[72] Exactly the same problem arises with a Kantian understanding of dignity. See, most recently, Doris Schroeder, 'Human rights and human dignity. An appeal to separate the conjoined twins', 329–31 ('The Kantian cul-de-sac'); Charles Foster, *Human Dignity in Bioethics and Law* (Oxford and Portland, OR, Hart Publishing, 2011), 38–9; Catherine Dupré, 'Unlocking human dignity. Towards a theory for the 21st century', *European Human Rights Law Review* 2 (2009), 190–205, at 193–4. Important clarifications at Gerhard Luf, 'Menschenwürde als Rechtsbegriff. Überlegungen zum Kant-Verständnis in der neueren deutschen Grundrechtstheorie', in Rainer Zaczyk et al. (eds), *Festschrift für E.A. Wolff zum 70. Geburtstag am 1.10.1998* (Berlin et al., Springer, 1998), 307–23, at 321; see also Oliver Sensen, *Kant on Human Dignity* (Berlin and Boston, De Gruyter, 2011), 202–12.
[73] See Goos, *Innere Freiheit*, 142–57.
[74] Deutscher Bundestag and Bundesarchiv (eds), *Der Parlamentarische Rat 1948–1949. Akten und Protokolle, Band 5, Ausschuss für Grundsatzfragen*, 73, my translation.
[75] See, most recently, Rolf Gröschner et al. (eds), *Des Menschen Würde—entdeckt und erfunden im Humanismus der italienischen Renaissance* (Tübingen, Mohr Siebeck, 2008).

was dignity, its nature was reason, and its consequence was autonomy'.[76] However, in practice, those people who are unable to think or do anything, not even to participate in culture, need to be protected.[77] In his remarkable book *Soul Hunger: The Feeling Human Being and the Life Sciences*, the Swiss psychiatrist Daniel Hell has pointed out that depressed people 'are often left with only a feeble experience of their corporeality. This experience cannot be turned into something positive, but it is the only thing of their own they have left.' Sometimes, though, depressed persons discover 'unexpected avenues of experience' because of their depression:

> They may sense that what made that possible was a first-person perspective that others don't know ... A deeper understanding of depression may help in developing a passion for the 'weak subject', that is, to discard the image of a person who is weighted down by the excessive demands of the postmodern conception of man as creator, designer and engineer of reality. Seeing a totally independent and isolated ego as questionable, the subject must not perish. It may come to understand itself as a creature that, as a natural 'living being', depends on many necessities, but still senses that it has personal value or—in the ancient way of speaking—a soul.

Hell concludes: 'Is it inconceivable that it is only the image of an ego perspective in another person that establishes the quality of humanness?'[78]

One can probably go one step further: Dignity as first-person perspective in the broadest possible sense can be understood as something that an embryo already 'has', and that even survives the death.[79] Prenatal psychologists like Inge Krens and neurobiologists like Gerald Hüther emphasize that even the fertilized egg 'unites both physical and psychological components. A human organism is not created by cells initially forming a body and the soul later eventually joining this entity. Body and psyche differentiate simultaneously and undividedly.'[80] Viktor Frankl points out in one of his books that the first-person perspective of another person is in the realm beyond physicality and sensuality even during their lifetime: 'We do not have it as we have an object, but we capture it because of sensory impressions.' Frankl uses the example of a famous opera singer: it does not matter if we listen to him in concert, on

---

[76] Charles Foster, *Human Dignity in Bioethics and Law* (Oxford and Portland, OR, Hart Publishing, 2011), 34. See also Mette Lebech, *On the Problem of Human Dignity. A Hermeneutical and Phenomenological Investigation* (Würzburg, Königshausen & Neumann, 2009), 87–90.

[77] Compare also Foster, *Human Dignity*: '[N]eat formulations don't do well when confronted with the messiness of real humans'; Dupré, 'Unlocking human dignity', 193.

[78] Daniel Hell, *Soul Hunger. The Feeling Human Being and the Life Sciences* (Einsiedeln, Daimon Verlag, 2010), 345–6.

[79] For further details, see Goos, *Innere Freiheit*, 148–57.

[80] Gerald Hüther and Inge Krens, *Das Geheimnis der ersten neun Monate. Unsere frühesten Prägungen* (Düsseldorf, Patmos Verlag, 2005), 36, my translation.

the radio, or even to a recording after his death. In each of these cases we do not only hear sound waves, but—conveyed by them—the singer himself. His uniqueness, his 'magic', endures.[81] Not later than 1971, the German Federal Constitutional Court ruled that it would be incompatible with the guarantee of human dignity in Article 1 of the Basic Law if a person could be humiliated or degraded after his or her death.[82] The duty of all state authority to respect and to protect human dignity does not end in death. In my view, this jurisdiction is entirely as intended by the framers.

Conclusion

We tend to assume that Article 1 German Basic Law is a specific result of Catholic and Kantian thought.[83] Indeed, the provision was interpreted like this very soon, especially and most influentially by the Catholic constitutionalist Günter Dürig in the 1950s. Decades later, Dürig admitted frankly and not without pride that he had successfully established a Christian-personalistic interpretation of the dignity Article.[84] However, in this regard, Article 1 differs significantly from the dignity references that can be found in the post-war constitutions of some German federal states. Although some Christian Democrats and National Conservatives in the Parliamentary Council tried to establish their idea of genuine, God-given freedom, phrasings like 'The dignity of man is founded on eternal, God-given rights' were repeatedly rejected by the other delegates.[85] Kant was not even mentioned during the framers' debates on Article 1.[86] The dignity debates were dominated by Carlo Schmid and The-

---

[81] Viktor Frankl, 'Der unbedingte Mensch' (1949), in Frankl, *Der leidende Mensch*, 3rd edn (Bern, Verlag Hans Huber, 2005), 65–160, at 132, my translation. Compare also Clemens Sedmak's reflections on mystery as a fundamental feature of an approach to human dignity, Chapter 33, this volume, 568.

[82] BVerfGE 30, 173, 194.

[83] See, for instance, Michael Rosen, *Dignity: Its History and Meaning* (Cambridge, MA, and London, England, Harvard University Press, 2012), 80–90; Rex D. Glensky, 'The right to dignity', *Columbia Human Rights Law Review* 43 (2011), 65–142, at 96: 'clear Kantian overtones of the conceiving of dignity as "inviolable"'.

[84] Günter Dürig, 'Dankrede am 65. Geburtstag', *Jahrbuch des öffentlichen Rechts der Gegenwart* 36 (1987), 91–103, at 100.

[85] See, in particular, the debate between the representatives Seebohm, Schmid, Heuss and Greve during the forty-second meeting of the Main Committee, Deutscher Bundestag and Bundesarchiv (eds), *Der Parlamentarische Rat 1948–1949. Akten und Protokolle, Band 14, Hauptausschuss*, 1289–92. Compare also Tine Stein, *Himmlische Quellen und irdisches Recht. Religiöse Voraussetzungen des freiheitlichen Verfassungsstaates* (Frankfurt and New York, Campus, 2007), 308–9.

[86] Compare also Möllers, 'Democracy and human dignity: limits of a moralized conception of rights in German constitutional law', 427: 'When interpreting a constitutional text, it is maybe best to do without a house philosopher.'

odor Heuss, a secularist and a Protestant, both highly educated. The two could easily convince their colleagues that Article 1 should be formulated in a way 'that one could comprehend theologically, another philosophically, another ethically'. In contrast to this, the meaning of the term 'dignity of man' did not remain undefined. The framers agreed that the 'dignity of man' was neither a more or less vague value assignment nor just the sum of the following basic rights but a real capacity of human beings, which had proved highly vulnerable during the Nazi regime: the inner freedom. Unlike other legal systems, the German Constitution thereby focuses particularly on the inner self and accents the interior component of the human personality.[87] To me, the potential of this Article in its original meaning has not been fully exploited yet.

---

[87] Compare also, from a comparative law perspective, Edward J. Eberle, 'Human dignity, privacy, and personality in German and American constitutional law', in Nikolaus Knoepffler, Peter Kunzmann, and Martin O'Malley (eds), *Facetten der Menschenwürde* (Freiburg and München Verlag Karl Alber, 2011), 102–40.

4

The Secret History of Constitutional Dignity

Samuel Moyn[1]

> IN THE NAME OF the Most Holy Trinity, from Whom all authority and to Whom, as our final end, all actions both of men and States must be referred,
>
> We, the people of Éire,
>
> Humbly acknowledging all our obligations to our Divine Lord, Jesus Christ, Who sustained our fathers through centuries of trial,
>
> Gratefully remembering their heroic and unremitting struggle to regain the rightful independence of our Nation,
>
> And seeking to promote the common good, with due observance of Prudence, Justice and Charity, so that the dignity and freedom of the individual may be assured, true social order attained, the unity of our country restored, and concord established with other nations,
>
> Do hereby adopt, enact, and give to ourselves this Constitution.
>
> Preamble, Irish Constitution of 1937

Introduction: dignity, Christianity, and democracy

In the prevalent narrative of public law after the Second World War, it is dignitarian constitutionalism—channelling Immanuel Kant's Enlightenment insistence on individual human worth into the United Nations Charter, the

---

[1] I am grateful to Josef Ansorge for doing much of the Irish research for this chapter, and to Yale Law School for funding his work, as well as to James Chappel for advice, and Sanford Diehl for supplementary help. A longer version of this chapter, with fuller attention to the drafting of the Irish Constitution and other further detail, is forthcoming in the *Yale Journal of Human Rights and Development Law*.

Universal Declaration, and the West German Basic Law, all three of which begin with the dignity of the individual as basic principle—that responded to the Holocaust as the nadir of Western civilization. Though it took some time, dignity then proceeded in the last few decades—in tandem with the larger fortunes of international human rights—to become a crucial watchword, going global in various constitutions and international treaties, and offering judicial guidance for the protection of basic values.[2] Certainly it is the case that interest in dignity swarms in legal cases and philosophical discussions today in ways that demand explanation.

Yet, as Jürgen Habermas has recently acknowledged, the appeal to dignity had not been required at any point for the constitutionalization of rights, either in 1776 in Virginia or in 1789 (or again in 1946) in France.[3] Conversely, West Germans writing the Basic Law were not yet concerned by the Jewish tragedy. And while it is true that Kant occasionally referenced dignity, none of his political disciples have made anything of this fact—and his current philosophical disciples only in the last few years. In any case, there were no Kantians in Germany of note after the Second World War, nor really anywhere else.[4] Contrary to familiar beliefs, it was not West Germany that first constitutionalized dignity as a leading principle anyway. That distinction belongs to the Irish.

In their 1937 constitution, the Irish gave it foundational placement, as a religiously inspired root concept connected (as in the later West German case) to the subordination of the otherwise sovereign democratic polity to God, and for many to the moral constraints of his natural law. This chapter takes up this neglected but revealing fact. It is critical, I contend in what follows, that dignity came to the world as part of the establishment of an alternative

---

[2] Samuel Moyn, *The Last Utopia: Human Rights in History* (Cambridge, MA, Harvard University Press, 2010).

[3] Jürgen Habermas, *The Crisis of the European Union: A Response*, trans. Ciaran Cronin (Cambridge, Polity Press, 2012), chapter 2, 'The concept of human dignity and the realistic utopia of human rights'.

[4] Q: Which of the following prominent philosophers who have published a major book, chapter, or article in the last ten years on dignity mentioned it before then? a) Seyla Benhabib, b) Ronald Dworkin, c) Jürgen Habermas, d) George Kateb, e) Avishai Margalit, f) Jeremy Waldron. A: g) none of the above. Kantians before the recent present, from Hermann Cohen to John Rawls, have done without the concept. Apparently the crucial pioneer in contemporary philosophical discussion is Thomas E. Hill, Jr, *Dignity and Practical Reason in Kant's Moral Theory* (Ithaca, NY, Cornell University Press, 1992). Before recently, the main thinkers of note to explore (let alone advocate) dignity were conservative. See, for example, Aurel Kolnai, 'Dignity', *Philosophy* 51 (1976), 251–71; Robert Spaemann, 'Über den Begriff der Menschenwürde', in Ernst-Wolfgang Böckenförde and Robert Spaemann (eds), *Menschenrechte und Menschenwürde: Historische Voraussetzungen, säkulare Gestalt, christliches Verständnis* (Stuttgart, Klett-Cotta, 1987); Hans-Georg Gadamer, 'Die Menschenwürde auf ihrem Weg von der Antike bis heute', *Humanistische Bildung* 12 (1988), 95–107.

constitutionalism—the constitutionalism of Christian democracy. So far as I know, there is no general historical study of its emergence; and though Ran Hirschl has contributed a valuable overview of what he provocatively calls 'constitutional theocracy', there is so far no recognition that it is the framework in which human dignity first became canonized.[5] This religious constitutionalism crystallized in the 1930s, when it seemed to many as if secular liberalism had no future. It was initially part of a replacement package for that secular liberalism (and remained so in Germany in 1949). The conventional narrative of the trajectory of constitutional dignity, in other words, is by and large false. Recovering the true sources of the constitutionalization of human dignity may, further, force a different light on a crucial phase in the norm's trajectory.

Around March 1937: Catholic dignity between corporatism and civil society

More specifically, anyone interested in human dignity as we know it should be interested in March 1937—when it made its spectacular entry into world politics, including constitutional politics.

That dignity long ago originated as one status word among others in a universe of aristocratic values is now undoubted, but this fact, or the 'democratization of aristocracy', does very little to explain the specifics of its ideological trajectory in the 1930s and 1940s—let alone since.[6] As late as the 1930s, in tune with its millennial prior trajectory, dignity attached to a huge range of objects, humanity rarely, and individual humanity extremely rarely, among them. There was thus little prior basis for the novelty that Ireland's constitution registered, whatever the minor circulation of the word in world affairs, including one or two constitutional articles, earlier. Then events in international Catholicism intervened, with the Irish constitutionalization of individual dignity as leading concept being one consequence.

In fact, dignity already had an important place in Catholic politics in March 1937, but it was radically different from the one it has had since then, thanks to the epoch-making reassignment from *groups* to *individuals* that the concept underwent. At the beginning of the month, thanks to Pope Pius XI's

---

[5] Ran Hirschl, *Constitutional Theocracy* (Cambridge, MA, Harvard University Press, 2010).
[6] See, for example, James Q. Whitman, '"Human dignity" in Europe and the United States: the social foundations', *Human Rights Law Journal* 25 (2004), 17–23, and, on Whitman's themes, the various essays culminating in Jeremy Waldron, *Dignity, Rank, and Rights*, ed. Meir Dan-Cohen (Oxford, Oxford University Press, 2012).

encyclicals *Casti connubi* (1930) and *Quadragesimo anno* (1931), dignity still attached primarily to collective entities like workers and religious sacraments like marriage. Though not utterly without precedent, it was in March 1937 that dignity attaching to individuals (more precisely, persons) crystallized as a visible ideological option. In the 1930s, no one could have guessed what would become of this option, in large part because the Irish Constitution's version of dignity reflected such a minority political choice in the landscape of political Catholicism. After all, the years during which it was framed were the period in which Catholic states were rising, typically based on corporatist rather than supplementary individualist notions.

These Catholic states remained true to the corporatist version of dignity, in which it was family or labour that was dignified, not persons (and thus not persons with rights).[7] Preceded by a year by António Salazar's Portuguese constitution, the purest move to constitutional corporatism occurred in Austria in 1934, which 'Austro-fascist' Catholic leader Engelbert Dollfuss consciously announced as enacting *Quadragesimo anno*'s corporatist principles. Not long afterwards, Spain, with its secular and indeed anticlerical constitution of 1931, fell prey to coup and dictatorship, and Francisco Franco introduced dignity to the quasi-constitutional documents of his regime in allegiance to reigning corporatist orthodoxy.[8] In the international Catholic context, the framing of the Irish constitution occurred in the shadow of this impressive wave of dignitarian corporatism.

Yet it also took place at a time of novel and at first brief and modest availability of a dignitarian alternative based on persons—an alternative it happened to register. The central source of the conceptual work to make possible the Irish Constitution's assignment of 'dignity' to the individual was in a raucous French dispute of the mid-1930s about the nature of Catholic politics, among those recovering from an earlier flirtation with far right politics and in a dispute with persisting reactionaries about what sort of response to offer to the secular liberalism that everyone thought was on its deathbed.

The leading historian of this dispute, James Chappel, has dubbed the conflict as one between corporatists (who in France would ultimately support the Vichy regime in the name of Christian principle) and 'civil society Catholics'. The intellectual debate and political controversy between these two groups assumed its classic form as a response to the Popular Front, for the dispute

---

[7] For the best survey in these years, see Tom Buchanan and Martin Conway (eds), *Political Catholicism in Europe, 1918–1965* (Oxford, Oxford University Press, 1996).
[8] See *Fundamental Laws of the State: The Spanish Constitution* (Madrid, SIE, 1967).

raging in 1934–6 was about what sort of alternative to offer to the frightening alliance of communists and socialists of the era.

These two groups of Catholics agreed on the rejection of the modern, liberal, secular republic in the name of the dispersal of authority to the 'natural' social hierarchy established by God, and descending through and including religious institutions, local communities, and patriarchal families. But where the civil society Catholics differed was in their assignment of importance to what they called 'the human person' as an element in the mix. The human person, a central icon of civil society Catholicism transnationally starting in 1934, would become the bearer of 'dignity'. Corporatists themselves, Chappel shows, referred to the human person too; just as some of their civil society foes ended up supporting the Vichy regime. But it seems clear that 'the dignity of the human person' mainly became a slogan for civil society Catholics attempting to stave off both secular liberalism with its destitute atomism and corporatist reaction, with its demand for integral religious politics or flirtation with 'pagan' regimes.[9]

In spite of the emergence of the civil society option, corporatist ideology offered the dominant version of political Catholicism until the outcome of the Second World War made Spain and Portugal seem not like the wave of an exciting future but a relic of past mistakes. Seriously outnumbered in spite of sharing many premises with their corporatist foes, civil society Catholics opened another path in the 1930s, which few took until later; individual dignity emerged, essentially, as a marker on that path. Consider as an example of civil society dissidence Joseph Vialatoux's speech, at the time of the finalization of the Irish Constitution, to the Semaines Sociales in Lyon (an annual summer camp of this faction). Its title: 'Dignity of the Group? Or of the Human Person?'[10]

'It may not be excessive', Vialatoux commented, 'to say that this very question defines the historical moment in which we live.' He inveighed against specifically biological and generally naturalistic approaches, which tended to view the human group as the locus of significance, arguing instead that Christianity brought the metaphysics of spirituality—which made the human person the site of dignity. Yet Vialatoux's preference for individual dignity, it bears noting, did not connote the corollary of 'human rights'. That revolutionary concept, in spite of its ostensible priority of persons, remained in what Vialatoux called a 'bastard union' with 'naturalist philosophy', and

---

[9] See James Chappel, 'Slaying the leviathan: Catholicism and the rebirth of European conservatism, 1920–1950' (PhD dissertation, Columbia University, 2012).

[10] Joseph Vialatoux, 'Dignité du groupe? Ou de la personne humaine?: Physique et métaphysique de l'ordre des valeurs', in *La Personne humaine en péril* (Lyon, Semaines sociales, 1938).

elicited the equally erroneous sequels first of secular nationalism then of counter-revolutionary racism. The 'dignity of the human person' was to be a response to all these mistakes. It was now critical to assert dignity against the 'depersonalized individual' of both revolutionary naturalism and counter-revolutionary naturalism. It would save the 'person' buried in revolutionary, secular politics from its own misguided proponents, and make it the foundation stone of a spiritual community rather than the materialist totalitarianism of communism and fascism alike.[11]

Vialatoux had posed his question about whether to give individual or group dignity priority in early 1937, but, far from crying in the wilderness against totalitarianism, by summertime when he gave his lecture it must have seemed as if the individualist option had garnered the highest possible support: from the Pope himself. It was for this reason above all—and not because of the Irish constitution—that March 1937 was a great month for civil society Catholics. That month, stung by the failure of earlier overtures towards and negotiations with Nazi Germany, Pope Pius XI condemned German incursion on church rights, and a week later issued his stirring encyclical *Divini redemptoris* 'on atheistic communism'. The dignity of the individual surged in world public discourse essentially because of this. It was hard not to see the sheer coincidence of these encyclicals as the Pope's own version of totalitarianism theory—though it remained utterly unclear what the proper alternative to 'totalitarianism' really was. Interestingly, however, 'dignity' was basic only in the second, anti-communist encyclical.

In fact, the failure to respect the dignity of the human person was repeatedly identified—and starting in March 1937 was to be so for decades—as communism's central error. Communism, the text reads, 'strips man of his liberty, robs human personality of all its dignity, and removes all the moral restraints that check the eruptions of blind impulse'. Simultaneously too authoritarian and too liberatory, communism reduced man to matter, and thus also interfered with the source of moral agency. That it 'denies the rights, dignity and liberty of human personality' also made it an affront to moral norms. Put differently, dignity offered an individualism that, far from atomizing humanity, offered the true first principle of community and society, for 'each individual man in the dignity of his human personality ... is supplied with all that is necessary for the exercise of his social functions'.[12] It was thus not strange that in Irish hands, individual dignity connected with the common

---

[11] Vialatoux, 'Dignité du groupe?', 123, 132–3.
[12] On the encyclical in the larger context of the Church's anticommunist politics, see Giuliana Chamedes, 'Reinventing Christian Europe: Vatican diplomacy, transnational anticommunism, and the erosion of the Church–state divide' (PhD dissertation, Columbia University, 2012), chapter 6.

good and theological virtues, since it shared in the consensus phobia of basing politics on an apparently destitute secular individualism.

Ignored in the contemporary literature on 'dignity', *Divini redemptoris* was epoch-making, for it gave the concept as an incident of individuals or persons by far its highest profile entry in world politics to that date. It also gave a lift to the civil society Catholics' insistence that dignity did not primarily attach to groups. And the crucial revisions of the Irish Constitution that led to the appearance of individual dignity in its preamble also occurred in this period—very precisely, in the immediate aftermath of the encyclical. This accidental coincidence forms the basis of my case about what dignity meant when it became an Irish touchstone, anticipating many later developments.

Ireland and the coming of religious constitutionalism

The many historians of Ireland's Constitution, notably the accomplished Dermot Keogh, have simply missed the relevance of its dignitarian turn. Unaware of Ireland's comparative priority when it comes to dignity, they have therefore failed to place the document in international context to explain this priority.[13] The Irish Constitution, of course, needs to be read in a number of contexts, of which the one I will emphasize—international Catholic thought and politics—is merely one. But it is this context that matters inasmuch as the Irish Constitution registered an international development that would later mark the UN Charter and the Basic Law—and thus make possible everything that followed based on their language.

Éamon de Valera, Fianna Fáil party leader and, from 1932, new Irish prime minister, wrote the Irish Constitution after brief and informal consultation with a tiny group of advisers, before unveiling his handiwork in April 1937 for approval. Though the wave of the Catholic future may well have seemed to be corporatist constitutionalism on the European continent at this moment, the Irish Constitution clearly could not go there—in spite of the hopes of some Irish Catholic integralists who were consulted during the process. An evanescent movement of Irish fascists known as the Blueshirts who trumpeted Catholic principle rose and fell in the mid-1930s; and around the same time as the Constitution was in preparation, Paddy Belton's fearsomely

---

[13] See, for example, Dermot Keogh and Andrew McCarthy, *The Making of the Irish Constitution 1937: Bunreacht na hÉireann* (Cork, Mercier Press, 1997), striking for its inattention to the preamble generally.

reactionary militant group, the Irish Christian Front, emerged.[14] But de Valera had no truck with these groups, nor with any other version of illiberal corporatism.

Indeed, the primary impulse for engineering a new constitutional process at all was negative. De Valera had long since committed himself vigorously to scuttling the Constitution of the Irish Free State of 1922 in the name of a new order. That the Anglo-Irish Treaty of 1921 had not allowed Ireland full sovereignty, and that the first constitution imposed a galling loyalty oath to the British crown (which de Valera deleted immediately in 1933), gave them so repulsive a stigma as to be unsalvageable.[15] The happenstance that the drafting of de Valera's long-sought replacement of the unacceptable text with a new one occurred in the winter and spring of 1936–7 proved fateful for the history of dignity, however. The process replaced a document of the so-called 'new constitutionalism' with a very different constitutional affair.

The Irish Constitution was not just a 'negative' success after all. The country's move beyond its prior dominion constitution to assert its 'rightful independence' reflected Catholic social thought in its positive outlook in a series of ways, and not surprisingly, given the centrality of Catholicism to Irish nationalism in the 1930s and long after.[16] De Valera, a devoted Catholic passionately committed to the greater presence of the country's dominant religion in the constitution, was above all a politician. He deftly manoeuvred to

---

[14] Fearghal McGarry, *Irish Politics and the Spanish Civil War* (Cork, Cork University Press, 1999), especially chapter 4.

[15] Leo Kohn, *The Constitution of the Irish Free State* (London, Allen and Unwin, 1934); for de Valera's views, see, for example, Ronan Fanning, 'Mr. De Valera drafts a constitution', in B. Farrell (ed.), *De Valera's Constitution and Ours* (Dublin, Gill and Macmillan, 1988), 34.

[16] In a recent piece on another subject, historian Perry Anderson makes the following pertinent and perhaps outrageous comparative remarks: 'In the history of 20th-century nationalism, there is a distinct sub-group in which religion played a central organising role from the start, providing so to speak the genetic code of the movement. The most significant cases are those which eventually founded stable parliamentary democracies. The three leading states of this type in the world today are Ireland, Israel and India. In all three, the nationalist party that came to power after independence—Fine Gael, Mapai, Congress—distanced itself from the confessional undertow of the struggle without ever being able to tackle its legacy head-on. In each case, as the ruling party gradually lost its lustre, it was outflanked by a more extreme rival that had fewer inhibitions about appealing directly to the theological passions aroused by the original struggle: Fianna Fail, Likud, BJP. The success of these parties was due not just to the faltering of the first wave of office-holders, but to their ability to articulate openly what had always been latent in the national movement, but neither candidly acknowledged nor consistently repudiated. They could claim, with a certain justice, to be legitimate heirs of the original cause. In each case, the setting was a parliamentary system, in which they operated constitutionally, if in each case with certain prewar sympathies for European fascism. ... The Irish reversion came within a decade of independence—its carrier was the genuinely more popular and radical wing of the national movement, with the greatest anti-colonial legitimacy—and enjoyed the longest ascendancy, only finally collapsing last year'. P. Anderson, 'After Nehru', *London Review of Books* (2 August 2012).

take account of the views of the episcopacy and various Catholic authorities, while also assuming final control of the details of drafting. In particular, de Valera saw the preamble as the place to achieve symbolic Christianization of the document, while specific articles would offer a considerable incorporation (though not total lock) of Catholicism on Irish politics. In this approach, de Valera may have been more canny than most comparative scholars of constitutions, who regularly slight preambles, though they are the most meaningful and memorable parts of founding texts to citizens.

In the preamble and in general, de Valera never wanted to go, nor could go, as far as reactionary or even doctrinally conservative Catholics desired. The constitutionalization of the freedom and dignity of the individual, in short, can be taken as a symbol of de Valera's larger balancing act, in which he crafted a Christian democratic synthesis throughout the document. In an era of the victory of Catholic corporatism or outright fascism, Ireland proved a peripheral laboratory of civil society Catholicism or even post-Second World War Christian Democracy. Keogh plausibly comments:

> De Valera had little or nothing in common with the authoritarian Catholic leaders of the 1930s. He did not make a fetish out of religion like the 'monkish' Salazar of Portugal. He was repelled by the extremism of General Francisco Franco's *cruzada*. De Valera exhibited none of the demagoguery practised by the Central European Catholic dictators of the 1930s ... [He was] both patriotic and loyally Roman Catholic, but in a very independent way.[17]

If it meant more than the anti-communist politics of *Divini redemptoris*, de Valera's registration of the dignitarian individualist rather than the dignitarian corporatist strand of political Catholicism of the moment encapsulates this broader stance. Negotiating between forsaken secular liberalism and rising Catholic reaction, it offered religiously inflected conservative democracy.

Comparison of de Valera's handiwork with the 1922 constitution he patriotically scuttled makes this graphically clear. The earlier document had been very much in the spirit of the liberal 'new constitutionalism' of the immediate moment after the First World War in its attitudes to church and state, religious pluralism, and gender; its 1937 replacement was a Christianizing document of a religious constitutionalism of religious democracy. Apparently, it was the first such document.[18] Its approach to property, for example, drew substantially on *Quadragesimo anno*, while its article on religion acknowledged

---

[17] Dermot Keogh, 'Church, state, and society', in Brian Farrell (ed.), *De Valera's Constitution and Ours* (Dublin, Gill and Macmillan, 1988), 104.
[18] Noel Browne, 'Church and state in modern Ireland', in Tim Murphy and Patrick Twomey (eds), *Ireland's Evolving Constitution, 1937–97: Collected Essays* (Oxford, Hart, 1998), 46–7.

the Catholic Church's 'special position'.[19] Its article on family and gender perhaps went furthest in qualifying the secular liberalism of the prior constitutional exercise.

Irish feminists, agitating for the group most obviously affected by such changes, registered its consequences immediately—though it is also true that Ireland never took up the fully maternalist turn of other places where Catholic social thought was enacted as authoritarian policy in this era.[20] The new draft constitution deleted the existing constitution's promise of equal rights without distinction to sex, which feminists feared might even strip women of the hard-won vote. (They succeeded in restoring the clause in ratification debates.) And, as ratified, the constitution's controversial Article 41 enshrined a traditionalist vision of the family. On a symbolic level, the article made clear that whatever the dignity of persons meant, it was inseparable from the centrality of families, which in turn depended on women's 'life within the home'. More substantively, the article constitutionally prohibited divorce (a prohibition lifted only six decades later in the constitution's fifteenth amendment).

Even as feminist complaints were marginalized, throughout this period (and indeed long after) a huge dispute swirled around the wording of Article 44, in which Cahill and others wanted to name the Catholic Church as the true Christian Church. But de Valera, in spite of his own apparent sympathies, ultimately understood he could not do so, setting out to balance Catholicism's pre-eminence with acknowledgement of minority faiths and religious freedom. It was, after all, a country with a Protestant population of 25 per cent (including the contested north, which the constitution claimed as part of the nation). Article 44 illustrated, once again, that the larger constitutional effort balanced between competing extremes of secular liberalism and religious authoritarianism.

It also caused no little difficulty for de Valera in his search for ecclesiastical imprimatur. In mid-April, two weeks before unveiling his handiwork to the public, he sent his emissary Joseph Walshe to Rome for endorsement. But Eugenio Pacelli, then the Vatican Secretary of State communicating for the already sick Pope whom he would succeed, refused to comply. Pacelli reminded Walshe that failure to acknowledge the Catholic Church as the true one was technically heretical, though Pacelli grasped that de Valera felt his

---

[19] Constitution of Ireland (1937), Article 44.
[20] This paragraph relies upon Maria Luddy, 'A "sinister and retrogressive" proposal: Irish women's opposition to the 1937 Draft Constitution', *Transactions of the Royal Historical Society* 15 (2005), 175–95. For comparison's sake, see Francine Muel-Dreyfus, *Vichy and the Eternal Feminine: A Contribution to the Political Sociology of Gender*, trans. Kathleen A. Johnson (Durham, NC, Duke University Press, 2001), especially part 3.

situation forced him into theological error. 'Ni approvo ni non disapprovo; taceremo' (I don't approve, but I also don't disapprove; I will remain silent), Pacelli told Walshe in the Pope's name—which was nonetheless a crushing result for de Valera, who had striven to explain to Rome that he was constrained by the fact of his Protestant minority from the more full-blown Catholic ideal he personally desired for the document. 'It did not shake him when I contrasted the expressly Christian character of our new Constitution with the liberalism [continental sense] of the old', Walshe reported back glumly.[21]

De Valera thus did not go as far as some of his Catholic advisers and ecclesiastical authorities desired. But he did intend the Irish Constitution to mark the appearance of a new sort of Christian state, and the preamble in which dignity now appeared had a special role here. In the pained negotiations with the Vatican, dignity—which did not come up—was not enough to convince Pius XI (or the future Pius XII, speaking in his name) to sign off. Nonetheless, during the ratification process some months later, when de Valera faced unexpected opposition to the constitution for its excessive secularism (rather than its excessive confessionalism), the Christian credentials of dignity proved helpful. In spite of the Pope's earlier reluctance, the Vatican paper *L'Osservatore Romano* providentially seemed to endorse the constitution. 'It differs from other constitutions', the paper noted, in an affirmation reported by the *Irish Press* that had a huge impact in placating the religious vote, 'because it is inspired by respect for the faith of the people, the dignity of the person, the sanctity of the family, of private property, and of social democracy. These principles are applied in a unique religious spirit, which animates the whole constitution.'[22] It seems that Ireland's pioneering venture in a religious constitutionalism, in which individual dignity came to the fore, was generally understood in these terms by its friends as well as by its critics.[23]

---

[21] Gerard Hogan (ed.), *The Origins of the Irish Constitution 1928–1941* (Dublin, Royal Irish Academy, 2012), 506 (Document 155, 22 April 1937).

[22] *Irish Press* (17 May 1937), as cited in Dermot Keogh, *The Vatican, the Bishops, and Irish Politics 1919–1939* (Cambridge, Cambridge University Press, 1986), 219.

[23] Compare with Arthur W. and Mary C. Bromage, 'The Irish Constitution: a discussion of its theoretical aspects', *Review of Politics* 2 (1940), 145–66. Certainly the document went far enough as to allow disputes to swirl for many decades around the degree to which Ireland had made natural law a constraint on democratic choices as well as judicial interpretation. Consider Vincent Grogan, 'The Constitution and the Natural Law', *Christus Rex* 7 (1954), 201–18; Declan Costello, 'The Natural Law and the Irish Constitution', *Studies* 45 (1956), 403–14; and John Maurice Kelly, *Fundamental Rights in the Irish Law and Constitution* (Dublin, Allen Figgis, 1961), especially 38–45.

From the Irish Constitution to the basic law

That some Catholics sought an alternative to authoritarian and fascist solutions by appealing to dignity in these years, of course, does not at all mean that the faltering republics of Europe were generally defended in their terms. It simply means that Catholics hewed out a conceptual possibility that was to have an unlikely fate in later history (up to and including our era). Secularists did not frame their republicanism in dignitarian terms, either before or after the Second World War. Further, during the war, just a few Catholics believed that allegiance to 'human dignity' entailed allegiance to 'human rights', which most Catholics following modern popes still considered the baleful child of the French Revolution and secularist evil, and which Catholics under authoritarian regimes were unsparingly told to spurn. Indeed, Catholic thinker Jacques Maritain, chief theoretician of civil society Catholicism and later premier interpreter of the Universal Declaration, did not connect dignity to 'human rights' until 1942 at the earliest.[24]

But between 1942 and 1945, as the Allied war effort after Stalingrad looked forward to its ultimate triumph, more and more Catholics in general linked 'the dignity of the human person' hewed out in the prior decade to 'human rights'—including, heroically, those few in the French Resistance who criticized the Vichy regime's popular claim to restore Catholic morality on religious grounds. More important, as the war wore on, Pius XII himself invoked the dignity of the individual human person in his most widely noticed remarks. He had done so as high Vatican official—even while remaining silent on de Valera's handiwork—already in 1937, accepting the language of *Divini redemptoris*.[25] In wartime, his public usage accelerated to a striking degree. The Pope's invocation of human dignity during the war provided a bridge between what might otherwise have been a passing peculiarity of a few dissident theorists, along with the Irish constitution, and the post-war trajectory of the concept.

Thanks to Pius XII, in fact, individual dignity became an incredibly common concept across the Atlantic during the later phases of the Second World War, though much more work remains to be done to excavate wartime usage. To take one of sundry examples, Edmund A. Walsh, American Jesuit (and

---

[24] See Daniele Lorenzini, *Jacques Maritain e i diritte umani: fra totalitarismo, antisemitismo, e democrazia (1936–1951)* (Brescia, Morcelliana, 2012), which goes far beyond a couple of earlier essays of mine on the same topic.

[25] See 'Lettre de S. Ém. le Cardinal Pacelli', in *La Personne humaine en péril*, which has a section on the 'Natural Dignity of the Person'.

founder of the Georgetown University School of Foreign Service which still bears his name), wrote in 1942:

> The conflict is between the rights of individual men, endowed with the dignity of the human personality and elevated to the adopted sonship of God, on the one side, and the dehumanised, totalitarian state of Fichte, Hegel, Treitschke, Nietzsche, Hitler and the Tanaka Memorial of Japan on the other. This means not a world campaign of conventional belligerents [but] a World Revolution seeking to capture the soul of humanity.[26]

How many people understood the global conflict as a crusade for dignity is unclear, but Catholics on the right side often did.

As in interwar debates, dignity in such usages carried with it a communitarian and religious streak intended to distinguish it from the secularism of nineteenth-century liberalism. Writing in *Fortune* magazine shortly after discovering the contiguity of dignity and rights, Jacques Maritain still castigated modern man for 'claim[ing] human rights and dignity—without God, for his ideology grounded human rights and human dignity in a godlike, infinite autonomy of human will'. But he now referred to the apparently alternative 'concept of, and devotion to, the rights of the human person' as 'the most significant political improvement of modern times'.[27] Notably in Pius XII's Christmas message to the world of 1944, human dignity in a similarly invidious conception teemed to a degree completely unprepared for by prior papal exhortation. A telos for and a check on democracy, and a commitment that would save it from levelling equality and secularizing materialism, dignity became one of Pius XII's key slogans, and would also play a central role in Cold War rhetoric throughout the Catholic universe and beyond.[28]

It was thus papal usage that proved of most direct relevance to post-war affairs—the bridge from the late 1930s to the late 1940s. The decisive waystation was the UN Charter. As political theorist Charles Beitz has recently discovered, it was Barnard College dean Virginia Gildersleeve, in her cosmetic work on South African Jan Smuts's draft of the UN Charter's preamble, who introduced the allusion to 'the dignity and worth of the human person'.[29] But

---

[26] Cited in Patrick McNamara, *A Catholic Cold War: Edmund A. Walsh, S.J., and the Politics of American Anticommunism* (New York, Fordham University Press, 2005), 114.

[27] Jacques Maritain, 'Christian humanism', *Fortune*, April 1942.

[28] For further details, see Giuliana Chamedes, 'Pius XII, rights talk, and the dawn of the religious Cold War', in D. Pendas (ed.), *Religion and Human Rights* (New York, Oxford University Press, forthcoming).

[29] Charles R. Beitz, 'Human dignity and human rights', working paper, which improves on the sketchy account in Christopher McCrudden, 'Dignity and the judicial interpretation of rights', *European Journal of International Law* 19 (2008), 655–724. Strangely, neither acknowledges the existence, let alone centrality, of papal usage in these years, though it is the obvious source of international invocations.

it is self-evident that the prominence of this notion in wartime—explaining its eligibility for Gildersleeve's fix—was thanks to the Pope more than all others, even all others combined, including in its connection to rights. (No American sources, in particular, conjoin human dignity and human rights earlier than or outside the framework of the Catholic sources mentioned above, and in the Pope's widely circulating language above all.)

The ground that human dignity provided human rights during the war is thus hard to describe as an unalloyed liberal victory. Dignity, it seems, helped wrest human rights from the French Revolution specifically and liberal secularism generally, in an era when both were so frequently represented in transatlantic public culture as stepping stones to totalitarianism. Not surprisingly, when conservative democracy came to post-war Germany, dignity could now have a crucial role, in constitutions that—like Ireland's before them—were grounded on the Christian God and human dignity together as the first principles of a new sort of democracy. This gesture occurred in Germany in the form of the several sub-federal *Länder* constitutions (especially the absolutely critical Bavarian constitution of 1946) before it was repeated in the Basic Law of the new federal republic.[30]

Implying Christian democracy, the Irish Constitution was thus in spite of its initially accidental and contingent breakthrough a premonitory document of the direction political Catholicism would eventually take after guns decided the larger direction of history. Drawing on the tradition established by his predecessor in his anti-communist breakthrough, dignity for Pius II by late wartime implied conservative democracy rather than authoritarian corporatism (or outright fascism). True democracy protected human dignity, the Pope warned, while false democracy sacrificed it on the altar of secularism, materialism, and relativism. Continental Europe followed this advice after the Second World War, with Western restabilization occurring under the auspices of conservative democracy supervised by a new sort of Christian political party, with Catholics in the lead. International institutions, once rejected by Catholics from the grassroots to the Pope as masonic rule, became prized sources of supra-sovereign moral norms. Dignity signalled these commitments.

---

[30] The preamble of the Bavarian 1946 text, written by Christian politician Alois Hundhammer, reads: 'Before the field of rubble, to which a state and social order without God and without knowledge and respect of human dignity have led the survivors of World War II …'

Conclusion: concepts, language, and politics

The Irish Constitution matters not intrinsically but instrumentally: in the current enthusiasm over human dignity, it decisively establishes both the right chronology and the 'original meaning' of its constitutionalization in the circumstances of religious democracy. It is, as it were, like a tape recorder that, because it was on at the right time, captures the moment in which an accident happened that still determines our discourse.

Needless to say, for the Catholic world and European politics generally, the Irish assignment of dignity to the individual human being in 1937—like the other tentative proposals of Christian democracy at the time—certainly did not settle matters. That took a war, in which illiberal corporatism was taken off the table as an option for political Catholicism, with much blood spilled in the process, though the survival of 'clerico-fascist' Spain and Portugal for many decades allowed some diehards to cherish the flame of reactionary dignity.

After the war, the peripheral Irish constitutionalization of individual dignity found a surer home, notably in West Germany, where a roughly similar sort of Christian democracy was founded. Constitutional dignity for individuals was thus invented as part of what became the unanticipated post-Second World War supremacy of Christian democracy. But one should understand this claim correctly. Dermot Keogh long ago proposed seeing de Valera as a 'Christian Democrat'.[31] The trouble with this otherwise illuminating interpretation is that there was no Christian democratic hegemony in Europe until after the Second World War—whose violence was required to open the possibility for its decades-long reign. But after it, de Valera's originally eccentric and peripheral synthesis of Catholicism and democracy suddenly became modish, and individualist dignity became a more prevalent foundation stone, in the Basic Law not least.

Obviously, those living under the regimes of the religious constitutionalism of Christian democracy could depart from original meanings, and unquestionably did so as the post-Second World War era wore on. This is especially true in a place like Germany (and Ireland too), where the huge influence of Catholicism on constitutional theory and practice has waned so substantially over the intervening decades that its original importance risks being forgotten or suppressed.[32]

---

[31] Dermot Keogh, *Ireland and Europe, 1918–1948* (Dublin, Gill and Macmillan, 1988), *passim*.

[32] For Catholicism in the early years of the Basic Law, see Hans Maier, 'Katholische Sozial- und Staatslehre und neuere Deutsche Staatslehre', *Archiv des öffentlichen Rechts* 93 (1968), 1–36, and now especially Frieder Günther, *Denken vom Staat her: Die bundesdeutsche Staatsrechtslehre zwischen*

In the history of words and concepts, including constitutional ones, genesis certainly does not account for use (let alone validity). As a result, dignity's functions today are no longer fully controlled by its original deployments. But my story does establish a starting point; and starting points sometimes remain relevant—as the starting point of individual human dignity does—since diverse Catholic voices remain central to the bitter contemporary struggles over its implications. History nevertheless shows that individual dignity could be given a liberal or conservative Catholic meaning, or an ecumenical Christian meaning, or (mostly later) a non-Christian meaning.

Looking around the world, no one would say that religious constitutionalism is a thing of the past, but it is fair to say that human dignity is no longer tightly, let alone exclusively, are tethered to its framework.[33] Starting points matter; but ultimately, both in theory and practice, they explain less and less as time passes about the course of the struggles that occur in their terms, whether at the level of constitutional keywords or constitutional politics generally.[34] In particular, therefore, my story not only acknowledges but insists that some rather recent account is required for the intense focus today on dignity.[35] In the academy, the belated and surprising return of Kantianism to prestige contributed something, to be sure, with the proviso that contemporary secular liberals claiming Kant's mantle did not turn to the touchstone of dignity until very late in their revivalism. The wave of recent constitutions invoking it—notably the South African—and the sudden relevance of international human rights law also clearly contributed to the salience of human dignity.[36]

Dezision und Integration 1949–1970 (Munich, Oldenbourg, 2004). For the Irish case, see, for example, John H. Whyte, *Church and State in Modern Ireland, 1923–1970* (Dublin, Gill and Macmillan, 1971), chapter 11.

[33] Some, to be sure, laud religious constitutionalism as an alternative to even less liberal politics, and perhaps as a transitional device towards even more liberal politics. Consider, for example, Jan-Werner Müller's argument that contemporary Islamism should take the same turn reactionary Catholicism once did thanks to Christian Democracy. In European history, however, religious constitutionalism *followed* secular constitutionalism in crisis circumstances; and it ascended compared with other options thanks to victory in war. More theoretically, the trouble with Müller's argument is the thought that formal constitutionalism is itself a causal factor of transformation; it might equally well lead to stabilization of 'constitutional theocracy', without further external intervention or political secularization. See, for example, Müller, 'From Christian democracy to Muslim democracy?', *Project Syndicate*, October 2008.

[34] For two later such struggles, see Reva B. Siegel, 'Dignity and sexuality: claims on dignity in transnational debates over abortion and same-sex marriage', *International Journal of Constitutional Law* 10 (April 2012), 355–79, emphasizing how dignity could be repurposed to serve various social agendas.

[35] For a start, see Oliver Sensen, 'Human dignity in historical perspective: the contemporary and traditional paradigms', *European Journal of Political Theory* 10 (2006), 71–91.

[36] Erin Daly, *Dignity Rights: Courts, Constitutions, and the Worth of the Human Person* (Philadelphia, PA, Pennsylvania University Press, 2012).

But such redeployment occurs through the muddying of multifarious contestation rather than the simplicity of first coinage. Stabilization (and therefore isolation) of meaning can occur at any point, but, especially when it comes to an open-textured term like 'dignity', is normally a daunting, partial, and temporary achievement. It is presumably easiest at the beginning rather than in the struggle for redefinition, for the same reason it is simplest to start with a blank canvas rather than attempt to alter an existing picture. The redefinitional struggle may make special sense or even count as a requirement, of course, when key words happen to have been embedded in authoritative legal documents like national constitutions and international treaties, notably to the extent that courts are willing to interpret them as of independent legal significance.[37] Continuing redefinition of existing words as partisan struggle continues is, indeed, a main business of politics.

The time may come, however, when it will seem wiser to coin new terms because disputes around the old ones are irresolvable. I believe that this stage has been reached with respect to 'human dignity', since it is too controverted to be available not simply for pristine use but even for meaningful invocation. Like an oversqueezed orange, dignity may have no more to give to any side in a struggle. No concept is useful or useless until someone tries to use it and succeeds or fails; the trouble with dignity is not that it is useless in theory but that the practice of political combat has made it much more so.[38]

Its beginnings were rather distinctive, then, compared with today. At a very different historical moment from ours, individual dignity originally entered world and constitutional politics as some Catholic actors struggled to establish it as a valuable tool; and the Irish constitution, like the German Basic Law that followed it, was a moment of relative success in this regard. Now it may be time to look for other things, especially as the persisting remnants and new versions of the religious constitutionalism of the 1930s command less and less respect.

---

[37] Famously, dignity in Germany was initially a *nicht interpretierte These* or strictly symbolic provision, but German judges departed from this original understanding long ago, and the Irish story is roughly similar. For some cases, see Teresa Iglesias, 'The dignity of the individual in the Irish Constitution: the importance of the Preamble', *Studies* 89 (2000), 19–34.

[38] See, notoriously, Ruth Macklin, 'Dignity is a useless concept', *British Medical Journal* 237 (2003), 1419–20.

5

Constructing the Meaning of Human Dignity: Four Questions

Catherine Dupré[1]

Introduction

HUMAN DIGNITY IS A multi-layered concept, with deep roots in history, philosophy, religion, politics, and law, to name but a few of the disciplines represented in this conference. While it is not easy to come up with a universally accepted legal definition of human dignity (it may in fact be neither possible nor desirable to do so), this chapter argues that it is nevertheless possible to identify a legal concept of dignity, particularly in Europe. In terms of positive law, this definition can be primarily located in the European Union Charter of Fundamental Rights (EU Charter), which came into force with the Lisbon Treaty in December 2009. This chapter proposes to use the EU Charter definition of human dignity as a tangible example of what dignity can be as a legal concept and as a helpful starting point to discuss four key questions that generally arise about constructing human dignity and understanding it. Each question is considered briefly in turn: What is human dignity? Who makes human dignity? When does dignity emerge as a legal concept? Why has dignity been crafted as a legal concept?

What is human dignity as a legal concept?

Human dignity has been a well-established legal concept since 1948, when it was enshrined under article 1 of the United Nations Universal Declaration of Human Rights,[2] and since then, it has been regularly enshrined in constitu-

---

[1] With thanks to Stephen Skinner for reading and checking an earlier draft of this chapter. The usual caveat applies.
[2] 'All human beings are born free and equal in dignity and rights. They are endowed with reason and conscience and should act towards one another in a spirit of brotherhood.'

tions around the world and in particular in Europe. The EU Charter provides one of the latest examples of codification of human dignity in a legal text, and is used here in order to illustrate how a (specific) legal definition of human dignity can be further discussed.

The EU Charter enshrines human dignity under its title I, which explicitly lists what are arguably the core components of human dignity in the EU: the principle of inviolability and a corresponding duty to respect and protect it (article 1), the right to life (article 2), the right to respect for physical and mental integrity (article 3), the prohibition of torture, and inhuman and degrading treatment or punishment (article 4), and the prohibition of slavery, forced labour, and human trafficking (article 5).[3] In addition to this core definition, the EU Charter contains two explicit mentions of dignity: the first relates to 'the rights of the elderly to lead a life of dignity and to participate in social and cultural life' (article 25), and the other protects 'the right to working conditions which respect [workers'] health, safety and dignity' (article 31).

While the EU Charter contains the first explicit mention of human dignity at the supranational level in Europe, this concept is not totally new to law in Europe.[4] It had already been substantially constructed by the European Court of Human Rights (ECtHR), which has made its commitment to protecting human dignity explicit since the 1990s.[5] In this respect, it has to be noted that the first title of the EU Charter endorses the first three substantive rights of the European Convention on Human Rights (ECHR). Moreover, the EU Charter develops the ECHR by adding the principle of inviolability, by granting the protection of mental and physical integrity (so far largely recognized under article 8 of the ECHR) a distinct normative basis under article 3 of the EU Charter, and by adding the specific prohibition on human trafficking. Finally, most EU Member States' constitutions enshrine human dignity under their human rights section, and have developed this concept through case law over the years.[6] In short, the European concept of human dignity is not only firmly established in (almost) all legal systems in Europe (both at national and supranational levels), but it has already reached a substantial normative density and complexity in its application in case law, included that of the European Court

---

[3] C. Dupré, 'Article 1: human dignity', in T. Hervey, S. Peers, J. Kenner, and A. Ward (eds), *A Commentary on the European Union Charter of Fundamental Rights* (Oxford, Hart Publishing, 2013), 319–41.
[4] C. Dupré, 'Dignité dans l'Europe constitutionnelle: entre inflation et contradictions', in J. Ziller (ed.), *L'Européanisation des Droits Constitutionnels à la Lumière de la Constitution pour l'Europe* (Paris, L'Harmattan, 2003), 121–35.
[5] *SW v UK*, 22 November 1995, application No. 47/1994/494/576, see also *Pretty v UK*, 29 July 2002.
[6] C. Dupré, 'Human dignity in Europe: a foundational constitutional principle', *European Public Law* 19 (2013 forthcoming).

of Justice.[7] As argued by Susanne Baer, it is best understood in a triangular connection with two other key values and rights of liberal constitutionalism, liberty and equality.[8]

This short answer to the 'what?' question does not however provide a full definition of human dignity as a legal concept; instead it establishes a point of reference and raises further questions of wider relevance. Four of them are briefly considered here. The most important question perhaps concerns the connections between the right to life and respect for human dignity. In this regard, the EU Charter arguably introduces a change in the hierarchy of rights established by the ECHR and the ECtHR, according to which, the right to life understood as sanctity of life takes priority over respect for dignity.[9] By contrast, in the EU Charter dignity comes before life, and this is arguably going to change the understanding and protection of the right to life, with the consequence that the concept of life in dignity might complement, and perhaps challenge, the principle of sanctity of life in ways that have yet to be explored and discussed. The second question is about the connections between dignity and work, which are made under article 5 of the EU Charter and article 4 of the ECHR,[10] as well as article 31 of the EU Charter. There is no doubt that protection of and respect for human dignity requires the prohibition of slavery, forced labour, and human trafficking. Arguably, however, protection of workers' dignity is not exhausted by the fact that they may not be subjected to these extreme violations. At the same time, while protection of dignity at work originally meant protection against sexual harassment, its full potential has yet to be explored, in particular perhaps in the light of domestic constitutions which have connected dignity and work with a decent income.[11] The third question arises out of article 25 of the EU Charter and the right of the elderly to a life in dignity. This involves in the first place some technical issues about determining a legal definition for the elderly (is it purely an age question?), as well as defining the legal boundaries of 'a life in dignity and independence and to participate in social and cultural life'. More importantly, perhaps, this provision possibly points towards a much more comprehensive protection of dignity, understood not just as its core elements under title 1 but as promoting a much more inclusive social model, in which everyone (and not just the elderly) could expect to lead a life of the quality described under

---

[7] L. Burgogne Larsen (ed.), *La Dignité Saisie par les Juges en Europe* (Bruxelles, Bruylant, 2010).
[8] S. Baer, 'Dignity, liberty, equality: a fundamental rights triangle of constitutionalism', *University of Toronto Law Journal* 59 (2009), 417–68.
[9] As very clearly illustrated in the *Pretty v UK* case.
[10] See Rebecca Scott, Chapter 2, this volume.
[11] For example, see article 36, Italian Constitution.

article 25. The fourth and last question considered here is one of method (and not substance), which is central to the interpretation and implementation of the EU Charter and is about integrating the various interpretations of human dignity, as developed in the ECHR and Member States' constitutional case law, particularly perhaps when they conflict. While this raises technical issues of EU law and human rights interpretation, the core question however is a political one: what kind of image of a human and of society being do Europeans want to create through their use of human dignity? Answering this leads to the questions below.

Who makes human dignity?

The question 'who makes human dignity?' presupposes that this is not a God-given quality and that it is a human concept, in other words, a social and political construct. In law, this question has largely focused on the role of judges in making dignity, with (rightly perhaps) some strong reservations about judges not being sufficiently well equipped or well positioned to construct this concept gradually through their case law.[12] It has to be remembered, however, that within the EU national judges are tied by a codified constitution (with the exception of the UK), the principle of primacy of EU law and of the EU Charter when applicable, and by ECtHR case law. As I have argued elsewhere, judges are also tied by a concept of a particular type of democratic civilization that has been developed in Europe in a conjunction of legal and political factors.[13]

Another group of dignity-makers has often been unnoticed by legal scholars, despite the fact that it arguably includes those who are perhaps the most important people in this process, namely the (alleged) victims of breaches of dignity. It is suggested here that any effort to define dignity further in law ought to find ways of including the victims, together with those who are most vulnerable and at risk of having their dignity violated. This can be done by paying closer attention to the applicants' arguments about, and construction of, human dignity in the context of human rights adjudication; by undertaking empirical studies to find out what a breach of human dignity feels like, and what causes it; or by including types of dignity narratives, such as personal testimonies and stories,[14] in legal discussion of this concept. From a

---

[12] C. McCrudden, 'Human dignity and judicial interpretation of human rights', *European Journal of International Law* 19 (2008), 655–724, and N. Rao, 'On the use and abuse of human dignity in constitutional law', *Columbia Journal of European Law* (2008), 201–55.
[13] C. Dupré, 'Dignity, democracy, civilisation', *Liverpool Law Review* (2013), 264–80.
[14] See Edwin Cameron, Chapter 27 in this volume.

CONSTRUCTING THE MEANING OF HUMAN DIGNITY 117

methodological point of view, any construction of a legal concept of human dignity ought to check that it passes what can be called the victim test, and explore whether or not it benefits the most vulnerable people and potential victims of dignity breaches.[15] After all, there is little point in constructing a legal concept of dignity which ignores the victims and is therefore bound to offer only limited protection.

When did human dignity emerge as a legal concept?

Dignity as a legal concept was certainly not made in one day.[16] The 'when?' question raises a complex issue. There is widespread agreement among lawyers that dignity's history ought to include non-legal elements, such as philosophy, with Kant's work being by far the most frequently cited.[17] Historical events also form part of its development, with the Second World War and the Holocaust being understood to have contributed significantly to the use of dignity in law. However, dating the beginning of a concept, as Gadamer reminded us, is not that simple, and it involves taking a political and philosophical stance on the concept's meaning and finality.[18] In relation to dignity, several beginning dates can be identified. For instance, as the concept of dignity is so tightly connected to human rights, 1789 might be a suitable starting date: despite the fact that the French Declaration of the Rights of Man and the Citizen did not include dignity in its current understanding, it arguably created the legal conditions for dignity to emerge as a legal concept later on. If we are looking for the first mention of dignity in a normative text, then 1848, with the adoption of the French decree prohibiting slavery, becomes a possible starting date.[19] The most generally mentioned starting dates are 1948 and 1949, but they leave out pre-war legal uses of the concept, such as the Irish Constitution

---

[15] See Clemens Sedmak, Chapter 33 in this volume.
[16] C. R. Miguel, 'Human dignity: history of an idea', *Jahrbuch des öffentlichen Rechts* 50 (2002), 281–99, and Michael Rosen, *Dignity: Its History and Meaning* (Harvard, Harvard University Press, 2012). In German, see J. Wetz (ed.), *Texte zur Menschenwürde* (Stuttgart, Reklam, 2011), and P. Kondylis, 'Artikel Würde' *Geschichtliche Grundbegriffe II–VIII, Band 7* (Stuttgart, Klett-Cotta, 1992), 637–77.
[17] G. P. Fletcher, 'Human dignity as a constitutional value', *University of Western Ontario* 22 (1984), 171–82, and T. E. Hill, *Dignity and Practical Reason in Kant's Moral Theory* (Ithaca, NY, and London, Cornell University Press, 1992).
[18] H. G. Gadamer, *Au Commencement de la Philosophie, pour une Lecture des Présocratiques* (Paris, Seuil, 2001).
[19] Decree of 27 April 1848, http://www.assemblee-nationale.fr/histoire/esclavage/decret1848.asp. See Rebecca Scott, Chapter 2 in this volume.

of 1937.[20] The last date that can be considered here is 2009, when the Lisbon Treaty came into force. This explicitly enshrined for the first time in Europe a normative definition of human dignity, binding both on the EU and its Member States (when they are implementing EU law).

The small sample of dates considered here demonstrates how significant dating the beginning of human dignity's construction as a legal concept can be for understanding and using it in law. For instance, using 1789 arguably leads to a definition of human dignity as a foundational principle of liberal democracy, strongly connected to claims of liberty and equality; using 1848 sheds light on the fundamental connection between dignity, humanity, work, and working conditions, and calls for other dates to be considered, such as 1919[21] or 1946;[22] choosing 1949 as a starting date has led to a construction of dignity as a negative concept, that is, a 'never again' response to the systematic denial and destruction of humanity, which leaves out its arguably much-needed positive and complementary dimensions; finally, a 2009 focus highlights the novelty of dignity, but risks misrepresenting it as a primarily EU-made concept, whereas the story is much more complex, involving Member States and the ECtHR as key actors, as well as their histories and contexts.

All these dates are not of course mutually exclusive, but rather point to the necessity of understanding dignity against a complex historical backdrop, bearing in mind that the development of a constitutional concept is not always linear and mono-directional, and that the exceptions and detours arguably deserve as much (if not more) scholarly attention than the apparently main direction.[23] Finally, dating the beginning of dignity and reconstructing its history require that the concept be methodologically positioned within a wider context and evolution. The dates suggested above are based on the assumption that the construction of dignity is part of the greater adventure of liberal

---

[20] W. Binchy, 'Human dignity as a constitutional principle', in O. Doyle and E. Carolan (eds), *The Irish Constitution: Governance and Values* (Dublin, Thomson Rond Hall, 2008), 307–26. See also Samuel Moyn, Chapter 4, this volume.

[21] Respectively adoption of the Weimar Constitution, which mentions human dignity in relation to the economic life (article 151, written under the direct influence of Lassale) and creation of the International Labour Organization.

[22] Article 36.1 of the 1946 Italian constitution reads: 'Workers are entitled to a remuneration commensurate with the quantity and quality of their work, and in any case sufficient to ensure to them and their family a free and dignified existence [un'esistenza libera e dignitosa].'

[23] Franco's constitution (1947 Fuero de los Espanoles) made 'respect for human dignity, integrity and the liberty of human person' its 'ruling principle'. Pétain's organic statute of 10 July 1940 (never enforced) was based on human dignity. See also the controversial Fundamental Law in force in Hungary since January 2012: C. Dupré 'Human dignity: Rhetoric, protection, instrumentalisation', in G. A. Tóth (ed.), *Constitution for a Disunited Nation. On Hungary's 2011 Fundamental Law* (Budapest, Central European University Press, 2012), 143–70.

democracy, a positioning that serves to understand the concept in a retrospective manner and to construct its history by a process of selection and inclusion (and thus exclusion) of key dates and events. The methodological awareness of dignity's positioning on a wider timeline is also crucial, of course, when understanding and constructing dignity in a prospective manner, that is, looking to the future and reflecting on the concept's possible implications, ensuring that this micro-narrative is not too inconsistent with the macro-narrative.

Why has human dignity been used as a legal concept?

The last question to be considered is the reason why dignity is being constructed and used as a legal concept when it is apparently such a difficult and controversial idea. The overall answer suggested here is that dignity is used to introduce change in the law, and this can be observed both at the level of constitution-making and at the level of human rights adjudication. The use of human dignity to break away from regimes of indignity and destruction of humanity is a well-known reason for enshrining it in constitutions adopted after a dictatorship, with the 1949 German Basic Law being the emblematic, but certainly not isolated, example.[24] In this context, human dignity can be understood as a solemn constitutional commitment 'never again' to deny people their humanity and to destroy it in a systematic manner. The connection between enshrining dignity and a new constitutional beginning has also spread beyond the context of post-dictatorial constitution-making, as illustrated by the 1994 Belgian constitution, the 2000 Finnish constitution, and the 2009 Lisbon Treaty (to the extent that it can be considered as founding the new constitutional order of the EU).

The more frequent, and perhaps the more difficult, uses of dignity have taken place in the context of human rights adjudication, and they have triggered a substantial amount of controversy and confusion owing to their apparent lack of logic and predictability. As frequently noted, human dignity has usefully filled in a gap in human rights protection that had not been addressed by the constitution or lawmakers in a given system. More importantly, perhaps (because less noticed), human dignity has arguably been used to introduce

---

[24] In Europe, the constitutions of Greece, Portugal, Spain, Hungary (1989), Bulgaria, Romania, Slovenia, Estonia, Slovakia, Lithuania, Czech Republic, Latvia, and Poland enshrined dignity to mark a break away from a regime of dictatorship. See C. Dupré, *Importing the Law in Post-Communist Transitions: The Hungarian Constitutional Court and the Right to Human Dignity* (Oxford, Hart Publishing, 2003). The South African constitution adopted at the end of the apartheid also enshrined dignity in a similar move away from the racist regime that had prevailed until then.

deep transformations at the heart of human rights understanding, reflecting more general social and cultural expectations and perceptions. Defining human dignity in this context involves assessing the change introduced by judicial reliance on it. This question has often been phrased and simplified in terms of whether or not dignity promotes a pro-life or a pro-choice stance on abortion, or a pro-assisted suicide or a pro-sanctity of life approach, to refer to what are perhaps two of the most controversial judicial usages of human dignity. These examples point to what is arguably the key question: the issue of fit of a new concept in an older or well-established system of rights and values. The tension between dignity of life and sanctity of life is an emblematic example. Understanding dignity and constructing it further in legal terms arguably requires movement beyond a (usually) conflictual approach to this type of tension and to reconsider critically the more familiar (and better established) concepts or rights with which dignity appears to conflict. A definition of human dignity can of course be found in the outcome of a particular dignity-based judgement. More informatively, however, it will be found in the degree of transformation that the established concept (e.g., equality, autonomy, or sanctity of life) has undergone by being interpreted through the prism of human dignity. The changes introduced by human dignity do not always trigger consensus, and should not be accepted without a sound degree of scepticism and criticism. Taking on board the potent transformative function of dignity and measuring it, however, also forms part of this concept's definition.

Therefore, it is suggested here that any scholarly definition or judicial use of dignity should pass a dual transformation test. Judges and scholars need to check whether reliance on dignity is not meaningless and redundant, and, for instance, better replaced by an easier and more familiar concept (e.g., respect, decency, or autonomy, to list a few words often used in conjunction with dignity). Moreover, they need to identify the change introduced as a result of using a human dignity argument, and to reflect on its short term (e.g., as limited to a given dispute), and wider impact and implications (e.g., on the whole thinking and practice of human rights).

Conclusion

This chapter has endeavoured to move beyond the emotionally and politically charged discussions that the mention of human dignity almost invariably triggers, by looking at how the concept has been constructed in the legal field. It has shown that the concept of dignity is firmly embedded in European law, with a plurality of histories, normative definitions, and actors who have contributed to its construction. The (brief) discussion of these four questions has shifted the focus of attention in seeking to understand dignity away from a search for a single definition to an awareness of dignity's context contingent and constructed—even 'under construction'—nature, with a diverse range of narratives and narrators involved in its legal formulation. Rather than being an obstacle to understanding, however, the unfinished nature of human dignity is a crucial sign of its dynamism and usefulness.

6

Human Dignity: Experience and History, Practical Reason and Faith

David Hollenbach

HUMAN DIGNITY HAS MOVED to the forefront of recent discourse about the normative standards that should govern human affairs. Since the promulgation of the Universal Declaration of Human Rights in 1948, the duty to respect the dignity of all human beings has come to be seen as the most fundamental duty that men and women owe each other in their interpersonal and social interactions. The concept of human dignity as a standard of morality is surely not an invention of recent decades. Some argue that it has deep roots in Greek philosophy and biblical religion. Others trace it back to medieval theories of natural law, to the French and American revolutions with their roots in Enlightenment reason, or to the anti-slavery movements of the nineteenth century. Nearer to today, the Nazi Holocaust of the Jewish people 'shocked the conscience' of humankind and has become a standard point of reference in reflection on the role that respect for human dignity ought to play in human affairs, as have the revulsion at the consequences of the two world wars, which made the twentieth century the bloodiest in European history. Post-war rejection of colonial domination and the struggle against Soviet tyranny further strengthened the emerging conviction that respect for the dignity of persons was a central social value.

Each of these explanations of why human dignity has become so central to normative approaches to social life has implications for what dignity means and how we interpret its requirements. This chapter will certainly not attempt to give a full treatment of human dignity's contemporary importance, meaning, and practical implications. Rather, by appealing to historical experience of the violation and attainment of dignity, some partial suggestions will be offered about how we might come to a better understanding of what it means and what it requires.

Objections to dignity

Despite the centrality of human dignity and human rights in contemporary social debate, some scholars have raised questions about whether the idea of human dignity is useful, and whether it will bear the weight placed on it in today's normative and ethical discourse.[1] For example, Ruth Macklin, a philosopher specializing in bioethics, has written an essay entitled 'Dignity Is a Useless Concept'.[2] She argues that dignity is too vague a standard to be useful in making judgements about difficult ethical matters. If dignity is to function effectively as a norm, we need to be able to determine with some precision when it is being violated. Macklin believes, however, that this is impossible because of the abstractness of the idea of dignity. Thus, she holds that respect for the liberal principle of autonomy is much more helpful than appeals to dignity, especially in domains as complex as contemporary biomedical ethics. In Macklin's view, therefore, appeals to an abstract concept of human dignity can be dispensed with in the field of bioethics without any notable loss.

Others have argued that appeals to human dignity should be avoided in secular or pluralistic societies because they depend on metaphysical or religious convictions that are not broadly shared in such societies. For example, irritation at the references to religious grounds for dignity in a volume of essays on *Human Dignity and Bioethics* produced by the US President's Council on Bioethics led evolutionary psychologist Stephen Pinker to write a dismissive essay entitled 'The Stupidity of Dignity'. Pinker sees the appeals to dignity in the Council's volume as an effort to 'impose a radical political agenda, fed by fervent religious impulses, onto American biomedicine'.[3] Indeed, he sees some of the understandings of dignity in this volume as a sign that the President's Council has been co-opted by a group seeking to impose a 'Catholic agenda' on US pluralism.[4]

In a similar way, Michael Ignatieff maintains that arguments in support of human rights should avoid appealing to dignity because such appeals overlap with contestable religious claims about the sacredness of human persons. In secular or pluralistic contexts, appeals to metaphysical or even religious convictions about human sacredness as the basis of human rights are not helpful.

---

[1] For an overview of and response to some of these objections see Mary Ann Glendon, 'The bearable lightness of dignity', *First Things* 213 (May 2011), 41–5.
[2] Ruth Macklin, 'Dignity is a useless concept', *British Medical Journal* 327 (20–7 December 2003), 1419–20.
[3] Stephen Pinker, 'The stupidity of dignity', *New Republic* (28 May 2008), 28. Michael Rosen notes this danger in a much less polemical way in Chapter 7, this volume.
[4] Pinker, 'The stupidity of dignity', 31.

Through the title of his book *Human Rights as Politics and Idolatry*, Ignatieff suggests that calling on a religious or quasi-religious interpretation of dignity to support human rights verges on being a form of idolatry. Some people may be quite ready to affirm dignity as another way of speaking about the sacredness of the person that they affirm on religious grounds; but those who do not believe in God will reject this, and see it as raising the human to a level it does not deserve, thus being a kind of idolatry. To be sure, Ignatieff wants to support human rights. But he believes we should forgo efforts to ground them on claims about a dignity or nature allegedly shared by all human beings. Support for human rights will be more secure if we avoid metaphysical or religious claims about their foundations and rely simply on historical, prudential, or pragmatic evidence that support for rights is desirable.[5] So human rights will be better served if we forgo appeals about their grounding. Again, we can dispense with the idea of dignity.

Still others object to dignity because they see claims to have identified a basis for human rights that is shared among all human beings as falsely universalizing what are in fact Western cultural and/or religious standards. Dignity could thus be used to try to justify the imposition of particular religious or cultural beliefs on those who do not share these beliefs. This argument has been raised in an Asian, Confucian perspective in a particularly pointed way by Lee Kwan Yew and from an African standpoint by Mahmood Mamdani.[6] In their views, seeking to advance human well-being by proposing a universalist understanding of human dignity and human rights carries overtones of colonial or imperial domination. People in diverse cultures are different enough from each other that it is dangerous to claim that one has identified a set of universal norms, such as human rights, that should govern how all people should be treated. Similarly, asserting a common human dignity supposedly shared by all people across cultural boundaries risks granting the interpretation of dignity in one cultural context a dominant and even repressive role in relation to other cultures.

The idea of human dignity, therefore, faces considerable challenges today. Some of the authors cited use harshly negative terms to characterize the role played by human dignity in contemporary discourse. Dignity is variously described as useless, stupid, idolatrous, and imperialistic. This is certainly not

---

[5] Michael Ignatieff, *Human Rights as Politics and Idolatry* (Princeton, NJ, Princeton University Press, 2001), 53–5.

[6] For Lee Kwan Yew's 'Asian values' argument, see Fareed Zakaria, 'Culture is destiny: a conversation with Lee Kwan Yew', *Foreign Affairs* 73:2 (March/April 1994), 109–26. The African postcolonialist stand is developed in a practical way in Mahmood Mamdani, *Saviors and Survivors: Darfur, Politics, and the War on Terror* (New York, Pantheon Books, 2009).

a promising situation. So should we abandon the effort to understand human dignity before spending any more time on such a debatable undertaking?

The context of dignity's recent emergence as a key social norm

By no means. I will argue that the concept of human dignity is not abstract and useless, insensitive to religious pluralism, or a potential threat to cultural difference. Such an argument can begin by giving some attention to the context of the emergence of the contemporary stress on human dignity and human rights.

First, we should note that the Preamble of the Universal Declaration states that it is affirming human dignity and human rights because of some utterly concrete evidence for why the idea is needed. The Declaration's starting point is what happens to human beings when dignity is *not* respected. Disregard for dignity, the Preamble states, has 'resulted in barbarous acts which have outraged the conscience of mankind'.[7] The reference is to the slaughter of six million Jews in the Holocaust, an abomination that the drafters hold to be utterly offensive to all but the socially obtuse. The importance of this context is reinforced by the fact that the 1948 Convention on the Prevention and Punishment of the Crime of Genocide was adopted by the UN General Assembly just one day before the Assembly proclaimed human dignity as the basis of human rights in the Universal Declaration.[8] The contrast between respect for dignity and descent into barbarisms like genocide indicates one of the most important functions of appeals to human dignity in recent discourse. Respecting human dignity means avoiding those violations of the human person that are so grave that all (or nearly all) persons see them as outrageous

---

[7] Universal Declaration of Human Rights, Preamble, http://www.un.org/en/documents/udhr.

[8] Samuel Moyn has argued that the Holocaust was at best tangential and perhaps even irrelevant to the drafting of the Universal Declaration. See Moyn, *The Last Utopia: Human Rights in History* (Cambridge, MA, Belknap Press of Harvard University Press, 2010), chapter 2. Moyn has quite effectively shown that the close linkage of human rights discourse and the Holocaust became much more explicit several decades after the Declaration was drafted rather than at the time of the drafting. However, the appeal to deeds that 'outraged the conscience of mankind' and the proclamation of the Universal Declaration just one day after the Genocide Convention suggests that the two are not as unrelated as Moyn maintains. Indeed, later appeals to the Universal Declaration to resist genocide would not be possible without the link between the two that is at least incipient in human rights discourse from the time of the drafting of the Universal Declaration. As will be clear from what follows, I diverge from Moyn in holding that changes in emphasis and even in the understanding of the content of human dignity do not necessarily imply radical discontinuity. 'Development of doctrine', as the term is used is Catholic theology, sees historical change, even dramatic change, as at least sometimes compatible with continuity in tradition. Moyn, on the other hand, sees change as most often suggesting discontinuity.

and shocking. The affirmation of human dignity as the basis of rights begins from objection to such outrages, and is proposed as an alternative to them. It points to the utterly concrete experience of those who suffered and died in the camps, who lost spouses, children, and parents to campaigns based on racist ideology, and who were forced to flee their homes as refugees and asylum seekers because of the efforts of an authoritarian demagogue to shape the world according to his deluded image of what it should look like. The affirmation of dignity in this context is far from an abstract norm that provides only ambiguous guidance. Rather, it is a normative declaration that such outrages should never happen. Indeed, dignity is proposed as a way of understanding our relation to each other that explains why we see such actions as outrageous.

The Preamble of the Universal Declaration invokes not only the Holocaust as the antithesis of its affirmation of dignity, but also the human destruction of two twentieth-century world wars. As an alternative to such destruction, the Declaration affirms that 'recognition of the inherent dignity and of the equal and inalienable rights of all members of the human family is the foundation of freedom, justice and peace in the world'. In addition, the Preamble notes the waves of anti-colonial sentiment that arose in India in the 1940s and spread across other parts of Asia and across Africa in the 1950s and 1960s. Respect for dignity, the Preamble maintains, is required if people are 'not to be compelled to have recourse, as a last resort, to rebellion against tyranny and oppression'. If respect for dignity and rights is lacking, oppression, grave injustice, and the violence of war can be expected to follow.[9] Respect for human dignity is seen as the antithesis of the evils that flow from oppression and violence.

This kind of appeal to human dignity can be called the 'Kantian moment' in discourse about human dignity. For Kant, the fundamental standard of morality is that all human beings be treated with respect, as ends in themselves rather than only as means to be used for some other purpose. The value of a human being—the person's dignity—is beyond price. Things with price can be exchanged for each other in the marketplace, but humans, having dignity, are valuable in themselves and thus cannot be simply traded one for another.[10] The response due to human dignity is respect for the inherent worth

---

[9] Moyn also rejects this linkage of the Universal Declaration to subsequent anti-colonial movements. See *The Last Utopia*, chapter 3. My divergence from Moyn again rests on noting that subsequent appeals to the Universal Declaration by anti-colonialists would not be possible without this incipient anti-colonial affirmation in the Declaration itself.

[10] Immanuel Kant, *Grounding for the Metaphysics of Morals*, trans. James W. Ellington, 3rd edn (Indianapolis, IN, Hackett, 1993), 40–1 [434–5].

of the person, not the kind of fairness that is involved in setting a just price for a commodity being exchanged in the marketplace.

One aspect of Kant's understanding of dignity, therefore, is that it affirms *who counts* when we are distributing the benefits of our life together in political, social, and interpersonal interaction. It concerns the scope of the community that the standards of morality should govern. Who are included in the 'we' that are to be governed by the standards of morality being proposed? The idea of dignity insists that the most fundamental moral 'we' includes *all* human persons. *All* deserve to be treated in a way that takes account of their common humanity.

Dignity is used in a similar way by the Universal Declaration of Human Rights. The Declaration affirms the reality of a global community to which *all* human beings belong.[11] This is evident in the way the terms 'all', 'everyone', and 'no one' are used throughout the Declaration to indicate the subjects of the enumerated human rights. All persons possess human rights without distinctions based on 'race, colour, sex, language, religion, political or other opinion, national or social origin'.[12] The idea that *all* persons share human dignity, therefore, relativizes all in-group/out-group boundaries. It challenges understandings of religious, national, or cultural identities that suggest only those people who possess that identity have the kind of worth that is deserving of respect.

The use of the idea of human dignity in contemporary human rights discourse thus follows Kant's lead not only in affirming the existence of universal moral obligations but also in closely linking these obligations with the requirement of respect for humanity as such. In response to the realities of the Holocaust, the violence of world wars, potential harms that can be caused by anti-colonial struggles, and the oppression of would-be revolutionary states such as those that formed the Soviet bloc, contemporary appeals to human dignity affirm both the universal reach of moral obligation beyond all in-group/out-group divides and the duty to treat every human being with the respect due to their irreplaceable worth.

---

[11] Though Moyn is right that anti-colonial movements of the 1950s and 1960s sought national self-determination by states, the Universal Declaration affirms human rights in a way that goes beyond such a state-centred understanding of self-determination. Jacques Maritain, who contributed to the philosophical underpinnings of the Universal Declaration, makes a forceful argument that rights must reach beyond state sovereignty. See his *Man and the State* (Chicago, University of Chicago Press, 1951), chapter 2 and 194–201.

[12] Universal Declaration of Human Rights, article 2.

An inductive understanding of dignity

It is true, of course, that Kant's moral philosophy is not without problems. But I believe there are alternative routes to the affirmation that all persons are due the respect that Kant calls for that do not depend on the whole of his systematic moral philosophy. Let me suggest the very general outlines of one such approach. The approach to understanding human dignity I would propose avoids Kant's effort to deduce an understanding of dignity from the preconditions of rational thought. Rather, it follows a more inductive approach that begins in human experience. Because of this, it can be called a more Aristotelian approach to an understanding of human dignity. Aristotle sought to identify the concrete dimensions of the good life in an inductive way by considering evidence from all the societies known to him.[13] In like manner, we can seek to determine what sort of respect is due to human beings, and thus what their dignity requires, by paying attention to the diverse religious, cultural, and political communities of our world, and observing how they believe persons should be treated. This will surely show considerable pluralism regarding how people think they should be treated and how they should treat others. In the midst of this pluralism, however, through practical reflection on the agreements, disagreements, and relative strengths of these diverse conceptions of dignity, some common standards may emerge. Such an inductive, experience-based approach may lead to transcultural agreement on at least some of the most basic requirements of respect for human worth. In fact, this is just what happened when people from many diverse traditions reached consensus on the most basic requirements of dignity when they drafted the Universal Declaration in 1948.

Using a phrase borrowed from Margaret Farley, one can call the requirements of respect for dignity 'obligating features of personhood'.[14] One might also call them obligating features of human dignity. These are dimensions of personal dignity that indicate not only *that* we should show respect towards one another but *what* it will mean to show such respect. Farley identifies two such features: autonomy (the capacity to be self-determining and not have one's life simply shaped by other persons or external powers), and relationality (the fact that persons cannot survive, thrive, or even exist as persons without some fundamental relatedness to other persons).[15] Because autonomy

---

[13] See especially Aristotle, *Nicomachean Ethics*, book X, chapters 4–6.
[14] This phrase, and some of the analysis that follows, is drawn from Margaret A. Farley, 'A feminist version of respect for persons', *Journal of Feminist Studies in Religion* 9:1–2 (Spring-Fall, 1993), 183–98.
[15] Margaret A. Farley, 'A feminist version of respect for persons', 187, 189.

can be interpreted in an excessively individualistic way, I would prefer to call the first of these features of personhood 'freedom' rather than 'autonomy'. In addition, I want to add 'basic needs' such as the need for food or health care as a third obligating feature of personhood that will help specify the meaning of human dignity and what respect for dignity requires.

The importance of these freedoms, relationships, and needs as crucial features of personhood emerges from reflection on the experience of what it is to be human. Long ago, Aristotle drew from experience the conclusion that human beings are different from both beasts and from gods, and should be treated differently from both beasts and gods.[16] This conclusion surely remains intelligible and valid today, even in the midst of our experience of cultural diversity. It points to some key ways in which our human personhood generates both negative and positive obligations in our interaction with each other. Not being a beast is having a capacity for self-transcendence that is unique to beings with consciousness or spirit. It is a key index of the distinctive worth of human personhood, and it points to a central aspect of how humans can reasonably expect to be treated by each other. We should support one another in undertaking activities of the spirit, such as growing in knowledge and exercising freedom. In addition, this capacity of human consciousness to move beyond itself is evident in the formation and sustaining of personal relationships in friendship and love. Respecting humanity requires, as a minimum, that we refrain from denying each other the most basic freedoms and relationships of these kinds, unless we have solid justification for doing so.

To respect a person's ability to know, make choices, and form bonds of relationship and love is to respect the claim of what she is and to acknowledge what she can become. Similarly, a second person is capable of experiencing that claim precisely because the second person also possesses the capacity for self-transcendence. This other person is not confined within the limits of his self-consciousness but can genuinely encounter the other as a fellow human being. Thus, one human being *is* a kind of *ought* in the face of another. Each person's capacity for self-transcendence makes a claim on the other's capacity for self-transcendence. One person's ability to know and understand calls out for acknowledgement in the understanding shown by others. One person's freedom places requirements on the freedom of another. One person's capacity

---

[16] That human beings are neither beasts nor gods and should be treated accordingly is a presupposition of ethical politics. See Aristotle, *Politics*, Book I, chapter 3 (1253ª). Martha Nussbaum takes this as a fundamental presupposition of her 'capabilities approach' to ethics in social and economic life. See, for example, Nussbaum, 'Human capabilities, female human beings', in Martha Nussbaum and Jonathan Glover (eds), *Women, Culture, and Development: A Study of Human Capabilities* (Oxford, Oxford University Press, 1995), 61–104, at 73.

to form bonds of relationship with others calls for acknowledgment and support through the concern of others.[17] These affirmations lead to a vision of the human race as a genuine moral community with reciprocal obligations among all its members. This is a cosmopolitan vision of a universal human community. Along with its respect for cultural differences, it also holds that basic common standards of dignity can be identified across cultures.

Aristotle also held that human beings are not gods, that the human good is that of a bodily being and has material conditions. Human dignity can only be realized if these material conditions are present, and it cannot be realized if they are lacking. Dignity requires not only that one's freedom and relatedness be secured and protected; it also requires food, shelter, bodily integrity, medical care in sickness, and a number of other material supports. Therefore, it can be reasonably affirmed that we have some responsibilities to enable one another to share in the material goods and physical, bodily activities that are among the conditions required for living with dignity. Again, at the minimum we have a duty not to deprive one another of these material basics.

Respect for all three of these features of personhood—freedoms, relationships, and basic needs—were evidently seen as required by human dignity by the drafters of the Universal Declaration. They saw dignity not as an abstract standard but as a way of referring to those inductively identified characteristics of personhood that make concrete demands for respect on other persons and on social institutions. Some, perhaps many, of these characteristics were identified through their absence. Thus, the experience of the effects of denial of freedoms because of religion, ethnicity, or race led to the affirmation that respect for freedom and dignity is due to all persons independent of their religious, ethnic, or racial identity. Further reflection on experience led a more inclusive list of the features of personhood that must be respected if persons are to be treated as such. These include the freedoms that enable one to be a self-determining person of one's own: freedom from slavery or arbitrary arrest, freedom of movement, thought, conscience, religion, expression, and assembly. They include patterns of relationship that enable people to participate actively in the interpersonal and social interactions that are necessary for the well-being both of individual persons and of the communities of which they are members. Finally, they imply that respect for persons and their

---

[17] See William Luijpen, *Phenomenology of Natural Law* (Pittsburgh, PA, Duquesne University Press, 1967), chapter 6, 'Justice as an anthropological form of co-existence', especially 180. For approaches that are both similar and interestingly different from this, see Jean-François Lyotard, 'The other's rights', in Stephen Shute and Susan Hurley (eds), *On Human Rights: The Oxford Amnesty Lectures 1993* (New York, Basic Books, 1993), 135–47, and Jacques Derrida, *Of Hospitality* (Stanford, CA, Stanford University Press, 2000).

dignity requires securing basic levels of subsistence, meeting other bodily needs such as the requirements of basic health, and the protection of persons through respect for their bodily integrity.

These forms of freedom, relationship, and need-fulfilment are seen to be essential to human well-being through reflection on experience, especially on the experience of their absence. Indeed, reflection on experience leads to the conclusion that some truly basic freedoms, relations, and needs are required if persons are to live lives that can be judged to meet the minimum requirements of humanity. In other words, the most basic freedoms, relationships, and needs are essential to the attainment of human dignity. They specify in a concrete way what is required if human dignity is to be respected. They are obligating features of human dignity. Their fuller development leads to the articulation of human rights that specify the minimum standards for the protection of human dignity.

Demands of dignity through practical reason

This specification of the dimensions of human dignity in the Universal Declaration's catalogue of human rights was an example of practical reason in action. Jacques Maritain, who participated in the drafting of the Declaration, saw the process as a vivid illustration of how practical reason can lead people from diverse religious and cultural traditions to agreement on moral values even when their understandings of ultimate meanings are different. Maritain observed that the drafters could 'agree about the rights but on condition that no one asks us why'.[18] Representatives of diverse religious and cultural traditions might be unable to reach agreement on the requirements of human dignity if they sought to deduce them from ultimate beliefs about the world and God. But this did not prevent the attainment of practical agreement on dignity and rights. Through practical reason, it was possible to reach common practical ideas that led to 'the affirmation of a single body of beliefs *for guidance in action*'.[19] That the reasoning involved was practical rather than theoretical did not mean that the agreement reached was simply fortuitous, accidental, or even irrational. The agreement on dignity and rights was in fact a vivid example of human reason in action—practical reason reflecting on human experience. Thus, the understanding of human dignity attained by the drafters of the Universal Declaration was not simply an expression of their preferences,

---

[18] Jacques Maritain, 'Introduction', in *Human Rights: Comments and Interpretations*, symposium edited by UNESCO (New York, Columbia University Press, 1949), 9.

[19] Maritain, 'Introduction', in *Human Rights: Comments and Interpretations*, 10, emphasis added.

biases, or cultural dispositions. In light of the shared experience and reflection that led to it, this understanding of dignity can be called reasonable.

In other words, there can be *good reasons* for conclusions about practical affairs, even when their ultimate significance is interpreted differently in diverse religious and cultural traditions. We can give *reasons* for affirming that human beings should not be slaughtered because they are Jews or Armenians or Rwandan Tutsi, that they should be allowed to express their religious beliefs and intellectual convictions in freedom, that they should not be excluded from participation in political community or denied access to work, that their need for food or health care should be met when their community has the capacity to do so. The reasons we provide will take the form of a statement like this: our experience has led us to the practical conclusion that treating a person as a human being requires this. We have learned from experience, and it is reasonable for us to affirm that these freedoms, relationships, and needs are obligating features of human dignity. Thus, if we are to treat people as they deserve, we must respect this dignity in its multiple dimensions. We have a duty to respect the human rights that spell out these features of dignity in more detail when we have the capacity to do so.

The interaction of practical and theological interpretations of dignity

Thus, practical reason can lead to shared understanding of the dimensions of human dignity and rights across the boundaries of different religious traditions and cultures. This is one of the most important contributions of the human rights ethos in a world simultaneously aware of its diversity and its increasing global interdependence. Because religious traditions articulate understandings of the ultimate meaning and purpose of human activity, however, they will surely affect people's motives for respecting dignity and, in the end, will influence how believers interpret the full meaning of dignity and rights. At the same time, because understandings of human dignity and rights arrived at through practical reasoning specify morally obligatory duties, they will have an impact on the ways religious traditions are interpreted. In other words, there is a mutually illuminating movement between the conclusions reached by practical reason about dignity and rights and the more theoretical orientations provided by the doctrines and beliefs of religious traditions.

This mutual illumination is evident in the way Catholicism grounds its affirmation of human dignity both in a theological understanding of the creation of human beings in God's image and in a more secular, philosophical understanding of human capacities. The theological approach begins from the biblical teaching in the book of Genesis that human beings are created in the image and likeness of God (Gen. 1:26). Persons possess a worth that deserves to be treated with the reverence shown to that which is holy. In the thirteenth century, Thomas Aquinas expressed this biblical perspective in a way that has notable parallels to Kant's affirmation that persons are ends in themselves. Aquinas wrote that of all the creatures in the universe, only humans are 'governed by divine providence for their own sakes'.[20] In addition, Catholicism also draws on the further theological conviction that human beings have been redeemed and recreated in Christ to call for an even greater level of respect for dignity.[21] These theological warrants lead to a strong commitment to defend human dignity, a commitment that the Second Vatican Council saw as flowing from the gospel that is at the heart of Christian faith.[22]

The Catholic tradition also holds that human dignity can be recognized by all human beings and makes claims upon all, both Christian and non-Christian. This is very much in line with Catholicism's long-standing, natural law-based conviction that ethical responsibilities can be grasped by human reason and philosophical reflection on what it is to be human. Thus, in addition to its explicitly theological grounding for human dignity, the Catholic tradition offers secular warrants for its affirmation of human dignity. The Second Vatican Council not only invoked the theological theme of creation in the image of God as the basis of dignity but also argued that this dignity can be seen in the transcendent power of the human mind. Through their intellects, human beings transcend the material universe, and the mind's capacity to share in divine wisdom gives humans a worth that reflects God's. For the Council, human dignity is also manifest in the capacity of the human conscience to search for moral truth, and to adhere to it when it has been found. Obedience to the dictates of conscience—which is the deepest core and sanctuary of a person—'is the very dignity of the human person'. The Council further held that dignity is evident in the excellence of human liberty. Freedom is 'an exceptional sign of the divine image within the human person'. The dignity of freedom requires that persons act with free choice, and that they seek to direct their freedom through knowledge of the true good.[23]

---

[20] Thomas Aquinas, *Summa Contra Gentiles*, Part I, chapters 112 and 113, trans. in *Basic Writings of Saint Thomas Aquinas*, vol. 2, ed. Anton C. Pegis (New York, Random House, 1945), 220 and 223.
[21] John XXIII, *Pacem in Terris*, no. 10, and Vatican Council II, *Gaudium et Spes*, no. 22. Both in David J. O'Brien and in Thomas A. Shannon (eds), *Catholic Social Thought: The Documentary Heritage*, expanded edn (Maryknoll, NY, Orbis Books, 2010).
[22] Vatican Council II, *Gaudium et Spes*, no. 41.
[23] Vatican Council II, *Gaudium et Spes*, nos 15–17.

These three secular warrants for human dignity—the transcendence of the mind, the sacredness of conscience, and the excellence of liberty—are all aspects of the power of human reason that is a prime manifestation of the likeness of humans to God. But because intellect, conscience, and liberty are rationally knowable through reflection on experience, they possess a certain autonomy from the doctrinal beliefs of the Church. This relative autonomy of the secular philosophical warrants for human dignity enabled thinkers such as Maritain and John Courtney Murray to rely upon them as a kind of fulcrum for the lever of their successful efforts to persuade the church to abandon its nineteenth-century rejection of the rights to freedom of conscience and religion. In the nineteenth and early twentieth centuries, several popes had seen modern arguments for freedom of religion and thought as manifestations of relativism, and thus as threats to the truth of Christian faith. Before and at the Second Vatican Council, however, Maritain and Murray successfully argued that, through the reflection of practical reason on the historical experience of modern democratic life, these freedoms could be seen to be true expressions of human dignity.[24] Thus, practical reflection on experience led to a dramatic development of the Catholic stance on religious freedom and related human rights. It brought the Second Vatican Council not only to reject the nineteenth-century papacy's suspicion of human rights but to the ringing positive statement that 'the right to religious freedom has its foundation in the very dignity of the human person as this dignity is known through the revealed word of God and by reason itself'.[25]

The reciprocal movement between practical and theoretical reason, or between practice and faith, can therefore lead a religious tradition like Catholicism to reconsider and perhaps to revise its understanding of what humanity requires. The movement can also go the other way. It can lead a religious tradition to critique the understanding of human dignity prevailing in a culture or society by drawing on its deeper religious convictions to highlight aspects of human dignity that are being overlooked or denied. This critique of practical understanding in light of the convictions of faith has been evident in the way the Catholic tradition has stressed the communal and social dimensions of human

---

[24] For the way John Courtney Murray's argument for religious freedom drew on practical reflection on historical experience, see his *The Problem of Religious Freedom* (Westminster, MD, Newman Press, 1965), esp. 17ff.

[25] Vatican Council II, *Dignitatis Humanae (Declaration of Religious Freedom)*, no. 2, in Walter M. Abbott and Joseph Gallagher (eds), *The Documents of Vatican II* (New York, America Press, 1966). Michael Rosen discusses the importance of this development of Catholic thought on human dignity and rights perceptively in his *Dignity: Its History and Meaning* (Cambridge, MA, Harvard University Press, 2012), 47–54, 90–100. For my own treatment of the historical development of Catholic thought on dignity and rights, see my *Claims in Conflict: Retrieving and Renewing the Catholic Human Rights Tradition* (New York, Paulist Press, 1979).

dignity in contrast with the more individualistic approaches common in much of the modern West. The Catholic tradition, for both theological and secular reasons, insists that human dignity cannot be reduced to an individualistic understanding of freedom. Freedom can only be realized in relationship and interaction with other persons. The ongoing exercise of personal freedom depends on the social interaction and social institutions that support such freedom.

The theological stress on the social dimensions of human dignity has several sources. The biblical story narrates how God's covenant draws those with faith into community and makes them 'a people'. Both the Hebrew Bible and the New Testament teach that the commandment to love one's neighbour as oneself is a key norm in social life, thus making the call to solidarity central for both Jews and Christians. The Christian eschatological hope that human destiny is realized in a communion of saints reinforces these communal dimensions of human personhood. Further, Catholic tradition sees the image of God in persons as a reflection of a God that Christians believe is a Trinitarian union of three persons who are interrelated in mutual love. The God of Christian faith is not a monadic being isolated in sublime solitude but is radically relational. As images of this Trinitarian God, human persons are also relational. Human beings achieve their dignity only in communal solidarity with each other. As the Council put it, 'God did not create the human being as a solitary ... For by his innermost nature the human being is a social being, and unless he relates himself to others he can neither live nor develop his potential.'[26]

This theological understanding of human dignity as a relational reality also has secular warrants. For example, Vatican II cites Thomas Aquinas's appropriation of Aristotle's philosophical defence of the 'social nature' of the human person, which implies that the development of the person and the advance of society 'hinge on each other' and that each person 'stands completely in need of social life'.[27] Thus, on both theological and secular grounds, the dignity of the person can only be achieved when persons enter into fraternity and community with each other. Human dignity is not realized by persons acting autonomously on their own but through collaboration and solidarity. An individualistic ethic is thus inadequate in light of Catholicism's relational

---

[26] Vatican Council II, *Gaudium et Spes*, no. 12. On this theme, see International Theological Commission, *Communion and Stewardship: Human Persons Created in the Image of God* (2004), especially chapter 2, online at the Holy See, www.vatican.va/roman_curia/congregations/cfaith/cti_documents/rc_con_cfaith_doc_20040723_communion-stewardship_en.html, and more recently, Jack Mahoney, *Christianity in Evolution: An Exploration* (Washington DC, Georgetown University Press, 2011), chapter 2.

[27] Vatican Council II, *Gaudium et Spes*, no. 25.

understanding of human dignity. Protection of human dignity and realization of the common good go together. Neither personal flourishing nor communal well-being can be secured without the other.

This relational understanding of the image of God and of human dignity has important practical implications, particularly for the way human rights are understood. During the Cold War, the West was inclined to conceive human rights largely in individualistic terms, and to give priority to the civil and political rights to freedom of belief, speech, and association, as well as due process of law. The negative rights not to be interfered with often took primacy in the West in its ideological struggle with the Soviet bloc. In contrast, Eastern bloc nations and some in the southern hemisphere adopted ideologies stressing social interdependence and the priority of community provision over individual initiative. This led to granting priority to social and economic rights, such as those to adequate food, work, and housing.

The Catholic affirmation of the importance of freedom and the simultaneous claim that freedom is dependent on and realized in community leads to a rejection of the need to choose between the two types of rights. Neither individualistic understandings that see human rights primarily as rights to be left alone nor collectivist approaches that subordinate persons to the community in a totalitarian way are adequate. The Catholic tradition holds that opposition between individual freedoms on the one hand and mutual solidarity in society on the other is a false dichotomy. Persons can live in dignity only when they live in a community of freedom—a community in which both personal initiative and social solidarity are valued as essential aspects of human dignity.

Thus, the Catholic tradition will challenge understandings of human rights that stress solely the protection of individual freedom in an economy based entirely on the free market. The free market can be productive and lead to economic growth. But the communal understanding of human dignity means that the participation of all persons in the social and economic life of society must be protected. If persons are left out of such participation, the market may need to be regulated or limited in order to guarantee the basic requirements of their dignity. In the context of current economic problems that have pushed many into poverty and unemployment, Pope Benedict stressed this when he stated that 'the worldwide financial breakdown has ... shown the error of the assumption that the market is capable of regulating itself, apart from public intervention and the support of internalized moral standards'.[28] This does not,

---

[28] Benedict XVI, Address to the Pontifical Academy of Social Sciences, 30 April 2010, http://www.vatican.va/holy_father/benedict_xvi/speeches/2010/april/documents/hf_ben-xvi_spe_20100430_scienze-sociali_en.html.

of course, mean that the Church endorses total state control of the economy. The communal understanding of dignity calls for a prudent blend of freedom and regulation in order to secure the agency of all through their participation in the dynamics of social and economic life. It calls for an approach to dignity and rights in which persons have political space for action (civil and political rights) and also the material and institutional prerequisites of communal life that make such action possible (social and economic rights). Thus, both civil-political and social-economic rights are required if human dignity is to be respected in its multiple aspects. This has opened the way for the Church to become an active voice for human dignity in the face of the problems raised both by free markets and by more centralized political systems as well.

Catholic understandings of human dignity and rights are thus shaped both by an inductive use of practical reason reflecting on experience and also on a more theoretical or imaginative vision of humanity shaped by Christian faith. Practical reason and faith play interacting roles in shaping the understanding of dignity. This interaction is itself a historical process. It led to notable revisions in the Catholic stance towards human rights, including religious freedom and democracy, where the Church moved from strong opposition to full support in the century from 1865 to 1965. This raises the question of whether further developments in the Catholic understanding of dignity and rights might be expected in the future. It also suggests that the question of possible continuing development in how dignity is understood needs to be faced in other religious traditions and in secular traditions as well.

Let me conclude by suggesting that the inductive role played by practical reason in formulating the concrete demands of human dignity means that we should expect our understanding of human rights to continue to change and develop. The historical nature of practical reason's reflection on experience can help us understand how the Catholic understanding of human dignity has developed in such notable ways over the past few centuries. It also suggests that we can expect developments in the Catholic understanding of human dignity and rights in the future. For example, recent Church teachings on the equality of men and women is often accompanied by an affirmation of a complementarity of male and female gender roles that leads to a rejection of some of the rights claimed by persons involved in same-sex relationships. Similarly, recent Church teachings reject some innovative forms of medical and technological support for human reproduction as threats to human dignity.[29] Clearly, affirming same-sex relationships and some forms of technologically assisted reproduction as supportive of human dignity would require notable shifts in

---

[29] International Theological Commission, *Communion and Stewardship*, nos 81–94.

aspects of the Catholic moral tradition. Though this is not the place to assess these matters, developments in Catholic thought on such issues should not be ruled out a priori, for Catholic understandings of the requirements of human dignity have clearly changed in a number of other domains. These changes occurred when practical reason indicated they would serve the human good and promote human dignity. So, today, we need similar reflection on how human dignity might be affected by new practices in these areas.

In a recent reflection on the role of Islam in the world today, Pope Benedict stressed the role of reason in assessing whether particular religious visions of the moral life are to be judged to truly reflect God's intent for humanity. The Pope noted that some Muslims appeal to the Qur'an and to Islamic tradition to justify Muslim resort to holy war to advance the spread of Islam. But the Pope saw such resort to violence as contrary to God's intent precisely because it rejects the use of reason as a key component of authentic faith. Quoting the fourteenth-century Byzantine emperor Manuel II Paleologus, the Pope stated that 'Not to act reasonably, not to act with *logos*, is contrary to the nature of God.'[30] In appealing to what he calls 'rationality of faith', the Pope was certainly not reducing faith to what can be known within the limits of reason alone. But he was clearly rejecting Muslim forms of holy war or *jihad* that fail to meet the kind of reasonable standards for the use of force that have become embodied in the tradition of just war, which combines practical human reasonableness with the Christian vision of the dignity of the person.

I would suggest that the Catholic tradition will be true to itself by being ready to apply similar standards of the 'rationality of faith' to the assessment of how human dignity is supported or threatened by the impact of shifting gender roles on same-sex relations, by technological interventions in human reproduction, and by other new and perhaps controversial forms of human interaction. Inductive reflection by practical reason on these issues may well lead us to conclude that traditional practices are the appropriate ways to continue to support human dignity. But it is possible that such reflection may suggest that change in traditional standards is the best way to secure human dignity. Human dignity raises ongoing challenges for all traditions of moral reflection. We can expect Catholicism to be an active participant in the efforts to respond to these challenges.

---

[30] Benedict XVI, 'Faith, reason and the university: memories and reflections', address at meeting with representatives of science, University of Regensburg, 12 September 2006, http://www.vatican.va/holy_father/benedict_xvi/speeches/2006/september/documents/hf_ben-xvi_spe_20060912_university-regensburg_en.html.

PART II

Dignity Critiques

7

Dignity: The Case Against

Michael Rosen

I GAVE THE BENEDICT LECTURES at Boston University on the subject of dignity in 2007. Shortly before the first lecture, I was talking to a leading moral philosopher I know. He regretted that he wouldn't be able to come to the lectures but wished me luck, and added: 'I hope you give it a good kicking'. Well, I don't think that I did that in those lectures or in the book that emerged from them,[1] so perhaps today is as good a time as any to remedy the omission.

Let me start, though, by noticing that my friend's animus against dignity is widely shared among philosophers, in my experience, and goes back a long way. Why should that be so?

This brings me to the first charge against dignity:

Dignity is humbug

Schopenhauer put the idea with characteristic vigour:

> That expression, *dignity of man*, once uttered by Kant, afterward became the shibboleth of all the perplexed and empty-headed moralists who concealed behind that imposing expression their lack of any real basis of morals, or, at any rate, of one that had any meaning. They cunningly counted on the fact that their readers would be glad to see themselves invested with such a *dignity* and would accordingly be quite satisfied with it.[2]

A shibboleth is a kind of tribal password. Schopenhauer's objection to dignity, however, is that it is a deceptive facade. Although the word 'dignity' carries associations of grandeur and elevated status, where we would expect a substantial structure—the foundation for morality—there is, in fact, an empty space. The impressiveness of the facade diverts our attention from the vacuum behind it.

---

[1] *Dignity: Its History and Meaning* (Cambridge, MA, Harvard University Press, 2012).
[2] A. Schopenhauer, *On the Basis of Morality* (Indianapolis, IN, Hackett, 1965), 100.

A few years ago, the University of Oxford in a piece of what all evidence suggests was quite inadvertent managerial brilliance instituted a system by which its overstretched and under-rewarded college fellows could apply for what it calls 'Titular Professorships'—a title which carries no financial benefit or reduction in burden. And yet, as it turned out, this chance to pin medals on one's own chest had considerable appeal to Oxford academics, and they (with the notable exception of the Philosophy Faculty, I should say) threw themselves into the practice with enthusiasm. This, or so Schopenhauer is suggesting, is how dignity functions.

Yet, even if dignity is a Potemkin village of vain pretensions, is it a good idea to expose it? The idea that illusions are essential to the political order runs through the Western tradition of political thought from Plato. According to Bacon, for example, even beneficent innovation in politics is to be distrusted, 'because it unsettles what is established; these things resting on authority, consent, fame and opinion, not on demonstration'.[3]

Nietzsche took this view. He believed[4] that the 'brutal truth' that 'slavery is of the essence of culture' must be concealed by sentimental illusions such as 'the rights of man', 'equality', and the 'dignity of labour':

> Such phantoms as the dignity of man, the dignity of labour, are the needy products of slavedom hiding itself from itself. Woeful time, in which the slave requires such conceptions, in which he is incited to think about and beyond himself! Cursed seducers, who have destroyed the slave's state of innocence by the fruit of the tree of knowledge! Now the slave must vainly scrape through from one day to another with transparent lies recognizable to every one of deeper insight, such as the alleged 'equal rights of all' or the so-called 'fundamental rights of man', of man as such, or the 'dignity of labour'.[5]

Better, in other words, for a heartless world to seem to have a heart than for its heartlessness to be plainly apparent.

But is that so? One description I used above for dignity was 'facade'—a significant metaphor, as it turns out. The idea that facades are false fronts, bogus and misleading, does not seem even to have entered speech before the beginning of the twentieth century. But the coming of architectural modernism—Loos's famous 'House without Eyebrows' on the Michaelerplatz in Vienna and his slogan 'Ornament is crime'—changed that. The force of the modernist revolt against facades was undoubtedly amplified by the First World War. The image of a thrusting modern, capitalist

---

[3] Bacon, *Novum Organum*, XC.
[4] Or, at least, believed in 1871, when he wrote the essay 'The Greek State'.
[5] 'The Greek State', in *Early Greek Philosophy and Other Writings*, trans. M. A. Mügge (New York, Russell & Russell, 1964), 4–5.

society concealed within buildings whose exteriors were presented within the static vocabulary of a nostalgic classicism parallels all too closely an industrialized war in which mass slaughter was carried on alongside the dignified flummery of emperors, hussars, and gallant, courtly ritual. Not only is the Nietzschean idea of philosophers as epistemic aristocrats a morally repellent form of arrogance, but, or so it seems, cynically sustaining illusory facades of dignity increases the destructiveness of the forces thereby concealed.

When everybody's somebody, nobody's anybody

Let me return now to Schopenhauer's suggestion. What gives dignity its imposing or impressive appearance? Earlier, I used the phrase 'grandeur or elevated status'—it wasn't accidental. If we look at the history of the word 'dignity', we notice that many of the words that are now translated into English as dignity were associated with rank and majesty—royal or divine.

Now one might argue that, if dignity is a matter of rank, then the attribution of dignity to human beings should not be measured by whether there is anything corresponding to it. It is a self-enacted status claim. Statuses are not God-given facts (*pace* Pope Leo XIII) but agreed social conventions. It is sufficient therefore that the status claim should be commonly accepted for it to be valid. 'Dignity' does not need to denote anything, just as (one might point out if in Wittgensteinian mood) there is no fact beyond social acceptance that underlies the chess piece with a horse's head being entitled to move in an 'L'-shape. At this point, however, a new objection to dignity presents itself. If there is nothing to dignity but conventional status, what significance can it still have to attribute to all human beings, just in virtue of being human, a status that was originally reserved only for a privileged portion of them? As the Grand Inquisitor says in Gilbert and Sullivan's *The Gondoliers*, 'when everybody's somebody then no one's anybody'.

But, of course, in the case of Schopenhauer's quotation, something more *is* being indicated. The idea is that dignity offers a foundation, drawn from Kant, for that complex of humanitarian ideas about equality and human rights about which Nietzsche thought the nineteenth century needed to conceal the ugly reality. Let us call this the idea of dignity as an inner transcendental kernel; which hich brings me to a third charge against dignity.

There is no inner transcendental kernel

What does Kant mean by dignity? It is important to realize that, for Kant, dignity is the name of a kind of value. All values fall into two classes, he says in the *Groundwork*—'In the kingdom of ends everything has either a *price* or a *dignity*' (Ak. 4:434). While whatever has a price can be replaced by an equivalent, 'what ... is raised above all price and ... admits of no equivalent has a dignity' (Ak. 4:434). Only one thing has dignity, however, says Kant: 'morality, and humanity insofar as it is capable of morality, is that which alone has dignity' (Ak. 4:435). This, then, is our inner transcendental kernel.

The epistemological and metaphysical difficulties in the way of establishing the existence of such an inner transcendental kernel have made it a matter of philosophical controversy (British understatement). Here I want to ignore those difficulties to note one thing: even if we concede the existence of an inner transcendental kernel, it is not clear what follows from that regarding the way in which individuals should be treated or should behave.

The inner transcendental kernel fails to guide our conduct

Consider. Dignity is something that inheres in me in virtue of my personhood. While it is possible to reason instrumentally about those things that have a 'price', my dignity cannot be increased or diminished, however I am treated. Indeed, according to Kant, dignity inheres in my *person*, not my physical body—it cannot even be destroyed by the loss of my life. So what possible guidance could my possession of it give to moral decision-making?

Of course, Kant does think that he can offer a framework for decision-making, although what that is has also proved controversial (more understatement). The dominant view among contemporary Kantians—see, for example, Christine Korsgaard, Onora O'Neill, or Derek Parfit—is that Kant endorses a consent principle.[6] But that cannot be right—unless Kant's claims about what particular ethical judgements follow from his principle are so flagrantly in contradiction with that principle as to beggar belief. What could be more obviously capable of being consented to than that people should have the right to end their own lives? Yet Kant denies this with a vehemence that would do credit to a Catholic bishop. Indeed, pretty much the same thing goes for all the duties that Kant considers as 'duties to oneself'. I have offered what I believe

---

[6] Parfit is not a Kantian—but he spends a huge effort elaborating what he claims to be the 'Kantian' principle of consent.

to be a superior interpretation of Kant's thought in my book, and shall not rehearse it here. I only note that it is a consequence of my interpretation that we shall look in vain in Kant for an objective algorithm for moral decision-taking. If you want an equivalent to the utilitarian's greatest happiness principle, you will be disappointed, I believe.

Given all the difficulties and controversies surrounding Kant's moral philosophy, it is surprising that dignity should have become so prominent in modern law and political discourse. In the light of this, we might suspect that what is behind dignity is not just Kantianism. Which brings me to a fourth objection.

Dignity is a Trojan horse for religiously inspired attacks on equality

The history of dignity and the history of Western Christianity are bound up with one another. Which is not at all surprising, of course, given how far the history of Western social thought has been, effectively, that of Christianity. Certainly, three of the most important historical strands of meaning for dignity (dignity as elevated social status; dignity as a status pertaining to human beings as such; and dignity as a form of speech and bearing that is 'dignified') can be found already in Cicero, but after that, it's pretty much Christianity all the way to the eighteenth century.

One effect of the Christian heritage has been to cast doubt on the status conception of dignity—sometimes in the form of the claim that dignity (worldly status) is of no value, and sometimes as the idea that there is another, truer, unworldly dignity, distinct from worldly status. What is important for my purpose now, however, is the idea of dignity as (in Aquinas's words in *On the Sentences*) 'something's goodness on account of itself'.[7] Stretching back to Aquinas, then, is a view of dignity as intrinsic value, such that *anything* that is capable of having an intrinsic value has dignity. For Kant too, as we have seen, dignity is a matter of intrinsic value—but it is found only in 'morality, and humanity insofar as it is capable of morality'. For Aquinas and his successors, however, dignity and human dignity are not co-extensive; many other kinds of being—including, indeed, abstract entities like thought or social relationships—are capable of having dignity.

In the nineteenth century—particularly under Pope Leo XIII—this Catholic dignity discourse became of very great significance. For Leo, the idea of

---

[7] *Scriptum super libros Sententiarium*, Book III, distinction 35, question 1, article 4, solution 1c.

dignity was part of a view of the world that vindicated hierarchy—in Church, society, and family:

> For, He who created and governs all things has, in His wise providence, appointed that the things which are lowest should attain their ends by those which are intermediate, and these again by the highest. Thus, as even in the kingdom of heaven He hath willed that the choirs of angels be distinct and some subject to others, and also in the Church has instituted various orders and a diversity of offices, so that all are not apostles or doctors or pastors, so also has He appointed that there should be various orders in civil society, differing in dignity, rights, and power, whereby the State, like the Church, should be one body, consisting of many members, some nobler than others, but all necessary to each other and solicitous for the common good.[8]

Like Kant, the nineteenth-century Catholic view was that human beings have dignity in the sense of an inner transcendental kernel of intrinsic value. But, unlike Kant, this was a characteristic that was not unique to human beings, held in isolation, but came to them from their place in a divinely ordained hierarchy.

As in the case of Kant, however, the question arises: what are the ethical consequences of something being a bearer or embodiment of dignity? And, as in the case of Kant, the answer is that this is something that cannot be pursued as an end to be maximized. The difference is that the answer, for Catholics, must come from the eternal truths of natural law and the teachings of revealed religion that are consonant with it. For Leo XIII (as for his predecessor Pius IX and successor Pius X), it was clear that the central message of Catholic social teaching is the need for a properly ordered and respectful hierarchy in society—something that quite explicitly counters the democratic tendencies of the French Revolution, with its principles of popular sovereignty and equal rights. It is in this context that we encounter dignity in the Catholic thought of that time.

Yet, for whatever reasons, by the end of the Second World War, the immutable truths of natural law turned out to be far less hostile to doctrines of social equality and rights than they had been thought to be in the previous century. It is in that light that we can appreciate the appearance of dignity in the important human rights documents that appeared in the five years after the end of the conflict. I am thinking in particular of the Universal Declaration of Human Rights (1948) and the *Grundgesetz* (Fundamental Law) of the Federal Republic of Germany (1949), both of which have dignity in the most prominent position possible and connect it explicitly with rights and (in the case of the Universal Declaration) equality. (The very first sentence of Article 1 of the Universal Declaration reads 'All human beings are born free and equal in dignity and rights'; while Article 1 of the *Grundgesetz* states that 'Human

---

[8] *Quod Apostolici Muneris* (1878), 6.

dignity is inviolable. To respect it and protect it is the duty of all state power. The German people therefore acknowledge inviolable and inalienable human rights as the basis of every community, of peace and of justice in the world.')

Now, the alert Schopenhauerian might think that the first article of the Universal Declaration confirms the suspicion that talk of dignity is vacuous. What would be lost if one were just to say 'All human beings are born free and equal in rights'? (Indeed, one might suspect that more words could be dropped from that sentence without loss of content.) But the German case is more challenging. Clearly, it requires two things—first, an account of how human dignity is to be protected from violation (if dignity is really an inner transcendental kernel, then what on earth would 'violate' it?) and, second, an explanation of how it is to be connected with 'inviolable and inalienable' human rights? We are returned, are we not, to the Kantian problem.

But perhaps this is not such a great problem. After all, as I have suggested, the end of the Second World War saw an agreement between liberal democratic humanism and the Catholic Church on the basic doctrines of social equality and rights. If the inclusion of 'dignity' alongside 'rights' in the Universal Declaration adds little content, at least it serves to give expression to that very significant coming-together. Surely, tolerating a little bit of humbug is a small price to pay for something so important.

Yet this would, I fear, be over-optimistic. First of all, the adoption of dignity—whether inspired by Kantianism or Catholicism—still leaves the question: what follows from this as a matter of practical ethical decision-making? And here, it is clear, there is both agreement and disagreement between liberal democratic humanism and Catholicism. While post-war Catholics have (with exceptions, of course—but then what generalizations about political attitudes do not have exceptions?) been prepared to endorse principles of democracy and equal rights, the differences between Catholicism and liberal humanism on questions of bioethics are very, very stark.

Which leads me to another objection to dignity.

Dignity is an attack on autonomy

In 2003, Professor Ruth Macklin published a trenchant editorial in the *British Medical Journal* headlined 'Dignity is a useless concept. It means no more than respect for persons or their autonomy.'[9] According to Macklin, dignity

---

[9] Ruth Macklin, 'Dignity is a useless concept', *British Medical Journal* 237 (20 December 2003), 1419–20.

has no positive role to play: 'appeals to dignity are either vague restatements of other, more precise notions or mere slogans that add nothing to the understanding of the topic'. Macklin's dismissal of dignity has been echoed by a number of other authors, notably the linguist and psychologist Steven Pinker, whose article 'The stupidity of dignity' echoes Macklin's charge. For Pinker, autonomy, understood as 'informed consent', is all that bioethics needs.[10] On this view, dignity is redundant, mere window dressing for a more fundamental idea. But is dignity simply a more elaborate way of saying autonomy?

The question is made more complicated by the presence in the background of Kant. On the one hand, Kant makes a clear and explicit connection between dignity and autonomy: '*Autonomy* is … the ground of the dignity of human nature' (Ak. 4:436). Yet he just as clearly prohibits a whole range of actions to which human beings may plausibly give informed consent. The explanation, of course, is that what Kant on the one hand and Macklin and Pinker on the other mean by autonomy is quite different.

On the most obvious interpretation, autonomy means that the self is sovereign—it is, in that sense, a law unto itself. And this idea—that to be autonomous means, essentially, to be able to do as one chooses—is at the heart of the modern idea of autonomy. That is, however, far from being Kant's idea. The Kantian 'self-given law' that governs human beings is law only because it is purged of any association with the arbitrary choices of individuals. It is the choice (if choice it is at all) of our higher, inner, noumenal selves. Hence, suicide, the failure to develop our capacities, and sexual activity outside marriage are all violations of our duties to ourselves for Kant:

> Self-regarding duties … are independent of all advantage, and pertain only to the worth of being human. They rest on the fact that in regard to our person we have no untrammelled freedom, that humanity in our person must be highly esteemed, since, without this, man is an object of contempt, which is an absolute fault, since he is worthless, not only in the eyes of others, but also in himself. The self-regarding duties are the supreme condition and *principium* of all morality, for the worth of the person constitutes moral worth. (Ak. 27:343 (*Moral Philosophy: Collins*))

The modern conception of autonomy that centres on the sovereign choice of the individual does not have to deny the very existence of duties to oneself (though Bernard Williams, famously, dismisses them as 'fraudulent items'), but what it certainly denies is the right of the state to override individuals' choices in the name of such duties.

---

[10] Steven Pinker, 'The stupidity of dignity', *The New Republic* (28 May 2008), 28.

Is this what dignity does? If one looks solely at the USA, this would seem implausible. Consider the celebrated 'Philosophers' Brief' on assisted suicide.[11] The six philosophers (Dworkin, Nagel, Nozick, Rawls, Scanlon, and Thomson) argued that the patient-plaintiffs in the case before the Supreme Court had what they termed a 'constitutionally protected liberty interest' in hastening their own deaths. Such a 'constitutionally protected liberty interest' could be inferred, they argued, from the Court's own jurisprudence. Significantly, they appealed to the Supreme Court's decision in *Planned Parenthood v. Casey* (505 U.S. 833, 851 (1992)), in which the Court had referred to 'the right of people to make their own decisions about matters involving the most intimate and personal choices a person may make in a lifetime, choices central to personal dignity and autonomy'. Dignity, then, in the view of the Court at that time, appeared to be synonymous with (or closely parallel to) autonomy, and required individuals to be allowed the power of choice over matters that they consider to be of the highest importance to themselves.

But this autonomy-friendly conception of dignity is not the only one to be found in modern jurisprudence. The clearest example to the contrary is the well-known case of M. Manuel Wackenheim—the French dwarf who was prohibited on grounds of the violation of dignity from participating in a dwarf-tossing contest. I shall not retrace the details of M. Wackenheim's path from administrative court to *Conseil d'État* to the Human Rights Committee of the UN, but note two things. First, that dignity was invoked to override M. Wackenheim's vigorously asserted choice and, second, that—the presence of dignity in a central position in the preamble to the International Covenant on Civil and Political Rights notwithstanding—M. Wackenheim's own claim that the ban on dwarf-tossing actually violated his dignity was not given weight. It seems, then, that so far from protecting individuals' autonomy, dignity, in this case at least, was being used by the courts to override it on the following schema:

1. Dwarf-tossing is undignified
   Therefore:
2. Dwarf-tossing violates the dignity of those who participate in it
   However:
3. Dignity is inviolable
   So:
4. The fact that dwarf-tossing is an activity that has been freely chosen by the participants is no reason to permit it.

---

[11] *New York Review of Books* (27 March 1997).

And this brings me to the final objection to dignity that I shall consider in this chapter:

Dignity is used by courts as a licence to illegitimately overrule democratic authority

Democratic countries with courts that practise judicial review of legislation face what is commonly called the 'counter-majoritarian difficulty'—by what right do they override decisions that can claim legitimacy by deriving from the decision of a popularly elected legislature? If that objection is to be met—or so the classical argument goes—it is because courts represent the means by which the rights of individuals can be protected against the (potential) 'tyranny of the majority'.

Now if dignity as an inner transcendental kernel of human value is indeed the magic bean out of which has sprung forth all the rich foliage of human rights, as the *Grundgesetz* and the International Covenant on Civil and Political Rights assert,[12] then it can be used to justify intervention by courts to override the legislature.

On the other hand, if the claim that there is a path from the inner transcendental kernel to specific rights is unsustainable, then it would appear that courts are operating freelance, and that their decisions—rhetorically framed in the grandiloquent language about dignity as they may be—lack basic moral legitimacy. Of course, this is an enormously difficult charge to evaluate—how could one hope to prove it one way or the other? Yet there are reasons to be suspicious, to say the least. The two leading candidates for a route from dignity to specific rights—Kantianism and Catholic natural law theory—are each (understatement yet again) open to dispute. Moreover, how could it be legitimate for democratic societies, in which the fact of moral pluralism appears to be fundamental, to plump for either one of these controversial comprehensive moral theories and impose it on their citizens?

Looking at the practice of courts that have used dignity to override democratic authority or individual choice does not eliminate those suspicions. The case of M. Wackenheim is plainly a case where the requirement of being *dignified* is taken to have the force of dignity in the sense of an inner transcendental

---

[12] The preamble to the ICCPR asserts that 'in accordance with the principles proclaimed in the Charter of the United Nations, recognition of the inherent dignity and of the equal and inalienable rights of all members of the human family is the foundation of freedom, justice and peace in the world ... [and] these rights derive from the inherent dignity of the human person'.

kernel—something that may (indeed, must) be defended with the authority of the state, irrespective of the will of the individual concerned. Similarly, the notion of dignity has been invoked by the German Constitutional Court in two decisions on abortion that clearly contradict the will of the legislature, vetoing legislative proposals for the (limited) legalization of abortion in both 1975 and 1993. Of course, abortion is a moral issue on which societies divide. Yet in 2005, over 60 per cent of Germans agreed with the proposition 'If a woman does not want children, she should be able to have an abortion'. That the notion of dignity should have been used in this way by the courts to override the moral judgement of this substantial majority as expressed through their legislative representatives ought to be extremely troubling to democrats.

Nor is it just the places where dignity has been appealed to by courts in support of their decisions that are of concern. Looking at the jurisprudence of the *Verfassungsgericht*, it is noteworthy too that the courts have conspicuously *failed* to intervene in the name of dignity in what might have been thought to be obvious cases of attacks on individuals' basic rights. For instance, in the so-called *Abhörurteil* of 1970, the Court refused to intervene to control extensive surveillance by the state of citizens' private communications on the grounds that this could not be a violation of dignity, since it did not amount to behaviour that expressed 'contempt for the value that the human being has in virtue of being a person' (BVerfGE, 30, 1). (This narrowing, we might note, plainly contradicts the idea of dignity as the inner transcendental kernel from which human rights in general are derived that is the clear implication of the first paragraph of the German *Grundgesetz*.)

Conclusion

So, would we be better off without dignity?

This is, I think, a misplaced question. Dignity is surprisingly deeply entrenched in our moral discourse: it is not going anywhere any time soon. What it does lack, however, is a single, well-defined core of meaning, and that ambiguity leaves it open to exploitation. In my view, there are four main, distinct, conceptually divisible strands.

1. There is the idea of dignity as rank or status—an idea that can be complicated by the idea that dignity is a status that all human beings share (but then, what does that amount to?), or that worldly status is not the same as real status—status seen from the point of view of religious faith

2. There is the idea of dignity as an inner transcendental kernel that allegedly founds—generates and justifies—the rich diversity of human rights
3. There is the idea of dignity as the quality of action or bearing that goes with being *dignified*—a valuable quality, no doubt, but not something that all human beings have, inalienably, in common
and
4. There is the idea that human beings should be treated *with dignity*—that it is important that the state does not just act in ways that are consonant with their welfare and allow them to exercise rational control over their own destinies but that it also acts in ways that express respect for them as human beings.

While we could not—and should not attempt to—get rid of dignity from public discourse entirely, democrats should certainly try to hold those who invoke dignity to account by requiring them, at the least, to specify the sense in which they are doing so. Perhaps then they will be in a better position to resist the use of dignity as a cloak behind which interested parties seek to impose moral prescriptions that lack the legitimacy of a popular mandate.

8

Socio-Economic Rights, Basic Needs, and Human Dignity: A Perspective from Law's Front Line

Conor Gearty

IN THIS CHAPTER, I reflect on how the idea of human dignity works in British law. My starting point will be three relatively recent cases, in each of which the underlying idea of dignity was certainly present but unable (as we shall see) to do the kind of work that might be expected of such a powerful moral notion. In the second part, I will think about why this was so, and argue that the relatively subsidiary (or, indeed, non-existent) role played by dignity even in cases such as these (in which the dignity of each of the claimants was so obviously engaged) is the right approach for the judges to have taken. In other words, I will be saying that the term is too vague and uncertain to be able to be effective on its own via judge-made law alone. I will be contrasting political and legal conceptions of dignity, and arguing that the idea belongs more in the former than the latter arena—at least so far as Britain is concerned. It follows that I am opposed to too much dignity-talk in British law, and will explain why as best I can in this second section. In the third and final part, I describe the way in which I believe the principle of human dignity can best be realized in our legal system via (as I shall argue) a combination of a legislative emphasis on particulars combined with a careful judicial deployment of the language of human rights. These two operate together to provide a better way for the term to do its work than through the sort of judicial short cut that is opened up by the notion of a constitutional right to human dignity, or some such equivalent guarantee.

In what follows I should be clear that I am talking only about Britain, though it may be that the points I make have a more general application. I feel that they do, but I leave to others more specialist than I to judge the extent to which the general principles developed here can be considered to have a wider reach. In saying this I am not (only) reflecting the modesty of my aims; I am making an indirect point about the seductiveness of 'going global' with one's views about dignity, of being tempted into regarding the conclusions one has drawn from one's own experience as necessarily of universal application—a particular risk so far as an abstract concept like dignity is concerned.

Three cases

The appellant in the first of our cases, *R (McDonald) v London Borough of Kensington and Chelsea*,[1] had once been 'the prima ballerina of Scottish ballet'.[2] In September 1999, when aged fifty-six, she suffered a severe stroke, and this left her with limited mobility as well as other disabilities. Just short of seven years later, she fell, breaking her hip in several places, and further falls led to further periods of hospitalization. The problem 'at the centre of these proceedings', however, related to the fact that she suffered from 'a small and neurogenic bladder which makes her have to urinate two to three times a night'.[3] In the words of the judge who gave the lead opinion in the case, Lord Brown:

> Up to now she has dealt with this by accessing a commode with the help of a carer provided by the respondent Royal Borough as part of a package of care services to ensure her safety. For some years past, however, the respondents have been proposing instead that the appellant should use incontinence pads or special sheeting (hereafter 'pads') which would avoid the need for a night-time carer. The respondents say that this would provide the appellant with greater safety (avoiding the risk of injury while she is assisted to the commode), independence and privacy, besides reducing the cost of her care by some £22,000 per annum. The appellant, however, is appalled at the thought of being treated as incontinent (which she is not) and having to use pads. She considers this an intolerable affront to her dignity. Whether night-time care can be provided on this revised basis is the critical issue in these proceedings.[4]

The Supreme Court, by a majority, and upholding an earlier decision of the Court of Appeal, found that it could. The respondent authority had not acted unlawfully in assessing the appellant's needs, and while '[t]here is, of course, a positive obligation under article 8 [of the European Convention on Human Rights[5]] to respect a person's private life … it cannot plausibly be argued

---

[1] [2011] UKSC 33.
[2] [2011] UKSC 33, para. 1 per Lord Brown.
[3] [2011] UKSC 33, para. 1.
[4] [2011] UKSC 33, para. 1.
[5] Part of UK law: see the Human Rights Act 1998, s 1 and sched. 1.

that such respect was not afforded here'.[6] Nor did the submissions rooted in recently passed disability discrimination legislation upon which the appellant relied convince the majority, a 'hopeless' argument as Lord Brown rather brutally described it.[7]

The dissenting opinion came from Baroness Hale of Richmond, the only woman on the bench (and still the only woman on the Supreme Court). The 'really serious question' raised by the case was whether it is 'lawful for a local authority to provide incontinence pads (or absorbent sheets) for a person who is not in fact incontinent but requires help to get to the lavatory or commode?'[8] Eschewing the argument as it had unfolded in the case before her, Lady Hale chose 'to address the question we might have been asked',[9] namely whether an earlier House of Lords decision allowing resources to be taken into account in relation to decisions like this was good law.[10] But even without tackling that precedent, a way of supporting the appellant could be found via traditional public law: the local authority's insistence on regarding her as having a need different from that which she really had was *Wednesbury* unreasonable.[11] The United Kingdom was not a place where 'we ... oblige people who can control their bodily functions to behave as if they cannot do so, unless they themselves find this the more convenient course'.[12] This was because '[w]e are, I still believe, a civilized society'.[13] Furthermore, the majority opinion may well produce a downward slide towards the wholly unacceptable:

> A person in [the appellant's] situation needs this help during the day as well as during the night and irrespective of whether she needs to urinate or to defecate. Logically, the decision of the majority in this case would entitle a local authority to withdraw this help even though the client needed to defecate during the night and thus might be left lying in her faeces until the carers came in the morning. This is not Ms McDonald's problem at the moment, but her evidence leaves one in no doubt that this is one of her fears. Indeed, the majority view would also entitle an authority to withdraw this help during the day. The only constraint would be how frequently (or rather how infrequently) it was deemed necessary to change the pads or sheets, consistently with the avoidance of infection and other hazards such as nappy rash. The consequences do not bear thinking about.[14]

---

[6] [2011] UKSC 33, para. 19 per Lord Brown.
[7] [2011] UKSC 33, paras 22 and 24.
[8] [2011] UKSC 33, para. 61.
[9] [2011] UKSC 33, para. 69.
[10] *R (Barry) v Gloucestershire County Council*, [1997] AC 584.
[11] [2011] UKSC 33, para. 78
[12] [2011] UKSC 33, para. 79.
[13] [2011] UKSC 33, para. 79.
[14] [2011] UKSC 33, para. 77.

This comment provoked a strong reaction from Lady Hale's colleagues.[15] At the heart of this case was the question of how far ideas of dignity (or indeed, more to the point here, indignity) should be allowed to drive the analysis, forcing the law into a shape that worked better from a dignified perspective. Here was not a person whose lack of consciousness was an issue and whose dignity could be challenged on this basis: Ms MacDonald knew exactly what was going on.[16] Lord Brown's description of the facts acknowledges the appellant's view that she has suffered 'an intolerable affront to her dignity' and Lady Hale talked about our being 'still ... a civilised society'. The majority allowed dignity little leeway for intrusion, whereas Lady Hale placed it centre stage—and it is worth noting that the 'it' here is not so much the appellant's view of her treatment as Lady Hale's (objective) assessment of it (and her judgement as to where it might lead). Since the meaning of dignity was not exclusively determined (or even overly influenced) by the appellant's view of her plight, her problem ended up being that only one judge was sufficiently affronted on her behalf to force dignity to the forefront of the legal analysis of the case, driving (as dignity tends to do) all before it. For the remaining four, dignity (whatever the view they might take of its absence on the facts before them) was hidden from sight by the legal scaffolding that surrounded the case by the time it reached their court.

Now the second decision, a case in which I myself appeared as an advocate, just before Christmas 2011, *DM v Doncaster Metropolitan Borough Council*.[17] Here, an aged wife found that as a joint account holder she was being charged for the cost of care given to her husband in a care home into which he had been placed under powers of compulsion first introduced in 2007 (as a result of a European Court of Human Rights ruling as it happens).[18] DM argued that it was unfair that she and her husband should find their whole life savings being dissipated to pay for the costs of accommodation that was desired by neither of them, especially when such costs would have been met by the State had the husband been either sectioned under mental health legislation and/or released from such a sectioning into after-care accommodation.[19] In a careful judgment, Mr Justice Langstaff located the basis for the costs squarely in the legislation under scrutiny, which was made up not only of the

---

[15] See [2011] UKSC 33, paras 28–33 (Lord Walker), para. 27 (Lord Brown), paras 57–60 (Lord Dyson).

[16] In discussion at the conference, Avishai Margalit made the important point that dignity should not be made to depend on the success of one's conscious self.

[17] [2011] EWHC 3652 (Admin); (2012) 15 CCLR 128.

[18] *HL v United Kingdom* European Court of Human Rights app 45508/99, 5 October 2004, http://www.bailii.org/eu/cases/ECHR/2004/471.html.

[19] As to the latter situation as a result of *R (Stennett) v Manchester City Council*, [2002] UKHL 34.

recently enacted deprivation of liberty laws but also the National Assistance Act of 1948, under which it had been provided that care be generally paid for by those who receive it where it had been sought from the local authority by someone who could afford it.[20] The judge found no foundation in law for rewriting the legislation to bring it into line with the imperative of non-discrimination that had been identified on the claimant's behalf.

There being no legal space for it, dignity could not be mentioned in court, but it was implicitly manifest throughout the proceedings. Here was a couple, married for some sixty years, whose last years were now to be blighted by separation and penury. On the other hand, the paying provisions dating from 1948 had been partly introduced in order to assure dignity to those forced by circumstance to rely on state support, the idea being that they would be thereby able to retain that level of independence that was judged by our then legislators to be an important part of their sense of self. Here we have a very good example of what Paolo Carozza has described as 'the way that participation in political life, in a very substantive sense ... (arguing, voting, organizing, persuading, legislating) is constitutive of our understanding of dignity'.[21] In 1948, dignity was thought to require an obligation to pay, whereas in 2011, what I was trying (obliquely and unsuccessfully) to get the judge—Baroness-Hale-like—to foreground was a different kind of dignity, one that saw payment not as a route to dignity but rather an affront to it. But why should my advocate's vision of what was required trump that of Parliament? Did it make a difference that it was a legislative act of so long ago? If we were to have had a right to dignity available, which version of the term's meaning would (or should) have mattered more, that of 1948 or one more amenable to the minds of today (or at least my kind of mind of today)?

Now the third decision, the very well-known assisted 'right-to-die' case of *R (Purdy) v Director of Public Prosecutions*.[22] In all discussion of this case outside the courtroom the emphasis is on dignity and dying. But when the case reached the House of Lords (as the UK's supreme judicial body then was), their lordships hardly mentioned dignity at all: their concern revolved around the much narrower points of, first, the remit of s 2(1) of the Suicide Act 1961 and, second, the extent to which the respondent in the case before them (the DPP) was obliged as a matter of law to construct an offence-specific policy setting out the factors that should be taken into account by him and his team in deciding whether or not it was in the public interest to bring a prosecution

---

[20] See National Assistance Act 1948, part III.
[21] In conversation at the conference.
[22] [2009] UKHL 45.

under this section, in the event that assisted suicide of the sort being contemplated by the appellant and her husband were carried out.[23] Resiling from an earlier collective ruling (in *R (Pretty) v Director of Public Prosecutions*[24]), their lordships now took the view that the guarantee of the right to respect for privacy in article 8 of the European Convention on Human Rights (implemented across the UK in October 2000) encompassed within it a right to respect for just this sort of life and death decision. It followed that Ms Purdy and her husband were entitled to have this right to respect for their privacy taken into account when decisions were being made by the DPP as to what to do about their proposed actions by way of enforcement of the criminal law.

The difference between the two decisions was not just seven years (which in this field of seemingly fast-changing moral attitudes is a long time) but also the Strasbourg court's ruling in the *Pretty* case when the matter had reached it, to the effect that its judges were 'not prepared to exclude' the application of article 8. This was because the applicant before them was 'prevented by law from exercising her choice to avoid what she considers will be an undignified and distressing end to her life'.[25] The Strasbourg court had even gone so far as to stress that 'The very essence of the Convention is respect for human dignity and human freedom'.[26] Despite all this, and to the untrained eye perhaps surprisingly, neither in *Pretty* in Strasbourg nor in *Purdy* in the House of Lords did the supplicants get any kind of mandate to act on their perceived moral imperative, *Pretty* because the restrictions imposed by law on those who assist suicide were judged (in the language of article 8) 'necessary in a democratic society ... for the protection of the rights of others'; and in *Purdy* because all that was being sought was an order to the DPP to produce guidance on his prosecution policy (on which point, certainly, Ms Purdy was successful). So while dignity may have underpinned the right before each court, adding impact to it, it remained in the background, a source of/explanation for a right rather than a right itself. And because it was 'only' a principle behind a right in this way, the fact that the right could be qualified did not mean that dignity was being ignored or that indignity was being imposed. Having jumped forward to give the Convention right energy, dignity fell back into the shadows and so was able to avoid seeming to have been rejected. This is as it should be. As with the *McDonald* and *DM* cases, dignity is not something we should be casually seen to be disregarding, whereas the right to privacy—with its

---

[23] [2009] UKHL 45, para. 28, per Lord Hope.
[24] [2002] 1 AC 800.
[25] *Pretty v United Kingdom* app 2346/02 (29 April 2002), http://www.bailii.org/eu/cases/ECHR/2002/427.html, para. 67.
[26] *Pretty v United Kingdom* app 2346/02, para. 65.

qualifications and acceptance therefore of proportionate intrusions—could be much less damagingly overridden.

Against justiciable dignity

Matthias Mahlmann has asked an interesting question about the 'conditions for the usefulness of a legal concept'.[27] One such requirement that strikes me as immediately relevant is a correct level of specificity. Here is Christopher McCrudden on human dignity, summarizing his path-breaking *Human Dignity and the Judicial Interpretation of Human Rights* (first published in July 2008):

> The Universal Declaration on Human Rights was pivotal in popularizing the use of 'dignity' or 'human dignity' in human rights discourse. This article argues that the use of 'dignity', beyond a basic minimum core, does not provide a universalistic, principled basis for judicial decision-making in the human rights context, in the sense that there is little common understanding of what dignity requires substantively within or across jurisdictions. The meaning of dignity is therefore context specific, varying significantly from jurisdiction to jurisdiction and (often) over time within particular jurisdictions. Indeed, instead of providing a basis for principled decision-making, dignity seems open to significant judicial manipulation, increasing rather than decreasing judicial discretion. That is one of its significant attractions to both judges and litigators alike. Dignity provides a convenient language for the adoption of substantive interpretations of human rights guarantees that appear to be intentionally, not just coincidentally, highly contingent on local circumstances. Despite that, however, I argue that the concept of 'human dignity' plays an important role in the development of human rights adjudication, not in providing an agreed content to human rights but in contributing to particular methods of human rights interpretation and adjudication.[28]

I will pick up and elaborate on the final sentence here in the third part of this chapter: like McCrudden, I believe in the underlying power of the language of dignity when localized and stripped of any direct reach into the facts before a court.

Both McCrudden and Michael Rosen in his recent book[29] write about the 1975 and 1993 decisions of first West Germany's and then Germany's

---

[27] In conversation at the conference.
[28] *Human Dignity and the Judicial Interpretation of Human Rights*, University of Oxford. Legal Research Paper Series no. 24 of 2008, http://papers.ssrn.com/sol3/papers.cfm?abstract_id=1162024. The extract in the text is the abstract to that paper.
[29] Michael Rosen, *Dignity: Its History and Meaning* (Cambridge, MA, Harvard University Press, 2012).

top constitutional court on the question of the consistency of the state's abortion law with its constitution, a basic law that (unusually) contains an explicit guarantee of dignity that is not capable of being altered or deviated from.[30] On both occasions the court has turned to this language of dignity to guide it to its conclusion. But as McCrudden has remarked, '[o]nce dignity entered the balancing calculus on the side of the life interest, the conclusion that the protection of the foetus's life must receive priority over the women's freedom was inevitable'.[31] And according to Rosen in 1993, the court 'affirmed its previous position in equally forceful language' when it declared that human dignity was 'already an attribute of unborn human life, not just human life after birth or with a developed personality'.[32] But then what happened? Here is Rosen's summary:

> The court's rigoristic stance regarding the extension of human dignity to foetuses at all stages of development is strongly out of line with German public opinion. A 2005 poll showed 64 per cent of the German public agreeing with the statement 'If a woman does not want children, she should be able to have an abortion' ... The outcome has been a remarkable compromise ... The court, while re-affirming that abortion is illegal (*rechtswidrig*) has nevertheless accepted that abortion should not be punishable (*strafbar*) provided that it takes place in defined circumstances (generally, within the first twelve weeks and after the pregnant woman has participated in an independent counselling session).[33]

Now I would suggest that this is the sort of legal manoeuvre likely to give dignity a bad name. It was not only that the court saw fit to impose its own view of dignity on the legislature—a body of elected representatives which had not, after all, set out to affront dignity but had wanted rather to reflect in the country's laws a different view of what the term was thought to entail. But it was also that, having done so, and faced with an immovable German opinion, the court wobbled, and compromised on what it had said dignity required. This is what happens when courts get involved in deciding what dignity is, treating it as a truth to be discovered and then imposed rather than a point of view to be argued for and deliberated on.[34]

I want now to introduce two ideas which I have already anticipated in part one and which are central to this chapter (and to which I return in part three). First, dignity cannot afford to be qualified in the way that other interests and

---

[30] Article 1(1): 'Human dignity shall be inviolable. To respect and protect it shall be the duty of all state authority.'
[31] *Human Dignity and the Judicial Interpretation of Human Rights*, 68.
[32] Rosen, *Dignity*, 102.
[33] Rosen, *Dignity*, 103–4.
[34] See, in the context of the USA and abortion law, Reva Siegel, Chapter 30, this volume.

even human rights can be. Having identified what dignity entails, it cannot then be overridden by proportionate attacks on it, as ordinary rights can be. That is one of the reasons that judges steer clear of the term or downplay it. We don't—and *contra* Aharon Barak (to whom I return) shouldn't—think of dignity as something which people have conditionally, the way they have rights to free speech or privacy, which are however capable of being set aside in the interests of the community. To note briefly another German case, also in Rosen: that of Wolfgang Daschner, the deputy chief of police in Frankfurt who had threatened to subject a suspect to very severe pain if he did not reveal the whereabouts of a boy he was presumed to have kidnapped (and whom it was credibly believed would die if not found quickly).[35] Even on such terrible facts, the relevant regional court convicted the police chief, albeit fining rather than imprisoning him. Once dignity is engaged, all bets are off (at least so far as culpability is concerned, whatever is thought about punishment). Second, there is this other feature of dignity-language: while there can be different versions of dignity, no deal can be done between them. The term is rooted in truth, not a passing point of view. Since there are these different meanings, and since they are not tradable, a decision has to be made between them—and so the key question is, who makes that decision? I don't think that, in the UK's democracy at least, it should be the courts. The German compromise stands as a very specific warning on this precise point, with the political version of what dignity entailed in relation to abortion standing outside the court's insistence on its perspective, a clumsy overlaying of a political on a constitutional truth.

Building on these two points, let me now elaborate a little more on my objections to the idea of justiciable human dignity before turning in the final section to what I think of as the proper role of dignity in English/British law. Extreme affronts to dignity can be dealt with via prohibitions on torture, inhuman and degrading treatment, slavery, and the like; indeed, when Deputy Police Chief Daschner's case reached the Strasbourg court (on the application of the man who had been threatened with ill-treatment), it was as an orthodox human rights case that it was processed (albeit presenting, it is true, a most unusual set of facts). And importantly, it is exactly these prohibitions on torture, slavery, and so on (which we might call 'applied-dignity' rights) that come without exception or qualification. In contrast to these stark ethical commands, there are the more general understandings of dignity, those not concerned with the crudities of torture or slavery or the like but designed as Paolo Carozza has put it to protect 'the human capacity for relationality …

---

[35] Although as it transpired he was already dead. See *Gäfgen v Germany* (2010) 52 EHRR 1.

and human flourishing'.³⁶ These are best realized by rigorously focused legislative interventions aimed at supporting and protecting particularized aspects of what dignity is thought to require. Neither of these approaches needs a justiciable language of dignity to make it work. Either the criminal law covering breach of a core negative human right (not to be tortured, and so on; not to be enslaved) does the business, or specific legislation focused on the good life achieves this outcome; neither need (or, I am tempted to add, should) mention dignity.

There is a middle ground which seeks to deliver dignity by producing neither specific legislation nor an overarching right to dignity as such but rather through enactment of a set of broadly based social and economic 'rights' which it then falls upon the courts to drive forward. This is attractive to many as a way of avoiding burdening the judges with 'dignity' issues, while at the same time depoliticizing the requirements of the good life, turning such necessities into entitlements to be asserted against political decision-makers, rather than matters of the importance of which these legislators need to be convinced. Certainly, social and economic rights are creatures of a vision of dignity which is attractive, focusing as it does on the universal entitlements to which we all should have access if we are to live successful (and therefore dignified) lives. But there are risks in this seduction.

The UK Parliamentary Joint Committee on Human Rights has elaborated on what it has called the three 'most common objections' to the entrenchment in law of social and economic rights.³⁷ First it observed that social and economic rights would be 'too vaguely expressed' and would 'only raise expectations and encourage time-consuming and expensive litigation against public bodies'.³⁸ Second, echoing McCrudden's remark already quoted, the move 'hands too much power to the courts and so is undemocratic'.³⁹ Third, such an adjudicative power would involve 'the courts in making decisions about resources and priority setting that they are ill-equipped to take'.⁴⁰ Several additional points of objection can be added to these. There is, fourthly, the strong emphasis on the individual that is inherent in the whole idea of justiciability, with its inevitable focus on particular claimants at the expense of the wider public interest. This might be laudable in the arena of traditional

---

[36] In conversation at the conference.
[37] I have developed the argument that follows in greater detail in C. Gearty and V. Mantouvalou, *Debating Social Rights* (Oxford, Hart Publishing, 2011).
[38] Joint Committee on Human Rights, *A Bill of Rights for the UK?* (Twenty-ninth Report of Session 2007–8, HL 165, HC 150) paras 183–4.
[39] *A Bill of Rights for the UK?*, paras 185–7.
[40] *A Bill of Rights for the UK?*, paras 188–91.

litigation where two parties jostle to secure a reading of a specific law (or prior agreement) in their favour, but it fits less well when such proceedings are being regarded by one of the parties as a device through which to smuggle into court the interests of thousands of invisible claimants, however meritorious the moral arguments being made via their representative litigant might be. Judges are suspicious of 'test cases', not necessarily because they are opposed to the outcome that the litigant before them is pursuing on behalf of others so much as on account of the self-evident lack of fit between the narrow realm of such litigation and the broader issues that they are being asked covertly to deal with in such proceedings.

This mismatch is compounded, fifthly, by the inappropriateness of the adversarial model to the resolution of broadly framed issues of social and economic rights which go well beyond the litigant before the court. We have already seen that human dignity may not be controversial as an idea but what it entails undoubtedly is, and so I have argued that it is in the political realm that issues about the content of an agreed commitment to dignity should be played out. It is exactly the same with social and economic rights. The court is simply not the right site to decide these things at such a high level of abstraction, and the more you fiddle with its procedures to make it the right place (special briefs on the impact on the 'dignity' or 'social rights' of the individual of this or that change; advice from philosophers; readings from other jurisdictions on social and economic rights), the more any such tribunal looks less and less like a court and more and more like an executive office, but without the usual democratic necessities of electoral legitimacy and public accountability. And without a proper enforcement arm as well, a sixth objection to assigning the concretization of the meaning of dignity and/or social and economic rights to the judicial branch emerges. Who is to follow-up the court's decision to see that it has been effectively implemented? What happens when unexpected glitches in effecting a court's orders are encountered? We should recall here how the German system has accommodated the court's rulings on abortion but in a way that has involved the drawing of practical lines which have seemed at odds with the judges' apparently powerful rhetoric on dignity and on life.

A seventh objection is almost embarrassing to mention, so old-fashioned does it seem: beware of empowering judges lest you give them an aggressive tool with which to hinder (rather than to facilitate) progress. Human dignity in the hands of the rich can become an agent of reactionary defensiveness, mustered to preserve privilege under the guise of a natural entitlement. If proof were needed, we can reflect on how judges across what is now the democratic world greeted the advances—on votes for women; on workers' rights;

on race discrimination; on the restriction of property and contract rights—that made that democracy possible.[41] Sometimes the dignity of all tomorrow has required some unfairness today, in the form of affirmative action programmes and the like, designed to rectify historic disadvantage. Reformers coming from outside the rights tradition would have no difficulty with this—of course the known few must suffer for the benefit of the future unknown many, and the fact that there is a withdrawal of the privileges of the minority now so as to assist in the future flourishing of all is of the essence of policy-making: this is exactly what planners ought to be doing. But to judges, schooled in the application of justice not by reference to broad societal goals but in accord with what precisely configured individual cases before them appear to require by reference to clear and enforceable laws, this seems a monstrous injustice. If they have the dignity weapon to hand, or even social rights that can trump the legislature, it may be impossible for them to forbear from their deployment.

Doing dignity

Jeremy Waldron has spoken of dignity as a 'sort of value, or principle, or policy deeply … within the law … established like a legal principle or deep policy of the law, not laid down in any text, but something to which the legal system has committed itself to in the way it commits itself also to other elements of public morality in the way that we reason'.[42] So in *McDonald*, 'one could imagine a court saying what [Waldron understands] Baroness Hale did say, that when we have to choose between two possibilities, even if we are not explicitly instructed to do so by the legislator, the role of dignity is as important as any other deep legal value, bubbling up implicitly pervasively in the law even if it's not textually mandated'. These are very helpful comments towards understanding what I believe to be the proper role of dignity in English law. There is a significant democratic dimension to this discussion, and it flows from what I have been saying in part two: visions of dignity already drive a very great deal of legislation, even if the legislation or even the debates preceding it are not framed in exactly this way, with the term merely, as Waldron puts it, 'bubbling up implicitly'.

One of the more distressing features of human rights lawyers is their tendency towards moral exclusivity; that without them ideas of dignity have

---

[41] The field of work detailing this point is now very large. A broad overview is Ran Hirschl, *Towards Juristocracy. The Origins and Consequences of the New Juristocracy* (Cambridge, MA, Harvard University Press, 2004).

[42] Transcript of conversation at the conference.

no space in the legal firmament, implicitly as well as explicitly. Indeed, when the agitation for a British bill of rights was at its height, in the early 1990s, it was sometimes as though the country's law had been immersed in an 'ethical aimlessness'[43] which had taken no account of principle before the arrival of the human rights cavalry. Even with due allowance being made for the need to talk up the problems that were said to require new legislation, this was always something of an exaggeration. In fact, ideas of human dignity have played a large part in the creation of the Britain that we know and appreciate today. Examples of this are the National Assistance Act 1948, which figured in the *DM* case, and the national health legislation, which was engaged in *McDonald*, and even (I would also say) the Suicide Act, which was the source of the *Purdy* litigation. Writing a book in 2004 on the then fairly new Human Rights Act I devoted a chapter to the 'Principle of Human Dignity', which began with what I consciously regarded as a salute to the achievements of the democratic legislature:

> from the landslide election of Henry Campbell-Bannerman's Liberals in 1905, it could be said that the dignity of the person was, with the defence of the realm, one of the two great legislative preoccupations of the twentieth century. The famous Trades Disputes Act of 1906 made possible trade union activism which transformed the lives of many working men and women, and legislation of this type continued until the mid-1970s. Winston Churchill's initiatives on national insurance and hours of work in 1911 were similarly radical for their day ... Highlights in any such narrative would include the Education Act 1944, the National Health Service Act 1946, the New Towns Act 1946, all of which initiatives came with the radical impetus of war behind them, demanding a better deal for those who had taken such risks in combat, and for the families they had left behind at home ... The trend persisted into the immediate post-war period ... though other even bolder assertions of dignity were to follow, such as the Housing (Homeless Persons) Act, enacted in 1977.[44]

Just because something does not advertise itself as rooted in dignity does not mean that this is not the basic idea that informs it, 'bubbling up implicitly'. The social democratic vision of the person—flourishing within a community; part of but not slave to the market; respecter of property but not of needless accumulation; secure from 'cradle to grave'—comes out of a sense of what it means to be a person, to lead a successful, a dignified, life.[45] But as we have

---

[43] 'The problem with the unwritten common law is that it has been ethically aimless': Lord Lester of Herne Hill, BBC News Human Rights Forum, 6 October 2000, http://news.bbc.co.uk/1/hi/talking_point/forum/954831.stm.
[44] C. A. Gearty, *Principles of Human Rights Adjudication* (Oxford, Oxford University Press, 2004), 88–9 (footnotes omitted).
[45] See Ronald Dworkin, *Justice for Hedgehogs* (Cambridge, MA, Harvard University Press, 2011).

seen in part two, there are other views of what dignity demands: the signifier floats not just in law but (especially perhaps) in politics as well. Thus, a different account of the human takes one down a path of autonomy and self-reliance, with richer readings of dignity playing second fiddle to demands for liberty and individual freedom; to such versions of what is essential, the 'cosseting' entailed in social democratic readings of dignity is anathema. The beauty of the democratic approach to dignity is that it manages the differences and resolves them, not in the form of a win for this or that approach but in the shape of several concrete versions of what dignity is found to entail, specific to particular moments and situations. Not only do these outputs not need the dignity label attached to them, they need not even be complementary: different versions of dignity can collide with each other, jostle against each other, contradict each other—all so long as none claims the prize of *true* dignity, for down that route lies an absolutism that does not fit with the contingency that is part and parcel of all parliamentary truth. This is a different kind of truth, the 'dignity of legislation' as Jeremy Waldron has put it.[46]

And legislation can provide for human rights as well. This is what the UK parliament did when it enacted the Human Rights Act 1998 (the HRA). The purpose of this measure was to introduce the European Convention on Human Rights and Fundamental Freedoms into domestic law. As we have seen, on the estimate of the Convention's own court (the European Court of Human Rights) this is a charter whose very essence is 'respect for human dignity and human freedom'.[47] Despite the grandeur behind this informing ethic, there are to be found in this Convention few if any of the social and economic rights the judicial enforcement of which we saw in part two to be somewhat problematic. Nor did the parliament that enacted the largely civil and political rights that are present in the HRA intend itself or its successors to be bound by it. The Act contains no clause purporting to entrench itself in law for all time.[48] It deliberately declines to empower judges to overturn Acts of Parliament on the basis of a conflict with the rights that are set out within it, the most that is achievable being an unenforceable 'declaration of incompatibility' which the executive and legislative branches are then bound to think about but not necessarily to act on.[49] So, just as in ordinary legislation, the version of dignity which finds expression in the language of human rights in the Convention (and therefore in the HRA) is in this important sense provisional: it is Parliament's best guess *at that moment* as to what dignity entails, and reflects its

---

[46] Jeremy Waldron, *The Dignity of Legislation* (Cambridge, Cambridge University Press, 1999).
[47] *Pretty v United Kingdom* app 2346/02, para. 65.
[48] Rather the reverse: see HRA s 3(2).
[49] HRA ss 4, 10, and sched. 2.

judgement that the fleshing out of what dignity requires in this way will be invariably right—albeit (of course) it is an elaboration that is always reversible, either generally through repeal of the HRA or specifically by directly ignoring its provisions in specific instances.

Some well-known examples can serve as illustrations. In *R (Limbuela) v Secretary of State for the Home Department*,[50] the House of Lords held that the Home Secretary had an obligation to provide support for asylum seekers since not to do so and thereby to ensure their destitution (subject to charitable intervention) would amount to degrading or inhuman treatment, contrary to article 3 of the Convention. This was not some free-floating intervention by their lordships: the relevant statutory provision had specifically required that all state action be consistent with the Convention rights of those adversely affected by such executive decisions.[51] Where Parliament has not mandated such overarching intrusiveness, the courts are able only to issue their unenforceable declarations, even where the matter under consideration is such a serious intrusion into one's life as indefinite detention without charge (as in the Belmarsh detention case)[52] or one's permanent listing on a sexual register without the possibility of review.[53] These are all cases engaging the idea of dignity, albeit (to say it yet again) indirectly via a particular right rather than as a right in itself. A last example, from Strasbourg this time, is the recent case of *MS v United Kingdom*,[54] in which prolonged detention in a police cell of a mentally ill man (beyond seventy-two hours) was found by the European Court of Human Rights to have breached his article 3 right not to be subjected to inhumane treatment, the Court noting that 'the mentally ill are in a position of particular vulnerability, and clear issues of respect for their fundamental human dignity arise whenever such persons are detained by the authorities'.[55]

It might at this point be thought: why not go the whole hog, cut out the linguistic middle-man, and simply apply a right to dignity unhampered by all this needless rights-specificity? This takes us back to the critique in part two, of course. But it is also to misunderstand the role of rights language, in law if not in ethical life: talk of specific rights allows for a balancing that direct dependence on a right to dignity could (as I have earlier said) simply not afford to countenance. Whereas for many rights we are familiar with (and not offended by) the notion of a legitimized departure from its ethical demands

---

[50] [2005] UKHL 66.
[51] Nationality, Immigration and Asylum Act 2002, s 55(5)(a).
[52] *A v Secretary of State for the Home Department* [2004] UKHL 56.
[53] *R (F) v Secretary of State for the Home Department* [2010] UKSC 17.
[54] App. 24527/08 (3 May 2012): http://www.bailii.org/eu/cases/ECHR/2012/804.html.
[55] App 24527/08 (3 May 2012), para. 39.

where this is judged to be (in the language of the European Convention) 'necessary in a democratic society' for this or that legitimate reason, or otherwise (to use another Europeanism) 'proportionate', the notion of our dignity being instrumentalized in this way is something that we would find hard to bear. This is why the Germans ended up with an absolute right to dignity: how can it not be unqualified in a civilized society? In contrast to this, in each of the cases with which we started (*McDonald*, *DM*, and *Pretty/Purdy*), the defeat of dignity was masked by the deployment of the language of human rights, coming as it did not only with assertions of right but with legitimate societal overrides as well. Fine-sounding though it is, an effect of taking a rights-based absolutist approach is to impose great pressure on the meaning of dignity, on the remit of the term itself, since there is a temptation to sneak in utility via a dilution in what we say the term embraces or requires. The German abortion issue comes to mind again in this regard. Something like this happens with the closest thing to dignity that traditional rights instruments have, the right not to be subjected to torture or inhuman or degrading treatment, a right that is absolute in a dignity-like way and therefore does not have the sort of societal override that we saw in *McDonald*, *DM* and *Pretty/Purdy*. It has been precisely the lack of balancing in this provision so far as suspected international terrorists are concerned which has been the main cause of disgruntlement with the HRA in UK political circles.[56] And even where the issues are not this hot, as in the *MS* case just mentioned, controversy encircles such ethical dogmatism: the UK courts had found no breach of article 3 when the case had been before them, and a leading commentator in this jurisdiction has attacked the Strasbourg ruling as 'a prime example of using Article 3 as a social and economic right, not a basic civil right, and thus extended leaves publicly funded authorities to carry out difficult jobs with threats of litigation looming on all sides'.[57]

Of course, some might argue that it is not at all problematic to subject dignity to the balancing test deployed when considering whether to allow a right to this or that (free speech, say, or privacy) to be overridden by the more urgent of the exigencies of any given moment. I understand Barak to be taking this line, both in this volume and in his earlier work on proportionality.[58] On this account, there is no difficulty about even central ethical concepts like dignity and the prohibition on torture being subjected to a proportionality test,

---

[56] *Othman (Abu Qatada) v United Kingdom* app. 8139/09 (17 January 2012), http://www.bailii.org/eu/cases/ECHR/2012/56.html.
[57] R. English, UK Human Rights Blog 3 May 2012: http://ukhumanrightsblog.com/2012/05/03/delay-in-transferring-mental-health-patient-for-treatment-amounted-to-inhumane-treatment/.
[58] Aharon Barak, Chapter 20, this volume. See also the same author's *Proportionality: Constitutional Rights and Their Limitations* (Cambridge, Cambridge University Press, 2012).

under which their demands might be departed from if the situation is thought urgent enough. I disagree with this approach, not just because of the reasons rehearsed in this chapter but because of my concern that it would achieve exactly the opposite of what it intends, in other words that by providing a stop-gap override permitting torture, for example, and/or affronts to dignity, it would legitimize as right and proper what should always be regarded as outside the pale of civilized living. Indignity is not the same as discrimination, something we can justify in some cases while continuing to abhor in others. Nor is it like free speech, a guarantee that must yield from time to time to the greater public good. Dignity is about what we are as persons. In the German torture case, Daschner needed to be punished despite our empathetic understanding of his plight—the case was not just about its facts; it was about how we as a community treat people.

Law does not eliminate political argument, the debate about hard choices; it merely relocates these conflicts. Litigating dignity provides no true answers, just passing victories for this or that side. Of course, it could be validly said in response to this (and echoing Clemens Sedmak) that the vulnerable are left exposed.[59] This is true as a subset of a general point about democracy, that we are all as individuals at risk from majoritarianism. The task is to contribute to the achievement and/or preservation of a healthy dignity-respecting society, one in which all are well catered for. Now perhaps this might entail laws like the HRA, a measure that handcuffs future legislatures while giving them the key at the same time—hoping they will choose not to unlock themselves and do bad things, or that at least they will have second thoughts while reaching for the key and forcing it into the lock. But it is a liberal daydream to suggest that a culture going downhill to indignity can be other than briefly interrupted by a bench of judges waving some piece of paper as a reminder of what by now only they believe were 'better' days. Keeping us civilized is a democratic task. In the UK, and perhaps in every democracy, this is primarily the work of our elected representatives, not our judges. They must work out what they mean by dignity and then put it into effect, either specifically or through general 'human rights' legislation if this can be made to work (as arguably the HRA does, in the UK). Our job as democratic stakeholders is to fight for the vision of dignity in which we believe and not rely on others—even benign judges—to deliver it for us.

---

[59] Clemens Sedmak, Chapter 33, this volume.

9

The Triple Dilemma of Human Dignity: A Case Study

Christoph Möllers

Introduction

THE FOLLOWING IS A CASE study that aims to argue systematically against applying the principle of human dignity in a legal order that respects individual rights. Our case, a decision of the European Court of Human Rights (ECtHR) on the right to privacy, will be used as an example of the dilemmas the application of human dignity in a legal system can create. The first part of this chapter presents the facts of the case, section two its solution by the ECtHR and possible alternative solutions. In section three we will identify three basic contradictions within the discourse of human dignity that appear in our case: contradictions among various concepts of the meaning of human dignity, different relational approaches to the scope of this guarantee, and the claims to generality and applicability of human dignity. The chapter ends with a short plea for less demanding and less general solutions for the judicial protection of human rights (section four).

The case: *KU v Finland*: the facts and the decision

In a case decided in 2008,[1] the ECtHR was confronted with the following facts. A photo and a physical description of a twelve-year-old boy (henceforth the victim) were posted on an online dating site and used as a sexual advertisement by a third person (henceforth the perpetrator) without knowledge or consent of the victim or his parents. The father of the victim asked the police to identify the perpetrator. The Internet service provider denied the police access to his files, considering itself bound to national laws of data protection.

---

[1] *KU v Finland*, Application no. 2872/02, 2008.

All attempts by the police and the prosecution to obtain the data failed at all three levels in the national court system of Finland. The national courts unanimously held that there was no statutory basis allowing the service provider to disclose the information or entitling the police to seize it from the provider. According to then-applicable Finnish law, this kind of information could only be seized to pursue certain defined criminal offences, none of which were relevant in this case. The manager in charge of the dating service could not be prosecuted because the prosecution of the alleged offence was at the moment of the prosecution already time-barred.

The ECtHR decided that the posting of a sexual solicitation of a twelve-year-old fell under Article 8 of the European Convention of Human Rights (ECHR), the right to privacy and family life:

> The Court reiterates that, although the object of Article 8 is essentially to protect the individual against arbitrary interference by the public authorities, it does not merely compel the State to abstain from such interference: in addition to this primarily negative undertaking, there may be positive obligations inherent in an effective respect for private or family life (see *Airey v Ireland*, judgment of 9 October 1979, Series A no. 32, § 32). (para. 42)

The court concluded that under Article 8 of the ECHR, Finland was obliged to provide a legal framework allowing the police to identify the name of the perpetrator:

> The Court considers that practical and effective protection of the applicant required that effective steps be taken to identify and prosecute the perpetrator, that is, the person who placed the advertisement. (para. 49)

Why this case?

As the reader will have noticed, in its reasoning the ECtHR makes no reference to the notion of human dignity. Human dignity is not even an explicit right of the ECHR, though it has been used by the ECtHR, especially in cases concerning cruel punishment.[2] But the fact that the ECtHR did not mention human dignity should not irritate the reader. When trying to explore a conceptual problem, we do not depend on the semantic use of human dignity in a specific positive legal order,[3] at least not as long as we can argue that the problems of our case are usually discussed within the framework of human

---

[2] Christopher McCrudden, 'Human dignity and judicial interpretation of human rights', *European Journal of International Law* 19:4 (2008), 655–724, at 683.
[3] For the problem of conceptualism in comparative law: Christoph Möllers, *A Concept of Separated Powers* (Oxford, Oxford University Press, 2013), Introduction.

dignity. This is also the case here. The case concerns different questions that are regularly addressed as ones of human dignity: sexual autonomy,[4] the right to privacy,[5] and the question of whether the state has a duty to protect these rights.[6]

The chapter uses this case as an example to illustrate three conceptual contradictions that the idea of an overall notion of human dignity entails: The contradiction between a sphere of protected privacy and the development of a social personality, between individual autonomy and the protection by public authorities (which can be reframed as a contradiction between reading human dignity as a right or reading it as a value), and between the interpretation of human dignity as a general political compromise formula and its use to decide individual cases.

To develop these points, our case may be interesting and illuminating for two reasons: first, because of its triadic structure. Three parties are involved in the simplified version of the case that we will analyse here. Also, all three are in a certain sense judged upon by the ECtHR. There is the juvenile victim whose identity was falsely posted on the Internet, the unidentified perpetrator, and the state, which has, in effect, no choice other than to offer a solution to the conflict by acting or declining to act.[7] The second reason for the case's relevance lies in the different normative roles that perpetrator and victim are playing. Since the victim has been involuntarily exposed to the public, his protected capability to socialize has thereby been compromised. The perpetrator remains anonymous, but this anonymity may be worth being protected as well. In many cases, dignity issues confront other, colliding normative claims. In relatively few cases, like this one, can competing claims be justified by a common reference to human dignity.

The constellation of the case and its possible solutions

Among the virtually infinite number of possible legal reactions to our case, three types of solutions can be singled out. The first would leave the actors alone with the exception of using private law remedies, remedies that would not work in our case because of the anonymity of the perpetrator. The second

---

[4] This is a topic in the case law of, for example, the USA and Hungary
[5] This is a topic in the case law of Germany.
[6] This is a topic in the case law of Germany, the ECtHR, and the ECJ.
[7] For the insight that non-action by the state is nothing neutral: Cass. R. Sunstein, *The Partial Constitution* (Cambridge, MA, Harvard University Press, 1998); for the relation between action and non-action see below *infra The substantial question: private intimacy or social persona?*

would explicitly prohibit and penalize the action of the perpetrator by means of public and criminal law, yet abstain from any obligation to keep track of online activities by which the crime was committed. This was the national legal order's solution when the case was decided. A third solution would indeed oblige the state to provide instruments through which the perpetrator could be identified and punished. This was the court's solution.

One important characteristic of the case lies in the fact that solutions one and two do not help the victim at all. For this constellation, they are simply of normative—one might also say expressive—value. Such an expressive function may be important for the legal community, but it cannot help to redefine the relationship between victim and perpetrator. Another, less obvious but equally relevant, characteristic of the case is that solution three not only helps the victim secure a concrete remedy from the perpetrator but also necessitates a whole bundle of state measures that infringe on the rights of virtually everybody else. In order to track the perpetrator, all of his Internet communication would have to be secured and traced back. Such measures would include an obligatory saving of files by Internet providers, comparable to the much disputed Data Retention Directive of the European Union that has been the object of constitutional litigation in different member states—litigation in which the notion of human dignity has played an explicit role.[8]

To a certain degree, this rather dramatic consequence is owing to particular technicalities of Internet communication, but not entirely: similar trade-offs can be observed with other instruments of criminal prosecution, for example the analysis of DNA. One could think of a comparable case constellation in which a raped woman asks for a remedy that would allow the offender to be identified. Introducing such instruments into a criminal justice system would mean making everybody identifiable for the sake of prosecuting the crimes of some. The sheer number of persons affected by such measures is not necessarily troublesome for an absolute concept of human dignity.[9] One violation of human dignity may claim a higher normative value than the violation of many

---

[8] Directive 2006/24/EC of the European Union, for a critical analysis see Francesca Bignami, 'Privacy and law enforcement in the European Union: the data retention directive', *Chicago Journal of International Law* 8:1 (2007), 233–55. The German Federal Constitutional Court uses the notion of human dignity to define absolute limits of the same instruments that the ECtHR finds must be applied in our case; see footnote 20.

[9] Such an absolute concept is claimed by the German constitutional doctrine, but an analysis of the case law proves this claim to be mistaken: Michael Rosen, *Dignity: Its History and Meaning* (Cambridge, MA, Harvard University Press, 2012), 100–7.

other only relative rights.[10] Still, as we will see, human dignity could appear on both sides of this equation.

A triple contradiction within human dignity

We may distinguish rather crudely between two basic approaches in the contemporary discourse on human dignity: The first tries to develop a correct systematic understanding of the concept by arguing from political theory or international or constitutional law.[11] The second looks at the variety of interpretations in a kind of second-order observation, searching for internal contradictions and historical path-dependencies.[12] It seems that both approaches have their merits and cannot be substituted for each other. There is no choice between the quest for good reasons for a certain understanding of a norm on the one hand and, on the other, the reflective observation of the way the norm is used and changing.[13] This chapter follows the second approach.[14] In the next section we will analyse some of the internal tensions within common understandings of human dignity. But it is equally important to mention that this second way of dealing with human dignity is applied here to a case and the reasoning of a court: Courts, unlike theorists, have no choice but to make a decision and to give their own reasons for it. Therefore, the way courts treat concepts like human dignity belongs decidedly to the first approach. Courts are not entitled to reflect on the contingencies of the reasons they apply. We must take this institutional necessity into account when we have a closer look at what I call the triple contradiction within human dignity.

---

[10] For an argument in favour of an absolute right: Alan Gewirth, 'Are there any absolute rights?', in J. Waldron (ed.), *Theories of Rights* (Oxford, Oxford University Press, 1984), 91–109.
[11] A more recent example is George Kateb, *Human Dignity* (Cambridge, MA, Belknap Press of Harvard University Press, 2012), or Jürgen Habermas, 'Das Konzept der Menschenwürde und die realistische Utopie der Menschenrechte', *Deutsche Zeitschrift für Philosophie* 58:3 (2010), 343–57.
[12] Rosen, *Dignity* and James Q. Whitman, '"Human dignity" in Europe and the United States: the social foundations', in George Nolte (ed.), *Europe and US Constitutionalism* (Cambridge, Cambridge University Press, 2005), 108–24.
[13] An attempt to square this circle is Hans Joas, *Die Sakralität der Person* (Berlin, Suhrkamp Verlag, 2011).
[14] For the author's account of the first approach, a systematic understanding: Christoph Möllers, 'Democracy and human dignity—limits of a moralized conception of rights in German constitutional law', *Israel Law Review* 42 (2009), 417–39.

The substantial question: private intimacy or social persona?

It is a truism that the concept of human dignity protects something that is specific to humans. The basic dilemma in this assumption is that human dignity is supposed to protect individual persons, but that many of the defining characteristics of human beings function only as social capabilities: language, deliberation, critique, pride.[15] Here lies, beyond the shop-worn question of how to relate individual and collective preferences, a much more interesting and relevant cognitive problem: it is far from clear where the individual self ends and where the social context begins. Even the human body itself draws an unreliable line: by taking DNA samples from suspects, we refuse to define an absolute corporeal limit to individual freedom. This dilemma was already vivid in the early, quite collectivist jurisprudence of the German Constitutional Court,[16] and is still present in many contemporary legal interpretations of human dignity. It seems to boil down to two protective ideals: on the one hand the ideal of the autonomous subject with a space of his or her own which is protected from any disturbance, and on the other the ideal of the social persona whose dignity enables successful participation in a community.

The first model may be rooted in a Kantian tradition, though it probably cannot be based on a plausible reading of Kant's own philosophy.[17] In this reading, human dignity refers to a qualification of the subject as such, to its ability to make free and reasonable decisions. Obviously, for a strictly Kantian account there is nothing here to be protected by law, as the ability to reason falls outside the realm of the external causal world in which the law, unlike moral obligations, has its place. But in a different interpretation, the protection of human dignity may be understood as referring to the practical conditions of a rational personality. In this reading, human dignity is a qualification of every human being independently of his or her social context. This may also mean that human dignity guarantees a place of intimacy in which every human being must be left alone. In a more concrete interpretation, this may provide for a space that is shielded from scrutiny by the state or other persons: intimate notes in diaries are one example, a collection of traces on the Internet that allows reconstruction of a whole personality may be another.

---

[15] For a good reflection: Lea Ypi, 'Self-ownership and the State: a democratic critique', *Ratio* 24: 1 (2011), 91–106.

[16] BVerfGE 4, 1, for a sharp critique from the perspective of individualistic Protestant theology: Graf.

[17] For a close analysis: Dietmar von der Pfordten, *Menschenwürde, Recht und Staat bei Kant* (Paderborn, Mentis Verlag, 2009). Even an author like Rosen, critical of a legislative approach to human dignity, never wonders in his analysis of Kant how the important distinction between moral and legal philosophy relates to the application of human dignity as a legal instrument.

We saw that the second understanding posits that human dignity refers to the ability to participate in a social environment. It is the possibility of socializing in the widest sense that is protected by human dignity here. In this interpretation, the old feudal meaning of dignity, which may have played an important role for the different developments of the legal concept in and outside continental Europe,[18] comes to the fore. In this understanding, dignity protects the conditions of social recognition by others. Or, to use an old-fashioned word, it protects the honour of everybody, allowing them to expect a certain respect from all other members of the community. Concrete examples of this kind of protection include the guarantee of a minimum standard of living that exceeds what is needed for mere survival, or the justification of the prohibition of consented yet demeaning treatment, such as the French case of dwarf-throwing, or those of demeaning caricatures in Germany.[19]

The extent to which these two interpretations of human dignity contradict or even mutually reinforce each other is a difficult and highly contested question of political philosophy. Maybe it takes an autonomous subject to become a functioning social persona and vice versa. One could also read this discussion as a version of the debate between liberals and communitarians, which in a certain way is the Anglo-American sequel to the argument between Kantians and Hegelians. But this is not our problem here. Often, lawyers can and should ignore the underlying fundamental issue in favour of the concrete problem. And, as we have already seen, at least in our case there is a conflict between the spheres of two different persons, who, indeed, brings to light the contradicting interpretations of their claim to human dignity that cannot be understood as mutually reinforcing. In other words, in this case human dignity plays a zero-sum game. While the victim needs the protection of his or her social persona, which is threatened by its inaccurate depiction on the Internet, the perpetrator needs a room of privacy that is, at least, protected even if he commits a crime within it. A solution that has to take sides for only one of the two persons is obviously easy to find. But this misses, as we have seen, the very problem of the case. We have already noted that every decision of the case that has a specific legal relevance for the victim, and not just a normative-symbolic meaning for the legal community, must use sanctions that allow the perpetrator to be identified. But every technique of identification would have problematic implications for the status of the perpetrator as well as for the whole legal community: it would require a potentially complete de-anonymization of online communication and state authority to seize it.

---

[18] Whitman, 'Human dignity'.
[19] An excellent critique of the latter can be found in Rosen, *Dignity*, 75–7.

The scope of such a system of control would not only be remarkable; it would also strike directly at the second understanding of human dignity, which seeks to provide everybody with a space of his or her own. The monitoring of a person's entire online activity could produce a complete picture of his or her personality, including the most intimate details and an overview of the person's daily life that could match the most precise and frank autobiography. One might therefore argue, as has been done, that such a regulation could in itself violate human dignity: in the words of the German Federal Constitutional Court reviewing the European Data Retention Directive and referring to human dignity: 'That the use of liberty by the citizens must not be detected and registered in total belongs to the constitutional identity of the Federal Republic of Germany.'[20] It seems that both understandings of human dignity clash in this case, private autonomy versus the social persona—but they can only clash if there is not only a normative assessment of the facts of the case but also a normative obligation to act. This leads us to our next question.

The relational question: subjective right or objective value?

So far, we have discussed a normative tension within the substantive scope of human dignity. We have assumed that from the perspective of the victim the social persona is at risk, but have also noticed that a regime of sanctions could in this case lead to a likewise grave and broad loss of rights that belong to the perpetrator's and third person's human dignity. We did not, however, pose the question of whether the violation of human dignity should require such a sanction. The idea that rights provide not only a space of freedom but also include a state duty to protect is common to some human rights systems but unknown to others. As we have seen, in our case the ECtHR endorsed a strong duty to protect, deducing from the right to privacy a rather broad regime of supervision by the state.

The question of protection adds a second tension to the concept of human dignity. Apart from the question of its substantive meaning, there appears the question of the scope of the right. We will present two different ways to frame this problem:

1. The objective effect of a right creates new obligations and may also serve as a justification to abridge the rights of a third party. This is nothing new to the doctrine of human dignity.[21] But why can we refer in our case to

---

[20] BVerfGE 125, 260 (324).
[21] McCrudden, 'Human dignity and judicial interpretation of human rights', 702–5.

an objective effect of the right in question? A subjective right entitles a legal subject in relation to another person who is correspondingly obligated by this right. In our case, the victim's right to privacy, in the reading of the Court, obliges the state to intervene in a course of action attributed to a third person, for whom the state is not responsible.[22] The case gives no strong reasons for this interpretation. It is presented instead as a self-evident move, though this is neither true for the comparative law of human rights nor for the jurisprudence of the ECtHR, which makes mixed and unsystematic use of an objective interpretation of basic rights.

Only an objective reading of the right to privacy allows an obligation of the state *to abridge the rights* of the perpetrator (and of every other participant in online communications). Obviously, this is a demanding and not unproblematic reading of a right. It destroys the asymmetry between the empowered individual persons and the state in favour of a more complex and less individualistic construction. It is one of the ironies of this approach that on the one hand it may claim to give an especially broad effect to human dignity, but that on the other hand it leads inevitably to a balancing approach in its application that has to define the scope of human dignity in relation to other claims. This is not the place to endorse or criticize balancing,[23] but it is clear that a broad interpretation of human dignity that permits case constellations in which two persons claim their right to human dignity at one another's expense excludes an absolute interpretation of this right.[24]

The same point can be made with regard to the distinction between values and rules. If human dignity is part of a legal order and not just a moral demand, does it take the form of a rule or a principle, respectively a value? An important part of the post-war jurisprudence of basic rights on both sides of the Atlantic has tried to establish models of rights as principles, not as rules.[25] Amongst the complicated arguments for this understanding, the higher normative rank of principles compared with other legal norms and the specific methodological approach their interpretation requires seem to be the most

---

[22] Gewirth, 'Are there any absolute rights?', 104.
[23] Ralf Poscher, 'The principles theories. How many theories and what is their merit?', in M. Klatt (ed.), *Institutionalized Reason* (Oxford, Oxford University Press, 2012), 218–47.
[24] The way this tension is solved in German law, where both objective effect and absoluteness of human dignity is claimed, seems rather like a trick. Human dignity is often interpreted 'in connection with' another right that can be balanced. Critical: Möllers, 'Democracy and human dignity—limits of a moralized conception of rights in German constitutional law'.
[25] Most notably Ronald Dworkin, *Taking Rights Seriously* (Cambridge, MA, Harvard University Press, 1977), and Robert Alexy, *Theorie der Grundrechte* (Frankfurt am Main, Suhrkamp, 1986), though both with attempts that lead (allegedly for purely jurisprudential reasons) to differing results that come quite close to their respective own national legal orders.

important. For our context, it is crucial to observe an asymmetric relation between two systematic questions: though it does not seem to be necessary that a model of rights as principles implies an objective and balancing interpretation of this right (Dworkin's theory is the counter-example), the same is not true vice versa. Any objective and balancing understanding of rights can hardly conceive of them as rules: rules have the form of a conditional sentence in which there is hardly room for a balancing test.[26]

For our case, the question of whether the ECtHR treated the right of privacy as a rule or a principle cannot be answered easily. One of the remarkable features of this decision is that it argues as if a rule were applied, though what the court actually did looks rather like an incomplete form of balancing: Without much of a legal argument, the Court devised a duty for the state to sanction a violation. But in accepting this duty the court had to introduce a second individual person into the legal argument, a person who also can claim Convention rights, the perpetrator. Therefore, the Court should have taken into account the rights of the perpetrator. In fact, these rights are part of an implicit balancing effort by the Court in which their weight equals zero. Again it is important to see that the form of the balanced value is at least not open to an approach that assumes an absolute protection through a certain right.[27] That may lead to the perverse effect, for example in German constitutional law, that for the assessment of the human dignity of a given person, the normative demands of other persons may be more important than his or her own consent.[28]

There is a second aspect to our point. One neglected problem of human rights theory is how to coherently sanction its violation. If human dignity is considered to be a particular right that enjoys a central position in a system of legal guarantees or even a normatively higher rank than other rights, should it not be protected more aggressively? Or should its violation not be sanctioned more harshly than the violation of other rights?

Normally, in constitutional orders in which rights are protected, the violation of a right is not necessarily sanctioned beyond the mere invalidation of this violation. A violation of my freedom of speech entitles me to a remedy that ends the infringement, but not necessarily to any other sanction. The ECtHR's reading of Article 8 of the ECHR is, therefore, not self-evident: if there had been no instrument to stop the posting of the victim's name, this would have

---

[26] Frederick Schauer, 'Balancing, subsumtion, and the constraining role of legal text', in M. Klatt (ed.), *Institutionalized Reason* (Oxford, Oxford University Press, 2012), 307–18.
[27] For an Alexian reading of the German human dignity clause see Nils Teifke, *Das Prinzip Menschenwürde* (Tübingen, Mohr Siebeck, 2011).
[28] Critical: Rosen, *Dignity*, 107.

been a problem of an appropriate remedy. But it does not seem equally compelling that every violation demands a positive legal sanction beyond this.

But maybe there are particular demands for specific violations of human rights. That this could be correct becomes plausible when we regard the rights to life and bodily integrity, which are protected by many national and international human rights catalogues. A violation of the right to life, the killing of a person, is de facto universally and severely sanctioned by private and criminal law, though only in certain qualified circumstances (responsible action of the perpetrator), and not or rarely in others (state of war beyond specific war crimes and crimes against humanity). One of the open problems of the legal doctrine of human dignity is the uncertain relation between the alleged rank of the right, the subjective necessity of sanctioning any intentional violation of it, and the severity of this sanction in relation to other sanctions. If torture is a violation of human dignity (which, within the very contested interpretation of its meaning, is perhaps the least contested case), and if human dignity can even be a higher ranking right than human life, than it seems plausible that the sanction of an intended violation of human dignity has to be at least as harsh as the sanction of an intended violation of life, that is, some kind of murder.

For our case this could mean that an appropriate sanction of the perpetrator would be in the range of the sanction of a murder. But this seems somewhat counter-intuitive, and this intuition is probably confirmed by much of the practice of criminal law, which does not recognize a crime that specifically violates human dignity. Even in Germany, in the constitutional order that seems to hold the protection of human dignity in the highest regard as an element of the unalterable core of the constitutional order, the same intuition is at work. It was generally acceptable, and not even a matter of public debate, that a person who had violated the human dignity of another person, as happened in the case of a police officer who threatened to torture a suspect (Daschner), was given only a relatively mild sentence for a minor physical injury.[29] The normative dissonance between this practice and the alleged rank of human dignity leads to a more general point. The connection between the protection of a right and the sanctioning of its violation is, perhaps for good reasons, rather weak. But many legal philosophers from Gustav Radbruch to Robert Alexy liked to identify the degree of unjustness of a flagrant violation of human rights by states like Nazi or East Germany with the injustice of these violations remaining unsanctioned. This is an approach one could call the remedial fallacy: though it is gravely unjust to intentionally kill somebody

---

[29] Mild beyond the additional justification that his threat had the aim to save the life of an abducted child.

and probably also unjust not to sanction the killer, any flat identification of the degree of injustice of the one deed with the other omission seems implausible. Obviously, the deed is morally worse than the omission.

If it is not necessary to sanction every intentional violation of a right for the sake of respecting this right, and if we see a legal practice at work that tends to sanction violations of human dignity less severely than other rights violations, then we might wonder how this reflects on the status of this guarantee compared with other rights.

Finally, we have already seen that in a strictly Kantian (probably as well as in a convincing Christian) reading, human dignity cannot be violated. Has the victim in our case, or any other victim of cruelty or a specifically degrading behaviour, lost his or her dignity? This seems dubious. At least in a moral sense, this would do too much honour to the perpetrator.[30] But if a legal reading of human dignity depends on at least some legal implications, we might deduce a more general conclusion. While an objective interpretation of human dignity, including a duty to protect, leads to a weaker concept of its substance, it is already a *legal* reading that must accept something that does not necessarily have to be: that humans can lose their dignity, and that this loss must be sanctioned by law.

The practical question: general rights and specific cases

One of the key assumptions in the discourse on human dignity is that it serves as a kind of incompletely theorized agreement,[31] as the expression of a consensus agreed upon for differing or even contradictory reasons. The post-war constellation on the international level and in many states in which secularists and the devout, Westerners and Easterners, capitalists and communists, had to formulate common founding documents is the most important example of this form of compromise. Given that this reconstruction reveals a historical experience, the question remains of what it means for the practice of the law,

---

[30] This is, by the way, what a close reading of the German codification of human dignity means: 'The dignity of the human being is untouchable (*unantastbar*). It cannot be violated.' The framers of the *Grundgesetz* did not suggest the same with regard to freedom of speech or the right to life and bodily integrity. It entails the argument that human dignity was meant as a moral assumption for the following rights, not as a right itself. The framers seemed to have a more nuanced concept of the relation between law and morals than the moralizing constitutional court following them. A good historical account is Christoph Goos, *Innere Freiheit: Eine Rekonstruktion des grundgesetzlichen Würdebegriffs* (Göttingen, Vandenhoeck & Ruprecht, 2011).

[31] Cass R. Sunstein, *Legal Reasoning and Political Conflict* (Cambridge, MA, Harvard University Press, 1998).

particularly for the decision of cases. What is the incomplete theory in this reconstruction? What reasons are beyond such a theory, and how do they relate to each other?

The considerable difference between the political process of finding a compromise formula for an international treaty or a constitution and the decision of a controversial case seems to escape this description. A look at Cass Sunstein's concept of incompletely theorized agreements (a jurisprudential version of John Rawls's idea of an overlapping consensus) may illustrate the point. It is far from clear that the reference to human dignity in a judicial decision is really an incomplete agreement in his sense. When the framers of a constitution decide to enshrine Sunday in the constitution as a holiday, they may do so following an agreement between Christian Churches and trade unions. This agreement is incompletely theorized as both parties have completely different, either spiritual or social, motives. But the result is uncontested, and the meaning of the resulting rule clear. When human dignity became a part of constitutions and international treaties, there was an agreement on the expression 'human dignity', but certainly none on its meaning for deciding concrete cases. And would it not be strange if a formula meant to convey an uncontroversial term into a controversial context could be used to decide concrete cases in an uncontroversial manner? In fact, the reference to human dignity instead of a more concrete less fundamental rule in order to solve a case just seems like the kind of fully fledged theoretical argument that Sunstein recommends be avoided.

It is, therefore, no accident that the universal acceptance of human dignity did not lead to common results.[32] To name just two examples from the western hemisphere: some states have outlawed capital punishment as a violation of human dignity, others practise it; some states see the right to abortion as part of women's dignity, but at least one state deduces from human dignity a duty to criminalize abortion.

These contradictions are well known and well documented.[33] The question is how they can be reconciled with the idea of a core meaning and a peripheral variation.[34] It seems they cannot. The concept of a consensual centre and a peripheral contestation fails if we can identify contradictory meanings within the concept. If we accept that human dignity entails a duty to

---

[32] One Arendtian claim that could be developed at this point is that one needs a political community to effectively protect human rights, a claim that seems to be supported by much of human rights practice. In such a community, one may find a consensus for, for example, a more liberal or a more paternalistic concept of human dignity that works its way through cases.
[33] McCrudden, 'Human dignity and judicial interpretation of human rights', 697–8.
[34] McCrudden, 'Human dignity and judicial interpretation of human rights', 711.

protect that widens the scope of intrusion into individual rights, what 'limits to state action' might mean remains contested.[35] If we accept that human dignity gives a right to a community identity, it is far from clear that it can serve as a universal category.

Our case may again serve as an illustration. To define a core concept, the question to be answered is: what is the common core of two differing interpretations of human dignity in which the first protects the social persona of the victim and the second protects the communicative intimacy of the perpetrator? No doubt a smart constitutional theorist could devise a formula to reconcile this contradiction, but exactly qua this reconciling propriety, such a formula could not help decide our case.

The regulatory use of human dignity

The organizational sociologist Karl Weick once remarked that simplicity, precision, and generality of a scientific explanation can only be had in a mutual trade-off.[36] The same is true for norms, and the use of human dignity in cases like ours may well serve to highlight this point. The inclusion of human dignity produces a high level of normative generality at the expense of precision, and it creates a remarkable demand for complexity in the legal argument. As a matter of regulatory strategy, this does not seem to be a good road to take. While it may be important to make the concept of human dignity serve as a formula that designates a general underlying normative assumption of a constitutional order, it is something completely different to define such an assumption as the basis for the decision of cases. Finnish legislators had a regulatory concept when they limited access to certain data relevant to the prosecution of particular crimes. This concept may be contestable, but it seems to have looked at the different rights at stake. We can find such a fine-grained solution neither in the ECHR nor in the reasoning of the ECtHR in our case. To be sure, one virtue of human rights is to offer simple solutions. There is nothing to say against an absolute protection of freedom of speech or an absolute prohibition of racist discrimination. But even though cases concerning these rights are often contested, the basic intuition in which direction the mentioned rights drive the legal argument is clear. The same is not true for the notion of human dignity. On the contrary, human dignity, as a master norm of constitutionalism, invites us to take a holistic approach, one that may be fine

---

[35] McCrudden, 'Human dignity and judicial interpretation of human rights', 679.
[36] Karl Weick, *The Social Psychology of Organizing*, 2nd edn (New York, McGraw-Hill, 1979), 35–41.

for understanding the internal tensions of liberal constitutionalism, one that gives both actors in our case, the victim as well as the perpetrator, their share of a right. But human dignity is definitely not the kind of norm that helps us to prevent states or private individuals from acting in a particular way. A legal order that attempts to outlaw a certain behaviour, like torture, by its officials and its citizens has to define this behaviour as precisely as possible. The reference to human dignity will not help fulfil this task.

10

Dignity Rather than Rights

John Milbank

Dignity and rights: fusion and instability

THERE IS LITTLE AGREEMENT on the usage of 'dignity', in particular its relationship to rights. For some, the recent use of dignity is a useful supplement to, or at least ornament for, the language of rights. For others, dignity tends to dilute the rights of individuals and must, therefore, be resisted and rejected, especially when dignity is allied with a religious vision. Still further, a small intellectual minority (myself included) see dignity as a more valid alternative to rights.

Before 1948, human dignity and rights were scarcely invoked together. It was only with the UN Declaration of Human Rights and the old German Federal Republic's provisional (in view of the division of the country) *Grundgesetz* that we really began to see a yoking of the two.[1] This post-1948 shift can be understood in terms of a double rejection, both of totalitarian suppression of human freedom and of unprecedentedly brutal treatment of certain classes of human beings. But, more precisely, one can understand this yoking in terms of the coming together of two quite different and indeed fundamentally opposed traditions of political and ethical reflection.

The first is the liberal, eventually secular, tradition of human rights that had been made the basis of the American Constitution and more fitfully of the various French constitutions since the Revolution.[2] For this tradition, the high status of human beings is self-given, whether because they 'own themselves' (the Lockean tradition of 'possessive individualism') or because they are divinely constituted as originally free and must therefore accord themselves a sacred respect as the trustees of an untradable liberty (the Rousseauian

---

[1] See Michael Rosen, *Dignity: Its History and Meaning* (Cambridge, MA, Harvard University Press, 2012), 38–47, 77–104.
[2] See Samuel Moyn, Chapter 4, this volume. See also Michael Rosen, 'Dignity past and present', in Jeremy Waldron (ed.), *Dignity, Rank and Rights* (Oxford, Oxford University Press, 2012), 89–98, and Chapter 18, this volume.

tradition). In either case, rights are derived from the exercise of subjective freedom or from human autonomy, and require no other foundation. Little or no mention is made of dignity.

The other tradition is largely Catholic, though it has many parallels in other Christian denominations. It concerns a defence of human existence in all its modes in terms of the category of dignity. In this discourse, which arose in the nineteenth century, there is a fluctuation between the notion of respect for the dignity of the human person as such and respect for various human roles such as, above all, the 'dignity of labour'. Such fluctuation, as I shall explain in this chapter, is both endemic to and coherent within the entire notion of dignity as it had been inherited from Classical, Patristic, and Medieval times. For this reason, this tradition could hold together respective emphases upon the dignity of the human as such, the dignity of roles, and of groups.

Attempting to mediate between these traditions, and the unlikely marriage of dignity and rights, was Kantian thought, especially in Germany. For Kant had assumed and further spiritualized Rousseau's approach to right and liberty: we do not own our own freedom, which is a divine gift, trumping the mutability and tradeability of the material sphere. Hence it is morally illicit to commit suicide, tell a lie, or surrender to sensuality for its own sake. Just for this reason Kant had spoken of human dignity or *würde*.[3]

However, I agree with both Samuel Moyn and Michael Rosen that this fusion is much more unstable than has often appeared to be the case. After 2001, we have witnessed a second upsurge of 'dignity' discourse. Arguably, this has qualified rights discourse. The reasons for this second wave are somewhat more obscure, but it can plausibly be taken that they parallel the post-1948 invocation. People have been horrified by the scant respect for human life, human suffering, and the accepted modes of human existence and human interaction exhibited both by terrorists and states since 9/11. There exists an anxiety that rights supposedly based upon autonomy and contract can logically be suspended in the case of 'terrorists' who refuse that contract. Refugees who have been accidentally placed outside state and legal contract often seem to fall beyond the sway of rights. And in either case, loss of rights seem to result in a loss of humanity, a casting out into a limbo unworthy of either the respect we accord to humans or the sympathy we sometimes accord to animals. For even though rights are deemed 'natural', if no pre-political divine establishment and enforcement of rights is admitted, then natural rights must, paradoxically, be positively instituted by human law. They are only natural in

---

[3] See Immanuel Kant, *Groundwork of the Metaphysics of Morals* (Cambridge, Cambridge University Press, 2012).

the Hobbesian sense of being founded upon a supposedly natural condition of pre-contractual egotism, which was not, in itself, a state of right. In a usually inchoate and inexplicit way, the resurgence of appeal to dignity besides rights or even as the foundation of rights seems to register an anxiety about the limits of secular recognition of human worth as rights.

But the instability of the alliance between rights and dignity also concerns the nature of Catholic social teaching. Blending corporatist and personalist understandings, Catholic social teaching stressed, and continues to stress, valuing the person as rationally free and as possessing an irreplaceably specific character, or role. 'Character', as Aristotle, Cicero, and Aquinas made clear, is not just given by nature but is also habitually acquired, ascribed, and chosen. It therefore does not exist outside relationality and social reciprocity. One does not, as in liberal thought, respect a man as man per se, a bearer of abstract rights.

This difference of understanding could be construed as an internal and external contrast. One could say that the liberal view sees dignity as an internal phenomenon of concealed willing, while the Catholic view sees dignity as an external phenomenon of human position within the cosmic order and equally of individual human position within the social order. In that sense, internal versus external would seem to express two divergent conceptions of dignity. However, this is far too simplistic. First, modern conceptions of dignity after all split internally between interior and exterior in their own specific way. And second, so do ancient and medieval ones, but in a different way. Exploring this split, I will try to show that the key contrast turns out to be a modern incapacity to mediate the internal and external, compared with the ancient perspective, especially in its Catholic Christian variant as inherited in later Catholic social teaching.

Internal and external dignities

Liberal dignity as duty or utility

First, the modern division and disjunction of the dignified. Take the notion of 'dying with dignity'. This refers in part to the interior dimension of human life: our capacity for a rational exercise of freedom. A dignified death is, supposedly, a death whose place and hour has, in theory, been freely chosen by the individual who is mortally ill, at a point before he has lost all capacity for autonomous decision, and so, for this perspective, all dignity.

Yet dignity with respect to death also refers in part to the most external circumstances of human life. A 'dignified death' is taken to be one that involves a minimum of pain, discomfort, physical mess, or distressing circumstances.

This split clearly reflects a more general modern division between deontological and utilitarian approaches to ethics—especially if we take the 'utile' to refer in the widest possible sense to the convenient and pleasurable. Thus, the same duality of dignity is extended from death to life in general. On the one hand, to live with dignity is to live not in any sense as a slave but as an autonomous being who has chosen or at least assented to her career, dwelling-place, friendships, and economic contracts. On the other hand, a dignified life is taken to be one where we enjoy enough food, decent shelter and clothing, protection from the natural environment, mechanized transport, access to professional healthcare, educational expertise, and informational and social media.

Again we see the contrast between, and yet typical combination of, the deontological and the utilitarian. Deontological aspects of dignity more readily apply to human adults, while utilitarian ones extend to children, and to a lesser degree are extended to certain animals. Michael Rosen struggles to explain how he personally requires a dignified treatment of dead bodies in secular terms outside these ethical frameworks—that is to say, even when no human freedom is at issue and no pleasure or displeasure to the living.[4] More to the point might be the observation that in fact respectful treatment of the dead (as of the dying) is increasingly violated in secular society.

It is therefore not simply the case that liberalism thinks of dignity as internal or invisible right, while Catholicism thinks of dignity as external or visible status. For it also turns out that liberalism combines the invisible dignity of right with the visible dignity of style and convenience. A lack of integration between the two is revealed in the fluctuations of public policy, where we possess no criterion by which to decide whether to concentrate on making people freer or more comfortable, ecstatically liberated or soberly healthy. In consequence, we often end up contradictorily pursuing libertinism in one domain and Spartan discipline in others: for example, liberalizing drug laws while extending draconian bans on smoking, or permitting adult pornography while forbidding children from even touching each other (as debated in a number of Australian schools today). The greatest synthesis we can ever achieve is a banal one that divides and rules the two incompatible modern ethical theories: people are thus rendered freer 'to choose' between ferociously marketed different versions of comfortable indulgence and programmes for self-discipline.

---

[4] Rosen, *Dignity*, 129–60.

However, the political legacy that Catholicism inherited had, from the outset, its own mode of doubling dignity between the visible and the invisible. The Latin *dignitas* lies close to the word *decus*, meaning 'ornament' or 'honourable reward', and also to *decorum*, meaning 'socially acceptable ethical style', and ultimately to the Greek *dokein*, meaning 'to show', and *doxa*, meaning 'shining manifestation', glory or honour, inherently proceeding or bestowed from without. Yet on the other hand, as Mette Lebech points out, *dignitas* also translates the Greek *axia*, meaning not just fundamental worth but also 'first principle', as in our derivative 'axiom'.[5] Hence the scholastics translated the Greek *axia* in logical and mathematical contexts as *dignitas*. So for Aquinas, for example, *dignitas* means both something good in itself and something taken to be true in itself.[6]

This suggests something like a paradox of dignity. The dignified is self-standing and independent; as such, it is sufficient to itself and so reserved. Yet the dignified is equally what gloriously shows itself, and even that which receives a supplement of honour from others. It is at once (like the number one in ancient mathematics) that which requires no addition, and yet is the very principle of addition. In fact, we still tend to register a paradox when we ascribe dignity: dignified motion, for example, is a motion that somehow moves without deserting a statue-like immobile erectness; a dignified gesture is one that somehow combines reserve—or non-gesture—with expression that necessarily negates reserve. Like sublime speech in rhetoric (which is itself traditionally dignified speech in contrast to the charm and delight of conversation), the dignified gesture makes a simpler and greater impact precisely through the exercise of restraint.

And this paradox is no trivial thing: instead dignity as both reserved and manifest would seem to have been the very heart of the classically syncretic ideal of the fully rounded man (*sic*)—the individual of wise contemplation who bestows his gifts of wisdom through practical action in the city. Yet this ideal was but precariously held together, as we can see if we examine the respective roles of *axia* in Aristotle and *dignitas* in Cicero.

Ancient dignity as reserved and expressed

For Aristotle, different political constitutions can be defined in terms of their 'axiomatic' preferences, or of what for them counts as dignity. For a democ-

---

[5] Mette Lebech, 'What is human dignity?', in Mette Lerbech (ed.), *Maynooth Philosophical Papers* (Maynooth, Maynooth University Press, 2004), 59–69.
[6] See Lebech, 'What is human dignity?', and Rosen, *Dignity*, 16–17.

racy it is simply free birth; for an oligarchy possession of wealth; for an aristocracy possession of virtue.[7]

Aristotle at times appeared to understand virtue in terms of the flourishing of an individual who attains an inner balance of the emotions and between emotions and reason. If, for example, an individual needs friends, it is to amend his loneliness and to enjoy utility, companionship, and agreement concerning the good. Yet this seeming individualism is massively qualified by Aristotle's statement that complete virtue involves also the virtuous treatment of others for their own sakes. The stated implication is that entire virtue is justice in a more general sense than specific justice, which is concerned with the distribution and exchange of inherently incommensurable resources.[8] In this sense, for Aristotle as for Plato, an originally 'manly' virtue of martial or philosophical restraint (inner, invisible dignity) gives way to a more relational understanding of virtue as work, justice, gift, and mutual dependency (external, visible dignity).

Aristotle defines *axia* not as a lonely principle but as something on which other truths and goods depend and to which it gives rise: it is 'a term of relation: It denotes having a claim to goods external to oneself' and supremely to the best mode of tribute, which is honour.[9] As Robert L. Gallagher argues in a remarkable recent essay, Aristotle actually calls into question virtue as an axiomatic standard if by that we understand an inert, already achieved status.[10] Aristotle no more accords to that any political or economic worth than he does to the given achievement of birth or of income. Instead, he understands specifically political virtue as an *ergon*, or as the exercise of a function or role—socially speaking a *leitourgia*, which the Latins translated as *officium*.

As Gallagher points out, Aristotle in the *Eudemian Ethics* includes justice within friendship rather than the other way around: 'the whole of justice is in relation to a friend, for what is just is just for certain persons, and persons who are partners, and a friend is a partner, either in one's family or in one's life'.[11] So for Aristotle it is not merely that justice trumps personal virtue and so politics ethics, but also and almost inversely, justice turns out to be always to do with a series of specific 'civic friendships' of many variously appropriate kinds, and the *polis* to be the open totality of the asymmetric reciprocities between incommensurable goods and persons that composes specific

---

[7] Aristotle, *Nicomachean Ethics*, V.iii, 7–8.
[8] Aristotle, *Nicomachean Ethics*, V. ii, 6–10.
[9] Aristotle, *Nicomachean Ethics*, IV, 11, 10.
[10] Robert L. Gallagher, 'Incommensurability in Aristotle's theory of reciprocal justice', *British Journal for the History of Philosophy* 20 (2012), 667–701.
[11] Aristotle, *Eudemian Ethics*, VII, x, 5.

justice.¹² It is as if the private gives way to the public, but then the public itself restores the intimate—now as relational and mutual rather than self-enclosed. It follows that if specific justice concerns economic and legal contracts it is answerable to a more general justice, which is for Aristotle none other than the life of paradoxically obligatory generosity and graciousness, where public statues of the Three Graces remind every citizen always to return favours with interest and to themselves offer endlessly new favours, which establish new reciprocal obligations.¹³

For Aristotle, then, dignity is not something inert and altogether reserved. It must in part be reserved to ensure further giving in the future and protect against foolish lavishness.¹⁴ But dignity much more consists in the operations of exchange through work and gift. Every exchange between incommensurable goods and roles, like that between a shoemaker and an architect, to give Aristotle's own prime example, involves an unmeasurable, ineffable, but real judgement of just exchange.¹⁵

As Gallagher argues, Aristotle's reasoning here shows that if one begins by *admitting* the real social situation of difference and inequality, then one can seek to qualify this through an ethos that honours material benefactors. As today, the architect has more prestige than the shoemaker, according to virtue. Architecture is a more variously demanding and paradigmatically more architectonic role. Within this hierarchy, the shoemaker will, Aristotle contended, seek to gain a disproportionate benefit or 'profit' (which for Aristotle always denoted an excessive share in any transaction). Aristotle's solution here is to allow this imbalance to pertain, but to compensate this in terms of a greater 'honouring' of the higher party by both the beneficiary and the public at large.¹⁶ Rather than the multi-billionaire's compensation for past iniquities of effectively coerced exchanging, we see generosity prepared always to raise the relatively poor in material terms met by an endless reconstrual of its own prestige in terms of a relatively immaterial honour. Human dignity as unequal and differential status paradoxically *promotes* human equalization, as Gallagher concludes his article.

For Aristotle, the exercise of dignity consists in the rendering of a social role (*leitourgia*) and performance of a social work (*ergon*). This is a measured generosity, entailing the internal, invisible reserve that is also an external, visible expressive act—the restraint of a reserved capacity for future giving

---

¹² Aristotle, *Nicomachean Ethics*, V, v, 6–7.
¹³ Aristotle, *Nicomachean Ethics*, V, v, 6–7.
¹⁴ Aristotle, *Nicomachean Ethics*, IV in general.
¹⁵ Aristotle, *Nicomachean Ethics*, V, iv, 2–8.
¹⁶ Aristotle, *Nicomachean Ethics*, VII, x, 10–13.

and relating as well as expressive reciprocity. The context for this exercise, or exchange, is the constitution of *diakosounē* (justice) within the *polis*. It is the city which integrates the external dignities of performed offices to form a functioning whole. And this functionalist understanding is qualified by the circumstance that the just city is itself defined as the open-ended sequence of personal relationships.[17]

Nevertheless, Aristotle's integration of invisible and visible dignity remained imperfect. We see an unresolved tension between virtue and justice, *aretē* and *diakosounē*. The aim of the best, aristocratic polity, according to Aristotle, is to produce virtue in its citizens. Yet virtue is defined by Aristotle in terms of an internal psychic balance of functions. This focus on inward prudential integration, against exchange itself, creates a tension with justice. Further, justice itself can take on the idea of 'the division of labour' or the proper *remaining* of psychic functions and social roles in their fixed, hierarchic social places. Such an understanding could, as Plato discussed in the *Republic*, reduce reason (*nous*) to a superior *force* restraining the desires of the soul, just as the military restrains the working classes in the city. *Phronesis* could then become, as with the sophists, self-preservation and the smooth functioning of individual strength; justice in the city was the preservation of the city against external enemies.

Plato was more able to overcome these possibilities. For Aristotle, the ethical was a purely human and political affair; in consequence, true friendship only pertains between adult male participants in the political process. The Aristotelian city, composed of a network of reciprocities, does not extend beyond the city walls. But for Plato, practical wisdom was identical with the theoretical contemplation of transcendent goodness. We are good insofar as we relate to the divine, and we participate in the divine by communicating this goodness as adult men not just to other adult men (as for Aristotle) but also to women, children, and animals. Human friendship participates in the higher friendship of the gods to us and with each other. *Phronesis* consequently escapes the framework of a fixed hierarchic space (the city walls) in favour of time—the always fluid discerning of the right time and places for certain appropriate actions.[18]

When we reach Cicero, however, we find that this aporetic split between inner and outer dignity (virtue and justice) was considerably magnified. On the one hand Cicero pointed towards a proto-modern founding of order upon

---

[17] Aristotle, *Eudemian Ethics*, VII, x, 5–20; *Nicomachean Ethics*, VIII–IX.
[18] Plato, *Republic, passim*; Zdravko Planinc, *Plato's Political Philosophy: Prudence in the Republic and the Laws* (London, Duckworth, 1991); Adrian Pabst, *Metaphysics: The Creation of Hierarchy* (Grand Rapids, MI, William B. Eerdmans, 2012), 5–112.

the individual subject. On the other hand, towards a new sense of cosmopolitan order appealing beyond legality to the laws of nature and to shared human customs and reciprocities that had never been confined by the merely political. In terms of the notion of *axia* or *dignitas*, one can read this as a postpolitical division between a sheerly inward principle of reserve and a radically exteriorized principle in which 'polity' is newly extended to coincide with cosmos. Stoicism was the philosophy which articulated this split: dividing the ethical between an apathetic indifference of the individual on the one hand, and a dutiful submission to the public demands of *leitourgia* or *officium* on the other.

Cicero's *De Officiis* is fundamentally ambivalent as to the relationship between an internal dignity of reserve or resignation and an external dignity of right action. This book, he said, concerns the lesser wisdom of practical involvement.[19] In that sense, the dignity of office which he discusses would seem to be a dignity of *decus* or of outward fittingness. However, he argues that this is guided by a relatively inward *honestum*. Even though this term itself has etymological connotations of an outwardly facing honour (as Aquinas later emphasizes),[20] as compared with the pure reserve of genuine wisdom, *honestum* is something like a severe adherence to duty.[21] Cicero continues in a traditional way to insist that no genuine *decorum* and even no genuine *utile* can be independent of *honestum*.[22] However, he always protests too much, because he is uneasily aware that he is in danger of splitting the two apart

This ambivalence allows a certain opening towards modern ethical duality. Cicero begins to suppress teleology in favour of a contrast between duty (*officium*) and utility (*utile*). For him, a perfect coincidence of duty with outcome is achieved by the attitude of inward resignation precisely because of its *indifference* towards result. Wisdom fully coincides with the *utile* or 'expedient' because it unites a man with all the vagaries of cosmic fate. To take this stance is implicitly to reject Plato and Aristotle's teleological notion that virtues are habits which tend of themselves to certain outcomes rather than others—and which we may sometimes be forced to follow rather than merely expedient (utilitarian) outcomes.

In this, Cicero already threatened to make subjective right the foundation of political order. His proclamation of the *dignitas* of man (*sic*) as such is an advance over Aristotle insofar as this allows him to begin to envisage the achievement of virtue by all, whatever their roles, and the duty of sympathy

---

[19] Cicero, *On Duties*, III, iv, 15–16.
[20] Thomas Aquinas, *Summa Theologiae*, II. II. q. 145 a. 1; a. 3 resp.
[21] Cicero, *On Duties*, I, xxvii, 93–7.
[22] Cicero, *On Duties*, III, viii, 35.

with man as such. But this comes at the price of an abstraction, which in the long term will lead to empty liberal formalism. Like Aristotle, he allowed that there were pre-political communities involving justice and friendship. He agreed with the Greek philosopher that the basis of these communities lay not just in human beings fulfilling their material needs but also in enjoying friendship. However, unlike Aristotle he declared (no doubt in conditions of increasing international anarchy) that the specific reason for the founding of city-states was the securing of private property.[23] In his insistence on the absoluteness of the latter (later criticized by St Augustine), the general wrongness of theft even in dire need, and the non-commutability of debts, Cicero comes across as proto-liberal and proto-capitalist.[24] His internationalism is already predicated upon a respect for person and property that begins to equate the two. In this instance, the practical translation of the deontological axis of his political thought, as later in the end with Kant, is the sacralization of private ownership. Sacralization, because political duty now refers to property as axiomatic *principium* instead of according property on just and principled lines as granted on certain conditions and in relation to the performance of certain responsibilities.

The Christian mediation between interior and exterior dignity

Following this trajectory, we face the following question: is it possible to affirm the dignity of human beings in universal and yet effectively concrete terms, and thereby to hold together absolute invisible value with specific visible valuation?

In order to do so, one must ensure that citizenry of the *cosmopolis* is not given simply by natural birth outside cultural and political relation. In doing so, Cicero seemed to shift from a concern for ethical character to the givenness of the mere individual and his 'own'. Nevertheless, Christian theology was able to adopt and borrow from Cicero (among other sources) his understanding of character as *persona*. As for Aristotle, Cicero saw 'personhood' as arising in part from universal human nature, in part from natural aptitudes, in part from accorded social role, and in part from habitual personal effort.[25]

In this respect, *persona* in Cicero would seem to mediate between invisible and visible in a way that *dignitas* fails to do. It is therefore fascinating

---

[23] Cicero, *On Duties,* II, xxi, 73; xxii, 78.
[24] Cicero, *On Duties,* II, xxiv, 94; III, vi, 28–31.
[25] Cicero, *On Duties*, I, xxx, 107; xxxii, 115.

to realize that in some medieval texts these two terms become practically synonymous.[26] This implies that now 'axiomatic' value had been accorded to 'personhood', a notion presupposing a merging of universal natural birth with cultural and political birth. And for this in turn to have become possible there had to emerge a political society that understood itself from the outset and intrinsically as cosmopolitan. For then universal citizenry ceases to be merely formal and abstract, without thereby sinking back into the atavistically particular.

This new universal polity was, of course, the *ecclesia*, the Church. Here there was a city without earthly walls in which, in consequence, the network of friendship (agapeic-erotic) is truly open-ended and indeed infinite, even though membership is constituted by an always specific if dynamic and fluctuating (both horizontally and vertically) emplacement. Thus St Ambrose was able to rewrite and qualify Cicero's *De Officiis* in newly ecclesiastical terms.[27]

Through the *ecclesia*, citizenry is now personhood and personhood citizenry: at once cosmic, social, and mystical-liturgical. The dignified status of human existence as such has become 'personal' because we play the role, wear the mask (the original meaning of *persona*) of God, who is himself personal and interpersonal, and in whose image we are created. Aquinas, in contrast to liberal thought which seeks to guarantee universality by reaching for a universal status behind any performed role (the rational human individual, for example), prefers to run with original etymology by conceiving a universal and cosmic drama where the authentic remains the merely assumed. He sustains the close new association of *dignitas* with *persona*, and mediates the notion of dignity by treating the category of *persona* as itself something that analogically shifts between natural and social status. He declares that *persona* originally meant the mask of high-ranking persons in classical plays, then was transferred to mean high-ranking dignitaries in the Church, and was finally applied to the high role played by all human beings. That this exalted status is nevertheless an assumed role is guaranteed by the fact that Aquinas thinks we may legitimately kill those who have effectively surrendered their humanity.[28] As with Aristotle, the ontological remains pragmatic: if we no longer perform human works, then we literally *are not* or are only vestigially human, at least as far as the other human eye can discern.

However, relationship to God as constitutive of the human person can seem to betoken another mode of refusal of outward dignity. If we are to

---

[26] See Lebech, 'What is human dignity?'.

[27] See Mark Jordan, 'Cicero, Ambrose and Aquinas "On Duties", *or* the limits of genre in morals', *Journal of Religious Ethics* 3 (2005), 485–502.

[28] Thomas Aquinas, *Summa Theologiae*, I, q. 29 a. 3 ad 3 and aa 1–3; II.II q. 64 a.2 ad 3; q. 102 aa 1–3.

honour humans as being in the image of God, then surely we are never honouring human beings as such, only God through human beings, and maybe through their most interior aspect of reason. Protestant Christianity has often expressed this sort of idea. But Aquinas refuses it: just as a sign to be a sign must also be something in itself, so also an image to be an image must be a reality in its own right. So if human beings are fit to be in the image of God, then they can be accorded honour for a dignity that they possess in a certain sense as properly their own.[29] The logic of the image therefore tends to integrate invisible and visible dignity; we must first 'stay with' the image in order to 'pass through' it to God.

Moreover, the notion of iconicity that is here involved disallows the disjunction of inward reason from outer corporeality through which character shines forth: each person in their face and body radiates a scintilla of the divine wisdom. In concrete terms, this means that a messy, suffering, human body can be in an evil-suffused world the most potent witness to human dignity. Or the dignity with pathos of the innocent, wondering, receptive child. (It is extraordinary that Michael Rosen thinks that children do not possess dignity when their unselfconsciousness ensures they can possess it far more naturally than can adults.[30])

This sense of personhood and dignity as the performing of a role, whether cosmic or cultural, continues in the Christian tradition, lying notably at the heart of Pico della Mirandola's treatise, posthumously entitled *Oration on the Dignity of Man*.[31] It is erroneous to imagine that this work pre-announces a modern liberal constructivism, because its entire *topos* and conclusions are all anticipated in writings of the Church Fathers. Humanity is a *Proteus*: lacking any specific attribute of his own, his specificity is paradoxically to combine in himself, at the centre of the cosmos, the material, animate and spiritual, along with the ruling, knowing, and loving functions of the three angelic orders of the Thrones, Cherubim, and Seraphim. Between all these attributes he is free to choose. This is in part indeed a matter of creative construction with respect to the operation of natural magic, but herein our co-creation with God is as much a matter of discovery as invention, as we both shape and release hidden natural powers. This 'Renaissance' dimension of Pico's work is itself unfolded in wholly orthodox Catholic terms, but at the heart of human choice lies for him a more traditional selection of our destiny among pre-given locations. Our real dignity is our capacity to elect to be united in the love of the

---

[29] Thomas Aquinas, *Summa Theologiae*, II.II. q. 101, a.3 ad 3.
[30] Rosen, *Dignity*, 77.
[31] Giovanni Pico della Mirandola, *Oration on the Dignity of Man*, trans. Francesco Borghesis et al. (Cambridge, Cambridge University Press, 2012).

Cherubim to God. And while this is our highest destiny, it can in reality only be granted to us by God as an act of grace.

So for Pico, human dignity lies finally in the divinely gracious gift. Dignity is something that we are granted, that we have borrowed. Since we do not possess dignity in ourselves or because of any inalienable property, it would seem questionable, for this outlook, to locate dignity in the conception of a human being as 'an end in itself', as does Kant. By contrast, for Christian tradition, human beings as divine images are more fundamentally means for other human beings to pass with them but also through them to God. Nor are we ends to ourselves, but rather destined for the contemplation of God, while the human race as a whole is a means first to display and then to restore the divine glory.

As in the case of right divorced from status, it can seem that the Kantian conception is far more likely to secure human dignity than any notion which confines human beings to means, in however refined a way. Is not Kant ensuring that human beings can never be treated as commodities or instruments? But to the contrary, the idea of the human being as in himself a dignified *principium*, a first and final reality, is merely the reverse aspect of the reduction of everything, including human beings *qua* workers, to commodity status. For the fungibility of *everything else* requires that the owning subject be absolutely non-fungible, non-exchangeable, entirely free for the mere sake of freedom, in order that his property-owning be freed of every condition, however honourable. The human subject who can never be treated as a means to an end that exceeds him is a subject that transcends all shared social purpose, but a subject that *qua* occupier of a social office can be (along with the commodified material earth) *all the more exploited* if ethics cannot be concerned with the discrimination of appropriate and inappropriate mediations which human beings can perform and be subject to.

An inheritance: corporatism *and* personalism

This emphasis on the dignity of role, understood in terms of personhood, continued through to Catholic social teaching in the nineteenth century, and still continues to this day. Indeed, this continuation could be described as a complementary union of corporatism and personalism.

It is wrong to say that Catholic corporatism contained no personalist dimension, or that the dignity of the group was entirely disconnected from the dignity of the person (even in the nineteenth century). Moyn is right that Catholic thought during the 1930s and the 1940s gradually moved from a corporatist stress on the dignity of groups (notably in its fascist version) to a personalist stress on the dignity of the individual.[32] Nevertheless, it would have been impossible to speak of the dignity of labour, in the nineteenth-century corporatist mode, without invoking the dignity of the human person. The dignity of labour announces that labour is an authentic way to be human—not to be a labourer, which would be tautologous.

The dignity of the human being as such was less spoken of in this era. This is because neo-Thomistic thought, in keeping with both Aristotle and Aquinas, did not think of human universality as something that could be atomically and empirically instanced as an abstract property that is literally the same and equal in all. Such is the approach of liberalism, tending towards valuing the person as an abstract bearer of free will. Rather, 'human' was understood as something always analogically differentiated in various conditions of life, including diversity of gender, talent, and ascribed and elected social role. In other words, Catholic social teaching realistically considered that it would be vacuous to focus in practice on the dignity and rights of human beings as such, and not on the several dignities of human being in their various functions as they actually are in the specifically modern world.

In respect of any consequent shift towards personalism, corporatism may have been more muted in Catholic social teaching and practice since the Second World War, but it has never gone away. In recent papal social teaching, the stress on the vocational and its (non-liberal) political relevance has been paramount. The doctrine of subsidiarity remains corporatist, since it seeks to devolve central sovereign powers to groups which are vocational as well as voluntary, with groups regarded as interlocking in function and as contributing to the flourishing of the political whole.

Further, and contra Rosen, Catholic social thought has never abandoned its predication upon metaphysical and social hierarchy. Subsidiarity is clearly a hierarchical doctrine, since it teaches that political, social, and economic functions should be fulfilled at the most appropriate levels, and preferably at the lowest ones. Such a conception assumes that there is a socio-political pyramid with rule at the top only authenticated by its guardianship of the common good under both divine grant and popular assent. (Derivation only from the latter, as with liberalism, has *never* been papally conceded.)

Indeed, we have never abolished and *could* never abolish dignity as hierarchical status in favour of dignity as equal human worth based on right. To try to do so is instead to give more worth to the ever more worthless. It remains a mystery to our media commentators and to many academics that Britain, since

---

[32] Samuel Moyn, Chapter 4, this volume.

the 1950s, has become less deferential, yet more economically and socially unequal. They are unable to see the obvious: namely that a collapse in deferential respect for the dignity of representative status and virtuous achievement *necessarily* results in increased inequality because *axia* will not tolerate a vacuum: where worth is no longer regarded, only money retains any value.

Against this, we can only acclaim human dignity as universal human talent and capacity for wisdom, love, and grace, and seek to elevate all in these respects, if we accord also more honour to those in whom these things are more expressed and realized, and diverse honours to the diverse but equally necessary modes of living dignified lives. To do so is the precondition for requiring that those so honoured go on giving to the community, in every sense, more than is expected from others.

Personalism and corporatism have, accordingly, always been complementary rather than in tension with each other. The simple core of corporatism, at one with Christian political thinking, entails a rejection of the separation of political from socio-economic powers. To nurture the person one must nurture social groups and economic vocations. In order to widen personal political participation or democracy, one must ensure that every individual can exercise political influence through the workplace and with those with whom he shares a common purpose.

It might seem as if stressing the dignity of a person's role would run the danger of subordinating her to her function for the social organism. However, the Aristotelian and Thomistic tradition, inherited through Catholic social teaching, defines the purpose of the social and political whole as securing reciprocal justice and the always specific virtuous flourishing of each of its members. Indeed, one can turn the tables on liberalism here: if we mainly respect a man as a man *per se*, then this formalism can readily turn out to be compatible with all and every exploitation of him *qua* worker, son, father, and so on. In consequence, these functions do indeed get reduced to merely instrumental functions of a machinic totality. Functions cease to be personally infused if, with false idealism and piety, we try to divorce personhood from function or, better, from 'role'.

We are left then with a final question: How is one to square these conclusions with the very evident embrace of liberal democracy by the Catholic Church and the papacy since the Second World War?

Three comments are in order here: first, there is a genuine and valid recognition that liberalism does, indeed, especially given a poor degree of consent about the common good, afford some protection against the worst intrusions upon the freedoms of some by the freedom of others. It is mature and balanced to say that liberalism offers a certain political good, but that this remains insufficient. Second, modern Catholicism tends to read individual rights in personalist terms, which regard the individual not in isolation but as the most basic rung in a subsidiarist vision that is in continuity with older distributist notions. What an individual can do for herself, own for herself, grow for herself, make for herself, she should. Inversely, she should be able to appeal against an oppressive group, just as a group has the right to appeal against an oppressive higher body and ultimately the state. The state itself should sometimes kenotically reach down to protect the individual person against the group, or smaller groups against greater ones, as in the protection of small businesses against greater ones and against monopoly. This was traditionally the populist argument for the need for monarchy as against merely aristocratic power: the One must sometimes defend the Many against the virtuous Few turned corruptly oligarchic.

But the third comment is to recognize that indeed some Vatican II documents did concede too much to liberal democracy.[33] This was understandable, given the reaction to totalitarianism and the apparently optimistic prospects for this ideology in the early 1960s. Neither the growth of a brutal economic neoliberalism, nor the rise of a cultural liberalism that would eventually threaten the very character of our shared human existence was envisaged. It is, however, clear that papal and the most sophisticated academic Catholic thought has gradually backed away from this excessive embrace.

At times, papal and other Catholic writings seem to adopt the language of rights in liberal, Kantian terms, which would suggest a grounding in autonomy, with dignity redundant as ground if also invoked as a supplement. This results sometimes in contorted attempts to defend the unborn and the dying in terms of a rights-talk that is predicated upon the autonomy of the adult human. (And it has to be added here that sometimes a rights perspective leads bizarrely to an *excessive* conservatism in these areas, which is more restrictive than the usual medieval positions—for example with respect to abortion.) However, perhaps more frequently, rights are fortunately so qualified by the modern Catholic Church as scarcely to mean rights in the modern sense at all.[34] They are deemed to correlate with the equally foundational duties of others, or else to coincide with equally foundational obligations of the rights-holder. One is led to the view that, in the face of the dominance of the human rights agenda

---

[33] See Tracey Rowlands, *Culture and the Thomist Tradition after Vatican II* (London, Routledge, 2002).

[34] See the ongoing discussion in Zachary R. Calo, 'Catholic social thought, political liberalism and the idea of human rights', *Journal of Christian Legal Thought* (Fall, 2011), 1; Christopher McCrudden, 'Legal and Roman Catholic conceptions of human rights: convergence, divergence and dialogue?', *Oxford Journal of Law and Religion* 1 (2012), 185–201.

(and the frequently noble causes that it espouses), the Catholic Church tends apparently to adopt it, but in reality smuggles in ancient objective *ius* under the guise of modern subjective right. In substantive terms this means that it is indeed allowed that one can have a legitimate subjective claim to an objective *ius*, but not that such a *ius* is *ever* derived from human self-willing alone, even if the adjudication of rights accords (as did Aquinas, and more than Aristotle) such a capacity a high moral and legal relevance.[35]

The essential continuity of modern Catholic social teaching suggests that the alliance of rights with dignity, adopted after 1948 but arguably now under question, is an unnatural one. For if before 1948 secular rights discourse almost never mentioned dignity, then equally Catholic dignity discourse scarcely mentioned rights in the modern subjective sense. It follows that perhaps the most crucial remaining question mark over the post-war liberal-tending legacy in Catholic thought remains to do with human rights. In reality, the rejection of liberalism by Catholic thought with respect to issues of life, death, sexuality and gender does not indicate a residual disagreement with liberalism in just these areas, nor a 'different' Catholic understanding of subjective right, but rather exposes to view the fact that Catholicism, and its development of 'dignity', remains at bottom incompatible with liberal notions of rights and democracy. The Catholic Church would be far better able to explain itself, and to explain the genuine core radicalism (after some needed theoretical pruning) of its positions in these areas, if it consistently abandoned rights in favour of dignity and criticized the abuses of justice consequent upon the hegemony of rights with respect to more political and economic issues also. This would expose to view what has always secretly been the case: that 'rights' and 'dignity' stand for two radically opposed political philosophies, and indeed for the two *most* opposed political philosophies: the politics of the moderns and the politics of the ancients.

---

[35] See John Milbank, 'Against human rights: liberty in the Western tradition', *Oxford Journal of Law and Religion* 1 (2012), 203–34.

Part III

Theological Perspectives

11

Dignity, Person, and *Imago Trinitatis*

James Hanvey

THEOLOGICAL REFLECTION comes to the theme of dignity with a long, complex, and rich tradition of understanding.[1] Theology can never be a purely speculative science; it is always ordered to the historical existence and witness of the Church. For this reason, tradition is as much about change and development as it is about continuity and conservation. This can be seen in the way in which the understanding of human dignity has been even more explicitly part of the Church's teaching through the cultural changes of the nineteenth and twentieth centuries, especially the atrocities which mark the latter and still continue.

In this chapter, I wish to explore key aspects of theological discourse on dignity as it occurs in the Catholic tradition. While acknowledging that in a book chapter this must be indicative rather than exhaustive, my hope is that it will help to illuminate the Catholic understanding of dignity and hence the various ways in which is conceptually deployed and realized in practice. Whether we accept that human dignity has any meaning or not, or we believe that other concepts can do a better job with fewer philosophical commitments and less metaphysical pain, we all acknowledge that it is a concept that we cannot ignore. Its importance does not lie so much in its articulation but in its personal, social, and political use. It is one of those concepts or beliefs which shapes our lives and relationships, and therein lies our need to understand the significance of its meaning and appeal.[2]

Two preliminary observations by way of an apologia may be in order.

---

[1] For a useful general overview of the different 'frameworks' (Charles Taylor) and phenomenological exploration of the history and meaning of 'dignity' across differing fields of discourse, see Mette Lebech, *On the Problem of Human Dignity: A Hermeneutical and Phenomenological Investigation* (Würzburg, Königshausen, & Neumann, 2009); also *Human Dignity and Bioethics:Essays Commissioned by the President's Council on Bioethics* (Washington DC, The President's Council on Bioethics, March 2008).

[2] See Jack Mahoney, *The Challenge of Human Rights* (Oxford, Blackwell Publishing, 2007), 144ff.

The problem of translation

We have become familiar with the terms 'Church' and 'religion', but if they are used as purely social or political descriptors they tend to distort rather than illuminate. We may feel that we have named a reality, but that does not necessarily mean that we have understood it. Indeed, our naming may block understanding or translate realities into systems that are strategies of conceptual if not social and political subjugation. When religion is translated into a secular framework of thought, it is named, but it is also given a particular understanding from within that system which may or may not bear much relationship to the life and the experience of those who live and create it. Indeed, the naming may well be a conscious elimination—demythologization—of those things which in fact sustain the life. The same may be the case when religion reads the secular. This is even more complex when we come to concepts that are used across many different discourses and are embedded in histories and systems of thought and practice. Such is the case with dignity.

The way in which dignity has been deployed across a wide field of discourses, at least in Western cultures, it seems principally, but not always, to be attached in some way to the idea of the human. One usually does not have to probe very far behind arguments about dignity to find a deeper argument (and assumptions) about what it means to be human and the relationships, entitlements, rights, and responsibilities that might follow from this. It is at this level that Catholic theology is a significant critical voice. It performs a dual purpose: internally, it expresses the logic of the believing community's faith to itself, testing its coherence and exploring the frontiers of its experience of the reality it names God in and through its own historical existence. In this way the community of faith, the Church, holds itself accountable to the truth it believes itself to have received and desires to live. As well as helping to mediate the faith of the community to cultures which do not share or understand its faith, theology also mediates to the community the sources of knowledge, critique, insight, or wisdom which it finds in cultures as well. At its best, this mediation is not a one-sided apologetics but a genuine dialogue, which allows itself to be shaped not only by the knowledge of what it brings but also by the understanding it discovers and receives from others. In this activity, all parties need to be aware of their hermeneutical commitments and horizons.

A life-world

Roman Catholicism is not a movement, an idea, or an institution; it is a world. For all its institutional form and swagger, it is a complex, dynamic, universal, and personal reality which extends in history. It understands itself to be a Church, which means that it does not see itself as self-founding. Rather, it understands itself to be 'gathered' by the Holy Spirit that it may not only participate in the life of Christ—whom it believes to be risen and active in all history—but from whom it has received its mission to make him known. This mission is not one of a political or cultural imperialism, although in different centuries it has unfortunately been co-opted to these designs; it is essentially one of service.[3] Insofar as the love of God is inseparable from the love of neighbour, the Church is at the service of the whole of humanity; it is not conditional upon having faith in Christ or belonging to the Church. Its service is not only practical but also intellectual: it is concerned that humanity should understand its own nature, meaning, and purpose, with a view to creating societies and cultures where all men and women can flourish.

There are two dimensions to this mission which are not easily understood, and can lead to misunderstanding about the responsibility the Church has to the integrity of its own discourse and the creativity which is required by fidelity to the revelation which it believes it holds. First, the Church does not believe that it is the master (or mistress) of its own speech. It is always accountable to God, to the community, and to the world to which it has to speak about this God.[4] Second, if the understanding of God which it possesses is true, if God has become human in Jesus of Nazareth, and if this Jesus is risen from the dead, and if the Spirit of God is now given as God's own witness to himself in Christ, then we cannot look upon the world with the same eyes and understanding as someone who does not have this knowledge in faith. It is not so much that we inhabit different worlds, but our understanding of it, its limits and possibilities, its meaning and purpose will be radically different. How then to think and speak of this new reality? How are we changed by it? So, the Church is constantly engaged in constructing a metaphysics of the Incarnation and hence a metaphysics of the human person and all that this entails. It understands this to be an impossible task, but it is also one that is generative and compels an engagement with other ontological and epistemological systems. This is to say nothing about whether it is engaged upon the most creative intellectual, imaginative, and spiritual adventure, or if it is a presumptive 'foolishness upon stilts'. We will not understand what dignity might mean in the Catholic theological tradition if we do not appreciate its

---

[3] The pastoral constitution of the Church in the modern world (Gaudium et Spes), Vatican Two, Decrees of The Ecumenical Councils, vol. 2, ed. Norman P. Tanner, SJ (Washington DC and London, Sheed and Ward and Georgetown University Press, 1990) §40ff.

[4] *Donum veritatis. The ecclesial vocation of the theologian* (The Congregation for the Doctrine of the Faith, Vatican, 1990).

metaphysical context. In other words, 'human dignity' stands within a tradition of thought which shapes its understanding. Although it will have many features in common with other ways in which it is thought, it will nevertheless be developed and changed in the light of Christian faith. If we are to understand how human dignity is used and the range of meanings it might have within the discourse, we need to be attentive not only to its own internal logic or grammar but to how it is historically situated. When this does not happen, then there is a danger of misunderstanding—sometimes serious misunderstanding—and consequently the loss of the subsequent goods that genuine dialogue may bring. I think this danger is present in two recent stimulating and influential treatments of dignity.

In different degrees and with different sensibilities, both Michael Rosen and Jeremy Waldron recognize the significance of Catholic thought in understanding human dignity.[5] However, neither attempts to situate the use of dignity within the tradition of Catholic philosophical and theological discourse. Briefly, we may take Rosen as a good example of the difficulties we have been identifying.

To frame his discussion, Rosen argues that dignity typically has three ways of being understood: as social position, as intrinsic value, not restricted to human beings, and as a value which belongs particularly to human beings. The third he largely attributes to Kant, but he strangely attributes the second to Aquinas, which he then takes to be the Catholic position. Leaving aside Rosen's interpretation of Kant, which I think is insightful, he bases his reading of Aquinas on one text from Thomas's *Commentary on the Sentences* to the effect that 'dignity signifies something's good on account of itself'.[6] He understands this in terms of the intrinsic value which gives a thing its place in creation. But one text from the *Sentences* seems a slim base on which to rest the reading, not only of Aquinas on human dignity but that of the whole Catholic tradition.

Aquinas mentions 'dignity' or its cognate at least 1,760 times in his writings.[7] It certainly is a way of speaking about intrinsic value, but it is not used

---

[5] Michael Rosen, *Dignity: Its History and Meaning* (Cambridge, MA, Harvard University Press, 2012). Jeremy Waldron, *Dignity, Rank, and Rights*, ed. Mier Dan-Cohen. (Oxford, Oxford University Press, 2012). In this chapter I concentrate on Rosen's presentation of Catholic thought on dignity because it offers the better illustration of how the tradition can be inadequately read.
[6] Rosen, *Dignity*, 16–17.
[7] Servais Pinckaers, 'Aquinas on the dignity of the human person', in John Berkman and Craig Steven Titus (eds), *The Pinckaers Reader, Renewing Thomistic Moral Theology* (Washington DC, Catholic University of American Press. 2005) Original essay, '*La dignité de l'homme selon Saint Thomas d'Aquin*' *Dignitate Hominis* (Freiburg im Breisgau, Verlag Herder, 1987), 144–63. Citing R. Busa, 146. My debt to Pinckaers in treating of this theme in Aquinas will be obvious.

in the undifferentiated way asserted by Rosen. He seems unaware of the ways in which Aquinas grounds the dignity in an ontology of the human person received in terms of the theology of the Trinity. In its highest and most complete use it applies to God, but it is an especial quality of the human person—*'persona est nomen dignitatis'*.[8] Moreover, Rosen fails to notice that there is a dynamic and moral aspect to dignity in Thomas's treatment which becomes significantly developed in the transcendental Thomism of theologians such as Joseph Maréchal. This combines with the recovery of patristic sources, particularly through the ressourcement movement, to produce a creative philosophical and theological anthropology which informs Catholic thinking and the Church's engagement with the contemporary secular world.[9] As a result, even though Rosen claims to be offering a history of dignity and its meaning, he fails to appreciate the way in which dignity is used within Catholic discourse, leaving many significant aspects unexplored, even when they might benefit his own thesis.[10]

That Rosen has his own a priori reading of the Catholic tradition becomes evident in his treatment of Pope Leo XIII and John Paul II. For example, without regard to the historical context of the argument, he selects a text from Leo XIII's *Quod Apostolici Muneris* (1878) to illustrate the anti-egalitarian use of dignity which appears to characterize Catholic thought.[11] To this end,

---

[8] I Sent. 10.1.5. also *Summa Theologiae* 1 29 a 3ad 2 in the context of the appropriateness of speaking of God as a 'person', 'Et quia magnae dignitatis est in rationali natura subsistere, ideo omne individuum rationalis naturae dicitur persona, ut dictum est. Sed dignitas divinae naturae excedit omnem dignitatem, et secundum hoc maxime competit Deo nomen personae.'

[9] On the recovery of the patristic sources, in addition to Henri de Lubac's seminal, *Catholisime* (Paris, Cerf. 1937), see Jean Mouroux's *Sens chrétien de l'homme* (Paris, Aubier, 1945). For a comprehensive treatment of ressourcement and its impact see *Ressourcement, A Movement for Renewal in Twentieth Century Catholic Theology*, ed. Gabriel Flynn and Paul D. Murray (Oxford, Oxford University Press, 2012).

[10] Cf. Aquinas, *Summa Theologiae* I–II, 85. The difference between Catholic and Protestant prelapsarian anthropologies has a significant effect upon the thinkers of Protestant Enlightenment, for example Hobbes and Kant.

[11] Rosen, *Dignity*, 48. It may be helpful here to make the distinction between intrinsic and extrinsic uses of 'dignity': a distinction which is already present in Cicero's uses, that is, that which is common to all men and marks them out from animals, and that which belongs to a particular role or individual excellence. The former applies to that which is inviolable and inalienable and the latter to social differentiation, rank, and office, hence responsibility. It is clear, even from the text which is quoted, that Leo is defending the 'dignity' of particular roles and offices in society. This is within the context of the social and political revolutions of the nineteenth century and the Church's opposition to socialism, communism, and certain ways of understanding democracy. Its basic objection to the theory of democracy lies in the source of power and hence accountability. The Church rejects the view that the ultimate source of power and political legitimacy is the people rather than God, whose laws, accessible through reason and natural law, even governments are obliged to obey. Rosen misses the significance of personalist and neo-Thomist movements on Catholic social thought, especially in the area of the

Rosen wants to attribute an anti-egalitarian position to Catholicism. It is significant that Rosen misses the encyclical's use of this sort of distinction a few paragraphs before his quotation, where the equality is strongly affirmed: 'the equality of men consists in this: that all, having inherited the same nature, are called to the same most high dignity of the sons of God, and that, as one and the same end is set before all, each one is to be judged by the same law and will receive punishment or reward according to his deserts'.[12] This is a comprehensive statement of equality, but especially of ultimate accountability in which responsibilities and corresponding rights may be applied. Rosen does not discuss the considerable arguments against slavery and in favour of social and economic justice mounted by Leo XIII in other writings which are developed out of the same understanding of dignity. This is especially in evident in *Rerum Novarum*, where 'the inviolable right to innate dignity of the individual person was the principle underlying the whole encyclical'.[13] There is a similar problem with Rosen's use of texts from John Paul II. I think this lack of an attentive critical engagement is a loss for both sides, but especially for

---

meaning of 'person', which allows Catholicism and Catholic thinkers to play such a significant role in the formulation of the Universal Declaration of Human Rights and in the German Grundgesetz. For the latter, the role of figures such as Konrad Adenauer is recognized, but for Jacques Maritain's influences see Edward M. Andries, 'On the German Constitution's fiftieth anniversary: Jacques Maritain and the 1949 Basic Law (Grundgesetz)', *Emory International Law Review* 13 (1999), 1–76.

[12] *Quod Apostolici Muneris* §5. The encyclical deals with the claims of socialism, communism, and nihilism, which are seen as political and social threats as well as philosophical challenges. It is part of Leo XIII's extensive programme to balance social order which must ultimately be accountable to the Divine Law entailing the common good with the requirements of political and economic justice. Here, Divine Law should be read not only in terms of Revelation but in terms of the whole natural law tradition, and especially in the significant body of political theory developed not only from Thomism but also in the Salamanca school, to name but two influential sources. The Encyclical aims to correct and refute the 'socialists' use of the *imago Dei* to conclude that 'no respect or honour' is owed to public authority and that laws have no claim other than by consent. One also needs to exercise considerable caution in applying contemporary political understands to the nineteenth-century movements. On the significance of the School of Salamanca in political and economic thought, see André Azevedo Alves and José Manuel Moreira, *The Salamanca School* (New York and London, Continuum, 2010). For a study of the way in which the question of political authority and rights—even the right to overthrow a tyrant—has developed in Catholic political thought, see Harold E. Braun, *Juan de Mariana and Early Modern Spanish Political Thought* (Aldershot, Ashgate, 2007), and Harro Höpfl, *Jesuit Political Thought, The Society of Jesus and the State 1540–1630* (Cambridge, Cambridge University Press, 2004).

[13] John Molony and David Thompson, 'Christian social thought', in Sheridan Gilley and Brian Stanley (eds), *Cambridge History of Christianity*, vol. 8: *World Christianities 1815–1914* (Cambridge, Cambridge University Press, 2006), 150. See also the encyclicals *In Plurimus* (1888), Catholicae *Ecclesiae* (1890), and especially *Graves Communi* (1901) for a more nuanced and accurate understanding of the nineteenth-century Church's position regarding egalitarianism than is provided by Rosen. See Paul Misner, *Social Catholicism in Europe* (New York, Crossroads Publishing Company, 1991), for a treatment of these themes and the development of Catholicism's developing positions in their historical context.

Rosen's own proposal that dignity is 'the sense of being treated with respect for one's humanity'.[14] This seems to be a precarious exhortation to some quasi-mystical notion, a '*Gefühl*'. Essentially, it leaves unanswered and largely unexamined the very premise on which it is based, that is, humanity. Yet this is the substance of the Catholic tradition.[15]

Person and *imago Dei*: *imago Trinitatis*

It is clear that the Catholic understanding and use of 'dignity' is grounded in an ontology of the human person.[16] The most complete statement of this position is in the documents of Vatican II, especially *Gaudium et Spes* and *Dignitatis Humanae*.[17] They represent a development not only contained in *Pacem et Terris*, the encyclical of John XXIII, but which also can be traced in the wartime radio addresses of Pius XII.[18]

Disputes about the Catholic position and the arguments it draws from dignity are actually disputes not only about its ontology but about whether

---

[14] Rosen, *Dignity*, 157. Rosen seeks to find a role for dignity which is not dependent upon God or what he calls Platonism—'timelessly valuable things to which we must act with respect or reverence' (156). He fails to appreciate that Catholic thought on dignity not only offers theological reasons but reasons that can, I believe, function independently of theological premises but are developed on the basis of an analysis of the intrinsic value of the human person which is part of the position that Aquinas wishes to establish. Non-Catholic readers of the discourse forget that Catholicism not only argues from faith but also from reason, especially through its natural law traditions.

[15] See Thomas Nagel, 'The taste for being moral', *New York Review of Books* 59:19 (6 December 2012), 40–2.

[16] For a useful examination of the Catholic tradition on Human Rights grounded in the notion of human dignity see Walter Kasper, 'The theological foundations of human rights', *The Jurist* 50 (1990) 148–66; also Michael Novak, 'The Judeo-Christian foundations of human dignity, personal liberty and the concept of the person', *Journal of Markets and Morality* 1:2 (October 1998), 107–21, but note that Novak does not distinguish the Protestant and Catholic approaches and their different theologies of the impact of sin upon the *imago* and human freedom. This is critical for understanding why the two approaches are developed in different ways. On the difference between Protestant and Catholic understandings of the *imago Dei* see Josef Fuchs, SJ, *Natural Law: A Theological Investigation*, trans. Helmut Reckter SJ and John A. Dowling (Dublin, Gill and Son, 1965), 59ff. On the significant shifts in the reformers' reading and the consequences that they drew see Heiko A. Oberman, 'The pursuit of happiness: Calvin between Humanism and Reformation', in John O'Malley et al. (eds), *Humanity and Divinity in Renaissance and Reformation: Essays in Honor of Charles Trinkaus* (Leiden, E. J. Brill, 1993), 262–74.

[17] Tanner, Ecumenical Councils, vol. 2. *Gaudium et Spes*, §12ff Note that there are several different usages of 'dignity' even within the Constitution, for example 'The dignity of marriage' §47; *Dignitatis Humanae* (On Religious Freedom) §1–3, 9–12.

[18] See The Church and Human Rights, Working Paper no. 1, 2nd edn, Pontifical Commission Iustitia et Pax (Vatican City, Typis Polyglottis Vaticanis, 2011), especially 15–27. Also International Theological Commission, *The Dignity and Rights of the Human Person* (Vatican, 1983).

ontology is possible at all. However, if dignity is not to be grounded in an ontology of the person, what is to prevent it simply being reduced to contingent social and cultural values which can be quickly manipulated? If dignity is a way of marking rank and worth, who decides how, when, and to whom or what it is to be applied? Legal provision is precarious at best, evidenced by the infamous ruling of the American Supreme Court on the status of Dred Scott in 1857. It is but one classic example, but many contemporary examples could also be cited. The grounding of dignity in the ontology of person is, therefore, an attempt to protect the value of all human beings and of holding all societies accountable.[19]

The most common theological route to an understanding of dignity is through the idea of the *imago Dei*—'the image and likeness of the Divine with which each human being is endowed'.[20] This is based on the text from Genesis 1.26. Given Judaism's prohibition against any images of the Divine, it is a most remarkable text that already signals the status of the human person within the created order.[21] It immediately links humanity and God in the most intimate of relationships. Not only is the human person summoned to honour and reverence the *imago Dei* manifest in the whole person (body and soul), but anyone who destroys or degrades another human being is also dishonouring or committing sacrilege against God. It is not difficult to see how for both Judaism and Christianity the *imago Dei* establishes the unique ontology of the human person and also allows each tradition to develop a rich understanding of responsibilities and duties towards oneself and others.[22]

Undoubtedly foundational, in discussions on human dignity the text of Genesis has difficulties. The *imago Dei* tends to be read and interpreted as if it is understood in the same way by all religious traditions. This is clearly not the case: as the history of the discourse shows, the Christian reading develops into the *imago Trinitatis*. Not only does this distinguish it from Islam and Judaism but it also provides an anthropology with different potentials. While the *imago* remains foundational and normative, other ontological arguments have been

---

[19] Oskar Negt argues that Cicero was the first to make this move in order to provide a stable ground of accountability or duty in a time when he believed his society to be in crisis. See 'The unrepeatable: changes in the cultural concept of dignity', in Regina Ammicht-Quinn et al. (eds), 'The discourse of human dignity', *Concilium* 2 (2003), 25–34, 27–8.

[20] See *Gaudium et Spes*, §12–19; 'The Church and human dignity', 37–45; Kasper, *Theological Foundations*, 153–4.

[21] For a detailed discussion of the relevant scriptural texts see G. W. Randall, *In His own Image and Likeness, Humanity, Divinity and Monthesism* (Leiden, Brill, 2003).

[22] From the Jewish perspective, see Y. Michael Barilan, 'From imago dei in the Jewish-Christian tradition to human dignity in contemporary Jewish law', *Kennedy Institute of Ethics Journal* 19:3 (2009), 231–59.

developed out of the nature of the human person in itself. Moreover, within the Christian tradition these anthropologies have significant differences, especially on the consequences of sin for the *imago*. This has consequences for the ways in which theological and practical responses to the loss, preservation, and defence of dignity are worked out.

Imago Trinitatis: towards ontology of the dignity of the human person

It was the Roman lawyer Tertullian who gave the West its formula for expressing the Christian idea of a Trinitarian God: *una substantia, tres personae*.[23] As Joseph Ratzinger notes, 'it was here that the word "person" entered intellectual history with its full weight for the first time'.[24] However, it is Augustine who is the most significant thinker for our purposes. If much of the contemporary discussion of human dignity develops from Renaissance thinkers, their recovery of the Augustinian tradition of the *imago Dei* 'offered a possibility for a renewed conception of the dignity of man, of man as a god on earth and not as an object of nature'.[25]

Augustine's insight was to see that the *imago Dei* of Genesis had now to be read as the *imago Trinitatis* if Christian revelation was to be coherent. In exploring the full radical implications of this coherence, he was to open up a new chapter in philosophical and theological anthropology which was dominant in the West until comparatively recent times. His opus on the Trinity (*De Trinitate*) is Augustine's masterclass in logic, philosophical speculation, and biblical hermeneutics.[26] Yet from the beginning, Augustine conceived it as a

---

[23] *Adversus Praxean* 2 3–7. Tertullian, edited with an introduction, translation, and commentary by Ernest Evans (London, SPCK, 1948). Part of the problem with the use of 'person' in theology is that it has different meanings when it refers to the Trinity and to human beings. The use must be analogical; if it is used univocally then one produces tritheism rather than a Trinity. This problem with the highly specialized use of 'person' with regard to the Trinity is recognized by two major influential thinkers in contemporary theology: Karl Barth, *Church Dogmatics*, vol. 1 §9.2. ET (Edinburgh, T. & T. Clark, 2009), and Karl Rahner, *The Trinity* III. E. trans. Joseph Donceel (London, Burns and Oates, 1970).

[24] Joseph Ratzinger, 'Concerning the notion of person in theology', *Communio: International Catholic Review* 17 (1990), 439–54, at 440.

[25] Charles Trinkaus, 'In our image and likeness. humanity and dignity', in *Italian Humanist Thought*, vol. 1 (Chicago, University of Chicago Press, 1970), 119.

[26] For an excellent treatment of Augustine's approach to the Trinity see Lewis Ayres, 'Augustine's Trinitarian theology', in *Augustine and His Critics*, ed. Robert Dodaro and George Lawless (London, Routledge, 2000), 51–76; also M. R. Barnes, 'Re-reading Augustine's theology of the Trinity', in S. T. Davies, D. Kendall, and G. O'Collins (eds), *The Trinity: An Interdisciplinary Symposium on the Doctrine of the Trinity* (Oxford, Oxford University Press, 1999).

search whose outcome could only be tentative. Indeed, in Book 15, reviewing the fruits of his intellectual labours, he critiques them as inadequate.[27] The significance for our discussion lies in Book 8. The first seven books are devoted to an exploration and defence of the logical and creedal coherence of the Christian belief in God as Trinity. In Book 8 he sets out on a more radical path. If Christian revelation is true, and God is a Trinity and the human person is made in the image of God, then we must in some way be able to discover the *imago Trinitatis* in the human person. If we cannot, then the coherence of revelation and its truth become questionable. Working with the Trinitarian formula articulated by Tertullian (one God in three 'persons'—Augustine is happy to admit the problematic nature of 'person' in this context), he explores various triads that also describe some sort of unity. They all fall short of the logic that the doctrine of the Trinity demands. Finally, he settles upon the least unsatisfactory, namely, the famous human trinity of 'memory, understanding and will' (*memoria, intelligentia, voluntas*).[28] This opens the way for a new Christian anthropology which subsequent centuries will develop.

There are two critical aspects of Augustine's treatment which need to be remembered if we are not to misread him. The first concerns mind. Why he regards memory, understanding, and will as strong candidates is because they are the actions of the one mind. They do not constitute three independent subjects but are a dynamic relational action in which and through which mind manifests itself.[29] To borrow a term from later scholastic thought, mind subsists in the action of memory, understanding, and will.

For Augustine, memory is not just recall of the past but the way in which the world is represented to us interiorly so that it may be known.[30] Here, as elsewhere, he is relying upon the Neo-Platonist tradition but also shaping it to Christian needs. If memory is the capacity we have to know, then our understanding is our ordering to know Truth, and our will is our ordering in freedom to act in our choice of the Good. Love is a central governing interior power for Augustine, and our understanding and will, indeed our whole being, is directed by love: knowing and willing is a loving of the true, the good, and the

---

[27] *De Trinitate*, Bk XV. 6, 10ff.
[28] As well as the need to find some 'imago' of the Trinity in the human person, Augustine's search for suitable analogies is also constrained by a logical need, namely, finding ways of adequately representing unity and multiplicity through God's simplicity.
[29] Augustine's discovery of the relational nature of 'persons' in the Trinity (*De Trinitate*, Book V, 5.6–7) is not sufficiently emphasized in many standard treatments, which are too much influenced by older and now untenable critiques of his Trinitarian theology as stressing the unity of God over the Trinity.
[30] See Augustine, *Confessions*, Book X. For Augustine, Memory is a sort of 'Chora'—a great source of ideas, images and emotions and, in some sense, the origin and possibility of our knowing and loving. Hence it stands as an image of the mystery of the Father.

beautiful. It is a mistake to think of Augustine working with a static ontology. It is part of his creative genius responding to the intelligibility of Revelation to see essence (*substantia*) expressing itself in existence. This is especially the case in the human person. For Augustine, therefore, the *imago Trinitatis* is not simply something which we have, it is something which we live; indeed, it is that which gives us the capacity to do so. If we think of dignity in this context, then it is not only a quality possessed or attributed but a manifestation of our person in our way of living.[31]

The second aspect concerns the way in which mind realizes itself in pursuit of the True and the Good. Ultimately, mind is only fully expressive of the *imago Trinitatis* when it is seeking or ordered to God, who is Goodness and Truth. This also applies to our seeking to love God's image in our neighbours.[32] In other words, Augustine offers a fully theological anthropology— we cannot know or become ourselves without in some way being in relation to God. If the first part of his treatment of the *imago* could allow for a plausible argument that Augustine stands behind the Enlightenment and Modernity, the second part could, with equal plausibility, make him one of its greatest contestants regarding coherence of its self-founding claims. This may offer some explanation for the tensions within the Catholic tradition and the various ways in which it responds to secular modernity.[33]

Although Augustine himself regarded his trinity of memory, understanding, and will as completely inadequate, it nevertheless offered a highly suggestive account of the human person and our relation to God's own life. Though criticized—I believe unfairly—by the Eastern Orthodox traditions— Augustine has proved to be a rich source of theological and philosophical speculation. He has not always been well used, and his legacy within Catholicism and Protestantism has frequently been controversial and problematic. Nevertheless, Augustine, to borrow a phrase of Michel Foucault, is one of the 'founders of our discursivity'.

It is not necessary for our purposes to follow all the twists and turns of the *imago* other than to identify two strands which are important in an appreciation of dignity in the Catholic ontology of the person.

---

[31] For a useful succinct treatment of the issues in Augustine's understanding of the human person as an *imago Trinitatis* see John M. Rist, *Augustine, Ancient Thought Baptized* (Cambridge, Cambridge University Press, 1994), 145–6.
[32] Rist, *Augustine*, 167–8.
[33] This is more evident in the continuing influence of Augustine's *City of God* and his distinction of the earthly and heavenly cities.

Rationality/freedom and relationality

Even from this brief sketch we can see how strongly the theme of rationality or understanding and freedom feature in the Augustinian account. This becomes even more pronounced in Aquinas.[34] As we have indicated, he inherits Augustine's insight regarding the way in which the *imago Trinitatis* informs our understanding of the dignity and unique status of the human person. Increasingly, this comes to be located in human rationality and freedom. Boethius's classic definition of the human person as 'an individual substance in a rational nature'(*naturae rationalis individua substantia*) is the one with which Aquinas chooses to work.[35] Even though it is more difficult to integrate into Trinitarian usage, it allows for greater anthropological development and precision.[36]

In Aquinas, person comes to signify what is unique, individual, and incommunicable. In this sense, it takes over the meaning of the Greek idea of *hypostasis* deployed, especially by the Cappadocians, in clarifying the uniqueness of the Trinitarian relations. For Aquinas, person 'designates an individual so excellent that it possesses a rational nature'.[37] In his thought, dignity is located in the ontology of the person worked out through the doctrine of the Trinity and Christology. Why is it fitting that the Son of God (the Logos) should take on *human* nature? Aquinas argues that human nature is the proper object of the Incarnation of the Logos for two reasons: dignity of human nature and its need.[38]

Dignity lies in human nature's rational capacity, the ability to know and love God, the Augustinian *imago Dei*. The need of our human nature flows from original sin's crippling effect, which diminishes our dignity though it does not destroy it completely.[39] Not only is our dignity redeemed through the Incarnation, it is elevated so that it is even more splendid than before. As Pinckaer argues, quoting Aquinas, one of the reasons for the Incarnation

---

[34] The significance of Aquinas for contemporary Catholic thought is due to Leo XIII, who in his encyclical *Aeterni Patris* (1879) established Aquinas as the principal authority for Catholic theology and philosophy, hence the renewal of Thomism in the twentieth century as his thought was brought into dialogue with modern schools of philosophy.

[35] Aquinas, *Summa Theologica* I–II.85; 73.2; 73.4.

[36] For the most complete discussion of Aquinas's treatment see Gilles Emery, OP, *Trinity in Aquinas* (Michigan, Sapientia Press, 2003), especially 137ff.

[37] Pinckaers, 'Aquinas on the dignity of the human person', 149. See Aquinas, *Summa Theologica* I q 29. 2, which Aquinas will wish to apply to God. However, we must always keep clearly in mind that 'person' when used of the Trinity is not the same as 'person' when applied to human beings. The use is always analogical.

[38] Aquinas, *Summa Theologica* III.4.1; Sentences Bk. III.2.1. also ST III.2.2. ad 2.

[39] Aquinas, *Summa Theologica* III.4.1; also ST I.93.

is 'to teach us about the great dignity of human nature, so that we will avoid marring it by sin'.[40] This brings out an important aspect of dignity, implicit in Augustine but missing in much of the contemporary treatment. The dignity of the human person has a teleology: the final consummation of human dignity consists in the beatific vision.[41] When seen within this teleological horizon, person grounded in the *imago Dei* is not a static reality but one that possesses dynamism. There is a sense in which the human person is a person becoming through the realization of their dignity. Hence, the other main element in the notion of person must be freedom.[42] This is not, of course, the concept of freedom introduced by nominalism that was to become transformed into the modern notion of autonomy. For Aquinas, 'free will is the faculty of reason and will, through which the good is chosen with grace assisting or evil with grace desisting'.[43] Freedom is not the capacity to do whatever we choose but rather to choose that which is true and good; it exists for excellence, and thus it serves and expresses our human dignity.[44]

There is another aspect of the Augustinian-Thomist tradition which it is important to recognize. While it clearly values reason as evidence of the *logos spermatikos*, it does not exalt it as does the Stoic-Kantian tradition. For both Thomas and Augustine, reason is always ordered to the true and the good, which is ultimately God's self, it is not an independent self-grounding faculty, and the dignity of the human person is not exhausted by it. Even if it were such a faculty, it is one that is deeply disordered and unstable. Reason is not immune from sin, which also has epistemological consequences that not only prevent us from knowing truly but also distort our judgements about what it is we do know. Although reason may be necessary to secure human dignity, it cannot be sufficient. This points us to the deeper insights of the Trinitarian *imago*, namely that the dignity of the human person is ultimately grounded in relationality: first to God, and then to each other. Indeed, knowing and loving are relational acts. As well as being a personal reality, dignity must then have a proper theological and social dimension.[45]

---

[40] Pinckaers, 155. Compare with ST III.1.2.
[41] Aquinas, *Summa Contra Gentiles*, Book IV, ch. 54.
[42] *Pace* Rosen, this is why it is necessary for Aquinas to establish a hierarchy of beings according to the power they possess over their actions. *Summa Theologica* I–II.6.1. As Pinckaers remarks, 'It is precisely this control that constitutes the perfection of the person and underlies his definition', 149.
[43] Aquinas, In Sent. II.24.3.
[44] It is out of this tradition and its development that John Paul II and Benedict XVI speak in order to recover an ancient and alternative discourse on freedom for the post-Enlightenment world.
[45] Rist, *Augustine*, draws attention to the impact of Stoicism on Augustine, especially through Cicero, but also brings out where he parts company with them. See 168ff.

All of these elements in the Augustinian-Thomistic understanding of human dignity are present in varying degrees in the Catholic tradition. They undergo significant development as they are brought into debate with contemporary schools of thought. This can be seen in Vatican II's authoritative treatment of the dignity of the human person in Vatican II, *Gaudium et Spes*.[46] As well as giving us a dynamic approach to the dignity of the human person, *imago Trinitatis* also opens up its relational nature. This has been developed in significant ways by Catholic thinkers like Maritain and Pope John Paul II, to explore the spiritual dignity of the human person, interiority, and its ethical implications.

If the thought of Maritian was influential in this development before the Council, then Pope John Paul II is significant for the post-conciliar development. If Maritain brings Aquinas and the Catholic tradition into a fruitful dialogue with personalism, Karol Wojtyła does so with phenomenology. As we have seen, for Aquinas the dignity of the human person as *imago Dei* was found principally in a dynamic rationality and freedom of the human person. Both Maritain and Wojtyła take this up, but also stress the 'spiritual' nature of the human person.[47] For both, self-communication that we can recognise in the inter-relational dynamic of the three persons of the Trinity is also integral to the human person as *imago Trinitatis*. It is the *imago Trinitatis* that discloses the dynamic of love at the centre of the person which constitutes subjectivity, 'Thus subjectivity reveals itself as self-mastery for self-giving ... by spiritually existing in the manner of a gift'.[48] Of course, this had not been lost in either Augustine or Aquinas, but it surfaces now with new emphasis, because both writers want to find ways of resisting the instrumentalization of the human person by fascism and totalitarianism. Maritain seeks to understand the uniqueness of the person in terms of community and the common good, while Wojtyła develops the notion of solidarity and interiority. Solidarity also entails the just sharing of human goods and those goods necessary for human life; it entails the ability to participate in society. This aspect of solidarity allows it to be developed into another basis for human rights, because rights

---

[46] Tanner, Ecumenical Councils, vol. 2. *Gaudium et Spes*, §12ff.

[47] Key texts of Maritain in this context are *Humanisme Intégral* (Paris, 1936), *Le Personne et le Bien Commune* (Paris, 1947). See also Michael A. Smith, *Human Dignity and the Common Good in the Aristotelian-Thomistic Tradition* (Lewiston, NY, Mellen University Press, 1995), especially part 1.

[48] Jacques Maritain, *Challenges and Renewals* (South Bend, IN, University of Notre Dame Press, 1966), 74–5. Cited by W. Norris Clarke, SJ in his excellent discussion of Aquinas's notion of person and its implication in *Person and Being, The Aquinas Lecture 1993* (Milwaukee, WI, Marquette University Press, 1993), 77.

'are the minimum condition for participation'.[49] Another important feature of Woytyła's thought, especially developed during his pontificate, is the dignity of the human body. It represents a very significant enrichment of Catholic discourse on the dignity of the human person.[50]

In all these developments, the redemptive or soteriological dimension has not been lost. Indeed, it is a major feature of the treatment of the dignity of the human person in contemporary Catholic thought that the redemptive movement—the preservation of human dignity and its restoration—explores the implications for society and its structures as well as for the individual.

This new emphasis on the social dimension of dignity is also grounded in the *imago Trinitatis*. It has been a significant recovery in Catholic thought, especially in its understanding of the ontology of the human person. We can see this in two theologians who, though widely different, nevertheless seek to deepen our notion of the person through a Trinitarian perspective. Joseph Ratzinger (Pope Benedict XVI) argues that Augustine, for all his insight, 'commits a decisive' mistake in developing his psychological model of the Trinity.[51] The problem here is that the *imago Trinitatis* is located in one faculty when it needs to be applied to the human person as whole. For Ratzinger, we lose the relationality and the dynamism that the *imago Trinitatis* requires. He

---

[49] Meghan J. Clark, 'Integrating human rights', *Political Theology* 8:3 (2007), 299–317, at 308. See also D. Hollenbach, *Claims in Conflict: Retrieving and Renewing the Catholic Human Rights Tradition* (New York, Paulist Press, 1979). It seems to me that there are considerable opportunities for fruitful engagement between the Catholic tradition and the 'capacities' approach of Martha Nussbaum and Amartya Sen. The various aporias of Nussbaum's approach in *Human Dignity and Political Entitlements*, particularly in her need both to recognize rationality as core but also resolve the problems of its hegemony in defining the human person, are dealt with, to some extent, in the Catholic approach. See Nussbaum, *Human Dignity and Bioethics: Essays Commissioned by the President's Council on Bioethics* (The President's Council on Bioethics, Washington DC, March 2008), ch. 14.

[50] The principal texts for K. Wojtyla before he became Pope are: *Person in Community, Selected Essays*, trans. Theresa Sandok, OSM (New York, Peter Lang, 1993), *The Acting Person*, trans. from the Polish by Andrzej Potocki (Dordrecht, Boston, D. Reidel Pub. Co., 1979), also his texts as Pope, especially the encyclicals. 'The Theology of the Body' was delivered by John Paul II in a series of 129 Wednesday Audiences 1979–84. See *Man and Woman He Created Them: A Theology of the Body*, trans. Dr Michael Waldstein (Reading, Pauline Books and Media, 2006), also C. Curran, *The Moral Theology of John Paul II* (Washington DC, Georgetown University Press, 2005). This offers a clear exposition and critique of the phenomenological approach. For a succinct review of magisterial teaching, especially recently developed by John Paul II, see J. Brian Benestad, *Church, State and Society, An Introduction to Catholic Social Doctrine* (Washington DC, University of America Press, 2010), 35–47.

[51] Cardinal Joseph Ratzinger, 'Concerning the notion of Person in theology', *Communio* 17 (Fall, 1990), 439–54, 447. Also his commentary on *Gaudium et Spes*, 'The dignity of the human person', in Herbert Vorgrimler (gen. ed.), *Commentary on the Documents of Vatican II* (London and New York, Burns & Oates/Herder and Herder, ET, 1969), 115ff. esp. 122–3.

approaches this through the significance of the person of Christ for the meaning of the human person:

> He [Christ] is not only an example that is followed, but he is the integrating space in which the 'we' of human beings gathers itself towards the 'you' of God. Something emerges here that has not been sufficiently seen in modern philosophy, not even in Christian philosophy. In Christianity there is not simply a dialogical principle in the modern sense of a pure 'I-Thou' relationship, neither on the part of the human person that has its place in the historical 'we' that bears it; nor is there such a mere dialogical principle on God's part who is, in turn, no simple 'I', but the 'we' of the Father, Son and Holy Spirit ... This Trinitarian 'we', the fact that God exists only as a 'we', prepares at the same time the space of the human 'we'.[52]

The social reality of the human person had already been emphasized in Vatican Two, but Ratzinger is making its theological foundation more explicit.[53]

In a more extended way, Catherine La Cugna, exploring the implications of the doctrine of the Trinity for our understanding of the human person and society, draws out the relational dynamics of equality, mutuality, and reciprocity, which she argues characterize the intra-relationality of the 'persons' of the Trinity.[54] She argues that these must be applied to persons in their relations if we are to realize the full implications of the *imago Trinitatis*. In different ways, Ratzinger and La Cugna represent a development within the tradition of the *imago* which has significant implications for the ways in which we understand the nature and dignity of the human person. They also wish to emphasize the socially transformative implications of the ontology of the human person which the *imago Trinitatis* contains.

There is another aspect of this recovery of the relationality of the human person which, I believe, has far-reaching consequences for the way in which we understand the dignity of the human person and are committed to it. If it is the case that we only realize the fullness of personhood in and through our relationality—the 'we'—then this must mean that dignity too has a social dimension. In some way our dignity, qua our person and identity not just our status, is held in and by the 'we' of our relationships, personal and civic. In terms of theology, we encounter here the reality of solidarity which has both natural and supernatural dimensions. The natural dimension is that moral obligation which we owe every human being in virtue of our common humanity. Supernaturally, it is the *communio* which unites all humanity in some way to

---

[52] Ratzinger, 'Concerning the notion of Person in theology', 453.
[53] *Gaudium et Spes*, especially §12; 24–5.
[54] Catherine Mowry LaCugna, *God for Us. The Trinity and Christian Life* (New York, HarperCollins, 1991, pbk 1993), especially 272–5, 281–3, 400ff.

the grace of Christ and is realized in the Church. The Church recognizes this *communio* as extending beyond space and time for its members, but given its own theology, it must also recognize this for all humanity. In this it discloses a fundamental aspect of the dignity of the human person for society as well: the dead can make a claim upon us for justice and respect. I think this is a significant witness to solidarity/*communio* in the secular sphere based upon its ontology of the human person.

Our obligation to the dead is more than *pietas*; it is a command which comes from the *imago* itself.[55] Where that *imago* remains degraded or humiliated, then so do we all; society itself remains unhealed, and it must bear the legacies of unreconciled histories. When forgetfulness or silence is accepted, the relationality of our being in the present is weakened, and we are rendered ontologically insecure. For then history belongs only to the powerful, whereas one of the most important features of dignity is the absolute claim it makes whether we are weak or strong. The ontology of the person provides a way of understanding how love (even of one's enemies) and forgiveness can also extend beyond the limits of time and space. There is a possible solution to the problem of deliberate and unintentional amnesia (forgetfulness, or suppression and distortion of memory) through anamnesis (remembrance) grounded in an understanding of the human person. By the restoration of their dignity, which needs also to recognize their histories, not only are the dead honoured but society itself is healed, and creative potentials of the future for humanity are released.

The other dimension of this relationality is the way in which our identity—our history, our life, and its value—is held by others and recognized by them. This again touches not only upon our personal value but our ontological security. Hence, even when we lose the capacity to reason or decide for ourselves, not only do we still retain our dignity—our absolute value—but others can carry our dignity for us in their care, respect, and preservation of our rights. If there is no 'we' which can make that claim upon us personally and as society, then persons are ultimately instrumentalized. No matter how subtle or bureaucratically softened the process may be, instrumentalization is always a humiliation; in such a society all are diminished.[56]

---

[55] In the Christian tradition this also extends to the bodies of the dead. This is further reinforced not only as respect for God's material creation but also for the Incarnation and the resurrection. Here, the question of reciprocity is also present, because for Christianity the person's life and identity continues after death, as does their active membership of the communio of the Church.

[56] Zigmunt Bauman develops this insightful and important thesis regarding bureaucracy in his book *Modernity and the Holocaust* (Ithaca, NY, Cornell University Press, 1989). For a discussion of the person who 'lacks dignity' see Paul Valadier, 'The person who lacks dignity', *Concilium* 2 (2003), 51–6.

Notwithstanding the circumstances of any given time, the fact that the dignity of the human person is not only ontologically grounded but expressed in the liturgical and existential praxis of a community such as the Church, gives accountability a historical reality that resists erasure. That each generation, present, past, and future, can be judged in its light also alerts us to the fact that dignity plays a role which goes beyond mere idealistic aspiration. It holds the place for the memory of what the human person and human society are called to be. Whether we express this dynamic as a theology or as a secular humanism, it reveals itself to be a moral task which is both personal and social. In this sense, dignity is the epiphany of the person in our relationships and in all our social systems—national and international; it is a way in which we are able to resist de-humanization. It not only keeps open the space of the 'I' but also of the other 'Thou'; it refuses to let us forget who we are before and for each other.

Concluding observations

It seems to me there are three brief points which arise out of this necessarily selective exploration of the Catholic tradition of the dignity of the human person.

The soteriological aspect of human dignity

The first is to emphasize that richness of the discourse and the way in which it continues develops through the internal theological conversation and also as it meets other sources. If it is to be engaged, then it is important to do justice to its complexity if one is to maximize the benefits. It will be clear from the way in which dignity is grounded in the ontology of the person that the locus of rights is in the person and not in a legal system. As Maritain observes, rights are not granted by society but recognised as universally valid, 'and which no social necessity can authorize us even momentarily to abolish or disregard'.[57] Rights, then, become the ways in which the dignity of the person is recognized in society. Dignity preserves the priority of the person over the dangerous impersonal demands of society.

Human dignity not only has a part to play in a secular theodicy which seeks to prevent, minimize, or overcome the effects of evil, it is part of a soteriology which runs through the whole of Christian understanding. Even from the brief indications given here, we can see how dignity is understood as

---

[57] Jacques Maritain, *Man and State* (Washington DC, Catholic University of America Press, 1998), 96.

a dynamic reality: something which we are and possess, but also something which we are called to realize both in ourselves and in others. This highlights the soteriological nature of human dignity for Catholic thought. Soteriology is the unfolding of the economy of salvation, the way in which God, through Christ, is at work in our world to restore and raise up our dignity as the *imago Dei/imago Trinitatis*. This is a work in which we are not merely passive objects but active agents—for our very participation and cooperation are already part of the way in which God recognizes our dignity. Moreover, the very fact of the cross in which we are presented with the abject humiliation of Christ is simultaneously the witness that God makes to the indestructibility of our dignity. For this reason, Christianity knows that no matter how humiliated or degraded the human person has become, his or her dignity is always held secure in the crucified Christ. In this way, the Cross not only secures our dignity but also subverts all attempts to destroy it.

Dignity as task

The 'soteriological' dimension of dignity has practical and effective consequences. Again, the recognition of human dignity cannot be a passive recognition. To be effective, it must be translated into structures which recognize and preserve the conditions in which people can flourish—can practise their dignity in the sense of striving for human excellence. This is the striving for the virtuous life across all the fields of human endeavour. Dignity cannot be only a claim we make upon each other or upon society; it must be one that we make upon ourselves, especially in the service of the good of others and of our societies. From a Christian point of view, we cannot do this unaided; we need God's grace. Whether we accept this premise or not, it is surely possible to establish a creative partnership between all who desire the common good. Kasper acknowledges that rights in some way grounded in a universal recognition of human dignity need to find expression in practical structures.[58] How we create these structures and the values which they enshrine emerges out of the philosophical, political, and theological discussion which our concern for dignity requires us to pursue. Although the outcomes are tested and developed in practice and in theory, they require communities to embody and espouse them. In other words, the idea of dignity needs to be incarnated: embodied in the *habitus* of a community so as to become part of its social memory. I believe that the Church is such a community; it is one of the principal agents within culture which carries that memory or *habitus* for all women and men. The significance of the Church

---

[58] Kasper, *Theological Foundations*, 149.

lies in the way in which it mediates the sacred and the secular worlds. Given that its commitment to human dignity does not ultimately rest on any philosophical system, political or social hierarchy of power, but on what it understands to be Revelation, then the Church must be one of the consistent carriers of this foundational value. It does not mean that its understanding of human dignity cannot change, rather that out of its commitment it is obliged to seek ever more coherent and persuasive ways of defending human dignity theoretically, politically, socially. If it truly perceives the dignity of each person, *imago Trinitatis*, then the Church must recognize and live this *ad intra* as well as *ad extra*.

The nature of dignity as mystery

In theological discourse, mystery is not an intellectual dead end; it is a point of departure. Mystery is the capacity for inexhaustible meaning, and so the fact that we cannot settle the question of dignity is not a reason to abandon it but to attend to it more closely. It may well be that it names something for us which is essential, without which our person and our society would be impoverished, if not endangered. Human dignity, as we have argued, does not devalue the dignity of other things whether they are other forms of life or matter. The teleology of dignity is theologically expressed as our vocation as persons to act in ways consonant with our dignity—bearers of the *imago Dei/imago Trinitatis*, which is also the *imago Christi*. It entails an ethical relationship to oneself as well as to others: to act towards them so as not to diminish our dignity, and to recognize the dignity which they also have. Far from placing us 'above' creation, this inserts us more deeply into it, opening up the realm of our responsibilities for all creation. In doing so, it commits us to the search for meaning, structures, actions which in some way enshrine dignity. To this extent, dignity has a heuristic function; it is part of our own search for the meaning of who we are and the sort of societies we are called to create. Our dignity as persons requires of us an intellectual, moral, ethical, and spiritual search. This cannot be undertaken without openness to new ways of understanding what the dignity of the human person might mean, and what we need to do to preserve and nourish it.[59] Human dignity is both our *terminus a quo* and our *terminus ad quem*; in the words of the psalmist: 'What is man [*sic*] that you remember him and the son of man that you visit him? You have made him little less than the angels, with glory and honour you crown him.'[60]

---

[59] See Maureen Junk-Kenny, 'Does theology need a theological foundation?', *Concilium* 2 (2003), 63–4.
[60] Psalm 8:5.

12

Human Dignity and the Image of God

Janet Soskice

IN PRESS REPORTS, CHRISTIAN, and especially Roman Catholic, teachings on issues of life and death make their appearance as so many staccato dictates emanating from the moon or (from what is for Fleet Street an even more remote and inexplicable place of origin) the Vatican. Catholics (good Catholics) follow these dictates unwittingly because that is what it means to be a good Catholic. There is, then, little point in asking good Catholics what they think about things since they don't think; they only follow and adhere.

In fact, Christian teaching, including Catholic teaching, is rooted in centuries and even millennia of reflection on God, the world, and the human condition (anthropology). These beliefs and teachings have in turn give risen to deeply felt convictions about respect for the unborn, the elderly, the ill, imprisoned, and the dying that are by no means knee-jerk. In this chapter I want to explore Christian teaching about God, Christ, and creation, particularly as they reflect on the dignity of human beings made 'in the image of God'.

Creation and salvation

The Christian God (and traditionally the Jewish and Muslim God) creates all that is, including space and time. This means that everything ('all that is') is good.[1] Contrary to what might be our lived experience, God has made and loves his creation, and evil has, at least in the classical theology of Augustine and Aquinas and others, no ontological reality of its own, but must be seen as lack. In creating 'all that is', God both loves and is close to his creatures (spiritual, rational, vegetable, and mineral) immediately as their Creator. Since God created time, creation is not what happened some distant ages ago, but from

---

[1] It is better to say that God creates 'all that is' than to say God creates 'the world' or 'the Universe', because in this teaching, were there for instance to be multiverses, God would be the creator of them, too. God creates simply everything, and everything that is not God is a creature.

God's point of view 'now'. God is at this very moment holding all that is in being, and were God not to do this for even a micro-second it would not be. God is accordingly entirely intimate to creatures, closer to me than my own hands and feet, as Augustine and John Henry Newman would say.

All things have their being in and from God (without themselves 'being God'—this is not a kind of panentheism). All things find their destiny, or *telos*, in the divine love. Living beings, unlike stones, are also moving and growing beings. Irrational living beings, like flowers, will unwaveringly follow their own good by a 'natural love'. Sunflowers will turn to the sunlight because naturally they seek to flourish. Human beings, as reasoning beings, are capable of going wrong in spectacular ways, but nonetheless they too seek to flourish. Thus 'salvation' is derived from '*salus*', health. Aquinas argued that all human beings seek their salvation, or, as *salus* is sometimes translated, their 'human flourishing'. For Aquinas, even in their animal natures human beings are rightly guided by 'natural love'. It is, for him, our misuse of reason, and not our bodily natures, which leads us astray. Dante is a powerful exponent of this view, and I can do no better than direct the reader to a speech in the *Purgatorio* where Virgil contrasts 'natural love' and 'mind love', and the comment on this of the translator, Robin Kirkpatrick,

> *The natural love can never go astray.*
> *The other, though, may err when wrongly aimed,*
> *or else through too much vigour or the lack.*

Kirkpatrick writes:

> To speak of a 'natural' love would, according to some moralists, imply a base instinct that should in some way be repressed by the conscious mind. But this is not at all Dante's view. Natural love is the instinctual will, the urge to live and to sustain oneself in the existence that the Creator has first granted. This form of love operates in all created things—whether rational or animal or vegetable—and provides an unwavering compass point, directed always towards the development of life, which is never capable of going astray. Desire here, as throughout the *Paradiso* also, is seen as being, on every level, the innate drive that impels all existing things—whether bees as they make honey or fire as it rises (*Purgatorio* 18:28) or fire rising in flame (*Paradiso* 1: 115–17)—towards their proper goal, which is to nurture the full capacity for life with which they have been endowed. All things in existence desire what is good. And 'good' means nothing more nor less that the nourishment that is appropriate to any particular form of life.[2]

---

[2] Robin Kirkpatrick, Introduction to *Dante Purgatorio*, trans. Robin Kirkpatrick (London, Penguin, 2007), xxxii.

Human beings, having free will, can go astray, but they can also, as Kirkpatrick points out, 'seek fulfilment in the sphere of intellectual good with the same zeal that the bee (or even, say, beetroot) seeks fulfilment in its own sphere of existence. If the human being succeeds in this, it will then freely be given credit for collaboration with the creation that the Creator intended it to enjoy. No bee or vegetable will receive such credit. (Nor will any bee or vegetable be condemned for failing to pursue its existential destiny.)'[3]

To seek God, to seek to flourish, and to seek the good are for Dante and Aquinas, whom he here follows, entirely natural to us. Nature is not, of course, for these thinkers something existing alongside of and in some way independent of God, as we seem to find in Newton or in Locke. Christians do not believe in 'nature' in its early modern sense but in 'creation'. Human nature is the nature created by God and the moral life is not rule following, but formation in virtue always brings us closer to our own good. Philosophical readers will recognize this as the Thomistic and Aristotelian synthesis that Alasdair Macintyre has done much to recover. In its theological form it is profoundly organic and teleological. Life, all creation, finds its wholeness and life in and from God.

The 'sanctity of life' and the 'image of God'

All life, all creation, is loved by God, and the lives of irrational creatures seem, from the biblical record, to matter to God. In that sense, all life has a 'sanctity'. Laws on the slaughter of animals in the Old Testament and modern Jewish and Muslim practice reflect the honour which animal life should be accorded even while taking it. The reason given for prohibition on drinking blood in Leviticus 17 is that blood is 'the life' of the animal.

The media and even the Churches, when addressing the question of Christian teachings on life and death, often today invoke the notion of 'the sanctity of life'. As well as being ambiguous (are animals included? what about viruses?), this phrasing has, as far as I can see, no fixed biblical root or deep presence in historical theology. Where reverence for human life is concerned, the directive biblical teaching is that the human being is made 'in the image of God', a teaching drawn from Judaism but which becomes much more potent in Christian teaching. I will return to the *imago Dei* later, but for the moment note that it has been the basis in Christian teaching for regarding

---

[3] Robin Kirkpatrick, Introduction to *Dante Purgatorio*, xxxiii.

every human being, no matter how poor, burdened, restricted, ragged, or dissolute, as entirely distinctive and worthy of reverence.

Disability and the end of life

The New Testament has a complex attitude to physical disability, illness, suffering, and death. These are not to be seen as punishment for sin. The decisive text for this has been the Gospel of John 9.2, where the disciples ask Jesus, 'Rabbi, who sinned, this man or his parents, that he was born blind?', to which Jesus answers, 'Neither this man nor his parents sinned; he was born blind so that God's works might be revealed in him' (Jn. 9.2–3, NRSV).[4]

On the other hand, death is an enemy, and one that Paul believes Jesus Christ, in dying and being raised from the dead, has defeated (2 Tim. 1.10). The Easter services in Christian churches proclaim that by his dying Christ conquered death. The author of the letter known as Hebrews identifies death with the devil, arguing that Jesus shared our flesh and blood, 'so that through death he might destroy the one who has the power of death, that is, the devil, and free those who all their lives were held in slavery by the fear of death' (Heb. 2.14). Pain in the New Testament appears not as the will of God but the work of the devil (although God mysteriously 'allows' pain). A general picture may be discerned of a world that is disordered, out of line, and which suffers and groans, awaiting its day of salvation. Individual suffering is not necessarily to be explained by individual wrongdoing, but our individual wrongdoings contribute to corporate disorder.

The ministry of Jesus was characterized by healings from sickness (Matt. 9.35), raising from the dead, and casting out of unclean spirits. According to the Gospel writers, his disciples were called to share this work (Matt. 10.1), even to the point of raising the dead.

It is probably anachronistic to think that the marvel of these healings lay, for the gospel writers and their audiences, in their apparent violation of the laws of nature. At the time of Jesus and Paul, the general public had no difficulty believing in miraculous cures. The Gospels themselves suggest that people other than Jesus and his followers could heal and cast out demons. The significance of Jesus's healing miracles for the New Testament writers lies not in their uniqueness but in their perceived role as signs of the in-breaking

---

[4] It is interesting that it is Jesus's own disciples, and not the Pharisees or some other rival group, who are represented as presenting Jesus with this unsatisfactory either/or. This seems to show that it was by no means a silly question.

of a new reign (or kingdom) of God, with Jesus as the anticipated Messiah. Thus when, in Matthew's Gospel, the imprisoned John the Baptist sends his followers to ask Jesus, 'Are you the one who is to come, or are we to wait for another?', Jesus answers with direct reference to the Old Testament prophet, Isaiah: 'Go and tell John what you hear and see: the blind receive their sight, the lame walk, the lepers are cleansed, the deaf hear, the dead are raised, and the poor have good news brought to them' (Matt. 11.2–5).[5] The disciples share in this healing ministry.

But healing is not only by prayer and miracle. The Parable of the Good Samaritan of Luke 10 was of decisive importance to the theologians of the early church. In this story, a traveller is beaten up and left for dead on the road to Jericho. A priest and a Levite, both members of respected Jewish groups, pass the wounded man without wanting to be bothered by stopping. A member of the despised Samaritan community then comes along, takes compassion on the victim, binds his wounds and makes arrangements for him to be looked after at an inn at the Samaritan's own expense. In conclusion, Jesus asks his disciples which one of these men was the neighbour to the fallen man. The story was important in early Christian teaching not least because it was understood to speak allegorically about Jesus himself: Jesus himself was seen to be the one who stopped to assist the man who had been beaten, robbed, and left half dead on the road to Jericho. The oil and wine used by the Samaritan to dress the wounds anticipate the bread and wine of the Christian sacraments. Jesus was the 'true Physician' whose gifts of bread and wine (his body and blood) were the true medicaments. Other medications, however, were equally important, and on a less allegorical level the Parable of the Good Samaritan was, and is, understood to suggest that care for the stranger should be blind to merit, kinship, or gain. Nor is there any question of the Samaritan requiring of the victim (presumably a Jew, since he was coming down from Jerusalem) any conversion, or even thanks. This was the answer Jesus gave to the question 'And who is my neighbour?' (Lk. 10.29). In many ways Christian admonitions to care of the poor, suffering, and needy were simply continuations of Jewish ones: care for the widows and orphans, the stranger ('hospice' and 'hospital' derive from the Latin for hospitality), but the early Christians also believed that Jesus would return, even within their lifetime, to inaugurate his new kingdom, and consequently felt an 'end of times' urgency which informed their practice.

---

[5] Compare Isaiah 29.18–19; also the Magnificat of Luke 1.

This was noted by others. The philosopher and convert Aristides, in an Apology delivered on behalf of the Christians to the emperor in the first part of the second century gives this summary of life among the Christians:

> when they see a stranger, they take him in to their homes and rejoice over him as a very brother; for they do not call them brethren after the flesh, but brethren after the spirit and in God ... And if there is among them any that is poor and needy, and if they have no spare food, they fast two or three days in order to supply to the needy their lack of food. They observe the precepts of their Messiah with much care, living justly and soberly as the Lord their God commanded them.[6]

The end of time was delayed, but care for the poor and sick continued. Guenter Risse in his history of hospitals, *Mending Bodies, Saving Souls*, discusses at length the calamity that hit Edessa, in what is now Eastern Turkey, in 499. Droughts, agricultural failure, and plagues emptied the villages. Those who could walk fled to the cities, where they begged and died in great numbers. The bishop, Eusebius, went personally to the emperor in Constantinople to appeal emergency funds and supplies for these newcomers, who were to be found 'wailing by night and day from the pangs of hunger, and their bodies wasted away ... the whole city was full of them and they began to die in the porticoes and in the streets'.[7] Joshua the Stylite, who chronicled the unfolding disaster, wrote of dead bodies of women and children in the streets, and that two priests 'established an infirmary among the buildings attached to the Great Church of Edessa. Those who were very ill used to go in and lie down there; and many bodies were found in the infirmary in which they were buried.'[8] Despite this and other measures from church and community leaders and Greek soldiers, many of those in the infirmaries still 'died by a painful and melancholy death', although surrounded by those devoted to their care'.[9]

Christ, the image of the invisible God

Christians believe that Jesus was not just a messenger of God or another prophet but God Godself, dwelling with humankind in the flesh. St Paul in his letters reconfigured the notion of *imago Dei* received from the Book of

---

[6] 'The Apology of Aristides', in *Ante-Nicene Christian Fathers*, vol. 10, ed. Allan Menzies (Edinburgh: T&T Clark, 1897), 277.
[7] William Wright, *The Chronicle of Joshua the Stylite*, cited by Guenter B. Risse, *Mending Bodies, Saving Souls: A History of Hospitals* (Oxford, Oxford University Press, 1999), 71.
[8] Wright, *The Chronicle of Joshua the Stylite*, cited by Risse, *Mending Bodies, Saving Souls*, 74–5.
[9] Wright, *The Chronicle of Joshua the Stylite*, cited by Risse, *Mending Bodies, Saving Souls*, 73.

Genesis along the lines of this new faith. The Book of Genesis taught that the human being was made 'in the image of God'. Paul takes this teaching in a new direction by identifying Jesus as the true image, indeed 'the image of the invisible God' (Col. 1.15; see also 2 Cor. 4.4).

The nature of the 'image of God' has been glossed in different ways by theologians, and indeed by rabbis. Since it is not in the virtue of the body that the human being is 'in the image of God', some have focused on rationality, others on our capacity for speech. However, it is evident that these capacities have not been judged definitive in the individual case, since even the prelinguistic infant and dying elderly person in extreme decline has been held to be 'in the image of God'. A certain vagueness is indeed desirable and ineliminable in the notion—it is not in virtue of possessing a particular set of qualifications that the human individual is in the image of God. *Imago Dei* would seem to be, as is perhaps the notion of human dignity itself, a placeholder concept *par excellence*, and nothing wrong with that if what is needed from a concept is placeholding.[10]

Among the Eastern Orthodox, one reading of the *imago Dei* is that, since God is mystery, so the human being made in the image of God is also mystery. This reading is supported Christologically by the Western theologians like Bernard of Clairvaux who cite I John 3.2. 'My dear people, we are already the children of God but what we are to be in the future has not yet been revealed; all we know is, that when it is revealed we shall be like him because we shall see him as he really is.' The idea is that as the fullness of Christ, the true image, is not yet known, nor yet is our own true nature.

Decisively for the moral and social life, it was held that whatever is done for anyone in need is done for Christ. A central text here has been Matthew 25, sometimes called the Last Judgement. In the course of a long sequence of teaching on the kingdom of heaven, Jesus says:

> Then the king will say to those at his right hand, 'Come, you that are blessed by my Father, inherit the kingdom prepared for you from the foundation of the world; for I was hungry and you gave me food, I was thirsty and you gave me something to drink, I was a stranger and you welcomed me, I was naked and you gave me clothing, I was sick and you take care of me, I was in prison and you visited me'. (Matt. 25.34–6)

Jesus tells his puzzled audience that whatever service they do for the 'least of his brethren' they do for him. This scripture has been foundational to the

---

[10] Here I am one with David Gushee in wanting to avoid a list of qualities that 'qualifies' a human being for respect. And in case *imago Dei* is mistakenly taken as suggesting that human beings are more spiritual than other creatures, it is worth reminding ourselves that, classically, angels were thought to be entirely spiritual creatures but never, like human beings, held to be in the image of God.

Christian conviction that one should see Christ in every person in need. The encounter of St Francis with the lepers, the founding of the hospice movement by Cicely Saunders (an evangelical Anglican), and the work of Mother Theresa of Calcutta are three memorable instances.

Jesus, understood by Christians to be the author of life (the one through whom all things were made according to the Prologue to John's Gospel) did not save himself from death. Indeed, he died a particularly painful and humiliating death. This tortured death is often represented in Christian art, sometimes to the consternation of modern viewers. One of the most shocking images is that on the Isenheim altarpiece (1512–16) of Matthias Grünewald. When the altarpiece wings are closed, the viewer is confronted with a savage portrayal of lifeless Christ on the cross: his body is not only wounded but gaunt, pallid, and covered with sores. The distortion of the body, almost to the point of decomposition, is far in excess of the trauma a body would suffer in death by crucifixion. Yet we cannot 'see' this painting without knowing that the altarpiece was painted for a hospice chapel. The order of monks to whom it belonged, the Antonites, was founded to care for the sick, especially by establishing hospices. At Isenheim, the community was famous for their work with those suffering from skin diseases and especially *ignis plaga*, or St Anthony's Fire—ergotism. By the late sixteenth century, the cause of this disorder was known to be poisoned rye, but at the time Grünewald executed his commission its cause was unknown. Victims had blackened limbs, gangrenous hands and feet, and suffered deforming muscular spasms.[11] Before this altarpiece, the ailing could map their own physical distress and disfigurement on that of the body of their crucified God—as could those who were caring for them. When the panels were opened they could see a gloriously risen Christ, his skin freed from sores, though the body still bearing the wounds of his crucifixion.

Resurrection and life after death

Death is not the end in the Christian story. For the writers of the Gospels, and especially for St Paul and the theologians of the early church, the resurrection of Jesus from the dead was the essence of the 'good news', and bound up with the promise that his followers, too, would be raised to eternal life. The Book of Acts describes the disciples, after the death of Jesus, proclaiming the

---

[11] Andrée Haym, *The Isenheim Altarpiece: God's Medicine and the Painter's Vision* (Princeton, NJ, Princeton University Press, 1989), 20–1.

resurrection of the dead in Jesus (Acts 4.2). St Paul makes the resurrection of Jesus central to his teaching and to Christian hope: 'If Christ has not been raised,' he writes in I Corinthians, 'your faith is futile and you are still in your sins' (I Cor. 15.17). For Paul, belief that Jesus was the promised Messiah was inseparable from belief in his Resurrection, and Christian hope for life after death was inseparable from belief that Jesus was the Messiah.

It is not clear exactly when the notion of the resurrection of the dead first became a debating point amongst the Jews as certainly it was between the Pharisees (who favoured the notion) and the Sadducees (who did not) at the time of the writing of the Gospels. Jon Levenson argues persuasively that the early rabbis were keen to find endorsement for the belief that the just would be raised on Judgement Day, and that they did so believing this to be in line with received Jewish teaching—even mandated by Torah.[12] A Jewish text written in the late second century BCE, 2 Maccabees, tells the harrowing story of a mother arrested with her seven sons whom the king attempts to force to eat pork. They declare that they would rather die than break the laws of their ancestors, and one by one are tortured and slain in front of their mother. The first, before having his limbs cut off and being fried alive in a pan, cites Moses: the LORD 'will have compassion on his servants' (2 Mac. 7.6); the second, before dying in a similarly dreadful way, says that 'the King of the universe will raise us up to an everlasting renewal of life, because we have died for his laws' (2 Mac.7.9); and so on, each expressing belief in resurrection to life.

It is not a coincidence that the same period in which we see evidence of belief in the 'raising of the dead' also saw developments in Jewish thought on creation, and particularly the consolidation of the belief in *creatio ex nihilo*. This teaching underscores that God freely creates everything, including time and space. We find in 2 Maccabees fairly clear insistence on the staples of *creatio ex nihilo*, in consort with growing interest in the possibility of resurrection—the mother of the seven martyred sons, for instance, expressly identifies the God who creates with the God that can restore to new life. In 2 Maccabees 7.28–9, she encourages her youngest son: 'I beg you, my child, to look at the heaven and earth and see everything that is in them, and recognize that God did not make them out of things that existed. And in the same way the human race came into being. Do not fear this butcher, but prove worthy of your brothers. Accept death, so that in God's mercy I may get you back again along with your brothers.' The connection is between a God who creates and a God

---

[12] Jon D. Levenson, *Resurrection and the Restoration of Israel: The Ultimate Victory of the God of Life* (New Haven, Yale University Press, 2006), 26–33. See also Tom Wright, *The Resurrection and the Son of God* (London, SPCK, 2003).

who saves. Just as God made all that is in the first place, so God can raise from the dead.[13] The themes were not new—the Book of Psalms and Isaiah both have creation as a central theme, and connect it with restoration and justice. The God who creates can save.[14] For the modern reader it is also worth emphasizing that belief in life after death, while it may be *inconceivable* (so is the 'state' of the Universe before the big bang) is not *incoherent*. A related parallel is this: it is impossible to answer the question 'why is there something rather than nothing?' but this is not an absurd question. It is a metaphysical (not a scientific) question, which believers answer by saying that they believe in a Creator. Indeed, it would seem to me curious if someone had no difficulty believing that God made all that is, including space and time, but drew the line at believing in life after death. After making space and time, the resurrection of the dead would seem to be a modest operation.

It was in this context of Messianic expectation, persecution, and hope that Christianity was born. For the writers of the New Testament, and especially for Paul, belief in the resurrection of the dead is of a piece with expectation for a Messiah who was to bring justice to the poor and food for the hungry—the themes of the Magnificat, the song sung by Mary, mother of Jesus, in the opening chapter of the Gospel of Luke. Luke and the other gospel writers draw on Isaiah for 'prophecies' of the one who restore sight to the blind and make the lame walk again. Jesus's miracles, including those in which he raises people from the dead, show him as participating in the power of the Creator (Lazarus in John 11, Jairus's daughter in Luke 8). The Prologue to John's Gospel goes so far as to identify Jesus with the creative power of God as the Word, through whom all things were made.

Resurrection in the New Testament is thus not best seen as a private reward for a the individual life lived well but as a sign of the even greater glory of the coming of the kingdom of God, a time of healing and justice when even the dead are not forgotten—thus St Paul:

> For I am convinced that neither death, nor life, nor angels, nor rulers, nor things present, nor things to come, nor powers, nor height, nor depth, nor anything else in all creation, will be able to separate us from the love of God in Christ Jesus our Lord. (Rom. 8.38–9)

The collective 'us' is important here, for Paul sees all the faithful as members of the one body of Christ, stones that go to build a living temple to be

---

[13] Islamic texts use the same argument.

[14] This hope is in the Jewish prayer, the *Amidah*, which according to Rabbinic law is to be said three days each weekday and four times on Sabbath: 'You are mighty forever, my Lord, You are the one who revives the dead, powerful to save (YOU make the wind blow and the rain fall) ... Faithful you are to revive the dead. Blessed are You, O Lord, who revive the dead.'

the dwelling place of God. In Romans, Paul suggests that the redeeming of our bodies might be but a part of a restoration of creation: 'We know that the whole creation has been groaning in labour pains until now: and not only the creation, but we ourselves, who have the first fruits of the Spirit, groan inwardly while we wait for adoption, the redemption of our bodies' (Rom. 8.22–3).

Jesus tells his disciples to 'cure the sick, raise the dead, cleanse the lepers, cast out demons', and, as they go, to 'proclaim the good news, "The kingdom of heaven has come near"' (Matt. 10.7–8; compare Lk. 10.9). Caring for the sick, the outcast, the poor is *not what one does to earn one's way into an afterlife* but a sign that, however partially, the follower of Christ is already in some way sharing in the kingdom of God. In its biblical context, the Christian belief in the resurrection of the body is not to be uncoupled from hope for the coming of the kingdom, and the exercise of justice and mercy in working for this great end.

Conclusions and applications

This, then, is a sketch of the scriptural and theological background to Christian teachings on human dignity in matters of life and death—and not just that, for we can see that care of the outcast, the impoverished, the disabled, and imprisoned arises from the same interanimating beliefs. These beliefs, which traverse the grand narrative of creation and redemption, are entirely central to Christian faith and hope. While there are correspondences between ancient philosophical wisdoms and Christian teaching, the revolution affected by Abrahamic teaching in the world of classical antiquity cannot be exaggerated.

Creation is a case in point. Neither Plato nor Aristotle have a creator God. Both are monotheists of a sort, but neither has anything like the Jewish or Christian creator. Aristotle's God is more like a mathematical theorem running alongside the universe. The Christian God by contrast (and where I say Christian read Christian, Jewish, and Muslim) has no need to create, and creates all that is freely and out of love. Aristotle's God has no knowledge of particulars, is not personal in any sense, and certainly not 'loving' (grossly anthropomorphic in Aristotle's austere scheme). The Abrahamic teaching that God creates everything has the radical implication that God is always already there—at every place, in any time—present to every creature all of which only and always have their being from God.

Of course Christians were keen to marry their wisdom with the best of what they found around them from the philosophers, but they transformed them in the process. The Hippocratic oath could be embraced but it was also supplemented. David Albert Jones points out in his chapter in this volume that the ancient philosophers had views about human dignity, friendship, and so on, but they certainly did not hold that all human beings were of equal dignity. Aristotle thought women had only undeveloped souls, and slaves no souls at all. Cicero may have shared with other ancients the idea of *philanthropia*,[15] but he also held that a man could only be friend to someone who was his social and economic equal, and certainly not with a slave or a woman. Thomas Jefferson may have thought it was self evident that all men were created equal, but a short read of the authors of classical antiquity might have robbed him of this confident assertion. It is not at all self-evident that all men are created equal—and even Jefferson and the drafters of the Declaration didn't effectively include women.

Christianity, for all its shortcomings, brought into antiquity and the subsequent Western intellectual tradition a radical notion concerning the dignity of all human beings, even if the societal ramifications have taken time to unfold.[16] Indeed, it is difficult to see how so counter-intuitive a notion as that of the equal dignity of all human beings could have entered the Western intellectual bloodstream apart from the influence of this Abrahamic strand, and sometimes hard to see how it can be maintained apart from it.[17]

The human being, each human being, whether a king or a milkmaid, is loved by God in their own particularity. Each life is a gift, and each human person is one who is in the image of God, in whose face we should see the face of Christ—witness the St Christopher legend, and many other similar tales of assisting Christ unawares.

As God is mystery, so each human being made in the image of God is a mystery. It is this, not respect for nature, which is the bedrock for Christian teachings about matters of life and death: debates about abortion, assisted suicide, and, we could add, euthanasia (for which I believe there is a growing pressure) and infanticide.[18] A 'respect for nature' is perfectly compatible with eugenic policies that sterilize or kill the infirm, the disabled, or members of ethnic minorities. Indeed, respect for nature and purity of bloodline

---

[15] D. A. Jones, 'Is the creation of admixed embryos "an offense against human dignity"?', *Human Reproduction and Genetic Ethics* 16:1 (2010), 101.

[16] Slavery continued in Christian antiquity, but slaves were held to be spiritual equals and have souls and entitlement to good treatment.

[17] I am speaking of the Western tradition deliberately, because other traditions have developed, independently, strong traditions of veneration for life, for instance the Jains. Greece and Rome were considerably more elitist.

[18] That the Christian position for this complex question cannot always be simply read off this conviction is evident in the different Christian stances taken on questions of contraception and abortion.

has frequently been invoked to endorse such measures. A respect for nature underlies some animal rights or deep green groups who, at least in rhetoric, are happy to countenance the elimination of many resource-grabbing human beings. Peter Singer's willingness to countenance infanticide for unwanted children is of a piece with his championing of animal life.[19]

From the Christian point of view, every human being is in the image of God and thus to be respected as a sacred mystery. God has brought them into being and is working his purpose out in their life. Of course 'the' Christian position on many complex issues can't always simply be read off this conviction, and here I think the notion of *imago Dei* and the attendant mystery that implies has many advantages over the idea of 'sanctity of life'. From the Catholic perspective, we must rest with the mystery of the origins of life. We do not rest easily with mystery, yet rest we must. When do the individual egg and sperm become not just human life but a single human life? At conception? After the possibility of twinning has past? We don't know, and from the Roman Catholic point of view it does not matter, since this life has come as a gift and should be accepted in its mysterious unfolding as gift.

We need also to keep in mind the reality and prevalence of miscarriages. I have had a miscarriage at an early stage of pregnancy, and learned then that these are very common. I was told that the 'product of conception' I had carried could never have been a baby, although it was a human conception, of course. It was a loss, a very great loss, and there were many tears, for my husband and I had already been thinking that seven months or so from that time we would have a baby. But it was not, at this stage, the death of a child. Nor indeed does the Catholic Church mark miscarriage as such. The fact that no liturgy has been developed and put in place for early miscarriage may be taken as a indicator that the Church has always noted the ambiguities of early pregnancy—and not simply because it was not clearly understood, in medieval times, that the early embryo was human.

This loss, which often takes place at three months of gestation, is often known only to the couple and even more frequently, we are told, not even known to the woman herself if the fertilized egg is lost in the first month. Given the frequency of early miscarriage, it is almost impossible, religiously, to regard it as a God-directed slaughter of the innocents. Instead, it seems more natural to say that the mystery of this new life is beyond us. In my case, had the pregnancy which miscarried gone to full term I would not have conceived

---

[19] See Helga Kuhse and Peter Singer, *Should the Baby Live? The Problem of Handicapped Infants* (Oxford, Oxford University Press, 1985), 124. I have written about this in Janet Soskice, *The Kindness of God* (Oxford, Oxford University Press, 2007), ch. 3, 'Creation and relation'. Chapter 2 of that book concerns the *imago Dei*.

the daughter I now have, since the successful pregnancy began during what would have been the term of the previous, miscarried one.

From a Catholic perspective, respect for the earliest life as 'in *imago dei*' means living with the mystery of a divine gift, even where we cannot see how this is so. The same sense of mystery and dignity which causes us to respect the early embryo should protect the convicted murderer whose sins and supplications are known, in the end, only to God. It should cause us to pause before the senile and demented and the drug-addicted for the same reason, and lead us to clothe the poor, aid the sick, and visit the prisoner, for these, too, are 'the least' in which nonetheless Christ is present.

Sergio Dellavalle has expressed concern about the 'possible parochialism' of the language of *imago Dei*. I grant that the notion, especially as expanded in terms of the face of Christ, is specific to a faith tradition and in that sense parochial. Were the nature of the parochialism such that it restricted need to care and attention only to those who were members of the Christian community, this would be an abhorrent teaching. But it does not and never has restricted the command to care just to Christians. I personally prefer the honesty, as a Christian, of invoking an openly Christ-focused notion *imago Dei* over the seemingly more neutral (but actually opaquely religious) 'sanctity of human life', a notion which trades (but how?) on some religious legacy but which is now so broad as to be used by all.[20] Furthermore, the idea of *imago Dei*, especially as developed with reference to Christ as the image after whom all human beings are made, keeps in place the sense of mystery and modesty before 'the other' which should be at the ground of our respect for the dignity of other persons. On the other hand, sanctity of life, especially as currently volatilized in American political debate, runs the risk of becoming one of those hegemonic concepts so feared by Costas Douzinas. It is better, in my view, to admit a parochialism at the outset—to say this comes from my Christian and Catholic convictions—than to cloak a religious view in would-be universal secularity. It should be clear that to focus on the *imago Dei* is in no way to depart from the Catholic teaching that all human life is to be protected, but equally it should guard against an unbalanced focus on life issues (that is, beginning and end of life) at the cost of ignoring the wider needs of those 'divine images' whose struggling lives are lived out before us.

Of inestimable importance to the Christian message, a lesson it takes from Judaism and underscored in this chapter, is attention to particularity.

---

[20] Emily Jackson, in her reply to my paper at the conference, mentioned Ronald Dworkin as invoking a shared conviction in the intrinsic sanctity of human life, based not only in religious views but derived from the miracle of creation. Both 'sanctity' and 'creation' would seem to be used figuratively here, since it seems on the face of it incoherent to speak of a 'creation' without a 'creator'.

Here one could especially think of assisted suicide. For a Christian, there is no point in a life which is without hope or without the possibility of growth. God's grace knows no bounds, and blessings may come from situations of what look to us to be direst despair.[21] Christians cannot expect the rest of the population to share this belief, but they may at least be able to understand where it comes from.

Each individual, whether Christian or not, believer or not, an AIDS sufferer or not, senile or not, is in the image of God and must be respected as such. As with some other religious traditions, loss of sight and speech is not understood as failure to somehow be present. No individual life should be judged, even by its bearer, to be worthless. This is not to say that extraordinary measures should be made to keep a dying person alive. Yet a dying person, however frail, silent, and physically or mentally disabled may be 'living and active' in ways invisible to us but apparent to God. The song of the elderly Zechariah speaks of being delivered by God to 'serve him without fear, in holiness and righteousness before him all the days of our life' (Lk 1.73–5). Death is not to be avoided at all cost. The most extreme serving of God recorded in the New Testament is the death, or passion, of Christ on the cross. It is a matter of Christian faith that all human life, no matter how weakened or debilitated, is still a life in which grace is at work—a belief that needs to be cherished in our performance-driven society.

---

[21] Of course, in public debate we are not dealing with a population that is Christian. In the secular sphere I would certainly invoke, to support prohibition of euthanasia, duty of care to the physicians and the vulnerability of the elderly to the pressure to end their lives.

13

Dignity as an Eschatological Concept

David Walsh

AN ESCHATOLOGICAL CONCEPT IS one that cannot be fully known because we live within it. One day its meaning will be disclosed, but for now we see through a glass darkly. Human dignity is such a concept because it says what we cannot fully say: that is, that each human being is inviolable. There is a zone of inviolability we must not cross because it would be to deny the very meaning of what it is to be a person. As one who holds his or her existence in his or her own hands, we must not take that away by treating them as objects of control. Autonomy is too thin a word for what autonomy identifies. It is the whole metaphysical significance of the person that is at issue when we confront the question of human dignity. Our difficulty is that we live in a world without metaphysics, and therefore have to say what cannot be said.[1] This chapter takes up the challenge by pointing to eschatology as the horizon of saying because it is the horizon of our existence. We begin by reflecting on what it means to live within an understanding we do not fully penetrate, and thereby enlarge the possibility of truth. Then we examine the regime of rights that is our authoritative moral language, yet one that acknowledges its own incompleteness. When pressed to explain what rights are imputed to defend, our 'rights-talk' can only point to the dignity of the person. This is why the topic

---

[1] George Kateb takes up a similar challenge in his essay on *Human Dignity* by insisting that we must be able to ground the conviction in wholly secular terms. The project is admirable but its completion would require a more expansive language than seems to be available, although he does approach it in invoking Emerson's characterization of every person as an 'infinitude'. The difficulty is that he immediately dismisses the notion of immortality as a subjective longing for endless life, rather than a glimpse of the true infinite that exceeds the mere extension of temporality. But is not that glimpse itself the proof of immortality? Kateb can, in other words, account for everything but his own convictions. 'We need to stay true to what we know—the immensity beyond immensity of space and time and the universe's purposeless waste—because that knowledge is an incomparably superior encouragement to wonder.' In light of that true immortality we disdain the false immortality of mere endless life. *Human Dignity* (Cambridge, MA, Belknap Press of Harvard University Press, 2011), 125, 215. As with so many 'secular' accounts, Kateb's explains everything except the source of his own perspective. Only infinity can apprehend the finite.

of human dignity has in the last few decades surfaced with new prominence. The problem, third, is that dignity proves more elusive than its invocation might suggest because it protects what is most invisible of all. That is, the true self that even the person him- or herself never fully apprehends. In avoiding metaphysics we have evoked it even more deeply. We cannot finally deny, fourth, that dignity derives from the transcendence of the person by which each of us approaches the transcendence of God. Human dignity names our capacity to go beyond the claim to dignity through total self-emptying. It is thus what constitutes the transcendence of the person and can therefore never really be lost. That is why, most of all, it must be preserved, as the framework of rights has continually sought to do.

Primacy of the practical

We begin by noting that the notion of dignity has migrated from a social setting where the assertion of status was all important to one in which it is precisely the capacity to transcend any status claim that is the central issue. Rather than a world immanent concept, dignity has become an eschatological proclamation. Each one of us exceeds the whole world, because we are called to exceed all limits in self-giving. There is no worldly limit to our capacity to love. It is that eschatological flash that we glimpse when we glimpse the reality of the person, or rather, the non-reality of the person who transcends every boundary assigned in advance. The inexhaustibility of the person, the inwardness within which everything is contained, is familiarly intuited in the persons we know. We might say that we hardly know them until we encounter them as individual abysses of unknowability. This is why we cannot know persons except personally. Then we at least gain a sense of each person's unique unfathomability. The problem is that we have no philosophical language that can access that mutuality of persons that is more than words can say. Even worse, philosophy has often despaired of the task. It concedes the death of metaphysics, the opaqueness of the language of substance as well as the language of God, and betrays a singular lack of interest even in attempting to say what cannot be said about itself. Wittgenstein is one of the few exceptions, at least in calling attention to the problem.[2] But this is where

---

[2] This is the famous observation with which he opens and closes the *Tractatus Logico-Philosophicus* by insisting that 'what we cannot talk about we must pass over in silence'. Unfortunately most of his readers fail to notice that this non-saying is in effect a saying. Certainly he has not passed over in silence.

politics enters the scene. In the political realm, philosophical limits cannot define the human limits. We cannot await the theoretical breakthroughs that would prove sufficiently compelling, but must forge a meaning from the remnants that still retain the evocative moral authority that wins our consent. In politics we do not agree on foundations and then erect the principles by which a publicly representative order is affirmed. Theoretical comprehension arises, like the owl of Minerva, only late in the day, and even then does not entirely detach itself from the principles whose emergence has been the condition of its own possibility. Before we reflect on whence we have come and who we are, as well as whither we are going, we are already bound by certain moral and political convictions with which we cannot dispense. Truthfulness cannot be grounded unless we are already prepared to do so truthfully. Loyalty cannot be discussed unless we are already pledged to its indefeasibility. This is why politics is always in advance of its philosophy and the prayer life of the Church is prior to its theology. What theoretical reflection provides is not the first principles of what it examines but a meditation on what it finds as already obliging its own exercise. Philosophy can never contain that wherein it too is contained. It is bound by the primacy of the practical that receives its public authorization only within politics.

A case in point is the unsurpassability of human rights. The mutual recognition of rights is not only entailed within the logic of discourse in general, as Jürgen Habermas suggests, but it is even more deeply entailed within the moral imperative of the human community.[3] It is difficult, if not impossible, for us to conceive of a human community that would not value each and every member as unique, irreplaceable, and immeasurable. Of course, we know of societies that devalue and dehumanize their members, but we cannot regard them as anything but perverse. What is decisive, however, is that we cannot conceive of any higher notion of community than the one that puts the neediest member first, that is, the one whose rights are in any instant most in need of defending. This does not mean that every member is preoccupied with the protection and the assertion of their individual rights. On the contrary, the reciprocity that a regime of rights requires consists in the mutual self-restraint by which the rights of all are recognized. Rights are permissive; they are not unlimited claims. We are free to exercise them or not, but we are not free to abrogate them in others. It may indeed be that in defending my rights I defend the rights of all, and that when the rights of one are threatened the rights of all are placed in jeopardy, but this is not a prescription for collective self-interest.

---

[3] Jürgen Habermas, *The Theory of Communicative Action*, trans. Thomas McCarthy, vols 1 and 2 (Boston, Beacon, 1984 and 1989).

Our interests are served only within a regime founded on fairness, because it is only then that the right to what each is owed is sufficiently guaranteed. Interest is served only when justice takes precedence. A system of rights is the way in which this relationship gains recognition. Its discovery, however, has largely been the fruit of historical practice for which the theoretical justification has continued to lag.[4] The pattern is detailed in Brian Tierney's *The Idea of Natural Right*, which traces the rise of natural rights largely outside medieval political theory to show that rights can be invoked within any expansive legal framework.[5] The canonists distinguished between the ownership of property and its use, and thereby established the notion of a right from which others could be excluded. It was only a small step for William of Ockham to establish the idea of a right that could not be alienated in his dispute with Pope John XXII over Franciscan poverty. The most that the vow of poverty could entail is a renunciation of the legal right to property, since the natural right to the use of property for life could never be renounced. From there, the idea migrated to the conciliarist disputes in which the right of the Church, and of any community, to govern itself could not be renounced. This in turn created difficulty for the Spanish monarchy in the sixteenth century, when Vitoria and the Spanish scholastics insisted that conquest of the Americas had not abrogated the natural rights of the Indians to property and self-government. In other words, long before political theory had begun its quest for the foundations of rights, the discourse had emerged in practical disputes in which inalienability had become starkly visible.

Dignity as the invisible source of rights

To call these 'subjective rights', as even Tierney does, is to suggest that they have no other basis than the mere assertion of claims. But they are not subjective in this relativist sense. Rather, they are simply the result of adopting the

---

[4] The prioritization of practice over theory, as well as the characterization of political principles as abbreviations, has long been associated with the thought of Michael Oakeshott, especially in *Rationalism and Politics* (Indianapolis, Liberty Fund, rev. ed., 1991). It is doubtful, however, that Oakeshott would have applied his notion to the language of rights, although, I would argue, that a more thorough application of the primacy of practice would have required it. His closest approach is in the notion of a 'civil association', which he distinguishes sharply from an 'enterprise association' in *On Human Conduct* (Oxford, Clarendon Press, 1975).

[5] Brian Tierney, *The Idea of Natural Rights* (Atlanta, Scholars Press, 1997), provides the historical account, but we can also see Rawls's principle that 'the right is prior to the good' as its philosophical counterpart. John Rawls, *A Theory of Justice* (Cambridge, MA, Belknap Press of Harvard University Press, 1971).

perspective of the person affected, the individual subject whose humanity is under threat. In effect, they are objective rights, the ineradicable rights that attach to a human being simply in virtue of his or her humanity without subtraction or addition. When all else is lost or renounced, they are the rights that remain to denote the inexhaustible reality of the person. The problem is that the source of that inexhaustibility remains strangely invisible. We are hard pressed to locate what cannot be located or to measure what cannot be measured. It is only in the heightened vitality of the disputes, in which the notion of natural rights arises, that their imprescriptible reality is clearly glimpsed. Once the high drama of defence has passed, rights recede into the inaccessible. It is no wonder that they generate a rich trail of theoretical adumbrations even if none have succeeded in establishing their formulations definitively. More recently, that awareness of intellectual fragility has begun to surface within the practical realm in which the priority of rights must be implemented. It is no accident that the UN Universal Declaration of Human Rights simultaneously avoids any indication of the source of justification of rights while also invoking the substantive notion of human dignity as their background. The same pattern is repeated in other contemporary constitutions, notably the German and Israeli ones, in which the protection of rights is deemed to be insufficient protection for what must be protected. Over the past twenty-five years the theme of dignity has become pervasive in charters and courts as they concede the insufficiency of a rights jurisprudence. Dignity is required to name what must be preserved over and above the preservation of rights. Only if it is named can the source of rights be adequately guarded.

The difficulties that this movement beyond the specificity of rights generates are readily accepted as the price that must be paid for what is priceless.[6] It is an impressive testament to deeper resonances within liberal discourse. Where philosophy has failed and religion has been unable to generalize its insights, the law must invoke what cannot readily be invoked. Dignity is surely the most elusive concept of all. Its presence within legal briefs and judicial opinions signals a felt need that is otherwise utterly unmet within the public square. Somehow the harm that the deprivation of rights inflicts must be resisted not just in the name of what is right but in relation to what the right seeks to shield. That evolution was amply displayed in the thought of Immanuel Kant, who was the one who introduced the notion of universal human dignity, in contrast to prior conceptions of dignity as specific to a particular office or station in life. Where previously dignity was precisely what attached to the role a

---

[6] See the very fine overview in Christopher McCrudden, 'Human dignity and judicial interpretation of human rights', *European Journal of International Law* 19 (2008), 655–724.

person played in society, now it would arise from the person who stood apart from the multiplicity of roles in which he or she might appear. Rather than the dignity of what is visible, Kant would turn our attention towards the dignity that exceeds all visibility. Kant may not be thinking juristically, but the same inexorability is at work in both cases. When we think about the respect that is owed to each human being, we realize that it cannot be limited to the finite contribution each has made. When they are no longer marked by their role, we are required even more to respect the person who played it. Entitlement to dignity is by virtue of his or her humanity. The sharp distinction we had made between social status and human status begins to melt away as we realize that the latter is the ground of the former. There are no pure role-players.[7] All are persons who first possess the dignity of persons.

It is their integrity as persons, their inwardness, that the notion of dignity seeks to guard. Rights are merely the external defences against the infringement of what is, strictly speaking, internal. This is, of course, what makes the protection of dignity so notoriously difficult, because what may be an infringement to one may not be so to another. Dignity is not contained in any of the codifiable attributes that make a legal code possible. What may be an insupportable burden to one may be a matter of indifference to another. A prohibition against turbans falls more heavily on Sikh men than on the rest of the gender, just as a ban on headscarves affects Muslim women differently from other women. In each case, it is not the specific character of the burden that is at issue but the way in which it infringes upon the inner freedom of the person to be him- or herself. Without intending it, requirements that on the face of it may be trivial or neutral can have the effect of abrogating the most sacrosanct imperative of self-determination. Of course, each individual remains capable of an interior refusal to obey, but this cannot be manifested within the external world. They are deprived of the possibility of presenting themselves in public, which is more than the loss of what they would present. It is a denial of the self as the source of all self-presentation. To denigrate or diminish that innermost self, the self from which all self-expression arises while it itself remains beyond expression, is to strike at the core of the person. It is to deny the dignity of that which enacts its own being. This is the awesome stature of the person for whom no one is entitled to speak but the person him- or herself. The person denied does not disappear but is prevented from appearing. It is the

---

[7] This is an insight that has remained latent from the beginning in the Greek word *prōsopon*, from which our word 'person' is derived. Originally it meant the mask that the actor wore, so it already called attention to the invisible one who was always there behind the mask, but could not be presented as such. We have yet to develop a philosophical account of the person that is adequate to this paradoxical reality. A forthcoming work, *Politics of the Person*, is aimed at meeting this challenge in part.

objectification of what cannot and should not be objectified. But what of the possibility that the person might choose that path of diminished personhood?

Dignity as invisible

This was the great difficulty that Kant intuited and struggled against. Indeed, his whole discourse about human dignity can be read as a protracted effort to heighten the awareness of dignity as a bulwark against its deliberate devaluation.[8] Even when we must allow ourselves to be used as objects, as in his strangely objectivist conception of marriage, we must take steps to ensure that the person is not reduced to that status. Marriage is the only way that the sexual relationship of men and women can affirm that they are more than what they do.[9] In marriage the partners are received as wholes and never as parts. The person who presents him- or herself to the other is acknowledged as what can never be fully presented. That is what is absent from the contract of prostitution. Even the term carries disavowal within it, for in that case the partners have only presented themselves in the form of economic exchange. Any service that entails the whole person cannot be reduced to the coin of barter. Persons can engage in economic exchanges precisely because they cannot exchange themselves. An economy requires persons who stand outside it as enactors of the freedom that makes it all possible. The person who remains beyond every action can neither be subsumed into the transaction nor excluded from it. Dignity is the path by which what cannot be said, what can neither be preserved nor abolished, is irrefutably displayed. Autonomy, Kant discovered, cannot be exercised in disregard of its own meaning. What remains to be discovered is how self-determination is bounded by what makes it possible.

In the absence of any comprehensive philosophical defence of the dignity of the person, we must be particularly alert to the insights that are generated in the field of practice. Real life controversies, especially as they are encountered in courts of law, are an invaluable guide, for they arise not only from the law but also from the most elementary human responses. What cannot be

---

[8] Something similar may be said about the heroic resistance against the devaluation of liberty undertaken by Tocqueville in the name of liberty. 'It is easy to see that what is lacking in such nations [who have chosen a comfortable slavery] is a genuine love of freedom, that lofty aspiration which (I confess) defies analysis. For it is something one must *feel* and logic has no part in it. It is a privilege of noble minds which God has fitted to receive it, and it inspires them with a generous fervour. But to meaner souls, untouched by the sacred flame, it may well seem incomprehensible.' *The Old Regime and the French Revolution*, trans. Stuart Gilbert (Garden City, NY, Doubleday, 1955), 169.
[9] Kant, *The Metaphysics of Morals*, trans. Mary Gregor (Cambridge, Cambridge University Press, 1996), §24–7.

concealed or denied is very often what makes its way into raw judicial decisions. One thinks of the famous dwarf-tossing case in which no amount of protest of liberty interests could override the sense that here a human had been utterly reduced to an object.[10] Could the assimilation to a piece of inert matter have gone any further? Perhaps only mutilation or the sale of body parts could suggest a further disdain and, characteristically, have also prompted a similar revulsion. At such points, all that is interior to a person seems to have been drained away. These are practices we would have difficulty contemplating even in relation to a corpse, so that it is inconceivable that they should be perpetrated on one who is alive. It is the loss of the person with whom one can relate that is the most devastating. Like torture or degradation, we can only engage in such practices when we have been able to cast aside any suggestion that this other is an other, another human being.[11] Even killing can often retain more of a sense of the nobility of the other as a worthy opponent who must not be gratuitously or inhumanly mistreated. Crimes against humanity that 'shock the conscience' are terms arising from such historical moments of revulsion, and, like many things said in the heat of emotion, they do not necessarily accurately reflect their own genealogy. The formulations suffer from an excessive abstraction, as if humanity could be assaulted or conscience shocked in general. The truth is that it is only individual human beings that can be killed, and we can be revolted only by the destruction of each unspeakably precious life. This is why the aggregate number of exterminations and casualties numb the imagination. We can be stirred to indignation only when we behold the misery of a single one. What is true of one is true of all, that each one carries a whole interior world within, and that it is the denial of that that is the ultimate indignity. Their suffering has ceased to count. Thus, it is not that they suffered but that they are no longer regarded as persons. The ultimate indignity points us towards what dignity is intended to guard.

Such a route is needed because dignity names what is invisible. The person is the source of all that is visible about the person but remains therefore beyond visibility. We often resort to the notion of a 'transcendent core' of the person to suggest what it is that dignity seeks to protect, but that language has understandably lost its evocative power. This is not necessarily to be regretted because the term is a contradiction. A core indicates an irreducible bedrock, while transcendent suggests that it lies beyond all fixity. Besides, we have

---

[10] Michael Rosen, *Dignity: Its History and Meaning* (Cambridge, MA, Harvard University Press, 2012), covers this and other relevant cases in chapter 2.

[11] Primo Levi, *If This Is A Man* and *The Truce*, trans. Stuart Woolf (Boston, MA, Little, Brown, 1991), and the discussion by Dustin Howes, '"Consider if this is a person": Primo Levi, Hannah Arendt, and the political significance of Auschwitz', *Holocaust and Genocide Studies* 22 (2008), 266–92.

become accustomed to conceiving of the philosophical alternatives as either deontological or consequential, both alternatives that eschew any appeal to ontology. What we have not considered is that the dignity of the person may not need any grounding in terms of ontological status. Just as the person lies beyond any social status, and thus can be regarded in relation to their human dignity quite apart from the dignity of their particular office or role, so the person can be seen as standing outside all ontological status, as incapable of containment within any horizon to which they may be assigned. Indeed, persons can consider their ontological status precisely because they are not simply confined to it. Dignity can be gained or lost because we are beyond dignity as such. We have already seen that the person is what eludes all the enactments and expressions to which he or she gives rise. There would be no 'giving rise' if there was not first what is not given rise to. Now we must be prepared to take the next step to which we have been led. We must dispense with the metaphysical crutch that there is nevertheless some innermost core, some primordial stuff, from which the person emerges and on which he or she is grounded. The extraordinary thing about persons is that they hold their existence in their own hands. They can give themselves or they can withhold themselves, so that nothing else can bear responsibility for them. Even God is not responsible for them, for he has left them free. Nothing is prior to the person who thus shares in the primordiality of God. In other words, the status of the person is of that which is beyond all status. Whatever is adduced as the ground of the value of the person, even the love of God, remains available to the person to be accepted or rejected. The demise of ontology (itself a hybrid invention) is therefore not to be lamented, for it always stood in the way of glimpsing that which it sought to articulate. Metaphysics (another surrogate) must finally yield to eschatology as we admit that the person arises from what is not, as befits the proper meaning of what is transcendent.

Persons transcend all saying and doing

Perhaps it is time too to shed the connection that the term human dignity has with any notion of status. Granted that it has already eliminated the vestiges of special status in favour of a universalization of simply human status from which no one is excluded. But this still may suggest something too worldly. It leaves something tangible, even if it is universally human, on which the person may stake his or her dignity. In doing so, however, we betray the dignity of the person which does not turn on any particular features or qualities the person may possess. Even the dignity of a rational being, so important to

Kant, seems to suggest that it must be accorded only so long as we retain the capacity to reason. This is, of course, the error into which the inclination to define what it means to be a person, and therefore an agent of dignity, inevitably leads. It is not what we intend in invoking the term human dignity, for we mean precisely the opposite of any scale of measurement. Even those who fall short of displaying their full personhood are somehow persons, and we affirm this in according them the dignity of persons. We do not ask them to produce proof of personhood. Instead, we are inclined to conclude that they most of all are persons, for they allow us to relate directly to them in all their invisibility. By saying nothing they have said everything. They show that above all persons are, most of all when they are not expressed in anything present. Even without consciousness, they give themselves through their breathing until they yield up their last breath. Theirs is the dignity of having given all, and we realize that there is nothing in which they can be contained. This is why we reverence their remains as what still speak to us even after the person is gone. Not even death can defeat the person who, somehow, is deathless. This is why the distinctive mark of all human societies is remembrance of the dead. We are inclined to think that thinking about the afterlife is the result of religion, but it is really the converse. Religion arises because we already know about the afterlife through our experience as persons who are never fully here and therefore are never fully departed.

To be a person is to be transcendent. We therefore know about the transcendent, God, only because we participate in that mode of being. Whatever we have said or done we have gone beyond it as that which can never be identical with the said or done. Persons thus exist nowhere. It is futile to ask for a metaphysics of the person, as if anything more substantive could explain the transcendence of the person. We can understand metaphysics, the possibility of transcendence, because we are persons capable of containing the whole world inwardly only because we are not present within it. This is the *imago Dei*, although the formula already suffers from the defect of suggesting that there is a likeness for what has no likeness. But the term also works because it shows that we have been able to glimpse the transcendent by virtue of our own transcendence. God can be known only by persons who are Godlike. That is their dignity. They are beyond any claim to dignity in this world. It is the dignity of those whose dignity does not turn on any display of dignity. They hold their dignity within their own hands and can freely take it up or surrender it. For this reason it does not arise from our acknowledgement. They cannot lose it, although we may fail to acknowledge its imperative. The dignity of persons is that they are deathless, that they stand outside all that they are. They cannot lose what never is. This is why, no matter what indignity they may suffer, they can never lose their dignity. Of course a human being may lose control, may be overwhelmed by suffering and devastation, but that is only a possibility for one who is not defined by that extremity of misery. Only persons can suffer because they are not identical with pain. Animals are engulfed in their pain. This is why we put them out of their pain. We cannot do that for a human being who always remains beyond the pain he or she undergoes. This is why they have faith, a faith by which their suffering is transcendence.[12]

It is exemplified by Christ, who not only lays aside the dignity of God to become man but even sets aside the prerogatives of a human being through his death on the cross. It is a death utterly without dignity because it is public. Crucifixion is certainly among the most excruciating ways to die, but it is intensified when it is undergone before a hostile public gaze.[13] The innermost agony of the person is exposed. That moment when the person is at his most vulnerable, the precious loss of life that must be shielded from the stare of indifferent onlookers, has been ripped open. What should be observed only by those who can share in the suffering of the dying is exhibited for all to see. Not only is death inflicted but the person is annihilated as a person. The interior life is denied, for it is objectified. Like one of Francis Bacon's carcass paintings, everything says this was not a human being. Of course that is precisely Bacon's point, that we cannot look upon a human being in that way. Yet that is the way willingly undergone by Jesus. He not only suffered and died, but did so in such a way that he abandoned all human dignity. Yet he simultaneously regained all that had been lost. In giving himself up, shedding not only the last drop of blood but also the last vestige of human dignity, Christ showed the real character of human dignity. It is the dignity of yielding up one's dignity completely. It is the dignity of God that carries nothing of self-concern within it but freely gives itself on behalf of all. No greater triumph over evil is possible than the divine action in which God sacrifices himself completely. Nor is there any greater meaning to human dignity than the capacity to share in that total outpouring that is the life of God. This is why human dignity is an eschatological concept. It cannot be described in the terminology of this world for it has exceeded every finite measurement. It is the dignity of the immeasurable, the dignity of that which has renounced all claims to dignity. That is its dignity. It is the dignity of what is beyond dignity.

---

[12] This idea is well developed in the theological personalism of Benedict XVI. 'Faith is not simply a personal reaching out towards things to come that are still totally absent: it gives us something.' *Spe Salvi (Saved in Hope)*, 2007, §7.

[13] 'The cross is the giant leap toward the radical internalizing of the concept of dignity, toward the awareness of something in the phenomenon of dignity at once veiled and unveiled.' Robert Spaemann, *Love and the Dignity of Human Life* (Grand Rapids, MI, Eerdmanns, 2012), 31.

This does not of course mean that it is only in the renunciation of dignity that dignity is realized. An even worse implication would be to suggest that dignity must not be safeguarded because it cannot ultimately be lost. The highest aspiration of our humanity would be taken as an invitation for its worst desecration. What could be worse than the blatant disregard of the best? Generosity is not an invitation to robbery. It may indeed be, as Plato saw, that the evildoers are even more severely injured than those whom they injure, but we cannot countenance their actions without complicity in them. Dignity, the dignity that cannot be lost, must be saved most of all. The challenge is to find a means of saving it when it appears to have no worldly presence at all. Dignity may be eschatological, but it is not for that reason any the less real or any the less present. We encounter it in every person towards whom we are charged with protecting their inviolability. Their self-presentation must be sacrosanct. No one can subsume the innermost self from whom all their existence flows. To do so would be to abrogate their existence as persons, that is as beings who have no existence but what they put themselves into. Their interiority must be guarded as the highest, uncontainable in anything but itself. But this means that we must be hesitant in imposing our judgement of what dignity requires in place of the person's own. We can easily see that there are many situations that might be deemed undignified or even degrading to outsiders but not to the responsible individuals themselves. Human dignity cannot be so serious that it prohibits all undignified behaviour—a bar that would eliminate many of the activities in which we engage. Nor can human dignity lack the highest seriousness of the capacity to surrender all claims to dignity, to exercise dignity in its most transcendent form. The turning point in each of these cases is to judge the validity of the claim to be exercising the highest form of self-responsibility.

The eschatological moment in which the whole of a person's existence is contained is neither private nor solitary. It is the meeting place of all human beings past, present, and future under the gaze of irremovable judgement. All have become judges who must place themselves in the position of the other. We cannot avoid rendering a judgement on the judgement that the person him- or herself must render. Have I put myself wholly into this action? If I have, then there is nothing that can diminish the dignity invested. Even letting oneself be demeaned to the level of an inanimate object can be accepted so long as it is a full expression of the self. But that does not mean that we must support every degradation to which a person may volunteer. It is only those losses to which a person has wholly submitted that can be regarded as retaining the dignity of a human being. The whole person must be given in the action. That is not possible if the indignity is merely an economic transaction, for no one can give him- or herself for the sake of an object. One can only give oneself for the sake of a person, including one's own person. Then one is giving what cannot be given and yet must be given in a human relationship. In an economic exchange at most we can give our time, ourselves in part. Material transactions are somehow beneath the dignity of persons who reside forever outside them. It is only if the meaning of an action rises above the economic level that it is an appropriate communication of the person as such. This is why it is possible to sacrifice oneself for another but it is impossible to sell oneself to another. Paradoxical as it may be, one can give away what cannot be sold. That which is priceless cannot be bought. Anything into which the person places the whole self, that is, precisely what cannot be contained in anything finite, must not be reduced to the terms of conveyance. The person always communicates by going beyond all that is said. By contrast, an exchange is what can be reduced to the terms of a contract. Marriage is virtually an overturning of its contract because it is unconditional. Organ donation is bedevilled by the same impossibility of reducing it to an economy. It may indeed be the case that everyone else in an operation gets paid but the donor, but has not the donor demonstrated that he or she has given more than can be repaid, in giving life? The dignity of the immeasurable cannot be measured.

Rights as guarding the invisible

The person who exceeds all that is given must nevertheless be preserved in his or her excessiveness. Has the giving been in the name of what cannot be given or only in the guise of what can be given and which is thus not given at all? It is in that eschatological arc that the dignity of the person lies. Is the uncontainable self contained in the action? That is the only relevant question, for we cannot prejudge in advance what form the gift of self may assume. This is why it is difficult to judge an affront to dignity, although it is not by any means impossible. We know what the gift is when we receive it. All we have to do is oppose its being counterfeited. This may still not forestall the possibility that counterfeit can be employed as the only available medium of truth. Humiliation may be redeemed by the giving that transfigures it or by the laughter that detonates it. We cannot fix the criteria of authenticity in advance of the event, but we can insist on its applicability. In doing so, we have established a boundary of dignity that, while it may be breached, has nevertheless marked what must be defended. Dignity, in the end, recedes into the indefinable, but that is why it must nevertheless be defined. We cannot protect the dignity that includes the possibility of its own self-abandonment as its highest possibility, but it is just for that reason that we must make the attempt. Law must define the indefinable in the only way that it can. It must acknowledge that law itself is overtaken by the dignity of the self that exceeds its own dignity. The legislation of dignity cannot in the final analysis escape the eschatological character of its subject. Law too must exceed its own limits.

It must acknowledge that human dignity cannot be alienated even when it is legally alienated. This is the core of the famous dispute of the Franciscans with Pope John XXII, when it was precisely their determination to renounce all that brought inalienability into focus. They could only alienate a legal right to property but never the inalienable right to the means necessary for life. Law encounters the limits of law in the notion of natural rights. They are not subject to the conveyance of law. Dignity as the unfathomable depth of the person, the container of the interior presentation of self, is the flash of transcendence that is glimpsed in the prohibitions against the violation of human rights. What is not present anywhere may nevertheless be intuited in the barriers it provokes. The discovery of natural and human rights is just such a moment. It is the point at which the law acknowledges its insufficiency as law. That is, that it is itself measured by an order of right beyond it. Law cannot be used to alienate the inalienable. On the contrary, it is pledged to preserve what it cannot but preserve. Dignity has been invoked as what exceeds a mere catalogue of rights, but it is in their recognition that dignity looms as the inexhaustible source. What cannot be alienated cannot be fully named. Rights are not the same as dignity, for dignity requires us to go beyond the mere acknowledgement of rights, but rights are the epiphany of the dignity of the person. Rights are inviolable. They cannot be balanced against some larger social good, nor is there a point at which the individual ceases to count as much as others or even as much as all others. Infinity cannot be calculated. It is that affirmation of the incalculability of each one that is the primary legal affirmation of human dignity. When it has said more than can be said, what more can the law say? It has wholly subordinated itself to the dignity of the person who is alone capable of giving him- or herself on behalf of the whole. Rights are our refusal to trade in the untradeable. It is in the defence of rights that dignity is resplendent.

14

The Vanishing Absolute and the Deconsecrated God: A Theological Reflection on Revelation, Law, and Human Dignity

Tina Beattie

THE THEME OF THIS BOOK raises a crucial question which is addressed in several chapters, including the session to which my own chapter refers. What do we mean when we use words such as 'human' and 'dignity', and what relationship do those words have to one another in the quest for justice? These are historically contingent words which shift in meaning depending on their contexts, and our concepts of justice shift with them.

This chapter is developed from my response to papers delivered at the original conference by Costas Douzinas, David Gushee, and Dieter Grimm (Gushee's and Grimm's revised versions are included in this book,[1] and Douzinas's approach was based on a previously published book),[2] positioned within my own disciplinary perspective of theology. I weave together strands from different theoretical and philosophical arguments to create a loosely woven theological tapestry—incomplete and full of gaps as every theological reflection must be, if it is to avoid the hubristic violation of the mystery before which it positions itself. This mystery is not only the mystery of the divine but also, and perhaps more importantly, the mystery of the human, that imaginative ape which suffers yearning and sorrow because somewhere along the evolutionary process its soul jumped the tracks of the finite and it began to imagine and to fear the prospect of its own death: 'In the day that you eat thereof you shall surely die', God cautioned the innocents in Eden, warning

---

[1] Dieter Grimm, Chapter 21, this volume; David P. Gushee, Chapter 15, this volume.
[2] Costas Douzinas, *Human Rights and Empire: The Political Philosophy of Cosmopolitanism* (Abingdon, Routledge-Cavendish, 2007).

them against eating the deadly fruit of the tree of the knowledge of good and evil (Gen. 2:17).[3]

The theme of original sin is not popular today, even although its evidence is all around us. Like that other old warning that you cannot serve both God and Mammon (Matt. 6:24), liberal optimists flourish best when they ignore these uncomfortable biblical cautions. However, I want to suggest that much postmodern theory is implicitly informed by a pessimistic view of the human condition, which could be seen as the secular derivative of the doctrine of original sin. Whatever we call it, this is the apprehension that our lives are haunted by a perpetual sense of alienation and suffering, and that all our institutions and relationships bear the taint of violence in some form or another. I ask what the Christian dialectic of sin and grace can contribute to our understanding of this affliction of our species, in a way that might open up a precipitous path of justice between the nihilism of some postmodern theorists, and the complacency of their more optimistic liberal counterparts.

It is with this in mind that I begin with a discussion of Douzinas's postmodern critique of the concept of human dignity and its Christian influences, which I explore in the context of Giorgio Agamben's idea of *homo sacer*.[4] I then consider Gushee's quite different interpretation of the significance of the biblical understanding of the human as sacred, and I relate this to the natural law tradition. This brings me to a critical evaluation of human dignity as an absolute right enshrined in the German Basic Law, which is the topic of Grimm's chapter. Finally, I weave all these themes into a short theological reflection on Christ as *homo sacer*.

Universal humanity and *homo sacer*

Douzinas focused on the problematic claims of human rights and the concept of the human that informs them. He argued that Christianity's universalization of the term 'human' has lent legitimacy to the West's missionizing and colonizing violence, up to and including the imposition of secular concepts of universal human rights by various forms of political, military, and economic coercion. The concept of universal humanity elides difference, sets up one norm (that of the Western Christian tradition and its secular derivatives) as the

---

[3] All biblical references are to the King James 2000 Bible.
[4] Giorgio Agamben, *Homo Sacer: Sovereign Power and Bare Life*, trans. Daniel Heller-Roazen (Stanford, CA, Stanford University Press, 1998, first pub. 1995).

standard for all others, and widens the gap between normative and empirical humanity.

Douzinas invites comparison between his critique of human rights and Agamben's idea of *homo sacer*.[5] This is an enigmatic concept in ancient Roman law, in which the Latin *sacer* has a more ambivalent meaning than the word 'sacred'. It means 'set apart', and it refers both to those who are exempt from the law because they are over and above it (the sovereign as lawgiver outside the law),[6] and to those who are excluded from the law because they are beneath it. Paradoxically, both of these positions are also defined within the law, insofar as it is the law itself that authorizes the exception enacted in its name.

Agamben applies the term '*homo sacer*' to the one who is excluded by law from the benefits, protections, and rights of modern liberal society, so that he or she exists in a condition of 'bare life'. In Greek philosophical terms this constitutes the biological organism whose life (*zoē*) has not yet become the particular form of life (*bios*) constituted by incorporation into the social body (the *polis*). In the ancient world, such life could not be sacrificed (the divinized sovereign above the law cannot be sacrificed under the law, and the bare life beneath the law lacks the significance to be a worthy sacrifice), but it could be destroyed with impunity.

For Agamben, this figure of *homo sacer* as the exception outside the law produced by the law is the originary embodiment of Western political relationships. In modernity, it acquires deadly significance because of the fusion of 'bare life' and politics.[7] There is no longer any distinction between organic life and political life, so that our bodies become colonized by the political order through the modern idea of autonomy. This gives me sovereignty over myself, but I always risk being reduced to 'bare life' if that self-sovereignty should be taken from me by mental or physical incapacity, or by political or legal intervention:

> It is as if every valorization and every 'politicization' of life (which, after all, is implicit in the sovereignty of the individual over his own existence) necessarily implies a new decision concerning the threshold beyond which life ceases to be politically relevant, becomes only 'sacred life', and can as such be eliminated without punishment. Every society sets this limit; every society—even the most modern—decides who its 'sacred men' will be. It is

---

[5] See Douzinas, *Human Rights and Empire*.
[6] Agamben develops this idea in engagement with the work of Carl Schmitt. See Carl Schmitt, *Chapters on the Concept of Sovereignty*, trans. George Schwab (Cambridge, MA, MIT Press, 1985).
[7] These arguments can also be approached from a Foucaultian perspective. Compare with Stephen Morton and Stephen Bygrave (eds), *Foucault in an Age of Terror: Essays on Biopolitics and the Defence of Society* (Basingstoke and New York, Palgrave Macmillan, 2008).

even possible that this limit, on which the politicization and the *exception* of natural life in the juridical order of the state depends, has done nothing but extend itself in the history of the West and has now—in the new biopolitical horizon of states with national sovereignty—moved inside every human life and every citizen. Bare life is no longer confined to a particular place or a definite category. It now dwells in the biological body of every living being.[8]

The fusion between biological life and politics eliminates the space of ambiguity between *zoē* and *bios* within which a living body might experience a limited freedom, before or beyond its inscription within the law. In terms of our humanity, we are now all or nothing—fully human or not human at all—and there is no protection for any form of in-between organic human life that is not politically constituted and legally sanctioned. For Agamben, the Nazi death camps are the defining example of the biopolitics of modernity—he calls them 'the "*Nomos*" of the modern'[9]—but he also discusses the American response to 9/11 and Guantanamo Bay in similar terms.[10]

Douzinas's critique of the concept of universal humanity refers to the normative human inscribed within the proliferating complexity of the concept of human rights, as every possible activity becomes incorporated and legislated for or against within the language of rights. The universal human encapsulated within the concept of human rights is life as *bios*—the biopolitically constructed and codified citizen who conforms to the conventions and laws of society, and who is bodily mapped and trapped within the rights that accrue to the modern subject by virtue of being designated and legally recognized as 'human'.

What Douzinas refered to as 'empirical humanity'[11] could be described as bare life or *zoē*. It is life as it is experienced on the margins of the normative or outside the sphere of the law. Such life offers a certain freedom from the rules, but it is always at risk of being violated, eliminated, or ignored in order to eradicate every exception that would threaten the universal norm. A human body that is not ensnared within the bureaucracy of laws, rights, policies, surveillance, and accountability enjoys what might seem to many of us a lavish freedom, but that body enjoys such freedom only on condition that it also forfeits its right to protection. Human life has value if and only if it conforms to the rules.

Yet there are two problems with Douzinas's account of history and the human condition. First, in his damning evaluation of the Western Christian

---

[8] Agamben, *Homo Sacer*, 81.
[9] Agamben, *Homo Sacer*, part Three, section 7, 95–101.
[10] Agamben, *State of Exception* (Chicago, University of Chicago Press, 2005).
[11] In discussion at the conference.

legacy, Douzinas himself falls into the trap of eliding all that is particular, empirical, and diverse by way of a universalizing hypothesis that fabricates and then condemns a normative metanarrative of Christian history and its concept of the human. He elides the robust particularity and revolutionary spirit, which have been as much a part of the Christian story as imperial conquest and tyranny. Christianity takes many forms—it tells many stories, inspires many dreams, awakens many desires, and weaves together friends and strangers across boundaries of time and place in multiple and diverse configurations of culture, faith, and practice. These complex and prismatic realities disappear before the cold glare of scientific rationalism, they are flattened out and rendered anachronistic by the universalising claims of human rights; but they also dematerialize before the deconstructive gaze of the postmodern sceptic.

The second problem is with Douzinas's deferred utopianism, and with his advocacy of the revolutionary potential of the Freudian death drive, which is pacified by the securities and happiness promised (but never delivered) by universal human rights. The death drive enables us to go to the revolutionary frontiers of the secure, the familiar, and the defended in order to expose ourselves to the vulnerability of encounter, risk, and transformation. It is the opposite of the pleasure principle, which orientates us towards stasis, comfort, and complacency. But the death drive is also capable of arousing sadomasochistic impulses, which are the dark underbelly of the politics of revolution and anarchy. As philosopher John Gray argues, the utopian revolutions and progressive ideologies of modernity have tended to disintegrate into savage and sometimes genocidal regimes.[12] In Louis Wolcher's critique of the relationship between law and violence, he argues persuasively that humanity is universal only in its capacity to suffer.[13] The attempted elimination of suffering can thus be seen as a horror coiled within every utopian quest, because it is only possible to eliminate suffering if we eliminate the humans who suffer or who are deemed to cause others to suffer, and thus there is no end to the killing that can be justified in the pursuit of utopia.

So my appeal to Douzinas is to practise more thoroughly what he preaches, to let go of the need to find a universalizing historical metanarrative which only perpetuates the suffering and exclusion that it seeks to address. The myth of progress still lurks within such postmodern deconstructive strategies, for

---

[12] John Gray, *Black Mass: Apocalyptic Religion and the Death of Utopia* (London and New York, Penguin Books, 2008).

[13] See Louis E. Wolcher, *Law's Task: The Tragic Circle of Law, Justice and Human Suffering* (Aldershot and Burlington, VT, Ashgate Publishing, 2008). Wolcher engages with Douzinas in Louis E. Wolcher, 'The problem of the subject(s)', in Anne Wagner and Jan M. Broekman (eds), *Prospects of Legal Semiotics* (London and New York, Springer Dordrecht Heidelberg, 2010), 145–70.

they share with modernity the belief that only the future can be redeemed, only the future can be struggled towards. The past is what hinders and oppresses us, and we must shake off its claims upon us as we surge towards the brave new world of nihilistic postmodern utopianism, even if this is infinitely deferred.

To say this is not to deny that the ideology of neo-liberalism demands resistance and transformation, but it is to insist that the fragile hopes of the future cannot be articulated without also attending to the fragile memories and untold stories of the past which are discovered within religious traditions. Johann Baptist Metz, a German theologian writing out of the context of the Holocaust, speaks of the 'dangerous memories' which interrupt progressive accounts of history by calling attention to the silenced voices and unheeded cries of suffering that constitute the human story.[14] The 'dangerous memory' of Christ's crucifixion and resurrection calls Christians to attend to the voices of the victims of history, and it exposes the culpability of all who, claiming to be Christian, have ignored or encouraged the suffering inflicted in their name. However, many of those silenced and forgotten voices are themselves anonymous Christian saints and martyrs—only the few are named and remembered—and the wholesale condemnation of Christianity by postmodern thinkers such as Douzinas perpetuates this act of silencing.

The human as sacred

Let me turn now to Gushee's quite different evaluation of the Christian legacy. Gushee argues that dignity is too thin a concept when compared with the rich meaning of human sacredness inherent in the biblical tradition. While acknowledging the abuses that have been part of Christian history, he nevertheless argues that the Bible offers a paradigmatic account of the sacredness of the human which sanctifies each and every human, guaranteed by God as 'the ultimate source of law in Israel', in the context of an essentially egalitarian understanding of divine law. Modern Western culture has squandered this rich biblical legacy through its compromises with power, violence, and injustice. The idea of sacredness has been replaced by the relatively thin secularized concept of human dignity, grounded in reason not in revelation, and it was discarded altogether by Nietzsche and his followers.

---

[14] See Johann Baptist Metz, *Faith in History and Society: Toward a Practical Fundamental Theology*, trans. David Smith (New York, Seabury, 1980).

So there is a hermeneutical conflict in the versions of Western religious history and its influences offered by Douzinas and Gushee. For Douzinas, Christianity is part of the problem; for Gushee it is part of the solution. For Douzinas, Hegelian, Marxist, Nietzschean, and Freudian perspectives offer an indispensable vantage point from which to criticize liberal legal and political philosophy. For Gushee, Nietzschean nihilism is symptomatic of the failure of post-Christian societies. The task of Christian intellectuals is to retrieve the richness of the biblical understanding of human sacredness as a resource for a deeper ethos than human dignity.

However, Gushee risks minimizing the failure of historical Christianity to make good on its claims of justice and equality. No other religion—including Islam—has been used to justify violence, conquest, and inequality quite so effectively as Christianity. If Douzinas needs to be more attentive to the redemptive vision of peace empirically realized in individual Christian lives, Gushee needs to be more attentive to the ways in which these redemptive fragments cannot be pieced together to form a coherent picture of Christian justice. They remain what they are—neglected memories that shimmer amid the rubble of the past, so that only through the careful sifting of historical despair are we able to extract the nuggets of hope. 'Bare life'—the life chosen by Christians who willingly transgress in order to express solidarity with Christ in the poor, the marginalized, and the criminalized—cannot be institutionalized or legitimated, for then it ceases to be 'bare life' at all. It must remain the exception if it is to challenge the system.

Before I turn to consider the idea of human dignity as an absolute in the context of Grimm's chapter, I want to bring a theological perspective to bear on the foregoing. What follows is necessarily underdeveloped, but I hope it gives a sense of what theology might bring to this discussion so far.

Amor mundi and *contemptus mundi*

There is a tension in Christianity between two broad traditions which flow in and out of one another in various configurations and forms of political, ethical, and theological expression. *Amor mundi*, love of the world, seeks an ephemeral flourishing within the material conditions of earthly life in recognition that creation is good and loved by God. *Contemptus mundi*, contempt for the world, seeks detachment and transcendence in relation to a natural order that is mired in sin and enslaved by violence. At the risk of extreme oversimplification, and with many exceptions on both sides, Catholic theology has tended towards the former and Protestant theology towards the latter. The tradition that emphasizes the destructive effects of original sin on the human capacity for natural justice is often—and not entirely accurately—associated with Augustine who, writing in the fifth century during the collapse of the Roman Empire, viewed the earthly city as a symbol of violence and oppression, blighted by sin and incapable of offering its inhabitants the justice and peace of the City of God.[15] In some Protestant theologies, this Augustinian pessimism evolves into a sweeping indictment of all attempts to discern justice and goodness within the natural order of a graced creation. Grace comes only through faith in Jesus Christ as revealed in the Bible, and this is the only hope of human salvation. Postmodern pessimism can be understood as the distant heir to Augustinianism and the theologies of the Reformation, although shorn of their themes of judgment and redemption.

Gushee's fundamentally positive evaluation of the biblical tradition in relation to the social order invites comparison with the Catholic understanding of natural law associated with Thomas Aquinas and scholasticism. The natural law tradition posits a fundamental continuity between grace and nature, reason and revelation, so that the relationship between theological and philosophical approaches to knowledge is complementary rather than contradictory. It is predicated upon a vision of cosmic justice which filters through all the levels of the created order, which manifests itself to human understanding through the use of reason and conscience, and which makes it possible for human authorities to enshrine just laws within their societies and institutions in a way that maintains the social conditions necessary for the good of each and the good of all. The idea of natural law has played a central role in the formation of Catholic concepts of justice, law, and ethics because of the belief that all nature, including human nature, participates in the divine law, and original sin has damaged but not destroyed our natural capacity for justice. To give a brief example of this, I want to refer to the Vatican II document on religious liberty, *Dignitatis Humanae*.[16]

This is a revolutionary document in the Catholic theological tradition, because for the first time it not only recognizes but also defends the right to religious freedom, and it does so in the context of human dignity. It starts by acknowledging that a sense of human dignity is becoming an increasingly important aspect of modern consciousness, and it cites the right to religious freedom as a primary concern in this context. Human dignity derives from

---

[15] See Augustine, *Concerning the City of God against the Pagans*, trans. Henry Bettenson (London and New York, Penguin Books, 2003).

[16] Pope Paul VI, '*Dignitatis Humanae*: On the Right of the Person and of Communities to Social and Civil Freedom in Matters Religious', 7 December 1965, http://www.vatican.va/archive/hist_councils/ii_vatican_council/documents/vat-ii_decl_19651207_dignitatis-humanae_en.html.

the fact that we are 'beings endowed with reason and free will and therefore privileged to bear personal responsibility' (#2). This entails an obligation to seek the truth, and this in turn requires 'immunity from external coercion as well as psychological freedom' (#2). The document defends the primacy of conscience and the freedom from coercion and force which this demands.

Dignitatis Humanae begins with an appeal to natural law, before focusing more closely on how this is to be understood in terms of biblical revelation. It affirms that:

> the highest norm of human life is the divine law—eternal, objective and universal—whereby God orders, directs and governs the entire universe and all the ways of the human community by a plan conceived in wisdom and love. Man has been made by God to participate in this law, with the result that, under the gentle disposition of divine Providence, he can come to perceive ever more fully the truth that is unchanging. (#3)

After setting out this inclusive vision informed by natural law, the document moves on to bring a particular theological slant to its understanding of the human condition:

> God calls men to serve Him in spirit and in truth, hence they are bound in conscience but they stand under no compulsion. God has regard for the dignity of the human person whom He himself created and man is to be guided by his own judgment and he is to enjoy freedom. This truth appears at its height in Christ Jesus, in whom God manifested Himself and His ways with men ... Not by force of blows does His rule assert its claims. It is established by witnessing to the truth and by hearing the truth, and it extends its dominion by the love whereby Christ, lifted up on the cross, draws all men to himself. (#11)

This weaving together of scripture and natural law is a distinguishing feature of the Catholic theological tradition, but there are different interpretations of natural law in modern Catholic thought. New natural law theorists, such as Christopher Tollefsen and Robert George, appeal to natural law to underwrite an absolutist ethical vision, concerned almost exclusively with sexuality, procreation, and marriage rather than with wider issues of social and economic justice.[17] Against such readings, scholars such as Jean Porter[18] offer a more contingent and contextualized interpretation, arguing that natural law in the classical theological tradition has little content. It is a general set of prin-

---

[17] For an excellent critique, see Russell Hittinger, *A Critique of the New Natural Law Theory* (South Bend, IN, University of Notre Dame Press, 1989).
[18] Jean Porter, *Natural & Divine Law: Reclaiming the Tradition for Christian Ethics* (Grand Rapids, MI, and Cambridge, William B. Eerdmans, 1999); *Nature as Reason: A Thomistic Theory of the Natural Law* (Grand Rapids, MI, and Cambridge, William B. Eerdmans, 2005).

ciples capable of accommodating a diverse range of philosophical, religious, and social constructs within its understanding of reason. Such interpretations support a liberal social ethos, requiring only such laws as are necessary to maintain public order, and with a high regard for the primacy of individual conscience.

From this classical natural law perspective, the critique of modernity offered by thinkers such as Douzinas and Agamben would be too negative. One could even argue that postmodern nihilism may be rather more attractive to Western intellectuals than to people trapped within the anarchic violence of failed states and lawless regimes—which is where the postmodern condition most fully embodies its chaos within human affairs. Those who live in the midst of violence well understand Augustine's widely quoted insight that 'The peace of the whole universe is the tranquillity of order.'[19] However, less widely quoted is what follows, when Augustine discusses the plight of those who lack such tranquillity: 'because their wretchedness is deserved and just, they cannot be outside the scope of order. They are not, indeed, united with the blessed; yet it is by the law of order that they are sundered from them.'[20]

Here, we glimpse the darker side of the function of law which Wolcher describes as being to '*divide* the vast realm of universal human suffering into parts: the legal and the illegal, the just and the unjust, the inevitable and the avoidable, and so forth'.[21] Augustine's earthly city is not a place of egalitarian justice but of hierarchical order, in which the forces of violence must be kept at bay by the power of law, lest they overwhelm our fragile capacity for peace and flourishing.

At its best, then, the law maintains social equilibrium by offering some level of coherence and predictability to ward off the threat of random violence and arbitrary punishment, but it can only do so by mastering the threat of violence. Ultimately, however, the Christian understanding of original sin as the loss of original justice means that there will always be a conflict between human laws and divine justice. In the Bible, the justice of God is not that of impartiality but, as Gushee suggests, of weakening the strong and strengthening the weak. This is what the psalmist means when he says of God:[22]

> He shall judge the poor of the people,
> he shall save the children of the needy,
> and shall break in pieces the oppressor.

---

[19] Augustine, *The City of God*, Part II, Book XIX, Chapter 13, 870.
[20] Augustine, *The City of God*, Part II, Book XIX, Chapter 13, 870.
[21] Wolcher, *Law's Task*, xx.
[22] Psalm 72:4, 12.

> For he shall deliver the needy when he crieth;
> The poor also, and the one that hath no helper.

This partiality towards the poor—what liberation theologians call God's preferential option for the poor—is not how human laws function. As Anatole France famously wrote, 'The law, in its majestic equality, forbids the rich as well as the poor to sleep under the bridges, to beg in the streets, and to steal bread.'[23] The justice of God takes up the cause of the *homo sacer*, and it can only be fleetingly glimpsed in the lives of those who transgress, those who willingly step across the dividing line between life and death, between insider and outsider, between those under the law and those outside the law, in order to uphold a law beyond the law on the side of those excluded by the law. In the words of theologian John Caputo:

> If justice is 'beyond' the law, that is not because justice is too big for the law but too little, because it has to do with the fragments and remains, the *me onta* who are before the law, beneath the law, too trivial or worthless or insignificant for the law to notice, with rags and litter, the nobodies, the outsiders.[24]

In a creation loved and sustained by God, Christians are called to recognize grace in ordinary human affairs, and to work with those who seek justice within the existing order. However, they are also called to be attentive to those who are excluded by that order, which requires a precipitous balancing act between conformity and transgression. It is a call to be in the world but not of the world, in a way which risks rejection and punishment (e.g. Jn 15:19). I turn now to Grimm's chapter, to develop these ideas in the context of the idea of human dignity as an absolute right, under the German Basic Law. What follows is highly tentative, informed by my reflections on extensive discussions during the conference but offering only a hesitant critique of what I find to be an impossible proposition—namely, that the law can name and defend an absolute.

Human dignity—a vanishing absolute

Article 1(1) of the Basic Law declares that 'Human dignity shall be inviolable. To respect and protect it shall be the duty of all state authority.'[25] Grimm

---

[23] Anatole France, quoted in Wolcher, *Law's Task*, 70.
[24] John D. Caputo, *More Radical Hermeneutics: On Not Knowing Who We Are* (Bloomington, IN, Indiana University Press, 2000), 139.
[25] 'Basic Law for the Federal Republic of Germany', translated by Professor Christian Tomuschat and Professor David P. Currie at the website *Bundesministerium der Justiz*, http://www.gesetze-im-internet.de/englisch_gg/index.html.

points out that human dignity is the only absolute right in the Basic Law, for the obvious reason that one cannot have two absolutes. All other rights can in certain circumstances be limited or interfered with, but 'dignity as an absolute right always trumps'. This means that it must be narrow in scope. It can and does influence other laws, but it must be sufficiently narrowly defined to enable it to be enforced.

It became clear in discussions during the conference that German judges will go to almost any lengths to find a legal alternative to claims made under Article 1(1) of the Basic Law, because of the near-impossibility of applying it in practice. This leads me to suggest that, if everyone has an absolute right to dignity, it turns out that nobody has an absolute right to dignity. But in fact, this absolute right does not apply to everyone. It is a right which applies only to those living under German law, and therefore it is a German right, not a human right. As Grimm explains, the Basic Law is addressed to Germans in public office and to state agents, it is binding only for the German state, and its beneficiaries are the citizens or the inhabitants of Germany.

For dignity as an absolute right to be invested universally in the human, it would have to trump every other law which threatens human dignity anywhere at any time in any circumstances. German law would have to act *in loco dei* if it were really to absolutize human dignity. Moreover, because the law always requires an exception to define its limits, there would have to be a category of outsiders. To reiterate, if everybody has absolute dignity, nobody has absolute dignity. So, despite the best intentions of those who drafted the Basic Law in the wake of Nazism, the term 'human dignity' smuggles into German law the right to define not only dignity but also the human according to its terms of inclusion and exclusion, and thus it cannot avoid reinstating the conditions which made the death camps possible. To say this is not to deny that there are many legal, political, and ethical factors working to safeguard the future against such a possibility, but I am expressing doubt as to whether the idea of an inviolable right to dignity can contribute to that endeavour. As Douzinas suggests, the definition of the rights-bearing human as endowed with inviolable dignity universalizes what is in fact a very particular and limited concept of who counts as human, and in that process it creates the abjected and dehumanized empirical others who fall outside its normative definition of the human.

My second, related question is that of language and the law. Grimm makes the point that the legal definition of dignity is enshrined within the law itself. Whatever theological or philosophical roots that word might have, its incorporation into law severs it from other sources of meaning. If we reflect on what this means, however, we can see that those outside the narrow remit of the authority of German law have no claim to dignity, because the law only recognizes claims framed in its own terms of reference. So any appeal to the law to recognize intrinsic human dignity on the basis of a philosophical or theological claim would fall on deaf ears. In co-opting the word 'dignity', the law also drains it of any alternative meaning. 'Bare life' is mute before the law.

This power of the law to legitimate its claims by emptying words of all their historical references and ideological inscriptions is the target of postmodern critiques of the law, such as those offered by Wolcher and others. Although the idea of the lawgiver outside the law collapses with the shift from a theocratic to a democratic order, such critics argue that the law continues to derive its power from unacknowledged religious associations, so that in one form or another what Lacan refers to as the 'unconscious God' of modernity underwrites the power of the law with the threat of some unspeakable violence.[26] Postmodern theorists would insist that only by tracing the linguistic ambiguities inherent in all claims to truth is it possible to recognize the extent to which the language of the law is freighted with historical injustice and quasi-religious meanings. With that in mind, I return to the question of what Christian theology might bring to this conversation.

The deconsecrated God

In this concluding section, I sketch what it might mean to identify Christ with *homo sacer*. Although it seems an obvious comparison, Agamben himself does not develop the potential of this association.[27] John Milbank is one of the few theologians who explores its potential, although he does so in the context of a more historically focused analysis of the status of *homo sacer* under Roman law than I offer here.[28]

If Christianity is to respond to critics such as Douzinas, if it is to move towards the kind of vision articulated by Gushee, then it might draw on its own marginal and neglected theological resources in order to identify Christ as

---

[26] For more on this, see Tina Beattie, *Theology after Postmodernity: Divining the Void* (Oxford and New York, Oxford University Press, 2013). See also Jacques Derrida, 'Force of law: the "mystical foundation of authority"', in G. Anidjar (ed.), *Acts of Religion* d. (London, Routledge, 2002, first pub. 1998), 228–98; Annabelle Mooney, 'Death alive and kicking: Dianne Pretty, legal violence and the sacred', *Social Semiotics* 18:1 (2008), 47–60.

[27] For a theological development of the ideas explored in *Homo Sacer*, see Giorgio Agamben, *The Kingdom and the Glory: For a Theological Genealogy of Economy and Government*, trans. Lorenzo Chiesa with Matteo Mandarini (Stanford, CA, Stanford University Press, 2011, first pub. 2007).

[28] See John Milbank, 'Christ the exception', *New Blackfriars* 82:969 (2001), 541–56.

homo sacer, so that Christ would be most starkly encountered in those abandoned, condemned, or betrayed by the law. This means, first and foremost, the abrogation of the idolatry of power that has been perpetuated through theology itself, in what feminist and liberation theologians have long argued is the unholy alliance between patriarchal and/or imperial domination and Christianity's God. Only if theology radically deconstructs all its own hubristic claims can it provide the kind of critique of modernity that Gushee proposes. Only then might theology remind the law that the language of the absolute is not within its control. As *Dignitatis Humanae* says, 'God respects human dignity.'

The language of the absolute cannot be co-opted by law, because the absolute is what remains when law has done its work. It is the exception that restrains the reach of the law. It is the justice that is discovered when the law draws a line in the sand and withholds its protection and reigns in its power. Any term used by the law is contingent and relative, including dignity. If dignity is absolute, then it is all or nothing, and I am suggesting that only when it becomes nothing under the law does absolute human dignity, respected by God, become an imperative that transcends every law and every context. Those who turn away in disgust, blame, or shame from the *homo sacer* are turning away from God as revealed in the suffering humanity of Christ, who was born of a virgin outside the laws of nature, and was tortured and killed in an act of mob violence outside the laws of religion and politics. Christianity as a religion belongs within the natural order of human laws and institutions, but it reveals its truth only in the radical act of the transgressive individual who follows Christ into the wilderness, to discover him in the refugee, the prisoner, the infant born into poverty, the criminal tortured and crucified.[29] 'And the King shall answer and say unto them, "Verily I say unto you, Since you have done it unto one of the least of these my brethren, you have done it unto me"' (Matt. 25:40).

The language of kingship is significant here. As *homo sacer*, Christ must be both sovereign and outcast. The distinction between divine sovereignty and human abjection must be collapsed, if sovereignty beyond the law is to empty itself into the bodies of those beneath the law—those who constitute 'bare life'. Milbank asks, 'what is the point of identifying oneself with bare life in order to escape earthly sovereignty, only to fall into the hands of cosmic tyranny?'[30] If the idolatry of power invested in the idea of God is to be

---

[29] These ideas invite development in engagement with René Girard's idea of Christ as the scapegoat. See René Girard, *Things Hidden Since the Foundation of the World* (London and New York, Continuum, 2003, first pub. 1978).

[30] Milbank, 'Christ the exception', 551.

challenged, then the idea of God must be deconstructed. If Christ is only the victim, then Christianity's God becomes the most vicious and abusive tyrant of all. Again, feminist theologians have pointed out the extent to which the Christian idea of God as an angry father who will only be appeased by the torture and death of his son is a violent theology with deadly political and ethical implications. Rather, to quote Milbank again, we must ask what solidarity with Christ means, if we recognize him as 'the God abandoned as *homo sacer* upon the cross'.[31]

Gushee argues that every human is sacred from the perspective of divine law, but if everybody is sacred nobody is sacred. Where, then, is the exception that delineates the sacred? Let me suggest that, if the crucified Christ is *homo sacer*, and if he is fully divine as well as fully human, then on the cross God becomes the exception to the sacred. In Christ, God is profaned, and every human sacrifice in the name of God, or in the name of any secular equivalent that has usurped the place of God and still demands such sacrifice (the state, the market, the law itself), is unmasked as the idolatry that it is. Original sin then becomes associated with the sin of idolatry which violates the first commandment: 'You shall have no other gods before me' (Ex. 20:3). This idolatry would refer to every human concept of God that justifies violence against another human in the name of the idolatrous constructs of the divine which have legitimated so much of Christianity's bloody history. Every human is sacred, because God is not sacred. No human can be violated, killed, or abused in the name of God, because to violate a human is to violate God. God is the exception, the excluded other who makes the human sacred—who divinizes the human, according to classical theology—by the emptying out of sacred divinity into the sacred humanity of Christ (a theological term known as kenosis).

When Christianity says that the fully human body on the cross is fully divine, it provides a theological response to the problem of law and sovereignty, and it gives material, historical expression to that idea of divine justice expressed by the psalmist, which turns all our human laws and institutions inside out. If, as Wolcher argues, ethical reflection on good and evil justifies the infliction of suffering on those who are deemed to be evil, then the first task of Christian ethics is, according to Dietrich Bonhoeffer, to invalidate the knowledge of good and evil that is acquired through rebellion against God in the Book of Genesis.[32] Christ drains away the divine legitimation of the law by saying that outside every possible law, outside every possible act of sover-

---

[31] Milbank, 'Christ the exception', 551.
[32] See Dietrich Bonhoeffer, *Ethics* (New York, Simon & Schuster, Touchstone edn, 1995, first pub. 1949), 231. See also the discussion in Stephen Plant, *Bonhoeffer* (London and New York, Continuum, 2004), 90–1.

eignty or autonomy, God is to be found as the most vulnerable, the most destitute, the most profaned, the least sacred thing in all creation—the infant born among the animals, and the human corpse on the cross: 'He is despised and rejected of men; a man of sorrows, and acquainted with grief: and we hid as it were our faces from him; he was despised, and we esteemed him not' (Isa. 53.3). The greatest good is revealed in the greatest evil, and the ancient rupture in human knowing is healed so that justice might once again be possible.

Jon Sobrino is a Jesuit priest and liberation theologian from El Salvador. In his book *The Crucified Christ*, he revisits the questions of liberation theology from the perspective of a double grief. First, he is grieving over the failure of liberation theology, after the collapse of communism and the rise of global capitalism destroyed the utopian dreams of a socialist future informed by a Marxist critique of economics and a Christian affirmation of the God of the poor. Second, he is grieving over the murder by the Salvadoran military of six fellow Jesuits, his housekeeper, and her daughter while he was out of the country. Here is what Sobrino says about the crucifixion:

> The cross reveals, not power, but impotence. God does not triumph on the cross over the power of evil, but succumbs to it. The faith-interpretation ... sees in this the love of God in solidarity, to the end, with human beings, but what appears on the cross on the surface is the triumph of the idols of death over the God of life. The idea that in the battle of the gods the true God could lose and through that defeat prove himself the true God requires us to rethink his transcendence.[33]

Christianity has indeed been a religion of empire, power, and conquest, but beyond its corrupted laws and institutions, there are the 'bare lives' of those who have followed a different way. These are the saints and martyrs—most of them buried in unmarked graves—who willingly stand alongside the unwilling victims of history, who recognize that 'bare life' is God's life, and there and nowhere else is it possible to affirm the absolute dignity of the human, beyond the power of any law and beyond the politics of any state.

---

[33] Jon Sobrino, *Jesus the Liberator: A Historical-Theological Reading of Jesus of Nazareth*, trans. Paul Burns and Francis McDonagh (Tunbridge Wells, Burns & Oates, 1994), 248.

15

A Christian Theological Account of Human Worth

David P. Gushee[1]

Introduction

THIS CHAPTER TAKES THE somewhat contrarian perspective that the concept of 'human dignity' is a half-secularized remnant of an earlier Jewish and Christian concept best labelled as *the sacred worth of the human person in the sight of God*, or more simply, the sacredness of human life. I will invest the majority of these pages in excavating the original biblical sources, in part so that the memory of them is not altogether lost, and in part to make a peculiarly Protestant and revelational contribution to the contemporary conversation centring on the term 'human dignity'.

On the language of sacredness

It is not uncommon even today to hear Jews and Christians and sometimes others claim that 'human life is sacred' or speak of 'the sanctity of human life'. Common usage of these phrases reveals both high passion and limited cognition. It seems reasonable as a first step to seek a deeper understanding of what might once have been meant, or might still be meant, when such terms are used.

The *Oxford English Dictionary* (OED) offers the following definitions for 'sanctity':

1. holiness of life, saintliness
2. the quality of being sacred or hallowed; sacredness, claim to (religious) reverence; inviolability.[2]

---

[1] Much of the material in the chapter overlaps with and was drawn from my new book *The Sacredness of Human Life* (Grand Rapids, MI, Eerdmans, 2013).
[2] *The Oxford English Dictionary*, 2nd edn (Oxford, Clarendon Press, 1989), 441–2.

But the OED's more extensive definition of the word 'sacred' yields a striking discovery. This English adjective actually emerges from an obsolete verb, *sacre*, which meant to consecrate, sacrifice, make holy; to dedicate (a person) to a deity, to make a class of things sacred to a deity.[3] The adjective 'sacred', derived from sacre, carries forward this range of meanings. A sacred thing is an object or being that someone (or Someone) has *made sacred*, for example, dedicated, consecrated, venerated. The adjective (sacred) now assumes the action of the lost verb (sacre), but because we have lost the verb it is easy to lose a sense of *agency*—of who (if anyone) bears responsibility for having consecrated or *made sacred*.

Sanctity carries a particular *moral* connotation—such as purity, holiness, or virtue—subtly linking the term to character qualities *achieved by the person* who has attained sanctity. *Sacredness*, by contrast, clearly reflects an *ascribed status*, referring to something or someone having received a special status through consecration by another. Sacredness is the more apt term in getting at what the biblical traditions have sought to say about human worth.

My explorations of a variety of cases in which an object, place, or person has been ascribed sacred status reveals a pattern I call the *sacredness paradigm*. It is not inextricably tied to belief in God, though most often in history it has been religiously motivated and rooted. It goes something like this:

1. One from among a class of ordinary things (we will call it X from among a large group of x's) is lifted up from the midst of its ordinary companions and designated as of elevated rank or special status;
2. The consecration, hallowing, or sacralizing of this now-sacred X is undertaken by some agency, whether collective or individual, human or divine, whose authority to make such a designation is accepted by the community affected;
3. A variety of reasons can exist for why this particular X is declared sacred, but for those making and acknowledging the designation the reasons are compelling;
4. This special/sacred status evokes in relation to X an attitude or posture of awe, veneration, or reverence;
5. This attitudinal posture is (expected to be) accompanied by concrete moral obligations within the community to treat X with due respect and even special care, and in particular to prevent any *desecration* of X;

---

[3] *OED*, 338–9.

6. This moral obligation to preserve what is often called the 'inviolability' of the sacred X is normally accompanied by negative sanctions for those who do violate the sacred.

When religious people today use the phrase 'sacredness of human life' they are not saying that some class of human beings is sacred and to be viewed and treated as in steps 1–6 above. They are instead saying that *each and every human life* is thus designated. Every human being x is to be set apart as a sacred X, and this by divine command.

This move conforms to the sacredness paradigm above, while departing from it in one crucial way. It conforms because those who make a claim that every human being is sacred intend something like the six steps I have identified in the sacredness paradigm. The only difference is in the first step. No longer is *one* from among a class of ordinary things lifted up above the others and designated as sacred. Now each and every member of the class *human being* is thus elevated. The great innovation in Jewish and Christian thought was *not at all* the ascription of sacred worth to some class or category of human beings. This was already common in ancient civilization, usually with reference to the royal classes. What was new (and revelatory) was the way the sacred texts of Judaism and Christianity bore witness to the divine ascription of such sacred worth to *all human beings*. Visible in their sacred texts and apparent (sometimes in glimpses) in the practice of these biblical religions was a sacredness-of-human-life ethic that is carried forward today among some of the practitioners of these biblical faiths.

In view of the sacredness paradigm, I define the still-extant Christian sacredness-of-human-life theology/ethic as follows:

> To say that each human life (or human life, as such) is sacred, is to claim that God has consecrated each and every human being--without exception and in all circumstances—as a unique, incalculably precious being of elevated status and dignity. Through God's revelation in Scripture and Incarnation in Jesus Christ, God has declared and demonstrated the sacred worth of human beings and will hold all human beings accountable for responding appropriately. Such a response begins by adopting a posture of reverence and by accepting responsibility for the sacred gift that is a human life. It includes offering due respect and care to each human being that we encounter. It extends to an obligation to protect human life from wanton destruction, desecration, or the violation of human rights. A full embrace of the sacredness of human life leads to a full-hearted commitment to foster human flourishing.

And I claim that while there may be a variety of paths to developing such an exalted view of the worth and proper treatment of the human being, the source of such a theology and ethic (in Western civilization, at least) can be traced to the sacred texts of Judaism and Christianity, and the religious traditions which produced and were nurtured by them.

Biblical foundations

The sacred scriptures of the Hebrew Bible and New Testament have for millennia borne witness to (belief in) the God-given sacredness of each human life. This is not to say that this witness is unequivocal, or that countervailing elements cannot be found in sacred scripture. Here, of course, a Christian theology of divine revelation and scriptural authority is relevant, though any kind of extensive articulation of such a theology goes beyond the scope of this chapter. Suffice it to say that I believe the Bible contains traces of what God communicated to Israel, the church, and humanity, as well as plenty of evidence of that divine communication being heard and misheard, obeyed and disobeyed. I believe biblical traces of the sacredness-of-life norm represent divine revelation well heard and sometimes well obeyed, and that it is therefore appropriate to test biblical and post-biblical texts and traditions by the criteria established by this ethical norm.

The Hebrew Bible offers at least four bodies of material that bear witness to a sacredness-of-life ethic: (1) its creation theology; (2) its depiction of God's compassionate care for human beings, especially suffering people; (3) its covenantal/legal materials; and (4) its prophetic vision of a just wholeness for Israel and all creation. Ultimately, the conviction that human life is sacred receives its firmest grounding in the Bible's revelation of the character, activity, and decision of God, which lies at the root of all its prescriptions related to how human beings should be perceived and treated. Let me elaborate briefly here on a few key elements of each of these four bodies of material.

God as creator of humanity

Most Christian declarations about life's sacredness begin with the claim that human life is sacred because it was created in God's image. Genesis 1–2 tells us that humans do not come from nowhere but are the creative handiwork of God. This claim by itself elevates human worth.

Further, God is *equally* the Creator of *all* humans. All references to humanity in Genesis 1 are references to all humanity, and the blessings and tasks given to human beings are given to all. There is one God who makes one humanity. This is a pivotal element of biblical creation theology, and it contributes at least an implicit primal human *equality* and unity.

The creation narrative found in Genesis 2, believed by biblical scholars to be the older account, adds another important element. It tells a story in which God begins to create humanity by creating a first man. The first woman is then formed out of the first man. From these first parents come absolutely everyone else. In this sense we are all kin, all part of one vast human family. Genesis 2 thus teaches a *primal human kinship, unity and equality* by narrating a story in which all human beings come from one common ancestor, or couple. These claims help equalize human status and teach us to value human beings far beyond those most closely connected to us.

The claim that human beings are made in the 'image (and likeness) of God' (Gen. 1:26–7) has perhaps attracted a disproportionate amount of theological-ethical attention. It is an important claim, to be sure, but its intended original meaning is uncertain and cannot always bear the theological-ethical weight that it has been asked to bear. With trepidation, I accept the conclusion that the biblical writer probably did intend for 'image of God' to signal some kind of resemblance between God and humans. This resemblance may include recognition of human intellectual, spiritual, and/or moral capacities over and against what were presumed to be the lower capacities of the non-human animals.

But a 'capacities' rendering of the divine image has proven vulnerable, and not just to the problem of setting up a persistent humans-over-animals dichotomy. Its vulnerability has resurfaced whenever claims about the supposed intellectual, spiritual, or moral incapacity of individuals or groups have been made. These issues have proved to be deeply problematic both in terms of various kinds of historic ethnocentrisms as well as in relation to contemporary bioethical concerns. This is one reason why it is probably better today to understand the image of God as having to do with our exalted *responsibilities* rather than capacities—humans 'image' God to one another and to the rest of creation through our representation of God's royal rule on earth. This seems a natural inference from the text of Genesis 1 itself, given the direct connection between the declaration of the image of God in humanity and the command to exercise dominion over the creatures.[4] The latter is a kind of royal function, with the significance here that *all* human beings, not just kings and queens, carry this kind of 'royal' authority on earth.

---

[4] Christopher J. H. Wright: 'The two affirmations are so closely linked in the text that there can be no doubt that they are meant to be related', *Old Testament Ethics for the People of God* (Downers Grove, IL, Intervarsity Press, 2004).

God as sustainer, rescuer, and liberator

The Hebrew Bible teaches that God sustains, cares for, rescues, and acts to liberate human beings made in the divine image. Despite our ascribed grandeur we are physically vulnerable creatures, subject to great misery and suffering. The Bible records that God's universal sustaining care for creation, including humanity (e.g., Gen. 9:8–17) took a more focused form in God's compassionate response to the suffering of God's people Israel when they were enslaved and threatened with the mass murder of their children in Egypt (Ex. 1–19). The numerous biblical examples of God's care for needy and suffering human beings have impressed themselves deeply on the consciousness of peoples and cultures affected by the biblical witness.

It is hard to overstate the significance of the Exodus narrative in particular. For the Jewish people, this founding narrative of God's compassionate deliverance has been fundamental. Its echoes resound through later biblical writings and in every generation of Jewish life. 'You shall remember that you were a slave in the land of Egypt and the Lord your God redeemed you' (Dt. 15:15). This memory instructs Israel as to the character of her God: one who keeps covenant promises, one who looks with compassionate love on Israel, and one who delivers Israel when it appears that all is lost. God is a God of justice who fights for Israel's liberation when she is victimized. This foundational understanding of God's character also demands of Israel that her way of life as a people reflects responsive covenant fidelity, compassionate love, and justice, central themes in both the law and the prophets. This Exodus-shaped vision has been embraced by many suffering peoples in human history. Michael Walzer has shown the endless fecundity of the Exodus texts for inspiring social revolutions in the name of justice.[5]

God as lawmaker and judge

The biblical narrative moves from Exodus to Sinai, from God's miraculous deliverance of the covenant people to God's articulation of the laws that shall govern Israel. It is highly significant that God is depicted as the ultimate source of law in Israel, and God holds this covenant people accountable for obedience. If God is the source of law—cultic, civil, criminal, social welfare, moral, all these dimensions flow together here—then the full weight of God's sovereign majesty and power falls upon the laws thus offered. The law therefore carries a great holiness and authority.

---

[5] Michael Walzer, *Exodus and Revolution* (New York, Basic Books, 1985).

The very idea that there is a divinely given moral law that governs Israel—and more than Israel—is itself a major contribution to a sacredness-of-life ethic. It means that God sets the terms for how human beings must relate to both the Divine Person and human persons. Human moral obligation is ultimately rooted in God's will.[6] 'The foundation for all morality ... is the character and will of God [who] is supreme and without any competitors ... there will be no higher standard of obligation.'[7] Such an ethic is thus starkly differentiated from any ethic based merely on personal preference, social power, unaided human reason, or communal tradition. God's revealed will establishes a transcendent reference point by which all life is to be governed and by which all human laws and actions can be evaluated and critiqued.

This elevation of a transcendent legal/moral standard over human life creates or reinforces momentum towards human equality before the law. In many cultures, especially in the ancient world, the ruler defined the law and was above the law. But the kings of Israel were accountable to the same divinely given moral law that governed everyone else. David Pleins has written, 'We ... see in these formulations of the Ten Commandments the makings of a subtle critique of monarchy and an attempt to limit its powers ... [here] each and every member of the community has a religious, moral and social duty toward the nation's deity.'[8] The many kings who were tempted to forget that their will was not absolute in Israel often ended up paying a serious price for their pride and disobedience. The only context in which that could happen was in a society that believed in divinely given moral law and the accountability of all to God's law, with a socially acknowledged role for prophets who could demand compliance in God's name.

The power of law to level the playing field in human life has the effect of weakening the strong and strengthening the weak. The standard is clear: all stand equal before the law and before those human courts charged with enforcing it. If any member of a particular political community is understood to have moral and legal rights, all have such rights.[9] One way that we come to know that all human beings, of all classes and races, are to be perceived as sacred and treated with respect is because we see it happen in the administration

---

[6] See Richard J. Mouw, *The God Who Commands* (South Bend, IN, University of Notre Dame Press, 1991); compare with Remi Brague, *The Law of God: The Philosophical History of an Idea*, trans. Lydia G. Cochrane (Chicago, University of Chicago Press, 2007).

[7] Walter J. Kaiser, Jr, *Toward Old Testament Ethics* (Grand Rapids, MI, Zondervan, 1983), 85.

[8] J. David Pleins, *The Social Visions of the Hebrew Bible* (Louisville, KY, Westminster John Knox, 2001), 48.

[9] The question then becomes who counts as a member of a political-legal community. The first step is to say 'every member of this political community stands equal before the law'. The second step is to include more and more people in the agreed political community.

of the law—if the law is functioning properly. In Israel, where law was seen as divinely given, a failure to administer justice in this way was treated as a direct affront to the God who authored the law.

Certainly Old Testament law had gaps and problems. But the texts contain striking elements, especially in Ancient Near Eastern context, that move in the direction of the comprehensive valuing of human life. Even today, even in societies that long ago abandoned a theocratic understanding of governance or of law, biblical law has left its impact on the construction of societies valuing the rule of law and attempting to include every citizen as an equal before the law.

God as the deliverer who brings shalom at last

One of the Old Testament's key resources for a sacredness of life ethic is found in the demand, and the yearning, for a transformed world of justice and peace. The concept of shalom names that state of affairs in which human beings flourish in community and the sacredness of each and every human life is finally honoured. It means an end to our 'division, hostility, fear, drivenness, and misery'.[10] The Hebrew prophets (our key source for the shalom vision) both demand shalom *now* and yearn for it *then*, when the time comes that God finally prevails.

Ethicist Karen Lebacqz has argued that an ethic of justice is often developed most profoundly amid the experience of a particular injustice.[11] Likewise, the prophetic yearning for shalom begins with the particular, especially Israel's experiences of wrenching violence and injustice. Prophets speak about shalom for Israel from within the cataclysm of war (e.g., Jer. 33). From exile, they speak of the land and people of Israel coming back from the dead (Ezek. 36–7), in a kind of 'new exodus'.[12] They yearn for a New Jerusalem, from within the experience of Jerusalem's destruction (e.g., Isa. 65). The prophetic writings left a legacy both of particularity and universality—they speak to specific events, injustices, and dreams of the Jewish people while also still having the moral power to evoke demands and yearnings on the part of millions of people for the kind of world that they envision.

The narrowest translation for the Hebrew word shalom is 'peace', as in the opposite of war, and peace as commonly understood is certainly an

---

[10] Walter Brueggemann, *Living Toward a Vision: Biblical Reflections on Shalom*, 2nd edn (New York, United Church Press, 1982), 16.
[11] Karen Lebacqz, *Six Theories of Justice: Perspectives from Philosophical and Theological Ethics* (Minneapolis, MN, Augsburg Fortress, 1987).
[12] Waldemar Janzen, *Old Testament Ethics* (Louisville, KY, Westminster John Knox, 1994), 170.

ingredient of it. The prophets demand peace from the covenant people Israel when they decry Israel's violence and murder (Micah 7:2–3), and her turn to military alliances and military might (e.g., Isa. 31:1, Hos. 1:7; Micah 5:10).[13] They yearn for peace as an end to war when they envision a time when 'there shall be endless peace' (Isa. 9:7) and 'they shall beat their swords into ploughshares, and their spears into pruning hooks' (Mic. 4:3; also Zech. 9:9–10). Shalom means peace, as in straightforward security from physical threats to bodies, homes, and communities. God promises just such a 'covenant of peace' (Ezek. 34:25; Isa. 65:25; Num. 25:12). 'Violence shall no more be heard in your land, devastation and destruction within your borders' (Isa. 60:18). Security is so complete that 'your gates shall always be open; day and night they shall not be shut' (Isa. 60:11). Eventually, shalom in this sense is so complete that God 'will destroy on this mountain the shroud that is cast over all peoples ... he will swallow up death forever' (Isa. 25:7). Shalom, as Irving Greenberg has put it, means 'the triumph of life' and 'the overcoming of death'. This is the mission of God in the world and, in Greenberg's view, remains the task of both Judaism and Christianity.[14]

In summary, the Hebrew Bible bears witness to a divinely declared elevation of the grandeur and worth of each human life, while also containing numerous exhortations to a corresponding moral behaviour on the part of humanity, and especially the covenant people Israel. Such elevated status and appropriate respect are not merited by something good or inherently valuable about humanity. There is no talk of something like intrinsic human dignity. Human life is valuable because God values it, and God's valuing is clear as God creates, sustains, liberates, governs, delivers and redeems, even in the face of human defiance and disobedience. Human life must be treated with respect because God requires it, and because it is the only proper response to the revealed will of God.

The New Testament builds upon and extends these themes from the Hebrew Bible, through its focus on the earthly ministry of Jesus Christ, on the implications of his Incarnation, and on the way of life of the community of faith gathered in his name.

---

[13] Walter Brueggemann, *A Social Reading of the Old Testament: Prophetic Approaches to Israel's Communal Life* (Minneapolis, MN, Fortress Press, 1994), chapter 15.
[14] Irving Greenberg, *For the Sake of Heaven and Earth: The New Encounter Between Judaism and Christianity* (Philadelphia, PA, Jewish Publication Society, 2004), 18, 39.

The earthly ministry of Jesus Christ

The strands of text and tradition cited in the last section flow forward into this one because Jesus was a faithful son of Israel and a creative expositor of Israel's best traditions. Jesus carried forward in profound ways all four themes noted above. He articulated a creation theology affirming God as Creator and God's sustaining care for human beings, while employing his power over creation to manifest that care in healing, rescuing, and raising people from the dead. He taught and exemplified the compassionate deliverance for suffering people that God had exhibited to Israel, and he offered such deliverance through suffering love rather than violence. He offered a rendering of Jewish legal and ethical norms that affirmed and heightened the protections offered there to human life. And he both articulated and embodied the prophetic vision of an eschatological shalom in God's coming future.

Jesus elevated the sacredness of life through his resolute rejection of violence and his teaching of the way of peacemaking. Jesus rejected the sad and terrible cycle of human violence in a context of Jewish subjugation under the Roman boot that offered daily incitement to violent resistance. The early church became convinced that such violence did not fit a community seeking to imitate and obey Jesus, and for centuries became known for its rejection of violence.

A key element of the sacredness of life is its expansive inclusiveness. Every life counts; every individual is welcomed; no groups are diminished vis-à-vis other groups; no categories of people are privileged over others. Jesus embodied that inclusiveness throughout his ministry. His example pushed Christians towards the development of love for 'each and every' human being, without exception, as a fundamental element of a Christ-following way of life. Numerous examples could be cited of his expansive embrace and valuing of the marginalized ones of his own context: women, the sick, the disabled, children, the poor, Samaritans, Roman soldiers, and so on. The early church became known for the radical expansiveness of its community and its hospitality.

Jesus also taught about a God of radical forgiveness and love. Acutely clear about human rebellion against God, even so Jesus declared that God loves each and every person. He spoke about how God loves not just those who love the Father but those who are his enemies (e.g., Mt. 5:43–8), calling any who would claim to be God's children to love enemies in the same manner.

Jesus said that God pays attention even to the life of a sparrow, and all the more attends to providing for our material needs—therefore freeing us to trust

God and serve others (Matt. 6:26). He describes God as like a loving Father who can be counted on to 'give good gifts to his children', which authorizes and encourages us to ask for what we need and trust that it will be given to us (Matt. 7:7–11; Lk. 11:13, 18:1–8). He said that God is like a shepherd who goes after the one lost sheep even if he has the ninety-nine at hand (Luke 15:3–7).

Jesus frequently offered reminders of God's special care for those who especially need it—the children, the poor, the abandoned, the sick, the hungry. These reminders were often accompanied by teachings requiring all who would be his followers to imitate this preferential love or face judgment for failing to do so (e.g., Matt. 25:31–46). Love attends especially to those who need love the most, and God will hold us accountable for doing so.

John's Gospel has either Jesus or the narrator sum up this theme in words memorized by many thousands of Christians: 'For God so loved the world that he gave his only Son, that whoever believes in him should not perish but have everlasting life' (Jn. 3:16). The bottom line of the New Testament is this divine saving love for the world; for humans; for each and every human. This is the ultimate foundation of Christian belief in the sacredness of human life. In its origins, all Christian claims about 'life's sacredness' or 'human dignity' are in fact theological claims that *for God's sake, and in obedience to God, we must prize and protect the life of human beings*.

The meaning of the Incarnation of Jesus Christ

Christianity's theologians, beginning in the pages of the New Testament, have seen significance for human worth not just in the ministry of Jesus Christ but in the very fact of Jesus Christ. They have pondered the implications of God-becoming-human in Jesus, his terrible, atoning death, his resurrection, and his ascension.

Christian theologians have often been moved to proclaim that if God became human in Jesus, the status of the human changes. No human can be seen as worthless. No human life can be treated cruelly or destroyed capriciously. Human dignity can never again be rejected, or confined to only a few groups or individuals of supposedly higher rank. The Incarnation elevates the status of every human being everywhere on the planet at any time in human history. It elevates the worth of every human being at every stage of their lives, because the arc of Jesus's own life included every stage of existence, from conception to death and even resurrection, which is our own destiny in Christ.

God not only took flesh in Jesus Christ, God sacrificed that flesh at Golgotha. This staggering New Testament claim deepens belief in the extent of

God's love and care for humanity. God stopped at nothing to reach out to humanity. The intensity of this conviction is deepened when Christians emphasize that Christ died for *each and every human*, friend and foe, good and evil. Belief in the sacredness of life is deepened considerably by reflection on the ultimate nature of the price God paid at the Cross. The incalculably terrible suffering and death of Jesus Christ, and what it says about how very much God values each and every human being, has contributed profoundly to a Christian moral tradition that exalts the immeasurable worth of the human being.

The resurrection of Christ signifies the victory of God over evil, including the evil that took Jesus to the Cross. In the Resurrection, God triumphs, and God signals that in the end he will triumph over Satan and all forces that bring suffering and death; even death itself is destroyed (1 Cor. 15:25).[15] The sacredness of life, when fully realized, will be part of this ultimate victory of God over the evil that has harmed and destroyed human lives. In the Incarnation, the One through whom all things were made, the one who sustains and holds together the creation itself, became flesh, took on human life. At the Cross this human being suffered and lost his life, for us. But in the Resurrection, Jesus lives again; God wins; and therefore life wins. God is for life.[16]

The historic confession of the Church is not just that Jesus rose from the dead but that he ascended to heaven, where he now sits at the right hand of the Father, and from which he shall come to judge the living and the dead. Remembering that the Jesus who rose from the dead was fully God and fully human, this means, as Karl Barth puts it, 'The real mystery of Easter is not that God is glorified in it, but that man is exalted, raised to the right hand of God and permitted to triumph over sin, death and the devil.'[17] God stoops low so that humanity can be exalted even to the right hand of God. Human beings must be viewed and treated as those whose divinely intended destiny is to dwell eternally along with Jesus the Son in the presence of God the Father. Humanity was made for an eternal destiny; this theme is often sounded in Christian declarations on the sacredness of human life.

---

[15] I first encountered this formulation in J. Christiaan Beker, *Paul the Apostle: The Triumph of God in Life and Thought* (Philadelphia, PA, Fortress Press, 1980). Since then it has become a familiar concept, linked to the kingdom of God.

[16] This theme has perhaps never been expressed more profoundly than by Pope John Paul II, in *The Gospel of Life* (New York, Times Books, 1995), chapter 2.

[17] Karl Barth, *Dogmatics in Outline* (New York, Harper & Row, 1959), 115.

The ministry of the early church

What ultimately emerged in early Christianity were congregations gathered around this Jesus Christ, believing that in their own early experience of transformed human relations lay the beginnings of the redemption of the world. Christ came, died, and rose again. The world at large remained in the grip of dark forces, of principalities and powers, and evidenced evil at every turn; and yet in Christian churches new seedlings of eschatological community could be found—and must be protected. Here rich and poor, young and old, male and female, Jew and Greek, slave and free, celebrated God's transforming love in Jesus Christ. And before this love all stood equally needy, equally blessed, and equally grateful. Until Christ returned, these communities would seek to live in love towards one another and to all. Instructed to avoid all forms of malice and ill-will to anyone, Christians would instead seek and contribute only good to their neighbours—beginning with their near neighbours in Christian community but extending far beyond 'the household of faith'. They would do so until Christ returned, the hope of which was often invoked as ground and motive for their extraordinary way of life.

From sacredness of life to human dignity

The scriptures of the Hebrew Bible and New Testament, and the Jewish and Christian theological traditions reflected and rooted therein, offer what can only be described as 'thick', particularistic theological accounts of human worth. Faith communities immersed in these sacred texts were the bearers over many centuries of a profound sacredness-of-human-life theological-ethical tradition that deeply shaped every culture in which Judaism and Christianity left a deep mark.

Eventually, however, the cultural imprint of these thick religious traditions began to fade or to be explicitly rejected, first in Europe and eventually beyond. One major reason they faded is because Christians, in particular, radically failed to live out their own ethical vision. Christianity's moral vision became compromised by its partnership with political power and its tragic participation in injustice and violence both in Europe and wherever Europeans went. One could hardly begin to name all of these moral failures, but one especially poignant place to start is with the long, terrible record of Christian anti-Semitism. Amid this and so many other terrible moral failures, the credibility of Christianity was badly damaged, and its powerful leading role in European civilization was rejected both politically and intellectually.

The story of secularization is a complex and disputed one, and there were many reasons why Christian intellectual influence faded in the West. But my own explorations lead me to a couple of very basic conclusions relevant to this subject. One is that Western philosophers and moralists remained deeply affected by the Christian theological-ethical substrate of Western culture even when they sought mightily to shift the foundation of epistemological and moral claims to reason rather than revelation. Thus, at least until well into the nineteenth century, Europe's leading moralists retained an articulation of human worth that was still elevated and profound. But they did so while shearing that ethic from its original theological foundation. Thus, there was still such a thing as exalted human worth, now often labelled as human dignity. But it was dignity, not sacredness, and it was grounded in reason, not revelation.

Eventually, more radical thinkers, such as Friedrich Nietzsche, rejected not only the theological *foundation* of 'human dignity' in divine revelation, but *the moral claims themselves*. The moral vision he substituted for the ethic represented by a term like human dignity was, in my view, a quite disastrous one. And he was not the only one who took such a path. The path taken by Nietzsche and his enthusiasts does raise the question of whether, in the end, the ethic of human dignity is secure apart from its original theological foundations. Certainly Nietzsche believed that the ethic could not survive without its theological underpinnings, and he was more than happy to bury both.

I am persuaded that *human dignity* as deployed in ethical discourse today remains a relatively thin secularization of an originally thick, theocentric claim about *sacred human worth*, the reasons it should be recognized, and the moral obligations that attend such recognition. Human dignity has the great value of being a useful crossover term functioning as a kind of secular cognate to sacredness of human life. By now it has its own formidable intellectual history yielding considerable good fruit in philosophy, law, and culture. It has the perhaps indispensable virtue in a globalized world of being able to bridge diverse religious, political, legal, and intellectual communities. But human dignity cannot fully convey the depth of theological meaning carried by the earlier religious language of human life's God-declared sacredness. It does not fully capture the central convictions of the Christian tradition when it comes to human worth. The best contemporary contribution of the Christian tradition to this discussion of human dignity, then, may well be to retrieve the richest possible exposition of the sacredness-of-human-life vision which preceded it and quietly continues to underwrite it today.

Part IV

Philosophical Perspectives

16

Human Dignity and the Foundations of Human Rights

John Tasioulas[1]

Introduction

THE EXPRESSION 'HUMAN DIGNITY' is nowadays commonly found in close proximity to that of 'human rights', not only in official legal and political documents but also in the discourse of political activists, lawyers, philosophers, and ordinary citizens. We can distinguish at least three functions that invocations of human dignity perform in connection with human rights. The first is simply to refer to the set, however composed, of genuine human rights. This usage is premised on the assumption—unfortunately, seldom defended or even explicitly identified as such—that human dignity and human rights either bear an identical sense or are extensionally equivalent in the standards that come under them. So, for example, some international lawyers interpret the Universal Declaration of Human Rights—which refers in its preamble to the 'recognition of the inherent dignity and of the equal and inalienable rights of all members of the human family'—as asserting precisely such an intensional or extensional equivalence.[2] This seems to me the least interesting, and perhaps the least tenable, of the three deployments of human dignity.

In a second, and more interesting, usage, human dignity fixes the distinctive significance and content of human rights as compared with other ethical-political standards, including moral and legal rights that are not human rights. In this vein, Jürgen Habermas contends that the idea of human dignity is a 'portal' or 'conceptual hinge', one that discharges a 'mediating function' between a morality of duties that pervades all human life, on the one hand, and the limited schedule of enforceable legal rights properly enacted by a

---

[1] My thanks go to Robert George, Avishai Margalit, Peter Schaber and Effy Vayena for helpful comments on earlier drafts of this chapter.
[2] See, for example, J. Tobin, *The Right to Health in International Law* (Oxford, Oxford University Press, 2012), 56.

democratic constitutional state, on the other. So understood, human dignity is a threshold at which the operative grounding values—the morality of equal respect—give rise to the rights that individuals can claim in virtue of their status as citizens of a democratic state.[3] Habermas's specification of the threshold constituted by human dignity—the enforceable legal rights properly claimable by democratic citizens—remains largely formal, offering little in the way of substantive criteria for determining the content of those rights. Perhaps the rights are to be agreed upon by democratic citizens through processes of collective deliberation.[4] But this in turn leads to the familiar conundrum that at least some human rights are arguably conditions of democratic deliberation, in which case they have a status independent of the outcome of any deliberative process. Presumably, Habermas's elusive thesis of the 'co-originality' of human rights and democracy is in part addressed to this problem.[5]

A third deployment of the notion of human dignity goes deeper, treating it as a grounding value of human rights, perhaps even as their exclusive normative basis. Hence, the 1966 Covenants on Civil and Political Rights and on Economic, Social, and Cultural Rights both assert that the rights they enumerate 'derive from the inherent dignity of the human person', an assertion reiterated by the UN General Assembly in 1986 (GA Res. 41/120) and echoed by numerous international, regional, and domestic human rights instruments.[6] It is this third, justificatory, deployment of the idea of human dignity that I wish to explore in this chapter.

Before doing so, however, it is worth dwelling on what the justificatory project, at the broadest level, involves. To begin with, what is to be justified are 'human rights', where these are understood to be individual moral rights possessed by all human beings simply in virtue of their humanity. We possess these rights not because of any personal achievement or social status, nor because they are conferred upon us by a positive legal order or social conventions, but simply in virtue of our standing as human beings. Second,

---

[3] J. Habermas, 'The concept of human dignity and the realistic utopia of human rights', in his *The Crisis of the European Union: A Response* (Cambridge, Polity Press, 2012), 81–7.

[4] Habermas, 'Concept of Human Dignity', 87.

[5] J. Habermas, 'On the internal relation between the rule of law and democracy', in his *The Inclusion of the Other: Studies in Political Theory* (Cambridge, MA, MIT Press, 1998), 259–62. Beyond the reservations noted above, one can question Habermas's conception of human rights as inherently oriented towards legalization (or, a fortiori, constitutionalization), see, for example, Amartya Sen, 'Human rights and the limits of law', *Cardozo Law Review* 27 (2006), 2913–27, and J. Tasioulas, 'On the nature of human rights', in G. Ernst and J.-C. Heilinger (eds), *The Philosophy of Human Rights: Contemporary Controversies* (Walter de Gruyter, 2012), 17–59, 40–3.

[6] Christopher McCrudden, 'Human dignity and the judicial interpretation of human rights', *European Journal of International Law* 19 (2008), 655–724.

the process of justification is primarily a matter of deploying ordinary moral reasoning, or natural reason in the terminology of an earlier tradition. Moreover, in common with most of the central figures in that tradition, I take it that the justification sought does not stop short of establishing the objective truth of certain positive propositions about human rights. These two features characterize what, at least until recently, was the orthodox understanding of human rights, an understanding that treats the concept of human rights as substantially equivalent to that of natural rights.

In the last decade, however, both limbs of the orthodox conception have come under sustained attack from proponents of political conceptions of human rights, most of whom take their cue from John Rawls's brief and scattered remarks on the subject in *The Law of Peoples*.[7] These critics spurn orthodoxy because of its supposed blindness to the political functions that are integral to the contemporary concept of a human right. Typically, some version of one or both of the following two broad functions are invoked. Internally, respect for human rights is at least a necessary condition for the legitimacy of the state; unless a state complies with human rights, its laws will not bind its subjects. Externally, human rights operate as standards whose violation, if extensive and persistent, can trigger a defeasible case for some form of international intervention or other manifestation of concern. Some advocates of the political conception also follow Rawls in abandoning the second limb of the orthodox conception. They insist that in an ideologically pluralistic world, an adequate justification of human rights cannot appeal to any 'comprehensive doctrine', including the idea that there are objective moral truths, regarding which 'reasonable', or at least 'not fully unreasonable', societies are prone to disagree. Instead, human rights are to be justified by a special mode of 'public reason' that is discontinuous from ordinary, truth-oriented moral reasoning.

Having marked this disagreement between orthodox and political understandings of human rights, I now set it aside and proceed on an orthodox footing, taking human rights to be broadly equivalent to natural rights.[8] In any case, none of the philosophers I shall discuss follows Rawls in abandoning the second tenet of the orthodox conception, which is the crucial one for our purposes.

---

[7] John Rawls, *The Law of Peoples* (Cambridge, MA, Harvard University Press, 1999), 10, 27, 37, 42, 65, 68–9, 78–81.
[8] I have made a case for orthodoxy about human rights elsewhere, including 'On the nature of human rights', 43–56, and 'Towards a philosophy of human rights', *Current Legal Problems* 1–30 (2012), 18–25.

Divine love and human interests

Is there anything more than a rhetorically induced feel-good factor to the familiar claim that human rights are grounded in human dignity? Is the latter notion doing any real work here, or is it just a placeholder for some justification that the speaker vaguely implies exists but has done absolutely nothing to specify? At the limit, is the appeal to human dignity in reality serving as a means of evading the question of foundations? One route into these questions is to see how much progress we can make towards justifying human rights without overt reliance on the notion of human dignity. Now, the idea of human dignity refers to some intrinsic value inhering in the status of being human, a value that is equally shared by all human beings but which somehow elevates them above all non-human animals. At this level of abstraction, one might wonder how human dignity could possibly fail to be a foundation of human rights. To get a clearer idea of how this might be thought to be so, let us consider two putatively alternative grounds for human rights: love and interests.

By love, I mean divine love. Of course, there exist theistic interpretations of human dignity that trace our special inherent worth to some salient respect in which human beings, unlike other creatures, bear the image of God: for example, in virtue of our capacity for abstract rational thought or self-determination. Such approaches struggle to embrace members of the species *Homo sapiens* who were born lacking these capacities or who have subsequently irretrievably lost them. But if human rights are rights possessed by all human beings, how can our Godlike status confer them upon those with severe mental disabilities or sufferers from advanced senile dementia? This line of thought has recently led Nicholas Wolterstorff to invoke God in a different way, one with its own distinct theological lineage. In his view, all human beings possess all human rights not because of some valuable quality inhering in each of those humans, not even one in virtue of which they resemble God, but because they are special objects of God's love. Moreover, since God loves each individual human being equally, even the most disabled human possesses exactly the same human rights as the most gifted members of the species.[9]

Even by Wolterstorff's own reckoning, and bracketing the contestable assumption of God's existence, this argument grounds very few human rights. So few, indeed, that there is a genuine question whether he is addressing the same subject matter as the mainstream human rights culture. And the problems run deeper still. If human beings are specially loved by God, one might

---

[9] N. Wolterstorff, *Justice: Rights and Wrongs* (Princeton, NJ, Princeton University Press, 2008), 352–61.

plausibly suppose that this is in virtue of qualities they possess that render them, as opposed say to earthworms, fitting objects of such love. In the absence of these qualities, God's love would seem to be arbitrarily bestowed. But if humans possess such qualities, why do they not directly ground human rights without the mediation of God's love? Perhaps the answer is that these qualities are not sufficiently impressive, considered by themselves, to do so. But even if we are persuaded by this response, there is a further question about whether this is a justification of the right kind. Human rights are supposed to pay tribute to the value of each individual human being, but on this account they are ultimately ways of respecting God. Human beings are, in consequence, radically decentred within human rights morality: they are not the ultimate source of the moral concern it embodies. This is analogous to the way in which, according to Wolterstorff, eudaimonistic justifications of human rights, which appeal to the flourishing of those bearing the duties generated by rights, unacceptably downgrade the status of the right-holder as the source of human rights. The suspicion that things have gone awry here is heightened by Wolterstorff's key illustration of how love bestows special worth, which is that of an ordinary individual acquiring a higher social status as a result of being befriended by the monarch. Treating such an individual with special respect, however, is ultimately a way of honouring the monarch, not the person himself.

We turn now to the second justificatory pathway to human rights, the one that invokes universal human interests. The idea here is that there are certain interests, the fulfilment of which standardly improves the quality of a human's life. Human rights on this view do not merely characteristically protect human interests—such as our interests in not being tortured, in subsistence and education, in being able to practise one's religion or to have a family, and so on—they also owe their very existence to the way they serve these interests. The fact that human rights characteristically further and protect human interests is, therefore, not a brute coincidence; it is explained by the grounding role of such interests in arguments for human rights. This is not the place to offer anything like an adequate account of universal human interests; instead it is enough to notice three features. First, they are universal interests, possessed by all human beings simply as human beings (inhabiting, we might add, some broadly defined historical epoch). Second, they are objective in status: they are interests of human beings whether or not those human beings believe them to be interests of theirs or desire their fulfilment. Finally, there is a plurality of interests that can give rise to human rights. In grounding human rights, we can avail ourselves of diverse aspects of the human good, provided they are genuinely universal: interests in knowledge, friendship, play, achievement, autonomy, and so on. Indeed, any given human right will typically be grounded in a cluster of affected interests.

Now, it is vitally important to appreciate that this interest-based approach does not simply identify human rights with universal interests. Not that such an identification would be utterly implausible. After all, it offers a benign way of explaining the endless proliferation of human rights claims. And it also provides one means of vindicating items in key human rights instruments that are often disparaged by sceptics, such as the controversial human right to 'highest attainable standard of physical and mental health'—for surely this is something in which we each have an interest.[10] Nevertheless, reducing human rights to universal interests is a category error. Interests belong to the domain of prudence or well-being, which concerns what makes a life better for the person living it, whereas human rights are moral standards that impose duties on others, where the violation of the duty entails *wronging* someone in particular—the right-holder. Our interests, by contrast, can be impaired in all sorts of ways without any *moral* wrongdoing being in the offing, let alone a directed wrongdoing of this specific kind. Lawyers have long understood this, as the distinction between *damnum* and *injuria* attests.

A central question confronting the interest-based account of human rights is that of spelling out how we may advance from premises about universal human interests to conclusions about human rights. The correct, albeit highly schematic, answer is: only insofar as universal human interests, in the case of each human being and without the added support of others' interests, generate a duty to serve these interests in some way.[11] Hence, a human right exists when in the case of all people their personal interests suffice to impose duties upon others to serve their interests by securing the object of the right. The object may be as various as access to clean water, a fair trial, freedom from torture, or basic education, depending on the particular right in question. So, the vital consideration is the duty-generative capacity of individuals' interests. And duty here has to be understood in a quite specific sense. It is not just a reason, or even a moral reason, but a specific kind of moral reason. It is categorical, in that it applies to us independently of how we happen to be motivated. It is exclusionary in its force, in that it is not simply to be counted in favour of, or against, a certain action, but also neutralizes at least some countervailing reasons. And, finally, it is a reason whose transgression merits an array of moral responses, such as resentment on the part of the victim, guilt

---

[10] Article 12 (1), International Covenant on Economic, Social and Cultural Rights (1966).
[11] For the leading exposition of the interest-based approach to moral rights generally, see Joseph Raz, *The Morality of Freedom* (Oxford, Oxford University Press, 1986), chapter 7.

on the part of the perpetrator, and blame or sometimes even punishment on the part of third parties.

Of course, the preceding response demands supplementation by a lot of substantive judgment in order to yield answers to specific practical problems. However, it is probably in vain that we hanker after some simple argumentative bridge, a comprehensive and readily applicable *ex ante* set of criteria, that enables us to cross the Rubicon from interests to duties that are the counterparts of rights. There is no prospect of any philosophical formula upstaging sound practical judgment attuned to the specificities of each case. Nevertheless, we can still acknowledge at least two thresholds that must be crossed in progressing from universal interests to human rights. I shall label them the thresholds of *possibility* and *burden*.

Passing the first threshold requires that it be possible to serve the putative right-holder's interest through the putative duty. The kind of impossibility that prevents an interest from generating a duty can vary from case to case. Sometimes it is logical: there can be no duty to provide everyone with an 'above average' standard of living. Sometimes it is a matter of scientific law: there can be no duty to enable men to give birth. And sometimes it is a matter of contingent empirical fact: given the scarcity of available resources, there can be no duty to provide everyone with the option of a Rodeo Drive lifestyle. Sometimes, more interestingly, the impossibility takes a more directly normative form, one whereby the relevant interest cannot be served specifically by means of the recognition of a *duty*. For example, a duty to love another romantically is arguably self-defeating, given that romantic love is the spontaneous outgrowth of another's feelings and desires. But even assuming that it is possible to serve an interest by means of a putative duty—as may be the case with the duty corresponding to the supposed right to 'the highest attainable standard of physical and mental health'—a second threshold must be negotiated. This registers the burdens that the duty would impose not only on the latter's putative bearers but also on our capacity to realize other values, including other rights. This is the main reason for scepticism about a human right to the highest attainable standard of health, at least on anything approximating a literal construal. Even if it is possible, given realistically available resources, to achieve the highest attainable standard of *health*—or, more modestly, of *health care*—in the case of all human beings, doing so would be so burdensome in relation to our capacity to realize other values, including other human rights, that individuals' interest cannot yield any such corresponding duty.

Of course, the idea of burden needs to be handled with great care. In particular, there is the delicate matter of distinguishing between the burdens that bear on the existence and content of a putative right, and those that at best count against complying with an existing right when reaching an all-things-considered decision regarding what to do. Any account that does not treat every human right as absolute, hence as never justifiably overridden by other considerations, must make room for this distinction. So, for example, in judging whether there is a human right to antiretrovirals, one cannot simply take as given the price that pharmaceutical companies, motivated by profit-maximization and asserting rights conferred by patent laws, charge for such drugs. Those prices are the upshot of policies formed within a market system and an intellectual property regime that may themselves be morally deficient in salient respects. Nevertheless, even if HIV-sufferers do have a human right to antiretrovirals, their high market price may justify a poorer country in adopting a policy of not (fully) complying with that right, given the many other pressing claims on its severely limited resources. Here, the high market price justifies non-compliance with a genuine human right, rather than preventing the human right from coming into existence in the first place or diluting its content.

Much more needs to be said about the transition from interests to duties. It can be a complicated process partly because of its holistic character. We cannot satisfactorily establish the existence and content of any one human right without also considering the implications for the existence and content of other putative human rights. Moreover, it is unlikely that the process of delineating and assigning counterpart duties is ever entirely a matter of pure moral reasoning. In order for human rights to be effective, action-guiding standards, they will often require a more determinate specification than unaided moral reasoning can generate from its own resources.[12] Hence the need to some form of social fiat, such as convention or positive law, to supplement the deliverances of natural reason. However, if it can be successfully executed, the interest-based account of human rights promises to make sense of a phenomenon that eluded Wolterstorff: namely, the status of the right-holder as the ultimate source of the moral claim embodied in his right. The duties associated with rights are *directed*, they are *owed to* someone in particular: the right-holder. In consequence, if a duty that is a counterpart to a right is violated, the right-holder is the immediate victim, and hence is in a special position to complain, to feel resentment. And the reason for this is that the duty has its origins in his interests alone. Perfect duties, corresponding to rights, contrast with imperfect

---

[12] For the spectrum of questions that have to be addressed in a tolerably full specification of rights, see J. M. Finnis, *Natural Law and Natural Rights*, 2nd edn (Oxford, Oxford University Press, 2011), 218–19.

duties, such as the duty to be charitable, which are owed to no one in particular, and hence are not associated with rights.

Deontology and personhood

Are we now in sight of at least the rough outlines of a satisfactory account of the foundations of human rights, one that dispenses entirely with human dignity? We cannot safely conclude that we are until two powerful onslaughts from the partisans of dignity have been withstood. Call them the *deontological* and the *personhood* objections. I shall consider them as they emerge, respectively, out of important recent writings on human rights by Thomas Nagel and James Griffin.

The first objection contends that the grounding of human rights cannot be primarily in interests, because the moral logic of rights is radically distinct from that of interests. Regarding the latter, the utilitarian is correct: the aggregate fulfilment of interests is to be maximized across all persons. In this process of aggregation, some people's interests may have to be sacrificed in order to promote the fulfilment of others' interests. The logic of rights, however, erects powerful, if not always absolutely insurmountable, obstacles to such interpersonal trade-offs. Nagel calls this feature of rights their 'agent-relativity': '[Rights] prohibit us from *doing* certain things to anyone but do not require that we count it equally a reason for action that it will prevent those same sorts of things from *being done* to someone but not by oneself.'[13] The right not to be murdered imposes a duty on each of us to refrain from murdering others. But this duty is not eliminated or overridden simply because murdering one innocent person is the only way of preventing the murder by someone else of two other innocents. Instead, it imposes on us duties *personally* to respect the life of each and every right-holder, so that compliance with the duty cannot be traded off in this way across persons. The agent-relativity of the duties imposed by rights finds its counterpart in the special status—'inviolability'—that such rights confer on their holders. It is this notion of status, which encapsulates the resistance of rights to trade-offs, that we can reasonably translate as human dignity. The inference that Nagel draws is that the primary basis of human rights is in our moral status, not our interests.

Nagel's argument evidently latches onto an important aspect of the logic of rights, one that interest-based theorists deny at their peril. However, Nagel

---

[13] T. Nagel, 'Personal rights and public space', in his *Concealment and Exposure* (Oxford, Oxford University Press, 2002), 31–52, at 35.

gives this feature the label 'agent-relativity' partly because he repeatedly stresses a self-other asymmetry in its formulation: *I* may not torture one innocent in order to prevent two other innocents being tortured by *another*. But arguably the self-other asymmetry, even if it is morally salient, is not the crux of the matter. I also may not torture one innocent person even if, through some convoluted but highly predictable train of events, this would prevent *me*, at some later stage, torturing two others. I therefore prefer to speak of the resistance of rights to trade-offs within a simple aggregative calculus, rather than to their agent-relativity, as constituting the nub of the deontological objection.[14]

But what is the content of Nagel's alternative justification, according to which human rights are aspects of our status as members of the moral community? Nagel's reply, in effect, is that this status comes down to the fact that we possesses certain rights, a fact that testifies to the fundamental, non-derivative standing of human rights in our moral thought. Human rights are grounded in our status as members of the moral community, but that very status is a matter of possessing certain rights. This circularity might be thought a steep price to pay in order to secure the resistance of human rights to trade-offs. Of course, there will be some points in our ethical thought at which we strike bedrock, leaving us only with an appeal to self-evidence, in the sense that properly understanding a certain principle provides sufficient warrant for believing it. So the appeal to underived moral norms is not in itself objectionable. But it does leave it rather mysterious why standard human rights protect some very important human interests; can this be a mere coincidence so far as the existence of the former is concerned? Moreover, such rights fundamentalism seems to short-circuit the potential for rational debate about which human rights exist, a debate conducted in significant part by reference to the moral significance of the interests served by putative rights.

The deontological objection, as we find it in Nagel, confronts us with a hard choice: either surrender the resistance to trade-offs characteristic of human rights or else accept them as fundamental moral standards for which a non-circular justification is unavailable. But, in the end, this is a false choice. We should not accept his premise that the moral logic appropriate to interests is exclusively one of aggregation. In the outline sketch of the interest-based account of human rights given above (see 'Divine love and human interests'), rights were not identified with interests, nor was there any hint that the reasoning advancing us from interests to duties can be subsumed under some

---

[14] I leave unaddressed, in this connection, the extent to which this resistance to trade-offs is well captured by some version of the principle of double effect which accords moral significance to the distinction between what one intends in acting and what one accepts as a side effect of so acting.

overarching aggregative principle. More generally, there are many teleological approaches to ethics, going all the way back to Plato and Aristotle, that make considerations of human good central to the justification of moral standards without endorsing the kind of crude aggregative reasoning that Nagel describes. One way of putting this is to say that the moral significance of interests finds expression not just in reasons to *promote* the fulfilment of those interests but also to *respect* them. And respecting them crucially includes not directly acting against the duties such interests generate, even if doing so would promote overall compliance with the very same duties.[15] However, this distinction needs to be handled with care, since nothing in the idea of promoting interests, as articulated so far, commits us to the thesis that a principle of maximizing overall utility is even *one* of the demands of morality. It may indeed be that such a principle is incoherent or otherwise unsustainable.[16]

And there are yet further difficulties with Nagel's status-based approach to human rights. Surely the whole of morality, so far as it concerns humans, reflects our status as members of the moral community. Subjecting people to punishment in the case of serious wrongdoing is one important way in which we pay tribute to their status as members of the moral community. Nevertheless, many of us baulk at the claim that offenders have a *right* to be punished. How, then, are we to differentiate rights from other elements of morality that are not rights-involving, such as demands of charity or ideals of moral perfection? The interest-based theorist has an answer to this question: the part of morality that concerns rights has a distinctive kind of justification; that is, the interests of the right-holder suffice, without the benefit of the additional weight of others' interests, to generate duties. How can Nagel differentiate the part of morality that concerns human rights from that which does not?

The start of one reply is to identify our moral status, or human dignity, with one particular value among others, but to deny that the realization of this value is something that generally enhances the quality of our lives. This is the account of human rights advocated by Amartya Sen, according to whom human rights are exclusively grounded in the value of freedom, but freedom in the relevant sense is not aptly characterized as one of our interests.[17] This sort of view fits with, and helps make sense of, Nagel's tendency to focus on human rights that are not readily conceived as enhancing the quality of the

---

[15] See also James Griffin, *On Human Rights* (Oxford, Oxford University Press, 2008), chapter 3, for a discussion of a teleological but non-consequentialist approach to human rights, and also the remarks in John Tasioulas, 'Taking rights out of human rights', *Ethics* 120 (2010), 647–78, at 675–8.
[16] See, for example, J. M. Finnis, *Natural Law and Natural Rights*, 110–18, and D. Wiggins, *Ethics: Twelve Lectures on the Philosophy of Morality* (London, Penguin, 2006), chapter 8.
[17] Amartya Sen, *The Idea of Justice* (Cambridge, MA, Harvard University Press, 2009), chapter 17.

right-holder's life, such as the right to consume pornography or publicly deny the Holocaust. In my view, which cannot be defended here, Sen's argument involves an implausible understanding of the value of freedom and its relation to well-being, and of how interests are served by rights on an interest-based account. Let me consider, instead, how the appeal to freedom might drive the second objection to the interest-based approach, which I call the *personhood* objection.

This objection can be seen as emerging from an alternative, personhood account of the foundations of human rights. On this view, whose leading contemporary exponent is James Griffin, human rights are grounded in the value of personhood or normative agency. Persons are normative agents, beings with the capacity to choose a conception of the good life from a range of valuable options (autonomy) and to pursue their choices free of interference (liberty). Personhood distinguishes us from non-human animals, hence it offers a salient and historically resonant interpretation of human dignity.[18] The personhood account opposes the deontological view, because it conceives of personhood as an important set of interests; but it also opposes the interest-based view, because it allows only the values of personhood—autonomy and liberty—directly to ground human rights, but not other universal human interests such as achievement, enjoyment, knowledge, or the avoidance of pain.

One problem with the personhood view is that it issues in counter-intuitive and precarious justifications of paradigmatic human rights.[19] For instance, Griffin contends that torture is a human rights violation because, and only because, of the way it attacks our capacity to 'decide for ourselves or to stick to our decision'.[20] Certainly, this is a major part of the story. But there are many other ways of undermining people's decision-making capacity, such as injecting them with mind-altering drugs. Part of what makes torture a graver human rights violation is that it achieves its purpose through the infliction of severe pain; and the avoidance of severe pain is another universal interest, along with the interest in freedom. The human right not to be tortured seems to draw its force from a number of interests that are threatened by torture, not just freedom. Another problem is that the personhood account, at least as developed by Griffin, is that it limits the subjects of human rights to 'the sub-class of human normative agents'.[21] This disqualifies an alarming number of human beings from having any human rights—all those members of the species who

---

[18] J. Griffin, *On Human Rights* (Oxford, Oxford University Press, 2008), 32–3, 36.
[19] For a fuller discussion of many of the points made in the rest of this section, see John Tasioulas, 'Taking rights out of human rights', 658–68.
[20] J. Griffin, *On Human Rights*, 52.
[21] J. Griffin, *On Human Rights*, 50.

are not, or are no longer, normative agents: not only foetuses but also newborn babies, infants, and those suffering from serious mental disabilities or in persistent vegetative states.[22] Of course, Griffin allows that there are other moral norms that prohibit the maltreatment of human beings who are non-agents. By his reckoning, wantonly killing an infant or an Alzheimer's patient is murder, a wrong far graver than most human rights violations, even though in neither case is the killing a human rights violation. Yet it is that last point that is extremely difficult to swallow, since murder is a paradigmatic rights violation. To say, in response, that the murder of non-agents violates their rights, but is not a *human rights violation*, is to rely on what looks, from an orthodox point of view, like an artificial distinction between universal moral rights and human rights.

The interest-based account of human rights offers a way of overcoming both of these problems. Since a plurality of interests can underwrite human rights, there is no need to construct counter-intuitively roundabout justifications of rights that appeal exclusively to our interest in normative agency. And, for the same reason, we are better placed to ascribe human rights to human beings who do not have substantial (present) interests in autonomy and liberty: the interest of infants and Alzheimer's patients in avoiding painful and degrading treatment is enough to render their torture a human rights violation. However, we should do well to register a powerful motivation that leads Griffin to the personhood view. He believes that the contemporary discourse of human rights is in an intellectually debased condition, to such an extent that the phrase human right has become virtually criterionless. And he claims that the pluralistic, interest-based approach connives at this debasement, exacerbating the problem of indeterminacy by allowing a plurality of interests to factor into the grounding of human rights. The upshot, he contends, is that a pluralistic view fails to respect the difference between human rights and the elements of a good human life, depriving the language of human rights of its distinctive significance.[23]

This personhood objection, however, is misplaced. Although I do not share Griffin's bleak assessment of contemporary human rights discourse, he is certainly justified in calling for greater intellectual discipline in arguments about the existence and content of human rights. But the interest-based account adequately meets the call; or, to put it more cautiously, it fares no worse than the personhood account in doing so. Pluralism does not license us to infer the existence of a human right to X wherever there is a universal

---

[22] J. Griffin, *On Human Rights*, chapter 4.
[23] J. Griffin, *On Human Rights*, 55.

human interest in X. Instead, we have to ask whether for all human beings that interest generates a duty with the same content, and in asking that question we must, among other things, negotiate the two thresholds. It is the combination of universality and threshold requirements that instils the necessary intellectual discipline, not an *ex ante* restriction on the kinds of universal interests that may have a rights-generative role. Indeed, Griffin himself needs to appeal to a threshold at which personhood interests generate rights, since not everything that furthers a personhood interest—however great the cost—is something to which there is a right.[24] So, the pluralistic account respects the distinction between rights and their grounding interests in precisely the same way as the personhood account: by appealing to a threshold at which the relevant interests generate duties. If a workable threshold exists for the personhood account, there is no reason why it should not equally operate within a pluralistic account.

The need for human dignity

If the interest-based account of human rights withstands the deontological and agency objections, should we deny human dignity a place at the foundation of human rights? Should we go further and join its legion of critics, from Arthur Schopenhauer to Steven Pinker, who insist that human dignity either reduces to some other value—such as autonomy—or else operates as rhetorical camouflage for the speaker's unspoken moral prejudices, often religious in origin?

No; this is not where the path we have followed has led. The situation is considerably more nuanced. Deontological theorists who claim that an interest-independent conception dignity furnishes a complete grounding of human rights are mistaken. But those who argue that human dignity is really just one component of well-being among others—the interest in freedom or normative agency—also go astray. Instead, an alternative position to both views is preferable. There is a meaningful notion of human dignity, and it is the notion of an intrinsically valuable status rather than of one human interest among others. It does lie at the foundations of human rights, but only because it is foundational to interpersonal morality generally. But, contrary to both Nagel and Griffin, it does not exhaust the foundations of human rights. In other words, human dignity by itself cannot generate anything like the familiar schedule of human rights. Instead, it characteristically operates in intimate union with

---

[24] Griffin uses the notion of 'practicalities' to articulate the nature of this threshold, *On Human Rights*, 37.

universal interests in grounding human rights norms. The resultant view of the grounds of human rights is doubly pluralistic: it affirms both moral (equal human dignity) and prudential (universal human interests) elements among the grounds of human rights, and it embraces a plurality of universal human interests as potentially human rights-generative.

The idea of human dignity is the idea of an intrinsically valuable status that merits our respect, a status grounded in the fact of being a human being. What it is to be a human being, what is the ontological basis of this valuable status, is an inexhaustible topic. But in broad outline it is to belong to a species which is in turn characterized by the possession of a variety of features: a characteristic form of embodiment; a finite lifespan of a certain rough magnitude; capacities for physical growth and reproduction; psychological capacities, such as perception, self-consciousness, and memory; and, specifically rational capacities, such as the capacities for language-use, for registering a diverse range of normative considerations (including evaluative considerations, prudential, moral, aesthetic, and others besides), and for aligning one's judgments, emotions, and actions with those considerations.[25] Call this the human nature conception of human dignity, insofar as it grounds the value of human dignity in the characteristic elements that constitute human nature.

Some important consequences follow from this understanding of human dignity. First, human dignity inheres in a human being from the moment of their coming into existence as an individual human being until their death (and in some ways retains significance beyond their death), and this is so irrespective of the choices (e.g., to engage in wrong-doing, to neglect developing or exercising their capacities) or condition (e.g., embryonic, diseased, comatose) of the human being in question at any stage of their life. Second, since what matters is the possession of a human nature, the value of human dignity remains constant across different persons despite other ethically significant variations among them. A human being with impaired rational capacities shares in human dignity to the same extent as one with ordinary rational capacities; the same applies to those endowed with superior rational capacities, or who have developed them to a greater extent, as compared with others. Third, in the case of all human beings, their dignity confers on them a special

---

[25] For broadly similar views of human dignity, see P. Lee and R. P. George, 'The nature and basis of human dignity', *Ratio Juris* 21 (2008), 173–93, and J. M. Finnis, 'Equality and differences', *Solidarity: The Journal of Catholic Social Thought and Secular Ethics* 2 (2012). However, there are some important differences worth noting, especially with Lee and George, of which I here mention only two. First, I want to separate much more sharply than they do the attribution of human dignity and the attribution of human rights. Second, unlike them, I am not inclined to make possession of a rational nature a necessary condition for the capacity to have moral rights. A further apparent difference is noted in 'Invariant dignity, variable rights'.

value, and therefore justifies according them special consideration, as compared with all non-human animals. What practical implications this special value has, in concrete cases, is a matter for substantive argument. Fourth, human dignity consists in an equality of basic *moral* status among human beings. Affirming its existence does not, in itself, amount to any claim about social, political, or legal status.[26] In contrast to Jeremy Waldron's recent conjecture, human dignity so conceived is not principally a juridical notion that attributes to all human beings a 'high-ranking legal, political, and social status'.[27] Historically, defenders of human dignity, or the basic moral equality of humans, such as the Stoics, Locke, and Kant, have embraced profoundly inegalitarian doctrines as to social, political, and legal status. These doctrines include the exclusion of women and those without property from political participation, and even some forms of slavery. But even if these inegalitarian practices violate human dignity, it again takes a substantive argument to establish that this is so: the claim of human dignity—of basic moral equality among human beings—is not in its essence a claim about legal or political status.

Someone might object that this articulation of human dignity simply identifies another interest, our interest in having and maintaining a distinctively human nature. Hence, it does not take us beyond the orbit of a resolutely interest-based view. Although this objection may well deploy the idea of interest in a perfectly intelligible way, ultimately it misfires. This is because there is a categorical difference between asking what kind of nature a being possesses and consequently what kind of respect it merits, on the one hand, and what interests it has, on the other. Indeed, it is impossible to even make a start on answering the second question without having some independent grasp of the answer to the first. This distinction between nature/status and interests survives the realization that a fully adequate specification of the nature and value of human status must ultimately make reference to the array of goods that the exercise of their essential capacities enables human beings to realize, and vice versa. This substantive interdependence is perfectly consistent with the distinctness of the concepts involved.[28]

---

[26] This distinction is marked by Rawls, who insists on the difference between 'equality as it is invoked in connection with the distribution of certain goods, some of which will almost certainly give higher status or prestige to those who are more favoured, and equality as it applies to the respect which is owed to persons irrespective of social position'. John Rawls, *A Theory of Justice* (Oxford, Oxford University Press, 1999), 447.

[27] Jeremy Waldron, *Dignity, Rank, and Rights*, ed. Meir Dan-Cohen (Oxford, Oxford University Press, 2012), 47.

[28] John Finnis has stressed both the link between capacities and goods and yet also the meaningfulness of the distinction between dignity and human interests in accounting for the basis of human rights:

Still, even though status is distinct from interests, we do not need to invoke human dignity as an extraneous add-on to the interest-based account of human rights that I sketched. Human dignity was already there in the interest-based account, staring us in the face, as it were, but not in the guise of one interest among others. There are at least two levels at which it figures. The first relates to the capacity of human beings to be right-holders. It is plausibly regarded as at least a necessary condition for any individual's capacity to have rights, leaving aside the case of non-artificial entities such as corporations, that their existence and well-being is of intrinsic and non-derivative value. Their existence and well-being must be of value in itself, and not simply in virtue of their causal consequences, and this intrinsic value must not be entirely dependent on the constitutive role that the putative right-holder plays in the existence or flourishing of some other individual.[29] Possessing the value of human dignity may be conceived as one way, if not the only way, of meeting this general condition for having the capacity to possess rights.

Human dignity, on this view, goes beyond merely endowing its possessors with moral considerability. Non-human animals and even plants or inanimate aspects of nature may be appropriate objects of moral concern despite lacking human dignity. Nor is human dignity helpfully interpreted as a condition for possessing any moral rights at all. To my mind, there is no compelling reason to deny that non-human animals possess the capacity to have some moral rights, a capacity that can be articulated in terms of their own species-specific dignity. Instead, human dignity encapsulates the distinctive moral standing of our fellow humans, a standing that differentiates them from non-human animals, thereby imparting a special moral significance to their existence and the fulfilment of their interests. It is a status that informs all human rights morality, but only because it is at the root of interpersonal morality in general. But it helps explain why human beings, in particular, have the capacity for rights.

There is a second, more complex, contribution that human dignity makes to the morality of human rights. It is essential to making sense of the idea that human rights are resistant to trade-offs, which is the feature of such rights emphasized by the deontologist. Human rights embody the idea that each human individual, considered in themselves, is an ultimate and distinctive object of

---

'Just as immaturity and impairment do not, in one's own existence, extinguish the radical capacities dynamically oriented towards self-development and healing, so they do not in the lives of other persons. *There* is the ontological unity of the human race, and radical equality of human persons which, taken with the truths about basic human goods, grounds the duties whose correlatives are human rights.' J. M. Finnis, 'Equality and differences', *Solidarity: The Journal of Catholic Social Thought and Secular Ethics* 2 (2012), 3.

[29] Joseph Raz, *The Morality of Freedom* (Oxford, Oxford University Press, 1983), 176–80.

moral concern. Insofar as it takes the form of respect for individuals' rights, associated with perfect duties that are *owed to* the right-holder, this concern surely tracks back to the fact that the individuals in question have interests. This was the key insight of the interest-based account of human and, more generally, moral rights. But people are not simply the 'locations' at which the satisfaction or frustration of free-floating interests happen to be instantiated. The individuals with these interests count in themselves, and not because the satisfaction or frustration of their interests is ultimately assimilated to some overarching aggregative concern. Their counting in this way is the starting-point in making sense of the resistance to trade-offs that status-based theorists wrongly suppose necessitates the abandonment of an interest-based approach to human rights.[30]

It follows from this view that although human dignity is an indispensable basis for human rights—a condition for their possession and a ground, together with universal interests, of their attribution—its normative significance is not exhausted by human rights. It is a broader notion than human rights, with the result that human dignity may be at stake in contexts and in ways not adequately captured by the idea of human rights, and even when no human rights issue arises. That human dignity may be disrespected without any human rights violation having occurred is a phenomenon for which we need to make conceptual space. When neo-Nazis desecrate Jewish graves there is, among other things, an affront to the dignity of the deceased. The desecration expresses the Nazis' view that the deceased were not fellow human beings, or not fellow human beings who count equally with themselves. And yet, we can regard this as an attack on the human dignity of the deceased without supposing their rights have been violated, perhaps because we believe that only living beings can have interests and that rights are characteristically grounded in interests. Here, although considerations of dignity are present and generate duties, the link with interests, which is paradigmatically in place in the discourse of rights, has arguably been severed.[31]

---

[30] For example, J. M. Finnis, *Natural Law and Natural Rights*; Philippa Foot, 'Morality, action and outcome', in T. Honderich (ed.), *Morality and Objectivity* (London, Routledge, 1985); D. Wiggins, 'Solidarity and the root of the ethical', The Lindley Lecture (University of Kansas, 2008).

[31] For a related discussion of dignity and treatment of human corpses, see M. Rosen, *Dignity: Its History and Meaning* (Cambridge, MA, Harvard University Press, 2012), chapter 3. However, I think that Rosen concludes too quickly that human dignity is not foundational for human rights. Partly this is because he considers it only as furnishing a comprehensive foundation, which it does not. But partly it is also because he sees dignity as giving rise principally to symbolic duties to act in certain ways that *express* respect, and correctly notices that most paradigmatic human rights violations as not fundamentally symbolic in character (see 157–8). But even if human dignity, by itself, mainly grounds prohibitions against symbolic wrongs, it does not follow that it has no important role to play, in tandem

Or, to take another example, a man whose beliefs and behaviour are impeccably liberal may be appalled to find himself upset that a black family has moved into his neighbourhood. This upset may be the product of the man's upbringing in a racist culture, an upbringing that has left a deep imprint on his psyche, one that he sincerely and vehemently condemns and disowns on those occasions when it rises to the surface of consciousness. But even if his upset manifests a failure on his part adequately to register the human dignity of his neighbours, again it does not automatically follow that he is violating their rights. This need not be, as in the previous case, because his upset does not threaten to impact detrimentally on their interests: perhaps it does, in that it causes him to be frosty or unhelpful in his dealings with them. Nonetheless, it might well be thought that there is no violation of a *duty* in this case. Recall the two thresholds that need to be crossed before any interest generates a right. One obstacle is the idea that our visceral emotional responses are not adequately subject to the control of our will. But even if it were psychologically possible to exert such control, the kind of mental self-policing that this requires is arguably excessively burdensome to generate an obligation to undertake it for the sake of the benefit to be secured to the putative right-holders. Here the affront to dignity is not a human rights violation because the link to duty is broken.

Invariant dignity, variable rights

I conclude by drawing out briefly some implications that the doubly pluralist account of the foundations of human rights has for their scope. Recall that Wolterstorff rejected dignitarian accounts of the foundations of human rights on the basis that they cannot confer human rights on those human beings who lack the valuable capacities that ground dignity. For Wolterstorff this is a fatal flaw, because he adopts a strict interpretation of the orthodox view of human rights described at the outset (see 'Divine love and human interests'). On this interpretation, all human beings must possess exactly the same set of human rights, irrespective of divergences in their capacities.[32] Taking this uniformity constraint seriously leads Wolterstorff to endorse an ultra-minimalist

---

with interests, in justifying standard human rights. To this extent, Rosen's scepticism about the human rights-generative powers of dignity over-reaches.

[32] Article 2 of the Universal Declaration of Human Rights may seem to reflect this strict interpretation in stating that 'Everyone is entitled to all the rights and freedom set forth in this Declaration', but this assumes that 'everyone' here means all members of the human species. However, the inadmissible bases of distinction set out in that article make no explicit reference to disabilities of any sort.

schedule of human rights, that is, one that excludes practically all the familiar socio-economic rights. Indeed, this minimalism is so severe that it falls foul of Wolterstorff's own desideratum on an adequate philosophical account of human rights: that it exhibit a significant degree of fidelity to widespread understandings of the sorts of rights that count as human rights.[33]

Does the account of the foundations of human rights sketched in this chapter enable us to meet Wolterstorff's uniformity constraint while simultaneously respecting the fidelity desideratum? So much seems to be implied by two other defenders of the human nature view, Patrick Lee and Robert George, according to whom '[s]everely retarded human beings have the same nature and thus the same basic rights as other humans'.[34] Now, Wolterstorff rejects the human nature view on the basis that membership of a species with a certain nature is a property insufficiently 'impressive' to undergird the doctrine of human rights, since those who possess this nature include 'human beings who are seriously lacking in capacities on account of human nature being malformed in their case'.[35] But there is no question of deriving human rights from possession of a human nature alone. We also have to attribute to people a standard profile of universal human interests before we can derive human rights. Human dignity, I have argued, works in tandem with interests in generating human rights.

Can the appeal to dignity and a plurality of universal interests satisfy both Wolterstorff's uniformity criterion and his fidelity desideratum? The only way it has any hope of doing so is if the primary duties associated with human rights can take a conditional form. The human right to a fair wage for work done, for example, is a right that imposes a duty to pay others a fair wage on condition that the latter have actually undertaken some work. Likewise, the human right to a fair trial imposes a duty to try offenders fairly on condition that they face the prospect of public condemnation and punishment for supposed wrongdoing. Wolterstorff rejects such conditional specifications of human rights on the grounds that they would permit us to reinterpret any right as a human right. But I have argued against this claim elsewhere: human rights are incompatible with some, but not all, conditional specifications of their duties. In particular, the conditions specified in the duties must refer

---

[33] 'Should the schedule of natural human rights that one arrives at ... diverge markedly from standard lists of human rights, one would have reason to wonder whether one's endeavour was seriously flawed in some way'. Wolterstorff, *Justice: Rights and Wrongs*, 320.

[34] Lee and George, 'The nature and basis of human dignity', 176. Though perhaps the reference to 'basic' rights is salient. In personal correspondence, Robert P. George has indicated that his position allows for the possibility that some human beings do not possess all of the rights enumerated in the standard schedule of human rights.

[35] Wolterstorff, *Justice: Rights and Wrongs*, 352.

only to circumstances that are not unduly remote for all human beings given the socio-historical conditions in relation to which the content of the right has been framed.[36] The conditions of having carried out work or being liable to punishment are not remote in this way; the conditions of being a monarch or having authored a work of genius, by contrast, are remote.

However, even if we permit conditional specifications of human rights, steadfast adherence to the uniformity constraint would seemingly rule out many standard human rights. This is because the conditions specified in their primary duty could never realistically be fulfilled in the case of some human beings. For example, the duties associated with rights to education or to work may incorporate conditions, for example that a certain level of education is to be made available on condition that the right-holder is capable of benefiting from it, or that the right-holder is to be given the opportunity to carry out meaningful productive activity on condition they are willing and able to do so. But consider now a human being in a persistent, and irreversible, vegetative state. The likelihood that they will ever in their lifetime have the actual capacity to satisfy either condition is vanishingly small to non-existent. More radically, it seems far-fetched to attribute to such an individual the standard profile of universal human interests. At this point, we face two alternatives. One is to cleave to the uniformity constraint, and insist that it makes sense to attribute all standard human rights to someone in a persistent vegetative state, even though many if not most of these rights make reference to conditions that the putative right-holder is incapable of satisfying during their lifetime. But this view seems to deprive human rights of their practical significance, since many rights will make absolutely no practical difference to how we treat their holders in any circumstances reasonably accessible to us. To avoid this normative inertness, I prefer to embrace the other alternative, which abandons the uniformity criterion. On this view, it is not the case that each human being possesses all of the standard human rights. Instead, this is true only of 'ordinary' human beings, who form the central cases of human rights-holders. Other human beings, such as sufferers from advanced senile dementia or those in a persistent vegetative state, will enjoy some human rights (e.g., the right to life or the right not to be tortured) but not all (e.g., the right to work or the right to political participation).

On the resultant view, all human beings possess human dignity in equal measure. But which human rights they possess depends also on their interests

---

[36] John Tasioulas, 'On the nature of human rights', in G. Ernst and J-C. Heilinger (eds), *The Philosophy of Human Rights: Contemporary Controversies* (Berlin and Boston, Walter de Gruyter, 2012): 17–59, at 37–9.

and the threshold considerations whereby those interests generate duties. In the case of ordinary human beings, without impaired capacities, we can employ a standardized profile of human interests and generate the standard list of human rights. But some human beings are so impaired in their capacities to realize their human nature that it is implausible to attribute to them all these rights, either because they lack the relevant interests or because in their case the threshold conditions for the generation of a duty are not satisfied. They will have only a subset of the standard human rights. This position avoids ascribing human rights that are normatively idle, yet at the same time respects the idea that all human beings have an equal measure of human dignity. It can do so because it distinguishes human rights from human dignity, and treats the latter as only one element in the grounding of human rights.

17

In Defence of Human Dignity: Comments on Kant and Rosen

Thomas E. Hill, Jr.

FOR MANY YEARS, IMMANUEL KANT has been recognized as the most important philosopher to defend the idea that human dignity is at the core of our shared moral beliefs and practices. His influence is undeniable, but his critics have been many. Michael Rosen is among the most articulate and informed critics. In his chapter for this volume[1] and his recent book *Dignity: Its History and Meaning*,[2] Rosen traces the history of the idea of dignity from Stoic philosophers to Kant and beyond, along the way calling our attention to separate strands of thought and apparent objections. He makes the history accessible and the objections vivid. His brief historical survey should help to awaken public interest in the topic, and his thought-provoking commentary should be a welcome challenge to scholars, theologians, and philosophers who take human dignity to be a coherent and defensible concept. Lawyers and judges, especially where human dignity is written into their constitution, should find Rosen's work a valuable exploration of theoretical questions that underlie their practical problems in trying to find reasonable applications. Philosophers inspired by Kant will be especially keen to examine critically his extended treatment of dignity in Kant's philosophy, and perhaps to propose a Kantian response.

To disclose my own history and perspective, I belong to the large group of philosophers inspired by Kant even though (like Rosen) I am critical of Kant at many points. My brief remarks here are not intended as a full review of the topic or of Rosen's contributions, but I do want to offer some supplement to Rosen's treatment of Kant and some response to the objections that he raises. I will comment very briefly on the following issues: (1) the alleged neglect of dignity among contemporary philosophers; (2) the indeterminacy

---

[1] Michael Rosen, Chapter 7, this volume.
[2] Michael Rosen, *Dignity: Its History and Meaning* (Cambridge, MA, and London, Harvard University Press, 2012).

of the idea of dignity and consequently its liability to abuse; (3) the apparently disconnected strands of thought commonly associated with dignity; and (4) the alleged inadequacy of Kant's conception of human dignity for practical applications (e.g., vagueness and absolutism). Rosen's most important objection, however, concerns Kant's basis for affirming the dignity of every human person. That is, (5) Kant's apparent attempt to ground human dignity on the premise that there is in each person an awesome 'transcendental kernel' of a noumenal *we-know-not-what*. The problem is that this would mean that Kant derives his ethical belief from unsupportable, non-empirical metaphysics.

Preliminary points: contemporary resources and potential abuse of theories

The first point is a minor one. In a short survey for a general audience, Rosen understandably wanted to avoid the distractions of scholarly controversy, and in this he succeeds very well. He acknowledges that discussions of how to interpret Kant's moral philosophy, for example his idea of moral duty, are 'densely populated', but he chooses not to engage with this literature in order simply to propose 'in an exploratory spirit' a 'radically unorthodox' interpretation.[3] New proposals should be welcome, but his further suggestion that contemporary philosophers have neglected Kant's idea of dignity may be misleading. As he says, there has not been 'a large systematic body of contemporary philosophical literature' in this area,[4] but virtually every major commentary on Kant's ethics presents a view of the place and arguments for dignity, and commentators often treat this as a core concept. Rosen's choice not to engage in scholarly disputes makes sense, given his aims, but readers should be aware of the relevant literature on the topic.[5]

---

[3] Rosen, *Dignity*, xv.
[4] Rosen, *Dignity*, xiv.
[5] See, for example, Richard Dean, T*he Value of Humanity in Kant's Moral Theory* (Oxford, Clarendon Press, 2006), Robin Dillon, *Dignity, Character, and Self-Respect* (London, Routledge, 1995), Alan Donagan, *The Theory of Morality* (Chicago, The University of Chicago Press, 1977), Thomas E. Hill, Jr, *Dignity and Practical Reason in Kant's Moral Theory* (Ithaca, NY, Cornell University Press, 1992), *Respect, Pluralism, and Justice: Kantian Perspectives* (Oxford, Oxford University Press, 2000) and *Virtue, Rules, and Justice: Kantian Aspirations* (Oxford, Oxford University Press, 2012), Oliver Sensen, *Kant on Human Dignity* (Berlin and Boston, Walter de Gruyter, 2011), Allen Wood, *Kant's Ethical Thought* (Cambridge, Cambridge University Press, 1999) and *Kantian Ethics* (Cambridge, Cambridge University Press, 2008), and Jeffrie G. Murphy, 'The elusive nature of human dignity', *The Hedgehog Review* 9:3 (Fall 2007), reprinted in Jeffrie G. Murphy, *Punishment and the Human Emotions* (Oxford and New York, Oxford University Press, 2012). Two further sources discussed briefly by Rosen are Christine Korsgaard, *Creating the Kingdom of Ends* (Cambridge, Cambridge University

Second, as Rosen notes, a persistent and troublesome problem with the idea of dignity as it appears in many contexts is that it sounds high-minded and inspirational but is so indefinite that it can serve as a banner for many different and conflicting causes.[6] Indefinite ideals are liable to abuse because there are no fixed criteria to prevent unscrupulous debaters from appealing to the ideal to sanctify their self-serving projects. There is a similar liability in political rhetoric about 'freedom' and 'democracy' when these terms are used apart from contexts that can give them specific meaning. No moral concept or doctrine, of course, can be defined so specifically that it will be completely immune from misuse and abuse. The problem often lies with the aims and motives of those who would rather exploit an indefinite concept than look for or construct a more determinate interpretation. If, however, the concept of dignity is left completely indefinite, it cannot serve the guiding function that Kant and others thought that it could have. This is the more important problem to which I turn in the next two sections.

Can diverse ideas of dignity be coherently unified?

Turning to the third issue, different strands of thought are commonly associated with *dignity*, as Rosen explains: (a) a rank or status, (b) intrinsic value, (c) 'measured and self-possessed behaviour', and (d) respectful treatment.[7] Moral philosophers who affirm human dignity should specify strands they intend, and, if there are several, they should indicate how they fit together in a coherent systematic theory. In Kant's work, I think, all these elements are present, but the relationships among them are not obvious. To explain how they can fit together coherently is a challenge, but not an impossible task. All too briefly, as a first step I would say the following.

Regarding (a), in Kant's view, every human person has a *status* of dignity, which consists of rights, duties, and respect-worthiness that animals lack. It is the status of equality before the moral law and the status of a moral 'lawmaker', that is, a person who shares in the common practical reason that specifies what the basic law requires. The kinds of protections, responsibilities, and honour that are due to a person who has this status cannot simply be read off the word 'dignity', which (as Rosen reminds us) has a chequered history and multiple common uses. Instead, what is due depends on many complex

---

Press, 1996), and Onora O'Neill, *Constructions of Reason* (Cambridge, Cambridge University Press, 1989).
[6] Rosen, *Dignity*, chapter 1, esp. 1–5.
[7] Rosen, *Dignity*, 114.

factors that determine how the fundamental moral law (for Kant 'the Categorical Imperative') should be interpreted and applied.[8] On my reading, the status of human dignity is a moral standing that follows from the fundamental moral law. It is not a mysterious metaphysical 'kernel' from which we derive our belief in the moral law and its practical applications.

Regarding (b), Kant does imply that dignity is a status that can be expressed in terms of *intrinsic value* in a sense, though not necessarily in the senses most familiar to us. Persons with dignity are 'ends-in-themselves', and so are not to be treated merely as means or treated with indifference.[9] They are not 'ends to be produced' but exist as beings with a special status and value that Kant contrasts with 'relative value'.[10] As members of a possible 'kingdom of ends', their dignity is contrasted with mere price—'market price' and 'attachment price'.[11] Dignity is also described as an 'inner worth' and an 'unconditional and incomparable worth'.[12] This implies that dignity is a worth not dependent on a person's talents, accomplishments, class, race, gender, sexual orientations, or even moral record.[13] More strikingly, dignity is not merely 'above price' but it is also 'without equivalent'.[14] That is, dignity is not a commensurable value that permits trade-offs. Even if, tragically, we must sometimes make decisions that cannot protect all persons from assaults on their dignity, we cannot justify the sacrifice of any one simply by reasoning that two are worth twice as much as one, and so on. How the special value of dignity can function in practical applications is subject to interpretation, but Kant's own view can be best seen in his system of ethical principles in his late work, *The Metaphysics of Morals*, especially Part II. For now, however, the

---

[8] Kant expresses his understanding of the fundamental moral law in Immanuel Kant, *Groundwork for the Metaphysics of Morals*, ed. Thomas E. Hill, Jr and Arnulf Zweig (Oxford, Oxford University Press, 2002), 221–40 (4:420–40). Bracketed numbers refer to the volume and pages in the standard Prussian Academy edition. The formulation is the imperative to treat humanity in each person as an end in itself. This is at least an important aspect of human dignity, but the more specific duties, rights, and attitudes that recognition of human dignity requires must be derived from all aspects of the basic moral law together with general facts about the human condition.

[9] To treat someone merely as a means is to treat the person as a means but not at the same time as an end in himself. So 'treat not merely as a means' is not a standard independent of 'treat as an end in itself', contrary to what Rosen suggests. See Rosen, *Dignity*, 82–5. In addition, the latter goes beyond the former, forbidding indifference to other persons even if one is not using them as a means at all. See Kant, *Groundwork*, 231 (4:430), and Immanuel Kant, *The Metaphysics of Morals*, trans. Mary Gregor (Cambridge, Cambridge University Press, 1996), 157 (6:395).

[10] Kant, *Groundwork*, 228–30 (4:427–30).

[11] Kant, *Groundwork*, 235 (4:435).

[12] Kant, *Groundwork*, 236 (4:447).

[13] Kant shared many of the cultural biases of his time regarding race, gender, and sexual orientation, but these attitudes, I think, are incompatible with his basic moral theory.

[14] Kant, *Groundwork*, 235 (4:434).

more important question is the interpretation of 'intrinsic value' implied by dignity. It might seem that by attributing both a status and a value associated with dignity Kant conflates two distinct and independent ideas, but I think not. The key to understanding is that for Kant the moral law is prior to value ('the good') and determines what is objectively valuable.[15] That is, objective value claims are implicitly claims about what is or would be willed by persons who are fully governed by morally committed practical reason. In effect, then, to say that persons have the special intrinsic value of dignity is just to say that any fully rational and reasonable person would (and so we should) grant them the special status (rights, responsibilities, and honour) that the moral law (a law of reason) requires. Kant describes this status in abstract and relatively formal terms in his earlier work, and then, taking account of real human conditions, he develops a thicker, more substantive conception in his later work.[16]

Turning to (c), what Rosen calls 'measured and self-possessed behaviour' is the idea that one should act in a *dignified* way as befitting one's class and social status. Undeniably this idea was historically important and important to Kant in his personal life. His moral theory, however, transforms the idea, making it appropriate to his conception of all human persons as fundamentally moral equals with basic capacity and rational predisposition to relate to others with due respect for standards that can in principle be justified to all. Thus the relevant class and status is that of human beings with dignity, and the 'dignified' behaviour that this calls for is whatever in context expresses one's valuing of this status. Although Kant does not make the point explicitly, the relevant standards for dignified behaviour must include the duties to oneself not to debase humanity in one's person—by servility, lying, gluttony, drunkenness, or any sexual practices incompatible with respect for oneself and others.[17] There is no obvious conflict between this idea of being dignified and other aspects of dignity described above, and arguably the status and value aspects of dignity support the prescription to behave in a dignified way in Kant's limited sense.

Finally, regarding (d), Kant held that we acknowledge the dignity of humanity by *treating every person with respect*.[18] Respect for the moral law demands basic respect for every human person, no matter how disliked, useless,

---

[15] Immanuel Kant, *Critique of Practical Reason*, trans. Mary Gregor (Cambridge, Cambridge University Press, 1997), 50–8 (5:57–67).
[16] The earlier work intended here is Kant's *Groundwork* (1795) and the later work his *The Metaphysics of Morals* (1797–8). See also Hill, *Respect, Pluralism, and Justice*, chapter 5, 119–51.
[17] Kant, *The Metaphysics of Morals*, 176–88 (6:421–37). Kant condemns 'unnatural' sexual practices as incompatible with proper respect for one's humanity, but this may have been partly owing to the assumption (common in his day) that these led to permanent damage to one's rational capacities.
[18] Kant, *The Metaphysics of Morals*, 462–213 (6:462–8).

or misbehaving. The respect in question is not the special honour and deference we give to those in high office or those who are especially talented or accomplished. It is rather an expressed recognition, appropriate to the context, that the person has the fundamentally equal status and value of dignity as determined by the moral law, that is, (a) and (b) above. The duty to respect others is not (as some suggest) the general requirement to treat persons with dignity as ends-in-themselves, but rather a derivative and more specific duty comparable to the duties of love, gratitude, and friendship.[19] Kant also thought that self-respect is important. A kind of respect for oneself as a person with rights and responsibilities is virtually inevitable, Kant thought, but we should also try to conduct ourselves in a manner worthy of this status, that is, in self-respecting ways. Again, this is an aspect of human dignity that fits well with the other aspects that we have considered.

Problems of application: indeterminacy and absolutism

A theory with a vague, 'squishy', indeterminate idea at its core not only is likely to be exploited but also, more importantly, it frustrates the efforts of well-meaning followers to use it in practical contexts.[20] This apparently is the current fate of dignity in legal systems of Europe, Israel, and elsewhere. Kant discusses dignity so infrequently and abstractly that critics understandably find it unready for use in guiding decisions in particular troublesome cases.[21] To assess the charge that Kant's conception of dignity is too indeterminate to provide any guidance would require a fuller examination of Kant's texts than is possible here, but readers can find detailed attempts to explain the practical implications of Kant's conception in recent commentaries.[22] The place to look for Kant's own (rather belated) efforts to apply his theory is primarily *The Metaphysics of Morals*. Here again and again he appeals to the dignity of humanity to underwrite self-regarding duties and duties to others. His arguments may fail to convince, but they reveal more determinacy in his idea of dignity than one might initially suspect. In general, we should recognize that Kant

---

[19] Kant, *The Metaphysics of Morals*, 198–208 (6:448–61) and 215–17 (6:459–73).
[20] The charge that dignity is a 'squishy' notion comes from Steven Pinker, 'The stupidity of dignity', *The New Republic*, 28 May 2008. Quoted by Rosen, *Dignity*, 120.
[21] Oliver Sensen reports that Kant used the expression 'dignity' 111 times in his entire published work and only 8 times in conjunction with 'worth' or 'value'. Sensen, *Kant on Human Dignity*, 144.
[22] See the references in footnote 4. My own attempts to draw out the practical implications of Kantian dignity in *Dignity and Practical Reason*, chapter 2, 38–66, *Respect, Pluralism, and Justice*, chs 3–5, 59–152, and *Virtue, Rules, and Justice*, chapters 8 and 13, 186–202 and 297–319. Allen Wood's account is in his *Kantian Ethics*, especially chapters 5, 85–105, and chapter 9, 158–181.

was a systematic moral theorist whose references to dignity were not free-floating but embedded in a theoretical network of ideas, including conceptions of a person, the will, autonomy, and practical reason that do not completely match ours. As John Rawls explained and illustrated in his own work, abstract ideals (like human freedom, equality, and dignity) require a more concrete interpretation to be developed in a systematic theory that can generate practical applications. As Rosen in effect acknowledges in his own discussion of Kant, one-shot intuitive objections are unlikely to bring down a major moral theory. What is needed is to understand, offer our best reconstructions, and compare the theory as a whole to available alternatives.

Among the most persistent objections to Kant's idea of human dignity is that it generates apparent conflicts of duty. Dignity is presented as an absolute status or value, never to be violated and always to be respected. In the real world, however, life can present us with tragic choices in which what seems demanded in order to respect the dignity of one person would violate the dignity of others. Especially in Kantian ethics, 'ought' implies 'can', and so if we cannot respect the dignity of all then this cannot be our duty.[23] Examples abound. It seemed impossible during the Second World War to rescue oppressed people from the indignities inflicted on Jews and others without bombing raids that burned to death innocent children. Mothers submitted to debasing prostitution to keep their families from starving. A secret agent in a just cause might have joined the enemy in degrading mockery and racial slurs to avoid detection long enough to gather and pass on information vital to protecting others. Dwarf-tossing intuitively seems demeaning, but many would say that to override the dwarf's voluntary consent is disrespectful. Resolution here is not easy, maybe even impossible, but a distinction may help to preserve Kant's central thesis even if it does not square with some of his own particular moral beliefs. As I explain elsewhere,[24] what should be regarded absolutely inviolable is the general principle that human dignity is always to be respected, but specific derivative principles that would honour human dignity under ideal circumstances cannot always be satisfied in particular tragic cases. In this situation, we must not resort to unconstrained consequentialist decision-making but, instead, try to judge what best respects the more specific values (and their priorities) that the dignity principle aspires to protect—the values, for example, of life, freedom, non-degradation, mutual respect, and

---

[23] For discussion of Kantian responses to such conflicts, see 'Moral dilemmas, gaps, and residues', in Thomas E. Hill, Jr, *Human Welfare and Moral Worth: Kantian Perspectives* (Oxford, Oxford University Press, 2002), chapter 2, 362–402.

[24] Hill, *Dignity and Practical Reason*, chapter 10, 196–226, and *Virtue, Rules and Justice,* chapter 8, 185–202.

happiness (insofar as it can be achieved by permissible means). Principles for ideal conditions may be subject to exceptions in real world conditions so long as the exceptions are justifiable from the same moral standpoint that incorporates the dignity principle. Hard cases cannot be avoided, but moral theories should aim to describe the moral perspective that a conscientious person should take in trying to resolve them. Also, a reasonable reconstruction of Kant's basic moral standards does not necessarily justify his belief in absolute prohibitions regarding particular issues, such as lying, revolution, and 'unnatural' sexual practices. Kant, like great theorists of all kinds, was not necessarily the best judge of how his theory applies to particular cases. The challenge for those inspired by his thought is to reconstruct how the best insights, reflectively modified, can be unified and defended.

Metaphysics or morals?

The most persistent obstacle to acceptance of Kant's conception of morality is the widely shared impression that it is hopelessly mired in an obscure and untenable metaphysics. Rosen focuses this general concern on Kant's idea of the dignity of humanity, especially insofar as this dignity—seen as an inner 'transcendental kernel'—is taken to be the metaphysical basis of Kant's practical affirmation of dignity as fundamental feature of a rational morality. The concern is understandable, but in my opinion misguided. Granted, when Kant tried boldly and honestly to reconcile his deepest moral and religious convictions with his earlier radical explanation of the foundations of empirical knowledge, he was led to write of 'things-in-themselves', noumena, 'an intelligible world' beyond empirical understanding. What Kant meant remains controversial, but few philosophers today, I think, see compelling reasons to accept the most radical conclusions to which Kant apparently felt driven. Kant's solution, however, has been interpreted in many ways, the most plausible of which emphasize that Kant used metaphysical 'Ideas' without intending to assert more than can be affirmed from the practical standpoint. More importantly, Kant did not base his argument for believing in human dignity on premises about noumena, the intelligible world, and so on, but rather used these Ideas to reconcile his prior moral conclusions (about dignity, duty, moral worth, etc.) with the earlier argument that all empirical phenomena must be regarded as governed by natural causes.[25]

---

[25] Any moral theorist except the most extreme naturalistic reductionist has the challenge to reconcile ordinary ideas of intending, doing things for reasons, having moral obligations, and so on, with com-

To explain, I will first distinguish Kant's normative claims about dignity as a moral status and value from some other claims with which it might be confused. Then I will sketch briefly Kant's strategies to defend his claims. These strategies include 'analytical' arguments based on common moral convictions that he takes to be undeniable.[26] He also offered a 'synthetical' kind of argument (from free will to morality), but again that argument apparently turned out to rest on our moral convictions. Finally, I will explain why I think Kant's arguments have been mistakenly thought to derive ethics, including dignity, from metaphysics.

Kant's assertion that humanity (so far as it is capable of morality) has dignity is a strong moral claim. The same is true for the similar contentions that humanity in each person is an end in itself,[27] and that persons (as ends in themselves in a kingdom of ends) have dignity, 'an unconditional and incomparable worth'.[28] Moral claims, on Kant's analysis, are ultimately about what is unconditionally (categorically) rational to do or, as we might say, what we have overriding reason to do even though we might fail to do what reason requires.[29] As often noted, Kant's conception of full rationality in the practical sphere includes what we might call being 'reasonable', that is, not merely intelligent pursuit of one's own ends but also constraining oneself by principles that take into account the interests and wills of others. To say that we morally 'ought' or 'must' refrain from acting in certain ways entails that there are compelling reasons to refrain, whether or not it serves our contingent ends or promotes our happiness. Particular judgments of this kind presuppose that there are fundamental rational principles that stand behind the particular moral 'ought' judgments, explaining why the particular moral judgments are warranted in the circumstances. Kant's claims that humanity has dignity, persons are ends in themselves, and so on, are part of his attempt to express those fundamental rational principles that particular moral judgments presuppose.

These various expressions of the moral and unconditionally rational requirement to treat humanity with dignity must be distinguished from other claims with which they might be confused. For example, they are not reducible to empirical hypotheses that human beings with a certain level of testable intelligence and competence at practical tasks do in fact behave, speak, and

---

plete deterministic causation in nature, if that is taken for granted. Admitting, with Kant, that there is much we do, and perhaps cannot, know and explain seems at least a reasonable aspect of a thoughtful response.

[26] Kant, *Groundwork*, 194 (4:392).
[27] Kant, *Groundwork*, 229 (4:428–9).
[28] Kant, *Groundwork*, 234–6 (4:433–6).
[29] Kant, *Groundwork*, 214–22 (4:412–21).

feel in certain predictable ways. Kant (like Aquinas and many others) did believe that competent adult human beings implicitly recognize the rationality of basic moral principles and are inevitably motivated by them to some degree, even if they choose not to conform. In effect, Kant had a model of what it is to be a rational agent with certain vulnerabilities that are common to human beings. Anyone who is a rational agent of that kind, he argues a priori, is subject to the moral law (including its requirement to respect human dignity), but his belief that the model applies to virtually all flesh and blood human beings—that they are rational agents in his sense—is a quasi-empirical belief. The model cannot make sense of the behaviour of trees, cockroaches, lions, and maybe some human sociopaths, but Kant thought it fitted real human beings as he knew them. The belief that real human beings in fact acknowledge the moral law is, of course, not the same as the moral law itself—a normative or prescriptive principle implying that it is rationally required to act in certain ways (if one can). Finally, the normative principle prescribing respect for human dignity does not itself assert anything that belongs to metaphysics, as this is traditionally conceived. Metaphysics so conceived is about the world *as it is*, and it is the product of theoretical reason. Ethics is about our aims and choices *as they ought to be*, and it is the product of practical reason. Metaphysics, using reason theoretically beyond what we can experience, is severely limited, and can only establish possibilities of things we cannot know or comprehend but can only 'think' speculatively.[30] In sum, Kant's affirmation of human dignity is a normative claim about what is rationally imperative for those who have moral capacities. It is not an empirical claim, it is not an expression of Kant's belief that virtually all real human beings actually acknowledge the moral law, and it is not an assertion of metaphysics based on theoretical reason.

Kant's main strategy to identify and defend his supreme moral principle—the Categorical Imperative in all its forms—was to argue analytically that 'common rational knowledge of morality' presupposes the supreme principle as the basis for its particular judgments. Famously, in *Groundwork* I Kant starts from the proposition that only a good will is good without qualification. He then argues through a series of steps that the principle of a good will is to act only on maxims that one can will as universal laws. In *Groundwork* II he starts from the intuitively understood distinction between the imperatives of prudence and skill and the imperatives of morality. Analytical-style argument is supposed to reveal that particular moral imperatives, such as the

---

[30] This is a major conclusion of *Kant's Critique of Pure Reason* (1781 and 1787), trans. Norman Kemp Smith (New York, St Martin's Press, 1965).

duty not to make false promises, presuppose as their basis the same basic principle—that one ought to act only on maxims that one can will as universal laws. In addition, because the particular duty is understood as not conditional on whether the false promise would serve one's personal ends, the supreme principle, Kant argued, must express an unconditional (categorical) rational requirement. Then, again analytically relying on our common understanding of morality, Kant argues for the different formulations of the Categorical Imperative, which include the prescriptions associated with the idea of human dignity. It is unnecessary to examine the details of the arguments in order to see the main point: Kant does not argue from metaphysics to ethics but rather from common moral beliefs to the more comprehensive basic principle on which they are based.

In *Groundwork* III Kant proposes to supplement the analytical arguments by arguing synthetically to address the sceptical thought that morality might be merely an illusion,[31] that is, that all the moral requirements we take to be rational may not be so, at least not for us. He argues from definitions that supreme moral principle must be rationally valid even for imperfectly rational beings like us *if we have free will*. Then he argues that we cannot help but act 'under the Idea of freedom' and so we can reasonably take ourselves to be subject to the supreme principle. Surprisingly, he acknowledges that he seems to be arguing in a circle—from morality to free will and from free will to morality.[32] Why? The best explanation, I think, is that he suspected that we cannot help but act under the Idea of freedom because that is a presupposition of our prior understanding ourselves as moral agents. If so, again the argument would not be from metaphysics to ethics but from moral belief to a practical use of a metaphysical Idea—a free will that theoretical reason cannot confirm, refute, or even comprehend. Kant does go on to claim that he finds a way out of the circle in the distinction between 'the intelligible world' and 'the sensible world',[33] but the argument, I think, in the end, simply relies on our broader understanding of ourselves (not reducible to empirical propositions) as capable of active thinking—a practical presupposition rather than a metaphysical foundation. In his *Critique of Practical Reason*, Kant abandoned the *Groundwork* III argument that prompted the suspicion of circular reasoning. Instead he simply asserts consciousness of the moral law as a 'fact of reason'[34] which we cannot help but acknowledge when we see duty in conflict with self-interest, for example, when refusing a king's order to give false witness

---

[31] Kant, *Groundwork*, 245 (4:444–5).
[32] Kant, *Groundwork*, 248–50 (4:448–50).
[33] Kant, *Groundwork* , 250–2 (4:450–3).
[34] Kant, *Critique of Practical Reason* (5:32).

would endanger one's life. This all too brief sketch of Kant's argument here skips over much detail, but the main point should be evident. Kant bases his case for human dignity on moral grounds, not on metaphysics. He thought he had to use admittedly incomprehensible metaphysical Ideas (e.g., a noumenal free will) to square his moral conclusions with his earlier conclusions about deterministic natural causation in the empirical realm, but arguably we need not follow him there.

Finally, why would one suspect that Kant bases human dignity on metaphysics? I can think of three sorts of reasons, but none that I find compelling. First, the titles of two of his major works on ethics make reference to 'a *metaphysics* of morals', but this is misleading. Kant's *Critique of Pure Reason*, which he never repudiates, is a sustained critique of traditional metaphysics as speculative use of reason beyond possible experience. Later works argue for that the use of metaphysical Ideas is legitimate for practical purposes only—which do not include the traditional metaphysicians' survey of furniture of the universe. A metaphysics *of morals* is *metaphysics* in a special sense: a coherent system of rational moral principles.[35] Second, there are many passages, especially in works in which Kant presents his themes to a general audience,[36] where Kant's metaphorical language, if taken literally, seems to imply the metaphysical existence of strange entities 'inside' us. Rosen's repeated references to this 'inner kernel' aggravates the problem, suggesting that Kant foolishly thought that a surgeon might find it by opening up a patient's chest or, perhaps worse, that it is a lump of something invisible and intangible in there. Kant's points, as Sensen and others argue, are really about how we ought to treat ourselves and others who have rational moral capacities. Third, some scholars apparently accept a metaphysical realist picture of the 'awesome' value of humanity as Kant's bedrock foundation for ethics, taking this to be the key to his arguments for treating humanity as an end in itself.[37] Other scholars disagree, rightly I think, but readers will need to decide for themselves.

---

[35] A metaphysics is a 'pure philosophy', and a metaphysics *of morals* is concerned with 'laws of freedom', that is, 'laws according to which everything ought to happen' though may not. Kant, *Groundwork*, 189–90 (4:487–8). A metaphysics of morals is 'a system of a priori cognition from concepts alone' that is about choices (not nature). *The Metaphysics of Morals*, 10 (6:216–17). *The Metaphysics of Morals* in fact lays out what Kant took to be the first principles of a system of pure (a priori) moral principles as applied to general human conditions.

[36] These include Kant's *Lectures on Ethics,* ed. Peter Heath and J. B. Schneewind, trans. Peter Heath (Cambridge, Cambridge University Press, 1997), to which Rosen often refers, and Kant's Doctrine of Virtue in *The Metaphysics of Morals*.

[37] See Allen Wood, *Kantian Ethics*, Oliver Sensen, *Kant on Human Dignity,* Richard Dean, *The Value of Humanity in Kant's Moral Theory*, and Christine Korsgaard, *Creating the Kingdom of Ends*.

In sum, although undeniably there are problems in Kant's moral philosophy (as any other), not even his so-called 'metaphysics of morals' actually tries to base morals on metaphysics (as traditionally conceived). The central point is that as human beings with the capacity to be moral we must treat ourselves and all others with the respect, restraint, and positive concern that for Kant is encapsulated in the idea of human dignity. This is not something we should believe because we see that we literally possess an 'inner transcendental kernel' of some mystical thing but rather because, on due reflection, we can see that respecting human dignity represents (abstractly) a deeply embedded core presupposition of the common morality that we share, despite our legitimate disagreements regarding many particular issues. If a metaphysics class can help to dispel philosophical worries about the basics of how we should treat each other, then so much the better—but it should not be necessary. Our task is to live up to our implicit commitment to human dignity, which too easily we find excuses to ignore.

18

Citizenship and Dignity

Jeremy Waldron

Theories of dignity have to navigate their way between two apparently quite different conceptions. There is the old idea of dignity in the sense of the Roman *dignitas*—the status attached to a specific role or rank in a system of nobility and hierarchical office. Then there is the egalitarian idea of *human dignity*, understood as invested in every human person from the highest to the lowest, from the moral hero to the most despicable criminal. This human dignity is supposed to attach to everyone no matter what their rank or role, and it remains with them inalienably no matter what they do or what happens to them. Theorists of dignity manage the relation between these conceptions in one of two ways: either they tell a story about the human dignity conception superseding the *dignitas* conception after a long period of uneasy coexistence since the time of the Stoic philosophers; or they tell a story about the *dignitas* conception morphing into the more egalitarian conception, a story that does not involve severing the connection between dignity and rank but involves a sort of transvaluation of *dignitas*, associating a high ranking status—a sort of nobility for everyone—with humanity as such.[1]

Kant on the dignity of a citizen

The philosophy of Immanuel Kant is almost always associated with the second conception—dignity attaching to humanity as such. In the *Groundwork of the Metaphysics of Morals*, Kant says that humanity has dignity insofar as it is capable of morality, and he believes that this capability exists in all humans irrespective of rank or deed.[2] But Kant also uses the first conception of dig-

---

[1] For the first approach, see Teresa Iglesias, 'Bedrock truths and the dignity of the individual', *Logos* 4 (2001), 144. I have followed the second route in 'Dignity and rank', *European Journal of Sociology* 48 (2007), 201–37, and in *Dignity, Rank, and Rights* (Oxford, Oxford University Press, 2012), 30–6.
[2] Immanuel Kant, *Groundwork of the Metaphysics of Morals* in Immanuel Kant, *Practical Philosophy*, ed. Mary Gregor (Cambridge, Cambridge University Press, 1999), 84 (4:435 in the Prussian

nity—role-related *dignitas*. In his later political philosophy, he talks of legislative, executive, and judicial offices as dignities;[3] in a slightly different sense, he speaks of 'the distribution of *dignities*, which are eminent estates without pay, based on honour alone' as one of the rights of 'the supreme commander of a state'.[4] He describes nobility as a dignity which 'makes its possessors members of a higher estate even without any special services on their part',[5] and he seems obsessed with the question of whether dignity in this sense can be both hereditary and legitimate. But his conclusion that hereditary dignity must eventually fade away in a legitimate polity does not affect his willingness to talk about non-hereditary dignity or to associate dignity with hierarchy and with differential roles, privileges, and responsibilities.

So does Kant attempt to reconcile the two conceptions or bring them into relation with one another? He does not explicitly address the question of the relation between them. But one line at least seems to be thrown across whatever chasm separates the two. Having spoken of hierarchical dignities in *The Metaphysics of Morals*, he says this: 'Certainly no human being can be without any dignity, since he at least has the dignity of a citizen.'[6] In context, 'the dignity of a citizen' is presented as one *dignitas* among others, albeit a pervasive one. But it is said to be a *dignitas* to which every human being as such is entitled. The intriguing link that is established in this way between human dignity and *dignitas* seems to me to be worth exploring.

I want to take this exploration beyond the confines of Kant's philosophy. I want to consider its implications for human dignity generally, and for the connections between citizenship and dignity that have been established in the twentieth century as well as in the eighteenth. But first, it is worth noting some peculiarities of Kant's own account.

First, immediately after having introduced this connection between being a human being and having the dignity of citizenship, Kant qualifies the universality of the latter: 'The exception is someone who has lost it by his own crime.'[7] This is not portrayed as derogating from the universality of human dignity, for later in the same work he invokes human dignity to secure a modicum of respect for and to limit the punishments that may be imposed

---

Academy edition of Kant's *Works*).
[3] Immanuel Kant, *The Metaphysics of Morals*, in Kant, *Practical Philosophy*, 459 (6:315).
[4] Kant, *The Metaphysics of Morals*, 470 (6:328).
[5] Kant, *The Metaphysics of Morals*, 470 (6:328).
[6] Kant, *The Metaphysics of Morals*, 471 (6:329).
[7] Kant, *The Metaphysics of Morals*, 471–2 (6:329–30).

upon vicious criminals.[8] So it indicates a possible dissonance between the two concepts.

Second, as is well known, Kant imagines two grades of citizenship—active citizenship and passive citizenship—with the lower grade assigned to those who cannot present themselves in social, economic, and political life as fully independent of others. Only independent citizens—those who are not dependent directly on others for their livelihood—have 'the right to manage the state as active members of it', as voters or as jurors, for example.[9] If human dignity as such is connected to citizenship, it must presumably be connected to passive citizenship, and Kant says as much when he notes that the passive citizens' 'dependence upon the will of others and this inequality is, however, in no way opposed to their freedom and equality as human beings'. They are still entitled to be treated 'in accordance with the laws of natural freedom of equality', and treated indeed as persons who make up the people of the state, for whose sake and for whose moral co-existence civil society is established.[10]

It is important to see how uncomfortable Kant thought we should be about this idea of passive citizenship: 'the concept of a passive citizen seems to contradict the concept of a citizen as such'.[11] In the 'Theory and Practice' essay, Kant suggested that those whom he later called 'passive citizens' shouldn't be called citizens at all but '*cobeneficiaries*'.[12] But it is not just a matter of finding an appropriate label. I think Kant's view is that all humans are to be regarded in as active a light as possible in the commonwealth of which they are subjects, whether they can vote or not. There must always be some possibility of advancing from the passive ranks to the active ranks, similar to the requirements of equal opportunity or offices open to talents that Kant also insists upon.[13] Nobody is to be frozen into passive citizenship by birth or descent.

That anticipates a third distinctive feature of Kant's account of citizenship. Kant is a hypothetical contractarian. For Kant, anyone's citizenship connotes a sense of the appropriateness of treating them and dealing with them as though they were contracting founders of the state. Not that they actually

---

[8] Kant, *The Metaphysics of Morals*, 580 (6:463): 'I cannot deny all respect to even a vicious man as a human being; I cannot withdraw at least the respect that belongs to him in his quality as a human being, even though by his deeds he makes himself unworthy of it. So there can be disgraceful punishments that dishonor humanity itself (such as quartering a man, having him torn by dogs, cutting off his nose and ears).'
[9] Kant, *The Metaphysics of Morals*, 458–9 (6:315).
[10] Kant, *The Metaphysics of Morals*, 458 (6:315).
[11] Kant, *The Metaphysics of Morals*, 458 (6:314).
[12] Immanuel Kant, 'On the common saying: that may be correct in theory, but it is of no use in practice', in his *Practical Philosophy*, 294 (8:294).
[13] Kant, 'On the common saying', 292–3 (8:292).

were, but the Kantian principle is that they must be regarded in this light. 'The idea of an original contract is *only an idea* of reason, which, however, has its undoubted practical reality, namely to bind every legislator to give his laws in such a way that they could have arisen from the united will of a whole people and to regard each subject, insofar as he wants to be a citizen, as if he has joined in voting for such a will.'[14]

And though it is only hypothetical, it generates a test of the actual legitimacy of any measure: 'If a public law is so constituted that a whole people could not possibly give its consent to it … it is unjust.'[15] (Once again, the example he gives of a law discredited by this test is one providing for the establishment of a system of differential hereditary dignities.)

A fourth point: though Kant's authoritarianism is well known, it is not on account of his denigrating the idea of citizenship. Citizens are like framers and lawgivers: they are conceived to have made the state for themselves rather than to be merely the subjects of authoritarian imposition. They must defer to the state and to the law, but still their deference is to something conceived of as made by them: the compulsory character of the deference is a reflection of the fact that, even under ideal circumstances, the making and nourishing of a state by those who are to be its citizens is conceived as a moral necessity not as the exercise of an option. No one ever had the moral option to remain in a state of nature, and no one has the moral option to revert to it at least as long as a well-organized state subsists.

Fifth, the dignity of citizenship is constituted for Kant partly by the fact that being a citizen in a well-ordered state is something of an achievement—albeit a morally necessary one. Helping to form a state (or at least not obstructing its formation), integrating oneself into its life, and submitting to its laws, involves a sort of transformation akin to that envisaged by Rousseau in Book I, chapter 8 of *The Social Contract*.[16] Citizens—even passive citizens—are entitled to look on those who have not transformed themselves in this way as 'lawless savages'.[17] This does not detract from the human dignity of the latter, but it marks a sense in which mere citizenship may be seen as something higher even than the high dignity of human moral capacity as such.

Its elevation, however, is a matter of the realization of a potential; it does not reflect any sort of difference of kind among human beings. All humans have the obligation to enter into civil society arrangements, and by virtue of their moral capacities all humans have the ability to do so. The moral capacity

---

[14] Kant, 'On the common saying', 296–7 (8:297).
[15] Kant, 'On the common saying', 297 (8:297).
[16] Jean-Jacques Rousseau, *The Social Contract* (Harmondsworth, Penguin Books, 1968), 64–5.
[17] Kant, *Metaphysics of Morality*, 482 (6:343–4).

which is basic to humanity and its dignity is often described by Kant as a form of individual rationality. But we should remember that it is also characterized in political or quasi-political terms: one can think of oneself as 'a law-giving member in the kingdom of ends'. And this is my sixth point about the Kantian notion of citizenship. Kant uses this notion not only in his political philosophy but also as an image whose character is crucial for his moral philosophy. One thinks of one's relation to others in moral terms by reference to the idea of something like common citizenship: 'a systematic union of rational beings through common objective laws', made by the very beings who are to be subject to them.[18] Acting morally, one thinks of oneself as fit for this notional status 'which he was already destined to be by his own nature as an end in itself'.[19] '[T]he worthiness of every rational subject to be a law-giving member in the kingdom of ends' is the basis of our dignity and distinguishes each of us from 'all merely natural beings'.[20] Being thought of as a lawgiving member in a kingdom of ends is like being thought of as a sort of active citizen, who participates responsibly in the making of the laws and submits himself to them faithfully along with others. Kant ends his great passage on the kingdom of ends with a reference back to human dignity: 'The dignity of humanity consists just in this capacity to give universal law, though with the condition of being subject to this very lawgiving.'[21]

The relation that this establishes between Kant's moral and political philosophy is extremely interesting. On the one hand it indicates a sort of priority for the latter over the former (which is not the usual order of batting in Kant interpretation): we draw on certain political ideals to make sense of our moral capacities. And the idea of lawgiving and a systematic union under common laws must be worked out first and foremost in political philosophy before being used as an illuminating device in moral philosophy. But it is not just a device. As humans we have capacities that are already civic or citizenly in form even before we make ourselves into citizens in an actual polity. What each of us is essentially—in our moral character, in our pre-political capacities, and in our political environment—is a (potential) citizen. So our human dignity is in large part the dignity of (potential) citizenship. What we become when we make ourselves into and behave as good citizens in an actual polity is a realization of what we always were: persons capable of living with others under laws which each of us has joined in making for ourselves.

---

[18] Kant, *Groundwork*, 83 (4:433).
[19] Kant, *Groundwork*, 85 (4:435).
[20] Kant, *Groundwork*, 87–8 (4:438–9).
[21] Kant, *Groundwork*, 89 (4:440).

Finally, some Kantian points about universality and particularity. Actual political citizenship is membership of this or that particular community, which might seem to distinguish the citizen of one country from the citizens of other countries. Kant even makes a gesture to nativism when he says that 'those who constitute a nation can be looked upon analogously to descendants of the same ancestors'.[22] If we push this very far, we may have to abandon any idea of the dignity of citizenship as such, for what citizenship amounts to in one nation may be different from—and those who possess it may differentiate it sharply from—what citizenship amounts to in another nation. But Kant pulls back from this nationalism in several ways. He insists that the common ancestry conception of national citizenship is a myth. The only truth in it is that the citizens of a state are born of the same mother (the republic) and it is on this basis, not any atavistic basis, that they are to regard themselves as 'of equally high birth'.[23] He believes that the fundamental normative structure of each polity is the same: each state is to be a republic, and the necessity of establishing broadly republican institutions can be inferred from the a priori premises of political philosophy (premises that are also represented in the political imagery used, as I have said, in Kant's moral philosophy).[24] Even if the division of the world into separate states is important,[25] still citizenship—or at least the normative ideal of citizenship—is the same in all polities. Finally, we should not underestimate Kant's aspirations for universal citizenship—citizenship of the world.[26] Independent states need to transform their relations with one another from a state of anarchy to something like an ordering in a loose federation under common laws. This is an imperative not just for sovereigns but in a world of republics for citizens too: citizens of each nation have a responsibility to act politically in ways that make a 'cosmopolitan constitution' possible.[27] To the extent that they discharge this responsibility, they act not just as citizens of their own polity but as citizens of the world. Kant even speculates that it is only in this latter capacity that they bring about a harmony of politics with morals.[28] In this way, the dignity of citizenship can finally present itself as a realization of the dignity of a moral being.

---

[22] Kant, *Metaphysics of Morality*, 482 (6:343).
[23] Kant, *Metaphysics of Morality*, 482 (6:343).
[24] Immanuel Kant, *Toward Perpetual Peace: A Philosophical Project*, in Kant, *Practical Philosophy*, 322–3 (8:349–51).
[25] Kant, *Toward Perpetual Peace*, 336 (8:367–8).
[26] Kant, 'On the common saying', 281 (8:277).
[27] Kant, *Metaphysics of Morals*, 487–8 (6:350–1), and Kant, *TP*, 307 (8:310).
[28] Kant, *Toward Perpetual Peace*, 350 (8:385).

Citizenship and human dignity

I embarked on this long exploration of Kant's view of the dignity of citizenship because I think the subtle connections he establishes between the dignity associated with the political role of citizenship and the dignity of the human person in general resonate beyond the confines of his particular philosophy. They have implications for the way we think about human dignity in the modern world. I do not want to argue that human dignity and the dignity of citizenship are the same, or that the latter approximates the former. Still, when citizenship is taken to be an important status that, in one state or another, should be available to everyone, then what it amounts to may be a good guide to the way in which human dignity can be realized in a world of separate states.

Like Kant, then, I am assuming that citizenship is a certain sort of dignity. It is a status and, as I have argued elsewhere, dignity too is best understood as a status-term.[29] Like other status-concepts—bankruptcy, infancy, felony, royalty, membership in the armed forces—citizenship comprises a bundle of rights, powers, duties, and liabilities, determined in its content and application as a matter of law rather than as a matter of choice, and united by a underlying social concern focused on individuals of certain types or in certain predicaments. The dignity of citizenship just is this status, or this status of citizenship regarded in a positive light. Not every status is a dignity: dignity is usually associated with a status that is valued and particularly respected; we don't talk about the dignity of felony or bankruptcy. But the remarkable thing about citizenship as a dignity—something it shares in common with human dignity—is that it is a status that is cherished as special notwithstanding the fact that it is widely spread among the members of a community.

Of course citizenship is not just one thing; it changes over time.[30] And it differs, both in its implications and prerequisites, from one country to another. Countries differ on the basis on which they assign citizenship. In the USA, citizenship is assigned on the basis of place of birth—anyone born in the USA is entitled to citizenship of the USA—as well as descent from one or both citizen parents. Other countries—Germany until recently—have made it a matter of blood or descent alone. Countries make it easier or harder for those not initially entitled to citizenship to gain it by naturalization. And the implications are different. In the USA citizenship is necessary for the franchise; but in the UK the vote (and also the right of candidacy for a seat in Parliament) is extended

---

[29] See Waldron, *Dignity, Rank, and Rights*, 57–61 and 73.
[30] For a classic account see T. H. Marshall, 'Citizenship and social class', in his collection *Class, Citizenship and Social Development* (New York, Doubleday, 1964).

to residents who are citizens of other countries historically connected with the UK, such as Ireland or countries in the Commonwealth. Some countries (like Israel) impose a duty of military service on their citizens; most others these days do not, although citizens are on notice that they retain the right to do so.

But the differences are perhaps not as important as the similarities. Everywhere citizens have the right to enter and remain in the country of which they are a citizen. Everywhere citizens are entitled, where practicable, to protection by their country's diplomatic and consular staff when they are abroad. In most places citizens have the right to vote and to participate in politics (even if in some countries others have that right as well); both in theory and in practice, citizenship is the backbone of republican government and of democracy where it exists. As I have already indicated, citizens may also have duties to support the state: they may be liable for example to military conscription in time of war, and in some countries even routinely during peacetime. Everywhere they owe a duty of allegiance to the government of the country of which they are a citizen, and may be punished for treason if they aid their country's enemies.

These are the normal or normative incidents of citizenship. Together, as I said, they add up to a status in each polity that is special, equal, and pervasive. Citizenship is a high status: it comprises important rights like the franchise and the right to inhabit a certain country; even those incidents of it that involve duties or liabilities are in some sense valued by those who have them and coveted by those who don't. It is an equal status: by contrast with Kant's conception, citizenship in most countries does not admit of classes; the term 'second-class citizen', whenever it is used, is always a reproach against the society that is supposed to be imposing the distinctions it connotes.

Above all, citizenship is understood to be pervasive. In principle, the expectation is that all or most of those who make a life in a given country will be its citizens. In countries of immigration, it is expected that long-term resident aliens will take out citizenship in due course.[31] That citizenship is a high-status dignity does not mean it is the special right of a few or even of a large privileged class in a society. Instead, citizenship is supposed to indicate the general quality of the relationship between the state and those subject to its power. By and large, those subject to state power are not to be treated as mere subjects, but as active and empowered members of the political community for which the state is responsible. The close connection between the idea of citizenship and the idea of a popular republican or democratic constitution is

---

[31] In the USA, for example, courts have held that long-term resident aliens may not complain about certain discriminations in favour of citizens and those who have applied for citizenship if they fail to do so: see *Ambach v Norwick* 441 U.S. 68 (1979), at 81n and *Nyquist v Mauclet* 432 U.S. 1 (1977), at 10.

supposed to indicate—as a fundamental premise of any good polity—that the government is always accountable to those over whom it rules.

Of course most advanced democracies are countries of immigration, and they include a substantial population of non-citizens (visitors, guest-workers, resident aliens, and those who have entered the country illegally). It may seem that citizenship works as a sort of 'us versus them' concept, marking a contrast between a privileged status and a less-privileged one, and that it is valued by those who have it precisely because of this distinction. Certainly there is a contrastive element: for one, being a citizen of the USA is different from being a citizen of Canada, even if the rights, privileges, and responsibilities of citizenship are similar in both countries; for another, the rights and powers associated with citizenship are worth having in contrast, no doubt, to not having them. But it would be quite wrong to identify the value of the status of citizenship in a given country with any sort of positional advantage within a given community. Citizenship would not lose its value if everyone within the boundaries of a state were a citizen of that state: the right to remain, the right to vote, and so on would still have the same importance.

So much is this so that the term is often used loosely in political philosophy to refer to anyone who lives in a country and is subject to its government, whether a citizen in the strict sense or not. Though this usage has its dangers, it has its advantages too.[32] As I said earlier, citizenship connotes not only the rights, powers, and responsibilities of a privileged class but also the general quality of relationship between the state and those subject to its power. Most constitutional rights and other legal protections enjoyed by those who are, in the technical sense, citizens of a given polity are likely to be enjoyed by non-citizens too. In the USA, free speech, due process rights, equal protection, and anti-discrimination all apply more or less to anyone within the jurisdiction, and the spirit in which they apply is (roughly) the spirit of citizenship. The government is required to treat everyone in the country with respect, and it can be held to account for maltreatment of anyone, citizen or not. It is also required to show concern for the interests, well-being, and opportunities of everyone in its jurisdiction. This equality of concern and respect goes far beyond the dignity of citizenship in the narrow sense.

Does this mean that, in the looser sense, the dignity of the citizen merges with human dignity as such? Not quite. Even when it applies to all humans in a given country, the idea of the dignity of the citizen remains specific and relational: it directs us to something like a membership-relation or a

---

[32] For some concerns about this, see Gerald Neuman, 'Rhetorical slavery, rhetorical citizenship', *Michigan Law Review* 90 (1992), 1276.

constituent-relation between an individual and the government of the country where that individual resides. In principle, the idea of human dignity abstracts from that. It too is a status connoting equality and comprising a number of rights—we call them human rights. Though rights make no sense without correlative duties, and though the bearers of the duties correlative to human rights are usually states in the first instance, talk of human dignity is not already talk of a relation between particular persons and particular states. It makes sense to say that human dignity may represent a claim against all mankind, but it makes little sense to say that about the dignity of the citizen. Perhaps if we make it clear that we are talking—as we saw Kant sometimes talking—about citizenship of the world, then the distinction begins to blur. But, that apart, the dignity of the citizen perhaps represents one possible realization of human dignity. Everyone's having a state that is responsible for her and a particular political community to which she belongs is *a way* of realizing human dignity, maybe the best way; but it doesn't mean that human dignity and the dignity of the citizen are the same thing.

Dignity and the right to a nationality

In 1958, in the case of *Trop v Dulles*, the Supreme Court of the United States held that any provision for the loss of citizenship as a penalty for an offence would violate the Eighth Amendment's prohibition on cruel and unusual punishment. In finding this, the court made the following comment on the cruel and unusual punishment clause: 'The basic concept underlying the Eighth Amendment is nothing less than the dignity of man.'[33] Reference to dignity in Eighth Amendment cases is familiar to us from the death penalty jurisprudence of the 1970s, where the issue of dignity was connected to pain and degradation: '[A] punishment must not be so severe as to be degrading to the dignity of human beings ... The infliction of a severe punishment by the State cannot comport with human dignity when it is nothing more than the pointless infliction of suffering.'[34] It seems to be part of dignity's role to patrol the extremities of punishment; we saw this earlier in Kant's reference to 'disgraceful punishments that dishonour humanity itself'.[35]

But denationalization is not in itself painful or cruel in the ordinary sense. As Chief Justice Warren observed, '[t]here may be involved no physical

---

[33] *Trop v Dulles* 356 U.S. 86 (1958), at 100 (Warren CJ, for the Court).
[34] *Furman v Georgia* 408 U.S. 238 (1972) at 271 and 279 (Brennan J, concurring).
[35] Kant, *Metaphysics of Morality*, 580 (6:463).

mistreatment, no primitive torture'. So how exactly does the decision in *Trop v Dulles* connect with the principle of human dignity that the Supreme Court insisted underpinned the Eighth Amendment? The court's answer is an interesting one, and it helps us address one last important question: what is the relation between the dignity of citizenship and the human dignity that underpins human rights?

The court's connection between dignity and the deprivation of citizenship is oriented in the first instance to the likely hardships of denationalization. Taking a person's citizenship, said Chief Justice Warren, involves 'the total destruction of the individual's status in organized society':

> [I]t destroys for the individual the political existence that was centuries in the development. The punishment strips the citizen of his status in the national and international political community. His very existence is at the sufferance of the country in which he happens to find himself ... It subjects the individual to a fate of ever-increasing fear and distress. He knows not what discriminations may be established against him, what proscriptions may be directed against him, and when and for what cause his existence in his native land may be terminated ... He is stateless, a condition deplored in the international community of democracies. (101–2)

This is the basis on which Chief Justice Warren agreed with the court below that 'the American concept of man's dignity does not comport with making even those we would punish completely "stateless"—fair game for the despoiler at home and the oppressor abroad, if indeed there is any place which will tolerate them at all'.[36]

All this is true and important: respect for human dignity is incompatible with the creation of this sort of vulnerability. But it is hard not to read this passage also in the light of discussions of the significance of statelessness for human rights that were also taking place in the USA in the same period. Hannah Arendt's account was the most prominent. The stateless person, she said, was in a sort of legal limbo, a situation of constantly having to transgress the law, indeed a situation of being necessarily governed directly by police power rather than by the rule of law (which would have assumed that violations were the exception not the rule).[37] One might have thought, she said, that the situation of these people would have been covered at least by human rights; but it turned out that without a nationality, without an attachment to and recognition by the legal system of a state, human rights were worthless:

---

[36] As quoted by Warren CJ, in *Trop v Dulles*, 356 U.S. 86 (1958), at 101n.
[37] Hannah Arendt, *The Origins of Totalitarianism* (New York, Harcourt, Brace, Jovanovich, 1973), 287–8.

> The Rights of Man ... had been defined as 'inalienable' because they were supposed to be independent of all governments; but it turned out that the moment human beings lacked their own government and had to fall back upon their minimum rights, no authority was left to protect them and no institution was willing to guarantee them.[38]

Paradoxically, human rights worked only for those who were citizens of a state:

> [C]ivil rights—that is the varying rights of citizens in different countries—were supposed to embody and spell out in the form of tangible laws the eternal Rights of Man, which by themselves were supposed to be independent of citizenship and nationality. All human beings were citizens of some kind of political community; if the laws of their country did not live up to the demands of the Rights of Man, they were expected to change them, by legislation in democratic countries or through revolutionary action in despotisms.[39]

But if one were not a citizen of a community, there was no legal framework within which one could agitate for one's human rights. Because loss of national rights was identical with loss of human rights, it quickly became apparent that the most important right was the right to have rights, the right to be a member of an organized community where one's claims of right would matter.

No doubt Arendt's pessimism about human rights was exaggerated. But the connection she drew between human rights and the rights of the citizen is important. The great declarations and covenants of human rights associate rights very closely with human dignity, and it might seem that this association eclipses mere rights of citizenship. But it turns out both in practice and in theory that human rights are not normally secure unless they are incorporated in each country into the legal fabric that provides for citizenship.[40] In real terms, then, the dignity of the citizen will be a necessary concomitant of human dignity. And an exploration of the contours of civic dignity will be an indispensable part of our theory of dignity as it applies to human beings as such.

Rights and responsibilities

Aristotle famously maintained that a good citizen is one who knows how to rule and how to be ruled.[41] Citizens need to know both how to occupy politi-

---

[38] Arendt, *The Origins of Totalitarianism*, 268.
[39] Arendt, *The Origins of Totalitarianism*, 293.
[40] See, for example, International Covenant for Civil and Political Rights, Preamble and Article 2.
[41] Aristotle, *Politics* (Harmondsworth, Penguin Books, 1981), 181 (Book III, chapter iv, 1277a25).

cal office, as a juror, for example, or as a member of the legislative assembly (in modern democracies as a voter or as a representative); but they also need to know how to receive and act upon decisions made by others: how to obey laws whose enactment one opposed or how to accept the verdict of a court when it decides in favour of the other party. On this account, the virtues of citizenship include the virtues of submission and restraint.

Now virtue is not the same as dignity, but one of the distinctive things about the introduction of the concept of human dignity into modern legal and political discourse is that it is formally capable of grounding duties and responsibilities as easily as it grounds rights and liberties. I don't just mean that it grounds a duty to respect the dignity of others; though it does; any emancipatory concept like rights will generate correlative duties of that kind. I mean that dignity also generates certain responsibilities upon each person conceived as the bearer of dignity; it is not a wholly emancipatory concept.[42] Kant associated human dignity with certain duties to oneself—not only the sense of duty which lay at the core of the moral capacity that was the ground of dignity, but duties of self-respect and self-maintenance in regard to 'the dignity of humanity within us'.[43] Similar themes are sounded in modern legal discussions of human dignity. Each person is said to bear a certain responsibility to human dignity in her own person, which might call in question certain claims to freedom—the claim to be able to degrade oneself for money, for example, in prostitution or in various forms of demeaning display.[44]

In fact, the dignity of citizenship illustrates three, not just two, ways in which duties and responsibilities may be implicated. As well as (1) the duty to respect others' dignity (the duty that is correlative to the rights-based aspect of their dignity), there is also a distinction between (2) the duty to submit to law and to political defeat, on the one hand, and (3) the responsibility associated with the active exercise of citizenship rights, on the other.

Aristotle's contrast illustrates (2): one must know how to be ruled. This is particularly important in modern democracies, where individuals and parties take it in turns to rule and be ruled depending on the vicissitudes of the electoral cycle. We must reject any association of political defeat with degradation

---

[42] For a discussion of this, see Stephanie Hennette-Vauchez, 'A human *dignitas*? Remnants of the ancient legal concept in contemporary dignity jurisprudence', *International Journal of Constitutional Law* 9 (2011), 32.

[43] Kant, *Metaphysics of Morality*, 558–9 (6:436).

[44] See, for example, the discussion of dignity in the concurrence of Sachs and O'Regan JJ in the South African case of *S. v Jordan and others* (CCT31/01) [2002] ZACC 22, concerning prostitution, at §§77–84. See also the famous dwarf-tossing case from France: *Commune de Morsang-sur-Orge*, CE, Ass., 27 Octobre 1995, Rec. Lebon 372, http://www.conseil-etat.fr/fr/presentation-des-grands-arrets/27-octobre-1995-commune-de-morsang-sur-orge.html.

or humiliation. Submissive postures like obedience to the law and acceptance of political defeat are not incompatible with the dignity of citizenship; they are part of its essence.

But even when one is politically in the ascendant, the element of responsibility is still present. The rights and powers associated with citizenship are things one possesses not for one's own sake but for the common good, and that imposes a certain discipline upon the way in which one exercises them. This is what I meant by (3), the responsibility associated with the active exercise of citizenship rights. Elsewhere, I have argued that many rights are best conceived as responsibility rights—the right to be trusted with and to exercise a certain important responsibility in society or in a political system.[45] The rights of parents, for example, are best seen in this light; so are many of the role-related rights generated for particular offices by the hierarchical notion of *dignitas*, and so, I think, are the political rights associated with the dignity of citizenship. Part of the respect bound up with citizenship is our respect for the capacity of individuals to rise to the responsibility of looking beyond their own interests to policies, laws, and frameworks which respond fairly to the interests of all. Citizenship is a dignity because it credits its bearers with having what it takes to fulfil this role.

Contractarian respect

I have referred several times to the close connection between citizenship and democracy. I guess one can be a citizen in an absolute monarchy, but Aristotle was right to insist that 'our definition of citizen is best applied in a democracy'.[46] Even if one's single vote seems like a drop in the ocean, there is something powerful nevertheless in the thought that nothing but citizens' votes like mine determine the outcomes in this polity.

But the dignity of citizenship goes even deeper than this, and deeper too than respect for the capacity on which its responsible exercise depends. There are layers of respect beneath whatever democratic arrangements might exist for voting and other forms of political participation. The status of citizenship has a dignity that is not exhausted either by suffrage or by the rights and protections accorded in a constitutional democracy. It is the dignity of being one of those for whose sake the legal and political structures exist and by whose agency—along with that of millions of others—those structures are sustained.

---

[45] Jeremy Waldron, 'Dignity, rights, and responsibilities', *Arizona State Law Journal* 43 (2011), 1107.
[46] Aristotle, *Politics*, 170 (Book III, chapter i, 1275b5).

We distinguish between citizens and subjects, and when we do so we mean to emphasize that a citizen is not just one who is at the mercy of an independently existing state and for whose sake certain constraints and requirements are imposed upon that state. The state is to be treated as though it were a concoction of the citizens, something that they have made and that they sustain together for the benefit of them all. And so each of the citizens is to be treated as though she were a founding member of the state, a participant in the social contract by which it was established.

Of course these ideas are mythic. The citizen really *is* not much more than a subject. The state *is* an independently empowered entity that confronts the subject in her abject vulnerability. The subject, far from being a signatory to any social contract, *is* in fact more or less helpless in shaping its structures and laws. And it may seem that the most we can do is to try to mitigate this helplessness by arranging a modicum of protection for the subject and ceding a microscopic quantum of political power to the subject and calling that 'citizenship'. And yet, our commitment to the *dignity* of citizenship connotes a determination not to always see things in the light. Just as in times past we sacralized and dignified kingship, even though we all knew kings were really nothing but human animals like any others, so now we create an aura of dignity for the ordinary subject. She is to be saluted, respected, empowered, and answered to, as though this were her society (among others').

To dignify the status of a ruler, we used to tell stories about the God-given rights of kings; and similarly to dignify the status of citizen we tell ourselves stories about social contract. Of course, in both cases we know we are dealing with a fiction, but the fiction may be the best way of tracing the contours of respect that we think are required.[47] The strategy here is a version of the Kantian hypothetical contractarianism that we traced in the first section: though the original contract is just an idea of reason, its practical reality is to require lawmakers to enact only laws that could have been agreed to in an original contract.[48] But there is this difference: Kant uses this device primarily as a (negative) test or criterion for legitimacy. I am using it also to determine the overall attitude that should be taken towards the subject. Respecting her as a citizen means according her the respect that would be due to one of the framers of the country's legal and constitutional arrangements. Her concerns are to be answered, her questions are not to be brushed aside, her views are to

---

[47] See also John Rawls, *A Theory of Justice* (Oxford, Oxford University Press, 1999), 12, for an acknowledgement of this.
[48] Kant, 'On the common saying', 296–7 (8:297).

be respected along with those of everyone else. Whatever her actual political power amounts to, she has *standing* in these matters.

One way in which the dignity of citizenship, so understood, goes beyond what Kant calls 'a touchstone of any public law's conformity with right' has to do with issues of transparency and non-deception. The principles on which the polity operates are to be public; nothing about the operation of the polity is to depend on citizens generally or any group of citizens being deceived or being under a misapprehension about how it works. Again, the social contract idea gives us a useful image for expressing this: the publicness of legal and constitutional arrangements must be such that everyone has access to the knowledge about their operation that she would have if she had been one of the people who set the arrangements and to whose care its continuing operation was committed.[49]

The image is mythic, and no doubt in the real world knowledge and understanding of legal and constitutional arrangements will be different from person to person. Statesmanship may require difficult calculations barely intelligible to the ordinary citizen, and there may be very specific things that have to be kept secret from time to time. But the general principle, underpinned by elemental respect for the dignity of citizenship, is that everything is to be open for scrutiny and discussion so that the citizenry can form their own view of it, as though the polity and all political decisions being made in it were theirs. If there is a need for secrecy in any matter, then that need should be capable of being explained; if there are differences in citizens' understanding of political issues, then they should be left to take advantage of each other's expertise in open discussion rather than have the matter managed for them. Anything less than this is insulting—not necessarily to the intelligence of ordinary people, but to their dignity and entitlement as citizens.

I say this because one sometimes hears among political elites resonances of what Bernard Williams used to call 'government house utilitarianism':[50] we who know the truth (about climate change, for example) have the responsibility of packaging information and manipulating public opinion to bring about political outcomes that we calculate will yield the best results; it would be irresponsible, the argument goes, to just put the information out there without seeking to control the processes by which the population assimilates it. Such an approach might be efficient and responsible in consequentialist terms, but

---

[49] Compare with Rawls, *A Theory of Justice*, 115, and John Rawls, *Political Liberalism* (New York, Columbia University Press, 2005), 66–71. See also Jeremy Waldron, 'Theoretical foundations of liberalism', in his collection *Liberal Rights* (Cambridge, Cambridge University Press, 1993), 56–8.
[50] Bernard Williams, *Ethics and the Limits of Philosophy* (Cambridge, MA, Harvard University Press, 1985), 120–2.

it is incompatible with by the dignity of the citizenship. It is like the board of a corporation manipulating its shareholders or a university dean manipulating her faculty. The status of those whose polity it is imposes constraints on the way in which information may be restricted or packaged to best effect. Their dignity trumps the value of any consequences that may accrue from bypassing their participation in open and informed discussion.[51]

---

[51] I am grateful to Robert Keohane for some discussion of these matters.

19

Human Dignity, Human Rights, and Simply Trying to Do the Right Thing

Roger Brownsword

Introduction

THOSE WHO DEBATE the nature and requirements of human dignity and human rights, as well as the relationship between the two, seem to agree about very little. However, I take it that each and every disputant would agree that it is important that humans should try to do the right thing. The problem is that, as soon as we each articulate and elaborate the criteria that we believe to be appropriate for determining which actions are right and which wrong, we find that we are no longer in agreement. Still, we should not forget that, at root, we see humans as characteristically having the capacity for moral reflection, for moral judgment, and for action that is guided by moral reasons. In short, we agree that, characteristically, humans have the capacity for doing the right thing; we agree that they should try to do just that; and many will also agree that humans express their dignity precisely by acting on their moral judgments and doing what they judge to be the right thing for the right reason.

In these short reflections arising from the conference discussions, I am adopting a public regulatory perspective, and I am assuming a context of rapid technological development, particularly the development of biotechnologies. As the (US) President's Council on Bioethics has put it:

> we have entered upon a golden age for biology, medicine, and biotechnology. With the completion of (the DNA sequencing phase of) the Human Genome Project and the emergence of stem cell research, we can look forward to major insights into human development, normal and abnormal, as well as novel and more precisely selected treatments for human disease.[1]

However, this is by no means the full extent of the current development of novel technologies. Alongside biotechnology, there have been important de-

---

[1] President's Council on Bioethics, *Beyond Therapy*, 5–6.

velopments in both nanotechnologies and in neurotechnology. Thus, the council continues:

> Advances in neuroscience hold out the promise of powerful new understandings of mental processes and behavior, as well as remedies for devastating mental illnesses. Ingenious nanotechnological devices, implantable into the human body and brain, raise hopes for overcoming blindness and deafness, and, more generally, of enhancing native human capacities of awareness and action ... In myriad ways, the discoveries of biologists and the inventions of biotechnologists are steadily increasing our power ever more precisely to intervene into the workings of our bodies and minds and to alter them by rational design.[2]

When we add enabling developments in information and communication technology into this mix, we should not be surprised that, in the twenty-first century, it is technology that attracts so much of our regulatory attention.

I will start by responding to one of the key questions raised at the conference,[3] namely: why at this particular juncture in human history are we debating human dignity with such intensity? Why human dignity and why now? My answer, as I have already hinted, is that the development of new technologies is a critical driver of these debates. This is followed by some reflections on the way in which debates about the challenges to human dignity that are generated by developments in biotechnology put the ideal of regulatory coherence under stress. Even if there is coherence on the surface of regulation, we soon find the pressure points once we drill down.[4] Finally, I take up another cue from the conference. One way of putting this is to ask what kind of society it would be if human dignity disappeared from our regulatory discourse. What kind of dystopia would this be? In this part of the chapter, I identify two threats to human dignity that are immanent in modern regulatory thinking. One threat is the rise of a risk paradigm that marginalizes (and possibly excludes) moral considerations; and the other is an over-reliance on technological instruments such that the complexion of the regulatory environment denies humans the opportunity to express their dignity.

---

[2] President's Council on Bioethics, *Beyond Therapy*.
[3] A question again posed by Christopher McCrudden in Chapter 1, this volume, 2.
[4] This part of the paper can be regarded as in the nature of an extended footnote to Christopher McCrudden's masterly survey 'Human dignity and judicial interpretation of human rights', *European Journal of International Law* 19 (2008), 655.

Why human dignity, and why now?

Why are we debating human dignity? Why, at this particular time, do we think it is such an urgent issue? If the question is why we, the British, are now turning our minds towards our understanding of human dignity, then we might respond that this is a case of 'better late than never'. A dozen years ago, when the British were debating whether regulators should be authorized to license human embryonic stem cell research, the idea that research of this kind might compromise human dignity—an idea widely expressed elsewhere—had little or no resonance.[5] For the British now to be taking human dignity seriously is simply to catch up with those many others who, for some time, have recognized human dignity as a fundamental value. Indeed, whether we are viewing the regulatory landscape regionally (e.g., looking at the Council of Europe's Convention on Human Rights and Biomedicine) or internationally (e.g., in UNESCO's work and especially in the UNESCO Universal Declaration on Bioethics and Human Rights), human dignity is a prominent feature. Why is this so?

No doubt there are many stories to be told about the resurgent interest in human dignity.[6] However, it seems to me that one of the principal drivers is the latest round of science and technology, particularly bioscience and biotechnologies. Although a commitment to human rights places some conditions on the application of these new technologies, the restrictions usually hinge on obtaining the informed consent of the parties to whom the technologies are applied. For those who want stronger limits, human dignity (specifically, in a conservative, sometimes communitarian, sometimes Catholic, articulation) holds the key.[7] On this view, the fact that an agent consents to a procedure (say, human reproductive cloning) is irrelevant: human dignity is non-negotiable.

Accordingly, one of the principal reasons why we now have such an intense interest in human dignity is because the development of new biotechnologies challenges important values that many take to be central to our essential humanity.[8] To put the point sharply, we appeal to human dignity in order to stop science; or, at any rate, we appeal to human dignity to ensure

---

[5] Roger Brownsword, 'Stem cells, superman, and the report of the select committee', *Modern Law Review* 65 (2002), 568.
[6] See Christopher McCrudden, Chapter 1, this volume, 2.
[7] Roger Brownsword, 'Bioethics today, bioethics tomorrow: stem cell research and the "Dignitarian Alliance"', *University of Notre Dame Journal of Law, Ethics and Public Policy* 17 (2003), 15; and 'Stem cells and cloning: where the regulatory consensus fails', *New England Law Review* 39 (2005), 535.
[8] A well-known example is Francis Fukuyama, *Our Posthuman Future* (London, Profile Books, 2002).

that the regulatory environment sets clear and firm limits to the reach of science and to the use and exploitation of new technologies. If revolutionary developments in biotechnology, neurotechnology, and the like were not being announced, we would not have such anxieties; and human dignity would be less of a focus for our debates.[9] But we do seem to be on the cusp of various technological revolutions; and, like it or not, human dignity becomes central to our regulatory deliberations.[10]

Human dignity, human rights, and regulatory coherence

According to Article 2(d) of the UNESCO Universal Declaration on Bioethics and Human Rights 2005, one of the aims of the Declaration is:

> to recognize the importance of freedom of scientific research and the benefits derived from scientific and technological developments, while stressing the need for such research and developments to occur within the framework of ethical principles set out in this Declaration and to respect human dignity, human rights and fundamental freedoms.

Article 3.1 simply states that 'Human dignity, human rights and fundamental freedoms are to be fully respected.' Similar provisions, to repeat, are commonplace in regional and international instruments of this kind. What, though, does human dignity require us to respect?

In my introductory remarks, I suggested that reflections on human dignity and human rights are rooted in the idea that it is important that humans should try to do the right thing for the right reason—this is the governing aspiration of any moral community. It follows that all members of such a community (whether as regulators or as regulatees) should orient their actions to this ideal, trying to put in place a regulatory environment that reflects their best moral judgments. However, to embed human rights and human dignity in regulatory regimes is the beginning and not the end of the story because, as is all too well known, these concepts can be appealed to from radically opposed sections of the political spectrum. Putting the matter somewhat crudely, while liberals appeal to human dignity in order to extend and protect the sphere of individual choice, conservatives appeal to human dignity in order to set limits

---

[9] Compare Roger Brownsword, 'Brain science: in the regulatory spotlight', *Science in Parliament* 67:2 (2010), 18; and 'Regulating brain imaging: Questions of privacy and informed consent', in Sarah J. L. Edwards, Sarah Richmond, and Geraint Rees (eds), *I Know What You Are Thinking: Brain Imaging and Mental Privacy* (Oxford, Oxford University Press, 2012), 223.

[10] Generally, see Roger Brownsword, *Rights, Regulation and the Technological Revolution* (Oxford, Oxford University Press, 2008).

to what they see as the legitimate sphere of individual choice, or to emphasize the priority of community over individuality.[11]

At Oxford, we did not discuss the UNESCO Declaration. However, in almost every session, the differences between the liberal and the conservative takes on human dignity were played out. Had we debated the Declaration, those rival articulations surely would have been voiced. This is a thoroughly familiar story, but in what follows I want to draw out the way in which these differences can put pressure on the ideal of regulatory coherence. In order to do this, I will comment briefly on two much-debated recent European decisions in each of which human dignity is the key concept. These decisions are *Oliver Brüstle v Greenpeace E.V.*[12] at the European Court of Justice (ECJ) and *SH v Austria*[13] at the European Court of Human Rights.

First, in *Brüstle*, the ECJ (following the Opinion given by Advocate General Yves Bot) held that a patent should not be granted for biotechnological innovation where the research employed materials that were derived from human embryos that were necessarily destroyed. Seemingly, this decision was driven by the conservative view (embedded in Article 6 of Directive 98/44/EC on the Legal Protection of Biotechnological Inventions, and specifically in Article 6(2)(c)) that the use of human embryos as research tools compromises human dignity.[14] For those who do not share this view, the head-on objection is that this misunderstands the application of human dignity (or, at one step removed, that moral judgments of this contested kind simply should not be drawn down to exclude what would otherwise be a patentable invention). However, the objection that I am interested in following through is one that maintains that the *Brüstle* decision lacks regulatory coherence.

Stated formally, regulatory coherence demands that the provisions of a regulatory regime should not be contradictory. Actually, it would have been very easy for *Brüstle* to have set up such a contradiction, because the Enlarged Board of Appeal (EBA) at the European Patent Office had already decided, on materially similar facts, that a patent was excluded.[15] If *Brüstle* had ruled that the patent could stand, Article 6(2)(c) notwithstanding, when the EBA had ruled that the same provision excluded a patent in these circumstances, that

---

[11] See David Feldman, 'Human dignity as a legal value: Part I', *Public Law* (1999), 682, and 'Human dignity as a legal value: Part II', *Public Law* (2000), 61; Deryck Beyleveld and Roger Brownsword, *Human Dignity in Bioethics and Biolaw* (Oxford, Oxford University Press, 2001).
[12] Case C-34/10, [2011] OJ C 362, 10.12.2011.
[13] Application no 57813/00 (1 April 2010). The judgment of the Grand Chamber was given on 3 November 2011.
[14] Article 6(2)(c) provides that 'uses of human embryos for industrial or commercial purposes' shall be excluded from patentability.
[15] Case G 0002/06, 25 November 2008 (the Wisconsin Alumni Research Foundation case).

would have resulted in an obvious case of regulatory incoherence. Given that *Brüstle* did not hand down a decision that flatly contradicted some other part of the European patent regime, in what sense can it be charged with a lack of regulatory coherence?

The argument starts with observing that the research into Parkinson's disease undertaken by Oliver Brüstle was perfectly lawful in Germany; and we need no reminding that German law takes the protection of human embryos more seriously than almost anywhere else in Europe. Assuming that German law and EC law is all part of one regulatory regime, the question posed by the objectors is this: how can it be coherent to permit Brüstle to carry out research that uses materials derived from human embryos and yet to deny a patent on the products of that research for just the reason that human embryonic materials were utilized?

The answer to this question turns on characterizing the denial or exclusion of a patent in the right way. Patent law incentivizes or encourages research that promises to be of public benefit. Like IP law more generally, proprietary rights are granted (or at any rate should be granted) only where this accords with the public interest.[16] It follows that to deny a patent is not to prohibit the underlying research activity; rather, it is to decline to encourage it. So the *Brüstle* decision does not prohibit an activity that is permitted elsewhere in the regulatory regime; it is not contradictory in such a straightforward way. Nevertheless, the objectors will argue that it is incoherent to decline to encourage a research activity that is permitted—indeed, some might contend that, unless the research activity is prohibited, it is incoherent for regulators to do anything other than encourage it.[17] However, that surely is not correct. It seems to me that, *formally* at least, it is coherent to gloss a permission with a lack of encouragement. Contract law, for example, declines to enforce many everyday transactions (gambling being an obvious example) on the ground that they are contrary to morals, even though those transactions are permitted. In doing so, regulators signal that a transaction is permitted but not encouraged. Moreover, I suspect that liberal-minded parents often signal something rather similar to their teenage children. It follows that the *Brüstle* decision does not fail for a lack of regulatory coherence in a formal sense.

That said, the particular reasons relied on in *Brüstle* might fail to satisfy a standard of substantive regulatory coherence. In other words, even if *Brüstle* survives scrutiny at the formal level, it might fail for want of substantive

---

[16] Compare the critique in James Boyle, *The Public Domain* (New Haven, Yale University Press, 2008).
[17] See the range of criticisms of the Wisconsin Alumni Research Foundation case in Aurora Plomer and Paul Torremans (eds), *Embryonic Stem Cell Patents* (Oxford, Oxford University Press, 2009).

regulatory coherence. Developing this line of objection, the argument is that the European jurisprudence of human rights gives no support to the idea that human embryos have rights; and from this we can take it that the same jurisprudence gives no support for declining to encourage research that makes use of human embryos. Hence, *Brüstle* involves a more subtle kind of regulatory incoherence. What should we make of this?

Defenders of *Brüstle* will have to concede that in the key cases at Strasbourg the Court has held that human embryos (and foetuses) do not have rights under the Convention.[18] However, the inference that the European jurisprudence of human rights gives no support for discouraging research that makes use of human embryos is much more questionable. For example, defenders might point to Article 18 of the Convention on Human Rights and Biomedicine as a clear signal that the use of human embryos as research tools is to be discouraged.[19] Be that as it may, the more important point is that the Strasbourg jurisprudence does no more than deny that human embryos hold rights *directly* under the Convention. This leaves open the possibility that contracting states may grant indirect protection to human embryos, just as in many places protection is afforded to non-human animals. Provided that these indirect protections (motivated by the desire to do the right thing) are not incompatible with the rights directly recognized by the Convention, no regulatory incoherence arises.

This leaves one other dimension of incoherence. Suppose that two rather different accounts are offered in defence of the decision in *Brüstle*. One account is quite complex. In the spirit of human rights, it is said, some rights-committed communities might legitimately accord a degree of protection to human embryos (even though they are not direct bearers of human rights); and, respecting this kind of concern for human embryos, the ECJ declined to encourage the use of human embryos as research tools. The other account is much more direct: quite simply, where human embryos are used as research tools, human dignity is compromised and such research activities are not to be encouraged.[20] If the better interpretation of the European jurisprudence is that it is predicated on a liberal articulation of human dignity, then the former account has the better

---

[18] *Evans v United Kingdom* (Application no. 6339/05) Grand Chamber, 10 April 2007; *Vo v France* (Application no. 53924/00) Grand Chamber, 8 July 2004.
[19] Article 18 (1) provides that 'Where the law allows research on [human] embryos in vitro, it shall ensure adequate protection of the embryo'; and Article 18(2) prohibits the 'creation of human embryos for research purposes'.
[20] Similarly, two accounts might be given of the decision of the ECJ First Chamber in Case C-36/02, *Omega Spielhallen- und Automatenaufstellungs-GmbH v Oberbürgermeisterin der Bundesstadt Bonn*, 2004 ECR 1-9609 (14 October 2004).

credentials; for, on this reading, the latter account would involve a deeper kind of regulatory incoherence.[21]

Turning to the second case, *SH v Austria*, the legal issue was whether Austrian law prohibiting the use of third-party donation of gametes for the purposes of assisted conception is compatible with Article 8 of the European Convention on Human Rights (ECHR). It being agreed that Article 8(1) was engaged, the question was whether Austria could justify its impingement on privacy by reference to the considerations in Article 8(2).[22] By a clear majority, the lower Chamber ruled against Austria but, with some hesitation, the majority of the Grand Chamber held that Austria could justify its local law as falling within the margin of appreciation. Critics of the Grand Chamber's decision are likely to say that it over-extends the margin of appreciation, However, there are two ways in which we might launch such a criticism. One way is to say that, while the margin of appreciation quite rightly recognizes that there are some matters (such as the balance between competing rights) on which communities of rights might reasonably disagree, there are limits to reasonable disagreement on such matters—and, in the instant case, Austria unreasonably insisted on its restrictive position. The other way—and this is the way that is of present interest—is to say that there are some matters that are simply not arguable at all in relation to the margin of appreciation. In other words, some considerations are categorically excluded and simply should not figure where a contracting state pleads the margin of appreciation. Here, the objection to the Grand Chamber's view is that it allows Austria to rely on arguments that simply should be excluded.

How does this latter line of objection run? The key point is that Article 8(2) only supports a state's impingement on privacy where its regulatory objectives are legitimate relative to the purposes specified in Article 8(2). In the Austrian case, the restrictive approach was supported by reference to the protection of local 'morals'. Stated bluntly, Austria feared that if couples could make use of third-party sperm and egg donors (or suppliers), this would allow for couples to seek out 'desirable' donors who would contribute to the birth of children with desired profiles. On the conservative wing, such

---

[21] In support of such a liberal rights-driven interpretation, I would rely on arguments derived from Alan Gewirth, *Reason and Morality* (Chicago, University of Chicago Press, 1978).

[22] Article 8(2) provides: 'There shall be no interference by a public authority with the exercise of this right except such as is in accordance with the law and is necessary in a democratic society in the interests of national security, public safety or the economic well-being of the country, for the prevention of disorder or crime, for the protection of health or morals, or for the protection of the rights and freedoms of others.'

commodification of children is one of the clearest cases of compromising human dignity.²³ However, if Austria could plead such conservative dignitarian values within the margin of appreciation, this would mean that an illiberal conception of human dignity was being set up against the liberal conception on which some suppose the ECHR to be founded. Possibly Austria could find another justifying reason that would be more in line with the spirit of human rights; but in the absence of such an account it would seem that the case is open to the objection that it lacks substantive regulatory coherence.

On the face of it, both *Brüstle* and *SH v Austria* represent triumphs for a conservative articulation of human dignity. We cannot complain that judges in these cases are trying to do the right thing. However, where the jurisprudence has embedded a rather different articulation of human dignity, at first blush, the decisions seem to lack regulatory coherence. If there is a human rights-compatible justification for these decisions, as there might well be in *Brüstle*, then the jurisprudence is not fractured. However, if regulators license both articulations of human dignity, liberal and conservative alike, there is a serious regulatory problem.

These remarks invite further questions about the prospects for regulatory coherence in communities that are deeply morally divided.²⁴ The Directive at issue in the *Brüstle* case is a textbook example of a political accommodation between rival articulations of human dignity. While Article 6 registers the acute concerns of conservative dignitarianism, the Directive is otherwise geared to the liberal view that innovative research around the human genome should be treated as 'invention' rather than mere 'discovery' and, in principle, should be treated as patentable. Even the assumption that the ECHR is founded on a liberal understanding of human dignity might be challenged. To the contrary, the modern commitment to human rights might be seen as the agreed outcome of a range of quite different moral views.²⁵ When moral pluralism drives deep into the regulatory environment, even if regulatory instruments avoid obvious prescriptive contradiction, it seems that we must accept that they will have difficulty in keeping faith with the ideal of regulatory coherence all the way down.

---

[23] Compare Timothy Caulfield and Roger Brownsword, 'Human dignity: a guide to policy making in the biotechnology era', *Nature Reviews Genetics* 7 (2006), 72.

[24] See, further, Roger Brownsword, 'Regulating the life sciences, pluralism, and the limits of deliberative democracy', *Singapore Academy of Law Journal* 22 (2010), 801.

[25] Hans Joas, *The Sacredness of the Person: A New Geneaology of Human Rights* (Washington, Georgetown University Press, 2013).

What if we lost human dignity from our regulatory discourse?

Some of the interventions at the conference prompted the question: what if our regulatory discourse did not get to, or was not sufficiently sensitized to, the importance of human dignity? Here, I take it that the question is what our regulatory discourse would look like if it did not get to root moral questions. Although such amoralism writ large might seem an improbable scenario, there are two tendencies in modern regulatory thinking that push in this direction. One tendency is the focus on risk; and the other is the focus on effective interventions facilitated by the use of technological regulatory tools.

The risk paradigm

In its recent report on emerging biotechnologies, the Nuffield Council on Bioethics remarks that 'the most common concern about novel technologies is the difficulty of predicting the likelihood of unintended and undesirable consequences'.[26] Indeed, this is so, for one of the first questions is whether the technology is dangerous. Is there a risk to human health and safety or to the environment? If there is such a risk, the challenge then is to manage the risk through various precautionary measures to the point that we can say that the risk is now 'acceptable'. Immediately, two questions arise: acceptable to whom? and acceptable in what sense?

Where the risks and benefits of a new technology concern just one agent, A, and where A, having calculated both the risks and the benefits, then decides whether it is prudent to use the technology, this is a relatively easy case for regulators. However, if the pattern is different—if the risks fall on A and the benefits accrue to B, or if it is C who makes the decision—there are likely to be public regulatory decisions to be made.[27] Before these decisions are made, best practice demands that the issues should be debated in a way that fully engages the public. So, for example, when Professor Amy Gutmann was appointed to chair the (US) Presidential Commission for the Study of Bioethical Issues (and first tasked to report on the implications of synthetic biology), she declared that it was her intention to champion informed debate in the spirit of deliberative democracy.[28] And, in due course, when the Commission advised that the regulation of synthetic biology should be guided by a strategy

---

[26] Nuffield Council on Bioethics, *Emerging Biotechnologies: Technology, Choice and the Public Good* (London, Nuffield Council on Bioethics, December 2012), para. 3.8.
[27] See Jonathan Wolff, 'Five types of risky situation', *Law, Innovation and Technology* 2 (2010), 151.
[28] See Meredith Wadman, 'Bioethics gets an airing', *Nature*, 7 July 2010, http://www.nature.com/news/2010/070710/full/news.2010.340.html.

of prudent vigilance, it did so on the basis that decisions would be guided by deliberative democratic debate.[29]

Even if debates about acceptable risk are broad enough to encompass questions about the equity of distributing risks and benefits in a particular way,[30] moralists might object that the community has yet to address the fundamental questions. To be sure, in a moral community it matters that technologies are safe; and it matters that risks and benefits are fairly distributed. Nevertheless, the sense of 'acceptability' that really matters is a moral one. As Henk ten Have has rightly remarked, regulators need to engage with the view 'that unbridled scientific progress is not always ethically acceptable';[31] and, for some, the real issue with synthetic biology and other modern biotechnologies is not that they might be dangerous but that they might compromise human dignity.

The cautionary lesson to take from this is that an initial (and possibly exclusive) focus on risk tends to marginalize or even exclude moral considerations. Just because the risk is regulated so that it is 'acceptable' (particularly bearing in mind the negative impact on innovation), it does not follow that we are doing the right thing in developing and applying the technology. It follows that it is critical that regulators take care that, by framing the issues in terms of a calculation of risks and benefits, they do not ignore or downgrade those concerns that lie beyond the risk paradigm (as conventionally conceived).[32]

The complexion of the regulatory environment

For communities that have moral aspirations, for communities that take human dignity seriously, it is important that the regulatory environment recognizes the right values and puts moral requirements, permissions, and prohibitions in the right place. So much is trite. Much less obviously, though, it is also important that the 'complexion' of the regulatory environment is right, in the sense that it allows for humans to express their dignity by freely choosing to do the right thing for the right reason. One of the reasons why we might be nervous about the impact of the surge of new technologies is not so much that

---

[29] Presidential Commission for the Study of Bioethical Issues, *New Directions: The Ethics of Synthetic Biology and Emerging Technologies* (Washington, Presidential Commission for the Study of Bioethical Issues, December 2010).

[30] Maria Lee, 'Beyond safety? The broadening scope of risk regulation', *Current Legal Problems* 62 (2009), 242.

[31] Henk ten Have, 'UNESCO and ethics of science and technology', in UNESCO, *Ethics of Science and Technology: Explorations of the Frontiers of Science and Ethics* (Paris, 2006), 5ff, at 6.

[32] See Roger Brownsword, 'Human dignity and nanotechnologies: two frames, many ethics', *Jahrbuch für Recht und Ethik* 19 (2011), 429.

their application might compromise human dignity in the ways that we have already mentioned but that, as regulatory tools, they might reduce the scope for the expression of human dignity.

It is in the nature of a regulatory environment that there will be various signals that are intended to direct the conduct of regulatees; there will be various means of monitoring conduct to see whether the directions are being followed; and, where deviation is detected, there will be measures for correction. In such environments, regulators signal whether particular acts are permitted (even required) or prohibited, whether they will be viewed positively, negatively, or neutrally, whether they are incentivized or disincentivized, whether they are likely to be praised or criticized, even whether they are possible or impossible, and so on.[33]

One of the key points about the regulatory environment is that we may find regulators employing a range of mechanisms or modalities that are designed to channel the conduct of their regulatees. Some of these modalities may well be of a legal nature (whether in the form of hard or soft law). It is not that regulatory environments never feature legal signals; and, in many instances, it will be the legal signals that have the highest profile. Nevertheless, the regulatory repertoire goes well beyond legal signals—including, for example, social norms, the market, and architecture (or code).[34] The traditional signals, the signals of law and morality, are normative; but, with new technological instruments, some of the regulatory signals might be non-normative. For example, if a car is equipped with sensors that can detect alcohol in the driver, it might be designed to respond normatively (by advising either that it is not safe for the driver to proceed or that, morally, as a matter of respect for others, the driver ought not to proceed) or non-normatively (by simply immobilizing the car).[35] Implicit in these remarks we can detect the following three regulatory registers:

1. the moral register: here regulators signal that some act, x, categorically ought or ought not to be done relative to standards of right action (as in retributive articulations of the criminal law where the emphasis is on the moral nature of the offence); or

---

[33] Roger Brownsword and Han Somsen, 'Law, innovation and technology: before we fast forward—a forum for debate', *Law Innovation and Technology* 1 (2009), 1; and Roger Brownsword and Morag Goodwin, *Law and the Technologies of the Twenty-First Century* (Cambridge, Cambridge University Press, 2012).

[34] Seminally, see Lawrence Lessig, *Code and Other Laws of Cyberspace* (New York, Basic Books, 1999).

[35] Compare Mireille Hildebrandt, 'Legal and technological normativity: more (and less) than twin sisters', *TECHNE* 12.3 (2008), 169.

2. the prudential register: here regulators signal that some act, x, ought or ought not to be done relative to the prudential interests of regulatees (as in deterrence-driven articulations of the criminal law, where the emphasis is on the sanction that will be visited on offenders); or
3. the register of practicability or possibility: here regulators signal that it is not reasonably practicable to do some act, x, or even that x simply cannot be done—in which case, regulatees reason, not that x ought not to be done but that x cannot be done (either realistically or literally).

For moralists, regulators who are eager to improve on the effectiveness of their interventions by grasping new technological opportunities need to be watched carefully. In particular, we need to keep an eye on any changes in the registers that regulators employ because these changes can affect the complexion of the regulatory environment in none-too-obvious but critical ways.

First, where there is an increasing reliance on regulatory technologies (for example, CCTV, DNA profiling, RFID tracking and monitoring devices, and so on), there is a real likelihood that the strength and significance of the moral signal will fade.[36] Quite simply, with these technological instruments, the dominant signal to regulatees becomes a prudential one, accentuating that the doing of a particular act is contrary to the interests of regulatees (because, in the event of non-compliance, they will be detected and punished). And with this, as Beatrice von Silva-Tarouca Larsen perceptively observes, 'one should not rule out the possibility that an over-reliance on CCTV, with its emphasis on the instrumental appeal to desist from crime in order to avoid paying the cost, might entail a dilution of the moral reasons for desistence'.[37] Although such a dilution of moral reason is a cause for concern, so long as these technologies operate only in support of (rather than in place of) the criminal law, the more serious threat to moral community has yet to manifest itself.

That latter threat arises when regulatory technologies are employed to manage environments in ways that limit the options that are realistically available to regulatees. In such settings, the signal is no longer normative; rather it becomes that an act is either not practicable (such as trying to board an aircraft for an international flight without going through the security scans, or riding the metro without buying a ticket) or simply not possible.[38] In such strongly managed environments, the space for self-interested (prudential) reason is

---

[36] Compare Mark A. Rothstein and Meghan K. Talbott, 'The expanding use of DNA in law enforcement: what role for privacy?', *Journal of Law, Medicine and Ethics* 34 (2006), 153.

[37] Beatrice von Silva-Tarouca Larsen, *Setting the Watch: Privacy and the Ethics of CCTV Surveillance* (Oxford, Hart, 2011).

[38] Bert-Jaap Koops, 'Technology and the crime society: rethinking legal protection', *Law, Innovation and Technology* 1 (2009), 93.

squeezed, and more importantly it is the opportunities for acting on moral reason that are restricted. In such non-normative managed environments, how are aspirant moral humans to express the *dignity* of their actions? Where the regulatory environment is managed so that 'wrongdoing' is designed out, so that the only possible acts are those that conform to the approved regulatory pattern, how can human agents express the most basic of moral virtues by showing that they are doing the right thing for the right reason?

Arguably, there is a deep paradox in the idea that, in a community with moral aspirations, the regulatory environment must leave open the option of humans doing the wrong thing so that they can express their dignity by choosing to do the right thing. It might also seem absurd that regulators should eschew strategies that are effective in reducing risk to human health and safety by designing-in appropriate technological features; and it might seem implausible that regulating technologies will be used to the point that human dignity is crowded out in this way.[39] It is also arguable that, in the final analysis, provided that humans do the right thing it really does not matter whether they do it for the right reason.[40] Each of these points merits debate. However, unless we have the complexion of the regulatory environment on our radar, we might find that the conditions for simply doing the right thing for the right reason have changed without our noticing that this was happening.

Conclusion

At a time when technologies are growing like compound interest, we need to ask whether moral community is threatened by regulators who operate with a risk-management mentality. We also need to ask whether, in increasingly complex technological environments, there is a danger that we lose sight of the simple virtue of doing the right thing. If our current preoccupation with human dignity leads us to ponder such questions, then (*pace* the sceptics) we need to keep it in the regulatory foreground.

---

[39] For further reflections, see Karen Yeung, 'Can we employ design-based regulation while avoiding Brave New World?', *Law, Innovation and Technology* 3 (2011), 1; and Roger Brownsword, 'Lost in translation: legality, regulatory margins, and technological management', *Berkeley Technology Law Journal* 26 (2011), 1321.

[40] See, further, Roger Brownsword, 'Code, control, and choice: why east is east and west is west', *Legal Studies* 25 (2005), 1.

Part V

Judicial Perspectives

20

Human Dignity: The Constitutional Value and the Constitutional Right

Aharon Barak

The constitutional meaning of human dignity

HUMAN DIGNITY HAS A long intellectual history.[1] It has spawned conflicting understandings. What should judges do with this wealth of ideas when they are called upon to interpret the concept of 'human dignity', as part of a constitutional bill of rights? They certainly cannot ignore the rich history of human dignity. But neither can they be satisfied with the conclusion that it is a vague concept. Their judicial role obligates them to furnish content to vague concepts. This is what they have done in the past, giving meaning to vague concepts such as liberty and equality. They must do so again now when they encounter the concept of human dignity as part of their constitution. But how?

To answer this question, it is appropriate to distinguish, with respect to human dignity, between two fundamental constitutional situations. The first is where human dignity serves as a constitutional value but not as a constitutional right. The second is where human dignity serves not only as a constitutional value but also as a constitutional right.

Human dignity as a constitutional value

Human dignity as an express or implied constitutional value

A constitutional value is a value or a principle that is recognized expressly or impliedly by a constitution. Recognition is express if there is a specific provi-

---

[1] See Matthias Mahlmann, *Elemente einer ethischen Grundrechtstheorie* (Baden-Baden, Nomos, 2008), 97; Laurie Ackermann, *Human Dignity: Lodestar for Equality in South Africa* (Cape Town, Juta and Co., 2012), 17.

sion in the constitution regarding that value.[2] For example, the Constitution of Spain (1978)[3] provides that 'human dignity, the inviolable and inherent rights, the free development of the personality ... are the foundation of political order and social peace'. Recognition is implied when express recognition is absent, yet consideration of the constitutional text in its entirety leads to the conclusion that the value is included within the constitution. For example, the American Bill of Rights[4] and the Canadian Charter of Human Rights[5] have been construed to include an implied value of human dignity.

The role of human dignity as a constitutional value

Human dignity as a constitutional value[6] has several functions in the field of human rights.[7] It provides the theoretical foundation for human rights;[8] it assists in the interpretation of human rights at the sub-constitutional level; it is one of the values that every constitutional right is intended to realize; it plays a role in the limitations to constitutional rights and in determining the limits to

---

[2] See Constitution of the Republic of South Africa, article 1(a). 1996.

[3] Spanish Constitution (Constitución Española), section 10, 1978.

[4] See Erin Daly, *Dignity Rights: Courts, Constitutions and the Worth of the Human Person* (Philadelphia, PA, University of Pennsylvania Press, 2013).

[5] See Dierk Ullrich, 'Concurring visions: human dignity in the Canadian Charter of Rights and Freedoms and the Basic Law of the Federal Republic of Germany', *Global Jurist Frontiers* 3:1 (2003), 1–103.

[6] On constitutional values see Andras Sajo and Renata Uitz, *Constitutional Topography: Values and Constitutions* (2010); Stephen Gottlieb, *Public Values in Constitutional Law* (Ann Arbor, University of Michigan Press, 1993); T. R. S. Allan, 'Constitutional justice and the concept of law', in Grant Huscroft (ed.), *Expounding the Constitution: Essays in Constitutional Theory* (Cambridge, Cambridge University Press, 2008), 213; Mark Walters, 'Written constitutions and unwritten constitutionalism', in Grant Huscroft (ed.), *Expounding the Constitution*, 245; Jeffrey Goldsworthy, 'Unwritten constitutional principles', in Grant Huscroft (ed.), *Expounding the Constitution*, 277; Jeffrey Goldsworthy (ed.), *Interpreting Constitutions: A Comparative Study* (2006).

[7] See Henk Botha, 'Human dignity in comparative perspective', *Stellenbosch Law Review* 20 (2009), 171–220, at 177. See also Stuart Woolman, 'Dignity', in Stuart Woolman, Michael Bishop, and Jason Brickhill (eds), *Constitutional Law of South Africa*, 2nd edn (Cape Town, Juta and Co., 2006), 24–36; Christopher McCrudden, 'Human dignity and judicial interpretation of human rights', *European Journal of International Law* 19 (2008), 655–724; Matthias Mahlmann, 'Human dignity and autonomy in modern constitutional order', in Michel Rosenfeld and Andras Sejo (eds), *The Oxford Handbook of Comparative Constitutional Law* (Oxford, Oxford University Press, 2012), 370–96; Ackermann, *Human Dignity*; Daly, *Dignity Rights*.

[8] See Louis Henkin, *Human Dignity and Human Rights* (Jerusalem, Israel Academy of Sciences and Humanities, 1995), 14; Alan Gewirth, 'Human dignity as the basis of rights', in Michael J. Meyer and William A. Parent (eds), *The Constitution of Rights: Human Dignity and American Values* (Ithaca, NY, Cornell University Press, 1992), 10–28; McCrudden, 'Human dignity and judicial interpretation of human rights'.

such limitations; it plays a primary interpretative role in those cases where the constitution does recognize a constitutional right to human dignity.

The meaning of human dignity as a constitutional value

What is human dignity as a constitutional value? The answer provided by most supreme and constitutional courts in modern constitutional democracies is that human dignity means humanity:[9] Human dignity as a constitutional value is the humanity of each person as a human being; it is the freedom of choice of human beings and the autonomy of their will. It is their human identity. It is the freedom of each individual to write the story of his or her life. It is the freedom from humiliation and degradation. It is preventing anyone from turning into a means for the satisfaction of another's will. Human dignity functions within the bounds of society. It represents a holistic approach to the internal and emotional world of human beings, their social identity, and their relationships with others.[10] This, in my opinion, is the modern version of the idea that every man has the status and rank of a king.[11]

---

[9] *Nova Scotia (AG) v Walsh*, 2002, 4 S.C.R. 325, 378 (Can.) ('Dignity is by its very nature a loaded and value-laden concept comprising fundamental assumptions about what it means to be a human being in society. It is an essential aspect of humanity, the absence of which is felt by all members of society') (L'Heureux-Dube J); *Jordan v S.*, 2002 (6) SA 642 (CC), para. 74 (S. Afr.) ('Our Constitution values human dignity which inheres in various aspects of what it means to be a human being') (O'Regan J, Sachs J); *S v Makwanyane*, 1995 (3) SA 391 (CC), para. 308, 326 (S. Afr.); *Prinsloo v Van Der Linde*, 1997 (3) SA 1012 (CC), para. 31 (S. Afr.); *Government of the Republic of South Africa and Others v Grootboom*, 2001 (1) SA 46 (CC), para. 83 (S. Afr.); *National Coalition for Gay and Lesbian Equality v Minister of Home Affairs*, 2000 (2) SA (CC), para. 54 (S. Afr.); *Minister of Home Affairs v Fourie*, 2006 (1) SA 524 (CC), para. 50 (S. Afr.); *NM v Smith*, 2007 (5) SA 250 (CC), paras 131–2 (S. Afr.); HCJ 6427/02 *Movement for Quality Government in Israel v Knesset* 61(1) PD 619, 685 (2006) (Heb.) (Isr.) ('At the foundation of human dignity is the autonomy of the individual will, freedom of choice, and freedom of action of a human being as a free person. Human dignity bases its recognition upon the physical and intellectual integrity of the human being, his or her humanity, and his or her value as a person, without any connection whatsoever to the degree of benefit that he or she provides to others') (Barak P).
[10] See Catherine Dupré, 'Unlocking human dignity. Towards a theory for the 21st century', *European Human Rights Law Review* 2 (2009), 190–205; Ackermann, *Human Dignity*, 23; Mahlmann, 'Human dignity and autonomy in modern constitutional order'. Catherine Dupré, 'Human dignity in Europe: a foundational constitutional principle', *European Public Law* 19 (2013), 319–40.
[11] On human dignity as a status and rank, see Jeremy Waldron, *Dignity, Rank, and Rights*, ed. Meir Dan-Cohen (Oxford, Oxford University Press, 2012). See also James Q. Whitman, '"Human Dignity" in Europe and the United States: the Social Foundations', in George Nolte (ed.), *Europe and US Constitutionalism* (Cambridge, Cambridge University Press, 2005), 108–24; Stéphanie Hennette-Vauchez, 'A human *dignitas*? Remnants of the ancient legal concept in contemporary dignity jurisprudence', *ICON* 9:1 (2011), 32–56.

This concept of human dignity as a constitutional value, though based on dignity's long intellectual history, is characterized by its modern nature. We are concerned with the dignity of a person in today's society.[12] In many respects, there is an 'overlapping consensus'[13] between this understanding of humanity and the religious or the Kantian perspective on humanity.[14]

The understanding of human dignity as the humanity of the human being within the framework of society is not based on one or another political or moral theory, although it draws upon several. It is not focused only on the value of human dignity as the underlying purpose of civil and political constitutional rights. It is equally applicable as the underlying purpose of economic, social, and cultural constitutional rights. It gives the legislature discretion, yet it also recognizes the limitations imposed on the legislature (in the framework of proportionality).

In their judgments, judges will take into account the external and the internal contexts characterizing the specific legal system.[15] The external context consists of the historical and social background that led to the recognition of human dignity as a constitutional value. The internal context reflects the constitutional architecture. It comprises the structure of the constitution and the bill of rights, generally, and the normative status awarded to the value of human dignity within these constitutional documents, specifically. Differences in these contexts among the various legal systems can lead to differences in the understanding of the value of human dignity and the implications of that understanding. Having considered the external and internal contexts, judges

---

[12] HCJ 5688/92 *Vicselbaum v Minister of Defense*, 47(2) PD 812, 827 (1993) (Heb.) (Isr.): 'Human dignity is a complex principle. In formulating it, the attempt to adopt one or another moral or philosophical world view must be avoided. Human dignity must not be turned into a Kantian concept, nor an expression of one of the conceptions of natural law. The meaning of 'human dignity' should be determined based on the perspectives of the enlightened public in Israel, against the background of the purpose of the Basic Law: Human Dignity and Liberty. This concept rests upon the recognition that human beings are free to develop their body and spirit according to their will, within those social networks to which they are linked and upon which they are dependent. 'Human dignity' encompasses a broad range of aspects characterizing human beings' (Barak P).

[13] See John Rawls, *Political Liberalism* (New York, Columbia University Press, 1993), 144.

[14] See *Movement for Quality Government in Israel v Knesset*, p. 682: 'What is the scope of human dignity as a human right? Answering this question is no simple task. It derives both from the complexity of the concept of "human dignity" and from its position within Basic Law: Human Dignity and Liberty. The scope of human dignity shall be determined according to purposive interpretation. That interpretation will take into account, among other things, the structure of the Basic Law, its history, the precedents that have interpreted it in the past, its relations with other Basic Laws and comparative law. That interpretation will benefit from the religious roots of the concept of human dignity which are traced to Judaism ... it will be affected from its philosophical roots, namely from the work of Kant. However, it must always be borne in mind that human dignity should be understood on the background of the social reality in Israel and its basic values' (Barak P). See also, Ackermann, *Human Dignity*, 18.

[15] See *Government of the Republic of South Africa and Others v Grootboom*, para. 22 (Jacoob J).

will express their understanding of how the society in which they are ruling views the concept of human dignity. They thereby express its history and its basic and fundamental values. That is what judges do when they express their society's concepts of equality, liberty, freedom of expression, and the other values underlying constitutional rights. They are not expressing their own personal outlooks but rather the outlook of the society in which they operate. Judges will also use information drawn from other constitutional documents, such as the preamble to the constitution or the declaration of independence. They will be assisted by the case law dealing with the concept and other similar concepts. They will examine comparative constitutional law and international law. They will focus on the foundational values and concepts, rather than the passing spirit of the times. They will express the long-term beliefs of a society, not the temporary and fleeting. All of these elements together allow judges to give expression to a society's conceptions about the humanity of the person as a constitutional value.

This approach gives the constitutional value of human dignity a broad reach. Each constitutional right has a special purpose, reflecting its unique nature. Yet alongside these special purposes, constitutional rights also rest upon the general purpose of realizing the value of human dignity. The result is that the purposes of most constitutional rights partly overlap with each other, because what they share in common is the general purpose of realizing human dignity. The majority of this overlap is complementary in nature: the constitutional value of human dignity which is common to most constitutional rights serves to strengthen the unique constitutional value characterizing each specific right. However, to some extent this partial overlap is also contradictory: the general purpose of human dignity in one right may be in conflict with the special purpose of another right. Thus, when two constitutional rights clash, the value of human dignity may be found on both sides of the scale. Sometimes, within a given constitutional right, its special purpose may conflict with the general purpose of human dignity.

How can these cases of conflict be resolved? Must we balance among the conflicting purposes on the constitutional level? This interpretative balancing would have an impact on the scope of the various constitutional rights.[16] In my opinion, this type of balancing approach is inappropriate. Conflicting overlaps are a natural phenomenon in the realm of constitutional values. They do not reflect a mistake in the constitutional text. They reflect the richness of the humanity of the human being with all of its inherent contradictions.

---

[16] On interpretive balancing, see Aharon Barak, *Proportionality: Constitutional Rights and Their Limitations* (Cambridge, Cambridge University Press, 2012), 92.

Therefore, these conflicting partial overlaps should be left untouched, without a solution at the constitutional level. Let a thousand flowers of constitutional values (either complementary or contradictory) bloom at the constitutional level. Yet, simultaneously, a solution should be sought in the second stage of the constitutional analysis,[17] which takes place at the sub-constitutional level, through the law of proportionality.

Human dignity as a constitutional right

Recognition of human dignity as a constitutional right

Human dignity is recognized as a constitutional right in many modern constitutions.[18] In a few cases, even though there is no independent right to human dignity, such has been derived through interpretation from another independent right. This can be described as a constitutional 'daughter-right' to human dignity, derived from a constitutional 'mother right', which is specified in the constitution as an independent right. Such a right to human dignity has been recognised by the Supreme Court of India, deriving from the right to life.[19]

In most countries that recognize a constitutional right to human dignity, the right is not absolute. It is relative, and thus can be limited.[20] The ordinary rules that are applicable to limitations on a constitutional right also apply to limitations on the right to human dignity. In most constitutions, the law of proportionality provides that not every limitation of the right to human dignity is unconstitutional. Only a disproportionate limitation of human dignity is unconstitutional. German constitutional law is different, in that the right to human dignity is absolute, and the law of proportionality is inapplicable to it.

In most cases, the constitutional right to human dignity is not an eternal right. Rather, it is subject to change through a constitutional amendment,

---

[17] On the two-stage analysis, see Barak, *Proportionality*, 19.
[18] See McCrudden, 'Human dignity and judicial interpretation of human rights'.
[19] *Francis Coralie Mullin v Delhi*, AIR 1981 SC 746 ('We think that the right to life includes the right to live with human dignity and all that goes along with it, namely, the bare necessaries of life such as adequate nutrition, clothing and shelter and facilities for reading, writing and expressing one-self in diverse forms, freely moving about and mixing and commingling with fellow human beings. Of course, the magnitude and content of the components of this rights would depend upon the extent of the economic development of the country, but it must, in any view of the matter, include the right to the basic necessities of life and also the right to carry on such functions and activities as constitute the bare minimum expression of the human') (Bhangwati J).
[20] See Barak, *Proportionality*, 27, 32.

pursuant to the accepted procedures for doing so.[21] This is not the case, however, under German constitutional law, in which the constitutional right to human dignity is not subject to constitutional amendment.[22] In a number of constitutions, the right to human dignity is both a negative and positive right.[23] The state's obligations are not satisfied solely by refraining from imposing limitations on the right to human dignity (the negative aspect). The state must also take action to protect human dignity and to facilitate its realization (the positive aspect). The constitutional right to dignity is intended to ensure human beings' political and civil liberties as well as their social and economic freedoms.

The content of the constitutional right to human dignity: the scope of the right to human dignity

The scope of the human right to dignity

The scope of the constitutional right to human dignity will be determined by its underlying purposes. The central purpose is the fulfilment of the constitutional value of human dignity, that is, the humanity of the person as a human being. The scope of the constitutional right to human dignity is the same as the scope of the constitutional value of human dignity. However, the constitutional architecture may prevent this outcome, and may lead to the conclusion that the scope of the constitutional right to human dignity is narrower than the scope of the constitutional value of human dignity. This is the case of German constitutional law. First, we shall discuss the situations in which there is an overlap between the scope of the right and the scope of the value. Then we shall examine the exceptional case of the right to human dignity in German constitutional law.

The standard case: an overlap between the right and the value of human dignity

Ordinarily, the constitutional right to human dignity is relative. In this case, the constitutional value of human dignity serves as the general purpose underlying the right to human dignity. Against this background, the Supreme Court of Israel has held that the right to human dignity does not extend to cor-

---

[21] See, however, Aharon Barak, 'Unconstitutional constitutional amendment', *Israel Law Review* 44:3 (2012), 321–41.
[22] See The German Basic Law, article 79(3).
[23] See The German Basic Law, article 1(1); Constitution of South Africa, article 7(2); Basic Law: Human Dignity and Liberty, 5752–1992, SH No. 1391, 150, article 2, 4, 1992 (Isr.).

porations.[24] It further held, in a long series of opinions,[25] that human dignity extends to all those activities in which human beings must be recognized as free agents, developing their body and mind according to their own free will. Human beings' free will is an expression of their humanity, and of their desire to shape and guide their own lives and realize themselves. It is the right of all human beings to develop their own personality, character, lifestyle, identity, relationships with others, and world view. It is the right to decide with whom to share one's life, start a family, and raise children. It is the right to parenthood. It is the right to decide where to be and where to go. It is the right to enter into a contract, choose a name, grow a beard, have sexual relations, eat whatever one wants, and speak whichever language one chooses. It is the right to think and to want. It is the right to decide what to believe and what not to believe. It is the right to know who your father is, who your mother is, and where you came from. It is the right to raise, nurture, and educate our own children. It is the right to write the story of our own lives.

Free will is closely related to the autonomy of individual will. Its meaning is that human beings—each individual, and not another; each individual, and not the state—control their own fate. Human beings are the masters of their own bodies and the way they are treated. It is also the right to be left alone.

The humanity of human beings mandates the recognition of their worth as individuals, irrespective of the benefit they provide to society. A human being is not merely a means of generating profits for another person. All human beings are equal, and no one controls another's freedom of choice. Each person is a world unto herself, an end unto himself. People should not be held responsible for actions they have undertaken which were not of their own free will,[26] and the responsibility imposed upon them for their actions should not

---

[24] HCJ 4593/05 *Bank Hamizrachi v the Prime Minister* (20 September, 2006), Nevo Database (by subscription) (Heb.).

[25] See, mainly, FApp 355/05 *Anonymous v the Biological Parents* 60(1) PD 124 (2005) (Heb.); HCJ 366/03 *'Commitment to Peace and Social Justice Society' v Minister of Finance* 60(3) 464 (2005) (Heb.); *Movement for Quality Government in Israel v Knesset*; HCJ 7502/03 *Adalah v Minister of Interior*, 61(2) PD 202 (2006) (Heb.); HCJ 2245/06 *Dovrin v Israeli Prison Service* (13 June 2006), Nevo Database (by subscription) (Heb.); HCJ 2911/05 *Alhanati v Minister of Finance* 62(4) PD 406 (2008); HCJ 10203/03 *'Hamifkad Haleumi' v Attorney General* 62(4) PD 715 (2008) (Heb.); HCJ 4293/01 *'New Family' v Minister of Work and Welfare* (24 March 2009) Nevo Database (by subscription) (Heb.); HCJ 2605/05 *Academic Center for Law and Business v Minister of Finance* (19 November 2009) Nevo Database (by subscription) (Heb.); HCJ 466/07 *Gal'on v Attorney General* (11 January 2012) Nevo Database (by subscription) (Heb.); HCJ 6298/07 Rasler v. Knesset (21 February 2012) Nevo Database (by subscription) (Heb.); HCJ 1213/10 *Nir v Speaker of the Knesset* (23 February 2012) Nevo Database (by subscription) (Heb.); HCJ 10662/04 *Hassan v National Insurance Institute of Israel* (28 February 2012) Nevo Database (by subscription) (Heb.).

[26] See Mordechai Kremnitzer and Tatjana Hörnle, 'Human dignity and the principle of culpability', *Israel Law Review* 44:1 (2011), 115–41.

be based on vengeance, nor should a person be used only as a means of deterring others.

The humanity of human beings is their humanity within the society in which they live. It is not humanity on a desolate island. This is humanity which is built on the mutual relationships between the individual and other individuals, and between them and the state. Thus the need arises to guarantee the minimum subsistence level and the conditions of education, health, food, and work, which enable individuals to realize their free will and their autonomy. Thus the need arises to protect a person's reputation, and to ensure that people can participate in society by expressing themselves and influencing its direction. Discrimination against people infringes their identity. The humanity of human beings is realized when each is an equal among equals in the society in which they live. The humiliation and degradation of human beings limits their humanity

The special case of human dignity as a constitutional right in the German constitution

In German constitutional law – as in other constitutions – the value of human dignity means the humanity of the human being. It is the supreme value of the German constitution.[27] It is view human dignity as the spirit and the essence of the entire Constitution;[28] it is the epicenter of the constitutional structure;[29] it is the primary principle governing all parts of the Constitution. This supreme status reflects the idea that Germany has renounced its Nazi past and the grave violations of human dignity which characterized it,[30] and has placed the human dignity, which was desecrated by the Nazis, as its highest priority.

What is the status of the constitutional right to human dignity? It is an absolute right.[31] It is not subject to the rules of proportionality and the balancing which is undertaken in its framework. It is an eternal right. It is not subject to constitutional amendment. Thus, the scope of the constitutional right to

---

[27] See Mahlmann, *Elemente einer ethischen Grundrechtstheorie*, p. 179; Horst Dreier, in Dreier (ed.), *Grundgesetz. Kommentar, Band I, Artikel 1–19*, 2nd edn (Tübingen, Mohr Siebeck, 2004), Article 1, Abs. 1, margin no. 41. Bodo Pieroth and Bernhard Schlink, *Grundrechte, Staatsrecht II* 28th ed. (Heidelberg, C. F. Müller, 2012), margin no. 364.
[28] See BVerfGE 12, 45; BVerfGE 27, 1; BVerfGE 30, 173; BVerfGE 45, 187; BVerfGE 82, 60. See also Donald P. Kommers, *The Constitutional Jurisprudence of the Federal Republic of Germany* (Duke University Press, 2nd edn, 1997), 298.
[29] See BVerfGE 7, 198; BVerfGE 35, 202; BVerfGE 39,1.
[30] See Dreier, in Dreier (ed.), *Grundgesetz. Kommentar*, Article 1, Abs. 1, margin no. 22. Pieroth and Schlink, *Grundrechte, Staatsrecht II*, 28th edn (Heidelberg, C. F. Müller, 2012), margin no. 364.
[31] See The German Basic Law, Article 1(1). See also Mahlmann, *Elemente einer ethischen Grundrechtstheorie*, 228.

human dignity is narrow and limited. As human dignity is an absolute right, any limitation imposed on it is unconstitutional. Therefore, the scope of the right to human dignity cannot extend to all aspects of the humanity of human beings. Thus, under German constitutional law, the right to human dignity applies only subsistence levels for every person in society. The criterion for understanding the right to human dignity is that it is violated whenever a person is considered as mere means to achieving someone else›s goals. The right to human dignity, in German constitutional law, is limited to always considering each person as an end unto itself to those extreme situations in which the taboos relating to human existence are violated. This framework includes the prohibition of torture, the prohibition of humiliation and the ensuring of minimum and not as a means (an object). This is the 'object formula',[32] influenced by Kantian philosophy.

This understanding of human dignity is narrower than the understanding of human dignity as the humanity of the human being. The external interpretive context, encompassing the historical and social background, might have led to the identification of human dignity in German constitutional theory with the humanity of the human being. However, the internal interpretive context, which is concerned with the constitutional architecture, which endows the right to human dignity its absolute and eternal nature, leads instead to the detachment between the scope of the constitutional value of human dignity (humanity of the human being) and the scope of the constitutional right to human dignity (negating the consideration of a person as a mere means). Only those certain aspects of the value of human dignity which are related primarily to the viewpoint that humanity is an end unto itself and not a means, set the scope of the constitutional right to human dignity.

The area covered by the right to human dignity

(1) The area covered and the partial overlap problem

Owing to the broad extension of the constitutional value of human dignity, the constitutional right to human dignity also has a broad extension. This situation raises many questions. I will discuss only three methodological questions: First, is there any area of human behaviour which is exclusively protected by the constitutional right to human dignity? Second, what is the role of the constitutional right to human dignity in areas where there is a partial comple-

---

[32] See Mahlmann, *Elemente einer ethischen Grundrechtstheorie*, 195; Dreier, *Grundgesetz. Kommentar*, Article 1, Abs. 1, margin no. 53. Klein Eckart, 'Human dignity in German law', in David Kretzmer and Eckart Klein (eds), *The Concept of Human Dignity in Human Rights Discourse* (Martinus Nijhoff Publishers, 2002), 145–59, at 150.

mentary overlap between the right to human dignity and other constitutional rights? Third, what is the law when there is a partial conflicting overlap between the constitutional right to human dignity and other constitutional rights?

(2) The area exclusively covered by the right to human dignity

(i) The Architecture of the constitutional Bill of Rights: A comprehensive Bill of Rights (the case of South Africa)

The answer as to whether human dignity has a domain (or 'normative territory') to which it is exclusively applicable lies within the structure of each state's constitutional bill of rights. To the extent that a bill of rights is more comprehensive and richer with respect to the constitutional rights that have human dignity as one of their underlying purposes, the domain which human dignity exclusively applies to as a constitutional right will be diminished. Consider the Bill of Rights in the Constitution of South Africa.[33] It contains most of the (civil and social) constitutional rights recognized in comparative law. As a result, most situations falling within the scope of the right to human dignity also fall within the scope of other constitutional rights. For example, human dignity is one of the important components underlying the right to equality.[34] To the extent that discrimination affects this component, it is prohibited by both the constitutional right to equality and the constitutional right to human dignity. Thus, in the area of discrimination the right to human dignity does not exclusively apply. To what, if anything, then, does the constitutional right to human dignity exclusively apply in South Africa? Is there a 'normative territory' which belongs exclusively to human dignity? The answer is that its exclusive coverage applies only to those areas that are included within the constitutional right to human dignity, but do not fall within the scope of any other constitutional right. For example, the protection of a person's reputation[35] and the right to family life[36] are not recognized in the Constitution of South Africa as independent constitutional rights. These are the exclusive aspects of the constitutional right to human dignity in the South African Constitution.

The exclusive aspects of human dignity in a comprehensive bill of rights, such as South Africa's, may become broader or narrower in the future through

---

[33] See Ackermann, *Human Dignity*; Woolman, 'Dignity'.
[34] See *Ferreira v Levin*, 1996 (1) SA 984 (CC), para. 145; *National Coalition for Gay and Lesbian Equality v Minister of Home Affairs*, para. 125; Ackermann, *Human Dignity*, 183.
[35] See *Khumalo v Holomisa*, 2002 (5) SA 401 (CC), paras 23–7. See also Woolman, 'Dignity', 55–36.
[36] See *Dawood v Minister of Home Affairs*, 2000 (3) SA 936 (CC), para. 36; *Booysen v Minister of Home Affairs and Another*, 2001 (4) SA 485 (CC), para. 10; *Islamic Unity Convention v Independent Broadcasting Authority*, 2002 (4) SA 294 (CC), para. 10.

interpretation. Thus, changes in the understanding of the scope of the right to human dignity may be warranted because of unforeseeable scientific developments. For example, scientific developments in the fields of genetic engineering, cloning, and stem cell research are at the centre of bioethics. Certain aspects of bioethics are likely to fall within the scope of the right to human dignity, particularly if this right is interpreted as extending not only to an individual's dignity but also to the dignity of the human race as a whole.[37]

Theoretically, there may be a situation in which a constitutional charter of human rights is so extensive that it covers any and all behaviour that limits human dignity, even without a specific right to human dignity. This is likely to occur with a bill of rights that includes a 'basket clause', that is, a provision stating that any behaviour that limits the individual's freedom of choice and that is not covered by the other constitutional rights falls within the category of the basket right. In such a situation, in theory, the right to human dignity does not have any unique 'territory' of its own, because any behaviour limiting human dignity which is not included in any of the special rights falls within the bounds of the basket right.

This seems to be the case with the bill of rights in the Constitution of Germany, which recognizes the right to the development of one's personality.[38] This right has been interpreted as a basket right (*Auffanggrundrecht*). Any state action limiting an individual's freedom of choice not covered by one of the specific constitutional rights recognized in the German Constitution falls within the bounds of the right to the development of one's personality. This, then, appears to leave a narrow field of operation unique to the right to human dignity in the German Constitution. Essentially, that the right to human dignity in the German Constitution is perceived as protecting against the limitation of one of the other constitutional rights in a way that infringes the right to human dignity. Human dignity is thereby joined to one of the other rights recognized in the Constitution, and operates as a marker for the unconstitutional limitation of such a right. Such limitation is not subject to proportionality, as it reflects the absolute nature of the constitutional right to human

---

[37] On human dignity and bioethics see Deryck Beyleveld and Roger Brownsword, *Human Dignity in Bioethics and Biolaw* (Oxford, Oxford University Press, 2001); Leon Kass, *Life, Liberty and the Defense of Dignity: The Challenge of Bioethics* (San Francisco, CA, Encounter Books, 2002); Roger Brownsword, *Rights, Regulation and the Technological Revolution* (Oxford, Oxford University Press, 2008); President's Council on Bioethics, *Human Dignity and Bioethics* (Washington DC, President's Council of Bioethics, March 2008); Charles Foster, *Human Dignity in Bioethics and Law* (Oxford and Portland, OR, Hart, 2011). On human dignity and stem cell research see ADI 3510 (2008) cited in Daly, *Dignity Rights*, 119.

[38] See The German Basic Law, article 2(1). For the interpretation of this article see Mahlmann, *Elemente einer ethischen Grundrechtstheorie*, 377.

dignity in German constitutional law. This is the case when the restriction of a constitutional right turns the person who is harmed into merely a means of realizing the public interest (the 'object formula'). In other constitutions, it may be the right to liberty or the right to life[39] which fulfils this role of the basket right. However, even then, the existence of a separate constitutional right to human dignity is nevertheless important, for two reasons. First, the future is unknown. Developments may occur which will not fall within the bounds of the basket right, but which may find their place within the scope of the right to human dignity. Second, even if the constitutional right to human dignity does not have unique scope, the fact that a state action limits not only a specific constitutional right but also the right to human dignity carries legal significance. The existence of the constitutional right to human dignity gives special weight to human dignity, precisely because it is an independent constitutional right and not just a constitutional value.

(ii) The architecture of the constitutional Bill of Rights: a partial constitutional Bill of Rights (The Case of Israel)

In comparison to the abundance of constitutional rights in some constitutions, others contain only a partial bill of rights. This usually occurs for historical reasons. Consider a situation in which the rights that are recognized in a partial bill of rights also include the constitutional right to human dignity. Let us also assume that the right is not an absolute right, in other words, that it is subject to proportional limitations. In such a case, the 'normative territory' of the constitutional right to human dignity is wide in scope.

This is the normative reality in Israel. The constitutional bill of rights enshrined in the Basic Law: Human Dignity and Liberty, and in the Basic Law: Freedom of Occupation is limited. The reasons for this are historical and the process of constitution-making has yet to be completed. The bill of rights contains only the following express rights: the right to life, the right to the body, the right to human dignity, the right to property, the right to personal liberty, the right to freedom of movement into and out of Israel, the right to privacy, and the right to freedom of occupation. Many of the rights recognized in comparative law have not been recognized as independent constitutional rights. The Supreme Court has interpreted their absence from the bill of rights as having been intended to signal non-recognition of them as independent constitutional rights. However, it has not interpreted this as entirely negating their existence. It has recognized certain of their aspects within the framework

---

[39] See Constitution of India, article 21, 1950. See *also Francis Coralie Mullin v Delhi*; *Olga Tellis v Bombay Municipal Corporation*, AIR 1986 SC 180.

of the right to human dignity.[40] Against this backdrop, the Supreme Court has ruled that human dignity is a 'framework-right' or a 'mother-right'. In one of its cases, the Supreme Court discussed the characteristics of human dignity as such a right:[41]

> A feature of this type of right is that its express language does not specify the particular situations to which it applies. Its reach is open-ended ... The situations it covers may be deduced by interpreting the open-textured language of the Basic-Law, in light of its purpose. For convenience, these situations can be grouped into categories, such as the right to a humane existence with dignity ... the right to physical and mental integrity ... the right of an adult to adopt ... and so forth, as 'daughter-rights' derived from the mother-right ... Of course, determining the scope of the daughter-rights raises difficult questions of interpretation. So long as the Knesset has not distinguished these rights from the right to human dignity, as independent rights, there is no alternative to the interpretive process, centered on human dignity, which aims to determine the scope of this right, while trying to categorise the types of situations it covers. Of course, this categorisation can never encompass the full scope of the right to human dignity, nor is it intended to do so. It is intended as an aid in understanding the framework provision of human dignity.

According to this view, various daughter-rights are derived from human dignity (as a mother-right), and their joinder expresses the full scope of the mother-right. Indeed, in its extensive and comprehensive case law, the Supreme Court has derived a considerable number of daughter-rights from the mother-right of human dignity, including the right to protect one's personality; the right to protection of one's personal and social identity; the right to protection from humiliation and degradation; the right to family life and parenthood; the right to education; the right to social security; the right to food; the right to housing; the right to water; the right to health; the right to equality; the right to freedom of expression; the right to freedom of conscience and religion; the right to freedom of movement within Israel; the right to reputation; and the right to minimum subsistence in dignity. All of these daughter-rights—and this is not a closed list—reflect various aspects of the humanity of the human being. These rights have been recognized as both negative and positive rights. They cover both civil and social aspects, and they inherently include both the core of the right and its penumbra. Differences between the right's core and its penumbra are relevant in the second stage of the constitutional analysis, that is, in assessing the proportionality of the limitation. All of the daughter-rights have been recognized as an integral part of the right to human dignity. These

---

[40] See *Movement for Quality Government in Israel v Knesset*, 682–4.
[41] *Adalah v Minister of Interior*, 293–5.

are not implied rights. They are express rights which bear the same name as their 'mother'—human dignity.

The Supreme Court of Israel ruled that rights, which in a comprehensive bill of rights are recognized as independent rights but are not so recognized in its partial bill of rights, would be recognized as dignity daughter-rights only with respect to those aspects of the independent rights which have a close substantive relationship to human dignity. For example, not every form of discrimination that limits an independent constitutional right to equality will also limit equality as a daughter-right of human dignity. The right to live with dignity as a daughter-right of human dignity includes the right to a minimum subsistence level with dignity. This existence is closely related to human dignity. If the right to minimum subsistence with dignity were an independent right, then it would certainly extend over a broader area. This restriction of the scope of the right to human dignity is mandated by the method of purposive interpretation. Human dignity, as one of the constitutional rights in the bill of rights, cannot fill the entire space left uncovered by the partial bill of rights. As the Supreme Court stated in one case:[42]

> Human dignity does not refer to everything that is good and beautiful in life. Human dignity is not all human rights. We must distinguish between human dignity as an overall goal underlying all rights and human dignity as a constitutional right. Human dignity is not intended to make all other human rights redundant ... It inherently includes that which is intrinsic to it ... even if in a complete constitutional arrangement it would be included within the other explicit rights. The concept is that the purpose of the Basic Law cannot be turned into something which it is not, nor can one cram into human dignity all of the civil and social rights, to their full extent, which are accepted in advanced societies.

(3) Complementary overlap between the constitutional right to human dignity and other constitutional rights

Different aspects of the value of human dignity are protected by various constitutional rights. Yet these aspects are also entitled to protection within the scope of the right to human dignity. The result is a complementary partial overlap between the right to human dignity and other constitutional rights. What is the relationship between the right to human dignity and other constitutional rights within this complementary overlapping area? The fact that a complementary overlapping area exists should not result in any changes in the scope of the constitutional rights that overlap. There is no reason to withdraw the overlapping area from the scope of the right to human dignity,

---

[42] See *Movement for Quality Government in Israel v Knesset,* 684 (Barak P).

just as there is no reason to withdraw it from the scope of the other rights. The complementary overlap does not lead to any changes in the boundaries of any of the constitutional rights, because each right is independent with respect to the scope it requires for its underlying purpose. Each right is reinforced by the support given to it in the overlapping area.

But is it not the case that when there is a complementary overlap we in effect apply only the specific constitutional right, and not the constitutional right to human dignity? This kind of approach can be found in the case law of the Constitutional Court of South Africa.[43] In my opinion, in the case of a complementary partial overlap between the constitutional right to human dignity and other constitutional rights, each right must be considered separately. The constitutional right to human dignity must not be treated as a residual right, because this would be inconsistent with the centrality of the right to human dignity within the constitution, and it is inappropriate from a methodological perspective as well. The specific right does not detract from the general right to human dignity. Both are applicable to the limiting behaviour, each from its own perspective. The complementary overlap is not given normative expression on the constitutional level, but rather at the sub-constitutional level. A statute that limits a constitutional right in an area in which there is a complementary overlap will be constitutional only if it is proportionate. This proportionality must be examined separately for each of the constitutional rights, especially if the proportionality requirements for each right are different. However, even when a general limitation clause applies to all of the constitutional rights, any limitation must be analysed separately from the perspective of each of the constitutional rights. The reasons for this are two. First, the weight given to the public interest that justifies limitation on the constitutional right to human dignity may differ from its weight as a justification for a limitation on the particular constitutional right. Second, the weight given to the protection of the particular constitutional right (where human dignity might be limited at the penumbra) may be different from the weight given to the protection of the constitutional right to human dignity (where the limitation might be close to the core).

I would take a similar approach when the complementary overlap is between certain daughter-rights of human dignity. Thus, for example, the daughter-right to equality and the daughter-right to family life overlap when the limitation on family life is achieved in a discriminatory manner. Similarly, the daughter-right to equality and the daughter-right to education overlap when equality in education is limited. This overlap results in each daughter-right

---

[43] Woolman, 'Dignity', 36–24.

strengthening the other. Their integration does not result in new boundaries for the daughter-rights. It acts at the sub-constitutional level, in the framework of the law of proportionality.

(4) Conflicting overlap (collusion) between the constitutional right to human dignity and other constitutional rights

In some cases the constitutional right to human dignity conflicts with another independent constitutional right shaped as a principle. How should this conflict be resolved? At the constitutional level, the clash remains. The conflicting partial overlap does not modify the scope of either of the conflicting constitutional rights, just as in the case of a complementary partial overlap. This is the case whether the constitutional right to human dignity is a relative right (as in South African constitutional law and Israeli constitutional law) or an absolute right (as in German constitutional law). Accordingly, the result of the clash is relevant only at the sub-constitutional level. This follows from the understanding that a conflicting overlap between rights shaped as principles is not the result of a mistake, nor does it reflect a constitutional pathology. We do not expect the constitutional right that is overruled by another constitutional right to be wholly or partially withdrawn from the array of constitutional rights. Nor do we proclaim that the special right prevails over the general right. The conflicting overlap demonstrates the richness of the constitutional arrangement and the ongoing clashes among its components. The Israeli Supreme Court ruled in one case:[44]

> The hallmark of democracy is the wealth of rights, values and principles and the ongoing conflicts among them. More than once it has been said that constitutional rights, values and principles are in contradictory pairs. Resolution of these contradictions—which are natural in a democracy and give it its vitality—is not generally done by determining the scope of the rights, values and interests and withdrawing the aspects which do not prevail from the constitutional discourse and constitutional scrutiny. These conflicts are resolved by leaving them at the constitutional level, while determining the degree of protection given to the rights, values and interests that clash at the level of ordinary legislation.

According to this approach, when a statute limits one constitutional right (such as the reputational aspect of the right to human dignity) in order to protect another independent constitutional right (such as the right to freedom of expression) the constitutionality of the statute should be determined in the second stage of the constitutional analysis, where the proportionality of the

---

[44] See HCJ 1434/03 *Anonymous v Haifa disciplinary court of state employees*, 58(1) PD 538–9 (2003) (Heb.) (Barak P).

limitation is decided. This determination takes place at the sub-constitutional level. A statute that restricts one right in order to protect another is constitutional if it is proportional. Thus, even if the limiting statute is determined to be proportional, this result does not restrict the scope of the right that is limited, nor does it expand the scope of the right that is protected.

I would take a similar approach when two constitutional daughter-rights of the mother-right of human dignity conflict with each other. This may occur frequently under a partial constitutional bill of rights, which is the situation in Israel. For example, the daughter-right to reputation may conflict with the daughter-right to freedom of expression, when a statute protecting freedom of expression limits the protection of reputation. Similarly, the daughter-right to freedom of movement may conflict with the daughter-right to freedom of worship, when a statute imposes a limitation on freedom of movement in order to protect freedom of worship. Such a conflict, like clashes between independent constitutional rights, is not resolved at the constitutional level. At that level it remains. Human dignity will continue to reflect the various aspects that characterize it, whether complementary or conflicting. Resolution of the conflict takes place at the sub-constitutional level. Within the framework of proportionality, human dignity will be found on both sides of the scale. The main issue in the proportionality analysis will generally be the balance struck by the statute between the marginal social importance of preventing the additional limitation of one daughter-right of human dignity and the marginal social importance of protecting the conflicting daughter-right. This is done in the second stage of constitutional analysis, within the framework of proportionality.

Conclusion

Many legal systems incorporate the constitutional value of human dignity, and a number of constitutions recognize the constitutional right to human dignity. In these situations, judges have no choice but to interpret these concepts. The vagueness of the concepts does not permit judges to ignore them or to deal with them as they wish. The job of judges is to understand and apply them, in accordance with the rules of interpretation in their own legal system.

The accepted approach in some supreme or constitutional courts is that dignity means humanity. The role of judges who interpret the constitutional value or the constitutional right to human dignity is to give meaning to the concept of the humanity. In doing so, they must reflect the fundamental social perceptions underlying their constitution's structure.

What is the role of comparative law in the understanding of the constitutional value of human dignity and the constitutional right to human dignity?[45] I suggest that two conclusions may be drawn from this chapter. First, comparative law is of great importance for understanding the concept of human dignity and the ideas that are derived from it. Comparative law gives interpretative inspiration to those who are attempting to understand what human dignity is, especially those judges who must give meaning to human dignity on a daily basis. Comparative law expands the interpretative horison and thus enables each legal system to know itself better. Needless to say, however, that it is not binding. The second conclusion regarding the role of comparative law is that extreme caution should be adopted when referring to it. Every legal system has its own external context, which reflects its own historical and social background; every legal system has its own internal context, which reflects its constitutional structure and the normative status of the constitutional right to human dignity. These contexts influence each legal system's approach to the normative characteristics of human dignity. As a result, each legal system has its own understanding of the humanity of the person, the scope of the bill of rights, and the architecture that characterizes it. Hence, human dignity in a constitution where it is an absolute and eternal constitutional right (such as Germany's) differs from human dignity in a constitution where it is a relative right and subject to constitutional amendment (such as that of South Africa or Israel). The constitutional daughter-rights that may be derived from the constitutional mother-right to human dignity are influenced by the scope of the bill of rights. The daughter-rights of human dignity where a bill of rights is comprehensive (such as that of South Africa) differ from the daughter-rights of human dignity where the bill of rights is narrow (such as that of Israel). Constitutional architecture has an impact on constitutional interpretation.

During its long history, human dignity has been considered as a social, religious, and philosophical value. The consideration of human dignity as a constitutional value and constitutional right is relatively young. There is still substantial lack of clarity regarding the concept of human dignity and the conceptions which may be derived from it. There are great apprehensions about handing over responsibility for the interpretation of this concept and its derivative concepts to judges. Ultimately, however, insofar as it concerns the lack of clarity of the concepts and the apprehensions about judges, there is no significant difference between the right to human dignity and the rights to equality or liberty. Constitutional democracy has apparently already become accustomed to the idea that the rights to liberty and equality, for all of their

---

[45] See Ackermann, *Human Dignity*, 14, 21.

vagueness, are essential features of every constitutional bill of rights. A similar rule should apply regarding the right to human dignity.

In the coming years, the number of judgements interpreting the constitutional value and the constitutional right to human dignity will multiply exponentially. The current vagueness will be reduced, and limited primarily to peripheral cases or situations in which changes are taking place in society or science. The apprehensions will subside. Human dignity will eventually become a constitutional value and a constitutional right that is seen as self-evident. I hope that the other participants in this book, who are scholars from other disciplines, will discuss the similarities and differences between their views and mine. Through an understanding of each other's viewpoints, a suitable framework may be created for reducing the gaps and narrowing the differences of opinion. Ultimately, we share the common goal of understanding and protecting human dignity. I hope that this chapter has contributed to advancing this goal.

21

Dignity in a Legal Context: Dignity as an Absolute Right

Dieter Grimm

Dignity as legal notion

DOES IT MAKE A DIFFERENCE whether a term like 'dignity' appears in a theological or philosophical text or in a law? The answer requires a reflection on what distinguishes a law from those texts. The characteristic of a law, its specific way of existing, is its legal validity (*Geltung*). It commands, prohibits, or allows human behaviour with the force of law. It is neither a divine command nor a moral obligation, although such norms may be at the origin of a legal norm or coexist with it. The law is enacted by a public authority that has the legitimation to issue binding norms. These norms claim compliance. Non-compliance renders a behaviour illegal and usually entails organized sanctions by the public authority.

Accordingly, a law has certain addressees, a certain scope, and a certain purpose. It is oriented towards application to concrete cases. The question is either (proactively) which behaviour is required or forbidden in a certain situation or (retroactively) whether a certain behaviour was compatible with or a violation of a legal norm. Different from a command, laws cover a great variety of future situations, including situations that could not be foreseen by the author of the law. Therefore, legal norms are passed in more or less general and abstract terms. This hinders their immediate application to a set of facts. The application is rather preceded by a concretization, which, in turn, requires an interpretation of the relevant norm.

The interpretation bridges the gap between the general and abstract norm and the individual and concrete case by deriving a more precise standard from the text, which can then be applied to the facts. There is no application without prior interpretation. The correct way to interpret a legal norm cannot itself be regulated by law. It is often a matter of controversy. Controversial is the goal of interpretation. Is it the intent of the author of the law or is it an impersonal objective of the law? Controversial is the question whether the context of the law matters for its interpretation. And controversial is the method of interpretation—strictly literal or purposive or even consequentialist, to name some possibilities.

Interpretation is everywhere. If the term 'dignity' appears in a constitutional text, such as in the German Basic Law, more precisely in its Bill of Rights ('Human dignity is inviolable'), the question arises to whom it is addressed. Against whom is human dignity constitutionally protected? The text itself does not answer this question. This leaves room for more than one answer. The obvious answer might be that the norm is addressed to everybody. Nobody may violate another's dignity. The widely accepted answer in Germany is, however, that all holders of public authority in Germany or all state agents are the addressees of the norm. They are bound by it. They must not violate it.

Constitutions of other countries may regulate this in a different way. In Germany this restraint follows from the fact that the Bill of Rights, of which the guarantee of human dignity forms a part, is binding for the German State only, not for other states, which have their own constitutions, and not for German citizens or the inhabitants of Germany. They are the beneficiaries of the guarantee of dignity, not its addressees. Hence, only state agents can violate the constitutional guarantee. A private person may behave in a way inconsistent with the value that is constitutionally protected in the Bill of Rights. But such a behaviour does not amount to a violation of the constitutional norm, since individuals are not bound by it.

The legal text may, however, go beyond a mere prohibition. The Basic Law, for example, prescribes that the state has to respect and protect dignity. 'Respect' means the obligation of the state to refrain from actions that would violate someone's dignity. 'Protect' means that the state is under the additional duty to shield the beneficiaries of the guarantee from acts by third parties incompatible with their dignity.[1] But this does not change the previous statement that dignity as formulated in the German Constitution binds exclusively the state. Individuals are not bound by dignity as a constitutional norm, but they are submitted to the laws or acts that the state may issue in order to fulfill its protective duty.

If the purpose of the dignity clause of the constitution is to prevent violations of human dignity, it is necessary to know what dignity means and which acts form a violation of dignity. Again, the constitutional text does not answer these questions. Yet this is not a peculiarity of dignity. While ordinary

---

[1] See BVerfGE 1, 97 (104) [Hinterbliebenenrente].

laws often define the notions they use, such definitions are rare within bills of rights. They name the object of protection (the press, the art, property, the home, etc.), but leave it to the applicant of the law to ascertain whether a certain object of a state action is covered by that notion or not. Vagueness does not deprive a norm of its legal nature. Vagueness has to be reduced by way of interpretation.

The orientation towards application of the law to concrete cases and the necessity to end up with a decision distinguishes legal interpretation from interpretation of other texts. The cases may present problems which the lawmaker was not aware of or could not have been aware of. This does not excuse the law applicant from making a decision. The question cannot be left open. As long as a law has not been repealed it applies, no matter whether the circumstances have changed since its enactment. Likewise, it cannot be left open which out of two or more possible interpretations is the correct one. All may have their merits; but the law applicant must choose among them and give reasons for the choice.

There may be instances in which the consensus as to what constitutes a violation of dignity is broad. Torture, although by no means uncontroversial, is an example. In other instances it may be difficult to find a consensus. Two recent cases that the German Constitutional Court had to decide may illustrate the difficulty. Does a law that permits the German Air Force to shoot down a captured plane that is directed into a target where people live or work violate the dignity of the passengers?[2] Would it make a difference if only the hijackers were in the plane? Or does a certain diminution of social security benefits violate the dignity of those in need?[3] Can this depend on the means that a state has at its disposal?

We discuss these questions in an interdisciplinary context: dignity is not the property of one discipline only. Before becoming a legal term it was a theological and a philosophical notion; the framers of a constitution may have been inspired by philosophy or theology. Does this mean that the meaning of dignity in a legal document may be or even has to be determined with reference to theological or philosophical works? Let us leave the practical difficulties aside, although they are serious enough: Which participant in a legislative process was influenced by which philosophical or religious theory? How were they understood? What if various tendencies were competing with each other? How can one prove influence?

---

[2] See BVerfGE 115, 118 ff. [Luftsicherheitsgesetz].
[3] See BVerfGE 125, 175 ff. [Hartz IV].

It seems of greater importance, though, that the notion, be it theological or philosophical by origin, is transferred into a different context if becoming part of a legal document. This transfer disconnects it from its roots, not in a way that completely changes its meaning but in a way that any inference from a theological or philosophical understanding of dignity to its legal meaning is prohibited. Rather, the legal process in which the notion was enacted, the historical experience on which the framers built or to which they reacted, the interplay of the norm with other provisions in the same legal document is decisive. It may then come close to its philosophical or theological roots, but it is the result of an autonomous legal process.

Thus, the German Constitutional Court, when expounding the notion of dignity in the Basic Law, often used language that reminds of Kant's object formula:[4] 'So act that you use humanity, whether in your own person or in the person of any other, always at the same time as an end, never merely as a means'.[5] But the court never referred to Kant. Kant taught in the eighteenth and early nineteenth century, whereas the constitutional guarantee of human dignity was first adopted in a German constitutional text after the Second World War. In order to determine its legal impact within the Basic Law, it is more promising to ask what caused this step in 1949, 150 years after Kant. Why did many other countries follow forty years later?

This leads the interpreter to the historical context. It is a source of illumination but does not bind the law applicant. Originalist theories of constitutional interpretation, according to which a legal notion has to be understood in the way the framers understood it, are absent in Germany. Here the question is less how the framers understood the term but what purpose or what function a constitutional provision that guarantees human dignity is to fulfil in a specific legal order. This leaves room for an adaptation of a legal notion to changed situations or new challenges as long as the purpose or function is not altered by the law applicant. Not every change of meaning requires a constitutional amendment.

Regarding dignity in a German constitution drafted in 1948–9 it is of importance that before the enactment the Nazi regime had committed atrocities

---

[4] Immanuel Kant, *Groundwork of the Metaphysics of Morals*, in *The Cambridge Edition of the Works of Immanuel Kant* (Cambridge, Cambridge University Press, 1996), 80 (German Academy Edn, vol. 4, 429).

[5] Examples of the use of the object formula by the German Constitutional Court include BVerfGE 9, 89 (95) [Gehör bei Haftbefehl]; BVerfGE 27, 1 (6) [Mikrozensus]; BVerfGE 28, 386 (391) [Kurzzeitige Freiheitsstrafe]; BVerfGE 45, 187 (228) [Lebenslange Freiheitsstrafe]; BVerfGE 57, 250 (275) [V-Mann]; BVerfGE 72, 105 (116) [Lebenslange Freiheitsstrafe]; BVerfGE 96, 375 (399) [Kind als Schaden]; BVerfGE 109, 133 (149 f.) [Langfristige Sicherungsverwahrung]; BVerfGE 109, 279 (312) [Großer Lauschangriff].

unheard of in history, and the Basic Law's underlying motive can be summarized in the words 'Never again', meaning never again a self-destruction of democracy as in 1933, and never again a total neglect of human rights and of the recognition that every human being deserves as a part of mankind. This background may then serve as starting point in the determination of the meaning of dignity, and, as a matter of fact, the court started its explanation of 'dignity' by referring to the Nazi atrocities as the clearest examples of what the guarantee of dignity should prevent in the future.[6]

But this does not mean that the application of dignity is limited to cases of repetition of Nazi atrocities. It shows, however, that in the light of historical events that had been up to then unthinkable, more was at stake than a number of liberties, something that forms the common ground of the various constitutional rights and guides their understanding. Dignity thus added something to the traditional bills of rights, for which no necessity had existed in previous constitutions written in the light of their historical context. This surplus value has to be determined, taking into account which values other provisions of the constitution entrench and what dignity adds to them. From there, analogies may be drawn to new layers of meaning.

This shows at the same time that human dignity will not necessarily have the same meaning in every legal system. In countries with a racist past, for instance, dignity, if included in the constitution, will have a strong emphasis on equal treatment.[7] Differences exist also with regard to rank and function. Dignity may be regarded as a principle that informs the interpretation and application of rights; it may be regarded as one right among others or count as a preferred right. In a country with a rudimentary bill of rights, such as Israel, the main function of the constitutional guarantee of dignity may be to fill the gaps and to generate new rights based on the argument that they are implied in the notion of dignity.[8]

---

[6] In an early case regarding the prohibition of the SRP party (BVerfGE 2, 1), the Constitutional Court emphasized that the Basic Law established a constitutional order that is the opposite of the totalitarian state which rejects human dignity, liberty and equality (BVerfGE 2, 1 (12)). In another early case (BVerfGE 1, 97 (104)), the Constitutional Court said that the purpose of the human dignity provision in Article 1 Basic Law was the protection against 'Erniedrigung, Brandmarkung, Verfolgung, Ächtung usw' (humiliation, stigmatization, persecution, ostracism, etc.). Later, the Constitutional Court explicitly said that this enumeration resulted from the experience of atrocities during the Nazi regime (BVerfGE 109, 279 (312)).

[7] See Laurie W. H. Ackermann, 'Equality in the South African Constitution: the role of dignity', *Zeitschrift fuer Auslaendisches Oeffentliches Recht und Voelkerrecht* 63 (2000), 537.

[8] In some cases, the Israeli Supreme Court derived an equality right from the notion of human dignity: for example, HCJ 5394/92 *Hupert v Yad Vashem* 48(3) PD 353, 362 [1994]; HCJ 453/94 *Israel Women's Network v Government of Israel* 48(5) PD 510 [1994].

The German Constitution starts with a guarantee of human dignity. Although without impact on the legal validity, the prominent position of dignity helped the Constitutional Court to declare dignity the foundational value of the social order, a basic norm that appears behind the more concrete guarantees in the Bill of Rights, but also behind the structural and organizational provisions of the constitution such as democracy and the rule of law, yet a value that had to be made explicit after the Nazi government had departed from a shared moral consensus. The older rights then appear as more concrete expressions of the overarching idea of dignity, and have to be understood and applied in its light.

This overarching value may have had different origins and different connotations for different people, and even for different members of the constituent assembly, for some a Christian, for others a humanistic or enlightenment, for others a Marxist background. The constituent assembly as such did not decide on which tradition to build. It only decided to make dignity the foundational norm of the polity. The enactment as law neutralizes the ideological background. Thus, it would not be legitimate for the law applicant to define the meaning by adhering to one of the background theories. Consequently, inconsistency with one or another theory does not disqualify the legal reasoning by which meaning is given to the notion.

Generally speaking, every reference to non-legal sources of understanding the legal notion of dignity or every insight from other disciplines must be translatable into a legal argument, and fit into the legal environment in which dignity appears. Thus, a concept of dignity which relies on the belief that every man is created in the image of God would conflict with the secular nature of the state, and likewise the idea that some people are more dignified than others conflicts with the egalitarian nature of the Basic Law. Of course, what counts as a legal argument and fits into a specific legal context is contested and alterable, but the contest can only be decided within the legal system, not from outside.

Dignity as absolute right

In a legal context, rights are usually not absolute. Every right can be abused to harm others. Every right can enter into conflict with other rights or the same right of others. This is why, in a legal context, the question of limits or restrictions of rights plays an important role. Most constitutions contain limitation clauses. But the necessity of imposing limits on rights is independent of a specific permission in the constitution. Also, under a constitution that gives the legislature or executive no express permission to limit rights, like the US Constitution, limitations are inevitable. It becomes a matter of interpretation to determine legitimate limits and distinguish them from illegitimate ones.

The most important questions that arise in connection with the limitation of rights are as follows. Who is entitled to impose limits on the use of rights? For which purposes may limits be imposed? Which circumstances allow the limitation of rights? What means are appropriate to limit rights? How far may limitations go in restricting the use of a right? Are there limits of limitation? Is there a hierarchy of rights that helps to decide a conflict among various rights? How can one balance different rights? These are questions with which courts, especially courts with constitutional jurisdiction, are constantly concerned when they adjudicate in the field of constitutional rights.

In Germany, dignity is exempted from considerations like these. Dignity is regarded as an absolute right.[9] This preferred position is mainly based on a textual argument. Article 1 section 1 sentence 1 of the Basic Law declares that human dignity is '*unantastbar*'. This term is commonly translated as 'inviolable' ('*unverletzlich*'). Yet *unverletzlich* appears several times in connection with fundamental rights whereas *unantastbar* is used only in connection with dignity. The rights which are called 'inviolable' can nevertheless be limited by law. *Unantastbar* is stronger than *unverletzlich*. This difference gave rise to the interpretation of dignity as being absolutely guaranteed.

No other right in the Basic Law enjoys absolute protection. It may be that some rights are regarded as more important or more fundamental than others. In the jurisprudence of the German Constitutional Court one can find language that privileges the right to life. In the First Abortion Decision, the court writes: 'It does not require any further explanation that human life is among the highest values of the constitutional order of the Basic Law; it is the vital basis of human dignity and it is the prerequisite of all other fundamental rights.'[10] Yet, in spite of this assertion, the court denies that there is a hierarchy among fundamental rights, and even this right is not protected absolutely. It has a limitation clause.

What distinguishes an absolute right from relative rights? The difference lies in the extent of protection. Constitutional protection of a right does not mean that it is immunized from any restriction. It only means that restrictions need a constitutional justification. The protection of a right is usually but a

---

[9] See BVerfGE 75, 369 (380) [Strauß-Karikatur]; BVerfGE 93, 266 (293) ['Soldaten sind Mörder'], BVerfGE 109, 279 (312 f.) [Großer Lauschangriff].

[10] BVerfGE 39, 1 (42): 'Das menschliche Leben stellt, wie nicht näher begründet werden muß, innerhalb der grundgesetzlichen Ordnung einen Höchstwert dar; es ist die vitale Basis der Menschenwürde und die Voraussetzung aller anderen Grundrechte.'

relative one. There may be good reasons for restrictions. 'Absolute' means, to the contrary, that no restriction is permitted. Hence, different from all other rights, dignity is neither subject to limitation nor to balancing. This entails a different treatment of dignity compared with other fundamental rights. They may be limited under certain conditions, or have to give way to another right in the case at hand.

Therefore, the application of fundamental rights to concrete cases follows a two tiered approach. It is first examined whether the right was negatively affected by some state action (or omission). This presupposes a determination of the scope of the right and a qualification of the state action as infringement. Second, it is examined whether the infringement was justified according to the limitation clause of that right and (usually) the principle of proportionality. Lorraine Weinrib describes this approach as the post-war paradigm of fundamental rights jurisprudence,[11] originally developed by the German Constitutional Court and later adopted almost universally, albeit with the exception of the USA.[12]

If a right is regarded as absolute, the two tier approach does not apply. Every infringement is a violation. The question of justification does not arise. No intrusion, no limitation can be justified if dignity is at stake. The same is true for balancing. The balancing procedure, which applies if two constitutionally protected rights, goods, or interests enter into collision, implies that, depending on the circumstances that have to be taken into account, at times one right and at times the other right prevails. Dignity as an absolute right always trumps. If dignity is involved in a collision with another constitutionally protected right, good, or interest, no balancing takes place. The result is clear from the outset.

The decision to recognize a right as absolutely protected has some consequences that follow logically from the absoluteness. The first consequence is that not more than one right within a constitution can be treated as absolute. Only then is it possible that this right always trumps. If two or more rights are regarded as absolute and they enter into conflict (which cannot be excluded), one of them has to give way, which means that it is not absolute. If several rights are to enjoy a special protection, they may be treated as preferred rights, meaning that they will usually prevail in case of conflict, yet not

---

[11] Lorraine Weinrib, 'The postwar paradigm and American exceptionalism', in Sujit Choudhry (ed.), *The Migration of Constitutional Ideas* (New York, Cambridge University Press, 2006), 83, at 93. In some countries, such as Canada, Israel, and South Africa, the infringement is called 'violation', although only the second step shows whether the infringement was a violation.

[12] For the USA see, for example, Michael J. Meyer and William A. Parent (eds), *The Constitution of Rights. Human Dignity and American Values* (Ithaca, NY, Cornell University Press, 1992).

always. Dignity, under German constitutional law, is not a preferred right, it is an absolute right.

The second consequence is that dignity, if understood as an absolute right, cannot have a broad scope. The German Constitutional Court concedes all fundamental rights a rather broad scope. This can easily be done because these rights are subject to limitation. The first step of the two tier approach only opens the door for the constitutional evaluation of whether a limitation or an infringement was justified. One can therefore be generous on the first step. In the case of an absolute right, the infringement is identical with a violation. As a consequence, the scope of an absolute right must be narrowly defined in order to prevent unacceptable results. The narrow scope is the price of the elevation to an absolute rank.

The necessity of a narrow scope follows also from the fact that dignity as an absolute right stops any political discussion. If a politically desirable measure affects human dignity, the need for it may be as pressing as possible; the measure has no chance of being employed. Not even a constitutional amendment would help, since the so-called eternity clause of the Germany's Constitution (Article 79, section 3) immunizes dignity from change. Dignity is, therefore, a most effective weapon in a political struggle, and many try to bring their rejection or their approval of certain political plans under the umbrella of dignity, currently mainly in the field of reproductive rights and bioethical questions.

Consequently, dignity is frequently invoked before the Constitutional Court, but the court rarely found that a law or an act violated Article 1. The court has to think twice before it includes a certain aspect of personhood into the scope of Article 1 because the inclusion predetermines the result of the legal scrutiny. If the aspect enjoys the protection of dignity no limitation can be justified. This is, for instance, important regarding the relationship between dignity and the right to life. According to Article 2, section 2, sentence 1 of the Basic Law everybody has the right to life. But according to section 2, this right can be limited. The Basic Law recognizes that there are certain situations where the state may lawfully take someone's life.

This can only mean that taking someone's life does not per se violate the person's dignity; otherwise the constitution would contradict itself. There may, however, be instances where life is taken in a way that affects the person's dignity. The Constitutional Court assumed this, for example, in the First Abortion Decision[13] and recently in the Aviation Security Case[14] with regard

---

[13] BVerfGE 39, 1 (42 f.) [Schwangerschaftsabbruch I].
[14] BVerfGE 115, 118 (152 f.) [Luftsicherheitsgesetz].

to the innocent passengers and crew members, not with respect to the terrorists. In the court's view, the passengers and the crew members were treated as mere objects, whereas the terrorists only bore the consequences of their free decision to kill innocent people in order to promote their political interests.

The impact of human dignity is therefore reserved for gross assaults on humanity, which fortunately remain rare in the Federal Republic. Does this mean that dignity enjoys an extremely high rank but is of little practical impact? This might be so if all the minor impairments of liberty and equality were constitutionally irrelevant. But this is not the case. They are treated under the various constitutional rights that render broad, though not absolute, protection. In addition, the legal impact of dignity is not limited to direct application in cases of presumed violations. Dignity as the highest value of the constitutional order also has indirect effects when other provisions of the constitution are interpreted and applied.

Other than the relatively small number of cases where dignity appeared as the foremost criterion of the judgment, the cases in which dignity is used to inform the interpretation of other rights are quite numerous. The constitutional norm on which the decision is based is then formed by a combination of the right at stake and dignity ('in conjunction with'). Here, Article 1 usually extends the scope of the right or deepens its impact when it comes to balancing. The combined criteria seem to be a speciality of German constitutional doctrine. The combination of the dignity clause in the constitution with another fundamental right has often led to important changes in the law.

The combination of dignity and a more concrete basic right is not limited to certain rights. Every right has a dignity core, and this can become relevant when the principle of proportionality is applied. The closer the restriction of a right comes to its dignity core the higher the weight of the right in the balancing process. However, dignity is never on the side of one right only. An illustrative case is the frequent conflict between freedom of speech on the one hand and personal honour (as part of everybody's right to free development of his or her personality) on the other. Here, dignity does not only strengthen the honour side, as some legal scholars would have it, but also the freedom of speech side.

A third and last consequence of the absolute character of Article 1 is that dignity can only protect a person against being treated in a way that is contrary to his or her dignity. It cannot protect activities of a person. Any activity, any behaviour may cause harm to others or endanger important communal goods. If dignity as absolute right were to protect activities, it would be impossible to prevent or cure the harm, because this would require the limitation of the exercise of the right to dignity, which means that it could no longer be absolute.

The protection of activities of a person is therefore left to the more concrete rights, which are, however, subject to limitation and balancing.

Whether it is advisable to endow one right, dignity, with the legal quality of an absolute right, and to pay the price in the form of a narrow scope seems debatable. There is no universally valid answer to this question. As mentioned before, the historical experience that created a demand for an absolute barrier to government plays an important role. Countries without experiences of that sort may see no need to establish an absolute right. The fact that such a right must be construed narrowly seems acceptable the more all important aspects of humanity have found protection in other fundamental rights, and perhaps even in a residual right that protects the individual against threats unknown when the constitution was framed.

22

Human Dignity in the Jurisprudence of the European Court of Human Rights

Jean-Paul Costa[1]

THIS CONTRIBUTION AIMS TO describe the adoption and use of the concept of human dignity in the jurisprudence of the European Court of Human Rights, the oldest and most important international tribunal in the world dealing with human rights issues and cases. Dignity, or human dignity, is often the foundation of the legal reasoning of the Strasbourg Court in its rulings. It was not at all obvious that this would happen: the text of the European Convention on Human Rights,[2] on which the Court's jurisprudence is based, does not mention dignity at all. Despite this, the use of that concept is engaged in many types of human rights violations. But recourse to it is never self-evident in the choice of reasoning of the rulings made by the Court. That is why it is worth reflecting on that practice, and ultimately about the philosophical and legal links between human dignity and human rights.

A surprising absence in the basic text

The word 'dignity' is not only quoted but given pride of place in the first sentence of the Preamble of the 1948 Universal Declaration of Human Rights,[3] and it appears again in Article 1, and in Article 23.3 of the Declaration. It is less well known that the word had been already used, in one of its first sentences, by the American Declaration of the Rights and Duties of Man, adopted a few months *before* the Universal Declaration. Similarly, the two international Covenants of 1966, which develop, and make enforceable, the

---

[1] This contribution expresses the author's own personal ideas.
[2] Its official title is the Convention for the Protection of Human Rights and Fundamental Freedoms.
[3] 'Whereas recognition of the inherent dignity and of the equal and inalienable rights of all members of the human family is the foundation of freedom, justice and peace in the world …'

Universal Declaration's provisions, solemnly speak of the 'inherent dignity of the human person'.

While those instruments grant dignity a prominent role in the foundation of, or basis for, human rights, and while some European texts do the same (such as the European Social Charter, 1961, and, more recently, the Charter of Fundamental Rights of the European Union, 2000),[4] the European Convention on Human Rights, signed on 4 November 1950, is absolutely silent about dignity. Neither the Convention itself nor the Protocols to the Convention use that word or expression.

Why this is so is not clear. The *'travaux préparatoires'* of the Convention, especially the debates in the Consultative Assembly of the Council of Europe in 1949–50, do not provide an obvious explanation. The absence of dignity is surprising, the more so if one considers that the text of the European Convention is in many respects very close to that of the Universal Declaration. Most of the rights guaranteed in the Convention are analogous to at least a part of the rights proclaimed by the Declaration. One hypothesis—the author here expresses his own personal ideas—could be that the Convention is a more practical, pragmatic, and mechanism-oriented text than that of the Declaration: it created a commission and a court, and provided for procedural ways and means for bringing a case to Strasbourg, and how these cases have to be settled.

It is likely that the drafters nevertheless had the concept of dignity in their minds, especially because the very establishment of the Council of Europe in 1949 and the elaboration of the Convention, the first treaty prepared within its framework, were the work of persons firmly opposed to the atrocities and barbarity of the Second World War. The founding fathers of the European system of protection of rights and freedoms shared the same philosophy as the authors of the Universal Declaration. Very probably, however, their intention was not to use solemn, emphatic language, but instead to concentrate on more practical, even technical issues.

---

[4] Significantly, Chapter I of the Charter is dealing with 'Dignity'. It includes five articles. Article I reads as follows: 'Human dignity is inviolable. It must be respected and protected.' Articles 2 to 5 guarantee, respectively, right to life, including the prohibition of death penalty, right to the integrity of the person, including in the fields of medicine and biology, prohibition of torture and inhuman or degrading treatments, and prohibition of slavery and forced labour, including trafficking of human beings. The Charter, which has been legally binding for the member states of the EU since 1 December 2009, together with the entry into force of the Lisbon Treaty, is clearly more complete and modern than the European Convention of Human Rights, adopted half a century before it.

Re-appearance of dignity in the case-law

It is difficult to ascertain when, for the first time, the Convention bodies had recourse to the concept of dignity. In the *Court's* case law, the leading judgment is usually said to be *Tyrer v United Kingdom*,[5] a case about judicial corporal punishment inflicted on a fifteen-year-old pupil in the Isle of Man. According to the Court, the penalty, and the conditions of its execution, and their indignity, amounted if not to inhuman at least to degrading treatment under Article 3 of the Convention, which therefore had been violated. So *Tyrer* seems to be a pioneer judgment.[6]

However, in a report dated December 1973, more than four years before *Tyrer*, the European Commission of Human Rights had already addressed the issue of human dignity. The Commission stated that racial discrimination could constitute a breach of human dignity.[7] It is noticeable that discrimination, even on racial or ethnic grounds, normally constitutes a violation of Article 14 of the Convention (the principle of equality), not of Article 3, which prohibits torture and inhuman or degrading punishment or treatment. This very first example of the use of the term dignity shows that the Commission,[8] and the Court subsequently, have never restricted their recourse to dignity solely to Article 3, even if it is the field where it is most frequently applied. The approach followed by the Commission in that particular case, namely that racial discrimination is, or may be, an offence to human dignity, has been influential, and was eventually confirmed by the Court itself.[9] A noteworthy example is seen in the inter-state case of *Cyprus v Turkey*,[10] in which discrimination against the Karpas Greek Cypriots was held to constitute a 'violation of the very notion of human dignity', and breached Article 3 of the Convention.[11]

---

[5] 25 April 1978.
[6] *Tyrer* was followed, under Article 2 of Protocol 1, which protects the right to education, by *Campbell and Cosans v UK*, 25 February 1982, again about corporal punishment in a school, in Scotland.
[7] *East African Asians v UK*, opinion, 27 December 1973.
[8] The European Commission of Human Rights, which produced a high number of decisions, opinions and reports, and played a very important role in the first phase of the system based on the European Convention on Human Rights, disappeared in 1998 with the entry into force of Protocol 11 to the Convention. Protocol 11 has changed the Court into a single, permanent body. It is a radical modification of the system, the most important since 1950.
[9] See for instance *Nachova v Bulgaria*, Grand Chamber judgment, 6 July 2005; the complaints of the applicants were under Articles 2 and 3 of the Convention, and Article 14 as well.
[10] Grand Chamber judgment, 10 May 2001.
[11] *Cyprus v Turkey*, (§309 of the judgment).

Examples of recourse to human dignity: Articles 2, 3, and 4

Most of the cases where the Court has decided a case on the basis of an offence against human dignity are cases arising under Article 3. Many of these cases deal with disproportionate use of physical force against people in vulnerable situations, such as people arrested by the police or detained in a cell. The general principle is that when a person is deprived of liberty, any recourse to physical force which is not strictly necessary diminishes human dignity, and is in principle an infringement of Article 3.[12] So, for example, in *Tekin v Turkey*,[13] a person had been held in a cold, dark cell, and so mistreated that wounds and bruises were left on his body. In *Selmouni v France*, a person held in custody in a police station had been very seriously injured by the police officers.[14] In both cases, the Court used dignity language in holding that there had been a violation of Article 3.

The Court has also found that human dignity, and the principles of medical ethics, are breached in a case where a detained person, seriously ill with cancer, had been handcuffed when being transferred from prison to hospital.[15] More generally, persons in prison must benefit from extended rights to be well treated, precisely for human dignity's sake. The state must ensure that the conditions in detention are compatible with the respect for human dignity.[16] The case-law is so abundant[17] that an authoritative observer of the Court's jurisprudence has written an article, the title of which explains that the Court through its case-law, has effectively added an additional paragraph, 'Article *3 bis*', to the Convention.[18]

These are not the only prominent examples of the use of dignity in an Article 3 context. In a case about prostitution, in a strong *obiter dictum*, the Court said that it stated firmly that *forced* prostitution is against human dignity and

---

[12] *Ribitsch v Austria*, 4 December 1995, §38 (inhuman and degrading treatment).
[13] 9 June 1998 (inhuman and degrading treatment).
[14] Grand Chamber, 28 July 1999, especially §99 (torture).
[15] *Mouisel v France*, 14 November 2002 (inhuman and degrading treatment).
[16] *Kudla v Poland*, Grand Chamber judgment, 26 October 2000, §94. However, the Court did not find a violation of Article 3 in the case.
[17] See for instance *Frérot v France*, 12 June 2007, §§47 and 48, a case about full-body strip searches of a detainee, with visual anus inspection (degrading treatment). See also, for a body search of a man in jail, who was stripped naked before a woman, *Valasinas v Lithuania,* 24 July 2011 (degrading treatment).
[18] Prof. Fréderic Sudre, 'L'article 3 *bis* de la Convention européenne des droits de l'homme: le droit à des conditions de détention conformes au respect de la dignité humaine', in *Mélanges en hommage au Doyen Gérard Cohen-Jonathan* Brussels, Emile Bruylant, 2004, vol. 2, 1499ff.

against human rights.¹⁹ In a recent case, the Court has held that the Croatian authorities had breached Article 3 for not having protected a physically and mentally disabled person against repeated harassment.²⁰ As can be noticed, many violations found by the Court rely on the failure from the state to fulfil its *positive obligations*. Dignity is therefore an objective to be reached by state authorities, even where private people or organizations encroached upon it.

As regards Article 2 (right to life), there are a very few cases where human dignity is engaged. Nevertheless, at least two where it was engaged, both of them important, should be mentioned. In *Pretty v UK*,²¹ human dignity (especially a right to die with dignity) was invoked by the applicant, a woman suffering from progressive neurodegenerative disease who needed to be assisted by her husband if she was to commit suicide. But the Court, while expressing its strong sympathy towards the applicant, did not find a violation of either Article 2 or Article 3. In the case of *Vo v France*,²² the applicant, a pregnant woman, accidentally lost the six-month foetus, a baby girl, whom she was bearing, owing to a medical mistake. The Court recognized that 'the foetus/embryo belongs to the human race ... and requires protection in the name of human dignity'.²³ Nevertheless, it held, on legal/procedural grounds, that there had been no violation of Article 2 in the material case. It may seem paradoxical that human dignity is less present in Article 2 than in Article 3 cases, but such is the fact. The most likely reason is that both the applicants and the Court, *ex officio*, feel less need to invoke, or to have recourse to, human dignity in issues related to respect of life.

Under Article 4, which prohibits slavery, servitude, and forced labour, the small number of applications explains why the Court, at least until recently, has not needed to have recourse to human dignity. In fact, the first judgment concluding that there had been a violation of Article 4 on grounds of servitude, not merely forced labour, in the case of *Siliadin v France*,²⁴ concerned a case of 'domestic slavery', or the so-called 'modern slavery'. Not only did the Court hold that the treatment inflicted on the applicant, a fifteen-year-old girl coming to Paris from Africa, amounted not just to forced labour but to servitude. The Court went further by stating that the exploitation of a person

---

[19] *Tremblay v France*, 11 September 2007. Actually, the ECtHR, basing itself on the facts of the case, found no violation of Articles 3 or 4 of the Convention, considering that the applicant was not forced to prostitute herself. The judgment is available only in French on the ECtHR's HUDOC site.
[20] *Dordevic v Croatia*, 24 June 2012.
[21] 29 April 2002.
[22] Grand Chamber, 8 July 2004.
[23] *Vo v France*, §84.
[24] 24 July 2005.

in such circumstances was contrary to human dignity.[25] This important judgment was confirmed by the Court's judgment in the case of *Rantsev v Cyprus and the Russian Federation*,[26] a very serious case, in which a young woman was forced into human trafficking and transferred from Russia to Cyprus in order to become a prostitute. She eventually died in unclear circumstances. As regards trafficking of human beings, the Court decided that it is covered by Article 4 of the Convention, even if the Convention does not expressly mention it. Article 4 was found to have been violated in this case, and the judgment states that the phenomenon 'threatens the human dignity and the fundamental freedoms of its victims'.[27]

Examples of recourse to human dignity in the case of other Articles

Articles 5 and 6 protect the rights to liberty and security, and to a fair trial. Human dignity, as such, is not used by the Court in finding violations of these provisions, and it is very seldom invoked by the applicants. In the famous case of *John Murray v UK*,[28] the applicant tried in vain to convince the Court that the fact that adverse inferences were drawn at his trial from his failure to answer questions by the police amounted to a violation of Article 6. The Court's reasoning is that, provided proper safeguards are in place, there is no improper compulsion to self-incrimination. However, in his partly dissenting opinion, Judge Pettiti, joined by Judge Valticos, stated that, for an accused person, the right of choosing to remain or not to remain silent should be free, and that effectively requiring him to answer questions is contrary to human dignity.

Article 7 (no punishment without law), prohibits, in particular, retrospective application of criminal law. Human dignity was engaged in the important cases of *S.W.* and *C.R. v UK*,[29] where the issue involved the conviction and sentencing of two husbands for the offence of rape committed on their wives. The husbands argued before the British courts, and then before the Court in Strasbourg, that the punishment was not foreseeable; the common law, since the seventeenth century, considered that sexual intercourse by a man with his wife against her consent was not illegal. The Court's reasoning, in rejecting the applicants' arguments, is very much founded on human dignity, and equality between man and woman. Both applicants should have foreseen, at the end

---

[25] *Siliadin v France*, §142.
[26] 7 January 2010.
[27] *Rantsev v Cyprus and the Russian Federation*, §282.
[28] Grand Chamber judgment of 8 February 1996.
[29] Two judgments of 22 November 1995.

of the twentieth century, that the rule had to be changed, in particular with regard to human dignity.[30]

In the case of *K.A. and A.D. v Belgium*,[31] the applicants had been sentenced to penalties of imprisonment and suspended fines, for having committed cruel sadomasochist acts against the first applicant's wife; she had, in principle, consented to these practices, at least to a certain extent. The Court rejected the applicants' complaints, based on Articles 6, 7, and 8 of the Convention. It is striking that neither the defending state, nor even the Court, which could have raised the issue *ex officio*, had recourse to the human dignity argument, which would have been a strong ground for rejecting the application. Many commentators subsequently criticized the judgment for this surprising shortcoming in the reasoning, especially because the Court, while rejecting the case, emphasized the importance of the autonomy of the victim. The difference with the aforementioned *S.W.* and *C.R.* should be noted.

Insofar as Article 8 is concerned (right to respect for private and family life), the Court's recourse to the concept of human dignity is recent, but highly relevant. In the so-called 'transsexual' case of *Christine Goodwin and I. v UK*,[32] the Court emphasized the fact that 'the very essence of the Convention is respect for human dignity and human freedom'.[33] On this basis, the Court found a violation of Article 8 (and Article 12), owing to a refusal by state authorities to grant the applicants, who were post-operative transsexuals, the right to be registered on the registry of births with their new gender, and the right to marry members of their new opposite sex. As is well known, this judgment reversed previous judgments of the Court,[34] showing that its jurisprudence is not necessarily stuck to precedents and may evolve according to new legal and factual elements which occur in Europe (applying the doctrine that the Convention is a 'living instrument', already spelled out in *Tyrer*). The approach in *Christine Goodwin* was followed in a judgment against Lithuania.[35]

Curiously, the concept of human dignity was not invoked as such by the applicant in the case of *Chapman v UK*,[36] a 'Gipsy' case about housing and urban planning, and the denial of a home. Admittedly, the Court recognized that it is highly desirable that every human being has a place to call home in which to live in dignity.[37] But, taking into account that many people live

---

[30] *S.W.* and *C.R. v UK*, §44 of *S.W.*
[31] 17 February 2005.
[32] Grand Chamber judgment of 11 July 2002.
[33] *Christine Goodwin and I. v UK*, §90.
[34] *Rees v UK* and *Cossey v UK*, 17 October 1986 and 27 September 1990.
[35] *L. v Lithuania*, 11 September 2007.
[36] Grand Chamber judgment of 18 January 2001.
[37] *Chapman v UK*, §99.

without fixed dwellings, even in 'rich' countries, the Court eventually did not find a violation of Article 8 in the material case. This 'realistic' approach has outweighed considerations in favour of human dignity, despite the sensitivity of the condition of the Roma population.

Article 10 (freedom of speech) applications very seldom involve human dignity arguments. However, the issue was raised in an important judgment dealing with the prosecution of a journalist for not having censored violent statements by racist young people whom he had interviewed for a TV programme.[38] The majority of the Court found a violation of Article 10 by the state authorities. However, four dissenters, Judges Ryssdal, Bernhardt (both of them Court Presidents), Alphonse Spielmann and Loizou, expressed their disagreement with the majority's finding, observing that the racist comments of the Greenjackets (as the young people were called) were an attack on, and even a denial of, individuals' human dignity. The dissenters did not consider that the Court's approach was sufficiently protective of the rights of those whose dignity had been attacked, as prescribed by Article 10, §2.

Why does the Court use the concept of human dignity in some cases more than in others?

Again, the answer is not obvious. The judicial approach of the Court, preceded, as observed, by the Commission, generally appears to use the concept of human dignity to *reinforce* the reasoning leading to a violation of the Convention, while in a few cases dignity is used to reject complaints based on arguments contrary themselves to human dignity (as in the cases of *S.W.* and *C.R.*). In the latter cases, the Court's reasoning is close to recourse to Article 17, which prohibits abuse of rights, and is rarely invoked by the defending states or accepted by the Court.[39]

When the Court uses human dignity 'positively', in order to find a violation, it is clear that it applies it much more to serious violations, with Article 3 being especially privileged in this regard among all the provisions of the Convention. The very notion of inhuman and degrading treatment, and even more of torture, is in the Court's view manifestly contrary to human dignity. If dignity is 'inherent to the human person', as stated in the Universal

---

[38] *Jersild v Denmark*, Grand Chamber judgment of 29 March 1994.
[39] One of the few examples of application of Article 17 is the decision *Garaudy v France*, 24 June 2003. Owing to the prohibited aims (revisionism, in the background of a historical controversy about the *Shoah*), the Court rejected the claim of the applicant, founded on freedom of expression (Article 10).

Declaration and, even more specifically, in the two UN International Covenants, the punishments and treatments prohibited by the Declaration (Article 5) and the Covenant on Civil and Political Rights (Article 7), are clearly contrary to human dignity. Under those circumstances, the intention of the judges in Strasbourg becomes less mysterious. They have constantly thought and said that the Convention rights must be interpreted not only on the basis of the text of the Convention itself but also drawing on other international instruments (even if they are not strictly legally binding). The UN's most fundamental instruments are the best possible examples of these external sources of inspiration, and Article 3 of the European Convention is the easiest provision to link with human dignity, in the meaning of the Declaration and the Covenants.

In other words, the reappearance of the concept of human dignity in the Court's jurisprudence expresses a deliberate intention of building a bridge between the universal instruments and the silent European text, filling the gap or the vacuum created by the authors of the Convention. Admittedly, the first example, the Commission's use of dignity in dealing with the issue of racial discrimination, looks even bolder. But is this appearance of boldness really true? Yes and no: the United Nations texts proclaim, after all, that men are *equal* in dignity; racial discrimination breach that equality, and hence dignity itself.

Moreover, it is possible that there are *subjective* reasons, explaining why the judges sitting on the bench were, and perhaps still are, keen on referring to human dignity, even where such references were not indispensable. As regards the Commission's decisions and the Court's judgments dating back to before 1998, at the time of the 'old Court', several members of the Commission, and several judges too, were philosophically or ideologically 'Christian-minded', and some were even politically committed Christian Democrats. This perspective has probably been influential in the first Strasbourg rulings based on dignity, and eventually the case law of the Court had to follow those authorities. This is a personal hypothesis of the author, but one based on some experience, and based on discussions with former members of the Convention institutions.

Admittedly, technically speaking, it is not very clear why in some of the less 'serious' matters, the Court has recourse from time to time to the same concept, and why in other similar matters it does not. There is no clear answer. Probably, the special circumstances of some cases, and the insistence by the applicants on dignity when presenting their arguments to the Court, may explain why there is a selective use of the concept. Again, this is a hypothesis, but ultimately it may not be that important to know.[40]

---

[40] The secrecy of deliberations is in any event an obstacle to commenting about recent judgments.

Is there a link between human dignity and human rights?

Certainly, such a link does exist. Leaving aside the philosophical field, human beings are *legally* entitled to benefit from basic rights because of their inherent dignity, at least according to the most solemn human rights international instruments, including the Universal Declaration and the two international Covenants. But it would be difficult to pretend that *all* human rights are grounded in human dignity, or that a violation of *any* human right constitutes a breach of human dignity. One can argue that some technical violations do not normally conflict with dignity as such, but even then, depending on special circumstances, such technical violations could be contrary to human dignity. For example, the excessive length of proceedings in a domestic trial, leading to a denial of justice and finally to arbitrariness, may become a breach of dignity.[41]

This is not, however, the general stance of the ECtHR, at least in its present case law. According to that, only the most fundamental, vital rights are protected by human dignity. That seems reasonable. To infringe dignity, there must be in the acts committed against the victims something especially infamous, outrageous, or disgraceful. This can be logically explained. Historically, the introduction of human dignity in the international texts appeared just after the atrocities and very serious crimes of the Second World War. By contrast, dignity is absent from the classical domestic human rights declarations, such as the English and American Bills of Rights, and the French *Déclaration des droits de l'homme et du citoyen*. Besides, the concept itself would run the risk of becoming devalued, and eventually weakened, by excessive extension of its applications. This is not logical, and above all it is not desirable.

A last question is: is it thinkable that the Court would not refer, or would not have referred, to dignity at all? The answer must be yes, from a strictly legal viewpoint. But reference to human dignity, if it does not necessarily reinforce the legal reasoning, at least emphasizes the *value* of the human being, who is at the centre of a system aimed at protecting human persons against breaches of their fundamental rights. The Court is not merely adjudicating cases: it also has a pedagogical role, and by referring to dignity it thereby sends important signals to all respondent states.

---

[41] There are a few authorities in that respect. Nevertheless, see *Bock v Germany*, 29 March 1989: the Court observed in its judgment that during the lengthy period of proceedings, a serious doubt remained about the applicant's mental health, and that there was therefore an encroachment on his human dignity; clearly, this element was an aggravating circumstance; the Court very probably took it into account for assessing the just satisfaction to be granted to the applicant under Article 50, now Article 41, of the Convention.

PART VI

Applications

23

Justifying Freedom of Religion: Does 'Dignity' Help?

Julian Rivers

Introduction

LEGAL AND POLITICAL THEORISTS find freedom of religion intensely problematic. It is therefore not surprising that when judges find themselves interpreting and applying broad constitutional or human rights provisions protecting freedom of religion, the answers they give to fundamental questions of scope and justification are sketchy or non-existent. In its first case under article 9 ECHR, the European Court of Human Rights (ECtHR) describes freedom of religion as 'one of the foundations of a "democratic society"'.[1] It is 'one of the most vital elements that go to make up the identity of believers' and also a 'precious asset for atheists, agnostics, sceptics and the unconcerned'.[2] Although the case-law under the European Convention has developed extensively since that first decision in *Kokkinakis*, the ECtHR has hardly added to these preliminary foundational considerations. There is no doubt in the minds of the Strasbourg judges that freedom of religion is important, but exactly what it is and why it matters remains elusive.

Normative evasion is a familiar feature of US constitutional doctrine as well. There, the basic constitutional principles are well established, and it is possible to mask one's normative case in the guise of a purely descriptive account of religion. Given an unquestioned commitment to norms of non-establishment and free exercise, all we need to do is determine what is to count as 'religion'. But the moment one abandons historic literalism as a proper approach to constitutional interpretation, it becomes a category mistake to suppose that a semantic definition drawn from sociology or anthropology can fulfil the purposes of political morality. The question which needs

[1] *Kokkinakis v Greece*, (1994), 17 EHRR 397, para. 31.
[2] *Kokkinakis v Greece*, (1994), 17 EHRR 397, para. 31.

answering is a composite one: what is religion for the purposes of our current constitutional principles of free exercise and non-establishment? Answering that question presupposes a normative theory.[3] And such a theory can have a determining effect on how one views seminal decisions of the Supreme Court such as *Smith* on religious accommodations and *Hosanna-Tabor* on religious group autonomy.[4]

Without wanting to gloss over important differences between different states in the liberal democratic tradition, as well as a range of caveats and exceptions, we have inherited a tradition of religious liberty which embraces the following precepts: (1) religion should be voluntary, in the negative sense that no-one should be coerced by law to adopt or hold a religion, or to be associated with persons or organizations characterized by specific religious beliefs or practices without their consent; (2) religion should also be voluntary in a positive sense: people should be free to adopt religious commitments and practices subject only to basic neutral limits protecting the interests of others, and such personal religious commitments and practices should where possible be accommodated in public and semi-public settings; (3) no religion is as such contrary to the policy of the law; only specific practices contrary to a non-religious conception of the public interest should be subject to constraint; (4) co-religionists should be free to form religious groups, which should be autonomous in their own sphere, free from state regulation to a significant and even exceptional extent; (5) the powers and privileges of religious groups should be available to all religions on terms of equality, that is, according to criteria which are not themselves religious and which have a non-religious rationale; (6) public bodies should be non-religious, in the sense that there should be no religious bar to participation in them or benefit from them, and in the sense that they should not fulfil religious functions or purposes; (7) public and religious bodies should coordinate action and possibly even collaborate in areas of education and social welfare in a way which respects the authenticity of both the religious and the (non-religious) state partner; (8) religious people and places should receive special protection from hostile acts, such as desecration and blasphemy.[5]

---

[3] See also Timothy Macklem, *Independence of Mind* (Oxford, Oxford University Press, 2008), 120–4.
[4] *Employment Division, Department of Human Resources of Oregon v Smith* (1990) 494 US 872; *Hosanna-Tabor Evangelical Lutheran Church and School v Equal Employment Opportunity Commission* (2012) 565 US.
[5] This list is drawn from Julian Rivers, 'The right to religious liberty in English law', in W. Cole Durham, Ana Maria Celis and Silvio Ferrari (eds), *God in the Constitution* (Aldershot, Ashgate, 2013, forthcoming).

Growing religious pluralism within individual states also makes an international or globalized approach increasingly attractive in the domestic context. It holds out the promise of an ethical solution rooted in a fundamental commitment to the value of all human beings as equal in dignity and rights. Yet international human rights standards are often considerably lower than those secured in domestic constitutional systems.

First, the scope of conscientious objection and exemptions from general laws (precept (2) above) is protected in international human rights law to a very small extent.[6] Yet within the domestic law of many countries, part of an account of religious freedom includes many more examples of exemptions for the sake of conscience. Furthermore, the religiously informed conscience is sometimes privileged over non-religious moral commitments.[7]

Second, international human rights law is relatively weak on religious group autonomy (precept (4) above). Over the last decade or so, a substantial body of case-law and practice has grown up around the rights of religious organizations to form, register, hold property, appoint staff, and so on.[8] Yet the European Court has been unwilling to draw clear lines around the powers of self-government. Instead, it prefers to see the state as the neutral and impartial organizer of religious life.[9] Yet within domestic systems, it is easy to find more robust examples of self-government—instances which if absent the relevant religious groups would find it impossible to acquire by way of human rights argumentation.

Third, in the area of education and welfare, many states still operate schemes of collaborative or coordinated provision with religious bodies (precept (7) above). Of course, the liberal political tradition varies considerably in this area. But even the USA and France, which have high degrees of separation between religions and the state, accommodate chaplaincies in public institutions and permit religious schooling. But the human rights principle here is also equality-based, not liberty-based. There is no right to offer or receive such services.

Finally, there is a lively international debate about the extent to which domestic laws should contain special provision for the protection of religious

---

[6] In the European context, *Thlimmenos v Greece* (2001) 31 EHRR 15 and *Bayatyan v Armenia* (2012) 54 EHRR 15 represent first tentative steps.
[7] See, for example, the former exemption from trade union membership contained in Trade Union and Labour Relations Act 1974, sched. 1 para. 6(5).
[8] Julian Rivers, *The Law of Organized Religions: Between Establishment and Secularism* (Oxford, Oxford University Press, 2010), chapter 2.
[9] Development traced in Malcolm D. Evans, 'Believing in communities, European style', in Nazila Ghanea (ed.), *The Challenge of Religious Discrimination at the Dawn of the New Millennium* (Leiden, Martinus Nijhoff Publishers, 2003).

believers, or even religions themselves.[10] While the practical enjoyment of liberty may require the state to take positive steps to protect religious believers, such laws can also empower dominant religions to oppress minorities and restrict their freedom in other respects.

The thinness of the conception of freedom of religion in human rights law is not surprising, given the political need to secure wide consensus and the diversity of levels of protection worldwide. The question is whether the 'levelling down' inherent in human rights law is merely the practical consequence of political and religious diversity, or whether its ethical foundations also have a part to play. To put that question the other way round, is dignity capable of generating a theory of freedom of religion rich enough to explain and justify the constitutional traditions of liberal democracies?

Framing dignity: instrumentalism and theology

The search for a dignitarian justification of religious liberty takes place against the background of two groups of arguments which fail to satisfy the necessary conditions for such a justification.

One group of familiar arguments for religious liberty is instrumental. These arguments share the view that it is not in our collective interest to restrict religious liberty. First, there is the view which we can call Hobbist, although it is not Hobbes's own. People are apt to find legal constraints on the religion they follow particularly irksome and lacking in legitimacy. This is likely to lead to widespread public dissatisfaction and disorder. Wise governments avoid interfering with religion. The problem with this view is that it is contingent on the extent of state power and influence. There may well be cases in which the state can achieve its ends successfully regardless of the impact on religious believers. It is also particularly unhelpful as a constitutional theory, because when judges decide disputed cases of religious liberty they rarely do so under the threat of public disorder, and would be likely to resist strongly any suggestion that such consequences are relevant to their decision-taking. Furthermore, the losers in a regime of religious oppression are likely to be small minorities, which are relatively easy to suppress. The argument is purely pragmatic and largely implausible.

---

[10] See Sejal Parmar, 'The challenge of "defamation of religions" to freedom of expression and the international human rights', EHRLR 3 (2009), 353–75.

Locke is famously associated with an argument for religious toleration which can be read in two ways.[11] On one reading, Locke argues that the state is powerless to influence religious belief and therefore should not try. The empirical assumption of this argument is deeply implausible. Of course, in a very crude sense people do not believe things because the law tells them to. But there are both specific instances in which law can influence belief and a general point to be made in response. For example, banning a minority group (or, more likely, one of its distinctive practices) almost certainly has a delegitimizing effect on its social status and affects its ability to recruit. Teaching in schools according to a state-determined curriculum almost certainly has an effect on what people take to be true. More generally, the view that action always flows from belief is overly intellectual. It is at least as true that practice influences belief, so that if the state can change what people do, it will in due course come to change what they believe as well.

On the other reading, Locke is arguing that if the state cares about orthodoxy it ought also to care about the process by which one comes to believe. What matters is not simply correct belief but correct belief held in the correct way, namely by uncoerced individual commitment. Only a regime of religious liberty can ensure that people come to hold the correct beliefs in the correct way. This argument is also problematic. First, the content of the orthodoxy in question may not include (as Locke assumes it does) a requirement that belief be acquired in a certain way. If all that matters to the state is orthopraxy, there is no reason not to coerce. The argument either inappropriately universalizes Christian or even Protestant assumptions, or is merely *ad hominem* in a context of legally imposed Christian uniformity of public worship. But, second, the problems of religious liberty faced in modern liberal democratic states are not problems of state imposed orthodoxy. Rather, they are more typically problems involving non-religious state policies and regulatory oversight which burden certain religious believers or organizations. Within extreme limits, the modern state is simply not interested in what people believe or how they come to believe it.

Finally, we should note John Stuart Mill's utilitarian argument for religious liberty. A regime of liberty is more conducive to the emergence of truth, in all domains, than a regime of coerced orthodoxy. Moreover, it is not sufficient for liberty to be purely intellectual. People must be free to engage in 'experiments in living' that others may judge of their success. Thus, on the basis of a minimal concern for truth and human well-being, Mill is able to

---

[11] See John Horton and Susan Mendus (eds), *John Locke, A Letter Concerning Toleration in Focus* (London, Routledge, 1991).

erect a case for freedom of belief which spans both factual and evaluative claims, as well as freedom of action flowing from belief limited only by some relatively neutral conception of harm.

It should be remembered that Mill is attempting to defend a political theory, not a theory of personal or social morality. He has no problem with those individuals and groups who have committed to an experiment in living. His point is that the instruments of the state and the law should not be brought to bear negatively or positively on them. The true value of their experiment will become more apparent more quickly under a regime of liberty. Nevertheless, it remains the case that Mill's argument seems to mislocate the source of the values it seeks to defend. On his view, freedom of belief is not primarily valuable for the individual believer who is already committed but for the agnostic who is still trying to work out what to believe.

Another quite different set of arguments take as their starting point the impossibility of identifying religiously neutral justifications for religious liberty.[12] They seek instead to root religious liberty within a political theology.[13] It is no accident that religious liberty as a modern political principle emerged in mid-seventeenth-century Europe. It is the effect of splitting the Christian Church along doctrinal and ecclesiological lines on the basis of individual theological judgement. The Reformation took place in a context in which the Church had always asserted its separate political identity toroyal government but had become subject to the rise of royal absolutism. Out of that explosive and at times violent mixture emerged several connected political beliefs: a specific understanding of the nature of religion based on the existing diversity of Christian belief and practice; a commitment to churches as self-governing institutions; a growing view that states should tolerate (more or less) those who dissented from the majority form of Christianity; a belief in conscience as the decisive factor in individual religious allegiance; new institutions for education, healthcare, and social welfare which were at first religious in ethos

---

[12] See, for example, Steven Smith, *Foreordained Failure: The Quest for a Constitutional Principle of Religious Freedom* (Oxford, Oxford University Press, 1995). Harold Berman's argument from religion as a social precondition for liberty tends in the same direction: 'Religious freedom and the challenge of the modern state', *Emory Law Journal* 39 (1990), 149.

[13] Oliver O'Donovan, *The Desire of the Nations: Rediscovering the Roots of Political Theology* (Cambridge, Cambridge University Press, 1996). See also Julian Rivers, 'Liberal constitutionalism and Christian political thought', in Paul Beaumont (ed.), *Christian Perspectives on the Limits of the Law* (Carlisle, Paternoster Press, 2002). There is more cautious exploration of the tension between Christian and liberal approaches in Rex Ahdar and Ian Leigh, *Religious Freedom in the Liberal State* (Oxford, Oxford University Press, 2005). For a bolder thesis see John Milbank, 'Shari'a and the true basis of group rights: Islam, the West and liberalism', in Rex Ahdar and Nicholas Aroney, *Shari'a in the West* (Oxford, Oxford University Press, 2010).

but institutionally semi-detached from churches. These beliefs eventually bore fruit in a principled attempt to disentangle completely the respective spheres of religion and government.[14]

Moreover, this Christian theory of religious liberty can reach back behind a millennium or so of Constantinianism to the first centuries of the Christian Church as a minority disconnected from government power. It can present itself as primitive and—given the normative role of the first generation of the Christian Church—authentic. In due time, other religions came to be formed in this image. On this account, even the meaning of the term 'religion' emerges out of a universalized Christianity. More practically, taking on existing forms was the precondition of their enjoying the liberty already available to majority Christian denominations. Theories of religious liberty rely implicitly on this narrative; Locke's own theory is a signal example.[15] More apocalyptic versions of this approach suggest that reasonably widespread and diverse Christian belief and practice is the social precondition for the enjoyment of religious liberty generally, to which secularization poses a considerable threat.[16] Non-establishment can thus only be a surface phenomenon, masking what is an unavoidable ideological foundation to the modern liberal democratic state.

It is highly likely that the constitutional traditions we have inherited depend on a blend of theological and instrumental justifications. Take, for example, the Lockean argument associated with Frederick Schauer and Brian Leiter which focuses not on the *impotence* of the state in producing right belief in the minds of citizens but on its *incompetence* in determining what the content of right belief is.[17] It is admittedly implausible to suppose that political organs are institutionally designed to act as experts on questions of religious truth. Moreover, their suggestion connects to a familiar feature of case-law in which judges decry any ability to determine disputed questions of religious doctrine. This can have the effect of creating legally free spaces for religious belief and practice. In English law it is very difficult to get a defamation action going on the basis of a religious disagreement.[18] However, the same approach can also disempower religious groups, as when acts which would have had a legal effect absent a religious context, such as the formation of a contract

---

[14] See Rivers, *The Law of Organized Religions*, chapter 1, for the English legal dimensions of this development.
[15] On the religious foundations of Locke's work, see Jeremy Waldron, *God, Locke and Equality* (Cambridge, Cambridge University Press, 2002); David McIlroy, 'Locke and Rawls on religious toleration and public reason', *Oxford Journal of Law and Religion* 2:1 (2013), 1–24.
[16] In Germany, this thesis is associated above all with E-W. Böckenförde. See *Staat, Gesellschaft, Freiheit* (Frankfurt, Suhrkamp, 1976), 60.
[17] Brian Leiter, 'Why tolerate religion?', *Constitutional Commentary* 25 (2008–9), 1.
[18] *Shergill v Purewall* [2011], EWCA Civ 815.

or constitution of a trust, cease to be legally effective.[19] In order to generate familiar features of the law, such as the power of a religious organization to order itself in legally cognizable form under its own organs of government, the court needs to be willing to understand and, all caution and deference notwithstanding, even resolve disputed questions of religious authority and doctrine. The incompetence of the court needs to be bounded by a culturally specific sense of the nature and purpose of organized religions. And that is certainly not theologically neutral.

However, both instrumental and theological justifications—and various forms of their combination—are ruled out in a political context in which the law is opened up to considerations of fundamental political principle. The rhetoric of rights carries with it expectations of justification which are non-instrumental and which are rooted in ethical universalism, not religious particularism. These are the dual conditions for a dignitarian justification.

The good of religion

Theories which fulfil the conditions of non-instrumentalism and ethical universalism can be grouped into two: some seek to show that religion is a universal liberty-grounding good for human beings; others reduce freedom of religion to freedom of conscience or seek to dispense with it altogether.

Martha Nussbaum has recently presented an attractive account which seeks to show that religion is a universal liberty-grounding good.[20] She rejects as inadequate a number of suggestions. Religion is not necessarily about a person's relationship to God; it does not necessarily take a group or organized form; religious commitments are not always strongly felt or experienced as obligatory. The idea that religion concerns 'ultimate questions, questions of life and death, the meaning of life, life's ethical foundation and so forth' gets closer, but this is too dogmatic in a country in which sceptics doubt whether there are answers to such questions. Nussbaum prefers an approach which focuses on the faculty of conscience, but understood more broadly as 'the human capacity to reason, search and experience emotions of longing in respect of the search for ultimate meaning'. It is this faculty, and the space in which it operates, which demands political respect.

This seems to bring Nussbaum very close to John Finnis's account of religion as a rational basic good:

---

[19] *Khaira v Shergill* [2012], EWCA Civ 983.
[20] Martha Nussbaum, *Liberty of Conscience: In Defense of America's Tradition of Religious Equality* (New York, Basic Books, 2008), 164–74.

> Is it reasonable to deny that it is, at any rate, peculiarly important to have thought reasonably and (where possible) correctly about these questions of the origins of cosmic order and of human freedom and reason—whatever the answer to those questions turns out to be, and even if the answers have to be agnostic or negative?[21]

Timothy Macklem is critical of Nussbaum's strategy.[22] He highlights the dilemma represented on one hand by conventional approaches to the constitutional definition of religion and on the other by psychological approaches which define religion as anything that is of 'ultimate concern' to people. The former approach takes traditional religions as paradigmatic and others as protected to the extent that they resemble them. This type of approach is biased towards historically dominant religions and assumes religious value-monism, which he rejects as inappropriate for the modern secular state. Value is irreducibly plural. On the other hand, the line of thought starting with William James, which seeks a psychological explanation of the role of religious faith and ends up widening the definition to include any commitment that is of 'ultimate concern' (Paul Tillich) can only be understood as unacceptably subjectivist. Morality must be based on objective value-pluralism. Macklem suggests that Nussbaum makes no progress by straddling this dilemma and landing on a definition of religion which is merely the middle road between tradition and subjective experience.

Macklem's alternative is to locate the value of religion in faith, understood as non-rational belief. He clearly distinguishes faith from trust. 'Both faith and trust ... enable one to believe and to act in the absence of full reason to do so, but trust depends upon the presence of prior, albeit incomplete reasons, while faith does not depend upon reason at all.'[23] One might think that it is only trust that is valuable, enabling us to deal with ignorance on the basis only of partial reasons. But Macklem asserts that faith can be valuable for some people too. Reasons are not always present to everyone; faith is valuable if it serves a person's well-being in those dimensions of his or her life in which reasons are not available. Two examples he gives are of people who have faith in the resurrection of Jesus, which enables them to cope well with the mystery of death, and theists who think morality can only derive from the command of God.[24] Macklem himself does not think that death is mysterious and thinks that morality can be derived from rational reflection on what contributes to human well-being. But for people who do not agree, faith is valuable.

---

[21] John Finnis, *Natural Law and Natural Rights* (Oxford, Clarendon Press, 1980), 89.
[22] Macklem, *Independence of Mind*.
[23] Macklem, *Independence of Mind*, 136–7.
[24] Macklem, *Independence of Mind*, 145.

On this basis, Macklem defends a theory of freedom of religion. Freedom of religion is freedom for 'collective participation in institutions and practices that manifest a freely given personal commitment to a particular set of beliefs, commitment to which is capable of enhancing human well-being; beliefs that are not based on reason alone but are held at least in part on the basis of faith'.[25] By contrast, non-establishment follows not from its contribution to freedom of religion but from the partial nature of religious-based morals and the need to secure a secular foundation for public life. One further consequence, which Macklem does not note, is that freedom of conscience and freedom of religion become diametrically opposed. Like trust, conscience is part of our engagement with and practical response to reasons.

Macklem's approach seeks to defend the value of religion by reference to the functional role faith can have in a person's life. Andrew Koppelman generalizes and radicalizes such an approach, thus rejecting all essentialising views of what religion is good for. For him,

> Religion denotes a cluster of goods, including salvation if you think you need to be saved; harmony with the transcendent origin of universal order, if it exists; responding to the fundamentally imperfect character of human life, if it is imperfect; courage in the face of the heartbreaking aspects of human existence, if that kind of encouragement helps; a transcendent underpinning for the resolution to act morally, if that kind of underpinning helps; contact with the awesome and indescribable, if awe is something you feel; and many others. No general description of the good that religion seeks to promote can be satisfactory, politically or intellectually.[26]

This cluster of goods both serves to make religions special and to warrant their constitutional position. He thinks it is sufficient to move one beyond mere tolerance to a position of 'appraisal respect' for a person whose religious beliefs are different from one's own.

It is questionable whether either Macklem's or Koppelman's accounts of the good of religion can generate sufficient force behind a claim to a religious right. A person's non-rational belief may ground a weak prima facie duty not to interfere with actions derived from that belief, but the moment there is any reason to restrict action, the non-rational nature of the belief makes it impossible to weigh or evaluate. Or perhaps one falls back on purely subjective evaluations of how strongly a person feels about their belief. No solution to the clash of rights can carry any inter-subjective plausibility. Koppelman's pluralistic account suffers from the additional weakness that it is no longer

---

[25] Macklem, *Independence of Mind*, 141.
[26] 'How shall I praise thee? Brian Leiter on respect for religion', *San Diego Law Review* 47 (2010), 961, at 981–2, footnotes omitted.

clear that we are considering a single distinctive phenomenon of 'religion'. If the good of religion becomes excessively broad and plural, its value evaporates altogether.

Liberty without religion

Some theorists, perhaps motivated by the need to reflect the seriousness of a religious claim, seek to understand freedom of religion instead as a special case of freedom of conscience. Human rights texts put the two very close together, and John Rawls certainly seems to conflate them.[27] Michael Sandel also argues that freedom of conscience is the best candidate for an underlying theory of freedom of religion.[28] Arguments that (political and legal) freedom is good for religion lack a universal basis—it all depends on the religion in question—while arguments that neutrality or separation are good for the state depend on contentious empirical foundations. Focusing on autonomy in the sense of freedom of choice reflects a false view of the person as an unencumbered chooser of what to believe and how to live. Religion is not worthy of respect simply because it is chosen. Rather, freedom of conscience connects to the individual's grasp of truth and obligation. 'Where freedom of conscience is at stake, the relevant right is to exercise a duty, not make a choice.'[29]

Arguments from freedom of conscience are attractive, since there is general agreement that conscience might, but need not, be informed by a broader religious world view. The fact that an individual conceives of her moral commitment as an experience of the voice or requirement of God shows that it does indeed bear down on her with obligatory force. And the location of the substance of the moral commitment at stake in a broader account of the nature and place of human beings in the world warrants its plausibility as a genuinely moral commitment as opposed to mere idiosyncratic whim. But both of these requirements—a sense of obligatory force and a wider account of reality which makes the obligation identity-constituting—can be present and respected in non-religious ways of thinking. The state is therefore protected from distinguishing between religion and non-religion. At the same time, respect for the individual's conscience requires freedom of belief and action.

---

[27] John Rawls, *A Theory of Justice* (Oxford, Oxford University Press, 1972), 205–21.
[28] Michael Sandel, 'Religious liberty—freedom of conscience or freedom of choice?', *Utah Law Review* 3 (1989), 597. Michael Sandel, *Democracy's Discontent: America in Search of a Public Philosophy* (Cambridge, MA, Belknap Press of Harvard University Press, 1996), chapter 3.
[29] Sandel, 'Religious liberty', 611.

To such approaches, Koppelman makes two powerful responses.[30] The first probes the grounding of conscience's force. Koppelman suggests that once any external referent is removed from the idea of conscience, all that one is left with is volitional necessity. The idea here is that we respect the conscientious act because the actor felt compelled to take the stand he did. But volitional necessity is massively over-inclusive. The homicidal maniac also experiences volitional necessity. There must be some connection to objective value, some external referent by which to judge the validity of the experience of necessity. He finds the most plausible suggestion here to lie in Amy Gutmann's idea of the 'will to be moral'. 'The distinctively human effort to conceive and live an ethical life' is itself valuable, even when misdirected.[31] But this cannot be an absolute claim, and the limits to toleration can only be set by reference to what is *actually* an ethical life.

Koppelman's second response is to question how far freedom of conscience takes us. It can only explain a small part of freedom of religion jurisprudence. The category of conscience works well for acts which have a clear moral significance—acts, for example, involving the life or well-being of another human person. But religions cannot be reduced to acts of clear moral significance. Many core aspects of religious practice are engaged in habitually; others are better seen as matters of ritual; still others, such as the appointment of ministers, are essentially administrative and organizational. It seems odd to characterize all religious life in such highly moralized terms.

For many theorists, freedom of conscience is a given, and the really live question is whether there is any grounding for freedom of religion over and above that given.[32]

Ronald Dworkin is perhaps the most well known of those who think not.[33] Dworkin understands dignity to embrace two sub-principles: self-respect and authenticity. These lead us to accept a right to ethical independence, by which he means an anti-utilitarian political claim to judge for ourselves what makes our life go well, and to live accordingly. Ethics is sharply distinguished from morality, which concerns what we owe to each other.[34] This sets limits to our right to ethical independence. Religious freedom is just one aspect of the right

---

[30] Andrew Koppelman, 'Conscience, volitional necessity, and religious exemptions', *Legal Theory* 15:3 (2009), 215.
[31] Koppelman, 'Conscience', 239.
[32] Both Timothy Macklem and Brian Leiter are representative of this approach.
[33] Ronald Dworkin, *Justice for Hedgehogs* (Cambridge, MA, Belknap Press of Harvard University Press, 2011). From a legal perspective see Henrik Palmer Olsen, 'The right to freedom of religion: a critical review', *Scandinavian Studies in Law* 52 (2007), 227–54.
[34] See, for example, T. M. Scanlon, *What We Owe to Each Other* (Cambridge, MA, Belknap Press of Harvard University Press, 1998).

to ethical independence, religion being no different from other foundational ethical choices.[35] This suggests that a specific right to religious freedom is not necessary—or perhaps only pragmatically necessary if religious dimensions of ethical independence are particularly vulnerable. The work can be done by more general rights to privacy and to freedom of belief, expression, and association. Furthermore, the state has no right to impose on dissenters its dominant conception of a life lived well. The non-establishment principle is not merely institutional but also ideological.

Other recent and creative attempts to justify freedom of religion seem to be caught between the implicit adoption of some more or less inadequate account of the good of religion and the conclusion that religion has no special place within liberal political theory. For example, Christopher Eisgruber and Lawrence Sager are well known for their defence of an equality-based argument in which religious exemptions from general laws seek to redress the structural biases of surrounding cultural assumptions.[36] Yet in order to defend religious group autonomy, they argue that privacy arguments apply to religious groups to an extent that they do not apply to commercial or political contexts. Religion is distinctive in being both personal and organized. They claim that religious arguments for conscientious action are different from secular ones in that the state is unable to assess their validity. They are, therefore immune, from being discounted in quite the same way. Finally, their conception of non-discrimination requires reasonable accommodation, which presupposes a certain degree of sympathy for the burden the general law imposes on the individual believer. Indeed, they draw an analogy with disability discrimination and refer to religious commitments as a type of 'moral disability'. This is not meant in a pejorative sense, but simply to highlight the appropriateness of reallocating the burdens of religious practice by creating exemptions.

All these features of their argument suggest that in spite of their intentions, Eisgruber and Sager have not wholly escaped the assumption that religion occupies a special place in people's lives, which the political community must respect. Adopting an equality-based approach which consistently refuses to see religion as special produces exactly the reduction in religious liberty referred to at the start of the chapter. As Brian Barry shows forcefully, non-discrimination norms make it wrong to impose religious barriers to political or economic life; but they also make it wrong to take account of religion in conferring benefits.[37] When it comes to framing a law requiring the

---

[35] Dworkin, *Justice for Hedgehogs*, 376.
[36] Christopher L. Eisgruber and Lawrence G. Sager, 'The vulnerability of conscience: the constitutional basis for protecting religious conduct', *University of Chicago Law Review* 61 (1994), 1245.
[37] Brian Barry, *Culture and Equality* (Cambridge, Polity Press, 2001).

wearing of motorcycle helmets, why should a liberal, neutral state prefer male Sikh motorbike riders over those who just love the feel of the wind whipping through their hair?

Conclusion: the problem with dignity

In the face of such diversity, Kent Greenawalt meets the challenge of justifying religious liberty in a way which has been termed 'eclectic reasonableness'.[38] In his view, there is no core justification for freedom of religion. It matters for a variety of reasons, and that variation should not cause us concern, because the fact that it matters is sufficiently secure.

Eclectic reasonableness is undoubtedly a desirable characteristic of legislatures which have the luxury of agreeing on statutory solutions to political problems without needing to agree on their underlying reasons. For a court seeking to ground its judgments in abstract statements of political principle such a consensual solution is hardly satisfactory. Moreover, Greenawalt himself acknowledges that his eclectic reasonableness is vulnerable to external scepticism. He admits that it is entirely possible that his moderately 'progressive' conclusions on the meaning of the first amendment (i.e., a fairly strong reading of both the free exercise and non-establishment clauses) are derived from his weak Protestant Christian commitments.[39] But we should be more concerned by the internal scepticism which also follows. For example, in responding to criticisms that he is insufficiently committed to a jurisdictional approach to questions of Church autonomy, Greenawalt confesses himself 'moderately supportive' and willing to revise his position. Such flexibility is illuminating: reasonable people find it difficult to decide hard cases and are willing to reconsider their views. In the face of the levelling-down pressure from international human rights discourse noted at the start of this chapter, something more robust is needed.

The two main points of weakness in the emerging theory and practice of religious liberty concern the *weight* of religious claims and the *self-government* of religious individuals and groups.[40] As regards the question of weight, constitutional systems are increasingly recognizing the fact that judges are required to balance competing interests, both individual and collective, in order to resolve difficult cases. While the structure of the processes

---

[38] See, most recently, Kent Greenawalt, 'Fundamental questions about the religion clauses: reflections on some critiques', *San Diego Law Review* 47 (2010), 1131.
[39] Greenawalt, 'Fundamental questions about the religion clauses', 1144–5.
[40] See Julian Rivers, 'The secularisation of the British Constitution', *Ecclesiastical Law Journal* 14 (2012), 371–99.

of reasoning involved is becoming increasingly clear, substantive decisions rest on some sense of the relative importance of the interests concerned. The first challenge is to reverse a creeping trivialization of religious claims.

The second area of weakness concerns self-government. Along with the rest of civil society, organized religions are becoming submerged in a web of governmentality which undermines their capacity to act as counterweights to the state. The regulatory state is displacing the traditional public/private divide. We need also to recapture a sense of individual self-government which is broader than the traditional claims of conscience: the wearing of personal religious symbols provides a case in point. Freedom of religion needs to be understood not merely as a negative liberty, that is, as an absence of law to permit a sphere of religious endeavour (however defined), but also as a positive liberty, that is, as including the capacity of individuals to participate in shaping an individual and collective life *under law* which contrasts with the collective life mediated by the state.

The dignitarian justifications on offer so far seem unable to meet this challenge. And perhaps the problem lies with dignity itself—or at any rate the dominant conception of it.[41] For from Pico della Mirandola's famous oration onwards, dignity locates the source of value in the self-creating human person.[42] This autonomy has always carried within itself the seeds of a fundamental antagonism to religion.[43] In a postmodern context which idolizes self-constructed identities, religions can only be valuable as personal ideologies or world views. They have their value as the projections of individuals, not as (inevitably partial and flawed) responses to what is already externally given. It is hardly to be expected that this can ground the weight of religious claims, both to individual and collective self-government, which we have inherited. Indeed, it is not surprising that its role in human rights discourse so far has been rather to *limit* the right to freedom of religion.[44] If dignity is to do any serious justificatory work here, it will need to be conceived of quite differently.

---

[41] Michael Rosen points out the clear conflict between secular and Catholic conceptions: 'Dignity past and present', in Jeremy Waldron, *Dignity, Rank, and Rights*, ed. Meir Dan-Cohen (Oxford, Oxford University Press, 2012), 90–4.

[42] References in James Griffin, *On Human Rights* (Oxford, Oxford University Press, 2008), 30–2 and 151–2.

[43] Kant's words in the *Metaphysics of Morals* are illuminating: 'Kneeling down or prostrating yourself on the ground, even to show your veneration for heavenly objects, is contrary to the dignity of humanity.' Cited in Waldron, *Dignity, Rank and Rights*, 25.

[44] Christopher McCrudden, 'Dignity and Religion', in Robin Griffith-Jones (ed.), *Islam and English Law: Rights, Responsibilities and the Place of Shari'a* (Cambridge, Cambridge University Press, 2013).

24

Which Dignity? Which Religious Freedom?

Patrick Riordan

There are two levels of debate about dignity, especially as it is used to ground religious liberty. One level of debate concerns the ways in which legislation on rights appeals to dignity, and how lawyers draw on those legal resources for the resolution of cases. There is another more foundational level of debate grounding the concept of dignity in some anthropological, historical, philosophical, theological, or ontological account. This chapter engages in one such debate about how the concept of dignity used to ground religious liberty is itself conceptualized. Ronald Dworkin's redefinition of religious freedom, based on his particular understanding of human dignity, situates the debate (section one). Developing jurisprudence is following the track mapped out by Dworkin. Here the emphasis is on dignity as rooted in autonomy, and consequently religious freedom is valued as the exercise of autonomy. But if this is its value, does religious freedom require separate mention apart from other freedoms? Can more be said to comprehend human dignity? Possible answers relying on a more ontological account, drawing on Martha Nussbaum's invoking of Stoic philosophy in recounting the history of religious liberty in the USA, would have to be secured against challenges of essentialism, and the suspicion of disvaluing autonomy (section two). At the same time the phenomenology of religious experience suggests that religion is not adequately understood as a choice. Because of its foundational nature and the architectonic role it plays in people's and societies' lives, religion poses particular challenges for social order. Hence there are good grounds for fostering a distinctive understanding of religious liberty which does not reduce it to autonomy (section three). While the notion of religion as it arises in current jurisprudence is strongly coloured by the emphasis on autonomy, the recovery of a more ontological grounding for dignity may not require any change in the law as such, because of the law's distinctive purposes, but it could foster a richer public culture and political debate.

Dignity and liberty

What is the relationship between the dignity of the human person and the right to religious liberty? Dworkin challenges the view that religious liberty is in some way special. He bases his argument on the role played by dignity in grounding the claim to religious liberty. He asserts that 'For us, now, dignity provides the only available justification for freedom of religious thought and practice.'[1] Dworkin interprets dignity in terms of two principles of (a) self-respect and (b) authenticity. Self-respect is the requirement that each one takes his own life seriously.[2] Authenticity is the responsibility to shape one's life according to self-chosen standards.[3] From this basic conception of human dignity, Dworkin clarifies first the difference between ethics and morality, and second the political and legal implications of his stance. Ethics is interpreted as the concern with the quality of one's own life, what one owes to oneself in terms of self-respect and authenticity. Morality is the concern with what is owed to others, but for Dworkin, significantly, what is owed to others must be decided collectively within a political community.[4] Ethics and morality are linked: morality—what we owe to others—is essential to living well—what we owe to ourselves.[5]

Dignity requires independence. The principle of authenticity in particular requires that people should have a role in the decisions about how their behaviour is to be regulated. Each citizen would want the dignity of equal participation so that each one is given respect on an equal basis.[6] Autonomy is critical for authenticity, and so it is jeopardized by usurpation, when others' judgements about the goals and values of life replace one's own. Hence the importance of liberty. This liberty must be respected by a political community whose legitimacy is grounded in the equal care and respect due to persons.

Religious liberty is to be respected because the political community owes respect (including non-interference in the scope of autonomous action) to the independence of persons who take control of their own lives. Freedom of religion is conflated with freedom of conscience, freedom of thought and belief, and freedom of assembly. Dworkin links the freedom of religion to what he

---

[1] Ronald Dworkin, *Justice for Hedgehogs* (Cambridge, MA, Belknap Press of Harvard University Press, 2011), 376.
[2] Dworkin, *Justice for Hedgehogs*, 203.
[3] Dworkin, *Justice for Hedgehogs*, 204.
[4] Dworkin, *Justice for Hedgehogs*, 377.
[5] Dworkin, *Justice for Hedgehogs*, 419. See his earlier publication on abortion, *Life's Dominion* (London, Harper Collins, 1993), for his use of this distinction to determine that the question facing a woman considering abortion is not a moral but an ethical one.
[6] Dworkin, *Justice for Hedgehogs*, 391.

calls 'other foundational ethical choices—about reproduction, marriage, and sexual orientation, for instance'.[7] Since religious liberty is derived from the more general right to ethical independence, religion is to be seen as only one of many life-shaping commitments that people are in a position to make, and their dignity, their self-respect in taking responsibility for their decisions, is no different from one kind of life-shaping option to another.

Dworkin's evaporation of religious liberty by conflating it with liberty of conscience is an increasingly popular position among philosophers of law. This involves a significant realignment of the freedom of religion, raising the question of why it would deserve special mention in the First Amendment to the US Constitution and in many charters and codes of human rights. Is there more to human dignity than what Dworkin's account explains? And is there something distinctive about religion which makes it more than an example of another category of event, namely life-shaping choice?

Dworkin's position finds support in a surprising quarter. Charles Taylor, writing with Jocelyn Maclure in a recent work on secularism and freedom of conscience, downplays the distinction between religious beliefs and convictions of conscience.[8] They write with approval of the growing tendency of the US and Canadian courts to treat all sincerely held convictions as deserving of respect, whether religious or secular in nature. And they also recognize the similarity of their stance to that taken by Dworkin in an earlier publication.[9]

Taylor and Maclure note how the understanding of religious liberty being developed by the courts tends in the direction of the individualization (or Protestantization) of religion.[10] Their own account of religious liberty exhibits the same individualizing tendency. Their argument frequently includes a remark to the effect that religious beliefs and world-views are *chosen*, and to that extent they are seen as similar to other life-carrying beliefs.[11] In suggesting that 'public institutions and policies must be guided by the ideal of a society in which all individuals have an equal opportunity to choose their life plan and to implement it', they once again take for granted that life-plans are chosen.

Roger Trigg comments on some of the same cases discussed by Taylor and Maclure, but with a different emphasis. Trigg notes the same dynamic of individualization of religion and the concentration on the psychological

---

[7] Dworkin, *Justice for Hedgehogs*, 376.
[8] Jocelyn Maclure and Charles Taylor, *Secularism and Freedom of Conscience* (Cambridge, MA, Harvard University Press, 2011).
[9] They quote from Ronald Dworkin, 'Religion and dignity', in his *Is Democracy Possible Here?* (Princeton, NJ, Princeton University Press, 2006), 61, *Secularism and Freedom of Conscience*, note 8, 128.
[10] Maclure and Taylor, *Secularism and Freedom of Conscience*, 81–3.
[11] Maclure and Taylor, *Secularism and Freedom of Conscience*, 82.

stance of the believer, but he regrets the development because of its consequence of undermining the status of religious liberty in contrast to the respect given to equality. In the ongoing political movement to secure equality by eliminating discrimination, religious liberty is being interpreted in such a way that when the values conflict, liberty must always be compromised in favour of equality. The reluctance of courts on both sides of the Atlantic to make reasonable accommodation for exceptions on religious grounds entails the risk of discriminating against the religious side in such cases.[12]

Trigg draws attention to instances in which judges have taken it upon themselves to decide what is to count as religion. Judges in difficult cases have been reluctant in general to enter into theological debates about what constitutes religion, or true religion, and have tended to concentrate instead on the subjective stance of the plaintiff. In some such cases, sincerity in holding a belief is sufficient for the belief to count as religious. Trigg comments on one Canadian judgment in which 'a personal or subjective conception of religion, one that is integrally linked with an individual's self-definition and fulfilment, and is a function of personal autonomy and choice', is explicitly espoused in the judgment given.[13] Trigg notes how the judgment undermines any idea of a communal religion, so that it is not the shared belief and practice of some community which is under review but the sincerely held attitudes of an individual person. He sees this as particularly risky. If any belief is to be deemed religious simply on account of the sincerity with which it is held, then it becomes impossible to distinguish religious from other sincerely held opinions, and the freedom of religion is emptied of content. North American courts take a great risk in deciding to understand religion along these lines, but similar dangers are noted also in European and UK court judgments.[14]

These discussions are surveyed here, not to advocate one or other resolution of the cases mentioned, or even to generalize on how religious liberty should be protected in law. Instead, the point is to illustrate how a particular conception of dignity as linked to autonomy is operative in the developing legal understanding of religious freedom. A comparison with the related case of exemption on religious grounds from military service is revealing. Conscientious objection to military service or to engagement in fighting wars has achieved legal protection in the UK, the USA, and in many other jurisdictions. Formerly, objectors had no protection in law but faced prosecution for their failure in civic duty. Gradually, legislators provided protection allowing for

---

[12] Roger Trigg, *Equality, Freedom, and Religion* (Oxford, Oxford University Press, 2012), 117.
[13] Trigg, *Equality, Freedom, and Religion*, 104–5.
[14] Trigg, *Equality, Freedom, and Religion*, 95.

exemption, but originally on religious grounds only. In the course of time, the grounds for exemption were extended to include such reasons which performed in the lives of dissenters the same function which religious belief performed in the lives of believers. The right now accessible for all was originally won for all by religiously motivated people. Interestingly, the courts provided the extension of the exemption by acknowledging that religious belief functioned in a distinctive way in the lives of religious believers. By analogy with that distinctive function of religious belief, they acknowledged that ethical and humanist ideas could perform a similar function in the lives of those who espoused them.[15] The direction of development was clear. What is noticeable now in the arguments from Dworkin and others is that the direction of analogy is reversed: religious belief is to be understood by comparison with the role of life-shaping choices in the life of anyone. And so the question arises: would the judges who first drew the analogy accept the reversal of its direction, or would they consider that something essential had been overlooked? Is the role of religious belief in the life of a believer, as they had understood it, just the same as any life-shaping choice, or is there something distinctive to which they drew attention?

A broader understanding of dignity

How are we best to understand the relationship between human dignity and religious liberty? Martha Nussbaum's 2008 study, *Liberty of Conscience*, illustrates some of the positions and resources for this question as played out in the USA.[16] The non-establishment clause in the First Amendment to the Constitution has required the US political community from its origins to be explicit about the relationship of the state and its law to Churches and faith groups. The demands of a pluralist society require that the state not endorse the particular metaphysical or theological commitments of any one faith or Church. On what grounds, then, might it affirm a distinctive freedom of religion, irreducible to other freedoms, without violating this requirement?

---

[15] The decisive case was in 1965, *United States v Seeger*, in which the Supreme Court ruled that the words 'religious training and belief' must be interpreted to mean 'any sincere and meaningful belief which occupies in the life of its possessor a place parallel to that filled by the God of those qualifying for exemption'. Interestingly, the Military Selective Services Act (1940), which originally allowed for conscientious objection on religious grounds, explicitly ruled out such an interpretation: 'the term "religious training and belief" does not include essentially political, sociological, or philosophical views, or a merely personal moral code' (Section 6(j)).

[16] Martha Nussbaum, *Liberty of Conscience. In Defense of America's Tradition of Religious Equality* (New York, Basic Books, 2008).

Nussbaum makes the case that the strong evaluation of religious freedom among the US founder generation had two prominent sources. On the one hand, she discerns the influence of Stoic philosophy with its account of human nature. On the other hand, there is the Protestant Christian emphasis on conscience. These are not presented in her study as separate sources, since she identifies Stoic influence on the Christian Roger Williams, whose thought on the dignity of conscience influenced the language of the tradition.

Nussbaum finds a Stoic background to the fundamental ideas of the equal worth and dignity of human beings which permeated the debates at the time of the revolution in the USA. In that Stoic background, the notion of equal worth and dignity was explained in terms of a divine spark in each human being, evident in the human ability to distinguish right and wrong, and to form ethical judgements. This capacity found in everyone was deemed worthy of respect, and indeed reverence.[17] The required respect was to allow liberty, and to protect it against subjection to the arbitrary will of another. Hierarchy of any kind would allow some to dominate others, violating the dignity of the subjected persons, who would be no longer free to follow their own judgement. It is worth emphasizing the Stoic focus on capacity for judgement.

Nussbaum identifies 'world citizenship', or cosmopolitanism, as a second important Stoic idea at the heart of the dignity of human beings. The communality in possessing the capacity for ethical judgement links human beings in ethical responsibility, and the duties that arise from it transcend the divisions of people into different groups and parties, and even nations. Nussbaum argues that such awareness of a communality in a shared human nature freed the revolutionary generation from the assumption that a political community required the unifying force of a shared religion.[18] The young nation could not appeal to common ancestry, or ethnic identity, to allegiance to the land or to a shared religion, to find its common ground. That was provided, according to Nussbaum, by the shared conviction that people were united by the bonds of ethical obligation, rooted in the equal dignity of all as sharing a human nature.

These Stoic ideas were wedded to a distinctively Christian idea in the Protestant tradition, namely the dignity of individual conscience. Williams, the founder of the colony of Rhode Island, and the author of its charter, is taken by Nussbaum as the pre-eminent spokesman for religious liberty rooted in respect for the dignity of conscience. Rhode Island's charter in its various editions, renewed by King Charles II following the Restoration, ensured religious liberty in a manner which was recognized at the time as a radical

---

[17] Nussbaum, *Liberty of Conscience*, 78–9.
[18] Nussbaum, *Liberty of Conscience*, 82–3.

innovation.[19] Williams had fled persecution in Massachusetts and attempted in Rhode Island the construction of a form of public and common life which would not rely on persecution of dissidents. In his voluminous writings against persecution and in favour of religious liberty he debated with John Cotton of Massachusetts, who had defended the need to enforce orthodoxy. In surveying this debate, Nussbaum highlights two of Cotton's contentions which Williams had to counter. The first was the widely held view that people could not live at peace with one another unless they shared fundamental religious beliefs. This was the operative assumption in the resolutions of the Treaty of Westphalia (1648). Cotton's second argument was concerned with the required virtues of public officials: they would have to be morally upright to be trusted with public responsibility.[20] For these two reasons, Cotton was prepared to persecute those who by adherence to dissident views jeopardized the harmony of the community. He defended religious persecution as necessary for public order, and to cut away the diseased part of the community which was likely to infect the healthy remainder. In English publications in 1644 and 1653, Williams attacked this willingness to persecute as a 'bloody tenet', and established a different practice in Rhode Island, based on respect for conscience. On the required goodness of public officials, Williams distinguished different forms of goodness, and he denied that the civil integrity of public officials required of them a religious virtue.

Nussbaum argues convincingly that Williams, writing in the mid-seventeenth century, anticipates many of the arguments which Locke will make in his letters on Toleration forty years later. She also underlines the point that the kind of respect for conscience which Williams advocates is not based on scepticism about the capacity of human reason to attain the truth. Williams did not evade the dilemma posed for those who were convinced of the truth of their own convictions, and the error of others' views: how are their views to be respected when they are believed to be false? Nussbaum comments that what Williams emphasizes is not so much the ability to find the truth, although this is not denied, but the sincere quest for that truth.[21]

> The idea that we are all solitary travellers, searching for light in a dark wilderness, led to the thought that this search, this striving of conscience, is what is more precious about the journey of human life—and that each person—Protestant, Catholic, Jew, Muslim, or pagan—must be permitted to conduct

---

[19] Nussbaum, *Liberty of Conscience*, 48.
[20] Nussbaum, *Liberty of Conscience*, 61–3.
[21] Nussbaum, *Liberty of Conscience*, 52.

it in his or her own way, without interference either from the state or from orthodox religion.[22]

The argument, neatly summarized in this sentence, is for effective recognition of liberty of conscience, which is worthy of respect because of the significance of the search for truth in anyone's life. It is noticeable how intellectualist is the interpretation of religious conviction, in contrast to the current emphasis on choice. In emphasizing the sincere quest for meaning, Nussbaum is not denying the possibility of finding true answers. But the dignity of conscience is not dependent on its success. This search for meaning which lends intelligibility and a narrative structure to life is the reason why liberty must be fostered, not so much because the exercise of autonomy is fundamental to the living of a dignified life but because no meaning or set of beliefs can serve the relevant function unless it is grasped and affirmed by people themselves. The act of comprehension is primarily an act of reason and only secondarily an act of will. At stake is the search for an adequate meaning which can comprehend all of life; for the sake of this search, and for the implementation of its results in the living of a life, freedom must be protected. In this sense, Nussbaum's promotion of respect for autonomy is different. On her account, autonomy is not the basic value, but instead serves the more ultimate end of the answers which articulate the truth about the reality of human existence.

Nussbaum's lengthy study offers a distinctive account of religious liberty and its relation to dignity, which is significantly different to Dworkin's account. The valuing of conscience and the human moral capacity as marking out human dignity is open to an ontological account, especially because of the connection to Stoicism. The question of human nature, of the nature of conscience, and those moral powers which deserve respect is raised by this approach. The possibility that something distinctive about the freedom of religion can emerge from such exploration is left open.

Nussbaum notes the orientation of conscience to the truth, so that the kind of toleration which is aimed at in the tradition of religious freedom in her view does not depend on scepticism about the capacities or accomplishments of conscience. Instead, the constitutional tradition cautiously maintains a distance lest the state unwittingly endorse content which conscience should embrace only freely. The emphasis is again on content, more than on the freedom to pursue or embrace that content. Without this emphasis, it would be difficult to make sense of the very strong endorsement which Nussbaum gives to a stance taken by Jacques Maritain, in which the ground for toleration is not scepticism but love of truth and respect for human intellect and conscience as

---

[22] Nussbaum, *Liberty of Conscience*, 37.

capable of attaining truth. Maritain distinguishes different kinds of tolerance, and concludes in a passage which Nussbaum cites twice in full, both at the beginning and at the end of her study:

> There is a real and genuine tolerance only when a man is firmly and absolutely convinced of a truth, or of what he holds to be a truth, and when he at the same time recognises the right of those who deny this truth to exist, and to contradict him, and to speak their own mind, not because they are free from truth but because they seek truth in their own way, and because he respects in them human nature and human dignity and those very resources and living springs of the intellect and of conscience which make them potentially capable of attaining the truth he loves.[23]

Rethinking dignity and religion

Nussbaum's study provides pointers for the two key questions: what more needs to be said to comprehend human dignity, and what is distinctive about religious freedom. On the first question, an ontological account of human nature can complement the practical account of dignity proposed by Dworkin. On the second question, closer attention to the phenomenology of religion and to its social history provides reasons for considering religion to be different. Religious faith is not a choice like other choices, and it is of such significance in social life that it warrants particular attention.

Dworkin's interpretation of dignity is evidently one-sided. Dignity is rooted in the kind of being the human is, but the description of that kind of being is foreshortened to concentrate simply on the capacity of each one to take responsibility for themselves. Nussbaum's study of the American case revealed an alternative emphasis, on the human capacity for judgement. A more extensive account of human nature would expand this basis. A comparison of humanity with other kinds of animate and inanimate beings—the traditional approach of an Aristotelian ontology—can provide perspectives in which the broader grounds of human dignity can appear. Several debates reflected in the contributions to this volume can be read as exploring these grounds. David Walsh's reflections on the encounter with human reality for which he uses the language of epiphany raise questions of ontological grounding, as does Clemens Sedmak's appeal to interiority and to mystery. Simi-

---

[23] Quoted from Jacques Maritain, 'Truth and human fellowship', in Maritain, *On the Use of Philosophy: Three Essays* (Princeton, NJ, Princeton University Press, 1961), and Nussbaum, *Liberty of Conscience*, 23, and 333.

larly, in a theological context James Hanvey points out the need for a more ontological account of the *imago Dei*.

This task of providing an ontological account to substantiate the claims of human dignity will not be completed here. Indeed, many doubt whether it could be completed at all. The spectre of essentialism is raised, not least by moral theologians who criticize a type of physicalism used to generate detailed moral norms. While the dangers of distortion are very properly noted, the risks should not result in a refusal to engage with the questions raised. Nussbaum herself attempts to defend a form of essentialism which she calls 'Aristotelian Essentialism', while rigorously avoiding the associated dangers.[24] Another area of debate in which the notion of a human nature has been controversial, but has also been found to be indispensable, is the analytic philosophical reconstruction of Karl Marx's thought. While Marx himself and most Marxists avoided any discussion of human nature, even to the point of denying that there is any such thing, leading analytic interpreters of Marx point to the necessity of a conception of human nature in which some fundamental constants are recognized. For instance, G. A. Cohen, while noting that Marxists traditionally deny that there is a historically invariant human nature, affirms some facts of experience which provide him with sufficient basis to sketch an outline of a conception of human nature.[25] Other contributors to the analysis of Marx's thought defend their understanding of his account of human nature, while acknowledging how controversial this project is among Marxists.[26] In a theological context, Bernard Lonergan offers a reconstruction of traditional notions of human nature, while retaining the perspectives of historical mindedness.[27] From these discussions, it is evident that the dangers associated with the provision of an account of human nature are well recognized but that they are insufficient to block the effort. For an adequate understanding of human dignity, ontological questions about human nature should not be excluded. If pursued in the Aristotelian tradition, which is by no means the only relevant philosophical tradition for this project, they would note that humans are animals, but qualified with the adjective rational. For instance,

---

[24] Martha C. Nussbaum, 'Human functioning and social justice: in defence of Aristotelian Essentialism', *Political Theory* 20.2 (1992), 202–46. A similar argument is made when she attempts to defend a 'thick' account of the human good which avoids the threatening dangers by remaining 'vague'. See Martha Nussbaum, 'Aristotelian social democracy', in R. Douglass, M. Bruce, M. Gerald and H. S. Richardson (eds), *Liberalism and the Good* (New York, Routledge, 1990).

[25] G. A. Cohen, *Karl Marx's Theory of History: A Defence* (Oxford, Clarendon Press, 1979).

[26] Sean Sayers, *Marxism and Human Nature* (London, Routledge, 1998); John McMurtry, *The Structure of Marx's World-View* (Princeton, NJ, Princeton University Press, 1978).

[27] Bernard Lonergan, 'Natural right and historical mindedness', in F. Crowe (ed.), *A Third Collection. Papers by Bernard J. F. Lonergan SJ* (London, Geoffrey Chapman, 1985).

Aristotle's remark in his *Politics* that it is the capacity for reasoned speech which makes humans political animals does not deny the fact that many other gregarious animals rely on voice to communicate. We humans are of such kind that we rely on reason for a good functioning social order. This capacity for reason and for the purposeful ordering of our lives according to what we know and believe is what distinguishes us from the animals. This notion of humans distinguished from other animals, though animals themselves, is the idea of human dignity.[28] On this account, then, the aspect of human dignity of particular relevance to religious liberty is the human capacity to enquire, to wonder, to seek to understand. It is not only in being a certain kind of animal, a rational one, that the dignity of humans on the ladder of being consists; it lies also in possessing an openness to the most ultimate and comprehensive explanation of reality, whatever it turns out to be. This too constitutes an essential element of human dignity.

Beyond these suggestions for an alternative grounding of human dignity, following Nussbaum's Stoic account, the question remains concerning the distinctiveness of freedom of religion, and why it might merit separate mention alongside other freedoms. The stoic account emphasized conscience, one's capacity for and exercise of moral judgement. Aristotelians would expand this to include the capacity to enquire about ultimate causes and reasons, and to order one's life according to what one comes to know. They fulfil an architectonic function in human life. Dworkin had emphasized the life-shaping feature of choice, and so this architectonic function alone will not serve to distinguish religious liberty as warranting distinctive protection. Another feature of his description was to characterize religious faith as a matter of choice. Maclure and Taylor also seemed to support such a view. But is religious faith properly or adequately labelled an act of choice? The phenomenology of religious faith suggests that the believer is more likely to feel chosen, or called, than to consider herself as selecting a way of life which seems attractive for some reason. Insofar as it is experienced as obedience to God's will, submission to the divine command, which is a common feature in the three monotheistic world religions, it is not primarily experienced as choice but as response. And as response, it is likely to be expressed in terms of necessity, as when the analogy is drawn with falling in love. Alvin Plantinga attempts to provide a reflective account of this aspect by referring to it as properly basic: it is that

---

[28] It is fascinating to note how this idea, though linked to Greek philosophy, is included in the Hebrew literature, for instance in Psalm 8, but also in other passages such as the Genesis stories of creation.

which grounds other decisions and commitments rather than a choice which might be explained in terms of prior preferences or interests.[29]

Finally, consideration of the actual history of the First Amendment to the US Constitution or indeed the history of codes of human rights, points to the elements of experience which led the drafters to see in religious liberty a distinctive ground for recognition and protection beyond the general recognition and protection for liberties of conscience, speech, and assembly.[30] The drafters of the Constitution and its First Amendment recognized that religion posed a distinctive problem for the political community. The experience of persecution and enforcement of orthodoxy both in England and in the colonies of Massachusetts and Connecticut, Cotton's bloody tenet, reminded them that such practice is always a temptation for those who hope to achieve good by the use of state power. And so they chose to ensure two things in relation to religious freedom which perhaps did not require explicit mention in relation to other freedoms. First of all, it was necessary to ensure that the state did not trespass in an area of life in which it had no competence, namely religion, and that it did not favour the views and convictions of any particular group. Note how here again the issue is intellectualist rather than voluntarist: the state should not endorse views and convictions that are beyond its capacities to judge. At the same time, it was necessary to ensure that no religion or Church, no matter how well supported by the electorate, could assume the powers of the state by means of establishment, and thereby impose its doctrines and practices on others. That these were real possibilities was evident to the framers, who did not see similar dangers with other kinds of belief or practices.

Non-establishment is not simply a restriction on what the state may do, it is also a restriction on what any religion may aspire to. It may not seek or attain endorsement by the powers of the state. The non-establishment provision underlines the distinctiveness of religious freedom and marks it off from other freedoms of belief and conscience. The legislators have not seen the need to warn Congress against endorsing with state authority the views of any groups with firm convictions concerning, the economy, the protection of the environment, scientific exploration of nature, or other fundamental values. They recognized something which distinguished religion from these other matters of personal commitment and belief. However that distinctiveness might be described, at least they recognized that there were significant dangers for public life associated with it, against which they saw the need for protection.

---

[29] Alvin Plantinga, *Warranted Christian Belief* (Oxford, Oxford University Press, 2000).
[30] See Michael Perry, 'The constitutional law of religious freedom', chapter 1 of *Religion in Politics. Constitutional and Moral Perspectives* (Oxford, Oxford University Press, 1997).

Conclusion

This chapter distinguished two levels of debate, and attempted a discussion on one level. It resisted an interpretation of human dignity which privileged autonomy, an interpretation which is quite at home within the other level of debate. From within the parameters of its own discipline, the law in liberal democratic polities must privilege autonomy. The freedom of individuals to pursue their own good as they judge it to be is highly respected, and the law takes great care not to infringe on that sphere of freedom unnecessarily. This would be a danger in any instance in which the law would appear to enter into deliberations of people concerning their own good. Their own good they must judge for themselves, within appropriate limits. Those limits include the preservation of such a regime of legislation and adjudication which protects autonomy. Some such goods are to be upheld by the rule of law. When questions of human goods arise, therefore, it is not surprising that the legal perspective tends to bracket those questions and to treat them all together under the rubric of autonomy. Whatever the debates may be about the goods in question, the law concentrates its attention on the autonomy secured for individuals to identify and pursue their own good. It may seem, then, that all the relevant goods are protected indirectly, in protecting the freedoms of people to identify and to pursue their good.

This, of course, is an extreme simplification, but it may have some validity as identifying a spontaneous inclination of the legal perspective. It may explain the tendency to interpret Nussbaum's discussion of liberty of conscience as rooting the freedom in question in the good of autonomy. In fact, as argued above, her discussion suggests a more intellectualist interpretation. This discussion entails no need for a change in the attitude of the law towards freedom of conscience: it is autonomy which is to be respected by the law. But in the context of other discussions, those of philosophy and the political debate about the goods to be valued and pursued in common life, autonomy is not the only or the ultimate good. Where the perspective of the law colonizes the philosophical and political debates, the predominance of autonomy can seem to silence other perspectives. This is the danger with Dworkin's discussion of human dignity. The liberal philosophical tradition's focus on autonomy, reinforced by its alliance with a liberal legal perspective, can envisage only one possible candidate as a philosophical ground of human dignity.

What difference would it make, if grounds other than autonomy were accepted for human dignity? What kind of difference would qualify as relevant in such a question and its answer? Perhaps those alternative grounds would entail no significant change in the practices of the law: it should continue to guarantee protection for liberty and the autonomy of human subjects. But alternative grounds might well entail significant differences in other realms of common life, as in the shared understandings which sustain the public sphere and the political debates in which our polities pursue the ongoing concerns about the quality of our common life. Our resources for discussing the common good may well be handicapped by an inability to consider dimensions of the human good which are not adequately articulated in the notion of autonomy and the freedom secured for individuals to identify and pursue their own good. The quality of public discourse requires literacy and mastery of meaning and argument beyond those required within the discipline of the law.

In conclusion, it is argued that there is a dynamic of constriction in the meaning of religious liberty in present debates, and that this follows from a restrictive reading of dignity. The debates are not only academic (Dworkin) but also in the practice of courts (Taylor and Maclure, Trigg). The restrictive readings can be challenged, following Nussbaum's account of the history of religious liberty in the USA, relying on an ontological grounding of dignity, and a more phenomenologically grounded understanding of religion.

25

From *Imago Dei* to Mutual Recognition: The Evolution of the Concept of Human Dignity in the Light of the Defence of Religious Freedom

Sergio Dellavalle

Can religious freedom be founded on human dignity?

IF WE CONSIDER THE RELATIONSHIP between assertions of human dignity and the declaration of specific human rights in the main legal instruments of the international community, dignity appears to be an ontological foundation of all these rights. The conclusion that might be drawn is, therefore, that dignity can serve as an ontological basis also for the right to religious freedom. Yet such a claim is far from self-evident: rather, the ability of the concept of human dignity to deliver the necessary link between the legal discourses on religious freedom and the pre-legal conditions of peaceful and respectful human interaction depends largely on how the concept of dignity is interpreted.

Within the Western tradition, the concept of human dignity is historically related to the idea of human beings as *imagines Dei*. This connection, however, does not guarantee any convincing ontological, axiological, and epistemological basis for the principled defence of religious freedom.[1] If based on the vision of man as *imago Dei*, dignity depends on the acceptance of a particular relationship between the members of an individual religious community and a divine entity. From this perspective, humans who do not share the religious belief thought to be true by the members of the individual religious community tend to be marginalized, discriminated against, or even persecuted (as discussed in section one).

---

[1] The opposite approach is presented, in different nuances, by many authors included in this volume. See, in particular, the contributions by Julian Rivers (Chapter 23), Patrick Riordan (Chapter 24), and Joel Harrison (Chapter 26).

Modern rationalism and the philosophy of the Enlightenment have developed an alternative conceptual foundation for religious freedom, centred on the notion of tolerance. However, this approach has proven to be as inadequate as the belief-based vision for the purpose of understanding an idea of religious freedom conceived not only as a domain of 'negative freedom' but as an essential element of the self-realization of humans (as discussed in section two).

To overcome the deficits of both approaches, religious freedom should not only be regarded as permitting the members of an individual religious community to worship the divinity in which they believe in the way they prefer, but also—and even more so—as the condition under which humans may address fundamental existential questions through the exercise of social communication. As a consequence, the experience of faith shared by the members of every religious community should not just be 'tolerated' by legal and social norms and practices. Rather, it should be recognized as an essential enrichment of social interaction. On the basis of this paradigmatic shift, the deep involvement of faith communities in the existential issues that characterize religious experience would transcend the horizon of individual faith, transforming particular belongingness into a universal dimension of human communication, thus opening religious experience to intercultural dialogue (as discussed in section three).

The religiously-based approach: the ontological understanding of human dignity resulting from the understanding of man as the 'image of God'

In order to answer the question whether religious freedom can be grounded in the concept of human dignity, it is necessary, first, to consider briefly the historical roots of the concept and, specifically, its relationship with religious traditions and beliefs. There are good reasons to believe that a basic idea of human dignity can be found within the cultural inheritance of the great part of existing civilizations, and in particular of all world religions.[2] In non-theistic religions, such as Buddhism, human dignity can be generally related, as in nearly all moral theories, to the general capacity of humans to 'differenti-

---

[2] H. Küng, *Projekt Weltethos* (München, Piper, 1990); H. Küng (ed.), *Dokumentation zum Weltethos* (München, Piper, 2002).

ate between what is right and what is wrong'.³ In contrast, in the theistic religions—and particularly in monotheism—the exceptional worth of human beings depends directly on God's revelation and on the belief that God gave humans an exceptional position among all creatures.

The religiously based idea of human dignity, however, is always characterized by particular limitations. Starting with the non-theistic approach, the claim to human dignity in Buddhism is not only a relatively new phenomenon, with rather fragile roots in the tradition,⁴ but also embeds the human capacity to moral judgement into a holistic and organic view of the whole world, unlike reflexive moral theories. But if the worth of man is regarded only as a part of a whole in this sense, it becomes difficult to understand wherein lies the specificity of the human condition.

Turning now to the theistic traditions in general, and to monotheism in particular, the idea of a privileged relationship between humans and a personal God seems to be, at least at first glance, an excellent starting point to claim the uniqueness of man. However, what appears to be the specific strength of monotheism can also turn out to be its main weakness, especially as regards the attempt to found the protection of religious freedom on the centrality of human dignity.

In Judaism, for example, although respect for human dignity may supersede Rabbinic law, under certain circumstances, it can never be regarded as generally superior to the highest commandment, namely to honour God and his laws.⁵ Therefore, 'the principle of human dignity should not be used to disregard the laws of God'.⁶ The historical connection between human dignity and religious commandment is also evident in the Islamic tradition. Here we find, besides the doctrinal school of Ash'ariyyah which asserts that human dignity can be derived exclusively from Allah's will laid down in Holy Qur'an, the more rationalistic approach of the Mu'tazilah school, in which human dignity can be drawn from both the Holy Scripture *as well as* rational considerations, although these too should be confirmed in the holy texts.

But it is precisely this kind of final derivation of human dignity from God's will that is the root of the main problem that affects theistic conceptions of the allegedly unique worth of man. If man's distinctive value is drawn

---

³ Ven Dr K Sri Dhammananda, *Human Dignity in Buddhism*, http://www.dhammatalks.net/Books6/Bhante_Dhammananda_Human_Dignity_in_Buddhism.pdf.
⁴ D. Keown, 'Are there human rights in Buddhism?', *Journal of Buddhist Ethics* 2 (1995), http://jbe.la.psu.edu/index.html.
⁵ H. H. Friedman, *Human Dignity and the Jewish Tradition* (2008), http://www.jlaw.com/Articles/HumanDignity.pdf.
⁶ Friedman, *Human Dignity and the Jewish Tradition*, 3.

from an incontestably free decision of the Creator, it will be quite difficult to declare human dignity as an inherent quality of human ontological and social condition. But, if human dignity has to be derived from extra-human sources, it could hardly be regarded as an ultimate good, depending only on what human beings owe to themselves and to their fellow humans. Moreover, if the assertion and protection of human dignity hangs on the profession of faith in individual and distinct divinities by particular distinct religious communities, two further questions arise. First, how can a universal claim derive from the belief of a specific community in the incontestability of a particular revelation? Being based on faith, a dialogue on dignity could not reach beyond the scope of each community, becoming an internal debate within each specific religion. Second, what happens to individuals and peoples who do not belong to the religious community which is regarded by its members as the one and only possessor of religious truth and, therefore, of the true understanding of human dignity? Are those outside not in continuous danger of being persecuted or at least discriminated against?

These problems are perfectly exemplified by the Christian tradition. Christendom is beyond doubt the theistic religion that has most profoundly shaped the Western understanding of human dignity. Christian philosophy developed the idea of human dignity mainly from the vision of man as in the image of God, as first outlined by the Jewish tradition[7] and presented in the Old Testament.[8] In the Middle Ages, Thomas Aquinas made belief in man as in the image of God a central element of his moral theory.[9] This approach was then generally adopted by Catholic theology. According to the Catholic understanding, human dignity has not been corrupted by original sin and is therefore complete and integral in every human being. This embryonic universalism was reinforced by the belief—shared also by Protestant doctrines—that the Christian gospel is addressed to all humans. This universalistic perspective in moral philosophy and theology did not, however, deter Catholic countries from barbaric persecution and enslavement of non-Christian peoples. Nor did it prevent Catholic theologians and philosophers from sometimes crude,[10] sometimes subtle, justifications of discrimination and persecution.[11] Unlike in

---

[7] Friedman, *Human Dignity and the Jewish Tradition*.
[8] The Holy Bible, Gen. 1:26 f; Gen. 5:1; Gen. 9:6.
[9] Thomas Aquinas, *Summa theologica* (Chicago, W. Benton-Encyclopedia Britannica, 1980), II, I.
[10] Juan López de Palacios Rubios, *De las islas del mar océano* (1512–14; Mexico, 1954); Juan López de Palacios Rubios, *El Requerimiento* (1513), in M. Delgado (ed.), *Gott in Lateinamerika* (Düsseldorf, Patmos, 1991), 72ff.; Juan Ginés de Sepúlveda, *De justis belli causis apud indos* (1544–5; Mexico, Fondo de Cultura economica, 1941).
[11] Francisco de Vitoria, *De Indis recenter inventis*, ed. W. Schätzel (Tübingen, Mohr Siebeck, 1952), 92ff.; Francisco Suarez, *De Triplici Virtute Theologica, Fide, Spe & Charitate* (1621), in Francisco

Catholic doctrine, Protestant theologians generally assumed, following Martin Luther's interpretation,[12] that human dignity had been damaged by original sin and could be completely restored only in eschatological perspective. In the best case, the final re-establishment of the perfection of man's privileged nearness to God could be anticipated by strict observance of religious precepts within the communities of the 'elect'. This assumption favoured the establishment of social and legal rules that openly discriminated against members of other religious communities, and even more against atheists.[13]

From an historical perspective, the reference to man as in the image of God seems not to provide, therefore, a sufficient basis for a really universalistic understanding of human dignity,[14] nor a robust justification for religious freedom. This conclusion is not surprising since the idea of *imago Dei* links dignity to faith in a specific, individual God, always putting those who are outside this specific religious community into a condition of potential inferiority. Sometimes, the danger of discrimination could be successfully overcome, while remaining within a mainly religious perspective, by resorting to the use of natural reason, which is generally accepted by theistic religions. Moreover, path-breaking documents issued by both the Catholic Church and the Protestant Churches expressly outlined that 'the right to religious freedom has its foundation in the very dignity of the human person',[15] or reaffirmed the essential relationship between human dignity, freedom of expression, freedom of religion, and the privileged closeness of man to God.[16] Nevertheless, in most historic situations—and still quite often in the present—the assumption of the nearness of man to God did not—and still does not—adequately guarantee universalistic respect for human dignity or effective protection of religious freedom.

Suarez, *Selections from Three Works* (Oxford, Clarendon Press, 1944), 755ff., 826ff.

[12] Martin Luther, *Disputatio de homine*, in G. Ebeling, *Lutherstudien*, vol. 2 (Tübingen, Mohr Siebeck, 1989).

[13] See, in particular: *Massachusetts Body of Liberties* (1641), in W. H. Whitmore (ed.), *The Colonial Laws of Massachusetts* (Boston, Rockwell & Churchill, 1890), article 94, 1 and 3; *Fundamental Orders of Connecticut* (1637), in A. Rock (ed.), *Dokumente der amerikanischen Demokratie* (Wiesbaden, Limes, 1947), Preamble. The tension between the will to protect by civil laws the faith believed to be true, and the awareness of the necessity of an at least germinal guarantee of religious freedom, likely due to their own previous experience of persecution, is clearly expressed in the Puritan *Agreement of the People* of 1648–9 (in S. R. Gardiner, *The Constitutional Documents of the Puritan Revolution 1625–1660*, Oxford, Clarendon Press, 1979, 1st edn 1906), 350ff., articles Ninthly 1 and Ninthly 3.

[14] For a different interpretation, see the contributions to this volume by David Hollenbach (Chapter 6, this volume), David Walsh (Chapter 13), and Paolo Carozza (Chapter 36).

[15] Paul VI, *Declaration on Religious Freedom: Dignitatis Humanae. On the Right of the Person and of Communities to Social and Civil Freedom in Matters Religious*, 7 December 1965, 2.

[16] Community of Protestant Churches in Europe (CPCE), *Human Rights and Morality* (2009), http://www.leuenberg.net/sites/default/files/Human_rights_and_morality%20%28final%29.pdf.

This argument does not imply that it is impossible for an individual to derive a reason and an obligation to respect human dignity from the firm belief in what we regard to be a religious truth. The point is rather that, if we claim dignity exclusively on the basis of religious convictions, it will hardly be possible to convince non-religious individuals as well as members of other religious communities, who share a different faith, of the compelling quality of such an assertion. Belonging to a religious group or faith is ultimately a highly intimate question of conscience, and therefore a universalism based only on religious precepts is ultimately doomed to fail.

The autonomy-based approach: religious freedom as a result of toleration

One result of the ambiguities of the religiously based understanding of dignity and religious freedom has been that the case for liberty in worshipping God or in not worshipping any deity, depending on one's own conscience, has come to be based, since the end of the seventeenth century, on religiously neutral assumptions or on arguments explicitly contesting the centrality of religion in social life. This non-religiously based position was first introduced by John Locke in his Letter concerning Toleration (1689), and developed later into a legal and political position best known for its rigid defence of the separation between public and religious domains. From this perspective, the separation between public sphere and religion implies a substantial indifference by the public power towards religious issues, which are seen as essentially private questions. Locke makes a clear distinction between the nature and functions of the 'commonwealth', as the sphere of public relevance, and those of the 'church'.[17] In Locke's view, the commonwealth consists only in those institutions which guarantee the external conditions for individuals to develop themselves and pursue their interests. Individual actions undertaken to support such developments and improvements fall entirely into the private domain and are of no concern to public institutions. Practices and—in general—forms of social interaction focused on questions of existential significance are completely irrelevant for the public sphere. It is religious communities that have the task of taking care of those dimensions of human life which are, according to Locke's understanding, outside the horizon of public interest.

---

[17] John Locke, *A Letter concerning Toleration* (1689), in John Locke, *Works* (London, 1824), vol. 5, 10.

From this contrasting of public and religious spheres, Locke derives the central principle of his theory, that the state should never intervene in religious questions. Locke's innovative proposal was made possible by a paradigmatic revolution in the understanding of social order[18] initiated by Thomas Hobbes several decades before Locke wrote his Letter on toleration. This revolution marked the passage from a holistic to an individualistic conception of the ontological foundation of human society. In antiquity and during the Middle Ages, individuals were considered as though they would quasi-naturally belong to the social, political, and cultural community in which they had been born and lived. Thus, the community was regarded as not only genetically but also ontologically and axiologically superior to the individual. As a result, the main task of political life consisted in maintaining the cohesion of the community and not in safeguarding individual rights. With the beginning of the Modern Age, the philosophical and political climate changed. Individual rights came to the fore, so that individuals were not any more seen as part of a given and predetermined community but as single entities, endowed with rights, reason, and interests. On the basis of these qualities, they can—and, rationally, should—decide to come together to form a political community, as an act of free will, constituting a society of free individuals for the purpose of improving their life conditions and protecting their original rights more efficiently and reliably.

Through the contract theory of state, philosophers who embraced this individualistic paradigm of social order refounded the justification and legitimation of public power by ingeniously resorting to a traditional instrument of private law, the contract. In the liberal variant of contractualism, the essentials of which were laid down by Locke in his political philosophy,[19] individuals entrust legitimate public power created by the contract with little authority. According to the liberal view, the state should only guarantee the conditions of 'negative' liberty, that is, the private space within which individuals pursue their happiness and improve their material and spiritual lives. Religious experience in all its forms belongs to this space. Religion is relegated to the private sphere and divorced from any sense of public endorsement by the political organization of the community. By doing so, Locke's approach can safeguard religious freedom in a way that was unknown to traditions which had—and have—based it on the premise of man as in the image of God.

---

[18] On the fundamental elements of a theory of the paradigms of public order, see A. von Bogdandy and S. Dellavalle, 'Universalism renewed. Habermas' theory of international order in light of competing paradigms', *German Law Journal* 10:1 (2009), 5–29; S. Dellavalle, *Dalla comunità particolare all'ordine universale*, vol. 1: *I paradigmi storici* (Napoli, ESI, 2011).

[19] John Locke, *Two Treatises of Government* (1690; London, Awnsham-Churchill, 1698).

The conceptual move from the incontrovertible and revelation-based vision of man as in the image of God to this proposal of an effective-because-negative religious freedom is characterized by two important elements. First, human rights, and therefore also religious freedom, are no longer based on dignity as the ontological relationship between man and the 'whole' ('*holon*') (whether of society, of the religious community, or of the universe) but on the free will of individual subjects, and therefore on autonomy. Second, the liberty to worship God following one's own conscience no longer relies positively on an appreciation of the social and axiological value of reflections on the most deep and involving existential questions but ultimately on a negative indifference about these dimensions of human life for the construction of a functioning civil society. Precisely because of the alleged irrelevance of existential and religious dimensions of human life for politics, at least as long as the religious communities do not threaten the cohesion of citizens based on the contract,[20] questions concerning religion are left to the domain of negative liberty, in which men are free since the law is silent. As a result, religious pluralism should be tolerated, rather than positively protected.

Despite its numerous advantages compared with the previous religiously based understanding, the interpretation of religious freedom as a consequence of toleration, and not based on a recognition of the positive value of the plurality of religious discourses, is also characterized by serious deficits. The first problem arises if we consider that the political and juridical institutions are far less neutral than we usually believe; rather, they mirror the cultural, historic and religious tradition of a country. Thus, if the political and juridical institutions of the society do not actively safeguard the general conditions for the free exercise of religious and cultural practices, minorities are likely to be discriminated against in practice.

If this warning against the bias embedded in the alleged neutrality of institutions may be seen as a kind of truism, the second issue is much more complicated and contestable. We identified earlier a general assumption that the religious neutrality of political and juridical institutions depends on their indifference to existential discourses and, ultimately, on the irrelevance of these discourses for other domains of social life. But is it really true that political and juridical institutions cannot actively protect practices of cultural and religious groups without losing the impartiality that is constitutive of a liberal understanding of social life, provided that all groups that are not breaking fundamental laws of peaceful coexistence are equally protected? And is it really a throwback to old-fashioned bigotry if we claim that the whole of society,

---

[20] Locke, *A Letter concerning Toleration*, 45ff.

including also political and juridical institutions, benefits from the lively involvement of a large part of the community in serious and engaged discourse on the existential, moral, and religious dimensions of life?

Dignity as communicative autonomy and the tenets of recognition

In order to sketch the essential elements for a possible answer to the shortcomings of both the previously identified positions, that of religious freedom based on an ontologically founded idea of dignity and that of a merely negative toleration of religious pluralism, it is necessary to find a way beyond the dichotomy between dignity and autonomy, away from sheer tolerance to a more positive mutual recognition. The active protection of religious freedom can be justified by resorting to the idea of a universal human dignity only if we successfully meet the following challenges: a) the concept of human dignity should be separated from having any privileged connections to religious beliefs; and b) religious pluralism should not be seen as a fact that has to be accepted so as to avoid disruptive social tensions or because religious questions do not matter in the public sphere, but should be recognized as an added value for the richness of social discourse.

Relationship with religious beliefs

The religiously based conceptions of human dignity draw the unique worth of man from a source that, at least in the eyes of their supporters, is ontologically located outside human society. Furthermore, in theistic conceptions this source consists in the will of an individual—and thus a particular—deity. If the concept of human dignity is to overcome the shortcomings of heteronomy and particularism, it must be directly founded on human beings themselves, and human interaction as well as human society must be conceived as universal in their scope.

Both steps were undertaken for the first time in Western thought in Stoic philosophy.[21] Before the emergence of Stoicism, ancient philosophy had no clear perception of what can be called the universal worth of humans; indeed, individuals were recognized as valuable mainly as citizens of a *polis*. As a consequence, the only universal features of man were seen in his natural constitution and, to a certain extent, in his general moral dispositions. In contrast, the Stoic claim to the universality of human beings was founded on an inno-

---

[21] J. von Arnim, *Stoicorum veterum fragmenta* (Lipsiae, Teubneri, 1905).

vative understanding of the entire system of philosophical disciplines, from logics to ontology and from ethics to political philosophy. Stoic philosophers conceived human societies as ruled by a universal *nomos*, which, for its part, was directly linked to the *logos*. The logos, which was also universal, was regarded as the logical grammar of the whole world and—together with 'matter' ('ύλη)—as one of the ontological foundations of the universe. Because of this philosophical structure, humans have a unique value as the holders of reason, which is here linked to the essence of the *holon*. Furthermore, this value is a distinctive feature of every human being and has to be generally acknowledged. Beyond the borders of the single polity, men were ultimately regarded, from the Stoic perspective, as citizens of a worldwide cosmopolis. Concretely, the universalistic paradigm of social order is realized, in Stoic political philosophy, by assuming that human beings are distinguished by a general tendency to 'sociability' '*οίκέιωσις*). From this postulation derives the assertion that humankind as a whole builds a universal community on shared values and interests.

The Stoic perspective on human dignity seems to guarantee the fulfilment of the first condition of a convincing approach to developing a truly universalistic understanding of human dignity, namely that the unique value of man does not depend on faith and religious beliefs but on the inherent quality of human beings. This quality is explicitly universal, and the core element of the worldwide community of human beings is built on it.

Despite its important achievements, this Stoic understanding of human dignity suffers from at least three significant flaws. First, the claim to human dignity depends on a metaphysical postulation, namely that man is the highest expression of the 'objective' *logos* of the world, that is empirically impossible to prove. Specifically, if the worth of man derives from his privileged connection to the 'objective' rationality of the *holon*, every epistemological difficulty we may find in determining the 'objectivity' of such rationality would result in a setback of human dignity itself, and such difficulties are very likely to occur. Second, the assumption of the universal sociability of humans is a risky bet in a world that also evidences, besides solidarity, innumerable episodes of indifference and cruelty. If we really want to defend human dignity, we should avoid resort to overly optimistic presumptions and conceive of it as an endangered good, one which deserves to be protected precisely because it is not a naturally given brute fact but a highly sensitive result of civilization. Third, the holistic perspective of Stoicism largely ignores the centrality of individuals; human dignity is disconnected from the distinctive features of the individual use of theoretical and, above all, practical reason. If human dignity has to be understood as concrete, it should be linked to the specific quality of individual action—and not only to the metaphysical essence of man as a distant ontological being.

A first step towards a solution at least to the third problem was undertaken, in the early modern ages, by Giovanni Pico della Mirandola. Inspired by the newly awakened interest in the humanities in the era of the Renaissance, Pico located the uniqueness of man in his capacity to improve himself by acts of free will.[22] In Pico's understanding, human dignity does not arise just from the possession of *logos* by humankind as a whole, and hence from its advantaged ontological position within a rational cosmos. Rather, dignity emerges, as an individual entitlement, from what every single human being can make of this ontological status by means of his practical reason and behaviour.

Nevertheless, even if we admit that human dignity had been reassigned, within the humanistic perspective of the Renaissance, to the free will of individuals, partially overcoming one of the flaws that burdened the metaphysical conception elaborated by the Stoic philosophy, the two further shortcomings—namely the tendencies to a metaphysical explanation of the uniqueness of human beings as well as to the presupposition, in social philosophy, of an unprovable harmonious whole comprehending all humans—remained unresolved. To find a solution to these issues we have to skip many centuries of philosophical history, coming to what can be defined as the paradigmatic revolution towards a communicative understanding of social order.[23]

According to the communicative paradigm of social order,[24] communication always presupposes, in order to work, the mutual recognition by all participants in the discursive interaction. In other words, discursive communication can achieve its goal only if all those involved mutually assume that: a) from an objective perspective, the assertions are true (in the sense that the propositions are referred to real situations or facts); b) from a subjective perspective, the speakers act truthfully (in the sense that they are committed to fair-minded purposes, and are sincerely persuaded that their assertions meet the conditions for truth); c) from an intersubjective perspective, the speakers interact according to the principles of rightness (in the sense that they accept

---

[22] Giovanni Pico della Mirandola, *Oratio de hominis dignitate*, 19ff, Engl. from: E. Cassirer, P. Oskar Kristeller, and J. H. Randal (eds), *The Renaissance Philosophy of Man* (Chicago, University of Chicago Press, 1948), 223ff.

[23] Bogdandy and Dellavalle, 'Universalism Renewed', 20ff.

[24] K-O. Apel, *Transformation der Philosophie* (Frankfurt am Main, Suhrkamp, 1973); J. Habermas, *Theorie des kommunikativen Handelns* (Frankfurt am Main, Suhrkamp, 1981); J. Habermas, *Moralbewußtsein und kommunikatives Handeln* (Frankfurt am Main, Suhrkamp, 1983); J. Habermas, *Vorstudien und Ergänzungen zur Theorie des kommunikativen Handelns* (Frankfurt am Main, Suhrkamp, 1984).

that their assertions have to meet the criteria for a general and mutual acknowledgement by all participants in the communication).[25]

Against the background of the communicative paradigm, human dignity is not based on metaphysical assumptions but is concretely rooted in the normative pragmatics of human interaction. According to this understanding, human dignity is thus not an abstract principle but illustrates the actual *modus operandi* of human beings in their relations with each other. Moreover, dignity is here intersubjective in its essence, since it does not describe primarily a quality of individuals conceived as single and isolated subjects but an inherent feature of functioning and normatively non-curtailed social communications. In other words, dignity is the concept that denotes, in general, the mutual compliance with the conditions of recognition within the pragmatic context of social interaction.

If dignity is interpreted as grounded on the mutual respect of human beings as participants in a discursive interaction based on the criteria for a 'true' communication (truth, truthfulness, and rightness), the question arises as to whether and how dignity should be recognized and attributed also to fellow humans who do not want or are not capable of meeting those criteria. At least two cases are imaginable: the first concerns extraordinarily infamous criminals; the second concerns young children, as well as the mentally disabled or individuals with dementia. Can dignity, understood in a pragmatic and postmetaphysical way, be bestowed also on these categories of humans? The solution consists, first, in considering that communication and the recognition founded on it have not only semantic and pragmatic components but are also highly emotional processes. In this sense, although children, disabled individuals, or those with dementia may have insuperable difficulties in articulating arguments, they can nevertheless communicate—at least at an emotional level—in a way which may be far more respectful of truth, truthfulness, and rightness than the communication that takes place between fully 'rational' and mentally healthy adult humans. Second, when we communicate with other human beings, we do not ascertain only the reality of the discursive interaction. Rather, we are always aware of the possibilities that are enshrined in human interaction as well. These possibilities define what Apel called the 'ideal community of communication'.[26] This is always in tension with the 'real community' but is, nonetheless, indispensable for effective recognition in reality.

---

[25] Habermas, *Vorstudien und Ergänzungen*, 598ff; J. Habermas, *Nachmetaphysisches Denken* (Frankfurt am Main, Suhrkamp, 1988), 73, 76ff, 105ff, 123ff; J. Habermas, *Wahrheit und Rechtfertigung* (Frankfurt am Main, Suhrkamp, 2004), 110ff.

[26] Apel, *Transformation der Philosophie*, vol. 2, 358ff; K-O. Apel, *Diskurs und Verantwortung* (Frankfurt am Main, Suhrkamp, 1988).

Within the 'community of communication'—either real or ideal—humans, although not 'images of God' any more, are nevertheless always 'images of human beings', and ought to be treated as such. Therefore, the most infamous criminal also has to be considered a holder of the value of dignity, in spite of the wrong he has done and for the sake of the good that he, as a human, could have done or even may do in the future, however improbable that may seem.

A second question focuses on the circumstance that, in general, the assertion of human dignity necessarily places human beings in a privileged position compared with all other living creatures and, a fortiori, compared with the non-living universe. This assumption does not imply, nevertheless, that other creatures would not deserve respect for their lives or, at the very least, for their capacity to feel pain. From the perspective of a communicative understanding of human dignity, pleading for the uniqueness of humans only means that respect for other creatures or for the environment is justified, not through our belonging to the whole of the universe but otherwise: by taking into account the moral analogy of our relation to certain living creatures, the indispensability of a safe environment for the quality of human life, or the aesthetic uniqueness of our experience of nature.

From the perspective of the communicative paradigm, the concept of human dignity is integrated by two corollaries that are significant for the present inquiry. First, the boundary that traditionally divided dignity and autonomy is fading away: in the communicative understanding, indeed, autonomy—both individual and collective—is the condition for the realization of a non-metaphysical conception of dignity as the status of mutual recognition; and dignity is nothing less than the guarantee that autonomy does not degenerate into a mere solipsistic arbitrariness, since it always maintains standards of reciprocity and self-respect as prerequisites of a normatively fully fledged social interaction.

Second, the communicative paradigm allows us a better comprehension of the distinction between the religious dimension and the public sphere. According to the communicative understanding of social order, society is the sum of different forms of interaction, each of them centred on a specific discourse. These different forms of interaction operationalize diverse understandings of reason and eventually lead to separate normative results.[27] One of these forms of interaction concentrates on issues regarding the existential identity of the self and of the community. In this, individuals communicate with each other in order to clarify the sense of their lives as individuals and as a culturally specific group. The special context of this kind of communication is the re-

---

[27] J. Habermas, *Erläuterungen zur Diskursethik* (Frankfurt am Main, Suhrkamp, 1991), 100ff.

ligious, *Weltanschauung*-based, ideological or cultural community, held together by shared values aiming to give an answer to existential questions. The values elaborated in this kind of communication do not claim to be universal; rather, they express principles on which individuals choose to orientate their existence. The members of a religious group, for instance, may be deeply convinced that their beliefs are the best basis on which to find sense in their life, but no justification is given to impose these beliefs on members of other cultural or religious communities, for example through legal compulsion. In a liberal and post-metaphysical society, observance of particular principles of life conduct should not be demanded from all members of the society.

In contrast, we speak of a political dimension of the social discourse when the communication is about the political identity of the community, when the members of a society argue about the best ways to address shared issues of public concern. In this case, individuals are not searching for existential sense, nor is discourse centred on identity questions. Rather, discourse consists in elaborating, in an inclusive discussion, the best ways to achieve the good government of society, an order which offers to all citizens subject to it the best possible chances of self-realization and self-enhancement. This distinction between existential and political discourses makes it possible to distinguish clearly the religious from the public domain, without any possible confusion. Nonetheless, neither domain can be considered self-sufficient since each of them, despite its specificity, is interlinked with the other(s) through the role played by communicative rationality: through respect for objective truth, subjective truthfulness, and intersubjective rightness, communicative reason characterizes all spheres of human interaction in which strategic or functional thinking are not reason's last word.

Religious pluralism

If existential—and thus also religious—discourses are an essential component of intersubjective communication, what is it about the plurality of such discourses? Should such pluralism just be tolerated, or is it a value that should be protected? The question concentrates, essentially, on how 'toleration' should be understood. In Locke's view, toleration corresponds to a substantial indifference of the public sphere towards the religious dimension of individual and collective experience. In the history of political philosophy, however, we can find also another approach, which had been prominently set out, at the same time of Locke's writing, by Pierre Bayle. In his *Commentaire philosophique*, Bayle maintains that religious pluralism is not just harmless to political stability: on the contrary, it is a downright blessing for society. According to

Bayle's understanding, religions are in the same mutual relationship as 'artisans' who, though each of them concentrates on his own work, cooperate for the sake of the common good.[28] The different confessions enrich each other through each being stimulated by the others to seek for ever more profound, touching, and convincing answers to religious and existential questions.[29] As a result, religious plurality improves the scope and quality of existential and religious discourse within a society making it, at large, culturally livelier and ethically stronger. The condition for such a positive development—Bayle adds—is that public power should protect the distinct religious communities with the same energy and commitment.[30] The greater danger to society does not arise, therefore, from religious pluralism but from its opposite, from the use of persecution as the violent imposition of homogeneity.[31]

What Bayle is delineating here, therefore, is an ambitious theory of recognition, in which different religious communities reciprocally acknowledge the equal worth and dignity of their respective ways of worshipping God following their own conscience (or even of not worshipping any deity), creating in this way a common space of respectful communication between individual faith, religious identity of groups, and the common good above them all, in a virtuous circle.[32] From this perspective, religious freedom does not describe an empty place, indifferent to public power, but a value worth being actively defended and supported. If we accept that dignity is a communicative value and existential-religious discourses are an important component of social communication, we can assert, at last, that religious freedom is indeed based on the broader concept of human dignity, and that the defence of religious plurality is a fundamental task of any political and juridical institution that cherishes the cultural and ethical improvement of society.

---

[28] Pierre Bayle, *Commentaire philosophique sur ces paroles de Jésus-Christ: 'Contrains-les d'entrer'* (Cantorbery, Thomas Litwel, 1686; English: Indianapolis, Liberty Fund, 2005), 363 (English: 200).
[29] Bayle, *Commentaire philosophique sur ces paroles de Jésus-Christ*, 363ff (English: 200).
[30] Bayle, *Commentaire philosophique sur ces paroles de Jésus-Christ*, 364 (English: 200).
[31] Bayle, *Commentaire philosophique sur ces paroles de Jésus-Christ*, 364ff (English: 200).
[32] Drawing the concept from John Rawls's political philosophy, in *Political Liberalism* (New York, Columbia University Press, 1993), Martha Nussbaum characterizes such a condition as 'overlapping consensus' in *Liberty of Conscience. In Defense of America's Tradition of Religious Equality* (New York, Basic Books, 2008), 354ff.

26

'A Communion in Good Living': Human Dignity and Religious Liberty beyond the Overlapping Consensus

Joel Harrison[1]

THE APPEAL TO HUMAN DIGNITY within religious liberty discourse serves two related purposes. First, it points to at least one, arguably central, reason why religious liberty matters. Judge Marten in the European Court of Human Right's (ECtHR's) foundational Article 9 case, *Kokkinakis*, contended that freedom of thought, conscience, and religion are an essential part of respecting 'human dignity and human freedom'.[2] He continued: 'respect for human dignity and human freedom implies that the state is bound to accept that in principle everybody is capable of determining his fate in the way that he deems best'.[3] Other courts have reasoned similarly.[4] Second, it gives a basis for regulation. Maclure and Taylor refer to human dignity as a constituent, non-negotiable part of liberal democracies because, with other core principles, it provides such democracies with 'their foundations and aims'.[5] Knowing what is at stake when dealing with claims of religious liberty provides a shared basis, on this argument, for guarding against unwanted, unreasonable forms of religion. Thus, European and United Kingdom case law has held that before a claim-right in respect of religious manifestation can

---

[1] I am grateful to Claudia Haupt, Kent Greenawalt, William Partlett, James Nelson, and Yvonne Tew for comments on an earlier draft of this chapter.
[2] *Kokkinakis v Greece*, 1994, 17 EHRR 397, at 436.
[3] *Kokkinakis v Greece*, 1994, 17 EHRR 397, at 436.
[4] See, e.g., *R v Big M Drug Mart Ltd*, 1985, 1 SCR 295 at para. 94-5 (Dickson J) and *MEC for Education, Kawzulu-Natal v Pillay*, 2008, (2) BCLR 99 at para. 64 (CC) (Langa CJ).
[5] Jocelyn Maclure and Charles Taylor, *Secularism and Freedom of Conscience* (Cambridge, MA, Harvard University Press, 2011), 11.

be heard, the religion in question must first establish that it is compatible with human dignity.[6]

While these appeals to human dignity—as a basis for religious liberty and as its regulator—are not entirely settled in practice,[7] they often exhibit a common argument. Human dignity is understood as a central concept shaping the contours of religious liberty, in principle both acceptable to and supported by different traditions. This turns human dignity into a neutral concept, not housed solely in any particular religious tradition but potentially compatible with them. Its content is secular or political, focusing on the freedom of the individual to develop his or her conception of the good.[8]

This chapter identifies problems with this view of dignity and its relationship to religious liberty. Part I critically questions recent arguments from Jürgen Habermas, consistent with other writers, that different traditions can cohere around shared political or secular principles, including an understanding of human dignity, through acts of translation. I argue that the resulting abstract constitutionalism, construing human dignity in terms of equal concern and respect and moral autonomy supports a particular vision of political and social space in which religion occupies a sphere of choice, individual conscience, or style distinct from politics. Part II discusses problems this view of dignity holds for religious liberty, looking at recent writing from Ronald Dworkin. I contend that Dworkin's view of equal concern and respect potentially contributes to problems in religious liberty discourse by reinforcing a paradigm of individual wills being regulated by the state's overriding and uniform application of rules. Part III challenges the view of dignity put forward by Habermas and Dworkin by contrasting arguments from Christian personalism. Human dignity within this tradition of thought concerns a quest for what Jacques Maritain called a 'communion in good living'.[9] Building on this, religious liberty would concern not the pursuit of individual conceptions of the good but rather the formation of bodies or associations in which persons are understood as unique gifts.

---

[6] See *Campbell and Cosans v United Kingdom*, 1982, 4 EHRR 293 at para. 36 and *R (Williamson and Others) v Secretary of State for Education and Employment*, 2005, 2 AC 246 at para. 23 (HL) (Lord Nicholls of Birkenhead).

[7] See Christopher McCrudden, 'Dignity and religion', in Robin Griffith-Jones (ed.), *Islam and English Law* (Cambridge, Cambridge University Press, 2013), 90, at 98.

[8] See John Rawls, 'The idea of public reason revisited', in his *The Law of Peoples* (Cambridge, MA, Harvard University Press, 1999), 129, at 143.

[9] Jacques Maritain, *The Person and the Common Good* (London, Geoffrey Bles, 1948), 36–7.

Dignity: the difficulty of translation

Can a religious tradition ground an understanding of human dignity, while accepting human dignity as a critical regulating and secular norm that may stand over and against, or above, the same religious tradition? The question presents, in perhaps a newer form, a much debated problem in religious liberty discourse and political theory. In light of religious and ideological difference, scholars have sought agreement, an overlapping consensus, over what John Rawls called 'constitutional essentials' as the basis for negotiating, and permitting, such difference.[10] Human dignity has been proposed as one such, perhaps central, 'constitutional essential'.[11] The basic contention is this: different traditions or world views can agree on the value of human dignity, supporting a 'political' vision in which citizens respect each other's different conceptions of the good and equal rights.[12] From such an overlapping consensus, there can be agreement on certain prohibitions, for example, a prohibition on torture or religious coercion, even though, as David Hollenbach puts it, the 'ultimate significance' of such a prohibition 'is interpreted differently in diverse religious and cultural traditions'.[13] This overlapping consensus argument is, I contend, deeply problematic. Put simply, a religious tradition's own understanding of human dignity may be framed within a competing theopolitical vision, meaning that translation to a political conception entails a loss of meaning. In other words, human dignity if found within a religious tradition may stand over and above that religious tradition, but only in the sense that it challenges that tradition with its own voice—to live up to the fullness of its logics, language, and practices.

In his contribution to this volume, Paolo Carozza has noted several reasons to be sceptical of the overlapping consensus approach.[14] He argues that while there might be welcome practical agreement on the prohibition of certain practices, the extent of agreement is always contestable or potentially thin. What practices should be prohibited (beginning and end of life issues, for example), or their specific scope (what is 'coercion'?), are also subject to the pluralism that precipitates the search for an overlapping consensus.

---

[10] Rawls, 'Public reason', 133. For judicial articulations of this, see *Christian Education of South Africa v Minister of Education*, 2000 (4) SA 757, at para. 33 (CC) and *McFarlane v Relate Avon Ltd*, 2010, IRLR 872, at para. 23 (CA).

[11] See, for example, Maclure and Taylor, *Secularism and Freedom*, 11, and Jürgen Habermas, 'The concept of human dignity and the realistic utopia of human rights', *Metaphilosophy* 41 (2008), 464, at 469.

[12] See, for example, Maclure and Taylor, *Secularism and Freedom*, 12.

[13] David Hollenbach, Chapter 6, this volume.

[14] Paolo Carozza, Chapter 36, this volume.

Here, I want to develop further another point of scepticism Carozza raises: that the abstraction from 'deeper ethical sources' when formulating human rights norms leaves us only within forms of proceduralism.[15] A brief look at Habermas illustrates the problem, both for overlapping consensus arguments and, further, agreement over questions of religious liberty.

Recently, Habermas has stressed the state's interest in engaging religious sources that 'nourish its citizens' consciousness of norms and their solidarity'.[16] To what end? For Habermas, the democratic state's political legitimacy rests on a prior 'informal public sphere' in which citizens engage in a dialogue about basic commitments.[17] What results, Habermas argues, is a new form of 'solidarity'. Rather than the unity offered by 'transcendent authority', we find unity in abstract constitutionalism.[18] This is, notably, agreement on 'human dignity' understood as equal concern and respect for individuals' conceptions of the good.[19] For Habermas, then, religion is useful when it helps maintain human dignity, so understood. This, he argues, is a neutral and secular commitment 'transcending the semantic domains of particular religious communities'.[20] To transcend itself and reach this vision of human dignity, Habermas argues that a religion must translate its various forms, language, and argument into the secular idiom of equal concern and respect.[21] The religion thus comes to understand its own basic commitments as underpinning a more universal 'political' logic.[22]

The Habermasian, and like-minded, political understanding of dignity depends on the claim that there exists a form of reason, which, shorn of any religious baggage, will satisfy any right-minded individual.[23] Charles Taylor

---

[15] Carozza, Chapter 36, this volume.

[16] Jürgen Habermas and Joseph Ratzinger, *The Dialectics of Secularization: On Reason and Religion*, trans. Brian McNeil (San Francisco, CA, Ignatius Press, 2006), 46.

[17] See Jürgen Habermas, 'Religion in the public sphere', in Bryan S. Turner (ed.), *Secularization: Defining Secularization: The Secular in Historical and Comparative Perspective*, vol. 1 (London, Sage, 2010), 271, at 283.

[18] See Jürgen Habermas, '"The political": the rational meaning of a questionable inheritance of political theology', in Eduardo Mendieta and Jonathan Vanantwerpen (eds), *The Power of Religion in the Public Sphere* (New York, Columbia University Press, 2011), 15, at 21; and Habermas and Ratzinger, *Dialectics*, 32–3.

[19] Habermas, 'The political', 27, and Habermas, 'Human dignity', 469.

[20] Jürgen Habermas, 'Concluding discussion', in Eduardo Mendieta and Jonathan Vanantwerpen (eds), *The Power of Religion in the Public Sphere* (New York, Columbia University Press, 2011), 109.

[21] Habermas, 'The political', 26.

[22] See also Ronald Dworkin, *Is Democracy Possible Here? Principles for a New Political Debate* (Princeton, NJ, Princeton University Press, 2006), 65 (arguing that religious conservatives should understand the fusion of 'religion' and 'politics' as inconsistent with their own political morality).

[23] See Taylor's criticisms in Charles Taylor, 'Why we need a radical redefinition of secularism', in Eduardo Mendieta and Jonathan Vanantwerpen (eds), *The Power of Religion in the Public Sphere*

refers to this as 'ideological Esperanto'.[24] Habermas is confident that religious language can be translated into universal secular idiom, or at least that 'reasonable' religious language can be. But Taylor analogizes this apparent process to an older usage of translation—a bishop moving from one diocese to another.[25] Such a translation, he notes, entails 'jumping over the boundary. And, of course, something is left behind.'[26]

How is something 'left behind'? Consider non-coercion in worship. In *Dignitatis Humanae*, the Second Vatican Council declared that the human person 'has a right to religious freedom', supporting this claim by an appeal to the dignity of the person as a bearer of conscience.[27] For the Council, this expressed the belief that conscience, entailing a desire to seek truth and pursue the proper ends of life, is moved by and ordered towards God.[28] A person could not be forced against conscience into worship because this would defeat the ends of worship—a subjective assent to one's true end.[29] Assuming an absence of coercion, religious liberty is consequently consistent with governmental fostering of the religious life, understood as including the communal pursuit of justice and peace 'which have their origin in men's faithfulness to God'.[30] But this understanding of dignity, religious conscience, and the pursuit of true ends is not an anthropocentric right of self-expression.[31] It does not, in other words, readily translate into the autonomy-based understanding of dignity proposed in the political account of equal concern and respect. To translate in this manner removes all teleological grammar in favour of a political community whose end is defined, in a proceduralist mode, by an apparent absence of collective or common ends.

Habermas's construal of human dignity and the contrasting construal in *Dignitatis Humanae* can be understood in terms of what Taylor calls 'social imaginaries'. A social imaginary concerns 'the ways people imagine their

---

(New York, Columbia University Press, 2011), 34, at 53.

[24] Taylor, 'Why we need a radical redefinition of secularism', 58, note 13.

[25] Charles Taylor, 'Concluding discussion', 116.

[26] Charles Taylor, 'Concluding discussion', 117.

[27] Pope Paul VI, *Declaration on Religious Freedom,* Dignitatis Humanae: *On the Right of the Person and of Communities to Social and Civil Freedom in Matters Religious* (The Vatican, 7 December 1965), http://www.vatican.va/archive/hist_councils/ii_vatican_council/documents/vat-ii_decl_19651207_dignitatis-humanae_en.html, para. 2.

[28] Pope Paul VI, *Declaration on Religious Freedom*, para. 3.

[29] See also Pope John Paul II, Redemptoris Missio: *On the Permanent Validity of the Church's Missionary Mandate* (The Vatican, 7 December 1990), http://www.vatican.va/holy_father/john_paul_ii/encyclicals/documents/hf_jp-ii_enc_07121990_redemptoris-missio_en.html, para. 36.

[30] Pope Paul VI, *Declaration on Religious Freedom*, para. 6.

[31] See Russell Hittinger, '*Dignitatis Humanae*, religious liberty, and ecclesiastical self-government', *George Washington Law Review* 68 (2000), 1035, at 1046–7.

social existence, how they fit together with others, how things go on between them and their fellows, the expectations that are normally met, and the deeper normative notions and images that underlie these expectations'.[32] This produces a vision of social and political life, containing an implicit understanding of the ends of community. Both religious liberty and human dignity are likely to be central to this vision. How we imagine the relationships between persons, groups, the body politic, and the state, and all of these to the divine, is the substance of religious liberty discussion. Human dignity raises questions of personhood, the autonomy of individuals and their solidarity with one another, the limits of state power, the dignity of institutions, statuses, or groups, and our connectedness to the divine (whether positively, agnostically, or negatively). On Habermas's construal, dignity as equal concern and respect is the hallmark of the 'modern social imaginary': '[the] idea of society as existing for the (mutual) benefit of individuals, and the defense of their rights'.[33] What does this 'imaginary' mean for religious liberty? Dignity takes on the character of bulwark against any religious tradition that would attempt to provide a public vision of justice, solidarity, or the common good that claims an orientation towards true human ends. Further, dignity arguably contributes to understanding religion relativistically as one choice among others. This latter contention is the basis for a substantive critique of dignity in the modern social imaginary, the subject of Part II.

Human dignity: the individual's capacity for self-definition

Liberal theorists of religious liberty seemingly face a paradox. Religion is understood as *one equal option* among many in an age of pluralism. But we also give or have traditionally given pride of place in constitutional texts to freedom of religion. How can we justify this privilege? What is religious liberty for? In attempting to resolve, or rather dissolve, this paradox, several writers have recently contended that religion is a species of the wider category of freedom of conscience or self-definition, which, in turn, is understood as the hallmark of human dignity.[34] In itself, this is not entirely new. Commentators have often sought to justify religious liberty as a species of a more general

---

[32] Charles Taylor, *A Secular Age* (Cambridge, MA, Belknap Press of Harvard University Press, 2007), 171.
[33] Taylor, *A Secular Age*, 160.
[34] Along with Dworkin, discussed in this essay, see also Maclure and Taylor, *Secularism and Freedom*, 90, and Martha Nussbaum, *Liberty of Conscience: In Defense of America's Tradition of Religious Equality* (New York, Basic Books, 2008), 168–9.

concern for personal autonomy.³⁵ But, in this part of the chapter, I contend that there is an increasing awareness of the difficulty posed for religious liberty by such an account. In particular, that it potentially undermines religious groups and dissolves religion into what Taylor calls 'expensive taste'.³⁶

Dworkin notably has argued that religious liberty is only a species of 'ethical freedom'.³⁷ By 'ethical freedom' he means the freedom of the individual to develop 'convictions' which identify 'the value and point of human life and the relationships, achievements, and experiences that would realize that value in his own life'.³⁸ He argues that, as a matter of justice, the general principle of ethical freedom requires that the government be neutral as between individuals' choices of value.³⁹ Any special appeal to the value of religion—for example, the Italian authorities hanging crucifixes in public schools, considered in *Lautsi*,⁴⁰ or any form of unique protection—is discriminatory.⁴¹ The tolerant secular society does not attach any special value to religion; rather, he argues, what is required is respect for ethical choices or decisions as such.

His construal of human dignity flows from or reinforces this account of ethical freedom and political morality, rejecting a distinct account of religious liberty. In his recent *Justice for Hedgehogs*, Dworkin argues that human dignity consists of two ethical principles: self-respect and authenticity.⁴² Each person, he writes, must strive for his or her life to be a 'successful performance' (self-respect), identifying 'what counts as success in his own life' through the cultivation of a 'style' (authenticity).⁴³ Political morality consequently consists in respecting human dignity, understood as the individual's capacity to search for and make a judgement as to meaning. He rejects a religious understanding of dignity, often narrowly construing religion in a voluntaristic manner as entailing following the commands of God to act well, like a 'detailed moral rule book'.⁴⁴ In the absence of this command-based God, which cannot alone give rise to a moral obligation in any event, he asks what morality *really*

---

³⁵ See, for example, Carolyn Evans, *Freedom of Religion Under the European Convention of Human Rights* (Oxford, Oxford University Press, 2001), 32, and Lucy Vickers, *Religious Freedom, Religious Discrimination and the Workplace* (Oxford, Hart Publishing, 2008), 38.
³⁶ Maclure and Taylor, *Secularism and Freedom*, 69.
³⁷ Dworkin, *Is Democracy Possible Here?*, 61.
³⁸ Dworkin, *Is Democracy Possible Here?*, 72.
³⁹ Ronald Dworkin, *A Matter of Principle* (Oxford, Clarendon Press, 1986), 203, and Ronald Dworkin, *Justice for Hedgehogs* (Cambridge, MA, Belknap Press of Harvard University Press, 2011), 338.
⁴⁰ See *Lautsi v Italy*, 2012, 54 EHRR 3 (Grand Chamber).
⁴¹ Dworkin, *Is Democracy Possible Here?*, 61.
⁴² Dworkin, *Justice for Hedgehogs*, 203–4.
⁴³ Dworkin, *Justice for Hedgehogs*, 203–4.
⁴⁴ Dworkin, *Justice for Hedgehogs*, 194–5.

requires. '*We* are the planners', Dworkin writes.[45] And 'we' consists of a collection of individuals who are each an 'ephemeral singularity'.[46] Each person must, accordingly, as a matter of the ethics of human dignity, seek out a 'style' and 'strive for independence'.[47] To do so is to stand heroically in the face of death and a purposeless universe.[48]

We might consider that Dworkin's argument bears some resemblance to the claim, seen in *Dignitatis Humanae*, that truth requires subjective assent. He emphasises the need for 'moral responsibility' – a person must engage in a search for, reason out of, and integrate convictions that grip him or her as a worthy way of living well.[49] This amounts, he argues, to seeking truth; there *is* a way for the person to live a successful life.[50] And, further, he contends that the attempt to live well and go on, hopefully, to establish a good life can be distinguished from triviality – collecting matchbook covers is not 'good in that critical way'.[51] Much of this – including his discussion of the person's life as performance – could fit with a vision of conscience or the person as orientated towards a true end. But there are also points of contrast, and I suggest these might bear upon religious liberty discourse in problematic ways.

As Patrick Riordan discusses in his contribution to this volume, Dworkin's argument for the individual's 'ethical independence' places considerable emphasis on individual autonomy.[52] Dworkin gives primary attention to *the responsibility to inquire* into successful living, within which the bounds of triviality or possible good ends are not entirely clear. Further, authenticity, he argues, requires that the person escape domination by others.[53] This is not simply a concern for coercion. Rather, the person is robbed of authenticity if certain options for living 'otherwise available' are deemed unworthy or the subject of communal disapproval.[54] Combined, these contentions emphasise the individual's capacity for self-definition as the critical hallmark of dignity. And it is this emphasis, coupled with the contention that religion is another form of ethical choice (or even one that should be treated critically), that arguably reinforces contemporary difficulties evident in religious liberty discourse.

---

[45] Dworkin, *Justice for Hedgehogs*, 217 (emphasis in original).
[46] Dworkin, *Justice for Hedgehogs*, 198.
[47] Dworkin, *Justice for Hedgehogs*, 211.
[48] Dworkin, *Justice for Hedgehogs*, 217.
[49] Dworkin, *Justice for Hedgehogs*, 108.
[50] Dworkin, *Justice for Hedgehogs*, 121.
[51] Dworkin, *Justice for Hedgehogs*, 196.
[52] Patrick Riordan, SJ, Chapter 25, this volume, 422.
[53] Dworkin, *Justice for Hedgehogs*, 212.
[54] Dworkin, *Justice for Hedgehogs*, 212, 335.

Here, I point to two difficulties: first, a 'flattening' dynamic in respect of religious groups; and second, weightless diffuse spirituality.

Each individual is to be accorded equal concern and respect as the abstract bearer of a shared capacity to craft his or her own life. The tension this may cause—of individuals, or individuals collectively in the form of groups, encroaching on each other's autonomy—has, as Taylor has discussed, at times led to an insistence on the uniform application of rules against all groups, understood as promoting the individual's interest in equal citizenship through a central sovereign or general will.[55] Eliminating sites of difference, some have called this modernity's 'flattening' impulse.[56]

Consider *Schüth v Germany*.[57] The ECtHR decided that Article 8, the right to private and family life, had been violated when a Catholic parish dismissed its organist. Mr Schüth had left his wife and begun a new family life, from the Church's perspective, a relationship of commited adultery.[58] For the Court, Mr Schüth's right to continue this relationship outweighed the competing interests of the Church. This reflects, I suggest, an outworking of the self-definition conception as it relates to the group. The latter's life is understood as a vehicle for balancing individual rights. This might mean it can maintain its ethos, in respect of priests or leaders, for example.[59] But the inquiry requires the Church, as a general rule, to consider Mr Schüth's self-determination, whether and how this universal right can be limited.[60] On such a view, the group's ethos (fidelity and right relationship) is taken as ground for suspicion.

The controversy over Catholic adoption agencies can be read in a similar way.[61] Continuing provision of adoption services in the UK was made dependent on all providers not discriminating against prospective parents on the grounds of sexual orientation. The logic is clear. Group claims to religious liberty were dismissed despite any contribution to worthwhile ends, as

---

[55] See Charles Taylor, 'The politics of recognition', in Amy Gutmann (ed.), *Multiculturalism and the 'Politics of Recognition': An Essay by Charles Taylor* (Princeton, NJ, Princeton University Press, 1992), 25, 48–51, 60–1.

[56] See William T. Cavanaugh, '"A fire strong enough to consume the house": The wars of religion and the rise of the nation state', in John Milbank and Simon Oliver (eds), *The Radical Orthodoxy Reader* (London, Routledge, 2009), 314, at 326.

[57] (2011) 52 EHRR 32.

[58] *Schüth*, para. 11-3.

[59] See the companion case to *Schüth*, *Obst v Germany* App no 425/03 (ECtHR, 23 September 2010).

[60] *Schüth*, para. 53.

[61] See *Catholic Care (Diocese of Leeds) v Charity Commission for England and Wales*, 2010, PTSR 1074 (HC); *Catholic Care (Diocese of Leeds)* (Charity Commission, 21 July 2010), http://www.charity-commission.gov.uk/library/about_us/catholic_care.pdf; and *Catholic Care (Diocese of Leeds) v Charity Commission for England and Wales* CA/2010/0007 (Charity Tribunal, 26 April 2011).

the group was construed as subject to (a vehicle for) recognizing individual rights, represented by the state's universal rule.[62]

But what of the apparent respect for individual style offered in the capacity-based account of human dignity? Isn't this liberating? Here, I suggest, is a second difficulty worth noting: collapsing religion into a form of style, consistent with appeals to personal autonomy as *the* good, fits comfortably with a diffuse form of spirituality that is weightless against state interests. Dworkin himself wants to ward against triviality, but it is unclear how he maintains the boundary.[63] Consistent with this difficulty, the trajectory of how religion is understood in contemporary cultural and legal terms arguably reflects the modern focus on a capacity for self-definition. We now see the proliferation of individual belief narratives, cultivated by modern technology, the appropriation of religious symbols, the consumption of goods, and the discovery of an inner voice.[64] In religious liberty terms, this is reflected in a capacious understanding of religion and the centrality of individual sincerity (*I* believe I should or must wear a purity ring or *jilbāb*, or set-up my own private *succah*).[65] As Taylor notes, we can give a critical gloss to this contemporary spirituality. While couched in terms of individual authenticity, autonomy, or experience, it is, he argues, often stimulated by a consumer culture in which people are marshalled by corporations into 'mutual displays' of identity.[66] Indeed, if what matters is the abstract capacity for self-definition or the cultivation of identities, then this is at least consistent with the promotion of a ceaseless variety of options within a market. Again, we can see a flattening potential—the abstract maintenance of a capacity to choose is what matters. At this point, religious liberty faces a dilemma: what weight should be given to such diverse, potentially marketed expressions of style or choice when placed against state interests?[67]

---

[62] See further Julian Rivers, *The Law of Organized Religions* (Oxford, Oxford University Press, 2010), 288.

[63] See Cécile Laborde 'Protecting Freedom of Religion in the Secular Age' (*The Immanent Frame*, 23 April 2012), http://blogs.ssrc.org/tif/2012/04/23/protecting-freedom-of-religion-in-the-secular-age/. Laborde queries how Taylor and Maclure (who draw from Dworkin) can, within a subjective paradigm of individual sincerity or authenticity, identify strong evaluations, matters of conscience, or triviality. She contends there is a suspicion this 'piggy-backs' on Christian ethics.

[64] See Danièle Hervieu-Léger, 'In search of certainties: the paradoxes of religiosity in societies of high modernity', in Bryan S. Turner (ed.), *Secularization*, vol. 4: *The Comparative Sociology of De-Secularization* (London, Sage, 2010), 259–60.

[65] See, respectively, *R (Playfoot) v Governing Body of Millais School* [2007] HRLR 34 (Admin); *R (SB) v Governors of Denbigh High School*, 2007, 1 AC 100 (HL) ('*Begum*'); and *Syndicat Northcrest v Amselem*, 2004. 2 SCR 551.

[66] Taylor, *A Secular Age*, 483.

[67] See also the discussion in Julian Rivers, Chapter 23, this volume.

I am suggesting the individual capacity for self-definition understanding of human dignity has implications for state and, indeed, market power. On this basis, recent interest in revitalizing civil society or group-based understandings of religious liberty is understandable.[68] Rivers has argued that in the UK we need to recover a sense of organized religion as representing locations of authority that stand over against the state.[69] And, as he intimates in his contribution to this volume, this combines with thinking of religion differently to current thought: 'as (inevitably partial and flawed) responses to what is already externally given'.[70] Together this potentially envisages, I suggest, a shift in our social imaginary, how we understand the person, the group, the divine, and their relationship to state power under the rubric of human dignity and religious liberty. One avenue, the subject of Part III, is to explore arguments drawing from Christian personalism.

Human dignity: the person as gift

As a tradition of thought, personalism points to the uniqueness of the person, understood in communitarian terms.[71] It sits within a family of movements or political ideas: for example, solidarity, social pluralist theories, advocacy of intermediate associations, and subsidiarity.[72] In this section, I first provide a general sketch of the contrasting articulation of dignity found in Christian personalist writing. In particular, I will focus on one aspect: how this articulation construes the person as gift. This leads, I argue, to an associational account of religious liberty, one focused on religious organizations instantiating and encouraging a life of charity.

In *The Person and the Common Good*, Maritain aligned the dignity of the person with an eternal vocation: each person has unparalleled dignity because each person is ordained directly to God as his or her absolute end.[73] This does not mean, however, merely an extratemporal fate. Rather, Maritain, consistent with later Christian personalist writing, emphasized that ordination to God

---

[68] In the USA, see, for example, Richard Garnett, 'Do churches matter? Towards an institutional understanding of the religion clauses', *Villanova Law Review* 53 (2008), 273.
[69] Rivers, *The Law of Organized Religions*, 295.
[70] Rivers, Chapter 23, this volume.
[71] See Thomas D. Williams and Jan Olof Bengtsson, 'Personalism', in *The Stanford Encyclopedia of Philosophy* (Summer 2011), http://plato.stanford.edu/archives/sum2011/entries/personalism/.
[72] Williams and Bengtsson, 'Personalism'.
[73] See Maritain, *Person and the Common Good*, 12, 72.

is participation in the divine life.[74] God is Trinity: the continual offering of love or mutual bestowing of gifts between three 'persons'.[75] It is this life that persons can claim to participate in now. To be human, the personalist account argues, is to be caught up in the economy of God's life of gift (otherwise understood as grace).[76] This finds concrete reality in participation in a new body—the body of Christ.[77]

The Pauline understanding of the *ecclesia* is central to Christian personalist writing.[78] For St Paul, the vision of peaceful social life is one body—the body of Christ—made out of 'parts'.[79] The one God is manifested through a diversity of gifts exercised for a social whole, 'given for the common good' in Paul's words.[80] One person is characterized as the 'ear', another as the 'eye', the 'foot', the 'hand'.[81] Each person is valued as a unique, complete, and non-substitutable reflection or icon of God's grace, offered to others for the purpose of human flourishing.[82] Importantly, this is not a vision of individuals cohering to one single whole. Rather, personalists emphasize that individuals cohere in different, multiple bodies, parts outside the state. The purpose of political authority is to recognize these parts and strive for their coordination in light of the whole body's life, understood as pointing towards charity.[83] This entails an act of judgement, for if the diversity of talents or gifts is still to be one body there must be a discerning of right positioning or right order.[84] How,

---

[74] Maritain, *Person and the Common Good*, 30. See also Karol Wojtyla, 'On the dignity of the human person', in *Person and Community: Selected Essays*, trans. Theresa Sandok (New York, Peter Lang, 1993), 177, at 179.

[75] Maritain, *Person and the Common Good*, 40.

[76] See Simon Oliver, 'Christ and gift: introduction', in John Milbank and Simon Oliver (eds), *The Radical Orthodoxy Reader* (London, Routledge, 2009), 199, at 201.

[77] See John Milbank, 'Shari'a and the true basis of group rights: Islam, the West, and liberalism', in Rex Ahdar and Nicholas Aroney (eds), *Shari'a in the West* (Oxford, Oxford University Press, 2010), 135, at 155–6.

[78] See Milbank, 'Shari'a', 157.

[79] 1 Corinthians 12:12–14.

[80] 1 Corinthians 12:7.

[81] 1 Corinthians 12:15.

[82] See John Milbank, 'Against human rights: liberty in the Western tradition', *Oxford Journal of Law and Religion* 1 (2012), 203, at 218, and Karol Wojtyla, 'The person: subject and community', in *Person and Community: Selected Essays*, trans. Theresa Sandok (New York, Peter Lang, 1993), 220, at 245.

[83] See, for example, Jacques Maritain, *Man and State* (Washington DC, Catholic University of America Press, 1998), 23. Social pluralist writing also emphasizes the independence of associations. See Paul Q. Hirst, 'Introduction', in Paul Q. Hirst (ed.), *The Pluralist Theory of the State: Selected Writings of G. D. H. Cole, J. N. Figgis, and H. J. Laski* (London, Routledge, 1989), 1, at 17.

[84] See Oliver O'Donovan, *Common Objects of Love: Moral Reflection and the Shaping of Community* (Grand Rapids, MI, William B. Eerdmans, 2002), 31–2. As O'Donovan notes, this can be related to Voegelin's understanding of the community's 'transcendental representation'. See Eric Voegelin, 'The

in other words, do particular institutions or roles—like giving ourselves to one another in marriage, raising a family, becoming educators, or exchanging products and talents (including labour) on just terms—reflect this right order, undoubtedly in creative and different ways?

This vision of dignity—persons as reflections of God's grace, offering themselves as gifts to one another for the formation of a body—points, I suggest, towards religious liberty as fundamental to social life. Concluding Part II of this chapter, I raised the need to characterize religious organizations as representing, or instantiating an authority over against the state. This must mean pointing to a *desirable and true* vision beyond quotidian politics, beyond, that is, the regulation of individual interests through the state and market. The appeal to gift for the formation of a body participates in, I suggest, a recovery of Augustinian themes. Rowan Williams, for example, has argued that the West's historical and contemporary character has been shaped by a Christian conception of 'graded levels of loyalty'.[85] He contends that Christianity set forth a new body entailing the 'optimal exchange' of gifts.[86] This body, he argues, continues to offer a perpetual critique of politics or society understood as merely the 'negotiation of practical goods and balanced self-interests'.[87] It points, however dimly, towards a transcendent universalism, understood as 'solidarities' outside of the state and, ultimately, beyond human organization.[88]

Manifestly, this account draws from the language and shape of 'Church'. Seeking the divine in community with others is understood as encouraging more generally a life of charity in associational settings that have authority independent of state sanctioning. What then of plural religious traditions and beliefs? Any political and social vision will negotiate difference in terms of its constitutive elements—what the community stands for.[89] In the case of the personalist vision, this includes the dignity of the person as gift, a life of charitable association, and the feature of graded levels of loyalty. But the personalist vision also accepts arguably a greater degree of heterogeneity,

---

new science of politics', in *The Collected Works of Eric Voegelin: Modernity Without Restraint*, vol. 5 (Columbia, University of Missouri Press, 2000), 213.

[85] Rowan Williams, 'Secularism, faith, and freedom', in *Faith in the Public Square* (London, Bloomsbury, 2012), 23, at 29.

[86] Williams, 'Secularism, faith, and freedom', 25.

[87] Williams, 'Secularism, faith, and freedom', 35. See similarly Pope Benedict XVI, *Caritas in Veritate* (The Vatican, 29 June 2009), http://www.vatican.va/holy_father/benedict_xvi/encyclicals/documents/hf_ben-xvi_enc_20090629_caritas-in-veritate_en.html, paras 6, 3.

[88] Williams, 'Secularism, faith, and freedom', 31. Augustine referred to this, ineffably, as 'peace'. See Augustine, *Concerning the City of God Against the Pagans*, trans. Henry Bettenson (London, Penguin, 2003), Book XIX, chapter 13.

[89] See Maclure and Taylor, *Secularism and Freedom of Conscience*, 11.

manifested as a plurality of groups, than the equal concern and respect vision. Equal concern and respect renders groups as equivalent, and therefore arguably exchangeable vehicles for individual interests (or the inhibitor of such interests). The personalist vision advances an understanding of groups seeking the divine, and right living in light of this. While there remains a central religious case (rather than a fictitious general religion), those writing in a personalist vein accept that different groups—Muslim mosques or Jewish schools, for example—are reaching at similar goals and often contributing, albeit differently, to an organic whole or quest for human dignity.[90] This kind of conversation arguably already occurs among UK religious communities.[91]

In practical terms, how does this conception of human dignity impact on religious liberty cases? I suggest tentatively a number of possibilities. First, when faced with an individual claiming freedom to manifest a particular belief, we would be much more interested in how this individual claim fits within a wider religious community, rather than sincerity and self-definition.[92] Denbigh High School's consultative approach to determining appropriate modest dress for Muslim girls within the local community is favoured over Ms Begum's sincerely held belief that she must wear a jilbāb.[93] Second, intervening contrary to the self-government of religious associations would be based on whether dignity was being infringed, understood in terms of the group engaging in undesirable social ends that diminish human flourishing. Mr Schüth's claim would be dismissed.[94] To apply a rule requiring the Church to take account of Mr Schüth's right to continue in his new relationship (adultery in the eyes of the Church), even if in certain circumstances such a 'right' is balanced by Church autonomy, problematically undermines the life of the group, which is purposed towards virtuous social living. Third, participation in the provision of charitable care would not turn on the universal application of what Rivers critically calls an 'individualistic conception of provision'.[95]

---

[90] See Milbank, 'Shari'a', 143–4, and Maritain, *Man and State*, 170.

[91] On the presence of such a conversation, see Rex J. Ahdar and Ian Leigh, *Religious Freedom in the Liberal State* (Oxford, Oxford University Press, 2005), 145 (noting the defence of Anglican establishment by writers from other faith traditions). See also Luke Bretherton, *Christianity and Contemporary Politics* (Chichester, Wiley-Blackwell, 2010) 15, 80 (describing a postsecularist space, manifested in civil society, in which religious groups pursue goods in common; Bretherton also relates this to ideas of Christian hospitality and the City of God).

[92] This raises a question of how to identify the claims of a community, and whether courts remain or should remain hands off in respect of religious doctrine. See, for a US perspective, Kent Greenawalt, 'Hands off: When and about what', *Notre Dame Law Review* 84 (2009), 913.

[93] This fits aspects of the House of Lords' judgment in *Begum*; see, for example, para. 36 (Lord Bingham of Cornhill).

[94] See (2011) 52 EHRR 32, and earlier discussion.

[95] Rivers, *The Law of Organized Religions*, 288.

Different groups, such as Catholic adoption agencies and state agencies, could be seen as 'parts' with their own integrity pursuing a shared good (stable and loving child rearing) in different, but not incompatible, ways.[96] Fourth, while mindful of coercion of worship, the idea of right ordering or the common good means that a community will appropriately recognize in public life its shared meanings, representative objects, persons, and histories.[97] Such a shared meaning is likely to have a sacred import—a form of transcendental value beyond the lives of individuals alone. The Grand Chamber in *Lautsi* was, on this basis, right to leave to Italy the decision 'whether or not to perpetuate a tradition'.[98]

Conclusion

I have argued that the search for a neutral principle of human dignity as the source and regulator of religious liberty is illusive. Consequently, I raised two visions or imaginaries for discussion. The self-definition and equal concern and respect vision of dignity, I argued, is problematic for religious liberty. Potentially, it reduces religion to an abstract instance of the individual's capacity for self-definition in a market of choices and gives rise to a flattening impulse, in which the group, rather than being its own site of authority, is understood as the vehicle for abstract individual rights. In contrast, the personalist vision understands human dignity in terms of the person's status as a gift to others and social wholes. This recognizes that we cohere in different, multiple bodies. In religious liberty terms, the personalist account focuses on associating well—pursuing virtuous living, the love of God and of neighbour. Such bodies, seeking a common or right order discernible through our different talents and gifts, constitute their own authority, capable of offering resistance to the power of the state and market. This, it is hoped, is a faithful image of the person and a possible basis for a revitalized religious liberty discourse.

---

[96] See *Catholic Care (Diocese of Leeds) v Charity Commission for England and Wales*, 2010, PTSR 1074 (HC); *Catholic Care (Diocese of Leeds)* (Charity Commission, 21 July 2010), http://www.charity-commission.gov.uk/library/about_us/catholic_care.pdf; and *Catholic Care (Diocese of Leeds) v Charity Commission for England and Wales* CA/2010/0007 (Charity Tribunal, 26 April 2011), and the accompanying text to footnote 62. An argument of this nature is begun in Milbank, 'Shari'a', 144.
[97] See Oliver O'Donovan, *Common Objects of Love*, 31–2, and Voegelin, 'The new science of politics', 213.
[98] *Lautsi*, para. 68.

27

Dignity and Disgrace: Moral Citizenship and Constitutional Protection

Edwin Cameron[1]

Introduction and summary: explaining the role of dignity

WHY HAS DIGNITY TAKEN such a central place in South Africa's constitutional jurisprudence? And what does it tell us about the fact that South Africa's Constitution was the first anywhere that expressly outlawed discrimination based on sexual orientation, and one of the first to extend equal rights to marry to lesbian and gay couples? The puzzle is worth unravelling.

On a visit to the Constitutional Court of South Africa in February 2010, Professor Catharine MacKinnon, who described herself as the pioneer of the 'substantive equality' approach to rights, forcefully expressed her bemusement that the court's equality jurisprudence centred on the right to dignity.[2] MacKinnon has recognized that 'deprivation of dignity is often a powerful dimension of the substance of inequality and does some of its work'. But she has also asserted that ascribing dignity to humans, particularly when employed in the Kantian sense of their unconditional and incomparable worth,[3] is simply inadequate to address certain social practices or relationships that undermine it, or instances where individuals willingly relinquish it.[4]

---

[1] I am greatly indebted to my law clerks Samantha Bent, Michael Mbikiwa, and Claire Avidon for helping develop and set out the ideas in this chapter, and to Pia Dutton for helping to finalize it.
[2] Professor MacKinnon declared, 'As the pioneer of the substantive equality approach, I just don't get why anyone thinks dignity has to do the work' (Personal communication).
[3] Kant *Fundamental Principles of the Metaphysic of Morals*, trans. Thomas Kingsmill Abbott (1785).
[4] Catharine MacKinnon, 'Substantive equality: a perspective', *Minnesota Law Review* 96:2 (2011), 1–27, at 10. Professor MacKinnon castigates the US Supreme Court for failing to undertake a substantive equality analysis of the statute outlawed in the same-sex sodomy case, *Lawrence Texas*, 539 US 558 (2003). Implicit in her critique seems the belief that dignity, while serving a powerful rhetorical purpose, cannot replace a substantive equality analysis. See 'The road not taken: sex equality in Lawrence Texas', *Ohio State Law Journal* 65 (2004), 1081–95.

Yet there is sound reason why dignity, for all its indeterminacy, has taken so central a place in the formative jurisprudence of the court. It is to be found in South Africa's past of racial indignity—where racial subordination was both premised on and itself enacted shamefulness and disgrace. Apartheid laws deprived black South Africans of their citizenship, gave them education that was inferior to whites', segregated and confined them on land both urban and rural, and relegated them to poorer jobs and economic roles.

But those laws represented, and did, more. They derived from the view that black South Africans were subordinate and inferior humans, and treated them accordingly. They enunciated and practised the condition of 'non-whiteness' as legally shameful. I grew up in apartheid South Africa in a desperately poor and fractured white family. But I was glad not to be black. At home, at school, and on the street, my daily consciousness was imbued with a sense and gratitude that, at least, I was white. The shame of being black, not only with the legal impediments and subordinations that marked it, but with the stigmatized condition those impediments implied, was not mine. My humanness was superior: unshamefully white.[5]

In this way, apartheid laws damaged both white and black, by stigmatizing black people, placing a mark of shame on their race, and by injuring white people with a false conception of superiority.[6] This legacy re-emerges vividly in persisting, acrid controversy about race in South African society.[7]

But, like other, less racist, societies, apartheid created also a further category of subordination and shame: that of deviant sexuality. There, too, the law stigmatized and persecuted a condition that was seen as undesirably shameful: homosexuality and same-sex sexual conduct. Of that category I was shamefully part. I was gay in an otherwise heterosexual world, a world that would accommodate me only to the extent that I managed to pretend that I was straight.

---

[5] In a statement attributed to him in the *Boston Globe* of 25 October 1977, after his death, black consciousness activist Stephen Bantu Biko said, 'whites must be made to realize that they are only human, not superior. Same with blacks. They must be made to realize that they are also human, not inferior.' Sourced from http://en.wikiquote.org/wiki/Steve_Biko.

[6] Aubrey Masango, 'Constructive criticism: if we can't give it who can?' *Daily Maverick* (2 October 2012), highlights Steve Biko's description of the contorted sense of self apartheid could create: http://dailymaverick.co.za/opinionista/2012-10-02-constructive-criticism-if-we-cant-give-it-who-can.

[7] That this past still haunts us emerged in a recent controversy where an artist, Brett Murray, painted a portrait of President Jacob Zuma, which was displayed for sale in a commercial art gallery in Johannesburg. The portrait was based on a famous image of Vladimir Lenin. But, unlike the original, this portrait portrayed the figure represented with fully naked genitals. This elicited an impassioned reaction. The portrait was seen as shameful. It was criticized as degrading to the dignity of black people, and as rekindling the past where blacks were subordinated and shamed.

When it came to determining the ambit of constitutional protection, those negotiating for gays and lesbians could plausibly contend that including sexual orientation as a protected condition was analogous to including race—both conditions had been harshly stigmatized under apartheid, and both had been subjected to severe indignity. By this path, the generous embrace of equality and non-discrimination was extended to sexual orientation. That same spirit has been evident in the Constitutional Court's jurisprudence.[8] In this chapter, I argue that the inclusion of sexual orientation as a protected ground in South Africa's Constitution, and the court's vigorous assertion of sexual orientation equality, can be fully understood only by understanding the indignity apartheid's racialized assault inflicted on black South Africans. That this protection has been based so centrally on asserting the inherent dignity of all reflects the continuing palpability of a past of indignity and shame.

Legal stigma and moral citizenship

In 1963, in a justly famous analysis, the sociologist Erving Goffman identified the 'structural preconditions' of stigma as consisting in a trait or attribute that amounts to an 'undesired differentness'—one that contravenes society's expectations or the standards upon which collective identity is predicated.[9] Stigma arises because society, through its social settings, laws, cultural practices, and policies, creates a structure and language for categorizing people, and hence for identifying qualities that are regarded ordinary or 'natural'.[10] These take on a normative meaning, which entails that those who cannot meet them are 'discredited'.[11] Discrediting confers an inferior social status, and concomitantly, less power and access to resources.[12] This is the essence of social stigma, and it takes little imagination to see that apartheid legal institutions systematically 'discredited' black people.

At its most brutal, the legal apparatus of apartheid denied black South Africans the vote, land, freedom of movement, jobs, public office, educational

---

[8] *Minister of Home Affairs v Fourie*, (2005), ZACC 19; 2006 (1) SA 524; *National Coalition for Gay and Lesbian Equality v Minister of Home Affairs*, (1999) ZACC 17; 2000 (2) SA 1;.
[9] Erving Goffman, *Stigma: Notes on the Management of Spoiled Identity* (New York, Simon & Schuster, 1986), 5–6.
[10] Goffman, *Stigma*, 2.
[11] Goffman, *Stigma*, 2. See also Gregory Herek et al., 'Sexual stigma: putting sexual minority health issues in context', in I. Meyer and M. Northridge (eds), *The Health of Sexual Minorities: Public Health Perspectives on Lesbian, Gay, Bisexual, and Transgender Populations* (New York, Springer, 2007), at 1.
[12] Herek et al., 'Sexual stigma', 2.

opportunity, the capacity to learn in their own languages, and the liberty to choose their sexual partners and spouses. It deprived them even of their South African citizenship. The process of degradation of civic status started with the European settlement of South Africa in the seventeenth century.[13] Over time, successive white governments made laws that regulated both the public and the most intimate aspects of people's lives, and in particular, placed onerous restrictions on the movements, relationships, and economic choices of black people.[14]

Perhaps the most oppressive embodiment of this control was the pass laws,[15] which required black people at all times to carry a document that denoted permission to be in a particular city or location for a specific purpose. The pass came to symbolize the viciousness and pettiness of apartheid. To be caught without a pass was a crime. Many hundreds of thousands of black South Africans were arrested every year for violating these laws,[16] and sentenced to jail terms, generally short but often repeated. The very spectre of arrest dominated black urban life. In this way, apartheid made criminals of a large proportion of South Africa's adult population. The system of discrimination, constraint, and denial required black people to collide, at every turn, with an omnipresent legal machinery that regulated their lives. The laws sought to erect and entrench 'separateness'. Necessarily, they embodied a pervasive strategy of repression and domination.[17] But they did more than this. They branded black South Africans as inferior.[18]

---

[13] See Lawrie Schlemmer, 'The factors underlying apartheid', in Peter Randall (ed.), *Anatomy of Apartheid* (Johannesburg, Spro-Cas, 1970), 20–1 (noting that master-slave relationships beginning in Cape Colony of the seventeenth-century established blackness as a badge of inferiority that has persisted throughout the country's history). See also Nigel Worden, *The Making of Modern South Africa: Conquest, Apartheid, and Democracy*, 3rd edn (Chichester Wiley-Blackwell, 2000).

[14] 'Black', unless I mention otherwise (specifically where I quote Stephen Bantu Biko), refers to people characterized as 'Bantu' or 'African' by the apartheid-era government.

[15] For the history of 'passes' in South Africa, see Worden, *The Making of Modern South Africa*, 74–80. For a comprehensive overview, *see* Muriel Horrell, *Laws Affecting Race Relations in South Africa (To the End of 1976)* 171–95 (Johannesburg, South African Institute of Race Relations, 1978).

[16] See John F. Burns, '"Pass" laws, aspect of apartheid Blacks hate most, bring despair and pent-up fury', *New York Times* (24 May 1978). Burns notes that in 1977, of the more than 400,000 black people arrested for violating the pass laws, more than 200,000 black people received a jail sentence. See also Worden, *The Making of Modern South Africa*, 81, and Thomas Karis and Gail Gerhart (eds), *From Protest to Challenge: A Documentary History of African Politics in South Africa—Challenge and Violence (1882–1964)* (Stanford, Hoover Institute Press, 1977), 250–1.

[17] *See* Max Coleman (ed.), *A Crime Against Humanity: Analysing the Repression of the Apartheid State* 13–27 (Johannesburg, Human Rights Committee, 1998).

[18] For a judicial reflection on the apartheid era's systematic discrimination against black people, *see Brink v Kitshoff* NO 2996 (4) SA 197 (CC), para. 40.

The effect of apartheid's laws in 'discrediting' black people in this way was fiercely contested: indeed, it was the cause of an externally based liberation struggle and a massive internal rebellion. But the legal meaning of apartheid was to subordinate, discredit, and stigmatize blackness. That meaning inflicted injury on all who lived under it, black and white.

The injury was also subsumed internally.[19] The American W. E. B. Du Bois articulated how this may happen. He spoke of a world that yielded an African-American descendant of slaves 'no true self-consciousness, but only lets him see himself through the revelation of the other world';[20] thus creating a sense of 'measuring one's soul by the tape of a world that looks on in amused contempt and pity'. But whose tape is to be used in this measurement? This question was taken up fiercely and eloquently by Stephen Bantu Biko, the young activist beaten to death in police detention in September 1977. He saw black people's struggle against racial categorization, restriction, and control as being against 'forces that seek to use your blackness as a stamp that marks you out as a subservient being'.[21] He asserted a counter-consciousness, an assertive black consciousness, that sought 'to infuse the black community with a new-found pride in themselves, their efforts, their value systems, their culture, their religion, and their outlook to life'.[22] His vision recognized the psychic scarring of legal stigma, as well as the internal dimension necessary to true liberation: 'The interrelationship between the consciousness of the self and the emancipatory programme is of paramount importance.'[23] Biko proclaimed that the fundamental tenet of black consciousness was 'that the black man must reject all value systems that seek to make him a foreigner in the country of his birth and reduce his basic human dignity'.[24] Biko rightly saw that the primary impact of apartheid was as a systematized affront to racial dignity, and that its reclamation was a task both public and private, both external and internal. This is so because the effect of systematic degradation

---

[19] A profound analysis of racism and its internalisation is M Fakhry Davids, *Internal Racism: A Psychoanalytic Approach to Race and Difference* (London, Palgrave Macmillan, 2011).

[20] W. E. B. Du Bois, *The Souls of Black Folk* (1903), http://www.bartleby.com/114/1.html.

[21] Biko used the term 'black' as encompassing all South Africans of colour, including 'Africans', 'Indians', and 'Coloureds'. See Biko, *I Write What I Like* (London, Picador, 2004), 52.

[22] Biko, *I Write What I Like*, 53.

[23] Biko, *I Write What I Like*, 53. Biko also captured Du Bois's idea of the 'consciousness of the self', which had for centuries enabled black people to find the courage to endure as well as to lead ordinary, even normal lives in a society that was extraordinarily abnormal: Steve Biko, 'The definition of black consciousness', in *I Write What I Like*, 52–57. In *Native Nostalgia* (Auckland Park, South Africa, Jacana Media, 2009), 19, Jacob Dlamini challenges 'facile accounts of black life under apartheid that paint the forty-six years in which the system existed as one vast moral desert, with no social orders, and as if blacks produced no art, literature or music, bore no morally upstanding children ...'

[24] Testimony in *S v Cooper*, 3 May 1976 (the SASO/BCP trial)on.

persists even after legalized racial,[25] and other, stigmas are abolished.[26] They burden even without being internalized, merely because the perceptions might be applicable.[27]

But the apartheid state assailed not only race. It also demeaned on the basis of sexual identity. Sexual expression was severely policed. In 1927, the Immorality Act forbade extramarital sexual relations between white and African people. This was amended after 1948 to prohibit sex between whites and any other race. And further, in 1949, the Prohibition of Mixed Marriages Act was enacted. This not only prohibited marriage between white people and members of all other races but also declared illegitimate any children born of a marriage later deemed invalid.[28]

What was more, 'Apartheid South Africa exhibited a well-developed tradition of legally sanctioned discrimination against gays and lesbians. South Africa had gathered anti-homosexuality laws from each of its several legal traditions—all of which condemned homosexuality. The legal situation in pre-liberation South Africa was more harsh (de jure at least) than many of its neighbours. Whereas many Sub-Saharan nations have no explicit provisions related to homosexuality, South Africa has had condemnatory laws since colonization.'[29]

All sexual expression between men was proscribed. Laws against sodomy and 'unnatural offences' were fiercely enforced. In 1969, the apartheid parliament expanded the common law and legislative prohibitions on sex between men.[30] Right until the lag-years of apartheid, the apartheid parliament was

---

[25] In South Africa, research suggests that perceived discrimination, generally higher among historically stigmatized groups, results in higher psychological distress and other mental health effects: David R. Williams et al., 'Perceived discrimination, race and health in South Africa', *Social Science Medicine* 67:3 (2008), 441–52.

[26] In the USA, sociologist Claude Steele has described 'stereotype threat', in which the performance of African-Americans and women in the academic realm is directly affected by their awareness of negative stereotypes about their intellectual abilities: Claude M. Steele, 'A threat in the air: how stereotypes shape intellectual identity and performance', *American Psychologist* 52 (1997) 613, at 616–18; Claude M. Steele, 'Race and the schooling of Black Americans', *The Atlantic Monthly* (April 1992), at http://www.theatlantic.com/magazine/archive/1992/04/race-and-the-schooling-of-black-americans/6073/. *See also* Glenn C. Loury, 'Racial stigma and its consequences', *Focus* 24:1 (University of Wisconsin-Madison Institute for Research on Poverty, Fall 2005).

[27] *Steele*, 'Race and the schooling of Black Americans', 617.

[28] Act 55 of 1949. This was followed by the Immorality Amendment Act 21 of 1950; the Immorality Act 23 of 1957; and the Prohibition of Mixed Marriages Amendment Act 21 of 1968.

[29] Eric C. Christiansen, 'Ending the apartheid of the closet: sexual orientation in the South African constitutional process', *NYU Journal of International Law and Politics* 32:997 (2000), 14.

[30] In that year section 20A was added to the Immorality Act 32 of 1957. It criminalized any act, even in private, if 'calculated to stimulate sexual passion or to give sexual gratification' between 'men at a party', defined as any occasion where more than two persons were present.

considering further expansions of these crimes.[31] The symbolic effect of these laws was immense.[32] As the Constitutional Court later noted, their meaning was 'that in the eyes of our legal system all gay men are criminals'.[33] The resonance with the way the pass laws made most black South Africans criminals is intense.

In my adolescent and early adult years, I experienced the debilitating effect of this criminality. I felt shame at what I was: a gay man with intense yearning for same-sex companionship and expression. And I felt fear that its expression would lead to a life-ruining confrontation with the criminal law. Sexual stigma stems from social discomfort or disregard for non-heterosexual behaviour, identity, relationships, or communities.[34] It is oppressive and pervasive, and, as with race laws, it is exacerbated when the law brands the condition as inferior: when the law discredits it. As with the effects of racial subordination, the reparatory project is both private and public, both internal and external. And here the law is of immense importance. The capacity to function fully within the legal sphere, and to be viewed as a fully legal citizen, helps diminish internalization of dignity and shame. Biko's ideas were a premonitory articulation of what dignity has come to mean in South African constitutional jurisprudence: a rejection of any value system that reduces human worth. They also explain the central role of dignity in the South African constitutional order.

Dignity-based jurisprudence has helped to foster the notion of an inclusive moral citizenship in South Africa, unburdened by the humiliating exclusions and degradations of the past. That the equal protection of the laws should have been extended so comprehensively to gays and lesbians, no less than to South Africans oppressed by apartheid's suffocating racial codes, is one of the truly remarkable aspects of our transition. The explanation lies in the degrading experience of indignity under apartheid, which was in significant respects common to black South Africans and gays and lesbians. This argument can be advanced plausibly because gays and lesbians were deeply involved in fighting apartheid.[35]

---

[31] See Mark Gevisser and E. Cameron, *Defiant Desire: Gay and Lesbian Lives in South Africa* (New York, Routledge, 1995), 30–6, for the President's Council investigation designed to broaden laws against gays and lesbians.
[32] See *Khumalo v Holomisa*, 2002 (5) SA 401(CC) para. [27].
[33] *National Coalition for Gay & Lesbian Equality v Minister of Justice*, 1999 (1) SA 6 (CC) at para. 28.
[34] Gregory M. Herek, et al., 'Sexual stigma: putting sexual minority health issues in context', in I. Meyer and M. Northridge, *The Health of Sexual Minorities*.
[35] My colleague Justice Zak Yacoob observes that 'one of the most important reasons for the inclusion of protection for gay and lesbian people is that they participated in the struggle for democracy' (personal communication, 3 July 2012).

Dignity as both a foundational value and a fundamental right

In the Constitution of South Africa, human dignity is both a founding value[36] and a discrete right in the Bill of Rights.[37] In fact, in the interim constitution under which South Africa's transition to democracy took place, dignity was listed only as a fundamental right.[38] It was the Constitutional Court that declared, in its decision outlawing the death penalty, that dignity played a larger role than merely as a right: it was also the value on which the new democracy was founded.[39] As a direct response to *Makwanyane*,[40] the Constitutional Assembly, drafting South Africa's final constitution, listed dignity not only as a fundamental right, but also as a founding value. And dignity is one of only two rights—alongside the right to life—that is non-derogable.[41]

Dignity thus operates in the jurisprudence of the court in two ways: as a foundational value that informs the interpretation of all other rights; and as a fully justiciable right.[42] Dignity is relatively rarely invoked as a right in itself.[43] More often, it operates as a value infusing other rights, most particularly, perhaps, the right to equality.

Dignity has an important public dimension.[44] This is embodied in the status and protection that legal, social, and political institutions confer. These enable us, without fear of abuse, discrimination, or constraint, to engage *out in the world* in the commitments and activities that embody who we are and what we wish to become—to attain self-actualization, despite the accidents of our birth and notwithstanding any incidents of lifestyle. The court has thus held that the anti-discrimination provisions of the constitution provide 'a bulwark against invasions which impair human dignity', and that the commitment to

---

[36] Section 1 of the Constitution provides that the Republic of South Africa is one sovereign democratic state founded on the values that include 'Human dignity, the achievement of equality and the advancement of human rights and freedoms'.

[37] Section 10 of the Constitution provides that 'Everyone has inherent dignity and the right to have their dignity respected and protected'.

[38] [Interim] Constitution of the Republic of South Africa, Act 200 of 1993, section 10.

[39] *S v Makwanyane*, 1995, ZACC 3; 1995 (3) SA 391 (CC) para. 58 (Chaskalson P), para. 328 (O'Regan J).

[40] I am indebted for this to my colleague Justice Yacoob, who was closely involved in drafting the final Constitution as a member of the panel of independent experts advising the Constitutional Assembly.

[41] Constitution of the Republic of South Africa, section 37. In states of emergency, other rights are partially derogable.

[42] O'Regan J, for the Court, in *Dawood*. See Currie and de Waal, *The Bill of Rights Handbook*, 5th edn (Lansdowne, Juta, 2005), 275.

[43] See Stuart Woolman, 'Dignity', in Stuart Woolman, Michael Bishop, and Jason Brickhill (eds), *Constitutional Law of South Africa*, 2nd edn (Cape Town, Juta & Co., 2007), 36–19.

[44] This public dimension of dignity has been given a unique flavour in South African jurisprudence by imbuing it with *ubuntu*.

dignity underpins the commitment to avoid discrimination.[45] In this way, dignity is the basis of the court's anti-discrimination jurisprudence.

This in many ways follows societies that have vested dignity as a fundamental constitutional or jurisprudential value.[46] The German Constitution, a product of the Second World War, established the 'inviolability' of human dignity and obliged state institutions to 'respect and protect' it.[47] Although Canada's Charter of Rights and Freedoms does not specifically mention dignity, the jurisprudence of its Supreme Court has invoked 'respect for the inherent dignity of every human person' to ascribe meaning to those rights and freedoms.[48]

The dignity and equality jurisprudence of the South African Constitutional Court has derived much of its formal and conceptual structure from that of the Supreme Court of Canada.[49] But the evolution of dignity as a constitutional value in South Africa has deeper roots; and it is wrong to think it was simply appropriated from elsewhere.[50] It is best understood through the indignity that apartheid inflicted on most South Africans. Dignity is intrinsic to each person (and may inhere in all beings). It comprises the deeply personal understandings we have of ourselves, and our worth as individuals and in our material and social context. No law or social practice can strip away dignity, in this sense.[51] Apartheid was an assault on black South Africans' dignity, but its laws could not deprive them of their intrinsic human worth.

So the systematic humiliation and degradation that apartheid's legal structures inflicted on black people may not have detracted from their intrinsic human dignity. But it stemmed from an ideology of racial superiority that imputed to white skin colour and European culture a high value, while regarding black skin colour and African culture as inferior. This left a residue of indignity that was perceived and experienced as shameful. It is from this that

---

[45] *Harksen v Lane*, 1997, ZACC 12; 1998 (1) SA 300 (CC) para. 49.

[46] See Arthur Chaskalson, 'Human dignity as a foundational value of our constitutional order', *South African Journal on Human Rights* 16 (2000), 193, 196–8.

[47] *Deutscher Bundestag—Basic Law for the Federal Republic of Germany*, Article I.

[48] See *R v Oakes*, 1986, 19 CRR 308, 334–5.

[49] See *President of the Republic of South Africa v Hugo*, 1997, ZACC 4; 1997 (4) SA 1 (CC) para. 41, citing *Egan v Canada*, (1995) 29 CRR (2d) 79 at 104–5.

[50] See Rowan Philp, 'In love with SA's Constitution', *Mail & Guardian*, 24 February 2012, http://mg.co.za/article/2012-02-24-in-love-with-sas-constitution.

[51] See Jeremy Waldron, 'Dignity and defamation: the visibility of hate', *Harvard Law Review* 123 (2011), 1596, 1612. 'Philosophically, we may say that dignity is inherent in the human person—and so it is. No law or social practice can take it away. But as a social and legal status, dignity has to be nourished and maintained by society and the law, and this ... is a costly and difficult business and something in which we are all required to play a part. At the very least, we are required in our public dealings not to act in a way that undermines on another's dignity in this socio-legal sense ...'

the conception of apartheid's racism as disgraceful stems: that it sought to inflict a state of disgrace on people for no morally sound or rational reason.[52] South African constitutional jurisprudence has thus sought to abolish the impediments of the past by ensuring that self-worth is recognized and protected by the formal institutions of the state and its law. Those who suffered from a disgraceful past would be restored to grace. We have neither forgotten nor fully healed from our oppressive past. But our constitution has given full recognition to those previously shamed and disgraced by an oppressive system. It has created a legal framework to permit rights-assertions that have enabled people to express their anger, to demand recognition. And in doing so, it has provided the means for overcoming that past, and for asserting, at an individual and collective level, a sense of dignity. The experience of the shameful effects of racial and gender subordination impelled those envisioning the new constitutional order to include protection for a wide array of conditions that under apartheid were disabling. Over the last decade and a half, South African law has invoked dignity to proscribe the criminal inhibitions on same-sex conduct, and to allow the recognition of same-sex partnerships, adoption, procreation, and marriage.

Dignity has also enabled the court's jurisprudence to advance individual personhood, and to erase the residues of shame by bringing differences in sexual functioning out of the hidden realm of the private sphere. The court's decisions have thus subverted the notion that, to avoid shameful disparagement, individuals' activities and relationships must subscribe to uniformity. The court's jurisprudence has sought not merely to abolish the impediments of the past by ensuring that self-worth is recognized and protected by the state and its institutions. It has sought to create a normative framework in which South Africans can assert their personhood without the shameful stigmata of past subordination.

In short, the function of dignity in South African constitutionalism has been to repair indignity, to renounce humiliation and degradation, and to vest full moral citizenship in those who were denied it in the past.

---

[52] *S v Makwanyane*, 1995, ZACC 3; 1995 (3) SA 391 (CC), para. 262.

Arriving at same-sex marriage

The earliest judgment of the Constitutional Court saw an inextricable link between dignity and equality.[53] But the role of dignity is evidenced most strikingly in the jurisprudence on the equality of gays and lesbians.

Over the last thirteen years, our law has invoked dignity to proscribe the criminalization of sodomy as well as to allow for the recognition of same-sex partnerships, adoptions, and, most recently, marriages. The pronouncements on same-sex relationships and marriage cannot be fully appreciated without understanding the impact of apartheid's expansive racialized assault on the dignity of the majority of South Africa's people. More tellingly, the same-sex rulings may not have been possible had courts relied exclusively upon the rights of privacy and equality.[54] Dignity, both as a right and as a foundational value, has enabled our jurisprudence to bring people's differences out of the hidden realm of the private sphere, by undercutting the notion that individuals' activities and relationships must correspond with uniform norms.

The cases that led to constitutional recognition of same-sex marriage were themselves the product of a past that treated most South Africans as outcasts in their own country. Instead, the jurisprudence sought to affirm each individual's intrinsic worth, regardless of social station or public disapproval.[55] The court finally struck down the exclusion of same-sex couples from marriage, emphasizing the significant role of human dignity, equality and freedom.[56] The court highlighted 'four unambiguous features of the context in which the prohibition against unfair discrimination on grounds of sexual orientation must be analysed'. These are: the inappropriateness of entrenching a particular family form as the social and legal norm, given the constantly changing

---

[53] *S v Makwanyane*, (1995, ZACC 3; 1995 (3) SA 391 (CC), para. 11; *President of the Republic of South Africa v Hugo*, (1997, ZACC 4; (1997, (4) SA 1 (CC); *Brink v Kitshoff NO*, 1996 (4) SA 197 (CC); *Harksen v Lane*, (1997, ZACC 12; 1998 (1) SA 300 (CC); *Dawood v Minister of Home Affairs*, 2000 (1) SA 997 (C).

[54] See *Bowers Hardwick*, 478 US 186 (1986); *Lawrence v Texas*, 539 US 558 (2003). See also Jeffrey Toobin, 'Comment: learning from gay marriage', *The New Yorker* (8 February 2012), http://www.newyorker.com/online/blogs/comment/2012/02/ninth-circuit-overturns-prop-8.html; 'Same-sex marriage, civil unions, and domestic partnerships', *New York Times*, 8 February 2012, http://topics.nytimes.com/top/reference/timestopics/subjects/s/same_sex_marriage/index.html; Gay Moon and Robin Allen, 'Dignity discourse in discrimination law: a better route to equality?', *European Human Rights Law Review* (2006), 610.

[55] *National Coalition for Gay and Lesbian Equality Minister of Justice*, 1998, ZACC 15; 1999 (1) SA 6 (CC) (striking down sodomy ban); *Satchwell v President of Republic of South Africa*, 2002, ZACC 18; 2002 (6) SA 1 (CC) (equal pension benefits); *Du Toit v Minister for Welfare and Population Development*, 2002, ZACC 20; 2003 (2) SA 198 (CC): (joint adoption and guardianship of children).

[56] *Minister of Home Affairs v Fourie* 2006 (1) SA 524 (CC).

nature of familial formation; the need to recognize the past persecution of gays and lesbians; the fact that no comprehensive legal regulation of gay and lesbian family law rights existed; and the fact that our constitution represents a 'radical rupture' with a past based on intolerance and exclusion.[57]

These considerations stand in stark contrast to the views advanced by Professor Robert P. George in this collection[58] and elsewhere.[59] Professor George seeks to defend what he calls a 'conjugal' understanding of marriage—which defines marriage as 'the distinctive type of relationship that is ordered to, and would be naturally fulfilled by, the spouses having and rearing children together'.[60] This necessarily excludes from marriage those in same-sex relationships. While he claims that marriage has intrinsic rather than merely instrumental value, he regards its orientation to having children as a necessary element. I deal with these arguments only cursorily because, in my view, the impermissibility of same-sex marriage seems as difficult to propound on coherent and rational moral grounds as the impermissibility of interracial marriage.

Professor George's argument rests on the 'principle' of joint procreation. This notion as an animating justification for an exclusionary definition of socially recognized human bonds is grossly flawed.[61] First, it is over-inclusive—it 'demeans the marriages of many opposite-sex couples who do not give birth to biological children, including infertile couples, couples who have chosen not to have children, couples who have adopted, and couples who have used reproductive technologies to create their families'.[62] Second, it is arbitrarily stipulative. One can defend proscription of interracial marriage on the basis that marriage should be between people of the same race, but the stipulation is arbitrary. That marriage should be for procreation is equally arbitrary.

Professor George must either say that any loving relationship that exists upon an expressly non-child-bearing basis, whether same-sex or opposite-sex, cannot be a marriage; or he must divine some other basis on which to exclude same-sex couples from marriage. But he does neither. Instead, he reasons that

---

[57] The seven paragraphs that follow were inserted after the seminar at which the papers were presented, after discussion with the editor of this volume.
[58] See Robert P. George. 'What's sex got to do with it? Marriage, morality and rationality', in Jean Bethke Elstain and Robert P. George (eds), *The Meaning of Marriage* (New York, Scepter Publishers, 2010), 149–53.
[59] Sherif Girgis, Robert P. George, and Ryan T. Anderson, 'What is marriage?', *Harvard Journal of Law and Public Policy* 34 (2010), 245.
[60] Page 502, this volume.
[61] Kenji Yoshino, 'Lose the baseball analogy', *Slate* (21 December 2010), http://www.slate.com/articles/news_and_politics/jurisprudence/2010/12/lose_the_baseball_analogy.html.
[62] Kenji Yoshino, 'Lose the baseball analogy'.

infertile and otherwise childless opposite-sex couples retain a 'basic orientation' towards bearing and rearing children, even though they may never have children.[63] This is absurd, as well as arbitrary.

It is difficult to see why, given that procreation is no less biologically impossible in cases of infertility than in those of homosexuality, heterosexual intercourse by infertile couples is any more 'oriented' towards bearing children than that by same-sex couples. The only distinction, where procreation is impossible, is that heterosexual sex involves a penis in a vagina. It is ludicrous to suggest that this is an essential element of marriage.

Hence, Professor George is constrained to invoke arguments concerning the 'potential' and 'orientation' of opposite-sex coupling—because no other rational basis exists on which to make peno-vaginal coupling, as opposed to any other form of coupling, a matter of distinctive moment in marriage. Even where opposite-sex couples choose not to have children, it seems silly to say that it is the 'potential' for a relationship to produce children that is key to marriage. Opposite-sex couples, deeply committed and in love, who share a moral and ideological opposition to biological reproduction in our already overpopulated world, would rightly be shocked and perhaps affronted to learn that the true basis of their marriage is their unrealized biological ability to reproduce.

But all of this exposes a much deeper flaw in Professor George's posture. This is his attempt to impose rigid preconceptions on forms of human commitment, loving, sexual conjunction and partnership. This rigidity is precisely the evil that afflicted South Africa under apartheid, and which the dignity jurisprudence of its Constitutional Court has in its first two decades addressed. It is a like evil that this chapter addresses. In South Africa, a history of state-controlled racial rigidity—including strictly defined racial categories, for which separate and segregated institutions were specifically created—had a mutilating impact on black and white alike.

It is in part through understanding the pernicious effects of that rigidity that the court has so fully embraced positive assertion of sexual orientation equality and diversity today. Today's arguments opposing same-sex marriage invoke the same rigidities, the same illogicalities, and the same absurdities of racism in South Africa's discredited past.[64] They deserve the same moral opprobrium.

---

[63] Girgis, George, and Anderson 'What is marriage?', 257.
[64] Yoshino, 'Lose the baseball analogy', 65, refers to the US Supreme Court decision in *Loving v Virginia* 388 US 1, 87 S.Ct. 1817, 18 L.Ed.2d 1010, where the trial court had held that: 'Almighty God created the races white, black, yellow, malay and red, and he placed them on separate continents. And

The limits of dignity

There is substantial criticism of dignity as a basis on which to adjudicate rights. A main concern has been that dignity is fuzzy—often rife with ambiguity, and hence difficult to give a concrete meaning or effect as a realizable right.[65] One criticism is that using dignity can involve imposing a normative or ethical value onto individual behaviour or choice.[66] And this has happened. In *S v Jordan*,[67] the majority rejected all challenges to the criminal prohibition on sex work. The minority would have overturned the criminal ban on narrow gender discrimination grounds. That judgment also rejected dignity as a basis. The minority said this was because it was not the criminalization of sex work but the commodification of a sex worker's body—that is, the work itself—that undermines her dignity.[68] 'The very character of the work they [sex workers] undertake devalues the respect that the Constitution regards as inherent in the human body'.

The judgment has been heavily criticized for making an unsustainable distinction between sexual activity that is subject to criminal sanction, and therefore subject to intervention by the state, and that which properly merits sanctuary in the private realm.[69] Indeed, dignity's rhetorical and conceptual power may be inadequate to challenge narrow conceptions of naturalness or normalness. It has justly been said that *Fourie* idealizes marriage as the most appropriate way for two people to garner public recognition and legitimation of their relationship.[70] And critics warn that institutionalizing same-sex marriage may merely replace one set of repressive social norms with another legal sanction of sexual sameness or conformity, thus 'discrediting' those who do not conform.

---

but for the interference with his arrangement there would be no cause for such marriages. The fact that he separated the races shows that he did not intend for the races to mix.'

[65] See Stéphanie Hennette-Vauchez, 'A human *Dignitas*? Remnants of the ancient legal concept in contemporary dignity jurisprudence', *International Journal of Constitutional Law* 9:1 (2011), 32–57. Justice Laurie Ackermann identified this problem by highlighting the difficulty of distinguishing between dignity as a 'right' and as a 'value'. 'Equality and non-discrimination: some analytical thoughts', *South African Journal on Human Rights* 22 (2006), 597, 598–9. See also Tarunabh Khaitan, 'Dignity as an expressive norm: neither vacuous nor a panacea', *Oxford Journal of Legal Studies* (2011), 1–19.

[66] See Rory O'Connell, 'The role of dignity in equality law: lessons from Canada and South Africa', *International Journal of Constitutional Law* 6 (2008), 272.

[67] 6 SA 642 (CC) (2002).

[68] *Jordan,* para. 74: 'We do not believe that [the provision] can be said to be the cause of any limitation on the dignity of the prostitute. To the extent that the dignity of prostitutes is diminished, the diminution arises from the character of prostitution itself.'

[69] Currie and de Waal, *The Bill of Rights Handbook*, 444.

[70] Jaco Barnard-Naudé and Pierre de Vos, 'Disturbing heteronormativity: the "queer" jurisprudence of Albie Sachs', *South African Public Law* 25 (2010), 209, 222.

In *Le Roux v Dey*,[71] the court certainly frowned upon sexual display. The majority described an image published of the plaintiff, which he alleged was both defamatory and injurious to his feelings, as being of 'two promiscuous men who allowed themselves to be photographed in what can only be described as a situation of sexual immorality, which would be embarrassing and disgraceful to the ordinary members of society',[72] and thus defamatory. A minority, of which I was part, found for the plaintiff on the narrower basis of affront to feelings (*iniuria*), invoking infringement of dignity. We held that the plaintiff had suffered an affront to his subjectively experienced personal dignity.

Taken together, *Jordan* and *Le Roux* may offer evidence of conservatism about sexual expression. This may be contrasted with assertions elsewhere in the court's jurisprudence that no particular social norm for adult, consensual sexual expression should be entrenched.[73]

The possibilities of dignity

Notwithstanding this, dignity has enabled the court to secure a significant break from the past. As a value and as a right, dignity has affirmed and destigmatized those previously excluded. Crucially, it has also provided a framework for proscription of other forms of discrimination—for instance, against non-citizens—and for recognition of sexual expressiveness. It is against this backdrop, characterized by the internalization of stigma and disgrace for the majority of people in South Africa, that constitutionalism has sought to create a reparative legal framework—one in which injury to dignity can be repaired, and in which humanhood can be asserted.

The constitution here serves as a simple statement and thus an assertion of the dignity of all South Africans. In addition, its provisions provide symbolic affirmation, reinstatement, and reparation to those previously excluded, recognizing and affirming their diversity. It also provides a practical framework for the more difficult task of attaining internal dignity, and asserting it externally, by disclaiming stigma and disgrace, and affirming moral citizenship and worth.[74]

---

[71] 2011 (3) SA 274 (CC).
[72] 2011 (3) SA 274 (CC), para. 98.
[73] Sachs J in *Minister of Home Affairs v Fourie* at para. 47.
[74] It is this explanation I sought to advance to assuage Professor MacKinnon's expressed bemusement when she visited the court in February 2010—see the introduction and summary to this chapter.

The law cannot, on its own, create internal dignity or repair a history of degradation. Nor can it remove stigma or stop hatred. But it can reject branding people as subordinate and inferior, and thus making them objects of shame. The court's jurisprudence on the equality of gays and lesbians has addressed both social and legal equality, and sought to rectify the subordination of the past by enabling gays and lesbians to assert themselves as equal moral citizens who can fulfil their capacities as humans without shame. Dignity thus enables not conformity but rather the advancement of those aspects of our lives that have the potential to be distinct and extraordinary: traversing public spaces fearlessly, developing our minds and speaking freely, and perhaps finding love and generativity.

28

The Dignity of Marriage

Christopher Tollefsen

THE CONCEPT 'DIGNITY' SEEMS to many to capture something important about the nature of the human person, and to express in a summary way various ethical and political conclusions that follow from that nature. Representatives of the Catholic and natural law traditions are particularly associated with such appeals; Pope John Paul II's work, for example, is suffused with references to dignity, both as describing human nature and as a ground for opposition to various kinds of action, such as abortion, euthanasia, and sexual objectification.[1] 'Dignity' appears elsewhere in contemporary Church documents as well, including, notably, the documents of the Second Vatican Council.[2] It is a well-established part of the Church's approach to the anthropology of the human condition.

Somewhat less known, perhaps, is contemporary Catholic use of the word dignity to describe the institution of marriage. 'The dignity of marriage' is an expression found more than once in *Gaudium et Spes*,[3] and is repeated by the late Pope in *Familiaris Consortio*.[4] Similarly, the *Catechism* speaks of 'offences against the dignity of marriage', an expression that mirrors the numerous instances in which some form of action is said to be an offence against the dignity of the human person.[5]

---

[1] See, for example, Pope John Paul II, *Evangelium Vitae* (Vatican City, Libreria Editrice Vaticana, 1995).
[2] It is prominent in Vatican Council II, *Gaudium et Spes* (Vatican City, Libreria Editrice Vaticana, 1965).
[3] Ibid. The section titled, in the Vatican's English translation, 'Fostering the nobility of marriage and the family', should rather be 'Fostering the dignity ...', after the Latin, *De Dignitate Matrimonii et Familiae Fovenda*.
[4] See Pope John Paul II, *Familiaris Consortio* (Vatican City, Libreria Editrice Vaticana, 1981). John Paul speaks there of the need for the 'entire truth and the full dignity of marriage and the family' to be 'preserved and realized' (no. 5); the rest of the document identifies what this preservation and realization would entail.
[5] *Catechism of the Catholic Church*, nos 2380–91.

It might be thought that this is a merely metaphorical extension of the language of the dignity of the person; dignity seems an essentially personal quality, and not to be used literally to describe an institution or cooperative arrangement of persons. I will argue, however, that the language of dignity is meant and should be taken quite seriously; dignity is predicated of marriage by analogy with its predication of persons, but not merely by a metaphorical extension. We are meant to understand some quite specific points about marriage by the language of dignity, as to its nature, its origins, its end, and its role in ethical and political life.

The dignity of the person

Most generally, the term dignity indicates some way in which its possessor is excellent or has achieved excellence, or should be considered of value or worth, and should hence be accorded certain forms of respect. John Paul II, in his encyclical *Evangelium Vitae*, links the dignity of human life to its source as a free gift of God; and to its destination, for human beings are destined for life with God. Human dignity is also linked by the Pope to human *nature*: human beings are made in the image of God, insofar as they are possessed of freedom and rationality.[6] These three dimensions of dignity together lead to two more, which I will call the person's *ethical dignity* and his *political dignity*. Each of these, in turn, exists in two aspects, as a task that persons have to carry out, ethically and politically, and as a requirement that ethical and political forms of respect be accorded to the person. The task aspect can be indicated by the suggestion that some act is *beneath* a person's dignity; the requirement aspect by the suggestion that some form of treatment is *against*, or *contrary to*, a person's dignity.

The Pope's threefold schema of source, nature, and destination as providing the foundational account of human dignity is pervasively influenced by revelation and theology, though not entirely to the exclusion of the deliverances of reason and the natural law. This is true even of the most obviously religious claims, as, for example, that the human being is made by God and for God. There is an argument in natural reason to the existence of a creative

---

[6] See especially *Evangelium Vitae*, nos 34–8. As Luke Gormally points out, nature and destination are not entirely distinct, since what something is can be known fully only by knowing its end; I believe the same is true of the source claim, since human existence begins with God's deliberate choice, a choice which has an end; Luke Gormally, 'Pope John Paul II's teaching on human dignity and its implications for bioethics', in C. Tollefsen (ed.), *John Paul II's Contribution to Catholic Bioethics* (Dordrecht, NL, Kluwer Academic Publishers, 2004), 7–33, at 7.

and therefore personal being whose free choice causes human persons, and all else, to be; and that argument easily leads to a natural law counterpart to the claim that human beings are made *for* God, for if we are made by a personal being, for the sake of no benefit that could accrue to *that* being, then that being acted, it would seem, exclusively for *our* good, and that fact calls for a response of gratitude on the part of human beings, and an attempt at cooperation with that being—an attempt to form a kind of friendship with it.

Still, the fullest understanding of the source and destination claims emerges within a rich religious tradition that draws upon the resources of revelation, as, for example, by understanding the ultimate destination of human persons as including eternal life in the kingdom of heaven, a form of community with all persons, and as also including, through baptism, a share in the divine nature and life of the Trinity.[7]

To a greater extent, however, the claim that human beings have dignity because of their nature has been appropriated within the tradition of natural law thought. And so in what follows, I will concentrate primarily upon the claim that, as possessed of the capacities for freedom and rationality, human persons are made in the image of God and possess thereby a special, and, in earthly creation, pre-eminent form of dignity. I will show how this claim leads to both ethical and political assertions of dignity, and then turn to what I take to be analogues to these assertions in claims that can be made about marriage.

The nature of the human person, and human dignity[8]

Of all the various explanations of human dignity, the most familiar is the second, that man is made in the image of God. This claim has both descriptive and normative aspects; it can only be fully understood insofar as it is recognized to point ahead of man's given nature to the nature he should take on in action.

The descriptive aspect should be understood in the following way: man is made in the image of God precisely because his existence is that of a person. Man, that is, is possessed of reason and will, and is capable of rational thought

---

[7] This theological bent is reflected in the analogues, in marriage, to personal dignity as regards source and destination. The Catholic view that marriage is an institution directly created by God, and the Catholic understanding of the sacramentality of marriage, reveal the dignity of marriage in both its source and destination, yet from a distinctly theological perspective.

[8] The following three paragraphs, and one paragraph in the next section, are adapted from my discussion in Christopher Tollefsen, 'A Catholic perspective on human dignity', in Steven Dilley and Nathan Palpant (eds), *Human Dignity and Bioethics: From Worldviews to the Public Square* (New York, Routledge, 2012), 49–66.

and free choice.⁹ This dual emphasis is found in the documents of the Second Vatican Council: in *Dignitatis Humanae*, the council writes that our 'dignity as persons' is our existence as 'beings endowed with reason and free will and therefore privileged to bear personal responsibility'.[10] John Paul summarizes: 'The biblical author [in the book of *Sirach*] sees as part of this image ... those spiritual faculties which are distinctively human, such as reason, discernment between good and evil, and free will.'[11]

In these descriptions, we see an anticipation of the way in which the dignity of the person is normative, for reason and free will in us are necessary precisely so that we may bear that privilege of 'personal responsibility'. Thomas Aquinas identified this responsibility as our participation in God's eternal law; unlike the rest of earthly creation, which follows God's law by nature, human beings are given a share in divine reason, and the faculty of free choice, precisely so that they may guide and constitute themselves as the persons they are *to be* in accordance with God's plan.[12] In this active shaping of their own lives in accordance with reason, human beings are thus *like*—in the image of—the divine. Of course, the orientation of this power must be identified: what is the substantive content of the deliverances of reason? This is the ethical dimension of dignity, to which I now turn.

Ethical dignity

All of the three aspects of dignity, but especially the dignity of human nature, signal two further aspects of human dignity. The first is dignity in its ethical sense; the dignity of human nature points beyond itself towards a normative dimension: dignity is something both to be respected in the human person, but also, and equally importantly, something to be realized in action.

The former sense of ethical dignity is well known to those familiar with Catholic ethics. Abortion and euthanasia, for example, are understood as contrary to the dignity of the person insofar as they involve the intentional taking of innocent human life, which is to be respected at all times. Similar uses of dignity indicate that about the person which must always be respected, and are to be found in treatments of sinful social structures and political institutions, in

---

[9] See P. Lee and R. P. George, 'The nature and basis of human dignity', *Ratio Juris* 21 (2008), 173–93, for a defence of this view.
[10] Vatican Council II, *Dignitatis Humanae* (Vatican City, Libreria Editrice Vaticana, 1965), no. 2.
[11] John Paul II, *Evangelium Vitae*, no. 34.
[12] Thomas Aquinas, *Summa Theologica* (Chicago, W. Benton-Encyclopedia Britannica, 1980), I–II, Prologue.

Catholic appraisals of torture and terror bombing, and in Catholic discussions of sexuality: every form of treatment in which a person is instrumentalized or objectified, or in which the fundamental goods of the person are intentionally damaged or destroyed, are considered to be contrary to human dignity.

In the latter sense, human dignity, manifest in freedom and reason, comes with a task, a task understood in the Catholic and natural law tradition ultimately to be one of love, of freely giving of oneself to another, and others. The Second Vatican Council expresses the thought in this way: '[B]y his innermost nature man is a social being, and unless he relates himself to others he can neither live nor develop his potential.'[13] And the council goes on to say: 'man, who is the only creature on earth which God willed for itself, cannot fully find himself except through a sincere gift of himself'.[14]

We see here two things. First, the earlier point about one aspect of man's dignity being found in his source—that is, God's gratuitous creation—here is joined to the second point about man's dignity as being made in the image of God. God, in creating a being for its own sake, creates that being as *able to love*—that, we here find articulated, is what it means to *be* a being capable of existing for its own sake.[15] And it is thus only in loving that man realizes, or fulfils, the nature by which he has dignity. Thus, we could say that man's constitutive dignity—the dignity he has in virtue of what he is, and in virtue of which he is entitled to full moral respect—sets on him a requirement to strive for ethical, or, as Luke Gormally has called it, existential, dignity, the dignity of excellence *as* a being capable of love and self-gift.[16]

Of course, this leaves largely unstated what precisely it means to achieve excellence in love. By way of the very briefest possible summary, I will simply say that I take our normative task to be the protection of, and service to, the basic goods of human persons in *all* such persons; our fulfilment as a being called to love is to be found only in the communion that is instantiated through action for the good in the person of *others*; a life lived only for the good in one's person would be deficient precisely from the standpoint of human flourishing, failing to achieve some goods altogether, and achieving no good as successfully as it could be achieved in communion with others.

---

[13] Vatican Council II, *Gaudium et Spes*, no. 12.
[14] Vatican Council II, *Gaudium et Spes*, no. 24.
[15] For reflections on how this structure permeates all creation, see W. N. Clarke, SJ, 'Person, being, and St Thomas', *Communio* 19 (1992), 601–18.
[16] Gormally, 'Pope John Paul II's teaching', 15–16.

Political dignity

This social dimension of the human person, while essentially to be realized in upright action, also points towards the need for a politics of dignity, a way of understanding political action and institutions that does justice to the dignity of the human person in the dimensions just discussed. John Paul II is well known for his criticisms of a form of democratic politics (and similar criticisms of a form of unconstrained capitalism) that is entirely about the promotion of freedom at the expense of truth, a politics that distorts the existential task of man away from the gift of self and towards the satisfaction of the self.[17] The realm of the political is not coextensive with everything that is constitutive of genuine human well-being, nor is that realm itself a basic good of the human person; but an upright politics, one that achieves what we could call political dignity, is always in service of the real needs of the person. The achievement of such a politics is the task of the political dimension of our dignity; and a politics that positively thwarts human flourishing, both in its individual and social dimensions, is thus contrary to the demands of political dignity.

The nature of marriage

I turn now to the nature and the good of marriage; doing so will enable us to see the analogy of dignity as it extends from the personal to the marital. The account I shall give could be called, for reasons that will become clear, a comprehensive union account of the nature and good of marriage; again, for reasons that will become clear, it could also be called a conjugal account of the nature and good of marriage.[18]

That marriage involves a comprehensive union emerges from its guiding point, which is the intention of the spouses to enter into a *complete and mutual sharing of lives at all levels of their existence*. This point is expressed also by John Paul, who writes that men and women 'in matrimony give themselves

---

[17] The first criticism may be found in John Paul II, *Evangelium Vitae*; the second in John Paul II, *Centesimus Annus* (Vatican City, Libreria Editrice Vaticana, 1991).

[18] In addition to the work of John Paul II, my account draws from work by members of the so-called 'new natural law' theory. See, for example, Girgis, George, and Anderson, 'What is marriage?', *Harvard Journal of Law and Public Policy* 34 (2010), 245–87. There are differences, of emphasis at least, however, between different NNL theorists, as can be seen in the work of John Finnis, who is critical of the language of 'total' self-giving in John Paul II; see Finnis, 'Sex and marriage: some myths and reasons', in *Collected Essays,* vol. 3: *Human Rights and Common Good* (Oxford, Oxford University Press, 2011), 353–88.

with a love that is total and therefore unique and exclusive'.[19] And he writes too that marriage involves an 'ever richer union with each other on all levels'.[20] So marriage is both a union at 'all levels', and is also a total gift of self between the spouses.

These expressions require further explanation: how is the sharing of lives in marriage something that takes place at all levels? And how is that sharing something that is complete or, in the Pope's word, total? I intend to answer both questions in due course. But first, I want to address the question of the goodness of a union of this sort.

Friendship, I believe, is a basic human good: the mutual willing of one another's good is recognized by friends as good in itself, and not just for whatever beneficial consequences it brings. We just are better off, fulfilled, perfected, as human beings simply by having friends, and this is *why* we pursue friendship, even if the *what* of friendship precisely requires that one transcend one's concern for one's own good, and make our friends' good our own.

But our friendships are inevitably limited in many ways. We do not make full and total commitments to our friends to share everything; we have many friends; and the available union is physically limited: it extends only to our organic boundaries, and can go no further. Nor do we usually look for more: in seeking friends we do not seek all-encompassing union, and we are rarely if ever disturbed at the organic limitations that we experience with our friends.

Thomas Aquinas held that our non-inferential awareness of basic goods is furthered by some experiential data provided by our inclinations. And we do appear to have, as a species, a natural inclination that orients us towards an all-encompassing union different from friendship, namely erotic desire. Erotic desire could be characterized as a desire for possession, or complete oneness and unity with another; this desire is not reducible merely to a desire for sexual pleasure, though sexual desire is no stranger to erotic love. But the agent in its grip desires the *totality* of the other person.

Erotic desire thus gives us an orientation towards, though it is not identical to, a good of a sort that, in its all-encompassing nature, goes beyond ordinary friendship. And *this* form of union is, like friendship, *itself* recognized as something fundamentally, basically, good for human persons (and so recognized even, as it may be, by people with little *experience* of erotic desire). We are capable of recognizing the object of erotic desire—a complete sharing of two lives—as an essential and intrinsic aspect of human perfection in the same way that we recognize the objects of other natural orientations

---

[19] John Paul II, *Familiaris Consortio*, no. 19.
[20] Pope John Paul II, *Theology of the Body* (Boston, MA, Pauline Books, 1997), 70.

as fundamental goods: knowledge, friendship, play, life, and health, among others. So we should see marriage—the marital union, understood as a comprehensive union—as good just in itself, and as desirable for its own sake. Marriage, in other words, is a basic human good.

It is important to ask how sex is related to, or integrated into, this good, and this leads to the conjugal description of my account of marriage. Understood as a comprehensive union, marriage was seen to involve a complete sharing of two lives, a sharing we can recognize as intrinsically desirable: thus marital union is a basic human good, perfective of us as human persons. But that union was described by the Pope as existing 'at all levels' of the spouses' lives, and the explanation of this, I believe, makes essential reference to conjugal intercourse.

On every understanding of marriage, there is *some* kind of union: spouses make mutual commitments to one another to share their lives in at least a quotidian way: they undertake the project of a life together. More robustly, that union should, normatively, bring spouses together in various aspects of their existence: their character, heart, intelligence, will. Spouses are deficient in their realization of the good of marriage if their characters in no way complement or harmonize with one another; spouses whose projects are entirely at odds, or who believe nothing in common, are similarly deficient in their realization of the good of marriage. But all these forms of union do not take us much past the union of a friendship of virtue; it is, in fact, *only* sex that can do this, and thus only in sex that a married couple can achieve the form of comprehensive union unique to, and specificatory of, the good of marriage.

On the conjugal view, the marital commitment to a union at all levels finds its *realization* or *completion* in the act of sexual intercourse, an act in which spouses are joined in a bodily and organic fashion so as to become 'one flesh'. In sexual intercourse, an organic function for which each spouse is, on his or her own, physically inadequate, becomes possible, namely, the function of reproduction. Thus, insofar as they are united in sexual intercourse, the two spouses become one organism, not by way of dissolution of their separate bodily identities but by the extension of the unity, identified in the totality of their commitment to one another, all the way down to the physical reality of their persons. And this has a further consequence: spouses become one physical organism in sexual intercourse; but human persons are physical organisms, and so spouses can even be said to become one person—or perhaps one personal reality—in their sexual intercourse.

I said just now that sexual union realized or completed the marital commitment. The conjugal view thus contrasts sharply with any view that holds that the sexual act does no more than *express* that (or some other) commitment. It is true, of course, that sexual union at its best expresses marital love; but expression ultimately is controlled and guided by human choice, and what expresses one thing may, by the creative act of man, be transformed so as to express something else. If the expression of marital union is all that sex is by nature about, then why not think that sex could be used to express some other desire, form of union, or aspiration, in the way that metaphor transforms language's natural meaning to give us something 'new'?

Now this might be, in fact, all that sex 'does'. If so, then the claim of marriage to be in any sense a self-standing, basic good, is highly dubious: marriage would simply be some form of union plus sexual expressiveness. Something like this is the main contender to the comprehensive union view, yet I will argue later that only the conjugal account can really sustain the claims of dignity made by its defenders. But if sex completes—and uniquely completes—the commitment to union that makes a marriage to be, then there is no substitute for it as regards the demands of the union, and reason as well to think that sex is not so easily available for the realization of other purposes in detachment from the purpose of marriage; for when a human act is intrinsically oriented towards some human good, as belief is to truth, then deliberate detachment of that act from that good typically, and perhaps always, is, morally speaking, a misuse of the act in question.

The dignity of marriage

In the remainder of this chapter, I wish to trace out some of the consequences of the comprehensive, or conjugal, conception of marriage for thinking about the idea of dignity. Representatives of the religious and moral traditions that have given most attention to the conjugal conception have also spoken freely of the dignity of marriage; I will suggest that there is good reason for this, and will suggest also some of the consequences of this identification for moral and political life.

The nature of marriage and the image of God

Though I intend to make some claims about the dignity of marriage from the standpoint of natural reason, I begin with some points drawn from biblical revelation. In the second Genesis account, man is described as being made in the image of God. But in Genesis 1, man is said to be made in God's image *as male and female*. The meaning of this will be obscure from the standpoint that sees freedom and rationality as the essence of the *imago Dei*; or it will be understood as saying no more than that both men and women possess the faculties of freedom and reason. But a different perspective becomes available when it is understood that divine freedom and reason are identical also to the love that is God, a love that constitutes the relations between the persons of the Trinity by going out from the Father to the Son, and then from the two in the procession of the Holy Spirit.

Accordingly, beings made in the image of the divine are, as I have argued, beings who are made to love. And in their complementary maleness and femaleness, human persons are uniquely capacitated to love in a way that mirrors the divine love, both in the unity constituted by that love—the unity of the spouses—and in that love's fruitfulness in bringing forth new life. Nor is this capacitation disjoined from the paradigmatic features in virtue of which persons are said to be in God's image, for, by the account earlier, the comprehensive and conjugal union of spouses by which they image divine love is a good known to the human person by natural reason and available to the will for choice; indeed, recognition and choice of that good are perfections, actualizations, precisely of those capacities in virtue of which human beings are traditionally thought to be in the image of God, and hence to have dignity.

To reiterate: marital love is a profound imaging of the divine precisely because by their self-giving spouses realize a unity similar to that of the unity of the divine persons; they are one flesh, as the divine persons are one God.[21] And they mirror the fruitfulness of the divine love, a fruitfulness that exists both within the Trinity and in the relation of the divine to all creation, in the embodying of their love in another, that is, in the begetting of a child. And it is this likeness to (or imaging of) the triune divine life in both the loving unity and fecundity of spouses that is the deepest source, I believe, of the language identifying the dignity of marriage, with its close parallels to the language concerning the dignity of the person.

Gormally has summarized these claims in an important paper on human dignity in the thought of John Paul II:

> The complementarity of man and woman in the sexual relationship which is marriage is meant to reflect the Triune God's own life of self-giving love. The unitive and procreative dimensions of this relationship are a central manifestation in the created order of the truth that the fulfillment of the human person

---

[21] Important aspects of John Paul II's thought on this matter can be found in *Familiaris Consortio*, and also in his *The Theology of the Body*.

is to be found in the gift of self that is open to the other. Marriage belongs to the order of creation because that covenantal relationship, in which a man and a woman commit themselves unreservedly to each other, and to any new life which may be the fruit of their self-giving love, is fundamental to God's primordial design for the transmission of human life and the flourishing of human communities.[22]

Gormally's discussion here indicates that the dignity of marriage as it images God cannot be detached from the ethical dignity of marriage, a point to which I shall return. But it is important here to make good on an earlier claim. The dignity of the human person as made in the image of God is, obviously enough, a religious idea; yet it is available also from the standpoint of natural reason, for by reason we can recognize both the profoundly special nature of the human being as free and rational, and also recognize that such powers are 'God-like', even if there is no God. Similarly, that in marriage two persons are enabled to become one through a mutual capacitation of a life-giving power can also be recognized as profoundly special and unlike any other relationship, sexual or non-sexual, into which persons may enter; and it can also be recognized as 'god-like' *if* we recognize that a God, if such a being existed, would, in order to be perfect, be not just very loving but *identical* to His love; and also if we recognize the essential tendency of love-as-self-giving to be creative. The comprehensive or conjugal conception of marriage thus gives *us* an imaged understanding of God, a being we would understand the less were we not acquainted with the unity, fidelity, and fecundity of marriage.

The ethical dignity of marriage

The ethical dignity of the person was to be found both in the sense that the person deserved respect if the requirements of his dignity were to be met by others, and that the person was set a task in virtue of his dignity, a task through success in which the person would, as it were, live up to the demands of his dignity, and achieve moral, or existential, dignity. There are analogues to both senses of personal dignity in the dignity of marriage, though they are closely intertwined.

In fact, most of the primary ethical offences against marriage are committed by those charged with the ethical task of marriage. What constitutes that task, and what sets the standard by which offences are to be judged, is

---

[22] Gormally, 'Pope John Paul II's teaching', 13.

the nature of marriage. For as a comprehensive union fully realized in the conjugal act, marriage requires of spouses that they be exclusively faithful to one another until death. Accordingly, both adultery and divorce, not simply in the sense of civil divorce accompanying justified separation but in the sense of an attempt to sever the marriage bond, are both offences of the married and offences against marriage itself, failures to do the institution itself justice as well as, typically, failures to do justice to its members.

Moreover, and here more controversially, marital exclusivity and fidelity is expected, in the natural law and Catholic traditions, to be prepared for in the lives of all human persons by premarital chastity. The marital commitment calls for the greatest possible realization of oneness between spouses, in physical union; and, as the norm against adultery indicates, this oneness is not compatible with that oneness being shared by one spouse (or both, of course) with a third person. What is shared with that third person is no longer uniquely one to the married couple.

This demand for unique unity—it sounds redundant, but I think it is not, really—extends backward to the time before marriage. To *have* given one's capacity for bodily oneness to another before being married is incompatible with the demand of the marital commitment to become *one*—uniquely one—with one's spouse. And it is not simply a logical requirement: without repentance, one's prior willingness to become one with someone not one's spouse incapacitates one for making the choice—the commitment—that makes a marriage to be in the first place, for one is committed by one's choices—again, barring repentance—to making a gift of *less* than one's full capacity for oneness with one's spouse. Premarital sex is thus a kind of mutilation of one's moral capacity for the good of marriage, wrong in a way similar to the wrongs of other mutilations that render one incapacitated for a basic good.

But in being a failure to live up to the task of marriage, it is also, again, an offence against the dignity of marriage itself: widespread failure as regards this norm systematically undermines the institution, renders its nature and desirability opaque, and, in the practical consequences of the refusal to commit oneself in one's entirety to one and only one other that premarital sex involves, it seems to make both adultery and divorce more, rather than less, common. And the same is surely true of both non-mutual and non-marital kinds of sexual acts as well. For example, if, in marriage, one makes of one's body, insofar as it is a sexual body, a gift to one's spouse, pledging that body's capacity for unity with another exclusively to that spouse, then a willingness to make use of one's sexual capacity for one's *own* (solitary) enjoyment would appear to be a form of infidelity to one's spouse similar to the kind of infidelity that pre- or extramarital sex is.

The political dignity of marriage

I come now to the political dignity of marriage, a topic continuous with the constitutive and ethical dignity of marriage, for the ways in which marriage is excellent from the standpoint of the *polis* flow from its nature and its ethical requirements; and the political forms of disrespect that can be shown to the dignity of marriage also typically involve misunderstandings of the ethics of marriage. In this section, I first identify some of the ways in which the institution of marriage is political in a broad sense: a contributor to the social and political common good of a society. This contribution is the political task of marriage. I then identify three ways in which a political society can fail, in some cases radically, to respect the dignity of marriage.

The account I have given of the nature and good of marriage is one I have characterized as comprehensive and conjugal. But so far, it might seem that it is also private; why should any union, even one comprehensive and conjugal in nature, be thought to be of political significance? The answer to this question has been a staple of the philosophical consideration of marriage since Plato; but I will attempt to bring it out with some force through a thought experiment.

Suppose, then, that marriage was constituted around a different form of organic unity than that which I have identified. Suppose, for example, that at age thirty human beings ceased to be digestively adequate, and that a biological union of a digestive nature was the common, and perhaps even orgasmically pleasurable, form of union available to us in answer both to our desire for a more profound unity with another than ordinary friendships can provide, and to our need to digest our food adequately. Let us imagine that a social institution develops around this possibility, called marriage*. And let us further imagine that the question arises whether marriage* should be given the protection of the laws; or whether other relationships, perhaps not involving biological unity but nevertheless involving commitments to unity and some form of sexual pleasure, should be given equal standing in the law; or whether, perhaps, the institution of marriage should be considered an altogether private affair, of no significant political importance.

Would the (no doubt fantastic) scenario just described generate the sort of controversy that attempts to open up the definition of marriage in our actual world have? Would the social institution of marriage* be thought to possess the same degree of significance which defenders of traditional marriage claim is intrinsic to marriage as they understand it *simply* because it involved a form of biological union between the spouses? Would it be something that it made sense to think of having political *dignity*?

I think the answer here is no; there would be a reasonable inclination here, even on the part of supporters of marriage*, to think that perhaps there really was something merely biological about the one-flesh digestive union. No doubt this union would be special, and orgasmic pleasure is perhaps never to be sneered at. But this form of union nevertheless, I suspect, would not strike us as the foundational form of human relationships, precisely because, while digestive activities sustain and are of manifest importance in the biological and practical economies of human persons, these activities are not truly *creative*.

The biological union of man and woman in conjugal intercourse, by contrast, is not just, and really not *even*, the engagement of an organic function necessary for the survival of the parties engaged in it. It is, instead, the performance of a biological function that, when successful, introduces something new *into* the world; and not just some *thing* but, in fact, a new *person*. The creativity that sexual reproduction manifests is spectacular, in two directions. Looking back to its motivations, it is a creativity that flows from a mutual commitment that is perhaps the paradigmatic form of love, a commitment to make a complete gift of oneself to another.

But by *loving* one another as they have pledged to, spouses are enabled, not, obviously, in every case but generally and for the most part, to realize a form of creativity otherwise unavailable. And, looking forward, the creativity in question involves the creation of a sort of being the reality of which is uniquely commensurate to the reality of two loving persons, namely another *person*. That child-persons should be the fruit of marital love is thus essential to the personal significance of the biological union to the spouses, which is, by virtue of its origins and its ends, anything but 'merely' biological.

Looking now from an even broader perspective than what has been discussed here, we see that the social significance of this union goes well beyond the interests of the two parties in their creative capacity. For while the digestive union described above would maintain 'digestive spouses' in existence, the sexual union, insofar as it comes to its complete fruition, is the organic function responsible for the survival of both a political society, and even of the species. And, in the natural overflow of the commitment to be open to new life that is internal to the commitment to a mutual complete sharing of lives, there is also a further commitment not just to the procreation but to the rearing and education of children. There is a commitment to bringing these children to a point at which they too are capable of commitments, sociality, and, ultimately, marriage and parenthood.

There is a commitment, in other words, to perpetuating the foundational conditions necessary not just for the continuation of the species but for the continuation of civilization—ours, or any; this is the political task of marriage, or, put another way, the task side of the political dignity of marriage. And this, surely, is the source of the political significance of this institution, and is likewise the reason why the state justifiably takes an interest in the good and institution of marriage; for marriage is thereby of crucial importance to the political common good, as well as to the personal common good of spouses.

Now the ways in which a state must respect the dignity of marriage emerge more or less clearly to the extent that one acknowledges the ethical and especially political dignity of marriage, an acknowledgement that, I have argued, requires a prior understanding of the nature and good of marriage, and of the relationship between that good and the conjugal act. So I here identify, briefly, some of the ways that the state might fail to respect this dignity.

One way, I believe, is by eroding the institutional framework that makes it possible for participants in the good to recognize the stringency of the commitment involved in marriage and the consequent norm of permanence. There can be room, I believe, even in a civil law that respects fully the nature and norms—in a word, the dignity—of marriage, for civil divorce; but various of the actual forms of civil divorce that have been embraced, most especially no-fault divorce, make it increasingly difficult for spouses to understand what they are doing as oriented towards permanence.

A second way in which the dignity of marriage can be traversed politically is by the detachment of the political recognition that the institution is afforded from an acknowledgement of the way that the marriage is, by its nature, intrinsically oriented towards procreation. Most notably, this is done by the redefinition of marriage as something that requires only mutual commitment plus sexual expression, an understanding that, in its abandonment of the necessity of sexual complementarity in the spouses, similarly abandons a directedness towards procreation as intrinsic to what marriage is.

I believe that in doing so, the state in fact makes it opaque why marriage, as opposed to other relationships of mutual commitment, many of which involve no sexual forms of expression but are nevertheless expressive in other ways, should receive the special attention of the law. The state thereby also makes it more difficult to live in accordance with the conjugal conception in at least two ways. First, a grasp of that conception is made more elusive by the lack of widespread social recognition of that conception; and second, the choices and commitments necessary to undertake life in accordance with that conception are also made more difficult in a cultural context in which sexual intercourse is widely viewed merely as expressive and not genuinely unitive, a context in which, severed from the connection to children, sexual activity may be, and is by many, engaged in *at will*. The appeal of *this* conception to the young is obvious, and the achievement of working oneself out of one's ensnarement to this conception is rare, and often achieved only with great difficulty.

A third way in which the state fails to respect the dignity of marriage, ethical and political, concerns the state's relationship to education. The responsibility, and accordingly the right, of parents to educate their own children, or have them educated, in accordance with their own religious, moral, and metaphysical understandings, is a direct outgrowth of the commitment to union-open-to-new-life: that commitment would be truncated if it did not come also with the commitment to educate to maturity.[23] But states are to a considerable extent either oblivious or hostile to this most primordial right of parents to care for their children, and of children to be cared for by their parents. States that forbid home-schooling, or that make undue ideological requirements on children's education, or that take advantage of schemes for public schooling as a way of advancing world views contrary to that of many parents without providing ample opt-outs, and so on; all are failures to respect the dignity of marriage at the political level, both directly and indirectly, since such failures often make it more difficult for families to pass on the knowledge and virtues required for the forming of future families in a stable and morally upright way.

To all this, I will add in conclusion a fourth failing, less political than cultural but one directly analogous to a similar failing as regards personal dignity. The account of personal dignity given in the Catholic tradition focuses especially on human reason and freedom. But it was a frequent complaint of the late Pope that modern understandings of human dignity have focused too much on a conception of freedom divorced from truth: freedom merely as self-expression, self-assertion, and self-satisfaction. The Pope believed that such an understanding of freedom, and of the dignity of beings possessed of such freedom, was ultimately a great threat to the good of human persons, especially those not yet or no longer able to assert themselves against the desires of others. And so, in the Pope's view, the 'culture of death', with its commitment to abortion and euthanasia, was a natural outgrowth of this more limited conception of freedom and human dignity.

Culturally, a similar error pervades our understanding of the dignity of marriage. Marriage is understood as a paradigmatic expression of freedom, yet freedom to marry and freedom in marriage are understood in a thin and often normatively unconstrained manner. The account that I have given here,

---

[23] I have addressed this point at greater length in Christopher Tollefsen, 'John Paul II and children's education', *Notre Dame Journal of Law, Ethics, and Public Policy* 21 (2007), 159–89.

however, of the nature of marriage and of the dignity of marriage, can only emerge if the possibility of a *true*, and hence normative, conception of marriage is not closed off at the outset. But any such conception, if it exists, will inevitably be resistant to the claim that mere desire to participate in the institution of marriage should suffice as grounds for a right to participate. And it will likewise be resistant to the claim that the norms within marriage—of exclusivity, permanence, openness to children—are available to be rewritten in their entirety. An institution available for such restructuring at will is an institution with no real nature, and it is difficult, if not impossible, to see in what the dignity of such an institution could reside.

29

Response to Tollefsen and Cameron

Robert P. George

THE CHAPTERS BY CHRISTOPHER Tollefsen and Edwin Cameron offer deeply opposed positions on central issues pertaining to sexual morality and marriage. They are irreconcilable positions, so I will make no effort to reconcile them, or even to show that they are less distant from each other than first appears. Still, it is worth noting that both authors argue from an understanding of human dignity in which the obligation to respect dignity is an obligation to favour the well-being, the integral flourishing of the human person. The authors differ so fundamentally precisely because they have such profound differences about what constitutes and promotes the flourishing of human persons when it comes to sexuality and the choices people face and make in which sexual desire and judgements about what is intrinsically good and bad and right and wrong crucially figure. And I want to suggest, in a moment, that these differences reflect competing conceptions of the nature of the human person—that being whose integral good should be respected and favoured in all of our choosing and acting, if, as both Professor Tollefsen and Justice Cameron believe, we have an obligation to honour human dignity.

For all their differences, we see in the chapters by both of these authors arguments reflective of what John Rawls called 'comprehensive views'. Of course, Rawls himself hoped that for purposes of political theory and thus for legislation and the design and functioning of political institutions (at least where questions of constitutional fundamentals and basic justice are concerned), we could lay aside comprehensive views and operate across their borders by way of an overlapping consensus on a purely political conception of liberalism. And Rawls himself struggled mightily, even heroically, to show how that might be possible. But his case was most vulnerable precisely on issues of the sort we are grappling with in this conference on human dignity—issues that cannot be resolved without reflection and deliberation about the nature and worth of human persons.

We should not be surprised to find Professor Tollefsen and Justice Cameron arguing on the basis of comprehensive views. It is difficult to see how it could be otherwise once a social consensus on the nature, meaning, and purpose of an institution as fundamental as the institution of marriage has broken down—a breaking down that itself reflects the shattering of a fairly wide consensus in the domain of sexual ethics. Similarly, it is difficult to see how a purely political liberalism, or any rigorously anti-perfectionist theory of political morality, could handle questions such as abortion and euthanasia in circumstances in which reasonable people of goodwill do not, or no longer, agree on such questions as who is a member of the human community whose dignity is to be respected, and whose rights are to be protected, by the effective application and enforcement of principles of political justice.

And so we are brought to a conflict of understandings of the human good and its integral directiveness as shaped by principles of morality for the guidance of our sexual conduct as individuals and for our decisions as communities regarding the regulation, or possible regulation, of sexual behaviour. And we are brought to a profound disagreement about *what marriage is* and what posture towards it law and the institutions of the polity ought to take.

The debate about marriage is sometimes depicted as a dispute about 'who should be permitted to marry' or 'who should be permitted to marry whom'. This is deeply misguided. Those who characterize the debate in this way are, perhaps unwittingly, simply helping themselves to the answer they happen to prefer to the question they are evading: *What is marriage?* They are, in most cases, assuming that marriage is fundamentally a form of sexual-romantic domestic partnership—a particularly intense form of friendship, or, in the (approving) words of John Corvino, 'your relationship with your Number One person'. On the basis of this (ordinarily) undefended assumption, they then maintain that 'restricting' (as they characterize it) marriage to male-female relationships is a denial of 'marriage equality'. But the undefended assumption is precisely what is contested by defenders of the historic conception of marriage as a conjugal union. To leave it undefended, therefore, is to beg the question (however useful it may be as part of a political strategy to brand one's opponents as enemies of equality and promoters of prejudice).

Professor Tollefsen ably sets forth and defends the rational-moral foundations of the conjugal conception of marriage. It is an understanding of marriage as the distinctive type of relationship that is ordered to, and would be naturally fulfilled by, the spouses conceiving and bringing up children together—a type of relationship (unlike ordinary friendships, however intense they may be, and other private partnerships) in which society as a whole has a profound interest because of its child-rearing value and significance. Marriage is, according to the understanding Tollefsen defends, the union of husband and wife in a multi-level (biological, emotional, volitional, rational) sharing of life whose foundation and matrix is the bodily (or 'one-flesh') union made possible by the sexual-reproductive complementarity of male and female. Though marriage is naturally ordered to procreation and the rearing of children, it is *intrinsically* and not merely instrumentally valuable. It is not a mere means—to children, to pleasure, to the expression of tender feelings, or anything else. Therefore, as the law has historically recognized, acts of sexual congress that consummate and renew marriages—acts that fulfil the behavioural conditions of procreation—have their meaning and significance, and thus their integrity as a form of bodily communion, quite independently of whether the non-behavioural conditions of procreation happen to obtain. A marital act is an act that is per se apt for procreation—an act that unites spouses *biologically* (as 'one flesh'); but its quality as a marital act does not depend on whether procreation occurs, can occur, or is desired or intended. True biological unity is an aspect of *personal* unity because the body, far from being a mere extrinsic instrument of the person (where the person is identified exclusively with the conscious and desiring aspect of the self) is part of the personal reality of the human being—because the person is properly understood as a dynamic unity of body, mind, emotion, spirit.

On the conjugal understanding, marriage is, in a sense, a natural kind, and in an even deeper sense a rational kind, since it is a basic aspect of human well-being and fulfilment which, as such, provides a more than merely instrumental reason for choice and action. And so marriage is inherently, and not merely incidentally, a *sexual* partnership (a *bodily* union) and it is intrinsically shaped by norms of sexual exclusiveness and fidelity and a pledge of permanence of commitment. Unlike the 'sexual-romantic domestic partnership' conception of marriage, or any conception that treats marriage as essentially an emotional bond (and not one founded on true bodily union), the conjugal understanding can give an account of the rational basis of these norms as moral principles.

Of course, Justice Cameron's view differs radically from Professor Tollefsen's view. According to Cameron, sexual choices are above all matters of personal expression. Sexual desires and general orientations differ, and people have an interest in being able freely and without shame or stigma to act on these desires, so long as they respect the rights of others. In so acting, they express who they are, some aspect of their identities, their very selves. If, indeed, dignity is intrinsic to each person, as Justice Cameron and Professor Tollefsen agree it is, then, according to Cameron, 'it comprises the deeply personal understandings we have of ourselves and our worth as individuals and in our material and social context'. And so, in its public dimension, particularly as a value that infuses rights, especially the right to equality, respect for human dignity should enable people 'without fear of abuse, discrimination, or constraint, to engage out in the world in the commitments and activities that embody who we are and wish to become—to attain self-actualization, despite the accidents of our birth and notwithstanding any incidents of lifestyle'.

And so Justice Cameron's expressive individualist understanding of sexuality and Professor Tollefsen's natural law understanding represent competing visions of what makes for, and detracts from, human well-being and moral uprightness in a central area of human concern and striving. From Justice Cameron's point of view, dignity figures in a proper analysis of the problem as a principle prohibiting stigmatization of people for acting freely on sexual desires, and thus expressing who they are and what they wish to become. From Professor Tollefsen's point of view, dignity figures as the reality we honour in ourselves and others when we order desire to the demands of practical reason and moral uprightness in our personal choices and actions, and when we as communities privilege and protect the institution of marriage as a conjugal union.

As Justice Cameron's chapter makes clear, this is not, as it is sometimes depicted, a debate about whether to 'expand' marriage to accommodate same-sex partnerships while retaining the social normativity of marriage and the specific norms that have traditionally been regarded as giving marriage its shape and substance—norms of monogamy, exclusivity (fidelity), and the pledge of permanence of commitment. This is evident throughout his chapter, but clearest in his expression of concern that 'there may be a danger that institutionalizing same-sex marriage may replace one set of dangerous repressive social norms for another—the legal sanction of sexual sameness or conformity'. His is no mere proposal to jettison the idea of sexual complementarity as an essential aspect of marriage while retaining traditional norms of sexual ethics, such as those condemning promiscuity, multi-partner (polyamorous) sexual unions, and the like.

Of course, his reference to 'dangerous' and 'repressive' social norms reflects the broader set of understandings and commitments that inform Justice Cameron's expressive individualism as a comprehensive view. From Professor Tollefsen's perspective (and my own), those norms—monogamy, sexual exclusivity and fidelity, permanence of commitment—are the opposite of dangerous and repressive; they are ennobling and enriching. They are generated not by some desire for 'sameness' or 'conformity' for its own sake but by an understanding of the various aspects of human well-being and fulfilment integrally conceived. Indeed, far from being 'repressive', they liberate us by way of fidelity to reason from what I once heard Elizabeth Anscombe describe as the most humiliating form of indignity—slavery to desire.

Of course, where Professor Tollefsen sees slavery to self, Justice Cameron sees fulfilling self-expression and self-actualization. And so he views Professor Tollefsen, and the Catholic Church, as enemies of human flourishing—enemies who are guilty of crimes against humanity that are deeply analogous to the crime of apartheid. So, presumably, the reparative project that he would carry out in the name of human dignity would stigmatize and, in palpable ways, limit certain opportunities and liberties of Catholics, many Protestants, Orthodox Jews, Muslims, and others who hold views contrary to his on questions of sexual morality and the nature and proper definition of marriage. And this, too, I think demonstrates that this dispute really is profound and not resolvable at the level of shared principle. One hopes that that the struggle will be political, and not carried out by non-political or non-democratic means; and that even in the political struggle—and even when each side must, in conscience, speak hard words to the other—we can do it with civility and respect.

Justice Cameron makes it clear that he feels insulted and demeaned when someone like Professor Tollefsen asserts that sexual conduct outside the marital bond is morally wrong, and that marriage is a conjugal union. From his expressive individualist point of view, defenders of traditional sexual morality are enemies of personal self-realization, and thus of human dignity. I am sure that Professor Tollefsen feels no less insulted and demeaned—I certainly do—when someone like Justice Cameron equates the conjugal view of marriage and sexual morality with bigotry—indeed, with something as ugly and evil as apartheid. From a natural law point of view, expressive individualist ideology undermines human dignity by encouraging people to yield to unworthy desires, thus damaging their own integrity and contributing to the erosion of a cultural environment in which marriage and the norms of sexual exclusivity and fidelity essential to it can flourish.

Who is right? No one can answer that question for himself or herself without wading into the deep philosophical waters of debates about expressive individualism and the moral understandings that, since the 1960s, have been aggressively challenged in its name. Unfortunately, many people seem to want to dodge the hard questions, or excuse themselves from engaging in serious arguments about deep and difficult philosophical matters. They sometimes dismiss such arguments as 'convoluted' or claim that they are merely a cover for unworthy motives. At the same time, they help themselves to controversial premises needed to support the positions they prefer, then claim that it is all, really, very simple.

But it is not.

The foregoing commentary, which is essentially what I presented at the Oxford conference on human dignity at which Professor Tollefsen and Justice

Cameron gave their chapters, is an assessment of the papers as they were presented there. Professor Tollefsen's chapter remains substantially the same. But Justice Cameron, perhaps accustomed as a judge to having the final word, chose to revise his chapter to insert into it an attack on me personally. Regrettably, he deploys in that attack the same sorts of abusive terms and forms of rhetorical manipulation he used in his efforts to blacken Professor Tollefsen. It is an altogether unlovely and unedifying maneuver—quite unworthy of the ambitions of this volume to provide a model of civil and serious argumentation and debate among people of goodwill representing a range of viewpoints. But it does necessitate a response.

Justice Cameron opens his attack by informing readers that he is going to 'deal with' the arguments on the nature of marriage I have presented in various places; but then says he will do so only 'cursorily' because 'the impermissibility of same-sex marriage seems as difficult to propound on coherent and rational moral grounds as the impermissibility of interracial marriage.' This is a rhetorically sly way of excusing himself from the obligation to engage serious arguments against his view in a serious way. But even if we lay aside for a moment his efforts to link those with whom he disagrees to the vile phenomenon of racism, it is clear from his very terms of reference that he profoundly misunderstands the arguments he has promised to 'deal with.' The claim of his opponents is not about the *permissibility* of non-conjugal 'marriage'—it is about its *possibility*. It is not about who should be 'permitted' to marry or 'prohibited' from marrying; it is about *what marriage is*. My argument is that marriage is inherently a conjugal union, and that the alternative position (i.e., 'marriage' as a form of sexual-romantic companionship or domestic partnership) cannot account for the norms and other defining features of marriage that remain largely uncontested, even as we debate the validity of the norm of sexual complementarity.

In the debate over interracial marriages, at least in the United States, the question was precisely whether such marriages should be *permitted* or could rightly be *prohibited*. No one doubted that they *were* conjugal partnerships, and therefore entirely *possible*. Of course, racism alone could account for the view that such marriages should be forbidden and subjected to criminal prohibition. That is why we rightly condemn laws prohibiting marriage across racial lines as gravely unjust and an assault on human dignity. By contrast, as I have noted, the question at issue in the present debate is: *What is marriage?* Is it a conjugal partnership, or is it a form of sexual-romantic companionship or domestic partnership? If it is the former, same-sex and polyamorous partnerships cannot be marriages and should not be recognized as such. If it is the latter, they can be, and should be. So which is it?

Marriage, understood as a conjugal union and not as a mere form of sexual-romantic companionship or domestic partnership, is ubiquitous in human history. One finds it in the laws and customs of diverse cultures and religions, as well as in the thought of figures ranging from Plato, Aristotle, Xenophanes, Musonius Rufus, and Plutarch, to Augustine, Aquinas, Kant, Anscombe, and Gandhi. No one of whom I am aware even attempts to argue that the conjugal understanding of marriage arose in our law and culture or any others as a result of racism or animus of any type, including hostility to persons who experience same-sex attraction. Plainly it didn't. The legal treatment of sodomitical acts as non-marital has historically applied to opposite sex couples, *including those who are lawfully married.* Marriage was understood as consummated by and only by reproductive behaviour, that is, acts that fulfil the behavioural conditions of procreation (quite irrespective of whether the nonbehavioral conditions happen to obtain).[1] Such acts were understood as uniting spouses as a biological unit (and not merely as juxtaposing flesh to produce sexual pleasure), and this unity was understood to be foundational to marriage considered as a comprehensive union, that is, a unity of hearts and minds, but one that differed from other sorts of personal relationships by its extension into the bodily plane—the body being, as John Finnis explains, no mere subpersonal instrument, but part of the personal reality of the human being.[2] None of these ideas were manufactured as pretexts for excluding anyone from marriage.

Because the idea of marriage as a conjugal union was not developed to establish or reinforce a system of subordination and exploitation, we cannot dismiss it as inherently unjust in the way we rightly dismiss the prohibition of interracial marriages. So, in contending that the norm of sexual complementarity should be abolished, it is incumbent upon Cameron and those on his side to make a philosophical case for their view and to respond in a serious (and not merely 'cursory') way to the philosophical arguments adumbrated by those of us who defend the conjugal understanding of marriage. This includes meeting the challenges that remain utterly unaddressed by Cameron and others who seek to redefine marriage, namely, the challenges to identify

---

[1] Cameron seems to suggest that this view—which he characterizes in typically reductive fashion as 'sex involv[ing] a penis and vagina', then dismisses (without argument) a 'ludicrous'—is original with me or thinkers associated with me. Nothing could be farther from the truth. The identification of acts fulfilling the behavioural conditions of procreation as uniquely marital (and distinguishable from other acts of penetration or juxtaposition involving sexual organs) has been embodied in our law of marital consummation for centuries, and was established quite independently of debates about same-sex relations.

[2] See John Finnis, 'Law, morality, and "sexual orientation"', *Notre Dame Law Review* 69 (1994), at 1066.

principled grounds consistent with their view of marriage as sexual-romantic companionship or domestic partnership for holding that marriage is a permanent and exclusive union of two and only two persons. After all, if two men or two women can marry, then what sets marriage apart from other bonds must be *emotional intensity or priority*. But nothing about emotional union or intensity requires it to be pledged to permanence, as opposed to deliberately temporary (or binding only 'for as long as love lasts'). Nothing beyond mere sentiment or subjective preference would require it to be sexually 'closed' as opposed to 'open', or limited to relationships of two persons, as opposed to three or more in 'polyamorous' sexual ensembles. Indeed, there would be no ground for understanding marriage as a *sexual* partnership—one that requires consummation by sexual intercourse—as opposed to one integrated around any of a range of possible non-sexual shared interests or commitments (for example, playing tennis, reading novels, or supporting a favourite team). Nor would there be any basis for understanding marriage as a relationship that is inherently enriched by family life and shaped by its demands. Yet these have always been defining features and norms of marriage—features and norms that make marriage unlike (and unlike *in kind*, and not merely in degree of emotional intensity) other forms or companionship or domestic partnership.

Cameron simply refuses to engage the central question: *What is marriage?* But his delinquency goes beyond even this dereliction of scholarly duty. After thoroughly misstating—indeed, mangling—the basic arguments he promised to 'deal with', he makes matters worse by *not dealing with them*—even 'cursorily.' Instead of counterarguments designed to expose errors of fact or fallacious inferences in the views he attributes to his opponents, he provides a string of undefended assertions (as if he were pronouncing judgments from the bench or launching thunderbolts from Mount Olympus), relying on denunciation and adjectival insults ('absurd', 'ludicrous', 'silly', 'rigid', and on and on) as a substitute for argument. Does he suppose that his readers will be too dim to notice the absence of argumentation? Or does he imagine that those against whom he shamelessly deploys these tactics will be too polite—or intimidated—to respond? I'm afraid I am neither.

30

Dignity and the Duty to Protect Unborn Life

Reva Siegel[1]

THIS CHAPTER ANALYSES COMPETING claims on dignity in constitutional judgments about abortion that impose on government a constitutional duty to protect unborn life, with attention to the ways courts reconcile commitments to dignity as liberty, dignity as equality, and dignity as life. By appeals to dignity as liberty, I mean appeals to dignity that invoke values of autonomy and free development of personality; by appeals to dignity as equality, I mean appeals to dignity that invoke concerns about standing, status, and respect. By appeals to dignity as life, I refer to claims on dignity associated with the regulation of birth, sex, or death that protect or symbolically express the value of human life itself.

The chapter first considers rival claims on dignity in political debates that led to the constitutionalization of abortion in the 1970s. Against this backdrop, it examines two influential German judgments that interpret constitutional protection for dignity as requiring protection for unborn life. The two judgments, rendered over a twenty-year period, reflect an evolving view of how the state may express respect for human life—a judgment tied to evolving understandings about the respect owed women in making decisions concerning motherhood. Brief consideration of other duty-to-protect-life jurisdictions suggest great variation in the ways that legal systems coordinate respect for different kinds of human dignity implicated by the regulation of abortion.

In 1975, West Germany's Federal Constitutional Court interpreted the guarantee of dignity in the nation's Basic Law to impose a duty to protect unborn life, and struck down a statute that had balanced respect for women's autonomy and respect for life by allowing abortion after dissuasive counselling in the first twelve weeks of pregnancy.[2] Two decades later, after the

---

[1] This chapter draws on Reva Siegel, 'Constitutionalization of abortion', in Michel Rosenfeld and András Sajó, *Oxford Handbook of Comparative Constitutional Law* (Oxford, Oxford University Press, 2012), 1057.

[2] 39 BVerfGE 1 (1975) (*Abortion I*), translated in John D. Gorby and Robert E. Jonas, 'West German abortion decision: a contrast to *Roe v Wade*', *John Marshall Journal of Practice & Procedure* 9 (1976), 605.

reunification of Germany, the Federal Constitutional Court revisited its judgment, and allowed government to discharge the duty to protect life through a regime of counselling rather than the threat of criminal punishment.[3] The court allowed the substitution on the grounds that counselling might be more effective in protecting life, but the court's reasoning revealed that conceptions of dignity as liberty also played a role in the judgment. While in its first decision the Federal Constitutional Court reasoned that dignity as life trumps dignity as liberty/equality, in the second, the court began to acknowledge and accommodate different forms of dignity.

Liberalization of the German framework is often explained as a compromise associated with reunification. But the court's reasoning also reflects a changing view of women. Practical judgments about the appropriate way for government to discharge its duty to protect life *in utero* presuppose some view of women. For this reason, in judicial decisions, judgments about dignity as liberty are often nested inside judgments about dignity as life. To see this dynamic at work, I compare discussion of dignity in the first and second German judgment, and close by considering protection for dignity as liberty and dignity as equality in the case law of other jurisdictions that impose a constitutional duty to protect life on government regulation of abortion.

The complex role of dignity in the German abortion cases and in other duty-to-protect-life jurisdictions suggests that, over time, both the right-to-life movement and the women's movement have shaped the evolution of dignity in constitutional case law. Changing conceptions of women as deliberative agents seem to play a role in the abortion case law, even in jurisdictions that constitutionalize a duty to protect unborn life. Attention to the ways law coordinates competing claims on dignity in the abortion cases offers a fascinating window on the roles dignity can play in mediating conflict within a constitutional community.

Appeals to dignity in debates leading to constitutionalization of abortion

In the 1960s, public health arguments for liberalizing access to abortion began to spread in Western Europe and North America. Critics argued that poor women unequally suffered the health harms of criminalization, and doctors sought freedom to practice in circumstances in which the criminal law was

---

[3] 88 BVerfGE 203 (1993) (*Abortion II*), translation available at http://www.bverfg.de/entscheidungen/fs19930528_2bvf000290en.html (official court translation).

erratically enforced.⁴ By the end of the decade, however, a newly mobilizing women's movement had joined public health advocates in challenging the criminalization of abortion. No longer were reformers satisfied with liberalizing indications for abortion (exceptions to criminal bans on abortion, typically determined in the individual case by permission of a committee of doctors). They now sought repeal of indications legislation, and, at the very least, enactment of periodic legislation that would give to women capacity to decide whether to carry a pregnancy to term during the early months of pregnancy—legislation sometimes termed 'on demand', because it shifted control of the decision whether to carry a pregnancy to term to the pregnant woman who was no longer obliged to plead her case to a committee of doctors.⁵

Feminists challenged the criminalization of abortion on new grounds, arguing that laws criminalizing abortion violated women's dignity. The claim was both practical and symbolic. Under prevailing social arrangements, they argued, laws criminalizing abortion took from women decisions about their health, sexual relations, family needs, economic independence, and political participation. Laws criminalizing abortion thus reflected and perpetuated status-based controls over women's lives. These associations, once identified, escalated the practical and symbolic stakes of the abortion debate and transformed it into a site of struggle over women's citizenship.⁶ In 1969, Betty Friedan, president of the newly formed National Organization of Women, mobilized these arguments in a call for the repeal of laws criminalizing abortion, in the process fatefully reframing American policy debate over abortion

---

⁴ See Dagmar Herzog, *Sexuality in Europe: A Twentieth-Century History* (Cambridge, Cambridge University Press, 2011), 156–60; Linda Greenhouse and Reva B. Siegel, 'Before (and after) *Roe v Wade*: New questions About backlash', *Yale Law Journal* 120 (2011), 2028, 2036–46. See generally Christopher Tietze, 'Abortion in Europe', *American Journal of Public Health* 57 (1967), 1923.

⁵ In this era, many feminists challenged the use of criminal law to regulate women's abortion decisions, and sought to minimize the involvement of the medical profession as well. It is impossible to identify one position spanning movements and borders. But there was shared hostility to the use of criminal law and to doctors' committees to restrict access to abortion in early pregnancy.

⁶ See, for example, Herzog, *Sexuality in Europe*, 156–60; Machteld Nijsten, *Abortion and Constitutional Law: A Comparative European-American Study* (Florence, European University Institute, 1990), 30–1; Reva B. Siegel, 'The constitutionalization of abortion', in Michel Rosenfeld and András Sajó (eds), *The Oxford Handbook of Comparative Constitutional Law* (Oxford, Oxford University Press 2012), 1057, 1060–4; Reva B. Siegel, '*Roe*'s roots: the women's rights claims that engendered *Roe*', *Boston University Law Review* 90 (2010), 1875, 1879–86, 1900–7; Greenhouse and Siegel, 'Before (and after) *Roe v Wade*', 3029–46. See also, Myra Marx Ferree, William Anthony Gamson, Jürgen Gerhards, and Dieter Rucht, *Shaping Abortion Discourse: Democracy and the Public Sphere in Germany and the United States* (Cambridge, Cambridge University Press, 2002), 131–53; Dorothy McBride Stetson (ed.), *Abortion Politics, Women's Movements, and the Democratic State: A Comparative Study of State Feminism* (Oxford, Oxford University Press, 2003).

reform.⁷ Friedan insisted: '[T]here is no freedom, no equality, no full human dignity and personhood possible for women until we assert and demand the control over our own bodies, over our own reproductive process ... The real sexual revolution is the emergence of women from passivity, from *thing-ness*, to full self-determination, to full dignity ...'⁸

This feminist claim to dignity in making decisions about bearing children would be publicized through speak-outs and through civil disobedience. In France, 343 women declared that they had had abortions in a manifesto published in *Le Nouvel Observateur* in April 1971.⁹ Two months after publication of the French manifesto, Aktion 218, a women's organization in West Germany named for the code provision criminalizing abortion, published in *Der Stern* the names of 374 women who had had abortions. They denounced the law criminalizing abortion because it 'branded them as criminals', and in their manifesto declared: 'I am opposed to Paragraph 218 and for desired children.'¹⁰ In other nations, similar speak-outs followed.

Opponents of abortion reform appealed to dignity as well. In appealing to human dignity, opponents were not seeking abortion laws that would express respect for women's decisional authority but instead sought abortion laws that would express respect for the value of life itself. In 1970, the Central Committee of German Catholics, an association of Catholic laypersons, argued that decriminalizing abortion would violate West German constitutional guarantees of dignity: 'If becoming life is not protected, including with the means of the criminal law, unconditional fundamental principles of a society founded on human dignity are not assured for long.'¹¹

During the 1970s, these national and transnational debates led to the enactment of legislation in a number of countries that liberalized access to

---

⁷ Betty Friedan, President, National Organization for Women, Address at the First National Conference on Abortion Laws: 'Abortion: a woman's civil right' (February 1969), reprinted in Linda Greenhouse and Reva B. Siegel (eds), *Before Roe v. Wade: Voices that Shaped the Abortion Debate Before the Supreme Court's Ruling* (2012), 39–40, http://documents.law.yale.edu/sites/default/files/BeforeRoe2ndEd_1.pdf.

⁸ Greenhouse and Siegel, *Before* Roe v Wade, 39–40.

⁹ 'La liste des 343 françaises qui ont le courage de signer le manifest "je me suis fait avorter" ' [The list of 343 French women who have the courage to sign the manifesto 'I have had an abortion'], *Le Nouvel Observateur* (5 April 1971), 5 (author's translation).

¹⁰ Wir haben abgetrieben! [We Aborted] *Stern* (Hamburg) (6 June 1971), 16 (author's translation). See also Alice Schwarzer (ed.), *Frauen gegen den §218. 18 Protokolle, aufgezeichnet von Alice Schwarzer* [*Women Against §218: Eighteen Interviews, Recorded by Alice Schwarzer*] (1971), 146 (author's translation).

¹¹ Manfred Spieker, *Kirche und Abtreibung in Deutschland: Ursachen und Verlauf eines Konflikts* (2nd edn, 2008), 22–3 (author's translation).

abortion. Those frustrated in politics increasingly brought their claims to court, leading to the first constitutional judgments on abortion.[12]

Claims on dignity in the German abortion decisions

Beginning with the West German judgment in 1975, and accelerating over time, claims on dignity played an increasingly important role in the constitutional law of abortion. The West German judgment famously interpreted constitutional protection for human dignity to require protection for unborn life. Less appreciated is the way in which the court's judgment *also* reflected an engagement with the dignity claims of the West German women's movement.

In what follows, I consider how dignity figured in two German abortion judgments set almost twenty years apart. The first German judgment, from 1975, appealed to dignity as respect for life to strike down periodic legislation adopted in response to the Aktion 218 campaign. In 1993, after reunification, the Federal Constitutional Court qualified its judgment in ways that acknowledged competing claims on dignity.

In 1975, the Federal Constitutional Court held that West Germany's 1974 law, which decriminalized abortion during the first twelve weeks of pregnancy for women who received abortion-dissuasive counselling, violated the Basic Law.[13] The court reasoned that the duty of the state to protect unborn life was derived from the Basic Law's protection for life and for dignity: 'Where human life exists, human dignity is present to it; it is not decisive that the bearer of this dignity himself be conscious of it and know personally how to preserve it.'[14] Without deciding whether the unborn held a right to life, the court concluded that there was an objective dimension to the right to life that government was obliged to respect by law.[15]

---

[12] In the early 1970s, the US Supreme Court and four courts in Western Europe issued judgments on the constitutionality of the legal regulation of abortion. Nijsten, *Abortion and Constitutional Law*, 231–6.
[13] BVerfGE 1 (1975) (*Abortion I*), 605.
[14] BVerfGE 1 (1975) (*Abortion I*), 641 (citing Articles 2(2)(1) and 1(1)(2)).
[15] See BVerfGE 1 (1975) (*Abortion I*), 641–2. 'The question … whether the one about to be born himself is the bearer of the fundamental right, or on account of a lesser capacity to possess legal and fundamental rights, is "only" protected in his right to life by the objective norms of the constitution need not be decided here … the fundamental legal norms contain not only subjective rights of defense of the individual against the state but embody, at the same time, an objective ordering of values, which is valid as a constitutionally fundamental decision for all areas of law and which provides direction and impetus for legislation, administration and judicial opinions.'

The court famously justified its decision to strike down the 1974 statute liberalizing access to abortion by invoking the Holocaust.[16] Less well known is the court's engagement with feminist claims; the 1975 decision expressly repudiated feminist dignity claims. The Federal Constitutional Court warned the legislature not to 'acquiesce' in popular beliefs about abortion that might have developed in response to 'passionate discussion of the abortion problematic'.[17]

The court expressly rejected the parliament's efforts to devise a framework that respected the dignity of both women and the unborn. It rejected the view of legislators who sought to identify a period during pregnancy to respect 'the right to self-determination of the woman which flows from human dignity vis-à-vis all others, including the child's right to life', on the grounds that it was 'not reconcilable with the value ordering of the Basic Law'.[18] Given the overriding importance of the dignity of human life, the court concluded, 'the legal order may not make the woman's right to self-determination the sole guideline of its rulemaking. The state must proceed, as a matter of principle, from a duty to carry the pregnancy to term.'[19]

The Federal Constitutional Court not only rejected the parliament's efforts to coordinate dignity concerns of women and the unborn; the opinion went further, and denied that pregnant women had claims of deliberative autonomy concerning motherhood. The court recognized a constitutional duty to protect life that required government to 'proceed ... from a duty to carry the pregnancy to term', that is, to enforce women's duty to mother.

The court derived these duties from nature, reasoning that the duty to protect life was 'entrusted by nature in the first place to the protection of the mother. To reawaken and, if required to strengthen the maternal duty to protect, where it is lost, should be the principal goal of the endeavours of the state by the protection of life.' The duty to protect life obliged government to 'strengthen the readiness of the expectant mother to accept the pregnancy as her own responsibility'.[20] On this view, women naturally choose to protect unborn life; where nature falters, law must enforce choices women ought naturally to make.

---

[16] BVerfGE 1 (1975) (*Abortion I*), 662. The majority's reasoning was disputed by dissenting justices, who pointed out that National Socialists had criminalized abortion. BVerfGE 1 (1975) (*Abortion I*), 669–70.

[17] BVerfGE 1 (1975) (*Abortion I*), 661–2.

[18] BVerfGE 1 (1975) (*Abortion I*), 643 (citing German Federal Parliament, Seventh Election Period, 96th Sess., Stenographic Reports, 6492).

[19] BVerfGE 1 (1975) (*Abortion I*), 644.

[20] BVerfGE 1 (1975) (*Abortion I*), 644.

Yet, even as the court required government to enforce women's maternal duties, the court limited the kind of sacrifices government could exact from women, again appealing to judgments about what is normal for women. The court distinguished between the 'normal' burdens of motherhood, which government can exact by law, and extraordinary burdens of motherhood, such as those posing a threat to a woman's life or health, which the court ruled were non-exactable by law.[21]

The passages of the opinion explaining when and why the duty to protect life should be exacted by law turn on judgments about women's dignity, identifying circumstances in which government must respect women's bodily integrity and deliberative autonomy, circumstances when government may do so, and circumstances when government must not do so. The court explained that when a pregnant woman faced difficulties other than the 'normal' burdens of motherhood, her 'decision for an interruption of pregnancy can attain the rank of a decision of conscience worthy of consideration', and in these circumstances it would be inappropriate to use criminal law or 'external compulsion where respect for the sphere of personality of the human being demands fuller inner freedom of decision'.[22] By contrast, women who 'decline pregnancy because they are not willing to take on the renunciation and the natural motherly duties bound up with it' may decide 'upon an interruption of pregnancy without having a reason which is worthy of esteem within the value order of the constitution'.[23] The court recognized a woman's concern about continuing a pregnancy that posed a threat to her life or grave risk to her health as worthy of respect, hence warranting an exemption from legal compulsion. The court permitted the legislature to allow exceptions on several indications where pregnancy would pose similarly onerous burdens for women.[24] But even in these cases where law was to respect women's deliberative judgment, the state was nonetheless to provide dissuasive counselling to guide its exercise 'with the goal of reminding pregnant women of the fundamental duty to respect the right to life of the unborn, to encourage her to continue the pregnancy …'[25]

In the 1990s, the Federal Constitutional Court would reaffirm this understanding, but in a framework that indirectly afforded far greater recognition to women's autonomy in making decisions about motherhood. The reunification

---

[21] BVerfGE 1 (1975) (*Abortion I*), 647.
[22] BVerfGE 1 (1975) (*Abortion I*), 647.
[23] BVerfGE 1 (1975) (*Abortion I*), 653.
[24] BVerfGE 1 (1975) (*Abortion I*), 624, 647–8. The court gave the legislature discretion whether to allow abortion on eugenic, rape, and social emergency indications.
[25] BVerfGE 1 (1975) (*Abortion I*), 649.

of Germany required reconciling the law of East Germany, which allowed women to make their own decisions about abortion in early pregnancy, with the law of West Germany, which did not.[26] Germany enacted compromise legislation that allowed women to make their own decisions about abortion in the first twelve weeks of pregnancy after participating in a counselling process designed to persuade women to carry the pregnancy to term—a form of regulation presented as more effective in deterring abortion than a criminal ban and respecting both 'the high value of unborn life and the self-determination of the woman'.[27] The Federal Constitutional Court struck down the legislation, but shifted ground as it did so.

The court again rejected legislation on the periodic model, reasoning that 'a woman's human dignity and her ability to make responsible decisions herself' was not enough to justify limiting protection for unborn life, even during the early months of pregnancy.[28] The court invoked the harm principle, ('[l]egal protection presupposes that the law lays down conditions governing to what extent and how far one person can interfere with another and does not leave it to the will of one of the parties concerned')[29], and reasoned from women's natural duties in determining the principle's application, ('[a]lthough [a woman's constitutional rights] must accordingly be protected, they do not extend so far as to allow the constitutional duty to carry the child to term to be suspended even for a limited time').[30] In striking down the statute, the court emphasized that the legislature was obliged to clearly communicate the scope of the duty to protect by demarcating in law the obligations exactable of the pregnant woman herself, and also of others in a position to support her in carrying the pregnancy to term.[31] Preserving the law criminalizing abortion was an effective way to do this.

But, the court emphasized, the legislature was not obliged to protect unborn life through the threat of criminal punishment itself. The legislature might find that the threat of criminal punishment did not in fact deter abortion but merely drove the practice underground. With this understanding, the legislature could arrange a system of counselling to persuade pregnant women to carry to term, and so long as the counselling was effective to that end, the

---

[26] See Peter H. Merkl, *German Unification in the European Context* (University Park, PA, Penn State University Press, 1993), 176–80.
[27] 88 BVerfGE 203 (1993) (*Abortion II*), 37.
[28] BVerfGE 1 (1975) (*Abortion I*), 156.
[29] BVerfGE 1 (1975) (*Abortion I*), 156.
[30] BVerfGE 1 (1975) (*Abortion I*), 157; see also 644, 647, and 653. The court discusses 'the constitutional duty to carry the child to term' as enforcing the natural role and responsibilities of women.
[31] BVerfGE 1 (1975) (*Abortion I*), 173–4; see also 170–2.

legislature could even dispense with the threat of criminal punishment 'in view of the openness necessary for counselling to be effective'.[32]

The court presented this judgment as a practical judgment, but explained it in ways that reflected and expressed an evolving view of women. The court reasoned that the legislature might base its judgment about enforcing the duty to protect on the view that the state's efforts to protect unborn life were more likely to succeed if it sought to work with the mother and to secure her support.[33] The court presented this new account of the state's duty of protection as in 'conformity with the respect owed to a woman and future mother',[34] observing that the counselling concept endeavours to exact what the pregnant woman owes 'without degrading her to a mere object of protection', and 'respects her as an autonomous person by trying to win her over as an ally in the protection of the unborn'.[35]

While the court required adherence to its 1975 judgment, the court's willingness to accept the substitution of counselling for threat of criminal prosecution reflected a changing view of the citizen that abortion regulation addresses. In this emergent view, women citizens are persons who exercise autonomy even in the ways they inhabit family roles; that exercise of autonomy is sufficiently worthy of respect that women would be degraded if abortion law were to treat them as a mere object or instrument for bearing children. For practical and even demonstrative reasons, government might discharge its duty to protect life through deliberative rather than coercive interactions with women.

A dissenting opinion underscored this point:

> [T]he counselling regulation is not a frustrated escape from the frustrating failure of the indication solution. The new regulation is much more the result of an altered understanding of the personality and dignity of the woman. The judgment's finding that a woman is capable of a responsible choice regarding the continuation or interruption of her pregnancy must, however, have consequences for the interpretation of the constitution. In our opinion, it forces us to solve the collision between the human dignity of the unborn on the one hand, and the dignity of the pregnant woman on the other, by achieving a balance between the two. This did not occur in the judgment.

---

[32] BVerfGE 1 (1975) (*Abortion I*), 178.
[33] BVerfGE 1 (1975) (*Abortion I*), 183.
[34] BVerfGE 1 (1975) (*Abortion I*), 185.
[35] BVerfGE 1 (1975) (*Abortion I*), 214.

In the wake of the 1993 decision, abortion in Germany remains criminally prohibited except under restricted indications, but a woman who completes abortion during the first twelve weeks of pregnancy.[36]

Respect for women's dignity in jurisdictions enforcing a duty to protect life

Around the world, there are now many jurisdictions that have followed Germany in imposing on government regulation of abortion a constitutional duty to protect life. In duty-to-protect jurisdictions, courts employ a variety of approaches for coordinating constitutional protections for dignity as life and dignity as liberty. A look at several cases in duty-to-protect jurisdictions shows how practical judgments about the state's obligations to protect unborn life are entangled with questions about the state's obligations to respect women's decisions concerning motherhood.

Some constitutional orders enforce the duty to protect unborn life even more strenuously than the 1975 West German decision. In the Republic of Ireland, the constitution was amended in 1983 to provide: 'The State acknowledges the right to life of the unborn and, with due regard to the equal right to life of the mother, guarantees in its laws to respect, and, as far as practicable, by its laws to defend and vindicate that right.'[37] This framework for vindicating the rights of the unborn imposes on women a duty to carry pregnancy to term exactable by law under a far greater range of circumstances than does the first German abortion decision. The first German abortion decision reasoned that when a pregnant woman faces difficulties exceeding the 'normal' burdens of motherhood, her 'decision for an interruption of pregnancy can attain the rank of a decision of conscience worthy of consideration', and in these circumstances it would be inappropriate to use criminal law or 'external compulsion where respect for the sphere of personality of the human being demands fuller inner freedom of decision'.[38] Irish constitutional law does not seem to recognize pregnant women as having dignity as liberty in decisions respecting motherhood. When an adolescent who was pregnant by rape was enjoined

---

[36] See Strafgesetzbuch [StGB] [German Penal Code] para. 218a; available in English at http://www.gesetze-im-internet.de/englisch_stgb/englisch_stgb.html#StGB_000P218.

[37] Republic of Ireland, Eighth Amendment of the Constitution Act, 1983, 1983 Acts of the Oireachtas, 7 October 1983 (amending Irish Constitution, Article 40.3.3). Adopted in response to developments in Ireland, Europe, and the USA, the amendment was intended to clarify that the Irish constitution recognized a 'personal' right to life of the unborn, and not only the objective value of life.

[38] 39 BVerfGE 1 (1975) (*Abortion I*), 647–8.

from travelling abroad for an abortion, the Irish Supreme Court overturned the injunction, but without recognizing the young woman as having a right to resist bearing the child of her rapist; instead, the court released the young woman from the obligation to bear the child on the ground that the young woman's risk of suicide satisfied the standard of a 'real and substantial risk' to the pregnant woman's life.[39]

Ireland's approach is not shared in all duty-to-protect-unborn-life jurisdictions. In the wake of the first German decision, the Spanish Constitutional Court held that the government could include a rape indication in abortion legislation consistent with its duty to protect life. The Spanish court emphasized that in the case of rape 'gestation was caused by an act ... harming to a maximum degree [a woman's] personal dignity and the free development of her personality', emphasizing that 'the woman's dignity requires that she cannot be considered as a mere instrument'.[40] Even so, following the first German decision, the Spanish court reasoned that Spain was permitted, not required, to include the rape indication in its abortion legislation.

The Colombian Constitutional Court has also interpreted its constitution to require government to protect unborn life, yet reasoned about government's obligation to vindicate this duty quite differently. The Colombian court held that a statute banning abortion was constitutionally *required* to contain exceptions for several indications.[41] Failure to allow for abortion in cases of rape, the court explained, would be in 'complete disregard for human dignity and the right to the free development of the pregnant woman whose pregnancy is not the result of a free and conscious decision, but the result of arbitrary, criminal acts against her in violation of her autonomy'.[42] The court emphasized that '[a] woman's right to dignity prohibits her treatment as a mere instrument

---

[39] *Attorney General v X and others*, 1992, 1 IR 1, para [44]. In response to *X* and to the ruling of the ECHR in Case 14234/88, *Open Door and Dublin Well Woman v Ireland* [1992] ECHR 68, Ireland has amended its constitution to allow women to obtain information about and travel to abortion providers abroad—the statutory implementation of which the Irish Supreme Court upheld as constitutional so long as the information provided neither 'advocates' nor 'promotes' abortion. Article 26 and the Regulation of Information (Services outside the State for the Termination of Pregnancies) Bill 1995, In Re [1995] IESC 9; [1995] 1 IR 1 (12 May 1995).
[40] Tribunal Constitucional, STC 53/1985, Pt *11(b)*, 11April 1985, 1985–49 *Boletin de Jurisprudencia Constitucional 515 (Spain)*, http://www.boe.es/aeboe/consultas/bases_datos/doc.php?coleccion=tc&id=SENTENCIA-1985-0053. Official court translation, http://www.tribunalconstitucional.es/es/jurisprudencia/restrad/Paginas/JCC531985en.aspx.
[41] Corte Constitucional (Constitutional Court), 10 May 2006, Sentencia C-355/2006, 25, Gaceta de la Corte Constitucional (Colombia) (partial translation is available in *Women's Link Worldwide, C-355/2006: Excerpts of the Constitutional Court's Ruling that Liberalized Abortion in Colombia* (2007)).
[42] Corte Constitucional, 10 May 2006, 51.

for reproduction, and her consent is therefore essential to the fundamental, life-changing decision to give birth to another person'.[43]

A recent decision of the Argentinian Supreme Court is to similar effect. Invoking women's dignity, the court required the government to take positive measures to implement a rape indication in order to ensure that women who were raped could abort the resultant pregnancy if they so chose.[44]

An evolving understanding of women's dignity is reflected within the duty to protect, not only in judgments concerning the indications that are constitutionally permitted or required in abortion bans but also in judgments concerning the constitutionality of abortion-dissuasive counselling legislation, which, following Germany, a number of European countries have adopted.[45]

In Portugal, legislation that allows abortion during the first ten weeks of pregnancy after a waiting period and counselling 'aimed at providing the pregnant woman access to all relevant information necessary to make a free, genuine, and responsible decision' was recently upheld by the Portuguese Constitutional Court as an effective means of protecting life.[46] The counselling regime the court upheld was not expressly dissuasive.[47] The decision employed the reasoning of the 1993 German decision to dispense with the need

---

[43] Corte Constitucional, 10 May 2006, 53.
[44] Corte Suprema de Justicia de la Nación [CSJN] [Supreme Court of Justice of the Nation], 13/3/2010, 'F, A. L. s/ Medida Autosatisfactiva', Expediente Letra 'F', N 259, Libro XLVI (13 March 2012) (Argentina).
[45] A recent Spanish statute provides women access on the periodic model: the ability to decide during the first fourteen weeks of pregnancy (twenty-two weeks for health reasons) subject to a mandatory three-day period for reflection. Invoking 'dignity and the free development of personality', the preamble declares that 'women can make the initial decision about ... pregnancy and that the decision, conscious and responsible, will be respected'; at the same time, the preamble reasons, in the tradition of German law, that '[e]xperience has shown that protecting prenatal life is more effective through active policies to support pregnant women and maternity. Thus, protection of the legal right at the very beginning of pregnancy is articulated through the will of the woman, and not against it.' *See* Ley Orgánica 2/2010, de 3 de marzo, de salud sexual y reproductiva y de la interrupción voluntaria del embarazo, http://www.boe.es/aeboe/consultas/bases_datos/doc.php?id=BOE-A-2010-3514. See generally Albin Eser and Hans-Georg Koch, *Abortion and the Law: From International Comparison to Legal Policy* (The Hague, T.M.C. Asser Press, 2005) 285–91.
[46] Tribunal Constitucional, Acórdão no 75/2010, Processos nos 733/07 and 1186/07, 26 March 2010, Diário da República vol. 60, at 15566 (Portugal), http://w3.tribunalconstitucional.pt/acordaos/acordaos10/1-100/7510.htm (author's translation). See also. at 11.4.15.
[47] The court observed that the legislation directed that the pregnant woman would receive information concerning government assistance should she carry the pregnancy to term, and stated at 11.4.15 that: 'the body of information to be provided to the pregnant woman in a mandatory counselling process ... has the objective effect of promoting in her the consciousness of the value of the life that she carries in her (or, at least, it will clearly be perceived by her as an attempt to do so) ... The fact that the counselling process is not, expressly and ostensively, orientational does not impose, *ipso facto*, its qualification as merely informative and deprived of any intention to favour a decision to carry on with the pregnancy.'

for expressly dissuasive counselling of the kind mandated by the 1993 German decision, and invoked women's dignity as it did so:

> By abstaining, even at a communicational level, from any indication that might be felt by the woman as an external judgment imposing a particular decision, the legislator acted in line with the underlying reasoning supporting the decision not to punish abortion.
>
> This is based on the belief that only the free adhesion of the woman to carry on with the pregnancy guarantees, at this stage, the protection of the unborn life.
>
> . . .
>
> It is objectively founded for a legislator that has decided, also for reasons of efficiency, to trust in the sense of responsibility of the pregnant woman by calling her to cooperate in the duty of protection that belongs to the state, not to create a context of decision that may run counter to that purpose.
>
> The trust in the sense of responsibility of the woman and in her predisposition to be open to the reasons contrary to abortion would not be compatible with a tutelage and paternalistic approach. The protection of the woman's dignity is also affirmed by the way in which the counselling process imposed on her takes place.[48]

Portugal's abortion statute and the constitutional decision upholding it reflect an understanding of women's dignity that has evolved beyond the second German judgment. In Portugal, life-protective abortion counselling of pregnant women presupposes a particular view of women as decision-makers and ethical agents. On the court's account, counselling does not condescend to women or treat them paternalistically. In this constitutional order, government addresses women making decisions about motherhood as equal and self-governing citizens. As the court explains the counselling required by Portugal's abortion law, the counselling relationship simultaneously vindicates dignity as life, dignity as liberty, and dignity as equality. But the constitutional framework in Portugal yet remains at some distance from the women's dignity-periodic access cases of jurisdictions such as the USA and South Africa.[49] The Portuguese court ruled that a result-open counselling framework in the early period of pregnancy is constitutionally *permitted*, not required, as it would be in a traditional woman's rights framework.

---

[48] See Tribunal Constitucional, 11.4.16.
[49] See *Planned Parenthood of Southeastern Pennsylvania v Casey* 505 US 833 (1992); *Christian Lawyers Association v Minister of Health*, 2004, 4 All SA 31(T).

Conclusion

In explaining what government must or may do to meet its constitutional duty to protect life *in utero*, courts have imposed different kinds of affirmative obligations on government,[50] and, in particular, on women. Judicial accounts of how government must respect the dignity of life *in utero* entail nested judgments about how government may, or must, respect the dignity of women.[51]

In jurisdictions that follow Germany in imposing on governmental regulation of abortion a constitutional duty to protect life, there appears to be growing recognition that respecting dignity as life entails judgments about dignity as liberty and dignity as equality. It is not simply that pregnant women have lives to be protected too. It is that pregnant women understand themselves in relation to others in the community and so experience and respond to law in different ways than do the unborn. This understanding may have taken root in instrumental reason, as a set of judgments about the most efficient way to manage women who are pregnant, but over time instrumental judgments have engendered expressive judgments about the forms of respect owed women who are pregnant.

In the 1970s, some judges and advocates may have imagined the abortion conflict as a zero-sum game, in which courts enforcing the constitution would declare a winner. This understanding of constitutional law waned as conflict intensified and crossed borders. Over time, courts have approached the interpretation of constitutions with the aspiration to channel rather than settle conflict. In this process, some judges have begun to coordinate constitutional values, looking for forms of regulation that might be understood as manifesting respect for different claimants and for different conceptions of human

---

[50] The German court is clear that the duty to protect life imposes obligations on government as well as women. See BVerfGE 1 (1975) (*Abortion I*), 173–4; also 170–2. But there are limits to the obligations courts impose on government. The Irish court has distinguished between the affirmative obligations the right to life imposes on women and on government. See *Baby O & Another v Minister for Justice, Equality and Law Reform & Others*, 2002, IR 169 (unreported Supreme Court decision) (upholding Ireland's deportation of a pregnant Nigerian woman and finding 'the standard of ante or postnatal care available ... in Nigeria ... entirely irrelevant to the legality of her deportation').

[51] See, for example, Reva B. Siegel, 'Dignity and the politics of protection: abortion restrictions under *Casey/Carhart*', *Yale Law Journal* 117 (2008), 1694, 1762 (observing that the United States Constitution imposes limits on the ways government may regulate abortion to protect unborn life; '*Casey*'s undue burden framework insists that the state can express respect for the dignity of life only if it does so in ways that respect the dignity of women').

dignity. American law has evolved in the process,[52] as has law in Europe.[53] Those approaching constitutional law from this perspective do not imagine constitutional law on the behavioural model, as the kind of instrument that can impose outcomes, but instead on the hermeneutic model, as the kind of instrument that can engender values. Purposive constitutional interpretation of this type seeks not only to shape norms of social life but also to mediate conflict, and even to cultivate community, among agonists.

Consider again the recent history of dignity and the duty to protect life. Few judges have conferred on life *in utero* the rights of born persons—perhaps because of the entailments for women, perhaps because of the entailments for government, perhaps because of the entailments for politics.[54] More common is the declaration that respect for the dignity of life is an objective value that government is bound to respect.[55] Understood in this way, as a question concerning the values expressed and vindicated through law, respect for dignity as life, dignity as liberty, and dignity as equality do not stand in zero-sum conflict. As courts in a number of 'life-respecting' jurisdictions have concluded, laws manifesting respect for the dignity of life need not instrumentalize women. As a practical matter, laws manifesting respect for the dignity of life can address women as deliberative agents. As a demonstrative matter, laws manifesting respect for the dignity of life might address women as the kind of deliberative agents who are capable of respecting the dignity of life. In some jurisdictions, the law must do so.

---

[52] Siegel, 'Dignity and the politics of protection', 1749–53 (tracing the incorporation of dignity values into the American constitutional framework, and analysing standards authorizing dissuasive counselling and other life-respecting restrictions on abortion under *Casey/Carhart*).

[53] See *A, B and C v Ireland* (25579/05) ECtHR (2010) [235] (finding 'that there is indeed a consensus amongst a substantial majority of the Contracting States of the Council of Europe towards allowing abortion on broader grounds than accorded under Irish law', that at least thirty states in Europe allow 'abortion on request', that forty states allow abortion on 'health and well-being grounds', that only three states have more restrictive access to abortion services than Ireland); Siegel, *Constitutionalization of Abortion*, 1077: 'The emergence in the last two decades of fetal-protective justifications for providing women control over decisions concerning abortion is especially striking in light of the concurrent spread of woman-protective justifications for denying women access to abortion (e.g., banning or restricting abortion for the asserted purpose of protecting women from harm or coercion).'

[54] As previously noted, the German court is clear that the duty to protect life imposes obligations on government as well as women. See BVerfGE 1 (1975) (*Abortion I*), 173–4; also 170–2.

[55] See, for example, BVerfGE 1 (1975) (*Abortion I*), 641–2.

31

Is Dignity Language Useful in Bioethical Discussion of Assisted Suicide and Abortion?

David Albert Jones

Dignity talk in bioethics

IN THE LAST FIFTEEN YEARS or so, the term human dignity has come into increasing prominence in bioethical and human rights discourse, in law, and in public policy discussions. However, at the same time as there has been an increase in use of the term, there has also been a reaction against its use (or, at least, against certain current uses of the term). The case against dignity is made in the present volume by Michael Rosen, but he is by no means alone in raising such criticisms. John Harris has attacked the concept of human dignity as 'comprehensively vague',[1] while even defenders have wondered whether it is 'too nebulous to be of use' in bioethics.[2] Other critics have suggested that any substantive ethical content expressed in terms of human dignity can be reduced to considerations of autonomy or of well-being, and hence that the term human dignity 'can be eliminated without any loss of content'[3] and should be 'purged from bioethical discourse'.[4] Michael Rosen concurs with this judgment, suggesting not only that the positive content of dignity language is reducible to the good of liberty but also that this confused and undefined term in fact masks an attack on liberty by reactionary, religious, and/or anti-democratic forces in society.

---

[1] J. Harris, *Clones, Genes, and Immortality* (Oxford, Oxford University Press, 1998), 31.
[2] J. Johnston and C. Eliot, 'Chimeras and human dignity', *The American Journal of Bioethics* 1536-0075 3:3 (2003), 6–8.
[3] R. Macklin, 'Dignity is a useless concept', *British Medical Journal* 327 (2003), 1419–20.
[4] H. Kuhse, 'Is there a tension between autonomy and dignity?', in P. Kemp et al. (eds), *Bioethics and Biolaw* (Copenhagen, Rhodos International Science and Art Publishers and Centre for Ethics and Law, 2000), vol. 2, 74.

As many commentators have observed, the term dignity has been used in various senses.[5] Nevertheless, these variations in meaning do not necessarily imply equivocation. There are, rather, 'a family of concepts clustered around the practice of moral evaluation'.[6] Indeed, that the search for the essential characteristics of a concept should lead to a family of meanings is not a special feature of the word 'dignity'. It is, rather, a common property of meaning in ordinary language.[7]

In relation to bioethics and human rights, the concept of dignity is commonly invoked in at least two distinct ways.

In the first place it provides a basis for human rights in respect for other persons as persons. This is how the term is used in preambles to declarations of human rights or fundamental constitutions. Used in this way it does not serve to identify a particular aspect of the human good that is to be protected. It rather serves as a placeholder for the recognition of other persons as worthy of moral consideration, as making moral claims on us. This use is sometimes signalled by the terms 'inherent dignity'[8] or 'intrinsic dignity'.[9]

It is well known that those who drew up the Universal Declaration on Human Rights did not in fact agree on the character of this fundamental basis.[10] This lack of agreement is potentially a serious problem for use of dignity language, because how we understand human dignity will influence the way we understand those rights that are founded upon it. Nevertheless, any set of moral categories will involve analogous problems. For example, Jeremy Bentham notoriously dismissed human rights' talk as 'nonsense upon stilts',[11] while others have seen Bentham's own project of a consistent calculus of pain

---

[5] See, among other places, D. P. Sulmasy 'Dignity and bioethics: history, theory, and selected applications', in E. D. Pellegrino, A Schulman, and T. W. Merrill (eds), *Human Dignity and Bioethics* (South Bend, IN, University of Notre Dame Press, 2009); G. Vlastos, 'Human worth, merit, and equality', in J. Feinberg, *Moral Concepts* (Oxford, Oxford University Press, 1982), 141–52; J. Kilner, 'Human dignity', in S. G. Post (ed.), *The Encyclopedia of Bioethics* (New York, Macmillan Reference USA, 2004), 1193–200; L. Nordenfelt, 'The varieties of dignity', *Health Care Analysis* 12:2 (June 2004), 69–81; R. Horton, 'Rediscovering human dignity', *Lancet* 364 (2004), 1081–5; R. Van Der Graaf and J. J. V. Delden, 'Clarifying appeals to dignity in medical ethics from an historical perspective', *Bioethics* 23:3 (March 2009), 151–60; D. A. Jones, 'Is the creation of admixed embryos "an offense against human dignity"?', *Human Reproduction and Genetic Ethics* 16:1 (2010), 87–114.
[6] M. Meyer, 'The simple dignity of sentient life: speciesism and human dignity', *Journal of Social Philosophy* 32:2 (Summer 2001), 115–26.
[7] L. Wittgenstein, *Philosophical Investigations* (Oxford, Blackwell Publishing, 2001), paras 66–77.
[8] R. Andorno, 'Human dignity and human rights as a common ground for a global bioethics', *Journal of Medicine and Philosophy* 34 (2009), 223–40.
[9] Sulmasy, 'Dignity and bioethics'.
[10] Jacques Maritain, writing in the Introduction to a symposium held by UNESCO in 1948. The report is available at http://unesdoc.unesco.org/images/0015/001550/155042eb.pdf.
[11] J. Bentham, *Anarchical Fallacies* (Edinburgh, William Tait, 1843), article II.

and pleasure as both 'utterly impractical' and open to 'all manner of objections' as the basis for moral judgment.[12]

Furthermore, the attempt to eliminate any idea of intrinsic dignity reduces ethics to a system of procedural reasoning (based on rational consistency) or utilitarian reasoning (based on pleasures or preferences) or to some combination of the two. These forms of reasoning rule as inadmissible the claim that some actions or goals are worthwhile or honourable in themselves (*honestum*), but insist instead that every human good must be related to the useful (*utile*) or the pleasant (*delectatio*).[13] However, consistency in action is not sufficient to ground ethical reasoning. A cynical view of human nature may be consistent in expecting no respect from others and giving no respect to others. A Hobbesian view of human nature as a 'war of all, against all'[14] is consistent, but it excludes what is most worthy in human nature. Furthermore, it is not at all obvious why we should respect people's choices per se, if these choices are based merely on pleasure or arbitrary preference instead of anything worthwhile. The strongest modern defender of the value of autonomy was Immanuel Kant, but he was far from seeing every whim and desire as an exercise of autonomous choice.

The second use of the term dignity is not as a fundamental basis for morality but as a specific term to pick out certain human goods, and in particular the goods of honour or public acknowledgement. It is this second kind of use, sometimes termed 'attributed dignity',[15] that explains the use of dignity in relation to some issues more than to others. In its general (intrinsic) sense *every* act of injustice is a failure to respect or honour the injured person: a failure to acknowledge his or her dignity. On the other hand, some kinds of injustice, such as forcing someone to live or work in subhuman conditions, seem to contradict human dignity in a more specific way. This second attributed meaning is easier to grasp in transgression than in fulfilment. It is the good that is harmed by humiliation, by degradation, or by demeaning actions or social structures.

Dignity as an analogical concept

With the exception of very narrow technical terms, any word that is remotely interesting will be used in more than one context and with more than one

---

[12] J. Finnis, *Fundamentals of Ethics* (Washington DC, Georgetown University Press, 1983), 88.
[13] Aquinas, *Summa Theologiae* I, q. 2 art 6, cf. Aristotle, *Ethics* 8.3
[14] In the words of Thomas Hobbes, *De Cive* (1652), XII–XIII.
[15] See, among other places, Sulmasy 'Dignity and bioethics'.

sense: it will express a 'family of meanings'. Its use in different contexts is not equivocal nor is it simply metaphorical but it is what Thomas Aquinas called 'analogical'. The different senses of a word are related by analogy.

Analogical terms often have a central or fundamental meaning in relation to which other meanings are best understood. Thus, for example, 'healthy food' and a 'healthy complexion' are secondary to the health of the body. The central concept here is bodily health, and other meanings are related as causes of or signs of that health. It seems unarguable that the most fundamental meaning of human dignity is inherent or intrinsic dignity—the dignity we have on the basis of our shared humanity.[16] Nevertheless, Thomas Aquinas pointed out that the context in which we first learn a word does not necessarily provide its most fundamental meaning.[17] What is first in order of learning is not necessarily first in order of logic. This general truth is also applicable to the word 'dignity', and one may well agree with Waldron[18] that it is the second attributed sense, dignity as public status or acknowledgement, which was the first to appear historically,[19] and yet think that over time we have come to discover a more fundamental meaning.

The remainder of the chapter is concerned primarily with dignity in this secondary attributed sense in the context of debates over assisted suicide and abortion. This attributed use is not wholly separable from the more fundamental concept of intrinsic dignity. On the contrary, there must be some relation between dignity as public status and dignity as intrinsic. However, it may be that the more fundamental concept is more difficult to grasp, and thus a discussion of dignity in the practical context of bioethical debates over assisted suicide and abortion will both help illuminate those debates and also be a profitable entry into deeper philosophical reflection on intrinsic dignity.

Dignity, indignity, and assisted suicide

Dignity language is used on both sides of the assisted suicide and abortion debates. In relation to assisted suicide, the debate may be characterized as between those who favour the practice, understanding it to be the acknowledgement of human dignity ('dignity as liberty'), and those who oppose it,

---

[16] Sulmasy, 'Dignity and bioethics'.
[17] Aquinas, *Summa Theologiae* I, q. 13, art. 6 ad 1.
[18] Jeremy Waldron, *The Dignity of Legislation* (Cambridge, Cambridge University Press, 1999); Jeremy Waldron, 'How law protects dignity', NYU School of Law, Public Law Research Paper (Dec. 2011), No. 11–83.
[19] Jones, 'Is the creation of admixed embryos "an offense against human dignity?"'.

holding it to be a failure to acknowledge human dignity ('dignity as life'). Inasmuch as this is so, it may be thought that talk of dignity adds little to the debate not already provided by the moral principles of autonomy and respect for human life.

What is striking, however, is the prevalence of dignity language in this debate. This is evident in the name of the Swiss suicide organization Dignitas and in the name of the largest and oldest organization in the United Kingdom campaigning for the legalization of assisted suicide and euthanasia. This was founded in 1934 as the Voluntary Euthanasia Legalization Society. Aside from a brief period in which it was called Exit, this title was retained with minor variations (with or without 'voluntary', with or without 'legislation') until 2005, when it was renamed Dignity in Dying. The change of name avoids the stigma attached to the word euthanasia; it also represents a shift from concern about pain relief to concern about the dignity of choice and the indignity of disability and dependence. A similar pattern is seen in the name given to Oregon's Death with Dignity Act,[20] and in the names of other lobby organizations and books that favour legalizing assisted suicide. Thus, studies of terminally ill patients who request euthanasia show that the request is associated, among other things, with *fear of indignity*, loss of control, and cognitive impairment.[21] While the concept of dignity is invoked in favour of legalizing euthanasia and/or assisted suicide, it has also been invoked against such proposals. One common line of argument is that assisting suicide contradicts human dignity because it fails to respect the dignity of each human life. This has been termed 'dignity as life', but it would be a mistake to reduce it to concern for the dignity of so-called 'biological life' alone. It is, rather, an appeal to the fundamental sense of intrinsic dignity that is held to be the basis of equality and of all other rights. On this view, killing is not wrong only when it frustrates someone's previous desires (including the explicit or implicit desire to continue to live). Rather, killing contradicts the intrinsic dignity of human existence in all its aspects: both life itself and what life makes possible for the person and for other people. If one follows Kant, this

---

[20] Oregon Revised Statues 127.800–995.
[21] A. Chapple, S. Ziebland, A. McPherson, and A. Herxheimer, 'What people close to death say about euthanasia and assisted suicide: a qualitative study', *Journal of Medical Ethics* 32:12 (December 2006), 706–10; J. A. Rietjens, A. van der Heide, B. D. Onwuteaka-Philipsen, P. J. van der Maas, and G van der Wal, 'Preferences of the Dutch general public for a good death and associations with attitudes towards end-of-life decision-making', *Palliative Medicine* 20:7 (October 2006), 685–92. Both quoted in U. Schuklenk et al. 'End-of-life decision making' (The Royal Society of Canada Expert Panel, November 2011), www.rsc-src.ca.

will also be true of self-killing.[22] Understood in this way, suicide is seen not so much as a failure of courage[23] or a failure of obedience to God[24] or a failure of self-love[25] (though it may be seen as these things as well), but, more fundamentally, as a failure to respect the worth or dignity of humanity in one's own case. Since the 1960s, in many jurisdictions, attempting suicide has been dealt with by mental health care rather than by criminal sanction, but assisting suicide remains a serious offence because of the dignity of each life, even when that dignity is not recognized by the victim.

The claim that suicide, and assisting suicide, contradict intrinsic human dignity has been a popular argument among bioethicists and jurists, especially in contexts where a Kantian conception of dignity is found persuasive.[26] However, because this concept of intrinsic dignity is categorically different from the attributed dignity that touches upon issues of dependence and loss of control, it is difficult to resolve this argument without appropriate definitions of dignity. A systematic account of dignity may well favour resolution in the direction of intrinsic dignity,[27] but whereas there is agreement that there are many uses of the term dignity, there is no consensus as to how these uses are to be understood in relation to one another.

At a political level, those who invoke these two uses of dignity therefore tend to talk past one another. There is, however, a possibility for more direct engagement between protagonists of different views if one focuses on the attributed use of dignity. Those who invoke dignity in favour of assisted suicide typically characterize a life of dependence and disability as undignified: if the person in this state does not have access to assistance in suicide, then he or she is forced to endure the indignity of what is considered a subhuman condition of life. The emotional appeal to dignity-language by the proponents of assisted suicide is thus not only concerned with the dignity of autonomous choice, it is implicitly or explicitly framed as a choice that allows the person to escape a state of indignity. This is clear from the limitation almost universally placed on such proposals, that they should apply only to the choice to

---

[22] Kant, *Groundwork for the Metaphysics of Morals* (second German edn, 1785), 54, 67 (edn of the Royal Prussian Academy in Berlin), 422, 429. This is not to endorse Kant's account of human dignity more generally, only to acknowledge his perceptiveness in seeing that suicide is a failure to respect the worth or dignity of human life in one's own case.

[23] As argued, for example, by Aristotle, *Ethics* (London, Penguin Books, 1984), III.7, 1116a.

[24] As argued, for example, by Augustine, *Concerning the City of God*, I.20.

[25] As argued, for example, by Aquinas, *Summa Theologia* II.II, q. 64, article 5.

[26] L. Kass, 'Defending human dignity' in President's Council on Bioethics report *Human Dignity and Bioethics* (Washington DC, March 2008), Part 4, Chapter 12; majority opinion in *Rodriguez v British Colombia (Attorney General)*, 1993, 3 S.C.R. 519 [1993] S.C.J. No. 94. At para. 129.

[27] Sulmasy, 'Dignity and bioethics'.

die of those suffering from terminal and/or disabling conditions. They are not intended for the inconsolable jilted lover or the shamed public servant. They are not intended to cover all and every suicide attempt but specifically concern those where the condition of life is implicitly agreed to be intolerable. However, once this rationale is made explicit, it has clear implications for the *dignity of equality* of others who live with disability. If different rules apply to those who are dependent and disabled and to those who are healthy, then the law is failing to grant equal status to disabled citizens and those with a short life expectancy. In practical and political terms, the desire for euthanasia is inseparable from the fear of dependence and of loss of control, of incontinence and of dementia, in short, from the fear of disability. While this desire is expressed as a wish to 'die with dignity', it implies that living in certain conditions is, per se, an indignity. This implication has been recognised by the disability rights movement, which is why, along with physicians, it is groups who represent disabled people who have been among the most vocal in their opposition to legalizing euthanasia or assisted suicide.[28]

The use of dignity language in the debate over assisted suicide thus expresses ethical concerns that are irreducible to the issues of autonomy and public safety. The concept of dignity both adds conceptually to the debate and explains the emotional force of the appeal of, and of the opposition to, assisted suicide. A key question at issue is: what can be regarded as a dignified death? And concomitantly, what can be regarded as a dignified life? Nor from the fact that dignity is invoked on both sides of the debate does it follow that 'the concept of human dignity is an unsuitable tool for settling normative questions pertaining to end-of-life decision making'.[29] Rather, the appeal to dignity in opposition to assisted suicide both appeals to a more fundamental meaning of dignity (that of intrinsic dignity) and effectively answers the appeal to attributed dignity on its own terms. Opposition to assisted suicide is importantly motivated by the concern that the very act of judging life with impairment as a 'life unworthy to be lived' is discriminatory and humiliating towards those who live with impairment. It is, precisely, *a failure to respect human life with impairment*, and hence a failure not just of 'dignity as life' but of 'dignity as equality'.

---

[28] See, for example, the organizations Not Dead Yet and Not Dead Yet UK.
[29] Schuklenk, 'End-of-life decision making'.

The elision of assisted suicide and abortion

There is some similarity between debates surrounding assisted suicide and abortion, and these issues are sometimes elided for a variety of philosophical, cultural, or other reasons. However, such elision is often more confusing than enlightening.

It is true that the issues emerge from the same historical and political context. It is a remarkable coincidence that the Voluntary Euthanasia Legalization Society and the Abortion Law Reform Association were founded in England within months of each other (VELS in December 1935[30], ALRA in February 1936[31]), and there have been prominent advocates who have defended both causes. For example, Glanville Williams, former Professor of Law and Cambridge University, served at different times both as vice-president of the Voluntary Euthanasia (Legislation) Society and as president of the Abortion Law Reform Association. In 1957, before either practice had been decriminalized, he advocated the legalizing of both (and also infanticide, suicide, and assisted suicide) in his influential work *The Sanctity of Life and the Criminal Law*.[32]

Those who advocate for both abortion and euthanasia frequently frame these as related issues of personal choice or liberty, a theme that has sometimes been developed into a sustained argument.[33] As advocates of euthanasia and abortion frequently link the two issues, so opponents also link these issues. Thus, for example, Pope John Paul II, in his encyclical on the value and inviolability of human life, *Evangelium Vitae*, argues that the prolife movement has emerged as a counter movement both to the legalization of abortion and to attempts to legalize euthanasia: 'In view of laws which permit abortion and in view of efforts, which here and there have been successful, to legalize euthanasia, *movements and initiatives to raise social awareness in defence of life* have sprung up in many parts of the world'.[34] John Paul II, in common with Glanville Williams and Ronald Dworkin, accepts the link between these two issues but, rather than seeing them as essentially matters of choice, understands them as attacks on the inviolability of human life.

---

[30] R. Whiting, *A Natural Right to Die: Twenty-Three Centuries of Debate* (London, Greenwood Press, 2002), 41.

[31] See, S. Clegg and R. Gough, 'The struggle for abortion rights', in M. Lavalette and G. Mooney (eds), *Class Struggle and Social Welfare* (London, Routledge, 2000), 157.

[32] G. Williams, *The Sanctity of Life and the Criminal Law* (New York, Alfred A Knopf, 1957); D. A. Jones and J. Keown, 'Surveying the foundations of medical law: a reassessment of Glanville Williams's 'The sanctity of life and the criminal law', *Medical Law Review* 16:1 (2008), 85–126.

[33] As, for example, Ronald Dworkin, *Life's Dominion: An Argument about Abortion, Euthanasia, and Individual Freedom* (New York, Alfred A. Knopf, 1993).

[34] John Paul II, *Evangelium Vitae* (London, CTS, 1995) para. 27, emphasis in the original.

There are, therefore, aspects that link abortion and euthanasia (and assisted suicide), conceptually and historically. Nevertheless, it is equally important to note important distinctions between these two issues. Whereas both movements had their origin in the 1930s and they have shared some common proponents, some common opponents, some common arguments in favour, and some common arguments against, the movements have fared very differently. As of 2007, according to the UN, over 78 per cent of countries including over 61 per cent of the world population lived under laws that allowed abortion for social and economic reasons.[35] In contrast, in the same year, only two countries (The Netherlands and Belgium) had decriminalized euthanasia (and assisted suicide), and one country (Switzerland) and two states of the USA had legalized assisted suicide—representing in total less than 2 per cent of countries and less than 0.5 per cent of the world population. For whatever reason, most countries have liberalized abortion law and most countries have not liberalized laws on euthanasia or assisted suicide.

The two movements are also distinct politically. The movement to promote access to legal abortion has from the first been strongly associated with feminism. This is not to say that abortion advocacy represents all women, or even all feminists, but in political terms the core of the movement is women's groups. In contrast, euthanasia is not and historically has not been a core feminist issue, and many feminists have been cautious about changes in the law in this area.[36]

The two issues are also quite distinct in relation to disability. As outlined above, a change in the law on assisted suicide is opposed by many disability groups who object to the double standard implicit in proposed legislation—that there is a duty to prevent suicide attempts by healthy and able-bodied citizens, while requests from those with disabilities or severe ill-health will not be resisted but actively facilitated. In contrast, while it is also true that many in the disability rights movement object to abortion for reason of disability, these objections do not typically amount to opposition to legal access to abortion as such.

Assisted suicide and abortion can be framed as an argument as to whether choice can excuse or justify the taking of life, but both the choice in question and the life in question are somewhat different. The controversy over assisted suicide concerns the choice of someone to take his or her own life and the choice of a second person to facilitate this. The controversy over abortion

---

[35] United Nations Department of Economic and Social Affairs Population Division *World Abortion Policies 2007* (United Nations Publication ST/ESA/SER.A/264, 2007).
[36] See, for example, The Law Commission *A New Homicide Act for England and Wales? A Consultation Paper* (Consultation Paper No. 177, December 2005), para. 8.67.

concerns whether the choice of a woman can justify a second person to facilitate or assist in taking a life whose status is disputed (the foetus or unborn child) and who depends for survival on remaining in her body. The context and implications of these issues are distinct, and so it is possible for someone to be opposed to legalizing assisted suicide but in favour of legal access to abortion,[37] or indeed to be in favour of legalizing assisted suicide but opposed to unrestricted access to abortion.[38] More subtly, for someone who is opposed to both or who is in favour of both, it is important to recognize that these are nevertheless distinct issues which should be considered separately.

Dignity in the abortion debate

While the abortion debate is distinct from the debate over assisted suicide and euthanasia, dignity language has nevertheless also played a role in legal and ethical discussion of abortion. Here again the debate has sometimes been framed as a conflict between 'dignity as liberty' and 'dignity as life'. The appeal to dignity as liberty evokes the idea of enforced labour or servitude, in this case the idea of *enforced pregnancy*. However, the issue is very different from assisted suicide in that the solution in the case of abortion involves the destruction not of one's own life but of that of an 'other'. At the heart of the debates between individuals and nations over the ethics of abortion is the question of whether the unborn life is or is not to be regarded as possessing the dignity of a person (in the sense of an individual with full moral status). This question concerns the foundational sense of dignity—the question of whether the human embryo or foetus is an 'other' possessing inherent or intrinsic dignity and thus meriting legal protection.

The abortion debate, therefore, far more than the euthanasia debate, involves the question of who is to be counted as a person with rights. If this

---

[37] M. Spindelman, 'Are the similarities between a woman's right to choose an abortion and the alleged right to assisted suicide really compelling?', *University of Michigan Journal of Law Reform* 29:3 (Spring 1996), 775–856; C. N. Manning 'Live and let die?: physician assisted suicide and the right to die', *Harvard Journal of Law & Technology* 9:2 (Summer 1996), 513–45; K. Yuill, 'Why those who favour abortion rights should oppose the legalisation of assisted suicide', *Pro-Choice Forum Opinion, Comment & Reviews: Ethical Issues* (31 August 2001); K. Yuill, 'Assisted dying: a product of pessimism, book review of George Pitcher, *A Time to Live: The Cases Against Euthanasia and Assisted Suicide*', *Spiked Review of Books* (Friday 30 July 2010), http://www.spiked-online.com/site/reviewofbooks_article/9372/.

[38] See responses to 'Is there a philosophical difference between abortion and assisted suicide?', *Yahoo Answers*, http://answers.yahoo.com/question/index?qid=20101208052701AAZZnJD.

fundamental question is not resolved, then it is questionable how far the concept of dignity can bridge the gap.

One example of the use of dignity-language in support of a consensus position on abortion is described by Reva Siegel.[39] She has argued that, in a number of jurisdictions, consideration of the dignity of women has been used to shape the way that the state seeks to protect unborn lives. In states that recognize a duty on the state to protect the unborn child, an increasing number have moved to protect the child not through threat of prosecution but through provision of counselling. This move has sometimes been defended on the basis of efficacy: counselling has been presented as more effective a means of protecting the child (and its mother) from abortion. However, in addition to such pragmatic arguments, governments have sometimes also argued that it is more in keeping with the dignity of women to protect unborn life by persuasion and counselling rather than by the threat of legal sanction. In this way, appeal to dignity is regarded as the basis of a possible compromise position which grants legal status to the unborn while permitting legal access to termination of pregnancy.

Siegel has provided a useful example of the way dignity is sometimes seen as forming the basis of a practical consensus between positions which have hitherto been irreconcilable. However, the extent and sustainability of this purported consensus is very much open to question. While advocates of access to legal abortion will generally welcome statutory counselling when this supplants a total ban on abortion, the same advocates fight fiercely against statutory counselling in contexts such as the USA and the UK, where abortion is legally available. Similarly, opponents of abortion, where they seek statutory (as opposed to non-statutory) counselling, only seek it as a means to discourage abortion when a thoroughgoing ban is politically or legally unachievable. Thus, for advocates on both sides of the debate, statutory counselling is seen as a potentially acceptable middle position only en route to more consistent position (either more consistent liberty of action or more consistent protection of the unborn).

These political considerations are confirmed by philosophical reflection. Peter Singer, an advocate of unrestricted access to abortion, has argued convincingly that unrestricted access to abortion is philosophically defensible only on the basis that the unborn child is not a person. Appeals to privacy, as for example in the *Roe v Wade* decision, 'take for granted that abortion does not harm an "other"—which is precisely the point that needs to be proven

---

[39] R. B. Siegel, 'Dignity and the politics of protection: abortion restrictions under Casey/Carhart', *Faculty Scholarship Series*, Paper 1134 (2008), and Siegel, Chapter 30, this volume.

before we can legitimately apply the principle in the case of abortion'.[40] The importance of the status of the child is evident if one considers the related issue of infanticide. The English law, and that of several other jurisdictions, includes a statute on infanticide,[41] which allows offenders to avoid a charge of murder if they admit to infanticide. This provision recognizes the disturbed state of mind typically found in women who kill their own children. However, in the case of infanticide this mitigation does not serve completely to exonerate the act, and it offers no mitigation whatsoever to the guilt of professionals or others who may have failed to prevent these acts, let alone those who have facilitated them. It seems therefore that appeals to dignity as liberty as the basis for complete decriminalization of abortion mask an unacknowledged rejection of the equal human status of the unborn human life. If that status is acknowledged, then it will justify significant restrictions of liberty, for there can be no general legal or ethical liberty to kill an innocent 'other'.

Dignity and the instrumentalization of human embryos

Another way in which dignity is used in the search for new agreement in public policy debates at the beginning of life is by arguing that the dignity of human nature should be respected even if the embryo is not yet recognized as a person in the full sense. Human dignity is potentially a broader concept than human personhood. This is particularly evident in the debate over the use of human embryos in experimentation. A number of philosophers and jurists have objected to the instrumentalization (and, still more, to the commercialization) of human embryos without thereby committing themselves to acknowledging the human embryo as a person.[42] Respect for the dignity of human nature from its origin has helped secure agreement within Europe on the prohibition of creating embryos for research and of patenting technologies that rely on the destruction of human embryos, as evident in the Convention

---

[40] P. Singer, *Practical Ethics* (Cambridge, Cambridge University Press, 2011), 131, quoted in Charles C. Camosy, *Peter Singer and Christian Ethics: Beyond Polarization* (Cambridge, Cambridge University Press, 2012), 14. Here Singer is criticizing the claims of J. J. Thomson and others that free access to abortion would be justifiable even if, for the sake of argument, it were granted that the unborn child had the dignity and status of a person.

[41] Infanticide Act 1938.

[42] T. Banchoff, *Embryo Politics: Ethics and Policy in Atlantic Democracies* (Ithaca, NY, Cornell University Press, 2011), 97–119; M. Hauskeller, 'Believing in the dignity of human embryos', *Human Reproduction and Genetic Ethics* 17:1 (2011), 53–65; S. Rolf, 'Human embryos and human dignity: differing presuppositions in human embryo research in Germany and Great Britain', *The Heythrop Journal* 53 (2012), 742–54.

on Human Rights and Biomedicine[43] and the Brüstle decision.[44] Such reasons have also been invoked as the basis for international agreement on a ban on reproductive cloning and on germline genetic engineering.

The invocation of the dignity of human nature has secured a consensus within Europe that includes more than those who regard the human embryo as having the moral status of a person. Nevertheless, this line of argument is more convincing against a Kantian (or Heideggerian) background or within a natural law context or within a religious context. In a reductive English-speaking context, the appeal to human nature loses its objective weight and is easily regarded as symbolic, that is, as expressive merely of subjective feelings of offence.[45] It has seemed opaque to many English-speaking commentators and has been viewed with some suspicion by feminist critics,[46] even those who are cautious about new biotechnologies.[47] Furthermore, in the face of the perceived promise of biomedical benefits, this argument has inhibited but has not prevented use of embryonic stem cell lines.[48] Indeed, it is arguably this appeal to human dignity by bioethicists such as Leon Kass[49] in the context of the debate in the USA over embryonic stem cell research and therapeutic cloning that has led to the concept of human dignity being strongly contested. Far from being a mechanism for securing consensus and side-stepping the question of the status of the embryo, it has generated further controversy focusing precisely on this disputed status.

---

[43] Council of Europe, *Convention for the Protection of Human Rights and Dignity of the Human Being with regard to the Application of Biology and Medicine: Convention on Human Rights and Biomedicine*, CETS No. 164 (Oviedo: Council of Europe), Article 18.

[44] S. Sterckx and J. Cockbain, 'Assessing the morality of the commercial exploitation of inventions concerning uses of human embryos and the relevance of moral complicity: comments on the EPO's WARF decision', *SCRIPTed* 7:1 (2010), 83; C. Staunton, 'Brustle v Greenpeace, embryonic stem cell research and the European Court of Justice's new found morality', *Medical Law Review* (2012), doi:10.1093/medlaw/fws026.

[45] D. A. Jones, 'The "special status" of the human embryo in the United Kingdom: an exploration of the use of language in public policy', *Human Reproduction and Genetic Ethics* 17:1 (2011), 66–83.

[46] F. Baylis and C. Mcleod, 'Feminists on the inalienability of human embryos', *Hypatia* 20:1 (2006), 1–14.

[47] F. Baylis, 'Animal eggs for stem cell research: a path not worth taking', *The American Journal of Bioethics* 8:12 (2008), 18–32.

[48] Banchoff, *Embryo Politics*, 193–230.

[49] L. Kass, *Life, Liberty, and the Defense of Dignity: The Challenge for Bioethics* (San Francisco, CA, Encounter Books, 2002).

Conclusion

In sum, considering human dignity adds significantly to an understanding of the debate of assisted suicide. It both helps disclose the emotional attraction of assisted suicide and helps disclose an ethical problem with assisted suicide that runs deeper than the reiterated arguments about slippery slopes and non-voluntary euthanasia. On the other hand, the recognition of the dignity of women and the recognition of the dignity of human nature are of more limited value in controversies surrounding abortion and the embryo research debate. They may help garner support for policies such as statutory counselling for abortion, and they may provide a rationale for maintaining the ban on instrumental uses of human embryos. However, until there is agreement over the central question of the status of the disputed 'other', the justice of such policies cannot adequately be determined and thus deeper disagreement will, and indeed should, remain.

32

Dignity, Choice, and Circumstances

Denise Réaume

DIGNITY IS AT LEAST in part about choice.[1] It is bound up with autonomy, and autonomy is about being able to make choices about the character and direction of one's life. Yet many do not live in autonomy fostering circumstances, but must still make choices, choices that shape the ongoing quality and character of their lives, and may bring them into contact or conflict with legal institutions. Such choices and the circumstances that shape them are often the context of contests over social and economic rights, by which I refer loosely to the web of arrangements meant to secure decent living conditions and security of membership in a society. These issues can arise not only in the constitutional context but also in the interstices of ordinary lawmaking and adjudication.

All too often, legislators and judges take the easy way out in resolving such contests, ratifying the choices made by desperate people as though they were autonomous and free. In doing so, they sometimes claim to be respecting the dignity of those whose choices they treat as grounding responsibility. Alternatively, the law sometimes responds to bad choices by constructing a category of 'defective' people who must have decisions made for them. These unfortunates are treated as wards of the state rather than agents in their own right, and this is often described as responding to need. Rather than respecting dignity, both responses add insult to injury. The first assigns blame rather than investigating the obstacles to healthy choices and the role of the legal system in their manufacture and maintenance. The second shows some sympathy for disadvantageous circumstances, but at the cost of depriving people of a say in their lives.

Thus the law seems to be caught up in a dilemma. Either we honour the choices of those with the legal status to choose by imposing responsibility for

---

[1] I emphasize that dignity is *in part* about choice, for there are many life circumstances in which individuals are incapable of choice—the very young, those in a comatose state, those suffering serious dementia—in which facilitating choice is not the issue and yet there are claims of dignity demanding satisfaction. Nevertheless, being able to make decisions for oneself is an important part of our concept of dignity and deserves, I think, the kind of specific focus I give it here.

them, and in so doing refrain from responding to real need or doing something about the circumstances that foster bad choices, or we pay more attention to the circumstances of choice and give little weight to the exercise of agency, and thereby stigmatize certain people as incapable of choosing for themselves. Either way, we do harm to the ideal of honouring the capacity for choice that is part of the modern conception of human dignity. The only way out of the dilemma is, first, to address social conditions that deprive some people of the option of a fully autonomous life, and second, in the meantime, to recognize the capacity for agency that people have at whatever level they have it and seek to work with them at that level to improve their ability to make the decisions that affect the quality of their lives.

Through an examination of three brief case studies, this chapter illustrates very different legal contests in which the meaning of dignity is part of the debate. Governments tend to understand dignity as simple respect for choice, and when that seems implausible, they shift to patronizing people as incapable of choice. Both seem to be ways of avoiding accepting responsibility for the ways in which social and economic conditions supported by the state contribute to a state of affairs that deprives some of the conditions of autonomy. Against this, advocates for disadvantaged groups try to direct our attention to whether the conditions of choice are adequate to support dignity, but many legal systems present scant opportunity directly to shape disputes around this issue. In an inhospitable legal climate, there nevertheless emerges in these cases an understanding of how we might better support dignity even in trying circumstances without depriving people of all means of choice. The chapter sketches these contesting visions in order to demonstrate the need for a more nuanced way to talk about need and choice at the same time. That effort is both grounded in and contributes to the development of a richer conception of dignity that could guide legal reasoning across a variety of contexts.

Dignity, autonomy, and law

In its modern usage, dignity is bound up with our attribution of inherent worth to human beings. To ascribe dignity to human beings as a moral matter is to treat human beings as creatures of intrinsic, incomparable, and indelible worth, simply as human beings.[2] Because this notion of dignity is independent

---

[2] Aurel Kolnai, 'Dignity', in Robin S. Dillon (ed.), *Dignity, Character, and Self-Respect* (New York, Routledge, 1995), 56, nicely captures the non-derivative nature of this kind of worth: 'If Dignity means "being worthy of ...", the completion that most aptly suggests itself would seem to be "worthy of being appreciatively acknowledged *as* worthy to be thus acknowledged and appreciated, *sans plus*".'

of the empirical attributes of particular individuals—their talents, skills, and ambitions—it is akin to the attribution of status, packaging together a range of norms about rights and obligations, appropriate forms of treatment, and access to opportunities, goods, and benefits.[3] These make concrete the entitlements flowing from the attribution of dignity and thereby give it shape. The distinctive ethos of the modern era is to develop this conception of dignity in an egalitarian direction. The hierarchies of rank that have characterized other eras have been repudiated.[4] We now share a single status, are now all owed 'equal concern and respect' in Ronald Dworkin's words.[5]

Full equality of status at the formal level has been achieved at least since the eradication of slavery and the enfranchisement of all adult citizens.[6] However, as T. H. Marshall so aptly noted long ago, the content of the 'status' of bearer of dignity (Marshall would have said 'citizenship') has been evolving over the modern period, the rights entailed gradually being enriched to achieve a 'fuller measure of equality'.[7] No doubt Marshall imagined that the flowering of full citizenship would be a smoother, more linear process than it has been. As it has turned out, states have been quicker to universalize civil and political rights as part of our conception of dignity than to attend to the social and economic institutions that Marshall had in mind as necessary to the enrichment—one might say fulfilment—of that status.[8] Even when key benefits have been put in place, such as public education, labour rights, public health care, and social assistance, these have often not been entrenched; rather, governments have given themselves the freedom to stall progress, even

---

[3] Jeremy Waldron, 'Does "equal moral status" add anything to right reason', New York University School of Law, Public Law & Legal Theory Research Paper Series, Working Paper No. 11–52, available on SSRN: http://papers.ssrn.com/sol3/papers.cfm?abstract_id=1898689; Gregory Vlastos, 'Justice and equality', in Louis P. Pojman and Robert Westmoreland (eds), *Equality: Selected Readings* (New York, Oxford University Press, 1997), 126–7.

[4] Waldron, 'Does "equal moral status" add anything to right reason.' Waldron usefully distinguishes between conditional status and sortal status, the latter demarcating what is understood to be a distinction between types of people, rather than differences in condition. It is all too easy, though, for differences in condition to attract legal rules and structures that create something very close to a sortal status even as the legal system congratulates itself on having transcended this sort of thinking.

[5] Ronald Dworkin, *Taking Rights Seriously* (Cambridge, MA, Harvard University Press, 1977).

[6] This claim is, of course, too strong, since it brackets the situation of refugees and illegal immigrants, a key site of disputes over status and the meaning of dignity likely to occupy us for some time. Indeed, one might argue that a conception of dignity as a form of status fits too readily into statist conceptions of membership, reinforcing the outsider status of illegal immigrants. This raises important challenges for dignity, but ones beyond the purview of this paper.

[7] T. H. Marshall, *Citizenship and Social Class and Other Essays* (Cambridge, Cambridge University Press, 1950).

[8] See, for example, Bruno de Witte's tracing of the situation in Europe, 'The trajectory of fundamental social rights in the European Union', in Gráinne de Búrca and Bruno de Witte, *Social Rights in Europe* (Oxford, Oxford University Press, 2005), 153.

to turn back the clock by reducing or eliminating entitlements, and in recent decades have not been shy about using this freedom. Indeed, even entrenchment does not guarantee that effective implementation will follow.[9]

The extension of legal and civil rights to all is grounded in the value of personal autonomy, and the legal recognition of these rights has been part of the process of constructing the modern conception of dignity. The priority given to these rights reflects one particular aspect of autonomy, and builds it into the idea of moral status. These specific rights protect a range of important choices, and well before they were extended to all they had come to be bound up with what it means to be a full member of society, a bearer of dignity. To have any of these rights taken away would clearly be treated as an assault on one's dignity. To be treated as though incapable of making these sorts of choices was a mark of inferiority. Their extension was an important step towards a more egalitarian conception of dignity.

For example, what marked the division of men and women into two separate and hierarchically ordered classes of human being was the systematic denial of autonomy to women through the denial of these rights. Without the right to own property, to enter into contract, to vote, to enjoy decision-making power over person or family, to pursue education, to enter many parts of the paid workforce, women's lives were severely and comprehensively circumscribed, confined to a narrow range of roles that were socially and legally sanctioned. The distinct and lesser status to which women were assigned operated by formally denying many choices so that only specific others were available. As these constraints began to be seen as constraints, rather than as a reflection of women's nature, it became imperative to extend the basic roster of legal and civil rights to women. The removal of legal constraints opened up choice and allowed women more autonomy, and thereby signalled the legal system's respect for women as beings able to formulate and execute the full range of human plans and projects.

---

[9] De Búrca and de Witte, *Social Rights in Europe*. A small but stark recent example of the fragility of social and economic rights is provided by the Report of the UN Special Rapporteur on the right to food on his recent visit to Canada (6–16 May 2010). Olivier de Schutter recorded the widening gap between rich and poor and the rising rate of food insecurity in contravention of Canada's international human rights obligations. The report is available http://www.srfood.org/index.php/en/component/content/article/1-latest-news/2253-canada-national-food-strategy-can-eradicate-hunger-amidst-plenty-un-rights-expert. For his trouble, de Schutter was insulted by at least two federal cabinet ministers, his findings dismissed out of hand as illegitimate interference by an outsider. See CBC News, 'UN official sparks debate over Canadian food security' (16 May 2012), http://www.cbc.ca/news/canada/story/2012/05/16/pol-un-canada-food-security.html; Heather Scoffield, 'Ottawa shrugs off UN warning on hunger and nutrition', *Globe and Mail* (16 May 2012), http://www.theglobeandmail.com/news/politics/ottawa-shrugs-off-un-warning-on-hunger-and-nutrition/article2434556/.

In turn, this fostered in women a new sense of self-respect as the kind of person who could exercise these rights. Two aspects of personality reinforce one another here. Human beings are reflective beings, capable of making and changing plans, seeing themselves as individuals and in relationship with others. Thus, respect for identity is crucial to respect for dignity, and to demean characteristics integral to identity is a key form of indignity. We are also capable of formulating and acting on a conception of 'the good'. Thus, respect for people's ability to formulate and execute plans and projects is relevant to protecting dignity. These two aspects of personality are connected:[10] one develops an identity partly through the life one creates, and a conception of the good partly in the context of one's sense of who one is. Thus, to restrict the plans and dreams of individuals either creates a mean sense of self, if people have never been allowed to glimpse what is denied them, or demeans and demoralizes individuals who can see their way clear to a richer life that is denied them.[11] If this sort of comprehensive disrespect for dignity is organized so as to affect individuals who are recognized as members of a group of some sort, it is very easy to create new forms of second-class status, even without intending to or fully realizing it.

The elimination of formal structures of constraint is, of course, of crucial importance in the movement towards a universal conception of dignity. But it is trite political sociology that the end of legal prohibitions does not necessarily make opportunities available in fact. Legal rules and restrictions are hardly the only forces capable of creating a more or less comprehensive web of constraints that can confine the life choices and chances of some, and, in turn, cramp their sense of self. The construction of the welfare state was meant to deal with some of the other autonomy-restricting forces operative in the modern world—ignorance, poverty, ill health, exploitation. But the task was and is a large and complex one and the merry-go-round of life cannot simply be stopped until we have got it right. So legislators go on enacting laws prohibiting some behaviour, encouraging or mandating others, and judges go on deciding individual cases in accordance with such laws. Having made the mistake before of subjecting different classes of people to different rules, and thus creating different statuses, the new world view starts from the premise

---

[10] Martha Nussbaum makes a similar point in her identification of two human capabilities—affiliation and practical reason—that are 'of special importance, since they both organize and suffuse all the others, making their pursuit truly human': Martha Nussbaum *Women and Human Development: The Capabilities Approach* (Cambridge, Cambridge University Press, 2000), 82.

[11] Thus, Bernard Williams argues that respect for human beings as conscious being entails a prohibition on treatment that is exploitative or that destroys the capacity for reflection. Williams, 'The idea of equality', in Pojman and Westmoreland, *Equality: Selected Readings*, 95.

that everyone should be subjected to the same rules, more or less. This is meant to reflect their dignity, their equal moral status. As the project of reducing social and economic inequality stumbles uncertainly forward, or even slips back, formal equal treatment against the backdrop of ongoing conditions of inequality often helps reinforce inequality even as we continue, enthusiastically or grudgingly, as the case may be, to construct the kinds of social institutions that are meant to level the playing field.

Cécile Fabre makes a similar point. Meditating on the idea of treatment with 'equal concern and respect', she distinguishes between showing concern and showing respect.[12] The latter evokes the choosing side of our moral status; concern, on the other hand, speaks to having regard for the interests or well-being of all. Generalizing her point about European constitutions, we might say that modern societies tend more enthusiastically to embrace respect than concern as aspects of the dignity of human beings. They enact general rules proscribing and prescribing, thereby creating a legal framework within which choices are judged, but pay little attention to underlying conditions in which choices are made.

When legislators adopt a uniform rule applicable to all, they inevitably assume a set of standard characteristics for those they imagine to be subject to the law. This includes a level of control over one's actions and circumstances consistent with staying out of legal trouble. They assume that those subject to the law can stay on its right side if they would. They have in mind a hypothetical subject who can and should be guided by the law. But it is often the case that the attributes of this hypothetical subject turn out to mirror those of people who have enjoyed conditions of security, who have not been subjected to severe disadvantage and deprivation. It should not, therefore, be surprising that many who fall foul of such laws have not enjoyed the luxury of the level of security attributed to the reasonable subject. Some may work that much harder to conform to the law's strictures and manage to succeed, but some will inevitably be unlucky or unwise and will fail. When they do, they will often be treated simply as the authors of their own misfortune, to be held responsible for their own choices.

But, of course, legislation doesn't always enact uniform rules; nor do judges always insist on uniform application of the rules. Indeed, sometimes legislation is meant specifically to deal with circumstances that are thought to pertain only to a limited class of persons, including circumstances of disadvantage that impair the ability to lead an autonomous life. Such efforts might be seen as acknowledgement that background social and economic conditions

---

[12] Cécile Fabre, 'Social rights in European constitutions', in de Búrca and de Witte, *Social Rights in Europe*.

needed to support autonomy are either absent or ineffective. The need for such redress after the fact might send policymakers back to the drawing board to repair or extend the web of supports. In fact, laws and judicial decisions meant to address disadvantage often also ratify and entrench it, not by treating the agent as unconstrained and fully responsible but by attributing to the character of a group of people the incapacities imposed on them by circumstances. This is, of course, what the law used to do formally to women—treat various legal incapacities as a reflection of women's distinct nature, as the ground of their different treatment rather than the cause of their inferiority. The law no longer operates comprehensively to create different ranks, but it still operates on the margins to reinforce social forces that manufacture second-class citizens, persons deemed not capable of living up to the standards of full moral agents, persons whose lives must be run for them by people who know better. That this is a violation of dignity we can tell by what our own reaction would be to having important decisions simply taken out of our hands. It is easier to do this to others if we can attribute to them, as an ingrained defect, the effects of their disadvantaged circumstances.

Thus emerges the dilemma: if we simply treat people as responsible for their choices, we punish them for being the victim of autonomy stunting conditions; if we simply take away the power of choice when it is likely to be used badly, we deny the very capacity for choice, and run the risk of stigmatizing vulnerable groups as incapable of choice.

There is much to be said about the concrete forms that social and economic rights should take in order to be fully protective of human dignity. This is one way out of this dilemma, but that is not my area of expertise, and in many jurisdictions we are some way from seeing the kind of political will that encourages blue sky thinking. So, instead, I want to consider how our legal institutions operate in the absence of the kinds of protections that would concretely alleviate disadvantage and enable everyone to live an autonomous life, particularly through the lens of the conception of autonomy and dignity that this practice implies. In the absence of such protections, people bump into the legal system in all kinds of ways, big and small, and the system has to respond to the consequences of its defects. Having, in a sense, set people up for failure, the legal system must then decide how to treat those who fall down. These are opportunities to study the often impoverished story about autonomy and human dignity embedded in state policy. They also give us glimpses into a richer way to understand dignity even under conditions in which autonomy is impaired.

I will examine three vignettes drawn from Canadian law to illustrate the interplay of competing conceptions of dignity as they emerge in discrete legal contests. Litigation unfolds on the terrain established by the legislature, however generous or stingy that happens to be, however close to or far from the idea of a robust conception of human dignity. One may therefore look to the terms of the legislation itself to see what conception of dignity it embodies. However, through litigation in these contexts, we occasionally get further insight into the official conception of dignity in the form of the arguments governments make about the rationale or purpose of its legislation. Where an adequate social and economic rights framework is not in place and there exists no constitutional entitlement to it, those affected by inadequate provision must look for indirect ways to try to vindicate their dignity. Sometimes other human rights can be used as a lens through which indirectly to assess the effectiveness of the social safety net.

Though my vignettes are Canadian in their technical legal details, I expect that the general phenomenon is quite common. I start with two examples of litigation under Canadian human rights instruments that indirectly give us a window onto access to social and economic benefits and their connection to a conception of dignity. These openings at the margins tend to occur because of the invocation of s.7 of the Charter of Rights and Freedoms, which guarantees the right to life, liberty, and the security of the person, and equality rights provisions, whether contained in the Charter (s.15) or statutory human rights codes.[13] Judges are as important as legislators in constructing a conception of autonomy congruent with human dignity. Because this is so, I will also examine an issue in an area in which judges have traditionally been the primary lawmakers such that *they* must craft the response to human tragedy occasioned by a failure of the state to foster conditions of autonomy.

Representing human dignity: three vignettes

The Insite case[14]

Vancouver's downtown east side is a very rough neighbourhood. The Supreme Court of Canada described it as follows:

> The DTES [Downtown East Side] is home to some of the poorest and most

---

[13] For example, the Ontario *Human Rights Code*, R.S.O. 1990 c. H. 19, protects against discrimination on the basis of various traits, such as sex, race, religion, disability, sexual orientation, and national or ethnic origin in respect of employment, accommodation, and the provision of services.

[14] *Canada (Attorney General) v PHS Community Services*, 2011, 3 S.C.R. 134, commonly referred to as 'the Insite case' after the name of the safe injection site.

vulnerable people in Canada. Its population includes 4,600 intravenous drug users, which is almost half of the intravenous drug users in the city as a whole. This number belies the size of the DTES. It is in fact a very small area, stretching for a few blocks in each direction from its heart at the intersection of Main and Hastings.

There is no single reason for the concentration of intravenous drug users in this urban neighbourhood. Contributing factors include the presence of several single-room occupancy hotels, the de-institutionalization of the mentally ill, the effect of drug enforcement policies over the years, and the availability of illicit narcotics at street level.

The injection drug use problem of the DTES is not hidden. At any given time of day drug transactions can be witnessed in the open air on the very steps of the historic Carnegie Community Centre at Main and Hastings. In alleys steps away, addicts tie rubber bands around their arms to find veins in which to inject heroin and cocaine, or smoke crack from glass pipes.

The residents of the DTES who are intravenous drug users have diverse origins and personal histories, yet familiar themes emerge. Many have histories of physical and sexual abuse as children, family histories of drug abuse, early exposure to serious drug use, and mental illness. Many injection drug users in the DTES have been addicted to heroin for decades, and have been in and out of treatment programmes for years. Many use multiple substances, and suffer from alcoholism. Some engage in street-level survival sex work in order to support their addictions. It should be clear from the above that these people are not engaged in recreational drug use: they are addicted. Injection drug use is both an effect and a cause of a life that is a struggle on a day to day basis.

While some affordable housing is available in the DTES, living conditions there would shock many Canadians. The DTES is one of the few places where Vancouver's poorest people, crippled by disability and addiction, can afford to live. Twenty per cent of its population is homeless. Of those who are not homeless, many live in squalid conditions in single-room occupancy hotels. Residents of single-room occupancy hotels live with little in the way of security, privacy or hygienic facilities. The residents of one building often have to share a single bathroom. Single-room occupancy hotels are commonly infested with bedbugs and rats. Existence is bleak.[15]

The failures to construct a social safety net recorded here are deep and entrenched.

In the wake of a dramatic rise in the rate of drug-related HIV and hepatitis infections and the number of drug-related deaths in the 1990s, the city and the province of British Columbia decided to change strategy. Instead of treating intravenous drug use exclusively as a law and order issue, they decided to adopt a harm reduction strategy. Convinced that it was pointless simply to tell drug addicts to stop injecting drugs or risk being sent to jail, they decided

---

[15] *Canada (Attorney General) v PHS Community Services*, paras 4–8.

to open a safe injection site, Insite, where addicts could have the use of clean needles and the benefit of medical supervision. Insite does not provide the drugs and its staff does not administer them; it merely provides a safe environment for their use, and the availability of medical care in the event of mishap. The clinic is not for recreational users but for those suffering from addiction.[16]

Operation of the scheme requires the cooperation of the federal government because federal law criminalizes the possession of narcotics. This put the staff of Insite at risk of being charged simply by virtue of running the place where drugs are being used, and, of course, the users themselves could be subject to prosecution. But the Controlled Drugs and Substances Act[17] contains a ministerial power to exempt a person or establishment from the operation of the Act. Insite operated from 2003 until 2008 under the protection of an exemption; then the Minister of Health in a newly elected Conservative government rejected Insite's application for renewal of its exemption. That decision was challenged by Insite staff and clients claiming that the minister's refusal violated their right to life, liberty, and security of the person protected by s.7 of the Charter.

The minister's defence of his actions illustrates the approach to autonomy that simply refuses to take account of the compromised circumstances of choice of disadvantaged people. The argument was simple: whatever health risks drug users suffer in the absence of a safe injection site are not caused by the prohibition on the possession of drugs kept in force by the minister's refusal but by their decision to use illegal drugs.[18] Non-medicinal use of narcotic drugs is a criminal offence, and anyone in possession of prescribed drugs should bear criminal responsibility for his or her actions.[19] This was the position adopted despite the finding of the trial judge that addiction is an illness accompanied by the risk of serious infection and overdose.[20]

It is evident that the typical story of addiction in this neighbourhood shows it to be, at least in part, a product of a web of disadvantaging circumstances that might lead almost anyone to take to drugs. Once one becomes addicted, the spiral is inexorably downward absent assistance. Yet the federal government's response was to blame the people for their own predicament and leave them to a bleak future of incarceration, disease, and death. This is

---

[16] The Supreme Court notes, *Canada (Attorney General) v PHS Community Services*, at para. 17, that 'Users must be 16 years of age or over, must sign a user agreement, release and consent form, must agree to adhere to a code of conduct, and cannot be accompanied by children. Users must register at each visit to the site and each is asked to identify the substance that will be injected.'
[17] S.C. 1996, c. 19, ss. 4(1), 5(1), 56.
[18] *Canada v P.H.S. Community Services*, para. 97.
[19] *Canada v P.H.S. Community Services*, para. 102.
[20] *Canada v P.H.S. Community Services*, para. 27.

the response of a government with its back up. Unwilling to accept that there is any state responsibility for the conditions that foster addiction, the government had to shove all the responsibility onto addicts themselves.

Ultimately, the minister's complete deflection of causal responsibility was rejected by the court, which held that Insite's clients' security interests were impaired by the refusal to exempt the clinic from the operation of the Act.[21] The court went on to hold that this infringement was not in accordance with the principles of fundamental justice because the minister's decision was inconsistent with the public health objectives of the Act rather than in furtherance of them. All the evidence in the case supported the conclusion that Insite saved lives and reduced infection rates, and did so without increasing drug consumption.[22]

There is an important lesson about autonomy and dignity in the philosophy adopted by Insite. It is significant, I think, that the clinic has abandoned a strategy of merely assigning blame for drug use in favour of working through the capacity for agency exhibited by the addicted population, impaired though it is, to help DTES residents help themselves. Traditional approaches to addiction tend to combine criminalization with making treatment conditional on giving up drugs for good. Insite was part of a coordinated strategy to provide care at whatever stage the person is at in his or her battle with drugs. The idea is to promote better health in whatever way possible to enable those addicted to drugs to move towards dealing with their addiction at whatever pace is possible for them. The project now includes a detox facility to support those ready to try living drug free. This seems to me a better way to promote progress towards a fully autonomous life. It acknowledges the burdens that those addicted to drugs labour under but still treats them as capable of making decisions to advance their own well-being. It supports them in the effort to advance towards their own objectives rather than imposing society's objectives on them. Nor was the significance of this philosophy lost on its clients. As Dean Edward Wilson, one of the litigants, put it: 'Insite has given dignity to people who have to struggle to have their humanity recognized.'[23]

The Insite litigation offers us a stark contrast between a government policy that assumes autonomy and seeks to punish those who choose to break the rules and a philosophy that is determined to treat addicts as agents, although in need of assistance to enable them to choose well. The former refuses to acknowledge the systemic failures that help create addiction, and

---

[21] *Canada v P.H.S. Community Services*, paras 91–2.
[22] *Canada v P.H.S. Community Services*, para. 131.
[23] *Canada v P.H.S. Community Services*, para. 22.

can therefore only affirm the dignity of choice by punishing bad choices; the latter acknowledges the background problems and seeks to do what can be done in the circumstances to move people forward, while still affirming their dignity as agents.

Ontario (Director, Disability Support Program) v Tranchemontagne[24]

Welfare reforms in Ontario in the mid-1990s, not unlike many jurisdictions, created two streams of recipients. Recreating for the twenty-first century the Victorian distinction between the 'deserving and undeserving poor', those with disabilities of a certified type and severity were entitled to one scheme of benefits (ODSP),[25] while others were relegated to another (OW).[26] The former scheme was more generous in the level of support it provided;[27] the latter imposed the additional requirement of participation in treatment or training programmes in preparation for entering the workforce on pain of being cut off benefit altogether. The rules dividing potential income support recipients into one of these two classes excluded from eligibility for ODSP a group who would otherwise be classified as disabled, but whose only disability involved addiction to drugs or alcohol. These people were therefore lumped in with those subjected to the lower benefit levels and compulsory work-readiness programmes of OW. This exclusion from ODSP was challenged as discriminatory under the Ontario Human Rights Code in that it discriminated against those with a specific disability, treating them differently from other disabled persons.

Ultimately the complaint was successful, but the government's argument in defence of its legislation illustrates a variant on the ways that the meaning and value of autonomy is often distorted under the guise of protecting human dignity. Taking the legislation itself together with the government's defence of it at trial we see a mixture of punitive and patronizing impulses. Together they disguise rather than confront the real causes of poverty and offer insult to the actual capacities of its victims even as the government claims to help them.

---

[24] *Werbeski and Tranchemontange v Ontario (Director, Disability Support Program)* Ont. Social Benefits Tribunal, File No. 9910-07541R 0050-04579, aff'd, *Ontario (Director, Disability Support Program) v Tranchemontagne* (2009), 95 OR (3d) 327 (Ont. Div. Ct.), aff'd Ontario (Director, Disability Support Program) v Tranchemontagne, 2010 ONCA 593.
[25] Ontario Disability Support Program.
[26] Ontario Works.
[27] I should note that even the more generous ODSP could hardly be called generous. The full amount ($959 per month) left recipients below the poverty level. OW benefits were roughly 60 per cent of that ($535 per month).

The legislation was carefully tailored to remove from disability support only those whose sole source of disability was alcohol or drug addiction where the addictive substance was not a prescription drug. Reading between the lines, the message is clear: those who are addicted to a substance which they chose to consume rather than having become addicted as a side-effect of treatment for some non-self-inflicted injury or illness were to be treated as not 'really' disabled. Rather, they could be considered responsible for their predicament because of their earlier choice. In this respect, the legislation reveals an attitude similar to that of the federal government in refusing to permit the operation of Insite. But the government's response to the discrimination complaint adds a further layer that is revealing.

The court framed the test for discrimination as follows: did the legislation treat those with a particular disability differently from others so as to violate human dignity? The government argued that there was no violation of dignity in the exclusion of addicts from the more generous benefit scheme because they were included in a scheme that better met their needs. That is, the government claimed that it was taking account of the addicts' current circumstance of impaired autonomy and responding appropriately. The claim was twofold: first, the government claimed that all those who suffered only from addiction were capable of employment and therefore would be better off being required to participate in programmes designed to get them back in the workforce; second, the government claimed that a significantly lower monthly amount of support would preserve addicts from the temptation to spend some of their income on alcohol or drugs.

Notice how this scheme works: based on an apparent assumption of conditions that uniformly foster autonomy, consumption of non-prescription drugs and the abuse of alcohol is judged to be a bad choice. On the surface, the legislation might be read as saying that those who make such choices should simply be held responsible and denied full social assistance benefits. But, perhaps wary of appearing to adopt a punitive approach towards a group of disabled people, the government's justification of the scheme claimed to recognize their special needs—by taking decision-making about how to return to health and employability away from them. The policy implies that it is necessary to force addicts to participate in work-readiness schemes because they will not do so of their own choice; likewise, they must be deprived of the means of making further bad choices by being reduced to a subsistence level of income. Having made bad decisions in the past, the addict's agency is treated as a source of trouble to be controlled by the state. He is to have his choices made for him, and this is justified as an affirmation of his dignity by meeting his special needs.

To be sure, those suffering from substance addictions face formidable challenges in staying healthy and holding down a job. And it is not wrong for social programmes to take these challenges into account; indeed, it is necessary. But the dignity-affirming way to do so is to work through and with whatever capacity for agency the participant in the programme has to support the making of good choices rather than taking over the direction of their lives so that they can make no further mistakes. In this respect, the government of Ontario could learn something from the creators of the Insite clinic.

The full import of the combination of punitive and patronizing measures is brought home when we realize that this is the regime that applies to *all* non-disabled social assistance applicants. To claim discrimination, those suffering from addiction had to claim that as disabled people they should not be lumped in with the 'undeserving poor'. The Human Rights Code provided no remedy for others tagged as 'undeserving'. The scheme assumes that anyone able to work but not in paid employment must be forced to participate in work-readiness programmes to push them into the workforce, and in the meantime be given a meagre allowance so that they have a further incentive to take whatever work is available. Poor people are treated as incompetent in the first instance, needing the government to tell them how to achieve self-sufficiency. If they resist any of the 'advice', they are treated as dishonest or incorrigibly lazy. Nowhere in this picture is there a recognition of the way social and economic policy shapes the work opportunities of the poor. However, there is plenty of evidence that social assistance recipients are eager to work and to better themselves—the problem has more to do with a dearth of jobs that pay a living wage than with the fecklessness of the poor.[28]

Thus, the help offered becomes merely a test of the recipient's submission. Failure to comply becomes an excuse for punishment. The risk is that these layered forms of disrespect may contribute to the construction of a new type of second-class citizen. The mix of punitive attitudes and controlling impulses often embedded in social assistance legislation risks turning poverty into a status, a set of entrenched characteristics attributed to the poor, rather than a set of social and economic circumstances that inflict sub-standard living conditions on people. The law casts widespread aspersion on the choices and capacities for choice of poor people. These meanings are not lost on other members of the public, whose own prejudices are thereby reinforced. And because the poor are deemed to be unworthy of making their own decisions,

---

[28] See, for example, Janet Mosher, 'Welfare reform and the remaking of the model citizen', in Margot Young, Susan B. Boyd, Gwen Brodsky, and Shelagh Day (eds), *Poverty: Rights, Social Citizenship, Legal Activism* (Vancouver, UBC Press, 2007), 119.

they are subjected to harsh conditions designed to control them. These conditions reinforce their powerlessness. The low rates paid out to able-bodied recipients leave them constantly at risk of hunger, illness, and homelessness, and therefore ill-equipped for full participation in the work force. One mistake is likely to have catastrophic results. The job training they are offered typically prepares them only for the lowest paid jobs, jobs with no benefits, no security, and no hope for advancement. People are not lifted out of poverty; they are just removed from the welfare rolls. The government programme becomes part of the problem rather than part of a solution. Indeed, the lines drawn by the policy and pre-existing sources of inequality reinforce one another to entrench indignity, making it harder, not easier, for the poor to achieve control of their own lives.

The criminalization of victims of domestic violence[29]

My third example examines cases in which women have had to defend themselves against criminal charges when they have killed or attempted to kill an abusive partner. Here, the prohibition against violence is meant to be of general application, but there are several defences available which provide at least an opportunity to raise extenuating circumstances. This provides another context in which to examine how well the legal system responds to disadvantaged circumstances that are at least in part created by a social and economic rights vacuum. The state is not responsible for abusive spouses, but it is responsible for securing the safety of those at risk of violence, both through an appropriate police response to domestic violence and the provision of the assistance needed to enable abused women to extricate themselves from violent relationships. Most states fall seriously short in providing the needed support in both respects. This leaves the courts to clean up the mess when a woman takes matters into her own hands and uses violence herself when she can see no other way out. Should she be held responsible for her choice, or should her desperate circumstances be taken into account?

The Canadian case law in this area is instructive in several ways. Although the courts have shown a willingness to consider the specific context of domestic violence, the way they have done so has sometimes been to treat the accused's response as stemming from a weakness in her—understandable, perhaps, and therefore excusable, but nevertheless a defect *in her*. Downplayed in the analysis is the inadequacy of measures to protect women

---

[29] I am grateful to Martha Shaffer for alerting me to some of the complexities in the jurisprudential developments in this area.

from violence in the first place. If we can see our way clear to relieving her of responsibility by merely declaring her to be defective in some way, we do not have to consider the circumstances that give rise to the tragedy. In the meantime, little progress seems to be made in providing greater protection and facilitating escape. Therefore, the cases keep coming and, as will happen, they provide the courts with a series of difficult doctrinal issues within criminal law. It seems likely that sooner or later the ingenuity of the criminal lawyers will run out, leaving women subject to criminal punishment because they could find no legal way out of a violent relationship.

This issue first came before the Supreme Court of Canada in *R. v Lavallee*,[30] in which a woman who had shot and killed her abusive husband pleaded self-defence. Her counsel introduced expert psychiatric evidence ostensibly to assist the jury in understanding the psychological effects of long-term abuse.[31] Over the Crown's objections, he led evidence about what had been labelled 'battered woman syndrome' to help explain the accused's behaviour.[32] The Supreme Court held the evidence to be admissible because it could help disabuse the jury of common myths and stereotypes about domestic violence, such as the view that the abuse claimed could not have been very bad or the woman would have left, or that if she stayed anyway she must be a masochist.[33] That is, the court recognized that a jury might need help not to fall into the trap of assuming that a choice not to leave was free.

The court held that the evidence may be relevant to the question of whether the accused believed on reasonable grounds that it was not otherwise possible to preserve herself from death or grievous bodily harm.[34] In *Lavallee*, the expert psychiatric evidence described victims of abuse as suffering from 'learned helplessness'—the effect of repeated violence is to induce 'an amotivational state, if you will, where it feels there no power and there's no energy to do anything'.[35] The court held that this could help explain why the accused

---

[30] [1990] 1 S.C.R. 852.

[31] He thought, probably correctly, that he could not adduce evidence of the social and economic obstacles to leaving a violent relationship. Thanks to Martha Shaffer for pointing this out.

[32] Lenore Walker, *The Battered Woman* (New York, Harper & Row, 1979); Lenore Walker, *The Battered Woman Syndrome* (New York, Springer, 1984).

[33] *Lavallee*, [1990] 1 S.C.R. 852, 873.

[34] The court also held that the evidence was relevant to self-defence because it could inform whether the accused had a reasonable apprehension of death at the hands of the deceased, since evidence shows that the victim of abuse typically has a heightened sensitivity to the cycle of violence typical of the relationship. Where an outsider may not perceive the deceased's behaviour as threatening, the accused may know better.

[35] Quoted in *Lavallee* [1990] 1 S.C.R. 852, 884.

felt she could not just leave. In other words, the effect of the violence was to turn the accused into a kind of zombie, *unable* to choose to leave.

Ultimately, Angelique Lavallee was acquitted, but the limits of criminal law doctrine required presenting victims of domestic violence as suffering from a 'syndrome', a psychological condition explaining what to 'normal' people would seem like unreasonable behaviour. Although there is ample evidence that in many cases of domestic violence the victim really has no means of escape, this is not evidence that can be directly led in order to ground a self-defence plea. In fact, the only mention in the decision of the background circumstances that conspire to keep women in abusive relationships is Justice Wilson's brief mention that 'environmental factors may also impair the woman's ability to leave—lack of job skills, the presence of children to care for, fear of retaliation by the man, etc. may each have a role to play in some cases'.[36] Missing from the list are inadequate police response when women do complain of abuse, unavailability of emergency shelters for women and their children so that they have a safe place to go, assistance in finding permanent housing, and income assistance for those who are not in paid employment.[37] All these are plausible aspects of women's right to security of the person and the material conditions that would make it real. Yet they are beyond the purview of the decision about whether the defence of self-defence is available. So instead of being treated as someone who realistically took her circumstances into account and made a rational decision, an abused woman is excused because the abuse she had suffered made her unable to do that rational thing.

Indeed, since *Lavallee*, many feminist criminal law scholars have complained of the tendency of lower courts to treat 'battered woman syndrome' as a kind of disease which a women pleading self-defence must prove she suffered from, which disease is bound up with particular indicia of helplessness.[38] In other words, the idea that the accused must show that there is something wrong *with her* in order to use the defence had become built into the doctrine. Given the ways, historically, in which weakness in individual women has been readily converted into an integral aspect of all women's nature, this was especially dangerous. To its credit, the Supreme Court has tried to counter this tendency, Justice L'Heureux-Dubé, in *R. v Malott*, warning as follows:

---

[36] Quoted in *Lavallee* [1990] 1 S.C.R. 852, 887.

[37] Melanie Randall, 'Equality rights and the charter: reconceptualizing state accountability for ending domestic violence', in F. Faraday et al. (eds), *Making Equality Rights Real, Securing Substantive Equality Under the Charter*, 2nd edn (Toronto, Irwin Law, 2009), 275.

[38] See for example, Martha Shaffer, 'The battered woman syndrome revisited: some complicating thoughts five years after *R. v Lavallee*', University of Toronto Law Journal 47 (1997), 1; Isabel Grant, 'The "syndromization" of women's experience', in Donna Martinson et al., 'A forum on *Lavallee v R.*: women and self-defence', *UBC Law Review* 25 (1991), 23.

> By emphasizing a woman's 'learned helplessness', her dependence, her victimization, and her low self-esteem, in order to establish that she suffers from 'battered woman syndrome', the legal debate shifts from the objective rationality of her actions to preserve her own life to those personal inadequacies which apparently explain her failure to flee from her abuser. Such an emphasis comports too well with society's stereotypes about women.[39]

This shows some sensitivity to the constraints under which abused women act, and a willingness to treat their behaviour as 'objectively rational' in the circumstances. It tries to restore some dignity to abused women. However, it does not do justice to the complex agency displayed by women trying to protect themselves from violence in intimate relationships. They often put enormous energy into planning and strategizing to minimize the harm to themselves and their children.[40] This includes seeking help from the authorities, help that is all too often denied.

The Supreme Court seems to have glimpsed this heroic effort, and for that reason wants to avoid imposing criminal responsibility. However the fact remains that judicial decisions contain only the slimmest acknowledgement that environmental factors are pervasive and powerful, and some of them are the responsibility of the authorities to counteract. This larger context is crucial to moving in a direction that would meaningfully support women's autonomy. One demonstration of the inadequacy of finding what space there is in the criminal law of defences is that women in desperate circumstances do increasingly desperate things, and there is only so far that the criminal law can be stretched. The Supreme Court has just handed down a decision in the case of *R. v Ryan*,[41] in which the accused woman was charged with counselling a third party (who was in fact an undercover officer) to murder her abusive husband. Nicole Doucet (formerly Ryan) had recently separated from her husband after years of abuse, yet he continued to stalk her and threaten her and her daughter with death. She claimed that she made several reports to the police and other agencies of this threatening behaviour, but no action was taken. Each time she was told it was a 'civil matter'. In this case, there is a very direct link between the state's failure to protect and Doucet's decision to take matters into her own hands. But because she asked someone else to do the killing, it is not clear

---

[39] *R v Malott* [1998] 1 SCR 123, para. 41. Indeed, Justice L'Heureux-Dubé went on to draw attention to the brief passage quoted above from *Lavallee* referring to environmental factors helping to explain why women do not leave abusive relationships. This seems calculated, since it is fair to say that at the time that *Lavallee* was handed down, one might have been forgiven for not having noticed the passage at all.

[40] Martha R. Mahoney, 'Legal images of battered women: redefining the issue of separation', *Michigan Law Review* 90 (1991), 1.

[41] 2013 SCC 3.

that self-defence is available, leading the trial judge to acquit on the basis of duress. The Supreme Court rejected this line of defence, holding that duress applies only to morally involuntary actions; Doucet's husband did not compel her to attempt to inflict harm on him. Nevertheless, the court entered a stay of proceedings on the grounds that the law of duress had been sufficiently unclear that the trial had been conducted solely around its availability. The court did not think a new trial would be fair, citing the enormous toll that the abuse and the trial had taken on Doucet and 'the disquieting fact that, on the record before us, it seems that the authorities were much quicker to intervene to protect Mr. Ryan than they had been to respond to her request for help in dealing with his reign of terror over her'.[42]

Fascinating as all this may be in doctrinal terms, one nevertheless wants to weep at the prospect of another abused woman having to fight for her liberty and at the need to devote considerable ingenuity to her defence, when what is really needed is a strategy to force police and other social service agencies to take domestic violence seriously so that its victims don't have to kill and take their chances in a criminal prosecution.

Conclusion

Personal autonomy—being able to live self-directed lives—is integral to our conception of dignity. For its sake, states must attend to the materials and social conditions that make autonomy possible. The vignettes presented above are just three tiny examples of how, in the absence of the right kind of autonomy-protecting programmes, the legal system must deal with myriad controversies in which a hapless individual is visited with legal consequences more because he or she was unlucky enough to be caught up in a web of disadvantage than because of his or her own fault. A proper network of social and economic rights cannot prevent all bad things from happening, of course. But its absence seems to tempt governments to deflect blame from themselves to individuals, as in the Insite case, or to seek to control vulnerable individuals in the name of helping them, and in *Tranchemontange*, or risks pathologizing people who had no realistic option in order to avoid blaming them, as in the domestic violence context. These strategies threaten to warp our conception of autonomy and, along with it, our conception of dignity. We can hold onto an understanding of the larger task of putting autonomy-supporting social structures in place by trying to honour the capacity for choosing exhibited by

---

[42] *R v. Ryan*, para. 35.

people even in difficult circumstances. That capacity must be supported not only by the appropriate external conditions but also through its exercise, and that requires sometimes resisting the instinct to control and seeing the situation of choice from the perspective of the disadvantaged. If state actors make the effort to engage with the choices of people as they see them, they would daily be confronted with the gaps in the social safety net, and perhaps be more consistently motivated to do something about them.

33

Human Dignity, Interiority, and Poverty

Clemens Sedmak

Human dignity and 'blindness to the human aspect'

A COMMON EVERYDAY FORM of disregard and disrespect of human dignity is the way we treat those around us—as if they were things rather than people. The French socio-anthropologist Anna Sam describes how, in working as a cashier for several years in a supermarket, she was looked at and treated more as an item off the shelf than a living being.[1] She regarded the customer as the greatest 'burden' of the job since she was continually humiliated and looked down upon. Customers were oblivious to the fact that a human individual was operating the till—often ignoring her completely without so much as a look or a word. Payment for goods is frequently carried out like the transaction at a cashpoint machine, with no trace of realization that the cashier is a person, reduced to being part of the till she works at, a mere extension of the items in the trolley. William Vollmann, who has researched poverty in its many geographical contexts, talks of 'invisibility' as an operative word in characterizing poverty.[2] Poverty makes people invisible, and becomes itself invisible at the same time: those hit by poverty are neither seen nor noticed, and are ignored like beggars on a street. The German journalist Günter Wallraff found out for himself what it was like to be homeless, living on the streets, and sometimes even locked up in a storage container (at times without windows).[3] Florence Aubenas, who worked undercover as a low-paid cleaner for twelve months to find out what it is like to try to make a living, was told in an induction course that she should not expect anyone to pass the time of day with her as cleaner: this was something she would have to get used to.[4] A cleaner is seen as an extension of the furniture (s)he is cleaning: you probably won't knock it over

---

[1] A. Sam, *Checkout: A Life on the Tills* (London, Gallic Books, 2009).
[2] W. Vollmann, *Poor People* (San Francisco, CA, Harper Perennial, 2007), 103–22.
[3] G. Wallraff, *Aus der schönen neuen Welt. Expeditionen ins Landesinnere* (Köln, Kiepenheuer & Witsch, 2009), 49–96.
[4] F. Aubenas, *Le quai de Ouistreham* (Paris, Éditions de l'Olivier, 2010), 45.

or bump into it, but you won't need to say hello either. Such situations are all about attitude, an attitude which perceives others as things rather than beings.

It is exactly this attitude which the Israeli philosopher Avishai Margalit terms 'blindness to the human aspect'.[5] The distinguishing feature of this blindness is not being able to see beyond or below the external, outer shell of others, and fails to notice the individual as individual. 'Blindness of the human aspect' implies restricted or diminished awareness in the process of noticing 'being' in 'other', but does not depend on depth of perception alone; it is a purely cognitive process of construction. In line with such an understanding of the term, 'blindness' is a clinical condition or dysfunctional vision comparable to colour blindness. Margalit points out that this type of blindness suggests people look through others or ignore them as though they were not there, and is a key element of anti-colonial literature.[6] There may be a fundamental difference in seeing others as 'things' or in just looking straight through them, but the perceptive refusal to see other as being and not thing is the same. Both aspects of seeing—failure to see—are intrinsic in patterns of awareness and not rationally justifiable cognitive interpretations. 'Blindness of human aspect' may fail to register one individual or, as is more common, disregard groups of individuals, for example for racist or sexist reasons—perceiving these groups as outside the scope of what we might assess to be human being.[7] In other words, such blindness is caused by prejudice, which reduces individual *personae* to items on a shelf. It is an awareness engendering a frame of mind and type of action favoured by asymmetrical relationships. Those who run the greatest risk of falling victim to such a frame of mind are the socially vulnerable.

What becomes glaringly apparent in this everyday mode of conduct is that the root cause of treating others as mere things would seem to lie in the fact that we do not judge according to rational reasoning but according to the way we may see and perceive. In turn, this way of seeing is founded on particular patterns of experience which have been corroborated and endorsed again and again. Ludwig Wittgenstein voiced his views on the condition of perception in his *Investigations*, asserting that we invariably: 'see something as something else'.[8] In being aware of what we see, certain features come to

---

[5] Avishai Margalit, *The Decent Society* (Cambridge, MA, Harvard University Press, 1996), 96–103.
[6] Margalit, *The Decent Society*, 102.
[7] Compare with M. Krygier, *Civil Passions. Selected Writings* (Melbourne, Schwartz Publishing, 2005), 206–7.
[8] L. Wittgenstein, *Philosophical Investigations*, trans. G. E. M. Anscombe (Oxford, Basil Blackwell, 1967), 193–208; compare with C. Dunlop, 'Wittgenstein on sensation and "Seeing-as"', *Synthese* 60 (1984), 349–67.

the fore; only when other aspects are noticed and considered, is our awareness of that which is seen modified.[9] Such sentient awareness of aspects may suddenly flash before our eyes, 'half visual experience, half thought'.[10] However, visual experience cannot be simply governed by cognitive powers of decision. All too often, we do not consciously register the shift in our awareness of what we see.[11] Perception and interpretation—*construction*—are not two disparate acts, categorized under separate headings. They are one and the same thing: share a oneness inextricably linked with our own private language and patterns of behaviour and those same patterns we see in others. Thus, our sense of perception and the language we use to describe it create a unity in as far as our own judgment of what we see relies on language to voice and create that judgment. '*Sprachspiele*'—judgments rendered, based on visual aspects—are intrenched in language and extra-language elements from which they cannot be divorced.[12] Both are part of a 'form of life'.[13] Utterances—supposition expressed—on what we see before us, for example, referring to or describing colour, frequently border on the confines of logic and empiricism.[14] The complexity of terms and definitions of perception is no less vast than the phenomenon of form of life—*Lebensform*—and neither the one nor the other can be reduced by subjugating them to the disciplinary powers of rules. Any changes which occur must take place at a deeper level and infringe upon form of life.

For the purpose of our present discussion on human dignity, these considerations are threefold: firstly, the definition of the term human dignity will be examined via blindness of aspect as a genus of perception. Thus, the definition of human dignity as attendant on a specific disposition of awareness, or a particular way of seeing other as being, begs to be questioned. Secondly, perception, not irrelevant in our present discussion of the term human dignity, is embedded in a way of life and is dependent on precedent examples which nourish the attitude they foster. Thirdly, vulnerable individuals, rejected by social norms, run a higher risk of not being noticed in blindness of aspect.

---

[9] Wittgenstein, *Philosophical Investigations*, 196.
[10] Wittgenstein, *Philosophical Investigations*, 197.
[11] Wittgenstein, *Philosophical Investigations*, 199.
[12] L. Wittgenstein, *Remarks on Colour*, trans. L. L. McAlister, M. Schättle (Oxford, Blackwell, 1977), I,1; compare with M. McGinn, 'Wittgenstein's "Remarks on Colour"', *Philosophy* 66 (1991), 435–53.
[13] Wittgenstein, *Remarks on Colour*, III, 302.
[14] Wittgenstein, *Remarks on Colour*, I,32; III,19.

Human dignity and interiority

What happens exactly when someone is perceived and treated like a thing—an item off a supermarket shelf, an extension of the till, or simply a piece of furniture? What does it mean to see someone else as some*one* and not some*thing*? We assume a certain level of perception as our point of entry, which enables us to see other not only in physical externals but also the inner depth and nature beyond. In other words, the way we see a table differs considerably from how we perceive the depth and inner-being of other being. And it is exactly this difference which enables us to humiliate and degrade others. You cannot humiliate a table: you may decide to use it for something other than the purpose it serves, you may damage or destroy it, but there is no way you can debase it. The whole notion of debasement by its very nature assumes a notion of vulnerability, which goes far and beyond external injury and damage and presupposes a meta-level of being, by which, in principle, we can reflect upon our attitude not only towards others but also of self. These two aspects are comprised in what we might term interiority. Humans are beings which can only be described via language, which similarly presumes that beyond the aspect of the visually obvious there is a complex world of feelings and emotions, powers of thought and reflection at work under the surface. Such assumptions are imperative if we are to define self—Jerold Seigel puts forward the idea that reflexivity is the defining principle in constructing the modern concept of self.[15]

This perception of other as individual has become an integral part of our modern understanding of self. 'Inwardness' is the hallmark of modern identity,[16] as put forward by Charles Taylor in his in-depth study of the modern self.[17] Taylor draws our attention to the fact that seeing other as self with all his/her innermost complexities inherent in individual identity is a typically modern concept. Likewise, it is this depth and complexity of self which denies scientific definition wholesale, because the subject of any scientific study has to be identified and described objectively, regardless of subjective interpretation, regardless of point of reference, and regardless of framework environment. None of this can be applied in analysing self in other and, does

---

[15] J. Seigel, *The Idea of the Self. Thought and Experience in Western Europe since the Seventeenth Century* (Cambridge, Cambridge University Press, 2005), 7–17.

[16] Compare with K. Flasch, 'Wert der Innerlichkeit', in H. Joas and K. Wiegandt (eds), *Die kulturellen Werte Europas* (Frankfurt am Main, Fischer, 2005), 219–36.

[17] C. Taylor, *Sources of the Self. The Making of Modern Identity* (Cambridge, MA, Harvard University Press, 1994).

to a certain degree even elude any exhaustive examination of own self.[18] The feeling or notion of self must go beyond any neutral observation of being or categorization of the practicalities involved. Seeking to identify identity is an attempt to define a place from which I can make a statement, and which in turn I would like to be addressed. A key work in the historical development of understanding human interiority is Augustine's *Confessions*.

While this key work undoubtedly had a decisive influence on the notion of inwardness,[19] one might dispute how original Augustine's ideas were. Augustine describes both himself and humankind in general as beings that have infinite inner-depth and rich resources at their disposal. The imagery Augustine uses to illustrate inwardness of being is revealing: the house (C I,5), the heart as vessel (C X,35), arable land (C II,3), the image of the battleground (C VIII,8). While the image of the house, conveying the idea of untold rooms and space within, was outlined in the sixteenth century by Teresa of Avila in *The Interior Castle*, the image of a field to be ploughed suggests the labour and toil involved in attaining inwardness. The image of the battleground is perhaps the most dramatic, and reflects the battle being fought out within. This inner space of interiority is, according to Augustine, the 'core' of human being; it is that inner space in which we can find God and the place: 'where God makes himself known to me' (C I,2).[20] This inner space is also the seat of that sense which perceives the voice of God, 'et clamasti de longinquo: ego sum qui sum. et audivi, sicut auditor in corde' (C VII,10). This inner space is able to both hear and feel God; Augustine talks about: 'The ears of my heart' (C I,5). God is the true 'heart' of inward being, 'more inner than inner' (C III,6). This is how God knows us better than we can ever know ourselves, since fathoming the profundity of our own inwardness is beyond us. Inner-being resonates with the dynamics of our aspirations and desires, our past memories and the impact of decisions taken, the sense of joy and sense of despair. Thus, the soul as inner space can be depicted as active agent as well as backdrop and set where the events of life are staged and come to pass. As immeasurable as our inner being may be, it is not without structure: it is the seat of diverse

---

[18] Taylor, *Sources of the Self*, 2.2.

[19] Augustine, *Confessions*, ed. J. O'Donnell (Oxford, Oxford University Press, 1992). Compare with P. Carey, *Augustine's Invention of the Inner Self* (Oxford, Oxford University Press, 2000). Carey reconstructs the Platonic school of thought as seen by Augustine in order to examine the originality of Augustine's ideas. Carey depicts the soul according to Plato's idea of Hell and Plotin's 'sphere revolving around the inner source of intelligibility'—all metaphors of space with the inner palace as the key metaphor as used by Augustine whom he sees as a bridge between linking Plato and Descartes; compare with Michael Tkacz's review in *Journal of the History of Philosophy* 39:4 (2001), 584–5.

[20] 'Quis locus est in me, quoveniat in me deus meus? quo deus veniat in me, deus, qui fecit caelum et terram?' (C I,2).

powers (will, memory, reason) but also divergent moods and emotions (craving and lust, joy, fear, regret, and grief: C X,14). Of these, Augustine reserves a special place for memory—*memoria*—as part of inner-being in his tenth book.[21] Augustine maintains it is memory that drives the thinking process: thinking collects and orders random ideas (C X,11). He is continually amazed by that rich inner homogeneity of memory which harnesses the heterogeneity of thought. Memory plays a central role in Augustine's analysis of the heart of being and the core of interiority. In one place, he mentions having made the journey to the seat of the soul, 'which is in my own memory' ('intravi ad ipsius animi mei sedem (quae illi est in memoria mea, quoniam sui quoque meminit animus'; C X,25). Personal memory serves as meta-memory: 'I remember having remembered' (C X,13), and it is the place in which we are confronted by ourselves (C X,8).[22] Finding rapport with self is perhaps *the* cornerstone in a culture of interiority.

So saying, Augustine's *Confessions* present us with a rich tapestry of the wealth of inwardness which can bestow human life with depth and unique meaning.[23] Inwardly, our abilities and powers are caught up in a fight for prominence; and it is here that decisions are arrived at and taken; a process involving striving, judgment, and memory. However, the governing factor in both decision-making and ensuing action remains the structure of inner-being which can be moulded, fashioned, and shaped, and which is subject to inherent laws which can at the same time be specified. However, in any decision reached and any action taken, it is the structure and fabric of inner-being, moulded, fashioned and shaped by experience and subject to inherent laws, which governs resources of inner-being as inexhaustible as they may be remain inaccessible without the grace of God; he knows our soul better than we do ourselves, and it is this—His—knowing which can lead us as beings to truth and salvation. This concept of understanding will have an impact on the way we think about and regard ourselves; the way we think about self will also impact the way we define self-esteem or dignity. Seen in this light, self can be neither measured nor mapped, and remains an enigma to objective, scientific calculation. This would thus imply that the whole concept of

---

[21] Compare with R. Sorabji, *Self. Ancient and Modern Insights about Individuality, Life and Death* (Oxford, Oxford University Press, 2005), 99–100; N. Fischer 'Einleitung', in *Aurelius Augustinus, Suche nach dem wahren Leben* (Hamburg, Meiner, 2006), xiii–xci.

[22] 'Ibi mihi et ipse occurro, meque recolo, quid, quando et ubi egerim quoque modo, cum agerem, affectus fuerim' (C X,8).

[23] Compare with Charles T. Mathewes, 'Augustinian anthropology: interior intimo meo', *Journal of Religious Ethics* 27:2 (1999), 195–221. Mathewes points out that Augustine's seemingly incoherent anthropology does shed new light on our understanding of 'agency' and autonomy as seen as the basis of interiority.

subjectivity has to be redefined too. An active agent bases his or her actions on emotions, ideas, aspirations, ambitions, and perception, which can only be accessed and expressed in the complex language found in interiority.

Human dignity and vulnerability

In defining interiority, a new perspective in the understanding of vulnerability is also being created. Admission of human vulnerability has made a major contribution to ongoing discourse on human dignity, since its beginnings in the atrocities of the Second World War, and an attempt to eradicate an entire race of people.

I would now like to turn to the concept under discussion here—human dignity—and examine the association and correlation between the terms human dignity, interiority, and vulnerability, whereby the latter has little to do with the knowledge that 'something might happen'. It is more the 'capacity to be wounded';[24] in other words, a profound realization that one's own integrity is at risk of being broken. Vulnerability is realizing the tentative nature and fragility of our own identity;[25] it is an insight revealing that identity—that unique quality which makes us what we are—is something which can be injured, crushed or destroyed. Therefore, if that main characteristic of interiority, as set out above, is an integral part of what it is to be human and determines that universal image of human-being, then vulnerability is an essential aspect of humanness. Vulnerability lies in knowing that being human involves risks that cannot be reduced to zero, and that the human condition entails exposure to contingencies and stress. We may try to protect ourselves against the onslaughts risk might bring, and even though possible strategies in minimizing risk are disproportionate and reflect social standing, they are neither lasting nor perfect. We cannot take out insurance to prevent dementia, being involved in a car crash, or avoid natural catastrophes. Human dignity takes central stage when vulnerability overrides in a particular situation—a situation in which our concept of self is substantially challenged. Lisa Genova gives us a telling example in her novel *Still Alice*, in which the central figure, Alice, a fifty-year-old woman, is diagnosed with Alzheimer's. For a time, Alice defines herself in this situation of extreme vulnerability by disease, until she realizes that she is a human being beyond the confines of disease: wife,

---

[24] H.-M. Füssel, 'Vulnerability: a generally applicable conceptual framework for climate change research', *Global Environmental Change* 17 (2007), 155–67, at 155.
[25] Compare with F. Delor and M. Hubert, 'Revisiting the concept of "vulnerability"', *Social Science and Medicine* 50 (2000), 1557–70.

mother, daughter, grandmother-to-be, best friend, cousin, and so on. Even under the most adverse conditions, a human being remains a human being, to be treated with a sense of depth. Defining human dignity lies at the heart of our being both prepared and willing to see other humans as beings.

The concept of human dignity is linked with the concept of vulnerability in at least two ways: first, because the concept of human dignity has emerged in confrontation with the fragility of human existence; second, because situations of experienced vulnerability prove to be the acid test of human dignity in its entirety. This connection between human dignity and vulnerability is important, since the definition of human dignity itself has to rise to at least three challenges: of its becoming pretentious, too far removed from the realities of everyday life, and/or so controversial as to be abused. These three aspects could push the whole debate surrounding human dignity over the edge of relevance, forcing it into a state of neither here nor there. Pretension tends to take over on those special occasions, where human dignity is celebrated and praised to the skies in ostentatious language. In a well-known text, Karl Popper warns about the use and power of 'big' words, which in covering up ambiguity in effect mislead.[26] We stand in awe and allow ourselves to be browbeaten by big words; we are duped, and thus robbed of our faculties of objective reasoning. The concept of vulnerability can assist to keep the concept of human dignity on the ground, while it is operationalized—by looking at elementary aspects of life. Human dignity becomes paramount when eating, drinking, egesting, sleeping, personal hygiene habits become especially vulnerable, for example, in hospitals, prisons, care-homes; places in which simple, personal patterns of day-to-day life become an issue—a problem. The status of elementary aspects of life serves as a litmus test for the concept of human dignity. The second challenge allows us to try out the 'trap of abstraction', which suggests that human dignity may well be assigned to each and every human being, but each and every human being is nevertheless treated in a different way: in this sense the equality of dignity is not visible.

This temptation of abstraction has been voiced by David Foster Wallace as an embodiment of the more dangerous side of academic study, in that: 'it enables a tendency to over-intellectualize stuff, to get lost in abstract thinking, instead of simply paying attention to what's going on in front of me'.[27] Our definition of vulnerability will help us in assessing the above, and if we remember that those who are particularly vulnerable in any society are

---

[26] K. R. Popper, 'Against big words (a letter not originally intended for publication)', in his *In Search of a Better World Lecture and Essays from Thirty Years*, trans. L. J. Bennett (London, Routledge, 1994), 82–98.

[27] D. F. Wallace, *This Is Water* (Cologne, Kiepenheuer & Witsch, 2012), 47.

those who are engaged in low-paid, unskilled work, in other words excluded from—outsiders of that society. And this begs the question of how people are treated and how are they shown respect particularly in adverse circumstances, for example within the confines—at every level—of a prison or psychiatric hospital. The acid test of self-esteem may then be found in considering how societies treat those who are vulnerable within that society. The third point could be described as cases of controversy, which is a favourite rhetorical device, implemented to stop conversations by using the concept of human dignity. Others adopt a more cynical approach to the topic of human dignity, regarding any terminology as utterly superfluous. There is a danger of becoming accustomed to a routine language of human dignity. The German historian Christian Meier reminds us that written accounts of history after Auschwitz will demand the ability of a 'constant renewal of shock'.[28] Auschwitz must not be allowed to be become a routine norm. And the same could be said for the definition of human dignity: in appraising our own vulnerability, in understanding that self-esteem and respect of self lie at the heart of dignity, we adopt the attitude of a constant renewal of shock to avoid cynicism.

Thus, we might consider whether the definition of human dignity can be operationalized via our understanding of the term vulnerability. This would be additionally advantageous in that we could pinpoint concrete examples of how human dignity is approached and treated. In defining human dignity, we depend on examples which will impact and mould perception of its definition to guarantee its operationalization. Examples will always be found in those places where the vulnerable are hardest hit and the constant revisiting will adapt and adjust our perception. Jean Vanier discovered this for himself when in 1964 he gave up his academic career and set up a group home, the first of what would later become *L'Arche*. In setting up his first shared community, he invited two people with severe developmental disabilities to share his home with him. He knew he was letting himself in for a life with people who were especially vulnerable and who in the social hierarchy of things were at the very bottom. He wanted to enable these individuals to discover their own sense of self-esteem. His whole understanding of being and self was to be transformed over the next few years in the experience of day-to-day living with two very vulnerable individuals. He found out that encountering vulnerable people may be healing: 'If you enter into relationship with a lonely or suffering person you will discover something else: that it is you who are being healed. The broken person will reveal to you your own hurt and the hardness

---

[28] C. Meier, *Von Athen bis Auschwitz* (Frankfurt am Main, Fischer, 2002), chapter 5.

of your heart, but also how much you are loved.'[29] Vanier realized that in discovering his own vulnerability and in recognizing the mystery of each person he was moving towards an understanding of human dignity.

Vanier is moved by a firm belief in the mission and mystery of each person: 'There is a meaning to every life, even if we cannot see it. I believe that each person, in her unique beauty and worth, lives out a sacred story.'[30] Vanier sees each person with a particular 'secret and mystery', a particular journey, a particular vocation to grow. The deepest identity that we can discover is a sense of our own worth.[31] This worth is not to be realized *in spite* of our vulnerability but because of it. It is through our vulnerability that we can overcome roles and masks, and face ourselves and our mystery. If we deny our weaknesses and vulnerability, we deny a part of who we are. In recognizing our vulnerability, we discover our fundamental unity, our common humanity. The recognition of the vulnerability and the mystery of a person lead to the basis of what we share as humans, which is also the basis for important elements of human dignity based on a sense of that mystery and sense of vulnerability. If we treat human beings like objects, we fail to do justice to the fundamental dimensions of what it is to be human. Vanier speaks from his own experience: 'People with disabilities who have been rejected or abandoned rise up with new energy and creativity when they feel loved and respected ... The presence of someone who loves them reveals to them their value and importance.'[32] It is against this background that we can understand Desmond Tutu's famous insight that perpetrators by humiliating others also lose the sense of their own dignity.

In realizing his own vulnerability, Vanier gained deeper insight into his sense of dignity. Let us call this realization 'the wound of knowing', by which I mean the painful knowledge that individual identity is fragile: it is knowing that our identity is transient, and knowing that at any time we may find ourselves in a situation in which we are dependent on and in need of another or others; it may be a sudden stroke or unforeseen accident which makes this realization a revelation. Such knowledge implies a sense of humility, which in turn will foster organic solidarity, recognizing that we are all vulnerable. The main point here lies in the insight that the wound of knowing will not

---

[29] J. Vanier, *The Broken Body* (London, Darton, Longman & Todd, 1988), 74.
[30] J. Vanier, *Our Journey Home: Rediscovering a Common Humanity beyond Our Differences* (Maryknoll and New York, Orbis, 1997), 147.
[31] J. Vanier, *Drawn into the Mystery of Jesus through the Gospel of John* (New York, Paulist Press, 2004), 157.
[32] Vanier, *Drawn into the Mystery of Jesus*, 128.

undermine but strengthen the definition of human dignity even under the most adverse conditions: therein lies the ultimate test.

Poverty, self-respect, and human dignity

A definition of human dignity is both necessary yet jeopardized at the same time: exactly where 'blindness to the human aspect' prevails. Blindness of others is a pattern of perception which sees 'human' as a thing with no inner depth. Recognizing inner depth is the admission of the existence of vulnerability in some form or other: the definition of vulnerability can be operationalized via the defining terms of human dignity—the most stringent test of all. How are people treated when their vulnerability is increased? As we have already seen, the risk of such blindness is higher and is, indeed, more pronounced in asymmetrical relationships. Thus, the concept of human dignity becomes a 'concept of crisis' that can be brought to the discourse by way of a preferential option for dealing with vulnerable people.

Susceptibility to poverty is one such social condition in which vulnerability is acutely experienced. Many stories have been told and written about the hardships of poverty; one story might be about poverty as experienced when there is no income, no bread-winner, describing poverty in monetary terms. This objectified approach to poverty can be measured and administered by the welfare state. A second story might depict poverty as social exclusion, the exclusion from standardized cultural activities. This approach describes poverty as a relative, complex and non-static condition. A third story might characterize poverty as having robbed or deprived a person of abilities and skills; poverty in this approach can be reconstructed as a lack of genuine opportunities.[33] All these stories have one thing in common—they touch upon and care about identity of self: human identity. Poverty can deprive a person of their resources of identity, which will include recognition and appreciation, a sense of belonging, or robust concern; access to which will be that much more difficult in a life of poverty. Poverty as social exclusion will prevent access to identity-forming groups, undermining a sense of belonging; an existence hallmarked by poverty will be entrenched in acute shortages and insufficiency, which will exacerbate any chance of taking on responsibility, of making promises, and of entering commitments—thus undermining the possibility of robust concern as a resource of identity.

---

[33] Compare with Amartya. Sen, *Development as Freedom* (New York, Basic Books, 1999), chapter 4.

One moving and explicit example of the dynamics and ensuing erosion involved in resources of identity is that in *Boyhood*, the autobiography of the South African Nobel Prize winner J. M. Coetzee. He tells of his father, who loses his job and means of making a living as a lawyer. Even without employment, his father goes into town every day but comes back one or two hours later, then spends the rest of the day in bed doing the crossword puzzle in the local paper and drinking a bottle of brandy. Not only does the father withdraw from the family within the home, he also becomes an alcoholic, and hides any bills delivered by the postman. Soon the whole situation has escalated out of control, and the family loses almost everything they have. The son loses his sense of respect for his own father, and refers to him simply as 'this man'. The father in turn loses all sense of belonging and the respect of his family (his own son denies him participating in family affairs—refuses him membership), and loses all sense of responsibility and attendant structures it requires (he becomes increasingly listless and lethargic—he no longer cares about anything). The consequences are a sense of shame and humiliation.

The knock-on effect incumbent on losing one's job—as in similar situations of social exclusion—is increased vulnerability. Poverty, in depriving one of one's own resources of identity, jeopardizes the highest moral value there is: self-respect—which is basically the individual equivalent of the social definition of human dignity. In attributing dignity to a human being, the foundation stone of a reflexive relationship with self has been both granted and created. Self-respect is regard and esteem of self inherent in one's own being. Blindness—as outlined above—erodes another's sense of dignity as source of self-respect. These dynamics need to be incorporated in any discourse on human dignity for two reasons: first, it is only by granting socio-economic rights that a way of life anchored in human rights within a given community even under adverse conditions can be guaranteed; a society as experienced by Desmond Tutu will eat away at an individual sense of human dignity if allowed to push—force—individuals and groups of individuals into inhuman living conditions. Second, it is in exactly such inhuman living conditions that one has to ensure that those hit by abject poverty do not lose or are not denied resources of self-identity as a source of self-respect. One major source—and resource—of understanding the human condition in poverty is interiority, similar to the protagonist in Lisa Genova's novel—who can see herself with respect if she is treated with respect. The same applies to a poor person: s/he is first and foremos a living being and before and beyond 'being' poor. The dynamics of everyday economics underlie '(re-)structuring identity'. Abhijit Banerjee and Esther Duflo discovered the idea of access to good life rather than rational survival strategies in their study on poverty: 'When very poor people get a chance to spend a little bit more on food, they don't put everything into getting more calories. Instead, they buy better-tasting, *more expensive* calories.'[34] A concrete example:

> We asked Oucha Mbarbk, a man whom we met in a remote village in Morocco, what he would do if he had more money. He said he would buy more food ... We were starting to feel very bad for him and his family, when we noticed a television, a parabolic antenna, and a DVD player in the room where we were sitting. We asked him why he had bought all these things if he felt the family did not have enough to eat. He laughed, and said, 'Oh, but television is more important than food!'[35]

This statement reflects the idea of self-respect. Decisions made in how we spend money can be key decisions taken in how we see and interpret self and identity, since the things we buy are the things that help make us what we are—give us the identity we have. Goods that we buy, things that we own say a lot about our identity, as has been shown by the British anthropologist Daniel Miller in a study of street-life in London.[36] Goods help us to express our identity.

When people do not have to give up or forgo that deep inward sense of their own being even under the most gruelling conditions, they have a chance of coming out on the other side—surviving. The example of Ingrid Betancourt, held hostage for over six years in the Colombian jungle, illustrates just this. She explicitly and consciously held onto the concept of her own dignity to remain resilient under these conditions of extreme vulnerability.[37] Human dignity is not an extravagant issue reserved only for academic discourse but a mainstay of survival—falling victim to the trap of vulnerability or not and preventing other and self becoming blind to that being and self in other.

---

[34] A. Banerjee and E. Duflo, *Poor Economics* (New York, Perseus, 2011), 23.
[35] Banerjee and Duflo, *Poor Economics*, 36.
[36] D. Miller, *The Comfort of Things* (Cambridge, Polity Press, 2008).
[37] I. Betancourt, *Even Silence Has an End. My Six Years of Captivity in the Colombian Jungle*, trans. A. Anderson (London, Hachette, 2010).

34

Dignity as Perception: Recognition of the Human Individual and the Individual Animal in Legal Thought

Joseph Vining[1]

Human dignity and forms of thought

'TO THEIR MURDERERS THESE wretched people were not individuals at all. They came in wholesale lots and were treated worse than animals.' This was Telford Taylor, beginning the presentation of the 'Medical Case' at the Nuremberg Trials after the Second World War.[2] The 'Medical Case' was not about genocide or war or the conduct of war. It was about experimentation on human beings; and it was this trial that produced the 'Nuremberg Code', the first control of such treatment of human beings by one another.

The word 'individual' came naturally to Taylor the lawyer as a starting point, and with it the contrast with animals. The connection between what kind of treatment these units of flesh and blood might receive, and whether they were individuals 'at all', came naturally to him too.

Taylor's opening at Nuremberg echoed the Nazi representative Joseph Goebbels' explanation in 1938 of German programmes of eugenic sterilization and euthanasia, themselves experiments. 'Our starting point is not the individual', Goebbels said.[3] He knew that this was the critical point in thought and then action, and he knew just what Taylor meant later by 'individual'.

---

[1] In this chapter I have drawn particularly on material in my Giannella Memorial Lecture, 'The mystery of the individual in modern law', at the Villanova University School of Law, *Villanova Law Review* 52 (2007), 1. I am indebted to James Boyd White and Christopher McCrudden for their detailed and helpful comments.

[2] *Trials of War Criminals before the Nuremberg Military Tribunals under Control Council Law No. 10, October 1946–April 1949: The Medical Case*, vol. 1 (Washington DC, US Government Printing Office), 27–8.

[3] US Holocaust Memorial Museum, *Deadly Medicine: Creating the Master Race* (Chapel Hill, University of North Carolina Press, 2004), 8, citing Michael Burleigh and Wolfgang Wippermann, *The Racial State: Germany 1933–1945* (Cambridge, Cambridge University Press, 1991), 69).

With an inversion of a biblical passage that would be well known, Goebbels made explicit the implication of not starting with the individual: '[A]nd we do not subscribe', he said, 'to the view that one should feed the hungry, give drink to the thirsty or clothe the naked ... Our objectives are entirely different: We must have a healthy people in order to prevail in the world.'[4]

We know the word 'individual' in Taylor's reference, or in Joseph Goebbels', is not referring merely to a unit, something discrete, an atom, a particle. Moving from units separate but interchangeable to the particulars of the experienced world that are each and always unique does not take us to the individual either. It takes us only to the little pebble or the rusting old car which there is nothing in the universe exactly like. The uniqueness of a living thing is just that, of pebble or rusty car, if it is only the product of those familiar elements of genetic nature and environmental nurture, the two poles of modern inquiry typically presented as exhausting the sources of living particularity. Biological parlance has a special name for that product, the phenotype, which is the current state of the mutual interaction of internal system and external system. Seeing the individual is looking in reality to something else besides, a third element.

What did the twentieth century threaten in the deepest way? What were those who eventually prevailed at such staggering cost fighting to protect? What was the great twentieth-century struggle about? The individual, and spirit itself, seen in us in being seen as an individual. The individual and spirit: they are linked, and their absence together defines the world of those two books emblematic of what the twentieth century might have brought, *1984*[5] and *Brave New World*.[6]

The home in the secular world for both these, the individual and spirit, is the legal mind and the legal form of thought. Both these connect law with religious sensibility and its work in us and in the world—the sensibility that the human, the human at least, if not also the sentience of other creatures, is spoken to and touched from beyond the world of the here and now. And it is the legal mind, rooted in and the possession of people in circles out and out from those professionally involved with it, that can protect humanity and the rest of the sentient world from reliving the twentieth century in the twenty-first.

The presence of the individual in modern law runs counter to the thrust of what are called 'modern' efforts to understand the world. The individual

---

[4] US Holocaust Memorial Museum, *Deadly Medicine*.
[5] George Orwell, *1984* (London, Secker & Warburg, 1949).
[6] Aldous Huxley, *Brave New World* (London, Chatto & Windus, 1932).

is associated with openness, each individual new and a new source of understanding by others of the world, 'world without end', as the phrase goes; while modern thought presses towards finality of understanding, 'theories of everything', 'final theories'. The individual human being's use of language is a source of newness and meaning, with translation of it on a presupposition of identity despite difference—more than presupposition, a *sense* of identity—that makes each of us a gift to the other.[7]

The individual is the carrier of creativity in the actual world. Creativity comes into the world despite views of the world, voiced of course by individuals, that have no place for creativity, in which everything in the world, and all thought itself, is the product of units of some sort operating by rules of some sort, Newtonian or post-Newtonian. The modern future, it is said, must be in principle predictable as the product of what has gone before, probabilistically or otherwise, even if it cannot in fact be predicted because of non-computability or some other inadequacy in our technical equipment. There simply is no creative force operating at any level to point to or produce what comes in the world unfolding before us. But—we see it every day—with each of us there comes into being a whole world.

Individual animals

The recognition of individuality in animals illustrates what perception of the human individual does in thought and means in practice. Taylor spoke of the wretched in the laboratories at Dachau or Buchenwald as not individuals 'at all'. They were treated '*worse* than animals', 'as *less* than beasts'.[8] Nearly fifty years later in the USA, it appeared that chimpanzees had not proved as suitable a model as expected for AIDS research, both in themselves and because of their expense—and also, interestingly, because of widespread and persistent opposition to their use. The question what to do with those that remained came to the National Research Council Committee on Long-Term Care of Chimpanzees, and eventually to the US Congress.

The minority statement of the National Research Council Committee took the view that euthanasia of some was 'an appropriate strategy for maximizing the quality of life of the remaining population while facilitating the continued

---

[7] For some exploration, on my part, of the connection between the individual and the meaning of language, see Joseph Vining, 'Fuller and language', in Willem J. Witteveen and Wibren van der Burg (eds), *Rediscovering Fuller: Essays on Implicit Law and Institutional Design* (Amsterdam, Amsterdam University Press, 1999), 453–78.
[8] *Trials of War Criminals*, 27–8.

production of chimpanzees to fulfill critical needs in biomedical and behavioral research'. It observed, '[j]ust as the viability of the species rather than of individual animals is proposed as the primary motivation for management strategies in the zoo situation', here 'the long-term viability of the resource for addressing biomedical research needs should be the primary concern'.[9] The majority, however, observed that the 'phylogenetic status and psychological complexity of chimpanzees indicate that they should be accorded a special status with regard to euthanasia that might not apply to other research animals', and that while not '"the moral equivalent" of humans ... they are more like humans than other laboratory species might be with respect to some features relevant to the question of euthanasia'.[10]

This led to a US Senate Report adopting the majority position and to the federal Chimpanzee Health Improvement, Maintenance, and Protection Act of 2000,[11] which set up a federal sanctuary for them, and provided not only that once in the sanctuary they could not be transferred out and any experimentation on them would be subject to limitations more stringent than those governing experimentation on human children, but, further, that 'none of the chimpanzees may be subjected to euthanasia, except as in the best interests of the chimpanzee involved'.[12]

The 'best interests of the chimpanzee involved'. The animal emerges as an individual here, and, I may say, from time to time elsewhere in law even when the animal is phylogenetically 'below' the higher primates. The individual when recognized begins to block weighing of costs and benefits, justification by relative numbers, thinking in terms of systems and processes, 'at the start' to use Goebbels' phrase.[13] It is this blockage, this shift in *kind* of thinking, that is signalled when we begin to speak of an individual 'right'.

The connection between recognition of a being (including a being that is human) as an individual, and the possession of a 'right', an 'individual' right, draws on the image of property, the castle or the cottage, security within it,

---

[9] Commission on Long-Term Care of Chimpanzees, Institute for Laboratory Animal Research, Commission on Life Sciences, and National Research Council, *Chimpanzees in Research: Strategies for Their Ethical Care, Management, and Use* (Washington DC, National Academies Press, 1997), 88, 92.
[10] Commission on Long-Term Care of Chimpanzees, *Chimpanzees in Research*, 38–9.
[11] Senate Report No. 106-494, p. 2 (2000); Chimpanzee Health Improvement, Maintenance, and Protection Act, Pub. L. No. 106-551, §481C(d)(2), 114 Stat. 2753 (2000).
[12] Chimpanzee Health Improvement, Maintenance, and Protection Act §481C(d)(2)(I), §481C(d)(3); Code of Federal Regulations Part 46—Protection of Human Subjects, Subpart D—'Additional Protections for Children Involved as Subjects in Research', 45 Code of Federal Regulations 46.401-9. The protections for chimpanzees in sanctuary are both substantive and procedural. The ultimate protections for children are procedural only, coupled with a directive to be ethical.
[13] US Holocaust Memorial Museum, *Deadly Medicine*, 8.

and dominion over it. A 'right' is said sometimes to dispose of other considerations. Those who work with legal argument and legal reasoning know that a right is not a thing, bundled or unbundled, that one holds in one's hand in advance of legal argument or a legal proceeding. Lawyers know that whether or not one will be 'found' to have a right is determined by argument on the merits in which public values are considered, 'weighed' we say, and the value reflected in the putative right-holder's argument may not outweigh the rest. But in some cases what is represented by the words 'individual right' is dispositive and holds back the arguments of others. No torture is an example, if the individual is a human being.[14] No slavery—for instance under the Thirteenth Amendment of the United States Constitution—may be another, looked to recently when the US Patent Office declared unpatentable a proposed being that would be grown to maturity after blending human and chimpanzee genetic material.[15] In Canada, under charters of rights, no absolute denial of medical care to a human being in a time of pain may be another.[16] No human experimentation without true consent may be gradually emerging as another, now two generations after Nuremberg[17]—Article 3(b) of the 2005 UNESCO Universal Declaration on Bioethics and Human Rights provides that '[t]he interests and welfare of the individual should have priority over the sole interest of science or society'.[18]

When this happens, in the case of an animal or a human being, understanding what is happening must involve shifting focus to the recognition of the individual. It is not the possession of a right but the effect of perceiving one as an individual that holds back the claims of the rest of the world. Nor is it suffering that does it. We use metaphors of quantity as we contemplate and speak of suffering as more or less, as acute, extreme, unbearable, or mild.

---

[14] J. Herman Burgers and Hans Danelius, *The United Nations Convention Against Torture* (Dordrecht, Martinus Nijhoff, 1988), 114–19, 123–4.

[15] Rick Weiss, 'U.S. denies patent for a too-human hybrid', *Washington Post* (13 February 2005), A03; Aaron Zitner, 'Patently provoking a debate', *Los Angeles Times* (12 May 2002), A1 (discussing part-human, part-mouse hybrid); Consolidated Appropriations Act (United States), Pub. L. No. 108-99, §634, 118 Stat. 3, 101 (2004) (providing that no funds could be 'used to issue patents on claims directed to or encompassing a human organism').

[16] *Chaoulli v Quebec*, 2005, 1 S.C.R. 791. Cf. Case C-372/04, *The Queen, on the Application of Yvonne Watts v Bedford Primary Care Trust, Secretary of State for Health* (European Court of Justice, 16 May 2006), http://curia.europa.eu/en/content/juris/index.htm (addressing issue in European Union).

[17] For example, *Burton v Brooklyn Doctors Hospital*, 452 N.Y.S.2d 875, 881 (N.Y. App. Div. 1982); In re Cincinnati Radiation Litigation, 874 F. Supp. 796, 819–22 (S.D. Ohio 1995). The various utilitarian justifications for dispensing with true consent, such as scientific knowledge, medical advance, or military effectiveness, were forcefully argued at Nuremberg, and are argued still.

[18] General Conference of UNESCO, 33d Session, Universal Declaration on Bioethics and Human Rights, Article 3(2), 19 October 2005.

Metaphors of quantity appear again when we detach suffering from individual experience and seem to aggregate it. In utilitarian reasoning, the amount of suffering of one would be put against the amount of suffering that could be prevented or alleviated for others alive or to be born. But on any supposed calculus of suffering, the suffering of one would be a drop in the oceans of the world's present suffering, human, animal, that is now connected with life and that only death fully eliminates, and not even a drop but barely an atom when placed against the eons of suffering that might be alleviated or prevented in the future, human and animal. In fact, we can see that the suffering of one can be as great as the suffering of all the world, the point made in the proposed bargain for the happiness forever of all mankind in the passage preceding the Grand Inquisitor scene in *The Brothers Karamazov*[19] and made, I think, at every celebration of the Eucharist. But in seeing that, we are seeing the individual.

We can foreground what it is, in law, to recognize an animal as an individual, by asking the kinds of questions we used to hear in the mid-twentieth century as we were contemplating 'nuclear winter'. Would the death of all human beings be a loss? I think we would say yes, and not that humanity's passing would merely be evolution at work. Would the death of a group of human beings, leaving behind a 'remaining population' that might benefit from resources freed up, be a loss? Again, we would say yes. Would the death of a single human being be a loss? Again, we would say yes, a loss not only to other individuals who knew or individually valued him or her but to the world, and we express that in so many ways, not least the real impossibility, the acknowledged fiction, of calculating a measurement or monetary value of a single human life so that human lives could conceivably come in Taylor's 'wholesale lots'.[20]

So, in the same vein, would the death of all animals, or all of a kind of animal—extinction we call it—be a loss? If we said yes, rather than that this is only evolution at work, I think our minds would most likely be focused on the ecological and the environmental, on systems that support the systems within us. But is the death of a single animal a loss to the world? To the extent an animal is an individual at all, we may begin to feel pressure within and pull from without to say yes, as we do contemplating the death of a single human being.

---

[19] Fyodor Dostoyevsky, *The Brothers Karamazov*, trans. Constance Garnett (New York, Vintage Press, 1955), 219.
[20] *Trials of War Criminals*, 27–8.

The pressure and pull from recognition of the individual is there in the legal mind, and has its effect whether or not it holds back other concerns and claims in the definitive way it does when torture or slavery are proposed. It was natural to Taylor at Nuremberg to say 'not individuals *at all*' as he presented humans conceived as 'less than beasts'.[21] There is a metaphorical 'degree' in 'at all'—and in 'pressure' or 'pull'. But what is happening is blunting, slowing, and interfering with thinking that is quantitative, as so much of our thought is and necessarily is, capturing in definitions, categorising, unitizing, systematizing, and calculating. Modern thought—your mind and mine— moves quickly to systems, and to units that can fit into a system. The pressure recognition of the individual introduces is instead towards imaginative escapes, reconfigurations, compromises that are temporary, facing the tragic in tragic choices made, and moving into the world of remorse, forgiveness, and beginning again to which calculation is utterly foreign.

The effect is easily seen, familiar really, in criminal law both as formulated and as applied. Judges, prosecutors, juries, legislators all feel it. The classic holding back of what is proposed to be done to a human convict for purposes of general deterrence, the insistence that a criminal sanction be linked in some proportional way to the mind condemned, is a turning of decisional attention to the individual who is at the mercy of the decision-maker. When we say the 'retributive' purpose of a criminal sanction limits its utilitarian use, it is this to which we are referring. Procedure and procedural choices are affected throughout criminal law, as are the placing and relative heaviness of burdens of proof. 'Strict' or 'vicarious' criminal liability introduced in the aptly named public policy offences, apparently eliminating any inquiry at all into the mind and particular situation of an individual before criminal condemnation, is demonstrably moulded into liability that is neither strict nor vicarious. The more serious the proposed suffering of the individual, the greater is insistence on such inquiry, constitutionally pushed by the very notion of 'law' in 'due process of law' and in the USA by the constitutional word 'cruel'.

Then, on the animal side: in criminal law, inquiry into the justification for the actions of human beings accused of the felony of animal cruelty is pulled and moulded by the suffering of animals without regard to number. Medical and scientific experimentation is institutionalized and regulated by statute. In the USA the legal mandate runs to federal mini-agencies called Institutional Animal Care and Use Committees, established to approve or disapprove research proposals and 'represent society's concerns regarding

---

[21] *Trials of War Criminals*, 27–8 (emphasis added).

the welfare of animal subjects'.[22] It is a mandate to researchers as well, and it focuses on individual animals. The absolute number of animals suffering is to be reduced to the lowest number possible, not the percentage of the kind but the absolute number. Experimental technique and procedure are to be refined to lessen each animal's suffering. Then, as a training manual for members of the enforcement committees instructs, '[f]inally, there comes a point in a number of research studies in which further pain and suffering by the animal is unjustified, no matter how noble the cause. It is the [committee's] role to recognize when this point has come and end the research trial at this time.'[23]

In Canadian and US trusts and estates law, an animal moves on its owner's death out from under the general law of property and into the world of wills acts and probate codes. There are now cases in which courts have voided an order put into a will to destroy an animal left behind, fashioning something like a temporary judicial sanctuary for it, when a challenge to the order as against basic legal values is brought by an executor or an intervenor or, indeed, by the state attorney general.[24] The Uniform Trust Code in the USA now provides for trusts for an animal effective for its life, in which the animal is an equitable beneficiary, and persons interested in the animal's welfare are given standing to intervene and seek enforcement of the terms of the trust.[25] Time and again attention is paid to the individual animal, quite apart from any ecological, environmental, or species-preservation concerns. It is recognized, it presses, as if in law it can look you directly in the eye.

Consideration of the individual animal can help us focus upon and titrate out, as it were, the third element to which I have referred. What evokes the human response of 'respect' is not entirely contained in what we call 'the

---

[22] 7 United States Code §§2132(n), 2143(b)(1) ('Animal Welfare Act' of 1966 as amended); Congressional Finding (4) for Pub. L. No. 99–198, §§2142–6, 99 Stat. 1645 (1985).

[23] Sally K. Wixson, 'The role of the IACUC in assessing and managing pain and distress in research animals', in M. Lawrence Podolsky and Victor S. Lukas (eds), *The Care and Feeding of an IACUC: The Organization and Management of an Institutional Animal Care and Use Committee* (Boca Raton, FL, CRC Press, 1999), 115, 117. The Animal Welfare Act itself now prohibits, for any animal it covers, surgery using paralytics without anesthetics. The prohibition is absolute, without regard to motive or context. 7 United States Code §2143(a)(3)(C)(iv) (1985).

[24] For example, Capers Estate, 340 D. and C.2d 121, 135–38 (Orphan's Court PA, 1964); In the Matter of the Estate of Clive Wishart, 129 N.B.R.(2d) 397, 401–2, 408–9, 412–24 (New Brunswick Court of Queen's Bench [Canada], 1992), reviewing both US and Canadian law. For discussion, see Sonia S. Waisman, Pamela D. Frasch and Bruce A. Wagman, *Animal Law: Cases and Materials,* 3rd edn (Durham, NC, Carolina Academic Press, 2006), 587–98.

[25] Uniform Trust Code (United States) §408 (2005); Official Commentary to §408 ('The concept of granting standing to a person with a demonstrated interest in the animal's welfare is derived from the Uniform Guardianship and Protective Proceedings Act, which allows a person interested in the welfare of a ward or protected person to file petitions on behalf of the ward or protected person'.)

human'. 'The individual' is not merely an expression of human self-regard. Noting this can uncouple us somewhat from the growing question about what is human and what is not, being raised by experimental work with embryonic stem cells, genetic engineering, and the hybridization of human and animal systems. It can even buffer us from the impossible question of relative degrees of human-likeness in legal categorizations of animals based on likenesses between human and animal physical systems, which is cousin to the impossible question of degrees of perfection within humanness in current eugenic discussion of 'selection in' or 'termination' using the tools of reproductive technology.

The individual and the person

Consideration of the individual that is an animal also pulls us away from mistaking the recognition and experience of the individual for the experience of persons. An animal may be an individual but not a person. On the human side, a slave may be property, a thing bought and sold, flogged and kicked, not a citizen or a legal person, thought even to be 'not fully human', but a slave presses nonetheless for entry into the perceived world as an individual.[26] To allude again to the biological manipulation that is now possible, the temporal line often drawn between using a developing human unit in scientific experimentation, and staying the hand at using it in experimentation, is the fourteenth day of embryonic development.[27] One of the reasons advanced for that line is the possibility of twinning before fourteen days and the challenge it may pose to perception of an individual until that possibility is past.[28] For many who would adopt that line, the individual after fourteen days is not yet a person. Then at the end of life, the person may fade away. The individual

---

[26] For a sweeping examination of the normality of slavery before the recent past, and of what is seen when a slave is seen, and for the history of the development of perception leading to a prohibition of slavery that is 'absolute', see John T. Noonan Jr, *A Church that Can and Cannot Change: The Development of Catholic Moral Teaching* (South Bend, IN, University of Notre Dame Press, 2005), 3–123.
[27] Human Fertilisation and Embryology Act 1990, chapter 37, §3(3), (4) (Great Britain); National Research Council and Institute of Medicine, *Guidelines for Human Embryonic Stem Cell Research* (Washington DC, National Academies Press, 2005), 57 (United States).
[28] National Institutes of Health, *Report of the Human Embryo Research Panel*, vol. 1 (Bethesda, MD, National Institutes of Health, 1994), 45–7, 65, 67; Anthony Kenny, 'Life stories: when an individual life begins–and the ethics of ending it', *Times Literary Supplement* (25 March 2005), 3, 4 (quoting from Parliamentary Debates, 6th Ser., vol. 73, 15 February 1985, 682, remarks to the House of Commons by Kenneth Clarke, Minister for Health in Great Britain). The fourteen-day point is also the point after which appear 'the precursors of the brain and central nervous system'. National Research Council and Institute of Medicine, *Guidelines*, 55.

stays—whom you do not experiment on or 'harvest' from—though the person fades. The individual is centred on the flesh, though that is something with which we do struggle, the continuing challenge of gnosticism in Christianity being only a more than usually clear example of struggle with it.[29]

Questions about how to use the terms 'individual' and 'person' are unsettled, but the terms as used do reflect an underlying sense of the difference between a person and an individual, indeed the difference between a person centred on an individual's body and the individual enfleshed there.[30] A person, both in mundane or ordinary or daily or unself-conscious talk, and in the considered language of law, may be enfleshed. But a person need not be enfleshed and can speak through one or another individual. We can and do take on various legal identities without losing our individuality: they are not identities all our own. Persons join us together, and the standard assumption, that one can always be challenged when one speaks on behalf of a person who is not an individual, is evidence of such joining rather than separation. Identification with persons who are not individuals is what links us, in a real way, to future individuals beyond our span of life, even the distant future, with responsibility to them and hope for them. It is what links us, in obligation and gratitude, to individuals before our individual time, indeed what makes the past even relevant and interesting to us so that we are willing to spend precious individual time, the most wasting resource there is, working to determine what is authentic in our understanding of the past, and what is unreal.

As for the 'individual person', this is mutually developed in our conscious and unconscious understanding and experience over time. Other individuals continually sift and sort through what an individual says and does as an individual, identifying it with him or her as a person who exists over time, or putting it aside as mistake or inauthentic. We do the same with ourselves, doubting or trusting, persuading ourselves and believing. We sit in judgment on what we ourselves say and do.

The person perceived or heard is 'half-created' *over* time, real and alive to us because of our work, something of our own. The individual is always in the present. If time moves or if one moves through time, the individual is always with us. Anything said is always in the past, immediately so, evidence with which we work, but evidence only, not the same as what it is evidence

---

[29] Philip J. Lee, *Against the Protestant Gnostics* (New York, Oxford University Press, 1993); Walter Brueggemann, *Praying the Psalms*, 2nd edn (Eugene, OR, Cascade Books, 2007).

[30] I first worked on these problems, against the background of twentieth-century developments in 'standing', in Joseph Vining, *Legal Identity: The Coming of Age of Public Law* (New Haven, Yale University Press, 1978), 2–3, 6–7, 145–8, 179–81.

of. The individual here and now is silent and lives with us in silence. As 'starting point', the individual always remains central. The person prevents the individual as starting point, this ongoing centrality, from ending in radical ignorance and isolation, solipsism and relativism.[31]

Articulating perception

But again, the third element, beyond systems internal and external, is what gives the individual its distinctive force in perception and action. This is what so demands to be fitted into our ongoing effort to put together the bits and pieces of our experience into a coherence that does not close the eyes to any of it. Without this third element, the individual's place in the worlds of other individuals would not be begun to be understood. Even if there is no real possibility—precisely because of the recognition of the individual—of anyone's tying up understanding of individuality into a finished package by the end of his or her life in the world, still our trying to articulate the perception on which we act can serve a purpose. It helps each of us in opening a door, moving to the side of systems in general, and stepping once more into the parts of the mind where quantification and calculation lose purchase.

Some might reach for the term used in professional philosophy, 'agency', to refer to this third element. But agency is too pale and neutral a term to evoke the force that recognition of the individual has, and this is because agency in its connotations remains attached to its origins in philosophic discussion and to language there that speaks of properties of units and emergent properties of systems of units, envisioning capturing all parts of experience, unitizing them so that they can be put in classes and groups of the same, and then manipulating them in ways logical or otherwise—rather than listening to them. Agents need not call as individuals do, appeal, stop, reveal as individuals do. Agency tames experience.

What to call the third element? The American pragmatist Richard Rorty summed up in the most wonderful way much of what we try to talk about in his response to a 1999 request for reflections upon the coming third millennium. He looked to 'accomplishing' a 'thorough-going secularization' before the fourth millennium. 'It will probably take', he said, 'at least a thousand years for human beings to give up the last remnants of the idea that they

---

[31] 'Half-create' is Wordsworth's—'all the mighty world/Of eye and ear, both what they half-create,/ And what perceive'. William Wordsworth, 'Lines written a few miles above Tintern Abbey', in Stephen Gill (ed.), *William Wordsworth: The Major Works* (New York, Oxford University Press, 2000), 134.

contain a spark of the divine: to see Beethoven and Jefferson as animals with extra neurons.'[32] He went on to speak of individuals in modern history who have 'unwittingly collaborated with each other ... to force us' to this conclusion about the nature of the sources of life and thought given us when we enter the world for our time in it. Rorty, so oblivious, it seems, to the phenomenon of human law and its recognitions, and so oblivious to what might be his own commitment to law's recognitions, and certainly his dependence on them in his life taken as a whole, calls the third element a 'spark of the divine' in denying it to both human and animal.

We have called the third element spirit here, rather than spark of the divine. Sparks go out, spirit continues. Sparks are units, spirit is not capturable. And it is because spirit is not capturable and is not predictable, and takes form in the human world in language the meaning of which is the meaning of its utterer and itself irreducible to any system, that spirit stands against the full thrust of thought that is distinctively twentieth century.

Not against thought of a religious kind, that continued through the century, not against legal thought, that has if anything flourished[33] and become more central to human life as the number of human individuals has increased, and not against 'ordinary' thought of 'ordinary' individuals: spirit stands against thought that, because in its own terms it has no place for spirit, would squeeze spirit out from thought itself, against elite, informed thought that views success in manipulating the systems of the world to human ends as authority to teach the nature of the world as a whole. Distinctively twentieth-century thought is cosmological, agitatedly and aggressively so, and thus for many, not most but many, one aspect of the mystery of the individual in modern law is the individual being there at all after the twentieth century.

Full recognition of the individual human being may be described, and I think in a way not inconsistent with spirit being the third element, as accepting into one's world something analogous to the acceptance of the Big Bang into physics and into contemplation of the physical world. The individual is a singularity, a word nicely taken over by physicists from their own experience of being individuals—not a unit playing a part in the working of rules and quantities governed by rules. Each individual has a view of the reality of the world, the cosmos itself, that cannot be different from his or her view. One

---

[32] Richard Rorty, 'International books of the year—and the millennium', *Times Literary Supplement* (2 December 1999), 11.
[33] Steven D. Smith, *Law's Quandary* (Cambridge, MA, Harvard University Press, 2004). See Steven D. Smith, *The Disenchantment of Secular Discourse* (Cambridge, MA, Harvard University Press, 2010), 205–10, for further discussion of 'spirit' as used here.

cannot say, 'I see the world in this way or see this in the world, but what I see is mistaken or an illusion.' One sees it the way one sees it. One can struggle with doubt and be open to change if open-minded and working with perceptions that themselves open out into the new and surprising. But one cannot truthfully say to another, 'The way you see the world is true, not the way I see the world.' Even if one hears oneself saying such a thing, the world remains the way one sees it, and another individual, who is only one, trying to dismiss it with the word 'solipsism', is merely denying that one is an individual like himself or herself.

When individuals are recognized by one another they acknowledge this sense on the part of each that each is at the centre of the world. The 'public' value of an individual life is bedrock-natural rather than a mysterious anomaly. 'Not for all the world', we say, and thought of 'all the world' and reference to 'all the world' is a quite understandable and common response to a proposal that something be done to an individual, a meaningful response, not hyperbole or nonsense. It is this ontological or cosmological sense, not of the smallness of the individual among the billions but of the largeness of the individual up to the level of the largeness of the world itself, that lies behind the blocking or blunting or continuous creative compromise with the kind of thinking, often called rational, that must work with fungible units. Since each of us is an individual, a cosmology that has a place for us will always be truer, or closer to truth, or have a greater claim to truth, than any cosmology that does not.

All this comes before and is not supplanted by the joining of individuals in persons and in the experience of living value. The first question of understanding each of us faces is not how can I be an individual or how could there possibly be an individual, but how can there be more than individuals, as there is, and how, in what can only be continuous acts of generosity, do we each see we are one among many?

However paradoxical such a sense of reality or such a cosmology may appear to be, and whatever the way it differs from consistently radical subjectivity on the one hand and consistently impersonal objectivity on the other, this is the sense of reality displayed to each of us individuals in the practice of law, expressed by law, making law possible, underlying what lawyers do. As Stephen R. L. Clark says so nicely of objectifying visions:

> Fortunately—or providentially—our own sense of self, and our sense of significant others as individual selves, keeps breaking in. Our attention is always being drawn to individuals as something more than episodes or anecdotes within a single story. Instead of *one* world, there are, in a way, very many

though each unitary world experiences itself as a fragment or an echo of the wider realm.[34]

Trinitarian Christianity has its words for this, and in its ecumenical reach seeks to understand the words for it in other enduring religious teachings. It is an ontology that, in addition to recognizing the world of each individual, recognizes faith in a reality beyond the worlds of each individual, which each of us is a new window on and from and for which each of us is a voice when we are, as we say, 'really' ourselves, authentic, not pretending, not false—a reality in which move the persons who join us and who are half-created by us all, but only half-created—a reality on which our individual action, each of us one among the billions, may have a causal effect neither we nor anyone else can trace.

But all this, internal system, external system, the third element that moves a unique unit to individuality, the individual person and the person we half-create—all can be put aside, and still the individual remains. Happily or unhappily, anything I or anyone may say in description of the individual, or of the place of the individual in thought, is soft when it comes up against the hard reality of the individual. The world just is as you see it and not otherwise. When you speak about anything (including about the individual), you just are only one speaking. I am and you are prior to our understanding. The past does not produce us—we come before the past. The existence, nature, and effects of the past are matters for our individual judgment or persuasion throughout our lives. Whatever may be thought generally of creation, we each are created, for there is no other language of understanding that begins to reach us as individuals. The current language of emergent properties or of complex adaptive systems certainly does not.

Imaging dignity

Is spirit what is recognized in an animal also? Is it spirit or an analogue that should be given a different name? The third element that moves an animal to individuality, with effects on human action similar to those implied whenever we speak of human dignity, may not be the same as the third element in the human. But as we have noted, the line between what is human and what is not may also be less and less secure as experimentation in genetics proceeds. Depending upon how strong in our own minds the connection between genetic

---

[34] Stephen R. L. Clark, *Biology and Christian Ethics* (Cambridge, Cambridge University Press, 2000), 315–16. Clark speaks of this breaking in as a 'spiritual tension' that 'is echoed in the biological'.

patterns and being human is, the phrase 'dignity simply by virtue of being a human being' may lose some of its ontological support and usefulness as an articulation of perception. Dignity can in fact already be found used in various legal contexts in connection with an animal[35]—again, an animal and indeed a human being need not be a 'legal person' to be seen to be an individual.

Currently, much of what is perceived and seeks expression clusters around an animal's sentience, which is a legal term as much as it is a term in ordinary speech or in scientific investigation,[36] and which doubles as expression of a line between animals that are seen as individuals and animals that are not. The relation between an animal's sentience and our spirit remains to be seen. We have only begun to open our eyes to the creatures around us.

A book I published several years ago had the title *The Song Sparrow and the Child*,[37] with *Claims of Science and Humanity* as its subtitle. I contrasted the song sparrow with the child throughout, and then at the end touched on the question how great the difference really was and how long the difference will continue in our perception, thought, and action.

Once, while I was working on the book, I opened the US National Science Foundation's webpage setting out the call of scientific work, and there a song sparrow was on the screen, the first thing seen, with a reference to investigation of its neurobiological mechanisms.[38] Some of the methods of investigation are brutal. What is done to a song sparrow would not be done to a child today—though the twentieth century witnessed such things done to children where the individual was obscured from view. Song sparrows are of

---

[35] Christopher McCrudden, 'Human dignity and judicial interpretation of human rights', *European Journal of International Law* 19 (2008), 708–9 (legal use of 'dignity' also with reference to animals).
[36] Maine Revised Statute Annotated title 7 §3907 (2001) (United States) ('"Animal" means every living, sentient creature not a human being.'); Treaty of Amsterdam amending the Treaty on European Union, the Treaties establishing the European Communities, and certain related acts: Protocol on protection and welfare of animals annexed to the Treaty of the European Community Protocol, *Official Journal* C340, 10/11/1997, 0110 ('The high contracting parties, desiring to ensure improved protection and respect for the welfare of animals as sentient beings, have agreed ...'). See Simon Conway Morris, *Life's Solution* (Cambridge, Cambridge University Press, 2003), a detailed discussion of scientific contributions to recognition of 'sentience' in animals; Alasdair MacIntyre, *Dependent Rational Animals: Why Human Beings Need the Virtues* (Chicago, Open Court, 2001), for an introduction to work in philosophy on the human and the animal that seeks to take into account these contributions, and individuality; Philip Low et al., *The Cambridge Declaration on Consciousness*, Francis Crick Memorial Conference (7 July 2012), http://fcmconference.org/img/Cambridge DeclarationOnConsciousness.pdf, on consciousness in animals; Barbara Smuts, 'Reflections', in J. M. Coetzee, *The Lives of Animals* (Princeton, NJ, Princeton University Press, 1999), 107–22, on relationships between individual human beings and individual animals, and on human-animal intersubjectivity.
[37] Joseph Vining, *The Song Sparrow and the Child: Claims of Science and Humanity* (Notre Dame, IN, Notre Dame University Press, 2004).
[38] National Science Foundation (United States), http://www.nsf.gov/od/lpa/news/publicat/frontier/4-96/4sparrow.htm.

particular interest to science, in part because a young song sparrow comes to sing a song that is special not just to its kind but to its individual throat and tongue—rather like the language of each of us.

I left the song sparrow to do its own work in the book, and did not spell out all the reasons for the choice of this creature rather than another to compare with a child. The song sparrow presented itself, not exotic, as common as a child. Its smallness sat with the smallness of the child. It was a dependable example because well known, like the standard laboratory mouse. There was the echo of its music.

But beyond this, I can suppose also some part of the attractiveness of the sparrow was its resonance with the comparison of human being and sparrow in the Gospel of Matthew. Emblems take flight from their origins. Forgetting its origin, I had remembered the linkage in the form of a saying, 'Not a sparrow that falls but the eye of God is upon it', as in the refrain of the folk hymn that Mahalia Jackson and the blues singer Ethel Waters made a signature piece:

> Why should I feel discouraged?
> Why should the shadows come?
> Why should my heart be lonely,
> And long for heav'n and home?
>
> I sing because I'm happy.
> I sing because I'm free.
> His eye is on the sparrow
> And I know He watches me.[39]

If you go to the original in the Gospel, there will be found a comparison but not an equation. The actual words can be something of a surprise:

> Are not two sparrows sold for a farthing? And one of them shall not fall on the ground without your Father. But the very hairs of your head are all numbered. Fear ye not therefore, ye are of more value than many sparrows.[40]

A line is drawn between the sparrow and the human being, at least to begin with (as in fact we do). The translators' farthing was the smallest coin, a quarter of a penny (and I recall that when I first saw a modern farthing, before decimalization, it was stamped with the image of a small bird). An *a fortiori*

---

[39] Civilla D. Martin and Charles H. Gabriel, *His Eye is on the Sparrow* (New York, Hope Publishing, 1905); Donna Britt, *Amazingly, an American in Paris, Washington Post* (7 March 1977), D1, D6; H. C. Boyer, 'Commentary', in *Mahalia Jackson Gospels, Spirituals, and Hymns* (Columbia 47084, 1991), 25; Laurraine Goreau, *Just Mahalia, Baby* (Waco, TX, Word Books, 1975), 181, 561; Ethel Waters with Charles Samuels, *His Eye Is on the Sparrow: An Autobiography* (Garden City, NY, Doubleday, 1951).

[40] Matthew 10:29–31 (King James).

case builds on an image of the least. One sparrow was not worth even the smallest coin, in the market.

There is a further tension in the original. Every hair, every detail of life is significant; but there is more than a hint of determinism within a concern that would value us to the point of counting the hairs on our head. Again, like the line between sparrow and human being, we may think this not inappropriate as a reflection of our situation. The limit on what we can do and be, the fact that we are in systems, is part of what makes a scientist of all of us. Shakespeare plays on all this when Hamlet, going forward at the end and presenting us with decision at last, individual decision, famously remarks to Horatio, 'There's a special providence in the fall of a sparrow'.[41]

But I think that as the image of the sparrow has come down, it has more and more represented one of no importance becoming of transcendent importance. It had appeared long before the Gospel comparison, in the Psalms—the altar of God a nesting place for the sparrow.[42] Those who first sang 'His eye is on the sparrow' included many who knew what it was to be properties, fungible units in a system. Even the hard words of the Gospel shift to the single sparrow before returning to the many—there are 'two sparrows' bundled and sold for a farthing; it is 'one' who shall not fall. And the providence that Hamlet saw in the 'fall of a sparrow' was a special providence.

For me as for others, including the blues singers who returned to it so often, the image blends with the extraordinary statement of human equality and individual value further along in the Gospel of Matthew,[43] which we have seen quoted already. It is a radical passage, of which I think the sparrow can be taken as an emblem. It carries on the oldest prophetic tradition and demands what seems impossible. It is still today a source of that side of the political spectrum we call individualistic. It is read around the globe, in unlikely places, by Christian and non-Christian, by scientist and non-scientist. And, it must be said, it can have been a source of the kind of totalitarianism that begins in an effort to realize it, before closing into the total. It addresses both action and inaction, commission and omission, doing with the hand and staying the hand, almost as if in anticipation of modern dilemmas. There is hierarchy in it, a 'least'. But then something happens, and happens to 'one'. The words are worth reading, for the first time, or again. They end:

> I was an hungred, and ye gave me no meat: I was thirsty, and ye gave me no drink: I was a stranger, and ye took me not in: naked, and ye clothed me not:

---

[41] William Shakespeare, *Hamlet* 5:2 (New Haven, Yale University Press, 2003), 205, 217.
[42] Psalm 84 (King James).
[43] Matthew 25:42–5 (King James).

sick, and in prison, and ye visited me not. Then shall they also answer him, saying, Lord, when saw we thee an hungred, or athirst, or a stranger, or naked, or sick, or in prison, and did not minister unto thee? Then shall he answer them, saying, Verily I say unto you, Inasmuch as ye did it not to one of the least of these, ye did it not to me.

One of no importance, the least, can become of transcendent importance.

PART VII

Ways Forward?

35

The Good Sense of Dignity: Six Antidotes to Dignity Fatigue in Ethics and Law

Matthias Mahlmann

THERE ARE MANY ASPECTS of the idea of human dignity that are questionable and uncertain.[1] One thing, however, seems clear: the law of dignity at the national (constitutional, sub-constitutional or quasi-constitutional), supra- or international level[2] cannot be expected to disappear, turning out to be one of those ephemeral normative whims and fashions that—after catching the attention for a while—have no lasting impact on the reality of the law. The law of dignity is by now too firmly established as a building block of international human rights law for that. In addition, dignity has a distinct political dimension that points in the same direction: whatever the changing currents of ethical and legal debates may be, it is hard to imagine that any serious political initiative aiming to reform international human rights law by removing references to human dignity would have any chance of success.

So, even if one is sceptical about the merits of the idea, the task at hand is to make human dignity a workable legal concept, with a shape that fosters its central aims: the protection of the autonomy, equality, and respect that every human being is entitled to, while steering clear of illiberal ideologies or particularistic political agendas. In principle, this task is not new: it is the familiar task posed by any concept central to human rights law and the political order of democratic, national, and international constitutionalism—from liberty to democracy, from equality to the rule of law. Like dignity, each of these concepts is of crucial and persistent importance, in need of concretization, and

---

[1] As an excellent starting point for any reflection on dignity, see the list of questions identified by Christopher McCrudden, Chapter 1, this volume.
[2] For an overview, see Christopher McCrudden, 'Human dignity and judicial interpretation of human rights', *European Journal of International Law*, 19 (2008), 655–724, at 664; M. Mahlmann, 'Dignity and autonomy in modern constitutional orders', in M. Rosenfeld and S. Sajo (eds), *The Oxford Handbook of Comparative Constitutional Law* (Oxford, Oxford University Press, 2012), 370–96.

therefore in danger of being abused politically. To make some progress on this task ahead, six topics that merit particularly close attention will be considered.

Problems of genealogy

The first issue of importance for a constructive account of human dignity is the problem of genealogy. The question is: where does the idea of dignity come from? Has it deep roots in the history of ideas, in Stoicism, perhaps,[3] or some other ancient source,[4] and do these roots extend beyond the European context?[5] Or is dignity of more recent origins, dating from the humanism of the Renaissance[6], or the Enlightenment?[7] Or is it a very modern idea, as some argue, possibly bound up (as other human rights are supposed to be) with the rise of statehood and the nation?[8] The question of genealogy is a standard question in current debates, and not only because of the widespread purely historical curiosity about the trajectories of the history of ideas.[9] It has a specific undertone, the meaning of which is significant because it shows that the question of genealogy is intertwined with two different problems: the problem of the content of human dignity and of its legitimacy. The origin of dignity is of such intense interest because of the widespread assumption that a genealogical reconstruction will tell us something about the meaning of this difficult concept, as well as whether or not it is justifiably regarded as a centrepiece of human rights law. The cognitive interests differ: some look for the reasons for its strange appeal; others, on the other hand, attempt to reveal some darker secrets hidden in the corners of its history that may even tie it to certain suspi-

---

[3] See M. Pohlenz, *Die Stoa: Geschichte einer geistigen Bewegung*, 7th edn (Göttingen, Vandenhoeck & Ruprecht, 1992), 137; M. Mahlmann, *Elemente einer ethischen Grundrechtstheorie* (Baden-Baden, Nomos, 2008), 108ff.
[4] For example, Greek tragedies; see Mahlmann, *Elemente*, 105ff.
[5] A standard reference point from Confucianism is Mencius: see Mahlmann, *Elemente*, 115.
[6] Standard references are P. della Mirandola, *De hominis dignitate* (Hamburg, Meiner, 1990); F. Petrarcha, *De remediis utriusque fortunae* (München, Fink, 1975); G. Manetti, *De dignitate et excellentia hominis* (Hamburg, Meiner, 1990); see Mahlmann, *Elemente*, 136ff.
[7] Immanuel Kant, *Grundlegung zur Metaphysik der Sitten* (Berlin, Akademie Ausgabe, vol. 4, 1903), 428ff; see Mahlmann, *Elemente*, 144ff.
[8] Samuel Moyn, *The Last Utopia: Human Rights in History* (Cambridge, MA, Belknap Press of Harvard University Press, 2010), 30.
[9] See Samantha Besson and Alain Zysset, 'Human rights theory and human rights history: a tale of two odd bedfellows', *Ancilla Iuris* (2012), 204–19, for a review of contemporary discussion on human rights in general.

cious creeds or content.[10] The question of genealogy, however, concerns all these competing perspectives.

Of particular importance, currently, is the idea that human dignity is an important example of political theology: although apparently a political and legal term, it is to some a secularized theological idea.[11] This thesis can serve very different aims: to legitimize dignity by religious metaphysics or, on the contrary, to delegitimize it, because of its supposedly particularistic religious content. This thesis serves as well as the basis of the argument that certain cultures and religions (say, to take the most important example, Islam) have not developed and cannot develop this concept drawing on the internal resources of their cultural heritage and the doctrines of their faith.[12] Given these far-reaching implications, a clear understanding of the theoretical parameters of the genealogical reconstruction of dignity is of great importance.

But how to proceed? One crucial precondition of any historical reconstruction is a theoretical understanding of what one is actually looking for. This is important for the historical study of any subject, but is perhaps of particular importance for understanding dignity. This means that one should not look only for the *term* dignity (*dignitas*, *Würde*, *kavod*, etc.) but for historical manifestations of the *idea* designated by these terms. In these manifestations, the idea may not be called dignity at all. This may be the case because the same or a similar idea can be expressed by many different linguistic means and, of course, not necessarily according to the linguistic expectations of posterity. A language may even lack a term for what is referred to in English by the word 'dignity'. This is, however, of no importance, because the absence of such a term in a language is no indication that the idea is absent from the minds of the speaker or the listener in the relevant speech community. The theory of language has taught us that the relationship between language and thought is much more complicated than that.[13] In addition, there are modes of expression beyond language that may be quite relevant; for example, art. One

---

[10] Some even proposed a connection to Nazi ideology: James Q. Whitman, 'On Nazi "Honour" and the New European "Dignity"', in C. Joerges and N. Galeigh (eds), *Darker Legacies of Law in Europe* (Oxford, Hart, 2003), 243ff.

[11] On the idea of political theology with dubious conclusions, see Carl Schmitt, *Politische Theologie*, 2nd edn (München, Duncker & Humblot, 1934), 49ff.

[12] On the latter see Axel von Campenhausen, in Detlef Merten and Hans-Jürgen Papier (eds), *Handbuch der Grundrechte*, vol. 6/1 (Heidelberg, C. F. Müller, 2010), 136, paras 104–12: rights are intrinsically connected to the Christian, and less so the Judean, tradition, but are alien to Islam.

[13] For example, Noam Chomsky, *New Horizons in the Study of Language and Mind* (Cambridge, Cambridge University Press, 2000), 147ff.

can learn a lot about human dignity from Goya's etchings or Giacometti's sculptures.[14] If one wants to understand the history of human dignity, therefore, one has to look at many forms of human expression.

On the other hand, one should not be led astray by the use of the term dignity in contexts that are unrelated to questions of human rights—say, discussions about the dignity of institutions as such, because this may produce considerable confusion: whatever sense it may make to speak of the dignity of an institution, the content of this term in this context is evidently very different from the content of dignity as a right attaching to human persons.

A further point worth stressing is how important it is to steer clear of *intellectual elitism* in such an historical reconstruction, because this may turn out to lead to a theoretically and historically severely impoverished vision of the intricacies and the depth of what the idea of dignity is about. There is a danger in thinking that what Cicero, Aquinas, Kant, or Nietzsche said about human dignity is the thread from which the history of this concept is woven. But this is far from true, and not only because of the contribution that art has made. Take the example of the abolition of slavery, more particularly the slave narratives written at that time.[15] These narratives are loaded with powerful claims about the worth of a person, laying the ground for the abolition of an institution that involved 500 years of subjugation, death, and suffering, and without doubt (despite philosophical defences from Aristotle to Locke) one of the great injustices of human history.

That these claims of shared, equal personhood and worth were able to play a decisive role in shattering this massive social institution (though other factors were of great importance as well) indicates an important property of human dignity: it is subversive; it poses a radical challenge to illegitimate power, hierarchy, and privilege.

As importantly, these subversive ideas of the intrinsic worth of human beings were formed by enslaved persons without the need to have read (and, of course, any possibility of reading) Aquinas or Kant. This is hardly surprising. One does not have to be literate to know what dignity means. On the contrary, some of the most impressive illustrations of the content of human dignity are found in the lives of those quickly forgotten by history, those who nevertheless manifest courageously what the idea of dignity is really about.

---

[14] On Giacometti, see M. Mahlmann, Le Chariot—Bemerkungen zu den Grundlagen des Rechts', *Zeitschrift für Schweizerisches Recht* 131(2012), 123–44.
[15] See, for example, Frederick Douglass, *Narrative of the Life of Frederick Douglass, an American Slave* (New York, Penguin Press, 1845, 1982), 107ff. Another example is furnished by the preamble to the decree abolishing slavery in the French empire; see R. J. Scott, Chapter 2, this volume.

Abolitionism, the working class and women's movements, post-colonial struggles, or the fight against apartheid were not following simple, single-purpose, monolithic political agendas. As with any mass movement, their actions were marked by competing claims, ideals, and internal contradictions. They sometimes pursued aims, as a matter of tactics or strategy, that were not reconcilable with human rights in general or dignity in particular. But their rich and complicated histories embody claims about the intrinsic worth of individuals, irrespective of colour, of social status, of poverty, or of sex that it is important to recognize, however much they are sometimes made invisible by layers of ideology and political doctrine. We would not understand much about dignity without reflecting closely about these contributions,[16] because it is the fight for the freedom of slaves, for justice for the working class or the poor, for equality for women, and the everyday manifestations of what human life is about, that fill the concept with thick meaning rather than the language of Petrarch, Pico, Manetti, or the prose of the *Grundlegung zur Metaphysik der Sitten*, as majestic as these may certainly be.

For historical studies, this requires broadening perspectives, studying not only texts but also social practices, and particularly for a term like dignity the investigation of the axiological content of human struggles. Thus, to study the history of the idea of dignity one cannot focus only on terminologically expressive use; one has to look at the implicit presence of the idea of dignity. The history of human dignity is therefore rich indeed, and any simple account is prone to fail. This is particularly true for any essentialist theory of dignity that sees it as intrinsically connected to one culture or religion. Such arguments are rarely not tainted with a touch of partisanship, because the culture or religion that is regarded as the 'true' source of dignity is more often than not the one the genealogist of dignity herself belongs to. With an appropriately broad perspective, it quickly becomes evident that these arguments point in the wrong direction, because the idea of intrinsic worth belongs to the heritage of more than one faith and culture, however tentative, incomplete, and lacking consistent application,[17] forming nothing but a beginning, a step to the full reflective appropriation of this idea by human thought and practice.

---

[16] Moyn, *The Last Utopia*, 84ff. rightly draws attention—for example—to national independence as an aim of post-colonial movements. There was, however, more at stake, too, namely the right of *individual persons* not to be subjugated by foreign powers, thus to political autonomy and self-determination. These rights often drowned in post-colonial dictatorships; but this is no reason not to remember their significance.

[17] Good and classical examples are furnished by Kant, for example his account of the death penalty: *Die Metaphysik der Sitten* (Berlin, Akademie Ausgabe, vol. 6, 1907), 331ff.; of limited political rights of women and servants: *Die Metaphysik der Sitten*, 314; or on ethnic groups: *Vorlesungen über An-*

Problem of content

But what is this idea really about? This leads to the next problem, the problem of content. As with any term, dignity can be used in many ways and in many contexts. There are also many theories of dignity that invest it with a plethora of nuances of meaning.[18] However, the core idea behind the term for the human rights context is, it seems, that human beings, irrespective of other characteristics, possess an inalienable, supreme, intrinsic worth because of their humanity alone, and for no other reason than that. Human beings are last-order purposes of human (individual and institutional) action. This implies the protection of their status as autonomous subjects, as end-in-themselves, and respect for their humanity. It necessitates, furthermore, the prohibition of their instrumentalization, reification, or objectification.

These tenets describe the normative core meaning of the idea of human dignity. This core content *morally* binds individuals as much as institutions. These normative entitlements and constraints are partly or fully mirrored *in law* through the subjective (claim) rights of individuals, the obligations of (state or international) public authorities, the (direct or indirect) horizontal effect of human rights norms between private parties, and the duties to protect individuals against certain qualified harms, which are derived in different legal systems from dignity guarantees, the details depending on their respective legal framework.[19]

There are many possible examples to illustrate the normative point and meaning of this delineation of the content of human dignity. The fight for the abolition of slavery is one: at its core it was about the idea that human beings are to be respected as autonomous subjects, and that they cannot be legitimately turned into tools for the service of others, into the heteronomously dominated objects of exploitation for slave-holders. The women's movements furnish other examples. One normative centrepiece of the struggle for the emancipation of women was, and still is, the demand that women should not be reified or used as things for sexual gratification, domestic exploitation, political guardianship, or reproductive services, but respected as subjects.

---

thropologie. Die Vorlesung des Wintersemesters 1781/82 (Berlin, Akademie Ausgabe, vol. 27, 1997), 1187, which are not reconcilable with his own account of human dignity.

[18] For some examples see McCrudden, Chapter 1, this volume, and for a review of influential modern theories see Mahlmann, *Elemente*, 248ff.

[19] See Mahlmann, 'Dignity and autonomy in modern constitutional orders', 370ff. According to J. Habermas, 'Das Konzept der Menschenwürde und die realistische Utopie der Menschenrechte', *Deutsche Zeitschrift für Philosophie* 58 (2010), 343–57, at 347, human dignity forms the central connection of an egalitarian-universalist morality and law.

Virginia Woolf dryly demanded money and 'a room of one's own', a claim succinctly symbolizing this space for the lived subjectivity of women, not as an act of grace but as a right based on their intrinsic worth as human beings.[20]

This delineation of the content of dignity can form a critical yardstick for assessing normative arguments based on this idea, since it provides relatively precise tools with which to identify conceptions of dignity that are legally unsuitably or loaded with dubious ideology. A good example of its potential is the critique of theories that assert an axiological priority of goods over individual well-being, say the interest in the procreation of the human species to justify unequal treatment of homosexual and heterosexual couples.[21] Arguments of this sort have a distinctly bewildering character, because there is no reason to worry about the continuation of the human race, not least because of the joy that children give. But, this apart, to ascribe individual well-being second rank behind such aims is to violate the dignity of individuals, as they are not regarded as ends-in-themselves but rather as means that are subservient to supra-individual purposes like procreation. This kind of critique can have important practical legal implications, as is illustrated by the example of the conceptual and doctrinal sharpening of anti-discrimination law against unequal treatment of gay people through its interpretation and conceptualization in the light of dignity,[22] including the right to enjoy a legally recognized and protected form of partnership with the same rights (and duties) as heterosexual couples.

This idea of dignity can also furnish directions in the maze of genealogical reconstructions. It can help to calibrate research and help to distinguish ideas of lasting potential from those that wither away with the contingent prejudice that produced them—as the example of Kant's defence of the death penalty, the disenfranchisement of women, or the supposedly distinct properties of different ethnicities vividly illustrates.[23] All these positions are most succinctly criticized on the base of the dignitarian concept of protected human subjectivity, which Kant himself helped to formulate in clear and distinct terms.

This critical function shows why it is important to determine the positive content of dignity, and not only rest content with identifying (clear) violations

---

[20] Virginia Woolf, *A Room of One's Own* (London, Hogarth Press, 1929).

[21] For an example—now overruled by the Federal German Constitutional Court—from the German jurisprudence, BGH, 14 February 2007—IV ZR 267/04 para. 22; BVerwG 25 July 2007—6 C 27/06 para. 43.

[22] See, for example, SACC, *National Coalition for Gay and Lesbian Equality v Minister of Home Affairs and Others* (CCT 10/99) [1999]; ZACC 17; 2000 (2) SA 1; 2000 (1) BCLR 39 (2 December 1999).

[23] See Kant, *Die Metaphysik der Sitten*, 314, 331ff.; *Vorlesungen über Anthropologie. Die Vorlesung des Wintersemesters 1781/82*, 1187; see note 17, this chapter.

of dignity, such as indignity produced by humiliation. Although the latter approach has much heuristic and practical force and is successfully utilized in legal argument,[24] one has to have as clear as possible an understanding of its substantive content in order to be able to meet the many challenges dignity faces from genealogy and from the critical assessments of potentially highly politicized and ideologized dignity claims.

Interestingly, despite the variety of different approaches, many theoretical understandings and, from an international comparative perspective to a surprising degree, international case law and legal doctrine coalesce in certain crucial respects explicitly or implicitly around certain ideas: autonomous subjectivity, basic respect, non-instrumentalization, non-objectivication, and non-reification.[25] It is therefore far from true that dignity is in practice devoid of identifiable content, or has become an 'empty signifier',[26] or a rallying cry that accommodates all different points of views.

The historical record of the creation of the modern law of dignity also tells more complicated lessons in this respect than is sometimes recognized. When norms constitutive of modern dignity law were drafted, their content was certainly open to many questions and future interpretations.[27] A plurality of background ideas—from humanism, socialism and social democracy, to Christian personalism—played roles that are not easy to decipher and disentangle.[28] Post-war human rights are in any case deeply embedded in strategies of power, not least of Cold War politics, and ornamental rhetoric accompanying it and human dignity is not an exception to this. But the complex history of the creation of central norms of the new law of dignity, the machinations

---

[24] An example is the idea current in German legal doctrine of a determination of the content of dignity by its violation, *Inhaltsbestimmung vom Verletzungsvorgang her*. The first decision of the German Federal Constitutional Court on dignity proceded this way, see BVerfGE 1, 97 (104).

[25] Mahlmann, 'Dignity and autonomy in modern constitutional orders', 370ff.

[26] As Costas Douzinas formulated in the conference discussion.

[27] See, for the example of the Universal Declaration of Human Rights (1948), J. Morsink, *The Universal Declaration of Human Rights: Origins, Drafting and Intent* (Philadelphia, PA, University of Pennsylvania Press, 1999); M. A. Glendon, *A World Made New* (New York, Random House, 2002).

[28] It is therefore not convincing to ascribe one particular perspective, say Christian personalism, a decisive role. See, for example, E. Roosevelt's explanation of the lack of reference to God in the Universal Declaration, quoted in Glendon, *A World Made New*, 147f. for background. On the plurality of influences, which even were made explicit by the drafters (including prominent Christian Democrats like Süsterhenn) in the case of the German Grundgesetz, see the review of the historical records of the drafting process in Mahlmann, *Elemente*, 246 and notes. On the thesis of the central role of Christian personalism, see S. Moyn, 'Personalism, community, and the origins of human rights', in S-L. Hoffmann and S. Moyn (eds), *Human Rights in the Twentieth Century* (Cambridge, Cambridge University Press, 2011), 85ff, which has a very distinct political edge: 'human rights need to be closely linked, in their beginnings, to an epoch-making reinvention of conservatism', 87.

and plots of (sometimes ethically not particularly inspiring) actors,[29] the selectivity of political representation, and the exclusion of many people in colonized and externally dominated parts of the world from the drafting of modern human rights law,[30] did not prevent important seeds from being sown that had the potential to grow into something meaningful beyond the narrow-minded intentions and expectations of some of those who played an important role in their development.[31] The ascertainment of the worth of human beings created the normative nucleus for a crucial limitation of any relativizing of the value of individual human lives, whether by assertions of the supremacy of state power, the greatness of the nation, the importance of class interests, or the superiority of a race.[32] This was the message sent by the Universal Declaration and the constitutions where dignity gained a prominent place. And this was in spite of the particularistic and dubious motives of some, despite how difficult it was and is to be to draw practical conclusions from this idea in the legal, political, and social spheres, despite how endangered dignity is by moral and legal regressions (as in the international debate about torture), and despite how winding the path was from these seeds of subversion to the development of a more or less convincing doctrine of dignity law.[33]

---

[29] A prominent example is Jan Smuts and his influence on the Preamble of the UN Charter; see M. Mazower, *No Enchanted Palace* (Princeton, NJ, Princeton University Press, 2009), 28ff.

[30] Only a fraction of the states member of the UN today were part of the founding fifty-one states (including Poland). The drafters of the Universal Declaration were not representing more than a fraction of world cultures.

[31] Not surprisingly perhaps—legal texts are sometimes cleverer than their authors; see G. Radbruch, 'Rechtsphilosophie', in A. Kaufmann (ed), *Gesamtausgabe*, vol. 2 (Heidelberg, C. F. Müller, 1993), 345.

[32] There is a debate in recent scholarship on the history of human rights, which role the Holocaust played for the development of modern human rights law—a central (see Morsink, *The Universal Declaration of Human Rights*, 37 and passim) or none (see, for example, Moyn, *The Last Utopia*, 7). There are good reasons to think that it did play a meaningful role, especially if one looks beyond the sphere of power politics and their agents. For a short survey, see G. D. Cohen, 'The Holocaust and the "human rights revolution": a reassessment', in A. Iriye, P. Goedde, and W. Hitchcock (eds), *The Human Rights Revolution* (Oxford, Oxford University Press, 2012), 53ff; Morsink, *The Universal Declaration of Human Rights*, 37ff. The second recital of the Declaration is of interest in this respect, too.

[33] One of the drafters of the German *Grundgesetz*, later Federal President T. Heuss, is often quoted, though sometimes in a misleading way: that dignity is a *nicht interpretierte These*, a non-interpreted thesis. There were substantial contours around what dignity meant in the drafting process, including the substantial connection of human dignity and human rights, the priority of the individual over state interests, the importance of liberty or the unfolding of human personality in a community; see the review of the drafting record in Mahlmann, *Elemente*, Goos, in Chapter 3, this volume, for further discussion. Illustrative for some background consensus on dignity during the drafting process of the Universal Declaration is the rebuttal of the South African Delegation's attempt to water down the egalitarian conception of rights in the Declaration: see Glendon, *A World Made New*, 146.

To be sure, dignity continues to be a morally and legally highly contested territory. But how could it be different since major questions of human life are at stake? One should not draw wrong conclusions from the degree of factual disagreement on all levels of morality and the law about as to what the concept means. One sometimes encounters in some discussions about dignity a conclusion that the *factual (historical and/or contemporary) variety of understandings* of dignity (which is a clearly evident reality) means that there is an *intrinsic impossibility* of giving the idea any convincing meaning. This is a fallacious conclusion. The factual variety of interpretations is one thing, arguing that some interpretations of this reality are more plausible than others is quite another. The factual variety of interpretations presents us with a task; it implies nothing about the possibility of carrying it out. Disagreement exists about legal concepts that have been with us for thousands of years, for example the basic concepts of tort. The challenge is therefore not to stay stuck in descriptive accounts of variety (a state of affairs that nobody would seriously contest), analytically crucial as they certainly are, but to answer the question, whether there are possible reasons *normatively to prefer* one concretization over the other. This leads to the next question, the question of justification.

Problem of justification

Genealogy and legitimacy

There is no understanding of human dignity without also understanding the historical genealogies of this idea in various cultural contexts. But it is important to remember that genealogy cannot substitute for a theory of the validity of a normative idea. Whatever the historical trajectory of understandings and misunderstandings of dignity, one needs a justificatory theory that provides reasons for ascribing dignity to human beings. There are doubts in contemporary theory about the difference between genealogy and justification,[34] but this misses a central point: that there is the possibility of wrong, illegitimate developments and traditions, and it is possible to formulate a critique of these

---

[34] For a recent example, see H. Joas, *Die Sakralität der Person* (Berlin, Suhrkamp, 2011), 12ff, pursuing the project of an 'affirmative genealogy of the universalism of values', 15ff., 147ff. These doubts are not limited to normative theory, cf. the critique of Reichenbach's and Karl Popper's distinction of the context of discovery and context of justification, K. Popper, *Die Logik der Forschung* (Tübingen, Mohr, 1934); T. S. Kuhn, *The Structure of Scientific Revolution*, 2nd edn (Chicago, University of Chicago Press, 1970), 8; P. Feyerabend, *Against Method*, 4th edn (London, Verso, 2010), 149ff.

in a theory of justification that transcends the pure facticity of historical trajectories.

Another point is worth stressing: The validity of such a theory is independent of the self-understanding of actors. Their self-understanding does not provide for sufficient reasons to assume or deny a particular value status of human beings. Schopenhauer, whose critique of dignity has become a much quoted reference point of scepticism about dignity,[35] may have thought of himself in the framework of his metaphysical theory of the ontological unity of all being and a correspondent ethics of life denial and pity and not in terms of his dignity. If so – what is the consequence of this stance? Was he not, as is any human being, of intrinsic, supreme worth? Just because he was unconvinced by the idea of dignity in general and Kant's account of it in particular does not mean that he didn't possess this value-status.

This leads to the next point: the fact that the mainstream of a culture denies the dignity of persons and perhaps even violates dignity, such as members of European cultures did for hundreds of years externally through slavery, colonialism or imperialism, and internally through the treatment of women (among other examples), does not mean that the victims of these actions, although part of this culture and perhaps even sharing its basic values, did not possess dignity. On the contrary, despite the age-old denial of the intrinsic worth of women, the resulting practices of denial, and even the self-understandings of some women of their lower worth, women most certainly possessed dignity, even when it was denied to them.

Dignity refers, therefore, to a value-status that is not dependent on the subjective self-perception of an individual or the self-understanding of a particular culture. This is not an exotic proposition but one describing a common feature of human rights: the fact that from the standpoint of a certain culture or religion the legitimacy of freedom of religion is denied does not mean that a person belonging to this culture or religion—from the perspective of legal ethics and a theory of legitimacy and even less so in positive law—should not enjoy this freedom.

This point is not to be confused with two quite different questions: whether, first, the dignity of an individual can legitimately be protected against her will; and, second, how and by whom the content of dignity is to be determined. As regards the first question, one can hold that dignity is an intrinsic normative property of human beings irrespective of the particular self-understanding of that individual while maintaining, without contradiction, that this

---

[35] A. Schopenhauer, *Preisschrift über das Fundament der Moral* (Hamburg, Felix Meiner Verlag, 1979), 64.

nevertheless entails a prima facie duty to respect the freedom of the person to decide about her life herself. This is so because, as indicated above, part of what dignity protects is human autonomy. There are practically universally accepted limits to this autonomy: it is a standard norm of human rights law to prohibit slavery (indeed, on the level of public international law it is *ius cogens*), even when the slavery is voluntarily undergone. Given the reality of human trafficking, this is a practically highly relevant point. The autonomy of the individual is thus limited by non-derogable minimum norms of how to treat human beings. But below this threshold, hard as it is to determine where this line is to be drawn in practical cases such as dwarf-tossing[36] and laserdromes,[37] there is a very wide space of robustly secured self-interpretation without any constraints that is based on the autonomy of individuals protected by dignity. The kinds of constraints that dignity can legitimately impose on human liberty serve only to preserve that autonomy, so even if this use of dignity constrains individual action for the person's own good, it is not truly paternalistic.[38]

Legitimacy without metaphysics?

The second question of the method and agent of determining the content of dignity leads to the theory of legitimacy and its foundations. Should human dignity—given what has been said—be taken to be an objective ontological property of human beings? And, if so, does this not presuppose a considerable amount of metaphysics that is widely discredited by contemporary postmetaphysical ontology and epistemology? However, nothing of what has been said before presupposes such an ontological claim. To be sure, dignity is not a natural property of an entity like weight or length.[39] Rather, dignity is a predication of a value-status by a value-judgement of a human subject to an object of evaluation (another human being) according to normative principles of axiological ascription.[40] Normative predicates of this sort do not imply ontological propositions about an objective normative reality irrespective of human moral judgement. On the contrary, they can be interpreted with ontological plausibility as elements of mental reality, created by the internal resources of the human mind, supervening upon facts that are uncontested elements of the

---

[36] Conseil D'Etat, no 136727, 27 October 1995, *Commune de Morsang-sur-Orge v Société Fun Production et M Wackenheim*.
[37] ECJ, C-36/02 Omega (14 October 2004).
[38] On further constraints based on respect of worth see below the remarks on limitations.
[39] See J. Habermas, *Die Zukunft der menschlichen Natur* (Frankfurt am Main, Suhrkamp, 2005), 62.
[40] Mahlmann, *Elemente*, 262ff.

fabric of the outer world, such as the particular properties of human beings, without referring to objective (metaphysical) normative facts in the world.[41] Nor do normative predicates of this sort necessarily lead to ethical subjectivism if the principles of ascriptions enjoy more than subjective, and perhaps even universal, validity. Whether or not this is the case, it is a question of the theory of validity that provides the reasons for normative legitimacy of dignity-ascriptions.

This formulates the next question: How can one form such a theory of legitimation? What could it look like? There is a very substantial debate about this topic concerning the history of justifications of dignity and contemporary attempts in this respect.[42] There are at least three types of legitimation theories discussed that have something like a paradigmatic character, though they do not exhaust the theoretical space in which dignity is explored today.

First, dignity can be regarded as a *transcendent gift*. Dignity is bestowed from this point of view through some kind of act of grace. This is the mode of legitimation of human dignity used in religious ethics. A common metaphor in this respect is the idea that human beings are formed in the likeness of God.[43] This is formulated in Judaism[44] and by the concept of *imago Dei* in Christian thought,[45] although this idea appears in others contexts as well, such as in polytheistic antiquity.[46] This mode of justification sometimes betrays a rather low estimation of human nature. Without the transcendent gift, humans can be regarded as quite deplorable creatures, not least because the tragedy of the Fall left humans with a corrupted nature or,[47] in Luther's drastic words, in Satan's image (*imago diaboli*).[48] Second, dignity can be based on properties of human beings, and—since properties of human beings as such have no prescriptive implications—on *normative principles*, although perhaps this

---

[41] On the epistemological background of this non-referential theory of moral judgement, see M. Mahlmann, *Rechtsphilosophie und Rechtstheorie*, 2nd edn (Baden-Baden, Nomos, 2012), 252ff, 343ff.

[42] On the historical debate and contemporary problems, see Mahlmann, *Elemente*, 97ff, 248ff.

[43] See the second (later) account of creation in Gen 1:26, 27.

[44] See Y. Lorberbaum, 'Blood and the image of God: on the sanctity of life in biblical and early rabbinic law, Mmyth, and ritual', in D. Kretzmer and E. Klein (eds), *The Concept of Human Dignity in Human Rights Discourse* (Den Haag, Martinus Nijhoff Publishers, 2002), 55ff; Nathan Rotenstreich, *Man and His Dignity* (Jerusalem, Magnes Press, 1983).

[45] For a central example from scholastic thought see Aquinas, Summa Theologica, in *Die deutsche Thomas-Ausgabe*, vol. 13 (Heidelberg, Kerle, 1953ff), I–II, q. 64,2.

[46] See Ovid, *Metamorphosen* (Stuttgart, Reclam, 1997), I, 76–86, on the two possible versions of the creation of human beings.

[47] Compare with Aquinas, *Summa Theologica*, I–II, q. 82,1.

[48] M. Luther, *Über das 1. Buch, Mose. Predigten. 1527*, in *M. Luthers Werke, Kritische Gesammtausgabe*, 24. Band (Weimar, 1900), 51; Luther, *Predigten über das erste Buch Mose, gehalten 1523/24*, in M. Luthers Werke, Kritische Gesammtausgabe, 14. Band (Weimar, 1895), 111; Luther, *Vorlesungen über 1. Mose von 1535–45*, ibid., 42. Band (Weimar, 1911), 166.

is often not made explicit, such as, for example, those that render some and not other properties of human beings constitutive of dignity, or general ethical principles like those of justice. From this perspective, human nature is, despite its rather evident unpleasant and destructive side, something that—in the light of these normative principles—*by itself* can legitimize the predication of human dignity. Dignity is not regarded as a transcendent gift; it is the original, inalienable, and equal property of every human being. This is the mode of legitimation of secular humanism.[49]

The third mode of legitimation is in the form of radical social constructivism. In this approach, various theoretical origins are posited that not only assume the historical relativity of certain aspects of the idea of dignity, but take it at its core as nothing but a contingent product of discourse formations, final languages, social semantics, autopoietic systems, grand narratives, and the like.[50]

The necessity of justification

The problem of justification is central. The plausibility of any determination of the content of dignity is dependent on its theoretical justifiability. No conception of dignity will survive in morality and the law if no convincing reasons are at hand why dignity should be understood in this way and not another.

Reasoned justification can, in addition, not be suspended because of a reliance on an overlapping consensus, leaving competing thick theories or normative justification to the side.[51] Though, today, human dignity is taken to be a bedrock ethical and legal principle from many points of views, the contemporary political and social world is certainly far from any satisfactory practice of this idea. In addition, history has taught us that there is little reason to rely with calm confidence on the persistence of such an overlapping consensus. The firmly established consensus of today may be eroded by tomor-

---

[49] An argument based on human properties and normative principles of human moral understanding is fully immanent and secular—it may be unconvincing, but there is no necessary 'transcendent kernel' connecting it to religion. On the idea of an inner 'transcendental kernel' in Kant's philosophy (something different to a transcendent kernel, it appears), see Michael Rosen, *Dignity* (Cambridge, Harvard University Press, 2012), 31.

[50] Dignity in systems theory is a good example for this approach; see N. Luhmann, *Grundrechte als Institution* (Berlin, Duncker & Humblot, 1965) and the post-autopoietic-turn maintained functional interpretation of human rights, N. Luhmann, *Die Gesellschaft der Gesellschaft* (Frankfurt am Main, Suhrkamp, 1997), 1075ff. One may count Habermas's reconstruction of dignity as the product of reciprocal communicative structures of recognition as belonging to this kind of justification as well: see Habermas, *Die Zukunft der menschlichen Natur*.

[51] See John Rawls, *Political Liberalism* (New York, Columbia University Press, 1996), 144ff.

row, if the wayward tides of human history change. There is consequently no alternative to try to develop as good a justification of human dignity as possible in order to reaffirm the basis on which any consensus may rest, while recognizing the fallibility of any such human theoretical endeavour.

A task of particular importance in this respect concerns the theory of legitimation by secular humanism. There are at least two reasons why this approach is of considerable interest. A secular humanistic account of dignity is of importance, first, because it is necessary to lay the groundwork for a common understanding of dignity that can be potentially shared beyond religious or cultural borders. This is an indispensable aim in a pluralistic but profoundly interconnected contemporary world. From a secular perspective this reference to secular modes of justification is without alternative, and it is not at all new to religious thought. On the contrary, it is a traditional approach familiar for example to classical Natural Law doctrine: it is the theoretical move to legitimize norms under the hypothetical (and from the point of view of the religious theoretician, contrafactual) assumption of the non-existence of God, the famous *etiamsi daremus* ('daring to think') justification of Natural Law without reference to transcendent sources.[52] Religions have nothing to lose by this move, as understood by many religious thinkers. If some normative content is justified even without arguments stemming from a particular religion, this additional justification should only be welcomed from a religious point of view. In addition, religious ethics are not petrified entities; they are very much shaped by human reflection and thought that is by its very nature mundane, and has no direct humanely unmitigated access to the cognition of another world (one should not forget this in order to maintain an adequate sense of epistemological humility). The simple distinction between religious ethics and secular thought is therefore an artificial one in important respects.

This point is of some practical importance, given the political agents of the culture and social practices of human rights. Religions have most certainly been responsible for severe violations of human dignity: slavery and the attribution of certain roles to women are cases in point. But religions have also inspired, and do inspire, many people to pursue a quite different course by fighting (often most impressively) for the worth of human beings. A secular humanism is therefore a minimum core of a justificatory theory. It can, and should, however, be supplemented by additional arguments, not the least from the religious sphere, that can strengthen the idea of human worth.

---

[52] See H. Grotius, *De jure belli ac pacis* (Tübingen, Mohr, 1950), 11; F. Suárez., *De legibus*, II, VI, 3 (Madrid, Institutio Francisco de Vittoria, 1974).

Second, secular humanism has some interesting thoughts to offer. One potentially promising way to think about this matter is the following: Humans are not just the objects of an obscure, passively endured environment and life; they are subjects that try to understand and (re)create their world. They attempt aesthetically to appropriate their own much-faceted chatoyant existence, including also its rather sombre sides. Their subjectivity is the one of a being endowed with an emotionally richly textured mortal and consciously transient self. They are faced with the possibility and task of autonomous self-determination that may lead sometimes to felicitous decisions and sometimes to decisions that they have to pay dearly for. Human autonomy is exerted under moral rules that can motivate us to transcend narrow personal interests out of care for the well-being of others and respect for what justice demands. This very peculiar fabric of human existence does seem to provide some reasons to ascribe to human beings intrinsic worth because creative subjectivity; feeling, conscious, mortal, autonomous selfhood; or the ability to moral self-transcendence can be plausibly taken as crucial elements of the axiological principles underlying the justified predication of dignity.

Another argument stems from the observation that human beings are, as a matter of anthropological fact, a purpose for themselves. Human beings are radically equal in this respect: the life one enjoys is something equally valuable for any person. Given the demands of justice to treat equals equally, this status of a life being of intrinsic worth has to be universalized. It is therefore a justified universal right for all.

Arguments from humiliation can be reconstructed as the negative flipside of these thoughts. It has been observed, and with good reason, that human beings have a fine sense of self-respect.[53] To violate this self-respect by degrading treatment is to harm human beings in a way that justifiably cannot be inflicted on beings that are of intrinsic worth.

The same is true for violations of other basic human interests that do not involve, or do not only involve, humiliation—the pain of torture is humiliating, but there is also the subjection of another to sheer pain as well, and this in itself is not reconcilable with the worth of human beings.

From this perspective, human dignity seems to have a foundational role for human rights, though not every violation of any human right is a violation of human dignity, an important point that will be considered in more detail below. It seems hard to justify the protection of the personal, physical, and psychic integrity of persons, their liberty and equality, without an argument

---

[53] S. von Pufendorf, De Officio Hominis, in G. Hartung (ed), *Gesammelte Werke*, vol. 2 (Berlin, Akademie-Verlag, 1996), VII, §1.

for the intrinsic worth of humans. Why should one not allow violations of personal integrity, of liberty, of equality, if not every person possesses equal intrinsic value? Personal integrity, liberty, and equality all presuppose that the human beings to whom these basic goods belong do count normatively. If humans are of no normative importance, their basic goods can have none either, and human rights lose their justificatory point.

Who decides?

Who decides about the justified content of human dignity? The answer is an unsurprising one. The agent is the usual one of any project of human thought. There are no philosopher kings or queens; there is no dignitarian avant-garde that has an epistemological prerogative in this respect. The justification of dignity can only be the result of the renewed, failing, improved, fallible attempts of equal human beings in common to grasp what the normative core of their humanity is about.[54]

Problem of concretization

Ambit and limits

A problem that applied ethics and the law share in common is the concretization of human dignity. For the law, this is a decisive task if one wants to avoid the term becoming emptied of content or expanded beyond recognition with perhaps unwelcome consequences for the human rights order. What is needed is precision about the content of guarantees of dignity and precision about the limits of the scope of dignity, too. The latter is of as much importance as the former. One cannot shy away from the task of stating clearly what the protection of dignity does *not* demand.

To take an example: there are good reasons to think that guarantees of dignity can serve as justifications for legislative action against hate speech under certain well-qualified, contextualized conditions; if a minority is endangered in concrete circumstances, for example.[55] This does not mean, however, that it demands protection against any speech that is discriminatory, offensive,

---

[54] L. Wingert has coined the poignant phrase of the 'irreplaceability of the individual', the *Unvertretbarkeit des Einzelnen*, in the course of justification in this respect. See L. Wingert, *Gemeinsinn und Moral* (Frankfurt am Main, Suhrkamp, 1993), 179ff, 290.
[55] M. Mahlmann, 'Free speech and the rights of religion', in A. Sajó (ed.), *Censorial Sensitivities: Free Speech and Religion in a Fundamentalist World* (Utrecht, Eleven International Publishing, 2007), 41ff.

or stupid. Another example: dignity is a reason for the protection of equality through discrimination law but not every discrimination is necessarily a violation of human dignity, because a certain degree of interference must be a precondition of the assumption of a violation of human dignity if the term is to maintain any definable legal contours.[56]

This explains why one can assert the *foundational role* of human dignity for other human rights as referred to above but still maintain the position that not every human rights violation is at the same time a violation of the dignity of the person. There is no justification of the abstract, substantive prima facie legal positions provided by human rights without reference to the idea of the intrinsic worth of human beings, and thus to human dignity. That does not mean, however, that human rights do not, or could not, protect human interests beyond what dignity demands, for instance for the sake of furthering the demands of justice.

The content of guarantees of dignity outlined above adds substance to a system of human rights. It is not made redundant by a catalogue of classical human rights, protecting the right to life, basic liberties, equality, and some social rights. One reason is that the scope of dignity encompasses specific notions that are not fully covered by other rights. This concerns protected levels of respect for individuals and, crucially, matters of instrumentalization, objectification and reification. Another reason is that the idea of human dignity can be a decisive tool in the convincing interpretation of other human rights. It can remind the interpreter of a central dimension of any human right as a heuristic tool of legal humanism. The expansion of rights of persons of a homosexual orientation is a case in point.[57] The reference to dignity helped to pierce the veil of traditional prejudice and resentment, emphasizing how human beings are a purpose in themselves irrespective of their sexual orientation. It showed more clearly the point of equality clauses and anti-discrimination law: whatever one thinks about the sexual orientation in issue is irrelevant, since the point of such protections is not to promote any particular sexual orientation but to acknowledge the intrinsic worth of persons, their

---

[56] Not to take into account periods of employment completed by an employee before reaching the age of twenty-five in calculating the notice period for dismissal can be regarded with convincing reasons as discrimination on the ground of age, but it is hardly a violation of human dignity. See ECJ, Case C-555/07 *Seda Kücükdeveci v Swedex GmbH & Co KG*, para. 43 (19 January 2010). An interpretation of equality and non-discrimination clauses as in *Law v Canada*, 1999, 1 SCR 497 paras 52ff that interprets the equality guarantee as demanding a violation of human dignity is in danger of interpreting the equality guarantee too narrowly or human dignity too broadly. See Supreme Court of Canada, *R v Kapp*, 2008, SCC 41, para. 22 (22 June 2008).

[57] See, for example, SACC, *National Coalition for Gay and Lesbian Equality v Minister of Justice* (CCT 10/99) [1999]; ZACC 17; 2000 (2) SA 1; 2000 (1) BCLR 39 (2 December 1999).

right to develop their personality, and to lead the live they wish to lead, within commonly justified limitations. That human dignity is sometimes taken to be redundant is perhaps partly owing to its success: other norms have been loaded with the spirit of human dignity, and may therefore appear to supersede the norm that determined their acquired dignitarian meaning in the first place.

The concretization of the content of dignity, positive as well as negative, is also crucial for sharpening the critical function of dignity. Dignity is often referred to by those on different sides of the argument: the critique of torture is based on arguments of dignity and so are some of its defences, which argues that there is a duty to protect the dignity of the victims of the tortured persons.[58] Dignity is used, to take another example, to justify the fight against assisted suicide and to justify its permitted expansion. This constellation of rival claims based on the same right is the usual business of human rights law: arguments about headscarves in the classroom, to take just one example, are buttressed *and* challenged on the basis of freedom of religion: the freedom to manifest one's belief and to live according to its command, as well as the negative freedom of pupils not to become the patients of religious indoctrination. Only if there is a clear understanding of the content of dignity, its scope, and limits, can the merits of these rival claims be convincingly assessed.

Limitations

A central question in the process of concretization is the question of the limitations on rights. The regime of limitations determines what concrete content rights in any human rights code really have. For dignity, one important question is whether dignity is absolute[59] or relative.[60] There is a good case for taking human dignity to be absolute in relation to other rights: the use of a particular freedom or the protection of equality never justifies the violation of human dignity, understood in the (narrow) sense outlined above and with it the instrumentalization, objectivication, or reification of a human being, or the denial of her intrinsic human worth. There is one case, however, where the dignity of one person may collide with the dignity of another human being,

---

[58] For example, W. Brugger, 'Darf der Staat ausnahmsweise foltern?', *Der Staat* 35 (1996), 67ff.; W. Brugger, 'Vom unbedingten Verbot der Folter zum bedingten Recht auf Folter?', *Juristenzeitung* (2000), 165ff.

[59] Article 1 German Basic Law is the standard example of an absolute conception of a dignity guarantee; see Philip Kunig, in I. von Münch and P. Kunig (eds), *Grundgesetz-Kommentar* 6th edn (München, Beck, 2012), Article 1, para. 4.

[60] See Supreme Court of Israel, H.C. 5100/94, *Public Committee Against Torture in Israel v The State of Israel* (6 September 1999), para. 23.

and that is the case of abortion. That such a collision may occur seems rather plausible at least for late stages of a pregnancy, whatever one thinks about the exact beginning of human life and personhood. If, in such a situation, the life of an unborn child is ended to save the life of the mother, the child's life is not taken as an end-in-itself, whereas the mother's life would not be regarded as an end-in-itself if her life were sacrificed to save the life of the unborn child. This paradigmatic collision illustrates why the time-sensitive permission of abortion for certain qualified reasons (life, health, and existential well-being of the mother, or rape) has become a standard and well-justified form of regulation, details aside, in many parts of the world. These regulations draw the right conclusion for a tragic conflict: that it should not be deepened by ill-advised criminal sanctions.

The question of the subject of dignity is of great concern not only in the context of abortion, not least because of new biotechnological challenges. This is a highly contested and particularly difficult area. The traditionally intense debates should not, however, cloud the fact that—some widely implausible theories apart—there is much crucial common ground, as it is hardly contested that human beings when born are the subjects of dignity, and if one thinks of the fate of children in many regions of this world, this is not a minor thing to agree upon.[61]

Dignity can form a substantive right itself, for example by setting limits to criminal sanctions in the case of life-long imprisonment,[62] or it may enhance the scope of other positive legal rights, as illustrated by the previous example of equality guarantees and anti-discrimination law. It can constrain rights as well, for example by limiting the use of free speech laws, as already indicated. This dual role is also a common feature of human rights: any freedom gives rights to its bearer and may constrain the rights of others, for example through freedom of religion-based limits on indoctrination by others. Here, as in other areas, considerations of proportionality (under whatever name) rank high in determining an appropriately fine-grained solution.

There are many other areas—from social rights[63] to the democratic structure of a society[64]—that are within the ambit of what human dignity is about. In all these areas, much constructive work needs to be done. The principles of protected subjectivity and the worth of human beings, of non-instrumen-

---

[61] On the discussion in bioethics and the law on the beginning of life, see Mahlmann, *Elemente*, 293ff.
[62] See, for example, BVerfGE 45, 187.
[63] SACC, *Government of the Republic of South Africa and Others v Grootboom and Other* (CCT 11/00)[2000] ZACC 19; 2001 (1) SA 46; 2000 (11) BCLR 1169 (4 October 2000) para. 44.
[64] See BVerfGE 2, 1; 5, 85.

talization, non-objectification, and reification can, however, serve as useful yardsticks and signposts concerning how to proceed.

Problem of universality

A fifth problem that needs more thought is the problem of its universality. The idea of the universality of dignity is one of the basic assumptions of the modern architecture of human rights. In the realm of theory, however, relativism abounds. For some, it seems, relativism is even something of a truism, an indubitable truth only questioned by those who fancy that their parochial thought has universal scope.[65] Despite this widely shared stance, the situation seems more complicated than that. The history of ideas, if conceptualized as outlined above, teaches us an important lesson in this respect. Ideas about the intrinsic worth of human beings have been developed in very different cultural circumstances and against very heterogeneous backgrounds, whether polytheistic, pantheistic, monotheistic, atheistic, or agnostic. As far as the theory of validity is concerned, relativism is not very attractive either. Neither the anthropological assumptions nor the normative principles implied in promising a theory of justification of human dignity appear to be dependent on one particular culture. In short, the argument that only some human beings, say whites or men, enjoy properties that legitimately invest them with intrinsic worth, and that other groups of human beings, say, of a certain skin colour or women do not, has somewhat lost its centuries-old appeal. That it is just to treat equals unequally in Bombay but not in London is also considerably less plausible than a hundred years ago. There are even plausible theoretical options for the construction of a fallibilistic, but non-relativistic ethical epistemology to account for these observations. Consequently, if the arguments of the sort outlined above are roughly on the right track, there is a good case to be made that the universal practice of dignity rests on more solid theoretical grounds than many tend to believe.[66]

---

[65] A standard argument is to regard any universalism itself as a more or less ill-disguised form of particularism; for example J-F. Lyotard, *Le Différend* (Paris, Editions de Minuit, 1983), 208ff., on the French Assemblée Nationale, which imagined itself (wrongly) as humanity.
[66] See Mahlmann, *Rechtsphilosophie und Rechtstheorie*, 330ff. On the background theory of moral epistemology within a mentalist framework see M. Mahlmann, *Rationalismus in der praktischen Theorie*, 2nd edn (Baden-Baden, Nomos, 2009); M. Mahlmann, 'Ethics, law and the challenge of cognitive science', *German Law Journal* 577ff. (2007); J. Mikhail, *Elements of Moral Cognition* (New York, Cambridge University Press, 2011).

Problems of human appeal

The sixth and last problem concerns dignity's profound ethical, legal, and political appeal. Where does this attraction stem from? Why has it so profoundly caught the moral and legal imagination of modern civilization? Dignity is a concept of vexing complexity in certain respects. At the end, however, dignity makes an elementary point that may furnish the reason why some cannot help but succumb to its human charms. We may like it or not; we may think of ourselves as greater, more elevated, more admirable than others; we may even rise in the social hierarchy and gain power and privileges; but we will not escape dignity's central lessons. No one of us is better than any other and no one of us is worse because we all share something quite important during our limited time on this planet, with all our folly, our insights, our feelings, our sorrows, and our occasional wit: the equal worth of that mysterious, mind-boggling, cruel, tender, and unfathomably vast thing called a human life.

36

Human Rights, Human Dignity, and Human Experience

Paolo G. Carozza

MY PERSPECTIVE IN THIS chapter is that of a legal scholar and of a lawyer formed primarily in the common law tradition of practical reasoning—that is, someone whose central preoccupation is with facts and cases, with the raw material of human experience, and with drawing out of those concrete circumstances certain practical implications regarding the most reasonable way to order our relationships towards justice and the common good. That methodological starting point is in fact an important one for the central claim that I want to propose here: that in critical ways the foundation of law's preoccupation with the protection and promotion of human dignity needs to be forged in the crucible of human experience. It is an argument against treating human dignity as an abstraction, at least insofar as the concept has implications for the legal recognition of human rights. Relying methodologically on human experience as the touchstone of legal claims of human dignity has certain important implications for how we might structure global human rights law and how we can give content to it.

The very concrete claims of human dignity that are the daily fare of international human rights bodies are as varied as can be imagined. In my own direct experience as a member of one such institution,[1] many dignity claims were powerful and moving: the Peruvian mother of the disappeared; the Jamaican men kept indefinitely in overcrowded, small, dark, and unventilated police holding cells amid garbage and urine; the leader of the Paraguayan indigenous community whose children were dying from diarrhoea because they had no access to clean water. Some claims were far less compelling, such as the man who claimed that he had been subject to degrading treatment because his employer fired him for refusing to cut the long hair that was very

---

[1] I served as a member of the Inter-American Commission on Human Rights from 2006 to 2010, and as its president in 2008–9.

important to his personal aesthetic preferences.² Still other cases were neither easy nor clear: how does one assess the claims of dignity of an infertile woman who deeply desires to be a mother but was prohibited by law from using the *in vitro* fertilization technology that would have made it possible for her to bear children? In each of these cases, and in many others very similar to them, the petitioners and their advocates not only made claims that their rights under the American Convention on Human Rights were infringed but also that their human dignity was threatened or violated. When we examine how legal actors and institutions, using the language and artifacts of law, have responded to this array of different circumstances, we do not find a theoretical discourse on human dignity (at least, not one that is explicit or extended), but decisions that have tangible consequences stemming from the choice to recognize and protect certain kinds of claims, or to deny them.

As the other chapters of this volume have made abundantly clear, the pervasive invocation of the concept of human dignity today is accompanied by a wealth of different ideas about the meaning and scope of dignity within the plurality of moral and legal traditions of the human family. Those differences can be profound, and can have dramatically different implications for how we understand and protect dignity in law, as even a very compressed comparative survey of contemporary law reveals.³

At a very high level of generality, one can find human dignity invoked across legal systems of widely divergent traditions to denote two interrelated ideas: (a) an ontological claim that all human beings have an equal and intrinsic moral worth; and (b) a normative principle that all human beings are entitled to have this status of equal worth respected by others and also have a duty to respect it in all others. The normative principle includes within it the obligations of the state to respect human dignity in its law and policy as well. Based on this core common meaning of human dignity, there is broad consensus across legal systems that certain ways of treating other human beings ought always to be prohibited by law. Prohibitions on genocide, slavery, torture, forced disappearance, and systematic racial discrimination, for instance, represent some important examples of universal acceptance of the implications

---

[2] Of course there are many other circumstances where the cutting of hair can often be the basis for a very serious claim that human dignity is threatened, as in the forcible shaving of a detainee's head for purposes of humiliation, or a requirement that a Sikh cut his hair in violation of his religious obligations, but no such deeply rooted dignity claims were presented here.

[3] The following paragraphs are drawn largely from more extended discussions in Paolo G. Carozza, 'Human dignity in constitutional adjudication', in Tom Ginsburg and Rosalind Dixon (eds), *Comparative Constitutional Law* (Cheltenham, Edward Elgar Publishing Limited, 2011), 459–72, and Paolo G. Carozza, 'Human dignity', in Dinah Shelton (ed.), *Oxford Handbook of International Human Rights Law* (Oxford, Oxford University Press, 2013 forthcoming).

of the status and basic principle of human dignity. It is not surprising that in international human rights law many of these clearest instantiations of the requirements of human dignity also coincide with the strongest and exceptionless norms of international law, found for example in the definitions of crimes against humanity or *jus cogens*.

In the same way, the most widespread and evident use of dignity in human rights adjudication can be found in cases dealing with the protection of life itself and the integrity (physical or mental) of human persons. Cases are legion where inhuman and degrading treatment is found to violate the inherent dignity of the victims, and references to the requirements of human dignity pervade the case law of virtually all systems in these areas.[4]

Beyond that hard minimal core of the meaning of human dignity, legal experience reveals several areas where the meaning and use of dignity has less universal resonance but still fairly broad recognition and acceptance across several different legal traditions and systems. For instance, in many different jurisdictions courts discuss dignity as a value central to the definition and protection of individuals' social status and social roles. The German and South African Constitutional Courts have fined authors and publishers or even banned books because, although presented as works of fiction, they shared too many details about a particular individual's private life, in violation of their dignity.[5] French courts frequently require newspapers to pay damages after they publish stories or photographs about individuals without respect for their dignity.[6] This conception of dignity is not quite universal, however, and seems to be primarily employed within European courts and associated with the distinctively European conceptions of privacy (which are often quite different from those prevalent in the USA, for instance). Another group of cases shows certain courts employ dignity to address the sweeping conditions that shape the lives of entire communities living in poverty and extreme vulnerability. One sees this developed very clearly in the Inter-American human

---

[4] For just two among innumerable examples, see HC 5100/94 *Public Committee against Torture v Government of Israel*, 1999, available in English at elyon1.court.gov.il/files_eng/94/000/051/a09/94051000.a09.pdf; *Napier v The Scottish Ministers*, 2004, S.L.T. 555 (UK).

[5] BVerfGE 119, 1, available in English at www.bundesverfassungsgericht.de/entscheidungen/rs20070613_1bvr178305en.html; *NM v State (5) SA* [Constitutional Court of South Africa] 250 (CC) (S. Afr.) (2007).

[6] For example, Cour de Cassation [Appellate Court, France] première chambre civile [Cass. 1re. civ.]. 7 March 2006, F P+B, F. c/Sté Hachette Filipacchi associés.; Cour de Cassation [Appellate Court, France] deuxième chambre civile [Cass. 2e civ.], 4 November 2004, Cour de Cassation [Appellate Court, France] première chambre civile [Cass. 1re. civ.], 12 July 2001, SNC PrismaPresse et al. c/ Saada, dit Sarde.

rights system's cases on the 'right to a dignified life' of indigenous peoples,[7] or in the Constitutional Court of South Africa's decision requiring the government to devote substantial resources to developing and carrying out a plan to progressively realize the right to adequate housing.[8] Such situations involving the dignity of excluded groups are also related to the use of human dignity in cases invoking equality as necessary to the respect for human dignity in general. Based on the proposition that all people are inherently and equally entitled to human dignity, this view is especially developed in Canadian jurisprudence, has become common in South Africa, and can be found in some other jurisdictions as well.[9]

The partial overlap of understandings of dignity in these several areas shades to even greater disagreement as we approach those questions that touch on fundamentally contested visions of the meaning and destiny of human life, and especially the meaning and nature of freedom. At some level, almost all jurisdictions wrestle in complicated ways with the right relationship of dignity to autonomy, but there is no clear consensus even within single legal systems, let alone across different traditions. From one perspective, human dignity clearly demands protection of individual autonomy. For instance, many jurisdictions ground the autonomy of patients to make free and informed choices about their medical care in human dignity,[10] and a government that does not respect people's choices to shape their identities can thereby violate their dignity.[11] Yet, in contrast to that use of dignity, which empowers people to make free choices, dignity also plays a role in empowering government to *limit* the personal choices of their citizens. The French prohibition on dwarf-throwing is the most famous example of this,[12] but others abound. In Germany, a prohibition on peep shows has been found to be a valid protection of the

---

[7] For example, the case of *Yakye Axa Indigenous Community v Paraguay*, Judgment of 17 June 2005, Inter-Am. Ct. H.R. (2005), http://www.corteidh.or.cr/docs/casos/articulos/seriec_125_ing.pdf.

[8] *South Africa v Grootboom, SA* [Constitutional Court of South Africa] 46 (CC) (2000).

[9] For example, *Law v Canada (Minister of Employment and Immigration)* [1999] 1 SCR [Canadian Supreme Court] 497 ('the purpose of (equality rights) ... is to prevent the violation of essential human dignity').

[10] Cour de Cassation [Appellate Court, France] première chambre civile [Cass. 1re. civ.], 9 October 2001; A. C. c/ C.et al. [arrêt no. 1511 P+B+R] [Juris-Data no. 011237]. A summary of the decision is available at www.courtdecassation.fr/IMG/Civ%201,%209%20October%202001.pdf

[11] For example, the Hungarian Constitutional Court held that dignity includes an inalienable right to bear a name reflecting one's self-identity. Alkotmánybíróság [AB] [Hungarian Constitutional Court] 58/2001 (XII. 7). The European Court of Human Rights observed in *I v The United Kingdom* that 'society may be reasonably expected to tolerate a certain inconvenience to enable individuals to live in dignity and worth in accordance to the sexual identity chosen by them at great personal cost'. No. 25680/94, ECHR [European Court of Human Rights] 2002, para. 71.

[12] Conseil D'Etat [CE] [Highest Administrative Court, France], 27 October 1995, Commune de Morsang-sur-Orge. Available in French at http://www.rajf.org/article.php3?id_article=245.

human dignity of the (consenting) women being exhibited,[13] while the South African Constitutional Court upheld a ban on prostitution because the commodification of one's body necessarily diminished the human dignity of the prostitutes.[14] At times, this internal contradiction in the relationship between dignity and autonomy manifests itself dramatically. Even when safeguarding the dignity of having free choices, law frequently tempers autonomy by placing some restrictions on those choices that may be necessary to safeguard the dignity of others.[15]

At or even beyond the furthest margins of consensus over dignity, we find cases in which different courts, and indeed different judges within the same court, rely on human dignity to come to two entirely different conclusions even when dealing with strongly similar situations. Some of the most obvious examples include cases surrounding the beginning and end of human life—abortion and euthanasia or assisted suicide—as has been richly illustrated by the variety of perspectives on these issues found elsewhere in this book.

In short, there is a practical consensus around a core meaning of human dignity, lesser but discernible convergences of understanding around a cluster of key questions, values, and circumstances that are related to dignity, and some sharp disagreements and even contradictions that reflect not only the variety of intellectual and moral traditions in which the concept has its roots but also differences in the specific political, social, and cultural contexts in which the very broad principle gets instantiated. Probably the most persistent tensions have to do with those cases that inescapably deal with the relationship between dignity and competing notions of individual freedom, and with arguments about who counts as a human being with equal and inherent moral worth (e.g., the unborn or the terminally ill).

A problem then arises from the fact that the label 'dignity' gets used so broadly that it elides the differences between the core areas of practical agreement and the (sometimes intensely) disputed uses of dignity at or beyond the margins of consensus. That ambiguity is what allows use of the normative principle of human dignity to be so vulnerable to charges of inconsistency and even incoherence, and even to ideological manipulation. Where the term 'dignity' in fact tacitly reflects a particular view of human nature and human fulfilment—say, the difference between a neo-Kantian emphasis on radical

---

[13] 1981 BVerwGE 64, 274 [Federal Administrative Court].
[14] *Jordan v State*, 2002 (6) SA [Constitutional Court of South Africa] 642 (CC); (11) BCLR 1117 (CC).
[15] In most instances, when the conflict between dignity-as-liberty and dignity-as-constraint appears, the issue is not necessarily two competing definitions of dignity but rather the competing dignities of two different people whose interests may collide. This helps unravel the otherwise puzzling ability of courts to rely on dignity in support of either side of the abortion divide.

autonomy and a Judaeo-Christian vision of human freedom as intrinsically oriented towards relationship with others—arguments based on an unelaborated assertion of 'dignity' simply mask the differences. Whether intentionally or only passively, the language of dignity becomes a vehicle for the surreptitious imposition of one profoundly contested vision of human nature and human destiny over another.

That dynamic brings us, over and over again, to an impasse. How can we arrive at a more widely understood and shared conception of dignity, such that we can broaden the ways in which the law becomes a tool for protecting and realizing it, without running aground on the rocks of incommensurable moral and intellectual premises? We seem to be lacking the capacity to move forward.

We might be tempted to conclude that dignity as a legal concept is either trivial (in the sense of being so self-evident and undisputed that it adds nothing to the discussion—say, in the case of torture or slavery), or else so irreconcilably contested as to be useful only within very circumscribed and homogenous communities of discourse, if at all. If so, it might be better simply to reject it as vacuous and/or quite dangerous.[16] If we take that road, though, in reality we are also rejecting the good and important functions of the status and principle of human dignity. The ontological claim of human dignity helps sustain the very possibility of human rights as global principles that can and should help us condition sovereignty and hold accountable those who abuse power, especially the power of the state. Human dignity represents the ideal that there is a certain unity to the human person in which conflicting claims of rights need to be balanced and reconciled. The recognition of the equal and inherent worth of human persons is, today, the only widely shared suprapositive value with which positive law and legal systems worldwide are reasonably judged and critiqued. In short, without a commitment to the idea of human dignity, human rights law as it has been painstakingly constructed over the last seventy years would not exist.

This reminder of the connection of human dignity to the foundations of human rights law in general might also begin to suggest a way for us to take a step beyond the impasse. We find there a strong parallel between the problem of human dignity and the structural problem at the origin of international human rights law itself. To draw this out, we can first recapitulate

---

[16] See, for example, Mirko Bagaric and James Allan, 'The vacuous concept of dignity', *Journal of Human Rights* 5 (2006), 257–70; Justin Bates, 'Human dignity—an empty phrase in search of meaning?', *Judicial Review* 10 (2005), 165–8.

very briefly two well-established premises about contemporary international human rights.

First, at a conceptual level, human rights, in a way that is not dissimilar to what we see with human dignity, is not a single coherent idea, but represents the intersection of a variety of different traditions of thought, which in various degrees have mutually incompatible premises, especially premises about the nature and destiny of the human person.[17] This deep divergence of foundational premises was of course recognized from the beginning of the attempt to forge an international agreement on human rights in the mid-twentieth century, but—and here is the second of the background features of human rights that needs to be highlighted—the whole international human rights project was constructed on the basis of a deliberate abstention from strong agreement about foundational principles. The generation of jurists, scholars, and politicians who drew up and secured approval for the Universal Declaration of Human Rights knew very well that they all came to the discussion with profoundly incompatible first principles.[18] The basis for their consensus on a declaration of basic human rights was not a substantive agreement about foundations nor the discovery of a transcendent global ethic that unified them. Rather, their project was based on a more modest and limited aim: to reach a practical consensus on the articulation of human rights while setting aside the goal of attaining any thicker consensus about where those rights come from and why we should regard them as pertaining to human persons. The human rights enterprise is built on practical agreement, *tout court*.

Whenever he was asked how it was possible that adherents of such radically opposed philosophies could reach agreement on a declaration of fundamental rights, Jacques Maritain—himself a Catholic, Thomist philosopher, and diplomat who was heavily involved in the adoption of the Universal Declaration of Human Rights—liked to say, 'Yes, we agree about the rights, but on condition that no one asks us why. It is with the "why" that all the disagreements begin.'[19] Maritain and his colleagues did not regard this lack of consensus on foundations as fatal to the project. The fact that an agreement could be achieved across cultures on several practical principles was 'enough', Maritain wrote, 'to enable a great task to be undertaken'.[20]

---

[17] See, for example, Patrick Hayden (ed.), *The Philosophy of Human Rights: Readings in Context* (St Paul, MN, Paragon House, 2001).

[18] For a description of the diverging principles, see 'A rocky start', in Mary Ann Glendon, *A World Made New: Eleanor Roosevelt and the Universal Declaration of Human Rights* (New York, Random House, 2001), 36–46.

[19] Jacques Maritain, 'Introduction', *Human Rights Comments and Interpretations*, symposium edited by UNESCO (Westport, CT, Greenwood Press, 1973), 9.

[20] Maritain, 'Introduction', *Human Rights Comments and Interpretations*.

And, in fact, in the subsequent history of the human rights movement, that practical consensus has allowed for the construction of an impressive human rights edifice. Because we have a positive acceptance of a list of rights, the human rights movement has largely been able to focus on the practical work of 'translating' human rights into positive legal norms, formal international and constitutional instruments, and an institutional system, and then on the practical work of securing universal agreement to all that. This approach has had enormous success by many important measures. The crisis of humanity that was represented by the totalitarian movements of the twentieth century, and their violation of the most fundamental principles of justice and dignity on a massive scale, made clear the need to articulate certain universal basic principles of accountability. The genesis of the international human rights movement thus did respond to a genuine and profound human need and desire, and the strategy of practical agreement allowed a response to that need to emerge. Today, in consequence, there exists a certain core of rights that are basically recognized and accepted across a broad array of different political, economic, religious, and cultural realities, regardless of concurrent differences in any theoretical justification of them. There are national, regional, and global institutions whose work is sincerely, and sometimes influentially, directed towards promoting and protecting those fundamental rights, regardless of the divergent traditions to which they are being applied.

What does all this imply for the possibility of going forward in building a common understanding of human dignity? One immediately evident conclusion is that the arguments and difficulties about dignity are nothing other than the replication at a more general level of the same 'unfinished business' of foundations that is at the heart of the human rights project.[21] Human rights instruments bracket foundational questions but universally invoke human dignity as a generic placeholder for the something that gives human rights a deeper justificatory source.[22] But that only ensures that the underlying disagreement is semantically shifted from the foundation and meaning of human rights to the foundation and meaning of human dignity.

If it is true that we are facing the same structural problem, should we adopt a structurally analogous strategy to address it? Should there be (for purposes of law) a limited focus on whatever practical agreement can be identified around the principle of human dignity, abstaining from engaging and

---

[21] The phrase 'unfinished business' is borrowed from Mary Ann Glendon, 'Foundations of human rights: the unfinished business', *American Journal of Jurisprudence* 44 (1999), 1–14.

[22] For discussion of human dignity as a placeholder see Christopher McCrudden, 'Human dignity and judicial interpretation of human rights', *European Journal International Law* 19 (2008), 655–724, see especially p. 722.

deploying more fully theorized accounts about the status of dignity, where it comes from, and in what it consists? There is some merit in that proposal, and it begins to get at what I am trying to suggest in saying that we need to turn to concrete human experience in order to gain a fuller understanding of the meaning and implications of human dignity. One could even imagine that it might generate a great deal of constructive convergences in those areas where there are already the conditions present for a fairly large overlap among various understandings of dignity—the relationship of the principle of dignity to the need to protect persons from all forms of cruel, inhuman, and degrading treatment, for example.

But it is not yet enough. The strategy of practical consensus of Maritain and his contemporaries, for all its outward success, also suffers from some serious weaknesses and limitations. I have tried to diagnose them more fully elsewhere, so I will not rehearse the criticism in detail again here.[23] In synthesis, though, we can point to a number of persistent problems with the international human rights project that are all traceable in some degree to the thinness of the practical agreement on which it rests. It contributes to the wide and enduring gap between the formal international legal norms and instruments of human rights law on the one hand and the local social, political, and cultural realities in which they are supposed to be operative in practice on the other. It also ignores the fact that positive law, alone and without deeper ethical sources within a society, is insufficient to sustain the relationships of justice and solidarity and commitments to the common good to which we aspire. Both of these reasons contribute in some important degree to the very high degrees of non-compliance that we find in virtually all systems of international human rights law. Third, the absence of thicker substantive agreement about the sources and meaning of human rights has left a vacuum which has often been filled by bureaucracy and proceduralism. Finally and most importantly, in the end it is impossible to avoid, at least passively, making judgements and decisions on the basis of the deeper and more contested premises about the nature of the human person and the meaning of human life. Acknowledging practical agreement alone only obscures the deeper differences that in fact persist. Whenever we are faced with difficult judgements about, for example, the existence or recognition of a human right, its extension into new spheres and its relationship to other rights, its permissible limitations, we are implicitly relying on any number of prior assumptions about the person, society, the

---

[23] See Paolo G. Carozza, 'Human dignity and judicial interpretation of human rights: a reply', *European Journal International Law* 19 (2008), 931–44; Paolo G. Carozza, 'Il Traffico dei diritti umani nell'età post-moderna', in Luca Antonini (ed.), *Il traffico dei diritti insaziabili* (Soveria Mannelli, Rubbettino, 2007), 81–105.

state, freedom, law, and so on. Bracketing the underlying assumptions doesn't make them disappear, it only makes them less transparent, and therefore less subject to reasoned discussion and debate.

Maritain and his contemporaries knew this, and in fact said clearly that consensus around a limited set of practical principles did not obviate the more difficult task of seeking greater common understanding of the underlying reasons and foundations of human rights. The strategy of practical agreement, the philosopher Richard McKeon stressed, would merely provide a 'framework within which divergent philosophical, religious, and even economic, social and political theories might be entertained and developed'.[24] In other words, for the drafters and intellectual supporters of the Universal Declaration, the focus on practical agreement on principles and institutions was merely a method for moving beyond the roadblock of incommensurable premises. It was not presumed to be a sufficient permanent basis for the recognition and protection of universal human rights. Instead, it was to be a provisional and partial overlap of commitments on the basis of which we would need to work (hard) towards a deeper understanding of basis of that practice. At best, the effort to reach practical agreement was a method to provoke, to force open, a more vital debate about the foundations too.

Turning back to the present predicament of human dignity, then, what can we conclude on the basis of seven decades of experience pursuing a strategy of limited practical consensus on universal human rights? Focusing on our concrete human experiences of human dignity, and the convergences that we can find there, might be a very fruitful way forward; not, however, merely as a way of seeking practical agreement while setting aside the deeper and more difficult task of seeking a common substantive understanding of the meaning and requirements of human dignity. Focusing on our human experience of dignity cannot be the end point of our efforts but must rather be the *beginning* of a sustained and critical method of reasoning together, about which understandings of dignity, among the many deeply divergent approaches, corresponds best—which is to say most completely, most universally, most reasonably—to the reality of human life in all its complexity.

What is needed, then, is not only a focus on our shared concrete human experience of dignity but a focus that opens up the possibility of critical reasoning about how that experience of dignity deepens our understanding of what it is to be human, to have value, or, most to the point, to have a common, irreducible, and universal value as human persons. One can call this sort of

---

[24] *Human Rights: Comments and Interpretations* symposium edited by UNESCO (Westport, CT, Greenwood Press, 1973), 35.

shared and critical experience, taking up the suggestion of Luigi Giussani, 'elementary experience'.[25]

As Giussani explains:

> What constitutes this original, elementary experience? It can be described as a complex of needs and 'evidences' which accompany us as we come face to face with all that exists. Nature thrusts man into a universal comparison with himself, with others, with things, and furnishes him with a complex of original needs and 'evidences' which are tools for that encounter. So original are these needs or these 'evidences' that everything man does or says depends on them ...
>
> > The need for goodness, justice, truth, and happiness constitutes man's ultimate identity, the profound energy with which men in all ages and of all races approach everything, enabling them to an exchange, of not only things, but also ideas, and transmit riches to each other over the distance of centuries. We are stirred as we read passages written thousands of years ago by ancient poets, and we sense that their works apply to the present in a way that our day-to-day relations do not. If there is an experience of human maturity, it is precisely this possibility of placing ourselves in the past, of approaching the past as if it were near, a part of ourselves. Why is this possible? Because this elementary experience, as we stated, is substantially the same in everyone, even if it will then be determined, translated, and realized in very different ways—so different, in fact, that they may seem opposed.[26]

This 'complex of needs and evidences' characterizes what is irreducibly human in all of us, what moves us to act, and what propels us into a dynamic relationship with all of reality. It is something more basic, more fundamentally constitutive of our humanity than any of the multitude of specific cultural artifacts (including law) could be. It is part of what we presuppose, even unconsciously, whenever we say 'I' in a serious, self-aware way.[27]

There is much more to be said to develop and unpack that concept than I could do justice to here, but let me be quick to say what the appeal to elementary experience is *not*. It is not a new anthropological theory or a new theory of law or natural law; it is not a set of moral precepts to order human affairs; it is not a generic idea of humanity. It is something distinct from (even if inevitably related to) both theory and culture, and it inheres in the human being as a fact. It is a form of experience of what is human in which the evidence that

---

[25] Luigi Giussani, *The Religious Sense* (Montreal, McGill-Queen's University Press, 1997), 7. The idea, and its relationship to law, has been developed in a recent, short collection of essays: Andrea Simoncini, Lorenza Violini, Paolo Carozza, and Marta Cartabia, *Elementary Experience and Law*, Hans. Mariangela Sulhvan (Milan, Fondazione per la Sussidiareta, 2012).
[26] Luigi Giussani, *The Religious Sense* (Montreal, McGill-Queen's University Press, 1997), 7–10.
[27] Andrea Simoncini, 'Elementary experience and law: a "persistent" question', in *Elementary Experience and Law*, 2.

we run up against thrusts us into a comparison with our own needs desires, our own nature, our 'I'.[28]

This is not to suggest, of course, that elementary experience isn't translated inevitably into judgements, theories, and values, and together with other persons translated also into cultural projects, including law. But the connection to law must not be 'short-circuited', as Carmine Di Martino has written: 'We have to avoid the short circuit between the list of fundamental rights and the universal structure of experience. The irreducibility of the latter, continuously sought after by reason in an indomitable attentiveness to experience, necessarily demands a critical vigilance, even in the face of so-called universal rights.'[29] Or to put this point in another way, despite the way that we talk about the universality human rights, it is not really the rights that are universal so much as the human is, and the universality of rights follows from the prior universality of the human.[30] But the meaning of human here is not based on the abstract definition or some a priori anthropological or metaphysical claim. Our awareness of what is human emerges in experience, an experience capable of a critical judgement of what corresponds to what is irreducibly human—that is, in elementary experience.

And so it is with dignity, then: the meaning of dignity, if not consigned to the fragmented and incoherent babel of approaches that we see about us, if not reduced to whatever the conventional mentalities of the day inculcate upon us, if not blocked by the schematic opposition of conflicting theories and ideological prescriptions, has to emerge first from an encounter with what is most elementary to our humanity, an encounter that educates us to see in ourselves and in the other what is the worth, the value, the dignity of the human.

To bring this back to concrete cases, let me illustrate the method of elementary experience for a few moments by reference to some of the same real-life examples of dignity claims mentioned in passing at the outset of this chapter, and by reference to the way that I, as human subject, related to them. All of those cases—the mother of the disappeared, the indigenous leader, the infertile woman seeking help—presented me with the challenge of trying to grasp and enter into not just the technical questions of how the treaty norms might or might not apply to the case in question. More than that, they posed the challenge of how to enter into the human dimensions of the problem. What was I supposed to say to a woman whose son had disappeared, whose heart was crying out for justice, or to the woman who came to us out of the anguish

---

[28] Simoncini, 'Elementary experience and law', 3.
[29] Carmine Di Martino, 'L'incontro e l'emergenza dell'umano', in Javier Prades (ed.), *All'origine della diversita'. Le sfide del multiculturalismo* (Milan: Guerini e Associati, 2008), 100.
[30] Simoncini, 'Elementary experience and law', 5.

of not being able to conceive? Clearly, I could not pretend to be able to satisfy their needs, in any real or comprehensive sense. How could I even begin to understand the dimensions of the problem of the indigenous people of the Chaco, deprived of the very foundations of their cultural integrity and reduced to raising their children in a narrow strip of dry earth between the highway and the barbed wire that kept them out of their ancestral lands? Before being legal problems, these were problems that demanded a deep sympathy, not in a trite sentimental sense but in the sense of recognizing in their suffering the authenticity of their desires, and seeing in it the evidence of a universal need in which one becomes aware of the constitutive factors of one's own self as well as of the humanity of the other. In a phrase, the recognition of their human dignity emerged as elementary experience. Even more starkly illustrative of this dynamic was the day in which we visited the Jamaican police holding cell I referred to earlier. Immediately after that, I also paid a visit to a residential community of a religious order known as the Missionaries of the Poor. Here the brothers welcome into their care some of the most despised and outcast members of the Jamaican society: people suffering from AIDS, typically in advanced stages of the syndrome's development, and acutely disabled children. The first group are rejected by society not only for the virus they carry but also because they are automatically presumed to be gay in a society rife with hatred and violence against homosexuals, where we documented instances in which the police stood by and watched as gays were beaten and their homes destroyed. The second group consisted of children whose physical deformities and mental handicaps were so severe that it was difficult not to avert one's eyes. What made a simple gaze on the lives of all these residents possible for me was seeing the exceptional love, care, attentiveness, and even joy that the brothers, and the volunteer doctors and the AIDS patients and children so evidently shared with one another. The contrast with the jail, just an hour earlier, was staggering—there, men were herded together and standing in garbage and urine; here, everything was treated with care, with attentiveness to beauty, with tranquillity. Both, in vividly contrasting ways, constituted the awareness of the meaning of human dignity for me: the first in which I could not fail to be struck by the blatant denial of the most elemental humanity of these ordinary men; the second in which I could not help but be moved by the human love that affirmed the inestimable value of each and every single one of the lives in the brothers' care.

What lessons can be drawn from all that? First of all, that human dignity, as the fruit of the method of elementary experience, is first of all something that is discovered, not something deduced from a theory or from an intellectual or ontological premise. It is something concretely encountered in an

Other and recognized in oneself. And it emerges in particular in relationships of solidarity, of compassion (in the etymological sense), of gratuitousness. It is subjective, in the sense of inhering always in an embodied 'I' rather than in a disembodied discourse, yet it is in no way a relativistic thing; it is a hard fact. It is given, not made.

Can that elementary experience of the dignity of another (and of myself), with its inherently intimate relation to the particular human subject, also form the basis of a broader approach to dignity in law? In a way, focusing on the roots of our experience of dignity has moved us back towards the origins of law rather than removing us from relevance to law. Law, as a cultural practice that addresses certain basic human needs, draws on and responds to something that comes before it. So the method of elementary experience, as a way to comprehend and verify the meaning and implications of human dignity, certainly has relevance to the way that law ought to be structured to reflect and protect human dignity, and gives us a possible way to evaluate the law's effectiveness in securing that dignity. But, remembering Di Martino's cautionary observation cited earlier, we must not short-circuit the path from human experience to law, still less to specific rights and responsibilities. Even in the cases cited, the clear recognition of the ways in which the *status* of human dignity is indeed at stake, which allows us to enter into an important reflection on the right way to instantiate the *moral principle* of respect for human dignity, does not take us so far as to determine in any clear and unambiguous way how those cases ought to be decided as a matter of positive law. What kind of reparations should be due to the mother of the disappeared? Should the state be held directly responsible for the material conditions of the indigenous communities of the Chaco and the deaths of the children there? Does a recognition of the authentic expression of human dignity in the desire for biological motherhood necessarily mean that access to new reproductive technologies are the right response, even when other human lives in embryonic form may be put at grave risk of instrumentalization and destruction? There are obviously several steps of reasoning, and many prudential judgements, that must be undertaken before getting from the experience of an authentic claim of human dignity to the formal way in which human rights law should recognize and protect it. For this reason, I emphasized earlier that the method of elementary experience does not itself propose, or even lead directly to, any specific theory of law, old or new.

Nevertheless, at a macro level the method of human experience could have at least a few fairly direct implications for how we treat human dignity in law.

First, it supports the idea that law, especially the global law of human rights, ought to seek and build on the existence of a practical consensus around the status and principle of human dignity, just as Maritain and the generation of 1948 did in the forging of the Universal Declaration of Human Rights. That consensus would look to the concrete experience of human dignity that is shared across broadly diverse forms of human culture.

Second, we ought to be very cautious and restrained in the use of the concept of dignity in the law in ways that generate new rights or aggressively new understandings of rights, for it is more likely than not that these are not reflections of shared experience but instead assertions of contested, abstracted, and often ideologically charged theories of dignity.

Third, where there are sharply divergent understandings of dignity at issue, instead of bracketing and closing the disagreement, setting it to one side, we ought to use disagreement as a provocation to break open the discussion about the meaning and consequences of dignity. In other words, it is entirely good and right that the discourse of law (as represented not only by judges but also by citizens, advocates, scholars, and legislators) should engage in serious and sustained debate about dignity, seeking always to ground it in fact and experience, and asking what most genuinely corresponds to the most original needs and evidences of our common human nature.

Fourth, where there is not a strong practical agreement, grounded in concrete experience, we should tolerate, and indeed embrace, a generous pluralism of understandings across cultures and legal systems. The risk of a hegemonic imposition of one idea of dignity is great. Human rights, as expressions of some of the specific moral principles that flow from a recognition of the status of human dignity, therefore, need in important ways to protect the conditions for a thick and pluralistic discourse on questions of human dignity—thus, protecting the integrity of diverse ways of life, forms of human association, expression, and participation.

Fifth, there needs to be a special regard for the role that religious freedom, religious pluralism, and interreligious dialogue will play in generating the conditions for a thicker understanding of human dignity to emerge from elementary experience. The method I have described and proposed emphasizes the generative value of solidarity, compassion, love, and gratuitousness in human relationships, as well as the critical role played by our capacity for increased self-awareness in an encounter with an irreducible Other. All of these are among the everyday basic features of a wide variety of religious traditions. It is there, within them and among them, that we have some of the greatest cause for hope that we can find our way forward from the impasse in which we find ourselves now with respect to the meaning and implications of human dignity.

37

The Concept of Human Dignity: Current Usages, Future Discourses

Bernhard Schlink

Current usages

UNDERSTANDING HUMAN DIGNITY BEGINS with understanding the different usages of the concept of human dignity.

Human dignity is used as a flag under which people unite and fight for freedom, equality, and decent living conditions that enable them to take care of their needs. The flag summarizes and abbreviates what they are fighting for; respect for their human dignity to them means respect for their freedom, equality, and right to live under decent conditions, no less, no more.

Human dignity is also used as a foundational concept for human rights, as a concept that at least justifies and at best requires the existence of human rights. While the flag summarizes and abbreviates freedom, equality, and decent living conditions, that stand in and of themselves, the foundational concept is the basis without which human rights have no standing.

Human dignity is further used as a last resort, insisted upon when every other claim fails. The same person that understands that his or her claim for freedom, equality, and decent living conditions has no chance to succeed, and therefore gives up raising these claims, can still insist on respect for his or her human dignity, and challenge the ultimate humiliation of being tortured or enslaved or broken for use in a show trial.

It is only a small step from using human dignity as the foundational concept for human rights to using it as a mother right, from which human rights are derived as daughter rights. Under Chief Justice Aaron Barak the Israeli Supreme Court pursued this approach with particular diligence. It developed a jurisprudence that regards human rights that are explicitly granted in most other constitutions, but not in the Israeli constitution, as protected by the Israeli constitution anyway—protected by the constitutional protection of human dignity as a mother right. The protection of human dignity as a mother right can only be relative. In conflicts and collisions between citizens, or between citizens and the state, human rights must be curtailed; for the daughter rights to be limitable, the mother right must be limitable as well.

But human dignity can also be an absolute right, used as a legal last resort exempt from all governmental and administrative curtailing, from all legislative give and take, from all proportionality considerations and balancing, from all utilitarian calculation. Under the German Constitution the protection of human dignity is understood as such an absolute protection. Since a constitution must allow for the curtailing of human rights, the absolute protection of human dignity can protect only some core elements of human identity and integrity.

We have these different usages not because we cannot agree on one usage, but because they serve different purposes, show up in respectively different contexts and documents, and rely on different philosophical traditions and conceptions.

When people unite and fight under the flag of human dignity, what matters to them is success: freedom, equality, and decent living conditions. Whether the respect for their human dignity is owed to them because of their value, for instance their value as beings created in God's image, or because of their status, for instance their equal status as contributors to the commonwealth, or because of rights granted to them by nature or reason, is of minor importance; whatever supports their fight is welcome, from Christian liberation theology and Marxist revolutionary ideology to any philosophy of liberté, egalité, and fraternité.

When the goal is to establish a foundation for human rights or to find a mother that gives birth to human rights that the constitution fails to protect explicitly, the realm of philosophical traditions and conceptions to build on is somewhat narrower, but still includes, among others, Thomas Aquinas, John Locke, and Jean-Jacques Rousseau.

When the goal is to embue human dignity as a last resort and an absolute right that courts can enforce and the state will respect, it is an obvious move to turn to Kant, because he understands human dignity as an absolute that prohibits each and every instrumentalization and requires to treat everybody as a subject and nobody as an object.

With these different usages and their different philosophical traditions and conceptions it is no wonder that the human dignity discourse does not have one concept and conception of human dignity. One wonders whether there is even a need for one. Isn't it enough to be aware of the different usages and to know in what usage one is engaging?

Indeed, much of today's human dignity discourse can do without one, and even without any concept and conception of human dignity.

This becomes obvious when the discourse turns to specific problems and cases. The crucifix in the classroom, the teacher with a headscarf, religious sentiments that demand protection against anti-religious pronouncements, women's equality versus religious traditions, religiously required or supported polygamy, equal access to health care, the right to life, the right to die, assisted suicide, abortion, stem-cell research, how to implement equality after apartheid, how to deal with colonial or similar crimes of the past—whatever the topic is, today's discourse employs some human dignity rhetoric. But no important aspect of any of these problems and cases is lost when the discourse doesn't use this rhetoric and deals only with the specific rights and freedoms involved carefully and comprehensively. Using human dignity rhetoric may add some colour, but it doesn't add to unfolding and solving the problem or case.

There are exceptions. When the German constitution protects human dignity absolutely, it invites use as a trump card that ends human rights arguments. Once the card is played, we don't talk about the right of the pregnant mother versus the right of the unborn baby, the merits of stem-cell research versus its dangers, what torture yields and what damage it does, but whether the stem-cell and the unborn baby have dignity and whether torture is a violation of dignity. Another seeming, but not true, exception is Israel, where every freedom and equality issue has to be developed as a human dignity issue but is then dealt with as a mere freedom or equality issue. Where human dignity is not protected absolutely, human rights discourse doesn't benefit from human dignity rhetoric.

Three reasons to hold on

So why do we keep engaging in human dignity discourse? Why do we hold on to the concept?

There are several good reasons to do so. The first is that human dignity discourse bridges the gaps between the different usages. Those who use human dignity as a political flag under which to unite and fight for freedom, equality, and decent living conditions, may not care about the philosophical traditions and conceptions of human dignity; all they want is success. But once the fight or the success become flawed, once the fight becomes about equality and neglects freedom, or the success is one of freedom without equality, the flag of human dignity can serve as a reminder that the fight was about more, about a life in dignity, a life with freedom and equality and under decent living conditions. Similarly, the concept of human dignity can keep the idea of human rights rich and complex; once it is understood that human dignity can serve as the foundational concept for human rights, it follows that every aspect of a good life that is associated with human dignity must find its place in the system of human rights. And whatever the political agenda or legal system of human rights may be, it is important that they are confronted with the question whether they manage to fight off the ultimate humiliations that people experience as an assault on their last resort, their human dignity.

The second good reason is that there is actually an overlap between the different usages of human dignity and the different conceptions and traditions they build on. There is a common core. For all usages, human dignity is something that all humans share; it is indefeasible, it—we can phrase it positively—demands at least some basic respect for human autonomy, it—we can also phrase it negatively—prohibits at least ultimate humiliations.

This overlap or core has meaning, even though it is vague and its precise content is contested and disputed. I wish that everybody agreed that torture is one of the inacceptable and unconstitutional ultimate humiliations; unfortunately this point is still being debated. But at least it has to be discussed as an issue of human dignity and not just as an infringement of bodily integrity, like vaccinations and haircuts for drafted soldiers.

There is a third good reason for holding onto the concept of human dignity. It is a *Sehnsuchtsbegriff*, a concept that encompasses our longing for a better and fairer world where the recognition and protection of humans is not up for grabs and cannot be overpowered or outmanoeuvred or argued down. The longing, again, is vague, and it will never be fulfilled and will often be frustrated. But the concept is important. It brings together people of goodwill who all share that longing, though they may disagree on what human dignity means, demands, and prohibits; whether it has religious connotations or is a completely secular concept; whether it builds on the idea of virtue, on individual autonomy, on social status, or on some other basis. The longing is something over which they can meet and join in at least some steps towards a better and fairer world.

Future discourses

There is enough common ground for interdisciplinary discourse on human dignity. Lawyers and particularly those who are or were justices tend to focus on results in a way that philosophers sometimes find reductionist, and philosophers tend to dig and dig into problems in a way that sometimes feels unfocused to a legal mind. But it is clear what both sides bring to the discourse: lawyers their real cases and legal problems, philosophers their reflections on what humans are and what they owe each other. Jurisprudence and legal scholarship meet anthropology and ethics.

With theologians it is difficult, and the difficulties surfaced in the discourse between philosophers, lawyers, and Catholic theologians at the conference. Of course, theologians can also bring to the discourse their reflections on what humans are and owe each other. But since lawyers seek solutions for their cases and legal problems that are acceptable to religious and non-religious people alike, since lawyers and philosophers work under a secular premise, the specifically theological anthropological and ethical considerations are of limited interest.

What would be of interest Catholic theologians don't bring. The Catholic Church is an institution with a strong hierarchy, and strong instruments and routines of control, treating women and also gays and lesbians not as equals, demanding from its functionaries a chastity that often overburdens them, engaging in charitable institutions and activities that, like all charity, cannot do without an element of paternalism, nursing a culture of seclusion. That hierarchy, control, and paternalism are problems for autonomy and also for human dignity, that the rejection of equality is a problem for human dignity, that overburdening someone while at the same time giving him the opportunity to use paternalist dominance over the young and weak to relieve the burden creates problems for the human dignity of the young and weak, that a culture of seclusion is a problem when protecting human dignity against violations—all this is obvious. The scandals of the last decades show that the problems are real. As the challenges for human dignity that the state creates and that lawyers and philosophers and theologians discuss, looking at specific problems and cases, the challenges for human dignity within the Catholic Church and similar institutions, particularly but not exclusively of a religious nature, could equally be discussed interdisciplinarily. And both discourses could learn and profit from each other.

That the Catholic Church has its hierarchy, control, unequal treatment of women and others, celibacy, charitable paternalism, and culture of seclusiveness is not the issue. The issues are the dangers for human dignity that this creates; they have to be reflected upon and dealt with, not just as occasional accidents but as structural problems. The voice of the Catholic Church in the public discourse on issues of human dignity rings hollow when the issues of human dignity within the Church are not visibly reflected upon—as the structural problems that they are.

The future that one wishes the human dignity discourse to have would not only include the Catholic Church and its theologians in a deeper way but would also invite Jewish and Muslim contributions. It would ask what man's creation in God's image means for Jews and Christians alike and differently. It would ask the Muslim theologians what human dignity means to them and how they reconcile human dignity with the inequality of men and women and believers and nonbelievers. It would have to be a discourse on human dignity and tolerance and on universalism and particularism. It could at least build on a universal longing for a better and fairer world.

38

Discourses of Dignity

Gerald L. Neuman[1]

THESE REFLECTIONS ARE WRITTEN from the perspective of a legal academic, whose professional training relates to human rights as they are embodied in institutions of national and international law. In observing and participating in a cross-disciplinary conversation about human dignity, the concerns of my home discipline inevitably colour my perceptions. The contributions of other disciplines can improve our understanding of the principle of human dignity and its consequences in the world. The kind of understanding we seek, however, is not necessarily the same.

Cognate concepts

The participants in the conversation come from different disciplines and employ different discourses. The principle of human dignity operates as a different kind of proposition in the different discourses.

For historians, the principle of human dignity is an evolving theme in the history of ideas; they may trace its transformations and ramifications and revivals without taking any position on how the principle is best understood or whether it has any validity. For philosophers, the principle of human dignity potentially states a moral norm whose content, validity, and consequences should be explored. Some philosophers affirm and elaborate the principle; some philosophers analyse invocations of human dignity as covering a variety of asserted norms that may be inconsistent with one another; and some philosophers dismiss the very notion of human dignity as delusion or deceit. For theologians, if I have understood our discussions correctly, the principle of human dignity may be a proposition about the relationship between human beings and God. Different theologians offer different

---

[1] I should state that this chapter is written in my personal capacity, and not in my capacity as a member of the UN Human Rights Committee, and that it does not speak on behalf of that treaty body.

accounts of the aspects of this relationship that ground an affirmation that human beings possess dignity in the relevant sense.

For lawyers, on the other hand, the principle of human dignity appears as a positive legal norm in a particular legal system. The system in question may involve a national constitution, or the European Convention on Human Rights, or European Union law, or a global human rights instrument. The principle of human dignity has a textual existence that lawyers must recognize, and a normative force that must be constructed if not deduced.

Even within the different discourses, we know that there is disagreement among the participants. But certain common features may provide reassurance that many of us are talking about cognate concepts, even if some other participants deny the existence of human dignity, or interpret dignity in a manner antithetical to the human dignity principle.

The principle of human dignity asserts that human beings have intrinsic value. The principle emphasizes that *all* human beings have that intrinsic value, and that they cannot lose or forfeit it. The principle further maintains that certain forms of treatment of a person are inconsistent with that value, and therefore wrong.

We may disagree about why human beings possess intrinsic value, or about which forms of treatment are inconsistent with that value, while still ascribing to versions of the same principle. Those who assert that human dignity must be earned by virtuous conduct, or is unequally distributed, are talking about something else.

In the political sphere, the principle of human dignity also tells us that the state exists for the sake of individual human beings. They do not exist for the sake of the state.

From human dignity to human rights

The principle of human dignity serves as part of the foundation of human rights law, at least in the sense that recognition of this value gives us reason to construct a system of legal rights, calculated to protect individuals against treatment inconsistent with human dignity. We can call these legal rights *positive human rights*, as creations of positive law (positive being in contrast with unenacted moral human rights, rather than in contrast with negative human rights).[2] Human rights treaties, for example, normally set out a list of the posi-

---

[2] Lawyers sometimes distinguish between negative rights that impose duties of inaction and positive rights that impose affirmative duties of action, but that contrast involves a different meaning of positive.

tive human rights that the states that ratify the treaty agree to protect, and also articulate secondary legal rules regarding how the treaty itself will operate to facilitate that protection.

From the legal perspective, one can affirm that the human dignity principle provides the foundation of a system of human rights, without meaning to claim that each positive human right could be deduced rigorously from the principle of human dignity. Rather, the human dignity principle justifies concern about threats to the lives and interests of human beings, a concern that extends to all human beings. The international human rights system also rests on the conviction that empowering individuals, by configuring many of the rules that protect them as legal rights that they can assert, best serves their human dignity.

The articulation of positive human rights may be motivated by insights from other disciplines such as moral philosophy, political science, or religion. Nonetheless, the relationship between positive human rights and these non-legal principles is varied and complex. Some positive human rights provisions attempt to express moral norms directly in implementable language; some positive human rights provisions merely approximate moral norms that cannot be concisely summarized; some positive human rights provisions create institutions that were chosen by the drafters as means for the protection of other human rights rather than as direct embodiments of non-legal principles.

An analogous example from US constitutional history may illustrate this last point. When James Madison introduced his proposals for a Bill of Rights in the US Congress in 1789, he described the right to jury trial as a needed positive protection for natural rights rather than as a natural right itself: 'Trial by jury cannot be considered as a natural right, but rather a right resulting from a social compact, which regulates the action of the community, but is as essential to secure the liberty of the people as any one of the pre-existent rights of nature.'[3] Today, jury trial is not part of the international corpus of positive human rights, but a more generalized guarantee—the right to a 'fair and public hearing by an independent and impartial tribunal'—is included.[4] Many positive human rights are specific procedural rights, chosen for their predicted effects rather than for their own sake.

The element of choice in the design of positive human rights provisions also reflects the reality that human rights treaties are constructed by political processes. Crucial steps in the drafting and adoption of the treaties are

---

[3] 1 Annals of Cong. 437 (1789) (remarks of Rep. Madison).
[4] See Universal Declaration of Human Rights, article 10; International Covenant on Civil and Political Rights, article 14; European Convention on the Protection of Human Rights and Fundamental Freedoms, article 6.

performed by political interaction of representatives of governments, including negotiation and vote-taking, either at the inter-governmental level or within the framework of international organizations; ratification of the resulting treaties by particular states involves political processes at the national level. The authoritative character of positive human rights provisions comes not merely from the moral appeal of the norms but also from the political endorsement that the drafting and ratification processes provide.

Political processes often involve compromise, and the drafting of positive human rights provisions may involve compromises of principles as well as compromises of interests. Sometimes different normative premises held by different political actors produce a common consequence, and no compromise is necessary. At other times, good faith normative disagreements can be resolved only by adopting second-best formulations that do not fully satisfy either party's commitments. Thus, there are many ways to construct a positive human rights system, and perhaps all of them are imperfect.

As I have emphasized in other writing, the considerations just given call attention to three aspects of positive human rights norms that influence the interpretation of human rights treaties.[5] One is the consensual aspect, derived from the completed or ongoing political processes that give the norms their positive force. Another is the suprapositive aspect, recalling the non-legal normative principles—which may be multiple or contested—that motivate their adoption. A third, often overlooked, is the institutional aspect, responding to the need to elaborate positive human rights as legal rules in a manner that facilitates compliance by duty-holders and oversight of their compliance by monitoring bodies. For present purposes, the important point is that although non-legal principles may legitimately influence the interpretation of positive human rights, the relevant non-legal principles may be multiple or contested, and there are other aspects that influence interpretation.

Constitutions and human dignity

Other chapters in this book illustrate the diversity of legal systems that protect human dignity at the national level. In some countries, such as the USA, human dignity remains in the background as a value justifying the set of human rights, but does not operate as an applicable legal rule at all.[6] The Declaration

---

[5] Gerald L. Neuman, 'Human rights and constitutional rights: harmony and dissonance', *Stanford Law Review* 55 (2003), 1863.

[6] See Gerald L. Neuman, 'Human dignity in US constitutional law', in Dieter Simon and Manfred Weiss (eds), *Zur Autonomie des Individuums: Liber Amicorum Spiros Simitis 249* (Baden-Baden: No-

of Independence asserted a natural law theory of rights that was not expressly repeated in either the Preamble or the operative provisions of the Constitution. Human dignity surfaces in judicial reasoning to inform the interpretation of enumerated rights, particularly since the end of the Second World War, without producing any positive right or enforceable principle of human dignity.

In other countries, such as Germany, an express constitutional provision on human dignity is interpreted as a very specific norm, accompanying a thick set of other enumerated rights that already do most of the work of protecting human dignity. The structure of the *Grundgesetz* makes the human dignity provision in Article 1 unamendable, and its phrasing has been construed as making it absolute. These features make judges cautious about invoking the human dignity provision to deal with cases that other, less rigid provisions could resolve.[7]

The European Union Charter of Fundamental Rights, reflecting clear German influence, also devotes its first article to guaranteeing human dignity, described as 'inviolable', before proceeding to an extensive series of other rights.[8] While the Charter's acquisition of legal force under the Lisbon Treaty is too recent to provide sufficient data on how the European Court of Justice will interpret the provision, the success of Germany in spreading its textual model across the entire European Union appears highly consequential.

In some constitutional systems more sparsely endowed with enumerated rights, an express provision on human dignity has become the operative norm from which interpreters derive (or to which they attribute) the more specific rights needed for its protection. The human dignity provision thus plays the residual role that the due process clause has played in the USA, and that the clause on the free development of the personality has played in Germany. Justice Barak's chapter in this book describes how a human dignity guarantee has operated in this manner in Israel. Hungarian constitutional law of the 1990s provides another example, in which the constitutional court characterized the

---

mos Verlagsgesellschaft, 2000); Judith Resnick and Julie Chi-hye Suk, 'Adding insult to injury: questioning the role of dignity in conceptions of sovereignty', *Stanford Law Review* 55 (2003), 1921. For an update on quantitative data, see Leslie Meltzer Henry, 'The jurisprudence of dignity', *University of Pennsylvania Law Review* 160 (2011), 169.

[7] Aharon Barak, Chapter 20, this volume; Dieter Grimm, Chapter 21, this volume.

[8] See Martin Borowski, 'Artikel 1: Würde des Menschen', in Jürgen Meyer (ed.), *Charta der Grundrechte der Europäischen Union*, 3rd edn (Baden-Baden, Nomos Verlagsgesellschaft, 2011), 94, 105. The English and French texts use the same word, which has the same spelling in both languages. The official German text employs the term '*unantastbar*', taken from the *Grundgesetz* and connoting 'untouchable' or 'sacrosanct', rather than the equivalent '*unverletzlich*'.

human dignity clause as a 'mother right' or 'parent right' from which other unenumerated rights emerge.[9]

The positive legal meaning of human dignity as a term of art in legal discourse thus varies among these different kinds of systems, because the phrase serves different functions within their constitutional structures. The legal content of the term would vary from country to country, even if there were no disagreement about the corresponding concept in other discourses. In our interconnected world, these meanings will often be developed in different local contexts with attention to both local and transnational influences.

One could ask what role the cross-disciplinary conversation pursued in this volume has in this transnational process. To some extent, the participants leave the conference and go back home to their own disciplines. Academics may do their best and thickest work within their fields, where they best understand the methods and traditions. What problems are worth investigating, what counts as evidence, how hypotheses are phrased, what terms mean and what baggage they carry, who are authorities to be reckoned with—these and other questions will vary across disciplines, and also across subfields within disciplines, and often across national borders. Researchers studying the same social phenomena may describe their data in very different manners in order to render them subject to the methods of their fields. Communicating across disciplinary boundaries may require simplification and may produce misunderstanding.

Nonetheless, the translation across boundaries may point to possibilities. For example, the chapter by Professor Goos examines the secret history of the drafting of Article 1 of the *Grundgesetz*, and the particular conception of human dignity that he found there. This conception may or may not have authority within German constitutional law. This conception has no authority outside Germany, but it is available for consideration and appropriation, or for adaptation, if it seems to have genuine explanatory power elsewhere. A court contemplating the borrowing of this conception might ask such questions as whether the conception is consistent with the operative text or other expressions of political consent within its legal system, how the conception coheres with the system's suprapositive commitments, whether it facilitates the broad or narrow functional role that a positive human dignity norm serves within the system, and how the distinctions drawn by the conception lend themselves to application and enforcement within its institutions.

---

[9] See Catherine Dupré, 'Importing the law in post-Communist transitions: the Hungarian Constitutional Court and the right to human dignity (Oxford, Hart Publishing, 2003); Péter Paczolay (ed.), *Twenty Years of the Hungarian Constitutional Court* (Budapest, Constitutional Court of the Republic of Hungary, 2009), 56–60. Hungary adopted a new constitution in 2011, which need not be discussed here.

Universal human rights

The international human rights regime has a different origins story, which has been retold repeatedly. In the establishment of that regime, human dignity had a consensus-building function for participants from different geographical and ideological backgrounds. All agreed on the urgency of affirming the universal possession of human rights in the wake of violent ultranationalism and colonialism[10]—and it is worth pausing for a moment to emphasize colonialism as an antithesis of universality. In the present era, voices continue to insist that international human rights must be defensible in terms that could be globally accepted, and not merely on the basis of a current political consensus in Europe.

In the international human rights system, human dignity is mostly foundational but sometimes operative as an applicable norm. Human dignity appears in the nearly identical preambles of the two Covenants, the principal human rights treaties designed to give legal force to the aspirational Universal Declaration of Human Rights. In the International Covenant on Civil and Political Rights (ICCPR), human dignity then returns in Article 10(1), which requires that 'all persons deprived of their liberty shall be treated with humanity and with respect for the inherent dignity of the human person'.[11] The official interpretation of this provision by the relevant treaty body, the Human Rights Committee (HRC), requires that states provide humane conditions of confinement, taking into account international prison standards, and also that detainees should 'enjoy all the rights set forth in the Covenant, subject to the restrictions that are unavoidable in a closed environment'.[12] So construed, the provision does not provide much occasion for a priori reasoning about the entailments of the concept of human dignity.

Human dignity also plays a role in interpretation of other provisions of the ICCPR,[13] and sometimes supplies reasons to limit a claim of right, in the

---

[10] See Johannes Morsink, *The Universal Declaration of Human Rights: Origins, Drafting & Intent* (Philadelphia, PA, University of Pennsylvania Press, 1999), 36–7, 96–101.

[11] The *travaux préparatoires* of the ICCPR reveal that the latter phrase was added for clarity, given the difficulty of translating the phrase 'with humanity' into other official languages. See Marc J. Bossuyt, *Guide to the 'Travaux Préparatoires' of the International Covenant on Civil and Political Rights* (Dordrecht, Martinus Nijhoff Publishers, 1987), 224–5.

[12] Human Rights Committee, General Comment No. 21: Article 10 (Humane treatment of persons deprived of their liberty), paras 3 and 5, in Compilation of General Comments and General Recommendations Adopted by Human Rights Treaty Bodies, vol. I, 202–3, UN Doc. HRI/GEN/1/Rev.9 (Vol. I) (2008).

[13] See Human Rights Committee, General Comment No. 29: Article 4: Derogations during a state of emergency, para. 13(a), in Compilation of General Comments and General Recommendations Adopted by Human Rights Treaty Bodies, vol. I, 238, UN Doc. HRI/GEN/1/Rev.9 (Vol. I) (2008) (con-

name of the rights of others, as in the well-known decision upholding a prohibition on arranging the activity of dwarf-tossing as a sporting event.[14] Like other defenders of that decision, I do not agree with the criticism that the HRC misconstrued the concept of human dignity in order to impose on the complaining party, M. Wackenheim, a requirement that he behave in a 'dignified' fashion; rather, I believe that the committee correctly found that the state had reasonably chosen to suppress a practice that treated a vulnerable minority as objects to be abused, and that undermined societal respect for the human dignity of the group in general.[15]

In the International Covenant on Economic, Social and Cultural Rights (ICESCR), human dignity resurfaces in a variant form in Article 13 on the right to education, but the other provisions enumerating economic, social, and cultural rights define them without express reference to dignity.[16] It could be said that Article 13 is written at one remove from a substantive norm of human dignity, because it provides that 'education shall be directed to the full development of the human personality *and the sense of its dignity*, and shall strengthen the respect for human rights and fundamental freedoms'. The General Comment of the Committee on Economic, Social and Cultural Rights regarding Article 13 also invokes this phrase as part of its justification for construing the treaty as prohibiting corporal punishment in schools.[17]

More specific human rights treaties at the global level add a few more operative provisions referring to human dignity or its perception. The Convention on the Rights of the Child and the Convention on the Rights of Persons with Disabilities include some norms that focus on enhancing their beneficiaries' sense of their own dignity,[18] as well as a few regarding respect for

---

struing the derogation clause of the ICCPR in relation to the rights of detainees, in light of the principle of human dignity).

[14] See Communication No. 854/1999, *Wackenheim v France*, UN Doc. CCPR/C/75/D/854/1999 (2002).

[15] With regard to the committee's action, it may also be worth explaining that the committee merely held that France had not violated M. Wackenheim's rights under the ICCPR by prohibiting the event; the committee did not hold that the ICCPR required France to prohibit the event.

[16] Even the right to just remuneration, framed in the Universal Declaration in terms of 'remuneration ensuring for [workers and their families] an existence worthy of human dignity', was rephrased in Article 7 of the ICESCR as ensuring a '*decent*' living for themselves and their families', at least in English and in French (*décente*)—the Spanish text employs the phrase '*condiciones de existencia dignas*'. ICESCR Article 7(a)(ii).

[17] Committee on Economic, Social and Cultural Rights, General Comment No. 13, The right to education (Article 13), para. 41 and note 18, in Compilation of General Comments and General Recommendations Adopted by Human Rights Treaty Bodies, vol. I, 71, 77, UN Doc. HRI/GEN/1/Rev.9 (Vol. I) (2008).

[18] Convention on the Rights of the Child (CRC), articles 39 ('in an environment which fosters the health, self-respect and dignity of the child'), 40 ('promotion of the child's sense of dignity and

their human dignity by others.[19] The Convention for Protection from Enforced Disappearance restricts the use of information collected for the purpose of finding a disappeared person, to ensure that it does not have 'the effect of infringing the human rights, fundamental freedoms or human dignity of an individual'.[20]

What role can theologically based interpretations of human dignity play in filling out the meaning of these global human rights?

The global human rights instruments, which are the fullest exercise in universality, aim at the protection of the human dignity of all persons under all governments in all societies.[21] They speak to Christians and also to Muslims and Buddhists and Hindus, as well as to adherents of indigenous belief systems of many kinds, and to non-believers. They speak to societies with majorities of various kinds, and they are administered by international bodies whose members have diverse religious and non-religious commitments.

This diversity of addressees makes extremely visible the need for generalizable arguments of human dignity which do not ground their details in a single religious tradition. The international human rights system cannot favour one religion as such over another. I mean to assert not merely that the system should not but that it cannot. This proposition is not offered as a claim about political liberalism or as a theory of the secular state. Rather, this proposition reflects the basic fact that all religions in the world, including Christianity, are minority religions at the global level.

As Christians, we claim our international human rights in countries with non-Christian majorities on the same basis as non-Christians claim their international human rights in countries with Christian majorities. The HRC, applying the religious freedom article of the ICCPR in its decisions on individual

---

worth...'); Convention on the Rights of Persons with Disabilities (CRPD), articles 16 ('in an environment that fosters the health, welfare, self-respect, dignity and autonomy of the person ...'), 24 (education directed to 'the full development of human potential and sense of dignity and self-worth ...').

[19] CRC articles 23 ('that a mentally or physically disabled child should enjoy a full and decent life, in conditions which ensure dignity, promote self-reliance and facilitate the child's active participation in the community'), 28 ('that school discipline is administered in a manner consistent with the child's human dignity ...'), 37 ('Every child deprived of liberty shall be treated with humanity and respect for the inherent dignity of the human person ...'); CRPD, articles 1 ('promote respect for their inherent dignity'), 3 ('Respect for inherent dignity ... of persons'), 8(1)(a) ('foster respect for the rights and dignity of persons with disabilities'), 25(d) ('raising awareness [among health care professionals] of the human rights, dignity, autonomy and needs of persons with disabilities').

[20] International Convention for the Protection of All Persons from Enforced Disappearance, article 19(2).

[21] Human rights are understood as universal with regard to rights-holders, applying to all human beings within the state's power, but global human rights treaties are also designed to be universal with regard to duty-holders, capable of being applied to all states, and not just to those of a particular region or culture.

communications and concluding observations on country reports, insists on the protection of those rights on the same basis.[22]

Emphasizing the need for generalizable arguments does not imply that structures of reasoning first developed within a specific religious tradition should not be employed within the international human rights system, even if they remain persuasive after they have been adapted to an external context. The reasons may be capable of translation across the discursive boundary, into terms suitable for secular legal argument, without losing all their persuasive force. In the process, they will lose some of their richness, and it may be felt that they lose their original point. Whether it is worth the sacrifice involved, to achieve the material benefit for human dignity, is not for a lawyer to say.

Regional human dignity?

Thus far, I have addressed the interpretation of human rights treaties at the international, that is, global, level. The question remains whether different considerations apply at the regional level, in particular in Europe, the location that may hold greatest interest for readers of this volume. Does human dignity have a distinct regional meaning in the European human rights system that differs from its meaning in the international human rights system? That possibility should not be dismissed: if the legal content of human dignity can vary from one national constitutional system to another, then the legal content of human dignity norms may also vary as between more inclusive and more circumscribed human rights systems. Each system must apply its legal conception of human dignity universally, but the systems may differ in their legal conceptions.

Interestingly enough, the European Convention on Human Rights does not contain any operative provision that refers expressly to human dignity, either in the original text or in the subsequent Protocols to date; the first preambular reference to human dignity occurred in Protocol No. 13, adopted in 2002.[23] Nonetheless, the concept of human dignity has long been employed in the interpretation of the Convention. The advent of the German-style guaran-

---

[22] See, for example, Communication no. 1249/2004, Sister Immaculate Joseph v Sri Lanka, UN Doc. CCPR/C/85/D/1249/2004 (Human Rights Committee 2005); Communication nos. 1853/2008 and 1854/2008, Atasoy and Sarkut v. Turkey, U.N. Doc. CCPR/C/104/D/1853–1854/2008 (Human Rights Committee 2012); Concluding Observations of the Human Rights Committee, Islamic Republic of Iran, paras 23–5, UN Doc. CCPR/C/IRN/CO/3 (2011).

[23] Protocol No. 13 to the Convention for the Protection of Human Rights and Fundamental Freedoms, concerning the abolition of the death penalty in all circumstances, ETS No. 187, preamble para. 2 ('Convinced that everyone's right to life is a basic value in a democratic society and that the abolition

tee of human dignity in the EU Charter of Fundamental Rights will probably increase the reliance on arguments from interpretations of human dignity in the judgments of the European Court of Human Rights.[24]

Might theological understandings of human dignity play a more direct role in the elaboration of human dignity within the European regional system? As a non-European, I approach that question with the hesitancy of an external observer. The earlier comment that all religions have minority status on the global scene holds less force in Europe, at least if Christianity is considered as one religion, and if degrees of secularism are not taken into account;[25] even then, the Council of Europe does include countries where Christians amount to a minority. Whether and how the European Court of Human Rights achieves legitimacy for its interpretations with regard to the populations of these countries, and with regard to non-Christian minorities in other states, has been a matter of controversy within the court itself.[26]

An indirect route to influencing European human rights law may also be utilized, passing through the legal construct of the 'European consensus'.[27] Neutrally stated norms addressing human dignity may be enacted at the national level, taking a positive legal form that omits a description of their religious origin or the reasons why they obtained political support. As these enactments accumulate in multiple European states, they may lead to the recognition of a positive European consensus that informs the interpretation of the European Convention. Alternatively, texts negotiated at Council of Europe level are sometimes invoked as evidence of a European consensus. This method of interpretation does not operate mechanically, and it may be combined with or outweighed by other methods of argumentation. Still, on occasion it may transform religious norms into legal facts that generate other positive norms at the regional level.

---

of the death penalty is essential for the protection of this right and for the full recognition of the inherent dignity of human beings ...').

[24] See, for example, *M.S.S. v Belgium and Greece*, App. No. 30696/09, 2011- ECtHR, paras 252–64 (Grand Chamber); see also Vereinigung Bildender Künstler v. Austria, App. No. 68354/01 (2007) (dissenting opinion of Judges Spielmann and Jebens).

[25] I recognize that different Christian denominations have different traditions and different approaches to doctrinal authority, and that these divergences (as well as others) may result in different accounts of human dignity. As a nonspecialist, I will not attempt to describe them.

[26] See, for example, *Leyla Şahin v Turkey*, 2005-XI ECtHR, App. No. 44774/98 (Grand Chamber) (dissenting opinion of Judge Tulkens); *Şerife Yiğit v Turkey*, 2010- ECtHR, App. No. 3976/05 (Grand Chamber) (concurring opinion of Judge Kovler).

[27] See, for example, Christos L. Rozakis, 'The European judge as comparatist', *Tulane Law Review* 80 (2005), 257, 270–4; Paolo G. Carozza, 'Uses and misuses of comparative law in international human rights: Some reflections on the jurisprudence of the European Court of Human Rights', *Notre Dame Law Review* 73 (1998), 1217.

The mere existence of a European consensus, however, is not a strong argument for the subsequent transfer of an interpretation of human dignity from the European regional system to the international human rights system. Regional human rights norms do sometimes become starting points for interpretations of human rights treaties at the international level. In suprapositive terms, a European norm and the reasons supporting it may inspire a similar development if the reasons prove persuasive to a global audience. In institutional terms, a European norm may indicate a practical and effective solution to a human rights problem, and the solution may be sufficiently adaptable to non-European states to lead to its employment at the global level as well. But it is the rationale attributable to the norm, rather than the consensus that produced it, that would justify its global influence. That rationale must involve generalizable arguments that can be addressed to a religiously diverse humanity.

39

Dignified Disciplinarity: Towards a Transdisciplinary Understanding of Human Dignity

Alexandra Kemmerer[1]

'INTERDISCIPLINARITY' SHOULD NOT BE treated as a shibboleth or a sign of one's advanced thinking. Neither is it an incantation that will magically solve our problems. Interdisciplinarity is simply a means. But to what end? Pragmatically put, towards the ends of greater insight and greater success at problem solving. More fundamentally, however, interdisciplinarity is a means towards the end of preserving or achieving the good life in a complex, global, rapidly innovating society. That is, interdisciplinarity constitutes an implicit philosophy of knowledge—not an epistemology but rather a general reflection on whether and to what degree knowledge can help us achieve the perennial goal of living the good life. It is the newest expression of a very old question.[2]

Introduction

The conference from which this book evolved was in its subtitle characterized as 'an Interdisciplinary Conference'.[3] Interdisciplinarity has now (finally) also in the legal field become a buzzword, attracting funders and scholars alike.

---

[1] This chapter is based on conference comments that have been revisited and rethought during a research visit at the University of Michigan Law School and the Bentley Historical Library of the University of Michigan. I am grateful to the Rechtskulturen Fellows 2012–13 at Humboldt University Law School in Berlin and to Lucy Chebout for a living experience of reflexive disciplinarity. Two conferences on 'The Concept of Human Dignity', convened at the Wissenschaftskolleg in Berlin, provided important inspiration.

[2] Robert Frodeman, 'Introduction', in Robert Frodeman et al. (eds), *The Oxford Handbook of Interdisciplinarity* (Oxford, Oxford University Press, 2010), xxix–xxxix, at xxxii.

[3] See my short reflection 'Dignity is here to stay: revisiting understandings of human dignity at Oxford', http://www.verfassungsblog.de/de/dignity-stay-understandings-human-dignity-oxford/ (1 December 2012).

Yet, conceptually and methodologically the term remains often obscure and ambiguous—not unlike the concept of dignity itself. That obscurity prompts a more profound inquiry into the disciplinary approaches and engagements with the term and concept of human dignity that we find assembled here. While most contributions are confined to the analytical and theoretical framework of a single discipline or a particular field or subdiscipline, the shared communicative space of the book (and of the preceding conference) allows for comparisons and confrontations reaching beyond the respective disciplinary boundaries. Hence, how do these different and diverse approaches relate? How do they, when placed side by side, inform a more pluralistic and nuanced understanding of dignity as a concept? What makes all the difference, and justifies the costs and labours of bringing together scholars from diverse backgrounds?

For full disclosure, my interest in such questions is prompted by my experience in the development of a research network and postdoctoral fellow programme that aims to enhance, from a genuinely legal perspective, a recontextualization of law within the field of the humanities, the cultural and social sciences.[4] The programme, entitled RECHT IM KONTEXT, brings together scholars of law from a variety of disciplinary and regional backgrounds.

Conceptually, it is intended to bring together and integrate various disciplinary, systematic, and regional approaches, to create a space of reflection and communication. Fundamental questions of law, the public/private divide, the pluriverse of courts and the dilemmata of legal pluralism, for example, shall be renegotiated and reconnected with doctrine and methodology.

For reasons that will be further explained in the following, the term and concept of human dignity not only prompts reflection from a variety of disciplinary perspectives—it requires such a plurality of approaches in order to be adequately understood and examined. And it makes an excellent substantive issue for an exercise in scholarship reaching beyond the borders of established disciplines, fields, and subdisciplines.

This chapter focuses chiefly on the possibilities (and problems) of such research beyond disciplinary boundaries. After outlining a taxonomy that aims to clarify the sometimes obscure concepts of multi-, inter-, and transdisciplinarity in part two, part three highlights some of the learning experiences that the Oxford exercise provided, and argues that it contributes to an experience of disciplined disciplinarity or reflexive disciplinarity. Part four develops the concept of such reflexive, disciplined and hence dignified disciplinarity further, and outlines a methodological response to the challenges of

---

[4] http://www.rechtimkontext.de; http://www.rechtskulturen.de.

new research questions and necessary innovations, but also to the pluralism behind these challenges.

Beyond disciplinarity

As already mentioned, our dignitarian exercise was initially labelled as interdisciplinary. Yet, were we truly interdisciplinary when we met for two days at Oxford's Rhodes House in June 2012? An answer to that question requires, in the first place, some terminological clarification. What are we talking about when we talk about disciplinarity, and about trans-, multi-, and interdisciplinarity? And intradisciplinarity? And should we not simply respect disciplinary boundaries and our limited abilities to apply a variety of methodologies?[5] Maybe some epistemic humility would be appropriate, anyway, amid all these buzzwords.

At the outset, let us talk about disciplinarity. The story does not need to be retold here in detail.[6] In the seventeenth and eighteenth centuries, the increasing activities of ordering and collecting all available knowledge, the delineating and systematic arranging of topics, and the ever more intense interaction between participants in scientific communities resulted in a dramatic growth of science that finally led to a differentiation of knowledge into disciplines. While throughout the eighteenth century, books, articles, and even experiments were still addressed to the general public, the more specialized the communication among scholars became, the more it was addressed to themselves. This closure of communicative communities, expressed through specialized journals and in the organization of scholarly associations, turned communication inward, and led to a self-referentiality of disciplinary communities: 'The disciplinary community became the relevant public.'[7]

But as knowledge became abundant, the quest for interdisciplinarity represented the resurgence of interest in a larger view of things.[8] The expansion of knowledge production since the Second World War led to demands for more accountability—and was, in itself, often a site of new forms of interdisciplinary 'knowledge production', as in the field of area studies heavily

---

[5] For some well-reasoned warnings, see Eric Hilgendorf, 'Bedingungen gelingender Interdisziplinarität—am Beispiel der Rechtswissenschaft', *Juristenzeitung* (2010), 913–22.

[6] For an illuminating account, see Peter Weingart, 'A short history of knowledge formations', in Robert Frodeman et al. (eds), *The Oxford Handbook of Interdisciplinarity* (Oxford, Oxford University Press, 2010), 3–14.

[7] Weingart, 'A short history of knowledge formations', 6.

[8] Weingart, 'A short history of knowledge formations', 12.

subsidized and thereby triggered by Cold War philanthrophic actors such as the Ford Foundation, with a so far largely unexplored impact on the shape and disciplinary development of post-war international law and the new field of the law of European integration.[9]

The number of interdisciplinary activities saw an enormous growth over the latter half of the twentieth century. And, as Julie Thompson Klein puts it in her excellent taxonomic chapter in the recently published *Oxford Handbook of Interdisciplinarity*, they gave rise 'to new taxonomies that registered the genus "Interdisciplinarity", propelled by new species of integration, collaboration, complexity, critique and problem solving'.[10]

Now, how are we to classify these new species? How do we identify and distinguish multidisciplinarity, interdisciplinarity, transdisciplinarity, and the various variations of these core classifications?

It speaks for itself that the first major interdisciplinary typology was published in 1972, created for an international conference held in France in 1970 and co-sponsored by the Organisation for Economic Co-operation and Development (OECD).[11] Here, also, the notion of transdisciplinarity comes into play. Transdisciplinarity was defined as a common system of axioms that transcend the narrow scope of disciplinary world views through an overarching synthesis, such as anthropology construed as the science of humans.[12] It describes a broad field of a synoptic discipline, a team-based holistic approach to health care or climate change, or, more recently—and maybe we will hear more on this shortly—to the regulation of financial markets.[13]

In Julie Thomson Klein's taxonomy, transdisciplinarity is characterized as 'transcending, transgressing, transforming', while multidisciplinarity is 'juxtaposing, sequencing, coordinating'. Interdisciplinarity, however, comes

---

[9] For example, the Ford Foundation's Foreign Area Fellowship Program started in 1950. For more on Cold War philanthropic actors see John Krige and Helke Rausch (eds), *American Foundations and the Coproduction of World Order in the Twentieth Century* (Göttingen, Vandenhoeck & Ruprecht, 2012).

[10] Julie Thompson Klein, 'A taxonomy of interdisciplinarity', in Robert Frodeman et al. (eds), *The Oxford Handbook of Interdisciplinarity* (Oxford, Oxford University Press, 2010), 15–30, at 15.

[11] L. Apostel, G. Berger, A. Briggs, and G. Michaud (eds), *Interdisciplinarity: Problems of Teaching and Research in Universities* (Paris, Organisation for Economic Co-operation and Development, 1972).

[12] Thompson Klein, 'A taxonomy of interdisciplinarity', 24.

[13] Matthias Bergmann and Engelbert Schramm, 'Grenzüberschreitung und Integration: Die formative Evaluation transdisziplinärer Forschung und ihrer Kriterien', Matthias Bergmann and Engelbert Schramm (eds), *Transdisziplinäre Forschung. Integrative Forschungsprozesse verstehen und bewerten* (Frankfurt am Main and New York, Campus, 2008), 149–175, at 159.

with many faces: it is 'integrating, interacting, linking, focusing, blending', and it may either be complementing or hybridizing.[14]

Multidisciplinarity, from the OECD's definition on, has always been seen as an approach that juxtaposes disciplines. 'Juxtaposition fosters wider knowledge, information and methods. Yet disciplines remain separate, disciplinary elements retain their original identity, and the existing structure of knowledge is not questioned.'[15] It is evident that many so-called interdisciplinary conferences, courses, and curricula are actually multidisciplinary assemblages of presentations, classes, and courses with a clear-cut disciplinary identity—but there is no question that there is a clear distinction to be made between multidisciplinary and interdisciplinary approaches.

Things are more difficult when it comes to a clear definition of transdisciplinarity versus interdisciplinarity. Given the broad concept of interdisciplinarity and its many faces (as described by Julie Thompson Klein), I follow here Jürgen Mittelstraß's definition of interdisciplinarity.[16] For Mittelstraß, interdisciplinarity and transdisciplinarity are not alternative concepts. Transdisciplinarity, as he uses it, can merely be seen as a 'sharper version' of interdisciplinarity.[17] Mittelstraß writes: 'Interdisciplinarity, if understood correctly, does not wander between subjects or disciplines, or hovers (as does the absolute spirit) above subjects and disciplines. [Interdisciplinarity] merely transcends substantial and disciplinary narrowings where they are obstacles to problem analysis and research development; it is, in truth, transdisciplinarity.'[18]

Mittelstraß, in his definition of transdisciplinarity as the 'better interdisciplinarity', rightly highlights the transcendental character of transdisciplinarity. Disciplines and disciplinary boundaries are not ignored and left behind but merely transcended. Their identity and methodology is respected, but opened up to an outside perspective that allows at the same time for internal

---

[14] Thompson Klein, 'A taxonomy of interdisciplinarity'; see also Helga Nowotny, *Es ist so. Es könnte auch anders sein* (Frankfurt am Main, Suhrkamp, 1999), 105–8; Erich Jantsch, *Technological Planning and Social Futures* (London, Wiley, 1972).
[15] Thompson Klein, 'A taxonomy of interdisciplinarity', 17.
[16] Jürgen Mittelstraß, *Wissen und Grenzen. Philosophische Studien* (Frankfurt am Main, Suhrkamp, 2001), 89–107.
[17] Hilgendorf, 'Bedingungen gelingender Interdisziplinarität—am Beispiel der Rechtswissenschaft', 914.
[18] Translation from the German by A.K., see Jürgen Mittelstraß, *Wissen und Grenzen*, 92ff: 'Interdisziplinarität im recht verstandenen Sinne geht nicht zwischen den Fächern oder den Disziplinen hin und her oder schwebt, dem absoluten Geist nahe, über den Fächern und den Disziplinen. Sie hebt vielmehr fachliche und disziplinäre Engführungen, wo diese der Problementwicklung und einem entsprechenden Forschungshandeln im Wege stehen, wieder auf; sie ist in Wahrheit Transdisziplinarität.'

reflexivity. Transdisciplinarity, in such an understanding, could also be defined as permeability.[19] As a form of bridge-building, it allows for a redefinition of disciplinary fields from their disciplinary inside and for a reflexive use of disciplinary traditions, without an entire restructuring and a weakening of disciplinary boundaries.

It is a tool to redefine disciplinary fields. It is transcendent but not transgressive.[20] Beyond the traditional, linear mode of knowledge production emerges a new, second mode of heterarchical organic knowledge production.

Helga Nowotny, the President of the European Research Council, a sociologist and lawyer by training, has described that new mode of knowledge production with the metaphor of the rhizome—not unfamiliar to legal networkers drawing from Deleuze and Guatteri.[21] The rhizome, as Nowotny stresses, highlights the structures of closely connected networks of knowledge that transport questions, challenges, and solutions in all directions.[22]

Given its transcendent, yet not transgressing, character, I do think that our collective undertaking here has been a truly transdisciplinary endeavour. In the following, I will explain why, and point to present shortcomings and future challenges.

Dignity as a placeholder and a reflexive tool

I think the participants of the Oxford conference set out on a process of transcending and transforming, while not attempting to integrate and blend their disciplinary backgrounds, experiences, and methodologies. I learned, however, that the juxtaposition of contributions from a variety of disciplines did not and does not automatically lead to a transformation of the respective positions and to a more reflexive take on speakers' own positions. At times, there were decidedly hermetic papers, without an outside, not opening up to any interaction with the transdisciplinary world beyond their own disciplinary background, and hence indeed impermeable. But the broad majority of contributions presented at Oxford and now assembled here did open up, al-

---

[19] For an inspiring use of the concept of permeability in legal scholarship, see Mattias Wendel, *Permeabilität im europäischen Verfassungsrecht. Verfassungsrechtliche Integrationsnormen auf Staats- und Unionsebene im Vergleich* (Tübingen, Mohr Siebeck, 2011).

[20] For a transgressive understanding of transdisciplinarity, see Thompson Klein, 'A taxonomy of interdisciplinarity', 25.

[21] Alexandra Kemmerer, 'The normative knot 2.0: Metaphorological explorations in the net of networks', *German Law Journal* 10 (2009), 339–461, at 451.

[22] Helga Nowotny, 'Vom Baum der Erkenntnis zum Rhizom. Zur Dynamisierung der Wissensproduktion', *in Es ist so. Es könnte auch anders sein* (Frankfurt am Main, Suhrkamp Verlag, 1999), 87–122.

lowing for connections and interrelations that led to respective illuminations and enrichments.

I learned that case studies are not only what lawyers would regard as such but also conceptual studies, or just reflections on fundamentals again—and that sometimes the distinction between case studies and fundamental theories is not as clear-cut as one might think at first.

I learned that dignity has many faces. The concept may seem empty and vague,[23] or overloaded with normative gravity,[24] but it is also a *Sehnsuchtswort*,[25] an expression of longing for a distant truth. It is a placeholder, opening a discursive space to negotiate our various and diverse understandings of fundamental values and normative groundings, as Christopher McCrudden has emphasized in his seminal 2008 EJIL article.[26] Conor Gearty points to that placeholder function in his reference to 'dignitarian pluralism', allowing to voice and transcend our various time-bound conceptions of human dignity.[27]

But throughout discussions and papers, the concept of dignity turned also out to be a tool to establish and improve reflexive disciplinarity, a more profound understanding of disciplinary boundaries and of the respective methodological and epistemic frames in which we are thinking and writing.

In particular, the historical studies presented by Samuel Moyn,[28] Rebecca Scott,[29] and Christoph Goos[30] unveil the potentialities of dignity as a tool to enhance disciplinary reflexivity and to overcome disciplinary boundaries. Moyn's historical examination of the influence of Catholic social thought on the concept of dignity as enshrined in post-war human rights codices easily connected with theological and philosophical reflections presented by David Hollenbach[31] and Clemens Sedmak,[32] but also with Christoph Goos's historical account of the origins of dignity in the (pre-)history of the German Basic Law. Goos's chapter, in turn, resonated with the presentations from other public lawyers highlighting, from different angles, the German dignitarian 'Sonderweg' (Dieter Grimm, Christoph Möllers, Reva Siegel). Rebecca Scott's historical research on human dignity in anti-slavery discourses opened

---

[23] Conor Gearty, Chapter 8, this volume.
[24] Christoph Möllers, Chapter 9, this volume.
[25] Bernhard Schlink, Chapter 37, this volume.
[26] Christopher McCrudden, 'Human dignity and judicial interpretation of human rights', *European Journal of International Law* 19 (2008), 655–724.
[27] Conor Gearty, Chapter 8, this volume.
[28] Samuel Moyn, Chapter 4, this volume.
[29] Rebecca Scott, Chapter 2, this volume.
[30] Christoph Goos, Chapter 3, this volume.
[31] David Hollenbach, Chapter 6, this volume.
[32] Clemens Sedmak, Chapter 33, this volume.

up new vistas on current jurisprudence of the European Court on Human Rights. And these are just some examples. Readers will discover many more explicit and implicit cross-references, and hopefully feel encouraged to make their own connections.

Fruitful transdisciplinarity does not require explicitly comparative approaches in order to reach beyond mere juxtapositions. Whenever the specificities of an individual approach are made explicit and the limits of particular disciplinary approaches are respected, this leads in itself to a more profound understanding of that perspective—from inside but also from outside. It does not change our disciplinary identities—but it helps us to transcend them.

Reflexive disciplinarity as dignified disciplinarity

Transcending disciplinary boundaries is a challenge and a temptation,[33] and it requires, as Samantha Besson and Alain Zysset have demonstrated for the field of Human Rights History and Human Rights Theory, engaging with Hans Joas's recent study on the genealogy of human rights,[34] 'mutual taming and learning'.[35] Yet it allows us in the first place to tame our own disciplinary passions and biases, and to learn about our own limitations. A reflexive disciplinarity is a disciplined disciplinarity,[36] and allows for a contextualization of our understanding of human dignity.

We can learn here from the centuries-old experiences of disciplines with strong intradisciplinary traditions,[37] such as theology and law. Here, we find a treasure of experiences with intradisciplinary interactions and connections. Often, they are only dealt with rather intuitively, taken for granted. And certainly the interrelations of subdisciplinary fields require (and merit) more attention and effort than is dedicated to them at present. Intradisciplinarity, as

---

[33] Alexandra Kemmerer, 'The turning aside. On international law and its history', in Russell A. Miller and Rebecca M. Bratspies (eds), *Progress in International Law* (Leiden and Boston, Martinus Nijhoff, 2008), 71–94, at 79.

[34] Hans Joas, *Die Sakralität der Person. Eine neue Genealogie der Menschenrechte* (Berlin, Suhrkamp Verlag, 2012).

[35] Samantha Besson and Alain Zysset, 'Human rights theory and human rights history: a tale of two odd bedfellows', *Ancilla Iuris* (special issue: International Law and Ethics) (anci. ch) (2012), 204–19, at 219.

[36] On 'reflexive legal scholarship' (reflexive Rechtswissenschaft), see Susanne Baer, *Rechtssoziologie* (Baden-Baden, Nomos, 2012), 43–9, 58–81; see also Hilgendorf, 'Bedingungen gelingender Interdisziplinarität', at 913–22.

[37] For an intradisciplinary approach to legal scholarship, see Oliver Lepsius, 'Themen einer Rechtswissenschaftstheorie', in Oliver Lepsius and Matthias Jestaedt (eds), *Rechtswissenschaftstheorie* (Tübingen, Mohr Siebeck, 2008), 1–49.

transdisciplinarity, needs to be cultivated and nourished. It is a precondition for any fruitful transdisciplinary endeavour.

The conference has shown—and so do the contributions—that we will not agree on a common concept of human dignity. And why should we?

Sam Moyn has voiced the assumption that the great times of dignity may be over. In Germany, as in other places, we experience a certain dignity fatigue. And yet the term prompts discourse and interaction, and allows for spaces and habits to cultivate pluralism: substantive pluralism, when it comes to diverse values and choices. And disciplinary pluralism. Both concepts are closely interconnected.

If we are 'to ensure that dignity does not turn into a black box to hide prejudice or to allow cultural stereotyping',[38] we may indeed dive into intellectual history, but also open up to other transdisciplinary transgressions and irritations.

For any inquiry into the concept of human dignity, what Peer Zumbansen has recently written about the concept of governance is true—a concept no less vague and contested than human dignity:

> The significance of the term lies in its horizontal and vertical irritation of disciplinary discourse as it forces us, on the one hand, to think about the connections between 'different' analytical and conceptual frameworks and, on the other, to take seriously the exhaustion of individual disciplines' vocabulary and established patterns of construction.[39]

What is true for governance is also true for human dignity: 'The key to understanding (...) then lies in accepting its interdisciplinary and transformative natures.'[40]

Reflexive disciplinarity opens not only spaces of translation and innovation,[41] it also allows for contestation[42] and confrontation,[43] and for a renegotiation of conceptual frames.

---

[38] Susanne Baer, 'Dignity, liberty, equality: a fundamental rights triangle', *University of Toronto Law Journal* 59 (2009), 417–68, at 420.
[39] Peer Zumbansen, 'Governance: an interdisciplinary perspective', in David Levi-Faur (ed.), *The Oxford Handbook of Governance* (Oxford, Oxford University Press, 2012), 83–96, at 84.
[40] Zumbansen, 'Governance: an interdisciplinary perspective', 84.
[41] Joachim Nettelbeck, 'How to organize spaces of translation, or, the politics of innovation', in: Helga Nowotny (ed.), *Cultures of Technology and the Quest for Innovation* (New York and Oxford, Berghahn Books, 2006), 191–5.
[42] Zumbansen, 'Governance: an interdisciplinary perspective', at 92.
[43] For 'confrontation beyond comparison', see the approach of the program 'Rechtskulturen: confrontations beyond comparison' (www.rechtskulturen.de).

We may quarrel about the proper habitat of the concept of dignity, and about the necessity of a particular starting point for our analysis.[44] Why should we not, as Michael Rosen suggests, move back and forth between the legal context and the moral analysis?[45]

While I have reservations about Jeremy Waldron's claim 'that dignity is more at home in the law (including the philosophical and normative part of jurisprudence) than in morality considered apart from the law',[46] I am intrigued by his insistence on the necessity of a particular starting point. It is our reflexive disciplinary situatedness that allows for a more nuanced understanding of a rich and diverse concept such as dignity.

Human dignity as a concept does not—and should not—break down boundaries between otherwise distinct discourses, disciplines, and theories of normative orders. But it should be used to call our established reference frameworks into question and to encourage reflexive disciplinarity. If we cultivate reflexivity, any reference to the concept of human dignity prompts the inclusion of competing disciplinary interpretations, allowing us to cope in a more dignified manner with the challenges of pluralism and of competing values and traditions.

---

[44] See Jeremy Waldron, *Dignity, Rank, and Rights*, with commentaries by Wai Chee Dimock, Don Herzog, and Michael Rosen, edited and introduced by Meir Dan-Cohen (Oxford, Oxford University Press, 2012).
[45] Michael Rosen, in Waldron, *Dignity, Rank, and Rights*, 79–98.
[46] Waldron, *Dignity, Rank, and Rights*, at 133.

Select Bibliography

Books and reports

Ackermann, Laurie, *Human Dignity: Lodestar for Equality in South Africa* (Cape Town, Juta and Co., 2012).
Agamben, Giorgio, *Homo Sacer: Sovereign Power and Bare Life*, trans. Daniel Heller-Roazen (Stanford, CA, Stanford University Press, 1998, first pub. 1995).
Agamben, Giorgio, *State of Exception* (Chicago, University of Chicago Press, 2005).
Agamben, Giorgio, *The Kingdom and the Glory: For a Theological Genealogy of Economy and Government*, trans. Lorenzo Chiesa with Matteo Mandarini (Stanford, CA, Stanford University Press, 2011, first pub. 2007).
Ahdar, Rex J. and Leigh, Ian, *Religious Freedom in the Liberal State* (Oxford, Oxford University Press, 2005).
Alexy, Robert, *Theorie der Grundrechte* (Frankfurt am Main, Suhrkamp, 1986).
Alves, André Azevedo and Moreira, José Manuel, *The Salamanca School* (New York and London, Continuum, 2010).
Apel, Karl-Otto, *Transformation der Philosophie* (Frankfurt am Main, Suhrkamp, 1973).
Apel, Karl-Otto, *Diskurs und Verantwortung* (Frankfurt am Main, Suhrkamp, 1988).
Apostel, L., Berger, G., Briggs, A., and Michaud, G. (eds), *Interdisciplinarity: Problems of Teaching and Research in Universities* (Paris, Organisation for Economic Co-operation and Development, 1972).
Aquinas, Thomas, *Scriptum super libros Sententiarium* [Aquinas on Creation] trans. Steven E. Baldner and William E. Carrol (Toronto, Pontifical Institute of Mediaeval Studies, 1997).
Aquinas, Thomas, *Summa Contra Gentiles*, trans. in Anton C. Pegis (ed.), *Basic Writings of Saint Thomas Aquinas*, vol. 2 (New York, Random House, 1945).
Aquinas, Thomas, *Summa theologica* (Chicago, W. Benton-Encyclopedia Britannica, 1980).
Araújo, Joaquim Nabuco de, *O Abolicionismo* (1883, reprinted São Paulo, Publifolha, 2000).
Arendt, Hannah, *The Origins of Totalitarianism* (New York, Harcourt, Brace, Jovanovich, 1973).
Aristides, 'The Apology of Aristides', in *Ante-Nicene Christian Fathers*, vol. 10, ed. Allan Menzies (Edinburgh: T&T Clark, 1897), 277.
Aristotle, *Eudemian Ethics* trans. Brad Inwood and Raphael Woolf (Cambridge, Cambridge University Press, 2013).
Aristotle, *Nicomachean Ethics* trans. Roger Crisp (Cambridge, Cambridge University Press, 2000).
Aristotle, *Politics* (Harmondsworth, Penguin Books, 1981).

Arnim, Johannes von, *Stoicorum veterum fragmenta* (Lipsiae, Teubneri, 1905).
Aschenberg, Reinhold, *Ent-Subjektivierung des Menschen. Lager und Shoah in philosophischer Reflexion* (Würzburg, Königshausen & Neumann, 2003).
Aubenas, F., *Le quai de Ouistreham* (Paris, Éditions de l'Olivier, 2010).
Augustine, *Concerning the City of God against the Pagans*, trans. Henry Bettenson (London and New York, Penguin Books, 2003).
Augustine, *Confessions*, ed. J. O'Donnell (Oxford, Oxford University Press, 1992).
Augustine, *De Trinitate* [On the Trinity], Gareth B. Matthew (ed.), trans. Stephen McKenna (Cambridge, Cambridge University Press, 2002).
Azevedo, Elciene, *O Direito dos Escravos: Lutas Jurídicas e Abolicionismo na Província de São Paulo* (Campinas, Editora da Unicamp, 2010).
Bacon, Francis, *Novum Organum*, Lisa Jardine and Michael Silverthorne (eds) [The New Organon] (Cambridge, Cambridge University Press, 2000).
Baer, Susanne, *Rechtssoziologie* (Baden-Baden, Nomos, 2012).
Bamforth, Nicholas C. and Richards, David A. J., *Patriarchal Religion, Sexuality, and Gender: A Critique of New Natural Law* (Cambridge, Cambridge University Press, 2008).
Banchoff, T., *Embryo Politics: Ethics and Policy in Atlantic Democracies* (Ithaca, NY, Cornell University Press, 2011).
Banerjee, A. and Duflo, E., *Poor economics* (New York, Perseus, 2011).
Barak, Aharon, *Proportionality: Constitutional Rights and Their Limitations* (Cambridge, Cambridge University Press, 2012).
Barry, Brian, *Culture and Equality* (Cambridge, Polity Press, 2001).
Barth, Karl, *Church Dogmatics* (Edinburgh, T. & T. Clark, 2009).
Barth, Karl, *Dogmatics in Outline* (New York, Harper & Row, 1959).
Bauman, Zigmunt, *Modernity and the Holocaust* (Ithaca, NY, Cornell University Press, 1989).
Bayle, Pierre, *Commentiare philosophique sur ces paroles de Jésus-Christ: 'Contrains-les d'entrer'* (Canterbury, Thomas Litwel, 1686; Indianapolis, Liberty Fund, 2005).
Beattie, Tina, *Theology After Postmodernity: Divining the Void* (Oxford and New York, Oxford University Press, 2013).
Becker, Ernst-Wolfgang, *Theodor Heuss. Bürger im Zeitalter der Extreme* (Stuttgart, Kohlhammer Verlag, 2011).
Beestermöller, Gerhard and Brunkhorst, Hauke (eds), *Rückkehr der Folter: Der Rechtsstaat im Zwielicht?* (München, Verlag C. H. Beck, 2006).
Beitz, Charles R., *Human Dignity and Human Rights* (Oxford University Press, 2011).
Beker, J. Christiaan, *Paul the Apostle: The Triumph of God in Life and Thought* (Philadelphia, PA, Fortress Press, 1980).
Bell, Caryn Cossé, *Revolution, Romanticism, and the Afro-Creole Protest Tradition in Louisiana, 1718–1868* (Baton Rouge, Louisiana State University Press, 1997).
Benedict XVI, Address to the Pontifical Academy of Social Sciences, 30 April 2010,
Benedict XVI, *Caritas in Veritate* (The Vatican, 29 June 2009).

Benedict XVI, 'Faith, Reason and the University: Memories and Reflections', address at meeting with representatives of science, University of Regensburg, 12 September 2006.
Benedict XVI, *Spe Salvi (Saved in Hope)*, 2007.
Benestad, J. Brian, *Church, State and Society, An Introduction to Catholic Social Doctrine* (Washington DC, University of America Press, 2010).
Bentham, J., *Anarchical Fallacies* (Edinburgh, William Tait, 1843).
Berlin, Isaiah, *Liberty. Incorporating Four Essays on Liberty* (Oxford, Oxford University Press, 2002).
Betancourt, I., *Even Silence Has an End. My Six Years of Captivity in the Colombian Jungle*, trans. A. Anderson (London, Hachette, 2010).
Beyleveld, Deryck and Brownsword, Roger, *Human Dignity in Bioethics and Biolaw* (Oxford, Oxford University Press, 2001).
Biko, Steve, *I Write What I Like* (Johannesburg, Picador Africa, 2004).
Blackburn, Simon, *The Oxford Dictionary of Philosophy* (Oxford, Oxford University Press, 2008).
Böckenförde, E-W., *Staat, Gesellschaft, Freiheit* (Frankfurt, Suhrkamp, 1976).
Bonhoeffer, Dietrich, *Ethics* (New York: Simon & Schuster, Inc., Touchstone edn, 1995; first pub. 1949).
Bossuyt, Marc J., *Guide to the 'Travaux Préparatoires' of the International Covenant on Civil and Political Rights* (Dordrecht, Martinus Nijhoff Publishers, 1987).
Boyle, James, *The Public Domain* (New Haven, Yale University Press, 2008).
Brague, Remi, *The Law of God: The Philosophical History of an Idea*, trans. Lydia G. Cochrane (Chicago, University of Chicago Press, 2007).
Braun, Harold E., *Juan de Mariana and Early Modern Spanish Political Thought* (Aldershot, Ashgate, 2007).
Bretherton, Luke, *Christianity and Contemporary Politics* (Chichester, Wiley-Blackwell, 2010).
Brownsword, Roger, *Rights, Regulation, and the Technological Revolution* (Oxford, Oxford University Press, 2008).
Brownsword, Roger and Goodwin, Morag, *Law and the Technologies of the Twenty-First Century* (Cambridge, Cambridge University Press, 2012).
Brueggemann, Walter, *Living Toward a Vision: Biblical Reflections on Shalom* 2nd ed. (New York, United Church Press, 1982).
Brueggemann, Walter, *A Social Reading of the Old Testament: Prophetic Approaches to Israel's Communal Life* (Minneapolis, MN, Fortress Press, 1994).
Brueggemann, Walter, *Praying the Psalms,* 2nd edn (Eugene, OR, Cascade Books, 2007).
Buchanan, Tom and Conway, Martin (eds), *Political Catholicism in Europe, 1918–1965* (Oxford, Oxford University Press, 1996).
Burgers, J. Herman and Danelius, Hans, *The United Nations Convention against Torture* (Dordrecht, Martinus Nijhoff, 1988).
Burleigh, Michael and Wippermann, Wolfgang, *The Racial State: Germany 1933–1945* (Cambridge, Cambridge University Press, 1991).

Camosy, Charles C., *Peter Singer and Christian Ethics: Beyond Polarization* (Cambridge, Cambridge University Press, 2012).

Caputo, John D., *More Radical Hermeneutics: On Not Knowing Who We Are* (Bloomington, IN, Indiana University Press, 2000).

Carey, P., *Augustine's Invention of the Inner Self* (Oxford, Oxford University Press, 2000).

Cassirer, E. P., Kristeller, Oskar, and Randal, J. H. (eds), *The Renaissance Philosophy of Man* (Chicago, University of Chicago Press, 1948).

Chamedes, Giuliana, 'Reinventing Christian Europe: Vatican diplomacy, transnational anticommunism, and the erosion of the Church-State divide' (PhD dissertation, Columbia University, 2012).

Chappel, James, 'Slaying the leviathan: Catholicism and the rebirth of European conservatism, 1920–1950' (PhD dissertation, Columbia University, 2012).

Chomsky, N., *New Horizons in the Study of Language and Mind* (Cambridge, Cambridge University Press, 2000).

Cicero, Marcus Tullius, *On Duties* E. M. Atkins (ed.), trans. M. T. Griffin (Cambridge, Cambridge University Press, 1991)

Citizens' Committee, *The Violation of a Constitutional Right, Published by Authority of the Citizens' Committee* (New Orleans, The Crusader Print, 1893).

Clark, Stephen R. L., *Biology and Christian Ethics* (Cambridge, Cambridge University Press, 2000).

Clarke, W. Norris, SJ, *Person and Being, The Aquinas Lecture 1993* (Milwaukee, WI, Marquette University Press, 1993).

Cohen, G. A., *Karl Marx's Theory of History: A Defence* (Oxford, Clarendon Press, 1979).

Coleman, Max (ed.), *A Crime Against Humanity: Analysing the Repression of the Apartheid State* (Human Rights Committee, Johannesburg, 1998).

Commission on Long-Term Care of Chimpanzees, Institute for Laboratory Animal Research, Commission on Life Sciences, and National Research Council, *Chimpanzees in Research: Strategies for Their Ethical Care, Management, and Use* (Washington DC, National Academies Press, 1997).

Committee on Economic, Social and Cultural Rights, General Comment No. 13, The right to education (article 13), in Compilation of General Comments and General Recommendations Adopted by Human Rights Treaty Bodies, vol. 1, 71, 77, UN Doc. HRI/GEN/1/Rev.9 (vol. I) (2008).

Community of Protestant Churches in Europe (CPCE), *Human Rights and Morality* (2009), http://www.leuenberg.net/sites/default/files/Human_rights_and_morality%20%28final%29.pdf.

Congregation for the Doctrine of the Faith, *Donum Veritatis: The Ecclesial Vocation of the Theologian* (The Vatican, 1990).

Curran, C., *The Moral Theology of John Paul II* (Washington DC, Georgetown University Press, 2005).

Currie, I. and de Waal, J., *The Bill of Rights Handbook*, 5th edn (Lansdowne, Juta and Co., 2005).

Daly, Erin, *Dignity Rights: Courts, Constitutions, and the Worth of the Human Person* (Philadelphia, PA, University of Pennsylvania Press, 2012).
Davids, M. Fakhry, *Internal Racism: A Psychoanalytic Approach to Race and Difference* (London, Palgrave Macmillan, 2011).
Dean, Richard, *The Value of Humanity in Kant's Moral Theory* (Oxford, Clarendon Press, 2006).
Dellavalle, S., *Dalla comunità particolare all'ordine universal*, vol. 1: *I paradigmi storici* (Napoli, ESI, 2011).
Derrida, Jacques, *Of Hospitality* (Stanford, CA, Stanford University Press, 2000).
Deutscher Bundestag and Bundesarchiv (eds), *Der Parlamentarische Rat 1948–1949. Akten und Protokolle, Band 5, Ausschuss für Grundsatzfragen,* bearbeitet von Eberhard Pikart und Wolfram Werner (Boppard am Rhein, Harald Boldt Verlag, 1993).
Deutscher Bundestag and Bundesarchiv (eds), *Der Parlamentarische Rat 1948–1949. Akten und Protokolle, Band 9, Plenum,* bearbeitet von Wolfram Werner (München, Harald Boldt Verlag, 1996).
Deutscher Bundestag and Bundesarchiv (eds), *Der Parlamentarische Rat 1948–1949. Akten und Protokolle, Band 14, Hauptausschuss,* bearbeitet von Michael F. Feldkamp (München, R. Oldenbourg Verlag, 2009).
Dillon, Robin, *Dignity, Character, and Self-Respect* (London, Routledge, 1995).
Dlamini, Jacob, *Native Nostalgia* (Auckland Park, South Africa, Jacana Media, 2009).
Donagan, Alan, *The Theory of Morality* (Chicago, University of Chicago Press, 1977).
Dostoyevsky, Fyodor, *The Brothers Karamazov*, trans. Constance Garnett (New York, Vintage Press, 1955).
Douglass, Frederick, *Narrative of the Life of Frederick Douglass, an American Slave* (New York, Penguin Press, 1845, 1982).
Douzinas, Costas, *Human Rights and Empire: The Political Philosophy of Cosmopolitanism* (Abingdon, Routledge-Cavendish, 2007).
Dreier, Horst (ed.), *Grundgesetz. Kommentar, Band I, Artikel 1–19* 1st edn (Tübingen, Mohr Siebeck, 1996); 2nd edn (Tübingen, Mohr Siebeck, 2004), 3rd edn (Tübingen, Mohr Siebeck, 2013).
Du Bois, W. E. B., *The Souls of Black Folk* (1903).
Dupré, Catherine, *Importing the Law in Post-Communist Transitions: The Hungarian Constitutional Court and the Right to Human Dignity* (Oxford, Hart Publishing, 2003).
Dworkin, Ronald, *Taking Rights Seriously* (Cambridge, MA, Harvard University Press, 1977).
Dworkin, Ronald, *A Matter of Principle* (Oxford, Clarendon Press, 1986).
Dworkin, Ronald, *Life's Dominion: An Argument about Abortion, Euthanasia, and Individual Freedom* (New York, Alfred A. Knopf, 1993).
Dworkin, Ronald, *Is Democracy Possible Here? Principles for a New Political Debate* (Princeton, NJ, Princeton University Press, 2006).
Dworkin, Ronald, *Justice for Hedgehogs* (Cambridge, MA, Harvard University Press, 2011).

Eisgruber, Christopher L. and Sager, Lawrence G., *Religious Freedom and the Constitution* (Cambridge, MA, Harvard University Press, 2007).
Elliott, Mark, *Color-Blind Justice: Albion Tourgée and the Quest for Racial Equality from the Civil War to* Plessy v Ferguson (New York, Oxford University Press, 2006).
Elliott, Mark and Smith, John David, *Undaunted Radical: The Selected Writings and Speeches of Albion W. Tourgée* (Baton Rouge, Louisiana State University Press, 2010).
Emery, Gilles, OP, *Trinity in Aquinas* (Michigan, Sapientia Press, 2003).
Eser, Albin and Koch, Hans-Georg, *Abortion and the Law: From International Comparison to Legal Policy* (The Hague, T.M.C. Asser Press, 2005).
Evans, Carolyn, *Freedom of Religion Under the European Convention of Human Rights* (Oxford, Oxford University Press, 2001).
Feldkamp, Michael F. (ed.), *Der Parlamentarische Rat 1948–1949. Die Entstehung des Grundgesetzes* (Göttingen, Vandenhoek & Ruprecht, 1998).
Ferree, Myra Marx, Gamson, William Anthony, Gerhards, Jürgen, and Rucht, Dieter, *Shaping Abortion Discourse: Democracy and the Public Sphere in Germany and the United States* (Cambridge, Cambridge University Press, 2002).
Feyerabend, P., *Against Method*, 4th edn (London, Verso, 2010).
Figueira, Ricardo Rezende, *Pisando Fora da Própria Sombra: A Escravidão por Dívida no Brasil Contemporâneo* (Rio de Janeiro, Civilização Brasileira, 2004).
Finnis, John, *Fundamentals of Ethics* (Washington DC, Georgetown University Press, 1983).
Finnis, John, *Aquinas: Moral, Political, and Legal Theory* (Oxford, Oxford University Press, 1998).
Finnis, John, *Natural Law and Natural Rights* (Oxford, Clarendon Press, 1980; 2nd edn Oxford, Oxford University Press, 2011).
Fitzgerald, John J., *The Person and the Common Good* (South Bend, IN, University of Notre Dame, 1985).
Flynn, Gabriel and Murray, Paul D. (eds), *Ressourcement, A Movement for Renewal in Twentieth Century Catholic Theology* (Oxford, Oxford University Press, 2012).
Foster, Charles, *Human Dignity in Bioethics and Law* (Oxford and Portland, OR, Hart Publishing, 2011)
Fukuyama, Francis, *Our Posthuman Future* (London, Profile Books, 2002).
Gadamer, H. G., *Au commencement de la philosophie, pour une lecture des Présocratiques* (Paris, Seuil, 2001).
Galilei, G., *Lettere* (Torino, Einaudi, 1978).
Gearty, C. A., *Principles of Human Rights Adjudication* (Oxford, Oxford University Press, 2004).
Gearty, Conor and Mantouvalou, V., *Debating Social Rights* (Oxford, Hart Publishing, 2011).
Gevisser, Mark and Cameron, Edwin, *Defiant Desire: Gay and Lesbian Lives in South Africa* (New York, Routledge, 1995).
Gewirth, Alan, *Reason and Morality* (Chicago, University of Chicago Press, 1978).

Girard, René, *Things Hidden Since the Foundation of the World* (London and New York, Continuum, 2003, 1st edn 1978).
Girgis, Sherif, Anderson, Ryan T., and George, Robert P., *What is Marriage?: Man and Woman: A Defense* (New York, Encounter Books, 2012).
Giussani, Luigi, *The Religious Sense* (Montreal, McGill-Queen's University Press, 1997).
Glendon, Mary Ann, *A World Made New: Eleanor Roosevelt and the Universal Declaration of Human Rights* (New York, Random House, 2002).
Glover, Jonathan, *Humanity: A Moral History of the Twentieth Century* (Yale University Press, 2001)
Goerlich, Helmut (ed.), *Staatliche Folter, Heiligt der Zweck die Mittel?* (Paderborn, mentis Verlag, 2007).
Goffman, Erving, *Stigma: Notes on the Management of Spoiled Identity* (New York, Simon & Schuster, 1986).
Goldsworthy, Jeffrey (ed.), *Interpreting Constitutions: A Comparative Study* (Oxford University Press, 2006).
Goos, Christoph, *Innere Freiheit: Eine Rekonstruktion des grundgesetzlichen Würdebegriffs* (Göttingen, Vandenhoeck & Ruprecht, 2011).
Goreau, Laurraine, *Just Mahalia, Baby* (Waco, TX, Word Books, 1975).
Gottlieb, Stephen, *Public Values in Constitutional Law* (Ann Arbor, University of Michigan Press, 1993).
Graf, Friedrich-Wilhelm, *Missbrauchte Götter* (München, C. H. Beck, 2009).
Gray, John, *Black Mass: Apocalyptic Religion and the Death of Utopia* (London and New York, Penguin Books, 2008).
Gray, John, *Heresies: Against Progress and Other Illusions* (Granta, 2004).
Greenberg, Irving, *For the Sake of Heaven and Earth: The New Encounter Between Judaism and Christianity* (Philadelphia, PA, Jewish Publication Society, 2004).
Greenhouse, Linda and Siegel, Reva B. (eds), *Before* Roe v Wade*: Voices that Shaped the Abortion Debate Before the Supreme Court's Ruling* (Kaplan Publishing, 2010).
Griffin, James, *On Human Rights* (Oxford, Oxford University Press, 2008).
Grimm, Dieter, *Die Würde des Menschen ist unantastbar* (Stiftung Bundespräsident-Theodor-Heuss-Haus, 2009).
Gröschner, Rolf et al. (eds), *Des Menschen Würde—entdeckt und erfunden im Humanismus der italienischen Renaissance* (Tübingen, Mohr Siebeck, 2008).
Grotius, H., *De jure belli ac pacis* (Tübingen, Mohr, 1950).
Günther, Frieder, *Denken vom Staat her: Die bundesdeutsche Staatsrechtslehre zwischen Dezision und Integration 1949–1970* (Munich, Oldenbourg, 2004).
Häberle, Peter (ed.), *Entstehungsgeschichte der Artikel des Grundgesetzes. Neuausgabe des Jahrbuch des öffentlichen Rechts der Gegenwart Band 1*, 2nd edn (Tübingen, Mohr Siebeck, 2010).
Habermas, Jürgen, *Theorie des kommunikativen Handelns* (Frankfurt am Main, Suhrkamp, 1981).
Habermas, Jürgen, *Moralbewußtsein und kommunikatives Handeln* (Frankfurt am Main, Suhrkamp, 1983).

Habermas, Jürgen, *Vorstudien und Ergänzungen zur Theorie des kommunikativen Handelns* (Frankfurt am Main, Suhrkamp, 1984).
Habermas, Jürgen, *The Theory of Communicative Action*, trans. Thomas McCarthy, vols 1–2 (Boston, MA, Beacon, 1984 and 1989).
Habermas, Jürgen, *Nachmetaphysisches Denken* (Frankfurt am Main, Suhrkamp, 1988).
Habermas, Jürgen, *Erläuterungen zur Diskursethik* (Frankfurt am Main, Suhrkamp, 1991).
Habermas, Jürgen, *Wahrheit und Rechtfertigung* (Frankfurt am Main, Suhrkamp, 2004).
Habermas, Jürgen, *Die Zukunft der menschlichen Natur* (Frankfurt am Main, Suhrkamp, 2005).
Habermas, Jürgen, *The Crisis of the European Union: A Response*, trans. Ciaran Cronin (Cambridge, Polity Press, 2012).
Habermas, Jürgen, and Ratzinger, Joseph, *The Dialectics of Secularization: On Reason and Religion*, trans. Brian McNeil (San Francisco, CA, Ignatius Press, 2006).
Harris, J., *Clones, Genes, and Immortality* (Oxford, Oxford University Press, 1998).
Hayden, Patrick (ed.), *The Philosophy of Human Rights: Readings in Context* (St Paul, MN, Paragon House, 2001).
Haym, Andrée, *The Isenheim Altarpiece: God's Medicine and the Painter's Vision* (Princeton, NJ, Princeton University Press, 1989).
Hazareesingh, Sudhir, *Intellectual Founders of the Republic: Five Studies in Nineteenth-Century French Republican Political Thought* (Oxford, Oxford University Press, 2001).
Hehl, Christoph von, *Adolf Süsterhenn (1905–1974): Verfassungsvater, Weltanschauungspolitiker, Föderalist* (Düsseldorf, Droste Verlag, 2012).
Hell, Daniel, *Soul Hunger: The Feeling Human Being and the Life Sciences* (Einsiedeln, Daimon Verlag, 2010).
Henkin, Louis, *Human Dignity and Human Rights* (Jerusalem, Israel Academy of Sciences and Humanities, 1995).
Herzog, Dagmar, *Sexuality in Europe: A Twentieth-Century History* (Cambridge, Cambridge University Press, 2011).
Heun, Werner, *The Constitution of Germany. A Contextual Analysis* (Oxford, Hart Publishing, 2011).
Hill, Thomas E., Jr, *Dignity and Practical Reason in Kant's Moral Theory* (Ithaca, NY, Cornell University Press, 1992).
Hill, Thomas E., Jr, *Respect, Pluralism, and Justice: Kantian Perspectives* (Oxford, Oxford University Press, 2000).
Hill, Thomas E., Jr, *Virtue, Rules, and Justice: Kantian Aspirations* (Oxford, Oxford University Press, 2012).
Hirschl, Ran, *Constitutional Theocracy* (Cambridge, MA, Harvard University Press, 2010).
Hirschl, Ran, *Towards Juristocracy: The Origins and Consequences of the New Juristocracy* (Cambridge, MA, Harvard University Press, 2004).

Hirst, Paul Q. (ed.), *The Pluralist Theory of the State: Selected Writings of G. D. H. Cole, J. N. Figgis, and H. J. Laski* (London, Routledge, 1989).
Hittinger, Russell, *A Critique of the New Natural Law Theory* (South Bend, IN, University of Notre Dame Press, 1987).
Hobbes, T., *De Cive* (1652) Richard Tuck and Michael Silverthorne (eds) [On the Citizen] (Cambridge, Cambridge University Press, 1998).
Hogan, Gerard (ed.), *The Origins of the Irish Constitution 1928–1941* (Dublin, Royal Irish Academy, 2012).
Hollandsworth, James G., Jr, *The Louisiana Native Guards: The Black Military Experience during the Civil War* (Baton Rouge, Louisiana State University Press, 1995).
Hollenbach, David, *Claims in Conflict: Retrieving and Renewing the Catholic Human Rights Tradition* (New York, Paulist Press, 1979).
Höpfl, Harro, *Jesuit Political Thought, The Society of Jesus and the State 1540–1630* (Cambridge, Cambridge University Press, 2004).
Horrell, Muriel, *Laws Affecting Race Relations in South Africa (To the end of 1976)* (Johannesburg, South African Institute of Race Relations, 1978).
Horton, John and Mendus, Susan (eds), *John Locke, A Letter Concerning Toleration in focus* (London, Routledge, 1991).
Hufen, Friedhelm, *Staatsrecht II. Grundrechte*, 3rd edn (München, Verlag C. H. Beck, 2011).
Human Rights Committee, General Comment No. 21: Article 10 (Humane treatment of persons deprived of their liberty), paras 3 and 5, in Compilation of General Comments and General Recommendations Adopted by Human Rights Treaty Bodies, vol. I, 202–3, UN Doc. HRI/GEN/1/Rev.9 (vol. 1) (2008).
Human Rights Committee, General Comment No. 29: Article 4: Derogations during a state of emergency, para. 13(a), in Compilation of General Comments and General Recommendations Adopted by Human Rights Treaty Bodies, vol. 1, 238, UN Doc. HRI/GEN/1/Rev.9 (vol. I) (2008).
Hüther, Gerald and Krens, Inge, *Das Geheimnis der ersten neun Monate. Unsere frühesten Prägungen* (Düsseldorf, Patmos Verlag, 2005).
Huxley, Aldous, *Brave New World* (London, Chatto & Windus, 1932).
Ignatieff, Michael, *Human Rights as Politics and Idolatry* (Princeton, NJ, Princeton University Press, 2001).
International Theological Commission, *Communion and Stewardship: Human Persons Created in the Image of God* (2004), http://www.vatican.va/roman_curia/congregations/cfaith/cti_documents/rc_con_cfaith_doc_20040723_communion-stewardship_en.html.
International Theological Commission, *The Dignity and Rights of the Human Person* (The Vatican, 1983).
Jantsch, Erich, *Technological Planning and Social Futures* (London, Wiley, 1972).
Janzen, Waldemar, *Old Testament Ethics* (Louisville, KY, Westminster John Knox, 1994).
Joas, Hans, *Die Sakralität der Person. Eine neue Genealogie der Menschenrechte* (Berlin, Suhrkamp, 2012).

Joas, Hans, *The Sacredness of the Person: A New Genealogy of Human Rights* (Washington DC, Georgetown University Press, 2013).

John XXIII, 'Pacem in Terris', in David J. O'Brien and Thomas A. Shannon (eds), *Catholic Social Thought: The Documentary Heritage*, expanded edn (Maryknoll, NY, Orbis Books, 2010).

John Paul II, *Familiaris Consortio* (Vatican City, Libreria Editrice Vaticana, 1981).

John Paul II, *Redemptoris Missio: On the Permanent Validity of the Church's Missionary Mandate* (The Vatican, 7 December 1990).

John Paul II, *Centesimus Annus* (Vatican City, Libreria Editrice Vaticana, 1991).

John Paul II, *Evangelium Vitae* (London, CTS, 1995; Vatican City, Libreria Editrice Vaticana, 1995).

John Paul II, *The Gospel of Life* (New York, Times Books, 1995).

John Paul II, *Theology of the Body* (Boston, MA, Pauline Books, 1997).

John Paul II, *Man and Woman He Created Them: A Theology of the Body*, trans. Dr Michael Waldstein (Reading, Pauline Books and Media, 2006).

Joint Committee on Human Rights, *A Bill of Rights for the UK?* (Twenty-ninth Report of Session 2007–8, HL 165, HC 150).

Jüngel, Eberhard, *Zur Freiheit eines Christenmenschen. Eine Erinnerung an Luthers Schrift* (München, Chr. Kaiser Verlag, 1991).

Kaiser, Walter J., Jr, *Toward Old Testament Ethics* (Grand Rapids, MI, Zondervan, 1983).

Kant, Immanuel, *Fundamental Principles of the Metaphysic of Morals*, trans. Thomas Kingsmill Abbott (1785).

Kant, Immanuel, *Grundlegung zur Metaphysik der Sitten* (Berlin, Akademie Ausgabe, vol. 4, 1903).

Kant, Immanuel, *Die Metaphysik der Sitten* (Berlin, Akademie Ausgabe, vol. 6, 1907).

Kant, Immanuel, *Critique of Pure Reason* [1781 and 1787], trans. Norman Kemp Smith (New York, St Martin's Press, 1965).

Kant, Immanuel, *Grounding for the Metaphysics of Morals*, trans. James W. Ellington, 3rd edn. (Indianapolis, IN, Hackett, 1993).

Kant, Immanuel, *The Metaphysics of Morals*, trans. Mary Gregor (Cambridge, Cambridge University Press, 1996).

Kant, Immanuel, 'Groundwork of the metaphysics of morals', in *The Cambridge Edition of the Works of Immanuel Kant* (Cambridge, Cambridge University Press, 1996).

Kant, Immanuel, *Critique of Practical Reason*, trans. Mary Gregor (Cambridge, Cambridge University Press, 1997).

Kant, Immanuel, *Lectures on Ethics,* ed. Peter Heath and J. B. Schneewind, trans. Peter Heath (Cambridge, Cambridge University Press, 1997).

Kant, Immanuel, *Vorlesungen über Anthropologie. Die Vorlesung des Wintersemesters 1781/82* (Berlin, Akademie Ausgabe, vol. 25, 1997).

Kant, Immanuel, *Groundwork for the Metaphysics of Morals*, ed. Thomas E. Hill, Jr and Arnulf Zweig (Oxford, Oxford University Press, 2002).

Kant, Immanuel, *Groundwork of the Metaphysics of Morals* (Cambridge, Cambridge University Press, 2012).

Kant, Immanuel, *Toward Perpetual Peace: A Philosophical Project*, in Kant, *Practical Philosophy*, 322–3 (8:349–51).
Karis, Thomas and Gerhart, Gail (eds), *From Protest to Challenge: A Documentary History of African Politics in South Africa—Challenge and Violence (1953–1882)* (Stanford, Hoover Institute Press, 1977).
Kass, Leon, *Life, Liberty and the Defense of Dignity: The Challenge of Bioethics* (San Francisco, CA, Encounter Books, 2002).
Kateb, George, *Human Dignity* (Cambridge, MA, Belknap Press of Harvard University Press, 2012).
Kelly, John M., *Fundamental Rights in the Irish Law and Constitution* (Dublin, Allen Figgis, 1961).
Keogh, Dermot, *The Vatican, the Bishops, and Irish Politics 1919–1939* (Cambridge, Cambridge University Press, 1986).
Keogh, Dermot, *Ireland and Europe, 1918–1948* (Dublin, Gill and Macmillan, 1988).
Keogh, Dermot and McCarthy, Andrew, *The Making of the Irish Constitution 1937: Bunreacht na hÉireann* (Cork, Mercier Press, 1997).
Kohn, Leo, *The Constitution of the Irish Free State* (London, Allen and Unwin, 1934).
Korsgaard, Christine, *Creating the Kingdom of Ends* (Cambridge, Cambridge University Press, 1996).
Krige, John and Rausch, Helke (eds), *American Foundations and the Coproduction of World Order in the Twentieth Century* (Göttingen, Vandenhoeck & Ruprecht, 2012).
Krygier, M., *Civil Passions. Selected Writings* (Melbourne, Schwartz Publishing, 2005).
Kuhn, T. S., *The Structure of Scientific Revolutions*, 2nd edn (Chicago, The University of Chicago Press, 1970).
Kuhse, Helga and Singer, Peter, *Should the Baby Live? The Problem of Handicapped Infants* (Oxford, Oxford University Press, 1985).
Küng, H. (ed.), *Dokumentation zum Weltethos* (München, Piper, 2002).
Küng, Hans, *Projekt Weltethos* (München, Piper, 1990).
LaCugna, Catherine Mowry, *God for Us. The Trinity and Christian Life* (New York, HarperCollins, 1991, pbk 1993).
Lange, Erhard H. M., *Die Würde des Menschen ist unantastbar. Der Parlamentarische Rat und das Grundgesetz* (Heidelberg, Decker & Müller, 1993).
Larsen, L. Burgogne (ed.), *La dignité saisie par les juges en Europe* (Bruxelles, Bruylant, 2010).
Law Commission of England and Wales, *A New Homicide Act for England and Wales? A Consultation Paper* (Consultation Paper no. 177, December 2005).
Lebacqz, Karen, *Six Theories of Justice: Perspectives from Philosophical and Theological Ethics* (Minneapolis, MN, Augsburg Fortress, 1987).
Lebech, Mette, *On the Problem of Human Dignity: A Hermeneutical and Phenomenological Investigation* (Würzburg, Königshausen & Neumann, 2009).
Lee, Philip J., *Against the Protestant Gnostics* (New York, Oxford University Press, 1993).
Leo XIII, *Quod Apostolici Muneris* (1878).

Leo XIII, *Aeterni Patris* (1879).
Leo XIII, *Graves Communi* (1901).
Lessig, Lawrence, *Code and Other Laws of Cyberspace* (New York, Basic Books, 1999).
Levi, Primo, *If This Is A Man* and *The Truce*, trans. Stuart Woolf (Boston, MA, Little, Brown, 1991).
Lilje, Hanns, *Im finstern Tal* (Nürnberg, Laetare Verlag, 1947).
Locke, John, *A Letter Concerning Toleration* (1689), in John Locke, *Works*, vol. 5 (London, 1824).
Long, Anthony A., *Epictetus. A Stoic and Socratic Guide to Life* (Oxford, Clarendon Press, 2004).
Lorenzini, Daniele, *Jacques Maritain e i diritte umani: Fra totalitarismo, antisemitismo, e democrazia (1936–1951)* (Brescia, Morcelliana, 2012).
Lubac, Henri de, *Catholisime* (Paris, Cerf, 1937).
Luhmann, N., *Grundrechte als Institution* (Berlin, Duncker & Humblot, 1965).
Luhmann, N., *Die Gesellschaft der Gesellschaft* (Frankfurt am Main, Suhrkamp, 1997).
Luijpen, William, *Phenomenology of Natural Law* (Pittsburgh, PA, Duquesne University Press, 1967).
Luther, Martin, *Vorlesungen über 1. Mose von 1535–45*, in M. Luthers Werke, Kritische Gesammtausgabe, 42. Band (Weimar, 1911).
Lyotard, J.-F., *Le Différend* (Paris, Editions de Minuit, 1983).
McGarry, Fearghal, *Irish Politics and the Spanish Civil War* (Cork, Cork University Press, 1999).
MacIntyre, Alasdair, *Dependent Rational Animals: Why Human Beings Need the Virtues* (Chicago, Open Court, 2001).
Macklem, Timothy, *Independence of Mind* (Oxford, Oxford University Press, 2008).
Maclure, Jocelyn and Taylor, Charles, *Secularism and Freedom of Conscience* (Cambridge, MA, Harvard University Press, 2011).
McMurtry, John, *The Structure of Marx's World-View* (Princeton, NJ, Princeton University Press, 1978).
McNamara, Patrick, *A Catholic Cold War: Edmund A. Walsh, S.J., and the Politics of American Anticommunism* (New York, Fordham University Press, 2005).
Mahlmann, Matthias, *Elemente einer ethischen Grundrechtstheorie* (Baden-Baden, Nomos, 2008).
Mahlmann, Matthias, *Rationalismus in der praktischen Theorie*, 2nd ed. (Baden-Baden, Nomos, 2009).
Mahlmann, Matthias, *Rechtsphilosophie und Rechtstheorie* (Baden-Baden, Nomos, 2012).
Mahoney, Jack, *The Challenge of Human Rights* (Oxford, Blackwell Publishing, 2007).
Mahoney, Jack, *Christianity in Evolution: An Exploration* (Washington DC, Georgetown University Press, 2011).
Mamdani, Mahmood, *Saviors and Survivors: Darfur, Politics, and the War on Terror* (New York, Pantheon Books, 2009).

Manetti, G., *De dignitate et excellentia hominis* (Hamburg, Meiner, 1990).
Margalit, Avishai, *The Decent Society* (Cambridge, Mass., Harvard University Press, 1996).
Maritain, Jacques, *Challenges and Renewals* (South Bend, IN, University of Notre Dame Press, 1966).
Maritain, Jacques, *Humanisme Intégral* (Paris, Fernand Aubier Ed., 1936).
Maritain, Jacques, *Le Personne et le Bien Commune* (Paris, 1947)
Maritain, Jacques, *The Person and the Common Good* (London, Geoffrey Bles, 1948).
Maritain, Jacques, *Man and State* (Chicago, University of Chicago Press, 1951; Washington DC, Catholic University of America Press, 1998).
Marshall, T.H., *Citizenship and Social Class and Other Essays* (Cambridge, Cambridge University Press, 1950).
Martin, Civilla D. and Gabriel, Charles H., *His Eye is on the Sparrow* (New York, Hope Publishing, 1905).
Mazower, M., *No Enchanted Palace* (Princeton, NJ, Princeton University Press, 2009).
Medley, Keith Weldon, *We as Freemen: Plessy v Ferguson* (Gretna, LA, Pelican Publishing, 2003).
Meier, C., *Von Athen bis Auschwitz* (Frankfurt am Main, Fischer, 2002).
Merkl, Peter H., *German Unification in the European Context* (University Park, PA, Penn State University Press, 1993).
Merseburger, Peter, *Theodor Heuss. Der Bürger als Präsident. Biographie* (München, Deutsche Verlags-Anstalt, 2012).
Merten, Detlef and Papier, Hans- Jürgen (eds), *Handbuch der Grundrechte*, vol. VI/1 (Zürich, Dike, 2010).
Metz, Johann Baptist, *Faith in History and Society: Toward a Practical Fundamental Theology*, trans. David Smith (New York, Seabury, 1980).
Meyer, Michael J. and Parent, William A. (eds), *The Constitution of Rights: Human Dignity and American Values* (Ithaca, NY, Cornell University Press, 1992).
Mikhail, J., *Elements of Moral Cognition* (New York, Cambridge University Press, 2011).
Miller, D., *The Comfort of Things* (Cambridge, Polity Press, 2008).
Miller, William Lee, *Arguing about Slavery: John Quincy Adams and the Great Battle in the United States Congress* (New York, Random House, 1995).
Ministério do Trabalho e Emprego, *Manual de combate ao trabalho em condições análogas às de escravo* (Brasilia, Ministério do Trabalho e Emprego, 2012).
Misner, Paul, *Social Catholicism in Europe* (New York, Crossroads Publishing Company, 1991).
Mittelstraß, Jürgen, *Wissen und Grenzen. Philosophische Studien* (Suhrkamp, Frankfurt am Main, 2001).
Möllers, Christoph, *The Three Branches: A Comparative Concept of Separated Powers* (Oxford, Oxford University Press, 2013).
Morris, Simon Conway, *Life's Solution* (Cambridge, Cambridge University Press, 2003).

Morsink, Johannes, *The Universal Declaration of Human Rights: Origins, Drafting & Intent* (Philadelphia, PA, University of Philadephia Press, 1999).
Morton, Stephen and Bygrave, Stephen (eds), *Foucault in an Age of Terror: Essays on Biopolitics and the Defence of Society* (Basingstoke and New York, Palgrave Macmillan, 2008).
Mouroux, Jean, *Sens chrétien de l'homme* (Paris, Aubier, 1945).
Mouw, Richard J., *The God Who Commands* (South Bend, IN, University of Notre Dame Press, 1991).
Moyn, Samuel, *The Last Utopia: Human Rights in History* (Cambridge, MA, Belknap Press of Harvard University Press, 2010).
Muel-Dreyfus, Francine, *Vichy and the Eternal Feminine: A Contribution to the Political Sociology of Gender*, trans. Kathleen A. Johnson (Durham, NC, Duke University Press, 2001).
Münch, Ingo von and Kunig, Philip (eds), *Grundgesetz-Kommentar*, 6th edn (München, Beck, 2012).
Murray, John Courtney, *The Problem of Religious Freedom* (Westminster, MD, Newman Press, 1965).
National Institutes of Health, *Report of the Human Embryo Research Panel*, vol. 1 (Bethesda MD, National Institutes of Health, 1994).
National Research Council and Institute of Medicine, *Guidelines for Human Embryonic Stem Cell Research* (Washington DC, National Academies Press, 2005).
Nijsten, Machteld, *Abortion and Constitutional Law: A Comparative European-American Study* (Florence, European University Institute, 1990).
Nisbet, Robert, *The Quest for Community* (Oxford, Oxford University Press, 1953).
Noonan, John T., Jr, *A Church that Can and Cannot Change: The Development of Catholic Moral Teaching* (South Bend, IN, University of Notre Dame Press, 2005).
Nowotny, Helga, *Es ist so: Es könnte auch anders sein* (Frankfurt am Main, Suhrkamp Verlag, 1999).
Nuffield Council on Bioethics, *Emerging Biotechnologies: Technology, Choice and the Public Good* (London, Nuffield Council on Bioethics, December 2012).
Nussbaum, Martha, *Liberty of Conscience: In Defense of America's Tradition of Religious Equality* (New York, Basic Books, 2008).
Nussbaum, Martha, *Women and Human Development: The Capabilities Approach* (Cambridge, Cambridge University Press, 2000).
Nystrom, Justin, *New Orleans after the Civil War: Race, Politics, and a New Birth of Freedom* (Baltimore, Johns Hopkins University Press, 2010).
O'Donovan, Oliver, *Common Objects of Love: Moral Reflection and the Shaping of Community* (Grand Rapids, MI, William B. Eerdmans, 2002).
O'Donovan, Oliver, *The Desire of the Nations: Rediscovering the Roots of Political Theology* (Cambridge, Cambridge University Press, 1996).
O'Neill, Onora, *Constructions of Reason* (Cambridge, Cambridge University Press, 1989).

Oakeshott, Michael, *Rationalism and Politics* (Indianapolis, Liberty Fund, rev. edn, 1991).
Oakeshott, Michael, *On Human Conduct* (Oxford, Clarendon Press, 1975).
Official Journal of the Proceedings of the Convention for Framing a Constitution for the State of Louisiana (New Orleans, J. B. Roudanez, 1867–8).
Orwell, George, *1984* (London, Secker & Warburg, 1949).
Pabst, Adrian, *Metaphysics: the Creation of Hierarchy* (Grand Rapids, MI, Eerdmans, 2012).
Paczolay, Péter (ed.), *Twenty Years of the Hungarian Constitutional Court* (Budapest, Constitutional Court of the Republic of Hungary, 2009).
Palacios Rubios, Juan López de, *De las islas del mar océano* (1512–14; Mexico, 1954).
Perdigão Malheiro, Agostinho Marques, *A Escravidão no Brasil: Ensaio Historico-Juridico-Social*, part 1, section 70 (Rio de Janeiro, Typographia Nacional, 1866).
Perry, Michael J., *Religion in Politics. Constitutional and Moral Perspectives* (Oxford, Oxford University Press, 1997).
Perry, Michael J., *The Idea of Human Rights: Four Inquiries* (Oxford and New York, Oxford University Press, 1998).
Petrarch, F., *De remediis utriusque fortunae* (München, Fink, 1975).
Pfordten, Dietmar von der, *Menschenwürde, Recht und Staat bei Kant* (Paderborn, mentis-Verlag, 2009).
Pico della Mirandola, Giovanni, *Oration on the Dignity of Man*, trans. Francesco Borghesis et al. (Cambridge, Cambridge University Press, 2012).
Pieroth, Bodo and Schlink, Bernhard, *Grundrechte, Staatsrecht II* 28th edn (Heidelberg, C. F. Müller, 2012).
Planinc, Zdravko, *Plato's Political Philosophy: Prudence in the Republic and the Laws* (London, Duckworth, 1991).
Plant, Stephen, *Bonhoeffer* (London and New York, Continuum, 2004).
Plantinga, Alvin *Warranted Christian Belief* (Oxford, Oxford University Press, 2000).
Plato, *The Republic*, ed. G. R. F. Ferrari, trans. Tom Griffith (Cambridge, Cambridge University Press, 2000).
Pleins, J. David, *The Social Visions of the Hebrew Bible* (Louisville, KY, Westminster John Knox, 2001).
Plomer, Aurora and Torremans, Paul (eds), *Embryonic Stem Cell Patents* (Oxford, Oxford University Press, 2009).
Pohlenz, M., *Die Stoa: Geschichte einer geistigen Bewegung*, 7th edn (Göttingen, Vandenhoeck und Ruprecht, 1992).
Pontifical Commission 'Iustitia et Pax', The Church and Human Rights, Working Paper No. 1, 2nd edn (Vatican City, Typis Polyglottis Vaticanis, 2011).
Popper, K., *Die Logik der Forschung* (Tübingen, Mohr, 1934).
Porter, Jean, *Natural & Divine Law: Reclaiming the Tradition for Christian Ethics* (Grand Rapids, MI, and Cambridge, William B. Eerdmans, 1999).
Porter, Jean, *Nature as Reason: A Thomistic Theory of the Natural Law* (Grand Rapids, MI, and Cambridge, William B. Eerdmans, 2005).
President's Council on Bioethics, *Beyond Therapy* (New York, Dana Press, 2003).

President's Council on Bioethics, *Human Dignity and Bioethics: Essays Commissioned by the President's Council on Bioethics* (Washington DC, President's Council on Bioethics March 2008).

Presidential Commission for the Study of Bioethical Issues, *New Directions: The Ethics of Synthetic Biology and Emerging Technologies* (Washington, Presidential Commission for the Study of Bioethical Issues, December 2010).

Pufendorf, S. von, *De Officio Hominis*, in G. Hartung (ed), *Gesammelte Werke*, vol. 2 (Berlin, Akademie-Verlag, 1996)

Radbruch, G., *Rechtsphilosophie* (Leipzig, Quelle & Mayer, 1932).

Rahner, Karl, *The Trinity*. III. E. trans. Joseph Donceel. (London, Burns and Oates, 1970).

Randall, G. W., *In His Own Image and Likeness, Humanity, Divinity and Monthesism* (Leiden, Brill, 2003).

Rawls, John, *A Theory of Justice* (Oxford, Oxford University Press, 1999, first edn 1972).

Rawls, John, *The Law of Peoples* (Cambridge, MA, Harvard University Press, 1999).

Rawls, John, *Political Liberalism* (New York, Columbia University Press, 1993, 2005).

Raz, Joseph, *The Morality of Freedom* (Oxford, Oxford University Press, 1983).

Risse, Guenter B., *Mending Bodies, Saving Souls: a History of Hospitals* (Oxford, Oxford University Press, 1999).

Rist, John M, *Augustine, Ancient Thought Baptized* (Cambridge, Cambridge University Press, 1994).

Rivers, Julian, *The Law of Organized Religions: Between Establishment and Secularism* (Oxford, Oxford University Press, 2010).

Rosen, Michael, *Dignity: Its History and Meaning* (Cambridge, MA, Harvard University Press, 2012).

Rotenstreich, Nathan, *Man and his Dignity* (Jerusalem, Magnes Press, 1983).

Rousseau, Jean-Jacques, *The Social Contract* (Harmondsworth, Penguin Books, 1968).

Rowlands, Tracey, *Culture and the Thomist Tradition After Vatican II* (London, Routledge, 2002).

Sachs, Michael, *GG Grundgesetz Kommentar* (Verlag C. H. Beck, 2004).

Sajó, Andras and Uitz, Renáta *Constitutional Topography: Values and Constitutions* (Eleven International Publishing, 2010)

Sam, A., *Checkout: A Life on the Tills* (London, Gallic Books, 2009).

Sandel, Michael J., *The Case Against Perfection: Ethics in the Age of Genetic Engineering* (Cambridge, MA, Harvard University Press, 2009).

Sandel, Michael, *Democracy's Discontent: America in Search of a Public Philosophy* (Cambridge, MA, Belknap Press of Harvard University Press, 1996).

Sayers, Sean, *Marxism and Human Nature* (London, Routledge, 1998).

Scanlon, T. M., *What We Owe to Each Other* (Cambridge, MA, Belknap Press of Harvard University Press, 1998).

Schmid, Carlo, *Erinnerungen*, 3rd edn (Bern, München, Wien, Scherz Verlag, 1979).

Schmid, Carlo, *Protokoll der Verhandlungen des Parteitages der SPD vom 21 bis 25 Mai 1950 in Hamburg* (Frankfurt am Main, n.d.).

Schmitt, Carl, *Politische Theologie*, 2nd edn. (München, Duncker & Humboldt, 1934).

Schmitt, Carl, *Chapters on the Concept of Sovereignty*, trans. George Schwab (Cambridge, MA, MIT Press, 1985).
Schopenhauer, A., *On the Basis of Morality* (Indianapolis, Hackett, 1965).
Schopenhauer, A., *Preisschrift über das Fundament der Moral* (Hamburg, Felix Meiner Verlag, 1979).
Schuklenk, U. et al, *End-of-Life Decision Making* (The Royal Society of Canada Expert Panel, November 2011).
Scott, John and Marshall, Gordon, *A Dictionary of Sociology* (Oxford, Oxford University Press, 2009).
Scott, Rebecca J., *Degrees of Freedom: Louisiana and Cuba after Slavery* (Cambridge, MA, Harvard University Press, 2005).
Scott, Rebecca J. and Hébrard, Jean M., *Freedom Papers: An Atlantic Odyssey in the Age of Emancipation* (Cambridge, MA, Harvard University Press, 2012).
Seigel, J., *The Idea of the Self: Thought and Experience in Western Europe since the Seventeenth Century* (Cambridge, Cambridge University Press, 2005).
Sen, A., *Development as Freedom* (New York, Basic Books, 1999).
Sen, A., *The Idea of Justice* (Cambridge, MA, Harvard University Press, 2009).
Sensen, Oliver, *Kant on Human Dignity* (Berlin and Boston, MA, Walter de Gruyter, 2011).
Sepúlveda, Juan Ginés de, *De justis belli causis apud indos*, 1544–5 (Mexico, Fondo de Cultura Economica, 1941).
Silva-Tarouca Larsen, Beatrice von, *Setting the Watch: Privacy and the Ethics of CCTV Surveillance* (Oxford, Hart, 2011).
Simoncini, Andrea, Violini, Lorenza, Carozza, Paolo, and Cartabia, Marta, *Esperienza elementare e diritto* (Milan, Guerini e Associati, 2011).
Singer, P., *Practical ethics* (Cambridge, Cambridge University Press, 2011).
Smith, Michael A., *Human Dignity and the Common Good in the Aristotelian-Thomistic Tradition* (Lewiston, NY, Mellen University Press, c. 1995).
Smith, Steven D., *Foreordained Failure: The Quest for a Constitutional Principle of Religious Freedom* (Oxford, Oxford University Press, 1995).
Smith, Steven D., *Law's Quandary* (Cambridge, MA, Harvard University Press, 2004).
Smith, Steven D., *The Disenchantment of Secular Discourse* (Cambridge, MA, Harvard University Press, 2010).
Sobrino, Jon, *Jesus the Liberator: A Historical-Theological Reading of Jesus of Nazareth*, trans. Paul Burns and Francis McDonagh (Tunbridge Wells, Burns & Oates, 1994).
Sorabji, R., *Self: Ancient and Modern Insights about Individuality, Life and Death* (Oxford, Oxford University Press, 2005).
Soskice, Janet, *The Kindness of God* (Oxford, Oxford University Press, 2007).
Spaemann, Robert, *Love and the Dignity of Human Life* (Grand Rapids, MI, Eerdmanns, 2012).
Spieker, Manfred, *Kirche und Abtreibung in Deutschland: Ursachen und Verlauf eines Konflikts*, 2nd edn (Paderborn, Ferdinand Schöningh, 2008).
Stein, Tine, *Himmlische Quellen und irdisches Recht. Religiöse Voraussetzungen des freiheitlichen Verfassungsstaates* (Frankfurt and New York, Campus, 2007).

Stetson, Dorothy McBride (ed.), *Abortion Politics, Women's Movements, and the Democratic State: A Comparative Study of State Feminism* (Oxford, Oxford University Press, 2003).
Suárez, F., *De legibus*, II, VI, 3 (Madrid, Consejo Superior de Investigaciones Científicas, 1974).
Sunstein, Cass R., *Legal Reasoning and Political Conflict* (Cambridge, MA, Harvard University Press, 1998).
Sunstein, Cass R., *The Partial Constitution* (Cambridge, MA, Harvard University Press, 1998).
Taylor, Charles, *Sources of the Self. The Making of Modern Identity* (Cambridge, MA, Harvard University Press, 1994).
Taylor, Charles, *A Secular Age* (Cambridge, MA, Belknap Press of Harvard University Press, 2007).
Teifke, Nils, *Das Prinzip Menschenwürde* (Tübingen, Mohr Siebeck, 2011).
Tertullian, *Adversus Praxean*, edited with intro., trans. and comm. by Ernest Evans (London, SPCK, 1948).
Tierney, Brian, *The Idea of Natural Rights* (Atlanta, Scholars Press, 1997).
Tobin, J., *The Right to Health in International Law* (Oxford, Oxford University Press, 2012).
Tocqueville, Alexis de, *The Old Regime and the French Revolution*, trans. Stuart Gilbert (Garden City, NY, Doubleday, 1955).
Trials of War Criminals before the Nuernberg Military Tribunals under Control Council Law No. 10, October 1946–April 1949: The Medical Case, vol. 1, 27–8 (Washington DC, US Government Printing Office).
Trigg, Roger, *Equality, Freedom, and Religion* (Oxford, Oxford University Press, 2012).
Trinkaus, Charles, *In our Image and Likeness. Humanity and Dignity in Italian Humanist Thought*, vol. 1 (Chicago, University of Chicago Press, 1970).
UNESCO, *Human Rights: Comments and Interpretations* (London, Wingate, 1949).
United Nations Department of Economic and Social Affairs Population Division, *World Abortion Policies 2007* (United Nations Publication ST/ESA/SER.A/264, 2007).
United Nations Special Rapporteur, *Report on the right to food on his recent visit to Canada* (6-16 May 2010).
United States Holocaust Memorial Museum, *Deadly Medicine: Creating the Master Race* (Chapel Hill, University of North Carolina Press, 2004).
United States Senate, *Chimpanzee Health Improvement, Maintenance, and Protection Act,* Report No. 106–494 (2000).
Vanier, J., *The Broken Body* (London, Darton, Longman & Todd, 1988).
Vanier, J., *Our Journey Home: Rediscovering a Common Humanity Beyond Our Differences* (Maryknoll and New York, Orbis, 1997).
Vanier, J., *Drawn into the Mystery of Jesus through the Gospel of John* (New York, Paulist Press, 2004).
Vatican Council II, *Dignitatis Humanae (Declaration of Religious Freedom)* in Walter M. Abbott and Joseph Gallagher (eds), *The Documents of Vatican II* (New York, America Press, 1966); Decrees of The Ecumenical Councils. vol. 2, ed. Norman

P. Tanner, SJ (Washington DC and London, Sheed and Ward and Georgetown University Press, 1990).
Vatican Council II, *Gaudium et Spes* in David J. O'Brien and Thomas A. Shannon (eds), *Catholic Social Thought: The Documentary Heritage*, expanded edn (Maryknoll, NY, Orbis Books, 2010).
Vickers, Lucy, *Religious Freedom, Religious Discrimination and the Workplace* (Oxford, Hart Publishing, 2008).
Villey, Michel, *Critique de la Pensée Juridique Moderne* (Paris, Dalloz, 1985).
Vining, Joseph, *Legal Identity: The Coming of Age of Public Law* (New Haven, Yale University Press, 1978).
Vining, Joseph, *The Song Sparrow and the Child: Claims of Science and Humanity* (Notre Dame, IN, Notre Dame University Press, 2004).
Vitoria, Francisco de, *De Indis recenter inventis*, ed. W. Schätzel (Tübingen, Mohr Siebeck, 1952).
Vollmann, W., *Poor People* (San Francisco, CA, Harper Perennial, 2007).
Waisman, Sonia S., Frasch, Pamela D., and Wagman, Bruce A., *Animal Law: Cases and Materials,* 3rd edn (Durham, NC, Carolina Academic Press, 2006).
Waldron, Jeremy, *The Dignity of Legislation* (Cambridge, Cambridge University Press, 1999).
Waldron, Jeremy, *God, Locke and Equality* (Cambridge, Cambridge University Press, 2002).
Waldron, Jeremy, *Dignity, Rank, and Rights*, with commentaries by Wai Chee Dimnock, Don Herzog, Michael Rosen, ed. with introduction by Mier Dan-Cohen (Oxford, Oxford University Press, 2012).
Walker, Lenore, *The Battered Woman* (New York, Harper & Row, 1979).
Walker, Lenore, *The Battered Woman Syndrome* (New York, Springer, 1984).
Wallace, D. F., *This is Water* (Cologne, Kiepenheuer & Witsch, 2012).
Wallraff, G., *Aus der schönen neuen Welt: Expeditionen ins Landesinnere* (Köln, Kiepenheuer & Witsch, 2009).
Walzer, Michael, *Exodus and Revolution* (New York, Basic Books, 1985).
Waters, Ethel with Samuels, Charles, *His Eye Is on the Sparrow: An Autobiography* (Garden City, NY, Doubleday, 1951).
Weber, Petra, *Carlo Schmid 1896–1979. Eine Biographie* (Frankfurt am Main, Suhrkamp, 1998).
Weick, Karl, *The Social Psychology of Organizing*, 2nd edn (New York, McGraw-Hill, 1979).
Wendel, Mattias, *Permeabilität im europäischen Verfassungsrecht. Verfassungsrechtliche Integrationsnormen auf Staats- und Unionsebene im Vergleich* (Mohr Siebeck, Tübingen, 2011).
Wetz, Franz Josef (ed), *Texte zur Menschenwürde* (Stuttgart, Reclam, 2011).
Whiting, R., *A Natural Right to Die: Twenty-Three Centuries of Debate* (London, Greenwood Press, 2002).
Whyte, John H., *Church and State in Modern Ireland, 1923–1970* (Dublin, Gill and Macmillan, 1971)

Wiggins, D., *Ethics: Twelve Lectures on the Philosophy of Morality* (London, Penguin, 2006).
Wiggins, D., 'Solidarity and the root of the ethical', The Lindley Lecture (University of Kansas, 2008).
Williams, Bernard, *Ethics and the Limits of Philosophy* (Cambridge, MA, Harvard University Press, 1985).
Williams, G., *The Sanctity of Life and the Criminal Law* (New York, Alfred A. Knopf, 1957).
Williams, Thomas D., *Who is My Neighbor?: Personalism and the Foundations of Human Rights* (Washington DC, Catholic University of America Press, 2005).
Wingert, L., *Gemeinsinn und Moral* (Frankfurt am Main, Suhrkamp, 1993).
Witt, John, *Lincoln's Code: The Laws of War in American History* (New York, Free Press, 2012).
Wittgenstein, Ludwig, *Tractatus Logico-Philosophicus*, trans. D. F Pears and B. F. McGuinness (London, Routledge, 1961).
Wittgenstein, Ludwig, *Philosophical Investigations*, trans. G. E. M. Anscombe (Oxford, Basil Blackwell, 1967, 2001).
Wittgenstein, Ludwig, *Remarks on Colour*, trans. L. L. McAlister and M. Schättle (Oxford, Blackwell, 1977).
Wojtyla, K., *Person in Community, Selected Essays*, trans. Theresa Sandok OSM (New York, Peter Lang 1993).
Wojtyla, K., *The Acting Person*, trans. Andrzej Potocki (Dordrecht, Boston, MA, D. Reidel Publishing Company, 1979).
Wolcher, Louis E., *Law's Task: The Tragic Circle of Law, Justice and Human Suffering* (Aldershot, UK and Burlington, VT, Ashgate Publishing, 2008).
Wolterstorff, N., *Justice: Rights and Wrongs* (Princeton, NJ, Princeton University Press, 2008).
Wood, Allen, *Kant's Ethical Thought* (Cambridge, Cambridge University Press, 1999).
Wood, Allen, *Kantian Ethics* (Cambridge, Cambridge University Press, 2008).
Woolf, Virginia, *A Room of One's Own* (London, Hogarth Press, 1929).
Worden, Nigel, *The Making of Modern South Africa: Conquest, Apartheid, and Democracy*, 3rd edn (Chichester, Wiley Blackwell, 2000).
Wright, Christopher J. H., *Old Testament Ethics for the People of God* (Downers Grove, IL, Intervarsity Press, 2004).

Articles, Book Chapters

Ackermann, Laurie W. H., 'Equality in the South African Constitution: the role of dignity, *Zeitschrift fuer Auslaendisches Oeffentliches Recht und Voelkerrecht* 63 (2000), 537.
Ackermann, Laurie, 'Equality and non-discrimination: some analytical thoughts', *South African Journal of Human Rights* 22:9 (2006), 597, 598.
Allan, T. R. S, 'Constitutional justice and the concept of law', in Grant Huscroft (ed.), *Expounding the Constitution: Essays in Constitutional Theory* 213 (Cambridge, Cambridge University Press, 2008).

Anderson, Perry, 'After Nehru', *London Review of Books* (2 August 2012).
Andorno, R., 'Human dignity and human rights as a common ground for a global bioethics', *Journal of Medicine and Philosophy* 34 (2009), 223–40.
Andries, Edward M., 'On the German Constitution's fiftieth anniversary: Jacques Maritain and the 1949 Basic Law (Grundgesetz)', *Emory International Law Review* 13 (1999), 1–76.
Ayres, Lewis, 'Augustine's Trinitarian Theology', in *Augustine and his Critics*, ed. Robert Dodaro and George Lawless (London, Routledge, 2000).
Badura, Peter, 'Generalprävention und Würde des Menschen', *Juristenzeitung* 19 (1964), 337–44.
Baer, S., 'Dignity, liberty, equality: a fundamental rights triangle of constitutionalism', *University of Toronto Law Journal* 59 (2009), 417–68.
Bagaric, Mirko and Allan, James, 'The vacuous concept of dignity', *Journal of Human Rights* 5 (2006), 257–70.
Barak, Aharon, 'Unconstitutional constitutional amendment', *Israel Law Review* 44:3 (2012), 321–41.
Barilan, Y. Michael, 'From imago Dei in the Jewish-Christian tradition to human dignity in contemporary Jewish law', *Kennedy Institute of Ethics Journal* 19:3 (2009), 231–59.
Barnard-Naudé, Jaco and Vos, Pierre de, 'Disturbing heteronormativity: the "queer" jurisprudence of Albie Sachs', *SA Public Law* 25 (2010), 209, 222.
Barnes, M. R., 'Re-reading Augustine's theology of the Trinity', in S. T. Davies; D. Kendall, and G. O'Collins (eds), *The Trinity: An Interdisciplinary Symposium on the Doctrine of the Trinity* (Oxford, Oxford University Press, 1999).
Bates, Justin, 'Human dignity—an empty phrase in search of meaning?', *Judicial Review* 10 (2005), 165–8.
Baylis, F., 'Animal eggs for stem cell research: a path not worth taking', *American Journal of Bioethics* 8:12 (2008), 18–32.
Baylis, F. and Mcleod, C., 'Feminists on the inalienability of human embryos', *Hypatia* 20:1 (2006), 1–14.
Bergmann, Matthias and Schramm, Engelbert, 'Grenzüberschreitung und Integration: Die formative Evaluation transdisziplinärer Forschung und ihrer Kriterien', in Matthias Bergmann and Engelbert Schramm, *Transdisziplinäre Forschung. Integrative Forschungsprozesse verstehen und bewerten* (Frankfurt am Main and New York, Campus, 2008), 149–75.
Berman, Harold, 'Religious freedom and the challenge of the modern state', *Emory Law Journal* 39 (1990), 149.
Besson, Samantha and Zysset, Alain, 'Human rights theory and human rights history: a tale of two odd bedfellows', *Ancilla Iuris* (special issue: International Law and Ethics) (anci. ch) (2012), 204–19. .
Bettelheim, Bruno, 'Individual and mass behavior in extreme situations', *Journal of Abnormal and Social Psychology* 38 (1943), 417–52.
Bignami, Francesca, 'Privacy and law enforcement in the European Union: The Data Retention Directive', *Chicago Journal of International Law* 8:1 (2007), 233–55.

Biko, Steve, 'The definition of black consciousness', in *I Write What I Like* (Johannesburg, Picador Africa, 2004).
Binchy, W., 'Human dignity as a constitutional principle', in O. Doyle and E. Carolan (eds), *The Irish Constitution: Governance and Values* (Dublin, Thomson Rond Hall, 2008).
Birnbacher, Dieter, 'Ambiguities in the concept of Menschenwürde', in K. Bayertz (ed.), *Sanctity of Life and Human Dignity* (Amsterdam, Kluwer, 1996).
Bix, Brian, 'Natural law: the modern tradition', in Jules Coleman and Scott J. Shapiro (eds), *The Oxford Handbook of Jurisprudence and Philosophy of Law* (Oxford, Oxford University Press, 2002).
Bogdandy, A. von and Dellavalle, S., 'Universalism renewed: Habermas' theory of international order in light of competing paradigms', *German Law Journal* 10:1 (2009), 5–29.
Borowsky, Martin, 'Artikel 1: Würde des Menschen', in Jürgen Meyer (ed.), *Charta der Grundrechte der Europäischen Union*, 3rd edn (Baden-Baden, Nomos Verlagsgesellschaft, 2011).
Botha, Henk, 'Human dignity in comparative perspective', *Stellenbosch Law Review* 20 (2009), 171–220.
Boyer, H. C., 'Commentary', in *Mahalia Jackson Gospels, Spirituals, and Hymns*, Columbia 47084 (1991).
Bromage, Arthur W. and Mary C., 'The Irish Constitution: a discussion of its theoretical aspects', *Review of Politics* 2 (1940), 145–66.
Browne, Noel, 'Church and State in modern Ireland', in Tim Murphy and Patrick Twomey (eds), *Ireland's Evolving Constitution, 1937–97: Collected Essays* (Oxford, Hart, 1998).
Brownsword, Roger, 'Stem cells, superman, and the report of the Select Committee', *Modern Law Review* 65 (2002), 568.
Brownsword, Roger, 'Bioethics today, bioethics tomorrow: stem cell research and the "Dignitarian Alliance"', *University of Notre Dame Journal of Law, Ethics and Public Policy* 17 (2003), 15.
Brownsword, Roger, 'Code, control, and choice: why east is east and west is west', *Legal Studies* 25 (2005), 1.
Brownsword, Roger, 'Stem cells and cloning: where the regulatory consensus fails', *New England Law Review* 39 (2005), 535.
Brownsword, Roger and Somsen, Han, 'Law, innovation and technology: before we fast forward–a forum for debate', *Law Innovation and Technology* 1 (2009), 1.
Brownsword, Roger, 'Brain science: in the regulatory spotlight', *Science in Parliament* 67:2 (2010), 18.
Brownsword, Roger, 'Human dignity, biolaw, and the basis of moral community', *Journal International de Bioethique* 21 (2010), 21–40.
Brownsword, Roger, 'Regulating the life sciences, pluralism, and the limits of deliberative democracy', *Singapore Academy of Law Journal* 22 (2010), 801.
Brownsword, Roger, 'Human dignity and nanotechnologies: two frames, many ethics', *Jahrbuch für Recht und Ethik* 19 (2011), 429–39.

Brownsword, Roger, 'Lost in translation: legality, regulatory margins, and technological management', *Berkeley Technology Law Journal* 26 (2011), 1321.
Brownsword, Roger, 'Regulating brain imaging: questions of privacy and informed consent', in Sarah J. L. Edwards, Sarah Richmond, and Geraint Rees (eds), *I Know What You Are Thinking: Brain Imaging and Mental Privacy* (Oxford, Oxford University Press, 2012).
Brugger, W., 'Darf der Staat ausnahmsweise foltern?', *Der Staat* 35 (1996), 67.
Brugger, W., 'Vom unbedingten Verbot der Folter zum bedingten Recht auf Folter?', *Juristenzeitung* (2000), 167.
Calo, Zachary R., 'Catholic social thought, political liberalism and the idea of human rights', *Journal of Christian Legal Thought* 1 (2011).
Carozza, Paolo G., 'Uses and misuses of comparative law in international human rights: some reflections on the jurisprudence of the European Court of Human Rights', *Notre Dame Law Review* 73 (1998), 1217.
Carozza, Paolo G., 'Il Traffico dei diritti umani nell'età post-moderna', in Luca Antonini (ed.), *Il traffico dei diritti insaziabili* (Soveria Mannelli, Italy, Rubbettino, 2007).
Carozza, Paolo G.,'Human dignity and judicial interpretation of human rights: a reply', *European Journal International Law* 19 (2008), 931–44.
Carozza, Paolo G., 'Human dignity in constitutional adjudication', in Tom Ginsburg and Rosalind Dixon (eds), *Comparative Constitutional Law* (Cheltenham, Edward Elgar, 2011).
Carozza, Paolo G., 'Human dignity', in Dinah Shelton (ed.), *Oxford Handbook of International Human Rights Law* (Oxford, Oxford University Press, 2013 forthcoming).
Caulfield, Timothy and Brownsword, Roger, 'Human dignity: a guide to policy making in the biotechnology era', *Nature Reviews Genetics* 7 (2006), 72.
Cavanaugh, William T., '"A fire strong enough to consume the house": the wars of religion and the rise of the nation state', in John Milbank and Simon Oliver (eds), *The Radical Orthodoxy Reader* (London, Routledge, 2009).
Chamedes, Giuliana, 'Pius XII, rights talk, and the dawn of the religious Cold War', in D. Pendas (ed.), *Religion and Human Rights* (New York, Oxford University Press, forthcoming).
Chapple, A., Ziebland, S., McPherson, A., and Herxheimer, A., 'What people close to death say about euthanasia and assisted suicide: a qualitative study', *Journal of Medical Ethics* 32:12 (December 2006), 706–10.
Chaskalson, Arthur, 'Human dignity as a foundational value of our constitutional order', *South African Journal on Human Rights* 16 (2000), 193.
Christiansen, Eric C., 'Ending the apartheid of the closet: sexual orientation in the South African constitutional process', *NYU Journal of International Law and Politics* 32 (2000), 997.
Clark, Meghan J., Integrating human rights, *Political Theology*, 8:3 (2007), 299–317.
Clarke, W. N., SJ, 'Person, being, and St Thomas', *Communio* 19 (1992), 601–18.
Clegg, S. and Gough, R., 'The struggle for abortion rights', in M. Lavalette and G. Mooney (eds), *Class Struggle and Social Welfare* (London, Routledge, 2000).

Cohen, G. D., 'The Holocaust and the "human rights revolution": a reassessment', in A. Iriye, P. Goedde and W. Hitchcock (eds), *The Human Rights Revolution* (Oxford, Oxford University Press, 2012).
Costello, Declan, 'The natural law and the Irish Constitution', *Studies* 45 (1956), 403–14.
Dederer, Hans-Georg, 'Die Garantie der Menschenwürde (Article 1 Abs. 1 GG): Dogmatische Grundfragen auf dem Stand der Wissenschaft', *Jahrbuch des öffentlichen Rechts der Gegenwart* 57 (2009), 89–124.
Delor, F., and Hubert, M., 'Revisiting the concept of "vulnerability"', *Social Science and Medicine* 50 (2000), 1557–70.
Derrida, Jacques, 'Force of law: the "mystical foundation of authority"', in G. Anidjar (ed.), *Acts of Religion* (London, Routledge, 2002, first pub. 1998).
Dhammananda, Ven Dr K Sri, *Human Dignity in Buddhism*, http://www.dhammatalks.net/Books6/Bhante_Dhammananda_Human_Dignity_in_Buddhism.pdf.
Doemming, Klaus-Berto von, Füsslein, Rudolf W., and Matz, Werner, 'Entstehungsgeschichte der Artikel des Grundgesetzes', *Jahrbuch des öffentlichen Rechts der Gegenwart* neue Folge 1 (1951), 1–941.
Dreier, Horst, 'Menschenwürdegarantie und Schwangerschaftsabbruch', *Die Öffentliche Verwaltung* 48 (1995), 1036–40.
Dunlop, C., 'Wittgenstein on sensation and "seeing-as"', *Synthese* 60 (1984), 349–67.
Dupré, C., 'Dignité dans l'Europe constitutionnelle: entre inflation et contradictions', in J. Ziller (ed.), *L'européanisation des droits constitutionnels à la lumière de la constitution pour l'Europe* (Paris, L'Harmattan, 2003).
Dupré, C., 'Human dignity: rhetoric, protection, instrumentalisation', in G. A. Tóth (ed.), *Constitution for a Disunited Nation. On Hungary's 2011 Fundamental Law* (Budapest, Central European University Press, 2012).
Dupré, C., 'Article 1: human dignity', in T. Hervey, S. Peers, J. Kenner, and A. Ward (eds), *A Commentary on the European Union Charter of Fundamental Rights* (Oxford, Hart Publishing, 2013 forthcoming).
Dupré, C., 'Dignity, democracy, civilisation', *Liverpool Law Review* (2013 forthcoming)
Dupré, C., 'Human dignity in Europe: a foundational constitutional principle', *European Public Law* 19 (2013 forthcoming).
Dupré, Catherine, 'Unlocking human dignity: towards a theory for the 21st Century', *European Human Rights Law Review* 2 (2009), 190–205.
Dürig, Günter, 'Die Menschenauffassung des Grundgesetzes', *Juristische Rundschau* 6 (1952), 259–63.
Dürig, Günter, 'Der Grundrechtssatz von der Menschenwürde', *Archiv des öffentlichen Rechts* 81 (1956), 117–57.
Dürig, Günter, 'Zur Bedeutung und Tragweite des Art. 79 Abs. III GG', in Hans Spanner et al. (eds), *Festgabe für Theodor Maunz zum 70. Geburtstag am 1. September 1971* (München, Verlag C.H. Beck, 1971).
Dürig, Günter, 'Dankrede am 65. Geburtstag', *Jahrbuch des öffentlichen Rechts der Gegenwart* 36 (1987), 91–103.

Eberle, Edward J., 'Human dignity, privacy, and personality in German and American constitutional law', in Nikolaus Knoepffler, Peter Kunzmann, and Martin O'Malley (eds), *Facetten der Menschenwürde* (Freiburg and München, Verlag Karl Alber, 2011).
Eisgruber, Christopher L. and Sager, Lawrence G., 'The vulnerability of conscience: the constitutional basis for protecting religious conduct', *University of Chicago Law Review* 61 (1994), 1245.
Enders, Christoph, 'A right to have rights—the German constitutional concept of human dignity', *NUJS Law Review* 3 (2010), 253–64.
Epictetus, '*Discourses*', in Robert Dobbin (trans. and ed.), Epictetus, *Discourses and Selected Writings* (London, Penguin Books, 2008).
Evans, Malcolm D., 'Believing in communities, European style', in Nazila Ghanea (ed.), *The Challenge of Religious Discrimination at the Dawn of the New Millennium* (Leiden, Martinus Nijhoff Publishers, 2003).
Fanning, Ronan, 'Mr De Valera drafts a constitution', in B. Farrell (ed.), *De Valera's Constitution and Ours* (Dublin, Gill and Macmillan, 1988).
Farley, Margaret A., 'A feminist version of respect for persons', *Journal of Feminist Studies in Religion* 9:1–2 (Spring–Fall 1993), 183–98.
Feldman, David, 'Human dignity as a legal value: Part I', *Public Law* (1999), 682.
Feldman, David, 'Human dignity as a legal value: Part II', *Public Law* (2000), 61.
Finnis, J. M., 'Equality and differences', *Solidarity: The Journal of Catholic Social Thought and Secular Ethics* 2 (2012).
Finnis, John, 'Sex and marriage: some myths and reasons', in *Collected Essays*, vol. 3: *Human Rights and Common Good* (Oxford, Oxford University Press, 2011).
Finnis, John, 'Natural Law: the Classical Tradition', in Jules Coleman and Scott J. Shapiro (eds), *The Oxford Handbook of Jurisprudence and Philosophy of Law* (Oxford University Press, 2002), 1.
Fischer, N., 'Einleitung', in *Aurelius Augustinus, Suche nach dem wahren Leben* (Hamburg, Meiner, 2006).
Flasch, K., 'Wert der Innerlichkeit', in H. Joas and K. Wiegandt (eds), *Die kulturellen Werte Europas* (Frankfurt am Main, Fischer, 2005).
Fletcher, G.P., 'Human dignity as a constitutional value', *University of Western Ontario* 22 (1984), 171–82.
Foot, Philippa, 'Morality, action and outcome', in T. Honderich (ed.), *Morality and Objectivity* (London, Routledge, 1985).
Frankl, Viktor E., 'Der unbedingte Mensch' (1949), in Frankl, *Der leidende Mensch*, 3rd edn (Bern, Verlag Hans Huber, 2005).
Frankl, Viktor E., 'Homo patiens' (1950), in Frankl, *Der leidende Mensch*, 3rd edn (Bern, Verlag Hans Huber, 2005).
Friedman, H. H., *Human Dignity and the Jewish Tradition* (2008), http://www.jlaw.com/Articles/HumanDignity.pdf.
Frodeman, Robert, 'Introduction', in Robert Frodeman et al. (eds), *The Oxford Handbook of Interdisciplinarity* (Oxford, Oxford University Press, 2010).
Fuchs, Josef, SJ, *Natural Law. A Theological Investigation*, trans. Helmut Reckter, SJ and John A. Dowling (Dublin, Gill and Son, 1965).

Füssel, H-M., 'Vulnerability: a generally applicable conceptual framework for climate change research', *Global Environmental Change* 17 (2007), 155–67.
Gadamer, Hans-Georg, 'Die Menschenwürde auf ihrem Weg von der Antike bis heute', *Humanistische Bildung* 12 (1988), 95–107.
Gallagher, Robert L., 'Incommensurability in Aristotle's theory of reciprocal justice', *British Journal for the History of Philosophy* 20 (2012), 667–701.
Garnett, Richard, 'Do churches matter? Towards an institutional understanding of the religion clauses', *Villanova Law Review* 53 (2008), 273.
Gewirth, Alan, 'Human dignity as the basis of rights', in Michael J. Meyer and William A. Parent (eds), *The Constitution of Rights: Human Dignity and American Values* (Ithaca, NY, Cornell University Press, 1992).
Gewirth, Alan, 'Are there any absolute rights?', in J. Waldron (ed.), *Theories of Rights* (Oxford, Oxford University Press, 1984), 91–109.
Girgis, Sherif, George, Robert P. and Anderson, Ryan T., 'What is marriage?' *Harvard Journal of Law and Public Policy* 34 (2010), 245.
Glendon, Mary Ann, 'Foundations of human rights: the unfinished business', *American Journal of Jurisprudence*, 44 (1999), 1.
Glendon, Mary Ann, 'The bearable lightness of dignity', *First Things* 213 (May, 2011), 41–5.
Glensky, Rex D., 'The right to dignity', *Columbia Human Rights Law Review*, 43 (2011), 65–142.
Goldsworthy, Jeffrey, 'Unwritten constitutional principles', in Grant Huscroft (ed.), *Expounding the Constitution* (Cambridge, Cambridge University Press, 2008).
Gomes, Angela de Castro, 'Trabalho análogo a de escravo: construindo um problema', *História Oral* 11 (January–December 2008), 11–41.
Goos, Christoph, '*Wirtschaft und Freiheit in den Bauernkriegsartikeln: Verfassungshistorische Anmerkungen zu Artikel 2, 3, 11: Freiheit von Zehnt, Leibeigenschaft und Todfallabgaben*', in Görge K. Hasselhoff and David von Mayenburg (eds), *Die Zwölf Artikel von 1525 und das 'Göttliche Recht' der Bauern—rechtshistorische und theologische Dimensionen* (Würzburg, Ergon Verlag, 2012).
Gorby, John D. and Jonas, Robert E., 'West German abortion decision: a contrast to *Roe v Wade*' *John Marshall Journal of Practice & Procedure* 9 (1976), 605.
Gormally, Luke, 'Pope John Paul II's teaching on human dignity and its implications for bioethics', in C. Tollefsen (ed.), *John Paul II's Contribution to Catholic Bioethics* (Dordrecht, Kluwer Academic Publishers, 2004).
Graaf, R. Van Der and Delden, J. J.V., 'Clarifying appeals to dignity in medical ethics from an historical perspective', *Bioethics*, 23:3 (March 2009), 151–60.
Greenawalt, Kent, 'Fundamental questions about the religion clauses: reflections on some critiques', *San Diego Law Review* 47 (2010), 1131.
Greenawalt, Kent, 'Hands off: when and about what', *Notre Dame Law Review* 84 (2009), 913.
Greenhouse, Linda and Siegel, Reva B., 'Before (and after) *Roe v Wade*: new questions about backlash', *Yale Law Journal* 120 (2011), 2028.
Grogan, Vincent, 'The constitution and the Natural Law', *Christus Rex* 7 (1954), 201–18.

Habermas, Jürgen, 'On the internal relation between the rule of law and democracy', in Jürgen Habermas, *The Inclusion of the Other: Studies in Political Theory* (Cambridge, MA, the MIT Press, 1998).

Habermas, Jürgen, 'The concept of human dignity and the realistic utopia of human rights', *Metaphilosophy*, 41 (2008), 464.

Habermas, Jürgen, 'Das Konzept der Menschenwürde und die realistische Utopie der Menschenrechte', *Deutsche Zeitschrift für Philosophie* 58 (2010), 343–57.

Habermas, Jürgen, 'Religion in the public sphere', in Bryan S. Turner (ed.), *Secularization*, vol. 1: *Defining Secularization: The Secular in Historical and Comparative Perspective* (London, Sage, 2010).

Habermas, Jürgen, '"The political": the rational meaning of a questionable inheritance of political theology', in Eduardo Mendieta and Jonathan Vanantwerpen (eds), *The Power of Religion in the Public Sphere* (New York, Columbia University Press, 2011).

Habermas, Jürgen, 'Concluding discussion', in Eduardo Mendieta and Jonathan Vanantwerpen (eds), *The Power of Religion in the Public Sphere* (New York, Columbia University Press, 2011).

Habermas, Jürgen, 'The concept of human dignity and the realistic utopia of human rights', in Jürgen Habermas, *The Crisis of the European Union: A Response* (Cambridge, Polity Press, 2012).

Hauskeller, M., 'Believing in the dignity of human embryos', *Human Reproduction and Genetic Ethics* 17:1 (2011), 53–65.

Have, Henk ten, 'UNESCO and ethics of science and technology', in UNESCO, *Ethics of Science and Technology: Explorations of the Frontiers of Science and Ethics* (Paris, 2006), 5.

Heckel, Martin, 'Luthers Traktat "Von der Freiheit eines Christenmenschen" als Markstein des Kirchen- und Staatskirchenrechts', *Zeitschrift für Theologie und Kirche* 109 (2012), 122–52.

Hellman, John, 'The opening to the left in French Catholicism: the role of the personalists', *Journal of the History of Ideas* 34:3 (1973), 381.

Hennette-Vauchez, Stéphanie, 'A human *Dignitas*? Remnants of the ancient legal concept in contemporary dignity jurisprudence', *International Journal of Constitutional Law* 9 (2011), 32.

Henry, Leslie Meltzer, 'The jurisprudence of dignity', *University of Pennsylvania Law Review* 160 (2011), 169.

Herek, Gregory, et al., 'Sexual stigma: Putting sexual minority health issues in context', in I. Meyer and M. Northridge (eds), *The Health of Sexual Minorities: Public Health Perspectives on Lesbian, Gay, Bisexual, and Transgender Populations* (New York, Springer, 2007).

Hervieu-Léger, Danièle, 'In search of certainties: the paradoxes of religiosity in societies of high modernity', in Bryan S. Turner (ed.), *Secularization*, vol. 4: *The Comparative Sociology of De-Secularization* (London, Sage, 2010).

Heschel, Susannah, 'Human dignity in Judaism', paper presented at the Concept of Human Dignity in a Transatlantic Perspective: Foundations and Variations: A Berlin Dialogue on Transatlantic Legal Culture(s), Wissenschaftskolleg zu Berlin, 16–18 November 2011.

Hildebrandt, Mireille, 'Legal and technological normativity: More (and less) than twin sisters', *TECHNE* 12.3 (2008), 169.

Hilgendorf, Eric, 'Bedingungen gelingender Interdisziplinarität—am Beispiel der Rechtswissenschaft', *Juristenzeitung* (2010), 913–22.

Hill, Thomas E., Jr., 'Moral dilemmas, gaps, and residues', in Thomas E. Hill, Jr, *Human Welfare and Moral Worth: Kantian Perspectives* (Oxford, Oxford University Press, 2002).

Hittinger, Russell, '*Dignitatis humanae*, religious liberty, and ecclesiastical self-government', *George Washington Law Review* 68 (2000), 1035.

Holt, Thomas C., 'Marking, race-making, and the writing of history', *American Historical Review* 100 (February 1995), 1–20.

Horton, R., 'Rediscovering human dignity', *Lancet* 364 (2004), 1081–5.

Houzeau, Jean-Charles, 'Le journal noir, aux Etats-Unis, de 1863 à 1870 (1)', *Revue de Belgique* 11 (1872), 5–28.

Howes, Dustin, '"Consider if this is a person": Primo Levi, Hannah Arendt, and the political significance of Auschwitz,' *Holocaust and Genocide Studies* 22 (2008), 266–92.

Iglesias, Teresa, 'The dignity of the individual in the Irish Constitution: the importance of the Preamble', *Studies* 89 (2000), 19–34.

Iglesias, Teresa, 'Bedrock truths and the dignity of the individual,' *Logos* 4 (2001), 144.

Isabel Grant, 'The "syndromization" of women's experience', in Donna Martinson et al., 'A forum on *Lavallee v R.*: women and self-defence', *UBC Law Review* 25 (1991), 23.

Isensee, Josef, 'Würde des Menschen', in Detlef Merten and Hans-Jürgen Papier (eds), *Handbuch der Grundrechte in Deutschland und Europa, vol. IV: Grundrechte in Deutschland: Einzelgrundrechte I* (Heidelberg, C. F. Müller, 2011).

Johnston, J. and Eliot, C., 'Chimeras and "human dignity"', *The American Journal of Bioethics* 1536-0075 3:3 (2003).

Jones, D. A., 'Is the creation of admixed embryos "an offense against human dignity"?', *Human Reproduction and Genetic Ethics* 16:1 (2010), 87–114.

Jones, D. A., 'The "special status" of the human embryo in the United Kingdom: an exploration of the use of language in public policy', *Human Reproduction and Genetic Ethics* 17:1 (2011), 66–83.

Jones, D. A. and Keown, J., 'Surveying the foundations of medical law: a reassessment of Glanville Williams's *The Sanctity of Life and the Criminal Law*', *Medical Law Review* 16:1 (2008), 85–126.

Jordan, Mark, 'Cicero, Ambrose and Aquinas "on duties", *or* the limits of genre in morals', *Journal of Religious Ethics* 3 (2005), 485–502.

Junk-Kenny, Maureen, 'Does theology need a theological foundation?', *Concilium* 2 (2003), 63–4.

Kant, Immanuel, 'On the common saying: that may be correct in theory, but it is of no use in practice' in Kant, *Practical Philosophy*, 8, 294.

Kasper, Walter, 'The theological foundations of human rights', *The Jurist* 50 (1990) 148–66.

Kass, L., 'Defending human dignity', in President's Council on Bioethics report *Human Dignity and Bioethics* (Washington DC, March 2008), part 4, ch. 12.
Kemmerer, Alexandra, 'The normative knot 2.0: metaphorological explorations in the net of networks', *German Law Journal* 10 (2009), 339–461.
Kemmerer, Alexandra, 'The turning aside. On international law and its history', in Russell A. Miller and Rebecca M. Bratspies (eds), *Progress in International Law* (Leiden and Boston, MA, Martinus Nijhoff, 2008).
Kenny, Anthony, 'Life stories: When an individual life begins–and the ethics of ending it', *Times Literary Supplement* (25 March 2005), 3.
Keogh, Dermot, 'Church, state, and society', in Brian Farrell (ed.), *De Valera's Constitution and Ours* (Dublin, Gill and Macmillan, 1988).
Keown, D., 'Are there human rights in Buddhism?', *Journal of Buddhist Ethics* 2 (1995), http://jbe.la.psu.edu/index.html.
Khaitan, Tarunabh, 'Dignity as an expressive norm: Neither vacuous nor a panacea', *Oxford Journal of Legal Studies* (2011), 1–19.
Kilner, J., 'Human dignity', in S. G. Post (ed.), *The Encyclopedia of Bioethics* (New York, Macmillan Reference USA, 2004).
Kirkpatrick, Robin, 'Introduction' to *Dante Purgatorio*, trans. Robin Kirkpatrick (London, Penguin, 2007).
Klein, Eckart, 'Human dignity in German law', in David Kretzmer and Eckart Klein (eds), *The Concept of Human Dignity in Human Rights Discourse* (The Hague, Martinus Nijhoff Publishers, 2002).
Klein, Friedrich, 'Artikel 1', in Hermann von Mangoldt/Friedrich Klein, *Das Bonner Grundgesetz*, 2nd edn (Berlin und Frankfurt am Main, Verlag Franz Vahlen, 1957).
Klein, Julie Thompson, 'A taxonomy of interdisciplinarity', in Robert Frodeman et al. (eds), *The Oxford Handbook of Interdisciplinarity* (Oxford, Oxford University Press, 2010).
Kolnai, Aurel, 'Dignity', *Philosophy* 51 (1976), 251–71.
Kolnai, Aurel, 'Dignity', in Robin S. Dillon (ed.), *Dignity, Character, and Self-Respect* (New York, Routledge, 1995).
Kondylis, P., 'Artikel Würde', *Geschichtliche Grundbegriffe II–VIII, Band 7* (Stuttgart, Klett-Cotta, 1992).
Koops, Bert-Jaap, 'Technology and the crime society: Rethinking legal protection', *Law, Innovation and Technology* 1 (2009), 93.
Koppelman, Andrew, 'Conscience, volitional necessity, and religious exemptions', *Legal Theory* (2009), 215.
Koppelman, Andrew, 'How shall I praise thee? Brian Leiter on respect for religion', *San Diego Law Review* 47 (2010), 961.
Kraynak, Robert P., 'The influence of Kant on Christian theology: a debate about human dignity and Christian personalism: A response to Derek S. Jeffreys', *Journal of Markets and Morality* 7:2 (2004), 533.
Kremnitzer, Mordechai and Hörnle, Tatjana, 'Human dignity and the principle of culpability', *Israel Law Review* 44:1 (2011), 115–41.
Kressel, Beth, 'Creating "what might have been a fuss": litigating in defense of equal public rights in Reconstruction-era Louisiana' (forthcoming).

Kuhse, H., 'Is there a tension between autonomy and dignity?', in P. Kemp et al. (eds), *Bioethics and Biolaw* vol. 2 (Copenhagen, Rhodos International Science and Art Publishers and Centre for Ethics and Law, 2000).

Lebech, Mette, 'What is human dignity?', in Mette Lebech (ed.), *Maynooth Philosophical Papers* (Maynooth, Maynooth University Press, 2004).

Lee, Maria, 'Beyond safety? The broadening scope of risk regulation', *Current Legal Problems* 62 (2009), 242.

Lee, P. and George, R. P., 'The nature and basis of human dignity', *Ratio Juris* 21 (2008), 173–93.

Leiter, Brian, 'Why tolerate religion?', *Constitutional Commentary* 25 (2008–9), 1.

Lepsius, Oliver, 'Human dignity and the downing of aircraft: the German Federal Constitutional Court strikes down a prominent anti-terrorism provision in the new air-transport security Act', *German Law Journal* 7 (2006), 761–76.

Lepsius, Oliver, 'Themen einer Rechtswissenschaftstheorie', in Oliver Lepsius and Matthias Jestaedt (eds), *Rechtswissenschaftstheorie* (Tübingen, Mohr Siebeck 2008).

Lerche, Peter, 'Verfassungsrechtliche Aspekte der Gentechnologie', in Rudolf Lukes and Rupert Scholz (eds), *Rechtsfragen der Gentechnologie. Vorträge anläßlich eines Kolloquiums Recht und Technik—Rechtsfragen der Gentechnologie in der Tagungsstätte der Max-Planck-Gesellschaft 'Schloß Ringberg' am 18, 19 und 20 November 1985* (Köln, Carl Heymanns Verlag, 1986).

Locke, John, *Two Treatises of Government* (1690; London, Awnsham-Churchill, 1698).

Lonergan, Bernard, 'Natural right and historical mindedness', in F. Crowe (ed.), *A Third Collection. Papers by Bernard J. F. Lonergan SJ* (London, Geoffrey Chapman, 1985).

Lonergan, Bernard, 'Dimensions of meaning', in Frederick E. Crowe (ed.), *Collection: Papers by Bernard Lonergan, SJ* (New York, Herder and Herder, 1967).

Lorberbaum, Y., 'Blood and the image of God: on the sanctity of life in biblical and early rabbinic law, myth, and ritual', in D. Kretzmer and E. Klein (eds), *The Concept of Human Dignity in Human Rights Discourse* (Den Haag, Martinus Nijhoff Publishers, 2002).

Loury, Glenn C., 'Racial stigma and its consequences', *Focus* 24:1 (University of Wisconsin-Madison Institute for Research on Poverty, Autumn 2005).

Luddy, Maria, 'A "sinister and retrogressive" proposal: Irish women's opposition to the 1937 Draft Constitution', *Transactions of the Royal Historical Society* 15 (2005), 175–95.

Luf, Gerhard, 'Menschenwürde als Rechtsbegriff. Überlegungen zum Kant-Verständnis in der neueren deutschen Grundrechtstheorie', in Rainer Zaczyk et al. (eds), *Festschrift für E.A. Wolff zum 70. Geburtstag am 1.10.1998* (Berlin et al., Springer, 1998).

Luther, M., *Über das 1. Buch, Mose. Predigten. 1527*, in M. Luthers Werke, Kritische Gesammtausgabe, 24. Band (Weimar, 1900), 51.

Luther, Martin, '*Admonition to Peace*', trans. Charles M. Jacobs, revised Robert C. Schultz, in Robert C. Schultz (ed.), Helmut T. Lehmann (gen. ed.), *Luther's Works*, inc vol. 46: *The Christian in Society III* (Philadelphia, PA, Fortress Press, 1967).

Luther, Martin, *Disputatio de homine*, in G. Ebeling, *Lutherstudien*, vol. 2 (Tübingen, Mohr Siebeck, 1989).
Luther, Martin, *Predigten über das erste Buch Mose, gehalten 1523/24*, in M. Luthers Werke, Kritische Gesammtausgabe, 14. Band (Weimar, 1895), 111.
Lyotard, Jean-François, 'The other's rights', in Stephen Shute and Susan Hurley (eds), *On Human Rights: The Oxford Amnesty Lectures 1993* (New York, Basic Books, 1993).
McCrudden, Christopher, 'Human dignity and judicial interpretation of human rights', *European Journal of International Law* 19 (2008), 655–724.
McCrudden, Christopher, 'Legal and Roman Catholic conceptions of human rights: convergence, divergence and dialogue?', *Oxford Journal of Law and Religion* 1 (2012), 185–201.
McCrudden, Christopher, 'Dignity and religion', in Robin Griffith-Jones (ed.), *Islam and English Law* (Cambridge, Cambridge University Press, 2013).
McGinn, M., Wittgenstein's 'Remarks on colour', *Philosophy* 66 (1991), 435–53.
McIlroy, David, 'Locke and Rawls on religious toleration and public reason', *Oxford Journal of Law and Religion* 2:1 (2013), 1–24.
MacKinnon, Catharine, 'The road not taken: sex equality in *Lawrence Texas*', *Ohio State Law Journal* 65 (2004), 1081–95.
MacKinnon, Catharine, 'Substantive equality: a perspective', *Minnesota Law Review* 96:2 (2011), 1–27.
Macklin, Ruth, 'Dignity is a useless concept', *British Medical Journal* 237 (2003), 1419–20.
Mahlmann, Matthias, 'Ethics, law and the challenge of cognitive science', *German Law Journal* 577 (2007).
Mahlmann, Matthias, 'Free speech and the rights of religion', in A. Sajó (ed.), *Censorial Sensitivities: Free Speech and Religion in a Fundamentalist World* (Utrecht, Eleven, 2007).
Mahlmann, Matthias, 'Le Chariot—Bemerkungen zu den Grundlagen des Rechts', *Zeitschrift für Schweizerisches Recht* 131 (2012), 123–44.
Mahlmann, Matthias, 'Human dignity and autonomy in modern constitutional order', in Michel Rosenfeld and Andras Sajó (eds), *The Oxford Handbook of Comparative Constitutional Law* (Oxford, Oxford University Press, 2012).
Maier, Hans, 'Katholische Sozial- und Staatslehre und neuere deutsche Staatslehre', *Archiv des öffentlichen Rechts* 93 (1968), 1–36.
Manning, C.N., 'Live and let die?: Physician assisted suicide and the right to die', *Harvard Journal of Law & Technology* 9:2 (Summer 1996), 513–45.
Margalit, Avishai, 'Human dignity between kitsch and deification', in Christopher Cordner (ed.), *Philosophy, Ethics, and a Common Humanity: Essays in Honour of Raimond Gaita* (New York, Routledge, 2011).
Maritain, Jacques, 'Christian humanism', *Fortune* (April 1942).
Maritain, Jacques, 'Introduction', in *Human Rights: Comments and Interpretations*, symposium edited by UNESCO (New York, Columbia University Press, 1949).
Maritain, Jacques, 'Truth and human fellowship', in Jacques Maritain, *On the Use of Philosophy: Three Essays* (Princeton, NJ, Princeton University Press, 1961).

Marshall, T. H., 'Citizenship and social class', in T. H. Marshall, *Class, Citizenship and Social Development* (New York, Doubleday, 1964).

Martino, Carmine Di, 'L'incontro e l'emergenza dell'umano', in Javier Prades (ed.), *All'origine della diversita'. Le sfide del multiculturalismo* (Milan, Guerini e Associati, 2008).

Mathewes, Charles T., 'Augustinian anthropology: interior intimo meo', *Journal of Religious Ethics* 27:2 (1999), 195–221.

Menzies, Allan (ed.), 'The apology of Aristides', in *Ante-Nicene Christian Fathers*, vol. 10 (Edinburgh: T&T Clark, 1897).

Meyer, M., 'The simple dignity of sentient life: speciesism and human dignity,' *Journal of Social Philosophy* 32:2 (Summer 2001), 115–26.

Miguel, C. R., 'Human dignity: history of an idea', *Jahrbuch des öffentlichen Rechts* 50 (2002), 281–99.

Milbank, John, 'Christ the exception', *New Blackfriars,* 82:969 (2001), 541–56.

Milbank, John, 'Shari'a and the true basis of group rights: Islam, the West, and liberalism', in Rex Ahdar and Nicholas Aroney (eds), *Shari'a in the West* (Oxford, Oxford University Press, 2010).

Milbank, John, 'Against human rights: liberty in the Western tradition', *Oxford Journal of Law and Religion* 1 (2012), 203.

Modood, T., 'Anti-essentialism, multiculturalism and the "recognition" of religious groups', *Journal of Political Philosophy* 6 (1998), 378.

Möllers, Christoph, 'Democracy and human dignity: limits of a moralized conception of rights in German constitutional law', *Israel Law Review* 42 (2009), 416–39.

Molony, John and Thompson, David, 'Christian social thought', in Sheridan Gilley and Brian Stanley (eds), *Cambridge History of Christianity, World Christianities 1815–1914* (Cambridge, Cambridge University Press, 2006).

Moltke, Helmuth J. von, 'Letter of 10 January 1945', in Günter Brakelmann (ed.), *Helmuth James von Moltke: Im Land der Gottlosen. Tagebuch und Briefe aus der Haft 1944/45* (München, Verlag C.H. Beck, 2009).

Moon, Gay and Allen, Robin, 'Dignity discourse in discrimination law: a better route to equality?', *European Human Rights Law Review* (2006), 610.

Mooney, Annabelle, 'Death alive and kicking: Dianne Pretty, legal violence and the sacred', *Social Semiotics* 18:1 (2008), 47–60.

Mosher, Janet, 'Welfare reform and the remaking of the model citizen', in Margot Young, Susan B. Boyd, Gwen Brodsky, and Shelagh Day (eds), *Poverty: Rights, Social Citizenship, Legal Activism* (Vancouver, UBC Press, 2007).

Moyn, S., 'Personalism, community, and the origins of human rights', in S-L. Hoffmann and S. Moyn (eds), *Human Rights in the Twentieth Century* (Cambridge, Cambridge University Press, 2011).

Müller, Felix, and Richter, Tobias, 'Report on the Bundesverfassungsgericht's (Federal Constitutional Court) Jurisprudence in 2005/2006', *German Law Journal* 9 (2008), 161–93.

Müller, Jan-Werner, 'From Christian democracy to Muslim democracy?', *Project Syndicate* (October 2008).

Murphy, Jeffrie G., 'The elusive nature of human dignity', *The Hedgehog Review*, 9:3 (Fall 2007), reprinted in Jeffrie G. Murphy, *Punishment and the Human Emotions* (Oxford and New York, Oxford University Press, 2012).
Nagel, Thomas, 'Personal rights and public space', in T. Nagel, *Concealment and Exposure* (Oxford, Oxford University Press, 2002).
Nagel, Thomas, 'The taste for being moral', *New York Review of Books* 59:19 (6 December 2012), 40–2.
Negt, Oskar, 'The unrepeatable: changes in the cultural concept of dignity', in Regina Ammicht-Quinn et al. (eds), 'The Discourse of Human Dignity', *Concilium* 2 (2003).
Nettelbeck, Joachim, 'How to organize spaces of translation, or, the politics of innovation', in Helga Nowotny (ed.), *Cultures of Technology and the Quest for Innovation* (New York and Oxford, Berghahn Books, 2006).
Neuman, Gerald L., 'Rhetorical slavery, rhetorical citizenship', *Michigan Law Review* 90 (1992), 1276.
Neuman, Gerald L., 'Human dignity in US constitutional law', in Dieter Simon and Manfred Weiss (eds), *Zur Autonomie des Individuums: Liber Amicorum Spiros Simitis* 249 (Baden-Baden, Nomos Verlagsgesellschaft, 2000).
Neuman, Gerald L., 'Human rights and constitutional rights: harmony and dissonance', *Stanford Law Review* 55 (2003), 1863.
Nietzsche, F., 'The Greek state', in *Early Greek Philosophy and Other Writings*, trans. M. A. Mügge (New York, Russell & Russell, 1964).
Nordenfelt, L., 'The varieties of dignity', *Health Care Analysis* 12:2 (June 2004), 69–81.
Novak, Michael, 'The Judeo-Christian foundations of human dignity, personal liberty and the concept of the person', *Journal of Markets and Morality* 1:2 (October 1998), 107–21.
Nowotny, Helga, 'Vom Baum der Erkenntnis zum Rhizom. Zur Dynamisierung der Wissensproduktion', in Helga Nowotny, *Es ist so. Es könnte auch anders sein* (Frankfurt am Main, Suhrkamp, 1999).
Nussbaum, Martha C., 'Aristotelian social democracy', in R. Douglass, M. Bruce, M. Gerald, and H. S. Richardson (eds), *Liberalism and the Good* (New York, Routledge, 1990).
Nussbaum, Martha, 'Human functioning and social justice: in defence of Aristotelian essentialism', *Political Theory* 20:2 (1992), 202–46.
Nussbaum, Martha, 'Human capabilities, female human beings', in Martha Nussbaum and Jonathan Glover (eds), *Women, Culture, and Development: A Study of Human Capabilities* (Oxford, Oxford University Press, 1995).
Nussbaum, Martha, 'Human dignity and political entitlements', chapter 14 in *Human Dignity and Bioethics*: essays commissioned by the President's Council on Bioethics, Washington DC (2008).
O'Connell, Rory, 'The role of dignity in equality law: lessons from Canada and South Africa', *International Journal of Constitutional Law* 6 (2008), 272.

O'Malley, Martin, 'Dignity in US bio-ethics debate: needs Würde', in Christine Baumbach and Peter Kunzmann (eds), *Würde—dignité—godnosc—dignity: Die Menschenwürde im internationalen Vergleich* (München, Herbert Utz Verlag, 2010).

O'Malley, Martin, 'A performative definition of human dignity', in Nikolaus Knoepffler et al. (eds), *Facetten der Menschenwürde* (Freiburg and München, Karl Alber Verlag, 2011).

Oberman, Heiko A., 'The pursuit of happiness: Calvin between humanism and reformation', in John O'Malley et al. (eds), *Humanity and Divinity in Renaissance and Reformation, Essays in Honor of Charles Trinkaus* (Leiden, E. J. Brill, 1993).

Oliver, Simon, 'Christ and gift: introduction', in John Milbank and Simon Oliver (eds), *The Radical Orthodoxy Reader* (London, Routledge, 2009).

Olsen, Henrik Palmer, 'The right to freedom of religion: a critical review', *Scandinavian Studies in Law* 52 (2007), 227–54.

Parmar, Sejal, 'The challenge of "defamation of religions" to freedom of expression and the international human rights', *European Human Rights Law Review* 3 (2009), 353–75.

Pinckaers, Servais, 'La dignité de l'homme selon Saint Thomas d'Aquin', *Dignitate Hominis* (Freiburg in Breslau, Verlag Herder, 1987).

Pinckaers, Servais, 'Aquinas on the dignity of the human person', in John Berkman and Craig Steven Titus (eds), *The Pinckaers Reader, Renewing Thomistic Moral Theology* (Washington DC, Catholic University of American Press, 2005).

Pinker, Stephen, 'The stupidity of dignity', *New Republic* (28 May 2008), 28.

Popper, K. R., 'Against big words (a letter not originally intended for publication)', in K. R. Popper, *In Search of a Better World Lecture and Essays from Thirty Year*, trans. L. J. Bennett (London, Routledge, 1994).

Poscher, Ralf, 'The principles theories: how many theories and what is their merit?', in M. Klatt (ed.), *Institutionalized Reason* (Oxford, Oxford University Press, 2012).

Randall, Melanie, 'Equality rights and the charter: reconceptualizing state accountability for ending domestic violence', in F. Faraday, et al. (eds), *Making Equality Rights Real, Securing Substantive Equality under the Charter*, 2nd edn (Toronto, Irwin Law, 2009).

Rao, N. 'On the use and abuse of human dignity in constitutional law', *Columbia Journal of European Law* (2008), 201–55.

Ratzinger, Joseph, 'The dignity of the human person', in Herbert Vorgrimler, gen. ed., *Commentary on the Documents of Vatican II* (London and New York, Burns & Oates/Herder and Herder, 1969).

Ratzinger, Joseph, 'Concerning the notion of person in theology', *Communio: International Catholic Review* 17 (1990), 439–54.

Resnick, Judith, and Suk, Julie Chi-hye, 'Adding insult to injury: questioning the role of dignity in conceptions of sovereignty, *Stanford Law Review* 55 (2003), 1921.

Rietjens, J. A., Heide, A. van der, Onwuteaka-Philipsen, B. D., Maas, P. J. van der, and Wal, G van der, 'Preferences of the Dutch general public for a good death and associations with attitudes towards end-of-life decision-making', *Palliative Medicine* 20:7 (October 2006), 685–92.

Rivers, Julian, 'Liberal constitutionalism and Christian political thought', in Paul Beaumont (ed.), *Christian Perspectives on the Limits of the Law* (Carlisle, Paternoster Press, 2002).
Rivers, Julian, 'The secularisation of the British Constitution', *Ecclesiastical Law Journal* 14 (2012), 371–99.
Rivers, Julian, 'The right to religious liberty in English law', in W. Cole Durham, Ana Maria Celis, and Silvio Ferrari (eds), *God in the Constitution* (Aldershot, Ashgate, 2013 forthcoming).
Rolf, S., 'Human embryos and human dignity: differing presuppositions in human embryo research in Germany and Great Britain', *The Heythrop Journal* 53 (2012), 742–54.
Rorty, Richard, 'Human rights, rationality, and sentimentality', in Stephen Shute and Susan Hurley (eds), *On Human Rights: The Oxford Amnesty Lectures 1993* (New York, Basic Books, 1993).
Rorty, Richard, 'International books of the year—and the millennium', *Times Literary Supplement* (2 December 1999), 11.
Rosen, Michael, 'Dignity past and present', in Jeremy Waldron (ed. Meir Dan-Cohen), *Dignity, Rank, and Rights* (Oxford, Oxford University Press, 2012).
Rothstein, Mark A. and Talbott, Meghan K., 'The expanding use of DNA in law enforcement: what role for privacy?', *Journal of Law, Medicine and Ethics* 34 (2006), 153.
Rozakis, Christos L., 'The European judge as comparatist', *Tulane Law Review* 80 (2005), 257.
Rubios, Juan López de Palacios, *El Requerimiento* (1513), in M. Delgado (ed.), *Gott in Lateinamerika* (Düsseldorf, Patmos, 1991).
Sandel, Michael, 'Religious liberty—freedom of conscience or freedom of choice?', *Utah Law Review* (1989), 597.
Schaede, Stephan, 'Würde—eine ideengeschichtliche Annäherung aus theologischer Perspektive', in Petra Bahr and Hans Michael Heinig (eds), *Menschenwürde in der säkularen Verfassungsordnung. Rechtswissenschaftliche und theologische Perspektiven* (Tübingen, Mohr Siebeck, 2006).
Schaede, Stephan, 'Ban on anthropological images and human dignity: some theological remarks', paper presented at The Concept of Human Dignity in a Transatlantic Perspective: Foundations and Variations: A Berlin Dialogue on Trans atlantic Legal Culture(s), Wissenschaftskolleg zu Berlin, 16–18 November 2011.
Schauer, Frederick, 'Balancing, subsumption, and the constraining role of legal text', in M. Klatt (ed.), *Institutionalized Reason* (Oxford, Oxford University Press, 2012).
Schlemmer, Lawrie, 'The factors underlying apartheid', in Peter Randall (ed.), *Anatomy of Apartheid* (Johannesburg, Spro-Cas, 1970).
Schmiesing, Kevin, 'A history of personalism' (1 December 2000), available at SSRN.
Schroeder, Doris, 'Human rights and human dignity: An appeal to separate the conjoined twins', *Ethical Theory and Moral Practice* 15:3 (2012), 323–35.

Schwarzer, Alice (ed), *Frauen gegen den §218. 18 Protokolle, aufgezeichnet von Alice Schwarzer* [*Women Against §218: Eighteen Interviews, Recorded by Alice Schwarzer*] (1971), 146.

Scott, Rebecca J., 'Public rights, social equality, and the conceptual roots of the Plessy challenge', *Michigan Law Review* 106 (March 2008), 777–804.

Sedgh, Gilda, Singh, Susheela, Shah, Iqbal H., Ahman, Elisabeth, Henshaw, Stanley K., and Bankole, Akinrinola, 'Induced abortion: incidence and trends worldwide from 1995 to 2008', *The Lancet*, 379:9816 (18 February 2012), 625–32.

Sen, A., 'Human rights and the limits of law', *Cardozo Law Review* 27 (2006), 2913–27.

Sensen, Oliver, 'Human dignity in historical perspective: the contemporary and traditional paradigms', *European Journal of Political Theory* 10 (2006), 71–91.

Shaffer, Martha, 'The battered woman syndrome revisited: some complicating thoughts five years after *R. v Lavallee*', *University of Toronto Law Journal* 47 (1997), 1.

Siegel, Reva B., 'Dignity and the politics of protection: abortion restrictions under *Casey/Carhart*', *Yale Law Journal* 117 (2008), 1694.

Siegel, Reva B., '*Roe*'s roots: the women's rights claims that engendered *Roe*', *Boston University Law Review* 90 (2010), 1875.

Siegel, Reva B., 'Dignity and sexuality: claims on dignity in transnational debates over abortion and same-sex marriage', *International Journal of Constitutional Law* 10 (April 2012), 355–79.

Siegel, Reva B., 'Constitutionalization of abortion', in Michel Rosenfeld and András Sajó, *Oxford Handbook of Comparative Constitutional Law* (Oxford, Oxford University Press, 2012).

Smuts, Barbara, 'Reflections', in J. M. Coetzee, *The Lives of Animals* (Princeton, NJ, Princeton University Press, 1999), 107–22.

Sorabji, Richard, 'Epictetus on *proairesis* and self', in Theodore Scaltsas and Andrew S. Mason (eds), *The Philosophy of Epictetus* (Oxford, Oxford University Press, 2010).

Spaemann, Robert, 'Über den Begriff der Menschenwürde', in Ernst-Wolfgang Böckenförde and Robert Spaemann (eds), *Menschenrechte und Menschenwürde: Historische Voraussetzungen, säkulare Gestalt, christlisches Verständnis* (Stuttgart, Klett-Cotta, 1987).

Spindelman, M., 'Are the similarities between a woman's right to choose an abortion and the alleged right to assisted suicide really compelling?', *University of Michigan Journal of Law Reform* 29:3 (Spring 1996), 775–856.

Staunton, C., 'Brustle v Greenpeace, embryonic stem cell research and the European Court of Justice's new found morality', *Medical Law Review* 21:3 (2013), 310–19.

Steele, Claude M., 'Race and the schooling of Black Americans', *The Atlantic Monthly* (April 1992).

Steele, Claude M., 'A threat in the air: how stereotypes shape intellectual identity and performance', *American Psychologist* 52 (1997), 613.

Sterckx, S. and Cockbain, J., 'Assessing the morality of the commercial exploitation of inventions concerning uses of human embryos and the relevance of moral complicity: comments on the EPO's WARF Decision' *SCRIPTed* 7:1 (2010), 83.

Suarez, Francisco, *De Triplici Virtute Theologica, Fide, Spe & Charitate* (1621), in Francisco Suarez, *Selections from Three Works* (Oxford, Clarendon Press, 1944).

Sudre, Frédéric, 'L'article 3 *bis* de la Convention européenne des droits de l'homme : le droit à des conditions de détention conformes au respect de la dignité humaine', in *Mélanges en hommage au Doyen Gérard Cohen-Jonathan*, vol. 2 (Brussels, Emile Bruylant, 2004).

Sulmasy, D. P., 'Dignity and bioethics: history, theory, and selected applications', in E. D. Pellegrino, A Schulman, and T. W. Merrill (eds), *Human Dignity and Bioethics* (South Bend, IN, University of Notre Dame Press, 2009).

Sulmasy, Daniel, 'The varieties of human dignity: a logical and conceptual analysis', in *Medicine, Health Care and Philosophy* (March, 2012).

Tasioulas, John, 'The legal relevance of ethical objectivity', *American Journal of Jurisprudence* 47 (2002), 211.

Tasioulas, John, 'Taking rights out of human rights', *Ethics* 120 (2010), 647–78.

Tasioulas, John, 'On the nature of human rights', in G. Ernst and J-C. Heilinger (eds), *The Philosophy of Human Rights: Contemporary Controversies* (Berlin and Boston, MA, de Gruyter, 2012).

Tasioulas, John, 'Towards a philosophy of human rights', *Current Legal Problems* (2012), 1–30.

Taylor, Charles, 'The politics of recognition', in Amy Gutmann (ed.), *Multiculturalism and the 'Politics of Recognition': An Essay by Charles Taylor* (Princeton, NJ, Princeton University Press, 1992).

Taylor, Charles, 'Why we need a radical redefinition of secularism', in Eduardo Mendieta and Jonathan Vanantwerpen (eds), *The Power of Religion in the Public Sphere* (New York, Columbia University Press, 2011).

Tietze, Christopher, 'Abortion in Europe', *American Journal of Public Health* 57 (1967), 1923.

Tkacz, Michael, *Journal of the History of Philosophy* 39:4 (2001) 584–85.

Tollefsen, Christopher, 'John Paul II and children's education', *Notre Dame Journal of Law, Ethics, and Public Policy* 21 (2007), 159–89.

Tollefsen, Christopher, 'A Catholic perspective on human dignity', in Steven Dilley and Nathan Palpant (eds), *Human Dignity and Bioethics: From Worldviews to the Public Square* (New York, Routledge, 2012).

Toobin, Jeffrey, 'Comment: learning from gay marriage', *The New Yorker* (8 February 2012).

Ullrich, Dierk, 'Concurring visions: human dignity in the Canadian Charter of Rights and Freedoms and the Basic Law of the Federal Republic of Germany', *Global Jurist Frontiers* 3:1 (2003), 1–103.

Valadier, Paul, 'The person who lacks dignity', *Concilium* 2 (2003), 51–6.

Vialatoux, Joseph, 'Dignité du groupe? Ou de la personne humaine?: Physique et métaphysique de l'ordre des valeurs', in *La Personne humaine en péril* (Lyon, Semaines sociales, 1938).

Vining, Joseph, 'Fuller and language', in Willem J. Witteveen and Wibren van der Burg (eds), *Rediscovering Fuller: Essays on Implicit Law and Institutional Design* (Amsterdam, Amsterdam University Press, 1999).

Vining, Joseph, 'The mystery of the individual in modern law', *Villanova Law Review* 52 (2007), 1.
Vlastos, Gregory, 'Human worth, merit, and equality', in J. Feinberg, *Moral Concepts* (Oxford, Oxford University Press, 1982).
Vlastos, Gregory, 'Justice and equality', in Louis P. Pojman and Robert Westmoreland (eds), *Equality: Selected Readings* (New York, Oxford University Press, 1997).
Voegelin, Eric, 'The new science of politics', in *The Collected Works of Eric Voegelin*, vol. 5: *Modernity Without Restraint* (Columbia, University of Missouri Press, 2000).
Volkmann, Uwe, 'Nachricht vom Ende der Gewissheit', *Frankfurter Allgemeine Zeitung* (24 November 2003), 8.
Wadman, Meredith, 'Bioethics gets an airing', *Nature* (7 July 2010).
Waldron, Jeremy, 'Theoretical foundations of liberalism', in Jeremy Waldron, *Liberal Rights* (Cambridge, Cambridge University Press, 1993).
Waldron, Jeremy, 'Dignity and rank', *European Journal of Sociology* 48:2 (August 2007).
Waldron, Jeremy, 'How law protects dignity', NYU School of Law, Public Law Research Paper (December 2011), No. 11–83.
Waldron, Jeremy, 'Dignity, rights, and responsibilities', *Arizona State Law Journal* 43 (2011), 1107.
Waldron, Jeremy, 'Does "equal moral status" add anything to right reason', New York University School of Law, Public Law & Legal Theory Research Paper Series, Working Paper No. 11–52.
Waldron, Jeremy, 'Dignity and defamation: the visibility of hate', *Harvard Law Review* 123 (2011), 1596.
Walters, Mark, 'Written constitutions and unwritten constitutionalism', in Grant Huscroft (ed.), *Expounding the Constitution: Essays in Constitutional Theory* (Cambridge, Cambridge University Press, 2008).
Weingart, Peter, 'A short history of knowledge formations', in Robert Frodeman et al. (eds), *The Oxford Handbook of Interdisciplinarity* (Oxford University Press, Oxford 2010).
Weinrib, Lorraine, 'The postwar paradigm and American exceptionalism', in Sujit Choudhry (ed.), *The Migration of Constitutional Ideas* (New York, Cambridge University Press, 2006).
Whitman, James Q., '"Human dignity" in Europe and the United States: the social foundations', *Human Rights Law Journal* 25 (2004), 17–23.
Whitman, James Q., 'Human dignity in Europe and the United States', in G. Nolte (ed.), *Europe and US Constitutionalism* (Cambridge, Cambridge University Press, 2005).
Whitman, James Q., 'On Nazi "honour" and the new European "dignity"', in C. Joerges and N. Galeigh (eds), *Darker Legacies of Law in Europe* (Oxford, Hart, 2003).
Wihl, Tim, 'Wahre Würde: Ansätze zu einer Metatheorie der Menschenwürdetheorien', in Carsten Bäcker and Sascha Ziemann (eds), *Junge Rechtsphilosophie* (Stuttgart, Franz Steiner Verlag, 2012).

Williams, David R., et al., 'Perceived discrimination, race and health in South Africa', *Social Science Medicine* 67(3) (2008), 441–52.
Williams, Rowan, 'Secularism, faith, and freedom', in *Faith in the Public Square* (London, Bloomsbury, 2012), 23.
Williams, Thomas D. and Bengtsson, Jan Olof, 'Personalism', in *The Stanford Encyclopedia of Philosophy* (Summer 2011), http://plato.stanford.edu/archives/sum2011/entries/personalism/.
Witte, Bruno de, 'The trajectory of fundamental social rights in the European Union', in Gráinne de Búrca and Bruno de Witte (eds), *Social Rights in Europe* (Oxford, Oxford University Press, 2005).
Wixson, Sally K., 'The role of the IACUC in assessing and managing pain and distress in research animals', in M. Lawrence Podolsky and Victor S. Lukas (eds), *The Care and Feeding of an IACUC: The Organization and Management of an Institutional Animal Care and Use Committee* (Boca Raton, FL, CRC Press, 1999).
Wojtyla, Karol, 'On the dignity of the human person', in *Person and Community: Selected Essays*, trans. Theresa Sandok (New York, Peter Lang 1993).
Wojtyla, Karol, 'The person: subject and community', in *Person and Community: Selected Essays*, trans. Theresa Sandok (New York, Peter Lang, 1993).
Wolcher, Louis E., 'The problem of the subject(s)', in Anne Wagner and Jan M. Broekman (eds), *Prospects of Legal Semiotics* (London and New York, Springer Dordrecht Heidelberg, 2010).
Wolff, Jonathan, 'Five types of risky situation', *Law, Innovation and Technology* 2 (2010), 151.
Woolman, Stuart, 'Dignity' in Stuart Woolman, Michael Bishop, and Jason Brickhill (eds), *Constitutional Law of South Africa*, 2nd edn (Juta and Co., 2006).
Yadollahpour, Behrouz, 'Human dignity and its consequences in the Holy Qur'an', 2011 International Conference on Sociality and Economics Development, IPEDR vol. 10 (2011), 551.
Yeung, Karen, 'Can we employ design-based regulation while avoiding *Brave New World*', *Law, Innovation and Technology* 3 (2011).
Yoshino, Kenji, 'Lose the baseball analogy' *Slate* (21 December 2010).
Ypi, Lea, 'Self-ownership and the state: a democratic critique', *Ratio* 24:1 (2011), 91–106.
Yuill, K., 'Assisted dying: a product of pessimism, book review of George Pitcher, *A Time to Live: The Cases against Euthanasia and Assisted Suicide*, *Spiked Review of Books* (Friday 30 July 2010).
Yuill, K., 'Why those who favour abortion rights should oppose the legalisation of assisted suicide', *Pro-Choice Forum Opinion, Comment & Reviews: Ethical Issues* (31 August 2001).
Zakaria, Fareed, 'Culture is destiny: a conversation with Lee Kwan Yew', *Foreign Affairs* 73:2 (March/April 1994), 109–26.
Zitner, Aaron, 'Patently provoking a debate', *Los Angeles Times* (12 May 2002), A1.
Zumbansen, Peer, 'Governance: an interdisciplinary perspective', in David Levi-Faur (ed.), *The Oxford Handbook of Governance* (Oxford, Oxford University Press, 2012).

Tables of Cases, and Other Legal Authorities

Table 1. State constitutions and legislation

Brazil
Brazil Constitution 63, 72

Canada
Charter of Rights and Freedoms 362, 475
    Sec. 7 546, 548
    Sec. 15 546
Controlled Drugs and Substances Act S.C. 1996, c. 19,
    Sec. 4(1) 548
    Sec. 5(1) 548
    Sec. 56 548
Human Rights Code, R.S.O. 1990 c. H. 19 (Ontario) 546, 550, 552

France
Decree of 27 April 1848 61, 117
Organic statute of 10 July 1940 118

Germany
Weimar Constitution
    Art 151 5, 118
German Basic Law (Grundgesetz für die Bundesrepublik Deutschland [Grundgesetz] [GG]), 1949 5, 79–93, 96, 101, 108–9, 111, 119, 260, 270, 367, 382, 384–6, 510, 514, 655
    Art 1(1) xv, 79, 83-4, 92-3, 260, 270, 369, 385, 387, 475, 611
    Art. 2(1) 372, 389
    Art 79(3) 367
Strafgesetzbuch [StGB]
    Para. 218a 518

Hungary
Fundamental Law in force in Hungary since January 2012 118

India
Constitution of India, 1950
    Art. 21 373

Ireland
Constitution of Ireland (1937) 95–111, 117, 518
    Preamble 5, 95, 101, 103, 105
    Art. 44 104
    Eighth Amendment of the Constitution Act, 1983, 1983 Acts of the Oireachtas,7 Oct. 1983 (amending Ir. Const., Art. 40.3.3) 518

Israel
Basic Law: Human Dignity and Liberty, 1992 364, 373–380
    Art. 2 xv, 367
    Art. 4 367

Italy
Italian Constitution 1946
    Art. 36 115, 118

South Africa
Constitution [Interim] of the Republic of South Africa, Act 200 of 1993
    Sec. 10 474
Constitution of the Republic of South Africa, 1996 371–377, 467–481
    Sec. 1 362, 474
    Sec. 7(2) 367
    Sec. 10 474
    Sec. 37 474
Immorality Act 23 of 1957 472
Immorality Amendment Act 21 of 1950
    Sec. 20A 472
Prohibition of Mixed Marriages Act 55 of 1949 472
Prohibition of Mixed Marriages Amendment Act 21 of 1968 472

Spain
Franco's Constitution (1947 Fuero de los Espanoles) 98, 118
Spanish Constitution (Constitución Española), 1978
    Sec. 10 362
Spanish Ley Orgánica 2/2010, de 3 de marzo, de salud sexual y reproductive y de la interrupción voluntaria del embarazo 520

TABLES OF CASES, AND OTHER LEGAL AUTHORITIES 701

United Kingdom
Human Fertilisation and Embryology Act 1990
    Sec. 3(3) 581
    Sec. 3(4) 581
Human Rights Act 1998 168
Infanticide Act 1938 536
    Sec. 1 156
    Sch. 1 156
National Assistance Act 1948
    Part III 159, 167
Nationality, Immigration and Asylum Act 2002
    Sec. 55(5)(a) 169
Trade Union and Labour Relations Act 1974
    Sched. 1 para. 6(5) 407

United States
Agreement of the People of 1647 439
Animal Welfare Act, 7 United States Code, 99 Stat. 1645 (1985)
    Sec. 2132(n) 580
    Sec. 2142 580
    Sec. 2143
        2143(a)(3)(C)(iv) 580
        2143(b)(1) 580
    Sec. 2144 580
    Sec. 2145 580
    Sec. 2146 580
Chimpanzee Health Improvement, Maintenance, and Protection Act, Pub. L. No. 106-551, 114 Stat. 2753 (2000)
    Sec. 481C(d)(2) 576
    Sec. 481C(d)(2)(I) 576
    Sec. 481C(d)(3) 576
Code of Federal Regulations Part 46,—Protection of Human Subjects, Subpart D—'Additional Protections for Children Involved as Subjects in Research', 45 Code of Federal Regulations 46.401-.9 576
Consolidated Appropriations Act (United States), Pub. L. No. 108-99, 118 Stat. 3, 101 (2004)
    Sec. 634 577
Fundamental Orders of Connecticut (1637) 439
Maine Revised Statute Annotated title 7 (2001)
    Sec. 3907 587

Massachusetts Body of Liberties (1641) 439
Military Selective Services Act (1940)
    Sec. 6(j)) 425
Oregon Revised Statues 127.800–995 539
Uniform Trust Code (2005)
    Sec. 408 580

Table 2. International and regional treaties and conventions

Council of Europe
Convention for the Protection of Human Rights and Dignity of the Human Being with regard to the Application of Biology and Medicine: Convention on Human Rights and Biomedicine, CETS No.164 (Oviedo Convention) 3, 547
    Art. 18 351, 537
        Art. 18(1) 351
        Art. 18(2) 352
European Convention of Human Rights and Fundamental Freedoms, 1950 17, 50, 168, 393–402, 405
    Art. 2 397
    Art. 3 169, 395–7, 401
    Art. 4 115, 397–8
    Art. 6 639, 646, 647
    Art. 8 114, 156, 160, 170, 174, 183, 352, 399–400, 459, 638
    Art. 9 405, 451
    Art. 10 400
    Art. 14 394, 395, 639
    Art. 17 400
    Protocol 1 Art. 2 395
    Protocol 11 395
    Protocol 13 646

European Union
Directive 2006/24/EC of the European Parliament and of the Council of 15 March 2006 on the retention of data generated or processed in connection with the provision of publicly available electronic communications services or of public communications networks and amending Directive 2002/58/EC, *OJ L 105, 13.4.2006 , pp. 54–63* 176
Directive 98/44/EC of the European Parliament and of the Council of 6 July 1998 on the legal protection of biotechnological inventions, *OJ L 213, 30.7.1998, pp. 13–21*

Art. 6(2)(c) 349
European Charter of Fundamental Rights 113, 115, 394, 641, 647
    Chapter I 394
        Art. 1 114, 394
        Art. 2 114, 394
        Art. 3 114, 394
        Art. 4 114, 394
        Art. 5 114, 115, 394
        Art. 25 114
        Art. 31 114, 115
Treaty of Amsterdam amending the Treaty on European Union, the Treaties establishing the European Communities and certain related acts - Protocol annexed to the Treaty of the European Community - Protocol on protection and welfare of animals, Official Journal C340, 10/11/1997, p. 0110 584

United Nations
Universal Declaration of Human Rights, 1948 xx, 2, 4, 5, 16, 17, 27, 56, 96, 106, 123, 129, 131, 132, 148, 149, 161, 214, 249, 291, 305, 393, 394, 402, 525, 600, 601, 621, 624, 629, 643
    Preamble 126, 127, 393
    Art. 1 xv, 113
    Art. 2 128, 148
    Art. 5 401
    Art. 10 640
    Art. 23 393
International Covenant on Civil and Political Rights, 1966
    Preamble 151–2, 338, 643
    Art. 2 338
    Art. 7 401
    Art. 10 643
    Art.14 639
International Covenant on Economic, Social and Cultural Rights, 1966
    Art. 7 644
    Art. 12 (1) 296
    Art. 13 644
Convention on the Rights of the Child, 1989
    Art. 23 645
    Art. 28 645
    Art. 37 645
    Art. 39 644

Art. 40 644
Universal Declaration on Bioethics and Human Rights, General Conference of UNESCO, 33d Session, 19 October 2005
   Art. 2 348
   Art. 3 348
Convention on the Rights of Persons with Disabilities, 2006
   Art. 1 645
   Art. 8 645
   Art. 16 645
   Art. 24 645
   Art. 25 645
International Convention for the Protection of All Persons from Enforced Disappearance, 2006
   Art. 19(2) 645

Table 3. Cases and opinions

Argentina
Corte Suprema de Justicia de la Nación [CSJN] [Supreme Court of Justice of the Nation], 13/3/2010, 'F, A. L. s/ Medida Autosatisfactiva,' Expediente Letra 'F', N° 259, Libro XLVI (13 March 2012) 520

Canada
Canada (Attorney General) v PHS Community Services [2011] 3 S.C.R. 134 546
Chaoulli v Quebec, [2005] 1 S.C.R. 791 577
Egan v Canada (1995) 29 CRR (2d) 79 475
In the Matter of the Estate of Clive Wishart, 129 N.B.R.(2d) 397 (New Brunswick Court of Queen's Bench, 1992) 580
Law v Canada (Minister of Employment and Immigration), [1999] 1 S.C.R. 497 618
Nova Scotia (AG) v Walsh, [2002] 4 S.C.R. 325 363
R v Big M Drug Mart Ltd [1985] 1 S.C.R. 295 451
R v Kapp, 2008 SCC 41 610
R v Lavallee, [1990] 1 S.C.R. 852 554–6
R v Malott, [1998] 1 S.C.R. 123 555–6
R v Oakes (1986) 19 CRR 308 475
R v Ryan, 2013 SCC 3 556–7
Rodriguez v British Colombia (Attorney General), [1993] 3 S.C.R. 519 530
Syndicat Northcrest v Amselem [2004] 2 S.C.R. 551 460

Werbeski and Tranchemontange v Ontario (Director, Disability Support Program) Ont. Social Benefi ts Tribunal, File No. 9910-07541R 0050-04579, aff'd, Ontario (Director, Disability Support Program) v Tranchemontagne (2009), 95 OR (3d) 327 (Ont. Div. Ct.), aff'd Ontario (Director, Disability Support Program) v Tranchemontagne (2009), 95 OR (3d) 327 (Ont. C.A.) 550

Colombia
Corte Constitucional (Constitutional Court), May 10, 2006, Sentencia C-355/2006, 25, Gaceta de la Corte Constitucional (Colombia) 519

Court of Justice of the European Union
Case C-372/04, The Queen, on the Application of Yvonne Watts v. Bedford Primary Care Trust, Secretary of State for Health [2006] ECR I-4325 577
Case C-34/10, Brüstle v Greenpeace eV [2012] All ER (EC) 809 (ECJ) 349
Case C-36/02, Omega Spielhallen- und Automatenaufstellungs-GmbH v Oberbürgermeisterin der Bundesstadt Bonn, [2004] ECR 1-9609 351, 604
Case C-555/07, Seda Kücükdeveci v Swedex GmbH & Co KG [2011] 2 SMLR 27 610

European Commission and Court of Human Rights
A, B and C v Ireland (25579/05) (2011) 53 EHRR 13 523
Bayatyan v Armenia (23459/03) (2012) 54 EHRR 15 407
Bock v Germany (A/150) (1990) EHRR 247 402
Campbell and Cosans v United Kingdom (7511/76) (1982) 4 EHRR 293 395, 452
Chapman v United Kingdom (27238/95) (2001) 33 EHRR 18 399
Cossey v United Kingdom (10843/84) (1991) 13 EHRR 622 399
Cyprus v Turkey (25781/94) (2002) 35 EHRR 30 395
Dordevic v Croatia (41526/10) (2012) 15 CCL Rep 657 397
East African Asians v United Kingdom (1981) 3 EHRR 76 395
Evans v United Kingdom (6339/05) (2008) 46 EHRR 34 351
Frérot v France (70204/01) [2007] ECHR 396
Gäfgen v Germany (22978/05) (2011) 52 EHRR 1 83, 163
Garaudy v France (65831/01) [2003] ECHR 400
Goodwin v United Kingdom (28957/95) (2002) 35 EHRR 18 399
HL v United Kingdom (45508/99) (2005) 40 EHRR 32 158
I v United Kingdom (25680/94) (2003) 36 EHRR 53 618
Jersild v Denmark (A/298) (1995) 19 EHRR 1 400
Kokkinakis v Greece (A/260-A) (1994) 17 EHRR 397 405, 451

Kudla v Poland (30210/96) (2002) 35 EHRR 11 396
L v Lithuania (27527/03) (2008) 46 EHRR 22 400
Lautsi v Italy (30814/06) (2012) 54 EHRR 3 457, 465
Leyla Şahin v Turkey (44774/98) (2007) 44 EHRR 5 647
M.S.S. v Belgium (30696/09) (2011) 53 EHRR 2 647
Mouisel v France (67263/01) (2004) 38 EHRR 34 396
MS v United Kingdom (24527/08) (2012) 55 EHRR 23 169
Murray v United Kingdom (18731/91) (1996) 22 EHRR 29 398
Nachova v Bulgaria (43577/98) (2006) 42 EHRR 43 395
Obst v Germany (425/03) [2010] ECHR 459
Open Door and Dublin Well Woman v Ireland (14234/88) (1993) 15 EHRR 244 519
Othman (Abu Qatada) v United Kingdom (8139/09) (2012) 55 EHRR 1 170
Pretty v United Kingdom (2346/02) (2002) 35 EHRR 1 114–5, 160, 168, 170, 399
Rantsev v Cyprus (25965/04) (2010) 51 EHRR 1 398
Rees v United Kingdom (A/106) (1987) 9 EHRR 56 399
Ribitsch v Austria (1995) 21 EHRR 573 396
Schüth v Germany (1620/03) (2011) 52 EHRR 32 459, 464
Selmouni v France (25803/94) (2000) 29 EHRR 403 396
Şerife Yiğit v Turkey (3976/05) (2011) 53 EHRR 25 647
SH v Austria (57813/00) (2011) 52 EHRR 6 (Chamber); [2011] ECHR (Grand Chamber) 349
Siliadin v France (73316/01) (2006) 43 EHRR 16 397–8
SW v United Kingdom (A/335-B) (1996) 21 EHRR 363 114
Tekin v Turkey (22496/93) (2001) 31 EHRR 4 396
Thlimmenos v Greece (34369/97) (2001) 31 EHRR 15 407
Tremblay v France (37194/02) [2007] ECHR 397
Tyrer v United Kingdom (A/26) (1979-80) 2 EHRR 1 395, 399
Valasinas v Lithuania (44558/98) 12 BHRC 266 396
Vereinigung Bildender Künstler v Austria (68354/01) (2008) 47 EHRR 5 647
Vo v France (53924/00) (2005) 40 EHRR 12 351, 397

European Patent Office
Wisconsin Alumni Research Foundation, Case G 0002/06, Eur. Patent Off., 23–26 (Nov. 25, 2008) 349–50

France
Conseil d'Etat, 27 October 1995, Commune de Morsang-sur-Orge, no 136727, Rec. Lebon 372, Commune de Morsang-sur-Orge v Société Fun Production et M Wackenheim 40, 339, 604, 618

Cour de Cassation, deuxième chambre civile [Cass. 2e civ.], 4 November 2004, Cour de Cassation [Appellate Court, France] première chambre civile [Cass. 1re. civ.], 12 July 2001, SNC PrismaPresse et al. c/ Saada, dit Sarde 617
Cour de Cassation, première chambre civile [Cass. 1re. civ.], 7 March 2006, F P+B, F. c/Sté Hachette Filipacchi associés 617
Cour de Cassation, première chambre civile [Cass. 1re. civ.], 9 October 2001; A. C. c/ C.et al. [arrêt no. 1511 P+B+R] 618

Germany
BGH, 14 February 2007—IV ZR 267/04 599
BVerfG, 1 BvR 1783/05, vom 13.6.2007, Absatz-Nr. (1 - 151) 617
BVerfG, 1 BvR 1807/07 vom 19.2.2008, Absatz-Nr. (1 - 39) 83
BVerfG, 1 BvR 256/08 vom 2.3.2010, Absatz-Nr. (1 - 345) 180
BVerfGE 1, 299 80
BVerfGE 1, 97 [Hinterbliebenenrente] 382, 385, 600
BVerfGE 103, 142 79
BVerfGE 109, 133 [Langfristige Sicherungsverwahrung] 384
BVerfGE 109, 279 [Großer Lauschangriff] 384, 385, 387
BVerfGE 115, 118 [Luftsicherheitsgesetz] 83, 383, 389
BVerfGE 125, 175 [Hartz IV] 383
BVerfGE 2, 1 385
BVerfGE 27, 1 [Mikrozensus] 369, 384
BVerfGE 28, 386 [Kurzzeitige Freiheitsstrafe] 384
BVerfGE 30, 173 (Mephisto) 92, 369
BVerfGE 39, 1 [Schwangerschaftsabbruch I] 387, 389
BVerfGE 4, 1 178
BVerfGE 45, 187 [Lebenslange Freiheitsstrafe] 369, 384, 612
BVerfGE 5, 85 612
BVerfGE 57, 250 [V-Mann] 384
BVerfGE 72, 105 [Lebenslange Freiheitsstrafe] 384
BVerfGE 75, 369 [Strauß-Karikatur] 387
BVerfGE 88, 203 (Abortion II) 510, 516
BVerfGE 9, 89 [Gehör bei Haftbefehl] 384
BVerfGE 93, 266 ['Soldaten sind Mörder'] 387
BVerfGE 96, 375 [Kind als Schaden] 384
BVerwGE 25 July 2007—6 C 39.06 599
BVerwGE 64, 274 (Peep Shows) 619
Oberlandesgericht Frankfurt/Main, 1 U 201/11 of 10 October 2012 83

708 TABLES OF CASES, AND OTHER LEGAL AUTHORITIES

Hungary
Alkotmánybíróság [AB] [Hungarian Constitutional Court] 58/2001 (XII. 7) 618

India
Francis Coralie Mullin v Delhi, AIR 1981 SC 746 366, 373
Olga Tellis v Bombay Municipal Corporation, AIR 1986 SC 180 373

Inter-American Court of Human Rights
Case of Yakye Axa Indigenous Community v Paraguay, Judgment of June 17th, 2005, Inter-Am. Ct. H.R. (2005) 618

Ireland
Article 26 and the Regulation of Information (Services outside the State for the Termination of Pregnancies) Bill 1995, In Re [1995] IESC 9; [1995] 1 IR 1 519
Attorney General v X and others [1992] 1 IR 1 519
Baby O & Another v Minister for Justice, Equality and Law Reform & Others [2002] IR 169 522

Israel
HCJ 10203/03 'Hamifkad Haleumi' v Attorney General 62(4) PD 715 (2008) 368
HCJ 10662/04 Hassan v National Insurance Institute of Israel (Feb. 28, 2012) 368
HCJ 1213/10 Nir v Speaker of the Knesset (Feb. 23, 2012) 368
HCJ 1434/03 Anonymous v. Haifa disciplinary court of state employees, 58(1) PD 538–539 (2003) 377
HCJ 2245/06 Dovrin v Israeli Prison Service (Jun. 13, 2006) 368
HCJ 2605/05 Academic Center for Law and Business v Minister of Finance 368
HCJ 2911/05 Alhanati v Minister of Finance 62(4) PD 406 (2008) 368
HCJ 355/05 Anonymous v the Biological Parents 60(1) PD 124 (2005) 368
HCJ 366/03 'Commitment to Peace and Social Justice Society' v Minister of Finance 60(3) 464 (2005) 368
HCJ 453/94 Israel Women's Network v Government of Israel 48(5) PD 510 [1994] 385
HCJ 4293/01 'New Family' v Minister of Work and Welfare (Mar. 24, 2009) 368
HCJ 4593/05 Bank Hamizrachi v the Prime Minister (Sep. 20, 2006) 368

TABLES OF CASES, AND OTHER LEGAL AUTHORITIES   709

HCJ 466/07 Gal'on v Attorney General (Jan. 11, 2012) 368
HCJ 5100/94 Public Committee against Torture v Government of Israel (Sept. 6, 1999) 612, 617
HCJ 5394/92 Hupert v Yad Vashem 48(3) PD 353, 362 [1994] 385
HCJ 5688/92 Vicselbaum v Minister of Defense, 47(2) PD 812, 827 (1993) 364
HCJ 6298/07 Rasler v Knesset (Feb. 21, 2012) 368
HCJ 7052/03 Adalah v Minister of Interior, 61(2) PD 202 (2006) 368
HCJ 6427/02 Movement for Quality Government in Israel v Knesset 61(1) PD 619 (2006) 363

Portugal
Tribunal Constitucional, Acórdão no 75/2010, Processos nos 733/07 and 1186/07, March 26, 2010, Diário da República vol. 60, at 15566 520

South Africa
Booysen v Minister of Home Affairs and Another 2001 (4) SA 485 (CC) 371
Brink v Kitshoff NO 1996 (4) SA 197 (CC) 470, 477
Christian Education of South Africa v Minister of Education 2000 (4) SA 757 (CC) 453
Dawood v Minister of Home Affairs 2000 (1) SA 997 (C), 2000 (3) SA 936 (CC) 371, 474, 477
Du Toit v Minister for Welfare and Population Development [2002] ZACC 20; 2003 (2) SA 198 (CC) 477
Ferreira v Levin 1996 (1) SA 984 (CC) 371
Government of the Republic of South Africa and Others v Grootboom, 2001 (1) SA 46 (CC) 363-4, 612, 618
Harksen v Lane [1997] ZACC 12; 1998 (1) SA 300 (CC) 475, 477
Islamic Unity Convention v Independent Broadcasting Authority 2002 (4) SA 294 (CC) 377
Jordan v State 2002 (6) SA 642 (CC); (11) BCLR 1117 (CC) 363, 619
Khumalo v Holomisa 2002 (5) SA 401 (CC) 371, 473
Le Roux v Dey, 2011 (3) SA 274 (CC) 481
MEC for Education, Kawzulu-Natal v Pillay 2008 (2) BCLR 99 451
Minister of Home Affairs v Fourie [2005] ZACC 19; 2006 (1) SA 524 363, 469, 477, 480–1
National Coalition for Gay and Lesbian Equality v Minister of Justice (CCT 10/99) [1999] ZACC (17; 2000 (2) SA 1; 2000 (1) BCLR 39 (2 December 1999) 363, 371, 469, 473, 477, 599, 610
NM v. State 2007 (5) SA 250 (CC) 617

President of the Republic of South Africa v Hugo [1997] ZACC 4; 1997 (4) SA 1 (CC) 475, 477
Prinsloo v Van Der Linde, 1997 (3) SA 1012 (CC) 363
S v Cooper (the SASO/BCP trial), 3 May 1976 471
S v Makwanyane [1995] ZACC 3; 1995 (3) SA 391 (CC) 363, 474, 476–7
Satchwell v President of Republic of South Africa [2002] ZACC 18; 2002 (6) SA 1 (CC) 477

Spain
Tribunal Constitucional, STC 53/1985, Pt 11(b), April 11, 1985, 1985-49 Boletin de Jurisprudencia Constitucional 515 519

United Kingdom
A v Secretary of State for the Home Department [2004] UKHL 56 170
Catholic Care (Diocese of Leeds) Decision of the Charity Commission, 21 July 2010 459, 465
Catholic Care (Diocese of Leeds) v Charity Commission for England and Wales [2010] PTSR 1074 (HC) 459, 465
Catholic Care (Diocese of Leeds) v Charity Commission for England and Wales CA/2010/0007 26 April 2011 (Charity Tribunal) 459, 465
DM v Doncaster Metropolitan Borough Council [2011] EWHC 3652 (Admin); (2012) 15 CCLR 128 158
Khaira v Shergill [2012] EWCA Civ 983 412
McFarlane v Relate Avon Ltd [2010] IRLR 872 (CA) 453
Napier v The Scottish Ministers [2004] S.L.T. 555 617
R (Barry) v Gloucestershire County Council [1997] AC 584 157
R (F) v Secretary of State for the Home Department [2010] UKSC 17 169
R (Limbuela) v Secretary of State for the Home Department [2005] UKHL 66 169
R (McDonald) v London Borough of Kensington and Chelsea [2011] UKSC 33 156
R (Playfoot) v Governing Body of Millais School [2007] HRLR 34 (Admin) 460
R (Pretty) v Director of Public Prosecutions [2002] 1 AC 800 160
R (Purdy) v Director of Public Prosecutions [2009] UKHL 45 159
R (SB) v Governors of Denbigh High School [2007] 1 AC 100 (HL) 460
R (Stennett) v Manchester City Council [2002] UKHL 34 158
R (Williamson and Others) v Secretary of State for Education and Employment [2005] 2 AC 246 (HL) 452
Shergill v Purewall [2011] EWCA Civ 815 411

United Nations, Human Rights Committee
Committee on Civil and Political Rights, Concluding Observations of the Human Rights Committee, Islamic Republic of Iran, U.N. Doc. CCPR/C/IRN/CO/3 (2011) 646
Communication no. 1249/2004, Sister Immaculate Joseph v Sri Lanka, U.N. Doc. CCPR/C/85/D/1249/2004 (Hum. Rts. Committee 2005) 646
Communication No. 854/1999, Wackenheim v France, UN Doc. CCPR/C/75/D/854/1999 (2002) 40, 644
Communication nos. 1853/2008 and 1854/2008, Atasoy and Sarkut v Turkey, U.N. Doc. CCPR/C/104/D/1853-1854/2008 (Hum. Rts. Committee 2012) 646

United States
Ambach v Norwick, 441 U.S. 68 (1979) 334
Bowers v. Hardwick, 478 U.S. 186 (1986) 477
Burton v Brooklyn Doctors Hospital, 452 N.Y.S.2d 875 (N.Y. App. Div. 1982) 577
Capers Estate, 340 D. & C.2d 121 (Orphan's Court PA, 1964) 580
Employment Division, Department of Human Resources of Oregon v Smith, 494 U.S. 872 (1990) 406
Furman v Georgia, 408 U.S. 238 (1972) 336
Hall v Decuir, 95 U.S. 485 (1877) 69
Hosanna-Tabor Evangelical Lutheran Church and School v Equal Employment Opportunity Commission, 565 U.S. 132 S.Ct. 680 (2012) 406
In re Cincinnati Radiation Litigation, 874 F. Supp. 796 (S.D. Ohio 1995) 577
Lawrence v Texas, 539 U.S. 558 (2003) 467, 477
Loving v Virginia, 388 U.S. 1, 87 S.Ct. 1817, 18 L.Ed.2d 1010 (1967) 479
Nyquist v Mauclet, 432 U.S. 1 (1977) 334
Planned Parenthood of Southeastern Pennsylvania v Casey, 505 U.S. 833 (1992) 151, 521
Tachiona v Mugabe, 169 F.Supp 2d 259, 313 (S.D.N.Y. 2001) 41
Trop v Dulles, 356 U.S. 86 (1958) 336–7
United States v Seeger, 380 U.S. 163 (1965) 425

Index

9/11 190, 262

abolitionism 63, 74, 123, 596
abortion 1, 12, 14–15, 17, 21, 120, 204, 240, 483, 486, 498, 502, 509–23, 528, 612, 619, 633
    constitutionalization of 509, 510–13, 522–3
    counselling 509–10, 513, 515, 516, 517, 520, 521, 535, 538
    criminalization of 510, 511, 512, 516
    debates 82–3, 532–6, 538
    and disability 533
    government regulation of 510, 518, 522
    and law 37, 48–9, 153, 161–2, 165, 170, 185, 387, 389
    liberalized access to 510–11, 512–13, 533
Abortion Law Reform Association 532
adoption
    Catholic agencies 459, 465
    same-sex 476, 477, 478
adultery 459, 464, 494
Africa, anti-colonial sentiment 127
Afro-Creole activists (Louisiana) 64–5, 69, 77
Agamben, Giorgio 260, 261–2, 268, 271
agnosticism 405
AIDS
    care for sufferers 627
    research 575
Aktion 218 512, 513
alcoholism 551, 552
Alexy, Robert 183

Alzheimer's disease 90, 303, 565–6
Ambrose, St 199
American Civil War 64–5
American Convention on Human Rights 616
American Declaration of the Rights and Duties of Man (1948) 393
American Revolution 4, 123
amor mundi 265–9
ancient philosophers 193–8, 239–40
Anglo-Irish Treaty (1921) 102
animals
    boundary between humans and 74, 86, 130, 294, 302, 306, 307, 315, 430–1, 447, 573, 579, 581, 584, 586, 587–90
    cruelty to 579
    on death of owner 580
    dignity of 9, 192, 587
    individuality in 575–81, 587
    and pain 255
    research on 575–6, 579–80
    rights 241, 307
    and sanctity of life 21
    slaughter of 231
    status of 8
    sympathy for 190
Anscombe, Elizabeth 504, 507
anthropology xxii, 24, 47, 213, 216, 217, 218, 219, 220, 229, 405, 421, 608, 613, 625, 626, 635, 652
anti-colonialism 123, 127, 128, 560, 596
anti-essentialism 18, 19
anti-Semitism 287, 308
apartheid 468, 469–73, 475–6, 477, 479, 505, 596, 633

Aquinas, Thomas 23, 26, 134, 136, 147, 191, 193, 197, 199–200, 202, 205, 212–13, 220, 221–2, 229, 230, 231, 266, 322, 438, 486, 489, 507, 528, 596, 632
Arab Spring (2011) xix, xxiii
Arendt, Hannah 337–8
Argentina
  abortion law 520
  Supreme Court 520
Aristides 234
Aristotle 129, 130, 131, 136, 191, 193–6, 197, 198, 202, 203, 205, 231, 239, 240, 301, 338, 339, 340, 429, 430–1, 507, 596
Armenians 133
art, dignity and 595–6
artificial insemination 81
Aschenberg, Reinhold 88
Ash'ariyyah school 437
Asia, anti-colonial sentiment 127
assisted suicide xii, xxii, 1, 12, 120, 151, 159–60, 240, 243, 397, 619, 633
  dignity and 528–34, 538, 611
  see also euthanasia
asylum seekers 127, 169
atheism 405, 439, 645
Aubenas, Florence 559
Augustine, St 30, 198, 217–19, 220, 221–2, 223, 229, 230, 266, 268, 463, 507, 563–4
Auschwitz 52, 567
Austria
  constitutional corporatism 98
  ECtHR ruling 349, 352–3
authenticity 422, 457, 458
authoritarianism 330
  corporate 108
  religious 104, 106
autonomy 245, 251, 261, 302, 304, 368, 415
  and circumstance and choice 539, 544–5

and dignity xxii, 36–7, 38–40, 42, 149–52, 168, 178, 180, 192, 421, 424, 433, 440–3, 447, 452, 455, 509, 527, 530, 531, 539–46, 549, 557, 598, 600
  impaired 545
  of individuals 456, 457, 459, 608, 634
  limits of individual 604, 618–19
  moral 38
  of personality 81
  principle of 124, 129–30
  protection of 557, 593, 618
  radical 620
  and religious freedom 421
  of religious groups 406, 407, 417, 418, 419
  respect for 428, 433–4, 634
  rights based on 190, 204
  sexual 175
aviation security 383, 389–90
avoidant personality disorders 88
axia 193, 194, 197, 203

Bacon, Francis (artist) 255
Bacon, Francis (philosopher) 144
Badura, Peter 81, 82
Baer, Susanne 115
Banerjee, Abhijit 570–1
Banks, General Nathaniel 67
Barak, Aharon xxv, 12, 50, 51, 52, 53, 55, 163, 170, 361–80, 631, 641
barbarism 126
Barry, Brian 417
Barth, Karl 286
basic good 24, 25, 412, 487, 488, 489–90, 491, 494, 502, 609
basic needs 130, 131, 132, 164, 179, 192, 369, 370, 374, 615, 628
basket clauses/rights 372, 373
battered woman syndrome 555–6
Bavaria, constitution 7, 108
Bayle, Pierre 448–9

Beattie, Tina xxv, 11–12, 16, 31, 32, 51, 53, 259–74
Beethoven, Ludwig van 584
behaviour, dignified 315, 317, 644
Beitz, Charles 107
Belgium
　constitution 119
　euthanasia/assisted suicide 533
Belton, Paddy 101–2
Benedict XVI, Pope 26, 137
　and dialogue between faith and reason xii, xx–xxi, 139
　see also Ratzinger, Joseph
benefits, entitlement to 550
Bentham, Jeremy 526–7
Bergsträsser, Ludwig 85–6, 87–8
Berlin, Isaiah 87
Bernard of Clairvaux 235
Bernhardt, Judge 400
Besson, Samantha 656
Betancourt, Ingrid 571
Bettelheim, Bruno 88
Bible 29, 31, 123, 134, 136, 231, 264
　and God-given sacredness 278–87
Big Bang 584
Biko, Stephen Bantu 471, 473
Bill of Rights (Germany) 372, 382, 385, 386
Bill of Rights (Israel) 373–5, 385
Bill of Rights (South Africa) 371, 474
Bill of Rights (UK) 402
Bill of Rights (US) 362, 402, 639
bioethics 3, 22, 124, 149, 150, 279, 345–6, 347, 349–53, 354–5, 372, 389, 612, 628
　use of dignity in debates on 525–38
Birkenau 52
black consciousness 471
Blackburn, Simon 19
blasphemy 406
blindness, to human aspect 560, 561, 569–71
bloodline, purity of 240–1

Blueshirts 101
body parts, sale of 252
Boethius 220
Bonhoeffer, Dietrich 273
Bot, Yves 349
Brazil
　abolition of slavery 72, 74
　constitutional amendment 63, 76
　slave labour (*trabalho escravo*) 62–3, 72–7
British Medical Journal 149
Brown, Simon, Lord 156, 158
Brownsword, Roger xxv–xxvi, 345–58, 363
Brüstle, Oliver 349–51, 353, 537
Buchenwald 88, 575
Buddhism, and human dignity 436, 437, 645

Cahill, Edward 104
Cameron, Edwin xxvi, 13, 37, 467–82
　response to 501–8
Campbell-Bannerman, Henry 167
Canada
　animal rights 580
　Charter of Rights and Freedoms 362, 475, 546, 577
　citizenship 335
　dignity cases 546–57, 618
　religious freedom 423, 424
　Supreme Court 475, 554, 556, 557
capital punishment 185, 474, 599
capitalism 488
Caputo, John 269
Cardoso, Fernando Henrique 73
Carmouche, Pierre 70
Carozza, Paolo G. xxvi, 14, 56–7, 159, 163, 453–4, 615–29
case law 365, 411, 451
　abortion 510, 535
　Canadian 546–57
　ECtHR 169, 395–402, 405, 451, 459
　Israeli 374

case law *cont.*
  South Africa 376, 480–1
  United Kingdom 167, 169–70, 451, 1655–61
Casti connubi 98
Catechism 483
categorical imperative 316, 322, 323
Catholic Bishops' Conference of England and Wales xii, xx
Catholic Church
  and *amor mundi* 265
  anti-revisionism 18, 19, 23, 24, 25–6, 27, 28
  and celibacy 635
  debates on dignity xix–xx, xxi, 15–19, 57, 97–101, 133–9, 147–8, 190, 198–205, 209–28, 229–43, 266–9, 438, 439, 483–99, 635–6
  decline in secular power 17, 23
  forbidden medical procedures xi–xii
  human rights debates 16–18, 106, 137, 138
  interaction with secular culture 23, 213
  issues of human dignity within 635
  and liberal democracy 203–5
  and marriage 483–99, 488–99
  mission of 210–11
  moral voice 17
  revisionism 18, 19, 22–3, 24, 25–6, 27, 28
  scandals in 635
  and sexual orientation 23–4, 635
  and slave labour in Brazil 73, 75, 76
  social teaching 7, 24, 102, 148, 149, 191, 202, 203, 205, 655
  treatment of women 23, 635
Catholic states 98
CCTV 357
censorship
  and privacy 617
  and racism 400

Central Committee of German Catholics 512
Chapman v UK 399
Chappel, James 98, 99
character 191
Charter of Fundamental Rights of the European Union (2000) 394
chastity
  clerical 635
  premarital 494
chattel slavery 63, 72
children
  and dignity 90, 192, 200, 446, 644
  disabled 627
  and marriage 25, 478–9, 490, 492, 496–7, 498, 502, 503
Chimpanzee Health Improvement, Maintenance, and Protection Act (US) (2000) 576
chimpanzees 575–6
choices
  bad 539–40, 550, 551
  circumstances and 539, 544–5, 552–3, 556, 557–8
  pro-life vs pro-choice 120
  responsibility for 544, 545, 551, 553
Christ
  crucifixion 274
  earthly ministry 284–7
  as *homo sacer* 260, 271–4
  as image of God 234–6
  incarnation 283, 285–6
  resurrection 236–9, 264, 285, 286
  suffering of 236, 255, 264, 272, 286
Christian Democracy 7, 109, 401
  and constitutionalism 97, 103, 108
Christian personalism 26–8, 39, 92, 191, 201–5, 452, 461–5, 600
Christianity
  and dignity 15, 30–1, 198–201, 438–9, 645, 647
  and freedom and relationship with others 620

Christianity *cont.*
  and inclusiveness 284
  ministry of early church 287
  and optimal exchange of gifts 463
  partnership with political power 287
  and religious freedom 410–11
  and sacred worth of humans 275–88
  and social life 136
  and status concept of dignity 147
  violence and conquest in name of 260, 265, 274, 287
  see also Catholic Church; Protestantism
Christine Goodwin and I. v UK 399
Christopher, St 240
Churchill, Winston S. 167
Cicero xix, 147, 191, 196–8, 199, 240, 596
circumstances, and choice 539, 544–5, 552–3, 556, 557–8
citizenship 198, 199, 541
  active and passive 329, 331
  and apartheid 468, 470
  basis for 333–4
  and dignity 9, 42, 327–43
  for freed slaves 64, 66
  full moral 476, 481, 482
  loss of 336–7
  rights and responsibilities of 334, 335, 336, 338–40
  women's 511, 517
  world 426
civil rights 71, 170, 541–2
civil society 98, 99, 101, 330, 442, 461
Clark, Stephen R. L. 585–6
class interest 601
cloning 372, 537
coercion 49, 260, 267, 458
  religious 453, 455, 465
Coetzee, J. M. 570
Cohen, G. A. 430
Cold War 107, 137, 600, 652
collectivism 28

Colombia
  abortion law 519–20
  Constitutional Court 519–20
colonialism 31, 123, 125, 260, 265, 601, 603, 633, 643
comatose state 305
common good xi, 17, 95, 137, 148, 202, 203, 222, 227, 340, 434, 449, 456, 462, 465, 495, 497, 526, 527, 615, 623
communality 426
communication 445–8
communism 27, 28, 99, 100, 103
community 136–7, 138, 167, 178, 186, 203, 224–5, 226, 227, 242, 247, 287, 441, 461
comparative law 55, 181, 371, 373, 379
compassion 233, 237, 278, 280, 284, 628, 629
concentration camps 8, 52, 88, 127, 262, 270, 567, 573–4, 575
conception 241
conciliarism 248
concretization 593, 602
Confucianism 125
conscience
  convictions of 423
  freedom of 412, 414, 415–16, 422, 423, 425, 427–8, 431, 432, 433, 442, 451
  and religious belief 410, 440, 449, 455
  sacredness of 134, 135
conscientious objection 407, 424–5
consensus
  on basic requirements of dignity 129
  European 647–8
  on marriage 502
  overlapping 55–6, 184–5, 364, 453–4, 501, 606, 623
consent
  informed 150
  principle of 146

consent *cont.*
    and sexual expression 481
    to sexual intercourse 398
consequentialism 34–5, 253, 319, 342
Constantinianism 411
constitutional essentials 453
constitutional rights
    clash of 365, 370–1, 377–8
    complementary overlap of 370–1, 375–7
    human dignity as 366–80, 632
    limits on 366, 372, 377–8, 386–7
constitutional value, human dignity as 361–6, 370, 380, 390
constitutionalism
    abstract 452, 454
    corporatist 101
    dignitarian 95–6, 97
    liberal 115
    new 102, 103
    religious 97, 101–5, 109, 110, 111
constitutions
    and Christian democracy 97
    concept of dignity in European 114
    and dignity 640–2
    drafting of 50
    human rights and dignity as watchwords in 96, 119, 361–6, 382
    limitation clauses 386
    see also specific countries
consummation, of marriage 25, 503, 507, 508
contemptus mundi 265–9
contraception 21
contract law 350
contractarianism 340–3
contractualism 441, 442
control, loss of 530, 531
Controlled Drugs and Substances Act (Canada) 548, 549
Convention on Human Rights and Biomedicine 347, 536–7

Convention on the Prevention and Punishment of the Crime of Genocide (1948) 126
Convention for Protection from Enforced Disappearance 645
Convention on the Rights of the Child 644
Convention on the Rights of Persons with Disabilities 644
convictions, compulsion to act against 86
corporal punishment 86, 395, 644
corporations, and constitutional right to human dignity 367–8
corporatism 9–10, 97–102, 191, 201–3
    authoritarian 108, 109
Corvino, John 502
cosmology 584–5
cosmopolitanism 426
Costa, Jean-Paul xxvi, 50, 393–402
Cotton, John 427, 432
Council of Europe 347, 394, 647
counter-majoritarian difficulty 152
courts
    decision-making 177
    and ideas of dignity in British 158, 159, 160, 163
    use dignity to illegitimately overrule democratic authority 152–3, 164
    see also specific courts
creation 212, 228, 229–31, 237, 238, 239, 269, 278–9, 284
crimes of the past 633
criminal law 164, 176, 183, 357, 398, 473, 510–11, 579
criminals 446, 447
    homosexuals as 473, 476
Cuba, slavery in 63
cultural difference 126, 131
Cyprus v Turkey 395

Dachau 88, 575
Dante 230, 231

Daschner, Rudolf 163, 171, 183
data protection 173–4, 186
Data Retention Directive (EU) 176, 180
daughter-rights 366, 374–5, 376–7, 378, 379, 631–2, 642
de Valera, Éamon 101, 102–3, 104–5, 106, 109
death
    in Christian teaching 232–4
    dignity of deceased 90, 92, 192, 225, 254, 305, 308
    dignity in 71, 75, 159, 191–2, 204, 243, 531
    humiliation after 92
    life after 236–9, 254
    and remembrance 254
death drive 263
death penalty 185, 474, 599
decision-making 39, 564
    by women 542
    circumstances and bad 539–40
    consequentialist 319
    ethical 146–7, 149, 161
    individual capacity for 302
    judicial x, xi, 161
Declaration of Independence 240, 640–1
Declaration of the Rights of Man and the Citizen 117, 402
degradation xv, 49, 62, 70, 72, 74, 75, 76, 92, 114, 163, 169, 170, 184, 216, 225, 227, 252, 256, 303, 319, 369, 374, 400, 471–2, 473, 475, 482, 527, 615, 617, 623
dehumanization 27, 76, 107, 226, 247, 270
Deleuze, Gilles 654
Dellavalle, Sergio xxvii, 29, 37–8, 39, 47, 242, 435–49
Delp, Alfred 89
dementia xxii, 41, 90, 242, 311, 446, 565–6

democracy 12, 52, 193–4, 315
    checks on 107
    and citizenship 334–5, 339–40
    and civilization 171
    conservative 108
    and dignity 108, 152–3, 168, 171
    and freedom of religion 405
    and human rights 292
    liberal 118–19, 203, 406, 408, 409, 451
    participation in 203
    post-war Catholicism and 149
    promotion of freedom at expense of truth 488
    religious 109
denationalization 336–7
deontological ethics 34–5, 36, 192, 198, 253, 299–302, 304, 307
dependence 530, 531, 567
deportation 83
depression 91
Desdunes, Daniel 69
desecration 256, 276, 277, 308, 369, 406
despotism 87
destitution 169
desubjectification 88
Di Martino, Carmine 626, 628
dignitas 42, 193, 197, 198, 327, 328, 340
Dignitas 529
Dignitatis Humanae 17, 215, 266–7, 272, 455, 458, 486
dignity
    as absolute right 51–2, 168, 170, 269–71, 272, 319, 366–7, 369–70, 377, 386–91, 611, 632
    as analogical concept 527–8
    appearance of concept/word 5, 6, 61, 71, 96, 595–6
    applications 403–590
    attributed 41, 42, 527, 528, 530, 531

dignity *cont.*
  Catholic debates on xix–xx, xxi, 15–19, 57, 97–101, 133–9, 147–8, 190, 198–205, 209–28, 229–43, 266–9, 438, 439, 483–99, 635–6
  and choice and circumstance 539–58
  and citizenship 327–43
  cognate concepts 637–8
  communal understanding of 138
  concretization of 609–13
  consensus on 622–4, 628–9
  constitutional value and constitutional right 361–80, 390
  constitutionalization of 97, 155, 187, 509
  content of 598–602
  contradictions within 177–86, 192
  corporatist 97–101
  criticisms of 30–1, 33, 120, 124–6, 141–205, 315, 525, 623
  currency of discussion about 2–3, 245–6, 249, 346, 347–8
  definitions of xv, 111, 193, 270, 526
  different conceptions of 8–10, 46–7, 315–18, 327, 386, 435, 526–7, 598, 623, 626, 629, 631–6, 637–8, 650
  as divine gift 201
  as equal and inalienable property of all 311–12, 606, 618, 620
  as eschatological concept 245–58
  fatigue 593–614, 657
  foundations of 15, 47
  functions of 13–15
  genealogy of 594–7, 602
  hiding behind 657
  historical perspectives on 59–139, 637
  history of 3–8, 117–19, 595–7, 602
  human appeal of 614
  and human experience 615, 623, 624–9

  human nature concept of 305, 310, 430–1
  and human rights 43–7, 291–312, 345, 348–53, 393, 402, 480–1, 526, 593, 608, 610, 613, 615, 620, 631, 632, 634, 638–40
  individual 97–8, 106–7, 109
  interdisciplinary/transdisciplinary debate 58, 637–8, 642, 649–58
  internal and external 191–201
  intrinsic/inherent 41, 212, 214, 291, 305, 316–17, 362, 394, 400–1, 475, 526–7, 528, 529, 530, 617
  inviolability of 149, 151, 214, 269, 270, 319, 362, 382, 387, 475
  as invisible 251–3
  invoked by both sides in controversial debates 1, 13, 120, 177, 348–9, 389, 528, 530, 611, 619
  judicial perspectives on 359–402, 638
  justiciable 161–6
  justification of 602–9
  as last resort 631, 632, 634
  legal concept of 4, 113–21, 381–6, 593, 620, 628–9
  legal debates on 47–54
  legitimacy of 594, 595, 602–6
  liberal and conservative views of 348–9, 353
  limits of 480–1, 632
  of marriage 491–9
  meaning of 113–21
  modern law of 600–2
  as mystery 228
  negative understanding of xv, 8, 41, 118, 125, 634
  objective interpretation of 184
  philosophical perspectives on 33–43, 289–358, 637
  and politics 12, 21–2, 52–3, 454, 593, 633–4, 638

INDEX   721

power of concept 1
problems of application 318–20
as qualified right 51, 162–3
regional 646–8
regulatory aspects of 186–7, 345–58
and religious freedom 405–65
reserved and expressed 193–8
and rights 51, 189–205, 258, 480
and sacredness of life 287–8
scepticism of 33, 120
in social debate 124, 136, 212
stabilization of meaning 111
status of 617, 620, 623, 628, 629
subjectivity of xxii, 40
as task 227–8
theological perspectives on 15–33, 207–88, 637–8, 645–6
transcendent value xix, 7, 9, 16, 33, 39, 43, 145, 146–7, 152–3, 154, 246, 252, 314, 320, 324, 325, 465, 605, 606
universality of 608, 613
violation of 382, 383
who makes 116–17
Dignity in Care campaign xxii
Dignity in Dying xxii, 529
disability 156–8, 232–4, 239, 240, 397, 627, 644
and assisted suicide 531, 533
and benefits 550–3
and vulnerability 567–8
disadvantage
and life choices 544–5, 548, 558
and social and economic rights 553
disappearance, forced 615, 616, 626, 645
disciplinarity 651–4
reflexive 656–8
discrimination 13, 37, 48, 171, 369, 457, 609–10
disability 157, 531, 551
ethnic 395
gender 480

prohibition of 371, 474–5, 599, 612
racial 166, 395, 401, 467–72, 616
religious 406, 417, 424, 435, 438, 439
sexual orientation 13, 37, 467, 472–3, 504, 599, 627
disgrace 468, 476, 481
divine, relationship with the 33
Divini redemptoris 100, 101, 103, 106
divorce
civil 497
in Irish constitution 104
as offence against marriage 494
DNA 176, 178, 345, 357
Dollfuss, Engelbert 98
domestic slavery 397–8
domestic violence 553–7
Dostoyevsky, Fyodor 578
Doucet, Nicole 556–7
Douzinas, Costas 11–12, 30–1, 242, 259, 260, 261, 262–4, 265, 268, 270, 271
Dreier, Horst 82–3
drugs
addiction 546–50, 551, 552
availability of 298
care for addicts 242, 548, 549
harm reduction scheme 547–8
mind-altering 302
policy 192
use in interrogation 81, 88
Du Bois, W.E.B. 471
dual transformation test 120
Duflo, Esther 570–1
Dupré, Catherine xxvii, 5, 51, 113–21
Dürig, Günter 81, 82, 92
duty
agent-relativity 299
and citizenship 334, 339–40
requirements of 41
and rights 296–9, 301, 308, 309, 310, 311, 312
to oneself 146, 150, 317, 339

duty *cont.*
    to protect 180, 181, 184, 186, 204, 269, 382, 517, 522, 523, 535, 616, 628
    to respect others 318
dwarf-tossing 40, 151, 179, 252, 319, 604, 618, 644
Dworkin, Ronald 38, 151, 182, 416, 421, 422–3, 425, 428, 429, 431, 433, 434, 452, 457–8, 460, 532, 541

East Germany 183
Eastern Orthodox Church 219, 235
ecclesia 199, 462
eclectic reasonableness 418
economic rights 138, 545, 553, 557, 570
education
    and religion 406, 407
    right to 311, 644
    and state 498
Education Act (1944) 171
egg donors 352
Egypt, revolution 2011 xix
Eisgruber, Christopher 417
elderly
    care of the xxi–xxii, 242
    cost of care 158–9
    respect for 229
    rights to life in dignity 114, 115
Emancipation Proclamation (1863) 64, 65, 66
embryology 21, 82, 91, 241–2, 347, 349–53, 536–7, 538, 581, 628
Enlightenment 4, 12, 123, 219, 436, 594
Epictetus 86, 87
equality 144, 224, 240, 329, 368, 610, 631, 632, 633–4
    before the law 281, 544
    Catholic teaching on 138, 213–14
    commitment to 42
    concepts of 30, 361, 365
    and dignity 42–3, 48, 145, 318, 327, 371, 426, 509, 510, 531, 618
    discourse 18, 19
    God-given 278, 279, 589–90
    as key value 115, 118, 148
    moral 306
    protection of 593
    racial 18
    religiously inspired attacks on 147–9
    respect for 292, 422, 424, 426, 452, 459, 464, 544
    right to 371, 374, 379, 474, 616
    and sexual orientation 477, 482
    substantive 467
    see also social equality
erotic desire 489
eschatology 16, 245–58, 287, 439
essentialism 18–19, 39, 421, 430
eternal life 485
ethical dignity 484, 486–7, 493–4
ethical freedom 457
ethics
    Kantian 34, 322
    and morality 416, 422
    normative 34–6, 124
    religious 607
    see also bioethics; deontological ethics; medical ethics; virtue ethics
ethnic cleansing 133, 240
ethnocentrism 279
EU Charter *see* European Union Charter of Fundamental Rights
eugenics 240, 352–3, 573, 581
European Commission of Human Rights 395, 400, 401
European Convention on Human Rights (ECHR) (1950) 17, 50, 114, 115, 116, 160, 168, 169, 170, 174, 182, 183, 351, 393, 394, 395, 396, 398, 399, 401, 405, 638, 646, 647

European Court of Human Rights
(ECtHR) 1, 114, 115, 116, 118,
158, 160, 163, 168, 169, 170,
173–5, 180, 181, 182–3, 349,
352–3, 405, 407, 451, 459, 647,
656
  human dignity in jurisprudence of
    393–402
European Court of Justice 114–15,
  349–51, 641
European integration 652
European Research Council 654
European Social Charter (1961) 394
European Union
  binding definition of human dignity
    118, 641
  Charter of Fundamental Rights (EU
    Charter) 113, 114–16, 641, 647
Eusebius, Bishop 234
euthanasia xxii, 17, 240, 483, 486, 498,
  502, 529, 531, 532, 534, 538,
  573, 619
  animals 575–6
  see also assisted suicide
evangelicalism 28
Evangelium Vitae 484, 532
evolutionary psychology 124
excellence 22, 227, 487
existentialism 447–8, 449
Exit 529
Exodus 280
exploitation 77
extinction 578

Fabre, Cécile 544
facade, dignity as 144–5, 154
faith 413, 436, 438, 439, 440, 586
Familiaris Consortio 483
family
  dignity of 98
  in Irish constitution 104
family life
  and marriage 508

  right to 371, 374, 399, 459
Farley, Margaret 129
fascism 12, 27, 98, 100, 101, 106, 108,
  222
feminism 19, 48, 273
  and abortion debate 511–12, 514,
    533
  and domestic violence 555
  in Ireland 104
  and status of embryo 537
fertility treatment 138, 139, 352, 616,
  626–7
Fianna Fáil 101
Fichte, Johann Gottlieb 107
fidelity, marital/sexual 494, 503, 504,
  505
Figueira, Ricardo Rezende 75
financial crisis, global 137
Finland
  constitution 119
  ECtHR and data protection case
    173–5, 186
Finnis, John 20, 412–13, 507
First World War 144–5
foetus, status of 14–15, 21, 49, 162,
  241, 303, 305, 397, 534, 536,
  581
food 130, 131
forced labour 114, 115, 397–8
Ford Foundation 652
forgiveness 284
Foucault, Michel 219
framework-rights 374
France
  abolition of slavery in empire 4–5,
    61, 64, 117, 118
  abortion debate 512
  constitution 96, 189
  French Revolution 4, 106, 108, 117,
    118, 123, 189
  privacy laws 617
  Revolution of 1848 64
  separation of religion and state 407

France *cont.*
   Vichy regime 98, 99, 106
France, Anatole 269
Francis, Pope 26
Francis, St 236
Franciscans 248, 258
Franco, General Francisco 98, 103
Franco, Itamar 73
Frankl, Viktor 88, 91–2
free persons of colour
   in armed forces 66–8
   legally mandated segregation 62, 63
   stigmatization of 63–4, 66–71
free will 221, 323, 368, 369, 441, 442, 445, 452, 485–6, 603–4
freedom 37, 44, 221, 315, 323, 329, 348, 485, 631, 632, 633–4
   of association 137, 417, 422
   at expense of truth 488
   basic 132
   of choice 150, 192, 363, 368, 372, 421, 423, 424, 425, 428, 429, 431, 486, 527, 618–19
   conflicting notions of 619
   dependent on community 137
   of expression 49, 365, 374, 377, 417, 439
   God-given 92, 134, 189
   and human rights 301–2
   inner 9, 84, 86, 87, 89, 90, 93, 250
   intellectual 88
   meaning and nature of 618
   negative 436, 441, 442
   outer 84, 87, 89
   and personhood 130–1
   and social interaction 136
   of speech 137, 163, 170, 171, 186, 390, 612
   of thought 89, 451
   see also conscience; religious freedom
French Resistance 106
Freudianism 31, 263, 265

Friedan, Betty 511–12
friendship 25, 45, 192, 194, 196, 198, 199, 240, 295, 318, 485, 489–90, 495, 502
functionalism 196
fundamental rights jurisprudence 388
funerals 71, 75

Gadamer, H.G. 117
Galilei, Galileo 21
Gallagher, Robert L. 194, 195
Gandhi, Mahatma 507
Gaudium et Spes 17, 215, 222, 483
gay marriage *see* same-sex marriage
Gearty, Conor xvii, 12, 50, 155–71, 655
gender
   Catholic debates about 17, 23–5, 138, 139
   discrimination 480
   equality 18
   in Irish constitution 104
   transsexuals 399
Genesis 24, 29, 30, 31, 134, 217, 235, 273, 278–9, 491–2
genetic experimentation 1, 3, 372, 537, 577, 581, 586–7
Geneva Conventions 74
genocide 12, 126, 133, 263, 565, 616
Genova, Lisa 565, 570
George, Robert P. xxvii–xxviii, 20, 21, 24–5, 28, 267, 310, 478–9, 501–8
Germany
   abortion law 37, 48, 49, 82–3, 153, 161–2, 165, 170, 387, 389, 509, 512, 513–18
   Basic Law *see Grundgesetz*
   bill of rights 372, 382, 385, 386
   Christian democracy 109
   citizenship 333
   constitution 5, 249, 366–7, 372, 382, 386, 475, 632, 633

Germany *cont.*
　Constitutional Court 178, 180, 383, 384, 386, 387, 388, 389, 509–10, 513–17, 617
　constitutional debates 7–8, 49, 50, 85, 96, 97, 109, 642
　dignity as constitutional right 366–7, 369–70, 377, 379, 633, 641, 646
　dignity fatigue 657
　dignity in post-Nazi era 79–93, 108, 270, 369, 384–5, 386
　dignity as principle/absolute right 51–2, 170, 183, 189, 269–70, 386, 387, 475
　embryology 350
　human rights 89, 163
　influence of Catholicism on 109
　Länder constitutions 7, 108
　Nazis and church rights 100
　reunification and liberalization 510, 515–16
Gerstenmeier, Eugene 89
Gestapo 88
Gewirth, Alan 36
Giacometti, Alberto 595
Gilbert and Sullivan 42, 145
Gildersleeve, Virginia 107–8
Giussani, Luigi 625
gnosticism 582
God
　Church as accountable to 211
　compassion of 278, 280, 284, 285, 286
　and creation 229–31, 278–9, 284, 487
　as deliverer 282–5
　desacralized 16, 271–4
　divine love 294–5
　grace of 266, 462, 463
　as lawmaker and judge 280–2
　man made in image of *see imago Dei*
　natural social hierarchy established by 99
　non-existence of 607
　will of 28, 437, 486
Goebbels, Joseph 573–4, 576
Goerdeler, Carl Friedrich 88
Goffman, Erving 469
Gómez, Ángela de Castro 77
good, individual conceptions of the 452, 453, 460
good government 448
good will 322
Goodwin, Christine 399
Goos, Christoph xxviii, 4, 5, 7–8, 9, 50, 79–93, 642, 655
Gormally, Luke 487, 492–3
Goya y Lucientes, Francisco de 595
gratuitousness 628, 629
Gray, John 11–12, 263
Greek philosophy 123
Greenawalt, Kent 418
Greenberg, Irving 283
Greenjackets 400
Greenpeace 349
Griffin, James 35, 37, 299, 302–4
Grimm, Dieter xxviii, 50, 52, 53, 259, 260, 265, 269–70, 381–91, 655
Grisez, Germain 20
Grundgesetz xv, 5, 44, 72, 79–93, 96, 108, 109, 111, 119, 148–9, 152, 189, 260, 269–71, 382, 384–5, 386, 387, 389, 509, 513, 514, 641, 642, 655
Grünewald, Matthias 236
Guantanamo Bay 262
Guatteri, Félix 654
Gushee, David P. xxviii–xxix, 16, 28–9, 30, 31, 259, 260, 264–5, 266, 268, 271, 272, 273, 275–88
Gutmann, Amy 354, 416
gypsies 399–400

Habermas, Jürgen 11, 38, 47, 96, 247, 291–2, 452, 454–5, 456
haircuts 615, 634

Hale, Brenda, Baroness xv–xvii, xxix, 157–8, 166
Hampton, Alice 70
Hanvey, James, SJ xxii, xxix, 16, 30, 31, 32, 209–28, 430
happiness principle 147
Harris, John 525
Harrison, Joel xxix, 26, 38, 39, 40, 451–65
Have, Henk ten 355
headscarves 611, 633
healing 232–3, 284
health care 130, 131, 132, 297, 633
health and safety 358
Hegel, Georg Wilhelm Friedrich 107, 179, 265
Heidegger, Martin 537
Hell, Daniel 91
helplessness, learned 554–6
hepatitis 547
heteronomy 443
Heuss, Theodore 10, 80, 84–5, 92–3
hierarchy
    dignity as xvi, 42, 202, 327, 328
    divinely ordained 148
    of rank 541
    of rights 387
    and violation of dignity 426
hijackings 83, 383, 389–90
Hill, Thomas E. xxix–xxx, 34, 213–25
Hinduism, and dignity 645
Hirschl, Ran 97
Hitler, Adolf 107
HIV 298, 547
Hobbes, Thomas 191, 408, 441, 527
Hollenbach, David, SJ xxx, 8, 22–3, 26, 28–9, 31, 54, 55–6, 123–39, 453, 655
Holocaust 7, 89, 96, 117, 123, 126, 127, 128, 262, 264, 270, 514, 565
holy war 139

home, right to a 399–400
home-schooling 498
homelessness 559
homo sacer 260–4, 269, 271–4
homosexuality 468, 472–3, 599, 627
honour, personal 390
hospice movement 236
hospitality 233–4
hostages 571
Housing (Homeless Persons) Act (1977) 167
Houzeau, Jean-Charles 68
human beings
    intrinsic value of 29, 37, 41, 42, 84, 127–8, 147, 152, 225, 252, 253, 294, 295, 305–6, 307, 315, 316–17, 320, 324, 325, 437–8, 444, 467, 477, 503, 540, 568, 596, 597, 598–9, 601, 603–4, 607, 608–9, 610, 611, 613, 616, 619, 620, 624, 626, 627, 638
    nature of 305
    as sacred 264–5, 273, 275–88
    universality of 626
    what it means to be human 15, 54, 57, 130, 134, 210, 462, 560, 565, 568, 624
human dignity *see* dignity
Human Genome Project 345
human interests 295–312
human life *see* life
human nature 305, 310, 430–1, 484, 486, 527, 606, 619
human rights
    adjudication xi, 116, 119, 161, 164, 402, 480, 617
    Catholic tradition and 16–18, 106, 137, 138
    conflicts with 51
    and constitutional value of dignity 362–3
    different concepts of 621

INDEX 727

human rights *cont.*
  and dignity 43–7, 106, 108, 117, 120, 124–5, 126, 127, 189–205, 345, 348–53, 393, 402, 480–1, 610, 613, 615, 638–40
  dignity as foundation of 1, 3, 10, 43–4, 46–7, 145, 152, 249, 291–312, 526, 593, 608, 620, 631, 632, 634, 638–9
  history of 4
  and human interests 295–312
  and humiliation 41
  individual 137
  international 96, 643–6, 648
  inviolable and inalienable 89, 114, 149, 258, 291, 299
  justification of 292–9
  law 110, 620–1, 623
  legal debate 44
  limitable 632
  movement 621–2, 643
  and nationality 337–8
  political conceptions of 293
  positive 638–40
  regional 646–8
  and religious diversity 645, 648
  and religious freedom 408
  sanctioned violation of 182–3, 184
  secular 18, 260
  in social debate 124
  and solidarity 222–3
  and strategies of power 600
  theoretical underpinning of 2
  of those with impaired capacity 311–12
  and torture 37
  uniformity 309–10, 311
  universal 128, 643–6
  unsurpassability of 247
  violation of 44, 183–4, 293, 302, 303, 309, 393, 402, 610, 622
Human Rights Act (1998) 167, 168–9, 170, 171

human trafficking 114, 115, 398, 604
Humanae Vitae 20–1
humanism 600
  legal 610
  liberal democratic 149
  Renaissance 445, 594
  secular 226, 606, 607–8
humanity 211, 215, 627
  crimes against 252, 390, 617
  and dignity 321, 327, 363, 364, 365, 367, 369, 370, 378
  empirical 261, 262
  legal systems and understanding of 379
  normative 261, 262
  universal 260, 262, 263
  within society 369
humiliation 40–1, 42, 46, 49, 50, 77, 257, 369, 374, 527, 599, 608
  after death 92
  of Christ 227
  prohibition of 370, 634
  and racial segregation 71, 475
  and sexual orientation 473
  and slavery 62
  of those with impairment 531
  and torture 631, 634
  and working conditions 74
humility 568
Hungary, constitutional court 641–2
Hüther, Gerald 91
Huxley, Aldous 574
hybridization 581

iconicity 29, 30, 200, 462
identity
  and dignity 363, 618, 632
  and discrimination 369
  and goods 571
  and poverty 569–70
  respect for 543
  sense of 575
idolatry 125, 272–3

Ignatieff, Michael 124–5
illness 232–4, 236
  terminal 619
imago Christi 228
imago Dei 8, 16, 22, 29–30, 31, 38,
  134–5, 137, 199–200, 201, 216,
  217, 220, 221, 222, 227, 228,
  229, 231–2, 234–6, 240, 241,
  242, 243, 279, 386, 430, 435,
  436, 438–40, 441–2, 484, 485–6,
  491–3, 605, 632, 636
imago Trinitatis 216–19, 220, 221, 222,
  223–4, 225, 227, 228
immigration 334
Immorality Act (South Africa) (1927)
  472
imperialism 125, 263, 603
imprisonment 229, 239, 242, 396, 612,
  616, 627, 643
in vitro fertilization 82, 616
Incarnation 211, 220–1, 283, 285–6
inclusiveness 284
incontinence 156–8
independence, ethical 422–3
India
  anti-colonial sentiment 127
  Supreme Court 366
Indians, South American 248
indigenous peoples
  beliefs of 645
  rights of xix, 618, 627, 628
indignity 8, 40–1, 46, 68, 158, 171, 252,
  254, 529, 530
individualism 27, 194, 441
  possessive 189
  secular 101
individuals
  animals as 575–81
  autonomy of 456, 457, 459, 604,
  634
  capacity for self-definition 456–61
  centrality of 444
  conceptions of the good 452

  in modern law 574–5
  and the person 581–3
  rights of 441
  rights and state action 186
  sovereign choice of 150, 261
  treatment of 573–4, 575–81
inductive method 54–5, 56, 129–32,
  138
inequality 195
  and privilege 43
infanticide 240, 241, 532, 536
infants 303
infertility 479, 616, 626–7
Insite case 546–50, 552
Institutional Animal Care and Use
  Committees 579–80
institutions, dignity of 9, 596
instrumentalism 408–10, 412
instrumentalization 49, 222, 225, 487,
  600, 610, 611, 612–13
  of human embryos 536–7, 538
Inter-American Commission on Human
  Rights 615, 617–18
interdisciplinarity 651–3, 656–7
interiority 32–3, 40–1, 222, 256, 429,
  562–5, 570
intermediate associations 461
International Covenant on Civil and
  Political Rights (ICCPR) 151,
  152, 292, 393–4, 401, 402,
  643–4, 645–6
International Covenant on Economic,
  Social, and Cultural Rights
  (ICESCR) 292, 393–4, 401, 402,
  643, 644
International Labour Organization
  (ILO) 5, 72
Internet 173–4, 176, 178, 179–80
interrogation 81, 83, 163, 171
invisibility, and low status 559–60
Ireland
  abortion law 518–19
  Catholic politics in 97–9, 102–4, 108

Ireland *cont.*
   dignity in constitution of 5, 7, 95–106, 107, 108, 109, 111, 117–18
   Supreme Court 519
Irish Christian Front 102
Irish Free State, constitution 102
Irish Press 105
Isenheim altarpiece 236
Islam 216, 595
   and creation 229, 239
   and dignity 15, 437, 636, 645
   jihad 139
   role in world today 139
   and slaughter of animals 231
   women's dress 464, 611, 633
Isle of Man 395
Israel
   Basic Law xv, 44, 373, 374, 375
   Bill of Rights 373–5, 378, 385
   citizenship 334
   constitution 249
   constitutional law 377, 379
   and constitutional right to human dignity 367–8, 373–5, 631, 633, 641
   dignity as right 51
   God's covenant with 278, 280–3, 284
   Supreme Court 367–8, 373–5, 377, 631

Jackson, Emily 21, 49
Jackson, Mahalia 588
James, William 413
Jefferson, Thomas 240, 584
jihad 139
Joas, Hans 656
John Murray v UK 398
John Paul II, Pope 26, 213, 214, 222, 483, 484, 486, 488–9, 492, 498, 532
   see also Wojtyła, Karol
John XXII, Pope 248, 258
John XXIII, Pope 17, 215
Jones, David Albert xxx, 14–15, 34, 240, 525–38
Joshua the Stylite 234
Judaism
   concept of autonomy 546
   concept of freedom 620
   and creation 229, 239
   and dignity 15, 437, 636
   and Holocaust 7, 89, 96, 123, 126, 127, 128, 319
   and image of God 29, 216, 231, 438
   and resurrection 237–8
   and sacred worth of humans 277
   and slaughter of animals 231
   and social life 136
   see also anti-Semitism
Judgement Day 237
judges
   conservatism of 165–6
   interpretations of dignity 50, 53, 116, 155–61, 163, 164, 171, 361, 364–5, 378, 379
   and religious freedom 424
judicial perspectives on human dignity 359–402
justice
   cosmic 266
   divine 268–9
   human dignity and quest for 259
   reciprocal 203
   and virtue 194–6

Kant, Immanuel xix, 7, 8, 27, 33–4, 35, 92, 95, 96, 110, 117, 127–8, 129, 134, 143, 145, 146–7, 148, 149, 150, 152, 178, 179, 184, 190, 198, 201, 204, 212, 221, 249–50, 251, 254, 306, 339, 364, 370, 384, 467, 507, 527, 529–30, 537, 596, 597, 599, 603, 632
   criticism of 313–25
   Critique of Pure Reason 324

Kant, Immanuel *cont.*
  on dignity of citizenship 327–32, 333, 334, 336, 341–2
  Groundwork 146, 316, 318, 322–3, 324, 327
  The Metaphysics of Morals 316, 318, 328
Karpas Greek Cypriots 395
Kasper, Walter 227
Kass, Leon 537
Kemmerer, Alexandra xxxi, 58, 649–58
Keogh, Dermot 101, 103, 109
kidnapping 83, 163
Kirkpatrick, Robin 230–1
Klein, Julie Thompson 652, 653
knowledge 45
  production of 651–2, 654
Kokkinakis v Greece 405, 451
Koppelman, Andrew 414, 416
Korsgaard, Christine 146
Kreisau circle 89
Krens, Inge 91

La Cugna, Catherine 224
labour
  dignity of 22, 62–3, 72–7, 98, 114, 115, 118, 144, 190, 202
  rights 165, 167
Lacan, Jacques 271
Lamartine, Alphonse de 65
The Lancet 49
Langan, John, SJ 18, 25, 56
Langstaff, Mr Justice Brian 158–9
Lavallee, Angelique 554–5
law
  comparative 55
  dignity, autonomy and 540–6
  dignity used to introduce change to 119
  interpretation of 381–2, 383, 385
  judicial perspectives on dignity 359–402, 638
  legal debates on dignity 47–54

legal rights 542
legal scholars 116
legislation of dignity 9, 258
modern law of dignity 600–2
and morality 53
Old Testament 282
and philosophy 53–4
protecting dignity in 616
recognition/denial of claims 616
role of dignity in British 166–71
League of Nations 72
Lebacqz, Karen 282
Lebech, Mette 193
Lee Kwan Yew 125
Lee, Patrick 310
Leiter, Brian 411
Leo XIII, Pope xix–xx, 145, 147–8, 213–14
Lerche, Peter 82
Levenson, Jon 237
L'Heureux-Dubé, Justice 555–6
liberalism 30, 192, 203–4
  purely political 501, 502
  secular 97, 98, 99, 103–4, 107, 108
liberation theology 274, 632
libertinism 192
liberty 13, 48, 84, 115, 118, 135, 168, 302, 610
  concepts of 361, 365
  deprivation of 396
  dignity as 509, 510, 518, 528, 534
  dignity used to mask attacks on 525
  religious *see* religious freedom
  right to 373, 379, 398
  without religion 415–18
  see also freedom
life
  after death 236–9, 254
  biological 529
  dignity as 509, 510, 518, 529, 531, 534
  duty to protect 29, 509–10, 514, 515, 516, 517, 518, 519, 520, 521, 522, 523, 617

life *cont.*
  eternal 485
  intolerable condition of 531
  origins of 241
  pro-life vs pro-choice 120
  right to 44, 114, 115, 183, 373, 389, 474, 610, 633
  sanctity of 21, 28, 29, 31, 49, 115, 120, 124–5, 231, 241, 242, 275–88, 532
  see also abortion; assisted suicide; euthanasia
Lilje, Hanns, Bishop of Hanover 88
Limbuela, Wayoka 169
Lincoln, Abraham 65
Lisbon Treaty (2009) 113, 118, 119, 641
living conditions, decent 631, 632, 633–4
Locke, John 189, 231, 306, 409, 411, 427, 440–1, 448, 596, 632
Loizou, Judge 400
Lonergan, Bernard 18, 25–6, 430
Loos, Adolf 144
Louisiana, racial segregation 62, 63–71, 77
love
  capacity to 246, 487
  divine 294–5
  excellence in 487
  and marriage 489, 491, 492, 493, 496
Luke, St 238
Lula da Silva, Luis Inácio 73
Luther, Martin 86–7, 439, 605

McCrudden, Christopher ix–xiii, xxxi–xxxii, 1–58, 161–2, 164, 655
McDonald, Elaine 156–8, 166, 167, 170
Macintyre, Alasdair 231
McKeon, Richard 624
MacKinnon, Catharine 467
Macklem, Timothy 413–14
Macklin, Ruth 124, 149–50

Maclure, Jocelyn 423, 431, 434, 451
Madison, James 639
magisterium 17, 19, 20, 24
Mahlmann, Matthias xxxii, 8, 161, 593–614
majoritarianism 171
Malott case 555–6
Mamdani, Mahmood 125
Mandela, Nelson 1
Manetti, Giannozzo 597
Mangoldt, Hermann von 86, 88, 89
Manuel II Paleologus, Emperor 139
Maréchal, Joseph 213
Margalit, Avishai 8, 29, 30, 40–1, 46, 560
Maritain, Jacques 26, 27–8, 56, 106, 107, 132, 135, 222, 226, 428–9, 452, 461–2, 621, 623, 624, 629
marriage 9, 267
  concepts of 24–5, 251, 257, 501–8
  conjugal 24, 192, 478, 488–93, 494, 495, 496, 497, 502–3, 504, 505, 506, 507
  dignity of 491–9
  ethical choices 423
  ethical dignity of 493–4
  interracial 472, 478, 506, 507
  nature of 488–91, 494, 502, 506–7, 508
  political dignity of 495–9
  same-sex 467, 476, 477–9, 480, 504, 506, 507–8
Marshall, T.H. 541
Marten, Judge 451
Martinet, Louis 70, 71
Marx, Karl 430
Marxism 27, 31, 265, 274, 430, 632
mass movements 596–7
Massachusetts, religious persecution in 427, 432
materialism 27, 100, 107, 108, 257
Matthew, Gospel of 588, 589–90
medical care

medical care *cont.*
  denial of 577
  patient' choices about 618
medical ethics xx, 396
medical research 575–6
Meier, Christian 567
Mengele, Josef 52
mental disability 90, 158, 169, 303, 305, 310, 397, 446, 627
mental integrity, protection of 114, 617
metaphysics 34, 124, 125, 146, 209, 211–12, 245, 246, 253, 254, 314, 320, 321, 322, 324, 325, 444, 445, 603, 604–5
Metz, Johann Baptist 264
Middle Ages 4, 45, 199–201
Milbank, John xxxii, 45–6, 189–205, 271, 272, 273
military service, exemption on religious grounds 424–5
Mill, John Stuart 409–10
Miller, Daniel 571
mind, transcendence of 134, 135
minimal theism 33
miracles 232–3, 238
miscarriage 241–2, 397
Missionaries of the Poor 627
Mittelstraβ, Jürgen 652
Mobile Inspection Groups (Brazil) 73, 76
modernism 144–5
modernity 219, 263, 264, 271, 459
Möllers, Christoph xxxii, 49–50, 173–87, 655
Moltke, Helmuth von 89
monarchy 204, 281, 341
monogamy 494, 503, 504
monotheism 239, 431, 437
moral responsibility 458
moral status 36, 42, 45
morality
  basis of 413, 416
  and dignity 146, 327, 437
  disagreement about 602

and doing the right thing 345, 358
and ethics 416, 422
human dignity as standard of 123, 127, 128
Kant's views on 320–5
and law 53
political 457, 502
sexual 505
and will of God 281, 415
Mother Theresa of Calcutta 236
mother-rights 366, 374–5, 378, 631–2, 642
motorcycle helmets 418
Mounier, Edward 27–8
Moyn, Samuel xxxiii, 4, 5, 7, 8, 9, 12, 16, 89, 95–111, 190, 201, 655, 657
multidisciplinarity 57–8, 652–3
murder 183, 199, 252, 299
  see also abortion; assisted suicide; domestic violence; euthanasia; genocide; infanticide
Murray, John 398
Murray, John Courtney 135
Musonius Rufus, Gaius 507
Mu'tazilah school 437
mutilation 252
mutual aid 70–1
mutuality 30, 224, 246, 247, 369
mystery 11, 32–3, 57, 92, 228, 235, 241–2, 259, 429, 568, 584

Nabuco, Joaquim 74–5
Nagel, Thomas 151, 299–302
Najem, Nawara xix
nanotechnology 346
National Assistance Act (1948) 159, 167
National Health Service Act (1946) 167
National Organization of Women 511
National Research Council Committee on Long-Term Care of Chimpanzees 575

National Science Foundation (US) 587
nationalism 332, 601
   Irish 102
   secular 100
nationality, right to 336–8
nativism 332
natural disasters 565
natural law 19, 20, 23, 96, 123, 134, 148, 152, 266, 267–8, 483, 484, 485, 487, 494, 504, 505, 537, 607, 641
natural love 230
natural reason 33, 35, 298, 484, 491, 492
natural rights 4, 190–1, 248, 258, 293
naturalism 100
nature and nurture 32
Nazi regime 8, 27, 52, 88–9, 93, 100, 123, 183, 262, 270, 369, 384–5, 386, 573–4
neglect 40
neo-Kantianism 620
neo-liberalism 204, 264
neo-Nazism 308
neo-Platonism 218
neo-scholasticism 18
neo-Thomism 202
Netherlands, euthanasia/assisted suicide 533
Neuman, Gerald L. xxxiii, 57, 637–48
neurobiology 91
neurotechnology 346, 348
new natural law 20–2, 24, 26
New Orleans 64–5, 68, 70
New Towns Act (1946) 167
Newman, John Henry 230
Newton, Isaac 231, 575
Nichols, Vincent, Archbishop of Westminster xix–xxiii, xxxiii–xxxiv
Nietzsche, Friedrich 27, 31, 107, 144, 145, 264, 265, 288, 596
nihilism 31, 264, 265, 268

non-establishment 406, 425, 432
Nowotny, Helga 654
Nozick, Robert 151
Nuffield Council on Bioethics 354
Nuremberg Code 573
Nuremberg Trials 573–4, 577, 579
Nussbaum, Martha 412, 413, 421, 425–9, 430, 431, 433, 434

Obama, Barack xi
objectification 483, 487, 600, 610, 611, 613
obligations
   negative and positive 50, 130
   reciprocal 131, 195
   to the dead 225
   universal moral 128
oligarchy 194, 204
O'Neill, Onora 146
online dating services 173–4
Ontario Disability Support Program 550–3
Ontario Human Rights Code 550, 552
ontology 30, 38, 47, 199, 211, 213, 215–19, 220, 223, 224, 225, 226, 229, 253, 305, 421, 428, 429–30, 434, 435, 436–40, 441, 442, 443, 444, 445, 585, 586, 587, 603, 604, 616, 620
Oregon, Death with Dignity Act xxii, 529
organ donation 257
Organisation for Economic Co-operation and Development (OECD) 652, 653
original sin 220, 260, 266, 268, 438, 439, 605
Orwell, George 574
L'Osservatore Romano 105

Pacelli, Eugenio 104–5
   see also Pius XII, Pope
Pacem in Terris 17, 215

pain 232, 255, 302, 608
    relief 529
Parfit, Derek 146
Parkinson's disease 350
Parliamentary Joint Committee on
    Human Rights (UK) 164
particularism 443, 601, 636
pass laws 470
patent law 349, 350, 353
paternalism 40, 604, 635
Patristics 190, 213
Paul, St 232, 235, 236–7, 238–9, 462
peacemaking 284
peep shows 619
Pelletan, Eugène 65–6
perception
    and blindness to human aspect 561,
        562, 567–8, 569
    and the individual 583–6
Perry, Michael J. ix
persecution, religious 427, 435, 438,
    449
persistent vegetative state 303, 311
persona 198, 199
personalism 26–8, 39, 40, 92, 191,
    201–4, 222, 452, 461–5, 600
personhood 129–31, 146, 198–9, 200,
    224, 251, 254, 456, 476
    equal 596
    and human rights 302–4
    individuals and 581–3
    loss of 252, 255
    and transcendence 253–7
Petrarch 597
Pettiti, Judge 398
phenomenology, of religion 421, 429,
    431–2, 434
phenotype 574
philosophy
    and law 53–4
    perspectives on human dignity
        289–358
    and theology 57

physical integrity, protection of 114,
    131, 132, 617, 634
Pico della Mirandola, Giovanni 90–1,
    200–1, 419, 445, 597
Pinckaers, Servais-Théodore 220–1
Pinker, Stephen 124, 150, 304
Pius IX, Pope 148
Pius X, Pope 148
Pius XI, Pope 97–8, 100, 104, 105, 108
Pius XII, Pope 104, 105, 106, 107, 108,
    215
placeholder idea of dignity 11, 235,
    526, 654–6
Plantinga, Alvin 431–2
Plato 144, 194, 196, 197, 239, 256, 301,
    495, 507
Pleins, David 281
Plessy, Homer 69
pluralism 129, 303–4, 607, 657, 658
    dignitarian 655
    moral 353
    religious 124, 126, 407, 414–15,
        442, 443, 448–9, 463, 629
    social 461
Plutarch 507
police
    brutality 396, 471
    detention 396, 471, 615, 627
politics
    acceptance of defeat in 339–40
    bare life and 261–2
    and debates on dignity 165, 247
    and manipulation of public opinion
        342–3
    political dignity 484, 488, 495–9
    political theology 410–12, 595
    right to participation in 306
polyamorous partnerships 504, 506, 508
polygamy 633
poor
    care of the 233, 242, 268–9, 552–3
    deserving and undeserving 550, 552
    rights of the xix, 597

Popper, Karl 566
Popular Front 98
pornography x, 192
Porter, Jean 267
Portugal
  abortion law 520–1
  Constitutional Court 520–1
  under Salazar 98, 103, 109
postmodernity 260, 263, 264, 266, 268, 271, 419
poverty
  and invisibility 559–60
  and right to dignity 617–18, 627
  vow of 248
  and vulnerability 569–71
pregnancy 241–2
  enforced 34
  see also abortion
prenatal psychology 91
Pretty, Diane/*Pretty v UK* 160, 170, 397
prisoners of war 74
privacy, right to 160–1, 163, 170, 173, 174, 175, 178, 179–80, 181, 182, 352, 373, 399, 417, 459, 617
privilege 43
pro-choice 120
pro-life 120
problem-solving, utilitarian approach to 34
proceduralism 454, 455, 623
procreation 267, 599
  marriage and 25, 478–9, 490, 492, 496–7, 503
prohibition 453, 616
Prohibition of Mixed Marriages Act (South Africa) (1949) 472
promiscuity 504
property rights 49, 66, 72, 166, 198, 248, 258, 373
proportionality 170–1, 366, 372, 373, 376, 377–8, 612, 632
prostitution x, 319, 396–7, 398
Protestantism

contemptus mundi 265, 266
and dignity debate 275, 438–9
emphasis on individual conscience 423, 426
and image of God 200
in Ireland 104, 105
and revelation 28
psycho-technical methods, use in interrogation 81
public and private spheres 441, 448
punishment 301, 328–9, 336
  inhuman and degrading 114, 163
Purdy, Debbie 159–60, 167, 170

Quadragesimo anno 98, 103
Quod Apostolici Muneris 213–14

racial segregation 62, 66–71
racism 27, 127, 166, 309, 395, 401, 506, 601, 613
  and censorship 400
  counter-revolutionary 100
  see also apartheid; discrimination
Radbruch, Gustav 183
Rantsev v Cyprus and the Russian Federation 398
rape 176
  and abortion 518–20, 612
  of wives 398–9
rationalism 436
rationality 220–1, 235, 321, 322, 331, 485–6
Ratzinger, Joseph 217, 223–4
  see also Benedict XVI, Pope
Rawls, John 55, 151, 185, 293, 319, 415, 453, 501
reason
  practical 132–3, 135, 138
  theoretical 135
Réaume, Denise xxxiv, 13, 37, 50, 55, 539–58
reciprocity 30, 131, 195–6, 197, 203, 224
  dignity as xvi

Reconstruction Acts 68
redemption 134, 223, 239, 265, 287
reflexivity 562
Reformation 410
refugees 127, 190
regulatory discourse 186–7, 345–58
reification 598, 600, 610, 611, 613
relationality xxii–xxiii, 39–40, 129, 130–1, 136–7, 163, 221–2, 223–6, 620
relativism 108, 135, 248, 613
religion
    as act of choice 431, 432, 452, 460
    as central to social life 440
    as challenge to social order 421, 429
    and human rights 645
    individualization of 423
    non-theistic 436–7
    phenomenology of 421, 429, 431–2, 434
    shared understanding of dignity across different 133–9
    theistic 437
    theological perspectives on dignity 15–33, 207–88, 637–8, 645–6
    value of 412–15
    and violations of dignity 607
    voluntary nature of 406
religious constitutionalism 97, 101–5
religious freedom 9, 33, 37–9, 44, 49, 133, 137, 138, 266–7, 378, 603, 611, 612, 629
    concepts of 435–6
    and courts 423, 424–5
    and dignity 421–34, 435–49, 451–65
    dignity and justification of 405–19
religious groups 406, 407, 411–12, 417, 418, 419, 436, 440, 448, 449, 457, 459, 461, 464
reparations 628
reproduction
    ethical choices 423
    and marriage 490, 492, 496–7, 507
    technological support for 138, 139, 352, 389, 478, 581, 616, 626, 628
reputation, protection of 371
Rerum Novarum xix–xx, 214
respect xxiii, 28, 40, 41, 128, 129, 315, 382
    for animals 580–1
    for autonomy 428, 433–4, 634
    contractarian 340–3
    for dignity 115, 123, 126, 127, 129, 131, 190, 319, 322, 339, 348, 440, 451, 465, 486, 509, 593, 600, 628, 631, 632
    equality of 292, 422, 426, 452, 459, 464, 544
    for freedom 451, 604
    for human body 480
    for humanity 130, 317–18, 325
    for identity 543
    mutual 446, 616
    for privacy 160
    for religion 417
resurrection 236–9, 285, 286
revelation 28, 29, 31, 217, 219, 228, 275, 277, 288, 437, 438, 442, 484, 485, 491
revolution 263
RFID technology 357
Rhode Island, religious freedom in 426–7
right-to-die 159–60, 397, 633
rights
    absolute 386–91
    agent-relativity 299–300
    animals 575–81
    balancing of conflicting 181, 182, 365, 386, 387, 388, 391, 632
    and citizenship 338–40
    constitutional 365, 366–78
    dignity and 51, 189–205, 258, 480
    dignity as invisible source of 248–51

rights *cont.*
   and duty 296–9, 308, 309, 310, 311, 312
   enumerated 641
   extent of protection 387–8, 389
   as human rights 310
   inalienable 248, 258, 338
   limits on 366, 372, 377–8, 386–7, 388, 391, 611–13
   loss of 190
   of man 144
   mother/daughter- 366, 374–5, 376–7, 378, 379, 631–2, 642
   mutual recognition of 247
   negative and positive 367, 374
   objective 180–1, 205, 249
   preferred 388–9
   preservation by others 225
   as principles not rules 181–2
   subjective 45–6, 180–4, 197, 205, 248
   substantive equality approach to 467
   to nationality 336–8
   universality 626
   violation 388, 389
Riordan, Patrick, SJ xxxiv, 37–9, 46, 421–34, 458
risk paradigm 346, 354–5
Risse, Guenter 234
Rivers, Julian xxxiv–xxxv, 9, 33, 37–8, 39, 40, 48, 405–19, 461, 464
Roman law 4, 23
Rorty, Richard 43–4, 583–4
Rosen, Michael xxxv, 8, 9, 12, 30, 33–4, 41, 42, 51, 54, 143–54, 161–2, 163, 190, 192, 200, 202, 212–15, 525, 658
   criticism of Kant 313–17, 319, 320, 324
Rousseau, Jean-Jacques 189–90, 330, 632
Roussef, Dilma 73
Rwanda 133

Ryan, Nicole *see* Doucet, Nicole
Ryssdal, Judge 400

sacredness 275–8
sacrifice 257, 263
sadomasochism 399
Sager, Lawrence 417
Salamanca School of Dominicans xix, 248
Salazar, António 98, 103
salvation 223, 226–7, 230, 232, 238, 266, 414
Sam, Anna 559
same-sex marriage 24, 25, 477–9, 480, 504, 506, 507–8
same-sex relationships 138, 139, 467, 468, 469, 477
Sandel, Michael 415
sanitation 75
Saunders, Cicely 236
Scanlon, Thomas 151
scepticism 405, 418, 603
Schauer, Frederick 411
Schlink, Bernhard xxxv, 13–14, 44, 45, 631–6
Schmid, Carlo 85, 86, 89, 92–3
scholasticism 193, 218, 248, 266
Scholl, Sophie and Hans 89
Schopenhauer, Arthur 143, 144, 145, 149, 304, 603
Schüth v Germany 459, 464
scientific rationalism 263
scientific research
   regulation of 347–8, 349–53, 354–6, 581, 586
   use of animals in 575–6, 579–80
Scott, Dred 216
Scott, Rebecca J. xxxv, 4–5, 7, 8, 12, 13, 61–77, 655
Second World War 106–7, 319
   atrocities of 209, 384, 385, 394, 402, 565, 567, 573–4
   end of 148, 149

Second World War *cont.*
  papal invocation of human dignity in 106
  restabilization after 108
  supremacy of Christian democracy after 109
  and use of dignity in law 117
sectioning 158
secularism 31, 32, 105, 106, 108, 288, 411, 423, 583–4, 645, 646, 647
security, right to 398
Sedmak, Clemens xxxv–xxxvi, 26, 32–3, 39, 40, 57, 171, 429, 559–71, 655
segregation, racial 62, 468, 479
Sehnsuchtsbegriff 13–14, 634, 655
Seigel, Jerold 562
self, understanding of 562–5
self-defence, pleas of 554, 555, 557
self-definition 456–61, 465
self-degradation x
self-determination 39, 251, 512, 514, 516, 608
self-esteem 40, 567, 570
self-perception 603
self-presentation 250, 256
self-respect 318, 339, 422, 423, 457, 570, 571, 608
self-responsibility 256, 268, 339
self-sovereignty 261
self-transcendence 130
Selmouni v France 396
Sen, Amartya 301–2
senility 242, 311
Sensen, Oliver 324
Separate Car Act (Louisiana) 69–70
separation, marital 494
serfdom 86
sex workers 480
sexual harassment 115
sexual immorality 481
sexual intercourse 490–1
  extramarital 497–8, 505
  premarital 494
sexual offenders register 169
sexual orientation
  and adoption rights 459, 476
  Catholic debates over 17, 23–5, 483, 487
  constitutional protection 467–9, 477–8, 481–2
  dignity and expansion of rights 610–11
  discrimination 13, 37, 467, 472–3, 503, 599
  ethical choices 423
  and right to marry 467, 476, 477–9, 504
sexual solicitation 173–4
sexuality 267
  deviant 468, 472–3
Shakespeare, William 589
shalom 282–3, 284
shelter 131
show trials 631
sick, care of 233, 234, 236, 239, 242
Siegel, Reva xxxvi, 14, 37, 48, 49, 509–23, 535, 655
Sikhs 418
Siliadin v France 397
Silva-Tarouca Larsen, Beatrice von 357
sin, consequences of 217, 260
Singer, Peter 241, 535
slavery xix, 7, 8, 83, 86, 87, 144, 306, 581, 603, 607, 620, 631
  abolition of 4–5, 61, 117, 118, 541, 596
  anti-slavery texts/movements 5, 6, 64, 74–5, 123, 596, 597, 598, 655
  and concept of dignity 62
  contemporary 62–3, 397–8
  prohibition of 114, 115, 163, 397, 577, 579, 604, 616
  to desire 504
Smith, Peter, Archbishop of Southwark xx
smoking 192

Smuts, Jan 107
Sobrino, Jon 274
social assistance 550–3
social communication 436, 445–8, 449
social constructivism 606
social contract 330, 341, 342
social democracy 167–8, 600
social equality 64, 67, 69, 71, 148, 149
social identity 363
social imaginaries 455–6, 461
social injustice xix
social life 123, 136, 137, 235, 429, 440, 442, 462, 463, 487, 523
social persona 178–80, 186
social pluralism 461
social rights 138, 545, 553, 557, 570, 610, 612
social security benefits 383
social welfare 280, 406, 407, 410
socialism 99, 600
socio-economic rights 39, 50, 164–6, 170, 309, 545, 553, 557, 570
sodomy 472, 477
solidarity 136, 222–3, 224–5, 454, 456, 461, 463, 623, 628, 629
solipsism 585
Soskice, Janet Martin xxxvi, 16, 29, 34, 229–43
soteriology 223, 226–7
South Africa
　abortion law 521
　apartheid 468, 469–73, 475–6, 477, 479, 505
　Bill of Rights 371, 474
　constitution 110, 371, 467, 474, 476, 480
　Constitutional Court 467, 468, 469, 473, 474, 475, 477, 479, 480, 481, 617, 619
　constitutional law 376, 377, 379, 467–9, 473, 476, 477
　dignity as fundamental right and founding value 474–5, 477, 481
　dignity in jurisdiction of 618
　sexual orientation and discrimination in 13, 37, 467–9, 472–3
sovereignty 72, 102, 262, 272, 273, 620
　divine 272
　popular 148
　self- 261
Soviet Union
　tyranny of 123, 128
　West's ideological struggles with 137
Spain
　abortion law 519
　colonies in Latin America xix, 248
　constitutional corporatism 98, 109
　Constitutional Court 519
　dignity in constitution of 362
　under Franco 98, 103
sparrows 587–9
sperm donors 81, 352
Spielmann, Alphonse 400
spirit 584, 586, 587
spirituality, contemporary 460
Stalingrad, Battle of 106
state
　and dignity of marriage 497–8
　and duty to protect 180, 181, 184, 186, 204, 269, 382, 517, 522, 523, 535, 616, 628
　and education 498
　and individual will 452
　and limits to individual choice 618–19
　obligations of 369, 397
　power of 601
　and private realm 480
　and religion 407, 408–11, 425, 432, 440, 441, 456, 460, 461
　and respect for human life 509
　rise of the 594
　and taking of life 389
statelessness 337

status
  appropriate 8
  aristocratic 4, 8, 97, 194, 328
  and citizenship 333–6, 337, 340, 341
  and dignity 42–3, 97, 153, 195, 202–3, 246, 253, 305, 306, 315–16, 333, 363, 509, 541, 617
  dignity as high xv, 4, 42–3, 145, 147, 189, 327, 328
  dignity as public 528
  equality of 541, 544, 632
  of foetus 14–15, 21, 49, 162, 241, 303, 305, 397, 534, 536, 581
  of human embryos 368, 536–7
  inferior social 469, 470
  and interests 207, 306
  phylogenetic 576
  of the unborn 534, 536, 619
stem-cell research 3, 347, 372, 581, 633
stereotyping
  cultural 657
  of domestic violence 554
  of women 556
sterilization 240, 573
stigmatization 63–4, 66–71, 83, 468, 469, 471, 472, 473, 481, 482, 503, 504, 505, 545
Stoicism 197, 221, 306, 313, 327, 421, 426, 428, 431, 443–4, 445, 594
subhumans 81
subsidiarity 461
suffering 190, 200, 232, 233, 252, 255, 263, 264, 268, 279, 280, 284, 577–8, 580, 627
suicide 146, 150, 190, 529–30, 531, 532
  see also assisted suicide
Suicide Act (1961) 159, 167
Sunstein, Cass 185
surveillance 153, 357
Süsterhenn, Adolf 84, 85
Switzerland, assisted suicide 533, 539
synthetic biology 354–5

Tanaka Memorial 107
Tasioulas, John xxxvi, 33, 35–6, 37, 45, 46, 54, 291–312
Taylor, Charles 39, 423, 431, 434, 451, 454–6, 457, 459, 460, 562
Taylor, Telford 573–4, 575, 578, 579
technological advance 345–6, 347–53, 354–6, 358, 372, 536–7, 612
Tekin v Turkey 396
teleology 4, 35, 197, 221, 228, 231, 301, 455
Teresa of Avila, St 573
terrorism 190, 383, 390, 487
Tertullian 217, 218
test cases 165
test-tube babies 82
theology
  perspectives on dignity 15–33, 207–88, 637–8, 645–6
  and religious freedom 410–12
Thomism *see* Aquinas, Thomas
Thomson, Judith Jarvis 151
Tierney, Brian 248
Tillich, Paul 413
Tinchant, Private Édouard 67–8
Tinchant, Lieutenant Joseph 67
toleration, religious 409, 427, 428–9, 436, 440–3, 448, 636
Tollefsen, Christopher O. xxxvi–xxxvii, 9, 21–2, 25, 28, 267, 483–99
  response to 501–6
torture 23, 37, 42, 48, 81, 83, 88, 183, 252, 302, 400, 453, 487, 601, 608, 611, 620, 631, 633
  evidence obtained under 52
  prohibition of 114, 163, 171, 187, 370, 577, 579
totalitarianism 27, 100, 107, 108, 189, 204, 222, 589, 622
Tourgée, Albion W. 69–70
trade-offs 176, 186, 299, 300, 307, 308, 316
Trades Disputes Act (1906) 167

INDEX 741

Tranchemontagne case 550–3, 557
transdisciplinarity 652–4, 656
transport, racial segregation on 69
transsexuals 399
treaties
 human rights 638–40, 644
 human rights and dignity as
  watchwords 96
 interpretation of 640
 ratification 640
Treitschke, Heinrich von 107
Trévigne, Paul 68
trial
 by jury 639
 right to fair 398, 639
Tribune (New Orleans) 68, 69
Trigg, Roger 423–4, 434
Trinity/Trinitarianism 30, 136, 213,
  216–19, 220, 221, 222, 223–4,
  462, 485, 492, 586
Tyrer v United Kingdom 395, 399
Tunisia, revolution 2011 xix
Tutsi 133
Tutu, Desmond 570
twinning 581

ultranationalism 643
the unborn 90, 91, 162, 204, 229, 612,
  633
 duty to protect 509–23, 535
 status of 534, 536, 619
unconsciousness 41, 158, 254
unemployment 570
Uniform Trust Code (USA) 580
L'Union 64, 65–6, 68
United Kingdom
 abortion 532, 535–6
 adoption services 459
 assisted suicide 529
 Bill of Rights 402
 case law 155–61, 169–70, 451
 citizenship 333–4
 dignity and the law 155–71

religious freedom 424, 461, 464
United Nations
 Charter 95, 101, 107
 Committee on Economic, Social and
  Cultural Rights 644
 data on abortion 533
 General Assembly 126, 292
 Human Rights Committee (HCR)
  151, 643, 644, 645
 UNESCO 3, 347, 348, 349, 577
 see also International Covenants;
  Universal Declaration of Human
  Rights
United States
 abortion law 37, 48, 511–12, 521,
  523, 535
 animal rights 575–6, 579–80
 assisted suicide xxii, 529, 533
 Bill of Rights 362, 402, 639
 citizenship 333, 335, 336–7
 Civil War 64–5
 concept of individual dignity in
  Second World War era 106–7,
  108
 constitution 96, 189, 387, 405,
  640–1
 First Amendment 423, 425, 432
 health care reforms xi–xii
 interracial marriage 506
 President's Council on Bioethics
  124, 345–6, 354–5
 racial segregation 66–71
 religious freedom 421, 423, 424,
  425–7, 429, 434
 separation of religion and state 407
 slavery in southern states 63, 64–6
 Supreme Court 216, 336–7, 406
Universal Declaration on Bioethics and
 Human Rights (2005) 3, 347,
 348, 349, 577
Universal Declaration of Human Rights
 xv, xx, 2, 5, 16, 17, 27, 56, 96,
 106, 113, 123, 126, 127, 128,

Universal Declaration of Human Rights *cont.* 129, 131, 132, 148, 149, 161, 189, 249, 291, 393–4, 400–1, 402, 526, 601, 621, 624, 629, 643
universal human community 131
universalism 125, 260, 412, 438, 440, 443, 444, 636, 643
universals, abstract 11
utilitarianism 10, 27, 34, 147, 192, 197, 342, 409–10, 463, 527, 632
utopianism 11–12, 263, 264

vaccinations 634
Valticos, Judge 398
Vancouver 546–7
Vanier, Jean 567–8
Vargas, Getúlio 72
Vatican I 18
Vatican II 17, 22, 134, 135, 136, 204, 215, 222, 224, 266, 455, 483, 486, 487
Vialatoux, Joseph 99–100
Vichy regime 98, 99, 106
victim test 117
Vining, Joseph xxxvii, 9, 32, 573–90
violence
    colonial 31
    rejection of 284
virtue ethics 34–5, 36, 194, 196, 634
Vitoria, Francisco de 248
Vo v France 397
Volkmann, Uwe 83
Vollmann, William 559
Voluntary Euthanasia (Legalization) Society xxii, 529, 532
vulnerability 32, 90, 91, 93, 169, 263, 337
    and blindness of aspect 561, 562
    and human dignity 565–9
    recognition of 569

Wackenheim, Manuel 151, 152, 644
Waldron, Jeremy xxxvii, 8, 9, 13, 42, 53–4, 166, 168, 212, 306, 327–43, 528, 658
Wallace, David Foster 566
Wallraff, Günter 559
Walsh, David J. xxxvii, 16, 26, 31, 245–58, 429
Walsh, Edmund A. 106–7
Walshe, Joseph 104, 105
Walzer, Michael 280
war, state of 183
Warren, Earl, Chief Justice 336–7
water, access to clean 615
Waters, Ethel 588
the weak, dignity and 90–2
Weber, Helene 85, 90
Weick, Karl 186
Weimar Constitution 5
Weinrib, Lorraine 388
welfare state 543, 550, 569
Weltanschauung (world view) 448
Wessel, Helene 84
West Germany *see* Germany
Westphalia, Treaty of 427
white supremacists 62, 69, 70
William of Ockham 248
Williams, Bernard 150, 342
Williams, Glanville 532
Williams, Roger 426–7
Williams, Rowan, Archbishop of Canterbury 463
Williams, Thomas 26–7
Wilson, Dean Edward 549
Wilson, Justice 555
Wittgenstein, Ludwig 145, 246, 560–1
Wojtyła, Karol 222–3
    see also John Paul II, Pope
Wolcher, Louis 263, 268, 271
Wolterstorff, Nicholas 294, 295, 309–10
women
    and abortion 48–9, 153, 162, 185, 509, 511–12, 514–17, 535
    autonomy of 515, 517, 519, 542–3, 556

women *cont.*
    Catholic understanding of role of 23
women *cont.*
    changing view of 510
    and domestic violence 553–7
    equality of 23, 240, 306, 597, 633
    and infanticide 536
    in Irish constitution 104
    modest dress of Muslim 464, 611, 633
    position of 542–3, 603, 607, 613, 635, 636
    stereotyping of 556
    violations of 398–9
    voting rights 104, 165, 599
    women's movement 596, 597, 598–9

Woolf, Virginia 598–9
working class movements 596, 597
working conditions
    dignified 5, 7, 114, 115, 118
    and slave labour 63, 72–7
worship
    coercion of 453, 455, 465
    freedom of 378, 436, 440, 442, 455
    uniformity of 409, 449
Würde des Menschen 79, 81, 90

Xenophanes 507

Zysset, Alain 656

Printed and bound by CPI Group (UK) Ltd, Croydon, CR0 4YY